PEARCE & STEVENS'
TRUSTS AND EQUITABLE OBLIGATIONS

Pearce & Stevens' Trusts and Equitable Obligations

Eighth Edition

PROFESSOR WARREN BARR

LLB (Hons), LLM (Th), PFHEA

Professor in Law at the School of Law and Social Justice at the University of Liverpool; Ex-Director & Current Member, Charity Law and Policy Unit (Liverpool Law School); National Law Teacher of the Year 2006

DR JOHN PICTON

LLB (Hons), PhD

Senior Lecturer in Law at the Liverpool Law School, School of Law and Social Justice, University of Liverpool Member, Charity Law and Policy Unit (Liverpool Law School)

OXFORD
UNIVERSITY PRESS

OXFORD
UNIVERSITY PRESS

Great Clarendon Street, Oxford, OX2 6DP,
United Kingdom

Oxford University Press is a department of the University of Oxford.
It furthers the University's objective of excellence in research, scholarship,
and education by publishing worldwide. Oxford is a registered trade mark of
Oxford University Press in the UK and in certain other countries

Fifth edition 2010
Sixth edition 2015
Seventh edition 2018

Published in the United States of America by Oxford University Press
198 Madison Avenue, New York, NY 10016, United States of America

British Library Cataloguing in Publication Data
Data available

Library of Congress Control Number: 2022932809

ISBN 978–0–19–886749–4

Printed and bound by
CPI Group (UK) Ltd, Croydon, CR0 4YY

This edition is dedicated to those who matter most in our respective lives (you know who you are), and to the countless students of Liverpool Law School who have made teaching the subject matter contained in this book such a pleasurable and learning experience for us both.

New to this edition

- Updated structure and revised legal content throughout
- Consolidation of key elements of equitable remedies into a single chapter
- The impact of *Stoffel & Co v Grondona* [2020] UKSC 42 on illegality
- The impact of *Manchester Building Society v Grant Thornton UK LLP* [2021] UKSC 20 on trustee advisors
- Updated and expanded coverage on intestate succession
- An independent chapter on secret trusts
- Consideration of *Archibald v Alexander* [2020] EWHC 1621 (Ch) on orally declared trusts of land
- Updated coverage of ethical investments
- Updated coverage on limitation of actions, as a new self-standing chapter
- Updated and enhanced coverage of the use of trusts and equitable devices to grant an interest in the family home, as an example of the creativity of equity in society
- A new chapter dedicated solely to public benefit and significant updates around regulation of charities
- Updated coverage of the charitable *cy-près* doctrine and its ongoing reform

Preface

This edition of the textbook marks the first that has not seen the involvement of Professor Robert Pearce, one of the two founding authors of this work. This edition still bears his imprint, and much of the detailed and concise explanation of difficult legal principles that have been a hallmark of this book in all seven of the previous editions remains and has inspired the updates and changes made to this edition. We will be forever indebted to Robert for his work and hope that this new edition cements the reputation of this text with student and practitioner readers alike. Certainly, the addition of Dr John Picton as co-author continues the book's tradition of rigorous trust law scholarship. Alongside Professor Warren Barr, John is a member of the Charity Law and Policy Unit at Liverpool and has played an invaluable role in expanding new features and critical commentary.

In common with work on previous editions, we have taken the opportunity to again refresh the organization of material, seeing a growth in the number of parts (from nine to ten) and a redistribution of topics and chapters. We remain extremely grateful for the many comments we have received from readers and reviewers of the last edition, which has proved invaluable in improving the coverage of the text, and also making sure it is fit for purpose in the current legal world . We have also further integrated academic perspectives into the text. A book cannot simply grow if it is to remain both accessible and useful, so this edition has also seen some reduction in content from previous editions, notably around equitable remedies. Instead of previous, distinct chapters on the various equitable remedies, we have instead consolidated treatment into the key aspects of remedies into one chapter. This is not to deny the importance of equitable remedies in practice, but recognizes that these are not often taught in substantive detail in trusts courses in England and Wales. We have tried throughout the book to use language which is clear and easy to understand; to this end we have renamed some chapters and refreshed headings and sections within chapters to break up the text and help with navigation. We have introduced some amended figures to help explain difficult concepts, as we know they have proved popular, and have updated existing figures to represent changes in the law between editions.

Discussion of the use of trusts and estoppel in the family home is now part of a new section (Part IV, Equity in Action: The Family Home). The law relating to family homes, as we expected, has continued to develop and remains an important illustration of the creativity (and flexibility) of equity to adapt to societal changes, and the new treatment sets the law in context in Chapter 11, and adds a postscript to analyse the current state of the law in Chapter 15 from various perspectives.

Part V of this book seeks to demonstrate the role of equity in society, with a particular emphasis in Chapter 17 on wills and intestate succession. This edition also improves the coverage of charitable trusts in Part VI of the book, with the separation of charitable purposes into a new chapter (Chapter 20) and a separate discussion of the requirements of public benefit (Chapter 21). The increased importance of charities has been brought into sharp relief by the pandemic, and there has again been real challenges to effective regulation of charities and to the charity brand.

We are writing this while we are still in the grips of the Covid-19 pandemic, which, hopefully, will soon tip from pandemic to endemic across the world. Alongside the myriad impacts on the lives of citizens across the globe, the pandemic has also had a negative impact on legal litigation, though, as will be seen from updated coverage throughout this book, the move to online proceedings and judgments has meant that there has still been some substantial changes to some key legal rules. *Lehtimäki v Cooper* [2020] UKSC 33, a Supreme Court case, shows the ever-expanding reach of fiduciary obligations, this time to include the member of a charitable company. *Stoffel & Co v Grondona* [2020] UKSC 42 is the latest Supreme Court intervention on illegality. There has also been clarification around the running of time limits in limitation of actions from the Supreme Court in *Matthew v Sedman* [2021] UKSC 19. Indeed, the Supreme Court has been busy in many aspects of equity in the past few years. Innovation does not only happen in the Supreme Court. *National Bank Trust v Yurov* [2020] EWHC 1779 (Comm) provides an important example of lower-level innovation and experimentation in the context of tracing, and there are many other examples peppered across the chapters of this book.

We are grateful, as always, to the members of the editorial team at Oxford University Press who have given us support and advice throughout the preparation of this latest edition and the inevitable delays to production that came with many late changes to the law, the significant restructuring of content in this edition, and the reach and impact of the Covid-19 pandemic on all our lives.

This is the first edition of this book where both authors hail from the same school—the School of Law and Social Justice at the University of Liverpool. This is a 'Liverpool' edition. We work at a lively hub for research into equitable and property issues, where discussion of new legal developments is always in the air. We have benefited from our connections with the Liverpool Law Society (of which Warren is currently a Director) and take pride in our Property Law Annual Lecture and strong series of seminars and international symposia through the Charity Law and Policy Unit. We have benefited from the enthusiasm of students across our property modules, including a large cohort of direct entry students from colleges in Kuala Lumpur, Malaysia. From all these things, grows our enthusiasm for equity and property research, scholarship and teaching, which we hope we have effectively transmitted through the pages of this book.

We have attempted to state the law in this text as at 1 December 2021.

Warren Barr
John Picton
January 2022

Contents

Table of statutes xviii
Table of cases xxvii
Glossary of common terms lx

Part I The Importance of Equity

1 What is equity? 3
1 Introduction 3
2 The concept of equity 4
3 The origins of equity 4
4 Trusts and powers 10
5 Equity and property 15
6 Equitable remedies 22
7 The creativity of equity 22
8 The maxims of equity 22

2 Equitable obligations 26
1 Introduction 26
2 Trust funds 26
3 Trustees are subject to obligations 28
4 The rights of beneficiaries 32
5 Classification of equitable obligations 34
6 A practical guide to interpretation 42

3 Equity and the management of property 44
1 Introduction 44
2 Hiding the identity of the true owner of property 44
3 Transferring the ownership of property 45
4 Sharing ownership of property 46
5 Protecting equitable interests in property 47
6 Delegating management or allocation functions 48
7 Gifts to be applied for purposes 51
8 Gifts for charitable purposes 51
9 Collective investment 52
10 Property holding by clubs and societies 54
11 Trusts arising to protect legitimate expectations 55
12 Trusts that are remedial in effect 55

13 Trusts and tax planning 56
14 Arrangements without trusts 59

4 Equitable remedies in modern English law 66
1 Introduction to equitable remedies 66
2 Where equity intervenes 66
3 Rescission 67
4 Rectification 75
5 Specific performance 77
6 Injunctions 86

Part II Creating the Relationship

5 Certainty 115
1 Introduction 115
2 The three certainties 115
3 Certainty of intention 116
4 Certainty of subject matter 121
5 Certainty of objects 125
6 Contagious uncertainty 137

6 Constitution of trusts 139
1 Introduction 139
2 Two ways of creating a valid trust 139
3 Requirements of an express trust 141
4 Constitution of trusts 142
5 Constituting the trust by transfer 146
6 Ineffective transfers and declaration 154
7 Enforcing a trust 155
8 Exceptions to the rule that 'equity will not assist a volunteer' 157
9 Common law remedies for incompletely constituted trusts 165

7 Formalities 170
1 Introduction 170
2 Inter vivos declarations of trust 170
3 Declarations of trusts by will 174
4 Dispositions of subsisting equitable interests 174
5 Resulting and constructive trusts 184

8 Policy limits 185
1 Introduction 185
2 The rule against perpetuities 185
3 Conditional and determinable interests 188

Part III Resulting and Constructive Trusts

9	**Resulting trusts**	195
	1 Introduction	195
	2 What are resulting trusts?	195
	3 Distinguishing resulting trusts	196
	4 Rationale of resulting trusts	198
	5 Presumed resulting trusts	201
	6 Resulting trusts operating to reverse unjust enrichment?	221
	7 Automatic resulting trusts	225
	8 *Quistclose* trusts	230
	9 Charitable trusts	237
	10 Exhaustion of a fund	237
10	**Constructive trusts**	238
	1 Introduction	238
	2 The role of constructive trusts	240
	3 Preventing benefit from crime	242
	4 Common intention constructive trusts	248
	5 Enforcing bargains	250
	6 The 'remedial constructive trust'	254

Part IV Equity in Action: The Family Home

11	**The family home in context**	267
	1 Introduction	267
	2 The social and legal context	267
	3 The legal response	271
	4 Avoiding the need for judicial intervention	272
12	**Determining interests in the family home through trusts**	273
	1 The current approach	273
	2 Features of the current approach	276
	3 Express trusts	277
	4 Applying the current approach	280
	5 The practical impact of proprietary rights in the family home	294
13	**The evolution of rights in the family home**	297
	1 Introduction	297
	2 The deserted wife's equity	297
	3 A proprietary interest in the home	298
	4 Resulting trusts	298
	5 Common intention constructive trusts	304

14 Proprietary estoppel 316
1 Introduction 316
2 The nature of proprietary estoppel 316
3 Establishing the equity 317
4 Satisfying the equity 332
5 Bars to a remedy 343

15 Family homes: Postscript 344
1 Introduction 344
2 Attempts at reform 344
3 Criticism of the current law 346
4 A clash of legal cultures: property and family law 349
5 Concluding thoughts 350

Part V Equity in Society

16 Clubs and societies 353
1 Introduction 353
2 Types of clubs and societies 353
3 The problem of asset holding and management 354
4 Dissolution of clubs and societies 361
5 Surplus funds on dissolution 362
6 Critique 367

17 Wills and intestate succession 369
1 Introduction 369
2 Methods of making provision after death 369
3 Probate 373
4 Intestacy 373
5 Wills 377
6 Mutual wills 389

18 Secret trusts 401
1 Introduction to secret trusts 401
2 Types of secret trust 402
3 Requirements for the creation of secret trusts 403
4 Fully secret trusts 403
5 Half-secret trusts 407
6 The burden of proof required to establish a secret trust 408
7 Failure of secret trusts 409
8 Death or disclaimer of the secret trustee 410
9 Can a secret trustee benefit from a secret trust? 411

10 Justifying the enforcement of secret trusts 411
11 Date of accrual of the beneficial interest under a secret trust 415
12 Problems associated with the modern theory 416
13 The juridical nature of secret trusts 417

Part VI Charitable Trusts

19 The role and status of charities 421
1 Introduction 421
2 Charities in society 421
3 Mechanisms for charitable giving 426
4 The unity of charity 427
5 Regulation and control of charities 427
6 Negative perceptions of charity 428
7 Privileges enjoyed by charitable trusts 428

20 Charitable purposes 432
1 Introduction 432
2 Defining charitable trusts 432
3 Charitable purposes 436
4 Recognizing new charitable purposes 458
5 Charitable purposes overseas 460
6 Trusts with political objects 461
7 Interpreting charitable gifts 467

21 Public benefit 471
1 Practical impact of public benefit 471
2 What is 'public benefit'? 473
3 Public benefit in particular circumstances 490

22 Cy-près: redistributing funds and changing purposes 493
1 Introduction 493
2 Circumstances triggering cy-près application 496
3 Subsequent failure of charitable gifts in wills 499
4 Initial failure of charitable gifts in wills 500
5 Cy-près schemes 506
6 Failure of charitable appeals 508

23 Regulation and control of charitable trusts 510
1 Introduction 510
2 Features of the regulatory system 511
3 The Charity Commission 516

Part VII Allocation of Benefit

24 Choosing who benefits 535
1 Introduction 535
2 Certainty 535
3 Beneficial entitlement and ownership 535
4 Purpose trusts 537
5 Charitable and benevolent giving 545
6 The duty to act even-handedly 546

25 Fixed trusts 550
1 Introduction 550
2 Nature of a fixed trust 550
3 Uses of fixed trusts 551
4 Beneficial entitlement to defined interests 555
5 Certainty of objects 556
6 Execution and performance 556
7 Dealing with the equitable interest 557

26 Powers of appointment 560
1 Introduction 560
2 Nature of powers of appointment 560
3 Rights of the objects of powers 563
4 The validity of powers of appointment 563
5 Exercise of powers of appointment 564
6 Duties of the donee of a mere power of appointment 567
7 Failure to exercise a mere power 569
8 When is a power fiduciary? 572
9 Duties of the donee of fiduciary powers 574
10 Supervision by the court of fiduciary powers 575
11 Effect of failure to exercise a fiduciary power 577
12 Release of powers 577

27 Discretionary trusts 581
1 Introduction 581
2 The nature of discretionary trusts 581
3 The flexibility of discretionary trusts 582
4 The development of the discretionary trust 583
5 Types of discretionary trusts 583
6 Essential validity of discretionary trusts 585
7 Rights of beneficiaries of discretionary trusts 589
8 The duties of trustees of discretionary trusts 591

9 Protectors 592
10 Enforcement by the court 593

28 Powers of maintenance and advancement 594
1 Introduction 594
2 What are powers of maintenance and advancement? 594
3 Changes in the law 595
4 The trustees' power of maintenance 595
5 The trustees' power of advancement 599

29 Variation of beneficial interests 603
1 Introduction 603
2 Consensual variation 604
3 Variation under the inherent jurisdiction of the court 606
4 Miscellaneous statutory powers 609
5 The Variation of Trusts Act 1958 611

Part VIII Managing Trust Property

30 Management and delegation 625
1 Introduction 625
2 The extent of management powers 626
3 Delegation by trustees 630
4 Delegation at common law 631
5 A statutory right to delegate 633
6 The current statutory framework 634
7 Individual delegation 640

31 Investment 641
1 Introduction 641
2 The purpose of investment 642
3 Powers of disposal 643
4 Authorized investments 645
5 Widening of powers of investment 652
6 Theories of investment 654
7 Duties 656
8 Delegation 664

32 Appointing and changing trustees 667
1 Introduction 667
2 The original trustees 667
3 Retirement of trustees 670

4 Appointing new trustees 671
5 Trustee Act 1925, s 36 673
6 Trustee Act 1925, s 41 679
7 Trusts of Land and Appointment of Trustees Act 1996 683
8 Appointment of special trustees 685
9 The court's inherent jurisdiction 687

Part IX Controlling Trustees and Fiduciaries

33 Need for control 693
1 The need for control and accountability of trustees 693
2 The means of control 695
3 The duty to exercise discretions properly 699
4 Are trustees required to give reasons for their decisions? 705
5 Information about the trust 707

34 Remedies against the trustee for breach of trust 714
1 Introduction 714
2 Meaning of breach of trust 715
3 Compensation for breach of trust 724
4 Defences to liability for breach of trust 733
5 Contribution and indemnity where a trustee is liable 741

35 Fiduciary duties of trustees and other fiduciaries 744
1 Introduction 744
2 Fiduciary relationships 744
3 Fiduciary duties 752
4 Abuse of position 753
5 Unauthorized remuneration 755
6 Purchase of trust property by trustees 757
7 Bribes and secret commissions 760
8 Incidental profits 761
9 Opportunities 764
10 Use of confidential information 767
11 Liability for breach of fiduciary duty 769
12 Remedies for breach 774
13 Defences to an action for breach of fiduciary duty 782

36 Limitation of action 783
1 Introduction 783
2 Limitation of action for breach of trust 783

3 Laches 789

4 Limitation of action against unauthorized profits 791

Part X Recovering Trust Property

37 Remedies against strangers to the trust 797

1 Introduction 797

2 When can strangers be liable? 797

3 Trustees de son tort 801

4 Dishonest assistance in breach of trust 803

5 Proprietary remedies for receipt in breach of trust 814

6 Liability for unconscionable receipt 814

7 Mapping a way through personal stranger claims 829

38 Tracing 831

1 Introduction 831

2 What is tracing? 831

3 Tracing and claiming at common law 841

4 Tracing and claiming in equity 852

Index 881

Table of statutes

Page references in **bold** indicate where a statute has been set out in part or in full

Accumulations Act 1800 . . . 186
Administration of Estates Act 1925 . . . 375
s.33 . . . 374
s.46 . . . 373–5
s.46(1) . . . 376
s.46(1)(i) . . . 375
s.46(1)(vi) . . . 377
s.46A . . . 248
s.47(1)(i) . . . 248, 375
s.47A . . . 376
Sch.1A . . . 375
Administration of Justice Act 1982
s.17 . . . 381
s.20 . . . 386
s.20(1) . . . 75
s.21 . . . 386
s.55(1)(x) . . . 374
Administration of Justice Act 1985
s.50 . . . 674, 685, 686
Age of Legal Capacity (Scotland) Act 1991
s.2 . . . 378
Arbitration Act 1996
s.9 . . . 81
Armed Forces Act 2006
Sch.15 . . . 377

Building Societies Act 1986 . . . 61, 62
Building Societies Act 1997 . . . 61, 62

Chancery Amendment Act 1858 (Lord Cairns' Act) . . . 86, 92, 93
s.2 . . . 86
Charitable Trusts Act 1853 . . . 516
Charitable Trusts (Validation) Act 1954 . . . 470
Charitable Uses Act of 1601 (Statute of Elizabeth I) . . . 424, 432, 433, 436, 458–60
Charities Act 1960 . . . 516, 524
s.13 . . . 496
s.38(1) . . . 433
s.49 . . . 470
Charities Act 1992 . . . 516
Charities Act 1993 . . . 511, 512, 516, 646
s.3 . . . 434
s.3A(2)(a) . . . 434
s.3A(2)(d) . . . 434
s.4(1) . . . 434
s.32 . . . 512
s.33(1) . . . 514
Sch.2 . . . 434
Charities Act 2006 . . . 426–8, 431–4, 444, 446, 456, 458, 463, 464, 472, 476, 483, 490, 498, 511, 516, 521, 522, 524–6
s.2(2)(j) . . . 445
s.2(2)(m) . . . 433
s.2(4) . . . 433
s.4 . . . 472
s.4(6) . . . 472
s.5(2) . . . 455
s.73 . . . 526
Charities Act 2011 . . . 361, 427, 428, 431, 433, 434, 436, 438, 439, 441, 442, 446, 451–4, 460, 464, 471, 490, 509, 511, 516, 522–4, 527–9, 636, 694, 713
s.1 . . . 432
ss.1–5 . . . 432
s.2 . . . 432
s.2(1)(b) . . . 471
s.2(3) . . . 435
s.3 . . . 432, 433, 435, 546
s.3(1) . . . 436
s.3(1)(f) . . . 440
s.3(1)(g) . . . 451
s.3(1)(j) . . . 438, 448, 454
s.3(1)(m) . . . 433, 457, 458, 460
s.3(2) . . . 434
s.3(2)(b) . . . 446
s.3(2)(c) . . . 446
s.3(2)(c)(ii) . . . 447, 448
s.3(2)(d) . . . 451
s.3(2)(e) . . . 454
s.4 . . . 471
s.4(3) . . . 471
s.5 . . . 435, 455
s.5(3) . . . 455
s.6 . . . 451
Pt.2 (ss.13–21) . . . 511
s.13 . . . 511
s.13(4) . . . 511
s.14 . . . 428, 516
s.16(4) . . . 511
s.17 . . . 472
s.17(5) . . . 472
s.21(3) . . . 524
s.22 . . . 511, 524
Pt.3 (ss.25–28) . . . 511
s.25 . . . 524
s.26(1) . . . 524
s.29 . . . 492, 523
s.29(2) . . . 524
s.30 . . . 525
s.30(1) . . . 524
s.30(2) . . . 524
s.30(2)(b)–(d) . . . 524
s.34 . . . 525

s.34(1)(a) . . . 525
s.34(1)(b) . . . 525
s.35(1) . . . 524, 528
s.35(2) . . . 524
s.38(1) . . . 524
s.46 . . . 522
s.46(1) . . . 521
s.46(2) . . . 521, 524
s.47(2)(a) . . . 521
s.47(2)(b) . . . 521
s.47(3)(a) . . . 521
s.47(3)(b) . . . 521
s.48 . . . 522
s.60 . . . 521
Pt.6 (ss.61–116) . . . 429
s.62 . . . 497
s.62(1)(a)–(e) . . . 497
s.62(2) . . . **498**
ss.63–66 . . . 508
s.63(1)(a) . . . 509
s.63(1)(b) . . . 509
s.63(2) . . . 509
s.63A(3) . . . 509
s.64(1) . . . 509
s.64(2) . . . 509
s.65 . . . 509
s.67(3) . . . 506, 508
s.67A . . . 509
s.69 . . . 493
s.69(1) . . . **513**
s.69(2) . . . **513**
s.70 . . . 493
s.75A . . . 523
s.76 . . . **522**
s.76(1) . . . 522
s.76(3)(a)–(d) . . . 522
s.76(3)(e), (g) . . . 522
s.79 . . . 522
s.83 . . . 511
s.84 . . . 511, 518, 522
s.84A . . . 523
s.85 . . . 511, 522
s.96 . . . 662
ss.97–103 . . . 662
s.100 . . . 662
ss.101–103 . . . 662
s.104A . . . 663
s.110 . . . 523
s.110(2) . . . 524
s.110(3)(a) . . . 524
s.110(3)(b) . . . 524
s.115(1) . . . **513**–5
s.115(2) . . . 515, 523
s.115(3) . . . 515
s.115(7) . . . 523
Pt.8 (ss.130–176) . . . 528
s.130 . . . 528
s.131 . . . 528
s.132 . . . 528
s.133 . . . 528
s.135 . . . 528
s.136 . . . 528
s.144 . . . 512
s.146 . . . 529
s.162 . . . 529
s.164(1) . . . 529
s.164(3) . . . 529
s.170 . . . 528, 529
Pt.9 (ss.178–84) . . . 527
s.178(1) . . . 527
s.181 . . . 527
s.181A(7A) . . . 522
s.183 . . . 527
s.185 . . . 756
Pt.11 (ss.204–50) . . . 426
s.275 . . . 495
s.280 . . . 495
s.280A . . . 499
s.280A(5) . . . 499
s.280A(6) . . . 499
s.280A(7) . . . 499
s.280A(10) . . . 508
s.292A . . . 448, 663
s.292A(2) . . . 664
s.292A(4) . . . 448, 663
s.292A(5) . . . 664
s.292B . . . 663
s.292B(3) . . . 664
s.292B(4) . . . 663
s.292B(5) . . . 663
s.292C . . . 663
s.292C(2)(a) . . . 664
s.292C(2)(b) . . . 664
s.292C(2)(c) . . . 664
s.292C(3) . . . 664
s.292C(4) . . . 664
s.294 . . . 529
s.311 . . . 501
Pt.17 (ss.315–30) . . . 525
s.318 . . . 525
s.319 . . . 525
s.326 . . . 525
s.351(3) . . . 515
s.761A . . . 522
Sch.1 . . . 516
para 11 . . . 521
Sch.2 . . . 524
Sch.3 . . . 511, 524
Sch.6 . . . 525, 526
Charities Act 2022 . . . 527
Charities (Protection and Social Investment) Act 2016 . . . 427, 448, 511, 518, 522, 523
s.1 . . . 523
s.2 . . . 522
s.4 . . . 522
s.6 . . . 523
s.9 . . . 527
s.10 . . . 522
s.13 . . . 428
s.15 . . . 448, 663
s.15(2)–(4) . . . 664
Children Act 1989 . . . 271

Civil Liability (Contribution) Act 1978 . . . 742
s.1(1) . . . **742**
s.2(1) . . . **742**
s.2(2) . . . 742
s.6(1) . . . 742
Civil Partnership Act 2004 . . . 270
s.49 . . . 375
s.65 . . . 270
Common Law Procedure Act 1854 . . . 7
s.78 . . . 849
Companies Act 2006 . . . 59, 361, 746, 764, 766
Pt.10, Ch.2 (ss.170–181) . . . 60, 717
s.170(3) . . . 781
s.171(4) . . . 60
s.174 . . . 717, 781
s.174(2)(a) . . . 717
s.175(1) . . . **764**
s.175(2) . . . 764
s.175(4)(a) . . . 764, 773
s.175(4)(b) . . . 766
s.175(5) . . . 766
s.175(6) . . . 766
s.180 . . . 766
s.193 . . . 515
s.217 . . . 575
Pt.15 (ss.380–474) . . . 515, 528
s.750 . . . 718
ss.770–1 . . . 147
Pt.22 (ss.791–828) . . . 553
s.1157(1) . . . 737
Company Directors Disqualification Act 1986 . . . 527, 694
Constitutional Reform Act 2005
s.23 . . . 7
s.59 . . . 7
Consumer Credit Act 1974 . . . 74
Consumer Credit Act 2006 . . . 74
Consumer Rights Act 2015
s.58 . . . 79
Contempt of Court Act 1981 . . . 87
Contracts (Rights of Third Parties) Act 1999 . . . 82, 157, 165–7, 169, 252, 637
s.1(1) . . . 166
s.1(2) . . . 166
s.1(5) . . . 82, 166
s.7(3) . . . 166
s.10(2) . . . 165
Conveyancing Act 1881
s.43 . . . 595
s.52 . . . 579
Copyright, Design and Patents Act 1988 . . . 104, 147
s.1 . . . 147
Co-operative and Community Benefit Societies Act 2014 . . . 354
Co-operative and Community Benefit Societies and Credit Unions Act 2010 . . . 61
Corporation Tax Act 2010
ss.191–202 . . . 430
Credit Unions Act 1979 . . . 61
Criminal Procedure (Insanity) Act 1964
s.1 . . . 243

Data Protection Act 2018 . . . 711
Domestic Violence, Crime and Victims Act 2004 . . . 104

Education Act 1944 . . . 424
Electronic Communications Act 2000
s.8 . . . 177
Enduring Powers of Attorney Act 1985 . . . 63
s.3(3) . . . 640
Equality Act 2010 . . . 191, 486
s.4 . . . 191
s.193(4) . . . 468
Pt.15 (ss.198–201) . . . 215
s.199 . . . 215, 216
s.199(2) . . . 215
s.199(2)(a) . . . 215
s.199(2)(b) . . . 215
Estates of Deceased Persons (Forfeiture Rule and Law of Succession) Act 2011 . . . 243, 248

Family Law Act 1996 . . . 104
s.30(1) . . . 269
Family Law (Scotland) Act 2006 . . . 275, 345
Finance Act 1921 . . . 53
Finance Act 1940
s.43(1) . . . 590
Finance Act 2002
Sch 18 . . . 451
Finance Act 2004 . . . 53
Finance Act 2010 . . . 451
Financial Services and Markets Act 2000 . . . 62
s.19 . . . 641, 658
s.253 . . . 718
Fire and Rescue Services Act 2004
Pt.2 . . . 457
Forfeiture Act 1982 . . . 246
s.1 . . . 243
s.2(1) . . . 245, 246
s.2(2) . . . **247**
s.3(1) . . . 247
s.5 . . . 247
Friendly Societies Act 1829 . . . 61
Friendly Societies Act 1896 . . . 61, 364
s.49(1) . . . 61
Friendly Societies Act 1974 . . . 61, 354
Friendly Societies Act 1992 . . . 61, 354

Housing Act 1985 . . . 61
Housing Act 1988 . . . 61
Housing Act 1996
s.152 . . . 831
Housing Act 2004 . . . 61
Housing and Regeneration Act 2008 . . . 515
Human Rights Act 1998 . . . 99, 191, 513, 530
s.6(3)(b) . . . 530
s.12(3) . . . 99
Hunting Act 2004 . . . 543

Inclosure Act 1845 . . . 438
Income and Corporation Taxes Act 1988
s.339 . . . 430
s.592 . . . 53

Income Tax Act 1952
Pt.XVIII . . . 178
Income Tax Act 2007
ss.413–30 . . . 430
ss.520–22 . . . 430
Income Tax (Earning and Pensions) Act 2003
ss.713–15 . . . 430
Industrial and Provident Societies Act 1852 . . . 61
Industrial and Provident Societies Act 1862 . . . 61
Industrial and Provident Societies Act 1965 . . . 61
Industrial and Provident Societies Act 1978 . . . 61
Industrial and Provident Societies Act 2002 . . . 61
Inheritance and Trustees' Powers Act 2014 . . . 371, 373, 376, 595, 596, 600, 601, 607
s.3(1)(x) . . . 374
s.6 . . . 371
s.8 . . . 595
s.8(a) . . . 596
s.9 . . . 595, 600
s.9(3)(b) . . . 600, 601
s.10(2) . . . 600
s.10(3) . . . 600
s.10(5) . . . 595
s.10(6) . . . 601
Sch 2 . . . 371
Inheritance (Provision for Family and Dependants) Act 1975 . . . 247, 269, 371, 372, 375, 400
s.3 . . . 373
s.4 . . . 3
Inheritance Tax Act 1984
s.3A(5) . . . 618
s.23 . . . 430
s.76 . . . 430
s.142 . . . 611
Insolvency Act 1986 . . . 261
s.11(3)(d) . . . 261
Intestates' Estate Act 1952
Sch.2 para.5(2) . . . 376

Judicature Act 1925
ss.36–44 . . . 8
Judicial Trustees Act 1896 . . . 685
s.1 . . . 685, 686
s.1(1) . . . **686**
s.1(3) . . . **686**
s.1(5) . . . 686, 756
s.3 . . . 736

Land Charges Act 1972 . . . 295
s.11 . . . 295
Land Registration Act 2002 . . . 18, 146, 294
ss.4–5 . . . 295
s.27 . . . 295
s.29 . . . 296
s.30 . . . 296
Pt IV, ss.40–47 . . . 277, 296
s.116 . . . 296
Sch.3 . . . 296
Landlord and Tenant Act 1985 . . . 79
s.17 . . . 79
Law of Property Act 1925 . . . 47, 48, 308
s.1 . . . 19
s.1(3) . . . 370
s.1(6) . . . 47, 668
s.2 . . . 669, 694
s.2(1) . . . 17
s.20 . . . 203, 668, 675
s.27 . . . 669, 694
s.27(2) . . . 629
s.34(2) . . . 669
s.34(3) . . . 669
s.36(2) . . . 47
s.40 . . . 46
s.51(1)(b) . . . 565
s.52 . . . 146
s.52(1)(b) . . . 45
s.52(2)(d) . . . 17
s.53 . . . 141, 324
s.53(1) . . . 180, 184
s.53(1)(b) . . . **144**, 170–5, 177, 277, 278, 308, 370, 417, 418
s.53(1)(c) . . . **147**, 170, 173–9, 181, 183, 184, 209, 620, 621
s.53(2) . . . 172, 180, 181, 184, 417, 621
s.54(2) . . . 17
s.60(3) . . . **204**, 205
s.136 . . . 557
s.155 . . . 578–80
s.159(1) . . . 565
s.159(2) . . . 565
s.160 . . . 578
s.164 . . . **186**
s.175 . . . 597, 598
s.199 . . . 20, 820
s.199(1)(ii)(a) . . . 20
s.205(1)(ii) . . . 183
s.205(1)(xxi) . . . 295
Law of Property (Amendment) Act 1926 . . . 629
Law of Property (Miscellaneous Provisions) Act 1989 . . . 399
s.1 . . . 17, 565
s.2 . . . 78, 84, 181, 324, 392, 393
Law of Property (Miscellaneous Provisions) Act 1994
s.14 . . . 687
Law Reform (Contributory Negligence) Act 1945 . . . 743
Law Reform (Succession) Act 1995 . . . 376
Legal Aid, Sentencing and Punishment of Offenders Act 2012 . . . 520
Limitation Act 1980 . . . 24, 85, 783, 785–7, 791, 829
ss.2–4A . . . 783
ss.5–7 . . . 783
s.18 . . . 134
s.21 . . . 791, 792
s.21(1) . . . 793
s.21(1)(a) . . . 784, 791
s.21(1)(b) . . . 785, 791, 792
s.21(3) . . . 134, 783, 786, 787, 791
s.22 . . . 134
s.22(1)(a) . . . **787**
s.23 . . . 788

s.32 . . . 792
s.32(1) . . . **786**
s.32(1)(c) . . . 75
s.32(2) . . . 787
s.36 . . . 789
Local Government Finance Act 1988
s.43(5) . . . 430
s.43(6)(a) . . . 472
s.47 . . . 430
Lord Cranworth's Act 1860 . . . 595

Married Women's Property Act 1882 . . . 269
s.11 . . . 625
Marriage (Same Sex Couples) Act 2013 . . . 270
Matrimonial and Family Proceedings Act 1984 . . . 104
Matrimonial Causes Act 1973 . . . 104, 197, 269, 346, 349, 610
s.11 . . . 375
s.24 . . . 610
s.24(1)(a)–(b) . . . 610
s.24(1)(c)–(d) . . . 610
s.25 . . . 293, 346
s.37 . . . 176
Mental Capacity Act 2005 . . . 63, 379, 380, 678, 679, 684, 685, 735
s.1 . . . 64, 379, 684
ss.1–3 . . . 379
s.2 . . . 684
ss.9–14 . . . 63, 675
s.9(1) . . . 63
s.9(2) . . . 63
s.9(2)(b) . . . 63
s.10 . . . 64
s.18(1)(h) . . . 610
s.22 . . . 64
s.23 . . . 64
Pt.2 (ss.45–61) . . . 64
s.66 . . . 63
Sch.1 . . . 63, 64
Pt.1, paras 1–3 . . . 63
para.2(1)(c)(i), (ii) . . . 64
para.2(1)(e) . . . 64
para.2(2) . . . 63
Pt.2, paras 4–17 . . . 63
para.6 . . . 64
para.13 . . . 64
Sch.4 . . . 63, 640
Pt.1, para.1 . . . 678
Pt.4 . . . 63
Sch.5, para.11 . . . 63
Mental Health Act 1983 . . . 243, 610
Misrepresentation Act 1967
s.2(2) . . . 70

National Assistance Act 1948 . . . 424
National Health Service Act 1946 . . . 424
National Trust Act 1907
s.4(1) . . . 453

Parish Councils and Burial Authorities (Miscellaneous Provisions) Act 1970
s.1 . . . 540
Patents Act 1949 . . . 104
Patents Act 1977 . . . 104
Pension Schemes Act 1993 . . . 54
Pensions Act 1995 . . . 635, 665
s.29(1) . . . 694
s.32 . . . 695
s.33 . . . 718, 719
s.34 . . . 646, 665
s.35 . . . 646
s.36 . . . 646
Pensions Act 2004 . . . 54, 713
s.224 . . . 713
Pensions Act 2008 . . . 54
Pensions Act 2014 . . . 54
Pensions Schemes Act 2021 . . . 54
Perpetuities and Accumulations Act 1964 . . . 187, 538
s.1 . . . 187
s.3 . . . 187
s.13 . . . 186
Perpetuities and Accumulations Act 2009 . . . 185, 186, 429, 538
s.5 . . . 186, 187
s.7 . . . 187
s.7(4)(a) . . . 187
s.12 . . . 185, 188
s.14(4) . . . 186
s.15 . . . 185
s.16 . . . 187
s.18 . . . 187
Petroleum (Production) Act 1934 . . . 94
Powers of Attorney Act 1971 . . . 640
Proceeds of Crime Act 2002 . . . 107, 214, 519
Public Service Pensions Act 2013 . . . 54, 661
Public Trustee Act 1906 . . . 554, 686
s.2(1) . . . 686
s.2(3)–(5) . . . 687
s.4(1) . . . **687**
s.4(2) . . . 686
s.4(3) . . . 756
s.5(1) . . . **687**
s.5(3) . . . 687
s.9 . . . 756
s.13(1) . . . 713
Public Trustee (Fees) Act 1957 . . . 756

Race Relations Act 1976
s.34 . . . 468
Real Property Act 1845 . . . 17
Real Property Limitation Act 1874
s.8 . . . 787
Recognition of Trusts Act 1987 . . . 115
Recreational Charities Act 1958 . . . 454, 455, 516
Registered Designs Act 1949 . . . 104
Road Safety Act 2006
s.20 . . . 245
Road Traffic Act 2006
s.2B . . . 245

Sale of Goods (Amendment) Act 1995 . . . 123
Senior Courts Act 1981 (formerly Supreme Court Act 1981)
s.37 . . . 87

s.37(1) . . . 108
s.49 . . . 8
s.49(1) . . . 8
s.50 . . . 86, 92
s.72 . . . 111
Serious Crime Act 2007
s.32 . . . 354
Settled Land Act 1925 . . . 334, 369, 600, 610, 644
s.38 . . . 644
s.64(1) . . . 610
s.67 . . . 645
s.68 . . . 759
s.73 . . . 644, 651
s.75 . . . 651
s.94(1) . . . 629
Statute of Frauds 1677 . . . 175, 176
s.7 . . . 170, 171
s.9 . . . 176
Statute of Uses 1535 . . . 12, 13
Stock Transfer Act 1963
s.1 . . . 147
Suicide Act 1961 . . . 161
s.2(1) . . . 245
Superannuation Act 1972
s.7 . . . 661
Supreme Court of Judicature Act 1873 . . . 4, 7–9, 86
s.24 . . . 8
s.24(5) . . . 8
s.25 . . . 8
s.25(1)–(10) . . . 8
s.25(11) . . . 8, 22
Supreme Court of Judicature Act 1875 . . . 4, 7, 9, 86
Supreme Court of Judicature (Consolidation) Act 1925
s.45(1) . . . 109

Terrorism Act 2000
ss.15–18 . . . 519
Theft Act 1968
s.1(1) . . . **695**
s.5(2) . . . 696
s.15(1) . . . 846
s.28 . . . 243
Theft (Amendment) Act 1996 . . . 847
Torts (Interference with Goods) Act 1977
s.3 . . . 849
Town and Country Planning Act 1990
s.106 . . . 104
s.187(B) . . . 104
Trade Marks Act 1938 . . . 104
Trade Union and Labour Relations (Consolidation) Act 1992
s.221(2) . . . 100
s.236 . . . 103
Transparency of Lobbying, Non-Party Campaigning and Trade Union Administration Act 2014 . . . 465
Tribunals, Courts and Enforcement Act 2007 . . . 525
s.25 . . . 525
Trustee Act 1850 . . . 680, 682
Trustee Act 1888
s.4 . . . 738
s.6 . . . 743
s.8 . . . 787
Trustee Act 1893
s.8 . . . 738
s.10 . . . 674
s.45 . . . 743
Trustee Act 1925 . . . 595, 610, 627, 628, 633, 640, 681, 684, 736, 785
s.4 . . . 662
s.8 . . . 651, 662, 730, 738
s.9 . . . 730
s.14 . . . 628
s.14(2) . . . 629
s.14 (3) . . . 628
s.15 . . . 629
s.16(1) . . . 644
s.18(1) . . . 676
s.19 . . . 629
s.19(1) . . . 629
s.22 . . . 630
s.22(4) . . . 713
s.23 . . . 633, 819
s.25 . . . 640, 674
s.25(1) . . . **640**
s.25(2)(a) . . . 640
s.25(4) . . . 640
s.25(7) . . . 640
s.27 . . . 374, 819
s.30(1) . . . 723
s.31 . . . 595, 596, 597
ss.31–32 . . . 375
s.31(1) . . . 597
s.31(1)(i) . . . 595, 596
s.31(1)(ii) . . . 596
s.31(2) . . . 596, 598
s.31(2)(i)(b) . . . 599
s.31(2)(ii) . . . 599
s.31(3) . . . 597
s.31(4) . . . 596
s.32 . . . 595, 600
s.32(1) . . . 600
s.32(1)(a) . . . 600, 601
s.32(1)(b) . . . 601
s.32(1)(c) . . . 601
s.32(1A) . . . 601
s.32(2) . . . 600
s.33(1) . . . 50
s.33(1)(i) . . . **50**
s.33(1)(ii) . . . 51
s.34(2) . . . 669
s.36 . . . 670, 673–5, 677–80, 683–5, 689, 700
s.36(1) . . . 668, 673, 674, 676, 678–80, 684
s.36(1)(a) . . . 676, 677
s.36(1)(b) . . . 676
s.36(2) . . . **673**, 675
s.36(3) . . . **675**
s.36(6) . . . **677–9**, 689
s.36(6A)–(6D) . . . 678
s.36(7) . . . **679**
s.36(8) . . . 674, 676
s.37(1)(c) . . . 676

s.38 . . . 677
s.39 . . . 670, 671, 689
s.40 . . . 679
s.41 . . . 671, 673, 677, 679–83, 687, 688, 689, 705
s.41(1) . . . **679**
s.53 . . . 610
s.57 . . . 609, 646, 652, 653
s.57(1) . . . 609, 653
s.61 . . . 374, 716, 736, 738–40, 743
s.62 . . . 743
s.63 . . . 580
s.68(17) . . . 785
s.69(2) . . . 595, 596, 599
Trustee Act 2000 . . . 548, 552, 554, 608, 620, 627–30, 634, 635, 637, 640, 645–53, 655–8, 662–5, 723
s.1 . . . 629, 630, 638, 665, 718, 737
s.1(1) . . . 656, 717
s.3 . . . 644
s.3(1) . . . 648
s.3(3) . . . 651, 662
s.4 . . . 657
s.4(1) . . . 657
s.4(2) . . . 661
s.4(3) . . . 657
s.4(4) . . . 664
s.4(5) . . . 664
s.5 . . . 730
s.5(1) . . . 658
s.5(2) . . . 658
s.5(3) . . . 658
s.5(4) . . . 658
s.6 . . . 646
s.6(1)(a) . . . 651
s.6(1)(b) . . . 651
s.7 . . . 646
s.7(1) . . . 652
s.7(2) . . . 652
s.7(3) . . . 652
s.8 . . . 644, 651, 653
s.8(1)(a) . . . 644
s.8(1)(c) . . . 644
s.8(2) . . . 651
s.11 . . . 665
s.11(1) . . . 635
s.11(2) . . . 635
s.11(2)(a)–(d) . . . 635
s.12(1)–(4) . . . 636
s.13 . . . 636
s.13(1) . . . 665
s.13(2) . . . 636, 665
s.13(3)–(5) . . . 635
s.13(4) . . . 635
s.13(5) . . . 635
s.13(8) . . . 635
s.14 . . . 636, 638
s.14(2) . . . 636, 665
s.14(3) . . . 665
s.14(3)(a) . . . 637
s.14(3)(a)–(c) . . . 636
s.15 . . . 636, 665
s.15(1) . . . 665
s.15(2)(a) . . . 665
s.15(2)(b) . . . 665
s.16(1) . . . 552
s.17(1) . . . 554
s.18(1) . . . 554
s.19(2) . . . 629
s.20 . . . 629
s.21 . . . 638
s.22 . . . 638
s.22(1) . . . 666
s.22(2) . . . 666
s.22(4) . . . 666
s.23 . . . 639
s.24 . . . 639, 665
s.28 . . . 756
ss.28–30 . . . 608
s.28(3) . . . 756
s.29 . . . 756
s.29(1) . . . 756
s.29(2) . . . 756
s.30 . . . 756
s.31(1)(a) . . . 755
s.32 . . . 638
s.32(2) . . . 636
s.34 . . . 629
s.36(5) . . . 636
s.36(8) . . . 636
ss.36–8 . . . 646, 651
s.37 . . . 636
s.38 . . . 636
Sch.1 . . . 717
para.3 . . . 638, 665
para.5 . . . 629
Sch.2 . . . 638
Trustee Delegation Act 1999 . . . 640, 678, 694
s.1 . . . 675
s.6 . . . 640
s.7 . . . 670, 671, 694
s.9 . . . 640
Trustee Investments Act 1961 . . . 620, 644, 645, 649, 652, 653, 655, 657, 658
s.1(3) . . . 645
s.2(1) . . . 655
s.6(1) . . . 657
Trustee Investments Act 2000
Sch.1, Pt.II, para.13 . . . 651
Trusts (Capital and Income) Act 2013 . . . 547, 642, 657
s.1(1) . . . 548
s.1(2)(a) . . . 643, 657
s.1(2)(b) . . . 548, 657
s.1(3) . . . 643
s.1(4) . . . 547
s.2(1) . . . 549
s.2(2) . . . 549
s.2(5) . . . 549
s.3 . . . 549
s.4 . . . 663
Trusts of Land and Appointment of Trustees Act 1996 (TOLATA) . . . 294, 334, 369, 609, 610, 627–9, 640, 643, 644, 651, 653, 670, 677, 678, 683, 700, 759, 876
ss.1–5 . . . 47
s.1 . . . 369, 370, 555

s.1(1) . . . 644
s.2 . . . 369
s.2(1) . . . 610
s.4 . . . 627, 628, 644
s.6 . . . 627, 628, 641, 642, 644, 651, 653
s.8 . . . 627
s.9 . . . 636, 640
s.9A . . . 638, 640
s.11 . . . 628, 700
s.12 . . . 628
s.13 . . . 628
s.14 . . . 294, 628
s.15(1) . . . 294
s.19 . . . 671, 673, 678, 684, 689
s.19(1)(a) . . . 671, 684
s.19(1)(b) . . . 671, 684
s.19(2)(a) . . . 670
s.19(2)(b) . . . 673, 684
s.19(3) . . . 671, 684
s.19(3)(b) . . . 671
s.19(3)(c) . . . 671
s.19(3)(d) . . . 671
s.19(5) . . . 684
ss.19–21 . . . 700
s.20 . . . 673, 685, 689
s.20(1)(a) . . . 684
s.20(1)(c) . . . 684, 685
s.20(2) . . . 684
s.20(2)(a) . . . 685
s.20(2)(b) . . . 685
s.20(2)(c) . . . 685
s.21(5) . . . 671, 685
s.21(5)–(8) . . . 684
s.21(6) . . . 671, 685
s.21(7) . . . 671
s.36(1) . . . 294
Sch.3 . . . 629, 676
para.3(11) . . . 677

Unfair Contract Terms Act 1977 . . . 721

Variation of Trusts Act 1958 . . . 32, 38, 604, 606–8, 610–2, 619–21, 646, 652, 653, 680
s.1 . . . 614, 619
s.1(1) . . . 611
s.1(1)(a) . . . 614, 619
s.1(1)(a)–(c) . . . 616
s.1(1)(a)–(d) . . . 603
s.1(1)(b) . . . 614, 615, 619
s.1(1)(c) . . . 615, 619
s.1(1)(d) . . . 615, 619

Wills Act 1837 . . . 164, 377, 383, 385, 412, 413, 417, 418
s.7 . . . 378
s.9 . . . 174, 381, 388, 412
s.9(a) . . . 174
s.9(c) . . . 174
s.9(d) . . . 174
s.10 . . . 565
s.11 . . . 377
s.15 . . . 383, 414
s.18 . . . 387
s.18A . . . 388
s.20 . . . 388
s.21 . . . 385
s.22 . . . 388
s.24 . . . 385
s.33 . . . 386
s.33A . . . 248
Wills Act 1963
s.2 . . . 565
Wills Act 1968 . . . 383
Wills (Soldiers and Sailors) Act 1918 . . . 377
s.1 . . . 378

Australia

ACT Domestic Relationships Act 1994 . . . 344

New South Wales Conveyancing Act 1919–54 . . . 491
New South Wales Property (Relationships) Act 1984 No 147 . . . 344
s.20 . . . 344
Northern Territory De Facto Relationships Act 1991 . . . 344
s.4 . . . 345
s.5 . . . 345

Victoria Property Law (Amendment Act) 1987 No 91 . . . 344

Canada

Ontario Perpetuities Act 1966 . . . 544

Cayman Islands

Cayman Islands Special Trusts (Alternative Regime) Law 1997 . . . 544
s.7(1) . . . 544

United States

Restatement of Restitution
para.16 . . . **259**

Uniform Trust Code . . . 544

International

Convention on Jurisdiction and Enforcement of Judgments in Civil and Commercial Matters 1968
Art.16(1) . . . 33

European Convention on Human Rights and Fundamental Freedoms 1950 . . . 191
Art.8 . . . 89, 191, 530
Art.9 . . . 191

Art.10 . . . 99
Protocol 7, Art.5 . . . 215

Fourth Money Laundering Directive (2015/849/EU) . . . 45, 519

Hague Convention on the Law Applicable to Trusts and on their Recognition 1985
Art.2 . . . 115

Universal Declaration on Human Rights 1948 . . . 452

Statutory Instruments

Charitable Incorporated Organisations (Conversions) Regulations 2017 (SI 2017/1232) . . . 426
Charities (Accounts and Reports) Regulations 1995 (SI 1995/2724) . . . 528
Charities (Accounts and Reports) Regulations 2008 (SI 2008/629) . . . 471, 472
Annex A . . . 471
Charities (Failed Appeals) Regulations 2008 . . . 508
reg 2 . . . 509
regs 3–5 . . . 509
reg 8 . . . 509
Schs 1 . . . 509
Schs 2 . . . 509
Schs 4 . . . 509
Civil Procedure Rules 1998 (SI 1998/3132) . . . 88, 106, 109
r 25.1(1)(f) . . . 106
Civil Procedure (Amendment) Rules 2005 (SI 2005/352) . . . 110
PD10 para 7.1. . . . 110

Local Government Pension Scheme (Management and Investment of Funds) Regulations 2016 (SI 2016/946)
reg.7(2)(e) . . . 661

Money Laundering, Terrorist Financing and Transfer of Funds (Information on the Payer) Regulations 2017 (SI 2017/692) . . . 45, 519

Occupational Pensions Schemes (Investment) Regulations 2005 (SI 2005/3378) . . . 646
Open-Ended Investment Companies Regulations 2001 (SI 2001/1228) . . . 61
Open-Ended Investment Companies (Amendment) Regulations 2005 (SI 2005/923) . . . 61
Open-Ended Investment Companies (Amendment) Regulations 2009 (SI 2009/553) . . . 61
Open-Ended Investment Companies (Amendment) Regulations 2011 (SI 2011/3049) . . . 61

Perpetuities and Accumulations Act 2009 (Commencement) Order 2010 (SI 2010/37) . . . 185
Public Trustee Rules 1912 (SI 1212/348)
r 30 . . . 554
Public Trustee (Custodian Trustee) Rules 1975 (SI 1975/1189) . . . 554
Public Trustee (Custodian Trustee) Rules 1976 (SI 1976/836) . . . 554
Public Trustee (Custodian Trustee) Rules 1981 (SI 1981/358) . . . 554
Public Trustee (Custodian Trustee) Rules 1984 (SI 1984/109) . . . 554
Public Trustee (Custodian Trustee) Rules 1985 (SI 1985/132) . . . 554

Stamp Duty Land Tax (Open-ended Investment Companies) Regulations 2008 (SI 2008/710) . . . 61

Transfer of Functions of the Charity Tribunal Order 2009 (SI 2009/1834) . . . 525
Art.3 . . . 526
Tribunal Procedure (First-Tier Tribunal) (General Regulatory Chamber) Rules 2009 (SI 2009/1976) . . . 525
Tribunal Procedure (Upper Tribunal) Rules 2008 (SI 2008/2698) . . . 525
Trustee Investment (Division of Trust Fund) Order (SI 1996/845) . . . 655

Unfair Terms in Consumer Contracts Regulations 1999 (SI 1999/2083) . . . 73

Table of cases

1 Click Charitable Trust, The (2016) . . . 525

A v B (2016) Ch . . . 579, 580, 616
Aas v Benham (1891) CA . . . 746, 762
AAZ v BBZ (2016) Fam . . . 759
Abbey Malvern Wells Ltd v Ministry of Local Government and Planning (1951) . . . 439
Abbott v Abbott (2008) PC . . . 285, 291
Abbott Fund Trusts, Re; Smith v Abbott (1900) . . . 226–8, 363
Aberdeen Railway Bros v Blaikie (1854) HL . . . 761, 770
Abergavenny (Marquess) Estate Act Trusts, Re; Marquis of Abergavenny v Ram (1981) . . . 601
Abou-Rahmah v Abacha (2006) CA . . . 810
Abrahams, Re; Abrahams v Bendon (1911) . . . 598
Abrahams v Trustee in Bankruptcy of Abrahams (1999) . . . 206, 218
Abrahams' Will Trusts, Re; Caplan v Abrahams (1969) . . . 189, 562
Accles Ltd, Re; Hodgson v Accles (1902) . . . 755
Acro (Automation) Ltd v Rex Chainbelt Inc (1971) . . . 87
Adair v Shaw (1803) . . . 715
Adam and Co International Trustees Ltd v Theodore Goddard (a firm) (2000) . . . 676, 678
Adams, Re; Adams v Adams (1893) . . . 598
Adams and Kensington Vestry, Re (1884) CA . . . 117
Adams (Deceased), Re (1990) . . . 385
Adamson v Paddico (267) Ltd . . . *see* Paddico (267) Ltd v Kirklees Metropolitan Council
Adelaide Partnerships Ltd v Danison (2011) . . . 806, 807, 816, 824, 829
Adye v Feuilleteau (1783) . . . 731, 734
AEG Unit Trusts (Managers) Ltd Deed, Re; Midland Bank Executor and Trustee Co Ltd v AEG Unit Trust (Managers) Ltd (1957) . . . 53, 605
AG Securities v Vaughan (1990) HL . . . 278
Agip (Africa) Ltd v Jackson (1990); affd (1991) CA . . . 56, 750, 776, 804, 807, 816, 822, 839, 843–5, 853, 855, 857, 861, 871
Agnew v Belfast Banking Co (1896) CA . . . 161
Agricultural Credit Corpn of Saskatchewan v Pettyjohn (1991) CA . . . 875
AIB Group (UK) plc v Mark Redler & Co Solicitors (2013) CA; (2014) SC . . . 237, 714, 716, 727, 729, 731, 732
Airbus Operations Ltd v Withey (2014) QB . . . 750
Air Jamaica Ltd v Charlton (1999) PC . . . 201, 367
Airport Industrial GP Ltd v Heathrow Airport Ltd (2015) CH . . . 80
Aitken's Trustees v Aitken (1927) . . . 541
AK Investment CJSC v Kyrgyz Mobil Tel Ltd & Ors (Isle of Man) (Rev 1) (2011) . . . 78
Akers v Samba Financial Group (2017) . . . 17
Akita Holdings Ltd v Attorney General of The Turks and Caicos Islands (2017) PC . . . 775, 814, 815
Alexander v Alexander (2011) . . . 653
Alfa Finance Holdings AD v Quarzwerke GMBH (2015) . . . 83
Ali, Re (2012) (Admin) . . . 287
Ali v Dinc (2020) Ch . . . 205, 236
Ali v Khan (2002) CA . . . 205
Alireza v Radwan (2017) CA . . . 276
Alkin v Raymond (2010) . . . 683
Allan v Rea Brothers Trustees Ltd (2002) CA . . . 54
Allcard v Skinner (1887) CA . . . 71, 72, 74
Allen, Re; Faith v Allen (1953) CA . . . 137, 189
Allen v Distillers Co (Biochemicals) Ltd (1974) . . . 608
Allen v Jambo Holdings Ltd (1980) CA . . . 107
Allen v Rea Brothers Trustees Ltd (2002) . . . 735
Allen v Snyder (1977) NSWCA . . . 218, 260
Allen-Meyrick's Will Trusts, Re; Magnall v Allen-Meyrick (1966) . . . 562
Allfrey v Allfrey (2015) . . . 613
Alliance and Leicester Building Society v Edgestop Ltd (1994); affd on other grounds (1995) CA . . . 726
Allied Irish Banks Ltd v McWilliams (1982) . . . 218
Allnutt v Wilding (2007) CA . . . 76
Allsop, Re; Whittaker v Bamford (1914) CA . . . 739
Alternative Power Solution Ltd v Central Electricity Board (2014) PC . . . 98
Amalgamated Investment and Property Co Ltd (in liquidation) v Texas Commerce International Bank Ltd (1982) CA . . . 319
American Cyanamid Co v Ethicon Ltd (1975) HL . . . 95–100, 109
Ames' Settlement, Re; Dinwiddy v Ames (1946) . . . 225
Amin v Amin (2020) Ch . . . 284, 286–9
Amos (Deceased), Re (2020) Ch . . . 245
An Bord Bainne Co-operative Limited (Irish Dairy Board) v Milk Marketing Board (1984) . . . 90
Andrew's Trust, Re; Carter v Andrew (1905) . . . 227
Andrews v Andrews (2014) Ch . . . 75, 76
Anglo Financial v Goldberg (2014) Ch . . . 216
Anglo Swedish Society v IRC (1931) . . . 464
Anker-Petersen v Anker Petersen (1991) . . . 609, 652
Anson v Anson (1953) . . . 220
Anstis, Re; Chetwynd v Morgan (1886) CA . . . 559
Anthony v Donges (1998) . . . 123
Antoni v Antoni (2007) . . . 211, 216
Antrobus v Smith (1805) . . . 559
Application for Information about a Trust, Re (2013) . . . 710

Araci v Fallon (2011) . . . 98
Archer v Cutler (1980) . . . 73
Archibald v Alexander (2020) Ch . . . 171, 172, 286
Argyle (Duchess of) v Duke of Argyle (1967) . . . 24
Argyll v Argyll (1967) . . . 92
Arif v Anwar (2015) Fam . . . 277
Armitage, Re; Armitage v Garnett (1893) CA . . . 548
Armitage, Re; Ellam v Norwich Corpn (1972) . . . 668
Armitage v Nurse (1997) CA . . . 717–21, 784
ARMS (Multiple Sclerosis Research) Ltd, Re (1997) . . . 503
Armstrong v Reeves (1890) . . . 456
Armstrong v Sheppard & Short Ltd (1959) CA . . . 322
Armstrong DLW GmbH v Winnington Networks Ltd (2012) . . . 825, 832, 836, 838, 849, 873
Arnold, Re; Wainwright v Howlett (1947) . . . 42
Arnold v Britton (2015) CA . . . 73, 597
Aroso v Coutts (2002) . . . 203, 208, 209, 370
Arrow Nominees Inc v Blackledge (2000); revsd (2000) CA . . . 551
Arthur v Attorney General of the Turks and Caicos Islands (2012) PC . . . 722, 824, 826
Ashburn Anstalt v W J Arnold & Co (1989) CA . . . 78, 251
Ashburton (Lord) v Lady Ashburton (1801) . . . 606
Ashby, Re ex p Wreford (1892) . . . 50, 51
Ashton's Charity, Re (1856) . . . 608
Ashworth v Royal National Theatre (2014) . . . 78, 80
Aspden v Elvy (2012) . . . 281, 285, 292, 309
Associated Artists Ltd v IRC (1956) . . . 449
Associated British Ports v Tata Steel UK Ltd (2017) Ch . . . 115
Astbury v Astbury (1898) . . . 695
Aston Martin Lagonda Ltd v Automotive Industrial Partnership Ltd (2010) . . . 79
Astor's Settlement Trusts, Re; Astor v Scholfield (1952) . . . 51, 226, 538, 539, 543–5, 697
AstraZeneca AB v KRKA dd Novo Mesto (2015) CA . . . 99
Astro Exito Navegacion SA v Southland Enterprises Co Ltd (No 2) . . . 100
Attenborough (George) & Son v Solomon (1913) HL . . . 628
A-G v Alford (1855) . . . 733
A-G v Barton (1990) . . . 98
A-G v BBC (1981) CA; revsd (1981) HL . . . 100
A-G v Blake (2000) HL . . . 93, 94, 102, 747, 752, 753, 767, 768
A-G v Boultbee (1794); affd (1796) . . . 504
A-G v Brown (1818) . . . 512
A-G v Charity Commission for England and Wales (2012) . . . 474, 482, 483
A-G v Cocke (1988) . . . 786
A-G v Coopers' Co (1812) . . . 512
A-G v Dedham School (1857) . . . 512
A-G v Duke of Northumberland (1877); varied (1878) CA . . . 482
A-G v Earl of Lonsdale (1827) . . . 470
A-G v Governors of the Foundling Hospital (1793) . . . 512
A-G v Guardian Newspapers Ltd (1987); revsd (1987) CA; affd (1987) HL . . . 97
A-G v Guardian Newspapers Ltd (No. 2) . . . *see* A-G v Observer Ltd
A-G v Jacobs-Smith (1895) CA . . . 156
A-G v Leicester Corpn (1844) . . . 805
A-G v London Corpn (1790) . . . 496
A-G v Manchester Corpn (1893) . . . 101
A-G v Margaret and Regius Professors in Cambridge (1682) . . . 439
A-G v Middleton (1751) . . . 512
A-G v Nottingham Corpn (1904) . . . 101
A-G v Observer Ltd; A-G v Guardian Newspapers Ltd (No.2); A-G v Times Newspapers Ltd (No.2) (1988); on appeal (1988) CA; affd (1990) HL . . . 747, 767
A-G v Price (1810) . . . 482
A-G v Punch Ltd (2002) HL . . . 87, 89
A-G v Rathmines and Pembroke Joint Hospital Board (1904) . . . 101
A-G v Ross (1986) . . . 439, 489
A-G v St John's Hospital Bedford (1865) . . . 668
A-G v St Olave's Grammar School (1837) . . . 512
A-G v Sherborne Grammar Schools Governors (1854) . . . 507, 512
A-G v Smart (1748) . . . 512
A-G v Stephens (1834) . . . 669
A-G v Tancred (1757) . . . 439
A-G v Times Newspapers Ltd (1992) HL . . . 87
A-G v Vint (1850) Ch . . . 475
A-G v Wilson (1840) . . . 723
A-G v Wright (1988) . . . 99
A-G v Zedra Fiduciary Services Ltd (UK) (2020) Ch . . . 494
A-G for Hong Kong v Humphreys' Estate (Queen's Gardens) Ltd (1987) PC . . . 319, 326
A-G for Hong Kong v Reid (1994) PC . . . 747, 760, 776–80
A-G for New South Wales v Public Trustee (1987) NSWCA . . . 505
A-G for the Dominion of Canada v Ritchie Contracting and Supply Co Ltd (1919) PC . . . 101
A-G of Belize v Belize Telecom Ltd (2009) PC . . . 468
A-G of the Bahamas v Royal Trust Co (1986) PC . . . 469
A-G of the Cayman Islands v Wahr-Hansen (2001) PC . . . 458, 459, 469, 470
A-G of Zambia v Meer Care & Desai (2007) . . . 810, 811
A-G's Reference (No. 1 of 1985) (1986) CA . . . 696, 780, 851
Auden McKenzie (Pharma Division) Ltd v Patel (2019) CA . . . 774
Austerberry v Oldham Corp (1885) CA . . . 17
Avenon's Charity, Re (1913) (Ch) . . . 507
Avondale Printers & Stationers Ltd v Haggie (1979) . . . 260
Avonwick Holdings Ltd v Azitio Holdings Ltd (2020) . . . *see* Dargamo Holdings Ltd v Avonwick Holdings Ltd

B v B (1976) . . . 216
B v D (2014) CA . . . 79
Bacon, Re; Toovey v Turner (1907) . . . 676
Baden Delvaux and Lecuit v Société Générale pour Favoriser le Développement du Commerce et de l'Industrie en France SA (1983); affd (1985) CA . . . 804, 805, 807
Baden's Deed Trusts (No. 1), Re; sub nom McPhail v Doulton (1971) HL . . . 26, 35–43, 49, 115, 116, 127, 129–33, 135–7, 142, 564, 574, 576, 582–7, 591–3, 704, 820, 821, 825, 835
Baden's Deed Trusts (No. 2), Re (1972); affd (1973) CA . . . 126, 127, 129, 131, 132, 135–7, 583, 591
Bagshaw, Re; Westminster Bank Ltd v Taylor (1954) . . . 501
Bahin v Hughes (1886) CA . . . 741
Bahr v Nicolay (No. 2) (1988) . . . 252
Bailey & Anor v Angove's PTY Ltd (2016) SC . . . 231, 240, 257, 263
Baillie, Re; Fitzgerald v Noad (1886) . . . 418
Bainbridge v Bainbridge (2016) . . . 69, 70, 74, 859
Bainbrigge v Browne (1881) . . . 17
Baird v Wells (1890) CA . . . 104
Baird Textile Holdings Ltd v Marks & Spencer Plc (2001) CA . . . 325
Baker v Archer-Shee (1927) HL . . . 557
Baker v Baker (2008) . . . 371
Baker v J E Clark Co (Transport) UK Ltd (2006) CA . . . 721
Baldry v Feintuck (1972) . . . 463
Balfour's Settlement, Re; Public Trustee v Official Receiver (1938) . . . 51
Balkanbank v Taher (1994); on appeal (1994) CA . . . 99, 108
Ball v De Marzo (2019) . . . 290
Ball v Storie (1823) . . . 76
Ball's Settlement Trusts, Re (1968) . . . 613
Balmes Goods, Re (1897) . . . 384
Banco Exterior Internacional v Mann (1995) CA . . . 72
Banco Exterior Internacional SA v Thomas (1997) CA . . . 72
Bank of Credit and Commerce International (Overseas) Ltd v Akindele (2001) CA . . . 815, 817, 818, 820, 821, 823–5, 827
Bank of Credit and Commerce International SA v Aboody (1990) CA . . . 71
Bank of Cyprus UK Ltd v Menelaou (2016) CA . . . 200, 840
Bank of New Zealand v New Zealand Guardian Trust Co Ltd (1999) . . . 714, 729
Bank of Scotland v Brogan (2012) . . . 315
Bank of Scotland plc v Forrester (2014) Ch . . . 215
Bank Tejarat v Hong Kong and Shanghai Banking Corpn (CI) Ltd (1995) . . . 843–5, 848
Bankers Trust Co v Shapira (1980) CA . . . 857
Bankes v Salisbury Diocesan Council of Education Inc (1960) . . . 668
Banks v Goodfellow (1870) . . . 378, 380
Banner Homes Holdings Ltd (formerly Banner Homes Group Plc) v Luff Developments Ltd (2000) CA . . . 83, 252, 253, 254
Bannister v Bannister (1948) CA . . . 45, 172, 241, 251
Banque Belge pour l'Etranger v Hambrouck (1921) CA . . . 843, 846
Banque Financière de la Cité v Parc (Battersea) Ltd (1999) CA . . . 199, 222, 224
Barber, Re; Burgess v Vincome (1886) . . . 755
Barclays Bank Ltd v WJ Simms Son and Cooke (Southern) Ltd (1980) . . . 819, 859
Barclays Bank plc v O'Brien (1994) HL . . . 17, 19, 71, 72
Barclays Bank plc v Quistclose Investments Ltd (1970) HL . . . 56, 230–2, 234, 236
Baring's Settlement Trusts, Re; Barings Bros & Co Ltd v Liddell (1940) . . . 51
Barker v Baxendale Walker Solicitors (a firm) (2016) Ch . . . 593
Barker (George) (Transport) Ltd v Eynon (1974) CA . . . 27
Barlow v Grant (1684) . . . 227, 602
Barlow Clowes International Ltd v Eurotrust International Ltd (2006) PC . . . 806, 807, 809, 810, 822
Barlow Clowes International Ltd (in liquidation) v Vaughan (1992) CA . . . 866–8
Barlow's Will Trusts, Re (1979) . . . 126, 134, 135, 137, 189
Barnardo's v Buckinghamshire (2016) CA . . . 54, 597
Barnes v Addy (1874) . . . 799, 805
Barnes v Phillips (2015) CA . . . 285, 290, 292
Barnett v Cregg (2014) Ch . . . 788
Barney, Re; Barney v Barney (1892) . . . 802
Barnsley v Noble (2016) CA . . . 720, 759, 760
Barnstaple Boat Co Ltd v Jones (2007) CA . . . 786
Baron Vestey's Settlement, Re; sub nom Lloyds Bank Ltd v O'Meara (1951) CA . . . 597
Barralet v A-G (1980) . . . *see* South Place Ethical Society, Re
Barrett v Barrett (2008) . . . 207, 289, 299
Barrett v Bem (2012) CA . . . 381
Barrett v Hartley (1866) . . . 755
Bartlett v Barclays Bank Trust Co Ltd (Nos 1 & 2) (1980) . . . 639, 661, 696, 716, 717, 725, 731–3, 737, 739, 787
Basham (Deceased), Re (1987) . . . 319, 321, 328, 330, 332, 335
Bashir v Ali (2011) CA . . . 84
Basma v Weekes (1950) PC . . . 85
Bassett v Nosworthy (1673) . . . 156
Bateman v Davis (1818) . . . 725
Bateman's Will Trusts, Re; Brierley v Perry (1970) . . . 384, 405, 407
Bates, Re; Mountain v Bates (1928) . . . 549
Bates (Thomas) & Son Ltd v Wyndham's (Lingerie) Ltd (1981) CA . . . 76
Bathe, Re; Bathe v Public Trustee (1925) . . . 190
Bathurst (Deceased), Re; sub nom Bathurst v Chantler (2018) . . . 600
Bathurst v Bathurst (2016) Ch . . . 620
Bathurst (Countess) v Kleinwort Benson (Channel Islands) Trustees Ltd; sub nom Wesley v Kleinwort Benson (Channel Islands) Trustees Ltd (2004) RC (Guernsey) . . . 709

BCCI Ltd v Akindele . . . *see* Bank of Credit and Commerce International (Overseas) Ltd v Akindele
Beale v Kyte (1907) . . . 75, 77
Beale's Settlement Trusts, Re; Huggins v Beale (1932) . . . 609
Beaman v ARTS Ltd (1949) CA . . . 787
Beard, Re; Beard v Hall (1908) . . . 191, 192
Beard, Tr; Reversionary and General Securities Co Ltd v Hall (1908) . . . 604
Beatty v Guggenheim Exploration Co (1919) . . . 240
Beatty's Will Trust (No. 2), Re (1997) . . . 681, 683
Beauclerk v Ashburnham (1845) . . . 554
Beaumont, Re; Beaumont v Ewbank (1902) . . . 163
Beckett's Settlement, Re; Beckett (Deceased), Re; Eden v Von Stutterheim (1940) . . . 601, 605
Bective (Countess) v Hodgson (1864) HL . . . 598
Bedingfield, Re; Bedingfield v D'Eye (1887) . . . 755
Bedson v Bedson (1965) CA . . . 278
Behn v Burness (1863) Ex Ch . . . 70
Behnke v Bede Shipping Co Ltd (1927) . . . 78
Behrens v Richards (1905) . . . 90
Bellis v Challinor (2015) CA . . . 232–5
Bell's Indenture, Re; Bell v Hickley (1980) . . . 730
Belmont Finance Corpn Ltd v Williams Furniture Ltd (No. 2) (1980) CA . . . 733, 805, 815, 820
Benedetti v Sawiris (2013) . . . 199, 222, 254, 262, 814
Benjamin, Re; sub nom Neville v Benjamin (1902) . . . 133
Bennet v Bennet (1879) . . . 216, 217, 219
Bennett, Re; Gibson v A-G (1920) . . . 469
Bennett, Re; Sucker v A-G (1960) . . . 512
Bennett v Gas Light and Coke Co (1882) . . . 761
Bentley v Craven (1853) . . . 746
Bentley v Mackay (1851) . . . 155, 558
Bentley v Robinson (1859) . . . 742
Berg (E and L) Homes Ltd v Grey (1979) . . . 318
Bernal v Bernal (1838) . . . 482
Bernstein's Will Trusts, Re; National Westminster Bank Ltd v Board of Governors of United Liverpool Hospitals (1971) . . . 446
Berrisford v Mexfield Housing Co-Operative Ltd (2010) . . . 83
Berry v IBS-STL (2012) . . . 501
Best, Re; Jarvis v Birmingham Corpn (1904) . . . 469
Besterman's Will Trusts, Re (1980) . . . 440
Bestobell Paints Ltd v Bigg (1975) . . . 100
Beswick v Beswick (1968) HL . . . 78, 79, 157
Bevan v Webb (1905) . . . 762
Bhimji v Chatwani (1991) . . . 110
Bhimji v Salih (1981) CA . . . 328
Bhura v Bhura (2014) Fam . . . 215, 285
Bhushan v Chand (2015) Ch . . . 248, 249
Bieber v Teathers Ltd (2013) CA . . . 233–5
Bignold's Settlement Trusts, Re (1872) . . . 675
Billson v Crofts (1873) . . . 50
Binions v Evans (1972) CA . . . 240, 251, 258
Birch v Curtis (2002) . . . 392
Birch v Treasury Solicitor (1951) CA . . . 162, 163
Birdseye v Roythorne & Co (2015) Ch . . . 710
Birmingham v Renfrew (1937) AusHC . . . 391, 398, 399
Biscoe v Jackson (1887) CA . . . 504
Bishop, Re; National Provincial Bank Ltd v Bishop (1965) . . . 220
Bishop v Charity Commission (2015) . . . 464, 465
Bishop v Charity Commission (2016) . . . 464
Bishop Square Ltd v IRC (1999) CA . . . 180
Bishopsgate Investment Management Ltd (in liquidation) v Homan (1995) CA . . . 125, 869, 870, 871, 874
Bishopsgate Investment Management Ltd v Maxwell (No. 2) (1994) CA . . . 693, 718, 723, 725, 726
Biss, Re (1903) . . . 761
Bisset v Wilkinson (1927) PC . . . 70
Black v S Freedman & Co (1910) AusHC . . . 857
Blackwell v Blackwell (1929) HL . . . 401, 407, 411–3
Blair v Duncan (1902) HL . . . 469
Blathwayt v Baron Cawley (1976) HL . . . 190
Blausten v IRC (1972) CA . . . 579
Bloomsbury Publishing Group plc v News Group Newspapers (2003) . . . 87
Blue Albion Cattle Society, Re (1966) . . . 365
Blue Manchester Ltd v North West Ground Rents Ltd (2019) . . . 83
Blue Sky One Ltd v Blue Airways LLC (2009) . . . 209
Blue Town Investments Ltd v Higgs and Hill plc (1990) . . . 91
Blythe v Fladgate (1891) . . . 802
Boardman v Phipps (1964) Ch; (1967) HL . . . 695, 735, 754–6, 762, 764, 765, 767–73, 779, 780, 782
Bohm v Secretary of State for Communities and Local Government (2017) . . . 354
Bold v Hutchinson (1855) . . . 75
Boles and British Land Co's Contract, Re (1902) . . . 757, 758
Bolton v Curre (1895) . . . 743
Bonar Law Memorial Trust v IRC (1933) . . . 461
Bond v Walford (1886) . . . 226
Bonithon v Hockmore (1685) . . . 755
Bonnard v Perryman (1891) CA . . . 100
Booker McConnell plc v Plascow (1985) CA . . . 110
Booth v Booth (1838) . . . 742, 743
Borden (UK) Ltd v Scottish Timber Products Ltd (1981) CA . . . 842, 850
Borwick, Re; Borwick v Borwick (1933) . . . 190
Boscawen v Bajwa (1995) CA . . . 853, 862, 874, 875, 879
Bose Trusts, Re; Public Trustee v Butler (2012) . . . 132
Bouch v Sproule (1887) HL . . . 549
Boughton v Knight (1873) . . . 379
Boulter, Re; Capital and Counties Bank v Boulter (1922) . . . 190
Bourne v Keane (1919) HL . . . 541
Bourne v Lloyds TSB Bank plc (2015) CA . . . 159
Boustany v Piggott (1993) PC . . . 73
Bowden, Re; Hulbert v Bowden (1936) . . . 155
Bowes, Re; Earl Strathmore v Vane (1896) . . . 227, 359
Bowman v Secular Society Ltd (1917) HL . . . 442, 461, 462, 537–9, 697
Boyce v Boyce (1849) . . . 121, 123

Boyd v Ineos Upstream Ltd; sub nom. Ineos Upstream Ltd v Persons Unknown (2019) CA . . . 102
Boyes, Re; Boyes v Carritt (1884) . . . 225, 401, 405, 409
Boyle v Collins (2004) . . . 362
Boyse (International) Ltd v Natwest Markets Plc (2021) Ch . . . 787
BPE Solicitors v Gabriel . . . *see* Gabriel v Little
Brace v Duchess of Marlborough (1728) . . . 23
Bracewell v Appleby (1975) . . . 91
Bradbury v Taylor (2012) CA . . . 323
Braddon Towers Ltd v International Stores Ltd (1987) . . . 81
Bradshaw, Re; Bradshaw v Bradshaw (1902) . . . 566
Bradshaw v University College of Wales, Aberystwyth (1987) . . . 511, 512, 514
Brandt's (William) Sons & Co v Dunlop Rubber Co (1905) HL . . . 558
Brassey's Settlement, Re; Barclay's Bank Ltd v Brassey (1955) . . . 647
Bray v Ford (1896) HL . . . 754, 761, 769
Breadner v Granville-Grossman (2001) . . . 572, 576, 704, 715
Breakspear v Ackland (2008) . . . 705–10, 713
Breed's Will, Re (1875) . . . 602
Breen v Amalgamated Engineering Union (1971) . . . 104
Breitenfeld UK Ltd v Harrison (2015) Ch . . . 811, 812
Brickenden v London Loan & Savings Co (1934) PC . . . 728
Bridge Trustees Ltd v Noel Penny Turbines (2008) . . . 562, 575, 688, 704
Bridges v Bridges (1752) . . . 606
Bridge v Campbell Discount Co Ltd; sub nom Campbell Discount Co Ltd v Bridge (1962) HL . . . 267
Bridges v Kilburne (1792) . . . 317
Briggs v Gleeds (Head Office) (2014) Ch . . . 67, 672, 702
Brinks Ltd v Abu-Saleh (No. 3) (1995) . . . 776, 806
Brinks-MAT Ltd v Elcombe (1988) . . . 88
Brisbane City Council v A-G for Queensland (1979) PC . . . 455, 457
Bristol and West Building Society v May, May & Merrimans (a firm) (No. 1) (1996) . . . 727
Bristol and West Building Society v Mothew (t/a Stapley & Co) (1996) CA . . . 236, 722, 745, 751–3, 791
Bristol's Settled Estates, Re; Bristol v Jermyn (1964) . . . 610
British Airways Pension Trustees Ltd v British Airways plc (2001) . . . 553
British Airways Plc v Airways Pension Scheme Trustee Ltd (2017) Ch . . . 54, 597, 704
British Celanese Ltd v Montcrieff (1948) CA . . . 767
British Coal Corpn v British Coal Staff Superannuation Scheme Trustees Ltd (1995) . . . 652
British Columbia v National Bank of Canada (1994) . . . 869
British School of Egyptian Archaeology, Re; Murray v Public Trustee (1954) . . . 449
British Syphon Co v Homewood (1956) . . . 767
British Transport Commission v Gourley (1956) . . . 730
Broadland District Council v Brightwell (2010) CA . . . 87
Brockbank, Re; Ward v Bates (1948) . . . 32, 678, 700
Brogden, Re; Billing v Brogden (1888) CA . . . 716
Brook v Brook Bond (1963) . . . 554
Brook's Settlement, Re; Brook v Brook (1968) . . . 618
Brooks' Settlement Trusts, Re; sub nom Lloyds Bank Ltd v Tillard (1939) . . . 124, 536, 563, 568
Brooks v Brooks (1996) HL . . . 53, 610
Brooks v Muckleston (1909) . . . 790
Brooks v Richardson (1986) . . . 514
Brotherton v IRC (1978) CA . . . 599
Broughton v Broughton (1855) . . . 757
Brown, Re (1954) . . . 189
Brown v Burdett (1882) . . . 541
Brown v Dale (1878) . . . 365
Brown v Higgs (1800); affd (1803); on appeal (1813) HL . . . 35, 36, 42, 572, 583
Brown v Innovatorone (2012) . . . 234
Brown v IRC (1965) . . . 746
Brown v Litton (1711) . . . 756
Brown v Sansome (1825) . . . 733
Browne, Re; Ward v Lawler (1944) . . . 408
Browne v Whalley (1866) . . . 482
Browne's Policy, Re (1903) . . . 625
Brudenell-Bruce v Moore (2012) Ch . . . 760
Brudenell-Bruce v Moore (2014) Ch . . . 608, 682, 717, 729
Bryanston Finance Ltd v de Vries (No. 2) (1976) CA . . . 97
Buckinghamshire Constabulary Widows and Orphans Fund Friendly Society (No. 2), Re (1979) . . . 356, 360, 364, 365, 367
Budge v Gummow (1872) . . . 632
Bullard v Bullard (2017) Ch . . . 76, 77
Bulmer (HP) Ltd and Showerings Ltd v J Bollinger SA (1977) CA . . . 91
Bunn v BBC (1998) . . . 790
Bunn v Markham (1816) . . . 161
Bunter v Coke (1707) . . . 378
Burdick v Garrick (1870) . . . 785
Burgess v Wheate (1759) . . . 23
Burgess' Trusts, Re (1877) . . . 683
Burke, Re; Burke v Burke (1908) . . . 645
Burnden Holdings (UK) Limited v Fielding (2018) SC . . . 785, 792
Burney v Macdonald (1845) . . . 406
Burns v Burns (1984) CA . . . 207, 301, 311
Burns v Burns (2021) Ch . . . 812
Burrough v Philcox (1840) . . . 37, 42, 43, 570–2, 578, 583
Burroughs-Fowler, Re; Trustee of the Property of Burroughs-Fowler (a bankrupt) v Burroughs-Fowler (1916) . . . 50
Burrows and Burrows v Sharp (1991) CA . . . 338, 342

Burrows Investments Ltd v Ward Homes Ltd (2017) CA . . . 93
Bushnell, Re; Lloyds Bank Ltd v Murray (1975) . . . 462
Butler v Broadhead (1975) . . . 819
Butler v Butler (2006) . . . 14
Butlin-Sanders v Butlin (1985) . . . 73
Butlin's Settlement Trusts, Re; Butlin v Butlin (1976) . . . 629
Butts Park Ventures (Coventry) Ltd v Bryant Homes Central Ltd (2003) . . . 362
Byers v Samba Financial Group (2021) Ch . . . 817
Byron's Settlement, Re; Williams v Mitchell (1891) . . . 562

C, Re (a minor) (1991) CA . . . 89
C, Re (Children) (2016) . . . 104
C v C (Ancillary relief: Nuptial Settlement) (2005) CA . . . 610
C v S (1988); affd (1988) CA . . . 89, 104
Caborne, Re; Hodge and Nabarro v Smith (1943) . . . 189
Cadogan v Earl of Essex (1854) . . . 554
Caffoor (Trustees of the Adbul Caffoor Trust) v Income Tax Commissioner for Columbo (1961) PC . . . 481
Cain v Moon (1896) DC . . . 162
Callaway, Re; Callaway v Treasury Solicitor (1956) . . . 245
Calverly v Green (1948) AusHC . . . 218
Cambridge Nutrition Ltd v BBC (1990) . . . 95
Cambridgeshire Target Shooting Association (CTSA) v Charity Commission Appeal No CA\2015\0002 . . . 451, 479
Camdex International Ltd v Bank of Zambia (No. 2) (1997) CA . . . 107
Cameron v Murdoch (1983); affd (1986) PC . . . 332
Cameron (Deceased), Re . . . 217
Campania Colombiana de Seguros v Pacific Steam Navigation Co (1965) . . . 557
Campbell Discount Co Ltd v Bridge . . . *see* Bridge v Campbell Discount Co Ltd
Campbell v Griffin (2001) CA . . . 328
Campbell v Walker (1800) . . . 757, 759
Campden Charities, Re (1881) CA . . . 496
Canada Goose UK Retail Ltd v Persons Unknown (2020) CA . . . 102
Canadian Aero-Services v O'Malley (1973) CanSC . . . 750
Candy v Holyoake (2017) CA . . . 108
Cannon v Hartley (1949) . . . 82, 165
Capehorn v Harris (2015) . . . 276, 285
Carly v Farrelly (1975) . . . 260
Carl-Zeiss-Stiftung v Herbert Smith & Co (a firm) (No. 2) (1969) CA . . . 240, 821, 822
Carman v Bucci (2013) Ch . . . 235
Carne v Long (1860) . . . 355, 357
Carreras Rothmans Ltd v Freeman Mathews Treasure Ltd (In liquidation) (1985) . . . 231, 234, 236
Carr-Glyn v Frearsons (a firm) (1999) CA . . . 388, 637
Cartier v B Sky B (2016) . . . 104
Cartwright, Re; Avis v Newman (1889) . . . 102
Catchpole v Trustees of the Alitalia Airlines Pension Scheme (2010) . . . 325
Caterpillar Logistics Services (UK) Ltd v de Crean (2012) CA . . . 101
Catholic Care (Diocese of Leeds) v Charity Commission for England and Wales (2010) . . . 486
Catholic Care (Diocese of Leeds) v Charity Commission for England and Wales (2012) . . . 486
Cave v Robinson Jarvis & Rolf (2003) . . . 787
Cavendish v Mercer (1776) . . . 607
Cavendish Browne's Settlement Trusts, Re; Horner v Rawle (1916) . . . 167
Cawdron v Merchant Taylors' School (2009) . . . 437, 483
Cayne v Global Natural Resources plc (1984) CA . . . 97, 98
CBS United Kingdom Ltd v Lambert (1983) CA . . . 107
CD (A Child) v O (2004) . . . 616
Cedar Holdings Ltd v Green (1981) CA . . . 85
Chadwick v Collinson (2014) Ch . . . 245, 247
Chagos Islanders v A-G (2004) . . . 73, 792
Chaine-Nickson v Bank of Ireland (1976) . . . 710
Challinor v Juliet Bellis & Co (2011) . . . 233
Challinor v Juliet Bellis & Co (2013) . . . 233, 234, 236
Challinor v Juliet Bellis & Co (2015) CA . . . 235
Chambers ex p (1829) . . . 599
Chan Yuen Lan v See Fong Mun (2014) . . . 280
Chaplin (Deceased), Re (1950) Ch . . . 374
Chapman, Re; Cocks v Chapman (1896) CA . . . 661, 716
Chapman, Re; Freeman v Parker (1894) CA . . . 755
Chapman v Browne (1902) CA . . . 662
Chapman v Chapman . . . *see* Chapman's Settlement Trusts
Chapman v Gibson (1791) . . . 565
Chapman's Settlement Trusts, Re; Chapman v Chapman (1953) CA; affd sub nom Chapman v Chapman (1954) HL . . . 261, 606–9, 611, 616, 630
Chappell v Davidson (1856) . . . 99
Chappell v Times Newspapers (1975) CA . . . 24, 92
Charalambous v Charalambous (2004) CA . . . 611
Chardon, Re; Johnston v Davies (1928) . . . 605
Charitable Corpn v Sutton (1742) . . . 715, 716
Charity Commission v Framjee (2015) . . . 868
Charity Commission Poverty Reference case . . . *see* A-G v Charity Commission for England and Wales (2012)
Charles v Fraser (2010) . . . 392, 394
Charter plc v City Index Ltd (2008) CA . . . 742
Chase Manhattan Bank NA v Israel-British Bank (London) Ltd (1981) . . . 56, 67, 752, 839, 853, 854, 859
Chattock v Muller (1878) . . . 254
Chaudhary v Chaudhary (2013) CA . . . 219
Chaudhary v Yavuz (2011) . . . 251, 252

Chaudhry v Prabhakar (1988) CA . . . 62
Cheese v Lovejoy (1877) . . . 388
Cheese v Thomas (1994) CA . . . 71, 74
Cheltenham & Gloucester plc v Appleyard (2004) CA . . . 222
Cherry v Mott (1836) . . . 504
Chesterfield (Earl) Trusts, Re (1883) . . . 548
Chettiar v Chettiar (1962) PC . . . 221
Chetwynd's Settlement, Re; Scarisbrick v Nevinson (1902) . . . 688
Chichester Diocesan Fund and Board of Finance Inc v Simpson; Wintle v Diplock; sub nom Diplock, Re; (1941) CA; affd (1944) HL . . . 226, 469, 470, 539
Chichester (Lord) v Coventry (1867) . . . 25
Children's Investment Fund Foundation (UK) v A-G; sub nom Lehtimäki v Cooper (2017) Ch; (2020) SC . . . 562, 575, 576, 747
Chillingworth v Chambers (1896) CA . . . 734, 742, 743
Chinn v Collins (Inspector of Taxes) (1981) HL . . . 180, 181
Choithram (T) International SA v Pagarani (2001) PC (BVI) . . . 123, 144, 146, 154, 159
Chong v Alexander (2016) Ch . . . 253
Chrimes, Re; Locovich v Chrimes (1917) . . . 558
Christie Miller's Marriage Settlement Trusts, Re; Westminster Bank Ltd v Christie-Miller (1961) . . . 580, 614
Christ's College Cambridge Case; . . . *see* A-G v Tancred
Church of the New Faith v Commissioner of Pay-Roll Tax (1983) AusHC . . . 443
Churchill, Re; Hiscock v Lodder (1909) . . . 598
Churchill v Churchill (1867) . . . 566
Cia De Seguros Imperio v Heath (REBX) Ltd (2001) CA . . . 791
CIBC Mortgages plc v Pitt (1994) HL . . . 71, 72
Cigna Life Insurance New Zealand Ltd v Westpac Securities Ltd (1996) . . . 807
City Index Ltd v Gawler (2008) CA . . . 741, 824
Clapham (Deceased), Re; Barraclough v Mell (2005) . . . 720, 721, 737
Clarence House Ltd v National Westminster Bank Plc (2009) . . . 83, 552
Clark v Taylor (1853) . . . 504
Clarke, Re; Bracey v Royal National Lifeboat Institution (1923) . . . 437
Clarke, Re; Clarke v Clarke (1901) . . . 355
Clarke v Allen . . . *see* Clarke (Deceased), Re
Clarke v Corless (2009) . . . 308, 321
Clarke (Deceased), Re; Clarke v Allen (2019) . . . 70
Clarke v Dickson (1858) . . . 74
Clarke v Earl of Dunraven and Mount-Earl (The Satanita) (1897) HL . . . 357
Clarke v Harlowe (2005) . . . 278
Clarke v Heathfield (No. 2) (1985) . . . 688
Clarke v Lord Ormonde (1821) . . . 707
Clarke v Meadus (2010) . . . 240, 262, 279
Clarke v Ramuz (1891) CA . . . 250
Clarke v Royal Panopticon of Science and Art (1857) . . . 632
Clarke v Swaile (1762) . . . 760
Clarke v Turner (1694) . . . 37, 585, 593
Clarke Investments Ltd v Pacific Technologies (2013) . . . 82
Clarkson v Clarkson (1994) CA . . . 43
Clasper Group Services Ltd, Re (1989) . . . 827
Clavering v Ellison (1859) . . . 188
Clay v Pennington (1837) . . . 602
Clayton v Clayton [2016] 1 NZLR 551 . . . 120
Clayton v Ramsden (1943) HL . . . 189, 190
Clayton's case; . . . *see* Devaynes v Noble
Cleare v Cleare (1869) . . . 382
Cleaver, Re; Cleaver v Insley (1981) . . . 390, 391, 393–5, 397, 418
Cleaver v Mutual Reserve Fund Live Association (1892) CA . . . 242
Clegg v The Estate & Personal Representatives of Andrew Gregory Pache (2017) CA . . . 815
Clements, Re; Clements v Pearsall (1894) . . . 598
Clergy Society, Re (1856) . . . 505
Clissold's Settlement, Re (1864) . . . 683
Clitheroe (Deceased), Re (2021) Ch . . . 379
Clitheroe's Settlement Trust, Re (1959) . . . 614
Clore's Settlement Trusts, Re; Sainer v Clore (1966) . . . 602
Close Invoice Company Ltd v Abowa (2010) . . . 217
Clough v Bond (1838) . . . 715, 716, 726
Cloutte v Storey (1911) CA . . . 568, 700, 702
Clutterbuck v Al Amoudi (2014) . . . 551, 552
Clutton ex p (1853) . . . 683
Clydesdale Bank Plc v Stoke Place Hotel Ltd (2017) Ch . . . 815, 828
Coake, Re; Winckley v Winterton (1922) . . . 81
Coates (Deceased), Re; Ramsden v Coates (1955) . . . 130, 137
Coates to Parsons, Re (1886) . . . 677
Cobbetts LLP v Hodge (2009) . . . 746
Cobra Golf Inc v Rata (No 2) (1998) . . . 111
Coca-Cola Co v Gilbey (1995) . . . 110
Cochrane, Re; Shaw v Cochrane (1955) . . . 226
Cockburn's Will Trust, Re; Cockburn v Lewis (1957) . . . 674
Cockerell's Settlement Trusts, Re; Cockerell v National Provincial Bank Ltd (1956) . . . 609
Cockerill, Re; Mackaness v Percival (1929) . . . 189
Cohen, Re; Brookes v Cohen (1911) . . . 566
Cohen v Roche (1927) . . . 78
Coldunell Ltd v Gallon (1986) CA . . . 74
Cole (A Bankrupt), Re (1964) CA . . . 162
Coleman, Re; Henry v Strong (1888) CA . . . 51
Coleman, Re; Public Trustee v Coleman (1936) . . . 585
Coles v Trecothick (1804) . . . 760
Collard's Will Trusts, Re (1961) . . . 600
Collier v Collier (2003) . . . 213
Collier v M'Bean (1865) . . . 715
Collins, Re; Collins v Collins (1886) . . . 607
Collins v Brebner (2000) . . . 728, 729
Collins v Collins (2016) Ch . . . 616
Collyer v Isaacs (1881) CA . . . 558
Columbia Picture Industries Ltd v Robinson (1986) . . . 109, 110

Combe, Re; Combe v Combe (1925) . . . 571
Combs, Re (1884) . . . 680
Comiskey v Bowring-Hanbury (1905) HL . . . 118
Commercial Bank of Australia Ltd v Amadio (1983) AusHC . . . 73
Commerzbank Aktiengesellschaft v IMB Morgan plc (2004) . . . 857, 868
Competitive Insurance Co Ltd v Davies Investments Ltd (1975) . . . 821
Compton, Re; Powell v Compton (1945) CA . . . 481, 482, 485
Conservative and Unionist Central Office v Burrell (Inspector of Taxes) (1980) Ch; (1982) CA . . . 63, 233, 358, 360, 361
Constable, Re [1971] VR 742 . . . 429
Construction Industry Training Board v A-G (1971) Ch; (1973) CA . . . 439, 457
Consul Development Pty Ltd v DPC Estates Pty Ltd (1975) AusHC . . . 777
Conway v Fenton (1888) . . . 606
Conway v Ratiu (2006) CAS . . . 746, 747
Conybeare's Settlement ex p (1853) . . . 683
Coode, Re; Coode v Foster (1913) . . . 683
Cook v Deeks (1916) PC . . . 764
Cook v Thomas (2010) CA . . . 262, 321, 335
Cook (Inspector of Taxes) v Medway Housing Society (1997) . . . 647, 649
Cooke, Re; Winckley v Winterton (1922) . . . 566
Cooke v Head (No. 1) (1972) CA . . . 258
Cooke v Henry (1932) . . . 382
Cook's Settlement Trusts, Re; Royal Exchange Assurance v Cook (1965) . . . 156, 157, 166, 167, 168, 169, 559
Coombes v Smith (1986) . . . 326, 327, 331
Cooper, Re; Le Neve-Foster v National Provincial Bank Ltd (1939) CA . . . 405, 409
Cooper v Fanmailuk.Com Ltd (2009) CA . . . 197
Co-operative Insurance Society Ltd v Argyll Stores (Holdings) Ltd (1996) CA: revsd (1997) HL . . . 25, 78, 80–3, 85
Cooper's Conveyance Trusts, Re; Crowdson v Bagot (1956) . . . 499
Corbett v Corbett (1888) CA . . . 189
Cornish, Re ex p Board of Trade (1896) CA . . . 785
Corsellis, Re; Lawton v Elwes (1887) CA . . . 757
Costa & Duppe Properties Ltd v Duppe (1986) . . . 52
Costa Rica Railway Co v Forwood (1901) CA . . . 761
Costello v Costello (1994) CA . . . 334
Cotching v Bassett (1862) . . . 329
Cotton v Brudenell-Bruce, Earl of Cardigan (2014) CA . . . 734
Coulthard v Disco Mix Club Ltd (2000) . . . 786
Coulthurst, Re; Coutts & Co v Coulthurst (1951) CA . . . 437
Courage Group's Pension Schemes, Re; Ryan v Imperial Brewing and Leisure Ltd (1987) . . . 579
Courtauld's Settlement, Re; Courtauld v Farrer (1965) . . . 580
Courtwood Holdings SA v Woodley Properties Ltd (2016) Ch . . . 751
Cousins v Sun Life Assurance Society (1933) CA . . . 625
Coventry (t/a RDC Promotions) v Lawrence; sub nom. Coventry v Lawrence; Lawrence v Coventry (t/a RDC Promotions); Lawrence v Fen Tigers Ltd (2014) SC . . . 92, 93, 102
Cowan v Foreman (2019) . . . 3
Cowan v Scargill (1985) . . . 54, 642, 643, 658–60, 664
Cowan de Groot Properties Ltd v Eagle Trust plc (1992) . . . 746, 807, 821, 822
Cowcher v Cowcher (1972) . . . 22, 170, 259, 299, 340
Cox v Jones (2004) . . . 303, 313
Coxen, Re; McCallum v Coxen (1948) . . . 489, 490
Cozens, Re; Green v Brisley (1913) . . . 143
CPOD SA v de Holanda Jr (2020) Ch . . . 832
CPS v Piper (2011) . . . 292
Crabb v Arun District Council (1976) CA . . . 318, 334, 338, 339
Cradock v Piper (1850) . . . 757
Cradock v Witham (1895) . . . 676
Crane v Hegeman-Harris Co Inc (1939); on appeal (1939) CA . . . 75, 77
Cranston, Re; Webb v Oldfield (1898) . . . 478
Craven's Estate (No. 1), Re; Lloyds Bank v Cockburn (1937) . . . 160, 610
Crawshay (Deceased) (No. 2); Hore-Ruthven v Public Trustee (1948) CA . . . 569
Credit Agricole Corporation and Investment Bank v Papadimitriou PC (2015) . . . 21, 826, 836, 845, 861, 870, 874
Crédit Lyonnais Bank Nederland NV v Burch (1997) CA . . . 72, 73
Cream Holdings Ltd v Banerjee (2004) HL . . . 99
Creggy v Barnett (2016) CA . . . 792
Cresswell v Potter (1978) . . . 73
Crick v Crick (2015) CA . . . 682
Crippen's Estate, Re (1911) . . . 246
Criterion Properties plc v Stratford UK Properties LLC (2004) HL . . . 815, 825, 827
Crockett v Crockett (1848); revsd (1848) . . . 36, 583
Crockfords case . . . *see* Ivey v Genting Casinos (UK) Ltd (t/a Crockfords)
Croker v Marquis of Hertford (1844) . . . 384
Crosby v Church (1841) . . . 735
Cross v Cross (1983) . . . 85
Crossco No. 4 Unlimited & Ors v Jolan Limited and Ors (2011) CA . . . 253, 275
Crowden v QBE Insurance (Europe) Ltd (2017) Comm . . . 658
Crown Dilmun plc v Sutton (2004) . . . 768
Croxon, Re; Croxton v Ferrers (1904) . . . 191
Crystal Palace Trustees v Minister of Town and Country Planning, Re (1951) . . . 457
CTB v News Group Newspapers (2011) . . . 105
Cuddon v Tite (1858) . . . 250
Cullen v A-G for Ireland (1866) . . . 413
Cumberland Consolidated Holdings Ltd v Ireland (1946) CA . . . 250
Cunnack v Edwards (1896) CA . . . 363
Cunningham v Ellis (2018) . . . 786
Curley v Parkes (2004) CA . . . 207, 300, 301, 310
Curnick v Tucker (1874) . . . 117

Curnock v Inland Revenue Commissioners (2003) SC . . . 147
Curran v Collins (2015) CA . . . 290, 291
Curtis, Re; Hawes v Curtis (1885) . . . 218
Curtis v Pullbrook (2011) . . . 151, 152
Customs and Excise Commissioners v Bell Concord Educational Trust Ltd (1990) CA . . . 439
CVB v MGN Ltd (2012) . . . 105

D&D Wines International Ltd (In Liquidation); Angove Pty Ltd v Bailey (2016) SC . . . 779
Dadourian Group International Inc v Simms (No 2) (2006) CA . . . 106
Dadourian Group International Inc v Simms (Damages) (2009) CA . . . 106
Dale v IRC (1954) HL . . . 755
Dale (Deceased), Re; Proctor v Dale (1993) . . . 389–92, 398
Dalkilic v Pekin (2021) Ch . . . 785, 791
Dalriada Trustees v Faulds (2012) . . . 568, 647, 702
Daltel Europe Ltd v Makki (2006) CA . . . 108
Dalton v Latham (2003) . . . 245
d'Altroy's Will Trusts, Re; Crane v Lowman (1968) . . . 225
Daly v Sydney Stock Exchange (1986) . . . 858
Dance v Goldingham (1872-73) . . . 103, 715
D'Angibau, Re; Andrews v Andrews (1880); affd (1880) CA . . . 156, 559
Daniel v Tee (2016) Ch . . . 639, 657–9, 665, 703, 716, 802
Danish Bacon Co Ltd Staff Pension Fund Trusts, Re; Christensen v Arnett (1971) . . . 175, 177
Darashah v UFAC (UK) Ltd (1982) CA . . . 107
Daraydan Holdings Ltd v Solland International Ltd (2005) . . . 781
Darbey v Whitaker (1857) . . . 81, 823
Dargamo Holdings Ltd v Avonwick Holdings Ltd; Avonwick Holdings Ltd v Azitio Holdings Ltd (2021) . . . 70
Darlow v Sparks (1938) . . . 163
Davenport v The City of Westminster (2011) CA . . . 105
Davey v Bailey (2021) (Ch) . . . 160, 161, 163
David, Re; Buckley v Royal National Lifeboat Institution (1889) CA . . . 446
Davidson v Seelig (2016) Ch . . . 708
Davies v Davies (2016) CA . . . 319, 334, 336, 338, 340–3
Davies v HMRC (2009) . . . 404
Davis, Re; Hannen v Hillyer (1902) . . . 429, 505, 733
Davis (As Trustee in Bankruptcy of Jackson) v Jackson (2017) Ch . . . 224, 279
Davis v Hutchings (1907) . . . 739
Davis v Richards and Wallington Industries Ltd (1991) . . . 228, 366
Davisons Solicitors (a firm) v Nationwide Building Society . . . *see* Nationwide Building Society v Davisons Solicitors
Dawson, Re; Union Fidelity Trustee Co Ltd v Perpetual Trustees Co Ltd (1966) . . . 725, 726
Dawson-Damer v Taylor Wessing LLP (2017) CA . . . 706, 711
Day v Brownrigg (1878) CA . . . 89
Day v Day (2013) . . . 76
Day v Harris (2013) CA . . . 158
DC v AC (2016) Ch . . . 613
De Bruyne v De Bruyne (2010) CA . . . 563
De Bussche v Alt (1878) CA . . . 746
De Falco v Crawley Borough Council (1980) CA . . . 99, 100
De Francesco v Barnum (1890) . . . 80
De Mestre v West (1891) PC . . . 156
De Visme, Re (1863) . . . 217
Dean, Re Cooper-Dean v Stevens (1889) . . . 539, 540, 543
Decro-Wall International SA v Practitioners in Marketing Ltd (1971) CA . . . 79
Delamere's Settlement Trusts, Re; Kenny v Cunningham-Reid (1984) CA . . . 599
Delius (Deceased), Re; Emanuel v Rosen (1957) . . . 51, 449
Delta Petroluem (Caribbean) Ltd v British Virgin Islands Electricity Corp (2020) . . . 79
Den Norske Bank ASA v Antonatos (1998) CA . . . 111
Denby (William) & Sons Ltd Sick and Benevolent Fund (1971) . . . 361, 362
Dening v Ware (1856) . . . 156
Denley's Trust Deed, Re; Holman v HM Martyn & Co Ltd (1969) . . . 355, 359, 542, 543
Denne v Light (1857) . . . 85
Dennis v North Western National Bank (1957) . . . 201
Denny v Jensen (1977) . . . 338
Densham (A bankrupt), Re; ex p Trustee of Bankruptcy v Densham (1975) . . . 172, 438
Dent v Bennett (1839) . . . 72
Dent v Dent (1996) . . . 67
Der Merwe v Goldman & Ors (2016) . . . 68, 69
Derby & Co Ltd v Weldon (1990) CA . . . 106
Derby & Co Ltd v Weldon (Nos. 3 and 4) (1990) CA . . . 107
Dering v Earl of Winchelsea (1787) . . . 24
Derry v Peek (1889) HL . . . 70
Design & Display Ltd v Abbott (2016) CA . . . 222
Deslauriers v Guardian Asset Management Ltd (2017) PC (Trinidad and Tobago) . . . 142, 151, 152, 155
Deutsche Morgan Grenfell Group v IRC (2006) HL . . . 879
Devaynes v Noble (Clayton's case) (1816) . . . 866–8
D'Eye (Thomas v Mariner Properties Ltd), Re (2017) . . . 872
DHN Food Distributors Ltd v Tower Hamlets LBC (1976) CA . . . 180
Diageo North America Inc v Intercontinental Brands (ICB) Ltd (2010) CA . . . 104
Dick, Re; Knight v Dick (1953) CA . . . 569
Diggles, Re; Gregory v Edmondson (1888) CA . . . 117
Digital Equipment Corpn v Darkcrest (1984) . . . 99

Dillon, Re; Duffin v Duffin (1890) CA . . . 163
Dillwyn v Llewelyn (1862) . . . 317, 332, 337, 338
Dimes v Scott (1828) . . . 731, 732, 733
Dingle v Turner (1972) HL . . . 428, 431, 482–5
Diplock's Estate . . . *see* Ministry of Health v Simpson (1951) HL
Diplock, Re . . . *see* Chichester Diocesan Fund and Board of Finance Inc v Simpson
Dive, Re; Dive v Roebuck (1909) . . . 662, 738
Diwell v Farnes (1959) CA . . . 218
Dix v Burford (1854) . . . 716
Dobson v Griffey (2018) . . . 286, 287
Dodds v Walker (1981) HL . . . 784
Dodsworth v Dodsworth (1973) CA . . . 334, 335, 337
Doherty v Allman (or Allen) (1878) HL . . . 90, 102
Doleman & Sons v Ossett Corpn (1912) CA . . . 81
Dominica Social Security Board v Nature Island Investment Co (2008) . . . 647
Dominion Students Hall Trust, Re; Dominion Student Hall Trust v A-G (1966) . . . 496
Donaldson v Donaldson (1854) . . . 156
Donohue v Armco Inc (2001) Hl . . . 103
Doohan v Nelson (1973) . . . 218
Douglas, Re; Obert v Barrow (1887) CA . . . 456
Douglas v Andrews (1849) . . . 599
Douglas v Hello! Ltd (2001) . . . 99
Douglas v Hello! Ltd (No. 3) (2008) HL . . . 768
Dover v Buck (1865) . . . 760
Dover Coalfield Extension Ltd, Re (1907); affd (1908) CA . . . 763
Downshire Settled Estates, Re; Marquis of Downshire v Royal Bank of Scotland (1953) CA . . . 607, 609, 610
Drake v Whipp (1996) CA . . . 202, 207, 301, 303, 308
Drakeford v Cotton (2012) . . . 209
Dream Property Sdn Bhd v Atlas Housing Sdn Bhd (2015) . . . 254
Dreger Estate, Re (1994) . . . 217
Drew v Nunn (1879) CA . . . 63
Drewe's Settlement Trusts, Re (1876) . . . 683
Dreyfus (Camille and Henry) Foundation Inc v IRC (1954) CA; affd (1956) HL . . . 460
Driver v Yorke (2003) . . . 310
Druiff v Lord Parker (1868) . . . 75
Drummond, Re; Ashworth v Drummond (1914) . . . 355, 482
Dubai Aluminium Co Ltd v Salaam (2003) . . . 742, 801
Dublin Corpn v Building and Allied Trade Union (1996) Irish SC . . . 852
Duddy v Gresham (1878) . . . 190
Dudman, Re; Dudman v Dudman (1925) . . . 161
Dufficy v Mollica (1968) . . . 163
Duffield v Elwes (1823); on appeal (1827) HL . . . 163
Duffy, Re (2013) . . . 479, 484
Dufour v Pereira (1769) . . . 390, 391, 393, 686
Dugdale, Re; Dugdale v Dugdale (1888) . . . 189
Duggan v Governor of Full Sutton Prison (2003) . . . 120
Duggan v Kelly (1848) . . . 191
Dukeries Healthcare Ltd v Bay Trust International Ltd (2021) Ch . . . 702
Dullow v Dullow (1985) . . . 217
Dunbar v Plant (1997) CA . . . 244–7
Dundee General Hospital Board of Management v Walker (1952) . . . 701, 703, 704
Dunne v Mahon (2012) . . . 361, 364
Dupree's Deed Trusts, Re; Daley v Lloyds Bank (1945) . . . 450
Durant v Heritage and Hamilton (1994) . . . 332
Durham Bros v Robertson (1898) CA . . . 557
Durham Tees Valley Airport Ltd v BMI Baby Ltd (2010) CA . . . 83
Dury v Dury (1675) . . . 218
DWS (Deceased), Re (2001) CA . . . 242, 248
Dyer v Dyer (1788) . . . 202
Dyson v Lum (1866) . . . 759
Dyson Technology Ltd v Curtis (2010) . . . 863
Dyson Technology Ltd v Pellerey (2016) CA . . . 89

E v E (Financial Provision) (1990) . . . 610
Eades, Re (1920) . . . 469
Eagle Trust plc v SBC Securities Ltd (1992) . . . 807, 821, 822, 826
Earl v Hector Whaling Ltd (1961) CA . . . 75
Earl of Oxford's Case (1615) . . . 5
East, Re (1873) . . . 675
Eastern Capital Futures Ltd (In liquidation), Re (1989) . . . 867
Eaves v Hickson (1861) . . . 805
Eclairs Group Ltd v JKX Oil & Gas plc (2014) . . . 553
Ecobank Transnational Incorporated v Tanoh (2015) CA . . . 103
Ecology Support Services Ltd v Hellard (2017) Ch . . . 824, 828
Edge v Pensions Ombudsman (2000) CA . . . 546, 547, 560, 568, 704, 705, 715
Edgerton v Edgerton (2012) CA . . . 88
Edgington v Fitzmaurice (1885) CA . . . 70
Edward, Duke of Somerset v Fitzgerald (2019) Ch . . . 610
Edwards v Chesterfield Royal Hospital NHS Foundation Trust (2011) SC . . . 103
Edwards v Edwards (2007) . . . 71
Edwards v Jones (1835) . . . 559
Edwards v Society of Graphical and Allied Trades (1971); varied (1971) CA . . . 104
Egmont (Earl) v Smith (1877) . . . 250
El Ajou v Dollar Land Holdings plc (No. 1) (1993); revsd (1994) CA . . . 815–7, 820, 821, 828, 836, 838, 843, 856, 858
Eleftheriou v Costi (2013) . . . 234, 236
Elektromotive Group Ltd v Pan (2012) . . . 106, 107
Ellenborough, Re; sub nom Towry Law v Burne (1903) . . . 124
Elliott v Davenport (1705) . . . 386
Elliott v Hattens Solicitors (2021) CA . . . 783
Emery's Investments Trusts, Re; Emery v Emery (1959) . . . 221

EMI Ltd v Kishorilal Pandit (1975) . . . 109
Endacott, Re; Corpe v Endacott (1960) CA . . . 354, 449, 539, 541, 544, 545
Engelbach's Estate, Re; Tibbetts v Engelbach (1924) . . . 625
Engelwood Properties v Patel (2005) . . . 250
England, In the Matter of the Estate of Mary, Re (1830) . . . 602
Englewood Properties v Patel (2005) . . . 716
English v Dedham Vale Properties Ltd (1978) . . . 802
English Bridge Union Ltd v Revenue and Customs Commissioners (2015) TCC . . . 451
Enniskillen Trust, Re (2013) . . . 362
Environment Agency v Biffa Waste Services (2006) . . . 89
Equitable Live Assurance Society of US Policy and Mitchell, Re (1911) . . . 626
Erlam v Rahman (2016) Ch . . . 281
Erlanger v New Sombrero Phosphate Co (1878) HL . . . 790
Ernest v Vivian (1863) . . . 17
Errat v Barlow (1807) . . . 607
Errington v Errington and Woods (1882) . . . 9
Erskine 1948 Trust, Re (2012) . . . 124, 191
Erskine's Settlement Trusts, Re; Hollis v Piggot (1971) . . . 596
Essery v Cowlard (1884) . . . 226
Estate of Bravda (1968) . . . 383
Estate of Park, In the (1954) . . . 379
Estate of Walker, In the (1912) . . . 379
Esteem Settlement, Re (2004) . . . 119
Esterhuizen v Allied Dunbar Assurance Plc (1998) . . . 388
Evangelou v McNicol (2016) CA . . . 357
Evans (Deceased), Re; Evans v Westcombe (1999) . . . 733, 739, 740
Evans v Lloyd (2013) . . . 73
Evans v London Cooperative Society (1976) . . . 716
Evans Marshall & Co v Bertola SA (1973) CA . . . 79
Evening Standard Co Ltd v Henderson (1987) CA . . . 103
Evered, Re; Molineux v Evered (1910) CA . . . 565
Eves v Eves (1975) CA . . . 258, 259, 307, 311, 315, 326, 347
EVTR Ltd, Re; Gilbert v Barber (1987) CA . . . 231, 234, 236
Ewing v Orr Ewing (1883) HL . . . 25
Exler (Deceased), Re (2017) . . . 164
Experience Hendrix LLC v PPX Enterprises Inc (2003) . . . 102
Eykyn's Trusts, Re (1877) . . . 216, 217
Eynsham Cricket Club v HMRC (2017) TC . . . 451
Eyre, Re; Johnson v Williams (1883) . . . 579
Eyre, Re; Johnson v Williams (1917) . . . 598

Factortame Ltd v Secretary of State for Transport (No. 2); . . . *see* R v Secretary of State for Transport ex p Factorame Ltd No. 2
Falcke v Gray (1859) . . . 78
Faraker, Re; Faraker v Durell (1912) CA . . . 187, 487, 501, 502, 507
Farley v Westminster Bank (1939) HL . . . 444
Farmer v Dean (1863) . . . 759
Farrant v Blanchford (1863) . . . 736
Farrars v Farrars Ltd (1888) CA . . . 746
Farrar v Miller (2018) CA . . . 253
Fattal v Walbrook Trustees (Jersey) Ltd (2010) . . . 719, 720
Favor Easy Management Ltd v Wu (2012) CA . . . 282
Federal Republic of Brazil v Durant International Corporation (2015) PC . . . 778, 832, 861, 871, 872
Feeny and Shannon v MacManus (1937) . . . 365
Feldman (David) Charitable Foundation, Re (1987) . . . 657
Fellowes & Son v Fisher (1976) CA . . . 95, 98
Fenwick v Greenwell (1847) . . . 716
Ffinch v Combe (1894) . . . 385
FHR European Ventures LLP v Cedar Capital Partners LLC (2014) SC . . . 60, 239, 263, 760, 761, 773, 777–80, 782, 804, 856
FHR European Ventures LLP v Mankarious (2011) Ch; (2013) CA; (2014) SC . . . 241, 744, 746
FHR European Ventures LLP v Mankarious (2016) Ch . . . 301, 744, 778, 779, 781, 827, 829
Fielden v Christie-Miller (2015) CH . . . 325, 681
Figgis, Re; Roberts v MacLaren (1969) . . . 220
FII Group Test Claimants v HMRC . . . *see* Test Claimants in the Franked Investment Income Group Litigation v Revenue and Customs Commissioners
Filshie, Re [1939] NZLR 91 . . . 187
Financial Services Authority (FSA) v Sinaloa Gold plc (2013) SC . . . 108
Fine Lady upon a White Horse Appeal's Application for Registration as a Charity, Re (2003) . . . 449
Finger's Will Trusts; Turner v Ministry of Health (1972) . . . 502, 506, 507
First City Monument Bank Plc v Zumax Nigeria Ltd (2019) CA . . . 234, 239, 789
First National Bank plc v Achampong (2003) CA . . . 72, 294
First Personnel Services Ltd v Halfords Ltd (2016) Ch . . . 236
First Subsea Ltd v Balltec Ltd (2017) CA . . . 792
Fish Man Ltd (in liquidation) v Hadfield (2016) NZ HC . . . 872
Fisher v Brooker (2009) HL . . . 91, 791
Fisk v A-G (1867) . . . 504
Fitzgerald v Williams (1996) CA . . . 107
Fitzwilliam (Countess) v IRC (1992) CA; affd sub nom Fitzwilliam v IRC HL . . . 56
Fletcher v Bealey (1885) . . . 101
Fletcher v Collis (1905) CA . . . 735
Fletcher v Fletcher (1844) . . . 167, 168
Fletcher v Green (1864) . . . 723, 732, 735
Flight v Bolland (1828) . . . 84
Flight v Booth (1834) . . . 85
Flinn, Re; Public Trustee v Flinn (1948) . . . 444

Foakes v Jackson (1900) . . . 580
Football Association Premier League Ltd v British Telecommunications (2017) . . . 104
Force India Formula One Team Ltd v 1 Malaysia Racing Team Sdn Bhd (2012) . . . 93
Forder, Re; Forder v Forder (1927) CA . . . 51
Foreman v Kingstone (2004) NZHC . . . 709, 711
Forster v Hale (1798); affd (1800) . . . 170
Forster's Settlement, Re; Forster v Custodian of Enemy Property for England (1942) . . . 601
Foskett v McKeown (1997) CA; revsd (2000) HL . . . 206, 626, 778, 831–3, 838, 839, 848, 850, 853, 855, 856, 860, 861, 871–8
Foster v McNicol (2016) . . . 357
Foster Bryant Surveying Ltd v Bryant (2007) . . . 765
Fountaine, Re; Fountaine v Lord Amherst (1909) CA . . . 785
Fowkes v Pascoe (1875) CA . . . 206, 208, 210
Fowler v Barron (2008) CA . . . 280, 292
Fowler v Fowler (1859) . . . 75
Fox, Re; Wodehouse v Fox (1904) . . . 601
Fox v Fox (1870) . . . 103
Fox v Jewell (2013) CA . . . 387
Francis, Re; Barrett v Fisher (1905) . . . 762
Freedman v Freedman (2015) Ch . . . 69
Freeland, Re; Jackson v Rodgers (1952) . . . 159
Freeman's Settlement Trusts, Re (1887) . . . 683
Freeston's Charity, Re (1979) . . . 735
French Caledonia Travel, Re (2004) . . . 868
Friends' Provident Life Office v Hillier Parker May & Rowden (a firm) (1997) . . . 742
Frost v Wake Smith and Tofields Solicitors (2013) CA . . . 83
Fry, (Deceased), Re; Chase National Executors and Trustees Corpn Ltd v Fry (1946) . . . 149
Fry v Densham-Smith (2010) CA . . . 377, 392
Fry v Fry (1859) . . . 723, 730
Fry v Lane (1888) . . . 73
Fry v Tapson (1884) . . . 632, 633
FSHC Group Holdings Ltd v Glas Trust Corp Ltd (2020) . . . 76
Fuller v Evans (2000) . . . 596
Funnell v Stewart . . . *see* Le Cren Clarke, Re; Funnell v Stewart
Furniss (Inspector of Taxes) v Dawson (1984) HL . . . 56
Futter v Futter . . . *see* Pitt v Holt
Futter v Revenue Commissioners . . . *see* Pitt v Holt
Fyler v Fyler (1841) . . . 805

G v A (2009) . . . 234
Gabriel v Little; Hughes-Holland v BPE Solicitors; Gabriel v Little (t/a High Tech Design & Build Ltd); BPE Solicitors v Gabriel (2013) CA; (2017) SC . . . 234, 236, 728, 730, 815
Gadd, Re; Eastwood v Clark (1883) CA . . . 678
Gafford v Graham (1999) . . . 92
Gaiman v National Association for Mental Health (1971) . . . 104
Gallarotti v Sebastianelli (2012) CA . . . 197, 208, 299
Games v A-G (2012) (Isle of Man) . . . 503
Gandesha v Gandesha (2020) . . . 267
Gape, Re; Verey v Gape (1952) CA . . . 189
Gardner (No. 2), Re (1923) . . . 403, 416
Gardner v Parker (1818) . . . 161
Gardner v Rowe (1828) . . . 170, 171
Garland v Consumers' Gas Co (2004) . . . 255
Garnett, Re; Gandy v Macaulay (1885) CA . . . 736
Garrard v Frankel (1862) . . . 77
Garrett, Re; Croft v Ruck (1934) . . . 602
Gartside v IRC (1968) CA; revsd (1968) HL . . . 58, 536, 589–91
Gascoigne v Gascoigne (1918) . . . 221
Gaspar v Zaleski (2017) Ch . . . 279
Gasquoine, Re; Gasquoine v Gasquoine (1894) CA . . . 632
Geary v Rankine (2012) CA . . . 276, 280, 282, 285
Geddis v Semple (1903) . . . 406
Gee (Deceased), Re; sub nom Wood v Staples (1948) . . . 763
Gee v Pritchard (1818) . . . 6
Gelber v Sunderland Foundation (2018) Ch . . . 652, 653
General Nursing Council for England and Wales v St Marylebone BC (1959) HL . . . 440
Generator Developments LLP v Lidl (UK) GmbH (2018) CA . . . 253
George, Re (1877) CA . . . 598
Gestetner Settlement, Re; sub nom Barnett v Blumka (1953) . . . 40, 130, 561
Ghazaani v Rowshan (2015) Ch . . . 325
Ghost v Waller (1846) . . . 632
Gibbard's Will Trusts, Re; sub nom Public Trustee v Davis (1966) . . . 136, 137
Gibbon v Mitchell (1990) . . . 67
Gibbon's Trusts, Re (1882) . . . 679
Gibbons v Smith (2020) Ch . . . 367, 368
Gibson, Re (1949) . . . 382
Gibson v Revenue and Customs Prosecution Office (2008) CA . . . 219, 302
Gibson v South American Stores (Gath & Chaves) Ltd (1949) . . . 483
Gilchrist v HMRC (2014) . . . 548
Giles v RNIB (2014) . . . 76
Giles (CH) & Co Ltd v Morris (1972) . . . 80
Gill v Woodall (2009) . . . 321
Gillam v Taylor (1873) . . . 482
Gillett v Holt (1998) Ch; (2000) CA . . . 319, 322, 323, 326, 328–30, 333, 335, 341
Gillies v Keogh (1989) . . . 319
Gillingham Bus Disaster Fund, Re (1958); Bowman v Official Solicitor (1958); affd (1959) CA . . . 226, 228, 229, 363, 509
Gilmour v Coats (1949) HL . . . 441, 490, 491
Gisborne v Gisborne (1877) HL . . . 37
Gissing v Gissing (1969) CA; revsd (1971) HL . . . 170, 196, 206, 248, 259–61, 281, 287, 298, 299, 300, 305, 308, 309, 311, 313
GKN Bolts and Nuts Sports and Social Club, Re (1982) . . . 361, 362
Glegg v Bromley (1912) CA . . . 124

Glencore International AG v Metro Trading International Inc (No. 2) (2001) . . . 842
Global Energy Horizons Corporation v Gray (2015) Ch . . . 772, 776, 778
Global Marine Drillships Ltd v Landmark Solicitors LLP (2011) . . . 237
Glover v Barlow (1831) . . . 606
Godfrey, Re; Godfrey v Faulkner (1883) . . . 716
Golay's Will Trusts, Re; sub nom Morris v Bridgewater; Golay, Re (1965) . . . 123
Gold v Hill (1999) . . . 116, 407
Goldcorp Exchange Ltd (in receivership), Re (1995) PC . . . 56, 122, 234, 260, 745, 747, 748, 847, 856, 859, 867, 870, 874, 876
Goldtrail Travel Ltd (In Liquidation) v Aydin (2016) CA . . . 764, 805, 814
Gomez v Gomez-Monche Vives (2008) CA . . . 562, 574
Gonin, Re (1979) . . . 159, 160
Gooch, Re; Gooch v Gooch (1890) . . . 219
Good, Re; Harington v Watts (1905) . . . 457
Goodchild v Goodchild (1997) CA . . . 391, 394, 395, 397–9
Goodchild (Deceased), Re (2002) . . . 403
Goodhart v Hyett (1883) . . . 101
Goodman v Gallant (1986) CA . . . 278
Goodwin v News Group Newspapers Ltd (2011) . . . 105
Gordon v Gordon (1816) . . . 70
Gore v Mishcon de Reya (2015) Ch . . . 234
Gore-Grimes v Grimes (1937) . . . 217
Gorog v Kiss (1977) OntCA . . . 218
Gott v Lawrence (2016) Ch . . . 93
Goulding v James (1997) CA . . . 603, 605, 611–3, 619, 620
Gourju's Will Trusts, Re; Starling v Custodian of Enemy Property (1943) . . . 584
Governments Stock and Other Securities Co v Manila Railway Co (1897) HL . . . 27
Gow v Grant (2012) SC . . . 275, 339, 346
Gower's Settlement, Re (1934) . . . 610
Graham-York v York (2015) CA . . . 283, 291, 292
Grainge v Wilberforce (1889) . . . 174
Gramsci (Antonio) Shipping v Lembergs (2013) CA . . . 551
Grant v Edwards (1986) CA . . . 55, 248, 259, 307, 311–5, 326, 330, 331, 347
Grant v Williams (1977) . . . 333
Grant's Will Trusts, Re; sub nom Harris v Anderson (1980) . . . 358, 364
Gray, Re; Todd v Taylor (1925) . . . 457
Gray v Barr (1971) CA . . . 243–5
Gray v Gray (1862) . . . 37, 585, 593
Gray v Perpetual Trustee Co Ltd (1928) PC . . . 389, 391, 393, 394
Greasley v Cooke (1980) CA . . . 326, 330, 333, 338, 339
Green, ex p (1820) . . . 599
Green v Gaul; sub nom Loftus (Deceased), Re (2007) CA . . . 787, 789, 791, 793
Green v Russell (1959) CA . . . 626
Green v Whitehead (1930) CA . . . 632
Green GLG Trust, In the matter of (2002) . . . 701
Green's Will Trusts, Re; Fitzgerald-Hart v A-G (1985) . . . 456, 474
Greenwell v Greenwell (1800) . . . 607
Greenwich Healthcare NHS Trust v London and Quadrant Housing Trust (1998) . . . 94, 95
Greer v Downs Supply Co (1927) CA . . . 836
Gregson v HAE Trustees Ltd (2008) . . . 644, 657, 781, 782
Gresham Life Assurance Society ex p Penney, Re (1872) . . . 705
Gresham's Settlement, Re; Lloyds Bank Ltd v Gresham (1956) . . . 130
Gresport Finance Ltd v Battaglia (2016) Ch; (2018) CA . . . 792
Grey v IRC (1958); revsd (1958) CA; affd (1960) HL . . . 174–7, 184, 620
Griffiths v Hughes (1892) . . . 743
Griffiths v Williams (1977) CA . . . 320, 334, 338, 339
Grill v General Iron Screw Collier Company (1866) . . . 720
Grobbelaar v News Group Newspapers Ltd (2002) HL . . . 24
Gross v French (1975) CA . . . 217
Group Seven Ltd v Allied Investment Corporation Ltd (2013) . . . 107
Group Seven Ltdr v Nasir (2017) Ch . . . 811
Group Seven Ltd v Notable Services LLP (2019) CA . . . 808, 811–4, 816, 825
Grove-Grady, Re; Plowden v Lawrence (1929) CA; on appeal sub nom A-G v Plowden (1931) HL . . . 456, 474
Groveholt v Hughes (2012) . . . 252
Grundt v Great Boulder Pty Gold Mine Ltd (1937) . . . 328
Guardian Ocean Cargoes Ltd v Banco do Brasil SA (The Golden Med) (No. 3) (1994) . . . 733
Gubay, Deceased, Re (2017) Ch . . . *see* Willers v Joyce
Guest v Guest (2020) CA . . . 319, 342
Guibert's Trust Estate, Re (1852) . . . 683
Guild v IRC (1992) HL . . . 455, 468
Guinness plc v Saunders (1990) HL . . . 756, 770–3
Gulbenkian's Settlement Trust (No. 1), Re; sub nom Hacobian v Maun (1968) CA; affd Whishaw v Stephens (1970) HL . . . 39, 127, 129, 130, 131, 133, 135–7, 563, 576, 586, 587, 704
Gulf Oil (Great Britain) Ltd v Page (1987) CA . . . 100
Gully v Cregoe (1857) . . . 117
Gurney, Re (1893) . . . 785
Gurtner v Circuit (1968) CA . . . 78
Guthrie v Morei (2015) Ch . . . 386
Guthrie v Walrond (1883) . . . 598
Gwembe Valley Development Co Ltd v Koshy (2003) . . . 783, 786, 791, 793
Gwyon, Re; Public Trustee v A-G (1930) . . . 437

H (Minors) (sexual abuse: standard of proof), Re (1996) . . . 95
Haastrup v Haastrup (2016) Ch . . . 802

Haastrup v Okorie (2016) Ch . . . 802
Hadaway v Hadaway (1955) PC . . . 457
Hadden, Re; Public Trustee v More (1932) . . . 455
Hadley, Re ex p Hadley (1851) . . . 674
Hadmor Productions v Hamilton (1983) . . . 99
Hageman v Holmes (2009) . . . 748
Hagger, Re; Freeman v Arscott (1930) . . . 394, 395, 397, 686
Haines, Re; Johnson v Haines (1952) . . . 540
Hain's Settlement, Re; Tooth v Hain (1961) CA . . . 130
Haley v Bannister (1820) . . . 607
Halifax Building Society v Thomas (1996) CA . . . 260, 857, 858
Hall, Re; Public Trustee v Montgomery (1944) . . . 51
Hall v Hall (1850) . . . 103
Hall v Hallett (1784) . . . 760
Hall v Mayor of London (On Behalf of the Greater London Authority) (2010) CA . . . 102
Hallett's Estate, Re; Knatchbull v Hallet (1880) CA . . . 746, 838, 843, 862, 863, 866, 868, 869, 877, 878
Halley v The Law Society (2003) . . . 175
Halpin v Steear (1976) . . . 453
Halstead's Will Trusts, Re; Halstead v Halstead (1937) . . . 601, 602
Hambleden (Viscount) Will Trusts, Re (1960) . . . 620
Hambro v Duke of Marlborough (1994) . . . 610
Hamilton, Re; Trench v Hamilton (1895) CA . . . 117
Hamilton v Hamilton (2017) Ch . . . 210
Hammond v Mitchell (1992) . . . 307
Hammond v Osborn (2002) . . . 71
Hampstead and Suburban Properties Limited v Diomedous (1969) . . . 98
Hampton Capital Ltd, Re (2015) Ch . . . 822, 824, 825
Hampton Fuel Allotment Charity, Re (1989) CA . . . 513, 514
Hanbey's Will Trusts, Re (1956) Ch . . . 429
Hanchett-Stamford v A-G (2009) . . . 357, 358, 361, 364–6, 435, 456, 463
Hancock v Smith (1889) CA . . . 866
Hanlon, Re; Heads v Hanlon (1933) . . . 190
Haque v Raja (2016) Ch . . . 196, 281, 824
Harari's Settlement Trusts, Re; Wordsworth v Fanshawe (1949) . . . 647
Harding, Re; Harding v Paterson (1923) . . . 676
Harding v Glyn (1739) . . . 131
Harding v Harding (1886) . . . 156
Harding (Deceased), Re (2008) . . . 468
Hardoon v Belilios (1901) PC . . . 551, 755
Hardy v Motor Insurers' Bureau (1964) CA . . . 244
Harlequin Property (SVG) Ltd v O'Halloran (2013) . . . 234
Harpur's Will Trusts, Re (1962) CA . . . 512
Harries v Church Commissioners for England (1993) . . . 660
Harrison, Re; Smith v Allen (1891) . . . 723
Harrison v Randall (1851) . . . 715
Harrison (JJ) (Properties) Ltd v Harrison (2002) CA . . . 791
Harrison's Trusts, Re (1852) . . . 675
Harris's Settlement, Re; Dent v Harris (1940) . . . 601
Harrow LBC v Donohue (1995) CA . . . 90, 101
Hart v Hart (2017) CA . . . 276, 281
Hart v O'Connor (1985) PC . . . 73
Hart v Tribe (1854) . . . 36, 37, 583, 585
Hartigan Nominees Pty Ltd v Rydge (1992) . . . 706
Hartogs v Sequent (Schweiz) AG (2019) . . . 69
Hart's Will Trusts, Re; Hart v Hart (1943) . . . 554
Harvard Securities Ltd (In liquidation), Re; Holland v Newbury (1997) . . . 122, 148
Harvey, Re; Westminster Bank Ltd v Askwith (1941) . . . 609
Harvey v Oliver (1887) . . . 723
Harwood, Re; Coleman v Innes (1936) . . . 504, 505
Hasham v Zenab (1960) . . . 80
Haslemere Estates Ltd v Baker (1982) . . . 514, 515
Hastings-Bass, Re; Hastings-Bass v IRC (1975) CA . . . 573, 701, 702, 704, 705
Hauxwell v Barton-upon-Humber UDC (1974) . . . 511, 512
Havelock v Havelock; Allen, Re (1881) . . . 607
Hayes v Willoughby (2013) SC . . . 105
Hay's Settlement Trusts, Re (1982) . . . 39, 42, 132, 562, 564, 572, 574, 576, 587, 589, 591
Haywood v Cope (1858) . . . 250
Hazell v Hammersmith and Fulham LBC (1992) HL . . . 223
Head v Gould (1898) . . . 723, 741
Healey v Brown (2002) . . . 392, 398, 399, 403
Heap v Tonge (1851) . . . 559
Heath, Re; Public Trustee v Heath (1936) . . . 599
Heath v Rydley (1614) . . . 6
Heathcote v Hulme (1819) . . . 733
Heavey v Heavey (1971) . . . 218
Helena Partnerships v HMRC (2011) UT; affd (2012) CA . . . 460, 474–6
Helmet Integrated Systems v Tunnard (2007) . . . 749
Hemingway Securities Ltd v Dunraven Ltd (1995) . . . 100
Hemmens v Wilson Browne (a firm) (1995) . . . 121
Henchley v Thompson (2017) Ch . . . 801
Henderson, Re; Henderson v Henderson (1940) . . . 680, 687, 688
Henderson v Eason (1851) Ex Ch . . . 788
Henderson v Merrett Syndicates Ltd (1995) HL . . . 751
Henderson v Wilcox (2015) Ch . . . 246, 247
Henry v Armstrong (1881) . . . 155
Henry v Henry (2010) PC . . . 319, 330, 332, 339
Henty v Wrey (1882) CA . . . 569
Hepplewhite's Will Trusts, Re (1977) . . . 189
Hepworth v Hepworth (1870) . . . 216
Herrick, Re; Colohan v A-G (1918) . . . 462
Heseltine v Heseltine (1971) CA . . . 218
Hetherington (Deceased), Re (1989) . . . 492, 541
Hewett v First Plus Financial Group plc (2010) CA . . . 71
Hewitt v Kaye (1868) . . . 147
Hey's Estate, Re; Walker v Gaskill (1914) . . . 389

Heyworth's Contingent Reversionary Interest, Re (1956) . . . 610
Higginbottom, Re (1892) . . . 678
High Commissioner for Pakistan in the UK v Prince Muffakham Jah (2020) Ch D . . . 117
High Commissioner for Pakistan in the United Kingdom v Prince Mukkaram Jah, His Exalted Highness the 8th Nizam of Hyderabad (2016) Ch . . . 28, 199, 240, 783, 792, 802
Hill, Re; Fettes v Hill (1914) . . . 645
Hill v Gomme (1839) . . . 626
Hillier, Re; Hillier v A-G (1954); on appeal (1954) CA . . . 228
Hill's Trusts, Re (1874) . . . 683
Hillsdown Holdings plc v Pensions Ombudsman (1997) . . . 560, 567, 568, 822
Hilton v Barker Booth and Eastwood (a firm) (2005) HL . . . 746
Hinchinbroke (Lord) v Seymour (1784) . . . 569
Hinves v Hinves (1844) . . . 547
Hipkiss v The Charity Commission (2018) . . . 440
Hobourn Aero Components Air Raid Distress Fund, Re; Ryan v Forrest (1946); on appeal (1946) CA . . . 362
Hodges, Re; Davey v Ward (1878) . . . 703
Hodgson v Duce (1856) . . . 88
Hodgson v Marks (1971); revsd (1971) CA . . . 204, 224
Hoffman-La Roche & Co AG v Secretary of State for Trade and Industry (1975) CA: on appeal (1975) HL . . . 95, 96, 99, 100
Holder v Holder (1968); on appeal (1968) . . . 668, 735, 754, 758, 759
Holding and Management Ltd v Property Holding and Investment Trust plc (1990) CA . . . 755
Holiday Inns Inc v Broadhead (1974) . . . 254
Holiday Inns Inc v Yorkstone Properties (Harlington) (1974) . . . 746
Holland, Re; Holland v Clapton (1914) . . . 566
Hollis v Rolfe (2008) . . . 757, 759, 824
Holman v Howes (2005) Ch; (2007) CA . . . 294
Holman v Johnson (1775) . . . 211
Holmden's Settlement Trusts, Re (1968) . . . 621
Holt's Settlement, Re; Wilson v Holt (1969) . . . 180, 250, 611–3, 617, 621
Hood v Oglander (1865) . . . 189
Hooper, Re; Parker v Ward (1932) . . . 444, 540, 543
Hooper v Oates (2013) CA . . . 86
Hooper v Rogers (1974) CA . . . 101
Hope, Re; De Cetto v Hope (1899) CA . . . 645
Hope's Will Trust, Re; Hope v Thorp (1929) . . . 609
Hopkins, Re; Dowd v Hawtin (1881) CA . . . 675
Hopkins v Hopkins (1739) . . . 13
Hopkins' Will Trusts, Re; Naish v Francis Bacon Society Inc (1965) . . . 440
Hopkinson, Re; Lloyds Bank Ltd v Baker (1949) . . . 440, 462
Horcal Ltd v Gartland (1984) . . . 754
Hore v Becher (1842) . . . 736
Horler v Rubin (2011) . . . 824
Horley Town Football Club, Re (2006) . . . 358, 359, 365
Horlock, Re; Calham v Smith (1895) . . . 25
Houston v Burns (1918) HL . . . 469
How v Godfrey and White (1678) . . . 755
Howe v Earl of Dartmouth (1802) . . . 547, 548, 642, 643, 657, 731
Howell & Ors v Lees-Millais (2009) Ch . . . 43
Howes, Re; Howes v Platt (1905) . . . 203
Howlett, Re; Howlett v Howlett (1949) . . . 785
Hoyl Group Ltd v Cromer Town Council (2015) CA . . . 322, 332
HR Trustees Ltd v Wembley Plc (In liquidation) (2011) . . . 630
HSBC Bank plc v Dyche (2009) . . . 307
HTC Corporation v Nokia Corporation (2013) . . . 90, 93
Hubbard v Pitt (1976); affd (1976) CA . . . 95
Hudson v Parker (1844) . . . 382
Hughes, Re (1970) . . . 869
Hughes v La Baia Ltd (Anguilla) (2011) . . . 83
Hughes v Southwark LBC (1988) . . . 80
Hughes-Holland v BPE Solicitors . . . *see* Gabriel v Little
Huguenin v Baseley (1807) . . . 406
Hulbert v Avens (2003) . . . 731
Human Dignity Trust (HDT) v The Charity Commission Appeal number CA/2013/0013 . . . 452
Hume v Lopes (1892) HL . . . 644
Hummeltenberg, Re; Beatty v London Spiritualistic Alliance Ltd (1923) . . . 433
Hunt (Charles) Ltd v Palmer (1931) . . . 85
Hunter v Moss (1994) CA . . . 115, 122, 148, 876
Hunter Engineering Co Inc v Syncrude Canada Ltd (1989) . . . 255
Huntley Deceased, Re (2014) . . . 581
Hurst, Re; Addison v Topp (1890); on appeal (1892) CA . . . 554
Hurstanger v Wilson (2007) CA . . . 747
Hussain v Hussain (1986) CA . . . 99
Hussey v Palmer (1972) CA . . . 258, 259, 335, 337
Hutcheson v Popdog Ltd (2011) CA . . . 100
Hutchinson (Deceased), Re (1955) Ch . . . 374
Hutchinson and Tenant, Re (1878) . . . 117
Hutton v Watling (1948); affd (1948) CA . . . 78

IBM United Kingdom Ltd v Prima Data International Ltd (1994) . . . 111
ICDL GCC Foundation FZ-LLC v European Computer Driving Licence Foundation Ltd (2012) . . . 720
ICIC v Adham (1998) . . . 107
Iles v Iles (2012) . . . 739
Ilott v Blue Cross (2017) . . . 372
Ilott v Mitson (2009) . . . 372
Ilott v Mitson (2014) (Fam); (2017) SC . . . 372
Imageview Management Ltd v Jack (2009) CA . . . 746
Imperial Gas Light and Coke Co v Broadbent (1859) . . . 92
In Plus Group Ltd v Pyke (2002) CA . . . 758, 764, 766, 773

Income Tax Special Purposes Commissioners v Pemsel (1891) HL . . . 424, 434–6, 441, 445, 449, 472, 473, 482
Incorporated Council of Law Reporting for England and Wales v A-G (1972) CA . . . 459, 460, 475
Independent Schools Council v Charity Commission (2011) TCC . . . *see* R (Independent Schools Council) v Charity Commission for England and Wales (2012)
Independent Schools Council v HMRC (2011) UKUT . . . 439, 472
Independent Trustee Services Ltd v GP Noble Trustees Ltd (2009) . . . 748, 749, 825, 873
Indian Oil Corpn Ltd v Greenstone Shipping SA (Panama) (The Ypatianna) (1987) . . . 46, 842, 850
Industrial Development Consultants Ltd v Cooley (1972) . . . 746, 764, 765
Ineos Upstream Ltd v Persons Unknown . . . *see* Boyd v Ineos Upstream Ltd
Ingosstrak-Investments v BNP Paribas SA (2012) CA . . . 103
Insol Funding Company Ltd v Cowlam (2017) Ch . . . 171, 277
IRC v Baddeley (Trustees of the Newtown Trust) (1955) HL . . . 433, 454, 455, 468, 486
IRC v Broadway Cottages Trust (1954); affd (1955) CA . . . 37, 128, 130, 539, 585, 586, 587
IRC v Burrell (1924) CA . . . 548
IRC v City of Glasgow Police Athletic Association (1953) . . . 457, 489
IRC v Duke of Westminster (1936) HL . . . 56
IRC v Educational Grants Association Ltd (1967) CA . . . 481, 482
IRC v Holmden (1968) HL . . . 612, 621
IRC v McMullen (1979) CA; (1981) HL . . . 439, 450, 455, 468
IRC v Oldham Training and Enterprise Council (1996) . . . 437, 457, 458, 467, 475, 476
IRC v Silverts Ltd (1951) CA . . . 554
IRC v Temperance Council of Christian Churches of England and Wales (1926) . . . 461
IRC v White (1980) . . . 439, 449
IRC v Willoughby (1997) HL . . . 56
IRC v Yorkshire Agricultural Society (1928) CA . . . 457
Interactive Technology Corp Ltd v Ferster (2017) Ch . . . 774, 781
International Contract Co, Re; Ind's Case (1872) . . . 75
International Sales and Agencies Ltd v Marcus (1982) . . . 827
Intext Coatings Ltd v Deo (2016) NZ HC . . . 872
Investors Compensation Scheme Ltd v West Bromwich Building Society (1998) . . . 468
Inwards v Baker (1965) CA . . . 318, 320, 328, 333, 337, 338
Inwood v Twyne (1762) . . . 606
Ioakimidis' Policy Trusts, Re; Ioakimidis v Hartcup (1925) . . . 625
Iranian Offshore Engineering and Construction Co v Zavarei (2020) . . . 287
Ironmongers' Co v A-G (1844) HL . . . 496
Irvine v Sullivan (1869) . . . 411
Isaac v DeFriez (1754) . . . 482
Island Export Finance Ltd v Umunna (1986) . . . 766
Island Records Ltd ex p (1978) CA . . . 109
Istel (AT & T) Ltd v Tully (1993) HL . . . 111
ITC Film Distributors Ltd v Video Exchange Ltd (1982) . . . 110
Item Software (UK) Ltd v Fassihi (2004) CA . . . 746, 754
Itter (No 2), Re (1950) . . . 385
Ives (ER) Investments Ltd v High (1967) CA . . . 318, 328, 334
Ivey v Genting Casinos (UK) Ltd (t/a Crockfords) (2017) SC . . . 808, 811–3
Ivin v Blake (1994) CA . . . 207

J, Re (2018) CA . . . 104
Jackson, Re; Jackson v Talbot (1882) . . . 606
Jackson v Cator (1800) . . . 317
Jackson v Hamilton (1846) . . . 123
Jackson v Normanby Brick Co (1899) CA . . . 87
Jackson v Phillips (1867) . . . 466
Jacobs, Re; Westminster Bank Ltd v Chinn (1970) . . . 460
Jacobs v Seward (1872) HL . . . 788
Jaffray v Marshall (1994) . . . 730, 731
Jaggard v Sawyer (1995) CA . . . 92–4, 101
James, ex p (1803) . . . 754, 758, 760, 769, 771
James, Re; James v James (1935) . . . 158, 159
James v British General Insurance Co Ltd (1927) . . . 244
James v James (2018) Ch . . . 325, 341
James v Thomas (2007) CA . . . 287, 327
James v Williams (2000) CA . . . 785
James v Williams, Re; Weetman (Dec'd) (2015) . . . 682
Janus Capital Management LLC v Safeguard World International Ltd (2016) Ch . . . 749
Jarvis, Re; Edge v Jarvis (1958) . . . 756
Jasmine Trustees Ltd v Wells & Hind (A Firm) (2008) . . . 674, 676, 802
Jazztel Plc v Revenue and Customs Commissioners (2017) Ch . . . 75
Jefferys v Jefferys (1841) . . . 155, 156
Jefferys v Marshall (1870) . . . 676, 716
Jeffrey v Gretton (2011) . . . 661
Jenner v Turner (1880) . . . 190
Jennings v Rice (2002) CA . . . 319, 334, 336, 339–42
Jeune v Queen's Cross Properties Ltd (1974) . . . 82
Job v Potton (1875) . . . 788
Joel's Will Trusts, Re; Rogerson v Brundenell-Bruce (1967) . . . 599
Johnson, Re (1939) . . . 117
Johnson v Agnew (1980) HL . . . 67, 86, 93
Johnson v Ball (1851) . . . 225
Johnson's Will Trusts, Re; National Provincial Bank Ltd v Jeffrey (1967) . . . 189
Jones, Re (1953) . . . 189
Jones (No 2), Re (2014) Fam . . . 91
Jones, Re; Meacock v Jones (1932) . . . 598

Jones, Re; sub nom Richards v Jones (1898) . . . 123
Jones v AMP Perpetual Trustee Co NZ Ltd (1994) . . . 658, 659, 662
Jones v Badley (1868) CA . . . 406, 409
Jones v Canal and River Trust (2017) CA . . . 89
Jones v De Marchant (1916) . . . 850
Jones v Foxall (1852) . . . 733
Jones v Jones (1874) . . . 668, 669
Jones v Jones (1977) . . . 330
Jones v Kernott (2009) Ch; (2010) CA; (2011) SC . . . 24, 197, 201, 202, 207, 219, 248, 253, 262, 263, 273–6, 278, 280–5, 288, 290, 291, 297, 300, 302–4, 307, 309, 314, 315, 331, 346, 347, 348
Jones v Lock (1865) . . . 139, 143, 144, 147, 559
Jones v Selby (1710) . . . 161
Jones v Smith (1841); on appeal (1843) . . . 20
Jones (FC) & Sons v Jones (1996) CA . . . 833, 838, 843, 845–50
Jordan, Re (2014) . . . 505
Jordan v Holkham (1753) . . . 190
Joscelyne v Nissen (1970) CA . . . 75, 77
Joseph's Will Trusts, Re (1959) . . . 621
Joyce v Epsom & Ewell Borough Council (2012) CA . . . 332
JS, Re (2016) Fam . . . 378
JSC BTA Bank v Ablyazov (2010) CA . . . 108
JSC BTA Bank v Ablyazov (2013) CA . . . 106–8
JSC BTA Bank v Ablyazov (2015) SC . . . 107, 108
JSC BTA Bank v Solodchenko (2010) CA . . . 106, 107
JSC Mezhdunarodniy Promyshlenniy Bank v Pugachev (2016) Ch . . . 106, 565
JSC Mezhdunarodniy Promyshlenniy Bank v Pugachev (2017) Ch . . . 120, 708
Judkin's Trusts, Re (1884) . . . 598

K, Re (1985); affd (1986) CA . . . 244, 246, 247
Kammins Ballroom Co Ltd v Zenith Instruments (Torquay) Ltd (1971) HL . . . 318
Kane v Radley-Kane (1999) . . . 758, 759
Kanval v Kanval (2021) . . . 286
Karak Rubber Co Ltd v Burden (No. 2) (1972) . . . 807, 816, 820, 828
Kavanagh v Feegan (1932) . . . 382
Kayford Ltd (in liquidation), Re (1975) . . . 25, 115, 116, 173
Kay's Settlement Trusts, Re; Broadbent v Macnab (1939) . . . 166, 167
Keay & Anor v Morris Homes (West Midlands) Ltd (2002) CA . . . 84
Keech v Sandford (1726) . . . 745, 754, 761, 762, 769, 776
Keen, Re; Evershed v Griffiths (1937) CA . . . 225, 405, 407, 408
Keeping Kids Co, Re (2021) (Ch) . . . 510
Kekewich v Manning (1851) . . . 155, 558, 559
Kelly, Re; Cleary v Dillon (1932) . . . 540
Kelsen v Imperial Tobacco Co of Great Britain and Ireland Ltd (1957) . . . 94
Kemp v Burn (1863) . . . 710
Kemp v Kemp (1795) . . . 37, 585, 593
Kemp's Settled Estate, Re (1883) CA . . . 683
Kennaway v Thompson (1981) CA . . . 92
Kennedy v Kennedy (2014) . . . 69, 70
Kenward v Adams (1975) . . . 380
Kerr v Baranow (2011) . . . 255
Kerr's Will Trusts, Re (1877) . . . 566
Kershaw's Trusts, Re (1868) . . . 602
Ketley v Gooden (1996) CA . . . 91
Keys v Hore (1879) . . . 161
Khan v Meadows (2021) SC . . . 729
Khodai v Tamimi (2009) CA . . . 747
Khoo Cheng Teow, Re (1932) . . . 541
Khoo Tek Keong v Ch'ng Joo Tuan Neoh (1934) . . . 648, 651
Khrapunov v JSC BTA Bank (2017) CA . . . 87
Kilpatrick's Policies Trusts, Re; Kilpatrick v IRC (1966); affd (1966) CA . . . 599
King, Re (1917) . . . 512
King, Re; Kerr v Bradley (1923) . . . 500
King v Dubrey (2016) . . . 160, 161, 163, 164
King v Victoria Insurance Co Ltd (1896) PC . . . 557
King (Don) Productions Inc v Warren (No. 1) (1998); affd (2000) CA . . . 117, 145, 146, 168, 762
King-Ansell v Police (1979) . . . 190
Kings v Bultitude (2010) . . . 494, 497, 500, 506
King's Estate, Re (1888) . . . 408
Kings' Trusts, Re (1892) . . . 192
King's Will Trusts, Re; Assheton v Boyne (1964) . . . 674
Kinsley v The Commissioner of Police for the Metropolis (2012) . . . 99
Kirkham v Peel (1880); on appeal (1881) . . . 746, 767
Kirklees MBC v Wickes Building Supplies Ltd (1993) CA; revsd sub nom Kirklees Metropolitan Borough Council v Wickes Building Supplies Ltd (1993) HL . . . 95
Kitchen v Royal Air Force Association (1958) CA . . . 787
KLDE Pty Ltd v Stamp Duties Commissioner (Queensland) (1984) . . . 250
Kleanthous v Paphitis (2011) . . . 786
Kleinwort Benson Ltd v Glasgow City Council (1999) HL . . . 222
Kleinwort Benson Ltd v Lincoln City Council (1999) HL . . . 819
Klug v Klug (1918) . . . 699, 701, 704, 712
Knight v Biss (1954) . . . 218
Knight v Knight (1840); affd sub nom Knight v Boughton (1844) HL . . . 115, 116
Knipe v British Racing Drivers' Motor Sport Charity (2020) Ch . . . 505
Knocker v Youle (1986) . . . 614, 615
Knott v Cottee (1852) . . . 725, 730
Knox, Re; Fleming v Carmichael (1937) . . . 504, 505
Koeppler Will Trusts, Re; Westminster Bank Trust Co Ltd v Stack (1984); revsd (1986) CA . . . 462, 464, 466, 467, 502, 505
Koettgen's Will Trusts, Re; Westminster Bank Ltd v Family Welfare Association Trustees Ltd (1954) . . . 439, 481
Kolb's Will Trusts, Re; Lloyds Bank Ltd v Ullman (1962); on appeal (1962) CA . . . 620, 647, 653

Korkontzilas v Soulos (1997) CanSC . . . *see* Soulos v Korkontzilas
Krawczynska v Rozuk (2020) . . . 281, 316

Labrouche v Frey & Ors (2016) Ch . . . 325, 816, 841, 872
Labouchere v Earl of Wharncliffe (1879) . . . 104
LAC Minerals Ltd v International Corona Resources Ltd (1989) CanSC . . . 256–8, 745–7, 751, 767, 768
Lagunas Nitrate v Lagunas Syndicate (1899) CA . . . 761
Laing (JW) Trust, Re; Stewards' Co Ltd v A-G (1984) . . . 496, 497, 499
Laing's Settlement, Re (1899) Ch . . . 648
Lamb v Evans (1893) CA . . . 746
Lambe v Eames (1871) . . . 117
Lambert v Co-operative Insurance Society (1975) CA . . . 70
Lancashire Loans Ltd v Black (1934) CA . . . 72
Land v Land (2006) . . . 245, 247
Lander v Weston (1855) . . . 725
Lander v Whitbread (1982) . . . 460
Lands Allotment Co, Re (1894) CA . . . 785
Langton v Langton (1995) . . . 72
Lansdowne's Will Trusts, Re; Marquis of Lansdowne v Earl of Shelburne (1967) . . . 610
Larke v Nugus (2000) . . . 417
Lashmar, Re; Moody v Penfold (1891) CA . . . 174
Laskar v Laskar (2008) CA . . . 281
Last, Estate of, Re (1958) . . . 123
Latimer v Commissioner of Inland Revenue (2004) PC . . . 235
Lavelle v Lavelle (2004) CA . . . 211, 219
Law Society v Sephton & Co (2004) CA; (2006) HL . . . 786
Law Society of England and Wales v Habitable Concepts Ltd (2010) Ch . . . 827
Lawrence's Will Trusts, Re; Public Trustee v Lawrence (1972) . . . 562
Lawton, Re; Gartside v A-G (1936) . . . 669
Layton v Martin (1986) . . . 321, 326
Lazard Bros & Co Ltd v Fairfield Properties Co (Mayfair) Ltd (1977) . . . 85
Le Cren Clarke, Re; Funnell v Stewart (1996) . . . 433, 441, 445, 468, 477, 489
Le Foe v Le Foe (2001) . . . 303, 310
Leach, Re (1912) . . . 192
Lead Co's Workmen's Fund Society, Re; Lowes v Governor & Co for Smelting Down Lead with Pit and Sea Coal (1904) . . . 362, 365
Leaf v International Galleries (1950) CA . . . 74
Leahy v A-G for New South Wales (1959) PC . . . 355, 356, 359, 470, 491, 537
Leake (formerly Bruzzi) v Bruzzi (1974) CA . . . 788
Leaper, Re; Blythe v Atkinson (1916) . . . 163
Learoyd v Whiteley (1887) HL; sub nom Whiteley, Re; Whiteley v Learoyd (1886) CA . . . 631, 656, 716
Lee v Lee (1876) . . . 156
Lee v Sankey (1873) . . . 695
Lee v Showmen's Guild of Great Britain (1952) CA . . . 104
Leeds Industrial Co-operative Society Ltd v Slack (1924) HL . . . 92
Legard v Hodges (1792) . . . 558
Legg v Burton (2017) Ch . . . 396
Lehman Bros International (Europe) (2012) . . . 236, 862
Lehtimäki v Cooper (2020) . . . *see* Children's Investment Fund Foundation (UK) v A-G
Leigh v Dickeson (1884) . . . 788
Lemann's Trust, Re (1883) . . . 675
Lepton's Charity, Re; Ambler v Thomas (1972) . . . 498
Leslie (J) Engineers Co Ltd (In liquidation), Re (1976) . . . 819, 837
Leslie (R) Ltd v Sheill (or Shiell) (1914) CA . . . 857
Lester v Woodgate (2010) CA . . . 334
Letterstedt v Broers (1884) . . . 687, 688
Levi v Bates (2015) . . . 105
Levy Estate, Re (1989) OntCA . . . 460
Lewes v Lewes (1848) . . . 227
Lewis, Re; Lewis v Lewis (1910) . . . 763
Lewis v Tamplin (2018) Ch . . . 709
Lewis v Warner (2017) CA . . . 373
Leyton v Sneyd (1818) . . . 695
Lictor Anstalt v Mir Steel UK Ltd (2014) Ch . . . 252
Liddiard, Re (1880) . . . 683
Liden v Burton (2017) CA . . . 317
Lightbody's Trusts, Re (1884) . . . 683
Lightfood v Lightfoot-Browne (2005) CA . . . 310, 311
Lillingston, Re; Pembery v Pembery (1952) . . . 161, 162
Lim Teng Huan v Ang Swee Chuan (1992) PC . . . 326, 333
Lincoln v Windsor (1851) . . . 757
Lincoln v Wright (1841) . . . 742
Lind, Re (1915) . . . 124
Lindsay Petroleum Co v Hurd (1874) PC . . . 789, 790
Lindsay's Executor v Forsyth (1940) . . . 541
Lipinski's Will Trusts; Gosschalk v Levy (1976) . . . 227, 359, 364, 542
Lipkin Gorman v Karpnale Ltd (1991) HL . . . 222, 262, 693, 799, 803, 807, 819, 822, 838, 843, 847, 849, 851, 857, 876
Lister Ex p Bradford Overseers and Bradford Corpn, Re (1926) CA . . . 668
Lister & Co v Stubbs (1890) CA . . . 108, 777
Litchfield (Earl) and Williams, Re (1737) . . . 632
LIV Bridging Finance Ltd v EAD Solicitors LLP (In Administration) (2020) Ch . . . 728
Liverpool and District Hospital for Diseases of the Heart v A-G (1981) . . . 502, 512
Llewellin's Will Trusts, Re; Griffiths v Wilcox (1949) . . . 763
Llewellyn's Settlement, Re; Official Solicitor v Evans (1921) . . . 42
Lloyd v Attwood (1859) . . . 736
Lloyd v Cocker (1860) . . . 602

Lloyd v Dugdale (2002) CA . . . 251
Lloyd's v Harper (1880) CA . . . 168
Lloyds Bank Ltd v Bundy (1975) CA . . . 72
Lloyds Bank plc v Carrick (1996) CA . . . 25
Lloyds Bank plc v Duker (1987) . . . 546
Lloyds Bank plc v Rosset (1989) CA; revsd (1991) HL . . . 55, 248, 284–8, 290, 291, 303, 305–9, 311–5, 326, 328, 347
Lloyds TSB Bank Plc v Crowborough Properties Ltd (2012) Ch . . . 75
Lloyds TSB Bank Plc v Markandan & Uddin (A Firm) (2012) CA . . . 236, 716, 738, 743
Lobb (Alec) (Garages) Ltd v Total Oil GB Ltd (1983); on appeal (1985) CA . . . 73
Locabail International Finance Ltd v Agroexport & Atlanta (UK) Ltd (1986) CA . . . 100
Lock International plc v Beswick (1989) . . . 110
Locker's Settlement Trusts, Re; Meachem v Sachs (1978) . . . 584
Lockhart v Reilly (1856) . . . 741
Lodge v National Union Investment Co Ltd (1907) . . . 24
Lofthouse, Re (1885) CA . . . 703
Loftus (Deceased), Re . . . *see* Green v Gaul
Logstaff v Birtles (2002) . . . 746
Lohia v Lohia (2001) . . . 204, 205
Lonrho Plc v Al-Fayed (No. 2) (1992) . . . 722, 858
London and Blackwall Railway Co v Cross (1886) CA . . . 88
London and Marshonaland Exploration Co v New Mashonaland Exploration Co (1891) . . . 764
London and Quadrant Housing Trust v Prestige Properties Ltd (2013) CA . . . 107
London Borough of Islington v Elliott (2012) CA . . . 101
London Capital & Finance (In Administration) v Thomson (Michael Andrew) (2021) . . . 107
London County Council v A-G (1901) HL . . . 57
London Hospital Medical College v IRC (1976) . . . 446, 489
London Wine Co (Shippers) Ltd, Re (1975) . . . 121, 122, 875
Londonderry's Settlement, Re; Peat v Walsh (1965) CA . . . 705, 706, 708, 709
Long v Dennis (1767) . . . 189
Long v Lloyd (1958) CA . . . 74
Longridge on the Thames v Revenue and Customs Commissioners (2013) . . . 489
Longton v Wilsby (1897) . . . 762
Lord and Fullerton's Contract, Re (1896) CA . . . 668
Loscombe v Wintringham (1850) . . . 505
Lovesy v Smith (1880) . . . 76
Low v Bouverie (1891) CA . . . 710, 711
Low v Peers (1770) Ex Ch . . . 189
Lowick Rose LLP v Swynson Ltd (2017) SC . . . 200, 222, 840
Lowin, Re; Perpetual Trustee Co Ltd v Robins (1967) CA . . . 460
Lowson v Coombes (1999) CA . . . 213
Lowther v Bentinck (1874) . . . 602
LS Systems v Scott (2015) . . . 749
LSC Finance Ltd v Abensons Law Ltd (2015) Ch . . . 236
Lucan (Earl), Re; Hardinge v Cobden (1890) . . . 156
Lucas, Re; Sheard v Mellor (1948); revsd (1948) CA . . . 501
Lucasfilm Ltd v Ainsworth (2011) SC . . . 104
Lucie-Smith v Gorman (1981) . . . 250
Lucking's Will Trusts, Re; Renwick v Lucking (1967) . . . 638, 639, 662, 716, 717, 723
Luke v South Kensington Hotel Ltd (1879) CA . . . 695
Lumley v Ravenscroft (1895) CA . . . 84
Lumley v Wagner (1852) . . . 80, 103
Lupton v White (1808) . . . 862
Lyell v Kennedy (1889) HL . . . 802
Lynch v Burke (1995) . . . 202, 208
Lynch Estate v Lynch Estate (1993) Can . . . 391
Lyon (Alloro Trust) v Revenue & Customs (2007) . . . 592
Lyon v Fishmongers' Co (1876) HL . . . 102
Lysaght v Edwards (1876) . . . 250
Lysaght (Deceased), Re; Hill v Royal College of Surgeons (1966) . . . 486, 496, 669
Lyus v Prowsa Developments (1982) . . . 249, 251, 252

M v M (1980) . . . 218
M v M (2013) Fam . . . 205, 211
Mabank v Brooks (1780) . . . 386
Macadam, Re; Dallow and Moscrop v Codd (1946) . . . 762, 763
Macaulay's Estate, Re; Macaulay v O'Donnell (1943) HL . . . 355
Macduff, Re; Macduff v Macduff (1896) CA . . . 469, 474
MacJordan Construction Ltd v Brookmount Erostin Ltd (1992) CA . . . 122, 123
Mack v Lockwood (2009) . . . 247
Mackay, Re; Griessemann v Carr (1911) . . . 738
Mackay v Wesley (2020) Ch . . . 668
Mackenzie v University of Cambridge . . . *see* R (on the application of Mackenzie) v University of Cambridge
Macleay, Re (1875) . . . 189
Macmillan Inc v Bishopsgate Investment Trust plc (No. 3) (1995) CA . . . 18, 20, 835, 836, 873, 874
MacNiven (Inspector of Taxes) v Westmoreland Investments Ltd (2003) HL . . . 56
Maddock, Re; Llewelyn v Washington (1902) CA . . . 410, 411, 416
Madoff Securities International Ltd v Raven (2011) . . . 107, 864
Madoff Securities International Ltd v Raven (2013) . . . 784, 806, 815, 824
Maguire, Re (1870) . . . 505
Main v Giambrone & Law (2017) CA . . . 727–9
Mair, Re; Richards v Doxat (1935) . . . 609
Makin (William) & Sons Ltd, Re (1993) . . . 573
Malik v Kalyan (2010) CA . . . 339
Malik v Kettle (2020) (Ch) . . . 670
Malik v Trump (2016) QB . . . 354

Malins v Freeman (1836) . . . 84
Mallott v Wilson (1903) . . . 410, 668, 669
Manchester Building Society v Grant Thornton UK LLP (2021) SC . . . 729
Manchester Trust v Furness, Withy & Co Ltd (1895) CA . . . 836
Mandla v Dowell Lee (1983) . . . 190
Manifest Shipping Co Ltd v Uni-Polaris Insurance Co Ltd (The Star Sea) (2001) HL . . . 813
Manisty's Settlement Trusts, Re; Manisty v Manisty (1974) . . . 42, 562–4, 588, 703
Mansell v Mansell (1732) . . . 715
Manton v Manton (2021) Ch . . . 688
Mara v Browne (1895); on appeal (1896) CA . . . 743, 801, 802
Mara v Manning (1845) . . . 735
March v Russell (1837) . . . 734
Mardon's Estate, Re (1944) . . . 384
Mareva Compania Naviera SA v International Bulk Carriers SA (1975) CA . . . 106, 108
Mariette, Re; Mariette v Aldenham School Governing Body (1915) . . . 450
Marlborough (Duke) v Lord Godolphin (1750) . . . 35
Marley v Rawlings (2012) CA; (2014) SC . . . 382, 385, 386, 388, 401
Marr v Collie (Bahamas) (2017) PC . . . 196, 202, 205, 207, 219, 248, 282
Marren v Masonic Havens Ltd (2011) . . . 495
Marsden v Regan (1954) CA . . . 740
Marsh v Lee (1670) . . . 23
Marsh v Von Sternberg (1986) . . . 207, 301
Marshall v Crutwell (1875) . . . 220
Martin v Edinburgh District Council (1988) . . . 660
Maryon-Wilson's Estate, Re (1912) CA . . . 647
Mascall v Mascall (1984) CA . . . 45, 146, 149
Mason v Farbrother (1983) . . . 608, 609, 620, 642, 652, 653
Masri v Consolidated Contractors International Company SAL (2011) . . . 87
Massey v Midland Bank plc (1995) CA . . . 72
Massingberd's Settlement, Re; Clark v Trelawney (1890) CA . . . 730
Masters, Re; Coutts & Co v Masters (1953) . . . 756
Matchmove Ltd v Dowding (2016) CA . . . 241, 249, 316, 325
Matharu v Matharu (1994) CA . . . 327, 329, 333, 335
Mathew v TM Sutton Ltd (1994) . . . 747
Matthew v Sedman (2021) SC . . . 784
May's Will Trust, Re; May and Stanford v Burch (1941) . . . 680
M'Caig v University of Glasgow (1907) . . . 541
M'Caig's Trustees v Kirk-Session of United Free Church of Lismore (1915) . . . 541
McAlpine (Alfred) Construction Ltd v Panatown Ltd (2000) HL . . . 167
McCheane v Gyles (No. 2) (1902) . . . 723
McCormick v Grogan (1869) . . . 408, 409, 412, 857
McDonald v Horn (1995) CA . . . 54
McEacharn, Re; Gambles v McEacharn (1911) . . . 629
McGeorge, Re; Ratcliff v McGeorge (1963) . . . 596–8
McGovern v A-G (1982) . . . 461, 463–8, 477
McGrath v Wallis (1995) CA . . . 219, 220
McHardy & Sons (A Firm) v Warren (1994) CA . . . 303
McKillen v Misland (Cyprus) Investments Ltd (2013) . . . 83
McMahon v Kerry Country Council (1981) . . . 318
McMaster v Byrne (1952) PC . . . 746
McPhail v Doulton (1971) HL . . . *see* Baden's Deed Trusts (No. 1), Re
Mead, Re; Austin v Mead (1880) . . . 163
Mead's Trust Deed, Re; Briginshaw v National Society of Operative Printers and Assistants (1961) . . . 481, 482
Measures Bros Ltd v Measures (1910) CA . . . 92
Mediterranean Reffineria Sicilliana Petroli SpA v Mabanaft GmbH (1978) CA . . . 832
Medlock, Re; Ruffle v Medlock (1886) . . . 598
Medsted Associates Ltd v Canaccord Genuity Wealth (International) Ltd (2017) Comm; (2019) CA . . . 775
Meek v Kettlewell (1842); on appeal (1843) CA . . . 559
Mendes v Guedalla (1862) . . . 633
Menelaou v Bank of Cyprus UK Ltd (2015) CA . . . 222, 224
Merchant Navy Ratings Pension Fund, Re (2015) . . . 718, 753
Mercier v Mercier (1903) CA . . . 218
Merton LBC v Nuffield Health (2020) Ch; (2021) CA . . . 472
Merton's Settlement, Re; Public Trustee v Wilson (1953) . . . 568
Mesnard v Welford (1853) . . . 675
Messeena v Carr (1870) . . . 695
Metal Box case . . . *see* IRC v Educational Grants Association Ltd
Metall und Rohstoff AG v Donaldson Lufkin & Jenrette Inc (1990); varied (1990) CA . . . 239, 240, 822
Metropolitan Bank v Heiron (1880) CA . . . 777
Metropolitan Housing Trust Ltd v Taylor (2015) CA . . . 106
Mettoy Pension Trustees Ltd v Evans (1991) . . . 39, 43, 54, 572, 573, 576, 579, 581, 583, 584, 701, 704
Meux, Re; Gilmour v Gilmour (1958) . . . 610
Miah v Miah (2020) Ch . . . 287, 288
Michaels (M) (Furriers) Ltd v Askew (1983) CA . . . 87
Mid Suffolk DC v Clarke (2007) CA . . . 78, 88, 99
Midland Bank plc v Cooke (1995) CA . . . 202, 303, 309, 314
Midland Bank plc v Dobson (1986) CA . . . 170
Midland Bank plc v Wyatt (1995) . . . 118, 119
Midleton's Will Trusts, Re; Whitehead v Earl of Midleton; sub nom Midleton's Settlement, Re (1969) . . . 123
Miller v Jackson (1977) CA . . . 94
Miller v Miller (1735) . . . 162, 293

Miller's Deed Trusts, Re (1978) . . . 725, 726
Mills, Re; Mills v Lawrence (1930) CA . . . 571, 577, 579
Mills v Farmer (1815) . . . 512
Mills v Mills (2015) Ch . . . 759
Mills v Partridge (2020) Ch . . . 790
Mills v Shields and Kelly (1948) . . . 161
Mills v Shields (No. 2) (1950) . . . 163
Milroy v Lord (1862) . . . 139, 144, 145, 147, 154, 155, 559
Ministry of Health v Simpson; Diplock v Wintle; sub nom Diplock's Estate, Re (1951) HL . . . 125, 787, 799, 818, 819, 822, 835, 836, 839, 843, 852–4, 864, 866, 867, 874–6
Mitchell v Homfray (1881) CA . . . 74
Mitchell v Watkinson (2014) CA . . . 357
Mitford v Reynolds (1848) . . . 539, 540, 543
MM (A Patient) (2017) CA . . . 91
MN v OP (2019) CA . . . 611
Moate v Moate (1948) . . . 217
Moggridge v Thackwell (1803); affd (1807) HL . . . 511, 512, 634, 669
Moncrieff's Settlement Trusts, Re (Practice Note) (1962) . . . 615
Monk, Re (1927) CA . . . 494
Montagu, Re; Derbishire v Montagu (1897) CA . . . 606
Montagu's Settlement Trusts, Re (1987); Duke of Manchester v National Westminster Bank plc . . . 799, 818, 821–3, 826, 828, 835, 836
Monte Carlo Grand Hotel case . . . *see* FHR European Ventures LLP v Cedar Capital Partners LLC
Montefiore v Guedalla (1903) . . . 672
Montefiore (Sir Moses) Jewish Home v Howell & Co (No. 7) Pty Ltd (1984) . . . 503
Montfort (Lord) v Lord Cadogan (1810); varied (1816) . . . 716, 734
Moody, Re; Woodroffe v Moody (1895) . . . 598
Moon's Will Trust, Re; Foale v Gillians (1948) . . . 500
Moore, Re; Trafford v Maconochie (1888) CA . . . 189, 192
Moore v M'Glynn (1894) . . . 763
Moore v Moore (1874) . . . 163
Moore v Moore (2018) . . . 342
Moore v Williamson (2011) . . . 120
Moorgate Mercantile Co Ltd v Twitchings (1977) HL . . . 318
Morgan, Re; Cecil-Williams v A-G (1955) . . . 455
Morgan, Re; Dowson v Davey (1910) . . . 190
Morgan v Hinton Organics (Wessex) Ltd (2009) CA . . . 89
Moriarty v Atkinson (2008) CA . . . 874
Morice v Bishop of Durham (1804); on appeal (1805) . . . 125, 424, 429, 537, 585, 697
Morris v Morris (2008) CA . . . 287, 311, 338
Morris-Garner v One Step (Support) Ltd; sub nom. One Step (Support) Ltd v Morris-Garner (2016) CA (2018) SC . . . 86, 94
Morrison, Re; Wakefield v Falmouth (1967) . . . 502
Morse v Royal (1806) . . . 760
Mortgage Business plc v Conifer & Pines Solicitors & Essex Solicitors (2009) . . . 737
Mortgage Corporation v Shaire (2000) . . . 294
Moseley v Moseley (1673) . . . 37, 585, 593
Moss, Re; Hobrough v Harvey (1949) . . . 456
Moss v Cooper (1861) . . . 406
Mossop v Mossop (1989) CA . . . 217, 218
Moss's Trusts, Re (1888) . . . 674
Motivate Publishing FZ LLC v Hello Ltd (2015) Ch . . . 316, 325
Mount Pleasant Islamic Trust v Sykes (Valuation Officer) (2019) . . . 444
Mountford v Scott (1974); affd (1975) CA . . . 85
Moyle v Moyle (1831) . . . 716
Muir v IRC (1966) CA . . . 577, 579
Mulholland's Will Trusts, Re; Bryan v Westminster Bank Ltd (1949) . . . 757, 758
Muller, Re; Cassin v Mutual Cash Order Co Ltd (1953) . . . 203
Mulroy, Re; M'Andrew v Mulroy (1924) . . . 163
Mumford v Bank of Scotland (1996) . . . 72
Munch v Cockerell (1840) . . . 633
Municipal and General Securities Co Ltd's Trust, Re; Municipal and General Securities Co Ltd v Lloyds Bank Ltd (1950) . . . 52
Munir (A Bankrupt), Re Chughtai v Munir; sub nom Murphy v Munir (2021) . . . 119
Murad v Al-Saraji (2005) CA . . . 773
Murawski's Will Trust, Re; Lloyds Bank Ltd v Royal Society for the Prevention of Cruelty to Animals (1971) . . . 456
Murless v Franklin (1818) . . . 215
Murphy v Munir . . . *see* Munir (A Bankrupt), Re Chughtai v Munir
Murphy v Rayner (2011) . . . 323
Murphy's Settlements, Re; Murphy v Murphy (1998) . . . 710
Murray v Parker (1854) . . . 75
Muschamp v Bluet (1617) . . . 189
Muschinski v Dodds (1985) HCAus . . . 260
Mussett v Bingle (1876) . . . 540
Mussoorie Bank Ltd v Raynor (1882) . . . 117, 138
Mutton v Peat (1899); revsd (1900) CA . . . 866
MWB Business Exchange Centres Ltd v Rock Advertising Ltd (2016) CA . . . 328
Mylne, Re; Potter v Dow (1941) . . . 444

Napier v Public Trustee (Western Australia) (1980) . . . 218
Napier and Ettrick (Lord) v Hunter (1973) HL . . . 10
National Anti-Vivisection Society v IRC (1948) HL . . . 461, 477, 511, 512
National Bank Trust v Yurov (2020) . . . 840, 841
National Crime Agency v Dong (2017) . . . 205
National Grid v McKenzie (2009) Ch . . . 750
National Provincial Bank Ltd v Ainsworth (1965) HL . . . 16, 18, 21, 33, 297, 298, 348, 832
National Trustees Co of Australasia Ltd v General Finance Co of Australasia Ltd (1905) . . . 716, 739

National Union of Rail, Maritime & Transport Workers v Serco Ltd (t/a Serco Docklands) (2011) CA . . . 98
National Westminster Bank Plc v Lucas (2014) CA . . . 734
Nationwide Building Society v Davisons Solicitors; sub nom Davisons Solicitors v Nationwide Building Society (2012) CA . . . 237, 716, 738
Natwest Markets Plc v Bilta (UK) Ltd (In Liquidation) (2021) CA . . . 813, 814
Navitaire Inc v EasyJet Airline Co Ltd (No. 2) (2005) . . . 92
Naylor v Goodall (1877) . . . 695
Neale v Willis (1968) CA . . . 172
Nelson, Re; Norris v Nelson (1928) CA . . . 589, 605
Nelson v Nelson (1995) . . . 217
Nelson v Rye (1996) . . . 24, 779, 780, 786, 789, 790
Nestlé v National Westminster Bank plc (1993) CA . . . 642, 655, 657–9, 717, 726
Neville v Wilson (1997) CA . . . 78, 180, 181, 250
Neville Estates Ltd v Madden (1962) . . . 356, 357, 443, 490
New, Re; Leavers, Re: Morley, Re (1901) CA . . . 604, 606
New Zealand Netherlands Society Oranje Inc v Kuys (1973) PC . . . 746
Newen, Re (1894) . . . 672
Newey, Re (1994) . . . 392
Newgate Stud Co v Penfold (2004) . . . 719
Newham LBC v Ali (2014) CA . . . 104
Newlon Housing Trust v Al-Sulaimen (1999) . . . 176
Newman v Clarke (2016) Ch . . . 758
Newport Association Football Club Ltd v Football Association of Wales Ltd (1995) . . . 91
News Group Newspapers Ltd v Society of Graphical and Allied Trades 1982 (1986) CA . . . 358
Nicholls v Jessup (1986) . . . 73
Nicholson v Smith (1882) . . . 695
Niedersachsen, The (1983) . . . 106
Nightingale v Goulburn (1847) . . . 470
Nimmo v Westpac Banking Corp (1993) . . . 820
Ninian, Re (2019) Ch . . . 245
Nintento Co Ltd v Sky Uk Ltd (2019) (Ch) . . . 104
Nippon Yusen Kaisha v Karageorgis (1975) CA . . . 108
Niru Battery Manufacturing Company v Milestone Trading Ltd (2003) CA . . . 822
Niyazi's Will Trusts, Re (1978) . . . 437, 460
NML Capital Ltd v Argentina (2011) SC . . . 107
Noack v Noack (1959) . . . 218
Nordenfelt v Maxim Nordenfelt Guns and Ammunition Co Ltd (1894) HL . . . 102
Norfolk's (Duke) Settlement Trusts, Re; Earl of Perth v Fitzalan-Howard (1979); on appeal (1982) CA . . . 608, 609, 627, 755, 756
Norman v Federal Comr of Taxation (1964) AusHC . . . 124
Norris, Re; Allen v Norris (1884) . . . 672, 683
North v Loomes (1919) . . . 418
North American Land and Timber Co Ltd v Watkins (1904); affd (1904) CA . . . 784
North Devon and West Somerset Relief Fund Trusts, Re; Baron Hylton v Wright (1953) . . . 499
North Harrow Tennis Club, Re (2017) Ch . . . 365
North London Railway Co v Great Northern Railway Co (1883) CA . . . 89
North Shields Old Meeting House, Re (1859) . . . 608
North Shore Ventures Ltd v Anstead Holdings Inc (2011) CA . . . 72
Northall (Deceased), Re (2010) . . . 203
Northampton Regional Livestock Centre Company Ltd v Cowling (2015) CA . . . 753, 775, 778, 779
Northern Bank Ltd v Henry (1981) Irish SC . . . 20, 218, 835
Northern Developments (Holdings) Ltd, Re (1978) . . . 231
Nosnehpetsj Ltd (In Liquidation) v Watersheds Capital Partners Ltd (2020) . . . 152
Nottage, Re; Jones v Palmer (1895) CA . . . 450
Novoship (UK) Ltd v Mikhaylyuk (2012) . . . 804, 805, 811, 815
Novoship (UK) Ltd v Nikitin (2015) CA . . . 730, 775, 776, 814, 828
NR v AB (2016) Fam . . . 298, 301
NRC Holding Ltd v Danilitskiy (2017) Ch . . . 197
Nuffield Health v Merton LBC . . . *see* Merton LBC v Nuffield Health
NWL Ltd v Woods (1979) HL . . . 100
Nwosu v Nwosu (2018) Ch . . . 682

Oakes v Turquand and Harding (1867) . . . 74
Oatley v Oatley Powney (2014) Ch . . . 77
Oatway, Re; Hertslet v Oatway (1903) . . . 863
Oberman v Collins (2020) Ch . . . 287–9
Oddy, Re (1911) . . . 713
O'Donnell v Governor & Company of the Bank of Ireland (2014) . . . 290
O'Donnell v Shanahan (2009) CA . . . 746, 754, 764, 766, 774
Official Receiver v Brown (2017) Ch . . . 354
Official Solicitor to the Senior Courts v Yemoh (2010) Ch . . . 375
Ogden, Re (1933) . . . 461
O'Keefe v Caner (2017) Ch . . . 751
O'Kelly v Davies (2014) CA . . . 213, 292
Oldham, Re; Hadwen v Myles (1925) . . . 392–4, 398, 399
Oldham BC v A-G (1993) CA . . . 499, 608, 609, 627
Olins v Walters (2009) CA . . . 390, 392, 394, 395, 397
Oliver, Re; Theobald v Oliver (1927) . . . 787
Oliveri v Oliveri (1995) . . . 216
Omojole v HSBC Bank Plc (2012) . . . 225
One Step (Support) Ltd v Morris-Garner . . . *see* Morris-Garner v One Step (Support) Ltd
O'Neill v Holland (2020) . . . 284, 286, 288, 292, 307
OPO v Rhodes (2015) SC . . . 89
Oppenheim v Tobacco Securities Trust Co Ltd (1951) HL . . . 49, 479–82, 484, 485
ORB a.r.l. v Ruhan (2016) . . . 24, 872
Orde, Re (1883) CA . . . 683
O'Reilly v Alderson (1849) . . . 675

O'Reilly v Mackman (1983); revsd (1983) CA; affd (1983) HL . . . 90
Orme, Re; Evans v Maxwell (1883) . . . 216
Ormsby, Re (1809) . . . 755
O'Rourke v Darbishire (1920) HL . . . 708, 709
Orwell's Will Trusts, Re; Dixon v Blair (1982) . . . 762
Osborne v Amalgamated Society of Railway Servants (1911) CA . . . 104
Osoba (Deceased), Re; Osoba v Osoba (1979) CA . . . 227
O'Sullivan v Management Agency and Music Ltd (1985) CA . . . 72, 74, 733, 756, 771, 772
Oswald Hickson Collier Co v Carter-Ruck (1984) CA . . . 746
OT Computers Ltd (In Administration) v First National Tricity Finance Ltd (2007) . . . 127, 128, 135, 136
OT Computers Ltd (In Liquidation) v Infineon Technologies AG (2021) CA . . . 786
Otkritie International Investment Management Ltd v Urumov (2014) . . . 815, 825, 827
Ottaway v Norman (1972) . . . 398, 403, 404, 406, 409, 418
Ottley v Gilby (1845) . . . 710
Oughtred v IRC (1960) HL . . . 25, 78, 175, 179–81, 250, 621
Overton v Banister (1844) . . . 734
Ovey, Re; Broadbent v Barrow (1885) . . . 502
Owens v Greene (1932) . . . 209
Oxfam v Birmingham City DC (1976) HL . . . 472
Oxford Group v IRC (1949) CA . . . 469
Oxley v Hiscock (2004) CA . . . 197, 290, 303, 304, 314, 316

P&O Nedlloyd BV v Arab Metal Co (No. 2) (The UB Tiger) (2007) CA . . . 85
P&P Property Ltd v Owen White & Catlin LLP (2018) CA . . . 737
Padden v Bevan Ashford Solicitors (2011) CA . . . 73
Paddico (267) Ltd v Kirklees Metropolitan Council;Taylor v Betterment Properties (Weymouth) Ltd; sub nom Betterment Properties (Weymouth) Ltd v Dorset CC; Adamson v Paddico (267) Ltd; Paddico (267) Ltd v Adamson (2014) SC . . . 789
Padfield v Minister of Agriculture, Fisheries and Food (1968) CA; revsd (1968) HL . . . 712
Page, Re; Jones v Morgan (1893) . . . 785
Page v Hewetts Solicitors (2013) . . . 786, 791
Page One Records Ltd v Britton (t/a The Troggs) (1967) . . . 80, 103
Pain, Re; Gustavson v Haviland (1919) . . . 557
Pallant v Morgan (1953) . . . 238, 249, 252–4
Palmer v Simmonds (1854) . . . 123
Pan Petroleum Aje Ltd v Yinka Folawiyo Petroleum Co Ltd (2017) CA . . . 89
Panama, New Zealand and Australian Royal Mail Co (1870) . . . 399
Panatown Ltd v Alfred McAlpine Construction Ltd; . . . *see* McAlpine (Alfred) Construction Ltd v Panatown Ltd
Pankhania v Chandegra (2012) CA . . . 118, 278, 279
Paradise Motor Co Ltd, Re (1968) CA . . . 176, 216
Paragon Finance plc v DB Thakerar & Co (1999) CA . . . 239, 241, 242, 779, 785–7, 791, 800, 857
Parbulk II AS v PT Humpuss Intermoda Transportasi TBK (2011) . . . 106
Pardoe, Re; McLaughlin v A-G (1906) . . . 444
Park, Re (1932) . . . 562
Parker v Bloxam (1855) . . . 736
Park v Cho and others (2014) Ch . . . 515
Parker v British Airways Board (1982) CA . . . 18
Parker v Camden LBC (1986) CA . . . 100, 103
Parker v Parker (2003) . . . 328, 342
Parker v Taswell (1858) . . . 17
Parke's Charity, Re (1842) . . . 608
Parkes v White (1805) . . . 758
Parkin v Thorold (1852) . . . 25
Parr v Keystone Healthcare Ltd (2019) CA . . . 776
Parrott, Re (1881) . . . 683
Parsons, Re; Barnsdale and Smallman v Parsons (1940) . . . 680
Partington, Re; Partington v Allen (1887) . . . 741
Pascoe v Turner (1979) CA . . . 320, 329, 332, 337
Patel v Ali (1984) . . . 85
Patel v Barlow's Solicitors (A Firm) (2020) (Ch) . . . 234
Patel v London Borough of Brent (2003) . . . 776
Patel v Mirza (2013) . . . 211–4, 221, 234
Patel v Shah (2005) CA . . . 789
Patel v WH Smith (Eziot) Ltd (1987) CA . . . 90, 101
Paterson v Murphy (1853) . . . 558
Paton v British Pregnancy Advisory Service Trustees (1979) . . . 89, 104
Patrick v McKinley (2017) CA . . . 316, 324
Paul v Constance (1977) CA . . . 143, 144, 173
Paul v Paul (1882) CA . . . 155, 370, 603
Pauling's Settlement Trust, Re (No 1); sub nom Younghusband v Coutts & Co (No.1) (1963) . . . 14
Pauling's Settlement Trust, Re; Younghusband v Coutts & Co (1964) CA . . . 602, 605, 734, 735, 737, 739, 740, 743, 789
Payne v Tyler (2019) . . . 70
Peacock, Re; Midland Bank Executor and Trustee Co Ltd v Peacock (1957) . . . 245
Peacock v Evans (1809–10) . . . 24
Pearce v Beverley (2013) Ch . . . 860
Pearse v Green (1819) . . . 707
Pearson v Pearson (1965) . . . 218
Pechar, Re (1969) . . . 246
Peczenik's Settlement, Re; Cole v Ingham (1964) . . . 647, 648
Peel's Release, Re (1921) Ch . . . 185
Pegler v White (1864) . . . 85
Peggs v Lamb (1994) Ch . . . 494
Peires v Bickerton's Aerodromes Ltd (2016) Ch . . . 102
Pell Frischmann Engineering Ltd v Bow Valley Ltd (2009) PC . . . 93
Pemberton v Pemberton (2016) . . . 613
Penn v Lord Baltimore (1750) . . . 25, 78
Pennington v Waine (No. 1) (2002) CA . . . 150–2, 155, 551, 558

Penny v Avison (1856) . . . 733
Penrose, Re; Penrose v Penrose (1933) . . . 567
Perowne (Deceased), Re; Perowne v Moss (1951) . . . 571
Perrin v Lyon (1807) . . . 191
Perrins v Bellamy (1898); on appeal (1899) CA . . . 715, 737, 739
Perrins v Holland (2009); affd (2010) CA . . . 378, 380
Peter v Beblow (1993) . . . 257
Peter Pan Manufacturing Corpn v Corsets Silhouette Ltd (1964) . . . 767
Pettifor's Will Trusts, Re; Roberts v Roberts (1966) . . . 615
Pettingall v Pettingall (1842) . . . 539, 543
Pettitt v Pettitt (1970) HL . . . 206, 207, 218, 219, 248, 259, 279, 298, 299, 302, 304, 311, 330
Pettkus v Becker (1980) CanSC . . . 255
Pfeiffer (E) Weinkellerei-Weineinkauf GmbH & Co v Arbuthnot Factors Ltd (1988) . . . 23
Phayre v Peree (1815) HL . . . 761
Phillips, Re; Robinson v Burke (1889) . . . 565
Phillips v Lamdin (1949) . . . 250
Phillips v Phillips (1861) . . . 23
Phillips v Phillips (1885) CA . . . 762
Phillips v The Royal Society for the Protection of Birds (2012) . . . 494, 500
Phillips-Higgins v Harper (1954); affd (1954) CA . . . 787
Philpott v St George's Hospital (1859) . . . 507
Phipps v Ackers (1842) HL . . . 599
Phipps v Boardman . . . *see* Boardman v Phipps
Photo Production Ltd v Securicor Transport Ltd (1980) HL . . . 77
Pierce v Wood (2009) . . . 549
Pierson v Shore (1739) . . . 606
Piety v Stace (1799) . . . 733
Pilford v Greenmanor Ltd (2012) . . . 92
Pilkington v IRC (1964) HL . . . 600–2, 631
Piller (Anton) KG v Manufacturing Processes Ltd (1976) CA . . . 109
Pillmoor v Miah (2019) . . . 286–8
Pince v Beattie (1863) . . . 757
Pinfield v Eagles (2005) . . . 303, 313
Pinion (Deceased), Re; Westminster Bank Ltd v Pinion (1965); on appeal (1965) CA . . . 450, 474
Piper, Re; Dodd v Piper (1946) . . . 190
Pirbright v Salwey (1896) . . . 540, 543
Pitcairn, Re; Brandreth v Colvin (1896) . . . 547
Pitt v Holt; Pitt v Revenue and Customs Commissioners; Futter v Revenue and Customs Commissioners; Futter v Futter (2010); (2011) CA; (2013) SC . . . 22, 68–70, 82, 566, 568, 573, 576, 616, 701–5, 715–8, 745
Pitt Rivers, Re; Scott v Pitt Rivers (1902) CA . . . 409
PK Airfinance SARL v Alpstream AG (2015) CA . . . 233
Pleshakov v Sky Stream Corp (2021) (PC BVI) . . . 116, 117, 552
Plimmer v City of Wellington Corpn (1884) PC . . . 332, 338, 339
Plumptre's Marriage Settlement, Re; Underhill v Plumptre (1910) . . . 157, 559
PMPA v PMPS (1994) Irish HC . . . 874
Polly Peck International plc v Nadir (Asil) (No. 2) (1992) CA . . . 799, 807, 822
Polly Peck International plc (in administration) (No. 2), Re (1998) CA . . . 239, 240, 261
Popoff v Actus Management Ltd (1985) . . . 680
Powell v Benney (2008) . . . 331
Powell v Brent LBC (1987) CA . . . 80
Powell-Cotton's Resettlement, Re; Henniker-Major v Powell-Cotton (1956) CA . . . 608
Power, Re; Public Trustee v Hastings (1947) . . . 609, 648, 649
Power's Settlement, Re; Power v Power (1951) CA . . . 678
Powys v Blagrave (1854) . . . 102
Practice Direction (Injunction: Undertaking as to Damages) (1974) . . . 99
Practice Direction (Interim Injunctions) (2009) . . . 865
Pratt's Will Trust, Re; Barrow v McCarthy (1943) . . . 644
Preedy v Dunne (2016) CA . . . 325
Prendeville, Re (1990) . . . 408
Presant and Presant v Goodwin (1860) . . . 227
Prescott v Birmingham Corporation (1955) . . . 753
Prest v Petrodel Resources Ltd (2013) SC . . . 44, 60, 197, 205, 210, 267, 290, 298, 551, 782, 827
Preston v Luck (1884) CA . . . 95
Price, Re; Midland Bank Executor and Trustee Co Ltd v Harwood (1943) . . . 355
Price v Blakemore (1843) . . . 745
Price v Strange (1978) CA . . . 84
Price v William-Wynn (2006) . . . 566
Pride of Derby and Derbyshire Angling Association Ltd v British Celanese Ltd (1953) CA . . . 94
Prince Jefri Bolkiah v KPMG (a firm) (1999) . . . 104, 746
Printers and Transferrers Amalgamated Trades Protection Society, Re (1899) . . . 362, 365
Prison Charities, Re (1873) . . . 507
Pritt v Clay (1843) . . . 736
Protheroe v Protheroe (1968) CA . . . 762
Prudential Assuance Co Ltd v London Residuary Body (1992) HL . . . 22
Prudential Assurance Co Ltd v Newman Industries (No. 2) (1980); revsd (1982) CA . . . 766
Prudential Staff Pension Scheme, Re (2011) . . . 703
Pryce, Re; Nevill v Pryce (1917) . . . 166, 167
Public Guardian's Severance Applications (2016) . . . 29
Public Trustee v Cooper (2001) . . . 734
Public Trustee v IRC (1960) HL . . . 755
Pullan v Koe (1913) . . . 156, 157
Pulvertoft v Pulvertoft (1811) . . . 559
Purrunsing v A'Court & Co (a firm) (2016) Ch . . . 738
Pye v Gorges (1710) . . . 715

Qayyum v Hameed (2009) CA . . . 323, 329
Queensland Mines Ltd v Hudson (1978) PC . . . 766, 782

Quest Advisors Limited, Sharriba Ltd v McFeely (2011) CA . . . 86
Quick Draw LLP v Global Live Events LLP (2012) . . . 842
Quinn v Irish Bank Resolution Corporation Ltd (In Special Liquidation) (2015) . . . 212

R v Ahmad (2014) . . . 214, 215
R v Archbishop of Canterbury and Bishop of London (1812) . . . 706
R v Clowes (No. 2) (1994) CA . . . 117
R v District Auditor ex p West Yorkshire Metropolitan CC (1986) . . . 133, 142, 543, 564, 587, 589
R v Ghosh (1982) . . . 809
R v Preddy (1996) HL . . . 846, 847
R v Radio Authority ex p Bull (1998) CA . . . 461, 463, 466
R v Registrar General ex p Segerdal (1970) CA . . . 442
R v Secretary of State for the Home Department ex p Doody (1994) HL . . . 712
R v Secretary of State for the Home Department ex p Fayed (1997) CA . . . 712
R v Secretary of State for Transport ex p Factortame Ltd (No. 2) C-213/89 (1991) ECJ; appld sub nom R v Secretary of State for Transport ex p Factortame Ltd (No. 2) (1991) HL . . . 95, 97
R (Hodkin) v Registrar General of Births, Deaths and Marriages (2013) SC . . . 442, 443, 491
R (Independent Schools Council) v Charity Commission for England and Wales (2012) . . . 437, 472–4, 477, 487, 490
R (Khan) v Secretary of State for the Home Department (2016) CA . . . 88
R (McIntyre) v Gentoo Group Ltd (2010) . . . 530
R (Mackenzie) v University of Cambridge; sub nom. Mackenzie v University of Cambridge; R (Mackenzie v Chancellor, Master and Scholars of the University of Cambridge (2019) . . . 80
R (Preservation and Promotion of the Arts Ltd) v Greater Manchester Magistrates Court (2020) . . . 450
R (Palestine Solidarity Campaign Ltd) v Secretary of State for Housing, Communities and Local Government (2020) SC . . . 661
R (SB (Afghanistan)) v The Secretary of State for the Home Department (2018) . . . 97
R (Weaver) v London and Quadrant Housing (2009) CA . . . 530
Rabaiotti's 1989 Settlement, Re (2001) . . . 706, 709
Raby v Ridehalgh (1855) . . . 742, 743
Racal Group Services Ltd v Ashmore (1995) CA . . . 76
Radcliffe, Re; Radcliffe v Bewes (1892) CA . . . 578
Raine, Re; Tyerman v Stansfield (1929) . . . 598
Ralli's Will Trusts, Re; sub nom Calvocoressi v Rodocanachi (1964) . . . 123, 146, 153, 154, 158, 159
Ramsay (WT) Ltd v IRC (1982) HL . . . 56
Ramsden v Dyson and Thornton (1866) . . . 317, 318, 322
Ramsden v Hylton (1751) . . . 736
Randall v Errington (1805) . . . 760
Ranelagh's (Lord) Will, Re (1884) . . . 762
Rank Film Distributors Ltd v Video Information Centre (1982); on appeal (1982) CA: affd (1982) HL . . . 109, 111
Ransome, Re; Moberley v Ransome (1957) . . . 596
Ras Al Khaimah Investment Authority v Bestfort Development Llp (2017) CA . . . 107
Rasmanis v Jurewitsch (1970) . . . 246
Rasu Maritima SA v Persuahaan Pertambangan Minyak Dan Gas Bumi Negara (1978) CA . . . 107
Rawluk v Rawluk (1990) . . . 256, 257
Rawstron & Anor (Executrices of the Estate of Lucian Freud) v Freud (2014) Ch . . . 401
Raymond v Young (2015) CA . . . 93
Rayner v Preston (1881) CA . . . 250
RBC Trustees (CI) Ltd v Stubbs (2017) Ch . . . 76
Reade v Reade (1881) . . . 736
Reade-Revell, Re; Crellin v Melling (1930) . . . 598
Reading v A-G (1951) HL . . . 746, 747
Recher's Will Trusts, Re; National Westminster Bank Ltd v National Anti-Vivisection Society Ltd (1972) . . . 55, 356, 357
Reddel v Dobree (1839) . . . 162
Redland Bricks Ltd v Morris (1970) HL . . . 88, 90, 91, 100, 101
Redrow Homes Ltd v Martin Dawn (Leckhampton) Ltd (2016) Ch . . . 82
Rees' Will Trusts, Re; Williams v Hopkins (1950) CA . . . 411
Reeve v A-G (1843) . . . 669
Regal (Hastings) Ltd v Gulliver (1942) (1967) HL . . . 746, 754, 764, 765, 768–70
Regan Paul Properties DPF No. 1 Ltd, Re (2007) . . . 92
Rehman v Ali (2015) Ch . . . 249, 353, 362, 504
Reid v Thompson and M'Namara (1851) . . . 715
Relfo Ltd v Varsani (2014) CA . . . 871, 872
Remnant's Settlement Trusts, Re; Hooper v Wenhaston (1970) . . . 617
Rena K, The (1979) . . . 107
Rendell's Trusts, Re (1915) . . . 680
Rennell v IRC (1962); affd sub nom IRC v Lord Rennell (1964) HL . . . 156
Republic Bank Ltd v Lochan (2015) PC . . . 332
Resch's Will Trusts, Re; Le Cras v Perpetual Trustee Co Ltd; Far West Children's Health Scheme v Perpetual Trustee Co Ltd (1969) PC . . . 445, 446, 487
Revel v Watkinson (1748) . . . 607
Revenue and Customs v The Investment Trust Companies (2017) SC . . . 199, 224
Rhone v Stephens (1994) HL . . . 17
Rice v Rice (1854) . . . 23
Richard v Mackay (1997) . . . 675, 681, 683
Richards v Delbridge (1874) . . . 143, 146
Richards v Wood (2014) CA . . . 716
Richardson, Re; Pole v Pattenden (1920) CA . . . 787
Richardson v Chapman (1760) HL . . . 37, 585, 593, 761

Richardson v Richardson (1867) . . . 155
Riches v Hogben (1986) . . . 332
Ricketts v Ricketts (1891) . . . 742
Rider v Kidder (1805) . . . 218
Rider's Will Trusts, Re; Nelson v Rider (1958) . . . 645, 647
Ridgewood Properties Group Ltd v Valero Energy Ltd (2013) . . . 252
Ridgwell v Ridgwell (2007) . . . 611, 616–8
Ridsdel, Re; Ridsdel v Rawlinson (1947) . . . 630, 685
Rigby v Connol (1880) . . . 104
Riordan v Banon (1876) . . . 408
Riverlate Properties v Paul (1975) CA . . . 76
Roadchef (Employee Benefits Trustees) Limited v Hill (2014) . . . 702, 703, 705
Roberts, Re (Stenton v Hardy) (1963) . . . 501
Roberts (Deceased), Re; Public Trustee v Roberts (1946) . . . 216
Robinson, Re; Besant v German Reich (1931) . . . 460
Robinson, Re (1921) . . . 496
Robinson v Killey (1862) . . . 599
Robinson v Ommanney (1883) CA . . . 393, 395
Robinson v Pett (1734) . . . 755
Robinson v Robinson (1848); varied (1851) . . . 731
Robson v Flight (1865) . . . 631, 632, 668
Rochdale Canal Co v King (1851) . . . 329
Roche, Re (1842) . . . 675
Roche v Sherrington (1982) . . . 72
Rochefoucauld v Boustead (1897) CA . . . 170–2, 241, 412, 418
Rodwell, Re; Midgley v Rumbold (1970) . . . 225
Rookes v Barnard (1964) . . . 859
Roome v Edwards (Inspector of Taxes) (1982) HL . . . 613
Roper-Curzon v Roper-Curzon (1871) . . . 601
Roper's Trust, Re (1879) . . . 703
Ropner's Settlement Trusts, Re; Ropner v Ropner (1956) . . . 601
Roscoe (James) (Bolton) Ltd v Winder (1915) . . . 868
Rose, Re (Deceased); Rose v IRC (1952) CA . . . 148–52, 154, 158, 162, 241
Rose (Frederick E) (London) Ltd v William H Pim Jnr & Co Ltd (1953) CA . . . 75
Rosenzweig v NMC Recordings Ltd (2013) . . . 514, 515
Rosher, Re; Rosher v Rosher (1884) . . . 189
Ross v Caunters (1980) . . . 388, 637
Rostron v Guildford Borough Council (2017) Admin . . . 354
Rover International Ltd v Cannon Film Sales Ltd (1987) Ch; (1989) CA . . . 100, 819
Rowbotham v Dunnett (1878) . . . 406
Rowe v Hewitt (1906) . . . 104
Rowe v Prance (1999) . . . 144
Rowland v Witherden (1851) . . . 632, 633
Rowland v Blades (2021) Ch . . . 281, 282
Rowlandson v National Westminster Bank Ltd (1978) . . . 807, 820
Rowntree (Joseph) Memorial Trust Housing Association Ltd v A-G (1983) . . . 438, 445, 454
Royal Bank of Scotland v Chandra (2010); affd (2011) CA . . . 71
Royal Bank of Scotland v Etridge (No. 2) (2001) HL . . . 72
Royal Bank of Scotland Plc v Highland Financial Partners LP (2013) CA . . . 24
Royal Bristol Permanent Building Society v Bomash (1887) . . . 250
Royal Brunei Airlines Sdn Bhd v Tan (1995) PC . . . 60, 719, 782, 797, 803–11, 822, 823, 826, 827, 844
Royal Choral Society v IRC (1943) CA . . . 449
Royal College of Nursing v St Marylebone Corpn (1959) CA . . . 440
Royal College of Surgeons of England v National Provincial Bank Ltd (1952) HL . . . 440
Royal National Lifeboat Institution v Headley (2016) . . . 707, 710
Royal Society for the Prevention of Cruelty to Animals v A-G (2001) . . . 512, 514, 529, 530
Royal Society's Charitable Trusts, Re (1956) . . . 609
Royce, Re; Turner v Wormald (1940) . . . 444
Russ and Brown's Contract, Re (1934) CA . . . 85
Russell v Jackson (1852) . . . 406
Russell v Scott (1936) . . . 208, 209, 218
Russell-Cooke Trust Co v Prentis (2003) . . . 864, 866, 868
RVB Investments Ltd v Bibby (2013) . . . 79
Ryan v Mutual Tontine Westminster Chambers Association (1893) CA . . . 82
Rycroft v Christy (1840) . . . 558
Rymer, Re; Rymer v Stanfield (1895) CA . . . 504, 505

S v J (2016) Fam . . . 278, 291, 292
SAAMCo . . . *see* South Australia Asset Management Corporation v York Montague Ltd (1997)
Safe Business Solutions Ltd v Cohen (2017) Ch . . . 240
Sage v Hewlett Packard Enterprise Company (2017) CA . . . 87
Sainsbury v IRC (1970) . . . 536, 590
Sainsbury Plc v O'Connor (Inspector of Taxes) (1991) . . . 551
St Andrew's Allotments Association Trusts; Sargeant v Probert (1969) . . . 365
St Andrew's (Cheam) Lawn Tennis Club Trust (2012) . . . 229, 358, 360, 366, 470
St George (deceased), Re (1964) . . . 191
St Pancras and Humanist Housing Association Ltd v Leonard (2008) CA . . . 322
Sale Hotel and Botanical Gardens Co, Re; Hesketh's Case (1897); revsd sub nom Sale Hotel and Botanical Gardens Ltd, Re ex p Hesketh (1898) CA . . . 784
Salomon v A Salomon & Co Ltd (1897) HL . . . 60
Salting, Re; Baillie-Hamilton v Morgan (1932) . . . 609
Salusbury v Denton (1857) . . . 490
Salvation Army Trustees Co Ltd v West Yorkshire Metropolitan County Council (1980) . . . 329

Sampson, Re; Sampson v Sampson (1906) . . . 672
Sandbrook, Re; Noel v Sandbrook (1912) . . . 190
Sandeman (FS) & Sons v Tyzack and Branfoot Shipping Co (1913) HL . . . 46
Sanders' Will Trusts, Re; Public Trustee v McLaren (1954); on appeal (1954) CA . . . 437
Sanderson v Hi Peak Property Ltd (2014) Ch . . . 362
Sanderson v Walker (1807) . . . 760
Sanderson's Will Trust, Re (1857) . . . 227
Sandhu v Sandhu (2016) CA . . . 292, 298
Sans Souci Limited v VRL Services Limited (2012) PC . . . 89
Santander UK v RA Legal Solicitors (2014) CA . . . 237, 716, 736, 738–40
Sargeant v National Westminstr Bank plc (1990) CA . . . 759
Satnam Ltd v Dunlop Heywood & Co Ltd (1999) CA . . . 768, 807
Satterthwaite's Will Trusts, Re; Midland Bank Executor and Trustee Co Ltd v Royal Veterinary College (1966) CA . . . 504, 505
Saul v Pattinson (1886) . . . 579
Saunders v Vautier (1841) . . . 32, 53, 136, 359, 536, 542, 551, 556, 563, 589, 603–5, 612, 620, 670, 671, 678, 684, 685, 697, 700
Savile v Couper (1887) . . . 674
Sawyer v Sawyer (1885) CA . . . 742
Saxton's Estate, Re; Barclays Bank Ltd v Treasury Solicitor (1939) . . . 384
Sayer Trust, Re; MacGregor v Sayer (1957) . . . 128–30, 561
Sayre v Hughes (1868) . . . 217
Scandinavian Trading Tanker Co AB v Flota Petrolera Ecuatoriana (The Scaptrade) (1983) HL . . . 80
Scarisbrick's Will Trusts, Re; sub nom Cockshot v Public Trustee (1951) CA . . . 482, 483
SCF Tankers Ltd v Privalov (2017) . . . 108
Schebsman (Decd), Re ex p Offical Receiver; Trustee v Cardo Superintendents (London) Ltd and Schebsman (1944) CA . . . 168, 626
Schenk v Cook (2017) QB . . . 232, 748, 776
Schmidt v Rosewood Trust Ltd (Isle of Man) (2003) PC . . . 26, 39, 417, 565, 592, 593, 707–11
Schobelt v Barber (1996) . . . 246
Schrader v Schrader (2013) . . . 71, 380
Scott v Hanson (1829) . . . 85
Scott v National Trust for Places of Historic Interest or Natural Beauty (1998) . . . 430, 514, 529, 632, 634, 701, 706, 707, 712
Scott v Rayment (1868) . . . 81
Scott v Scott (2012) . . . 682
Scottish Burial Reform and Cremation Society v Glasgow City Corpn (1968) . . . 433, 434, 458, 459
Seale's Marriage Settlement, Re (1961) . . . 617
Searle v Law (1846) . . . 559
Seaton v Seddon (2012) . . . 786, 791
SEC v Chenery Corpn (1943) . . . 745
Secretary of State for Environment, Food and Rural Affairs (Respondent) v Meier (2009) SC . . . 91
Secretary of State for Trade and Industry v Rogers (1996) . . . 619
Sefton v Tophams Ltd (1965); on appeal (1965) CA; revsd sub nom Tophams Ltd v Earl of Sefton (1967) . . . 85, 92
Segelman (Deceased), Re (1996) . . . 75, 77, 437, 482, 483
Sehota (Deceased), Re; sub nom Kaur v Kaur (1978) . . . 375
Sekhon v Alissa (1989) . . . 217, 219
Selangor United Rubber Estates Ltd v Craddock (A Bankrupt) (No. 3) (1968) CA . . . 242, 746, 800, 801, 804, 807, 820
Selby v Alston (1797) . . . 13
Selby-Walker, Re; Public Trustee v Selby-Walker (1949) . . . 598
Sells v Sells (1860) . . . 76
Sen v Headley (1991) CA . . . 160–3
Series 5 Software Ltd v Clarke (1996) . . . 95, 96
Shafto's Trusts, Re (1885) . . . 676
Shah v Shah (2010) CA . . . 117
Shaker v Al-Bedrawi (2002) CA . . . 766
Shakespeare Memorial Trust, Re; Earl of Lytton v A-G (1923) . . . 449
Shallcross v Oldham (1862) . . . 761
Shalson v Russo (Tracing Claims) (2003) . . . 119, 848, 857, 868
Sharma v Farlam Ltd (2009) . . . 760
Sharma v Simposh Ltd (2013) . . . 214
Sharman's Will Trusts, Re (1942) . . . 668
Sharp v Sharp (2017) . . . 293
Sharpe, Re; Bennett, Re; Masonic and General Life Association Co v Sharpe (1892) CA . . . 790
Sharpe (A Bankrupt), Re; Trustee in Bankruptcy v Sharpe (1980) . . . 209, 239, 301, 311, 334, 337, 338, 340
Sharp's Settlement Trusts, Re; Ibbotson v Bliss (1973) . . . 599
Shaw, Re; Public Trustee v Day (1957); on appeal (1958) CA . . . 441, 475, 538, 539, 544, 697
Shaw v Applegate (1977) CA . . . 91, 318, 322
Shaw v Cates (1909) . . . 662, 738
Shaw v Foster (1872) . . . 250
Shaw's Will Trusts, Re (1952) . . . 477, 490
Sheffield v Sheffield (2013) . . . 557, 559
Shield v Shield (2014) CA . . . 249
Shelfer v City of London Electric Lighting Co (No. 1) (1895) CA . . . 91–3
Shell UK Ltd v Lostock Garage Ltd (1977) CA . . . 85, 92
Shelley v Shelley (1868) . . . 118
Shephard v Cartwright (1955) HL . . . 210, 211, 216
Shepherd Homes Ltd v Sandham (1971) . . . 100
Sheppard's Settlement Trust, Re (1888) . . . 676
Shergill v Khaira (2012) CA . . . 491
Sheridan v Joyce (1844) . . . 828
Sherrington v Sherrington (2005) CA . . . 382, 383
Shiloh Spinners v Harding (No. 1) (1973) HL . . . 17
Ship v Crosskill (1870) . . . 70
Shipwrecked Fishermen and Mariners' Royal Benevolent Society, Re (1959) . . . 609
Shotton v Hammond (1976) . . . 104

Shovelar v Lane (2011) CA . . . 387
Shrewsbury Grammar School, Re (1849) . . . 512
Sichel's Settlement, Re; Sichel v Sichel (1916) . . . 676
Sick and Funeral Society of St John's Sunday School, Golcar, Re (1973) . . . 229, 364, 365, 367
Sieff v Fox (2005) . . . 703
Siew Soon Wah v Yong Tong Hong (1973) PC . . . 333
Sifton v Sifton (1938) . . . 189, 191
Sigsworth, Re; Bedford v Bedford (1935) . . . 245, 246
Silver v Silver (1958) CA . . . 217, 218
Silverwood v Silverwood and Whiteley (1997) CA . . . 213
Simon v Byford (2014) . . . 378
Simpson v Bathhurst (1869) . . . 546
Simpson v Gowers (1981) . . . 201
Simpson v Simpson (1992) . . . 72
Simpson (Decd), Re (1977) . . . 380
Simson, Re; Fowler v Tinley (1946) . . . 444
Sinclair v Brougham (1914) HL . . . 23, 746, 839, 852, 853, 854, 858, 867, 877
Sinclair v Lee (1993) . . . 548, 549
Sinclair v Sinclair (2009) . . . 324
Sinclair Investments Holdings SA v Versailles Trade Finance Ltd (2005) CA . . . 748, 777, 782, 857
Sinclair Investments (UK) Ltd v Versailles Trade Finance Ltd (in administration) (2011), CA . . . 60, 780, 824, 862, 873
Singh v Ali (1960) . . . 214
Singh v Charity Commission and others (2016) . . . 515
Singh v Singh (2014) . . . 289, 292
Singha v Heer (2016) CA . . . 143
Singleton v Tomlinson (1878) HL . . . 384
Singularis Holdings Ltd (In Liquidation) v Daiwa Capital Markets Europe Ltd (2019) . . . 214
Sir Edward Heath Charitable Trust (2012) . . . 498, 627
Siskina (Cargo Owners) v Distos Cia Naviera SA (1979); on appeal sub nom Siskina (Cargo Owners) v Distos Cia Naviera SA (The Siskina) (1979) CA; revsd (1979) HL . . . 108
Skeats, Re; sub nom Thain v Gibbs (1936) Ch . . . 374
Skeats' Settlement, Re; Skeats v Evans (1989) . . . 672
Skinner, Re; Cooper v Skinner (1904) . . . 710
Sky Petroleum Ltd v VIP Petroleum Ltd (1974) . . . 79, 100
Slatter's Will Trusts, Re; Turner v Turner (1964) . . . 501
Sledmore v Dalby (1996) CA . . . 295, 335, 338
Sleight v Callin (2021) Ch . . . 736
Slevin, Re; Slevin v Hepburn (1891) CA . . . 494, 499
Smart's Goods, Re (1902) . . . 384
Smirthwaite's Trust, Re (1871) . . . 680
Smith, Re (1932) . . . 470
Smith, Re; Public Trustee v Aspinall (1928) . . . 536, 589, 605
Smith, Re; Smith v Thompson (1896) . . . 741
Smith v Anderson (1880) CA . . . 60
Smith v Day (1882) . . . 99
Smith v Grigg Ltd (1924) CA . . . 95
Smith v Houblon (1859) . . . 579
Smith v Inner London Education Authority (1978) CA . . . 97
Smith v Matthews; Matthews's Settlement, Re (1861) . . . 170, 171
Smith v Michelmores Trust Corporation Ltd (2021) Ch . . . 569, 589, 592
Smith and Service and Nelson & Sons, Re (1890) CA . . . 81
Smith & Smith v Smith (1869) . . . 382
SmithKline Beecham v Apotex Europe Ltd (2007) CA . . . 845
Smith v Stanley (2019) . . . 70
Smith's Will Trusts, Re; Barclays Bank Ltd v Mercantile Bank Ltd (1962) CA . . . 445
Snook v London and West Riding Investments Ltd (1967) . . . 118
Snowden (Deceased), Re; Smith v Spowage (1979) . . . 116, 117, 404, 409, 413
Soar v Ashwell (1893) CA . . . 802
Soar v Foster (1858) . . . 218
Societe Generale, London Branch v Geys (2012) SC . . . 80, 103
Society of Accountants and Auditors v Goodway (1907) . . . 90
Society of Architects v Kendrick (1910) . . . 90
Sofer v SwissIndependent Trustees SA (2020) CA . . . 720, 743
Soinco SACI v Novokurznetsk Aluminium Plant (1998); affd (1998) CA . . . 106
Solicitor (1951 M No. 234), Re (1952) . . . 680
Solle v Butcher (1950) CA . . . 24
Solomon v McCarthy (2020) . . . 172, 173, 282
Solomon, Re; Nore v Meyer (1912); on appeal (1913) CA . . . 662
Somerset, Re; Somerset v Earl Poulett (1894) CA . . . 743
Somes, Re; Smith v Somes (1896) . . . 573, 580
Sorochan v Sorochan (1986) . . . 256
Soulby's Trusts (1873) . . . 679
Soulos v Korkontzilas (1997) . . . 255, 256
South Australia Asset Management Corporation v York Montague Ltd (1997) . . . 728, 729
South Buckinghamshire DC v Porter (2003) HL . . . 105
South Place Ethical Society, Re; sub nom Barralet v A-G (1980) . . . 442, 459, 460, 489
South Somerset District Council v Hughes (2009) CA . . . 105
Soutzos v Asombang (2010) . . . 234
Space Investments Ltd v Canadian Imperial Bank of Commerce Trust Co (Bahamas) Ltd (1986) PC . . . 755, 869, 870
Spalding (GG) & Bros v AW Gamage Ltd (1915) HL . . . 104
Speechley v Allott (2014) CA . . . 672
Speight v Gaunt (1883) HL . . . 631–3, 639, 656, 696, 716
Spence, Re; Ogden v Shackleton (1979) . . . 497, 500, 502–5

Spence, Re; Quick v Ackner (1949) . . . 408
Spence v Crawford (1939) HL . . . 74
Spence v Union Marine Insurance Co (1868) . . . 46, 842, 847
Spencer's Settled Estates, Re (1903) . . . 683
Spiro v Glencrown Properties Ltd (1991) . . . 759
SPL Private Finance (PF1) IC Ltd v Arch Financial Products LLP (2014) Comm . . . 782
SPL Private Finance (PF2) IC Ltd v Farrell (2015) CA . . . 811
Sprange v Barnard (1789) . . . 123
Spread Trustee Company Ltd v Hutcheson (2011) PC . . . 720, 721
Spring v Pride (1864) . . . 757
Springett v Dashwood (1860) . . . 707
Springette v Defoe (1992) CA . . . 260, 301
Spycatcher . . . *see* A-G v Observer Ltd
Stacey v Elph (1833) . . . 668, 758
Stack v Dowden (2007) HL . . . 197, 202, 219, 248, 253, 262, 273, 274, 276–85, 287, 288, 290–2, 297, 300, 302–4, 307, 309, 313, 317, 331, 347, 348
Stafford v Stafford (1857) . . . 734
Stamford (Earl), Re; Payne v Stamford (1896) . . . 683
Stamp Duties Commissioner (Queensland) v Livingston (1965) PC . . . 538
Stamp Duties Commissioners v Byrnes (1911) . . . 220
Stanford, Re; Cambridge University v A-G (1924) . . . 500
Stanford International Bank Ltd (In Liquidation) v HSBC Bank Plc (2020) Ch; (2021) CA . . . 812
Staniland v Willott (1852) . . . 161–3
Stapleton, Re; Stapleton v Stapleton (1946) . . . 598
Stapylton Fletcher Ltd (In Administration Receivership), Re (1995) . . . 122
Star Energy Weald Basin Ltd v Bocardo SA (2010) . . . 94
Starglade Properties Ltd v Nash (2010) CA . . . 811, 812
State Bank of India v Sood (1997) CA . . . 694
Statek Corp v Alford (2008) . . . 722, 810, 816
Stead, Re; Witham v Andrew (1900) . . . 406
Steadman v Steadman (1976) HL . . . 312
Steed's Will Trusts, Re; Standford v Stevenson (1960) CA . . . 608, 611, 619, 620, 703
Steel v Wellcome Custodian Trustees Ltd (1988) . . . 620, 653
Steele v Steele (2001) . . . 868
Steele's Will Trusts, Re; National Provincial Bank Ltd v Steele (1948) . . . 118
Stemson's Will Trusts, Re; Carpenter v Treasury Solicitor (1970) . . . 501
Stenning, Re; Wood v Stenning (1895) . . . 866
Stephen (Harold) & Co Ltd v Post Office (1977) CA . . . 103
Stephens v Green (1895) CA . . . 558
Stevens, Re; (1892) . . . 479
Stevens v Bell (2002) CA . . . 54
Stewart, Re; Stewart v McLaughlin (1908) . . . 159
Stichting Shell Pensioenfonds v Krys (British Virgin Islands) (2014) PC . . . 103
Stickland v Aldridge (1804) . . . 403
Stilwell v Simpson (1983) . . . 326
Stockholm Finance Limited v Garden Holdings Inc (1995) . . . 197
Stocks v Wilson (1913) . . . 857
Stoffel and Co v Grondona (2020) SC . . . 214
Stone, Re; Perpetual Trustee v Stone (1970) . . . 460
Stone v Hoskins (1905) . . . 395
Stone v Stone (1869) . . . 716
Stoneham's Settlement Trusts, Re; Popkiss v Stoneham (1953) . . . 674, 676
Stones v Rowton (1853) . . . 672
Story v McLoughlin (2017) . . . 360
Stott v Milne (1884) CA . . . 755
Strafford (Earl) (Deceased), Re; Royal Bank of Scotland v Byng (1980) CA . . . 27, 629, 630
Strahan, Re ex p Geaves (1856) . . . 723
Strakosch (Deceased), Re; Temperley v A-G (1949) CA . . . 453
Stratford (JT) & Son Ltd v Lindley (1965) CA; revsd (1965) HL . . . 95
Strathcona (Lord) Steamship Co Ltd v Dominion Coal Co Ltd (1926) PC . . . 168
Stratulatos v Stratulatos (1988) . . . 335, 340
Strong v Bird (1874) . . . 158, 159, 414
Stuart, Re; Smith v Stuart (1897) . . . 736, 738
Stumore v Campbell & Co (1892) . . . 233
Subhani v Sultan (2017) Ch . . . 214
Sudbrook Trading Estate Ltd v Eggleton (1983) CA; revsd (1983) HL . . . 78
Suffert's Settlement, Re; Suffert v Martyn-Linnington (1961) . . . 615
Suggitt v Suggitt (2012) CA . . . 328, 341
Sullivan, Re; Dunkley v Sullivan (1930) . . . 547
Sullivan v Henderson (1973) . . . 85
Summer's Trusts, Re (1874) . . . 604
Sun Indalex Finance, LLC v United Steelworkers (2013) . . . 255, 257
Surrey County Council v Bredero Homes Ltd (1993) CA . . . 93, 94
Sutton, Re; Stone v A-G (1885) . . . 469, 679
Sutton v England (2011) . . . 609
Sutton v Sutton (1984) . . . 83, 84
Swain, Re; Swain v Bringeman (1891) . . . 787
Swain v Law Society (1983) HL . . . 129, 168
Swan (William Lawrence Greenwell) v Gibbs (Dominic Vaughan) (2020) Ch . . . 585, 613
Swindle v Harrison (1997) CA . . . 728, 746, 774
Swiss Bank Corpn v Lloyds Bank Ltd (1982) CA; affd (1982) HL . . . 79
Sybron Corpn v Rochem Ltd (1984) CA . . . 750
Symes v Green (1859) . . . 379

T (A Child), Re (2017) . . . 104
Tacon, Re (1958) . . . 500
Tahir v Faizi (2019) . . . 282
Tai Hing Cotton Mills Ltd v Kamsing Knitting Factory (1979) PC . . . 77
Tailby v Official Receiver (1888) HL . . . 558
Taittinger SA v Allbev Ltd (1994) CA . . . 87, 104

Tamares (Vincent Square) Ltd v Fairpoint Properties (Vincent Square Ltd) (2007) . . . 94
Tamplin v James (1880) CA . . . 84
Tancred v Delagoa Bay and East Africa Railway Co (1889) . . . 557
Tang Man Sit (Deceased) v Capacious Investments Ltd (1996) PC . . . 724, 781
Target Holdings Ltd v Redferns (a firm) (1996) HL . . . 237, 725, 727–32
Tasarruf Mevduati Sigorta Fonu v Merrill Lynch Bank & Trust Co (Cayman) Ltd (2011) PC (CI) . . . 39, 545, 561
Tate v Hilbert (1793) . . . 163
Tate Access Floors Inc v Boswell (1991) . . . 111
Tatham v Drummond (1864) . . . 456
Taylor, Re; Midland Bank Executor and Trustee Co Ltd v Smith (1940); affd (1940) CA . . . 355
Taylor, Re; Smart v Taylor (1901) . . . 598
Taylor v Dickens (1998) . . . 318, 322, 340
Taylor v HMRC (2008) . . . 404
Taylor v Plumer (1815) . . . 842, 843, 847, 849
Taylor v Tabrum (1833) . . . 716
Taylor v Taylor (1843) . . . 755
Taylor v Taylor (1956) . . . 334, 337
Taylor v Taylor (2017) Ch . . . 170, 171, 277, 278
Taylor Fashions Ltd v Liverpool Victoria Trustees Co Ltd (1982) . . . 318, 319, 322
Tee v Ferris (1856) . . . 406
Tegg, Re (1936) . . . 188, 190
Tempest, Re (1865-66) CA . . . 682, 683
Tempest v Lord Camoys (1882) CA . . . 37, 695, 699
Test Claimants in the Franked Investment Income Group Litigation v Revenue and Customs Commissioners (2012) . . . 879
Test Claimants in the Franked Investment Income Group Litigation v Revenue and Customs Commissioners [2020] . . . 68, 787
Thames Guaranty Ltd v Campbell (1985); affd (1985) CA . . . 77
Thavorn v Bank of Credit and Commerce International SA (1985) . . . 203
Thellusson v Woodford (1799) . . . 186
Themehelp Ltd v West (1995) CA . . . 97
Third Chandris Shipping Corpn v Unimarine SA (1979); affd (1979) CA . . . 106, 108
Thomas, Re; Thomas v Thompson (1930) . . . 609
Thomas v Thomas (1956) . . . 332
Thomas and Agnes Carvel Foundation v Carvell (2008) . . . 396, 686
Thompson, Re (1934) . . . 543, 544
Thompson v Finch (1856) . . . 741
Thompson v Foy (2009) . . . 321, 329, 333
Thompson v Hurst (2012) CA . . . 281, 300
Thompson v Mechan (1958) . . . 160
Thompson v Park (1944) CA . . . 337
Thompson's Estate, Re; Goff v Duffield (1928) . . . 163
Thompson's Settlement, Re; Thompson v Thompson (1986) . . . 754, 758, 759
Thompson's Settlement Trust, Re; Thompson v Alexander (1905) . . . 668
Thompson's Trustee in Bankruptcy v Heaton (1974) . . . 746, 762
Thomson, Re; Thomson v Thomson (1930) . . . 761, 762
Thomson v Eastwood (1877) HL . . . 736, 760
Thorne v Heard and Marsh (1895) CA; affd (1895) HL . . . 784, 785
Thorner v Major (2009) HL . . . 240, 261, 319–24, 328, 330, 335, 349
Thornton v Howe (1862) . . . 444
Thynne v Glengall (1848) . . . 25
Tierney v Tough (1914) . . . 362, 365
Tierney v Wood (1854) . . . 558
Tilley's Will Trust, Re; Burgin v Croad (1967) . . . 833, 874, 877
Timmis, Re; Nixon v Smith (1902) . . . 785, 787
Timpson's Executors v Yerbury (Inspector of Taxes) (1936) CA . . . 557
Tinker v Tinker (1970) CA . . . 217, 221, 302
Tinline v White Cross Insurance Association Ltd (1921) . . . 244
Tinsley v Milligan (1993) CA; affd (1994) HL . . . 196, 202, 204, 213, 214, 221, 299
Tito v Waddell (No. 2) (1977) . . . 116, 711, 715, 757
TMSF v Merril Lynch Bank . . . *see* Tasarruf Mevduati Sigorta Fonu v Merrill Lynch Bank & Trust Co (Cayman) Ltd
Tollemache, Re (1903) CA . . . 606
Tombstone Ltd v Raja (2008) . . . 87
Tomkin v Tomkin (2003) . . . 701
Torkington v Magee (1902); revsd (1903) CA . . . 557
Townley v Sherborn (1634) . . . 723
Transfield Shipping Inc v Chiping Xinta Huaya Alumina Co Ltd (2009) . . . 98
Trappes v Meredith (1871) . . . 51
Trenberth (John) Ltd v National Westminster Bank Ltd (1980) . . . 90
Trevor (J) & Sons v P R Soloman (1978) . . . 100
Tribe v Tribe (1995) CA . . . 213, 221
Trimmer v Danby (1856) . . . 540
Triplex Safety Glass Co Ltd v Scorah (1938) . . . 767
Trust of Arthur McDougall Fund, Re; Thompson v Fitzgerald (1956) . . . 462
Trustees of the British Museum v A-G (1984) . . . 620, 642, 653
Trustees of the Graphic Reproduction Federation v Wellcom London Ltd (2014) . . . 361, 362, 365
Trustor AB v Smallbone (No 2) (2001) . . . 827
Trusts of Scientific Pension Plan, Re (1989) . . . 54
Trytel, Re; sub nom Trustee of Property of Bankrupt, Ex p v Performing Right Society Ltd and Soundtrak Film Co Ltd (1952) . . . 124
T's Settlement Trusts, Re (1964) . . . 612, 617
TSB Bank plc v Camfield (1995) CA . . . 72
TSE v News Group Newspapers Ltd (2011) . . . 105
Tuck's Settlement Trusts, Re; sub nom Public Trustee v Tuck (1978) CA . . . 134, 135
Tufnell, Re; Byng v Tufnell (1902) . . . 785
Tufton v Sperni (1952) CA . . . 72
Tulk v Moxhay (1884) . . . 17
Turkington, Re; Owen v Benson (1937) . . . 359

Turner, Re; Barker v Ivimey (1897) . . . 736, 738
Turner v Corney (1841) . . . 631
Turner v Jacob (2006) . . . 863
Turner v Turner (1983) . . . 575, 576, 699
Turner's Will Trusts; District Bank Ltd v Turner (1937) CA . . . 596, 616
Turton, Re; Whittington v Turton (1926) . . . 191
Twentieth Century Fox Film Corp v Harris (2013) . . . 241
Twin Benefits Ltd v Barker (2017) Ch . . . 34
Twinsectra Ltd v Yardley (1999) CA; (2002) HL . . . 231–7, 719, 807–10, 815, 816, 818, 822
Tyler, Re; Tyler v Tyler (1891) CA . . . 429
Tyler's Fund Trusts, Re; Graves v King (1967) . . . 411
Tyrell v Bowden (2018) Ch . . . 316, 319, 322
Tyrrell v Bank of London (1862) . . . 777

UL v BK (2013) . . . 106, 109
Ulrich v Treasury Solicitor (2005) . . . 470
Ultraframe (UK) Ltd v Fielding (2005) . . . 765, 773, 804
Ulverston and District New Hospital Building Trusts, Re; Birkett v Barrow and Furness Hospital Management Committee (1956) CA . . . 226, 229
Ungurian v Lesnoff (1990) . . . 334
United Grand Lodge of Ancient Free and Accepted Masons of England v Holborn BC (1957) . . . 444
United Scientific Holdings Ltd v Burnley BC (1978) HL . . . 8, 9, 85
Unity Joint Stock Mutual Banking Association v King (1858) . . . 334
Universe Tankships Inc of Monrovia v International Transport Workers Federation (1983) HL . . . 358
University College of North Wales v Taylor (1908) CA . . . 384
University of London Charitable Trusts, Re (1964) . . . 662
University of Nottingham v Fishel (2000) . . . 749
Ust-Kamenogorsk Hydropower Plant JSC v AES Ust-Kamenogorsk Hydropower Plant LLP (2013) SC . . . 102
Utley, Re; Russell v Cubitt (1912) . . . 713
Uzinterimpex JSC v Standard Bank plc (2008) CA . . . 816

V v T (2014) Ch . . . 611
Vagliano, Re; Vagliano v Vagliano (1905) . . . 460
Vajpeyi v Yijsaf (2003) . . . 208, 209, 302
Vallance, Re (1876) . . . 462
Vallee v Birchwood (2013) . . . 160, 162
Valuation Commissioner for Northern Ireland v Lurgan BC (1968) CA . . . 455
Van Gruisen's Will Trusts, Re; Bagger v Dean (1964) . . . 618
Van Zuylen v Whiston-Dew (2021) Ch . . . 839
Vandepitte v Preferred Accident Insurance Corpn of New York (1933) PC . . . 168
Vanderpant v Mayfair Hotel Co Ltd (1930) . . . 102
Vandervell v IRC (1967) HL . . . 175, 177–9, 181, 198, 201, 225, 551, 556
Vandervell's Trust (No. 2), Re; sub nom White v Vandervell Trustees Ltd (1974); revsd (1974) CA . . . 7, 145, 182–4, 195, 200
Vane v Lord Barnard (1716) . . . 102
Vane v Vane (1873) . . . 784
Varsani v Jesani (1998) CA . . . 442, 498, 499, 508
Vatcher v Paull (1915) PC . . . 567, 568, 569
Vegetarian Society v Scott (2013) . . . 379
Venture, The (1908) . . . 206
Vernon's Will Trusts, Re; Lloyds Bank Ltd v Group 20 Hospital Management Committee (Coventry) (1972) . . . 502
Vernor-Miles and Ors v Charity Commission Appeal number: CA/2014/0022 (12 May 2015) . . . 459
Verrall, Re; National Trust for Places of Historic Interest or Natural Beauty v A-G (1916) . . . 453
Verrall v Great Yarmouth Borough Council (1981) CA . . . 78
Vestey, Re . . . *see* Baron Vestey's Settlement, Re
Vestey v IRC (1980) HL . . . 536, 563, 566
Vickery, Re; Vickery v Stephens (1931) . . . 633
Vinogradoff, Re; Allen v Jackson (1935) . . . 198, 203, 370, 668
Voyce v Voyce (1992) CA . . . 329, 332, 343
Voyle v Hughes (1854) . . . 558
VTB Capital Plc v Nutritek International Corp and Ors (2011) . . . 106
Vynior's Case (1610) . . . 387
Vyse v Foster (1872); affd (1874) . . . 758

W v Egdell (1990); affd (1990) CA . . . 853
W v G (1996) . . . 331
W (Algeria) v Secretary of State for the Home Department (2012) SC . . . 88
Wade v Cox (1835) . . . 736
Wakeham v Wood (1982) CA . . . 92, 103
Walbrook Trustees (Jersey) Ltd v Fattal & Ors (2007) Ch . . . 565
Wale, Re; Wale v Harris (1956) . . . 159
Walker and Hughes' Contract, Re (1883) . . . 676
Walker, Re (2014) Ch . . . 379
Walker, Re; Summers v Barrow (1901) . . . 604, 674
Walker v Boyle (1982) . . . 70, 84
Walker v Stones (2001) CA . . . 719, 720, 737
Walker v Symonds (1818) . . . 723, 734
Wallace's Settlements, Re (1968) . . . 618
Waller v Waller (1967) . . . 103
Wallersteiner v Moir (No. 2) (1975) CA . . . 733
Wallgrave v Tebbs (1855) . . . 405, 409
Wallis v Solicitor-General for New Zealand (1903) . . . 511
Walpole v Lord Orford (1797) . . . 391, 393
Walsh v Lonsdale (1882) CA . . . 8, 17
Walsh v Walsh (2017) . . . 144
Walsingham's Case (1578) . . . 11
Walton v Walton (1994) . . . 319, 332
Warburton v Warburton (1702) HL . . . 37, 585, 593
Ward v Turner (1752) . . . 162, 163

Ward-Smith v Jebb (1964); on appeal sub nom Jebb, Re; Ward-Smith v Jebb (1966) CA . . . 739
Ware v Cumberlege (1855) . . . 512
Warman International v Dwyer (1995) . . . 771
Warner Bros Pictures Inc v Nelson (1937) . . . 80
Warnes v Headley (1984) CA . . . 319
Warnick (Erven) BV v J Townend & Sons (Hull) Ltd (1979) HL . . . 104
Warren v Gurney (1944) CA . . . 220, 785
Wasserberg, Re; Union of London and Smiths Bank Ltd v Wasserberg (1915) . . . 162
Waterman's Will Trusts, Re; Lloyds Bank Ltd v Sutton (1952) . . . 717
Watkin v Watson-Smith (1986) . . . 73
Watson, Re (1904) . . . 710
Watson, Re; Hobbs v Smith (1973) . . . 444, 491
Watson (Probate), Re (2008) . . . 380
Watson v Croft Promosport Ltd (2009) CA . . . 86, 92
Watson v Kea Investments Ltd (2019) CA . . . 733
Watts v Spence (1976) . . . 85
Watts v Stewart (2016) . . . 513
Watts v Storey (1983) CA . . . 329, 331
Watt's Will Trusts, Re; Watt v Watt (1936) . . . 596
Waverley Borough Council v Hilden (1988) . . . 94
Wayling v Jones (1993) CA . . . 320, 322, 326, 327, 330, 334
Weatherhill v Pearce (1995) Ch . . . 383
Webb, Re; Barclays Bank Ltd v Webb (1941) . . . 625
Webb v Earl of Shaftesbury (1802) . . . 755
Webb v Kelly (1839) . . . 227
Webb v O'Doherty (1991) . . . 463
Webb v Webb (1992); on appeal (1992) CA; refd sub nom Webb v Webb C-294/92 (1994) ECJ . . . 33, 220
Webb v Webb (2020) (PC Cook Islands) . . . 119, 120, 561
Webster v Cecil (1861) . . . 84
Wedgwood, Re; Allen v Wedgwood (1915) CA . . . 456, 474
Weekes' Settlement, Re (1897) . . . 560, 561, 571, 572
Weir Hospital, Re (1910) CA . . . 496
Weir v Crum-Brown (1908) HL . . . 468
Weir's Settlement, Re; MacPherson and Viscount Weir v IRC (1969); on appeal (1969) CA . . . 590
Weld v Petre (1929) CA . . . 790
Weld-Blundell v Wolseley (1903) . . . 102
Wellbeloved v Jones (1822) . . . 512
Weller v Kerr (1866) HL . . . 579
Wellesley v Wellesley (1828) HL . . . 599
Welsh Hospital (Netley) Fund, Re; Thomas v A-G (1921) . . . 228
Wesley v Kleinwort Benson (Channel Islands) Trustees Ltd . . . *see* Bathurst (Countess) v Kleinwort Benson (Channel Islands) Trustees Ltd
Wesley, Bathurst v Chantler and others (2018) . . . *see* Bathurst (Deceased), Re
West, Re; Westhead v Aspland (1913) . . . 598
West v Knight (1669) . . . 470
West (Richard) & Partners (Inverness) Ltd v Dick (1969); on appeal (1969) CA . . . 25, 78
West Sussex Constabulary's Widows, Children and Benevolent (1930) Fund Trusts, Re; Barnett v Ketteringham (1971) . . . 228, 362, 363, 364, 367
Westdeutsche Landesbank Girozentrale v Islington LBC (1994) CA; revsd (1996) HL . . . 22, 29, 34, 56, 67, 121, 195, 198– 200, 222–4, 238–41, 243, 260, 261, 667, 722, 752, 817–9, 822, 834, 838, 847, 852–5, 857–9
Western Fish Products Ltd v Penwith DC (1981) CA . . . 267
Westminster Bank Ltd's Declaration of Trust, Re (1963) . . . 604
Weston, Re; Bartholomew v Menzies (1902) . . . 163
Weston's Settlements, Re; Weston v Weston (1969); affd (1969) CA . . . 603, 616, 617, 680, 681
Westpac Banking Corpn v Savin (1985) NZCA . . . 820
Wetherspoon (JD) plc v Van de Berg & Co Ltd (2009) . . . 804–6
Wheeler and De Rochow, Re (1896) . . . 675, 676
Whichcote v Lawrence (1798) . . . 759
Whitby, Re; sub nom Public Trustee v Whitby (1944) CA . . . 374
White, Re; White v White (1893) CA . . . 512
White v Barton (1854) . . . 668
White v Jones (1995) CA; affd (1995) HL . . . 388, 637
White v White (2001) . . . 293
White v William (2010) . . . 498, 507
Whitehead's Will Trusts, Re; Burke v Burke (1971) . . . 683
Whitehead's Will Trusts, Re; Public Trustee v White (1959) . . . 549
Whitelaw v Wilson (1934) . . . 244
Whiteley, Re; London (Bishop of) v Whitely (1910) . . . 629
Whiteley, Re (1887) . . . *see* Learoyd v Whiteley
Whitlock v Moree (2017) PC . . . 208
Whitney v Smith (1869) . . . 757
Whittaker v Kinnear (2011) . . . 321
Widdow's Trusts, Re (1871) . . . 604
Wightwick's Will Trusts, Re; Official Trustees of Charitable Funds v Fielding-Ould (1950) . . . 740
Wiles v Gresham (1854); affd (1854) . . . 731
Wilkes v Allington (1931) . . . 161, 163
Wilkes v Spooner (1911) CA . . . 21
Wilkes' (Beloved) Charity, Re (1851) . . . 700, 705, 706, 712
Wilkinson v Parry (1828) . . . 734
Williams v Barton (1927) . . . 760
Williams v Central Bank of Nigeria (2014) SC . . . 240, 242, 784, 789, 801, 802, 829
Williams v IRC (1965) CA . . . 124
Williams v Staite (1979) CA . . . 333, 337, 339
Williams' Trustees v IRC (1947) HL . . . 455, 458, 459, 468
Williams-Ashman v Price and Williams (1942) . . . 802, 816
Willers v Joyce; Willers v Gubay; Gubay (Deceased), Re No 2) (2016) SC; (2017) Ch . . . 592, 810

Willis, Re (1921) . . . 669
Willis v Kibble (1839) . . . 755
Willis Ltd v Jardine Lloyd Thompson Group Plc (2015) CA . . . 89
Willmott v Barber (1880); on appeal (1881) CA . . . 318
Willoughby v Willoughby (1756) . . . 23
Wills' Trust Deeds, Re; Wills v Godfrey (1964) . . . 43, 572, 577–9
Wilson, Re; Wilson v Wilson (1908) . . . 361
Wilson, Re (1913) Ch . . . 495
Wilson v Duguid (1883) . . . 42
Wilson v Law Debenture Trust Corpn plc (1995) . . . 705, 707, 712
Wilson v Moore (1833); affd (1834) . . . 723
Wilson v Turner (1883) . . . 595, 596
Wilson (Michael) & Partners Ltd v Emmott (2018) CA . . . 103
Winchelsea (Earl) v Norcloffe (or Norcliffe) (1686) . . . 606
Windeatt's Will Trusts, Re (1969) . . . 681
Windsor Steam Coal Co (1901) Ltd, Re (1928); affd (1929) CA . . . 785
Winkler v Shamoon (2016) Ch . . . 152, 154
Wippell (Deceased), Re (2018) Ch . . . 384
Wise v Jimenez (2014) . . . 234
Withers LLP v Langbar (2012) . . . 233
Withington v Withington (1848) . . . 675
Wodzicki v Wodzicki (2017) CA . . . 208, 282, 290
Wokingham Fire Brigade Trusts, Re; Martin v Hawkins (1951) . . . 229, 446
Wolff v Wolff (2004) . . . 67, 68
Wolverhampton and Walsall Railway Co Ltd v London and North Western Railway Ltd (1873) . . . 102
Wolverhampton Corpn v Emmons (1901) CA . . . 82
Wood, Re; Barton v Chilcott (1949) . . . 538
Wood v Commercial First Business Ltd (2021) CA . . . 775
Woodar Investment Developments Ltd v Wimpey Construction UK Ltd (1980) HL . . . 167
Woodard v Woodard (1991) CA . . . 162
Woodford v Smith (1970) . . . 104
Woodhams, Re; Lloyds Bank Ltd v London College of Music (1981) . . . 496, 497, 504
Woodhouse v Newry Navigation Co (1898) CA . . . 91
Woodin, Re; Woodin v Glass (1985) CA . . . 598
Woollerton & Wilson Ltd v Richard Costain Ltd (1970) . . . 90, 94
Woolwich Equitable Building Society v IRC (1992) CA; affd (1993) HL . . . 222
Worby v Rosser (2000) CA . . . 637
Wordingham v Royal Exchange Trust Co (1992) . . . 75
Worthington, Re; Leighton v MacLeod (1954) . . . 756, 757
Wortley v Birkenhead (1754) . . . 23
Wragg, Re; Wragg v Palmer (1919) . . . 648
Wren v Bradley (1848) . . . 189
Wright, Re (1954) . . . 500
Wright v Atkyns (1823) HL . . . 115
Wright v Carter (1903) CA . . . 72
Wright v Gater (2011) . . . 612, 618
Wright v Morgan (1926) . . . 757, 759
Wright v National Westminster Bank plc (2014) . . . 70
Wright v Pyke (2012) CA . . . 99
Wright v Snowe (1848) . . . 734
Wright v Wright (1750) . . . 558
Wrightson, Re; Wrighton v Cooke (1908) . . . 687, 688
Wroth v Tyler (1974) . . . 86
Wrotham Park Estate Co Ltd v Parkside Homes Ltd (1974) . . . 90, 93, 94, 629
Wyndham v Egremont (2009) . . . 613, 641

X v A (2006) . . . 602
X Trust, Re (2013) . . . 725

Yaxley v Gotts (2000) CA . . . 78, 314, 324, 333, 340
Yeates v Line (2012) . . . 393
Yeoman's Row Management Ltd v Cobbe (2008) HL . . . 252, 253, 262, 321, 324
Yong v Panweld Trading Pte Ltd (2012) SGCA . . . 785
Yonge v Toynbee (1910) CA . . . 63
York and North Midland Railway Co v Hudson (1853) . . . 767
Young, Re (1885) . . . 208
Young v Sealey (1949) . . . 209, 370
Young v Young (2013) Fam . . . 551
Young (Deceased), Re; Young v Young (1951) . . . 406, 414, 437
Yugraneft v Abramovich (2008) . . . 832
Yukong Line v Rendsberg Investments Corp (2001) . . . 108

Z v Z (2016) Fam . . . 565
Z Ltd v A-Z and AA-LL (1982) CA . . . 106, 107
Zabihi v Janzemini (2008) . . . 213
Zeital v Kaye (2010) CA . . . 149, 152
Zumax Nigeria Ltd v First City Monument Bank Plc . . . *see* First City Monument Bank Plc v Zumax Nigeria Ltd
Zyk v Zyk (1995) . . . 144

Glossary of common terms

Acquiescence assent to a set of events that can be express, or inferred from the conduct of a party.

Ad Valorem Tax a tax charged 'according to value' so proportionate to the value of the property.

Administrator a person appointed by the court to deal with the estate of a deceased person (a female administrator is known as an 'administratrix'); an administrator can also be appointed to wind up an insolvent company.

Advancement, power of enables the trustees to advance (make an immediate payment of) part of the capital to beneficiaries who are contingently interested in the trust fund, but who have not yet satisfied all the conditions for immediate payment.

After-Acquired property property acquired after a trust or settlement is created. To be distinguished from future property.

Agency an arrangement where one person (the agent) acts for another (the principal), and where the acts of the agent can bind the principal.

Annuity an annual payment made in return for the payment of a lump sum (unless the contract otherwise specifies, there is no right to the repayment of all or any part of the capital).

Assignment where one person transfers the whole of his/her entitlement to property to another, so that he/she retains no rights in the property whatsoever.

Attorney, power of a form of agency under which one person (the attorney) is empowered to act for another (the principal) in executing deeds or (in the case of a lasting power of attorney) making defined decisions on behalf of the principal; also the instrument conferring this authority.

Bankruptcy a legal process started by or against an individual (a 'bankrupt') who is no longer able to meet outstanding debts owed to creditors.

Bare trust a trust in which the trustees are only effectively nominees and must act according to the beneficiaries' instructions.

Beneficiary a person entitled to the benefit or enjoyment of the trust property held by the trustees.

Beneficial interest the nature of the equitable interest the beneficiary has in a trust.

Bequest a gift of personal property made under a will.

Bona fide in good faith.

Bona vacantia property which vests in the Crown, because no other owner can be established.

Capacity to be of the age of legal majority (18) and not to be suffering from a disability that prevents the person from understanding the transaction in question. Capacity is required for making binding legal arrangements such as entering into legally binding agreements or making a will. Also known as being 'sui juris' (in charge of one's own affairs).

Capital the property (or fund) held under a trust.

Cestui que trust a beneficiary under a trust.

Charge a security for the payment of a debt or the fulfilment of an obligation that operates over identified property (*see* mortgage).

Charity an organization or purpose which is recognized by law as being of such public benefit as to merit special treatment.

Chattel an item of personal property (*see* personal property).

CHOSE IN ACTION property (such as copyright or the right to payment of a debt) which has no physical existence but is enforceable through legal proceedings.

CIVIL PARTNERS partners in a registered same-sex relationship, which gives similar property entitlements as conferred on married couples.

CLAIMANT a person initiating an action in court (formerly known as a 'plaintiff').

COHABITANT a person living with another, in a close personal relationship, who is neither a registered civil partner nor a spouse. A cohabitant is sometimes referred to as a 'cohabitee'.

CONDITIONAL GIFT a gift which is dependent on a specified event occurring or thing being done (e.g., a gift to Charlie if she graduates with a degree in law).

CONSIDERATION the concept of value given in return for a promise or the transfer of property, which is a prerequisite to transform a promise into a binding contractual obligation at law. In equity, consideration has a slightly wider meaning and can include the reason why a transfer is made (such as love and affection), even if no value is provided.

CONSTRUCTIVE TRUST a trust that is implied or imposed by operation of law, in defined circumstances relating to unconscionable conduct by the parties.

CONTEMPT OF COURT conduct which impedes the court process. In the context of equity, this would usually consist of a failure to follow an order of the court, which may lead to a fine or a custodial sentence.

CONTINGENT INTEREST a right which is provisional because it is dependent on the happening of an event which has not yet taken place (e.g., a gift to Clarissa if she survives her mother who is still alive).

CONVEYANCE the transfer and vesting of title to, or the creation of an interest in, property (usually land).

COVENANT a contractual promise contained in a deed.

DEBT a sum of money due from one person (the debtor) to another (the creditor).

DEED a specialized form of document, which must declare on its face that it is a deed and must be signed by the parties in the presence of a witness.

DEHORS THE WILL literally, outside the will.

DEVISE a gift of real property made under a will.

DETERMINABLE INTEREST an interest that ends on the happening of an event, although the event may never occur (e.g., a gift of an annual sum to Davina until she qualifies as a solicitor).

DISCRETIONARY TRUST a trust in which the trustees elect how to distribute property among a class of potential beneficiaries (the objects of the discretionary trust), as they in their discretion think fit.

DISCLAIMER a refusal to accept either an office (such as the office of trustee) or a gift.

DISPOSITION a transfer of title to property.

DISTRIBUTIVE POWER power to allocate property either generally or to the members of a defined class (objects).

DONEE a person who receives either property or a distributive power.

DONOR a person who gives property by way of a gift or creates a distributive power in favour of the donee.

ELECTION a choice, e.g., to rescind a contract or keep it in existence, or to choose a particular remedy.

ENDOWMENT where property is given to provide a permanent fund or source of income.

EQUITABLE TITLE title to property that is only enforceable in equity, and is vested in the beneficiaries under a trust.

EQUITABLE INTEREST an interest that can only be enforced in equity.

ESTATE either describes the property assets of a deceased person or describes the ownership rights a person enjoys over land.

EXECUTOR a person who acts as personal representative of a deceased person in carrying out the terms of a will and who was named in the will. (A person acting as a personal representative who is not named in the will is known as an administrator.)

EXEMPTION CLAUSE a contractual term designed to exclude or reduce the liability of one or other parties.

EXPRESS TRUST a trust that is intentionally created.

FIDUCIARY a person who has undertaken an obligation of loyalty to another and is compelled to put that other person's interests before his/her own (e.g., director of a company is a fiduciary for the company shareholders).

FIDUCIARY OBLIGATIONS the duties imposed by equity on a fiduciary to make sure that they act in the best interests of the person to whom they stand as a fiduciary.

FUTURE PROPERTY rights to property that have not yet been acquired, but may be acquired in the future.

GIFT a gratuitous transfer of all title in property.

GRATUITOUS without receiving a legally recognized benefit in return.

HOLDING TRUST specific type of trust in which the trustees simply obey the orders of the principal, often used to conceal the true identity of the principal.

IMPLIED TRUST the label given to a trust that has not been formally declared by the parties, but is found to exist by the courts because the evidence indicates that the parties meant to create this kind of obligation (either through a resulting or constructive trust).

INALIENABLE unable to transfer e.g., inalienable property is property that may not be transferred.

INSOLVENCY a legal process started by or against a company that is no longer able to meet outstanding debts owed to creditors.

INSTRUMENT the legal document that creates an obligation or transfers an interest (e.g., a trust instrument is the document creating a trust).

INTANGIBLE without physical form, e.g., intangible property, such as shares in a company.

INTER ALIA among other things.

INTER VIVOS during one's lifetime.

INTESTACY the process relating to the distribution of an individual's property after death where an individual dies without leaving a will.

JUDICIAL TRUSTEE a person appointed by the court to replace a trustee or fiduciary who has acted improperly (e.g., personal representatives under a will).

KNOWLEDGE the state of mind or awareness of facts necessary to the imposition of liability.

LEASE an estate in land of limited duration (held by a tenant), which is created out of a large estate of another (the landlord).

LIEN a right to claim or hold another's property as security for a debt.

LIFE INTEREST an interest in property that lasts for the duration of the holder's life.

MAINTENANCE, POWER OF enables the trustees to apply the income generated by a trust fund for the maintenance of the beneficiaries, even where they are not as yet entitled to the capital of the fund.

MORTGAGE the creation of a specific form of charge (usually of land) to provide security for a loan.

MORTGAGEE the person or company that advances the loan and receives the mortgage charge as security.

MORTGAGOR the person or company that receives the loan and creates the mortgage charge over their property in favour of the mortgagee.

NOMINEE a person or company who holds the legal title to property and ostensibly the control of the property, but who must exercise it in accordance with the directions of their principal (person who appointed the nominee or persons to whom the nominees owe their duty).

NOTICE, DOCTRINE OF an equitable doctrine that affects the durability of equitable property rights. Notice can be either actual (being aware of rights) or constructive (the rights would have been revealed if reasonable enquiries had been made).

OBJECTS the persons who may benefit from property on the exercise of a distributive power or discretionary trust.

OPTION a right to elect to create a binding contract to purchase property, when exercised.

OVERREACHING a process by which the asset value of beneficial interests in land is transferred to the proceeds of sale, so that a purchaser takes free from the beneficial interests.

PARI PASSU a right to share in property equally and without preference.

PAROL oral (e.g., a parol evidence lease is one created without writing).

PER STIRPES meaning 'by root', so property left in a will moves down a family tree through lineal divisions.

PERSONAL PROPERTY rights or interests relating to property other than land.

PERSONAL RIGHTS *see* Rights in personam.

POSSESSION, INTEREST IN an immediate entitlement to rights or income in property (compare with an interest in remainder).

POWER an authority to do something (e.g., allocate property to beneficiaries).

PRINCIPAL person to whom obligations are owed under a relationship (e.g., agency, or fiduciary).

PRIORITY to enforce a claim to property in preference to others.

PRIVITY a rule of common law that provides that obligations can only be enforced by and against the parties to a transaction.

PROBANDUM something which has to be proved. The plural is probanda, so that if there are three probanda, there are three things to be proved.

PROBATECOURT authority approving a will given to an executor to begin the administration of a deceased person's estate.

PROPRIETARY RIGHTS *see* Rights in rem.

PROTECTIVE TRUST a specialized form of trust, which allows beneficiaries to receive income on the property, but preventing them from transferring the right to income to someone else (sometimes called a spendthrift trust).

REAL PROPERTY rights or interests relating to land.

RECEIVER a person appointed (usually by court order) to receive income payments from property (e.g., on the bankruptcy of an individual).

REMAINDER, INTEREST IN an interest granted to take effect on the expiry of an interest in possession (e.g., to Lucy for life, remainder to Raoul). The person entitled to a remainder is known as a remainderman.

RESIDUARY ESTATE the final property of a deceased person, once all debts have been paid and any specific gifts by will have been made.

RESTITUTION the body of law designed to prevent unjust enrichment of the defendant by the claimant.

RESULTING TRUST an implied trust in which the beneficial interest in property results (comes back) to the person who transferred the property.

RIGHTS IN PERSONAM rights that are enforceable only against the person granting them (also known as personal rights).

RIGHTS IN REM rights that are enforceable against the whole world, not just the person granting them (also known as proprietary rights).

SECRET TRUST a specialized form of trust used to provide for someone on death, which is secret because it does not appear in the will (fully secret) or does not disclose the beneficiaries (half secret).

SENIOR COURTS the new title of the High Court and Court of Appeal. Until the creation of the United Kingdom Supreme Court, these courts were known as the Supreme Court of Judicature.

SETTLOR the person who creates a trust by putting (settling) his property on trust.

SPOUSE a married partner.

STRANGER TO A TRUST a third party who is neither the trustee nor beneficiary under a trust, but who deals with trust property (e.g., a bank facilitating the deposit of trust funds in a trust account).

SUI JURIS to be of full legal capacity. *See* Capacity.

SUPREME COURT the court which in October 2009 replaced the House of Lords as the highest court in the United Kingdom.

TESTAMENTARY property transfers on death made by will (wills are also known as testaments).

TESTATOR a male person who executes (creates) a will (a female person is known as a 'testatrix').

TITLE a right to ownership of property.

TRANSFEREE person who receives a transfer of property.

TRANSFEROR person who transfers property to another.

TRUST although impossible to define accurately, it describes a form of property ownership in which the control and benefit to property are separated, with legal title and control vested in trustees who are compelled by equity to exercise such control for the benefit of the beneficiaries, who hold the equitable title.

ULTRA VIRES in excess of authority (beyond the powers of a body or person with limited authority).

VALUE payment, usually in money or money's worth.

VESTING the satisfaction of all the requirements necessary for a right to property to become unconditional; the completion of the transfer of property to a person, so that they can begin to enjoy the rights in that property.

VOID (AB INITIO) of no legal effect (from the outset).

VOIDABLE a transaction which can be set aside at the election of one party, but which is otherwise effective until set aside.

VOLUNTEER a person who has not given consideration for a promise to have property settled on them on trust.

WILL the instrument by which a person declares what their wishes are concerning their property after their death. The terms of the will do not take effect automatically, but have to be implemented by an executor or administrator.

PART I

The Importance of Equity

1. What is equity? ... 3
2. Equitable obligations ... 26
3. Equity and the management of property ... 44
4. Equitable remedies in modern English law ... 66

1

What is equity?

1 Introduction

This chapter answers the fundamental question posed by the title. Equity[1] is both a different system of law which recognizes rights and obligations that the common law does not, and a system which seeks to address the inherent gaps which can exist in following any set of rules. It is important to understand the historical origins to appreciate how the system operates today, but equity remains an active force. This chapter will also detail the historical development of the trust. Despite this focus on history, there should be no doubt that trusts are at the centre of much of our modern lives and also at the centre of a great deal of contemporary litigation.

One modern example of how Equity can reach unexpectedly into our lives, can be found in the recent case of *Cowan v Foreman*,[2] in which an elderly widow living in California had lost her husband. His estate had been worth £29 million on his death. He attempted to provide for her through establishing trusts. Under those trusts, although Mrs Cowan was a beneficiary, certain other people and her husband's charity had interests as well. While she did not initially question this trust arrangement, claiming that she did not understand its implications, she lost confidence and had a shock when her trustees queried her medical expense claims. In consequence, wishing to be free of the trust arrangement, she sought to contest her deceased husband's will and achieve outright provision from his estate. The Court of Appeal gave her permission to do so.[3]

Just as Mrs Cowan discovered when the trustees started intervening in her affairs, Equity can play a large, but sometimes unexpected, role in our modern lives. If we buy a house with a partner, we own the house using a trust. If we borrow to pay for it, the borrowing is secured by a charge (usually called a mortgage), the rules governing which were developed in equity. If we invest in a private or company pension, the chances are that this will be through a trust. If we make complex arrangements in a will, in many cases, this will involve a trust, and if we delegate the choice of those who can benefit under a gift by will, this will be achieved through a power of appointment, another great creation of equity. If someone threatens to abuse our human rights, for instance, by publishing scandalous material about our private lives, we may want to seek an injunction (another creation of equity) to prevent them. In short, equity, even if we do not always appreciate it, intrudes into many parts of our lives.

[1] For a succinct and engaging account of the development and contribution of Equity, see Hayton, 'The development of equity and the "good person" philosophy in common law systems' CPL [2012] Conv 263.

[2] [2019] EWCA Civ 1336.

[3] Mrs Cowan was able to make her claim with permission of the court under Inheritance (Provision for Family and Dependants) Act 1975, s 4 despite it being six months after the grant of probate, which is the usual time limit to contest a will.

2 The concept of equity

(1) A layperson's understanding

To the layperson the term 'equity' connotes justice and fairness, so that to act 'equitably' is synonymous with acting 'fairly'. For example, Psalm 96 speaks of God's justice in such terms:

> The LORD reigns.
> The world is firmly established, it
> cannot be moved;
> he will judge the peoples with equity.[4]

The idea of 'equity' has always been particularly associated with judicial decisions, and it emphasizes that cases should be decided in a way which is fair and right, so that justice is achieved between the parties. However, although the branch of English law known as 'equity' may have its origins in such concepts of fairness and justice, it carries a specific and technical meaning.

(2) A legal definition

Legally, the term 'equity' describes a particular body of law, consisting of rights and remedies, which evolved historically through the Courts of Chancery. Until the late nineteenth century, there were two parallel systems of law operating in England, each recognizing, upholding, and applying its own distinct rights and remedies. The common law courts applied the common law, and the Courts of Chancery applied equity. Although this division between courts was removed by the Judicature Acts of 1873 and 1875, those rights and remedies which are today described as 'equitable' were either originally developed by and enforced through the Chancery courts or have evolved by extension from such rights and remedies.

3 The origins of equity

(1) The common law

(a) History and emergence

Prior to the Norman Conquest of 1066, there was no developed legislature or judicature operating throughout England.[5] Instead, a system of 'custom' was applied by a variety of decision-making bodies, ranging from the King's Council to village meetings. Custom inevitably varied with geographical location. However, the notion had already begun to evolve that justice was the prerogative of the Crown. This laid the jurisprudential foundation for the emergence of the common law in the twelfth century. The focus of the common law was the *Curia Regis*, the King's Court. By 1234 the two common law courts, the Court of Common Pleas and the King's Bench, had developed.

(b) Writs, actions, and remedies

A plaintiff (now called a claimant) who wished to start an action in the Court of Common Pleas or the King's Bench needed to obtain a royal writ authorizing the commencement of

[4] Psalm 96 v 10: New International Version.

[5] See Holdsworth, *A History of English Law* (7th edn, London 1956), Vol 1, Ch V; Baker, *An Introduction to English Legal History* (2nd edn, Butterworths 1979), Ch 6.

proceedings. These writs were purchased from the King's Chancery. As plaintiffs sought redress for novel legal problems, new writs were developed to meet their needs, until the Provisions of Oxford in 1258 prevented the issue of new writs without the permission of the King's Council. This closed the categories of writ which were available, severely limiting the ability of the common law to develop effective redress for new types of case. The common law, therefore, became stultified and inflexible. Furthermore, the common law also offered only a limited range of remedies, predominantly monetary damages, to redress the wrong suffered by a successful plaintiff. This straitjacketing of the common law was the predominant motive for the emergence of 'equity' as administered by the Courts of Chancery.

(2) **The Courts of Chancery**

(a) The Chancery and the Chancellor

The Chancery was essentially a department of state. The Chancellor was the Keeper of the Great Seal, a Minister of the Crown who sometimes acted in a Prime Ministerial capacity to the King.

(b) Emergence of the judicial role of the Chancellor

Despite the development of the common law, justice remained a royal prerogative, and, therefore, the King retained a residuum of justice which enabled aggrieved parties to appeal directly to him for redress. These appeals were initially heard by the King in Council, but by the fourteenth century, they were delegated to the Chancellor, who acted on behalf of the King. By 1473 the Chancellor had begun to issue decrees by his own authority in his own name.

(c) Motivation for the emergence of the Courts of Chancery

The Chancery courts and their equity jurisdiction emerged because of the defects and rigidity of the common law, typified by the limited range of writs and the tendency to apply the strict rules of the common law even when this caused hardship, or seemed to do injustice, on the particular facts. For example, a debtor who had paid his debt but who had not ensured that his sealed bond was cancelled could be compelled by the common law to pay his creditor a second time, because the bond was incontrovertible evidence of the debt.

In contrast, the Court of Chancery developed as a court of 'conscience' to remedy these defects of the common law system. In the *Earl of Oxford's Case*,[6] heard in 1615, Lord Ellesmere explained why there was a Chancery:

> [M]en's actions are so diverse and infinite that it is impossible to make any general law which may aptly meet with every particular and not fail in some circumstances. The office of the Chancellor is to correct men's consciences for frauds, breaches of trust, wrongs and oppression of what nature so ever they be, and to soften and mollify the extremity of the law.

This corresponds with the conception of equity in classical writings, where Aristotle had defined 'equity' as 'a correction of law where it is defective owing to its universality'.

(3) **Character of the equity jurisdiction**

(a) A court of conscience

The Chancery Courts initially functioned as courts of conscience. In 1452 Fortescue CJ responded to a legal argument presented in the Court of Chancery: 'We are to argue

[6] [1615] 1 Rep Ch 1 at 6.

conscience here, not the law.'[7] The Chancellor decided cases on the basis of his own sense of justice. Inevitably, different Chancellors had different conceptions of justice so that, in Selden's well-known phrase, equity varied with the length of the Chancellor's foot.[8]

(b) Court of Equity

By the seventeenth century, the Chancellor[9] tended to be a lawyer rather than a churchman. Decisions were reported, leading to a system of precedent and the development of a settled body of law, with distinct rights and remedies, that was almost as rigid as the common law. The Court of Chancery was no longer a simple court of conscience, but a court of 'equity' in the technical sense. At the beginning of the nineteenth century the process was complete. Lord Eldon, Chancellor (1801–06 and 1807–27), reflected in *Gee v Pritchard* that:

> The doctrines of [the Court of Chancery] ought to be well settled, and made as uniform, almost, as those of the common law, laying down fixed principles, but taking care that they are to be applied according to the circumstances of each case. I cannot agree that the doctrines of this court are to be changed by every succeeding judge. Nothing would inflict on me greater pain in quitting this place than the recollection that I had done anything to justify the reproach that the equity of this court varies like the Chancellor's foot.[10]

(4) The relationship between equity and the common law

(a) Equity challenges the law

Initially equity avoided conflict with the common law and the common law courts. However, with two parallel systems of law administered by separate courts it was inevitable that there would be conflict as each struggled for dominance over the other. It had become frequent practice for the Court of Chancery to issue so-called common injunctions, either ordering a party to a dispute to restrain his action at common law or, if judgment had already been given in his favour by the common law court, to prevent him enforcing it. Refusal to obey these injunctions would be a contempt of court, deterred by the threat of imprisonment. These 'common injunctions' were a direct threat to the jurisdiction of the common law courts, which saw their supremacy as being at stake.

(b) Equity prevails

The threat, and with it the struggle between law and equity, came to a head in the early seventeenth century. Sir Edward Coke, the Chief Justice of the King's Bench, held that imprisonment for disobedience of the Chancery injunctions was unlawful, and ordered the release of those affected under the writ of habeas corpus.[11] The Chancery Court argued that the injunctions did not interfere with the common law, as any judgment still stood, but rather, concerned only the conduct of the parties. This jurisdictional civil war was finally ended in 1616, when James I issued an order in favour of the Chancery Court and the common injunctions. Despite some subsequent attempts to reverse this resolution,[12] the primacy of the Chancery Courts was well established by the end of the century.

[7] Mich 31 Hen VI, Fitz Abr Subpoena, pl 23.

[8] *Table Talk of John Selden* (F Pollock edn, 1927), p 43.

[9] The last non-legal chancellor was Lord Shaftesbury (1673–82).

[10] [1818] 2 Swan 402 at 414.

[11] See *Heath v Rydley* [1614] Cro Jac 335.

[12] For example, in 1690, a bill was introduced in the House of Lords enacting that no Court of Equity should entertain any suit for which the proper remedy was at common law. However, the bill was dropped when it was shown that it would make equity unworkable, which would lead to injustice.

(5) Equity in the eighteenth and nineteenth centuries

(a) Defects

Although the supremacy of equity was firmly established by the end of the seventeenth century, its administration was affected by severe procedural defects causing extreme delay. The Chancellor was the sole judge and the court officers abused their positions. The Chancery offices, in particular that of the Master, were lucrative for the holders. The offices were sold and the purchasers appointed by the Chancellor.[13] A fee system operated for tasks performed by the officers, leading to inefficiency. In 1824 these difficulties led to the establishment of a Commission headed by Lord Eldon, who was himself notorious for delay. At that time some £39 million (equivalent to around £4 billion today) was held by the court awaiting the outcome of its decisions.

The development and administration of equity and the common law in different courts also added confusion and great expense, since neither had full power to grant complete relief. A case could be started in the common law courts when it should have been started in Chancery, or may have had to be referred between courts during proceedings. The duration and expense of suit soon became intolerable 'equity had become a byword for delay and injustice'. Lord Denning, echoing the historic reputation of equity in more recent times, said: '[e]ven a court of equity would not allow him to do anything so inequitable and unjust.'[14]

(b) Reforms

In order to improve the administration of the equity jurisdiction a number of reforms were introduced.

(i) Reform of the personnel of the Chancery Courts

The number of persons competent to exercise the equity jurisdiction was increased with new judicial roles and a Court of Appeals in Chancery.

(ii) Limited reform of the jurisdiction of the Chancery Courts

The Common Law Procedure Act 1854 introduced changes marking a step towards the fusion of the common law and equity jurisdictions.

(6) The Judicature Acts 1873 and 1875

(a) Restructuring the system of the courts

The Judicature Acts effected a radical restructuring of the English court system. The Courts of Chancery, King's Bench, Common Pleas, Exchequer, Admiralty, Probate, and the London Court of Bankruptcy were consolidated and merged to form a single Supreme Court of Judicature,[15] now known as the Senior Courts of England and Wales,[16] divided into the High Court and the Court of Appeal. As a matter of convenience, rather than of jurisdiction, the High Court was organized into divisions, comprising the Chancery Division, King's Bench Division, Common Pleas Division, Exchequer Division, and the Probate, Divorce, and Admiralty Division.

[13] For up to £5,000 each; roughly equivalent to £350,000 in contemporary currency.

[14] *Re Vandervell's Trusts No.2* [1974] Ch 269.

[15] To be distinguished from the Supreme Court of the United Kingdom, established by the Constitutional Reform Act 2005, s 23, to replace the Judicial Committee of the House of Lords as the highest appellate court in the UK.

[16] Constitutional Reform Act 2005, s 59.

(b) Uniform jurisdiction given to judges of the Senior Courts

The central feature of the reform was that all the judges of the Senior Courts, irrespective of the division in which they sat, were to have both common law and equitable jurisdiction. This was achieved by the 1873 Act, s 24, which provided that all judges were to give effect to such equitable estates, rights, relief, defences, duties, and liabilities as would have been given effect by the Court of Chancery, and to recognize and give effect to all estates, titles, rights, duties, obligations, and liabilities existing by the common law.[17]

(c) Procedural implications of the reforms

The concurrent common law and equity jurisdiction conferred on the Senior Courts by the Judicature Acts revolutionized the process of litigation. It was no longer necessary to commence a separate action in the Chancery Court to gain recognition of an equitable right or to obtain an equitable remedy.

(d) Supremacy of equity enshrined

(i) Supreme Court of Judicature Act 1873, s 25

Common injunctions were abolished by the Supreme Court of Judicature Act 1873, s 24(5), since the concurrent jurisdiction granted to judges under s 24 rendered them unnecessary. The supremacy of equity was itself placed on a statutory footing by s 25, which, in addition to dealing with some specific instances,[18] also provided more generally that:

> in all matters not herein-before particularly mentioned, in which there is any conflict, or variance, between the Rules of Equity and the Rules of the Common Law with reference to the same matter, the Rules of Equity will apply.[19]

(ii) Operation of s 25(11)

Section 25(11) only operates if there is a genuine conflict between the rules of equity and the rules of common law. A good example is provided in the context of contractual terms as to the time when performance is expected. Whereas at common law requirements as to time were regarded as of the essence of the contract, in equity, they were not, so that a party in breach of a requirement of time was not entitled to repudiate the contract for breach. Outside of commercial contracts, where stipulations as to time are regarded as crucial, the equitable rule has been held to prevail over the common law rule where there is no express agreement that time is to be of the essence.[20]

(e) The fusion of law and equity

(i) The effect of the Judicature Acts

One question arising from the reforms instituted by the Judicature Acts is whether there has been a 'fusion' of law and equity. Jurisprudential debate has questioned whether there is now one single body of 'English law', which has its heritage in the rules, rights, and remedies of the previously distinct bodies of 'common law' and 'equity', or whether there has been a mere fusion of the administration of these two distinct bodies of law so that 'common law' and 'equity' are now administered by a single court replacing the pre-existing duality of courts.

[17] Judicature Act 1925, ss 36–44; Senior Courts Act 1981, s 49. [18] s 25(1)–(10).

[19] s 25(11). This provision is retained by the Senior Courts Act 1981, s 49(1), which provides that: 'wherever there is any conflict or variance between the rule of equity and the rules of the common law with reference to the same matter, the rules of equity shall prevail'.

[20] *United Scientific Holdings Ltd v Burnley Borough Council* [1978] AC 904. Another good example is *Walsh v Lonsdale* [1882] 21 Ch D 9, where the creation of an equitable lease where formalities for a legal lease were wanting allowed a remedy of distress for rent to be brought which would not have been applicable in a legal lease—see Stevens and Pearce, *Land Law* (5th edn, Sweet & Maxwell 2013), Ch 9.

(ii) Fusion of administration

Traditionalists hold that the Judicature Acts merely fused the administration of equity and the common law.[21] In the famous words of Ashburner the result is that:

> the two streams of jurisprudence, though they run in the same channel, run side by side, and do not mingle their waters.[22]

(iii) Fusion in substance

As time passed and the separate administration of law and equity became little more than a distant memory, an increasing number of judges advocated practical realism and declared that law and equity had been fused. In the middle years of the twentieth century, Lord Denning regarded law and equity as unified, and manipulated this as a justification for law reform. In *Errington v Errington and Woods*,[23] for example, he stated that 'law and equity have been fused for nearly eighty years'. Some twenty years later, members of the House of Lords expressed similar sentiments in *United Scientific Holdings Ltd v Burnley Borough Council*.[24] Lord Diplock specifically commented on Ashburner's metaphor:

> by 1977 this metaphor has in my view become both mischievous and deceptive. The innate conservatism of English lawyers made them slow to recognize that by the Supreme Court of Judicature Act 1873 the two systems of substantive and adjectival law formerly administered by the Courts of Law and Courts of Chancery . . . were fused. As at the confluence of the Rhone and Saone, it may be possible for a short distance to discern the source from which each part of the combined stream came, but there comes a point at which this ceases to be possible. If Professor Ashburner's fluvial metaphor is to be retained at all, the waters of the confluent streams of law and equity have surely mingled now.

(iv) A single coherent body of law

While the debate has not been settled clearly in favour of either view, it seems that the central problem is often the meaning invested in the term 'fusion'. If 'fusion' means that any distinction between equity and common law, and especially between equitable and legal rights and remedies, has been completely removed so that adjectivally the term 'equitable' has no continuing relevance, then it has not occurred. The law still distinguishes between legal and equitable ownership, the foundation of the trust concept which is the main subject of this book. However, it is also clear that English law no longer preserves the strict distinction between equitable and legal rules that was maintained before the Judicature Acts. The law has developed as a whole, so that there has been some synthesis of legal and equitable rights and remedies and cross-fertilization between them, and some of the old distinctions between rights and remedies historically equitable in origin and those historically of common law origin have ceased to be significant. The adjectives 'equitable' and 'common law' are useful to distinguish the different rights and remedies that make up English law but, as Lord Diplock observed in *United Scientific Holdings Ltd v Burnley Borough Council*:

> [To] perpetuate a dichotomy between rules of equity and rules of common law which it was a major purpose of the Supreme Court of Judicature Act 1873 to do away with, is, in my view, conducive to erroneous conclusions as to the ways in which the law of England has developed in the last hundred years.[25]

The approach which best represents the prevailing judicial attitude is that the long fusion of the administration of law and equity has produced a single, coherent body of rules

[21] See [1954] 70 LQR 326 (Lord Evershed); [1961] 24 MLR 116 (V T H Delaney); [1977] 93 LQR 529 (P V Baker); [1977] 6 AALR 119 (T G Watkin); [1994] 14 LS 313 (David Capper), at 315–17.

[22] Snell, *Principles of Equity* (2nd edn, Sweet & Maxwell), p 18.

[23] [1952] 1 KB 290 at 298. [24] [1978] AC 904. [25] [1978] AC 904 at 924.

which operate harmoniously together, even though some historically have their origin in equity and others in the common law and may still need to be considered separately.[26] In *Napier and Ettrick v Hunter*, Lord Goff considered the relationship between equitable proprietary rights and personal rights and obligations deriving from a contract of insurance:

> No doubt our task nowadays is to see the two strands of authority, at law and in equity, moulded into a coherent whole; but for my part I cannot see why this amalgamation should lead to the rejection of the equitable proprietary right . . .[27]

4 Trusts and powers

Although equity has a much broader influence than just in the management of property, its contribution to how property can be managed is particularly important. Especially important are trusts and powers.

(1) The trust

Trusts allow the ownership of property to be separated from its management. Where property is subject to a trust, equity treats the persons for whose benefit the trust exists as the owners of the property, even though they are not the owners of it at law. Where property is subject to a trust, there is a duality of ownership, or 'double dominium', and a distinction must be drawn between the legal ownership and the equitable ownership. This capacity for dual ownership at law and in equity is the most distinctive feature of English property law. It emerged as a product of the historical divide between equity and the common law. Duality of ownership of property is the essential characteristic of a trust. A person enjoying the legal ownership of the trust property is referred to as a 'trustee', and a person enjoying the equitable ownership is a 'beneficiary'.

(2) The importance of separation of ownership

What is important about separating the rights to property into legal and equitable ownership (strictly speaking legal title and equitable ownership) is that it enables the powers of management to be split from the beneficial enjoyment (see Figure 1.1). In addition, it

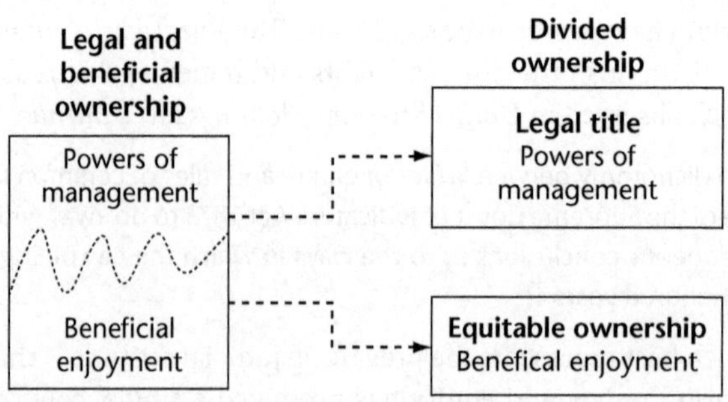

Figure 1.1 Separation of ownership

[26] See also Duggan 'Is Equity Efficient?' [1997] 113 LQR 601.
[27] [1978] AC 904 at 401.

allows much greater complexity in the division of beneficial enjoyment. The relationship between the legal owner and the equitable owner does, of course, have to be regulated, and equity does this through the trust.

(3) **How trusts emerged**

(a) **The feudal system of land holding**

An understanding of the origins of the trust[28] requires an elementary grasp of the feudal system of landowning operative during the medieval period.[29] All land was ultimately owned by the King, while others enjoyed the right to use it as tenants. Individuals were granted 'tenure' of land by their 'overlord', who would in turn enjoy tenure from his 'overlord'. These levels of tenure formed a feudal pyramid of landholdings stretching downwards from the King (who was at its pinnacle because he had no 'overlord'). The terms of 'tenure' defined the conditions under which the tenant was entitled to enjoy the land, generally requiring the performance of services on behalf of his lord. These might include the provision of military forces,[30] religious functions,[31] or agricultural services.[32] On the death of a tenant, the person who succeeded to his tenure and thereby inherited his position on the feudal ladder was required to make a payment to his overlord. These medieval inheritance taxes, termed 'feudal incidents', provided the Crown with a significant source of revenue. While tenure defined the terms under which land was held, the parallel doctrine of 'estates' determined the duration for which a grant of tenure was to last.[33] An estate in fee simple[34] was a grant of tenure for ever, and within the feudal structure the right to tenure of land in fee simple was tantamount to absolute ownership.

(b) **Development of the 'use'**

In the context of this feudal structure, the 'use', the ancestor of the modern trust, was developed by the Chancery courts. If land was conveyed to X 'to the use of Y', this had the effect that, while X became the owner of the land, X was obliged to apply it for the benefit of Y and was prevented from treating it as his own. X was termed the 'feoffee', and Y the 'cestui que use'. The common law did not recognize, and would not enforce, a 'use' of land, but rather, regarded the feoffee, in whom the legal estate was vested, as the absolute owner. From the perspective of equity, however, the feoffee was bound in conscience to apply the property for the benefit of the cestui que use, because of the undertaking he had given. The Court of Chancery was, therefore, prepared to enforce the use in personam, requiring the feoffee to apply the property vested in him to the benefit of the cestui que use. Equity did not deny the reality of the ownership of the feoffee at common law, but instead prevented him from exercising the entitlements concomitant with his legal ownership in a manner inconsistent with the interests of the cestui que use. Thus, the use

[28] See Holdsworth, *History of English Law* (7th edn, London 1956), pp 407–80; Baker, *Introduction to English Legal History* (2nd edn, Butterworths 1979), pp 210–19 and 242–4. See also [1998] 61 MLR 162 (Pottage).

[29] See Gray and Gray, *Elements of Land Law* (5th edn, Oxford University Press 2008), pp 64–8.

[30] The tenure of 'Knight's service', for example, which required the provision of armed horsemen for battle.

[31] 'Spiritual tenure'.

[32] Tenures in socage.

[33] See *Walsingham's Case* [1579] 2 Plowd 547 at 555: 'the land itself is one thing, and an estate in the land is another thing, for an estate in the land is a time in the land, or land for a time, and there are diversities of estates, which are no more than diversities of time . . .'

[34] To be distinguished from a 'fee tail' (or 'entailed interest'), which was only to last for so long as the grantee had lineal descendants, and the life interest, which was only to last for the length of the grantee's life.

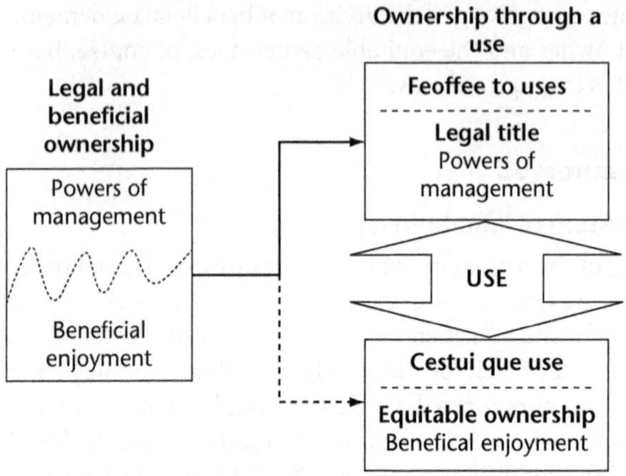

Figure 1.2 Separation of ownership and the use

shared a central characteristic of the modern trust, namely that the formal ownership of the property subject to it was separated from the right to enjoy the benefit derived from such ownership (see Figure 1.2). The use evolved as a popular mechanism for landholding because of the advantages it offered. It provided a means of making gifts to charities that were technically unable to own property. For example, the monastic order of St Francis was forbidden to own property by its rule, but land could be given to feoffees for its use. Though technically it would not 'own' the property, it would be entitled to derive the benefits flowing from such ownership. A landowner could also avoid the strict legal rules of inheritance by directing feoffees in his will to hold the land as he wished. The use also offered a mechanism for primitive tax-planning through the avoidance of feudal dues. If land was vested in a group of feoffees, who would never die as a group because each individual feoffee would be replaced on death, the legal title would never have to be passed by way of succession. The feudal incidents payable on inheritance would thus be avoided altogether.

(c) The development of the trust

The financial advantages attendant upon a use were so attractive to landowners that by 1500 the majority of land in England was held in use.[35] This inevitably led to a serious diminution in the King's feudal revenue. In order to close this tax-avoidance loophole, legislation (the Statute of Uses 1535) was introduced to abolish uses by 'executing' them, which means vesting the legal estate in the cestui que use. It did not take the ingenuity of lawyers long to find ways around the Statute of Uses and, indeed, to turn it to their advantage. The statute did not apply to uses where the feoffee had active duties to perform, for example the collection and distribution of profits and the management of an estate.[36] A further means to avoiding 'execution' of a use under the statute was to create a double use, termed a 'use upon a use', whereby the legal estate in land would be conveyed 'to X, to the use of Y, to the use of Z'. Although the first use would be executed by the Statute of Uses, so that Y would be treated as the legal owner, the second use remained unexecuted. The Court of Chancery would then enforce the second use, requiring Y to hold the land for the benefit of Z. This second use was termed a 'trust', providing the modern terminology.[37]

[35] YB Mich 15 Hen VII, 13, p 1, per Frowyk Sjt.

[36] A use of leasehold land, a term of years, was also not executed.

[37] In fact, the term was also used for a single 'use' prior to the development of the 'use upon a use'.

The 'use upon a use' was accepted as valid by the latter part of the sixteenth century,[38] by which time it had come to serve different social functions than the mere avoidance of feudal dues. Common objectives were to protect estates from spendthrift sons, and to enable married women to enjoy property independently of their husbands. The effect of the trust to avoid the execution of uses was so successful that in 1739 Lord Hardwicke was able to observe that the Statute of Uses 'has had no other effect than to add at most, three words to a conveyance'.[39] Although the trust had emerged as a recognized legal instrument by the end of the sixteenth century, it flourished in the nineteenth century, when it served as the foundation for property holding by families and as a device to preserve family estates.

(4) The modern trust

The cardinal features of a modern trust are very much the same as those of the early use from which it has developed. Under a trust, the legal and equitable ownership of the trust property are separated and held by different persons.[40] A trust arises where property is conveyed to or vested in the trustee by a settlor in such circumstances that equity will compel the trustee to administer the property for the benefit of the beneficiary.

(a) Separation of title under a trust

The legal title is vested in the trustee, who must apply the property for the benefit of someone else, the cestui que trust, more commonly termed the 'beneficiary', who is regarded as the equitable owner (see Figure 1.3). It follows from this separation of the legal and equitable ownership of the trust property that there is also a separation between the management responsibilities arising in connection with the property and its enjoyment.

(b) Trustee as legal owner

The trustee looks like the outright owner of the property. He has legal title vested in him, and as legal owner, the trustee controls the property.[41] He is usually entitled to decide

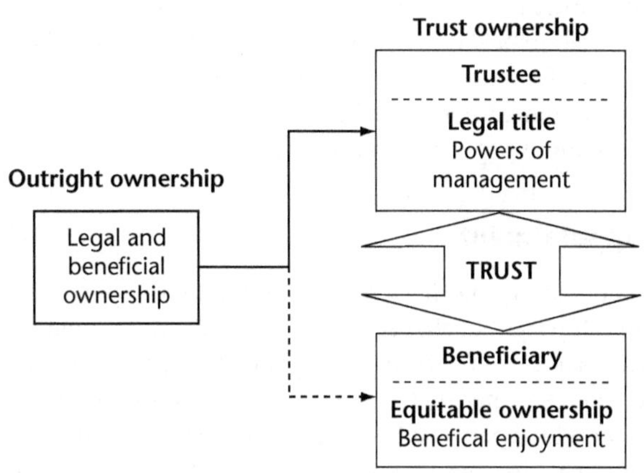

Figure 1.3 Separation of ownership and the trust

[38] See [1966] 82 LQR 215 (Barton); [1977] 93 LQR 33 (Baker).

[39] *Hopkins v Hopkins* [1739] 1 Atk 581. Lord Hardwicke was a better lawyer than a mathematician.

[40] *Selby v Alston* [1797] 3 Ves 339.

[41] It is possible that the trustee may have an equitable title only, which occurs where the property settled on the trust is equitable (technically, this is usually referred to as a sub-trust). In this case, the key points about control and separation of the benefit are exactly the same as where a trustee has legal title.

whether it should be retained or sold, and how it should be invested. In some types of trust the trustee even has the right to determine how the property should be distributed among a class of defined beneficiaries. However, he is compelled by equity to exercise this control over the property strictly for the benefit of the beneficiaries. He is not permitted to exercise his rights to deal with the trust property for his own personal advantage. Thus, he must (i) act only within the terms of the trust; (ii) act with reasonable care in performing his obligations; and (iii) act in the best interests of the beneficiaries. He must consider the interests of all the beneficiaries collectively, and not favour any one of them, sometimes referred to as his duty to consider the trust as a whole. This is particularly important where persons are entitled to the beneficial interest in succession, so that someone entitled for life does not get all the benefits of ownership to the exclusion of those beneficiaries entitled after the death of the currently entitled beneficiary.

(c) Beneficiary as equitable owner

The beneficiary has equitable ownership of the property, which identifies him as being entitled to the benefits of the property held under the trust.[42] The fact that the beneficiary has equitable ownership of the trust property differentiates the trust from a contract for the benefit of a third party. The beneficiary, as a property holder, has additional rights against other parties in addition to those against the trustee. The beneficiary's rights can be enforced not only against the trustee but also against any new trustees (as the trust property will be vested in them) or against third parties who receive the trust property in breach of trust. A beneficiary does not have control of the property, so although the beneficiary has rights against the trustee to make sure he performs his duties throughout the duration of the trust, he does not usually have the right to instruct the trustee in performing those duties.

(5) Impact of the trust

This capacity of the trust to separate the management of property from its enjoyment renders it a perfect vehicle to facilitate complex arrangements involving property. Its tremendous flexibility has enabled it to adapt through the centuries and into new social and commercial contexts. Maitland was of the opinion that the trust was 'the greatest and most distinctive achievement performed by Englishmen in the field of jurisprudence'. Trusts now underpin many aspects of modern life.

(6) Powers of appointment

Associated with the trust is another creation of equity, the power of appointment. A power of this kind is the right to choose who will benefit from property held by trustees. In a family context a testator (a person making a will) might wish to leave his house for the benefit of his widow for her lifetime, with instructions that on her death it is to be sold and the capital divided between his grandchildren in such shares as his widow may decide.[43] Although the widow has no right to the capital (a life interest gives her only the right to live in the house or to enjoy the income from any investments), she has the power

[42] It is possible for a person to be both trustee and one of the beneficiaries of the same property, in which case the person is compelled by equity to control the property for the benefit of all those sharing the beneficial ownership.

[43] For two examples of variants on this, see *Re Pauling's Settlement Trusts (No. 1)* [1963] EWCA Civ 5 and *Butler v Butler* [2006] IEHC 104.

to decide who should receive the capital within the identified class of objects or potential beneficiaries. Powers of appointment can be used in a more commercial context, for instance, in pension trust schemes. They can be given to the trustees, to a beneficiary, or to a third party. They can be unlimited, or restricted in their ambit, and they can be purely permissive or subject to a range of different levels of obligation.

The donor of a power (usually the person creating the trust which contains the power[44]) may give someone (the donee) a power of appointment in respect of specific property or a fund of property.[45] The donee may be the executor of a will, the trustee of a trust, or a third party. The donee is able to allocate the property by exercising the power and making appointments to the objects of the power (the named individuals or the description of individuals amongst whom the donee can make a selection). Unlike a trust, the donee of a power of appointment is under no obligation to exercise the power conferred upon him. It is discretionary rather than mandatory in character, although it is possible for the power to be fiduciary in nature, in which case it shares some of the obligatory characteristics of a trust.

5 Equity and property

(1) **What is property?**

Lawson and Rudden have commented that 'the law of property deals with the legal relations between people with regard to things'.[46] It addresses such questions as the following: Who owns the thing? What is the owner entitled to do with the thing he owns? How can the owner of the thing transfer it to someone else so that they become the owner in his place? Can the owner continue to assert his ownership of the thing even when a third person has taken it from him without permission, or against a person who has acquired the thing from such a third person?[47]

(2) **Proprietary rights**

Proprietary rights are those rights and entitlements which exist in reference to things.[48] The most important and absolute right is that of ownership, but there are many lesser interests that may be enjoyed in respect of an item of property. It has been said that the law of property is about the relationship persons enjoy with things:

> For serious students of property, the beginning of truth is the recognition that property is not a thing but a *power relationship*—a relationship of social and legal legitimacy existing between a person and a valued resource (whether tangible or intangible). To claim 'property' in a resource is, in effect, to assert a significant degree of control over that resource.[49]

More accurately, the law of property is about the relationship which one person has with other persons in regard to things.

[44] Where the donor has created a trust, the donor will also be the settlor of the trust.

[45] Thomas, *Powers* (Oxford University Press 1999).

[46] Lawson and Rudden, *The Law of Property* (Clarendon Press 1982), p 1.

[47] See further Lawson and Rudden, *The Law of Property* (Clarendon Press 1982), pp 1–38; [1998] 18 LS 41 (Rotherham); McFarlane, *The Structure of Property Law* (Hart 2008).

[48] See Eleftheriadis 'The Analysis of Property Rights' [1996] 16 OJLS 31; Chambers 'Proprietary Interests in Commercial Transactions' [1998] 18 OJLS 363.

[49] Gray and Gray, *Elements of Land Law* (5th edn, Oxford University Press 2008), p 88.

(a) Ownership

Ownership is the 'greatest possible interest in a thing which a mature system of law recognises'.[50] Lawson and Rudden identify three main elements of ownership:

(a) the right to make physical use of a thing;

(b) the right to the income from it, in money, in kind, or in services; and

(c) the power of management, including that of alienation.[51]

By virtue of ownership a person is entitled to do as he wishes with his property. He is even free to destroy it. He can give it away or sell it to a third person. The person who owns property is said to have 'title' to it, a term derived from the fact that he is 'entitled' to it. Of course, that ownership may be constrained by other rules of law, so, for example, a landowner may not lawfully build on his land without applying for planning permission. In many cases the ownership of property will be more complex. For example, there may be multiple owners of the thing, termed co-owners, who enjoy concurrent ownership, or there may be multiple owners with successive interests.

(b) Other rights in property

Although the most important right in property is ownership, there is a large range of other proprietary rights that a person may enjoy over a thing. Such subsidiary rights may qualify or limit the absolute entitlement of the owner to do as he chooses with the thing. This multiplicity of proprietary rights in the same thing is most clearly illustrated in the context of land. Norman may own a house, but this could be subject to a mortgage to Sparks Bank, to the right of a neighbour, Owen, to share the driveway, and to a tenant, Penelope, to live in the basement flat. In this simple scenario, Norman, Sparks Bank, Owen, and Penelope, all have different proprietary interests in the same land.

(c) The need to distinguish proprietary and personal rights

Not every agreement by an owner of property gives rise to proprietary rights or interests. For instance, if Kevin is a taxi driver and contracts to drive Michael to the airport, that does not give Michael any rights to Kevin's car. Michael has a personal right which is only enforceable against a specific individual.[52] Proprietary rights are described as rights in rem,[53] whereas personal rights are rights in personam.

(d) The defining characteristic of proprietary rights

In *National Provincial Bank Ltd v Ainsworth*[54] Lord Wilberforce identified the essential characteristics of a property right:

> Before a right or an interest can be admitted into the category of property, or of a right affecting property, it must be definable, identifiable by third parties, capable in its nature of assumption by third parties, and have some degree of permanence or stability.[55]

The central characteristic of a proprietary right is, therefore, that it is capable of enduring through changes in the ownership of the property to which it relates.

[50] Honoré, 'Ownership', in Guest (ed), *Oxford Essays in Jurisprudence* (Oxford University Press 1961).

[51] Lawson and Rudden, *The Law of Property* (Clarendon Press 1982), p 8.

[52] For a detailed treatment of the law relating to personal property, see Bridge, *Personal Property Law* (3rd edn, Oxford University Press 2002).

[53] Meaning 'in the thing', from the Latin word 'res', meaning 'thing'.

[54] [1965] AC 1175. [55] [1965] AC 1175 at 1248.

(3) Equitable rights and property

We have already seen that the trust allows a separation of control and benefit, and through it a separation of ownership. Equity has also created or recognized other rights in property.

(a) Equitable rights corresponding to legal rights

The common law only recognized the creation of proprietary rights if appropriate formalities were satisfied. This generally required the grant of the right using the special formality of a deed.[56] For example, under the Real Property Act 1845, a legal lease would not be created unless made by deed.[57] However, equity, which looks to the substance rather than the form of transactions, was prepared to recognize and enforce proprietary interests even if the requisite formalities for creation at law had not been observed. Equity regards a mere contract for a lease as creating an equitable lease despite the absence of a deed.[58] The difference between the legal and equitable form of these rights affects the quality of the right, not the nature of it. Thus, both a legal and an equitable mortgage, for example, give the mortgage holder the same rights and obligations. However, while both are proprietary interests capable of binding third parties, the circumstances in which they may bind third parties are different.

(b) Equitable proprietary rights without a legal equivalent

The creativity of equity also allowed it to develop proprietary interests that were not parasitic equivalents of corresponding common law rights. For example, in law the burden of a covenant affecting the use of freehold land is enforceable only against the original covenantor because of the doctrine of privity of contract.[59] However, following *Tulk v Moxhay*,[60] equity elevated freehold covenants restrictive of the owner's use of his land to the status of proprietary interests, with the consequence that they are capable of passing with the title of the land so as to bind subsequent purchasers.[61] Although there has been debate about the nature of the rights of a beneficiary of a trust,[62] the Supreme Court in *Akers v Samba Financial Group*[63] was willing to proceed 'on the basis of the "conventional" analysis that a trust creates a proprietary interest.'

(c) Mere equities

Equity further recognizes a category of entitlements described as 'equities' or 'mere equities'. This terminology is intended to distinguish them from complete equitable proprietary interests. They have been held to include the right to have a transaction set aside for fraud[64] or undue influence,[65] the right to have a document rectified,[66] and the deserted

[56] This originally required the document to be 'signed, sealed, and delivered'. Because of this, the grant was sometimes said to be made 'under seal'. See now Law of Property (Miscellaneous Provisions) Act 1989, s 1.

[57] See now Law of Property Act 1925, s 2(1). By s 52(2)(d) and s 54(2) there is no need for a deed for the creation of a legal lease for less than three years at the best rent which can reasonably be obtained.

[58] *Parker v Taswell* [1858] 2 De G & J 559; *Walsh v Lonsdale* [1882] 21 LR Ch D 9.

[59] *Austerberry v Oldham Corpn* [1885] 29 Ch D 750, CA; *Rhone v Stephens* [1994] 2 AC 310.

[60] [1848] 2 Ph 774.

[61] For some reason, English law has failed to recognize restrictions on the use of land as capable of existing as easements, the nearest equivalent right recognized by the common law.

[62] See the summary in *Akers v Samba Financial Group* [2017] UKSC 6 at 15.

[63] [2017] UKSC 6 at 16.

[64] *Ernest v Vivian* [1863] 33 LJ Ch 513.

[65] *Bainbrigge v Browne* [1881] 18 Ch D 188; *Barclays Bank v O'Brien* [1994] 1 AC 180.

[66] *Shiloh Spinners Ltd v Harding (No 1)* [1973] AC 691 at 721, per Lord Wilberforce.

wife's right to occupy the matrimonial home.[67] When mere equities relate to property, they have a limited capacity to affect third parties who acquire ownership of it, but they are not true interests in the property itself.

(4) Equity and the durability of proprietary rights

As has been noted earlier, one of the defining characteristics of a proprietary right is that it is capable of enduring through changes in the ownership of the thing to which it relates. Different rules developed in equity and the common law to govern the durability of their respective proprietary rights. In general, legal rights are more durable than their equitable equivalents. In relation to land, the traditional rules have been almost completely replaced by the new statutory scheme contained in the Land Registration Act 2002, but the rules developed by equity and the common law remain operative in relation to personal property.[68]

(a) Legal proprietary rights

Of all types of ownership and rights, legal ownership is the most durable, subject to a few exceptions at common law and to rather more which have been introduced by statute. The basic rule is that the ownership or rights of a legal owner will continue indefinitely until the owner has transferred them to someone else. Apart from those situations where a special rule applies,[69] the rule relating to legal ownership or rights is, therefore, that 'legal rights bind the world'. In consequence, where two people can assert a claim with a lawful origin, 'the first in time prevails'.

So, for example, if Alf steals a bicycle belonging to Mary and sells it to Peter, neither Alf nor Peter becomes the owner of the bicycle. It continues to belong to Mary. If Peter still has the bicycle in his hands, Mary can demand that it be returned to her, vindicating her continuing legal ownership. Only if the bicycle is destroyed will Mary's legal ownership be terminated, as there will no longer be any subject matter in which the right can continue to subsist.

(b) Equitable proprietary rights

(i) Priority between equitable interests

Equity followed the law when it was dealing with the relative status of claims based in equity. It, therefore, accepted the principle that competing claims should be judged on the footing that where they all had a lawful origin, 'the first in time prevails'.

(ii) The doctrine of notice

When it came to dealing with the relative status of rights, some of which were legal and some equitable, equity again adopted the root philosophy that they should be judged in accordance with the time order of their creation. However, this philosophy is applied with one very important qualification. A pre-existing equitable interest will cease to be enforceable against property which is acquired by a bona fide purchaser of a legal interest who was not aware at the time of its acquisition of the earlier equitable interest. This principle is known as the 'doctrine of notice'. For instance, in *Macmillan Inc v Bishopgate*

[67] *National Provincial Bank Ltd v Ainsworth* [1965] AC 1175.

[68] For personal property, see Worthington, *Personal Property Law* (Hart 2000), pp 457–73. In relation to real property, see Stevens and Pearce, *Land Law* (5th edn, Sweet & Maxwell 2013).

[69] When a chattel has been lost, a finder will not acquire a right to it superior to that of the legal owner—see *Parker v British Airways Board* [1982] QB 1004.

Investment Trust Plc,[70] the legal title to shares was transferred for value to a number of companies which were unaware that the shares were subject to a trust. The trust could not be enforced against them (although the beneficiaries retained remedies against the trustees).

The operation of the doctrine of notice to destroy equitable proprietary interests is rooted in concepts of good conscience, which lies at the heart of the equitable jurisdiction. In the view of equity, a person who was aware of a pre-existing interest subsisting in a property cannot acquire it free from such interest. He has no grounds for complaint when equity requires him to continue to give effect to it because he knew what he was getting. Only if he purchased the property without knowing of its existence is his conscience unaffected so as to justify the conclusion that he should not be bound by it. As Lord Browne-Wilkinson explained in *Barclays Bank plc v O'Brien*:[71]

> The doctrine of notice lies at the heart of equity. Given that there are two innocent parties, each enjoying rights, the earlier right prevails against the later right if the acquirer of the later right knows of the earlier right (actual notice) or would have discovered it had he taken proper steps (constructive notice). In particular, if the party asserting that he takes free of the earlier rights of another knows of certain facts which put him on enquiry as to the possible existence of the rights of that other and he fails to make such enquiry or take such other steps as are reasonable to verify whether such earlier right does or does not exist, he will have constructive notice of the earlier right and take subject to it.

(iii) Requirements of the equitable doctrine of notice

The equitable doctrine of notice only operates in favour of a person who can demonstrate that he was the bona fide purchaser of the legal ownership of the property for value without notice. Because a purchaser who meets this test takes free of any equitable interests in the property acquired, such a person is also referred to as 'equity's darling'. Each component element of this formula must be satisfied.

(iv) Bona fides

The doctrine of notice only operates in favour of a person who acted in good faith. However, this requirement adds little to the element that he must not have notice of the equitable interests in the property.

(v) Purchase for value

The doctrine of notice will only operate in favour of a person who purchased the property in which there was a pre-existing equitable interest for valuable consideration. The concept of consideration in equity is different to that at common law. In equity, nominal consideration, which would be sufficient to establish an enforceable contractual obligation at common law,[72] is insufficient. It follows from this requirement of valuable consideration that the doctrine of notice will never operate in favour of a volunteer. Thus, a person who receives property by way of gift or succession will always acquire the legal ownership subject to any pre-existing equitable interests.

(vi) Of the legal title

The doctrine of notice only protects a purchaser of the legal title to the property. In the case of land, the purchase must be of a legal estate or interest.[73] A person who purchases an equitable interest in property will, therefore, take subject to all other pre-existing

[70] [1996] 1 All ER 585. [71] [1994] 1 AC 180. [72] For example, a peppercorn.

[73] Under the Law of Property Act 1925, s 1, this means a fee simple absolute in possession (freehold) or a terms of years absolute (leasehold) or one of the subsidiary legal interests listed in the section.

equitable interests, since between competing equitable entitlements 'the first in time prevails'.

(vii) Without notice

Without notice[74] is the most important of the requirements. It concerns the extent to which the purchaser was aware or ignorant of the existence of any pre-existing equitable interests subsisting in the property acquired. Clearly, he will have 'notice' of such interests if he consciously knew of their existence, for example, if the seller had informed him. Such awareness is termed 'actual notice'. However, the concept of notice has been given a wider ambit in equity, so that a person is treated as if he was actually aware of all pre-existing equitable interests that he would have discovered if he had taken all reasonable steps to investigate the property concerned by making 'such inquiries and "inspections" as ought reasonably to have been made'.[75] This prevents a person claiming the benefit of the doctrine of notice simply by seeking to avoid receiving actual notice of such rights. Such deemed notice is termed 'constructive notice'. A person will also be treated as having notice if the purchase was conducted by an agent acting on his behalf if the agent had actual or constructive notice of the existence of the equitable interest. Such notice is termed 'imputed notice'.

(viii) Constructive notice

The rules on constructive notice have been developed most fully in relation to land. Although a different regime now applies to all land with registered title, the rule for unregistered land is that a person is to be treated as knowing everything that could be discovered from a full investigation of title to land and from an inspection of the land itself. It is now accepted that a less strict regime should apply to commercial transactions not involving land. In *Manchester Trust v Furness* Lindley LJ stated:

> The equitable doctrines of constructive notice are common enough in dealing with land and estates with which the Court is familiar; but there has always been repeated protest against the introduction into commercial transactions of anything like an extension of those doctrines and the protest is founded on perfect good sense. In dealing with estates in land title is everything and it can be leisurely investigated; in commercial transactions possession is everything and there is no time to investigate title; and if we were to extend the doctrine of constructive notice to commercial transactions we should be doing infinite mischief and paralysing the trade of the country.[76]

In *Macmillan Inc v Bishopsgate Investment Trust plc*[77] Millett J glossed this view, saying:

> It is true that many distinguished judges in the past have warned against the extension of the equitable doctrine of constructive notice to commercial transactions . . . but they were obviously referring to the doctrine in its strict conveyancing sense with its many refinements and its insistence on a proper investigation of title in every case. The relevance of constructive notice in its wider meaning cannot depend on whether the transaction is 'commercial': the provision of secured overdraft facilities to a corporate managing director is equally 'commercial' whether the security consists of the managing director's house or his private investments. The difference is that in one case there is, and in the other there is not, a recognised procedure for investigating the mortgagor's title which the creditor ignores at his peril.[78]

[74] See Law of Property Act 1925, s 199.

[75] Law of Property Act 1925, s 199(1)(ii)(a). See *Jones v Smith* [1841] 1 Hare 43; *Northern Bank Ltd v Henry* [1981] IR 1.

[76] [1895] 2 QB 539 at 545. [77] [1995] 3 All ER 747.

[78] Stevens 'Restitution or Property?' [1996] 59 MLR 741 at 769.

The position now appears to be that where there is an established procedure for investigating the validity of a transaction this should be followed, and the recipient will be treated as knowing anything that this would have disclosed. Beyond this, the question is what more will constitute constructive notice. The Privy Council looked at this issue in *Credit Agricole Corporation and Investment Bank v Papadimitriou*.[79] The question was whether a bank should be treated as having constructive notice of a trust affecting funds paid in by a client. It was held that the bank did have constructive notice because of the unusual circumstances. Lord Clarke said:

> The bank must make inquiries if there is a serious possibility of a third party having such a right or, put in another way, if the facts known to the bank would give a reasonable banker in the position of the particular banker serious cause to question the propriety of the transaction.[80]

Lord Sumption preferred to express the test slightly differently. For him:

> If even without inquiry or explanation the transaction appears to be a proper one, then there is no justification for requiring the defendants to make inquiries. He is without notice. But if there are features of the transaction such that if left unexplained they are indicative of wrongdoing, then an explanation must be sought before it can be assumed that there is none.[81]

Whilst there is probably no difference in substance between these two formulations of what constitutes constructive notice, it would be helpful to have a single expression of the test.

(ix) Destruction of equitable proprietary interests by the doctrine of notice

Where all the requisite elements of the doctrine of notice are satisfied, it operates so as to completely destroy any subsisting equitable interests in the property concerned. Even if the property is subsequently transferred to a person with notice of the relevant interest, it will not revive. This can be seen from the facts of *Wilkes v Spooner*.[82] Spooner was the tenant of a pork butcher's shop. Wilkes was the beneficiary of an equitable restrictive covenant, affecting the shop, preventing its use as a general butcher's. Spooner surrendered his lease of the shop to the landlord.[83] As the landlord was unaware of the restrictive covenant, he was protected by the doctrine of notice, with the consequence that his legal ownership was not encumbered by it. Subsequently, the landlord granted a new lease of the shop to Spooner's son, who had actual notice of the restriction. Since the doctrine of notice had operated so as to destroy the right altogether, he too acquired the shop free from the restriction.

(c) **Mere equities**

Mere equities relating to property are incapable of binding a person who purchases an interest in it, whether legal or equitable, irrespective of whether they have notice. As Lord Upjohn stated in *National Provincial Bank Ltd v Ainsworth*:

> I myself cannot see how it is possible for a 'mere equity' to bind a purchaser unless such an equity is ancillary to or dependent upon an equitable estate or interest in the land . . . a 'mere equity' naked and alone is, in my opinion, incapable of binding successors in title even with notice; it is personal to the parties.[84]

[79] [2015] UKPC 13. See Pearce, 'When must a bank repay stolen funds?' [2015] 79 Conv 521.
[80] [2015] UKPC 13 at 20. [81] [2015] UKPC 13 at 33. [82] [1911] 2 KB 473.
[83] The surrender of the lease satisfied the requirement that the landlord be a purchaser of a legal estate for value.
[84] [1965] AC 1175 at 1238.

6 Equitable remedies

The common law was very limited in the civil remedies it could offer. Apart from helping a landowner to recover possession of land, the common law would normally award only damages. Equity was very much more flexible, and, as well as ordering monetary compensation, could order specific performance compelling a person to do what they had promised, or an injunction restraining a person from doing something they should not. In addition, equity allowed a document containing a mistake to be rectified, and it would order accounts to be taken where this was necessary to ascertain how much one person owed another. These remedies are considered in more detail in Chapter 4.

7 The creativity of equity

Throughout its history, equity has been dynamic and has developed new solutions to meet the problems of the day. To borrow a favourite metaphor of Lord Denning, equity is not 'past the age of childbearing'.[85] Examples of new developments include 'superinjunctions' and the way in which equity has dealt with problems relating to ownership of the family home. However, there are constraints. One is the general reluctance of the courts to interfere with settled law. For example, in *Prudential Assurance Co Ltd v London Residuary Body*[86] the House of Lords refused to overrule the ancient common law rule that a lease must have an ascertainable maximum duration, despite the fact that it served no useful purpose and they could find no satisfactory rationale for its existence, because of fear that so doing might 'upset long-established titles'. Another constraint is an unwillingness to usurp Parliament by making new law which Parliament had not envisaged.[87] A third constraint is the desire to avoid uncertainty,[88] although there has been increasing use of the potentially vague concept of unconscionability as a test in recent Supreme Court decisions.[89]

8 The maxims of equity

The maxims of equity are an attempt to formulate the law in pithy principles. They are not binding rules, nor do they provide guidance for every situation in which equity operates. It can be seen from the following list of maxims that modern judges do sometimes refer to them as they decide cases. However there is also a sense in which the idea of maxims belong to another legal era. In a history of traditional legal writing, AWB Simpson describes how earlier textbook writers attempted to reduce the entire common law to maxims.[90] In those times, the concept was that all of English law could be presented in a

[85] Contrast the view expressed in 1953 by Lord Evershed that: 'the passing of the Judicature Act, and section 25(11) in particular, put a stop to, or at least a very severe limitation on, the inventive faculties of future Chancery judges.' [1953] 6 CLP 1 at 12.

[86] [1992] 3 All ER 504.

[87] *Westdeutsche Landesbank Girozentrale v Islington London Borough Council* [1996] 2 All ER 961 at 1021 per Lord Lloyd: 'To extend the equitable jurisdiction for the first time to cover a residual injustice at common law, which Parliament chose not to remedy, would, I think, be . . . a usurpation of the role of the legislature'. See also [1996] RLR 3 (Birks); [1996] LMCLQ 441 (Stevens).

[88] See *Cowcher v Cowcher* [1972] 1 WLR 425 at 430, where Bagnall J emphasized the need for 'sure and settled principles'.

[89] For instance, *Futter v Revenue and Customs* [2013] UKSC 26.

[90] Simpson, 'The Rise and Fall of the Legal Treatise: Legal Principles and the Forms of Legal Literature' (1981) 48 UCLR 632, 644.

neat and exhaustive list and that students or practitioners need only consult the list to find an answer to their legal query.

In the contemporary legal world, it would not be wise to try and structure an entire book around these maxims. While the maxims are sometimes useful, they are almost by definition a very abstract way of presenting the law. In this book, equity will be seen to emerge in concrete contexts such as disputes over the family home or litigation over charitable bequests. To understand how the case law develops it is necessary also to understand the circumstances in which cases are decided. By contrast, the maxims, being abstract principles, are necessarily removed from such contexts.

(1) **Equity will not suffer a wrong to be without a remedy**

This maxim provides the philosophical foundation of equity that, if possible, wrongs should be redressed by the courts. Equity developed as a response to defects of the common law to provide relief where none was available. For example, by means of a trust, equity enabled a beneficiary to enforce an obligation to use property in a particular way even though this obligation was not recognized at common law.

(2) **Equity follows the law**

This is arguably the most important maxim. The Court of Chancery did not override the courts of common law except to remedy an injustice, and could not depart from statute.[91] Equity does not unnecessarily depart from legal principles.[92] The fact that equity follows the law is well illustrated in the context of land by the fact that the equitable estates and interests largely correspond to those at law.

(3) **Where the equities are equal the law prevails**

This maxim means that where there are two persons with competing rights to the same item of property, one with a legal right and the other an equitable right, the legal right will take priority over the equitable right, even if the equitable right had pre-existed it. In *Wortley v Birkhead*,[93] Lord Hardwicke LC explained that this was 'by reason of that force [the Court of Chancery] necessarily and rightly gives to the legal title'.[94] In the context of land, issues of priority between competing rights, whether legal or equitable, are governed by statutory rules which have displaced the operation of this maxim and the next.

(4) **Where the equities are equal the first in time prevails**

This maxim means that if two parties have competing equitable rights in the same item of property, and neither has the legal estate, the right which was created first enjoys priority.[95] This maxim mirrors the common law rule as to priority between competing legal rights.

[91] See Gardner 'Two Maxims of Equity' [1995] CLJ 60.

[92] *Burgess v Wheate* [1759] 1 Eden 177 at 195, per Clarke MR; *Sinclair v Brougham* [1914] AC 398 at 414–15, per Lord Haldane LC.

[93] [1754] 2 Ves Sen 571 at 574.

[94] Compare also *Marsh v Lee* [1670] 2 Vent 337; *Pfeiffer (E) Weinkellerei-Weineinkauf GmbH & Co v Arbuthnot Factors Ltd* [1988] 1 WLR 150.

[95] *Willoughby v Willoughby* [1756] 1 Term Rep 763; *Brace v Duchess of Marlborough* [1728] 2 P Wms 491; *Rice v Rice* [1854] 2 Drew 73; *Phillips v Phillips* [1861] 4 De GF & J 208.

(5) He who seeks equity must do equity

This maxim looks to a claimant's future conduct. If a claimant seeks equitable relief, he must be prepared to act fairly towards the person against whom it is sought.[96] For example, if a purchase is set aside in equity, the purchase money must be repaid with interest.[97]

(6) He who comes to equity must come with clean hands

In contrast, this maxim looks to the past conduct of the claimant. If the claimant's conduct is tainted by illegal or inequitable conduct, he may be denied the relief to which he would otherwise be entitled. The maxim does not apply to conduct in general, but only where the 'grime on the hands' is sufficiently closely connected with the remedy sought.[98] In *Royal Bank of Scotland Plc v Highland Financial Partners LP*[99] Aikens LJ said:

> *Spry: Principles of Equitable Remedies* suggests that it must be shown that the claimant is seeking 'to derive advantage from his dishonest conduct in so direct a manner that it is considered to be unjust to grant him relief'. Ultimately in each case it is a matter of assessment by the judge, who has to examine all the relevant factors in the case before him to see if the misconduct of the claimant is sufficient to warrant a refusal of the relief sought.

In *Argyle (Duchess) v Argyle (Duke)*,[100] the plaintiff's adultery, which caused a divorce, was no bar to her claim for an injunction to restrain the defendant from publishing confidential material. However, in *Grobbelaar v News Group Newspapers Ltd*,[101] the House of Lords was reluctant to grant an injunction preventing a newspaper alleging that an international footballer had 'thrown' games because it had been proved that he had received bribes to fix the outcome of matches.

(7) Delay defeats equity

Equity will not assist a plaintiff who has failed to assert his rights within a reasonable time. This is the foundation of the equitable defence of laches, which was applied in *Nelson v Rye*,[102] where it was held that a musician could not claim an account of earnings wrongfully retained by his manager in breach of fiduciary duty because he had waited for more than six years before commencing an action. The operation of this defence must today be considered in conjunction with the statutory rules concerning limitation of actions under the Limitation Act 1980, considered in Chapter 36.

(8) Equality is equity

Where persons enjoy concurrent entitlement to identical interests in property, and there is no express provision, agreement, or other basis as to how it should be divided among them, equity prescribes that equal division should occur, so that each receives an equal share in the property, for example, where joint purchasers purchase land and there no express allocation of the equitable interest.[103]

[96] See e.g. *Lodge v National Union Investment Co Ltd* [1907] 1 Ch 300; *Solle v Butcher* [1950] 1 KB 671; *Chappell v Times Newspapers Ltd* [1975] 1 WLR 482.

[97] *Peacock v Evans* [1809–10] 16 Ves 512.

[98] *Grobbelaar v News Group Newspapers Ltd* [2002] 4 All ER 732 at 90. See also *Dering v Earl of Winchelsea* [1787] 2 White & Tud LC 488 at 489, and *ORB a.r.l. v Ruhan* [2016] EWHC 850 (Comm) at 99.

[99] [2013] EWCA Civ 328 at 159.

[100] [1967] Ch 302.

[101] [2002] UKHL 40.

[102] [1996] 2 All ER 186; Stevens 'Too Late to Face the Music? Limitation and Laches as Defences to an Action for Breach of Fiduciary Duty' [1997] Conv 225.

[103] See *Jones v Kernott* [2011] UKSC 53.

(9) Equity looks to the intent rather than the form

The principle behind this maxim was well stated by Romilly MR in *Parkin v Thorold*:

> Courts of equity make a distinction between that which is matter of substance and that which is matter of form; and if it finds that by insisting on the form, the substance will be defeated, it holds it to be inequitable to allow a person to insist on such form, and thereby defeat the substance.[104]

Therefore, it is not necessary to use the precise word 'trust' to create a trust, provided that in substance the settlor intended to subject the legal owner of the property to a mandatory obligation regarding its use.[105]

(10) Equity regards as done that which ought to be done

Where a contract is specifically enforceable, equity regards the promisor as having already done what he has promised to do, because he can be compelled to do it. Hence, a contract for the purchase of land,[106] or of unique personal property,[107] will give rise to an immediate constructive trust vesting the equitable ownership in the purchaser by way of a constructive trust at the very moment that the contract is entered.

(11) Equity imputes an intention to fulfil an obligation

Equity places the most favourable construction on a man's acts, so that if he does something which could be construed as fulfilling an obligation he owes, equity will regard it as having this effect. For example, if a debtor leaves a legacy to his creditor, this is presumed to be a repayment of the debt.[108] The doctrines of performance and satisfaction are founded on this maxim.

(12) Equity acts *in personam*

This maxim refers to the fact that equity enforces its decisions by means of a personal order against the defendant, for example, by an order to perform a contract, observe a trust, or refrain from some behaviour by means of an injunction. If the defendant breaches the order, he will be in contempt of court.[109] The court may exercise jurisdiction over any person within the power of the court,[110] even though the order may relate to property which is situated abroad.[111]

[104] [1852] 16 Beav 59 at 66. [105] *Re Kayford Ltd* [1975] 1 WLR 279.

[106] *Lloyds Bank plc v Carrick* [1996] 4 All ER 630.

[107] E.g. in *Oughtred v IRC* [1960] AC 206, where there was a contract for the purchase of a beneficiary's equitable interest in shares in a private company.

[108] *Thynne v Glengall* [1848] 2 HL Cas 131; *Chichester v Coventry* [1867] LR 2 HL 71; *Re Horlock* [1895] 1 Ch 516.

[109] See *Co-operative Insurance v Argyll Stores* [1997] 3 All ER 297 at 302–33.

[110] Namely, someone who is within the jurisdiction or on whom the court order can be served outside of it.

[111] *Penn v Lord Baltimore* [1750] 1 Ves Sen 444; *Ewing v Orr Ewing* [1883–84] 9 App Cas 34, HL; *Richard West & Partners (Inverness) Ltd v Dick* [1969] 1 All ER 289; affd [1969] 2 Ch 424, CA.

2

Equitable obligations

1 Introduction

Trusts and powers are two of the main elements in equity's toolkit for managing property. Their utility has been enhanced by the approach flagged by the landmark decision in *McPhail v Doulton*[1] of seeking to facilitate the wishes of a settlor rather than trying to shoehorn arrangements into preconceived categories. The result has been the recognition of a range of intermediate obligations, including the discretionary trust and fiduciary powers. Alongside this, equity developed the concept of the fund which has helped in the separation of beneficial ownership from asset management. Combined with all of this, equity has recognized the possibility that a settlement can include directions to trustees which are binding or discretionary, and also the power to make variations by adding or removing beneficiaries. The result has been that settlements can contain a range of flexibility which is far removed from a simple transfer of ownership from one person to another.

Schmidt v Rosewood Trust[2] provides an example of the flexibility which is possible with trusts. The case, which is considered more fully in relation to the right of a beneficiary to require trustees to disclose information about the trust, involved a settlement containing a discretionary trust in favour of a group of beneficiaries, and allowed the trustees not just to make distributions amongst those beneficiaries, but also to remove or add beneficiaries, and to accumulate income under the trust instead of distributing it.

2 Trust funds

(1) The concept of a 'trust fund'

Although a trust may exist in relation to a single, specific asset, such as a sum of money, a piece of land, or shares in a company, often the property to which the trust relates will comprise a wide range of different assets. In both cases, the trustees may be permitted to sell the assets and exchange them for new ones. For this reason the property subject to the trust is generically identified as the trust 'fund'.[3] Often the precise content of the fund will be fluid, because the individual assets comprising the fund are frequently being substituted by means of sale and reinvestment. For example, if trustees hold capital under a trust requiring them to invest it and pay any income to the beneficiaries, the capital need not necessarily remain in the same investments throughout the life of the trust.

[1] [1971] AC 424. [2] [2003] 2 AC 709.
[3] See Nolan 'Property in a Fund' [2004] 120 LQR 108.

Indeed, there will be some instances, such as with unit trusts and pension schemes, where the benefits of collective investment would largely be lost without a regular review of the investment portfolio. The trustees, therefore, have powers of disposition over the investments held and they will move or change those investments from time to time. Provided that the proceeds from the realization of any investment are immediately reinvested, the value of the investment portfolio will remain unchanged, apart from transaction costs and any gains or losses that have been made on individual investments within the portfolio.[4] The powers of the trustees are management powers which do not affect the rights of the beneficiaries, unlike powers of appointment, which allow the trustees (or others) to make decisions identifying beneficiaries or quantifying their rights.

This concept of trust assets forming a collective investment fund is a core principle in equity. It lies at the root of investment vehicles such as unit trusts and pension funds. In more domestic contexts, it provides a means by which parents with sufficient money to invest can make provision for their children, preserving wealth within the family, but giving flexibility to the trustees as to how it will be managed and invested. The fund concept has also been employed in a corporate context, where equity has recognized that it is possible to create a floating charge over the assets of a company. This operates to use the assets of the company as security for an obligation, in a similar way to that in which a house can be mortgaged to secure the repayment of a loan. Instead of freezing any particular asset (which is all that was allowed at common law), a floating charge treats all the assets of the company as a fund, and applies to the fund as a whole. So long as the company continues to trade in the ordinary course of business, so that assets disposed of are balanced by assets acquired, the company retains freedom of disposition over individual assets. Should the company cease to trade in the ordinary way, or if some other specified event occurs, then the charge settles and crystallizes by attaching to the specific assets then forming part of the fund.[5]

(2) **The product of trust property will also be trust property**

A feature of a fund is that it includes accretions, as well as substitutions. Property produced by trust property itself becomes subject to the trust. For example, if the trust property includes shares in a company, any dividends paid on such shares will also comprise trust property. It has already been noted that property acquired by the sale and reinvestment of trust property will belong to the trust fund. As an extension of this principle, any unauthorized profits earned by the exploitation of opportunities arising from the trust property will also be trust property. Where, for example, the trust property comprises shares in a company, those shares inevitably carry voting rights in the company general meeting, which are controlled by the trustees by virtue of their legal title to the shares. If a trustee is then appointed director through the use of those voting rights, any personal remuneration he receives in that capacity will prima facie constitute trust property.

(3) **Tracing and following trust property**

If a trustee, without authority, disposes of trust property, the beneficiary can usually choose between one of two options. The first is to follow the original property into the hands of the recipient and to enforce the terms of the trust against the recipient. This course of action is normally possible unless the property has ceased to exist, or the

[4] See, for example, *Re Earl of Strafford (Deceased)* [1980] Ch 28.

[5] *Governments Stock and Other Securities Co v Manila Railway Co* [1897] AC 81, at 86, per Lord MacNaghten; *George Barker (Transport) Ltd v Eynon* [1974] 1 All ER 900, at 905, per Edmund Davies LJ.

recipient is a bona fide purchaser for value. The second is to trace the property into what it has been exchanged for: so if the trustee wrongly sold shares and put the cash into a savings account, the beneficiaries could make a tracing claim against the funds in the savings account. In some cases, tracing and following can be combined.

In addition to these proprietary claims (i.e. claims to the trust property), the beneficiaries will have personal claims against the trustee for his or her wrongdoing, and may also have personal claims against a wrongdoing third party such as a recipient of the trust property who knew that it was subject to a trust or a person who has dishonestly assisted in the breach of trust.

3 Trustees are subject to obligations

(1) **The trust as a species of obligation**

The word 'trust' is used in a variety of contexts.[6] In this context, a trust is an obligation affecting property, and can best be regarded as a sui generis 'proprietary obligation'.[7] The essence of a trust is that the owner of specific property is subject to mandatory personal obligations governing how it should be used and applied. A trustee is someone who owns property subject to personal obligations to manage and apply it in accordance with the terms of the trust to the advantage of the beneficiaries thereof. He does not enjoy the right to treat the property as if it were his own. The precise nature of the trustee's obligations and duties in relation to the trust property are dependent upon the terms of the particular trust. His rights and duties may be both positive and negative—there are usually some things that a trustee should do in relation to the trust property, and others that he should not. The obligations imposed by a trust do not limit the capacity of the trustee to deal with the property. His unencumbered capacity to deal with the trust property derives simply from the fact that he owns it. The trust obligations merely dictate what he should or should not do, and dealings with the trust property in contravention of these obligations are not ultra vires and void. A trustee who deals with the trust property inconsistently with the terms of the trust will instead become personally liable to the beneficiaries for 'breach of trust' and, in the absence of any defences, will be required to compensate them for any loss they suffer in consequence. Even the Crown can be a trustee, although this will be unusual since the Crown can also hold property subject to governmental obligations rather than simply as a beneficial owner.[8]

(2) **Powers confer authority**

Unlike trusts, where the capacity of the trustee to deal with the trust property derives from his or her legal title, a person with a power of appointment normally has no direct control of property. Instead the instrument conferring the power authorizes the donee of the power to decide who will benefit from the property by giving a direction to the trustees of the settlement creating the power or to the administrators of the will containing

[6] See Bartlett 'When is a "Trust" Not a Trust? The National Health Service Trust' [1996] Conv 186.

[7] Hayton 'Developing the Obligation Characteristics of the Trust' [2001] 117 LQR 96; Parkinson 'Reconceptualising the Express Trust' [2002] 61 CLJ 657.

[8] *High Commissioner for Pakistan in the United Kingdom v Prince Mukkaram Jah, His Exalted Highness the 8th Nizam of Hyderabad* [2016] EWHC 1465 (Ch) at 47 et seq.

the power, as the case may be.[9] Having this power does not make the donee the owner of the property, and the power can only be exercised in accordance with the terms under which it was conferred. This means that if a donee purports to make a decision which is outside the terms of the power, that is, in principle, ultra vires and a nullity.

(3) The source of the trust obligations

A trust arises when property is held by trustees subject to obligations owed in favour of beneficiaries. Such obligations will arise where the outright owner of property deliberately subjects it to a trust, is presumed to have subjected it to a trust, or if a trust is imposed by law.

(a) Express intention to impose trust obligations

Property may be subjected to a trust obligation by the deliberate act of its owner. An outright owner[10] of property may create a trust either by subjecting himself to trust obligations, by declaring that he holds it for specified beneficiaries, or by transferring the ownership to someone else, specifying that they are intended to hold it on trust. For example, if Mike owns shares in a company and wishes to create a trust of them in favour of Norma, he can either declare himself a trustee of the shares or transfer them to Owen, directing him to hold them on trust for Norma. In either case the trust is said to be express, as it was created by the deliberate intention of the owner. The person creating an express trust is described as the 'settlor', as he is said to 'settle' the property on trust for the benefit of the beneficiaries.

(b) Implied intention to impose trust obligations

While the paradigm source of trust obligations is the express intention of the settlor, there are some circumstances in which equity presumes that a person intended to subject property to a trust, even though in fact no such intention was expressed. If a presumption of a trust arises, and it is not rebutted by counter-evidence that no trust was intended, the property will be subject to what is known as a resulting trust. Resulting trusts arise in two main circumstances, which were identified by Lord Browne-Wilkinson in *Westdeutsche Landesbank Girozentrale v Islington London Borough Council*:

> (a) where A makes a voluntary payment to B or pays (wholly or partly) for the purchase of property which is vested either in B alone or in the joint names of A and B, there is a presumption that A did not intend to make a gift to B; the money or property is held on trust for A (if he is the sole provider of the money) or in the case of a joint purchase by A and B in shares proportionate to their contributions . . .
>
> (b) where A transfers property to B on express trusts, but the trusts declared do not exhaust the whole beneficial interest.[11]

(c) Imposed trust obligations

In some cases property will be regarded as subject to trust obligations despite the lack of either express or presumed intention on the part of the owner because his unconscionable

[9] Powers of appointment need to be distinguished from powers of attorney (which are recognized at common law) and which are 'a formal arrangement whereby one person (the donor) gives another person (the attorney or donee) authority to act on the former's behalf and in their name'. See *The Public Guardian's Severance Applications* [2016] EWHC COP 10 at 9.

[10] This is where the owner has legal and equitable title to the property in his own right. If the owner only has equitable title, it is still possible to create a trust, normally referred to as a sub-trust.

[11] [1996] 2 All ER 961 at 990.

conduct demands that he be required to hold the property for the benefit of others. In such circumstances, the law imposes a constructive trust. The family home is often held on a constructive trust based on the common intention of the parties living there.

(4) The content of the trustees' obligations under the trust

The precise obligations imposed on any particular trustee will vary with the terms of the trust. In many cases the obligations of the trustees will be specified in the trust instrument by the settlor creating the trust. However, in the absence of any contradictory express terms, some powers and duties are granted and imposed by statute. Two main categories of obligation can be identified.

(a) The obligation to allocate the trust property

The most important obligation imposed by a trust is the obligation of the trustees to apply the trust property for the benefit of the beneficiaries in accordance with the terms of the trust. Under some trusts, the trustees have no part to play in deciding how the trust property should be allocated among the beneficiaries because the terms of the trust stipulate how the beneficial interest is to be shared. Such a trust is described as a 'fixed trust', because the settlor who created it has specified the respective entitlements of the beneficiaries in the terms of the trust, and the trustees' duty is merely to carry out his instructions. In other cases, the trustees have a role to play in determining how the beneficial interest is to be allocated. Rather than fixing the specific entitlements of the beneficiaries, the settlor may confer on the trustees the right to decide how the trust property should be allocated among a class of beneficiaries. Such a trust is called a 'discretionary trust' because the entitlement of any individual beneficiary to share in the trust fund is at the discretion of the trustees. Where property is held on trust for children who have not yet reached the age of majority, so that they do not enjoy vested interests in the trust property or the income generated from it, the trustees may enjoy the power to apply such income to their benefit, or even to allow them to receive part of the trust property itself ahead of time. These powers are respectively termed the power of 'maintenance' and the power of 'advancement'. These powers may be granted expressly to the trustees by the settlor creating the trust, but in the absence of an express grant they are conferred by statute.

(b) The obligation to manage the trust property

The second category of trustees' obligations concerns their duties to manage the trust property and to maintain the integrity of the fund. The trustees enjoy complete control of the trust property by virtue of their legal ownership of the assets that comprise the fund. Management functions include decisions on how the trust fund should be invested, and on whether assets held should be realized and the proceeds of sale reinvested. The precise scope of the trustees' management powers is determined by the terms of the particular trust. For example, the terms of the trust may expressly specify the investment powers that the trustees are to enjoy in relation to the trust property, perhaps limiting the type of investments that the trustees are entitled to make. In the absence of such express powers of investment, statute intervenes to grant the trustees standard investment powers. The trust may also specify the means by which new or replacement trustees can be appointed, and statute empowers the trustees to delegate some of their functions to an agent acting on their behalf.

(5) The mandatory character of the trustees' obligations

The obligations of a trustee are mandatory in nature. This means that trustees are required to carry the terms of the trust into effect. In the event that they fail to carry out their obligations, especially the obligation to allocate the trust fund among the beneficiaries, the court will intervene to ensure that the trust is carried out, either by ordering them to act as required by the terms of the trust or, if necessary, by finding an alternative means of enforcing the trust, for example, by appointing new trustees. In this sense trust obligations can be distinguished from powers of appointment, which are discretionary rather than mandatory in character. The mandatory character of trust obligations is also seen in the operation of the maxim that 'equity will not allow a trust to fail for want of a trustee'. If a settlor transfers property to a person who refuses to accept the office of trustee, or if he leaves property by will to a trustee who predeceases him, equity will not allow the trust to fail but will instead find an alternative person to act as trustee.

(6) **The trustees' liability for breach of trust**

If trustees act inconsistently with the terms of the trust, their breach of obligation will render them personally liable to compensate the beneficiaries for any loss caused by the breach.[12] The trustees may commit a breach of trust in four circumstances. First, they commit a breach of trust if they act in a manner inconsistent with the terms of the trust by doing something they were not authorized to do. Second, they commit a breach of trust by omission if they fail to do what the terms of the trust require them to do. Third, they commit a breach of trust if they fail to act with the requisite objective standard of care expected of them, namely, that of 'the ordinary prudent man of business' or with reasonable care. Fourth, trustees are subject to fiduciary duties, meaning that they have to put the interests of the trust and its beneficiaries above their own interests. Equity recognizes that trustees may be tempted to take advantage of their position as the legal owners of the trust property and utilize it to their own advantage, rather than in the interests of their beneficiaries. It, therefore, imposes a strict duty of exclusive loyalty on trustees, obliging them to act solely in the interests of their beneficiaries, and assumes that any personal profit derived from their position as trustee was only obtained by allowing their own interests to prevail over those of their beneficiaries. Trustees are obliged to make restitution to the beneficiaries of any unauthorized profits that they received by virtue of their position, or in circumstances where there was a mere possibility of a conflict of interest between their duty and their personal interests. Trustees will not be in breach of fiduciary duty if they act with the informed consent of all the beneficiaries.

(7) **Fiduciary powers**

A bare or mere power of appointment does not impose any duty on the donee, but simply authorizes the donee to choose who is to benefit. Even in this case, the donee must act within the limits of the power. If Hamid makes a will under which Natasha has a bare power to appoint property 'to such of Hamid's sons as Natasha sees fit', this would not allow Natasha to make an appointment in favour of one of Hamid's daughters. If the power is stated to be exercisable by deed, it cannot be exercised by a will, or vice versa. In addition to acting within the limits of the power, the donee cannot exercise the power for an improper purpose, for instance to make a profit for themselves which is not authorized by the settlement. That would constitute what is called a 'fraud on the power'.

However, it is possible for a power to share some of the characteristics of a trust, and to impose obligations on the donee. A power exercisable by trustees, for instance, is normally considered to be fiduciary, and the trustees will be expected to consider from time to time whether the power should be exercised. In the case of a trust power, or discretionary trust, the trustees may even be required to implement the power. The nature of

[12] The beneficiaries may also have a claim against someone who receives the trust property knowing of the breach or who dishonestly assists in the breach.

the duty on the donee will depend upon the terms in which a power was granted, or the circumstances of its creation.

4 The rights of beneficiaries

(1) Duties are owed to the beneficiaries

Obligations and rights are two sides of the same coin. The obligations of the trustees are owed to the beneficiaries of the trust.

With the exception of trusts for charitable purposes, and a very small number of other anomalous trusts for purposes, trusts must exist for the benefit of persons rather than purposes. The reason for this limitation is that only legal persons, whether human individuals, companies, or corporations, possess the necessary capacity to enjoy and enforce the obligation of the trustees. Therefore, a trust cannot be validly created for the abstract purpose of 'promoting good journalism' because there is no person to whom the obligation is owed, and no one who possesses sufficient *locus standi* to complain to the court if the trustees fail to apply the trust property to the specified purpose. In the case of charitable trusts, the trustees' obligations are supervised on behalf of the Crown by the Attorney-General and the Charity Commission.

(2) The beneficiaries can enforce the trust obligations

The prime entitlement of the beneficiaries of a trust is that the trustees carry out the terms of the trust. They are entitled to enforce the trust, either by preventing the trustees acting in breach or by requiring them to perform their obligations if they are refusing to do so. In effect, they are entitled to require full performance of the trust in their favour. Once property has been validly subjected to a trust in their favour, the beneficiaries are entitled to enforce it irrespective of whether or not they provided consideration in return for the creation of the trust.

(3) The beneficiaries can override the terms of the trust

Beneficiaries of a trust, acting unanimously, enjoy the right to override the terms of the trust as stipulated by the settlor if they are of full age and legally competent. They can demand that the trust be brought to an end in accordance with the rule in *Saunders v Vautier*.[13] They may not dictate to the trustees, however, as to the exercise of the trustees' powers under the terms of the trust.[14] Beneficiaries, individually or collectively, can authorize an act by the trustees which would otherwise be a breach of trust or a breach of fiduciary duty, but the trustees remain liable to any beneficiaries who do not give valid authorization. Similarly, the beneficiaries of a trust can countenance variations in its terms, again potentially undermining the wishes of the settlor embodied therein. The Variation of Trusts Act 1958 even permits the court to grant approval to variations on behalf of beneficiaries who are incapable of consenting for themselves, either because they lack the capacity to consent, are not yet in existence, or cannot be ascertained, provided that the proposed variations are for their 'benefit'.

[13] [1841] 4 Beav 115. [14] *Re Brockbank* [1948] Ch 206.

(4) The beneficiaries' proprietary entitlement

The beneficiaries of a trust enjoy more than merely personal rights to have the trust obligations carried out in their favour by the trustees. Despite some historical debate, the better view is that beneficiaries are also entitled to proprietary rights in the trust property.

(a) The beneficial interest as a mere interest in personam

Some have argued that the fact that the beneficial interest behind a trust is destroyed by the bona fide purchase of the trust property proves that it is a mere interest in personam. Maitland stated that equity had never regarded the beneficiary as 'owner' of the trust property, but only as entitled to enforce the personal obligation of the trustee to carry out the terms of the trust:

> [the trustee] is the owner, the full owner, of the thing, while the cestui que trust has no rights in the thing . . .[15]

More recent support for the view that beneficial interests behind a trust are mere rights in personam can be derived from the decision in *Webb v Webb*,[16] where the central issue was whether a father's assertion that his son held a holiday home in France on resulting trust for him, was a claim founded on a right in rem for the purposes of art 16(1) of the Convention on Jurisdiction and the Enforcement of Judgments in Civil and Commercial Matters 1968. Following the advice of Advocate-General Damon, the Court of Appeal held that the father's claim was not founded on a right in rem but merely on the existence of a personal fiduciary relationship. However, little weight should be placed upon this decision, as the classification of the nature of claims for the purposes of settling whether the English courts have jurisdiction when the property in dispute is situated abroad should not be determinative of the jurisprudential character of beneficial interests for domestic purposes.

(b) The beneficial interest as a proprietary interest in rem

In reality, it seems that the beneficial interest behind a trust is more than a mere personal interest enforceable against the trustee. A beneficiary's interest is enforceable against anyone acquiring the trust property except a bona fide purchaser for value, who is protected by the doctrine of notice. In this sense the beneficial interest shares the essential characteristic of proprietary rights identified by Lord Wilberforce in *National Provincial Bank Ltd v Ainsworth*,[17] namely, that they are capable of enduring through changes in ownership. Beneficial interests are certainly not as durable as legal ownership, but the mere fact that in some circumstances they are defeated by superior rights should not prevent the recognition that they are essentially proprietary in nature. Even Maitland later acknowledged that a beneficiary was entitled to more than a merely personal obligation:

> I believe that for the ordinary thought of Englishmen 'equitable ownership' is just ownership pure and simple, though it is subject to a peculiar, technical and not very intelligible rule in favour of bona fide purchasers . . . so many people are bound to respect these rights that practically they are almost as valuable as if they were dominium.[18]

[15] Maitland, *Equity* (Cambridge University Press 1936), p 17.

[16] [1994] QB 696; MacMillian, 'The European Court of Justice agrees with Maitland: Trusts and the Brussels Convention' [1996] Conv 125.

[17] [1965] AC 1175.

[18] Collected papers, Vol III, p 349.

The proprietary nature of the beneficial interest under a trust is also supported by the fact that the beneficiary is entitled to deal with it in ways characteristic of property owners. He can transfer his equitable interest by assignment, either by way of sale or as a gift. He can dispose of it by will, or in the event of his dying, intestate it passes to his heirs under the rules governing intestate succession. It can be used to provide security for a loan. He may be required to pay tax on its value. His rights, if he has a beneficial interest in land, are enforceable against third parties, subject to the limitations contained in the land registration rules. The proprietary character of the beneficial interest under a trust was clearly stated in *Westdeutsche Landesbank Girozentrale v Islington London Borough Council*,[19] where Lord Browne-Wilkinson said:

> Once a trust is established, as from the date of its establishment the beneficiary has, in equity, a proprietary interest in the trust property, which proprietary interest will be enforceable in equity against any subsequent holder of the property (whether the original property or substituted property into which it can be traced) other than a purchaser for value of the legal interest without notice.[20]

(5) **Objects of powers of appointment**

Powers of appointment may be general, special, or hybrid. A general power of appointment allows the donee to choose anyone to be a beneficiary, even himself or herself. A special power is limited to named individuals or a defined class or classes. A hybrid power excludes named individuals or a defined class or classes. The individuals or class or classes of person in whose favour the power can be exercised are not beneficiaries unless and until the donee exercises the power: until then they are described as objects of the power. The rights of objects of a power are less extensive than those of beneficiaries of a trust. The donee does not normally owe fiduciary duties to the objects,[21] although the objects have locus standi to apply to the court if they believe that the power has been improperly exercised. The objects do not have proprietary rights in the trust fund, because it is only if they are named by the exercise of the power that they acquire a right.

5 Classification of equitable obligations

(1) **Overview**

In the trust and the power, equity has developed two mechanisms which facilitate a separation between the three functions of the management and allocation of property and the right to the enjoyment of property. In the absence of either a trust or a power, these entitlements are enjoyed in a unitary manner by the owner of the property. With trusts and powers, one or more of these functions is separated from the others. However, despite a degree of functional similarity between trusts and powers, it was historically important to draw a sharp distinction between them. Conceptually, a power is purely discretionary, imposing no obligations upon the donee and conferring no proprietary rights upon the objects. In contrast, a trust is mandatory in character, imposing an obligation to act upon the trustees and conferring a proprietary entitlement to the trust fund upon the beneficiaries. Equity at one time tended to differentiate between trusts and powers by examining any given situation and characterizing the mechanism created as either a trust or a power. The rights and duties of the parties were thus determined by that characterization.

[19] [1996] AC 669. [20] [1996] AC 669, at 705.
[21] *Twin Benefits Ltd v Barker* [2017] EWHC 1412 (Ch) at 72.

Traditionally, the two mechanisms were, therefore, clearly distinguishable from each other. However, over time, such a simple bifurcation proved insufficiently flexible, and equity extended the boundaries of existing obligations and developed new obligations. As a result, the distinction between different categories of equitable mechanism may be extremely fine and very difficult to draw in practice. In the light of these developments, although convenient from the point of view of analysis, it is questionable whether it is still valid to regard the law as comprising a fixed group of categories of obligation into which each fact situation must be fitted, with the inevitable result that the categorization will determine the rights and duties. Instead, a 'scale' of equitable obligations has emerged, and the courts will be willing to construe any particular fact situation as falling somewhere along the scale, not necessarily within a fixed traditional category, and then finding the appropriate rights and duties. The shift has been from a 'black and white' categorization of equitable obligations as either trusts or powers, to a recognition that there is a 'greyscale' with an almost infinite variation between the two extremes.

(2) A traditional categorization

(a) Trust or power

Originally, a trust and power were seen as being conceptually distinct, with only a limited scope for overlap. In construing a document, it was, therefore, simply a question of determining whether an obligation fell within the category of a trust or power. This would be determined by a consideration of the language used in the instrument creating it. In some circumstances the characterization of an arrangement as a trust or a power would determine whether the arrangement was valid or invalid.

For both trusts and powers it is necessary for the court to supervise the arrangement by ensuring that the fund is allocated only to those who fall within the terms of the original disposition. This requires that the beneficiaries of the trust, or the objects of the power, be defined with sufficient clarity and certainty. If this certainty of objects is lacking, then the whole arrangement will be void. Until the decision of the House of Lords in *McPhail v Doulton*,[22] the test of certainty of objects for powers was more generous than the test of certainty for trusts. Thus, it was often the case that an arrangement would be valid if characterized as a power, but invalid if it was a trust.

(b) Limitations of a traditional categorization

One major limitation of the traditional categorization was the difficulty of determining whether a particular obligation was to be classed as a trust or a power, which could have such significant consequences for all the parties involved. The mere use of the words 'trust' or 'power' would not necessarily be conclusive, since what was important was the intention of the property owner creating the arrangement. If he intended to impose mandatory obligations, indicating that he expected the obligations to be carried out, a trust would be created, but if he intended to give discretion without imposing an obligation, then a power would be conferred. The difficulty lay in the fine distinction between these two alternatives. As Lord Wilberforce acknowledged in *McPhail v Doulton*, this is an area of 'delicate shading'.[23] No particular words were (or are) needed to create a trust or a power. There is, therefore, no easy way of telling whether a particular disposition (even if professionally drafted) creates a trust or a power, and the law reports are full of cases where even the courts have found it difficult to decide which is created in a given case.

[22] [1971] AC 424.

[23] [1970] 2 All ER 228 at 240. See also Sir Richard Arden MR in *Brown v Higgs* [1800] 5 Ves 495 at 505, citing *Duke of Marlborough v Lord Godolphin* [1750] 2 Ves Sen 61.

In *McPhail v Doulton* itself, the judge at first instance and the Court of Appeal found that the settlor had intended to create a power. These conclusions were influenced by the fact that the arrangement would be valid if characterized as a power, but void for want of certainty if it was a trust. The House of Lords ultimately held that the mandatory character of the language used indicated an intention to create a trust, but proceeded to revise the test of certainty applicable to trusts to ensure that it was not invalidated.

(c) Trusts combined with powers

The difficulty of making a distinction between trusts and powers is compounded by the fact that a power created inter vivos will always be associated with a trust.[24] This is because a power of appointment is essentially the right to give directions to trustees as to how or for whom they are to hold trust property. This can happen in one of several ways. First, trustees could be directed to hold property for whomever the donee of the power selects. In the absence of the power being exercised, there may be a defined trust in default of appointment. Second, there might be a fixed trust, subject to the donee of a power being able to divest the beneficiaries of their interests by exercising the power. Finally, there might be an obligation to make a selection, so that the 'power' is really itself a trust. In each case, the power of selection could be held either by the trustees of the trust fund themselves or by a separate donee.

(3) The evolution of intermediate obligations

The development of trusts and powers by equity was driven by the desire to enable property owners to deal with their property as they wish. The power enabled a property owner to delegate to another the control over the distribution of his property, within the limits he had specified. The trust enabled the owner of property to distribute his property to predetermined individuals by giving the legal title to a trustee and specifying the beneficial interests. However, as owners' intentions changed with time and they sought to distribute their property in more complex ways, a simple analysis of equitable obligations proved inadequate. Equity was able to develop new obligations which combined aspects of both the power and the trust. The prime example is the emergence of the discretionary trust. Despite its lengthy heritage, the effect of the development was not fully felt until the decision of the House of Lords in *McPhail v Doulton*.[25]

(a) Early developments akin to discretionary trusts

The existence of hybrid obligations was recognized by Lord Eldon LC in the leading case of *Brown v Higgs*:[26]

> There are not only a mere trust and a mere power, but there is also known to the court a power which the party to whom it is given is entrusted and required to execute; and with regard to that species of power, the court considers it as partaking so much of the nature and qualities of a trust, that if the person who has that duty imposed on him does not discharge it, the court will to a certain extent discharge the duty in his room and place.

Such an arrangement was demonstrated in *Crockett v Crockett*,[27] which followed the case of *Hart v Tribe*.[28] Within just a few years the concept was sufficiently clearly

[24] A power of appointment may also be contained in a will. The executors or administrators then stand in the position of the trustees of a settlement created inter vivos.

[25] [1971] AC 424.

[26] [1799] 4 Ves 708; reheard [1800] 5 Ves 495; affd [1803] 8 Ves 561.

[27] [1848] 2 Ph 553.

[28] [1854] 18 Beav 215. Sir John Romilly, who had been counsel in the *Crockett* case, was then Master of the Rolls.

established for Thomas Smith MR, in the Irish Court of Chancery, to describe it as a discretionary trust.[29]

However, as might be expected, the early development was uncertain. This is evident in the decision in *Burrough v Philcox*.[30] John Walton left property to his two children for life and granted them a power to dispose of it by will in favour of his nephews and nieces. His two children died without making any appointment, and the question arose whether the nephews and nieces could claim the property or whether it would pass to the residuary legatees of John Walton's will. The arrangement was clearly a power, but the court found that there was a general intention in favour of the class by John Walton, and since that intention had failed because a selection had not been made by his children, the court would carry into effect the general intention and divide the property equally between the nephews and nieces. The court chose to analyze this disposition as a power with a trust in favour of the class should the power fail to be exercised. It could equally well have been treated as a discretionary trust.

(b) The enforcement of hybrid obligations

While equity seemed willing to contemplate the emergence of mechanisms which were hybrid in nature, in that they were not exclusively mandatory or exclusively discretionary, there was uncertainty as to how the court could intervene if a trustee failed to exercise his discretion under a discretionary trust. For many years, judicial opinion was divided. In some cases, the courts had compelled a trustee to act,[31] or substituted its own judgment for that of a discretionary trustee who had failed to act.[32] In others, the court disclaimed the ability to substitute its own opinion for that of the trustee,[33] culminating in the condemnation of cases taking a flexible approach by the Court of Appeal in 1954 in *IRC v Broadway Cottages Trust*.[34] The orthodox view adopted in that case was that the court had no right to substitute its discretion for that of the designated trustees, should they fail or refuse to act. The discretion being conferred on and exercisable by the trustees alone, the court could not do anything other than authorize a distribution in equal shares. To this there might have been a limited exception that where the testator or settlor had laid down pointers or guides to the exercise of the discretion, this could form a basis for the exercise of a more flexible order by the court.[35]

(4) *McPhail v Doulton*: a twentieth-century watershed

The decision in the House of Lords in *McPhail v Doulton* marks the major break from the traditional dichotomy between trust and powers. Mr Bertram Baden settled property on trust to enable the trustees to make grants in favour of the staff of Matthew Hall and Co Ltd and their relatives and dependants. It was obvious that Mr Baden did not intend each and every member of staff and their dependants and relatives to have a share in the property left on trust, as there would simply not be enough for them each to receive any meaningful sum. The trustees were to have discretion which of the members of staff and their relatives and dependants were to benefit. The House of Lords held by a majority that

[29] *Gray v Gray* [1862] 13 I Ch R 404. [30] [1840] 5 My & Cr 72.

[31] See *Hart v Tribe* [1854] 18 Beav 215 at 217–18; *Gisborne v Gisborne* [1877] 2 App Cas 300, HL; *Tempest v Lord Camoys* [1882] 21 Ch D 571.

[32] *Moseley v Moseley* [1673] Cas temp Finch 53; *Clarke v Turner* [1694] Freem Ch 198; *Warburton v Warburton* [1702] 4 Bro Parl Cas 1; *Richardson v Chapman* [1760] 7 Bro Parl Cas 318.

[33] See, for example, *Gray v Gray* [1862] 13 I Ch R 404; *Kemp v Kemp* [1795] 5 Ves Jr 849.

[34] [1955] Ch 20, [1954] 3 All ER 120.

[35] See the dissenting judgment of Lord Hodson in *McPhail v Doulton* [1970] 2 All ER 228 at 234.

this was a trust and not a power. Most significantly, it held that if the trustees failed to exercise their discretion, the court could intervene to compel them, or to ensure by some other means that the trust was carried out. Lord Wilberforce stated that:

> The court, if called upon to execute the trust power, will do so in the manner best calculated to give effect to the settlor's or testator's intentions. It may do so by appointing new trustees, or by authorising or directing representative persons of the classes of beneficiaries to prepare a scheme of distribution, or even, should the proper basis for distribution appear by itself directing the trustees so to distribute.

(5) The contemporary classification of equitable obligations

McPhail v Doulton[36] overturned the orthodox view that there were a limited number of categories of equitable obligation and that regard would be had to the wishes of the settlor by allocating the arrangement that he had created into the most appropriate box or category. Some of the categories recognized before *McPhail v Doulton* did, of course, contain the potential for fine-tuning. The settlor could specify what discretions he was conferring upon his trustees, but the lack of anything but the crudest form of enforcement through equal division in the case of a failure by his trustees to exercise a discretion meant that the settlor's freedom of invention was comparatively limited. *McPhail v Doulton*[37] marked a watershed not merely because it changed the certainty requirement for discretionary trusts (explored in Chapter 5), but also because it altered the basis on which the courts would enforce fiduciary obligations. By recognizing that equal division was not the only remedy available where a trustee failed to act, the House of Lords opened the possibility of more varied and sophisticated obligations in equity. The possibilities opened up by the case have been confirmed and exploited since.

Writing extrajudicially and giving a critical take on the development of the Law of Trusts, Lord Walker has described *McPhail v Doulton*[38] as a key moment in the development of equity. At the start of his career, Chancery practice had not been a particularly lucrative line of work for lawyers as, 'fees were low, and it has to be said that standards were low. . .'[39] Alongside the introduction of the Variation of Trusts Act 1958 (discussed in Chapter 29), *McPhail v Doulton* should be understood as part of a 'shot in the arm' to the reach and relavance of equity. By making the rules more flexible, it became possible for wealthy individuals to try and arrange trusts so that their fianances were managed in a way that was more tax efficient. In turn, this generated considerable work for practitioners. It will be seen that the innovation in *McPhail v Doulton* is a far-reaching one. In this context, it is important to keep it mind that change in this area has been innovation through the case law, rather than through legislative law reform.

(6) Blurring distinctions

The historic categories of the mandatory fixed trust, discretionary trust, and mere power provided the beginnings of a broader scale of obligations developing as grey shades between the black and white of trusts and powers. *McPhail v Doulton* has led to the exploitation of more intermediate shades of grey. This has happened both by the evolution of new mechanisms filling the gaps between the old constructs, and also by expansion within the categories themselves (see Figure 2.1).

[36] [1971] AC 424. [37] [1971] AC 424. [38] [1971] AC 424.
[39] Walker, 'The Changing Face of Trust Law' (2017) 1 TLI 19, 19.

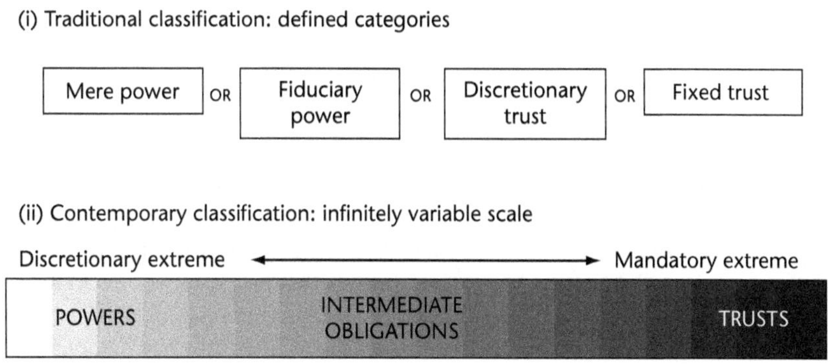

Figure 2.1 A scale of equitable obligations

(a) Exhaustive and non-exhaustive discretionary trusts

Within the category of discretionary trust, it is possible to distinguish between those under which the trustees are obliged to distribute the assets of the trust, and those where there is no such obligation. Since *McPhail v Doulton* the difference matters. The way in which the court is likely to intervene may differ markedly according to whether the trustees' obligation does or does not require the exhaustion of the trust fund.

(b) Enforcing fiduciary powers

In a similar vein, it has long been recognized that some powers are fiduciary, in the sense that the donee is unable to agree voluntarily or by contract not to exercise the power. It is said, to use the technical term, that the power cannot be released. That was as far as the court was willing to intervene when the traditional dichotomy between mandatory trusts and permissive powers held sway. However, in *Mettoy Pension Trustees Ltd v Evans*,[40] Warner J held that in some circumstances the courts might be willing to compel the donee of a fiduciary power to exercise it using the same methods of enforcement that were suggested by Lord Wilberforce as applicable to discretionary trusts in *McPhail v Doulton*.[41] The case, which has since been doubted, is fully discussed in a later chapter, but at this stage it is sufficient to recognize that this runs against the tenor of previous cases, which had maintained the orthodox position that the exercise of fiduciary powers[42] cannot be enforced by the courts.[43]

(c) Blurring of the traditional categories of trust and power

Discretionary trusts themselves represent a blurring between the distinct categories of the trust and power. The House of Lords in *McPhail v Doulton* described the arrangement which Bertram Baden had set up as a 'trust power'. That phrase encapsulates the hybrid nature of the discretionary trust, which draws in elements both of trusts, in the obligation which is placed upon the trustees, and of power, in relation to the discretions which are conferred upon the trustees and the lack of defined rights, even in default, upon the part of the beneficiaries. The decision in the *Mettoy Pension* case, if correct on this

[40] [1991] 2 All ER 513.

[41] [1971] AC 424. The Privy Council has confirmed that a power can be executed by the appointment of a receiver: *Fonu v Merrill Lynch* [2011] UKPC 17.

[42] As opposed to the consideration of the exercise of the power.

[43] *Re Gulbenkian's Settlement Trusts (No 1)* [1968] Ch 126; *McPhail v Doulton* [1971] AC 424; *Re Hay's Settlement Trusts* [1981] 3 All ER 786.

point, suggests a further blurring. Rather than there being a sharp conceptual distinction between discretionary trusts and fiduciary powers, the case recognizes that there is a 'grey area' where obligations are neither distinctly one nor the other, but where they enjoy characteristics of both. The subsequent decision of the Privy Council in *Schmidt v Rosewood Trust Ltd*[44] further confirms the blurring of the traditional distinction between trusts and powers. In this case it was held that no distinction should be drawn between the rights of the object of a discretionary trust or of a fiduciary power in regard to the entitlement to the disclosure of trust documents. Thus, a right that was formerly predicated upon the proprietary right of the beneficiary to the trust property was extended to the objects of a power of appointment who have no proprietary interest. In reaching this conclusion, Lord Walker referred to the way in which Lord Wilberforce had demonstrated in *McPhail v Doulton* that the differences between trusts and powers were 'a good deal less significant than the similarities'.[45]

(d) Blurring in practice: pension schemes

The increasingly sophisticated use of trusts and powers further suggests the inevitability of a blending and melding between some of the old categories. Take, for instance, the pension scheme. The trustees of a pension fund will generally be under a binding obligation to pay pension benefits to the widow or dependent children of a contributing member if he dies in service, that is, while still in employment. A capital sum will usually also be available. With most pension schemes, the trustees hold any capital sum upon discretionary trusts to distribute it among a class of beneficiaries including the member's near family, any dependants, and any person the member may have nominated. The trustees may also have powers to establish trusts containing discretions and powers where they are applying a lump sum on death in service. In considering what to do, the trustees may have received directions from the member. In one typical scheme, it is stated: 'In the exercise of their discretionary powers the Trustees may have regard to but shall not be bound by any wishes notified to them by the member.' In a single arrangement, therefore, one can find fixed trusts, discretionary trusts, powers, and directions with no express binding force alongside each other.

(7) Determining rights and duties

Given the blurring of the distinctions between the recognized equitable mechanisms and the difficulty of drawing conceptual distinctions between them, the traditional approach of categorizing obligations into a small number of well-defined categories seems inappropriate. In the past, there was a temptation to allow the classification of an arrangement to dictate the parties' rights and duties. However, this is a circular activity, and the fallacy of it is evident by examining an illustration. In *Re Gestetner Settlement*,[46] Harman J indicated that in addition to a discretionary trust where the trustees were under an obligation to distribute, there could also be a situation where trustees were simply under an obligation to consider whether a power to distribute should be exercised, without being obliged to part with any income or capital. This is sometimes described as a non-exhaustive discretionary trust, to distinguish it from the case where the trustees are under a duty to distribute and exhaust the fund (an exhaustive discretionary trust). In *McPhail v Doulton*, Lord Wilberforce drew a distinction between a discretionary trust (which he described as a trust power) and a mere power which was conferred on trustees. In the latter case, he stated that 'although the trustees may, and normally will, be under a fiduciary duty

[44] [2003] 3 All ER 76. [45] [2003] 3 All ER 76 at 66.
[46] [1953] Ch 672; [1953] 1 All ER 1150.

to consider whether or in what way they should exercise their power, the court will not normally compel its exercise'. Lord Wilberforce did not consider this to be a discretionary trust (or a trust power, in the terminology which he used in the case), but it is difficult to see how it differs in any real respect from a non-exhaustive discretionary trust.[47]

The extent of the obligation to review the range of objects can also vary. Again, in *McPhail v Doulton* Lord Wilberforce said that:

> as to the trustees' duty of enquiry or ascertainment, in each case the trustees ought to make such a survey of the range of objects or possible beneficiaries as will enable them to carry out their fiduciary duty. A wider and more comprehensive range of enquiry is called for in the case of trust powers than in the case of powers.

Earlier in his opinion, he had indicated that the distinction was a functional one:

> Such distinction as there is would seem to lie in the extent of the survey which the trustee is required to carry out; if he has to distribute the whole of a fund's income, he must necessarily make a wider and more systematic survey than if his duty is expressed in terms of a power to make grants . . . The difference may be one of degree rather than of principle; in the well-known words of Sir George Farwell, trusts and powers are often blended, and the mixture may vary in its ingredients.[48]

(8) **A scale of equitable obligations**

The mix of trusts and powers, and the nature of the obligations that can be imposed on the donee of a fiduciary power, makes it undesirable to insist upon a rigid classification. There are, moreover, difficulties in locating some arrangements clearly under one category or another. As the litigation in *McPhail v Doulton* indicates, what one person sees as a trust in favour of a class with a power to accumulate may by another be seen as a trust to accumulate with a power to make grants in favour of a class. The House of Lords recognized that the distinctions not only are fine but also are not determinative of the obligations of the donee or trustee. In the words of Lord Wilberforce:

> It is striking how narrow and in a sense artificial is the distinction . . . between trusts . . . and powers . . . And if one considers how in practice reasonable and competent trustees would act, and ought to act, in the two cases, surely a matter very relevant to the question of validity, the distinction appears even less significant. To say that there is no obligation to exercise a mere power and that no court will intervene to compel it, whereas a trust is mandatory and its execution may be compelled, may be legally correct enough, but the proposition does not contain an exhaustive comparison of the duties of persons who are trustees in the two cases.[49]

This marks a fundamental shift from a simple conceptual framework of equitable obligations, where characterization as either a trust or a power determines the rights and duties of the parties, to a functional analysis, where the courts will construe an arrangement in the way best capable of fulfilling the intention of the owner of the property. The absence of a rigid hierarchy of equitable obligations means that there is instead a wide spectrum of arrangements, the characteristics of which depend upon the terms and circumstances of their creation. Any classification can be adopted only as a matter of convenience as a way

[47] See, however, Hayton's definition of a non-exhaustive discretionary trust as one in which 'the trustees must distribute the income amongst class "A" only if they fail to exercise a power to withhold the income for some purpose such as accumulating it or using it for class "B"': Hayton and Marshall, *Cases and Commentary on the Law of Trusts* (11th edn, Sweet & Maxwell 2001), p 152, n 90.

[48] Farwell, *Farwell on Powers* (3rd edn, London 1916), p 10.

[49] [1970] 2 All ER 228, at 240.

of describing, rather than prescribing, the incidents of any particular arrangement. It is possible to describe some of the principal kinds of equitable obligation which are found in practice, although it is impossible to draw up a definitive list. However, some features of the scale of equitable obligations can usefully be identified.

(a) The mandatory extreme

At one end of the spectrum of equitable mechanisms for property management and holding is the bare trust. The trustee may well have no independent powers of management or investment, and the shares in which the property is to be enjoyed are predetermined. The freedom of the trustee is constrained, and control is at its highest. Yet even here the position may be qualified. For instance, it is not unusual for a trust providing for fixed successive interests to contain a power enabling the trustee to draw down some of the capital and to pay it by way of an advancement to a beneficiary who has only a presumptive interest in the fund. There may also be a power to make applications of income (and sometimes capital) for the education and maintenance of an infant beneficiary who would otherwise have only a deferred right to those funds.

(b) The discretionary extreme

At the other end of the spectrum is a mere power, the donee of which enjoys an unfettered discretion whether to exercise it and, if it is exercised, how to exercise it. Even here, however, the donee does not have complete freedom, for the court will ensure that the power is exercised only within its terms.

(c) Intermediate points on the scale

Between the black and white extremes of the bare fixed trust and the mere power there lies an almost infinite variety of intermediate arrangements. These include: trusts in favour of a fixed class, but with a power to make a selection between them in unequal shares;[50] a discretionary trust where the trustee is under an obligation to make a selection and which will be exercised by some means by the court if the trustee fails to exercise it;[51] a fiduciary power where the donee need not make a distribution but must at least consider periodically whether it should be exercised;[52] and a power or discretionary trust in favour of a class with a power to extend that class by appointing new members of the class.[53] Most of these possibilities can be combined in one form or another, creating a nearly infinite range of shades of grey.

6 A practical guide to interpretation

Whether a transaction—normally a written instrument—creates a trust or a power (or something in between) is a process of interpretation which is governed by the normal rules for interpretation. However, because the defining difference between the extremes of the scale of equitable obligations is that trusts impose mandatory, binding obligations whilst powers confer an authority without any binding obligation, it is possible to identify some practical pointers which may be helpful in distinguishing trusts and powers.

[50] *Wilson v Duguid* [1883] 24 Ch D 244 (where the gift to the class in equal shares was implied); *Burroughs v Philcox* [1840] 5 My & Cr. 72; *Re Llewellyn's Settlement* [1921] 2 Ch 281; *Re Arnold* [1947] Ch 131.

[51] *Brown v Higgs* [1803] 8 Ves 561; *McPhail v Doulton* [1971] AC 424.

[52] *Re Manisty's Settlement Trusts* [1974] Ch 17; *Re Hay's Settlement Trusts* [1982] 1 WLR 202.

[53] *Re Hay's Settlement Trusts* [1982] 1 WLR 202.

(1) Are mandatory expressions used?

It is not necessary for the word 'trust' to be used for a trust to be created. However, an instrument must impose an obligation if a person is to be a trustee. Words like 'shall' or 'must' point towards a trust, whilst words like 'may', 'might', or 'hope' incline more to a permissive power.[54]

(2) Is the power conferred on a trustee?

A discretionary trust combines the duties of a trustee with the discretion given by a power, and was, therefore, originally called a trust power. A power conferred on a trustee is more likely to be construed as subject to obligations than a power conferred on a person who is not also a trustee.[55]

(3) What happens if a discretion is not exercised?

If a power or discretion must be exercised, then it is not a mere power but a discretionary trust. If the gift conferring a power or discretion indicates what is to happen if the power is not exercised, then that is a factor (although not conclusive in itself) which suggests that there is no obligation to make a selection.[56] For instance if Abbie leaves a fund on trust 'to such of my children and in such shares as my husband Arthur may by deed or will appoint, and in default of any such appointment to my children equally', the existence of the specific direction as to how the property is to be held in the event of no appointment being made tends to suggest that Arthur is permitted to make a different allocation, but is not under an obligation to make a selection.[57]

It does not follow from the absence of a gift over in default of appointment that the power is in the nature of a discretionary trust. The failure to specify what will happen if the power is not exercised may be a simple omission, and in some cases, the court will imply a gift in default on the basis that there is a general intention that the class should benefit whether or not the power is exercised.[58] This is discussed in Chapter 5, which looks in more detail at powers of appointment and discretionary trusts.

[54] See the discussion in *McPhail v Doulton* [1971] AC 424.

[55] *Mettoy Pension Trustees Ltd v Evans* [1991] 2 All ER 513; *Clarkson v Clarkson* [1994] EWCA Civ 25.

[56] *Re Wills' Trust Deeds* [1964] Ch 219.

[57] See the settlement in *Howell & Ors v Lees-Millais* [2009] EWHC 1754 (Ch), where there was an express gift in default even though the wording of the power given to the trustees suggested that it was mandatory.

[58] *Burrough v Philcox* [1840] 5 My & Cr 72.

3

Equity and the management of property

1 Introduction

Trusts are more common in everyday life than most people realize, and this chapter provides some examples. They demonstrate that, like Molière's character in *The Bourgeois Gentilhomme* who exclaimed 'Good Heavens! For more than forty years I have been speaking prose without knowing it', the way in which trusts underpin much of the modern law of property is often unnoticed or under-appreciated. For instance, few people realize that the family home is, in most cases, held on trust.

While trusts first emerged in an entirely different social environment, they have proved extremely adaptable to modern family and commercial contexts and play a key role in the modern law of charities. Those who invest in a pension, a unit trust, or an ISA are likely to find that the underlying assets behind their investment are held under a trust. Persons with considerable wealth may utilize trusts to help in tax planning. The John Lewis Partnership is an example of a trust used in a commercial context: the company is owned by its employees through a trust for them set up by Spedan Lewis (the son of the store founder) as a social experiment with the radical philosophy that the business would thrive if its staff had an interest in its success.

2 Hiding the identity of the true owner of property

The fact that a trust enables the separation of the legal and beneficial ownership of property means that it can be used as an effective mechanism for hiding the identity of the true owner of property. If property is held on trust, it may appear to the world that the trustee is in fact the absolute legal owner, and others will have no knowledge of the existence of a trust. There is no obligation to publicly disclose the existence of a trust, and, therefore, this mechanism will be particularly important where the legal ownership is made public, such as in the case of land where the name of the owner is publicly available from the records kept by the Land Registry. An example of this kind or arrangement, known as a bare trust, being used to acquire property is *Prest v Petrodel Resources Ltd.*[1] A wealthy oil trader had used a number of companies to acquire or hold property for which he had paid. His wife claimed that these homes could be treated as part of his assets for the purposes of assessing his wealth on divorce. The Supreme Court held that, even though the corporate structures had been used for tax planning purposes rather than to avoid a divorce

[1] [2013] UKSC 34.

settlement, the assets could be taken into account as part of the divorce because they were held by the companies on trust for the husband. Similarly, if a man wishes to make provision for his mistress on his death without members of his family discovering that she exists, he can create what is called a 'secret trust',[2] where the property is left by will to a trustee, such as a friend, but the terms of the trust—or even the trust's existence—are not disclosed in the will, which would become a public document as a consequence of the probate procedure.

The ability of the trust to hide the identity of the true owner can often be employed to less palatable ends, such as financial crime (including money laundering) or terrorism.[3] They can also be used to conceal wealth, particularly in complicated off-shore arrangements to divest people from the burdens of wealth, such as taxation, whilst still ultimately sharing in the benefits of that wealth as beneficial owner.[4] As a direct result of high profile scandals,[5] there has been legislative intervention to curb these abuses, including requiring increased transparency as to the beneficial ownership of property under a trust.[6] This will doubtless have further implications in the future, but it is important not to judge the utility or value of any legal mechanism purely on the basis of how it may be employed in illegitimate and illegal activities.[7]

3 Transferring the ownership of property

One of the simplest dealings with real property is an outright transfer of ownership, whether by gift or sale. The requirements for effective transfer of ownership vary with the type of property involved. Some forms of property, including banknotes and ordinary goods like books and furniture (referred to as 'chattels'), can be transferred simply by handing over possession with the intention of transferring ownership. Other forms of property require more. The transfer of land, for instance, requires the transfer to be made in a prescribed form of deed, and the transferee must then be registered as the new owner by the Land Registry.[8]

Equity normally has no role to play in outright transfers, except where the form of property concerned is recognized only in equity, for example a transfer of a beneficial share in a trust fund. In some instances equity will treat an attempted transfer as effective, even though some of the special formal requirements for the transfer of that form of property have not been used. Equity will, for instance, treat a transfer of land as being effective for some purposes after all the necessary documents have been completed and signed, even though the statutory rules require the transfer to be registered.[9] Conversely,

[2] See Chapter 18.

[3] See Knobel 'Trusts: Weapons of Mass Injustice?' *Tax Justice Network*, February 2017.

[4] See Cotterell, 'Power, Property and the Law of Trusts: A Partial Agenda for Critical Legal Scholarship' in Fitzpatrick & Hunt, *Critical Legal Studies* (Blackwells 1987).

[5] See, for example, the Paradise Papers scandal in 2017, where the International Consortium of Investigative Journalists (ICIJ) investigated the hidden wealth of many of the world's most wealthy individuals. Details are available here: https://www.icij.org/ (accessed October 2021).

[6] For example, the Money Laundering, Terrorist Financing and Transfer of Funds (Information on the Payer) Regulations 2017 (SI 2017/692). For commentary on the EU Directive (2015/849) which underpinned these Regulations (but which included provisions not enacted in the Regulations), see Wong 'The New EU Anti-Money Laundering Directive: Farewell to transparency of UK Trusts' (2017) TLI 137.

[7] For a good summary of the detail of trusts and crime, see Tucker et al, *Lewin on Trusts* (20th edn, Sweet & Maxwell 2020), Pt 9.

[8] See Law of Property Act 1925, s 52(1)(b).

[9] *Mascall v Mascall* [1985] 50 P & CR 119 and further Chapter 6.

in some special cases, the principles of equity may become involved to deprive an apparent transfer of its full effect by imposing a resulting or constructive trust so that the original owner retains the equitable interest in the property transferred. For example, in *Bannister v Bannister*,[10] Mrs Bannister sold two cottages to her brother-in-law for one-third less than their full market value. He promised orally to let Mrs Bannister stay on in one of the cottages rent-free for the rest of her life, but four years later, he sought to evict her. The oral promise could not be enforced as a contract since it was not in writing, or proved in writing, as the statutory rules at the time required.[11] The Court of Appeal held that in view of the promise that the brother-in-law had made, he acquired the cottage as trustee during the life of Mrs Bannister. He could not evict her so long as she desired to occupy the cottage.

4 Sharing ownership of property

(1) Concurrent ownership of property

Trusts also provide a mechanism by which the ownership of property can be shared between a number of persons. Their interests are said to be concurrent because they are enjoyed at the same time. Co-ownership can be effected by means of either a joint tenancy or a tenancy-in-common.[12]

(a) Joint tenancy

Where the ownership of property is shared by means of a joint tenancy, all of the co-owners have identical rights to the property. Taken together, they are entitled to the whole of the co-owned property, but they do not have specific shares in it. In the event of the death of one joint tenant, his interest passes automatically to the other remaining joint tenants under the principle of survivorship. A joint tenancy can be converted into a tenancy-in-common in equity by means of severance, where the joint tenant severs his 'share', and the rules of survivorship no longer apply.

(b) Tenancy-in-common

Where the ownership of property is shared by means of a tenancy-in-common, the co-owners enjoy 'undivided shares' in the co-owned property. This means that they have specific notional shares in the property, which may be equal or unequal, and survivorship has no application. However, all the co-owners enjoy the right to use and enjoy the property, and no co-owner can regard part of it as representing his 'share' alone.

(c) Trusts and co-ownership

In relation to some property, the ownership can be shared concurrently by means of a joint tenancy or a tenancy-in-common without the need for a trust. For example, two students who purchase a car together may become the joint owners of it without a trust. In the case of personal property, the legal title may be held by co-owners either as joint tenants or as tenants-in-common. Where the chattels of two owners are commingled to form an indistinguishable whole (for instance, because their oil has been mixed in the same tank), they share the whole as tenants-in-common in proportion to their contributions.[13]

[10] [1948] 2 All ER 133. [11] Law of Property Act 1925, s 40.

[12] See Bevan, *Land Law* (3rd edn, OUP 2022) Ch 5.

[13] See *Spence v Union Marine Insurance Co* [1868] LR 3 CP 427; *Indian Oil Corpn Ltd v Greenstone Shipping SA* [1987] 3 All ER 893; cf *F S Sandeman & Sons v Tyzack and Branfoot Shipping Co* [1913] AC 680, HL.

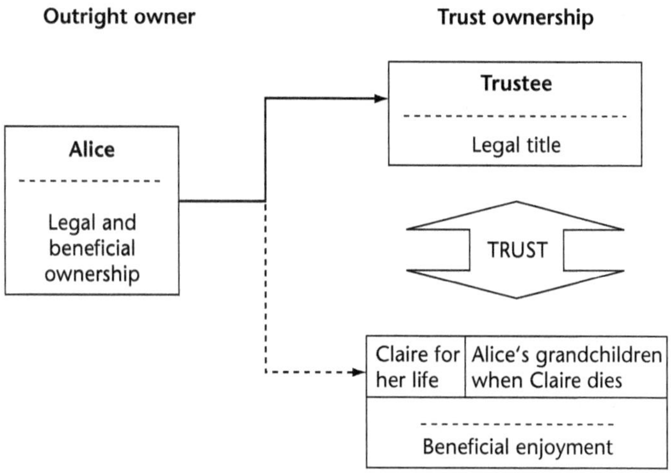

Figure 3.1 Creating successive interests using a trust

However, in general, the common law preferred the mechanism of a joint tenancy, and, thus, a tenancy-in-common is relatively rare without a trust. Where the property concerned is land, any form of co-ownership will inevitably give rise to a trust of land.[14] By statute the legal title to land can only be held by individuals or joint tenants,[15] and, therefore, a tenancy-in-common can only exist in equity. The only situation in which land will not be held on trust is where there is a single outright owner. This means that the trust is the foundation of most land holding under English law.

(2) **Successive ownership of property**

An owner of property may wish to divide the ownership of property so that it is enjoyed successively rather than concurrently. For example, imagine that Alice, an elderly lady with a significant shareholding, has one daughter, Claire, and three grandchildren. On her death she wants Claire to enjoy the income from the shares but, ultimately, she wants to ensure that they pass to her grandchildren. Alice can grant Claire a life interest in the shares that will entitle her to receive the income they produce for the duration of her life, but without any right to their capital value. On her death the shares will become the property of the grandchildren (see Figure 3.1). Such an arrangement, sharing the enjoyment of the property successively, can only be achieved by means of a trust, irrespective of whether the property concerned is land or personal property.[16]

5 Protecting equitable interests in property

(1) **The doctrine of notice**

As has been noted in Chapter 1, an equitable interest behind trust is treated as a proprietary interest, which means that, subject to the doctrine of notice and statutory rules, if the trustee has improperly parted with the property, the trust can be enforced against the

[14] See Trusts of Land and Appointment of Trustees Act 1996, ss 1–5.

[15] Law of Property Act 1925, ss 1(6), 36(2).

[16] It was once possible to create limited interests in land without using a trust, but since the Law of Property Act 1925, a trust is now required whenever limited interests in land are created. It has always been the case that limited interests in property other than land can only be created by means of a trust.

property in the recipient's hands. In the case of personal property and unregistered land (where title has not been registered at the Land Registry), the doctrine of notice governs priority. The doctrine of notice is considered in Chapter 1. For registered land (where title has been registered at the Land Registry) special statutory rules apply. These are fully explored in most land law textbooks.[17]

(2) **Overreaching**

Where a trustee sells or disposes of trust property in an authorized transaction, for instance, selling an investment in order to reinvest, the rights of the beneficiaries cease to apply to the original property, but attach instead to the proceeds of sale or disposal. This is a process known as overreaching, and it operates irrespective of whether the purchaser had knowledge, actual or constructive, of the existence of the trust. The Law of Property Act 1925 provides that where land is held on trust, the interests of the beneficiaries are automatically overreached if it is transferred to a purchaser who pays any purchase moneys arising to two or more trustees holding the legal title. This is the case even if the disposal is unauthorized, although since this constitutes a breach of trust, it exposes the trustee to personal liability.

6 Delegating management or allocation functions

Many of the most significant uses of trusts arise because they enable an owner to delegate some of the management responsibilities attendant upon the ownership of property to a third person who will become the trustee. In some cases such delegation will be chosen for reasons of convenience, while in others it may be a matter of necessity because the owner of property is incapable of managing it for himself.

(1) **Delegation for reasons of convenience**

The owner of property may choose to create a trust of his property for reasons of convenience. Thus, a person owning a substantial share portfolio may transfer his shares to his stockbroker or a professional trustee to facilitate dealing transactions. In the case of such a bare trust, the trustee may not enjoy any active powers of management over the trust property but will act on the instructions of the beneficiary.

(2) **Delegation of allocation**

An owner may know that he wants to transfer the ownership of his property but not yet know who he wants to transfer it to. By means of a discretionary trust or a power of appointment, the owner can effectively delegate the responsibility for choosing who should receive the ultimate benefit of his property to someone else.[18] Often, the donee of the power or the trustee of the discretionary trust will be in a better position than the original owner to determine how it should be distributed, either by reason of the time at which they can make the decision or because of their superior knowledge. For example, imagine that Hama has no children of his own but has a large number of nieces and nephews. He only has a small estate and he wants to ensure that his property goes to those who really need it. In his will, he can leave his property to his sister Fabbia for life, and on her

[17] See Bevan, *Land Law* (3rd edn, OUP 2022) Ch 2 (registered land), Ch 3 (unregistered land and notice).

[18] These functions are considered in detail in Chapter 24.

death, on trust for such of his nephews and nieces in such shares as she determines. By means of this discretionary trust, Hama has imposed a mandatory obligation on Fabbia to allocate the property among the class of his nephews and nieces, but has left her the decision as to which specific members of that class should benefit and to what extent.

Again, a discretionary trust or a power of appointment can be used on a larger scale. For instance, Zaheb is the owner of a large business with some 10,000 employees. He wishes to establish a fund to provide for the education of the children of his employees. Obviously, he cannot provide for them all, so he is able to create a trust in which the fund is transferred to trustees who have the discretion to select which of his employees' children should receive this benefit. The result is that only some of the 10,000 will benefit, but Zaheb has delegated to others the task of deciding those who will benefit.[19]

McPhail v Doulton[20] provides an example of such delegated allocation. Bertram Baden wanted to give property for the benefit of the employees and ex-employees, and their relatives and dependants, of a company he owned. Rather than determining how the property should be allocated, he left the property to trustees, giving them the discretion as to which of the potential beneficiaries should actually receive a share of the property (see Figure 3.2).

(3) **Providing for vulnerable individuals**

An owner may want to separate the legal and equitable ownership of property through a trust to gain the advantage of ensuring that the beneficial owner does not have control of the management of the property. There are a number of reasons why this may be the case.

(a) **The beneficiary cannot manage the property**

An owner may wish someone to enjoy the benefit of property who is not capable of managing it adequately for himself by reason of infancy or incapacity. Suppose that Rochelle has a disabled adult son for whom she wishes to make provision in her will. Rochelle knows that her son is unable to make decisions for himself. By means of a trust, Rochelle can nominate a trustee to hold the property for her son. The trustee will have the legal ownership of the money and will be able to decide how it should be invested and used. Rochelle's son will enjoy the equitable or beneficial ownership in the money.

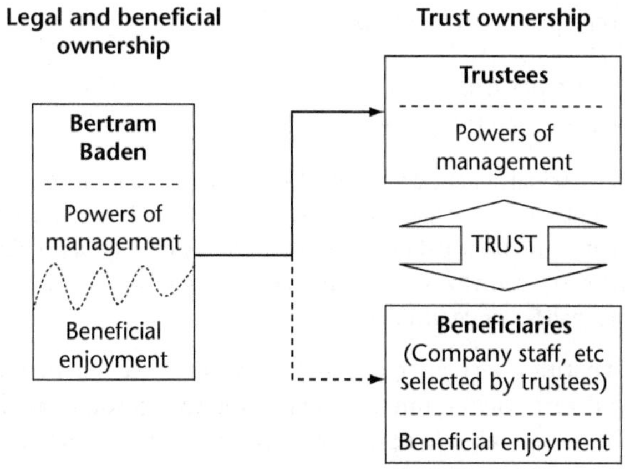

Figure 3.2 Delegating allocation using a trust: *McPhail v Doulton*

[19] For example, *Oppenheim v Tobacco Securities Trust Co Ltd* [1951] AC 297.
[20] [1971] AC 424.

(b) The beneficiary should not manage the property

An owner may also want to create a trust if he is concerned that it would be unwise to permit the beneficiary, although legally competent, to manage the property. In the Victorian period, the trust was often used to preserve the integrity of family estates from spendthrift heirs. A classic example can be found in Trollope's Victorian novel, *Dr Thorne*. There, a wealthy baronet, Sir Richard Scatcherd, dies, leaving a vast estate of some £300,000. His son, Sir Louis, was 21, a drunkard, and a spendthrift. In order to protect the estate, Sir Richard left his property to his close and trusted friend, Dr Thorne, so that the son would not have control of it but rather that Dr Thorne would manage the estate until Sir Louis reached 25, with the hope that by such age he would be a reformed character. Somewhat fortunately for the story, he died before reaching that age, leaving the heroine, Miss Thorne, to inherit the estate.

(c) Protective trusts

A spendthrift may also be protected from the dangers of his own bankruptcy by a special type of trust, the protective trust. Here, property is held by the trustees with a direction that the beneficiary is to receive the income from the trust. In the case of a conventional trust, if the beneficiary becomes insolvent, his trustee in bankruptcy will be entitled to receive the income from the trust. However, the terms of a protective trust provide that in the event of insolvency, the beneficiary's entitlement to the income automatically fails or determines, so that he is no longer entitled to it as of right. Instead, the income is to be held by the trustees under a discretionary trust to be used for the support of a range of persons, including the original beneficiary. This means that the trustee in bankruptcy will only receive the income if the trustees of the settled fund make an appointment to the bankrupt beneficiary. By this means the trust property and income are protected from the consequences of the beneficiary's bankruptcy.

It has been held that a settlor cannot create a trust to protect himself from his own bankruptcy.[21] However, a trust created by a third party that will protect the beneficiary from the consequences of his bankruptcy has been held to be valid.[22] Although a protective trust may be created expressly, a statutory form has been introduced. Section 33(1) of the Trustee Act 1925 provides that where any income is directed to be held on 'protective trusts' for the benefit of any person, then the property is to be held upon the terms set out in the section. These provide for a primary trust, and then a secondary trust that will only come into being if the primary trust fails.

(i) The terms of the primary trust

Section 33(1)(i) provides that the income will be held:

> Upon trust for the principal beneficiary during the trust period or until he . . . does or attempts to do anything, or until any event happens . . . whereby, if the said income were payable during the trust period to the principal beneficiary absolutely during that period, he would be deprived of the right to receive the same or any part thereof, in any of which cases . . . this trust of the said income shall fail or determine.

This primary trust entitles the principal beneficiary to receive the income from the trust, which entitlement determines automatically if he for any reason loses the right to retain it, for example, if he becomes bankrupt, in which case his trustee in bankruptcy would be

[21] *Re Burroughs-Fowler* [1916] 2 Ch 251.

[22] *Billson v Crofts* [1873] LR 15 Eq 314; *Re Ashby, ex p Wreford* [1892] 1 QB 872 QBD.

entitled to the income from the trust.[23] Other events have included the sequestration of the income[24] and the trustees impounding the income to repay capital wrongly advanced to the beneficiary.[25] In contrast, the fact that a beneficiary was resident in enemy-occupied territory, with the consequence that income could not be paid to her, was held not to be sufficient to determine the trust.[26]

(ii) The terms of the secondary trust

If the primary trust is determined, then the income is to be held on the terms of a secondary trust set out in s 33(1)(ii). This is a discretionary trust for the principal beneficiary and any spouse and issue, with an alternative secondary trust if there is no spouse or issue. Because the secondary trust is a discretionary trust, the principal beneficiary no longer has the right to the income of the trust, but the trustees may at their discretion give him some or even all of that income, or otherwise use it for the support of his family. At any event, it will be possible to ensure his family's support without the income being seized by his trustee in bankruptcy.[27]

7 Gifts to be applied for purposes

It is a general principle of property that only a legally recognized person[28] may be an owner. The owner of property might, however, wish to transfer it not to specified individuals, but for the carrying out of a specified purpose. Clearly, an owner can apply his own property in the furtherance of whatever purpose he chooses, but the problem arises when he wishes to oblige a transferee of the property so to apply it. While it might be thought that a trustee could be obliged to use trust property in furtherance of a specified purpose, equity has adopted the general rule that, subject to limited exceptions, a trust can only be validly created in favour of persons rather than purposes. A trust for the benefit of a pure purpose will be void. For example, in *Re Astor's Settlement Trusts*,[29] a trust was established for the purpose of the 'maintenance of . . . good understanding sympathy and co-operation between nations' and 'the preservation of the independence and integrity of newspapers'. This was held to be invalid, as it was a gift for a purpose and not persons.

8 Gifts for charitable purposes

The most important exception to the requirement of a beneficiary is that property can be transferred on trust for purposes that are regarded as charitable in law. For example, in *Re Delius*,[30] the widow of the composer Frederick Delius left her residuary estate[31] to trustees to promote the musical works of her late husband. This was upheld as a charitable

23 *Trappes v Meredith* [1871] 7 Ch App 248*Re Forder* [1927] 2 Ch 291.

24 *Re Baring's Settlement Trusts* [1940] Ch 737.

25 *Re Balfour's Settlement* [1938] Ch 928.

26 *Re Hall* [1944] Ch 46.

27 In some circumstance the trustee in bankruptcy will be entitled to income that is received by the bankrupt principal beneficiary as the assignee of his interests under the discretionary trust. See *Re Coleman* [1888] LR 39 Ch D 443; *ex p Wreford* [1892] 1 QB 872.

28 This includes a company which is treated as having legal personality and therefore the capacity to hold property.

29 [1952] Ch 534.

30 [1957] Ch 299.

31 The residuary estate is the balance of a deceased person's assets after their debts have been paid and all specific gifts by will have been made.

gift, even though there was no person who would directly benefit from this gift. Where the trust is charitable in status, it attracts certain privileges, both legal and financial. Charitable trusts are examined in detail in Part VI (Chapters 19–23).

9 Collective investment

(1) Lottery syndicates and investment clubs

Trusts are an effective vehicle by which individuals can pool their resources for collective investment, because the trust both enables the responsibilities for the management of property to be severed from its ownership and enjoyment and enables the ownership of property to be shared concurrently. One example of how trusts may be used in this way is the formation of a syndicate to enter the National Lottery. Rather than entering as single individuals, a group may combine to pool their resources and increase their chances of winning by buying multiple combinations of numbers that they could not afford individually. Fundamental to the operation of such a syndicate would be the collection of the 'stakes' from the members, the purchase of the tickets, and the distribution of any winnings. Since the ticket will be purchased in the name of only one member, that member will hold any winnings on trust for the members of the syndicate who have contributed, in proportion to the size of their stake.[32] An investment club can be set up in the same way, with investments being made on behalf of the group and held on trust for the group in the way the members have agreed. The club rules will need to provide for what is to happen if the members of the syndicate fail to reach agreement, if they wish to wind the club up, or if one of them wishes to resign.

(2) Unit trusts

Unit trusts have grown in significance since the middle of the last century as a means of making modest investments on the stock exchange or in other securities.[33] Suppose that Adrian has £1,000 to invest. He wishes to invest in stocks and shares, rather than to deposit his money with a bank or building society. He knows the dangers of dealing on the stock market and wants to be able to spread the risk of his investment over a variety of securities, but his investment is too small to enable that. By buying units in a unit trust, Adrian is able to join together with other investors so that collectively they can spread their investments. A fund management company takes subscriptions from Adrian and other individual investors. The subscriptions are pooled and used to purchase shares or to make other investments. These investments are held on trust by a custodian trustee (not normally the fund manager) in shares (units) proportionate to the amounts contributed by investors. The investors are thus able to share in a far wider portfolio than if they were to invest alone.

A unit trust is a complex form of equitable co-ownership.[34] Although it is possible for a unit trust to contain no power of reinvestment,[35] most unit trusts permit the fund manager to alter the portfolio of investments, although often within special limits. The number of units can be increased or reduced to allow new investors to subscribe, or to allow existing investors to withdraw.

[32] See Wilkinson, 'Running a Lottery Syndicate' [1995] NLJ 217.

[33] They have replaced endowment policies, which are regular savings contracts with an insurance company including life insurance. These served a similar purpose, but did not involve trusts.

[34] See *Costa & Duppe Properties Ltd v Duppe* [1986] VR 90.

[35] See *Re Municipal and General Securities Co Ltd's Trust* [1950] Ch 212.

The rights of investors in a unit trust are a mix of contract and trust. The investor has a contract with the investment company that defines the basis upon which units are bought and sold. The assets themselves are held on trust, with the ultimate beneficiaries being the contributors as a whole,[36] although it is common for the contract to state that the investor acquires no proprietary right in the underlying assets in which investments are made. The effect of this contractual term is that no individual participant in a unit trust can call for the vesting in him or her of the property held in the scheme, thereby excluding the operation of the rule in *Saunders v Vautier*.[37]

(3) **Pension schemes**

(a) Types of pension scheme

Pension schemes can take a variety of forms. The UK state old age pension and many public sector pension schemes are unfunded: the pensions are paid out of current taxation or revenue. Pension annuities are contractual arrangements in which an insurance company, in return for a lump sum, promises a pensioner a monthly or annual[38] payment for life. Other pension schemes work in a very similar way to unit trusts, enabling members of the scheme to pool their contributions for the purpose of making investments that will later pay the pensions.[39] These are known as 'funded' schemes, and may be either defined benefit or defined contribution (also known as money purchase) schemes. Most funded schemes are now defined contribution: the rights of each member reflect the value of the investments purchased through the contributions relating to that individual. The 'pension pot' thus generated can then be drawn upon in retirement, or used to buy an annuity. With a defined benefit scheme, the pension fund company guarantees a pension of a certain amount (typically a proportion of career average earnings) regardless of the value of the pension pot which the individual's contributions would have generated. That promise is contractual, but it is backed up by the fund generated by the accumulated investments made with pension contributions and usually by a 'balance of cost' promise made by the employer to make good any deficiency. Because of the open-ended nature of the employer's liability, most defined benefit schemes have been converted into defined contribution schemes over the last two decades.

(b) Pension scheme trusts

It would be possible for funded pension schemes to operate on an entirely contractual basis, but most are based upon a trust.[40] One substantial reason for this was that the tax privileges accorded to 'approved schemes' used to be available only to pension schemes established in this way.[41] The use of the trust as a means of providing for pensions enables the fund assets to be kept separate from the assets and liabilities of the employer. This offers some security in the event of the insolvency of the employer. The trust also means that where benefits are payable to someone other than the employee who is a member of the scheme, such as the employee's surviving spouse, the beneficiary has an enforceable claim which will not be barred by an absence of privity of contract.

[36] See *Re AEG Unit Trust Managers Ltd's Deed* [1957] Ch 415.

[37] [1841] 4 Beav 115.

[38] Hence the term 'annuity'.

[39] There can in addition be special arrangements such as an 'executive pension plan' for a single employee, as in *Brooks v Brooks* [1996] AC 375. In this case, the House of Lords considered that special features of this bespoke pension plan meant that it constituted a marriage settlement that could be varied on divorce.

[40] See Pollard, *The Law of Pension Trusts* (Oxford University Press 2013).

[41] Income and Corporation Taxes Act 1988, s 592, re-enacting a provision first found in Finance Act 1921, repealed by Finance Act 2004.

(c) Special features of pension trusts

Pension schemes are subject to a substantial body of statutory regulation[42] and supported by the Pension Protection Fund.[43] They are also subject to the general law of contract and trusts. Whilst in principle the ordinary principles of trusts law apply,[44] pension schemes have special characteristics, one of which is that the beneficiaries help to finance their own benefits. Even in a non-contributory scheme, the employer's payments are not bounty. They are part of the consideration for the services of the employee.[45]

The special features of pension schemes could be expected to produce some differences in the way in which trust law applies, and this is evident in the extensive special statutory rules and in some of the emerging case law.[46] In *Stevens v Bell*,[47] Arden LJ, giving the sole opinion of the Court of Appeal on a complex issue of interpretation of the Airways Pension Scheme, said:

> A pension scheme should be construed so as to give a reasonable and practical effect to the scheme. The administration of a pension fund is a complex matter and it seems to me that it would be crying for the moon to expect the draftsman to have legislated exhaustively for every eventuality.[48]

In reaching an interpretation which gives a reasonable and practical effect to the scheme, it is legitimate to take into account the fact that the members of the scheme have contributed to it, that the scheme may have been subject to a number of changes since it was set up, and that the scheme is likely to last for many years so that any changes to the rules need to be looked at in the context of circumstances at the time the change was adopted rather than related back to the time when the scheme was set up.

(d) Pension fund surplus

In a defined benefit pension scheme it is possible for the invested funds to be worth more than the actuarial cost of meeting pension liabilities. This gives rise to the difficult question of who is entitled to that surplus. This is considered in Chapter 9.

10 Property holding by clubs and societies

Clubs and societies that are not incorporated as companies are not capable of owning property in their own right, since they lack the necessary legal personality. This raises the question as to how the funds of the society are to be held. There has been considerable debate about this in the past, but since the last quarter of the twentieth century, the rules have been relatively settled. Cases decided earlier than this need to be treated with care. The current view is that in most cases the assets of a club can be treated as belonging to

[42] Contained in voluminous acts of Parliament including, for example the Pension Schemes Act 1993, the Pensions Act 2008, the Public Service Pensions Act 2013, the Pensions Act 2014, and the Pensions Schemes Act 2021.

[43] The Pension Protection Fund was created under the Pensions Act 2004 and is a statutory fund intended to protect members of defined benefit schemes if their pension fund becomes insolvent.

[44] See Sir Robert Megarry in *Cowan v Scargill* [1985] Ch 270 at 290; *Re Trusts of Scientific Investment Pension Plan* [1998] Lexis Citation 2681; *Allan v Rea Brothers Trustees Ltd* [2002] EWCA Civ 85 at 11.

[45] *McDonald v Horn* [1995] 1 All ER 961 at 973, per Hoffmann LJ.

[46] See e.g. *Mettoy Pension Trustees Ltd v Evans* [1991] 2 All ER 513. See also Hayton, 'Pension Trusts and Traditional Trust: Drastically Different Species of Trusts' [2005] Conv 229.

[47] [2002] EWCA 672.

[48] [2002] EWCA 672 at 28. See also *Barnardo's v Buckinghamshire* [2016] EWCA Civ 1064 at 8–10; *British Airways Plc v Airways Pension Scheme Trustee Ltd* [2017] EWHC 1191 (Ch) at 408–10.

the whole membership of the club, subject to the rules of the club.[49] Where the assets are vested in the members of the committee or some other group of individuals on behalf of the members of the club, those holding the club assets will be trustees for the members. The management of property by these groups, known as 'Unincorporated Associations', is explored in Chapter 16.

11 Trusts arising to protect legitimate expectations

Most of the situations examined concern the deliberate choice of a trust or power by an owner to achieve his objective. However, not every trust arises as a result of the owner's overt intention. For example, trusts commonly arise informally where a couple pool their resources in order to buy a home together, but the legal ownership of the home is put in the name of one of them alone. Often the couple will have given no thought as to how their arrangement would be characterized by the law. Provided that the couple had acted on a common understanding that they were intended to share the ownership of the property, the court will impose a trust to give effect to this intention. Even in cases where there is no clear agreement, a trust will be imposed if the contributions made by each of the couple are such that the only reasonable inference is that, if asked, the couple would have said they intended to be joint owners.[50] *Grant v Edwards*[51] is a clear example. Mrs Linda Grant left her husband and moved in with Mr George Edwards. A modest house was purchased with the aid of a mortgage to provide a home for the couple. The purchase was made in the name of George Edwards and his brother, Arthur. Mrs Grant's name was not included in the purchase, since Mr Edwards suggested that it might complicate her divorce proceedings. Mrs Grant helped with the purchase by contributing to the repayment of the mortgage and in other ways. The court imposed a trust on George and Arthur to give effect to the understanding that Mrs Grant would be entitled to a half-share in the net value of the house. Chapter 12 looks in detail at how equity supports the acquisition of rights in the family home in this and other ways.

12 Trusts that are remedial in effect

Trusts can be used deliberately, and may also be used to protect legitimate expectations. Equity also serves a powerful remedial function, however, by creating rights to correct wrongdoing. Although not universally accepted, some writers would characterize these proprietary rights as remedial or restitutionary trusts,[52] although the trust arises automatically to right the injustice, rather than being used by the judge as one tool in a portfolio of remedies. The use of remedial trusts has proved especially significant in the context of commercial transactions.

(1) Misappropriated property

Beneficiaries do not lose their proprietary rights in trust property which has been wrongly disposed of by a trustee unless the property is acquired by a bona fide purchaser for value. The trust property can be followed in its original form or traced through mixtures and substitutions. Equity's rules for asserting proprietary rights are more extensive

[49] *Re Recher's Will Trusts* [1972] Ch 526.

[50] *Lloyds Bank plc v Rosset* [1991] 1 AC 107.

[51] [1986] Ch 638.

[52] See, for example Birks, *An Introduction to the Law of Restitution* (Clarendon Press 1985).

than those of the common law (see Chapter 38 on tracing), which means that there is an advantage in a claimant establishing the existence of equitable proprietary rights. There are two important situations in which this can be done through a constructive trust, even though there is no express trust: where a person (such as a company director) has made unauthorized gains through a breach of fiduciary duty;[53] and probably also where a thief has misappropriated property, even if there was no prior fiduciary relationship.[54]

(2) **Avoiding the effects of insolvency**

Property held by someone on trust is not available to meet their own debts, even if they become bankrupt or insolvent: the beneficiary is entitled to it. So, if a trader becomes insolvent, a creditor will fare better if it can be established that they are the beneficiary under a trust of any assets still in the hands of the trader: the creditor can claim those assets in priority to any other claims which have to be paid out of the trader's general assets. Normally, any payment to a trading company will be treated as transferring outright ownership, but there can be special situations where a trust can arise. For instance, it has been held that a trust will arise in favour of a lender if a company receives money for a single specific purpose, agrees to hold that money separately unless and until it is used for that purpose, and agrees to return it if it is not so used.[55] It has also been held, in a questionable decision, that if a bank by mistake pays a debt twice, the recipient becomes a trustee of the overpayment.[56] Where a customer has ordered goods from a supplier, they may be held on trust for him if they have been separated from the bulk so as to be identifiable as his property.[57]

13 Trusts and tax planning

Trusts have evolved to enable owners to deal with their property flexibly. However, one of the major motivations for the use of trusts is that they can be used effectively and creatively to reduce taxation. They are an essential aspect of tax planning, which aims to achieve legitimate tax avoidance.[58] As Lord Tomlin said in *IRC v Duke of Westminster*:

> Every man is entitled if he can to order his affairs so that the tax attaching under the appropriate Act is less than it otherwise would be. If he succeeds in ordering them so as to secure that result, then, however unappreciative the Commissioners of Inland Revenue or his fellow taxpayers may be of his ingenuity, he cannot be compelled to pay an increased tax.[59]

This general principle has been qualified by more recent House of Lords' decisions which have held that where steps are inserted into a pre-ordained series of transactions which have no commercial or business purpose but are inserted solely to avoid tax, the transaction will be treated as a single whole and taxed as such.[60] This limitation applies to trusts.[61]

[53] *Agip (Africa) Ltd v Jackson* [1992] 4 All ER 451.

[54] *Westdeutsche Landesbank Girozentrale v Islington London Borough Council* [1996] AC 669.

[55] *Barclays Bank Ltd v Quistclose Investments Ltd* [1970] AC 567.

[56] *Chase Manhattan Bank NA v Israel-British Bank (London) Ltd* [1981] Ch 105.

[57] *Re Goldcorp Exchange* [1995] 1 AC 74.

[58] Tax avoidance is to be distinguished from illegitimate tax evasion. That is not to say that trusts are not employed for criminal ends.

[59] [1936] AC 1. See also *IRC v Willoughby* [1997] 1 WLR 1071.

[60] *W T Ramsay Ltd v IRC* [1982] AC 300; *Furniss v Dawson* [1984] AC 474; *MacNiven (HM Inspector of Taxes) v Westmoreland Investments Ltd* [2003] 1 AC 311. See Lord Walker, '*Ramsay* 25 Years on: Some Reflections on Tax Avoidance' (2004) 120 LQR 412.

[61] *Countess Fitzwilliam v IRC* [1992] STC 185.

A detailed consideration of taxation is outside the scope of this book,[62] but it is essential to have an elementary grasp of the tax structure. Trusts have historically been used to minimize liability to taxation. In consequence there has been an ongoing 'battle' with the government seeking to raise revenue. As a result, tax laws have become ever more complicated, and the scope to use trusts to reduce tax liabilities has diminished. There are still some instances where trusts can be used as part of tax planning, but expert advice or knowledge is required. There are three main types of taxation that will affect a trust: income tax, capital gains tax, and inheritance tax. Each will be briefly examined and their applicability to trusts considered.

(1) **Income tax**

(a) **Definition of income tax**

Income tax, as Lord Macnaghten somewhat unnecessarily pointed out,[63] 'is a tax on income'. However, income tax is not payable on a person's whole income, but only his 'taxable income'. There are a number of basic principles. Taxpayers can set some expenses against their income, and only the net figure is subject to tax. Most taxpayers are then given a personal allowance, which means that the first part of their income is not subject to any income tax. The rate of tax that is paid on the remainder of their income then increases, with higher rates of tax being paid on higher 'slices' of income. The levels of personal allowance, the percentage tax rate, and the levels at which these tax rates come into effect are varied frequently, often annually. Different types of income may be subject to different rates of tax, and some income is taxed before being received by the taxpayer. For instance, tenants paying a landlord who is resident overseas are required to deduct income tax from the rent and to pay the tax to HMRC.

(b) **Income tax and trusts**

In order to prevent trusts being used to avoid the payment of income tax, trustees are liable to pay income tax on the income of the trust. There is no personal allowance. The rate of tax depends upon the type of trust and the type of income.

(c) **The receipt of trust income by trust beneficiaries**

Complicated provisions govern the payment of income tax by beneficiaries receiving trust income. In most cases the beneficiaries are able to set off any income tax paid by the trustees against their own liability for income tax. In some cases it is possible for a beneficiary to claim a refund of tax paid by the trustees where this exceeds the beneficiary's own liability for tax.

(d) **Trusts as a means of avoiding income tax**

Trusts have in the past been used as an effective means of avoiding income tax. The scope for doing this has been much reduced by changes to the tax regime, with measures such as the introduction of a high rate of tax for discretionary trusts, which had previously been used by some settlors to allow the trustees to distribute income to beneficiaries who the settlor might otherwise have wanted to support out of taxed income, but who had a lower rate of taxation than the settlor. To further limit tax avoidance, income under a trust is treated as the income of the settlor unless the income arises from property in which the settlor has no interest. A settlor is treated as having an interest in property if that property

[62] See, for example, Loutzenhiser, *Tiley's Revenue Law* (9th edn, Hart Bloombury 2019).

[63] *LCC v A-G* [1901] AC 26 at 35.

or any property derived from it can or might be payable to or for the benefit of the settlor or the settlor's spouse in any circumstances whatsoever.

(2) Capital gains tax

(a) Definition of capital gains tax

Capital gains tax (CGT) is payable on the increase in value of 'chargeable assets' when they are realized. What is taxable is the difference in value of the asset between the date of acquisition and of disposal. Taxpayers are allowed an exemption for each year in which they pay CGT, the amount of which is varied from time to time.

(b) Capital gains tax and trusts

Capital gains tax cannot be avoided by settling property on trust. A settlor will be liable to pay CGT personally when he settles property on trust, as this is considered a disposal. In addition, trustees pay CGT on disposals by the trust. The trustees will be liable when they dispose of assets as part of the administration of the trust, and where the beneficiary becomes absolutely entitled to the property held on trust, other than by the death of the life tenant, which is a 'deemed disposal'. This deemed disposal means that capital gains tax is payable whenever a settlement is brought to an end and the property resettled, which increases the costs of terminating or resettling property.

(3) Inheritance tax

(a) Definition and history of inheritance tax

Inheritance tax (IHT) is, in essence, a tax payable on capital that passes on death, but it also applies to inter vivos gifts that were made less than seven years before the death occurred. It is something of a combination of two earlier taxes: estate duty and capital transfer tax. Prior to 1974 there was just one tax, estate duty, which was payable on death. Transfers inter vivos would be liable to estate duty if made seven years before the death. Estate duty was payable on the whole trust fund on the death of a life tenant, but was easily avoided by the creation of a discretionary trust where the beneficiaries had no interest in the fund itself.[64] In 1974 estate duty was replaced by capital transfer tax, which was to be payable on any transfer of capital either inter vivos or on death, although higher rates applied to transfers on death. In 1986 capital transfer tax was replaced by inheritance tax.

(b) The operation of inheritance tax

Inheritance tax is charged on 'transfers of value', in other words, transfers which diminish the value of the transferor's estate. Some transfers are 'exempt transfers' that are not liable to IHT. These include most transfers between spouses and relatively small gifts up to a specified annual limit. Where 'chargeable transfers' have been made, tax is payable on the cumulative total of all such transfers made within seven years of the taxpayer's death, but taper relief has the effect of reducing the rates of tax that apply to transactions made between three and seven years before death. Where a transfer has been made more than seven years before the taxpayer's death, the transfer is not subject to IHT.

(c) Inheritance tax and trusts

The rules relating to inheritance tax and trusts are complicated. There are four main occasions when IHT may apply to trusts: when assets are transferred into a trust; when a trust

[64] *Gartside v IRC* [1968] AC 553.

reaches a ten-year anniversary; when property is transferred out of a trust or the trust comes to an end; when a beneficiary with an interest under a trust dies; and when the settlor dies, if this is within seven years of assets being transferred into the trust. IHT rules were changed in 2006, and different rules may apply to existing trusts.

14 Arrangements without trusts

There is a temptation when studying the law of trusts to slip into 'trusts think' and to think of solutions solely through the prism of trusts. Much of the practical usage of trusts derives from their ability to separate the management responsibilities from the ownership of property. However, this ability is not unique to trusts, and continental legal systems developed without any direct equivalent of the trust. This section will examine briefly some situations in which trusts are used where alternative methods are possible.

(1) Bank deposits

It is a common misconception that when you deposit money with a bank, the bank 'looks after it for you' in a similar way to a trustee. That is not the case. Whilst it is possible for a bank to act as a trustee, it does not do so in relation to ordinary savings or current accounts. When you deposit money with a bank, the money becomes the bank's, free from any claim by the depositor. The bank gives in return a contractually binding promise to pay an equivalent sum to or by the depositor's instructions, with or without charges, and with or without interest, depending upon the terms of the contract. The bank is free to use the money deposited for its own purposes such as paying staff, or lending to others.

(2) Companies

(a) Joint stock companies

One means by which a separation between management and ownership of property can be made in practice is through companies. The capital for establishing a joint stock company[65] is provided by the shareholders who originally subscribed to the shares. They own the company. If it is wound up, any surplus funds remaining after the payment of the company's creditors will be distributed among them. Any profits that the company makes which are not capitalized by being retained to develop the business will also be distributed by way of a dividend to the shareholders. In a very real sense, therefore, the company belongs to the shareholders. It is they who benefit from its capital value and from the income that it produces. Yet the shareholders of a public company[66] will very rarely be involved in its day-to-day management. Instead, they will appoint directors at a general meeting to whom they delegate the everyday management of the enterprise. The directors (unless they are also shareholders) will not themselves have a stake in the assets of the company, although within the limits of the authority given to them they will be able to decide how the assets of the company should be used. The directors will, of

[65] These are companies created under the Companies Act 2006. The Act also allows the creation of companies limited by guarantee (a method used by not-for-profit organizations). Companies can also be established by Royal Charter.

[66] It is more likely with private companies that the same individuals will be both shareholders and directors.

course, be under an obligation to exercise their powers of management with reasonable care, skill and diligence,[67] as well as being required to act honestly and properly because of their fiduciary status[68] in equity.[69] These duties are owed, through the company, to the shareholders.

Companies have independent legal status, so that where a company acts as a trustee any liability for breach of trust falls on the company rather than its directors. It will rarely (if ever) be the case that it is possible to 'lift the corporate veil' to identify a company with its directors or controller (see *Prest v Petrodel Resources Ltd*[70]). Even though directors are in a fiduciary position, the duties they owe are to the company, and it is not possible for a party who has a claim against the company to enforce it against the directors personally, either directly or by what is sometimes called a 'dog's leg' claim in which the claimant seeks to enforce the claim through the company. However, there are a number of ways in which it is possible for a company director to be held personally liable. First, as in *Prest v Petrodel Resources Ltd*, it may be found that the company, although on its face having title to property vested in it, is not entitled to the beneficial ownership. Second, a company director who instigates or assists a breach of trust may be personally liable for dishonest assistance in breach of trust (see *Royal Brunei Airlines v Tan*).[71] Third, in exceptional circumstances, a director may assume direct fiduciary duties to people dealing with the company: this was the case in *Sinclair Investments (UK) Ltd v Versailles Trade Finance Ltd*[72] Fourth, where proprietary remedies are available against a company, these can be enforced against any recipient of the property except a bona fide purchaser for value without notice (this is possibly one of the reasons why the Supreme Court was willing to grant a proprietary remedy in the Monte Carlo Grand Hotel case (*FHR v Cedar Capital Partners LLC*[73])). Finally, even where a director has parted with assets received from a company in breach of trust or fiduciary duty, the director may be personally liable for knowing receipt of trust property if it would be unconscionable for him, given his knowledge of the circumstances, not to make recompense to the disappointed beneficiaries.

(b) Investment trusts

Despite the misleading nomenclature, these are not trusts at all, but companies quoted on the stock exchange whose purpose is not to trade directly, but instead to purchase shares in manufacturing or service companies. The word 'investment' is descriptive of the purpose of the corporation; the word 'trust' reflects the way in which joint stock companies were originally established, prior to modern company legislation permitting the statutory incorporation of companies. If the investments made by the company prosper, shareholders will receive dividends and see the value of their shareholding increase. Some investment trusts act as venture capital funds—providing capital for new or developing business ventures, and taking a stake in the companies in which they invest through shareholdings in them.

(c) Open-ended investment companies

Investment trusts are closed-ended in that the company issues a fixed number of shares. If an investor who originally subscribed for those shares decides to realize his investment,

[67] Companies Act 2006 Pt 10, Ch 2, ss 170–81.

[68] At one time they were considered to be trustees for the company (see *Smith v Anderson* [1880] 15 Ch D 247), but that is no longer the case: *Salomon v A Salomon & Co Ltd* [1897] AC 22.

[69] Regard is to be had under Companies Act 2006, s 171(4) to 'equitable principles in interpreting and applying the general duties'.

[70] [2013] UKSC 34. [71] [1995] 2 AC 378. [72] [2011] EWCA Civ 34.

[73] [2014] UKSC 45; Pearce, 'Bribes and Secret Commissions [2014] 26 Denning LJ 274.

he does so by selling his shareholding to a new investor. The company does not normally buy back the shareholding. Unless the company seeks exceptional power to buy back shares, or new shares are issued to raise additional capital, the number of shares issued remains unchanged.

Open-ended investment companies (or OEICs) operate differently.[74] The only purpose of an OEIC is to provide a vehicle for collective investment. The company issues shares to prospective investors, and uses the funds so raised to make investments through the purchase of shares and other securities. These assets are held by a depositary (effectively a custodian trustee) on behalf of the OEIC. New shares can be issued, or existing shares cancelled, to allow new investors to join, or existing investors to leave. The price at which the shares are bought or sold reflects the average asset value of the underlying investments.

(3) **Mutual societies**

Clubs and societies, which have already been considered above, can be forms of unincorporated association. It has been seen that, since they do not have legal personality, they cannot own property directly, and the current theory to explain their management of property is that their assets belong to all of the members collectively, but subject to the rules of the club. Most unincorporated associations are established for social purposes, but they can also exist as vehicles of altruism or as vehicles for running a social business or for investment. The Co-operative Group and some building societies began life as unincorporated associations. The lack of legal status presented difficulties for associations which wished to engage in commercial or quasi-commercial activities. To overcome these difficulties, legislation was enacted which enabled mutual associations, through a simple process of registration, to obtain limited independent legal personality, although they continued to be owned and governed by their members in accordance with their rules.[75] The legislation provided for a variety of different forms of association, for instance friendly societies set up to provide mutual insurance benefits;[76] and cooperative societies established to provide not-for-profit trading activities.[77] An example of the latter which is still in existence is the International Exhibition Co-operative Wine Society, which was set up in 1874 to supply good wines at fair prices to its members. Additional legislation covers specialist types of association, for instance credit unions,[78] building societies,[79] and housing associations.[80] Registration of an association as an industrial and provident society or as a friendly society was a convenient alternative to incorporation under the Companies Acts for mutual groups, many of which remain in operation today.

A difference between organizations incorporated under the Companies Acts and mutual organizations is that the subscribers to companies have shareholdings which they

[74] See the Open-Ended Investment Companies Regulations 2001, 2005, 2008, 2009, and 2011.

[75] See, for example, Friendly Societies Act 1896, s 49(1), which states: 'All property belonging to a registered society, whether acquired before or after the society is registered, shall vest in the trustees for the time being of the society, for the use and benefit of the society and the members thereof, and of all persons claiming through the members according to the rules of the society.'

[76] Friendly Societies Act 1829; Friendly Societies Act 1896. The current legislation is the Friendly Societies Act 1974 and the Friendly Societies Act 1992.

[77] Industrial and Provident Societies Act 1852; Industrial and Provident Societies Act 1862. See now the Industrial and Provident Societies Acts 1965 (as amended by the Industrial and Provident Societies Act 2002) and 1978.

[78] Now governed by the Credit Unions Act 1979 and the Co-operative and Community Benefit Societies and Credit Unions Act 2010.

[79] Building Societies Act 1986, as amended by the Building Societies Act 1997.

[80] Housing Acts 1985, 1988, and 2004.

can sell, whilst with mutuals, the assets belong to the members for the time being, and those members lose any claim to the assets when they leave the mutual.

(4) Building societies

Although they now operate in a very similar way to banks,[81] building societies were originally mutual organizations established for the purpose of enabling their members to build or acquire houses for residential use. The members would pool their savings. The fund thereby created would be used to make loans on mortgage to members for house purchase. Some building societies were set up for a limited period and were dissolved once the original membership had all acquired homes. Others were established on a permanent basis, and this was reflected in the name of the society, such as the Leeds Permanent Building Society.

Some early building societies took advantage of friendly society legislation, although they now have their own legislation.[82] Thus, they were able to obtain legal personality for the purpose of holding and managing property, for entering into contractual arrangements, and for bringing and defending legal actions. Nevertheless, as mutual organizations, they were—and in theory remain—controlled by their members (i.e. qualifying depositors and borrowers) without separate shareholders. The consequence of the controlling interest of the membership can be seen in what happens when it is proposed that a building society should merge with another, or be taken over by a public limited company. The members have to give their approval through a ballot to the proposed merger or takeover. Any payment made to the society will be distributed between the society's borrowers and depositors.

(5) Agency

(a) The agency relationship

The relationship of agency is the principal means by which the common law enables the management and enjoyment of property to be separated. For example, Jake is the owner of a car he wishes to sell. Rather than arranging a contract of sale himself, he can delegate the task to 'Honest Jill', who runs a local garage. He could authorize Jill to display the car on her forecourt and to sell the car to any purchaser prepared to pay more than a price arranged in advance. Here, Jake would be the principal and Jill would be acting as his agent. The relationship between the principal and the agent is contractual, and under this contract ownership in the car never passes to the agent (Jill). The agent is empowered to enter a contract with the purchaser on the principal's behalf, and property in the car will pass directly from the principal to the purchaser under that contract. Although he was not a party to the contract, the essence of agency is that it brings about a contract that is binding on the principal. Subject to any special arrangement between them, the agent owes a fiduciary duty to his principal to act honestly and properly (for instance, not to take a 'backhander' from the purchaser). An agent will be liable to his principal under the tort of negligence even where the agent is acting gratuitously.[83]

Agency is frequently found in commercial situations. All company directors are treated as agents of the company, authorized to make decisions and to enter into engagements on behalf of the company. The manager of a shop, and the sales staff in the shop,

[81] Northern Rock was a former building society that incorporated as a bank with public limited company status. Northern Rock ceased operations in 2012.

[82] Building Societies Act 1986 (as amended, including by the Building Societies Act 1997 and the Financial Services and Markets Act 2000).

[83] *Chaudhry v Prabhakar* [1988] 3 All ER 718, CA.

will be agents of the proprietor, whether that proprietor is an individual or a company. Agency also supports lasting powers of attorney, described below, and can be used in other contexts.[84]

(b) Automatic termination of agency

An agency is limited by the terms in which it was granted. The agent cannot enjoy a greater authority than the principal has given him, or than the principal himself enjoys. For this reason, if the principal loses his contractual capacity, the agent automatically loses his authority to enter into contracts with third parties that are binding on the principal. Thus, if the principal dies, or loses mental capacity, the authority of the agent is automatically terminated, whether or not the agent is aware of the principal's situation.[85]

(c) Powers of attorney

Where a principal wishes an agent to be empowered to enter into a transaction requiring a deed, the authority must itself be conferred by way of deed, termed a power of attorney. An agent so appointed is described as an attorney. The phrase 'power of attorney', as well as describing the deed and arrangement under which an agent is permitted to execute a deed on the principal's behalf, is also used to describe a general authority given by a principal permitting an agent to undertake any business concerning property on behalf of the principal. Such an authority could be given by a principal who was expecting to spend some time abroad, during which it would be impracticable for him to manage his own affairs.

(d) Lasting powers of attorney

(i) The need for lasting powers of attorney

Since a power of attorney is a form of agency, it will also terminate automatically if the principal loses his capacity. This poses particular difficulties if someone has been diagnosed as being in the early stages of dementia, and wants to grant someone she trusts, perhaps a child or other relative, a comprehensive power of attorney over her affairs to be used when she is no longer able to cope. An ordinary power of attorney would cease to be exercisable just at the point where it was most needed. For this reason, the enduring power of attorney was introduced by the Enduring Powers of Attorney Act 1985. From 1 October 2007,[86] this mechanism was replaced by the lasting power of attorney under the Mental Capacity Act 2005, ss 9–14, which is more comprehensive, as it allows the donor to choose someone not only to manage their financial affairs and property but also to make decisions concerning their health and welfare.[87]

(ii) Creation of lasting powers of attorney

A lasting power can only be created in accordance with the requirements set out in the Mental Capacity Act 2005, s 9(2); namely, that it must be created using the prescribed form and be registered with the Public Guardian,[88] the donees of the power must be properly

[84] See *Conservative & Unionist Central Office v Burrell* [1982] 1 WLR 522.

[85] See *Drew v Nunn* [1879] 4 QBD 661; *Yonge v Toynbee* [1910] 1 KB 215.

[86] Enduring powers of attorney granted before that period may still be used (Mental Capacity Act 2005, s 66 and Sch 4), provided they have already been registered (Mental Capacity Act 2005, Sch 5, para 11), or they are registered under the 2005 Act (Mental Capacity Act 2005, Sch 4, Pt 4).

[87] Mental Capacity Act 2005, s 9(1). It is also possible for the donor to appoint different persons to look after their property and their personal welfare.

[88] s 9(2)(b). The requirements for registration are set out in Sch 1 of the Act. Part 1 of Sch 1 (paras 1–3) relates to the form of the power of attorney and includes the requirement that the document creating the power contains explanatory information of the general effect of the power to make clear the effect to both the principal and to the attorney (see para 2(2)). Part 2 (paras 4–17) sets out the registration regime.

appointed,[89] and the donor must have the capacity to execute the power.[90] The instrument creating the lasting power of attorney must be certified—this replaces the requirement to have the signature of the donor and donee witnessed as under the enduring power of attorney.[91] The certifier must confirm that, in his opinion, the donor understands the purpose and scope of the document they are signing.

(iii) Supervision by the court

Clearly, the lasting power of attorney gives the attorney tremendous power over the affairs of the person who created it, and there is a real danger of abuse, particularly after the creator has become incapable and is not able to supervise the exercise of the power. For this reason, the Court of Protection[92] exercises a supervisory function and this explains why the lasting power of attorney must be registered to be effective. By ss 22 and 23, the court has powers in relation to the validity and operation of lasting powers of attorney, respectively.

(iv) Notice to named persons

When the attorney applies to the court for the power to be registered, he is under a duty to give notice to named persons in accordance with Sch 1 to the Act.[93] The Act allows the donor to nominate the 'named persons' he or she wishes to be notified,[94] and this will normally be used to allow relatives to be notified.[95] This would enable the relatives or other named persons (who will normally include those most likely to be affected by the way that the attorney deals with the donor's property), to object to the registration.[96]

(e) **Agency and equity**

Agency and powers of attorney are common law concepts, but both are supported by equity. The common law remedies for a failure by an agent or attorney to act in accordance with the terms of the authority conferred, or to break the duty of loyalty and care owed to the principal, are to deprive a purported but improper transaction of effect and to impose on the agent or attorney an obligation to compensate the principal in damages for any loss. In some cases a third party suffering loss will have a right of redress against the agent by way of damages for breach of warranty of authority. Equity recognizes agency by treating agents or attorneys, and company directors, as fiduciaries,[97] standing in such a position of trust with regard to their principal that they can be held liable to account for any abuse of their position. Thus, if they make an unauthorized profit, they can be obliged to hand the benefit over to their principal. In this respect, there is a clear analogy between the position of an agent and the position of a trustee.

(f) **Agency and ownership**

Although agency provides a means by which powers of management can be divorced from the rights of enjoyment of property, it is generally considered to leave ownership in the principal unless the agent exercises his authority to pass ownership to himself or

[89] Mental Capacity Act 2005, s 10.

[90] Capacity is presumed under the Act (s 1), but the court has power to act where the donor lacks capacity (see s 23).

[91] Mental Capacity Act 2005, Sch 1, para 2(1)(e).

[92] The Court of Protection is an office of the Supreme Court of Justice responsible for administering the affairs of those who are incapable of doing so for themselves by virtue of mental incapacity. See Mental Capacity Act 2005, Pt 2.

[93] Sch 1, Pt 2, para 6.

[94] Sch 1, Pt 1, para (2)(1)(c)(i).

[95] The donor does not have to name any persons: Sch 1, Pt 1, para (2)(1)(c)(ii).

[96] Mental Capacity Act 2005, Sch 1, Pt 2, para 13.

[97] See Chapter 34.

a third party. Even though the principal has conferred rights of disposal on the agent, this does not normally deprive him of his own rights of management and disposal. The agency is simply an authority which the principal gives to someone else to do some of those things which he can do himself. Moreover, apart from some limited exceptions, the principal retains the right to give instructions to the agent and to terminate the agency. The divorce between management and enjoyment is accordingly neither complete nor permanent.

(g) Mandate

Agency is normally used to permit someone entrusted by the principal to enter into contracts on behalf of the principal. The common law recognizes, however, a form of agency in which an agent is permitted to dispose of property belonging to the principal. This form of agency is known as mandate. For instance, Howard might authorize his wife, Winnie, to sign cheques payable from his own bank account. Similarly, Elizabeth, wishing to distribute a sum of money to the poor, might give a sum in cash to Philip, authorizing him to choose the recipients. In each case, the agent may not be entering into contracts with third parties but is given authority to transfer title in the principal's property to a third party. Unless and until this authority is exercised, the title in the property remains with the principal.

4
Equitable remedies in modern English law

1 Introduction to equitable remedies

Equitable remedies apply in all fields of law, from disputes over property or entitlement in contract and intellectual property, to preventing harm, or to the proceeds of wrongdoing being dissipated before a claim can be made against them. Equity evolved these remedies in the Court of Chancery to ameliorate the common law. Sometimes the remedies (like rescission) modified the harshness of the common law rules. Sometimes the remedies (like specific performance and injunction) provide alternative relief to the common law remedy of damages. Other remedies, such as those depriving a fiduciary of the profits of his or her wrongdoing, and the processes of following and tracing misappropriated property, are considered in later chapters of this book,[1] as well as the important mechanism for granting remedies, proprietary estoppel.[2] This chapter provides a summary of the key elements of the remedies of recission, specific performance, and injunctions. It is not intended as an exhaustive treatment.[3]

2 Where equity intervenes

(1) Remedies supporting the common law

Equitable remedies are available in a range of circumstances. First, equity has intervened to support the common law. This is particularly evident in the law of contract, where the remedies of specific performance and injunction can be used respectively to compel the performance of a positive obligation or to prevent a party from doing something which he has contracted not to do. The remedy of account also supports the common law. This remedy could be used, for instance, to assist in quantifying damages where a defendant has failed to pay a contractual royalty on a musical recording by verifying the total receipts from sales. Equitable remedies are also available in other areas of the common law, for instance, where injunctions are used to prevent the commission of a nuisance, to prevent interference with an easement, or to exclude an abusive spouse from the family home.

(2) Remedies ameliorating the common law

Equity's involvement has also been to ameliorate the common law. The common law would only rarely look at the circumstances which led to a contract being made, one

[1] Chapters 34, 37, and 38. [2] Chapter 14.

[3] See Spry, *Equitable Remedies* (9th edn, Sweet & Maxwell 2013).

exception being the doctrine of *non est factum* (it is not my act). The common law would not treat a signature as binding a person to a contract if they were only led to sign the document under the false impression that the document was something else (for instance, where a person signed a contract thinking they were doing so only as a witness not as a contracting party). In equity other vitiating factors will be sufficient to justify not holding someone liable under a contract, for instance, where the contract has been obtained as a result of a serious mistake or through undue influence or as a result of an unconscionable bargain.

(3) Remedies enforcing equitable obligations

Finally, equitable remedies are available in support of equitable obligations. By way of illustration, equitable compensation can be ordered where a trustee has caused loss to a trust or made an unauthorized profit. Where relevant, an equitable account can be ordered to verify the extent of the profit. A person in a fiduciary position, who owes duties of loyalty to another, can be prevented by injunction from acting in disregard of those duties.

3 Rescission

(1) Rescission for mistake

(a) Rescission of contracts

Rescission is the right of a party to a contract to have the contract set aside and to be restored to his former position as if the contract had never been made. There can be a number of reasons for rescission, including mistake, fraud, or lack of consent. The House of Lords held in *Johnson v Agnew*[4] that this type of rescission is to be distinguished from the situation (also called rescission) where a party is discharged from any obligation to perform the contract as a result of the breach of the other party. At common law a contract can be rescinded for *mistake* where the parties have made a mistake which negates agreement or which would make the performance of the contract as agreed impossible. Of course, there can only be rescission if the purported transaction would have otherwise had some binding effect; so, for example, an appointment of trustees by means of a defective deed was void and had no effect.[5]

(b) Rescission of voluntary transactions

It is possible for voluntary transactions to be set aside for mistake.[6] A person who has transferred property to another, or who has created a trust, may sometimes be able to have that transfer or trust set aside. The doctrines of resulting and constructive trusts[7] can have that effect. It has been held, for instance, that where a person transfers money to another in the mistaken belief that a debt is owing, when in fact it has been paid, then not only will there be a legal obligation on the recipient to repay, but also there may be an equitable obligation on the recipient which gives rise to a resulting or constructive trust.[8]

[4] [1980] AC 367 at 392.

[5] *Briggs & Ors v Gleeds (Head Office) & Ors* [2014] EWHC 1178 (Ch) (the decision concerned an unsuccessful set of arguments to remedy defects in the deed by means of estoppel).

[6] *Gibbon v Mitchell* [1990] 1 WLR 1304; *Dent v Dent* [1996] 1 WLR 683; *Wolff v Wolff* [2004] STC 1633.

[7] See Chapters 9 and 10 respectively.

[8] See *Chase Manhattan Bank NA v Israel-British Bank (London) Ltd* [1981] Ch 105 and the explanation of the case given by Lord Browne-Wilkinson in *Westdeutsche Landesbank Girozentrale v Islington LBC* [1996] AC 669.

It is also possible for a voluntary disposition to be rescinded or set aside as if it had never taken place. The rules applicable in this situation are not the same as those applicable to contracts.[9]

(i) Pitt v Holt

The leading authority for the application of the equitable rules is the decision of the Supreme Court in *Pitt v Holt*.[10] The alleged mistake in this case was that, in settling a damages award on a particular form of discretionary trust, the professional advisers had not appreciated that tax would be payable. Miss Pitt was successful on the ground of mistake, on the basis that the gravity of the mistake as to the adverse tax consequences was such that the settlement should be set aside. The Supreme Court made it clear that the test was not as onerous as that for contracts, since equity had always looked differently upon voluntary dispositions, even if made by deed.[11] It was no longer necessary to distinguish between the 'effect' of an alleged mistake, which may have been actionable, and the 'consequence' of the mistake, which would not, as had been the requirement previously.[12] The court indicated that 'the true requirement is simply for there to be a causative mistake of sufficient gravity'.[13] Whilst that would normally be 'a mistake either as to the legal character or nature of a transaction, or as to some matter of fact or law which is basic to the transaction',[14] it could also be a mistake as to the effects or consequences of the transaction, including, as we have seen, the tax consequences. In assessing what constitutes a mistake of sufficient gravity, the court indicated that it would be inappropriate to apply strict rules, and the test was instead what would make it unconscionable or unjust to leave the mistaken disposition uncorrected. That judgement would depend, not upon an elaborate set of rules, but a consideration in the round of the centrality of the mistake to the transaction in question, and the seriousness of its consequences.[15]

Whether it is unconscionable not to set aside a voluntary disposition must be viewed objectively, doing so primarily from the perspective of the recipient of the bounty.[16] It is not necessary for the recipient to have contributed to the mistake or to have been aware of it, although these factors may affect the assessment of what is conscionable.[17] The fact that the recipients are volunteers will militate against a finding that they should in conscience be able to retain a benefit once they realize that it was the result of a serious mistake;[18] they may, however, receive protection through the defence that before they should have realized that it was unconscionable to retain the benefits of the disposition they have materially changed their position.[19]

The jurisdiction applies only to correcting mistakes, and not to decisions made through ignorance or inadvertence, even if this ignorance was causative (in other words, directly influenced the decision). However, ignorance or inadvertence could lead to a conscious belief or tacit assumption which would be sufficient to constitute a mistake.[20]

[9] See *Der Merwe v Goldman & Ors* [2016] EWHC 790 (Ch) per Morgan J at 31.

[10] [2013] UKSC 26. No claim was pleaded in *Futter v Revenue Commissioners*, part of the same judgment of the Supreme Court. The case is important in relation to the duties of trustees and is considered in Chapter 33. See also *Test Claimants in the Franked Investment Income Group Litigation v Commissioners for Her Majesty's Revenue and Customs* [2020] 3 WLR 1369.

[11] [2013] UKSC 26 at 115. [12] See, for example, *Wolff v Wolff* [2004] STC 1633.

[13] [2013] UKSC 26 at 122. [14] Ibid. [15] [2013] UKSC 26 at 124–8.

[16] [2013] UKSC 26 at 124. See also *Der Merwe v Goldman & Ors* [2016] EWHC 790 (Ch).

[17] [2013] UKSC 26 at 114. [18] [2013] UKSC 26 at 124. [19] [2013] UKSC 26 at 124–5.

[20] [2013] UKSC 26 at 108.

(ii) The requirements for mistake

The requirements necessary to prove a valid mistake to allow recession have been usefully summarized in *Kennedy v Kennedy*[21] as follows:

> (1) There must be a distinct mistake as distinguished from mere ignorance or inadvertence or what unjust enrichment scholars call a 'misprediction' relating to some possible future event. On the other hand, forgetfulness, inadvertence or ignorance can lead to a false belief or assumption which the court will recognise as a legally relevant mistake . . .
>
> (2) A mistake may still be a relevant mistake even if it was due to carelessness on the part of the person making the voluntary disposition, unless . . . he or she deliberately ran the risk, or must be taken to have run the risk, of being wrong.
>
> (3) The causative mistake must be sufficiently grave as to make it unconscionable on the part of the donee to retain the property. That test will normally be satisfied only when there is a mistake either as to the legal character or nature of a transaction or as to some matter of fact or law which is basic to the transaction . . .
>
> (4) The injustice (or unfairness or unconscionableness) of leaving a mistaken disposition uncorrected must be evaluated objectively but with an intense focus on the facts of the particular case.

(iii) Taxation

Cases often involve questions of mistake as to taxation liability, often from schemes which are designed to minimize tax, which is permissible, but tip into artificial tax avoidance schemes, which are not. In *Freedman v Freedman*,[22] the relevant mistake pleaded was that the settlor's legal advisers did not appreciate that inheritance tax charges would result from the settlement, so that in practice the settlor would not be able to repay the loan. Proudman J held that the claimant had been given incorrect advice and, on the basis of that, mistakenly believed that the settlement would have no adverse tax consequences. In reaching her decision, Proudman J noted that it is 'likely that relief will not be given if the transaction is part of a tax avoidance scheme.'[23] In *Der Merwe v Goldman & Ors*,[24] mistake was again successfully applied to address the severe tax consequences of failing to be aware of a change to tax law operative at the time a voluntary settlement was made. In reaching judgment, Morgan J noted that the parties had actively thought that no inheritance tax charge would apply. It is not sufficient that ignorance of the law led to an incorrect assumption about the tax consequences of a transaction. Success in this case relied upon the fact that the claimant believed there to be no question of a charge to tax by reason of his actions, rather than a mistake that involved running a risk about a possible liability to pay tax. Given that, Morgan J held that it was irrelevant that the mistake was about taxation, and that an inheritance tax charge to the value of 20 per cent of the property, and further payments on each ten-year anniversary of 6 per cent of the value, was of sufficient gravity to merit the transaction being set aside.

Nevertheless, as noted in *Hartogs v Sequent (Schweiz) AG*,[25] it was emphasized that the principles in *Pitt* should not be 'viewed as an available "get-out-of-jail-free" card, which may be invoked whenever a taxpayer finds himself facing a charge to tax which has not been anticipated.'[26]

[21] [2014] EWHC 4129, followed in, for example, *Bainbridge v Bainbridge* [2016] EWHC 898.

[22] [2015] EWHC 1457 (Ch).

[23] [2015] EWHC 1457 (Ch) at [18]. This was based on an obiter comment of Lord Walker in *Pitt v Holt* [2013] UKSC 26 at [135].

[24] [2016] EWHC 790 (Ch).

[25] [2019] EWHC 1915 (Ch).

[26] [2019] EWHC 1915 (Ch) at [37], though, on the facts of the case, which involved an unexceptional tax planning scheme, recission for mistake was granted.

(iv) Only part of transaction affected

It is clear that mistake can be pleaded to sever part of a transaction from the whole, as in *Kennedy v Kennedy*[27] where a clause in a deed of appointment was set aside on grounds of mistake.

(v) Difficulties with the current principles

There is little doubt that the distinction between mistakes and ignorance has and will be a cause of difficulty in applying the new principles on rescission for mistake.[28] Perhaps more importantly, the vagueness of what makes it unconscionable not to rescind a transaction will make predicting the outcome of cases on mistake difficult. In recent years, factors have included the impact of incorrect, professional advice on decisions,[29] lack of clear explanation to the claimant of the impact of actions,[30] the extent of unintended tax liabilities,[31] the hardship that would be caused to the relevant claimant if recission through mistake was unsuccessful.[32] It is clear that the courts are grappling with the new life given to rectification by mistake through the relaxing of the rules in *Pitt v Holt*.

(2) **Rescission for misrepresentation**

(a) **Meaning of misrepresentation**

In *Behn v Burness*,[33] Williams J defined a representation in the context of the formation of contracts as 'a statement or assertion, made by one party to the other before or at the time of the contract, of some matter or circumstance relating to it'.

(b) **Rescission of contracts for misrepresentation**

A misrepresentation does not render a contract void, but the other contracting party may be entitled to rescind it where the making of the contract was induced by misrepresentation.[34] The representation must be of fact,[35] and not simply an expression of intention[36] or opinion.[37] Although there is no general duty on a contracting party to reveal all known relevant facts, in the case of some contracts, known as contracts *uberrimae fidei*, there is such a duty. These include contracts for insurance[38] and family settlements.[39] The right to rescind a contract applies both where the misrepresentation is fraudulent (which means a false statement made knowingly, or without belief in its truth, or reckless whether it is true or not[40]) and where the misrepresentation is innocent (where the party making the misrepresentation honestly believes it to be true).[41] By s 2(2) of the Misrepresentation

[27] [2014] EWHC 4129.

[28] See Mitchell, 'Rescission of Voluntary Settlements and Dispositions of Trust Property on the Ground of Mistake' [2017] Private Client Business 41, who broadly welcomes the development of being able to invoke mistake to avoid unintended tax consequences (see at pp 43–50).

[29] See *Bainbridge v Bainbridge* [2016] EWHC 898 (Ch); *Payne v Tyler* [2019] EWHC 2347 (Ch).

[30] *Wright v National Westminster Bank plc* [2014] EWHC 3158 (Ch) (unilateral mistake as to beneficial entitlements as to a trust and bank letter was not sufficient).

[31] *Smith v Stanley* [019] EWHC 2168 (Ch).

[32] *Clarke v Allen* [2019] EWHC 1193.

[33] [1863] 3 B&S 751.

[34] The representation does not 'have to be' cause of inducement, though it must have made a material contribution to the actions taken—see *Avonwick Holdings Ltd v Azitio Holdings Ltd* [2020] EWHC 1844 (Comm).

[35] *Ship v Crosskill* [1870] LR 10 Eq 73.

[36] *Edgington v Fitzmaurice* [1885] 29 Ch D 459, CA.

[37] *Bisset v Wilkinson* [1927] AC 177, PC.

[38] See *Lambert v Co-operative Insurance Society* [1975] 2 Lloyd's Rep 485, CA.

[39] *Gordon v Gordon* [1816] 3 Swan 400.

[40] *Derry v Peek* [1889] 14 App Cas 337.

[41] *Walker v Boyle* [1982] 1 All ER 634.

Act 1967, the court has the discretion to award damages in lieu of rescission for innocent misrepresentation and declare the contract subsisting.

(c) Rescission of voluntary dispositions for misrepresentation

It cannot be assumed that the rules relating to the rescission of voluntary dispositions for misrepresentation are the same as those for contracts. By analogy with the position in relation to mistake, it is likely that the test will be whether it is unconscionable for the disposition to remain uncorrected. This viewpoint is reinforced because in most if not all cases a misrepresentation causing or inducing a voluntary disposition will have led the donor into making a mistake. Rescission for that mistake will be possible under the rules just described: the fact that the beneficiary has induced the mistake will make it more likely that it will be unconscionable for the mistake not to be redressed.

(3) Rescission for undue influence

(a) Meaning of undue influence

Contracts or voluntary dispositions, including wills,[42] can be set aside where they have been induced by undue influence. The rules in both instances are broadly the same. The essence of undue influence is that the party making the contract or disposition was dominated by the other so that he was not acting of his own free choice.

(b) Actual undue influence

Actual undue influence arises where one party has in fact applied improper pressure to the other, which falls short of that necessary to constitute duress (which at common law is also sufficient to avoid a contract or disposition).[43] This may be through the exercise of conscious deception, although there will also be cases where a trusted adviser has broken his fiduciary duty of loyalty by preferring his own interests.[44] Merely failing to reveal material facts is insufficient by itself to amount to undue influence because negligence is not the same as a breach of the duty of loyalty,[45] but it was held to be a breach of duty where a husband had failed to inform his wife that he was engaged in a secret affair at the time of asking her to act as surety.[46]

In *Bank of Credit and Commerce International SA v Aboody*,[47] the court held that it was also necessary for the party alleging actual undue influence to demonstrate that they had suffered a 'manifest disadvantage' from the transaction, but this requirement was rejected by the House of Lords in *CIBC Mortgages plc v Pitt*.[48]

(c) Presumed undue influence

In some circumstances, the nature of the relationship between the parties itself gives rise to the presumption of undue influence, and the burden falls on the defendant to demonstrate that no such influence was exercised.[49] Examples of relationships where influence

[42] *Schrader v Schrader* [2013] EWHC 466 (Ch). For the principles applied to wills, see this case or *Edwards v Edwards* [2007] WTLR 1387.

[43] See e.g. *Cheese v Thomas* [1994] 1 All ER 35.

[44] *Royal Bank of Scotland Plc v Chandra* [2011] EWCA Civ 192 at 26.

[45] *Royal Bank of Scotland v Chandra* [2010] EWHC 105 (Ch) at 140, and *Royal Bank of Scotland Plc v Chandra* [2011] EWCA Civ 192 at 24.

[46] *Hewett v First Plus Financial Group plc* [2010] EWCA Civ 312.

[47] [1990] 1 QB 923, CA.

[48] [1994] 1 AC 200. See also *Barclays Bank v O'Brien* [1994] 1 AC 180.

[49] See *Allcard v Skinner* [1887] 36 Ch D 145. See also *Hammond v Osborn* [2002] WTLR 1125.

will be presumed include parent and child;[50] spiritual adviser and disciple;[51] doctor and patient;[52] married and cohabiting couples[53] or couples in a close, stable, sexual, and emotional relationship;[54] or between solicitor and client.[55] In the case of other relationships, for example, bank and customer[56] or pop artist and manager,[57] it may be possible to show that there was in fact a relationship of influence. Undue influence has increasingly been presumed where a relationship of confidence has been shown to have existed between family members or relations.[58] Similarly, the fact that a person agrees to act as surety of the debts of another will give rise to a presumption of a relationship of confidence if the surety gained no personal advantage from so acting.[59] In *Crédit Lyonnais Bank Nederland NV v Burch*,[60] the Court of Appeal held that an abuse of a relationship of confidence was presumed from the mere fact that a junior employee had executed an 'extravagantly improvident' unlimited guarantee of all her employer's debts, and that there was no need to show any sexual or emotional tie.

Rebutting undue influence is normally done by ensuring that the party subject to the influence has received independent legal advice. The other contracting party must also ensure that they have been informed of any unusual aspects of the transaction.[61]

(d) Influence exercised by third parties

A transaction can be set aside where the circumstances are such that the person benefiting from the transaction was aware of circumstances in which the other party may have been acting under the undue influence of a third party. Most typically this has occurred where a wife has executed some kind of financial guarantee of her husband's debts in favour of a bank, as in *Barclays Bank v O'Brien*,[62] where the bank had failed to take reasonable steps to satisfy itself that she had entered the transaction freely, it had constructive notice of the undue influence and she was therefore able to set the transaction aside.[63] A person will not be affixed with constructive notice of such undue influence if they ensure that the party they contract with received independent advice as to the effect of the transaction.[64] A creditor may also be put on notice where the undue influence has been exercised by a co-surety of the mortgagor, rather than the debtor.[65]

In *Royal Bank of Scotland v Etridge (No 2)*,[66] the House of Lords clarified the circumstances in which such surety transactions may be set aside. The Lords looked at eight cases in which a wife had agreed to a charge in favour of a bank to secure debts owed by her husband or a company that he controlled. In seven of these cases, the wife claimed

[50] [1934] 1 KB 380, CA.

[51] *Allcard v Skinner* [1887] 36 Ch D 145; *Tufton v Sperni* [1952] 2 TLR 516, CA; *Roche v Sherrington* [1982] 1 WLR 599.

[52] *Dent v Bennett* [1839] 4 My & Cr 269.

[53] *Barclays Bank v O'Brien* [1994] 1 AC 180.

[54] *Massey v Midland Bank plc* [1995] 1 All ER 929.

[55] *Wright v Carter* [1903] 1 Ch 27, CA.

[56] *Lloyds Bank v Bundy* [1975] QB 326, CA.

[57] *O'Sullivan v Management Agency and Music Ltd* [1985] QB 428.

[58] See, for example, *Simpson v Simpson* [1992] 1 FLR 601; *Langton v Langton* [1995] 2 FLR 890.

[59] *Barclays Bank v O'Brien* [1994] 1 AC 180; *CIBC v Pitt* [1994] 1 AC 200. But cf *Mumford v Bank of Scotland* 1996 SLT 392.

[60] [1997] 1 All ER 144.

[61] *North Shore Ventures Ltd v Anstead Holdings Inc* [2011] EWCA Civ 230.

[62] [1994] 1 AC 180.

[63] See also *Massey v Midland Bank plc* [1995] 1 All ER 929; *Banco Exterior Internacional SA v Mann* [1995] 1 All ER 936; *TSB Bank plc v Camfield* [1995] 1 All ER 951.

[64] See, for example. *Banco Exterior Internacional SA v Thomas* [1997] 1 All ER 46; *Crédit Lyonnais Bank Nederland NV v Burch* [1997] 1 All ER 144.

[65] *First National Bank v Achampong* [2003] EWCA Civ 487; *Enonchong* [2003] LMCLQ 307.

[66] [2001] 4 All ER 449. See Capper, 'Banks, Borrowers, Sureties and Undue Influence—A Half-Baked Solution to a Thoroughly Cooked Problem' [2002] RLR 100; Phang and Tijo, 'The Uncertain Boundaries of Undue Influence' [2002] LMCLQ 231.

that the charge was unenforceable against her because it was tainted by undue influence. In the eighth case, the wife who had agreed to a similar arrangement was suing a solicitor for breach of duty concerning the advice that he had given her. The House of Lords held that a bank would be put on inquiry whenever a wife offers to stand surety for her husband's debts. To avoid the transaction being impugned on the grounds of undue influence, the bank must merely take reasonable steps to satisfy itself that the practical implications of the proposed transaction have been brought home to the wife, especially the risks involved, so that she is able to enter the transaction with her eyes open as to its basic elements. This does not require a meeting between the bank and the wife. The bank is entitled to rely upon confirmation from a solicitor acting for the wife that he has advised her appropriately. A solicitor who fails to give the advice correctly is likely to be held liable for negligence.[67]

(4) **Setting aside unconscionable bargains**

Equity will set aside bargains that have been made in circumstances that can be regarded as 'unconscionable'. It is not enough that the bargain has disastrous and unanticipated consequences, because the general principle is that people are held to the bargain which they have made.[68] The scope of the doctrine is relatively narrow, and there are three requirements. The first is that the person seeking to avoid the disposition suffered from a significant disability[69] or disadvantage, such as someone who is a person of limited means and limited education.[70] Other kinds of disability or disadvantage may be relevant in the particular circumstances of a case.[71] This may include a mental incapacity such as senile dementia,[72] illiteracy, or unfamiliarity with a language or culture,[73] age,[74] or youth and inexperience.[75] The arrangement must be oppressive and must have been procured by the stronger party wrongly exploiting the weaker party.[76] This requires an assessment not just of the terms of the bargain (which must be oppressive or unfair, for instance by conferring no personal advantage on the weaker party[77]), but also of the behaviour of the stronger party ('which must be characterized by some moral culpability or impropriety').[78] The onus is on the person seeking relief to establish unconscionable conduct, namely that unconscientious advantage has been taken of his disabling condition or circumstances.[79] Such exploitation will not be demonstrated if the contracting party received independent legal advice before entering the bargain.[80]

Parliament has intervened with a regime of consumer protection, which extends to the regulation of terms in contracts,[81] and unconscionable terms in credit arrangements,

[67] *Padden v Bevan Ashford Solicitors* [2011] EWCA Civ 1616.

[68] *Arnold v Britton* [2015] UKSC 36 (an escalation clause in a contract to pay a service charge on a holiday chalet was enforceable even though it would give rise to an annual charge per unit of over £1 million).

[69] *Evans v Lloyd* [2013] EWHC 1725.

[70] *Cresswell v Potter* [1978] 1 WLR 255.

[71] *Chagos Islanders v Attorney General* [2003] EWHC 2222 (QB) at 559.

[72] *Archer v Cutler* [1980] 1 NZLR 386; *Hart v O'Connor* [1985] AC 1000.

[73] *Commercial Bank of Australia Ltd v Amadio* [1983] 46 ALR 402.

[74] *Watkin v Watson-Smith* [1986] The Times, 3 July.

[75] *Crédit Lyonnais Bank Nederland NV v Burch* [1997] 1 All ER 144 (a junior employee).

[76] *Boustany v Piggott* [1993] 69 P & CR 288 (bargain must be more than 'hard, foolish or unreasonable'). See Bamforth, 'Unconscionability as a Vitiating Factor' [1995] LMCLQ 538.

[77] *Crédit Lyonnais Bank Nederland v Burch* [1997] 1 All ER 144.

[78] *Alec Lobb (Garages) Ltd v Total Oil (Great Britain) Ltd* [1983] 1 WLR 87 at 94; *Hart v O'Connor* [1985] AC 1000; *Nichols v Jessup* [1986] 1 NZLR 226.

[79] *Commercial Bank of Australia Ltd v Amadio* [1983] 46 ALR 402 at 413, per Mason J.

[80] *Fry v Lane* [1888] 40 Ch D 312; *Butlin-Sanders v Butlin* [1985] Fam Law 126.

[81] See, for example, the Unfair Terms in Consumer Contracts Regulations 1999.

such as hire purchase agreements, are now regulated by the Consumer Credit Act 1974, as amended by the Consumer Credit Act 2006. Some unfair bargains may still escape, as is shown by the government consultation in 2017 on potentially unfair and unreasonable ground rent charges and other conditions on the sale of leasehold properties.[82]

(5) Limitations on the availability of rescission

There are a number of circumstances where it will not be possible for a claimant to rescind a contract.

(a) Restitutio in integrum is impossible

When a contract is rescinded, the parties must be returned to their former positions as far as is practically possible.[83] Hence, in *Clarke v Dickson*,[84] the court held that a party could not rescind a contract to purchase shares in a partnership that had been converted into a limited liability company. Equity approaches the question flexibly, and is particularly ready to grant rescission where there was fraud.[85] The overall objective is for the courts to do 'what is practically just'.[86] Thus, in *O'Sullivan v Management Agency and Music Ltd*,[87] a contract for the management of a popular singer (Gilbert O'Sullivan) was rescinded on the grounds of undue influence. The managers were allowed to retain a reasonable remuneration for the work they had done which had contributed to his success.

(b) Affirmation

A party cannot rescind a contract that he has subsequently affirmed. In *Long v Lloyd*,[88] a purchaser was taken to have affirmed a contract for the sale of a lorry when he used it a second time having discovered there were faults. He could not rescind on the grounds of the seller's misrepresentation. Similarly, a person cannot rescind a contract entered under undue influence if he affirms it after the influence has stopped.[89]

(c) Third-party rights

The right to rescind is lost once third parties have acquired rights in the property in good faith for value.[90] This is no longer an absolute bar, if the court can be persuaded to allow rescission alongside a backwards or reverse tracing claim, as was the case in *Bainbridge v Bainbridge*.[91]

(d) Delay

In *Allcard v Skinner*,[92] the plaintiff was held not to be entitled to rescind gifts of stock to a religious order five years after she left because of her delay. Lindley LJ stated that the victim must 'seek relief within a reasonable time after the removal of the influence'.[93] Similarly, in *Leaf v International Galleries*,[94] a plaintiff was not entitled to rescind a contract for innocent misrepresentation after a delay of five years. In the case of mistake

[82] Department for Communities and Local Government, 'Tackling Unfair Practices in the Leasehold Market. A Consultation Paper', July 2017.

[83] *Cheese v Thomas* [1994] 1 All ER 35 at 412, per Nicholls V-C. Moriarty, 'Equitable Compensation for Undue Influence' [1997] 114 LQR 9.

[84] [1858] EB & E 148.

[85] *Spence v Crawford* [1939] 3 All ER 271, HL.

[86] *Spence v Crawford* [1939] 3 All ER 271 at 288, per Lord Wright.

[87] [1985] QB 428.

[88] [1958] 2 All ER 402, CA.

[89] *Mitchell v Homfray* [1881] 8 QBD 587.

[90] See *Oakes v Turquand* [1867] LR 2 HL 325; *Coldunell Ltd v Gallon* [1986] 1 All ER 429.

[91] [2016] EWHC 898 (Ch). Backwards tracing is discussed in Chapter 38.

[92] [1887] 36 Ch D 145.

[93] [1887] 36 Ch D 145 at 187.

[94] [1950] 2 KB 86.

claims for rescission, the ordinary limitation period of six years from the date of payment could be extended by the Limitation Act 1980, s 32(1)(c), which provided that the limitation period would begin to run when the claimant discovered the mistake, or could with reasonable diligence have discovered it.[95]

4 Rectification

Rectification is a discretionary equitable remedy that allows for the correction of a document so that it reflects the real intention of the parties. It is an exception to the 'parol evidence rule' so that oral evidence may be admitted to demonstrate that a written instrument is incorrect. For example, in *Joscelyne v Nissen*,[96] the Court of Appeal ordered the rectification of an agreement between a daughter and her father, which they intended should include a provision that she was to pay the household expenses, which she had refused to pay, claiming that she was not required to do so on a true construction of the written agreement they had entered. A wide range of documents have been rectified, including a conveyance,[97] a bill of exchange,[98] a marriage settlement,[99] a transfer of shares[100] and, by statute, wills.[101]

(1) Requirements for rectification

(a) Mistake in written document

Rectification is only possible where a written document mistakenly fails to state what the parties had intended to agree. It is not necessary that the parties had actually entered a contract orally prior to the incorrect instrument. In *Joscelyne v Nissen*,[102] the Court of Appeal held that all that is necessary is a prior common intention as to what the written agreement was to be.[103] There are grounds for rectification if that common intention does not appear in the written document.[104] Rectification is only available for a mistake of the actual terms of the parties' agreement. Thus, in *Frederick E Rose (London) Ltd v William Pim Jnr & Co Ltd*,[105] rectification was not possible where the parties had entered a written contract for the sale of 'horsebeans', which they had mistakenly believed were the same as 'feveroles'. The contract was a correct record of their agreement. Rectification was similarly refused in *Lloyds TSB Bank Plc v Crowborough Properties Ltd*,[106] where a contract accurately recorded what the parties agreed, but did not have the effect either of them intended since they both shared a mistaken common assumption.

(b) Common mistake

Generally, an instrument will only be rectified if it records the agreement contrary to the intentions of both parties.[107] It is now clear that in assessing whether there has been a

95 *Jazztel Plc v Revenue And Customs Commissioners* [2017] EWHC 677 (Ch).
96 [1970] 2 QB 86. 97 *Beale v Kyte* [1907] 1 Ch 564.
98 *Druiff v Lord Parker* [1867–8] LR 5 Eq 131. 99 *Bold v Hutchinson* [1855] 5 De GM & G 558.
100 *Re International Contract Co* [1872] 7 Ch App 485.
101 Administration of Justice Act 1982, s 20(1). See *Wordingham v Royal Exchange Trust Co* [1992] Ch 412; *Re Segelman* [1996] Ch 171, [1995] 3 All ER 676; *Andrews v Andrews* [2014] EWHC 1725 (Ch).
102 [1970] 2 QB 86. 103 *Crane v Hegeman-Harris Co Inc* [1939] 1 All ER 662.
104 *Earl v Hector Whaling Ltd* [1961] 1 Lloyd's Rep 459. 105 [1953] 2 QB 450.
106 [2012] EWHC 2264 (Ch).
107 *Murray v Parker* [1854] 19 Beav 305; *Fowler v Fowler* [1859] 4 De G & J 250.

common mistake, the courts will consider what the parties' intentions actually were, and that there is no room for an objective assessment:

> [I]t is necessary to show not only that each party to the contract had the same actual intention with regard to the relevant matter, but also that there was an 'outward expression of accord'—meaning that, as a result of communication between them, the parties understood each other to share that intention.[108]

(c) Unilateral mistake

Rectification is not normally available where a mistake is unilateral.[109] However, rectification will be available if the party who was not mistaken had acted fraudulently[110] or is estopped from resisting rectification. In *Thomas Bates & Son Ltd v Wyndham's (Lingerie) Ltd*,[111] Buckley LJ stated that a person would be estopped from resisting rectification if he knew that the other party was mistaken about the inclusion or omission of a provision and failed to draw it to the other party's attention. He also thought that the party estopped needed to derive some benefit from the mistake, although the reason for this requirement is not self-evident.[112]

A line of authorities which suggested that the party who was not mistaken has the option of accepting rectification or rescission of the contract has been disapproved by the Court of Appeal in *Riverlate Properties Ltd v Paul*.[113]

(d) Rectification of unilateral instruments

The requirement of a common intention, or estoppel, does not apply where rectification is sought of a unilateral instrument such as a voluntary settlement, nor is there any need for an outward display of intention.[114] The principles were set out by Barling J in *Giles v RNIB*.[115] He set out four requirements:

(1) Clear evidence of the true intention of the person executing the instrument.
(2) A flaw in the instrument meaning that it does not give effect to that intention (it is not sufficient that the document fails to achieve the desired objective[116]).
(3) Some degree of precision about what was intended which is different from what was done.
(4) An issue capable of being contested.[117]

These principles were applied in *RBC Trustees (CI) Ltd v Stubbs*,[118] where Rose J held that a variation of trusts could be rectified because it did not merely revoke a life interest in the trust, but also revoked and resettled the trust funds omitting the life interest. The requirement of a contestable issue 'has been much criticised and . . . the purpose of it, and its actual content and scope, are by no means clear'.[119] Both Barling J and Rose J emphasized that there was no need for an actual dispute, and it was irrelevant if all parties agreed

[108] *FSHC Group Holdings Ltd v Glas Trust Corp Ltd* [2020] Ch 365 at [176]. See Davies, 'Rectification Rectified' (2020) 79 CLJ 8.

[109] *Sells v Sells* [1860] 1 Drew & Sm 42.

[110] *Ball v Storie* [1823] 1 Sim & St 210; *Lovesy v Smith* [1880] LR 15 Ch D 655.

[111] [1981] 1 All ER 1077, CA.

[112] [1981] 1 All ER 1077, CA at 1086.

[113] [1975] Ch 133. Applied in *Andrews v Andrews* [2014] EWHC 1725 (Ch).

[114] *Day v Day* [2013] 3 All ER 661.

[115] [2014] EWHC 1373 (Ch).

[116] See *Allnutt v Wilding* [2007] EWCA Civ 412.

[117] A requirement derived from the Court of Appeal decision in *Racal Group Services Ltd v Ashmore* [1995] STC 1151.

[118] [2017] EWHC 180 (Ch). See also *Bullard v Bullard* [2017] EWHC 3 (Ch).

[119] Ibid at 62.

to the rectification. Rose J suggested that a more than theoretical issue amounting to a material change would be sufficient.

The use of rectification to rewrite a trust instrument has drawn academic criticism, as 'the courts are constructing for settlors better trusts than they had made for themselves'.[120] While this is doubtless true, this is the result of the use of the remedy and, as we have already seen earlier in this chapter, the burden of proof to argue for rectification is set somewhat higher than for rescission through mistake.

(e) Burden of proof

For rectification the mistake must be established with 'a high degree of conviction'.[121] In *Joscelyne v Nissen*,[122] Russel LJ said that there must be 'convincing proof' of the mistake. Thus, in *Re Segelman*,[123] Chadwick J held that a testator's will should be rectified where extrinsic evidence of his intentions demonstrated convincingly that it had failed to carry out his intentions.

(2) Defences to rectification

Rectification will not be granted where it would affect the position of third parties who have acquired rights bona fides for value.[124] Delay may also bar a claim,[125] though this is not an absolute bar. In *Oatley v Oatley Powney*,[126] despite the borderline nature of the evidence for rectification, the remedy was granted despite a delay in bringing proceedings for rectification, as this has not caused any undue prejudice to granting the remedy.[127] The delay had also been explained by the difficulty that Mr Boyd had found in dealing with the matter before retiring from the firm and the time then taken to contact all the beneficiaries, find a litigation friend, and obtain independent advice before proceedings were initiated.

5 Specific performance

(1) Introduction

At common law the only remedy for breach of contract was damages. A defendant who had breached her contract could not be compelled to perform, but was liable to compensate the claimant for any loss the claimant suffered as a consequence of the breach.[128] Depending on the circumstances this would be either her 'expectation loss' (the extent to which she expected to gain from performance) or her 'reliance loss' (the extent to which she had incurred costs in reliance on the contract). The claimant was expected, at common law, to use her compensation to purchase alternative performance. She could buy replacement goods on the open market, or find an alternative supplier of services.[129]

In effect, the defendant can buy his way out of performance of the contract. However, the payment of damages might not always be an adequate remedy. This is when equity

[120] Douglas, 'Misuse of Rectification in the Law of Trusts' (2018) LQR 138 at 150.

[121] *Crane v Hegeman-Harris Co Inc* [1939] 4 All ER 68, CA.

[122] [1970] 2 QB 86, CA. See *Re Segelman* [1995] 3 All ER 676.

[123] [1995] 3 All ER 676 at 684.

[124] *Garrard v Frankel* [1862] 30 Beav 445; *Thames Guaranty Ltd v Campbell* [1985] QB 210.

[125] *Beale v Kyte* [1907] 1 Ch 564.

[126] [2014] EWHC 1956 (Ch). See also *Bullard v Bullard* [2017] EWHC 3 (Ch) (delay not a reason for failing to rectify even after 14 years because the problem had only recently come to light).

[127] Ibid at 115.

[128] *Tai Hing Cotton Mills Ltd v Kanmsing Knitting Factory* [1979] AC 91.

[129] *Photo Production Ltd v Securicor Transport Ltd* [1980] 1 All ER 556 per Lord Diplock.

intervenes.[130] By means of an order of specific performance the court can compel the defendant to perform his contractual obligations. The court is also willing to order specific performance of a contract to confer benefits on third parties,[131] although any action seeking specific performance must be brought by a party to the contract.[132] Like other equitable remedies, specific performance is an order made personally against the defendant,[133] and disobedience is classified as a contempt of court which can lead to imprisonment or other action.[134]

(2) **When is specific performance available?**

Specific performance is not generally available as a remedy for breach of contract. It is instead 'regarded as an exceptional remedy . . . in cases in which remedies available at common law were inadequate.'[135]

There are a number of well-recognized circumstances in which it is known that damages would not provide an adequate remedy so that specific performance is ordinarily available.

(a) **Contracts concerning land**

Land is always deemed to be unique as it is assumed that there is no identical market alternative, so that damages would 'constitute a wholly inadequate and unjust remedy for the breach'[136] That is why the normal remedy is by a decree of specific performance.

Specific performance is, therefore, available in respect of a contract for the sale of land, for the grant of an interest in land, or even for the grant of a licence to occupy land.[137] A contract for the sale of land, or the disposition of an interest in land, must be made in writing in accordance with the provisions of s 2 of the Law of Property (Miscellaneous Provisions) Act 1989. Specific performance will not, therefore, be available to enforce an oral contract in respect of an interest in land,[138] although such an agreement might give rise to a remedy by way of proprietary estoppel.

(b) **Contracts for the sale of unique personal property**

If an item of personal property is unique and there is no available alternative, the court may grant a decree of specific performance. For example, in *Falcke v Gray*,[139] Kindersley V-C would have granted specific performance of a contract for the sale of two oriental jars which were of 'unusual beauty, rarity and distinction' if he had not found that the consideration was inadequate.[140] A contract to sell shares may also be specifically enforceable if they are not available in the general market.[141]

130 *Hutton v Watling* [1948] Ch 26; affd [1948] Ch 398.

131 *Beswick v Beswick* [1968] AC 58; *Gurtner v Circuit* [1968] 2 QB 587.

132 *AK Investment CJSC v Kyrgyz Mobil Tel Ltd & Ors (Isle of Man)* (Rev 1) [2011] UKPC 7 at 22.

133 See *Penn v Lord Baltimore* [1750] 1 Ves Sen 444; *Richard West & Partners (Inverness) Ltd v Dick* [1969] 1 All ER 289.

134 See *Mid Suffolk DC v Clarke* [2007] 1 WLR 98.

135 [1997] 3 All ER 297 at 301. See also *Ashworth v Royal National Theatre* [2014] EWHC 1176 (QB) at 31, where specific performance to require the National Theatre Company to engage orchestra members in the play *War Horse* was refused; one of the grounds being that damages would provide adequate compensation.

136 *Sudbrook Trading Estate Ltd v Eggleton* [1983] 1 AC 444 at 478 per Lord Diplock.

137 *Verrall v Great Yarmouth Borough Council* [1981] QB 202. This is so even though a contractual licence does not create an interest in the land capable of binding successors in title of the licensor: *Ashburn Anstalt v Arnold* [1989] Ch 1.

138 *Yaxley v Gotts* [2000] Ch 162. See Chapter 14.

139 [1859] 4 Drew 651.

140 See also *Behnke v Bede Shipping Co Ltd* [1927] 1 KB 649 (contract for the sale of a steamship, which had unique and special value to the plaintiff). Contrast *Cohen v Roche* [1927] 1 KB 169 (eight 'Heppelwhite' chairs, which were not considered of any special value or interest by the court).

141 *Oughtred v IRC* [1960] AC 206; *Neville v Wilson* [1997] Ch 144.

(c) Practical unavailability of market substitutes

Specific performance has also been granted of contracts for the sale of goods that are not unique and are normally readily available in the market where special circumstances have meant that substitutes are in fact unobtainable. In *Sky Petroleum Ltd v VIP Petroleum Ltd*,[142] the plaintiff sought an injunction to prevent the defendants from breaching their contract as the exclusive supplier of petrol and diesel for the plaintiff's garages. Goulding J granted the injunction,[143] which had the same practical effect as specific performance of the contract, because the market in petroleum had changed considerably since the contract had been entered and the plaintiff had no market alternative.

(d) Quantification of damages would be difficult

Specific performance has been ordered of contracts to sell or pay annuities because the value of the rights is uncertain,[144] and of contracts to execute a mortgage for money already lent because the value of having security for the loan cannot be quantified.[145] Specific performance has also been awarded where the loss is difficult to prove,[146] or where the defendant is unlikely to be able to pay damages.[147] Where there is doubt, the burden is on the claimant to prove that damages are not an adequate remedy on the normal civil standard of the balance of probabilities. In *RVB Investments Ltd v Bibby*,[148] for example, Behrens J QC ordered specific performance of an obligation by an insolvent surety to execute and complete a lease. Damages would have provided an inadequate remedy, as the local authority was pursuing the claimant landlord for non-domestic rates, but would pursue the surety instead if the surety took the lease.

(e) Claimant entitled only to nominal damages

Specific performance has been ordered where the claimant would only be entitled to recover nominal damages for his loss.[149] Damages may also be nominal because of a term in a contract that restricts the damages recoverable for the breach. In such circumstances, it is possible for the claimant to argue that damages would not provide an adequate remedy.[150]

(f) Statutory rights to specific performance

A right akin to specific performance can be granted via statute. Hence, tenancies to which the Landlord and Tenant Act 1985 apply[151] provide a statutory right to specific performance of a landlord's repairing obligations in a lease.[152] This statutory right goes beyond the general equitable remedy in that it allows specific performance to be ordered 'notwithstanding any equitable rule restricting the scope of the remedy, whether on the basis of a lack of mutuality or otherwise.' Often the statutory right will simply be declaratory, adding nothing to the general operation of specific performance as an equitable remedy, as, for example, in the Consumer Rights Act 2015, s 58.

[142] [1974] 1 All ER 954.. See also *Aston Martin Lagonda Ltd v Automotive Industrial Partnership Ltd* [2010] All ER (D) 131; *Delta Petroluem (Caribbean) Ltd v British Virgin Islands Electricity Corp* [2020] UKPC 23.

[143] Injunctions are explored later in this chapter.

[144] *Beswick v Beswick* [1968] AC 58.

[145] *Swiss Bank Corpn v Lloyds Bank Ltd* [1982] AC 584.

[146] *Decro-Wall International SA v Practitioners in Marketing Ltd* [1971] 1 WLR 361.

[147] *Evans Marshall & Co v Bertola SA* [1973] 1 All ER 992.

[148] [2013] EWHC 65 (Ch).

[149] See, for example, *Beswick v Beswick* [1968] AC 58 (contract made for widow's benefit between nephew and testator would have yielded nominal damages if widow sued as personal representative, as testator had suffered no loss).

[150] See *B v D* [2014] EWCA Civ 229 at 30, per Stuart-Smith J.

[151] This applies to all short leases for residential property and tenancies agreed for a period of less than seven years or on a periodic term.

[152] Landlord and Tenant Act 1985, s 17.

(g) Anticipatory performance

It is possible to bring a claim through specific performance before the relevant date for performance arises; so in anticipation of that performance.[153] It now appears that specific performance may be pleaded in anticipation of a breach of a contractual obligation to secure performance of that application if it appears likely that the relevant party will fail to perform it by the agreed deadline in the contract.[154]

(3) Contracts where specific performance is not available

(a) Contracts of personal service

Equity will not specifically enforce a contract of personal service requiring the defendant to work for the claimant for a variety or reasons,[155] one of them because this would infringe his liberty.[156]

Conversely, it is not open to an employee to obtain an order of specific performance to make an employer engage their services.[157] The court will also normally refuse to grant an injunction to give effect to a contractual provision that the defendant is not to work for anyone else, as this would indirectly amount to specific performance of the contract.[158]

However, the rule is not absolute. In *CH Giles & Co Ltd v Morris*,[159] Megarry J explained that, in some circumstances, specific performance might be available because 'the matter is one of the balance of advantage and disadvantage in relation to the particular obligations in question'.[160]

(b) Contracts to carry on a business

In *Co-operative Insurance v Argyll Stores (Holdings) Ltd*,[161] the House of Lords held that specific performance should not be granted of a contract to carry on a business. The defendants operated a Safeway supermarket in a Sheffield shopping centre. In their lease they had covenanted to keep the premises open for 'retail trade'. Following a review of their national operations, the defendants decided to close the store, along with other loss-making supermarkets. The plaintiff landlords sought specific performance of the covenant for the remainder of the lease, which had over nineteen years left to run. The House of Lords held that specific performance should not be ordered, reiterating that there was

[153] See *Hasham v Zenab* [1960] AC 31 (PC), which held that a claim could be brought before the relevant date for performance arose.

[154] *Airport Industrial GP Ltd v Heathrow Airport Ltd* [2015] EWHC 3753 (Ch), where an order was made to complete a multi-storey car park, which had been delayed, and the deadline in the contract was extended for two years to have the work carried out. The courts will not always be so willing to allow an order which requires supervision of specified works rather than a particular result, as we shall see later in this chapter.

[155] *Societe Generale, London Branch v Geys* [2012] UKSC 63. For an account of the reasons, see Lord Sumption (dissenting on the result) at 119.

[156] *Lumley v Wagner* [1852] 1 De GM & G 604; *De Francesco v Barnum* [1890] 45 Ch D 430.

[157] *Ashworth v Royal National Theatre* [2014] EWHC 1176; *MacKenzie v The University of Cambridge* [2019] EWCA Civ 1060 (no specific performance granted to re-engage an employee, even though they had been unfairly dismissed).

[158] *Page One Records Ltd v Britton* [1967] 3 All ER 822; *Scandinavian Trading Tanker Co AB v Flota Petrolera Ecuatoriana, The Scaptrade* [1983] 2 AC 694.

[159] [1972] 1 WLR 307.

[160] See also *Warner Bros Picture Inc v Nelson* [1937] 1 KB 209, where the film star Bette Davis (married name Nelson) was compelled to work for Warner Brothers for the remainder of her contractual period with the movie studio; *Powell v London Borough of Brent* [1987] IRLR 446; *Hughes v London Borough of Southwark* [1988] IRLR 55.

[161] [1997] 3 All ER 297.

a 'settled practice'[162] to this effect and also that such an order requiring the defendant to conduct an activity would require constant supervision by the court. Lord Hoffmann also considered that the grant of an order might 'cause injustice by allowing the claimant to enrich himself at the defendant's expense' by requiring the defendant to run a business at a loss far greater than the claimant would suffer by reason of the breach of contract,[163] and that from the wider perspective of public policy it was not in the public interest 'to require someone to carry on business at a loss if there is any plausible alternative by which the other party can be given compensation'.[164]

(c) Contracts for partnership

Such contracts will not be specifically enforced unless the partners have begun to act upon their agreement.[165]

(d) Contracts to transfer goodwill

The court will not specifically enforce a contract to transfer merely the goodwill of a business,[166] unless annexed to an agreement to sell the premises or other assets of the business.

(e) Contracts to exercise a testamentary power of appointment

The court will not grant specific performance of a contract to exercise a testamentary power in favour of a specific person because this would undermine the intention of the person who had granted the power (the donor) that the donee should be able to exercise it until his death.[167]

(f) Contracts referring to arbitration

The court will not specifically enforce a contract to refer a matter to arbitration,[168] but it may stay proceedings under s 9 of the Arbitration Act 1996. This will indirectly enforce the agreement because the claimant will have no option other than to seek arbitration if he wishes to obtain a remedy. A decision made by an arbitrator can be enforced by means of specific performance.

(4) Other obstacles to ordering specific performance

Most of the instances just considered are contracts of types which the courts will normally decline specifically to enforce. There are some other reasons why specific performance may be refused.

(a) Agreements made without consideration

It is an established principle that equity will not assist a volunteer,[169] as specific performance may only be obtained by a person who has provided valuable consideration under the contract. Accordingly, specific performance may not be obtained by a volunteer who

[162] [1997] 3 All ER 297 at 301, citing *Braddon Towers Ltd v International Stores Ltd* [1987] 1 EGLR 209.

[163] [1997] 3 All ER 297 at 304, approving the comments of Millett LJ who dissented in the Court of Appeal [1996] Ch 286 at 303–5.

[164] [1997] 3 All ER 297 at 305.

[165] *Scott v Rayment* [1868] LR 7 Eq 112.

[166] *Darbey v Whitaker* [1857] 4 Drew 134: the reason is because of the uncertainty of the subject matter.

[167] *Re Coake* [1922] 1 Ch 292.

[168] *Re Smith and Service and Nelson & Sons* [1890] 25 QBD 545; *Doleman & Sons v Ossett Corpn* [1912] 3 KB 257.

[169] A volunteer is someone who has not provided valuable consideration for the benefit they are seeking equity to enforce—see Chapter 6.

is a party to a covenant, even though a promise made by deed may be binding and enforceable at common law, owing to the presence of a deed.[170]

Although the Contracts (Rights of Third Parties Act) 1999 provides that a third party who is entitled to enforce a contract may obtain any remedy 'that would have been available to him in an action for breach of contract if he had been a party to the contract', it seems that a volunteer third party will still be unable to obtain specific performance. Section 1(5) provides that the 'rules relating to . . . specific performance . . . shall apply accordingly', thereby incorporating the long established rule that a volunteer may not obtain specific performance.

(b) Claimant in breach

If the claimant is in breach of an essential term of the contract (such as by not being ready to pay the full purchase price on completion of a contract for the sale of land after time has been made of the essence), then specific performance will not be available.[171] Nevertheless, just because there is a breach of a non-essential term in a contract does not prevent the party in breach from obtaining specific performance of a different provision in the contract.[172]

(c) Contracts requiring constant supervision

In *Ryan v Mutual Tontine Westminster Chambers Association*,[173] the defendants, who were the lessors of a block of residential flats, covenanted to provide a resident porter who would be in constant attendance. The Court of Appeal held that this covenant could not be specifically enforced because 'the execution of it would require constant superintendence by the court, which the court in such cases has always declined to give'.[174] This rationale was questioned by the House of Lords in *Co-operative Insurance v Argyll Stores (Holdings) Ltd*.[175] Lord Hoffmann said such refusal was not because the court itself would have to supervise the execution of the order, but because the court might have to give an 'indefinite series of rulings' whether the order had been kept or broken.[176] This would be expensive both in costs to the litigants and in court time.[177]

Lord Hoffman nonetheless drew a distinction between results and activities:

> This is a convenient point at which to distinguish between orders which require a defendant to carry on an activity, such as running a business over a more or less extended period of time, and orders which require him to achieve a result. The possibility of repeated applications for rulings on compliance with the order which arises in the former case does not exist to anything like the same extent in the latter. Even if the achievement of the result is a complicated matter which will take some time, the court, if called upon to rule, only has to examine the finished work and say whether it complies with the order.[178]

This distinction between activities and results explains why the courts have decreed specific performance of building contracts[179] and repairing covenants,[180] since the

170 *Futter v Revenue and Customs* [2013] UKSC 26 at 115. Equity does not consider the presence of the seal on a deed to provide valuable consideration for any of the promises contained therein—see *Cannon v Hartley* [1949] Ch 213.

171 *Clarke Investments Ltd v Pacific Technologies* [2013] EWCA Civ 750.

172 *Redrow Homes Ltd v Martin Dawn (Leckhampton) Ltd* [2016] EWHC 934 (Ch).

173 [1893] 1 Ch 116.

174 [1893] 1 Ch 116 at 123, per Lord Esher MR.

175 [1997] 3 All ER 297; Jones, 'Specific Performance: A Lessee's Covenant to Keep Open a Retail Store' [1997] CLJ 488.

176 [1997] 3 All ER 297 at 302.

177 [1997] 3 All ER 297 at 303.

178 [1997] 3 All ER 297 at 303.

179 *Wolverhampton Corpn v Emmons* [1901] 1 KB 515.

180 *Jeune v Queens Cross Properties Ltd* [1974] Ch 97.

performance of such obligations requires a result to be achieved. In practice, however, the dividing line is not always so clear, and even where an order to achieve a result is made, the court may, for example, give leave to appeal should, in practice, the work prove impossible or impracticable in the future.[181]

(d) **Contractual terms are insufficiently precise**

An agreement which is too vague to be contractually enforceable cannot be specifically enforced,[182] although, even absent a contractually enforceable obligation, it is possible for specific performance to be used to enforce a constructive trust.[183] Where specific performance is used in support of a binding contract, the terms must be sufficiently precise to enable an order to be drawn clearly defining what the defendant must do to comply.[184] The degree of certainty of the obligation in question is only a factor to be taken into account by the court in relation to the exercise of its discretion, and where the claimant's merits are strong the courts have 'shown themselves willing to cope with a certain degree of imprecision in cases of orders requiring a result'.[185] Indeed, if an obligation can be performed in a variety of ways the court can 'in order to give its order specificity and effectiveness . . . spell out what performance is required in the particular circumstances of the case.'[186]

(e) **Illegal, unlawful, or immoral contracts**

The court will not grant specific performance if the contract is illegal, unlawful, or contrary to public policy.[187] Specific performance will not be available where this would contravene a statutory provision.[188] Similarly, specific performance to transfer shares will not be ordered where this is contrary to the articles of association of the company concerned,[189] nor will a contract to assign a lease be enforced if this would be in breach of covenant.[190] An obligation which is not recognized by law, such as a contract to create a lease for an uncertain term, cannot be enforced by means of specific performance.[191]

(5) **Mutuality**

Despite earlier cases suggesting that the court could not grant specific performance in favour of a claimant unless it could also have granted specific performance in favour of

[181] See *Blue Manchester v North West Ground Rents Ltd* [2019] EWHC 142 (TCC) (enforcement of a repairing covenant, which gave L 18 months to design and implement a scheme to replace temporary glass panels in a hotel building).

[182] *Frost v Wake Smith and Tofields Solicitors* [2013] EWCA Civ 772 at 9 and 17.

[183] *Banner Homes Group plc v Luff Developments Ltd* [2000] Ch 372 at 397 per Chadwick LJ.

[184] *Co-operative Insurance v Argyll Stores (Holdings) Ltd* [1997] 3 All ER 297 at 303 per Lord Hoffman; *Durham Tees Valley Airport Ltd v BMI Baby Ltd* [2010] EWCA Civ 485 at [90], per Toulson LJ; *Blue Manchester v North West Ground Rents Ltd* [2019] EWHC 142 (TCC) at [109] per Stephen Davies J.

[185] *Co-operative Insurance v Argyll Stores (Holdings) Ltd* [1997] 3 All ER 297 at 304.

[186] *Alfa Finance Holdings AD v Quarzwerke GMBH* [2015] EWCH 243 at [8–9].

[187] *Sutton v Sutton* [1984] Ch 184 (an ante-nuptial agreement to settle property on divorce was not enforced as it would be against public policy to do so).

[188] *Hughes v La Baia Ltd (Anguilla)* [2011] UKPC 9. In this case the legislation (regulating land ownership by aliens) did not affect the enforceability of private rights.

[189] *McKillen v Misland (Cyprus) Investments Ltd* [2013] EWCA Civ 781.

[190] See *Clarence House Ltd v National Westminster Bank Plc* [2009] EWCA Civ 1311 at 45.

[191] See *Berrisford v Mexfield Housing Co-operative Ltd* [2010] EWCA Civ 811 (this point was not considered on appeal).

the defendant,[192] the current view is that lack of mutuality is not an absolute bar to specific performance. In *Price v Strange*,[193] Goff LJ stated the 'true principle' is that:

> one judges the defence of want of mutuality on the facts and circumstances as they exist at the hearing, albeit in the light of the whole conduct of the parties in relation to the subject matter, and in the absence of any other disqualifying circumstances the court will grant specific performance if it can be done without injustice or unfairness to the defendant.[194]

The defendant had agreed to grant the plaintiff a new lease of premises he occupied if he carried out some internal and external repairs. At the time of trial, the plaintiff had completed the internal repairs and had only been prevented from completing the external repairs by the defendant, who had done them herself. In these circumstances, the Court of Appeal ordered specific performance, even though at the date of the agreement the defendant could not have compelled the plaintiff to carry out his promises to repair. There was no risk of hardship to the defendant in granting specific performance because the plaintiff's contractual undertakings had been performed.

(6) Defences to specific performance

Even though the contract may be one where specific performance would be available, there are a number of defences available to a defendant.

(a) Absence of necessary formalities

Specific performance will not be available to a claimant where a contract was entered without the necessary formalities, for instance where a contract for the grant of an interest in land has not been made in writing as required by s 2 of the Law of Property (Miscellaneous Provisions) Act 1989.[195]

(b) Misrepresentation by the plaintiff

Any misrepresentation by the plaintiff to the defendant, whether innocent or fraudulent, which would entitle the defendant to rescind the contract, will be a defence to an action seeking specific performance.[196]

(c) Mistake

Where the defendant has made a mistake, which does not prevent the formation of a contract, this will generally be no defence to specific performance.[197] However, the court may refuse the order if it would cause the defendant 'a hardship amounting to injustice'.[198] In *Webster v Cecil*,[199] for example, the defendant vendor offered to sell land for £1,250 by mistake instead of £2,250. The plaintiff purchaser must have known that it was a mistake, because earlier the defendant had refused to sell for £2,000. The plaintiff accepted the offer of £1,250 by return of post. The defendant realized his mistake and immediately told the plaintiff. The plaintiff claimed specific performance of the contract, but the court refused specific performance.

192 See, e.g., *Flight v Bolland* [1828] 4 Russ 298; *Lumley v Ravenscroft* [1895] 1 QB 683.

193 [1978] Ch 337. See also *Sutton v Sutton* [1984] Ch 184.

194 [1978] Ch 337 at 357.

195 See, for example, *Keay & Anor v Morris Homes (West Midlands) Ltd* [2012] EWCA Civ 900.

196 *Walker v Boyle* [1982] 1 WLR 495.

197 See *Bashir v Ali* [2011] EWCA Civ 707.

198 *Tamplin v James* [1880] LR 15 Ch D 215 at 221, per James LJ. Compare *Malins v Freeman* [1836] 2 Keen 25.

199 [1861] 30 Beav 62.

(d) Hardship

Specific performance is a discretionary remedy, and the courts may refuse to grant it if it would cause great hardship to the defendant[200] or a third party.[201] In *Patel v Ali*,[202] Mr and Mrs Ali had entered into a contract to sell their house to Mr and Mrs Patel. Mr Ali was then adjudicated bankrupt and spent a year in prison. Mrs Ali was diagnosed as having bone cancer, had a leg amputated just before the birth of her second child, and then subsequently had a third child. In these circumstances, Goulding J refused an order for specific performance on the grounds of the hardship to the plaintiffs. He stressed that:

> The important and true principle . . . is that only in extraordinary and persuasive circumstances can hardship supply an excuse for resisting performance of a contract for the sale of immoveable property . . .[203]

(e) Misdescription of the property

If the property has been misdescribed in a contract for sale, the defendant will be entitled to rescind the contract[204] and resist a claim for specific performance if the property he would be forced to buy was different in substance.[205] The purchaser may, however, choose to take the interest under the contract subject to an abatement of the purchase price in compensation.[206] If the misdescription is slight, so that the purchaser receives substantially what he is entitled to under the contract, the court will order specific performance, subject to the vendor compensating the purchaser, as for example in *Scott v Hanson*,[207] where there was a contract for the sale of 14 acres of water meadow, but only 12 could be so described.

(f) Delay

Equity does not normally regard time as of the essence of a contract[208] and, therefore, specific performance may be granted after the due date for performance. Although there is no statutory time limit to a claim for specific performance,[209] the claimant must not delay unduly because specific performance will not be ordered if, in view of the delay, it would be unjust to either of the parties.[210] A failure to perform a contract by its due date is a breach for which common law damages may be payable whether or not specific performance is available.[211]

[200] *Denne v Light* [1857] 8 De GM & G 774; *Pegler v White* [1864] 33 Beav 403; *Mountford v Scott* [1975] Ch 258; *Shell UK Ltd v Lostock Garage Ltd* [1977] 1 All ER 481; *Cross v Cross* [1983] 12 Fam Law 182.

[201] *Earl of Sefton v Tophams Ltd* [1965] Ch 1140; *Sullivan v Henderson* [1973] 1 WLR 333; *Watts v Spence* [1976] Ch 165; *Cedar Holdings Ltd v Green* [1981] Ch 129.

[202] [1984] Ch 283.

[203] [1984] Ch 283 at 288. See also *Co-operative Insurance v Argyll Stores* [1997] 3 All ER 297.

[204] *Flight v Booth* [1834] 1 Bing NC 370; *Charles Hunt Ltd v Palmer* [1931] 2 Ch 287.

[205] *Re Russ and Brown's Contract* [1934] Ch 34.

[206] *Basma v Weekes* [1950] AC 441.

[207] [1829] 1 Russ & M 128.

[208] *United Scientific Holdings Ltd v Burnley Borough Council* [1978] AC 904. See the discussion of when time will be of the essence by Carter, Courtney, and Tolhurst, 'An assimilated approach to discharge for breach of contract by delay' [2017] CLJ 63.

[209] The normal six-year limitation period under the Limitation Act 1980 does not apply, even where the specific performance claim includes claims for damages for breach of contract—*P&O Nedlloyd BV v Arab Metals Co (No 2)* [2007] 1 WLR 2288.

[210] *Lazard Bros & Co Ltd v Fairfield Properties Co (Mayfair) Ltd* [1977] 121 Sol Jo 793.

[211] *United Scientific Holdings Ltd v Burnley Borough Council* [1978] AC 904.

(7) Damages in lieu of specific performance

(a) Jurisdiction to award damages

The Court of Chancery was given the power to award damages in lieu of specific performance by s 2 of the Chancery Amendment Act 1858.[212] This had the procedural advantage that if a plaintiff was not awarded specific performance, he would not have to start a separate action for damages in the common law courts. After the Judicature Acts of 1873 and 1875, there was no need to rely on the earlier provision, except where damages would not have been available at common law. The Chancery Amendment Act 1858 has been repealed, but its provisions are preserved in the Senior Courts Act 1981, s 50.

(b) Assessment of damages

It is almost certainly the case that the measure of damages is the same, whether based on common law principles or awarded in lieu of specific performance.[213] Megarry J, in *Wroth v Tyler*,[214] sought, by holding that the measure of damages was different, to avoid the old rule that common law damages have to be assessed at the date of breach, but that old rule has now been discredited.[215] In the words of Lord Reed in *One Step (Support) Ltd v Morris-Garner*:[216]

> . . .[I]t is necessary to treat with care Lord Wilberforce's remark in *Johnson v Agnew* [1980] AC 367, 400 that he found in Lord Cairns' Act 'no warrant for the court awarding damages differently from common law damages'. . ..Lord Wilberforce's words should not be read out of context and taken to imply that damages awarded in substitution for an injunction must necessarily be measured in the same way as damages recoverable at common law. That is hardly to be expected, given that the damages are available on a different basis, in different circumstances, and in respect of different types of wrong (past, on the one hand, and future or continuing, on the other).

(8) Effect of order of specific performance

Once an order for specific performance has been granted, the supervision of the contract's performance is in the hands of the court, and the pursuit of alternative remedies such as rescission or cancellation is only possible with the approval of the court.[217]

6 Injunctions

(1) Introduction

Injunctions can be used for a wide variety of purposes, and their scope has evolved considerably over the years. Traditionally, injunctions have been used to prevent breaches of contract or breaches of restrictive covenants affecting land or to restrain the continuation of a public or private nuisance.[218] The late twentieth century saw the development of freezing and search orders. This century has seen the emergence of privacy

[212] Referred to as Lord Cairns' Act. [213] *Johnson v Agnew* [1980] AC 367 per Lord Wilberforce.
[214] [1974] Ch 30. [215] *Hooper v Oates* [2013] EWCA Civ 91.
[216] *One Step (Support) Ltd v Morris-Garner* [2019] AC 649 at [47].
[217] *Quest Advisors Limited Sharriba Ltd v McFeely* [2011] EWCA Civ 1517 at 41.
[218] *Watson v Croft Promo-Sport Ltd* [2009] EWCA Civ 15.

orders, superinjunctions, and notification orders. Injunctions normally order a person[219] to refrain from doing something, such as preventing the sale of a non-alcoholic drink described as 'elderflower champagne'[220] because this would constitute passing off the product as genuine 'champagne'.[221] In some exceptional circumstances, an injunction can have a mandatory effect, operating like specific performance to compel the defendant to do something.

Failure to comply with an injunction will constitute a contempt of court, which may lead to sanctions including imprisonment[222] (the Contempt of Court Act 1981 provides for committal for up to two years), sequestration of property,[223] or a fine.[224] There is also a jurisdiction to award damages.[225] A third party who aids and abets a breach of an interlocutory injunction will also be guilty of contempt,[226] and third parties who nullify the effect of an injunction, for example, by publishing information which others have been ordered not to publish, will be in contempt of court by virtue of their knowing interference with the administration of justice.[227]

The power to grant injunctions, which was originally inherent in the judiciary, is now also conferred by a number of statutory provisions, the most important being s 37 of the Senior Courts Act 1981, which provides that the court can grant an injunction if 'just and convenient'. The discretion given to the judges by this provision must be exercised on settled principles. What follows in the rest of this chapter is very much in outline only, as injunctions, particularly their detailed use in the emerging law of privacy, are deserving of their own chapter.

(2) Types of injunction

(a) Prohibitory and mandatory

A prohibitory injunction orders a person to refrain from, or to discontinue, a wrongful act. A mandatory injunction requires a person to perform some act, and is often given after the wrong has been done and orders its reversal. For example, if a defendant is about to build a structure in circumstances that would be wrongful, a prohibitory injunction would order him not to build. However, if the structure had already been built, a mandatory injunction would order the building to be pulled down.[228] Originally all injunctions had to be given in a prohibitory form, but for over a century, an injunction which is mandatory in substance will be given in a mandatory form.[229]

(b) Perpetual, interlocutory, and interim

A perpetual injunction is granted to defend a claimant's rights after a full hearing. It is a final remedy, even if it does not last for ever as its name might suggest. An interlocutory

[219] An injunction may also be granted against an unnamed person (*Bloomsbury Publishing Group plc v News Group Newspapers* [2003] 1 WLR 1633) or against the members of a class or organization (*M Michaels (Furriers) Ltd v Askew* [1983] The Times, 25 June).

[220] 'Elderflower champagne' is a traditional home-made country drink for which recipes are readily available on the Internet.

[221] *Taittinger SA v Allbev Ltd* [1994] 4 All ER 75.

[222] See, e.g. *Sage v Hewlett Packard Enterprise Company* [2017] EWCA Civ 973 (committal for twelve months for 'flagrant and inexcusable behaviour').

[223] See, e.g. *Tombstone Ltd v Raja* [2008] EWCA Civ 1444.

[224] See, e.g. *Masri v Consolidated Contractors International Company SAL* [2011] EWHC 1024 at 349.

[225] *Khrapunov v JSC BTA Bank* [2017] EWCA Civ 40 at 40.

[226] *Acro (Automation) Ltd v Rex Chainbelt Inc* [1971] 1 WLR 1676.

[227] *AG v Times Newspapers Ltd* [1992] 1 AC 191; *AG v Punch* [2003] 1 AC 1046.

[228] For an example, see *Broadland District Council v Brightwell* [2010] EWCA Civ 1516.

[229] Since *Jackson v Normanby Brick Co* [1899] 1 Ch 438.

injunction is granted in order to preserve the status quo pending a full trial and before the parties' rights have finally been established. An interim injunction is a short-term expedient, often granted where time and urgency require a decision to be made without a hearing.

(c) Injunctions without notice

In urgent cases a claimant will be able to apply for an injunction without giving notice to the defendant (formerly called an ex parte injunction).[230] Where such an injunction is granted, the defendant will subsequently have the opportunity to have the order set aside or varied. Such an injunction should never be given without a limit of time and the opportunity for the respondent to contest the decision. The applicant is also required to draw the judge's attention to all material information, not merely supplying documents without identifying their significance.[231] An ex parte injunction will normally be discharged if it was obtained without full disclosure.[232]

(d) Quia timet injunction

A quia timet[233] injunction is an injunction to prevent a threatened infringement of the claimant's rights that has not yet taken place.[234]

(e) Superinjunction

A superinjunction is an order preventing the disclosure of information which also prohibits disclosure of the existence of the injunction. Most cases involve the protection of privacy, but they may also be used in other situations. In *W (Algeria) v Secretary of State for the Home Department*,[235] it was suggested that in exceptional circumstances, which would be very rare indeed, a superinjunction may be justified to prevent disclosure of the identity of a witness who was otherwise likely to face recriminations.

(f) Undertakings to the court

The need for an injunction can sometimes be avoided by the party concerned giving an undertaking to the court that he will, or will not, do something. Such an undertaking is binding in a similar way to a court order, since a failure to comply will constitute a contempt of court.[236] The breach of an undertaking can be enforced in the same way as the breach of an injunction.[237]

(3) General principles governing perpetual injunctions

(a) Damages would be an inadequate remedy

An injunction will only be awarded if damages would prove an inadequate remedy.[238] That will frequently be the case where there is a continuing infringement of the claimant's rights. An injunction is not available for a past infringement that will not be repeated. Damages may be inadequate simply because the defendant has no means of paying them.[239] Where the court is being asked to enforce an express negative contractual

[230] The change was introduced by the Civil Procedure Rules (CPR) 1998.

[231] *R (Khan) v Secretary of State for the Home Department* [2016] EWCA Civ 416 at 40.

[232] *Brink's Mat Ltd v Elcombe* [1988] 1 WLR 1350.

[233] The name comes from the Latin and means 'he who fears'.

[234] See *Redland Bricks Ltd v Morris* [1970] AC 652.

[235] [2012] UKSC 8.

[236] See *Edgerton v Edgerton* [2012] EWCA Civ 181, where a freezing order was discharged on the giving of an undertaking having similar effect.

[237] *Mid Suffolk District Council v Clarke* [2006] EWCA Civ 71 (fine imposed and committal considered).

[238] *London and Blackwall Rly Co v Cross* [1886] 31 Ch D 354.

[239] *Hodgson v Duce* [1856] 28 LTos 155.

obligation, the requirement to prove damage does not apply because of equity's perception that it is unconscionable for the defendant to ignore his bargain.[240]

(b) An infringement of the claimant's rights

In *Paton v British Pregnancy Advisory Service Trustees*, Sir George Baker P stated:

> the first and basic principle is that there must be a legal right enforceable in law or in equity before the applicant can obtain an injunction from the court to restrain an infringement of that right.[241]

In that case, the court refused to grant a husband an injunction to prevent his pregnant wife having a lawful abortion because he had no right that was thereby infringed.[242] In *Day v Brownrigg*,[243] the Court of Appeal refused to grant an injunction restraining the defendant from giving his house the same name as that of the plaintiff, his next door neighbour, because this did not infringe any of the plaintiff's legal or equitable rights. Where rights conflict, the court must weigh and balance the conflicting rights. For instance, in *Jones v Canal and River Trust*,[244] Mr Jones was using a canal boat as his home, but had moored it in contravention of the licence from the canal authority. The court had to balance his rights under Art 8 of the European Convention on Human Rights against the authority's duty to manage the waterway by enforcing licence conditions. Mr Jones' rights could not be dismissed summarily.

In some cases, using what is known as the springboard principle, future actions will be prohibited, even if they are lawful, in order to prevent a defendant from taking advantage of previous unlawful activities: 'the question of springboard relief is whether the effect of past wrongdoing continues to confer a present and future benefit on the wrongdoer which the court should prevent.'[245]

(c) Clarity of order

Just as with an order for specific performance, the terms of an injunction must be sufficiently clear to allow those affected to know when they have infringed the terms of the order. As Lady Hale and Lord Toulson said in *OPO v Rhodes*:

> Any injunction must be framed in terms sufficiently specific to leave no uncertainty about what the affected person is or is not allowed to do.[246]

Clarity can be achieved by reference to objective standards, or to the opinion of an expert.[247] When enforcing an injunction, whilst the normal principles of construction of legal instruments apply:[248]

> the terms in which it was made are to be restrictively construed. Such are the penal consequences of breach that the Order must be clear and unequivocal and strictly construed before a party will be found to have broken the terms of the Order and thus to be in contempt of Court.[249]

240 *Dyson Technology Ltd v Pellerey* [2016] EWCA Civ 87 at 34.

241 [1979] QB 76. See also *North London Rly Co v Great Northern Rly Co* [1883] 11 QBD 30, CA; *Re C* [1991] 2 FLR 168.

242 See also *C v S* [1988] QB 135.

243 [1878] 10 Ch D 294.

244 [2017] EWCA Civ 135.

245 *Willis Ltd v Jardine Lloyd Thompson Group Plc* [2015] EWCA Civ 450 at 22.

246 [2015] UKSC 32 at 79, citing Lord Nichols' similar statement in *Attorney General v Punch Ltd* [2002] UKHL 50 at 35.

247 *Morgan v Hinton Organics (Wessex) Ltd* [2009] EWCA Civ 107 approving *Environment Agency v Biffa Waste Services Ltd* [2006] EWHC 3495 (Admin).

248 *Sans Souci Limited v VRL Services Limited* [2012] UKPC 6.

249 Flaux J in *Pan Petroleum Aje Ltd v Yinka Folawiyo Petroleum Co Ltd* [2017] EWCA Civ 1525 at [41].

(d) Grant of an injunction is discretionary

The award of an injunction is at the court's discretion, like any equitable remedy, although a party who establishes an infringement of his right should be granted an injunction unless there are special circumstances.[250] An injunction will not be available in circumstances where no common law or equitable redress is possible, for instance, where a statutory duty provides an exclusive enforcement mechanism:[251]

> The claim for an injunction does indeed enable the court to exercise a discretion, but only as to the choice of remedy, i.e. damages or injunction, not as to granting any remedy at all.[252]

(i) Prohibitory injunctions

Some prohibitory injunctions are in practice available almost as of right.[253]

The fact that a claimant has only suffered nominal or very small damage from the infringement of his right does not prevent the court awarding an injunction,[254] although it is a factor to be taken into account.[255] In *Behrens v Richards*,[256] Buckley J refused an injunction against the defendants who were trespassing on the plaintiff's land because their use of a path caused no damage. However, a more strict approach to trespass was taken in *Patel v WH Smith (Eziot) Ltd*,[257] where the Court of Appeal held that only in very rare cases would an injunction be refused to restrain a continuing trespass.[258]

(ii) Mandatory injunctions

Lord Upjohn stated the principle in *Redland Bricks Ltd v Morris*:

> the grant of a mandatory injunction is . . . entirely discretionary and unlike a negative injunction can never be 'as of course'. Every case must depend essentially upon its own particular circumstances.[259]

He held that the question of the cost to the defendant to do the works necessary was an element to be taken into account in determining whether an injunction should be granted. For this reason, the House of Lords refused to grant a mandatory injunction requiring the defendants to perform remedial work costing some £35,000 to their land, to provide support for the plaintiff's land which was only worth £1,500. In *Wrotham Park Estate Co Ltd v Parkside Homes Ltd*,[260] Brightman J refused to grant a mandatory injunction requiring the demolition of houses which had been built in contravention of a restrictive covenant because he felt that it would be 'an unpardonable waste of much needed houses'.[261] Obviously, the defendant's conduct is a major factor that will be taken into consideration in determining whether a mandatory injunction should be awarded. As Lord Upjohn said in *Redland Bricks Ltd v Morris*:

> where the defendant has acted without regard to his neighbour's rights and has tried to steal a march on him or has tried to evade the jurisdiction of the court or . . . has acted wantonly

[250] *HTC Corporation v Nokia Corporation* [2013] EWHC 3778 (Pat) at 8; *Harrow London Borough Council v Donohue* [1995] 1 EGLR 257.

[251] *O'Reilly v Mackman* [1983] 2 AC 237.

[252] *An Bord Bainne Co-operative Limited (Irish Dairy Board) v Milk Marketing Board* [1984] 2 CMLR 584 at 15.

[253] *Doherty v Allman* [1878] 3 App Cas 709 at 720 per Lord Cairns LC.

[254] See, for example. *Woollerton & Wilson Ltd v Richard Costain Ltd* [1970] 1 WLR 411.

[255] *Society of Architects v Kendrick* [1910] 26 TLR 433; *Society of Accountants and Auditors v Goodway* [1907] 1 Ch 489.

[256] [1905] 2 Ch 614.

[257] [1987] 2 All ER 569. See also *Trenberth (John) Ltd v National Westminster Bank Ltd* [1980] 39 P & CR 104.

[258] Trespass to land is a tort.

[259] [1970] AC 652 at 665.

[260] [1974] 1 WLR 798.

[261] [1974] 1 WLR 798 at 811.

> and quite unreasonably in relation to his neighbour he may be ordered to repair his wanton and unreasonable acts by doing positive work to restore the status quo even if the expense to him is out of all proportion to the advantage thereby accruing to the plaintiff.[262]

(e) Court order unlikely to be ineffective

Since 'the court should not normally make orders which it does not intend, or will be unable, to enforce',[263] there may be cases where an injunction should not be granted because of the likelihood that it will be disregarded and the lack of practicable means of enforcement (perhaps because the defendant has no means and is unlikely to be committed to prison for contempt). However, the grant of an injunction may still be merited if it has some deterrent effect and there is some prospect of enforcement, for instance through a suspended order of imprisonment.[264] In *Secretary of State for Environment, Food and Rural Affairs (Respondent) v Meier*[265] the Supreme Court approved the grant of an injunction to prevent travellers trespassing on Forestry Commission land even though it was unlikely that the injunction would be enforced by imprisonment or sequestration of assets.

The court is, therefore, likely to respond robustly to a defendant who:

> says it cannot be performed or will not be performed . . . There is a sound practical reason why the court should adopt that approach, for otherwise one is simply giving the potentially obdurate the opportunity to escape the penalties for contempt by persuading the court not to make the order in the first place.[266]

(f) Delay and acquiescence

The court may refuse an injunction if the claimant has delayed for an inordinate time,[267] although where an injunction is refused for reasons of delay, a claimant may be entitled to damages in lieu.[268] His failure to seek interlocutory relief may also be relevant to a refusal to grant an injunction.[269] Equally, there will be no injunction if the claimant has acquiesced and waived his rights.[270] In *Fisher v Brooker*,[271] one of the composers of Procol Harum's iconic song 'A Whiter Shade of Pale' (which was first released in 1967) sought to enforce his rights in 2005. His rights as a co-composer had never previously been acknowledged, and he had, therefore, received no royalties. The House of Lords held that he was not debarred by the significant length of time from bringing an action, although the delay would be relevant in deciding whether to grant an injunction against future exploitation of the work. The Lords' view was that in order for delay to justify a denial of equitable relief, some sort of detrimental reliance would usually be needed.[272]

[262] [1970] AC 652 at 666. See *Woodhouse v Newry Navigation Co* [1898] 1 IR 161, CA.

[263] *Secretary of State for Environment, Food, and Rural Affairs v Meier* [2009] UKSC 11 at [80], per Lord Neuberger.

[264] See *Secretary of State for Environment, Food, and Rural Affairs v Meier* [2009] UKSC 11 at [16], [39], and [81].

[265] [2009] UKSC 11. At [17] and [32] per Lord Rodgers.

[266] Sir James Munby in *MM (A Patient)* [2017] EWCA Civ 34 at 13, citing his own statement in *Re Jones (No 2)* [2014] EWHC 2730 (Fam) at 15.

[267] *H P Bulmer Ltd and Showerings Ltd v J Bollinger SA* [1977] 2 CMLR 625, CA (where, technically, the opinions expressed were obiter). Cf *Newport Association Football Club Ltd v Football Association of Wales Ltd* [1995] 2 All ER 87, where, on the facts, there was not felt to be unreasonable delay.

[268] *Shelfer v City of London Electric Lighting Co (No 1)* [1895] 1 Ch 287; *Bracewell v Appleby* [1975] Ch 408; *Ketley v Gooden* [1996] EGCS 47.

[269] See *Shaw v Applegate* [1977] 1 WLR 970, CA.

[270] *Blue Town Investments Ltd v Higgs and Hill plc* [1990] 1 WLR 696.

[271] [2009] 1 WLR 1764.

[272] [2009] 1 WLR 1764 at 64, per Lord Neuberger.

(g) Claimant must come with 'clean hands'

A claimant will only be granted an injunction if he himself comes seeking the aid of equity with 'clean hands'. Breach of his own obligations or unfair conduct[273] will disentitle him to relief, as will his own refusal to carry out his future obligations.[274]

(h) Damages in lieu of an injunction

Under the Chancery Amendment Act 1858 (Lord Cairns' Act), the court has jurisdiction to award damages in substitution for the award of an injunction. The jurisdiction remains, despite the repeal of this Act.[275] In general, the courts will only award damages in substitution in exceptional circumstances.[276]

(i) When damages will be awarded

For many years the generally adopted 'good working rule'[277] as to when damages should be awarded in substitution was that set out by AL Smith LJ in *Shelfer v City of London Electric Lighting Co (No 1)*:

(1) If the injury to the plaintiff's legal rights is small; and
(2) is one which is capable of being estimated in money; and
(3) is one which can be adequately compensated by a small money payment; and
(4) the case is one in which it would be oppressive[278] to the defendant to grant an injunction.[279]

The rule was accepted by the Court of Appeal in *Kennaway v Thompson*,[280] where the court reversed the decision of the judge at first instance to award damages in substitution because the first three criteria of the rule had not been met. Similarly, it was applied by the Court of Appeal in *Jaggard v Sawyer*,[281] (a case involving trespass) although Millett LJ emphasized that it provided 'only a working rule and does not purport to be an exhaustive statement of the circumstances in which damages may be awarded instead of an injunction'.[282] Other factors may be taken into account: for example, delay in bringing an action,[283] or a willingness, expressed in pre-trial correspondence, to accept financial compensation.[284]

In *Coventry v Lawrence*,[285] the Supreme Court considered that the guidelines set out in *Shelfer* were too prescriptive.[286] Lord Neuberger thought that while the starting point should be that an injunction should normally be available, 'the court's power to award damages in lieu of an injunction involves a classic exercise of discretion, which should

273 *Shell UK Ltd v Lostock Garage Bros Ltd* [1977] 1 All ER 481. The conduct must concern the subject matter of the dispute in relation to which the injunction is sought: *Argyll v Argyll* [1967] Ch 302.

274 *Measures v Measures* [1910] 2 Ch 248; *Chappell v Times Newspapers Ltd* [1975] 1 WLR 482.

275 Senior Courts Act (formerly the Supreme Court Act) 1981, s 50; *Leeds Industrial Co-operative Society Ltd v Slack* [1924] AC 851, HL.

276 *Imperial Gas Light and Coke Co v Broadbent* [1859] 7 HL Cas 600; *Shelfer v City of London Electric Lighting Co (No 1)* [1895] 1 Ch 287, CA; *Sefton v Tophams Ltd* [1965] Ch 1140.

277 See *Watson v Croft Promosport Ltd* [2009] 3 All ER 249; *Regan Paul Properties DPF No 1 Ltd* [2007] Ch 125.

278 It has been suggested that the test for this is whether the remedy is disproportionate to the wrong: *Navitaire Inc v EasyJet Airline Co Ltd (No. 2)* [2005] EWHC 282 (Ch), [2006] RPC 4.

279 [1895] 1 Ch 287.

280 [1981] QB 88. See also *Wakeham v Wood* [1982] 43 P & CR 40, CA.

281 [1995] 2 All ER 189.

282 [1995] 2 All ER 189 at 208.

283 *Pilford v Greenmanor Ltd* [2012] EWCA Civ 756.

284 *Gafford v Graham* [1999] 77 P & CR 73.

285 [2014] UKSC 13. This case is also known as *Lawrence v Fen Tigers Ltd.*

286 [2014] UKSC 13 per Lord Neuberger at [119–23]; Lord Sumption at [161]; Lord Mance at [167]; Lord Clarke at [171]; Lord Carnwath at [239].

not, as a matter of principle, be fettered'.[287] The *Shelfer* tests should be treated only as guidelines which should not be mechanically applied, and they did not exclude the importance of having regard to any other relevant factors.[288] A particularly important factor was the public interest. The court should have regard to such matters as how many people are adversely affected by the activity complained of, and also to the positive effects of the activity, such as providing employment or leisure activities. Lord Sumption (who was not supported on this point by the majority of the court) would have started from the proposition that damages should normally be treated as an adequate remedy for cases involving a nuisance where the activity had required and had received planning permission. The Supreme Court recognized that the new, less directive principles would have to be developed on a case-by-case basis in future decisions.

(ii) The measure of damages

The quantum (measure) of damages that may be awarded in lieu of an injunction has been a matter of some controversy. In *Johnson v Agnew*,[289] the House of Lords held that, where damages would have been available at common law, the court only possessed the jurisdiction to award damages on the same compensatory basis. However, in some cases, the courts awarded damages in lieu of an injunction or specific performance even where there had been no obvious loss, suggesting that equity might adopt a measure of damages different from that at common law. In *Wrotham Park Estate Co Ltd v Parkside Homes Ltd*,[290] for example, Brightman J refused an injunction to demolish houses built in breach of covenant, but granted the plaintiff damages in substitution. The plaintiff had suffered no loss in terms of a reduction in value of his land, so as the common law rule on damages was understood at the time, damages would have been purely nominal. Nevertheless, substantial damages were awarded, equivalent to the sum of money that might reasonably have been demanded by the plaintiffs for relaxing the restrictive covenant. This type of damages are sometimes described as damages for loss of a bargaining opportunity, or as 'negotiating damages'[291] or 'gain-based' damages.[292] In *Surrey County Council v Bredero Homes Ltd*,[293] Dillon LJ questioned whether this measure of compensation was consistent with *Johnson v Agnew*. Subsequent decisions have resolved the conflict by holding that damages for loss of a bargaining opportunity are compensatory and can be awarded at common law.[294] The hypothetical negotiation method of calculating damages continues to be used at first instance[295] and has been endorsed by the Court of Appeal[296] and the Privy Council.[297] The significant difference is that in equity, where damages are awarded in lieu of an injunction, they can compensate for future as well as for past losses.[298] Lord Nicholls explained in *A-G v Blake*[299] that although Lord Cairns' Act did not alter the measure to be employed in assessing damages, it did enable the court to award damages in respect of the future as well as the past, so that the damages awarded in lieu of an

[287] [2014] UKSC 13 per Lord Neuberger at [120]. [288] [2014] UKSC 13 per Lord Neuberger at [123].

[289] [1980] AC 367. [290] [1974] 1 WLR 798.

[291] *Force India Formula One Team Ltd v 1 Malaysia Racing Team Sdn Bhd* [2012] EWHC 616 (Ch), [2012] RPC 29 at 383–6. [292] *Coventry v Lawrence* [2014] UKSC 13.

[293] [1993] 3 All ER 705. [294] See *Jaggard v Sawyer* [1995] 2 All ER 189.

[295] *Gott v Lawrence* [2016] EWHC 68 (Ch) 75–81.

[296] *Burrows Investments Ltd v Ward Homes Ltd* [2017] EWCA Civ 1577; *Raymond v Young* [2015] EWCA Civ 456 at 13.

[297] *Pell Frischmann Engineering Ltd v Bow Valley Ltd* [2009] UKPC 45.

[298] *HTC Corporation v Nokia Corporation* [2013] EWHC 3778 (Pat); *Jaggard v Sawyer* [1995] 2 All ER 189 at 201–2, per Sir Thomas Bingham MR. [299] [2000] 4 All ER 385.

injunction could include losses likely to follow from the anticipated future continuance of the wrong as well as losses already suffered:

> The Court's refusal to grant an injunction means that in practice the defendant is thereby permitted to perpetuate the wrongful state of affairs he has brought about.[300]

The House of Lords has, therefore, approved *Wrotham Park Estates,* and doubted *Surrey County Council v Breredo Homes.*[301] The same general approach was approved by the Supreme Court in *Star Energy Weald Basin Ltd v Bocardo SA,*[302] although in that case, damages were limited by the Petroleum (Production) Act 1934 to the current market value of the rights lost by the claimants.

In *One Step (Support) Ltd v Morris-Garner,*[303] the Supreme Court upheld the use of negotiation damages as one (but not the only) means of quantifying the loss which a person suffers where damages are awarded in substitution for specific performance or an injunction. It considered that the method was less widely available for assessing common law damages for breach of contract, but could still be an appropriate tool for arriving at a valuation of a lost asset where the claimant has been deprived of a valuable asset: the rationale being that the wrongful use of the property has prevented the owner from exercising a valuable right to control its use, and the wrongdoer should therefore compensate the owner for this loss.

(i) Suspension of injunctions

In some circumstances the court will suspend an injunction so that it does not have immediate effect.[304] This may be because it may not be possible to immediately cease the infringing activity. In *Pride of Derby and Derbyshire Angling Association Ltd v British Celanese Ltd,*[305] for example, the Court of Appeal suspended an injunction made against the defendants who polluted a river with sewage, giving them time to remedy the nuisance they were causing. In *Waverley Borough Council v Hilden,*[306] Scott J suspended an injunction requiring travellers to remove their caravans from an unauthorized site for three months to give them 'a reasonable time to comply with the order'. However, the courts have disapproved of the suspension granted in *Woollerton and Wilson Ltd v Richard Costain Ltd,*[307] which amounted to a licence for the defendants to continue trespassing in the plaintiff's airspace.[308]

(j) Declarations

In *Greenwich Healthcare National Health Service Trust v London and Quadrant,*[309] Lightman J held that the court has power to grant a declaration that a defendant will not be entitled to an injunction if the claimant engages in a particular course of conduct. The case concerned re-development of a hospital, which would infringe a right of way[310]

[300] [2000] 4 All ER 385 at 394.

[301] See *Tamares (Vincent Square) Ltd v Fairpoint Properties (Vincent Square Ltd)* [2007] 1 WLR 2148, where similar principles were applied in deciding the measure of damages to be awarded for interference with a right to light to a building.

[302] [2010] UKSC 35. [303] [2018] UKSC 20.

[304] See, for example, *Miller v Jackson* [1977] QB 966, CA; *Waverley Borough Council v Hilden* [1988] 1 WLR 246.

[305] [1953] Ch 149. [306] [1988] 1 WLR 246. [307] [1970] 1 WLR 411.

[308] See *Jaggard v Sawyer* [1995] 2 All ER 189 at 199. Contrast *Kelsen v Imperial Tobacco Co of Great Britain and Ireland Ltd* [1957] 2 QB 334.

[309] [1998] 3 All ER 437.

[310] This ownership was by means of an easement, which is an interest in land enjoyed by one landowner (the dominant owner) over the land of another landowner (the servient owner). See further Bevan, *Land Law* (3rd edn, OUP 2022) Chapter 11.

belonging to the defendant and Lightman J was prepared to make the declaration that any future breaches of the right would be limited to redress by means of damages. Lightman J observed:

> The jurisdiction of the court to grant declarations must extend to entitlement both to proprietary rights and to particular remedies. Circumstances may exist when a declaration, e.g. that a defendant is not entitled to specific performance, rectification or an injunction, is necessary if a period of damaging (or indeed paralyzing) uncertainty is to be voided, and indeed the occasion for an unwarranted ransom demand is to be removed. The law is sufficiently adaptable to grant declarations which are necessary to dispel uncertainties and remove obstacles to progress and legitimate activities.[311]

(4) **General principles governing interlocutory injunctions**

Unlike permanent injunctions, which are granted to protect a claimant's established rights, an interlocutory injunction is granted to preserve the status quo between the claimant and the defendant before their respective rights can be determined at trial. As Lord Wilberforce said in *Hoffmann-La Roche (F) & Co AG v Secretary of State for Trade and Industry*:

> The object is to prevent a litigant, who must necessarily suffer the law's delay, from losing by that delay the fruit of his litigation.[312]

At a hearing relating to an interlocutory injunction the court will not normally be concerned with resolving doubts raised by conflicting affidavit evidence.[313]

(a) **When should an interlocutory injunction be granted?**

The principles by which the court should determine whether to grant an interlocutory injunction were outlined by Lord Diplock in the leading case of *American Cyanamid Co v Ethicon Ltd*[314] Subsequent cases have held that the principles are not 'rules', but rather, guidelines with room for flexibility.[315] It was initially considered that in *American Cyanamid*, the House of Lords had rejected earlier authorities holding that a claimant was required to demonstrate a prima facie case before an interlocutory injunction could be granted[316] in favour of a lower threshold which required the claimant merely to demonstrate that there was a 'serious question to be tried'. However, in *Series 5 Software Ltd v Clarke*,[317] Laddie J questioned this orthodoxy and provided a reinterpretation of *American Cyanamid* requiring the court to take into account the strength of the parties' respective cases on the evidence. He especially pointed to the decision of the House of Lords in *Hoffmann-La Roche (F) & Co AG v Secretary of State for Trade and Industry*,[318] which had been decided a few months before *American Cyanamid*, but which was not cited in the subsequent case. There, Lord Diplock had suggested that the award of an interlocutory injunction was conditional upon the claimant demonstrating a 'strong prima facie case

311 [1998] 3 All ER 437 at 444. 312 [1975] AC 295 at 355.

313 *Re H (Minors) (sexual abuse: standard of proof)* [1996] AC 364 at 589.

314 [1975] AC 396, HL; see, for example, C Gray, 'Interlocutory Injunctions since Cyanamid' [1981] 40 CLJ 307.

315 See, e.g. *Cambridge Nutrition Ltd v BBC* [1990] 3 All ER 523, CA; *Factortame Ltd v Secretary of State for Transport (No 2)* [1991] 1 All ER 70; *Kirklees MBC v Wickes Building Supplies Ltd* [1993] AC 227.

316 *Preston v Luck* [1884] 27 Ch D 497; *Smith v Grigg Ltd* [1924] 1 KB 655, CA; *JT Stratford & Son Ltd v Lindley* [1965] AC 269. Compare also *Fellowes & Son v Fisher* [1976] QB 122; *Hubbard v Pitt* [1976] QB 142.

317 [1996] 1 All ER 853. 318 [1975] AC 295.

that he will be entitled to a final order'.[319] Having concluded that the prospects of success at trial were relevant, Laddie J indicated the matters that he thought the court should take into account in deciding whether to grant an injunction:

(1) The grant of an interlocutory injunction is a matter of discretion and depends on all the facts of the case.
(2) There are no fixed rules as to when an injunction should or should not be granted. The relief must be kept flexible.
(3) Because of the practice adopted on the hearing of applications for interlocutory relief, the court should rarely attempt to resolve complex issues of disputed fact or law.
(4) Major factors the court can bear in mind are (a) the extent to which damages are likely to be an adequate remedy for each party and the ability of the other party to pay, (b) the balance of convenience, (c) the maintenance of the status quo, and (d) any clear view the court may reach as to the relative strengths of the parties' cases.[320]

He refused to award an interlocutory injunction despite the fact that the plaintiff's case was 'arguable in the sense that it is possible that the facts at the trial may support the allegation it makes' because he was 'not impressed with its strength'.[321] Laddie J's view has been praised as restoring judicial discretion to an area that was in danger of becoming 'so encrusted with expectations as to how that discretion should be exercised that it too had established a tyranny'.[322] Subsequent decisions have mostly taken *American Cyanamid* as the starting point, but some have recognized that there are circumstances where the strength of the parties' relative cases should also be a factor.

(b) The *American Cyanamid* guidelines

Applying *American Cyanamid*, the following factors must be taken into account by the court to determine whether an interlocutory injunction should be granted.

(i) 'A serious question to be tried'

Although the claimant does not need to establish a prima facie case, Lord Diplock held that 'the court . . . must be satisfied that the claim is not frivolous or vexatious; in other words that there is a serious question to be tried'. Only if the plaintiff fails to show any real prospect of succeeding in his claim at trial should the court refuse the injunction without going on to consider the balance of convenience.

(ii) The 'balance of convenience'

Once the claimant has shown that there is a serious issue, the court must weigh the balance of convenience between granting and refusing an injunction, and the effect that this would have on the respective parties if the issue was determined in favour of that party at trial. The court must assess the adequacy of damages as a remedy for any loss the parties may suffer in consequence of the grant or refusal of an injunction. Lord Diplock explained the issues to be considered:

> [T]he court should first consider whether, if the plaintiff were to succeed at the trial in establishing his right to a permanent injunction, he would be adequately compensated by an award of damages for the loss he would have sustained as a result of the defendant's continuing to do what was sought to be enjoined between the time of the application and the time of

[319] [1975] AC 295 at 360–1. [320] [1996] 1 All ER 853 at 865. [321] Ibid at 867.

[322] Phillips, 'Interlocutory Injunctions and Intellectual Property: a review of *American Cyanamid v Ethicon* in the Light of *Series 5 Software*' [1997] JBL 486 at 487, reviewing the cases decided since *Series 5 Software*.

> the trial. If damages in the measure recoverable at common law would be adequate remedy and the defendant would be in a financial position to pay them, no interlocutory injunction should normally be granted, however strong the plaintiff's claim appeared to be at that stage. If, on the other hand, damages would not provide an adequate remedy for the plaintiff in the event of his succeeding at the trial, the court should then consider whether, on the contrary hypothesis that the defendant were to succeed at the trial in establishing his right to do that which was sought to be enjoined, he would be adequately compensated under the plaintiff's undertaking as to damages for the loss he would have sustained by being prevented from doing so between the time of the application and the time of the trial. If damages in the measure recoverable under such an undertaking would be an adequate remedy and the plaintiff would be in a financial position to pay them, there would be no reason upon this ground to refuse an interlocutory injunction.[323]

He concluded that where the factors appear to be evenly balanced, 'it is a counsel of prudence to take such measures as preserve the status quo'. This exercise of weighing the 'balance of convenience' has also been described as the 'balance of the risk of doing an injustice',[324] or, in other words, finding the balance of convenience requires that the balance of inconvenience between the parties be considered.

One of the constraints faced by the Home Secretary seeking to remove illegal immigrants is that an injunction against removal may be sought. These cases present real problems for the courts because the consequence of removal may be severe, but equally, 'there is a strong public interest in permitting a public authority's decision to continue'.[325]

(iii) 'Other special factors to be taken into consideration'

Lord Diplock also recognized that there 'may be many other special factors to be taken into consideration in the particular circumstances of individual cases'.[326] For example, in *American Cyanamid*[327] itself, where the plaintiffs sought an interlocutory injunction to prevent the defendants launching a surgical product claimed to be in breach of the plaintiffs' patent, a number of additional factors were taken into account, including the fact that the defendants as yet had no business which would be brought to a stop by the injunction; that the launch of the defendants' product would prevent the plaintiffs' patented product becoming established in the market; and that if the defendants' product was allowed on the market before trial and patients and doctors became used to it, it might be impracticable for the plaintiffs to insist on a permanent injunction at trial. For these reasons the House of Lords held that an interlocutory injunction should be granted. The public interest, and the interests of the public in general may also be factors to be taken into account in determining whether an interlocutory injunction should be granted.[328] In *Themehelp Ltd v West*,[329] the Court of Appeal was asked to grant an interlocutory injunction preventing the enforcement of a performance bond pending a fraud trial. The court was prepared to grant the order, but recognized that the situations in which such orders should be granted had to be considered with care lest they disturb the mercantile practice that performance bonds should normally be treated as autonomous guarantees that could be enforced regardless of any problems extraneous to the guarantee itself.

[323] [1975] AC 396 at 408.

[324] *Cayne v Global Natural Resources plc* [1984] 1 All ER 225 at 237, per May LJ.

[325] See the discussion of the issues in *R (SB (Afghanistan)) v The Secretary of State for the Home Department* [2018] EWCA Civ 215.

[326] *Bryanston Finance Ltd v de Vries (No 2)* [1976] Ch 63; *A-G v Guardian Newspapers Ltd* [1987] 1 WLR 1248.

[327] [1975] AC 396.

[328] See *Smith v Inner London Education Authority* [1978] 1 All ER 411, CA; *Factortame Ltd v Secretary of State for Transport (No 2)* [1991] 1 All ER 70 at 118–19, per Lord Goff.

[329] [1995] 4 All ER 215.

Goods commercially shipped in bulk are frequently paid for by means of what is known as an irrevocable letter of credit. This is an instruction to a bank to make payment when certain conditions are satisfied, for instance, when the bank is provided with a document certifying that the goods have been loaded on board the ship which is transporting them. In order to facilitate certainty that such payments will be honoured, the courts have adopted the principle that, even if liability to make the payment is disputed, the bank cannot refuse payment unless the demand for payment is made fraudulently and the bank is aware of the fraud. In *Alternative Power Solution Ltd v Central Electricity Board*,[330] the Privy Council held that before an interlocutory injunction to prevent a bank making payment under a letter of credit could be ordered:

> it must be clearly established at the interlocutory stage that the only realistic inference is (a) that the beneficiary could not honestly have believed in the validity of its demands under the letter of credit and (b) that the bank was aware of the fraud.[331]

This test, which requires a case which is stronger than a good arguable case, is a much stricter test than the test under *American Cyanamid* of a serious issue to be tried. Even when this test has been surmounted, it is still necessary to demonstrate that the balance of convenience requires the grant of an injunction, and this will very rarely be possible 'because the balance of convenience will almost always militate against the grant of an injunction.'[332]

(iv) 'Real prospect of trial'

Although an interlocutory injunction is intended to preserve the status quo before the final determination of the issue at trial, it is inevitable that in many cases the matter will go no further. In some cases, this will be because the parties settle on the basis of the injunction granted.[333] In others it is because the injunction would no longer be relevant. The application of the *American Cyanamid* principles assumes the prospect of a full trial in which the 'arguable case' will be tested. One response is to apply the principles only where a future trial is likely to take place.[334] Another is to require a stronger case to be demonstrated where a future trial is unlikely. For example, where an injunction is sought to prevent a strike, the impetus for the strike may have disappeared by the time a trial could take place. This will affect the balance between the parties, and 'in disputes of this nature it is incumbent on them [the courts] to have regard to the underlying merits of the claim'.[335]

(c) Other considerations

(i) Breach of a negative covenant

The balance of convenience does not normally need to be considered where an injunction is sought to enforce an express contractual undertaking not to do something.[336] As Jackson LJ said in *Araci v Fallon*:[337]

> Where the defendant is proposing to act in clear breach of a negative covenant, in other words to do something which he has promised not to do, there must be special circumstances

[330] [2014] UKPC 31. [331] [2014] UKPC 31 at [59]. [332] Ibid at 89.

[333] See *Fellowes & Son v Fisher* [1976] QB 122 at 133, per Lord Denning MR, who suggested that 99 cases out of 100 go no further than the grant of an interlocutory injunction. Reasons include the expense of litigation in both time and money.

[334] *Cayne v Global Natural Resources plc* [1984] 1 All ER 225 at 234. See also *Transfield Shipping Inc v Chiping Xinta Huaya Alumina Co Ltd* [2009] EWHC 3642 (Comm) at 51–2.

[335] *National Union of Rail, Maritime & Transport Workers v Serco Ltd (t/a Serco Docklands)* [2011] EWCA Civ 226 at 12.

[336] *Doherty v Allman* [1878] 3 App Cas 709 at 720 (Lord Cairns LC).

[337] [2011] EWCA Civ 668 at 39. See also *Hampstead and Suburban Properties Limited v Diomedous* [1969] 1 Ch 248 and *Attorney General v Barton* [1990] 3 All ER 257.

(e.g. restraint of trade contrary to public policy) before the court will exercise its discretion to refuse an injunction.

(ii) Freedom of expression

The principles by which it is determined whether an interlocutory injunction should be granted are different in cases involving a breach of confidence, privacy, or libel because of the effect of the Human Rights Act 1998, which incorporates into English Law Art 10 of the European Convention on Human Rights protecting freedom of expression. Section 12(3) of the Human Rights Act provides that the court should not grant relief unless it 'is satisfied that the applicant is likely to re-establish that the publication should not be allowed'. It follows that in such cases the courts must look at the strength of the claimant's case before granting an interlocutory injunction, and not simply apply the usual 'balance of convenience' test. An interlocutory injunction will therefore only be granted if the claimant can show that he would probably succeed at trail, unless the consequences of publication would be especially serious.[338] Even where the claimant can demonstrate the likelihood of success, the court may refuse an injunction and leave the claimant to a remedy in damages if the 'balance of convenience' favours refusing the award of an injunction.[339]

(iii) Approach on appeal

An appellate court will be slow to overturn the decision of a trial judge unless there is some error of law, the judge was mistaken about the facts, or there are new circumstances.[340]

(d) **Undertaking in damages**

On the grant of an interlocutory injunction the claimant is generally required to give an undertaking in damages to the defendant. By this undertaking, made to the court,[341] the claimant is liable to pay the defendant damages for any loss he has suffered as a result of the grant of the interlocutory injunction prior to the full hearing if at the subsequent trial it appears that the injunction should not have been granted.[342] In *AstraZeneca AB v KRKA dd Novo Mesto*,[343] an award of £27 million damages (said to be the largest award ever made by the Patents Court in a case of this kind) was upheld.

There is no need for an undertaking in damages in matrimonial proceedings,[344] or where the Crown seeks an injunction to enforce the general law[345] rather than its own proprietary right.[346]

(e) **Mandatory interlocutory injunctions**

The courts are more reluctant to award mandatory interlocutory injunctions, and it seems that a higher test may have to be satisfied than that set out in *American Cyanamid*,[347] which involved a prohibitory injunction. In *De Falco v Crawley Borough Council*,[348] Lord

338 *Cream Holdings Ltd v Banerjee* [2004] 3 WLR 918.

339 *Douglas v Hello! Ltd* [2001] QB 967. See Morgan, 'Confidence and Horizontal Effect; "Hello" Trouble' [2003] 62 CLJ 444.

340 *Hadmor Productions v Hamilton* [1983] 1 AC 191 at 220A (Lord Diplock); *Wright v Pyke* [2012] EWCA Civ 931; *Kinsley v The Commissioner of Police for the Metropolis* [2012] EWCA Civ 515.

341 Therefore, any breach is a contempt and not merely a breach of contract: *Hussain v Hussain* [1986] Fam 134, CA; *Mid Suffolk DV v Clarke* [2007] 1 WLR 980. Compare *Balkanbank v Taher* [1994] 4 All ER 239.

342 See *Chappell v Davidson* [1856] 8 De G M & G 1; *Smith v Day* [1882] 21 Ch D 421; *Digital Equipment Corpn v Darkcrest* [1984] Ch 512.

343 [2015] EWCA Civ 484.

344 *Practice Direction (Injunction: Undertaking as to Damages)* [1974] 1 WLR 576.

345 *Hoffman La Roche (F) & Co AG v Secretary of State for Trade and Industry* [1975] AC 295.

346 See *A-G v Wright* [1988] 1 WLR 164.

347 [1975] AC 396, HL.

348 [1980] QB 460, CA.

Denning MR held that a mandatory interlocutory injunction should not be granted unless the plaintiffs made out a 'strong prima facie case',[349] and in *Shepherd Homes Ltd v Sandham*,[350] Megarry J held that 'the case has to be unusually strong and clear before a mandatory injunction will be granted'. His suggestion that 'the court must . . . feel a high degree of assurance that at the trial it will appear that the injunction was rightly granted'[351] was approved and applied by the Court of Appeal in *Locabail International Finance Ltd v Agroexport & Atlanta (UK) Ltd*,[352] which felt that the statements of principle relating to mandatory interlocutory injunctions were not affected by *American Cyanamid*.[353] Where the requirements are met, the court will grant such an injunction.[354]

(f) Interlocutory injunctions in the context of trade disputes

By s 221(2) of the Trade Union and Labour Relations Act 1992, in determining whether to grant an interlocutory injunction, the court must have regard to the likelihood of the defendant establishing at trial that the action was in contemplation of a trade dispute and, therefore, entitled to statutory immunity. The defendant must be able to show a high degree of probability that the statutory defence will succeed if the consequences of refusing the injunction will be severe damage to the claimant.[355]

(g) Interlocutory injunctions in the context of libel

The courts will generally refuse to award an interlocutory injunction in cases of alleged libel if the defendant intends to justify (i.e. to prove the truth of the defamatory statement).[356] This has not been altered by *American Cyanamid*.[357]

(h) Impact on third parties

As indicated earlier, a party who has notice on an interlocutory injunction 'is at risk of being in contempt of court if he does something which effectively flouts or undermines the injunction'.[358]

(5) General principles governing quia timet injunctions

Quia timet injunctions are available where, although there has as yet been no infringement of the claimant's rights, such an infringement has been threatened or is apprehended. In *Redland Bricks Ltd v Morris*, Lord Upjohn distinguished two circumstances in which a quia timet injunction would be appropriate:

> first, where the defendant has as yet done no hurt to the plaintiff but is threatening and intending (so the plaintiff alleges) to do works which will render irreparable harm to him or his property if carried to completion . . . Secondly, the type of case where the plaintiff has been fully compensated both at law and in equity for the damage he has suffered but where he alleges that the earlier actions of the defendant may lead to further causes of action.[359]

[349] [1980] QB 460, CA at 478. [350] [1971] Ch 340 at 349. [351] [1971] Ch 340 at 351.

[352] [1986] 1 WLR 657.

[353] See also *Films Rover International Ltd v Cannon Film Sales Ltd* [1987] 1 WLR 670, where Hoffmann J held that a mandatory interlocutory injunction could be granted where refusal carried a greater risk of injustice than granting it, even though the 'high degree of assurance' test was not met.

[354] *NWL Ltd v Woods* [1979] 1 WLR 1294, HL.

[355] See *Sky Petroleum v VIP Petroleum Ltd* [1974] 1 WLR 576; *Astro Exito Navegacion SA v Southland Enterprise Co Ltd (No 2)* [1982] QB 1248; *Parker v Camden London Borough Council* [1986] Ch 162; *Hemingway Securities Ltd v Dunraven Ltd* [1995] 1 EGLR 61.

[356] *Bonnard v Perryman* [1891] 2 Ch 269, CA.

[357] *Bestobell Paints Ltd v Bigg* [1975] 119 Sol Jo 678; *J Trevor & Sons v P R Solomon* [1978] 2 EGLR 120; *A-G v BBC* [1981] AC 303; *Gulf Oil (GB) Ltd v Page* [1987] Ch 327.

[358] *Hutcheson v Popdog Ltd* [2011] EWCA Civ 1580 at 5. [359] [1970] AC 652 at 665.

In order for the court to grant a quia timet injunction, the plaintiff must satisfy a relatively high burden of proof that the threatened or apprehended infringement will occur. As Lord Dunedin said in *A-G for the Dominion of Canada v Ritchie Contracting and Supply Co Ltd*,[360] 'no one can obtain a quia timet order by merely saying "Timeo."'[361] In *A-G v Manchester Corpn*, Chitty J stated:

> The principle which I think may be properly and safely extracted from the quia timet authorities is, that the plaintiff must show a strong case of probability that the apprehended mischief will, in fact, arise.[362]

In *Redland Bricks Ltd v Morris*,[363] Lord Upjohn said that 'a mandatory injunction can only be granted where the plaintiff shows a very strong probability upon the facts that grave damage will accrue to him in the future.'[364] Russell LJ suggested a different formulation in *Hooper v Rogers*:

> In different cases differing phrases have been used in describing circumstances in which . . . quia timet injunctions will be granted. In truth it seems to me that the degree of probability of future injury is not an absolute standard: what is to be aimed at is justice between the parties having regard to all the relevant circumstances.[365]

Where the defendant cannot demonstrate a strong probability of the threatened or apprehended infringement, the court will refuse to grant an injunction. In *London Borough of Islington v Elliott*,[366] an injunction was sought to remove ash trees, which, if allowed to continue growing, would have undermined the foundations of the claimant's property. The injunction was refused because it would have involved expenditure by the defendant, it would be several years before the damage occurred, and the defendant had agreed to remove the trees before then.[367] In contrast, in *Goodhart v Hyett*,[368] the plaintiff owned, by virtue of an easement, a pipe running across the defendant's land. North J granted a quia timet injunction to prevent the defendant building a house above the pipe, because the plaintiff had shown that this would prevent him repairing the pipe.

(6) **Rights which will be protected by injunction**

Having examined the general requirements governing the grant of perpetual, interlocutory, and quia timet injunctions, it is appropriate to consider the most important practical circumstances in which they are available as a remedy.

(a) **Trespass**

A landowner will normally[369] be entitled to a prohibitory injunction to prevent trespassers entering his land, and a mandatory injunction ordering trespassers to be removed. These remedies are available even though he has suffered no damage from the trespass.[370] Injunctions have been used to end occupations of public spaces by protest groups, such

360 [1919] AC 999 at 1005.

361 'Timeo' means 'I am afraid' and comes from the same Latin verb as quia timet.

362 [1893] 2 Ch 87 at 92; *Caterpillar Logistics Services (UK) Ltd v de Crean* [2012] EWCA Civ 156 at 67.

363 [1970] AC 652.

364 See also *A-G v Manchester Corpn* [1893] 2 Ch 87; *A-G v Rathmines and Pembroke Joint Hospital Board* [1904] 1 IR 161.

365 [1974] 3 WLR 329 at 334.

366 [2012] EWCA Civ 56. See also *Fletcher v Bealey* [1885] 28 Ch D 688 at 698.

367 See also, for example, *A-G v Rathmines and Pembroke Joint Hospital Board* [1904] 1 IR 161; *A-G v Nottingham Corpn*, [1904] 1 Ch 673.

368 [1883] 25 Ch D 182.

369 *Jaggard v Sawyer* [1995] 2 All ER 189 is an example of an exception.

370 See, for example, *Patel v WH Smith (Eziot) Ltd* [1987] 1 WLR 853, CA; *Harrow London Borough Council v Donohue* [1995] 1 EGLR 257.

as the occupation of Parliament Square in 2010 by groups claiming to represent the Four Horsemen of the Apocalypse.[371]

(b) Nuisance

An injunction is an important remedy available to the occupier of land where the defendant is causing a private nuisance, or to a private individual who suffers particular damage from a public nuisance.[372] In *Peires v Bickerton's Aerodromes Ltd*,[373] for example, the claimant sought an injunction to prevent noise nuisance caused by helicopter training activities at an adjacent aerodrome. Peter Smith J, in delivering judgment for the claimant, granted an injunction which limited the frequency and duration of training at the aerodrome. This was designed to achieve a balance between the claimant's rights to undisturbed enjoyment of her property and the defendant's right to use its property for its own lawful enjoyment in carrying out the training activities. The grant of an injunction will not be an automatic response to a nuisance, if damages are considered an adequate alternative.[374]

(c) Waste

Waste is a tort committed when by any action or inaction, a tenant under a lease of land or a tenant of land with a life interest permanently alters the physical character of land in his possession. An injunction will be granted to restrain voluntary[375] and equitable waste,[376] but not ameliorative[377] or permissive waste.[378]

(d) Breach of contract

An injunction is an appropriate remedy against a party who is in breach of a negative contractual term.[379] In *Nordenfelt v Maxim Nordenfelt Guns and Ammunition Co Ltd*,[380] for example, the House of Lords granted an injunction to enforce a contractual stipulation that the defendant would not engage in the business of manufacturing guns or ammunition for 25 years after he had sold his patents and business to the plaintiffs.[381]

(e) Anti-suit injunctions

An arbitration clause can be enforced by an order prohibiting, staying, or requiring the discontinuance of court proceedings in the UK or overseas (an anti-suit injunction).[382] Similar

[371] *Hall v Mayor of London (On Behalf of the Greater London Authority)* [2010] EWHC 1613; [2010] EWCA Civ 817. Injunctions have also been used in other protest claims, such as anti-fracking demonstrations (*Ineous Upstrean Ltd v Persons Unknown* [2019] 4 WLR 100) or against the use of animal products (*Canada Goose UK Retail Ltd v Persons Unknown* [2020] 1 WLR 2803).

[372] *Lyon v Fishmongers' Co* [1975–6] 1 App Cas 662, HL; *Vanderpant v Mayfair Hotel Co Ltd* [1930] 1 Ch 138.

[373] [2016] EWHC 560 (Ch).

[374] *Coventry v Lawrence* [2014] UKSC 13.

[375] Any acts which positively diminish the value of the land, for example quarrying or cutting timber.

[376] Equitable waste is malicious or wanton destruction of the land or buildings exceeding the licence conferred by a clause exempting the tenant from liability for voluntary waste: *Vane v Lord Barnard* [1716] 2 Vern 738; *Weld-Blundell v Wolseley* [1903] 2 Ch 664.

[377] Where the land is improved: *Doherty v Allman* [1878] 3 App Cas 709.

[378] Defaults of maintenance and repair: *Powys v Blagrave* [1854] 4 De GM & G 448; *Re Cartwright* [1889] 41 Ch D 532.

[379] The term need not be expressed in a negative way, as the court will look to the substance and not the form: *Wolverhampton and Walsall Rly Co Ltd v London and North Western Rly Ltd* [1873] LR 16 Eq 433. In exceptional circumstances breach of a negative term of a contract may give rise to the restitutionary remedy of an account of profits: *A-G v Blake* [2001] 1 AC 268; *Experience Hendrix LLC v PPX Enterprises Inc* [2003] 1 All ER (Comm) 830.

[380] [1894] AC 535.

[381] A worldwide prohibition would normally be invalid as being in restraint of trade, but it was upheld in this case because of the international scale and nature of the businesses concerned.

[382] *Ust-Kamenogorsk Hydropower Plant JSC v AES Ust-Kamenogorsk Hydropower Plant LLP* [2013] UKSC 35.

principles apply to an injunction to prevent overseas litigation where there is an exclusive jurisdiction clause.[383] An injunction against enforcement (an anti-enforcement injunction) may be sought even after foreign proceedings have taken place.[384] It has been said that particular caution has to be exercised where proceedings in an overseas court are involved,[385] although there is also a view that the court is protecting the contractual rights of the claimant, rather than interfering with overseas courts (which it has no power to do).[386] Anti-suit injunctions can be used in other circumstances where the ends of justice require, for instance, to prevent a creditor of an insolvent company incorporated in one country taking proceedings in another country with the purpose of gaining unjustifiable priority.[387]

(f) Employment relationships

The courts are reluctant to grant mandatory injunctions in the context of industrial disputes, as Geoffrey Lane J said in *Harold Stephen & Co Ltd v Post Office*:

> It can only be in very rare circumstances and in the most extreme circumstances that this court should interfere by way of mandatory injunction in the delicate mechanism of industrial disputes and industrial negotiations.[388]

The court will not normally grant an injunction to enforce a contractual term in a contract for personal services that would indirectly amount to specific performance of the contract because the employee will have no option but to perform the contract or remain idle.[389] There are, however, some circumstances where injunctions will be used in support of an individual employment contract, for instance, to prevent a dismissal taking place until a required disciplinary procedure has been followed.[390] The court will also grant injunctions to enforce the terms of partnership agreements.[391]

(g) Restrictive covenants

The court may grant an injunction to enforce a restrictive covenant over land. In *Wakeham v Wood*,[392] for example, a mandatory injunction was granted requiring the defendant to demolish a building that obstructed the view of the sea from the plaintiff's house, contrary to a restrictive covenant.

(h) Breach of trust

The court will grant an injunction to restrain trustees from committing a breach of trust.[393]

[383] *Donohue v Armco Inc* [2001] UKHL 64; *Michael Wilson & Partners Ltd v Emmott* [2018] EWCA Civ 51.

[384] *Ecobank Transnational Incorporated v Tanoh* [2015] EWCA Civ 1309.

[385] *Ingosstrak-Investments v BNP Paribas SA* [2012] EWCA Civ 644.

[386] *Ecobank Transnational Incorporated v Tanoh* [2015] EWCA Civ 1309 at 83 and 92. The court recognized that if an order affected the execution of a judgment in the country of the court which made the order, this would be indirect interference (at 136).

[387] *Stichting Shell Pensioenfonds v Krys (British Virgin Islands)* [2014] UKPC 41.

[388] [1977] 1 WLR 1172 at 1180. See *Parker v Camden London Borough Council* [1986] Ch 162, CA, where the court was willing to grant a mandatory injunction for the defendants to turn on boilers where tenants had no heat or hot water, because of a boilermen's strike. There is thus a strong element of public policy to this decision.

[389] See *Lumley v Wagner* [1852] 1 De GM & G 604; *Page One Records Ltd v Britton* [1967] 3 All ER 822; *Evening Standard Co Ltd v Henderson* [1987] IRLR 64. See also Trade Union and Labour Relations (Consolidation) Act 1992, s 236.

[390] See *Societe Generale, London Branch v Geys* [2012] UKSC 63 at 73–4; *Edwards v Chesterfield Royal Hospital NHS Foundation Trust* [2011] UKSC 58, [2012] 2 AC 22.

[391] *Hall v Hall* [1850] 12 Beav 414.

[392] [1982] 43 P & CR 40, CA.

[393] *Fox v Fox* [1870] LR 11 Eq 142; *Dance v Goldingham* [1972–3] 8 Ch App 902; *Waller v Waller* [1967] 1 All ER 305.

(i) Intellectual property rights

An injunction can be granted to prevent a defendant using a description for a product which means that it is likely to be confused with another product,[394] from passing off a product so that it appears to have been produced by the plaintiff,[395] or from using his trade mark, or infringing his patent, his registered design, or his copyright.[396] This can also apply to foreign intellectual property rights.[397] A website-blocking injunction can also be used against Internet service providers (e.g. British Telecom or Virgin Media) to block access to certain websites which are infringing trademarks by selling counterfeit goods.[398] Such injunctions have also been used to block infringement of copyrighted material via streaming services.[399]

(j) Expulsion from clubs and societies

The court may grant an injunction to restrain the wrongful expulsion of a member from a club or professional association, for example, where the rules of natural justice have been breached.[400] The court will clearly act if the member has a proprietary interest in the club,[401] but even where there is no proprietary interest[402] an injunction is available to protect his right to work[403] or if a matter of public importance is involved.[404] One particular area where injunctions have been granted is to prevent wrongful expulsion from trade unions.[405]

(k) Family matters

The court has statutory jurisdiction under the Family Law Act 1996[406] to grant injunctions excluding a spouse or partner from the matrimonial home, and to restrain one spouse from molesting the other.[407] Injunctions (including non-molestation orders) may also be used to protect minors.[408] Breach of a non-molestation order is a criminal offence under an amendment to the 1996 Act made by the Domestic Violence, Crime and Victims Act 2004. In one rather unusual case, a mother was prevented by injunction from giving her daughter the forename 'Cyanide'.[409] An injunction cannot, however, be obtained by a husband or partner to prevent a woman having an abortion.[410] A detailed consideration of these issues is outside the scope of this text.

394 *Diageo North America Inc v Intercontinental Brands (ICB) Ltd* [2010] EWCA Civ 920; *Taittinger SA v Allbev Ltd* [1994] 4 All ER 75, CA.

395 *GG Spalding & Bros v AW Gamage Ltd* [1915] 32 RPC 273, HL; *Erven Warnick BV v J Townend & Sons (Hull) Ltd* [1979] AC 731.

396 See Trade Marks Act 1938; Patents Act 1949; Registered Designs Act 1949; Patents Act 1977; Copyright, Design and Patents Act 1988; *Prince Jefri Bolkiah v KPMG* [1999] 2 AC 222.

397 *Lucasfilm Ltd v Ainsworth* [2011] UKSC 39 (27 July 2011) at 110.

398 *Cartier v B Sky B* [2016] EWCA Civ 658.See also *Nintento Co Ltd v Sky Uk Ltd* [2019] EWHC 2376 (Ch).

399 *Football Association Premier League Ltd v British Telecommunications* [2017] EWHC 480 (Ch).

400 *Labouchere v Earl of Wharncliffe* [1879–80] 13 Ch D 346.

401 *Rigby v Connol* [1880] 14 Ch D 482.

402 See *Baird v Wells* [1890] 44 Ch D 661, CA; *Rowe v Hewitt* [1906] 12 OLR 13; *Lee v Showmen's Guild of Great Britain* [1952] 2 QB 329; *Gaiman v National Association for Mental Health* [1971] Ch 317.

403 *Edwards v Society of Graphical and Allied Trades* [1971] Ch 354.

404 *Woodford v Smith* [1970] 1 WLR 806.

405 *Osborne v Amalgamated Society of Railway Servants* [1911] 1 Ch 540; *Edwards v Society of Graphical and Allied Trades* [1971] Ch 354; *Breen v Amalgamated Engineering Union* [1971] 2 QB 175; *Shotton v Hammond* [1976] 120 Sol Jo 780.

406 Extending and replacing earlier legislation, including the Matrimonial Causes Act 1973 and Matrimonial and Family Proceedings Act 1984.

407 As in *Re J* [2018] EWCA Civ 115.

408 *Re T (A Child)* [2017] EWCA Civ 1889.

409 *C (Children)* [2016] EWCA Civ 374.

410 *Paton v Trustees of British Pregnancy Advisory Service* [1979] QB 76; *C v S* [1988] QB 135.

(l) Harrassment

An injunction can be used to prevent harassment.[411] The harassment does not have to be aimed directly at the claimant, provided that the claimant is directly and foreseeably affected by it.[412]

(m) Planning permission

Under s 187(B) of the Town and Country Planning Act 1990, an injunction can be used to support the planning laws, for example, where land is used in contravention of planning permission.[413] An example of an injunction being used in support of town and country planning is provided by *Newham LBC v Ali*,[414] where an injunction was granted to prevent the use of land as a mosque, contrary to a planning obligation made under s 106 of the Town and Country Planning Act 1990.

(7) Injunctions to protect privacy, and reputation

Three types of injunction which have achieved prominence (indeed, notoriety) in the first two decades of the twenty-first century are the privacy order, the anonymized injunction, and the superinjunction. These forms of injunction are granted mainly to protect the privacy of individuals, although they have been used to prevent the disclosure of sensitive commercial information.[415] A privacy order prevents the disclosure of private or personal information, often preventing the naming of the individual obtaining the order (an anonymized injunction). In some cases, even the disclosure of the existence of the injunction is prohibited (a superinjunction). Some of the most infamous anonymized injunctions have involved prominent footballers, such as Ryan Giggs[416] and John Terry,[417] but the disgraced former head of the Royal Bank of Scotland, Sir Fred Goodwin (later stripped of his knighthood), also successfully obtained an anonymized injunction preventing disclosure of an alleged extramarital affair which took place during the period leading to the collapse of the bank.[418]

Disclosure of the existence of this injunction in Parliament almost led to a constitutional crisis involving a conflict between Parliament and the courts.[419] Less controversial instances where anonymity orders may be made involve 'clinical negligence, or other causes of action related to medical and other highly personal information'.[420] Exciting those these uses are, they fall outside the remit of this treatment in this edition.

[411] *Hayes v Willoughby* [2013] UKSC 17. [412] *Levi v Bates* [2015] EWCA Civ 206.

[413] *South Bucks District Council v Porter* [2003] UKHL 26 [2003] 2 AC 558; *South Somerset District Council v Hughes* [2009] EWCA Civ 1245; *Davenport v The City of Westminster* [2011] EWCA Civ 458.

[414] [2014] EWCA Civ 676.

[415] The first known superinjunction, the *Trafigura* injunction, was not concerned with privacy, but prohibited disclosure of a legally privileged internal company report concerning alleged dumping of toxic waste. The case is discussed in the *Report of the Committee on Super-Injunctions: Super-Injunctions, Anonymised Injunctions and Open Justice*, May 2011 (the 'Neuberger Report') paras 6.1 to 6.4. There is no publicly available judgment.

[416] *CTB v News Group Newspapers Ltd* [2011] EWHC 1232.

[417] *TSE v News Group Newspapers Ltd* [2011] EWHC 1308.

[418] *Goodwin v News Group Newspapers Ltd* [2011] EWHC 1341.

[419] For an account of the use of these injunctions and the conflict between Parliament and the courts, see Pearce, 'Privacy, Superinjunctions and Anonymity: "Selling My Story Will Sort My Life Out"' [2011] Denning LJ 92–130.

[420] *CVB v MGN Ltd* [2012] EWHC 1148 (QB) at 25 (Tugendhat J), giving citations of examples.

(8) Freezing injunctions

(a) Definition

A freezing order or injunction[421] prevents a defendant (or a third party holding a defendant's assets)[422] from dissipating his assets or removing them from the jurisdiction so that there will be nothing remaining to satisfy a judgment that might be obtained against him at trial.[423] Originally, freezing injunctions were known as 'Mareva' injunctions, taking their name from the case in which they were first exercised, *Mareva Compania Naviera SA v International Bulk Carriers SA*.[424] The revised nomenclature was introduced in the Civil Procedure Rules.[425]

(b) Nature of the freezing injunction

The overriding purpose of a freezing order is 'to prevent the dissipation by a defendant of assets which would otherwise be available to satisfy a judgment in favour of the claimant'.[426] This has been described as the 'enforcement principle',[427] since 'the purpose of a freezing order is so that the court "can ensure the effective enforcement of its orders."'[428] A freezing injunction is granted in an interlocutory form and is usually obtained ex parte (i.e. on the application of the claimant without hearing the defendant). It should not be interpreted as a finding of guilt or impropriety on the part of the defendant.[429] The jurisdiction to make a freezing order carries the power to make whatever ancillary orders are needed to make it effective.[430] In *JSC Mezhdunarodny Promyshlenniy Bank v Pugachev*,[431] an injunction (a passport order) restraining the defendant from leaving the jurisdiction was granted in order to support a freezing injunction.

(c) When freezing injunctions will be granted

Three conditions have to be satisfied for a freezing order to be granted.[432] Firstly, there must be a 'good arguable case' that the claimant will obtain a judgment for damages in court proceedings.[433] A higher level of proof is required than is the case for ordinary interlocutory injunctions. In addition, the claimant must be frank about the strengths and weaknesses of the claim and any defence likely to be put forward by the defendant.[434] Secondly, there must be a real risk or danger that the defendant may take steps to ensure that the assets which would otherwise be available to meet the judgment 'are no longer available or traceable when judgment is given against him'.[435] Thirdly, there must be assets to preserve: 'it is not enough for a claimant to assert that a defendant is an

[421] For an approved specimen see *UL v BK* [2013] EWHC 1735 (Fam).

[422] See Devonshire, 'Third Parties Holding Assets Subject to a Mareva' [1996] LMCLQ 268.

[423] It has been suggested that the jurisdiction extends to future assets of a defendant as well as those in existence at the date that the injunction is granted: *Soinco SACI v Novokuznetsk Aluminium Plant* [1998] QB 406, per Coleman J.

[424] [1975] 2 Lloyd's Rep 509. [425] CPR r 25.1(1)(f).

[426] *JSC BTA Bank v Solodchenko* [2010] EWCA Civ 1436, [2011] 1 WLR 888 at 32 (Patten LJ).

[427] *JSC BTA Bank v Ablyazov* [2013] EWCA Civ 928 at 34.

[428] *Parbulk II AS v PT Humpuss Intermoda Transportasi TBK* [2011] EWHC 3143 (Comm) at [38] per Gloster J.

[429] *Metropolitan Housing Trust Ltd v Taylor* [2015] EWCA Civ 1595 at 18.

[430] *JAC Mezhdunarodniy Promyshlenniy Bank v Pugachev* [2015] EWCA Civ 139 at 47.

[431] [2015] EWCA Civ 1108. There have been several separate actions relating to this dispute.

[432] *Derby & Co Ltd v Weldon* [1990] Ch 48 at 57.

[433] *The Niedersachsen* [1983] 1 WLR 1412; *Elektromotive Group Ltd v Pan* [2012] EWHC 2742 (QB) at 33.

[434] *Third Chandris Shipping Corpn v Unimarine SA* [1979] QB 645; *Dadourian Group International Inc v Simms* [2009] EWCA Civ 169.

[435] *Z Ltd v A-Z* [1982] QB 558 at 585. *VTB Capital Plc v Nutritek International Corp and ors* [2011] EWHC 3107 (Ch) at 227–30.

apparently wealthy person who must have assets somewhere'.[436] A freezing injunction is available against both movable[437] and immovable property.[438] Originally, it was only available against assets within the jurisdiction, but today an order may be made with worldwide effect[439] and may probably also be made in respect of assets within the jurisdiction, even if the defendant is overseas and the order is made to support an overseas judgment.[440] Even where all the requirements for the grant of the order have been met, the grant of an injunction remains discretionary, and the judge must be satisfied that it would be just and convenient to grant the order.[441]

(d) **Operation of a freezing order**

Where a freezing injunction is granted, the defendant is entitled to draw upon his assets to fund his legitimate expenses,[442] including his reasonable legal expenses in defending the subsequent action, but is otherwise prohibited from removing from the jurisdiction, or from dealing with, disposing of, or reducing the value of his assets up to the sum specified in the order.[443] The standard form of a freezing order applies to all the assets of a defendant, which can include assets of which he is, ostensibly, only a trustee or nominee[444] or which are held by a company which he owns or controls.[445] The order does not, however, give the claimant security for the claim, for instance, through charging the assets.[446] The order does not apply to an unsecured loan facility, even though, by using such a facility, a defendant may increase his general indebtedness.[447] Nor does it apply to articles which have no commercial value.[448] Like other injunctions, the order should be restrictively construed because of its penal nature.[449] It had been suggested that 'the court will, on appropriate occasions, take drastic action and will not allow its orders to be evaded by manipulation of shadowy offshore trusts and companies formed in jurisdictions where secrecy is highly prized and official regulation is at a low level.'[450] This has been described

[436] *Ras Al Khaimah Investment Authority v Bestfort Development Llp* [2017] EWCA Civ 1014 at 39.

[437] 'Assets' include a wide range of chattels. See *Allen v Jambo Holdings Ltd* [1980] 1 WLR 1252 (aeroplanes); *The Rena K* [1979] QB 377 (ships); *Rasu Maritima SA v Persuahaan Pertambangan Minyak Dan Gas Bumi Negara* [1978] QB 644 (machinery); *CBS United Kingdom Ltd v Lambert* [1983] Ch 37 (jewellery, *objets d'art*, other valuables, and choses in action); *Darashah v UFAC (UK) Ltd* [1982] The Times, 30 March, CA (goodwill of a business).

[438] *Derby & Co Ltd v Weldon (Nos 3 and 4)* [1990] Ch 65 (disposition of a freehold interest in a house).

[439] *In Dadourian Group International Inc v Simms (No 2)* [2006] 1 WLR 2499 at 2502–8 the Court of Appeal laid down some guidance ('the Dadourian guidelines') on the factors the court should consider in deciding whether to grant a worldwide freezing order (WFO). See *London Capital & Finance v Thomson* [2021] EWHC 1833 where it was confirmed that a worldwide freezing order is not blocked by an extisting criminal restraint order (CRO) under the Proceeds of Crime Act 2002.

[440] *NML Capital Ltd v Argentina* [2011] UKSC 31 at 150. See also *Madoff Securities International Ltd v Raven* [2011] EWHC 3102 (Comm).

[441] *Elektromotive Group Ltd v Pan* [2012] EWHC 2742 (QB) at 88.

[442] Cf *Fitzgerald v Williams* [1996] 2 All ER 171, where the Court of Appeal held that a defendant was not permitted to draw on frozen funds, to which the plaintiff asserted a proprietary claim, unless he had no other funds on which he could draw.

[443] In an exceptional case there may be no such limit: *London and Quadrant Housing Trust v Prestige Properties Ltd* [2013] EWCA Civ 130.

[444] *JSC BTA Bank v Solodchenko* [2010] EWCA Civ 1436, [2011] 1 WLR 888.

[445] *Group Seven Ltd v Allied Investment Corporation Ltd* [2013] EWHC 1509 (Ch) at 80–1.

[446] *Z Ltd v A-Z* [1982] QB 558 at 571 and 585 (per Lord Denning MR and Kerr LJ).

[447] *JSC BTA Bank v Ablyazov (Rev 1)* [2013] EWCA Civ 928 at 102.

[448] In *Camdex International Ltd v Bank of Zambia (No 2)* [1997] 1 All ER 728. the Court of Appeal refused an order preventing the export of newly printed Zambian banknotes since they had no value until issued. It was inappropriate to use a freezing order merely to hold a defendant to ransom.

[449] *JSC BTA Bank v Ablyazov* [2015] UKSC 64 at 19.

[450] *ICIC v Adham* [1998] BCC 134 (Robert Walker J).

as the 'flexibility principle'.[451] The Supreme Court has rejected this approach, adopting a description given by counsel:

> the flexibility principle has no role in the construction of the Freezing Order as an order of the court. As Mr Crow colourfully put it, the flexibility principle is that the court must be agile in this game of cat and mouse between claimants and defendants to make sure that it is making new orders to meet new avoidance measures, but that is not a justification for the expansive interpretation of an order which has already been made.[452]

Failure to comply with a freezing order is a contempt of court and can lead to civil committal proceedings.[453]

(e) Undertaking in damages

A freezing injunction is not permanent, but is only intended to protect a claimant until the trial of the main issue. There is normally a requirement that the claimant undertakes to compensate the defendant if he fails to establish his case at trial.[454]

An undertaking to compensate affected third parties is also normally required, and in this case, there may be liability to 'innocent' third parties, even if the injunction is justified.[455] However, as was made clear in *Balkanbank v Taher*,[456] the undertaking is made to the court and not the defendant and the 'court has a discretion whether to order the plaintiff to pay damages where the defendants have sustained loss caused by the injunction'.[457] The court is not bound to order damages, and whether it does will depend on the circumstances of the case.[458] Where the injunction is sought by a public authority exercising its statutory functions, there is no general rule that an undertaking in damages is required, unless the particular circumstances require it.[459]

(f) Appointment of receiver

In exceptional cases a receiver can be appointed to administer the assets.[460]

(g) History

The freezing injunction is a relatively recent creation of equity.[461] It was traditionally thought that *Lister & Co v Stubbs*[462] prevented the court from granting the claimant such an injunction, but in *Nippon Yusen Kaisha v Kaageorgis* and *Mareva Compania Naviera SA v International Bulkcarriers SA*,[463] the Court of Appeal held that the court enjoyed the jurisdiction to grant just such an order under the predecessor to s 37(1) of the Supreme

451 *JSC BTA Bank v Ablyazov* [2013] EWCA Civ 928 at 36.

452 *JSC BTA Bank v Ablyazov* [2015] UKSC 64 at 18.

453 See *Daltel Europe Ltd v Makki* [2006] EWCA Civ 94.

454 *Third Chandris Shipping Corpn v Unimarine SA* [1979] QB 645; *The Financial Services Authority (FSA) v Sinaloa Gold plc* [2013] UKSC 11 at 15–18.

455 *The Financial Services Authority (FSA) v Sinaloa Gold plc* [2013] UKSC 11 at 18–19.

456 [1994] 4 All ER 239.

457 Per Clarke J. See also *Yukong Line v Rendsburg Investments Corp* [2001] 2 Lloyd's Rep 113 at 32–4. For an obiter discussion of whether an insurance policy provides sufficient fortification for an undertaking in damages, particularly where fraud is alleged, see *Candy v Holyoake* [2017] EWCA Civ 92.

458 The principles are discussed in *SCF Tankers Ltd v Privalov* [2017] EWCA Civ 1877.

459 *The Financial Services Authority (FSA) v Sinaloa Gold plc* [2013] UKSC 11.

460 *JSC BTA Bank v A* [2010] EWCA Civ 1141.

461 However, in *The Siskina* [1979] AC 210 Lord Denning MR suggested that the Mareva injunction was a 'rediscovery' of the earlier procedure of 'foreign attachment'.

462 [1890] LR 45 Ch D 1.

463 [1980] 1 All ER 213, [1975] 2 Lloyd's Rep 509. A 'Mareva' injunction was first granted in the earlier case of *Nippon Yusen Kaisha v Karageorgis* [1975] 1 WLR 1093.

Court Act 1981.[464] Lord Denning MR described the development of the order as 'the greatest piece of judicial law reform in my time'.[465]

(9) Search orders

(a) Definition

A search order prevents a defendant from destroying vital evidence before an issue comes to trial by requiring him to allow the plaintiff to enter his premises and search for, examine, remove, or copy articles specified in the order.[466] Previously, such injunctions were known as Anton Piller orders, and the new nomenclature was introduced by the Civil Procedure Rules. The rationale for the order was explained by Lord Denning MR in *Anton Piller KG v Manufacturing Processes Ltd*:

> such an order can be made by a judge ex parte, but it should only be made where it is essential that the plaintiff should have inspection so that justice can be done between the parties: and when, if the defendant were forewarned, there is a grave danger that vital evidence will be destroyed, that papers will be burnt or lost or hidden.[467]

The first such order was granted in *EMI Ltd v Kishorilal Pandit*,[468] and the first by the Court of Appeal in *Anton Piller KG v Manufacturing Processes Ltd*[469] They were approved by the House of Lords in *Rank Film Distributors Ltd v Video Information Centre*.[470] Search orders have been particularly appropriate in cases where it is suspected that 'pirating' of music or films has taken place.[471]

(b) Preconditions to the grant of a search order

Search orders are granted ex parte, as the element of surprise is essential to prevent defendants destroying or hiding the evidence. As was said in *Rank Film Distributors Ltd v Video Information Centre*:[472]

> If the stable door cannot be bolted, the horse must be secured . . . If the horse is liable to be spirited away, notice of an intention to secure the horse will defeat the intention.[473]

Given the powerful effect of the order, as well as the fact that it will be granted without hearing the defendant, the court has laid down relatively strict criteria that the claimant must satisfy. In *Anton Piller KG v Manufacturing Processes Ltd*,[474] Ormrod LJ said that there are 'three essential pre-conditions' for the granting of an order. To these a fourth requirement suggested by Lord Denning MR can be added.

(i) Strong prima facie case

There must be 'an *extremely* strong prima facie case'. This represents a much higher standard than that required for other interlocutory injunctions following *American Cyanamid*.

(ii) Serious potential damage

The damage, potential or actual, must be very serious for the applicant.

[464] Supreme Court of Judicature (Consolidation) Act 1925, s 45(1).

[465] Lord Denning, *The Due Process of Law* (Butterworths 1980), p 134.

[466] For an approved specimen, see *UL v BK* [2013] EWHC 1735 (Fam).

[467] [1976] Ch 55 at 61. [468] [1975] 1 All ER 418. [469] [1976] Ch 55. [470] [1982] AC 380.

[471] E.g. *Ex p Island Records Ltd* [1978] Ch 122, CA; *Rank Film Distributors Ltd v Video Information Centre* [1982] AC 380; *Columbia Picture Industries Ltd v Robinson* [1986] 3 All ER 338.

[472] [1982] AC 380. [473] [1982] AC 380 at 418, per Templeman LJ. [474] [1976] Ch 55 at 62.

(iii) Real possibility evidence will be destroyed

There must be clear evidence that the defendants have in their possession incriminating documents or things, and that there is a real possibility that they may destroy such material before any application inter partes can be made.

(iv) No real harm to the defendant

Lord Denning held that an order should only be granted when it 'would do no real harm to the defendant or his case'. In *Coca-Cola v Gilbey*,[475] Lightman J held that the risk of violence against a defendant if forced to disclose information will not generally justify the refusal to award an Anton Piller order. An order had been granted against the defendant, who had been involved in an operation to counterfeit Coca-Cola products, but he refused to disclose information concerning the operation because such disclosure would jeopardize his safety and that of his family. Lightman J held that such threats were 'a factor' to be considered when deciding whether to grant an order, but that in most cases it would be outweighed by the interests of justice:

> I cannot think that in any ordinary case where the plaintiff has a pressing need for the information in question, the existence of the risk of violence against the potential informant should outweigh the interest of the plaintiff in obtaining the information. In case of any unlawful threat or action directed at a party, a witness or their families, the rule of law requires that the law should in no wise be deflected from following its ordinary course and the court should proceed undeterred. Police protection is the appropriate remedy . . .[476]

(c) **Protection for the defendant**

Because of the 'draconian and essentially unfair nature of search orders from the point of view of the defendant',[477] there are a number of limitations and restrictions as to its execution intended to protect the defendant. Many of these were stated by Dillon LJ in *Booker McConnell plc v Plascow*,[478] and Scott J in *Columbia Picture Industries v Robinson*, who recognized that:

> a decision whether or not an Anton Piller order should be granted requires a balance to be struck between the plaintiff's need that the remedies allowed by the civil law for the breach of his rights should be attainable and the requirement of justice that a defendant should not be deprived of his property without being heard.[479]

Many of these limitations are incorporated in the standard form order issued under a Practice Direction under the Civil Procedure Rules 2005.[480]

(i) Service and explanation by a solicitor

The order must be served by an independent supervising solicitor accompanying the plaintiff,[481] who must also explain what it means to the defendant in everyday language.[482] If the premises are likely to be occupied by an unaccompanied woman and the supervising solicitor is a man, one of the persons accompanying him must be a woman.

[475] [1995] 4 All ER 711. [476] [1995] 4 All ER 711 at 716.

[477] *Columbia Picture Industries Ltd v Robinson* [1986] 3 All ER 338 at 371. See also *Lock International plc v Beswick* [1989] 1 WLR 1268; *Bhimji v Chatwani* [1991] 1 WLR 989.

[478] [1985] RPC 425, CA. [479] [1986] 3 All ER 338.

[480] PD10 *Practice Direction on Interim Injunctions* (1 October 2009), para 7.1.

[481] *ITC Film Distributors Ltd v Video Exchange Ltd* [1982] Ch 431.

[482] *Bhimji v Chatwani* [1991] 1 WLR 989.

(ii) Times of service

The order may normally only be served between 9.30 am and 5.30 pm on a weekday. This is to allow the respondent of the order to seek legal advice.

(iii) Application to vary or discharge

The defendant may apply to the court at short notice for variation or discharge of the order, provided that the plaintiff and his solicitor and the supervising solicitor have been allowed to enter the premises, although not commenced the search.

(iv) Items to be removed

No item may be removed from the premises until a list of the items to be removed has been prepared, a copy of the list has been supplied to the person served with the order, and he has been given a reasonable opportunity to check the list.

(v) Search in the presence of the defendant

The premises must not be searched, and items must not be removed from them, except in the presence of the defendant or a person appearing to be a responsible employee of the defendant.

(vi) Undertaking in damages

The claimant must make an undertaking in damages to compensate the claimant for any loss he suffers as a result of the carrying out of the order if the court decides that he should be compensated.

(d) **The privilege against self-incrimination**

In *Rank Film Distributors Ltd v Video Information Centre*,[483] the House of Lords held that a claimant would not be granted a search order requiring the defendants to answer questions or disclose documents that would have the effect of incriminating him, as he is entitled to the privilege against self-incrimination.[484] In *IBM United Kingdom Ltd v Prima Data International Ltd*,[485] Sir Mervyn Davies QC refused to set aside sections of a search order made against a company director from whom IBM sought damages for conspiracy to extract goods without payment because the solicitor serving the order had adequately explained his right to claim privilege against self-incrimination. However, this privilege was removed as regards proceedings for the infringement of intellectual property rights and passing off by s 72 of the Senior Courts Act 1981.[486] In *Cobra Golf Ltd v Rata*,[487] Rimer J, therefore, held that a defendant had no right to assert an entitlement to the privilege against self-incrimination where proceedings for civil contempt had been commenced by a manufacturer of golf equipment alleging that he had infringed their trade marks.

[483] [1982] AC 380.

[484] See also *Tate Access Floors Inc v Boswell* [1991] Ch 512; *IBM United Kingdom Ltd v Prima Data International Ltd* [1994] 4 All ER 748; *Cobra Golf Ltd v Rata* [1997] 2 All ER 150; *Den Norske Bank ASA v Antonatos* [1999] QB 271.

[485] [1994] 4 All ER 748.

[486] See *Istel (AT & T) Ltd v Tully* [1993] AC 45, HL.

[487] [1998] Ch 109.

PART II

Creating the Relationship

5. Certainty 115
6. Constitution of trusts 139
7. Formalities 170
8. Policy limits 185

5

Certainty

1 Introduction

Trusts and powers are the main instruments by which equity facilitates the management of property. The essential difference between a trust and a power is that the former imposes an obligation to deal with property for the benefit of others, whilst a power of appointment (as its name suggests) gives a person the opportunity to identify who will benefit from property. Since the landmark ruling of the House of Lords in *McPhail v Doulton*,[1] the courts have recognized that the two categories are not wholly distinct, and it is possible to combine trusts and powers in an almost infinite variety of forms. Thus in between the extremes of a trust which confers no discretion at all and a power which involves no obligation at all, there can be a trust with varying levels of discretion, and powers with varying levels of obligation. For an obligation to be legally enforceable, it must be defined with sufficient certainty to allow the courts to control it;[2] and a power conferring authority can only be exercised within the limits subject to which it is created. This range of different types of obligation has implications for the applicable tests for certainty. The court must know who is under an obligation; what the obligation is; to what property the obligation relates; and who can enforce the obligation. In the case of a power, the court needs to know who can exercise the power, how it can be exercised, and whether the power has been validly exercised.

2 The three certainties

Lord Langdale MR in *Knight v Knight*[3] said that a trust would only come into existence if there was certainty of words, certainty of subject matter, and certainty of objects.[4] Putting this more fully, three essential characteristics of trusts can be identified.[5] First, there must be a binding obligation on the trustees holding property. Second, a trust can only exist in relation to specific property. Third, the trustees must owe the obligations to legal persons who are entitled to enforce them. These persons are termed the beneficiaries of the trust, and they are entitled to the trust property in equity. These three elements all appear in the definition of a 'trust' in article 2 of the Hague Convention on the Law Applicable to Trusts and on their Recognition, incorporated into English law by the Recognition of Trusts Act 1987. If the three certainties are not satisfied, the arrangement lacks the clarity needed for legal enforcement.

1 [1971] AC 424.

2 The same issue applies to contracts: *Associated British Ports v Tata Steel UK Ltd* [2017] EWHC 694 (Ch).

3 [1840] 3 Beav 148 at 173.

4 See *Wright v Atkyns* [1823] Turn & R 143 at 157, per Lord Eldon.

5 See *Re Kayford Ltd (In Liquidation)* [1975] 1 All ER 604 at 607; *Hunter v Moss* [1994] 3 All ER 215 at 219.

3 Certainty of intention

(1) Intention to create a trust

(a) Meaning of the requirement

Lord Langdale MR in *Knight v Knight*[6] spoke of the need for 'certainty of words', but the modern meaning is better captured by the term 'certainty of intention'. The essence of the requirement is that an express trust will only arise if it can be shown that the recipient of property was intended to be subject to a trust obligation. Where the trust is created by a document, the intention is deduced by examining the words used in the document purporting to create the obligation. As Megarry J said in *Re Kayford Ltd (In Liquidation)*:

> the question is whether in substance a sufficient intention to create a trust has been manifested.[7]

There is no special formula or technical phrasing necessary to create a trust. A trust can be created without ever using the word 'trust'. In *Re Kayford Ltd (In Liquidation)* itself, a mail-order company was in financial difficulties and used a separate bank account to deposit money received from customers whose goods had not yet been delivered. When the company became insolvent the question arose whether the money in that account was held on trust for the customers, in which case it would not form part of the general assets of the company. Megarry J held that a trust had been created, stating:

> As for the requisite certainty of words, it is well settled that a trust can be created without using the words 'trust' or confidence or the like . . .[8]

Similarly, the use of the word 'trust' will not of itself indicate the existence of an intention to create a trust, since the word may not have been used as a technical legal term.[9]

Since there is no requirement for a particular formula or phrase to be used to create a trust, an intention to create a trust must instead be deduced from the use of language that makes it clear that the recipient does not hold property for their own benefit, but holds it for the benefit of others. The words must demonstrate an intention to impose a binding legal obligation on the recipient of property as opposed to a purely moral obligation; an intention that the objects of the trust will benefit come what may.[10] Finding an intention to create a trust is a question of fact that depends in every case on the construction of the particular language employed. However, some examples are useful to illustrate the approach of the courts. In *Re Snowden (Decd)*,[11] an elderly lady who could not decide how to leave her property among her nephews and nieces left it all to her brother, Bert, telling him that he would 'know what to do'. It was held that she had not intended to impose a mandatory obligation on him to hold the property on trust for her nephews and nieces, but merely expressed a moral obligation to distribute the property among her family. This can be contrasted with *Gold v Hill*,[12] where it was held that a man who orally directed the beneficiary of his life insurance policy to 'look after Carol [his former wife] and the kids' had intended to impose a mandatory obligation and created a trust. In *McPhail v Doulton*,[13] the House of Lords held that the mandatory character of the language used in a

[6] [1840] 3 Beav 148. [7] [1975] 1 WLR 279 at 282.

[8] [1975] 1 All ER 604 at 607. See, also, *Pleshakov v Sky Stream* [2021] UKPC 15 at [48] per Lord Sales: 'in relation to establishing certainty of intention to create a trust neither a written instrument nor any formal language is required'.

[9] See *Tito v Waddell (No 2)* [1977] Ch 106.

[10] There is, however, no need to find a contractual relationship between the settlor and the beneficiaries: *Pleshakov v Sky Stream* [2021] UKPC 15 at [47].

[11] [1979] 2 All ER 172. [12] [1999] 1 FLR 54. [13] [1971] AC 424.

deed establishing a fund to provide for the benefit of the employees and ex-employees of a company, and their relatives and dependants, meant that the deed created a trust and not a mere power. The deed stated that the 'trustees shall apply the net income of the fund in making at their absolute discretion grants' to the specified class. The presence of the word 'shall' demonstrated that the recipients were under a mandatory duty to make grants, although they had a discretion in deciding to whom the grants would go. In *R v Clowes*,[14] it was held that a trust had arisen where an investment company had declared in its brochure that all monies received from clients would be held in a designated client account and only used to purchase specified government stock. In *Shah v Shah*, Arden LJ demonstrated that the actions of the settlor provide an important context to decide the meaning of the language used as the court must consider 'the intentions of the maker as manifested by the words he has used in the context of all the relevant facts'.[15] Here, an incomplete transfer of shares was found to be held on a validly declared trust as the delivery of a signed letter alongside a shared stock transfer form bolstered language used in relation to the shares to demonstrate the required, mandatory duty. Similarly, in *Pleshakov v Sky Stream*,[16] the necessary intention to establish a bare trust of shares in Sky Stream for the benefit of Mr Pleshakov was inferred from the words and conduct of the parties at the time of the incorporation of Sky Stream and in the years that followed.

Even if the language used in an agreement is inadequate in itself to create a trust, a trust may be held to have been created if this would fulfil the settlor's overriding intention. In *Don King Productions Inc v Warren (No 1)*,[17] Lightman J held that such an intention could be deduced as a 'matter of business common sense' from the commercial background and the commercial purpose of agreements for the assignment of promotion and management of a number of boxers.[18] It is the intention of the settlor that matters; the actions of a proposed trustee in accepting or rejecting trusteeship has no bearing on a finding of an intention to create a trust.[19]

(b) **Precatory words**

In older authorities it was held that if a settlor or testator used certain key words or phrases, called 'precatory words', this would create a trust.[20] For example, if a testator had expressed his 'confidence', 'desire', 'wish', or 'hope' that a gift in his will be used in a particular way, this would be held to impose a trust on the recipient of the gift. The difficulty with this approach is that such words merely express the wish of the transferor or testator as to how he would like to see the property used. They imply at most a purely moral obligation[21] and not the legally enforceable obligation which is the essential characteristic of a trust.

The lack of an intention to impose a legally binding obligation was recognized in a number of late nineteenth-century cases, and it was held that a trust could no longer be created merely through the use of 'precatory words'.[22] In *Re Adams and Kensington*

[14] [1994] 2 All ER 316. [15] [2010] EWCA Civ 1408 at 13. [16] [2021] UKPC 15.

[17] [1998] 2 All ER 608; affd [2000] Ch 291, CA.

[18] [1998] 2 All ER 608; affd [2000] Ch 291, CA at 625.

[19] *High Commissioner for Pakistan in the UK v Prince Muffakham Jan* [2020] Ch 421 ar [244].

[20] Even if the terms of the gift seemed to be absolute: *Gully v Cregoe* [1857] 24 Beav 185; *Curnick v Tucker* [1874] LR 17 Eq 320. The Court of Chancery originally held that such words created a trust, because of historical reasons relating to the possibility of abuse by executors of wills.

[21] In *Mussoorie Bank Ltd v Raynor* [1882] 7 App Cas 321 at 331, the use of precatory words such as 'confidence' was described simply as an 'appeal to the conscience of the taker'. See also *Re Snowden (Decd)* [1979] Ch 528.

[22] See *Lambe v Eames* [1871] 6 Ch App 597; *Re Hutchinson and Tenant* [1878] 8 Ch D 540; *Mussoorie Bank Ltd v Raynor* [1882] 7 App Cas 321; *Re Diggles* [1888] LR 39 Ch D 253; *Re Hamilton* [1895] 2 Ch 370; *Re Johnson* [1939] 2 All ER 458.

Vestry,[23] for example, a testator left all his property to his wife 'in full confidence that she would do what was right as to the disposal thereof between his children'. The question was whether this language was effective to create a trust in favour of the children, or whether the wife took the property absolutely. The Court of Appeal held that the precatory words alone were insufficient to give rise to a trust. The position was summarized by Cotton LJ:

> I think that some of the older authorities went a deal too far in holding that some particular words appearing in a will were sufficient to create a trust. Undoubtedly confidence, if the rest of the context shows that a trust is intended, may make a trust, but what we have to look at is the whole of the will which we have to construe, and if the confidence is that she will do what is right as regards the disposal of the property, I cannot say that that is, on the true construction of the will, a trust imposed upon her.[24]

The consequence of these decisions is not that precatory words can never create a trust, but that such words are now just part of the evidence used to discover an intention to create a trust. A trust will be created if, on the proper construction of the whole instrument purporting to create a trust, including any precatory words, an intention can be found to subject the property to legally binding obligations.[25]

In the very unusual case of *Re Steele's Will Trusts*,[26] it was held that precatory words were sufficient to create a trust. A testatrix left a diamond necklace to her son by will. Her will contained a clause intended to make the necklace a family heirloom that ended with the expression 'I request my said son to do all in his power by his will or otherwise to give effect to this my wish.' This form of words had been copied exactly from the will in the earlier case of *Shelley v Shelley*,[27] where they had been held effective to create a trust. Wynn-Parry J concluded that although subsequent cases had held that mere precatory words were not sufficient to create a trust, the fact that the precedent of *Shelley v Shelley* had been followed verbatim afforded the strongest indication that the testatrix had intended to create a trust. Thus, the rationale for this decision was not the use of the precatory words per se, but the intention evidenced by following an established precedent for the creation of a trust of a family heirloom. It would be extremely foolish to attempt to create a trust in the same way.

(c) 'Sham' intention

The court may refuse to find that a trust was validly created if such an apparent intention to create a trust was a 'sham' because at the time it was made the owner had no real intention to subject his property to a trust and the purpose of the purported trust declaration was to give a false impression to third parties or the court.[28] In *Midland Bank plc v Wyatt*,[29] Mr and Mrs Wyatt were the joint legal owners of their matrimonial home. In 1987 they executed a formally valid declaration of trust of the house in favour of Mrs Wyatt and their daughters. The trust deed was dated 17 June 1987 and signed by both husband and wife, although Mrs Wyatt had not been aware of its effect. The declaration of trust was not acted upon in any way but was placed in a safe. Subsequently, Mr Wyatt obtained loans to finance his business, secured by his interest in the house. The banks

[23] LR [1884] 27 Ch D 394. [24] LR [1884] 27 Ch D 394 at 410.

[25] *Comiskey v Bowring-Hanbury* [1905] AC 84, HL. [26] [1948] Ch 603.

[27] [1868] LR 6 Eq 540.

[28] *Pankhania v Chandegra* [2012] EWCA Civ 1438 at 20. For a general description of when a document is a sham, *Snook v London and West Riding Investments Ltd* [1967] 2 QB 786 at 802. For a re-examination of the basis of shams, see Douglas and McFarlane, 'Sham Trusts' in Conway and Hickey, *Modern Studies in Property Law: Volume 9* (Hart 2017) 236.

[29] [1995] 1 FLR 696.

were unaware of the existence of the declaration. The declaration was only produced after the business had gone into receivership and the secured creditors sought a charging order against the house. D E M Young QC held that in these circumstances the purported declaration of trust in favour of the wife and children was a sham and had, therefore, been ineffective to divest the husband of the entire beneficial interest in the house:

> I do not believe that Mr Wyatt had any intention when he executed the trust deed of endowing his children with his interest in Honer House, which at the time was his only real asset. I consider the trust deed was executed by him, not to be acted upon but to be put in the safe for a rainy day . . . As such I consider the declaration of trust was not what it purported to be but a pretence or, as it is sometimes referred to, a 'sham' . . . Accordingly, I find that the declaration of trust sought to be relied upon by Mr Wyatt is void and unenforceable.[30]

Midland Bank plc v Wyatt concerned a situation where a settlor purported to declare himself a trustee. Where the settlor and the trustee are distinct, the trust will only be invalidated on the basis of a sham intention if the trustee either shared the intention of the settlor or was prepared to go along with the intentions of the settlor without knowing or caring about the tranasctions they were asked to carry out as trustee.[31]

In *Webb v Webb*,[32] the Privy Council emphasized that the finding of sham trust turned on the subjective intentions of the parties involved and should be distinguished from an 'objective nullity' which described the situation where the settlor had not divested himself of the beneficial ownership of the property.[33] The case involved a scheme by Mr Webb to put his assets beyond the reach of his divorcing spouse by purporting to create a trust over them, even though, in practice he retained control of the assets as settlor.[34] Mr Webb was sole trustee and one of two named beneficiaries of the trust (the other was his son). The trust deeds gave Mr Webb considerable powers, including a general power, not subject to his obligations as trustee, to appoint himself as sole beneficiary in place of the existing beneficiaries, under clause 10 of the trust deed. The net impact of this, and other powers, was to enable Mr Webb to secure the benefit of the trust assets for himself.

It was accepted, following findings at first instance and in the Court of Appeal, that the trusts were not shams, but the trust was still not validly created:

> There is, however, no inconsistency between the finding . . . that the trusts are not shams and a conclusion that Mr Webb's attempts to create the trusts have failed or are defeasible. Acceptance that Mr Webb intended to create trusts does not in any way preclude a finding that he reserved such broad powers to himself as settlor and beneficiary that he failed to make an effective disposition of the relevant property . . . These powers were therefore amply sufficient for Mr Webb to arrange matters in such a way that he alone would hold the trust property on trust for himself and no-one else, with the consequence that the legal and beneficial interest in all of that property would vest in him.[35]

Lord Kitchin noted that it mattered not whether the invalidity of the trusts came from the fact that Mr Webb, as settlor, had never divested himself of the property on trust, or

[30] [1995] 1 FLR 696 at 707.

[31] *Murphy & Anor v Munir & Ors (Re Muhammed Munir)* [2021] EWHC 278 (Ch); *Shalson v Russo (Tracing Claims)* [2005] Ch 281; *Re Esteem Settlement* [2004] WTLR 1.

[32] [2020] UKPC 22.

[33] [2020] UKPC 22 at [73] per Lord Kitchin, confirming the reasoning if the Court of Appeal in the same case.

[34] For critical commentary on the reasoning and practical impact of the decision, see Agnew 'The reservation of powers by settlors: intention and illusion' [2021] 80 CLJ 18.

[35] [2020] UKPC 22 at [87].

whether the powers reserved to him 'were so extensive that in equity he can be regarded as having had rights which were tantamount to ownership'.[36]

(2) **Lack of intention to create a trust**

(a) **No trust without intention**

If the words used in the instrument purporting to create a trust do not evince an intention to create a trust, then a trust cannot be created. If the words alleged to create a trust were associated with a transfer of the property inter vivos or by will, then in most cases, the transfer or will gift remains effective to transfer the property and the recipient acquires the property free of any trust. If the words were alleged to constitute a declaration of the settlor himself as trustee, but show no such intention, then the settlor remains the outright owner.

(b) **Something other than a trust intended**

When looking at certainty of intention in the context of trusts there is a temptation to assume that the only intention which can be in issue is an intention to create a trust. This temptation must be avoided, because the purpose of interpretation is to ascertain what the testator, grantor, or settlor intended.[37] Words used in a will, for instance, may fail to create a trust because no trust was intended, but the testator intended to make an absolute gift: if precatory words have been used, this may have been done deliberately with the intention of imposing only a moral obligation, not a legally binding obligation. Ascertaining intention can be particularly difficult where arrangements are made informally, with no written evidence. For instance, as will be seen in Chapter 12, where we look at rights in the family home, the arrangement under which a parent helps to finance the purchase of a house by one of their children could be interpreted as creating a trust under which the parent acquires a share of ownership or the right to live in the house with the child, but it could also be a repayable loan or a gift, or even an arrangement under which, without imposing any legally binding obligation, the expectation is that the child will look after the parent in some way in the future.

(c) **Importance of evidence**

Questions of intention can often turn on difficult, practical issues of evidence. In *Moore v Williamson*,[38] the question before the court was as to the ownership of one of the two shares in a company. Mr Moore, the claimant, alleged that one of the shares was held on trust for him by the defendant Jason Williamson on the basis of either an oral or written declaration of trust by Jason. Picking through a tangled web of evidence through unreliable and conflicting testimony from key and supporting witnesses, David Cooke J found that no written trust declaration ever existed. He did, however, find that Mr Moore had not intended to give up his previous interest in the business and that there had been an oral declaration of trust, based on express statements made by Jason to Mr Moore as to

[36] [2020] UKPC 22 at [89]. In other commonwealth jurisdictions, a concept of 'illusory trusts' appears to have arisen around trusts which prohibits settlor control of trusts: see *Clayton v Clayton* [2016] 1 NZLR 551; *JSC Mezhdunarodni Promyshlenniy Bank v Pugachev* [2017] EWHC 2426 (Ch). *Webb* does not clarify matters here—see, for example, Strachan 'Whither the "illusory trust"?' (2021) 127 LQR 206; Nitikman 'More about illusory trusts: is "tantamount" to ownership the same as "ownership"? The Privy Council takes a step too far' (2021) 27 Trusts & Trustees 69.

[37] See, for example, *Duggan v Governor of Full Sutton Prison* [2003] 2 All ER 678 (money held on account for a prisoner by a prison governor created the relationship of debtor and creditor, not that of trustee and beneficiary).

[38] [2011] EWHC 672 (Ch).

the ownership of the shares and evidenced by Mr Moore's continued involvement in the affairs of the new company.

4 Certainty of subject matter

(1) The requirement of certainty

(a) A trust can only exist in relation to specific property

The second of the three certainties is certainty of subject matter. A trust can only exist in relation to specific property: for a trust to be enforceable, the court must be able to ascertain with certainty what property is subject to the trust obligation. As Lord Browne-Wilkinson stated in *Westdeutsche Landesbank Girozentrale v Islington London Borough Council*: 'In order to establish a trust there must be identifiable trust property.'[39] An imprecise definition of the intended trust property will render the trust invalid for uncertainty of subject matter.

(b) No specific property has been identified

Since a trust cannot exist in abstract, but only in relation to specific assets, the failure to identify any specific property as the trust property will prevent the creation of a valid trust. in *Hemmens v Wilson Browne (a firm)*,[40] it was held that an agreement allowing a person to call for a payment of £110,000 at any time could not create a trust of such a sum arising over the solicitor's general assets because no specific property had been identified as the subject matter of the obligation. As Judge Moseley QC observed: 'there was no identifiable fund to which any trust could attach'.[41]

A similar problem prevented a trust arising in *Boyce v Boyce*.[42] A testator bequeathed his two houses to trustees, one to be held on trust for each of his two daughters. The terms of the trust required the trustees to convey to Maria whichever house she chose and then to convey the other house to Charlotte. However, as Maria had died during his lifetime the court held that no valid trust of either house was created in favour of Charlotte because it was impossible to ascertain which house she was intended to have.

(c) The trust property has not been earmarked or segregated

Boyce v Boyce shows that even where the source of trust property has been identified in general terms, it must be possible to separate out the specific property which is to be held on trust. Where only part of a larger bulk of property is to be held on trust, the trust may fail if there has been insufficient earmarking or segregation of the trust property.[43] In *Re London Wine Co (Shippers) Ltd*,[44] a wine merchant held large stocks of wine in various warehouses. When a customer ordered a consignment, it was intended that the bottles ordered should become the property of the customer, and that from that moment they would be held on trust for him by the company. However, there was no segregation of the bottles ordered from the general stocks until actual delivery to the customer. No beneficiary was able to identify which of the bottles were his or hers. In these circumstances, Oliver J held that the intended express trust of wine in favour of customers whose orders had not yet been delivered failed for lack of certainty of subject matter because the wine

[39] [1996] 2 All ER 961 at 988. [40] [1995] Ch 223. [41] [1995] Ch 223 at 232.
[42] [1849] 16 Sim 476.
[43] See Parkinson, 'Reconceptualising the Express Trust' [2002] 61 CLJ 657 at 667–76.
[44] [1975] 126 NLJ 977.

had not been appropriated from the general stock.[45] The same requirement was affirmed and applied by the Privy Council in *Re Goldcorp Exchange Ltd (In Receivership)*,[46] where a company dealing in gold and other precious metals had used investors' money to acquire bullion. The company had not appropriated or segregated any specific parcels of bullion to the individual purchasers, but rather held it in bulk. The Privy Council held that it was not held on trust for the investors. The customers were, therefore, limited to a contractual claim against the company for the return of their investment. A comparable problem arose in *MacJordan Construction Ltd v Brookmount Erostin Ltd*,[47] where a builder's employer was entitled by contract to retain 3 per cent of the contract price as trustee for a builder, to ensure that the work done was satisfactory. The employer became insolvent, but had failed to put aside a separate retention fund of specific money due under the contract. The trust failed because it was impossible to identify any specific money as subject to the trust obligation.

(d) **Trust of a share of a larger bulk**

A case which is difficult to explain is *Hunter v Moss*.[48] The Court of Appeal held that an oral declaration of trust by Mr Moss, who owned 950 shares in a private company, of 5 per cent of the issued share capital in favour of Mr Hunter, was not void for want of certainty of subject matter merely because the shares had not been segregated or appropriated. The issued share capital was 1,000 shares, so Moss held 50 of his shares on trust for Hunter. Since the shares had been sold, he was accountable for an equivalent percentage of the consideration received. The reason for this decision is not entirely clear. One interpretation is that the requirement of the appropriation of the trust property from a common stock only applies in the case of tangible property but has no application to intangible property, provided that there is an identifiable bulk from which the property allegedly subject to the trust can be drawn. This interpretation is inconsistent with the *MacJordan Construction* case. Another, more plausible, interpretation is that the declaration of trust was to be treated as of a fractional share of Mr Moss's holding, like a trust of a share in the family home. While it could be objected that, even in this situation, the shares could have been segregated, there could be technical problems with segregating the shareholding into two separate holdings—it was likely, for instance, that Mr Moss's holding was represented by a single share certificate. However, an analogy with trusts of land supports this interpretation. It is possible for a legal owner of a house to be a trustee of a proportional part of it for someone else. This is commonplace with family homes, where one partner may be registered as legal owner, but holds on a trust to share the property with the other partner, who has also contributed financially to the purchase, or who has been promised a share which gives rise to a trust interest. The trust does not require the house to be divided physically in any way.

Hunter v Moss was argued and decided before the decision had been given in *Re Goldcorp Exchange Ltd*. It has, therefore, been subjected to criticism[49] on the grounds that it is inconsistent with the ringing endorsement by the Privy Council of *Re London Wine Co (Shippers) Ltd*. However, in *Re Harvard Securities Ltd (In Liquidation)*, Neuberger J held that he was required to follow the decision in *Hunter*, and that it could be distinguished

[45] Compare *Re Stapylton Fletcher Ltd (In Administration Receivership)* [1994] 1 WLR 1181, where a legal tenancy in common was found because bottles of wine for a group of customers had been segregated from the bulk.

[46] [1995] 1 AC 74. [47] [1992] BCLC 350.

[48] *Hunter v Moss* [1994] 1 WLR 452; Hayton, 'Uncertainty of Subject-Matter of Trusts' [1994] 110 LQR 335; Martin, 'Validity of Trust of Unidentified Shares' [1996] Conv 223.

[49] See Goode, 'Are Intangible Assets Fungible?' [2003] LMCLQ 379.

from the earlier cases on the grounds that it concerned shares and not chattels.[50] It is submitted that this is not a strong ground for distinguishing the two cases, and that the better basis for making a distinction is that property is sufficiently identified if a trust is declared of a defined fractional share of a clearly identified whole. It should be noted in this context that as a consequence of the Sale of Goods (Amendment) Act 1995, purchasers of unascertained goods held in bulk become tenants in common of the legal title if the goods are interchangeable. Although this does not generate a trust, it ensures that the purchaser enjoys a proprietary interest in the goods purchased, with the consequence that they will enjoy priority over other general creditors if the seller subsequently becomes insolvent before the goods are segregated from the bulk.

(e) A definition is too vague

A trust will fail for uncertainty if the definition given lacks the clarity needed to identify the property intended to be subject to it. In essence, there must be no 'conceptual uncertainty' as to the subject matter of the trust. In *Palmer v Simmonds*,[51] for example, a testatrix attempted to create a trust of 'the bulk of my said residuary estate'. Kindersley V-C held that this did not create a trust because the term 'bulk' did not identify a definite, clear, and certain part of her estate. Similarly, in *Re Jones*,[52] it was held that a gift by a testator of the parts of his residuary estate which were not spent or disposed of by his wife did not create a trust.[53] In *Anthony v Donges*,[54] a husband made a gift to his wife by will of 'such minimal part of my estate of whatsoever kind and wheresoever situate save as aforesaid she may be entitled to under English law for maintenance purposes'. Lloyd J held that this provision was void for uncertainty on the grounds that it was impossible to determine what she was entitled to under English law for maintenance purposes.

(f) A mechanism allows the property to be identified

In contrast, if the property is capable of being ascertained from the definition used a valid trust will be created. In *Boyce v Boyce*,[55] discussed earlier in this chapter, if Maria had still been alive, her choice would have resolved the question of which house was held on trust for Charlotte. Similarly, Herman can create a trust by his will of 'the residue of my estate' because the residue can be calculated.[56] It is what is left of the estate after other bequests or testamentary gifts have been made. A more sophisticated operation of this principle is illustrated in *Re Golay's Will Trusts*.[57] Here, a testator provided in his will that a legatee was to receive a 'reasonable income' from his properties. Ungoed-Thomas J held that this was not uncertain because the term 'reasonable income' was sufficiently objective to be capable of quantification, noting that the court is regularly required to make objective assessments of what is reasonable.[58] In *T Choithram International SA v Pagarani*,[59] the Privy Council expressed no view as to whether a settlor's gift of 'all my wealth' was void for uncertainty, as the particular assets at issue in the case had been clearly identified by the settlor as being included in the gift, and they were, therefore, held on trust.

(g) Future property

It is impossible for a settlor to create a presently existing trust of future property. 'Future property' means property which a person does not presently own, but which he hopes or

[50] [1997] 2 BCLC 369, 381–4. [51] [1854] 2 Drew 221. [52] [1898] 1 Ch 438.

[53] See also *Sprange v Barnard* [1789] 2 Bro CC 585; *In the Estate of Last* [1958] p 137. The authorities on mutual wills are developing in a way which suggests that (at least in some cases) a valid trust can exist where a beneficiary has a limited entitlement to draw down capital. See Chapter 17.

[54] [1998] 2 FLR 775. [55] [1849] 16 Sim 476.

[56] *Re Midleton's Will Trusts* [1969] 1 Ch 600; *Re Ralli's Will Trusts* [1964] Ch 288.

[57] [1965] 2 All ER 660. [58] See *Jackson v Hamilton* [1846] 3 Jo & Lat 702. [59] [2001] 1 WLR 1.

expects will come into his ownership sometime in the future. Examples of future property include: the interest a person hopes to receive under the will or on the intestacy of a living person;[60] property a person may receive under the exercise of a special power of appointment;[61] future royalties (rather than the copyright in a work);[62] a part, rather than a share, of future income;[63] and damages expected to be recovered in future litigation.[64]

In *Re Ellenborough*,[65] Miss Emily Towry Law, who was the sister of Lord Ellenborough, had executed a settlement in 1893, granting trustees any property to which she might become entitled on the deaths of her brother and sister. When her brother died in 1902, she decided not to transfer the property to the trustees. Buckley J held that no trust had been created by the execution of the settlement. It amounted rather to a mere promise to create a trust. The trustees could not compel her to transfer the property to the trustees because no consideration had been given for the promise, and 'equity will not assist a volunteer'.[66] Similarly, in *Re Brooks' Settlement Trusts*[67] in 1929 a son assigned to trustees all the property which he might receive under the exercise of a power of appointment by his mother over property held on her marriage settlement. An appointment of £3,517 was made in his favour in 1939. Farwell J held that no trust had been created in 1929 because the property was a 'mere expectancy' and that since the settlement had been voluntary it could not be enforced.[68]

Future property should be distinguished from a residuary interest where a person has an immediate right to property, subject only to the expiry of another right. Since it is not 'future property', he may subject it to an immediate trust. For example, a landlord owning a freehold can create a trust of it, even if he has given a lease to a tenant. Similarly, if Yvette (who has just died) has left her house to her son Teddy, subject to her husband, Ed, having the right to live in the house for the rest of his life, Teddy has a vested interest, rather than a mere expectancy, which can itself be the subject matter of a trust. This appears to have been misunderstood by Mark Herbert QC, sitting as a Deputy High Court Judge, in *Re Erskine 1948 Trust*.[69] Under this trust, the settlor expressly provided that in certain circumstances, the funds would devolve to the 'statutory next of kin' of the principal beneficiary. As the judge accepted, the reference to the statutory next of kin was to be treated as if the words of the relevant Act had been incorporated into the settlement. Despite this, the judge thought—without citing any authority—that the next of kin had 'by definition'[70] only an expectancy. That aspect of his decision was erroneous, because their rights could not be destroyed by a new will. The reason why the next of kin (or a beneficiary under the will) of a living person have only an expectancy is because their expectations may be wholly defeated by the making of a will (or the changing of an existing will).

(h) Contract to create a trust

A person can contract to make a trust in the event of receiving property in the future, but this is not the same as creating an immediate trust.

60 *Re Ellenborough* [1903] 1 Ch 697; *Re Lind* [1915] 2 Ch 345.

61 *Re Brooks' Settlement Trusts* [1939] Ch 993.

62 *Re Trytel* [1952] 2 TLR 32.

63 *Williams v IRC* [1965] NZLR 395: the settlor assigned the first £500 of his income to a charitable purpose. The New Zealand Court of Appeal held that this was future property, because it was not certain there would be such income. If he had assigned a proportion of his annual income, this would have been valid.

64 *Glegg v Bromley* [1912] 3 KB 474.

65 [1903] 1 Ch 697.

66 The concept of the volunteer in equity is discussed in Chapter 6 on constitution of trusts.

67 [1939] Ch 993.

68 See also *Norman v Federal Comr of Taxation* [1964] ALR 131; *Williams v IRC* [1965] NZLR 395.

69 [2012] 3 All ER 532.

70 Ibid at 55.

(2) Effect of uncertainty of subject matter

(a) The trust fails

Uncertainty as to the subject matter of a trust prevents the trust taking effect. If it has been claimed that a settlor has declared himself to be a trustee, the settlor will remain outright owner free of any trust. If the uncertainty relates to property which has already effectively been given to a third party (for instance, where a gift of the settlor's entire estate has been made to a third party with a direction which applies only to an unascertained part), the effect of the trust failing will be to make the gift outright and free from a trust. Finally, if the uncertainty defines not only the property subject to a trust but also the property contained in a transfer, the uncertainty will prevent the transfer taking effect.

(b) Property ceases to exist

A trust will cease to exist if all the property subject to it is destroyed or dissipated.[71] As will be seen later, this does not prevent the trustee being liable if the loss of the trust fund is something for which the trustee is answerable.

5 Certainty of objects

(1) General

Certainty of objects is the third of the three certainties, and the one which gives rise to the greatest theoretical issues. It helps, in trying to pick a way through these theoretical issues, to remember that the reason for requiring the three certainties is that trusts are legally enforceable obligations. For an obligation to be enforceable, it needs to be sufficiently clear and defined to allow the courts both to determine whether the obligation has been broken, and to guide them as to the order for enforcement they should make. There also needs to be someone who is sufficiently interested in the trust to petition the court in the event of an alleged breach. The requirement of certainty of objects has two aspects:[72] for the one part the objects of the trust must be certain in the sense that the trustees must know (or be able to find out) the limits of their authority to use the trust fund. For the other part, the objects must be certain in the sense that, with the exception of charitable trusts (and the small number of anomalous unenforceable trusts which are valid as exceptions to the beneficiary principle), a trust will only be valid if it exists for the benefit of identified legal persons who possess the locus standi to enforce the trust obligations, and for whom the property is held. This second sense of the requirement of certainty of objects—also known as the beneficiary principle—will be explored later in the context of trusts for purposes. Our focus here is on certainty in the first sense: the need for the authority of trustees to be clearly defined. In most cases this will also centre on the beneficiaries since most trusts are established for the benefit of individuals. The beneficiaries must be defined in such a way that it is possible for the trustees, or in the event of their default the court, to know who they are. Problems of uncertainty generally arise where the beneficiaries are defined by means of a 'class definition'. Such a definition must be sufficiently certain, and the criterion used to identify the class sufficiently objective, to enable determination of who is within, and who is outside, the class, thus ensuring that allocations of trust property are only made to genuine beneficiaries.

[71] See *Re Diplock* [1948] Ch 465; *Bishopsgate Investment Management v Homan* [1995] 1 All ER 347.

[72] The leading case, *Morice v Bishop of Durham* [1804] 9 Ves 399, conflates these two requirements and consequently has been the cause of some confusion.

(2) Certainty for trusts, powers, and gifts

It is not just in relation to trusts that certainty of objects is an issue. Even a straightforward outright gift can only take effect if it is known who the recipient is. A gift in a will 'to my cousin Mary' will fail if there is no way of deciding which of two cousins with that name were meant by the testatrix (or if there is no one who matches that description). Powers of appointment are also subject to a requirement of certainty of objects, although the test here operates slightly differently from trusts. When a trust compels a trustee to make a distribution, the terms of the trust must be sufficiently clear to enable the trustee to perform that duty. Thus, as a simple matter of common sense, if the trustees have to divide a fund equally amongst the members of a group, the description of that group must be sufficiently clear to enable the trustees (or if the trustees fail to act, the court) to identify the exact number of individuals who are in that group. On the other hand, where a power of appointment contains no obligation on the donee to make an appointment, all that is needed is sufficient clarity to enable the court to review, after any appointment, whether it falls within the limits prescribed by the instrument creating the power.

(3) Conceptual and evidential certainty

In deciding what level of certainty is required for a trust or a power, the courts have distinguished between conceptual certainty and evidential certainty.

(a) Conceptual certainty

'Conceptual certainty' refers to the semantic clarity of the description of beneficiaries. If there is any ambiguity in the words used to define a class of objects or if the definition is not objective, so that the court or the allocator cannot determine without a doubt whether a person is within the class or not, it will be conceptually uncertain. For example, 'tall people' is conceptually uncertain, because there is no way of telling what is 'tall'. 'People over 6 ft' would be conceptually certain, because the method of measurement is not a matter of doubt or debate. Similarly, a class of 'old ladies', 'good friends', or 'regulars' at a local pub would be conceptually uncertain. In *Re Baden's Deed Trusts (No 2)*[73] Sachs LJ gave as examples of conceptually certain classes 'first cousins', 'members of the X trade union', and 'those who have served in the Royal Navy'. Browne-Wilkinson J expressed the problem clearly with regard to the word 'friends' in *Re Barlow's Will Trusts*:

> ['Friends'] has a great range of meanings; indeed its exact meaning probably varies from person to person. Some would include only those with whom they had been on intimate terms over a long period; others would include acquaintances who they liked. Some would include people with whom their relationship was primarily one of business; others would not. Indeed, many people, if asked to draw up a complete list of their friends, would probably have some difficulty in deciding whether certain of the people they knew were really 'friends' as opposed to 'acquaintances' . . .[74]

This requirement is, therefore, about the precision of language used to define the class of persons the settlor intends to benefit and it can be a difficult question, as it is concerned with linguistics and semantics. 'Nobel Prize winners' or 'David's descendants' would both be conceptually certain: there is no or very limited scope for debate as to what each of these descriptions means.

[73] [1973] Ch 9 at 20. [74] [1979] 1 WLR 278 at 298.

(b) Evidential certainty

This describes the extent to which the evidence in a particular case enables specific persons to be identified as members of a particular class of objects. For example, one could prove that one was a 'Nobel Prize winner' by providing the necessary documentary evidence that the prize had been awarded. In the case of 'David's descendants', although the test is conceptually certain—you are either one of David's children or grandchildren or you are not—until the advent of DNA fingerprinting there could have been evidential difficulties in individual cases of proving paternity. If the children have moved away from home and not kept in touch, there could also be difficulties in finding all of the descendants, although this is not strictly a question of certainty.

(4) No single test of certainty for all trusts

Because the requirement of certainty of objects flows from the need for trustees to know what their obligations are, and for the court to act in the event of breach, the requirement does not operate identically in every situation.

(a) Fixed trusts

Fixed trusts are those in which the shares of the beneficiaries are defined by the trust instrument. Trusts for an individual, and a trust to divide in equal shares are both examples. For all forms of fixed trust, the test for certainty of objects is the complete list or class ascertainability test. For many years there was no direct authority for this, but in *OT Computers Ltd v First National Tricity Finance Ltd*,[75] Pumphrey J, in considering that a proposed fixed trust of a supplier's deposit account was uncertain, stated that a complete list of beneficiaries was necessary so that the property could vest immediately under the trust:

> At this point, it is important to remember that the trust which is proposed is a fixed trust. Accordingly, it must be possible to identify each member of the class of beneficiaries. It is not sufficient to be able to say whether or not any identified person is or is not a member of the class entitled to be considered: the purpose of the trust in the present case is to vest an immediate interest in the suppliers in question.[76]

Significantly, Pumphrey J cited *McPhail v Doulton*[77] as authority for this statement of the law, demonstrating that the 'complete list' test has survived that decision, despite arguments to the contrary which are considered below.

(i) Trust for identified individual

Where a trust is created for an individual, that person must be described in such a way as to make that person identifiable. That requires conceptual certainty, but it also requires evidential certainty, as Lord Upjohn explained in *Re Gulbenkian's Settlements*:

> If a donor . . . directs trustees to make some specified provision for 'John Smith', then to give legal effect to that provision it must be possible to identify 'John Smith'. If the donor knows three John Smiths then by the most elementary principles of law neither the trustees nor the court in their place can give effect to that provision; neither the trustees nor the court can guess at it. It must fail for uncertainty unless of course admissible evidence is available to point to a particular John Smith as the object of the donor's bounty.[78]

[75] [2003] EWHC 1010 (Ch). [76] [2003] EWHC 1010 (Ch) at 21.
[77] Referred to as *Re Baden* [1971] AC 424. [78] [1970] AC 508 at 523.

If the beneficiary is identified by a description, rather than by name, then the description must have sufficient clarity to enable the individual to be identified. A gift in a trust in favour of 'the first woman to land on the moon' would satisfy this requirement. As will be seen later, a provision in a trust for 'any wife of Jewish faith' would, without more, probably fail since it is unclear what is meant by the description.

(ii) Trust for equal division

Where a trust requires provision to be made for a group in equal shares, it must be possible to draw up a 'complete list' of all the beneficiaries.[79] This is sometimes referred to as the 'class ascertainability' test. This means that the definition of the beneficiaries must be both conceptually certain and there must also be evidential certainty of who is within the class.[80] The reason for this is obvious: an obligation to divide the property in equal shares between the members of the class requires that the trustees should know how many there are in the class. The beneficiaries do not have to be named individually, but if they are identified by way of a description, (e.g. 'Wendy's children') it must be possible to identify each and every person who matches that description.

(iii) Other fixed trusts

It is possible for a trust to exist in favour of a class, but with unequal shares, for instance where a solicitor invests client money in a client trust account. In such a case, each client would be entitled to that share of the account which represents their individual investment. Both conceptual and evidential certainty will be required to prove a share in the fund. In *OT Computers Ltd v First National Tricity Finance Ltd*,[81] a proposed trust in favour of 'urgent suppliers' failed as it did not create a conceptually certain class. The case concerned the collapse of the Tiny Computer retailer, owned by the claimant, OT Computers Ltd. To protect its customers and suppliers from creditors in difficult trading conditions, the claimant had instructed the defendant bank to set up two separate bank accounts, one for customers and one for monies owed to its suppliers. The company also created two schedules, which listed the names of its customers and a selection of its suppliers, respectively. When the claimant company went into receivership, the defendant sought to reclaim a loan due to it from the money in the two deposit accounts. The claimant argued that trusts had been validly declared of the monies in the bank accounts. Pumphrey J upheld a fixed trust of the customer account, as all the beneficiaries could be clearly identified due to the payments made by them to the claimant company. However, in relation to the supplier account, the schedule did not list all suppliers, but referred instead to 'urgent suppliers'. Pumphrey J held that the term 'urgent suppliers' was an insufficiently conceptually certain description of a class, so that the trustees could not draw up a complete list. The term 'urgent' was simply too vague. The money in the suppliers account remained part of the company assets.

(iv) Evidential certainty

A 'complete list' of beneficiaries can only be drawn up if it is possible to identify each and every member of the class in fact. This means that there must be 'evidential certainty'. If the trust is created in favour of all the 'employees and ex-employees' of a company, it must be possible to identify each and every employee and ex-employee. In *Re Sayer*[82] a trust in favour of the employees and ex-employees of Sayers (Confectioners) Ltd was held

[79] *IRC v Broadway Cottages Trust* [1955] Ch 20, CA.

[80] Emery, 'The Most Hallowed Principle: Certainty of Beneficiaries of Trusts and Powers of Appointment' (1982) 98 LQR 551.

[81] [2003] EWHC 1010 (Ch).

[82] [1957] Ch 423.

void for uncertainty[83] because it was impossible to draw up a complete list of the persons employed by the company since its incorporation. The company had found it impossible to keep accurate records of its ex-employees.[84]

(v) When is certainty required?

The relevant date for the drawing up of the complete list is the date of execution of the trust, not the date of its creation.[85] Thus a trust may be created now for the benefit of persons as yet unborn or unascertained, but it must be possible to draw up a complete closed list on the due date of execution.

(b) **Powers of appointment**

Powers of appointment differ from trusts in that they do not require the donee of the power to distribute the property concerned. They authorize the donee to nominate a beneficiary. The power can only be exercised within the limits of the authority conferred by the instrument—normally a trust—creating it. Sufficient certainty is required to enable the donee to identify in whose favour an appointment can be made, and to allow the court to intervene, should the limits of the donee's authority be exceeded. It is possible for a power to be general, in other words, to contain no restrictions upon whom can be chosen as a beneficiary, but the class of objects can be restricted either by limiting the exercise of the power for the benefit of named individuals or a defined class of objects (this would be called a special power) or by excluding certain individuals or groups (this would be called a hybrid or intermediate power).

The supervisory jurisdiction of the court does not allow it to compel the exercise of a bare or mere power of appointment. The function of the court is restricted to interfering should there have been an excessive exercise of the power (i.e. an exercise beyond the limits of the authority which it confers). The court does not need there to be a complete list of objects or potential beneficiaries for it to do this; it is only necessary to determine of any individual in whose favour the donee has purported to exercise the power whether that individual is within the limits defined by the instrument creating the power.

The test of certainty for powers of appointment was laid down by the House of Lords in *Re Gulbenkian's Settlement (No 1)*[86] and is often described as the 'is or is not' test or, more formally, as the 'individual ascertainability' test. A special power of appointment was granted in favour of a class consisting of Nubar Gulbenkian, his wife and children, and 'any person or persons in whose house or apartments or in whose company or under whose care or control or by whom or with whom he may from time to time be employed or residing'. This was upheld as sufficiently certain. Lord Upjohn stated the relevant test of certainty:[87]

> a mere or bare power of appointment among a class is valid if you can with certainty say whether any given individual is or is not a member of the class: you do not have to be able to ascertain every member of the class.[88]

[83] *Re Sayer* involved what today would be regarded as a discretionary trust and the test adopted in the House of Lords in *McPhail v Doulton* [1971] AC 424, HL would now be applied. As interpreted in *Re Baden (No 2)* [1973] Ch 9, the trust would be upheld, as for a discretionary trust the class of beneficiaries must be 'conceptually' certain but need not be 'evidentially' certain.

[84] [1957] Ch 423 at 430: because of its large number of shops (seventy), and the nature of its workforce, which consisted of a large number of female shop assistants who tended to change employment frequently.

[85] See, for example, *Swain v Law Society* [1981] 3 All ER 797.

[86] [1970] AC 508.

[87] Lord Hodson and Lord Guest agreed with Lord Upjohn; Lord Reid delivered a similar opinion; Lord Donovan agreed with Lord Upjohn but reserved his opinion on whether the test proposed by the Court of Appeal that the power should be valid if it could be said of any one person that he was within the class, although he was 'inclined to share' Lord Upjohn's view.

[88] [1970] AC 508 at 521.

This test had been propounded by Harman J in *Re Gestetner Settlement*[89] and approved by the Court of Appeal in *IRC v Broadway Cottages Trust*.[90] Lord Upjohn rejected[91] a broader test of certainty put forward by Lord Denning MR in the Court of Appeal that a power of appointment would be valid if it could be said with certainty of any one person that he was clearly within the class, even if it may be difficult to say in other cases whether a person is within the class or not.[92] In *Re Gresham*[93] Harman J had held that a power with similar terms to that in *Re Gulbenkian* was void for uncertainty, but the Court of Appeal and House of Lords overruled the decision. Mere difficulty in determining whether an individual is within or without the class is not sufficient to invalidate the power, and the court can rule on borderline cases.[94] Only insuperable difficulty will render the power void for uncertainty.

The *Gulbenkian* test is consistent with established principle and logic. It requires that the court must be able to determine with absolute certainty whether any given individual is or is not a member of the class of potential objects. This is essential if the court is to determine whether the power has been exercised properly. If Toby grants Stephanie a power of appointment over his residuary estate in favour of 'old men', it would be impossible for the court to determine if an appointment in favour of Robert, who is 64, was excessive. It is not possible to say of every individual whether they are 'old' or not, because 'old' has no clear objective meaning: it would be different if the power was limited to 'men aged over 65' because that is an objectively clear criterion.

(c) Discretionary trusts

Some trusts combine the characteristics of trusts and powers. In the leading case of *McPhail v Doulton*,[95] the House of Lords was asked to rule on a settlement created by Bertram Baden, under which the trustees of a fund were to apply the income 'to or for the benefit of any of the officers and employees or ex-officers or ex-employees of the company [Matthew Hall & Co Ltd] or to any relatives or dependants of any such persons in such amounts at such times and on such conditions (if any) as they think fit'. The Court of Appeal had thought that if this was a trust, it was invalid because it would not have been possible to draw up a complete list of beneficiaries, but held it was valid because it was a power and it satisfied the 'is or is not' test. The House of Lords took a different view for reasons which are more fully explored in the chapter on discretionary trusts.[96] According to the Law Lords, taken as a whole the words of the instrument were mandatory: they imposed an obligation and, therefore, created a trust. However, the Court of Appeal had been wrong to consider that all trusts needed a complete list of beneficiaries. The question was whether the court could control the trust. In other words, the court must be in a position to make a valid judgment if it is alleged that the trustees have performed their duty wrongly, and must be capable of intervening in some effective way if it is alleged that the trustees have failed to perform their duty. Intervention by the court where trustees failed to act did not require equal division. There were other interventions open to the court such as appointing new trustees or making its own decision on the merits. In that light, it was unnecessary for there to be a complete list of all the beneficiaries, and the test

[89] [1953] Ch 672; followed by Roxburgh J in *Re Coates (Decd)* [1955] Ch 495 and Upjohn J in *Re Sayer* [1957] Ch 423.

[90] [1955] Ch 20. See also *Re Hain's Settlement* [1961] 1 WLR 440 at 445, per Lord Evershed MR.

[91] [1970] AC 508 at 134. [92] [1968] Ch 126 at 134. [93] [1956] 1 WLR 573.

[94] [1970] AC 508 at 523.

[95] [1971] AC 424. This decision is probably the most important case on the law of trusts decided in the twentieth century.

[96] This is looked at in more detail in Chapter 27 because the change in the certainty test is so closely concerned with the questions of the duties on the trustees and the powers of the court to intervene.

for certainty of beneficiaries in discretionary trusts should be 'similar' to that used for the certainty of objects of powers,[97] namely, that it must be possible to say of any given individual that he is, or is not, within the class. This is the 'individual ascertainability' or the 'is or is not' test. This requires that the class be specified with conceptual certainty. The case was remitted to the Chancery Division to apply the new test to the facts, and the application reached the Court of Appeal as *Re Baden's Deed Trusts (No 2)*.[98]

(d) **Problems with the individual ascertainability test**

(i) Is the test the same for both powers and discretionary trusts?

Lord Wilberforce stated in *McPhail v Doulton* that the test for discretionary trusts should be 'similar' to that for powers of appointment. That begs the question of how, if at all, it differs. It is generally assumed that the test is the same, but there may be as yet unidentified considerations which apply to trusts but not to mere powers.

(ii) Application of the test

The Court of Appeal were not of a single mind as to how the individual ascertainability test should be applied in *Re Baden's Deed Trusts (No 2)*.[99] The central question was whether the application of the 'is or is not' test adopted by the House of Lords from *Re Gulbenkian's Settlement Trusts*[100] requires positive proof of the negative limb, so that it can be categorically stated that any individual in the world 'is not' a member of the given class. Stamp LJ held that it must be possible to categorize *any* individual as being either inside the class or outside it.[101] On that basis, if he had not also considered that the expression 'relatives' should be treated as limited to the statutory next of kin,[102] the trust would have failed for uncertainty. The view of Stamp LJ appears to require both conceptual and evidential certainty, and if applied, it would ultimately be possible to draw up a complete list by surveying all potential objects.

The majority of the Court of Appeal took the view that the *Gulbenkian* test did not require that it could be proved that any given individual is not within the class. Sachs and Megaw LJJ emphasized the distinction between conceptual and evidential certainty, and neither believed that the test required evidential certainty. As Sachs LJ observed:

> the court is never defeated by 'evidential uncertainty', and it is in my judgment clear that it is conceptual certainty to which reference was made when the 'is or is not a member of the class' test was enunciated... The suggestion that such trusts could be invalid because it might be impossible to prove of a given individual that he was not in the relevant class is wholly fallacious...[103]

Both Sachs and Megaw LLJ took the view that since the words 'relatives' and 'dependants' were conceptually certain in their widest possible meanings, the trust was valid and not void for uncertainty. However, they took slightly differing approaches to the problem of 'evidential certainty' (see Figure 5.1).[104] Sachs LJ took the view that if a class was 'conceptually certain', then there was in essence no evidential difficulty because of the operation of a presumption that anyone not positively proved to be within the class is outside of it. The burden falls on potential claimants to prove they fall within the class.

[97] *Re Gulbenkian's Settlement Trusts (No 1)* [1968] Ch 126. [98] [1973] Ch 9.
[99] [1973] Ch 9. [100] [1970] AC 508. [101] [1973] Ch 9 at 28.
[102] At 28–9, following *Harding v Glyn* [1739] 1 Atk 469. [103] [1973] Ch 9 at 20.
[104] Criticized in Hopkins, 'Continuing Uncertainty as to Certainty of Objects of Trust Powers' [1973] CLJ 36.

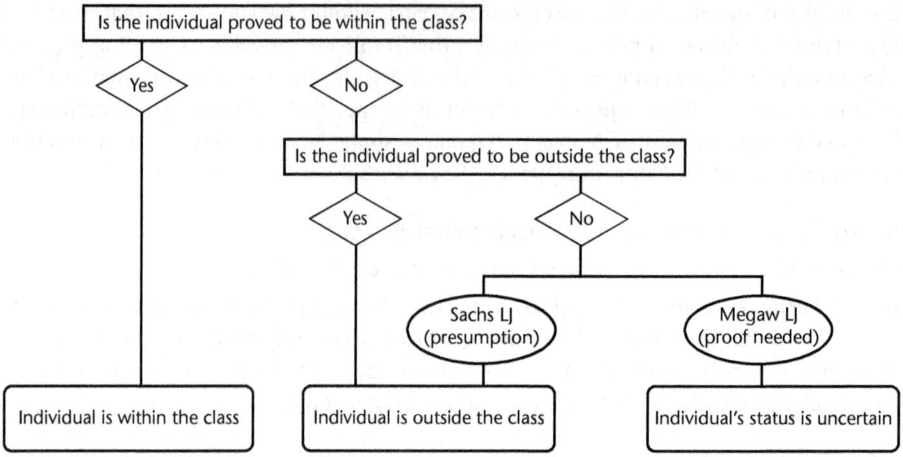

Figure 5.1 Dealing with evidential certainty

Megaw LJ did not employ such a simple evidential presumption, but pointed out that the test did not require the creation of a list of all the beneficiaries, since that test had been rejected by the House of Lords. Nor was the test satisfied if a single individual could prove that he or she satisfied the description, since that view had also been specifically rejected. He considered that there were three groups of persons: those positively proved within the class, those positively proved to be outside the class, and those about whom, if they were to be considered, it would have to be said they are not proven to be inside or outside the class. He concluded that:

> the test is satisfied if, as regards at least a substantial number of objects, it can be said with certainty that they fall within the trust; even though, as regards a substantial number of other persons, if they ever for some fanciful reason fell to be considered, the answer would have to be, not 'they are outside the trust', but 'it is not proven whether they are in or out'.[105]

The majority of the court, therefore, concentrated on the need to prove that individuals were within the description of the class, taking a pragmatic approach to the possibility that it might be difficult to make a conclusive decision as to whether other individuals were outside the class. All members of the court agreed that the terms 'dependant' and 'relative' should be interpreted in a way which was conceptually certain and made the trust valid.

Despite much academic debate, the difference of opinion between the members of the court in *Re Baden's Deed Trusts (No 2)*[106] has not given rise to any significant problems in subsequent cases.[107] This is, no doubt, because the decision in *McPhail v Doulton* makes two things clear. First, that the courts will seek to facilitate the intentions of the settlor rather than trying to shoehorn dispositions into rigid categories. Second, that the emphasis is on how the trustees should act and how the court should control them. In order to distribute the funds, the trustees of a discretionary trust do not need to know the identity of every member of the class, nor the exact number of the beneficiaries.[108]

105 [1973] Ch 9 at 24. 106 [1973] Ch 9.

107 See, for example, *Re Bose Trusts, Public Trustee v Butler* [2012] All ER (D) 40 where the case was cited without substantial discussion.

108 *Re Hay's Settlement Trusts* [1981] 3 All ER 786.

(iii) Other factors

Even where the test for certainty of objects has been satisfied, a discretionary trust may still fail if it is capricious in the sense that there is no discernible objective to guide the trustees in making their decisions, or if the class of beneficiaries is so large as to be administratively unworkable.[109] These two constraints, which will be explored in a later chapter,[110] are probably connected.

(5) Resolving uncertainty

(a) Ascertainment and Benjamin orders

What happens where a trust requires equal division between a group, but the whereabouts of one of the individuals are unknown? Suppose Frances leaves all her property to Eric on trust to be divided equally among her first cousins. This will create a valid fixed trust. The class is conceptually certain. Suppose, also that it is known that Francis had seven first cousins, but one of the seven, Graham, left for South America in 1987 and has not been seen or heard from since. Would the fact that it is not known whether he is alive or cannot be found, invalidate the trust? The phrase 'first cousin' is conceptually certain, but there is a problem of ascertainment.[111] This was addressed by Lord Upjohn in *Re Gulbenkian's Settlements*, where he said:

> If the class is sufficiently defined by the donor the fact that it may be difficult to ascertain the whereabouts or continued existence of some of its members at the relevant time matters not.[112]

Lord Wilberforce echoed this view in *McPhail v Doulton*:

> as to the question of certainty, I desire to emphasise the distinction clearly made and explained by Lord Upjohn, between linguistic or semantic uncertainty . . . and the difficulty of ascertaining the existence or whereabouts of members of the class . . .[113]

Problems of the ascertainment of beneficiaries will not render the trust void for uncertainty provided that in other respects the trust is valid. This is consistent with principle. If a complete list can be drawn up, then the minimum share to which each beneficiary is entitled is known and the fund can be allocated on that basis. In our example, because it is known that Francis had seven first cousins, each cousin is certainly entitled to a minimum one-seventh share in the fund, and Eric can allocate it on that basis. As to the seventh share to which Graham may be entitled, Eric can 'apply to the court for directions or pay a share into court'.[114] In the case of unascertainable beneficiaries who are thought to be dead, the court can make a 'Benjamin order'. This entitles the trustees to allocate the fund on the presumption that the beneficiary had predeceased the testator. In *Re Benjamin*[115] David Benjamin left his residuary estate to his children in equal shares. He had twelve children surviving him, but one had disappeared while on holiday in France a year before the testator's death. Joyce J held that, in the absence of any evidence to the contrary, he must be presumed to be dead and his share was to be allocated accordingly. If it subsequently turns out that the unascertained beneficiary is alive, he may trace his

[109] *McPhail v Doulton* [1971] AC 424; *R v District Auditor, ex p West Yorkshire Metropolitan County Council* [1986] RVR 24.

[110] See Chapter 27.

[111] It is open to debate whether this is an issue of evidential uncertainty. See Emery, 'The Most Hallowed Principle: Certainty of Beneficiaries of Trusts and Powers of Appointment' [1982] 98 LQR 551 at 556.

[112] [1970] AC 508 at 524.

[113] [1971] AC 424 at 457.

[114] *Re Gulbenkian's Settlement Trusts* [1970] AC 508 at 524, per Lord Upjohn.

[115] [1902] 1 Ch 723.

share of the fund into the hands of those who received it,[116] and the trustees are not liable for breach of trust. The court order protects them.

(b) Gifts subject to a condition

There are some ways in which a gift that would otherwise fail on grounds of uncertainty might be found to be valid. What might appear to be a gift to an ill-defined group, such as 'my old friends', could in some contexts be treated as a series of separate gifts that can be considered as if they stood alone. For instance, in *Re Barlow's Will Trusts*,[117] Helen Alice Dorothy Barlow died leaving a valuable collection of paintings. She gave instructions in her will that 'any members of my family and any friends of mine' could buy any of the paintings at the prices contained in a catalogue of valuations made some five years before her death. These prices were significantly below the value of the paintings after her death. Browne-Wilkinson J held that the instruction was not invalid for uncertainty. This was not a gift to a class. It was properly to be regarded as a series of individual gifts to persons answering the description of friend or family member. The test which applies to class gifts:

> has no application to a case where there is a condition or description attached to one or more individual gifts; in such cases, uncertainty as to some other persons who may have been intended to take does not in any way affect the quantum of the gift to persons who undoubtedly possess the qualification.

Accordingly, 'anyone who can prove that by any reasonable test he or she must have been a friend' of Helen Barlow would be entitled to purchase a picture. Anyone who did not satisfy this stringent test would not be entitled to take advantage of the option created by the will. Similarly, anyone who could prove a blood relationship to Helen Barlow would qualify as a family member. The fact that there might be considerable areas of uncertainty did not defeat the provision for those who clearly satisfied it. This solution could not apply where the size of each gift depended upon the number of individuals satisfying the description.

(i) Mechanism for resolving uncertainty

Another way in which problems of uncertainty can be resolved is where the gift itself provides a mechanism for resolving that uncertainty. Thus, a gift to 'intelligent people' would normally fail for lack of certainty because there is no clear definition of intelligence. However, a gift to people who, in the opinion of the President of Mensa, are intelligent, would probably be held to be valid. For instance, in *Re Tuck's Settlement Trusts*,[118] Sir Adolf Tuck, a Jew, was made a baronet in 1910. He wanted to make sure that future descendants inheriting the title of baronet remained in the Jewish faith. To this end, he specified that future baronets would inherit the funds he left by will only if they married a wife of Jewish blood, who at the time of her marriage 'continues to worship according to the Jewish faith'. He added that in case of dispute 'the decision of the Chief Rabbi in London shall be conclusive'. Eveleigh LJ in the Court of Appeal had some doubt as to whether the condition as to the Jewish faith would in itself have been sufficiently clear. However, the reference to the Chief Rabbi operated to make it clear: 'Different people may have different views or be doubtful as to what is "Jewish faith" but the Chief Rabbi knows and can say what meaning he attaches to the words.'[119]

There has been some debate about the reasoning lying behind this decision. Eveleigh J suggested that the Chief Rabbi would have a clear understanding of what was meant by the Jewish faith and could provide it if asked. But it is more than likely that, even for the

[116] Subject to the Limitation Act 1980, ss 18, 21(3), and 22.
[117] [1979] 1 WLR 278.
[118] [1978] Ch 49; [1978] 1 All ER 1047.
[119] [1978] 1 All ER 1047 at 1057.

Chief Rabbi, there could be areas of conceptual doubt. In that case, does reference to him for a decision resolve any uncertainty? It may be that providing for a decision to be made by a third party means that an inherently uncertain concept (for instance, who is intelligent?) is replaced by the certain test (e.g. those persons stated by the President of Mensa to be intelligent). In that case, what can be done if a decision is taken by the third party arbitrarily—for instance, if the President of Mensa states that someone is intelligent when they are clearly not? The courts are reluctant to see their jurisdiction ousted. If they retain a supervisory jurisdiction, then they need to be able to control the arbitrary exercise of the decision-making authority conferred on the third party. Yet they can only decide if the decisions he or she makes have been properly made if the test itself is sufficiently certain to be applied by the court. That takes us back to where we began.[120]

The answer to this problem is contained in the common-sense judgment of Lord Denning. Even if there is conceptual uncertainty, it can be cured by a provision stating that any uncertainty may be resolved by the decision of a competent third party:

> So long as he does not misconduct himself or come to a decision which is wholly unreasonable, I think his decision should stand . . . As this very case shows, the courts may get bogged down in distinctions between conceptual uncertainty and evidential uncertainty . . . The testator may want to cut out all that cackle, and let someone decide it who will really understand what the testator is talking about, and thus save an expensive journey to the lawyers and the courts. For my part, I would not blame him. I would give effect to his intentions.[121]

Table 5.1 Tests for certainty of objects

Obligation	Test of certainty	Authority	Requirements
Power	It must be possible to say whether any given individual is or is not a member of the class	*Re Gulbenkian* [1968] Ch 126	Conceptual certainty
Discretionary trusts	It must be possible to say whether any given individual is or is not a member of the class	*McPhail v Doulton* [1971] AC 424; *Re Baden (No 2)* [1972] Ch 607	Conceptual certainty
Fixed trusts	Complete list of all beneficiaries	*OT Computers Ltd v First National Tricity Finance Ltd* [2003] EWHC 1010 (Ch); [2007] WTLR 165	Conceptual and evidential certainty
Conditional gifts (conditions precedent)	Condition valid for those who can prove they satisfy the condition	*Re Barlow's Will Trust* [1979] 1 WLR 278	Individual proof

[120] It may be possible to classify this decision as one of evidential uncertainty, rather than conceptual uncertainty, but doing so does not resolve the issues raised earlier, as the same concerns about arbitrary decision-making by the nominated third party remain.

[121] [1978] 1 All ER 1047 at 1053–4.

(6) Topics of debate

(a) Should there be a single test for certainty of objects?

The 'complete list' test is almost universally accepted as the requisite test of certainty of objects for fixed trusts. However, it has been argued that the 'complete list' test is a 'heresy' that has grown from a misunderstanding of judicial statements,[122] and that the test for fixed trusts should be the same as that for discretionary trusts.[123] This argument runs against principle, logic, and authority, and fails to take sufficient account of the differences between the duty of trustees of a fixed trust to allocate the fund and that of trustees under a discretionary trust.[124] The 'complete list' test is supported both in principle and in logic. The very nature of the fixed trust where the beneficiaries are defined as a class requires that a 'complete list' be drawn up before the trustee can allocate the fund. If such a list cannot be drawn up, it is absolutely impossible for the trustee to carry out his duty to allocate the fund, or for the court to act on his default. Lord Upjohn expressed the problem clearly in *Re Gulbenkian's Settlement*:

> Suppose the donor directs that a fund be divided equally between 'my old friends', then unless there is some admissible evidence that the donor has given some special 'dictionary' meaning to that phrase which enables the trustees to identify the class with sufficient certainty, it is plainly bad as being too uncertain. Suppose that there appeared before the trustees (or the court) two or three individuals who plainly satisfied the test of being among 'my old friends', the trustees could not consistently with the donor's intentions accept them as claiming the whole or any defined part of the fund. They cannot claim the whole fund for they can show no title to it unless they prove they are the only members of the class, which they cannot do, and so, too, by parity of reasoning they cannot claim any defined part of the fund and there is no authority in the trustees or the court to make any distribution among a smaller class than that pointed to by the donor.[125]

These forcefully and persuasively expressed views are now supported by the decision in *OT Computers Ltd v First National Tricity Finance Ltd*,[126] explained above.

(b) An alternative test for powers

Following *Re Gulbenkian*,[127] *McPhail v Doulton*,[128] and *Re Baden (No 2)*,[129] the same requirement of conceptual certainty applies to fixed trusts, discretionary trusts, and powers of appointment. He proposed that:

> if the [donees] can say of a particular person: 'He is clearly within the category', the gift is good, even though it may be difficult in other cases to say whether a person is or is not within the category.[130]

In *Re Gibbards Will Trusts*[131] a testator gave his trustees a power of appointment over his residuary estate in favour of 'any of my old friends'. Plowman J concluded that 'there is not a sufficient degree of uncertainty about the expression'[132] to hold the power void

[122] Matthews, 'A Heresy and a Half in Certainty of Objects' [1984] Conv 22.

[123] Requiring only 'conceptual certainty' and not a 'complete list' to be in fact drawn up. See also Matthews, 'The Comparative Importance of the Rule in *Saunders v Vautier*' [2006] LQR 268 at 276: 'there is no sensible basis for applying a different test of certainty for different kinds of equitable owners. The size or stability of the equitable interest concerned is not a sufficient reason. All interests having a *Saunders v Vautier* value (however big or small) should be judged by the same criteria of certainty.'

[124] Martin and Hayton, 'Certainty of Objects—What Is Heresy?' [1984] Conv 304.

[125] [1970] AC 508 at 524. [126] [2003] EWHC 1010 (Ch); [2007] WTLR 165.

[127] [1970] AC 508. [128] [1971] AC 424. [129] [1973] Ch 9.

[130] *Re Gulbenkian's Settlement* [1968] Ch 126 at 134. [131] [1966] 1 All ER 273.

[132] [1966] 1 All ER 273 at 281.

for uncertainty. Similarly, in *Re Coates (Decd)*[133] a power to appoint a specified sum to 'friends' was upheld as valid. Roxburgh J held that the word 'friend' was not too vague, although he recognized that 'friendship' was a phrase 'particularly blurred in outline'.[134] Both cases would almost certainly now be decided differently. Definitions such as 'old friends' would probably not be sufficiently conceptually certain[135] under the test propounded in *Re Baden (No 2)*,[136] and *Re Gibbard*[137] was decided on the basis of the test rejected by the House of Lords in *Re Gulbenkian* that it must be possible to say of at least some persons that they are certainly within the class, even if it were not possible to say of others whether they are or not.[138]

Ultimately, it is a question of policy whether a purely discretionary power should fail for lack of conceptual certainty. If a donor grants a power to appoint his property in favour of his 'old friends', there will usually be some people who are without question within the class. Should the power fail and the donor's intention be defeated merely because there are others about whom it cannot be definitely stated whether they are 'old friends' or not? It would be more in keeping with the donor's intentions that appointments can be made in the donee's discretion to those who are definitely objects. An analogy can be drawn from the requirement of certainty applicable to a gift subject to a condition precedent. In *Re Barlow's Will Trusts*,[139] Browne-Wilkinson J held that such gifts are valid if 'it is possible to say of one or more persons that he or they undoubtedly qualify even though it may be difficult to say of others whether or not they qualify'.[140] If this approach was applied to powers of appointment it might provide a better balance between upholding the donor's intentions and ensuring that the court can supervise the execution of the power. The court will not intervene if the power is not exercised, so there is no possibility of the court exercising the power itself.[141] The court could prevent excessive exercise by upholding only appointments to those shown definitely to be within the class on any reasonable basis. In cases of doubt, the donee of the power could apply to the court for determination whether a person falls indisputably within the class. Such an approach would be entirely inappropriate for fixed or discretionary trusts, where the court may have to carry out the terms of the trust. For powers of appointment, it would provide a less stringent test than that declared by the House of Lords in *Re Gulbenkian*.[142] One disadvantage is that it would again create a distinction between the test of certainty applying to discretionary trusts and powers, which would make the question of whether a particular instrument creates a trust or a power far more significant, since that may determine its validity. That danger could be prevented by the court taking a strict view and not succumbing to the temptation of construing an invalid trust as a valid power.[143]

6 Contagious uncertainty

Although the certainties of 'intention' and 'subject matter' refer to different aspects of the trust relationship, they are not to be considered independently of each other. Doubt over the certainty of the subject matter of a trust will exacerbate any doubt over the certainty

[133] [1955] Ch 495. [134] [1955] Ch 495 at 499.

[135] See *Re Barlow's Will Trusts* [1979] 1 WLR 278 at 298, per Brown-Wilkinson J: '["Friends"] has a great range of meanings; indeed, its exact meaning probably varies slightly from person to person . . .'.

[136] [1973] Ch 9. [137] [1966] 1 All ER 273.

[138] Although it is notable that the majority of the Court of Appeal in *Re Baden No 2* adopted an approach not far different from this.

[139] [1979] 1 WLR 278. [140] [1979] 1 WLR 278 at 281, following *Re Allen* [1953] Ch 810.

[141] Unlike a discretionary trust. See *McPhail v Doulton* [1971] AC 424. [142] [1970] AC 508.

[143] As was taken in *McPhail v Doulton* [1971] AC 424.

of intention. This was recognized by the Privy Council in *Mussoorie Bank Ltd v Raynor*,[144] where the question at issue was whether the use of precatory words had been effective to create a trust:

> Now these rules are clear with respect to the doctrine of precatory trusts, that the words of gift used by the testator must be such that the court finds them to be imperative . . . If there is uncertainty as to the amount or nature of the property that is given over, two difficulties at once arise . . . the uncertainty in the subject of the gift has a reflex action upon the previous words and throws doubt upon the intention of the testator, and seems to show that he could not possibly have intended his words of confidence, hope, or whatever they may be . . . to be imperative words.[145]

[144] [1882] 7 App Cas 321. [145] [1882] 7 App Cas 321 at 331.

6

Constitution of trusts

1 Introduction

Because trusts impose legally binding obligations, they have to be defined with sufficient clarity for the trustees to understand their duties and for the courts to enforce them. We looked at this in Chapter 5. But that is not the only requirement. Trusts do not arise just because they provide a neat solution to a problem. This is well illustrated by an old case, *Jones v Lock*.[1] Jones was an ironmonger who had returned from a business trip to Birmingham. The nurse of his infant son complained that he had not brought anything back as a present for the baby. Jones then produced a cheque for £900, payable to himself, which was the result of his business negotiations and handed it to the baby saying: 'Look you here, I give this to baby; it is for himself, and I am going to put it away for him, and will give him a great deal more along with it.' A few days later he died. The question was whether in the circumstances the father had created a trust of the money represented by the cheque for the son. Jones had not effectively transferred the cheque to his son, as this would have required the father's endorsement (naming the son on the back of the cheque and signing it to confirm the transfer). Lord Cranworth LC held that there was equally no effective declaration of trust:

> the case turns on the very short question whether Jones intended to make a declaration that he held the property in trust for the child; and I cannot come to any other conclusion than that he did not. I think it would be of very dangerous example if loose conversation of this sort, in important transactions of this kind, should have the effect of declarations of trust.[2]

The proceeds of the cheque were not, therefore, held on trust, but formed part of the father's general assets.

2 Two ways of creating a valid trust

A trust can be created in two ways: by the owner of property becoming a trustee himself, or by transferring property to someone else, and at the same time imposing a trust on them (see Figure 6.1). These two methods were identified by the Court of Appeal in *Milroy v Lord*.[3]

(1) Declaration of self as trustee

A trust will be created if the person who holds the legal title to property free of any existing trust[4] effectively declares himself trustee of it in favour of specified beneficiaries. From the moment of the declaration, he will hold the property on trust, and, although he

[1] [1865] LR 1 Ch App 25. [2] [1865] LR 1 Ch App 25 at 28–9. [3] [1862] 4 De GF & J 264.

[4] If there is no trust already in existence, the person holding the legal title also holds the full beneficial title to the property, as the owner of the property.

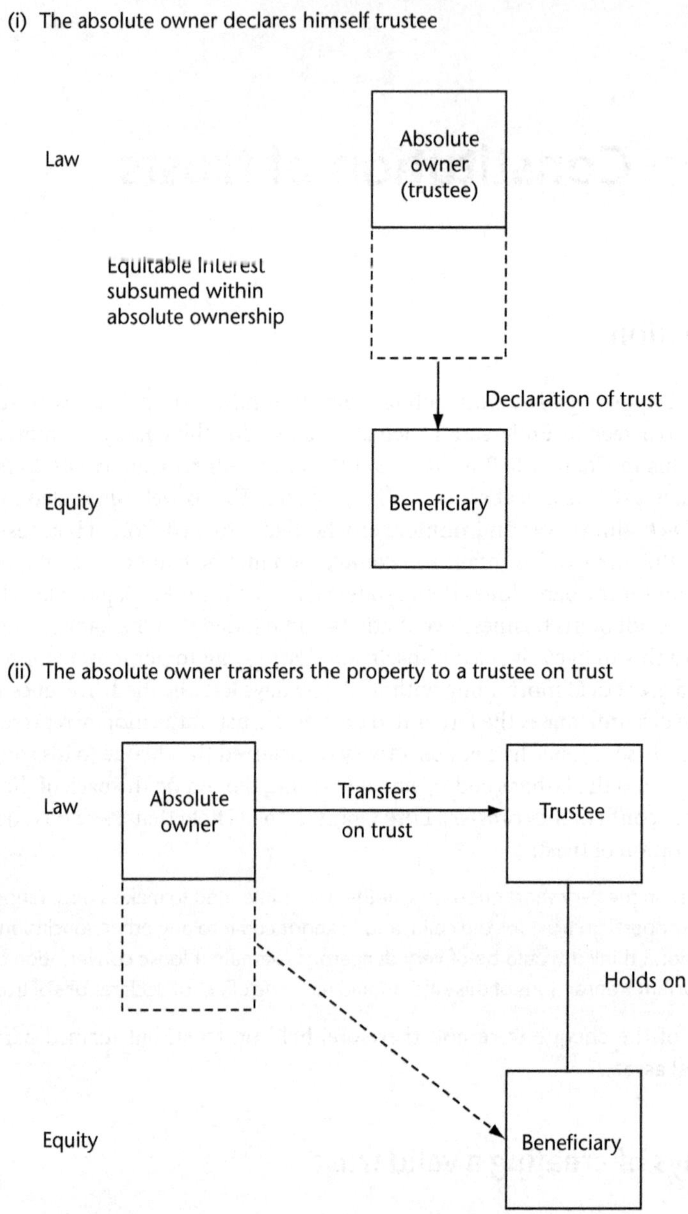

Figure 6.1 Creating a valid trust

retains the legal title, the beneficiaries will enjoy the equitable interest in the property. If a trust is created by such a declaration, there is no need for any transfer of the property. Instead, the owner has simply changed his status vis-à-vis the property from that of absolute legal owner to that of trustee. The owner is known as the settlor, because he settles the property on trust.

(2) **Transfer of the property on trust to trustees**

If the legal owner of property, the settlor, wishes to subject it to a trust in favour of beneficiaries, but does not wish to serve as trustee himself, he can create a trust by transferring the property to someone else, requiring them to hold it as trustee for the intended beneficiaries. In such circumstances, the original owner ceases to have any interest in the property, and the transferee of the property receives it as trustee subject to the trust obligations. After the transfer has occurred, the beneficiaries enjoy the equitable interest in the property.

3 Requirements of an express trust

Whichever method is used to create the trust, a number of requirements must be satisfied, including satisfying the 'three certainties' discussed in Chapter 5.

(1) Express intention to create a trust

Trusts can sometimes arise by implication or as constructive trusts. Express trusts are created deliberately. For this to happen, the owner of property must make it clear by a declaration of trust that the property is to be subjected to a trust obligation. As explained in Chapter 5, there must be certainty of intention.

(2) Trust property

A trust obligation can only subsist in relation to specific property which is to be subject to the trust. Mere intention to create a trust will be of no effect if the settlor does not also make it clear what property is to be held on trust. As explained in Chapter 5, there must be certainty of subject matter.

(3) Beneficiaries

There must also be certainty of objects. In addition to the requirement of certainty, as a consequence of what is known as 'the beneficiary principle', a trust can only exist in favour of individuals or legal persons. With some exceptions, the most notable of which is a trust for a charitable purpose, it is not possible to create a trust for abstract purposes with no ascertainable human beneficiaries.[5]

(4) Constitution

A trust will only come into existence if the property intended to be held on trust is vested in the trustee. The combination of declaring a trust and transferring property into it is known as constituting the trust. If these two steps are completed, the trust is described as completely constituted. If there was a declaration of trust, but no effective transfer, the trust relationship will not have come into being, and the trust is described as incompletely constituted.

(5) Formalities

Where the owner of property intends to create a trust of it during his lifetime, it may be necessary for him to comply with statutory provisions requiring the declaration to be made or evidenced by certain formalities. This is especially so if the intended trust property is land.[6] If these formalities are not followed, then the inter vivos declaration of

[5] There are some limited exceptions, referred to as 'trusts of imperfect obligation'—see Chapter 24.

[6] Law of Property Act 1925, s 53.

trust may be void or unenforceable and the trust will not come into existence. Where the owner intends to make a trust of property on his death, he must comply with the statutory formalities required for a valid will. Formalities also apply where an existing equitable interest under a trust is transferred to new beneficiaries.

(6) Capacity

The settlor must also have the legal capacity to settle property on trust. This requires the settlor to be of sound mind in relation to the transaction involved, and where a transfer is involved, to have the legal standing to make it. It should go without saying that a person can only create a trust of property over which they have a right of disposition. Pippy cannot create a trust of property belonging to Caroline (her partner) without Caroline's authority (such as a power of attorney or a power of appointment).

(7) Administrative unworkability and capriciousness

We shall see later (in Chapter 27) that a discretionary trust will be invalid if it is administratively unworkable because of the sheer size of the class of potential beneficiaries.[7] This means that an otherwise valid trust can be invalidated if it would be too difficult, expensive, or time-consuming for the trustees to make distributions within the class, even though the class is both conceptually and evidentially certain. There is also a poorly defined principle that a discretionary trust may be invalid if the objective of the trust is so unclear or capricious that the trustees are disabled from exercising their discretion.

4 Constitution of trusts

(1) Fully constituted trusts

A trust is described as fully constituted once there has been a valid declaration of trust and the trust property has vested in the trustee. Where a person already owns property and wants to become a trustee of it, only a declaration of trust is required for constitution. Where the owner wants to make someone else a trustee, both a declaration of trust and a transfer of the property are required for the trust to be fully constituted. To describe a trust as fully constituted means simply that the trust has in fact come into existence, because legal title to the property has been properly vested in the trustees and beneficial title in the proposed beneficiaries. Given that a perfect trust has been created, the settlor cannot reclaim the property at a later date.

(2) Incompletely constituted trusts

In contrast, if for any reason the settlor fails effectively to declare himself trustee of the intended trust property, or if the property is never transferred by the settlor to the intended trustee, the trust does not come into being. The settlor remains the owner of the property, and it is not held by him subject to the trust obligations. In consequence, the beneficiaries have no proprietary entitlement to the intended trust property. In such circumstances, the trust is described as 'incompletely constituted'.[8] This terminology may be confusing, as in fact no trust exists.

[7] *McPhail v Doulton* [1971] AC 424; *R v District Auditor, ex p West Yorkshire Metropolitan County Council* [1986] RVR 24.

[8] See *Deslauriers v Guardian Asset Management Ltd* [2017] UKPC 34, where, on appeal from the Court of Appeal of Trinidad and Tobago, the Privy Council found that a purported trust of land was incompletely constituted and upheld the trial judge's finding that an order for sale should be made of the relevant land.

(3) **Beneficiaries' remedies**

If a trust has been completely constituted, the beneficiaries have an equitable interest in the property, and may enforce the trust obligations. However, where a trust remains incompletely constituted, the background is often that a settlor has previously promised that he will create a trust in favour of the proposed beneficiaries, but he has not fulfilled his promise by making an effective declaration or transfer. In such circumstances, the main concern of the proposed beneficiaries will be whether they have any means of requiring the settlor to constitute the trust in their favour. The basic position is that the beneficiaries cannot force the settlor to constitute the trust if they are volunteers, owing to the rule that 'equity will not assist a volunteer'. Potential beneficiaries will be volunteers if they have not provided valuable consideration in return for the settlor's promise to settle the property on trust for them. It is worth noting that the majority of potential beneficiaries will be volunteers, as it is rare that a beneficiary pays for the benefit acquired under a trust. It will be seen that the general restriction against enforcing a promise to create a trust is subject to a number of limited exceptions. Alternatively, even if the beneficiaries are volunteers and not entitled to any equitable remedies, they may be able to seek common law remedies to compensate them for the loss they have suffered because the trust has not been constituted.

(4) **Requirements of effective declaration**

In *Re Cozens*, Neville J indicated what would be required by the court to establish that a settlor had declared himself trustee of his property:

> in each case where a declaration of trust is relied on the Court must be satisfied that a present irrevocable declaration of trust has been made.[9]

This emphasizes that an expression of intent to create a trust in the future does not create an immediate fully constituted trust. In *Richards v Delbridge*, Jessel MR made clear that the settlor does not need to use particular words or technical expressions to create a trust by declaration:

> he need not use the words 'I declare myself a trustee', but he must do something which is equivalent to it, and use expressions which have that meaning.[10]

The converse also applies, and the use of the word 'trust' does not mean that the true effect of an arrangement is to create a trust in the legal sense.[11] The principle is that 'there must be clear evidence from what is said or done of an intention to create a trust'.[12]

(5) **Formalities**

In general, an inter vivos declaration of trust will be valid and effective to create a fully constituted trust, even though it is made orally and without consideration.[13] No transfer of property is necessary; the settlor is simply changing the nature of his ownership of the property from owning it as himself to owning it as a trustee acting for named beneficiaries. The legal title does not move anywhere; the effective declaration of a trust separates the legal and equitable ownership of the property.

[9] [1913] 2 Ch 478 at 486. [10] [1874] LR 18 Eq 11 at 14.

[11] *Singha v Heer* [2016] EWCA Civ 424 at 31.

[12] *Paul v Constance* [1977] 1 WLR 527, CA per Scarman LJ.

[13] See *Jones v Lock* [1865] LR 1 Ch App 25 at 28, per Lord Cranworth LC: 'a parol declaration of trust of personality may be perfectly valid even when voluntary'.

However, in the case of land, s 53(1)(b) of the Law of Property Act 1925 provides:

> a declaration of trust respecting any land or any interest therein must be manifested and proved by some writing signed by some person who is able to declare such trust or by his will.

A purported declaration of a trust of land which is not evidenced in writing will generally be ineffective, although this general rule is subject to exceptions, which are discussed in Chapter 7.

(6) Cases illustrating effective declaration

It is ultimately a question of fact whether in any particular case an effective declaration of trust has occurred. A number of general indications can be drawn from the authorities.

(a) Loose conversation

Jones v Lock[14] (which was described in the introduction to this chapter) suggests that words spoken in what was merely 'loose conversation' will not amount to an effective declaration of trust because the necessary intention to create a trust is lacking.

(b) Words repeated over a period of time

Although isolated 'loose conversation' will not alone effect a valid declaration of trust, the courts recognize that 'family arrangements may have a certain informality of execution but are underpinned by a prior intention of joint benefit'[15] and that makes it easier to identify a trust from repeated, even if vague, statements that assets will be shared. *Paul v Constance*[16] is an example. Dennis Constance was separated from his wife and living with Doreen Paul. In 1974 he received £950 damages as compensation for an injury at work. He deposited the money in a bank account and on a number of occasions told Paul that the money was 'as much yours as mine'. Constance died without a will so that his wife, from whom he had not been divorced, was entitled under the inheritance rules to any property he owned at his death. The Court of Appeal held that she was not entitled to the money because it was held upon a validly declared express trust in favour of Paul. Scarman LJ said that although this was a borderline case and 'it is not easy to pin-point a specific moment of declaration', the 'use of those words on numerous occasions' between Constance and Paul was sufficient to constitute an express declaration of trust.

Paul v Constance was followed in *Rowe v Prance*.[17] Mr Prance and Mrs Rowe had conducted a relationship over many years. Although Prance had promised to divorce his wife to live with Mrs Rowe, he had remained married. He purchased a yacht where he said he would live with Mrs Rowe, and in which they could sail the world. The yacht was registered in his sole name, allegedly because Mrs Rowe did not have an Ocean Master's certificate. Over a period of time, Mr Prance regularly used the word 'our' in relation to the yacht. Nicholas Warren QC held that in these circumstances the yacht was held on trust by Mr Prance for himself and Mrs Rowe in equal shares.

(c) Words of gift by the settlor to himself

Choithram (T) International SA v Pagarani[18] was an unusual case which did not fall squarely within either of the methods of constitution identified in *Milroy v Lord*. A wealthy philanthropist ('TCP') wished to set up a charitable foundation to receive much of his wealth when he died. In February 1992, knowing that he was dying, he signed

[14] [1865] LR 1 Ch App 25.

[15] *Walsh v Walsh* [2017] IEHC 181 at 38 (trust of winning lottery ticket) citing *Paul v Constance* (below) and *Zyk v Zyk* [1995] Fam CA 135.

[16] [1977] 1 WLR 527. [17] [1999] 2 FLR 787. [18] [2001] 1 WLR 1.

a trust deed establishing the foundation. The deed stated that he was the settlor, and appointed seven trustees, of which he was one. After signing the deed, he orally stated that he was giving all his wealth to the foundation. He died a month later, but had not executed any share transfers to the foundation, nor had he executed a formal declaration of trust. The judge at first instance, and the Court of Appeal of the British Virgin Islands, held that no trust had been created, because of the absence of either an effective declaration or an effective transfer. The Privy Council allowed an appeal, advising that the settlor had constituted the trust. Lord Browne-Wilkinson explained that his words of gift to the foundation could only have been intended to establish a trust:

> Although the words used by TCP are normally appropriate to an outright gift–'I give to X'–in the present context there is no breach of the principle in *Milroy v Lord* if the words of TCP's gift (ie to the foundation) are given their only possible meaning in this context. The foundation has no legal existence apart from the trust declared by the foundation trust deed. Therefore the words 'I give to the foundation' can only mean 'I give to the trustees of the foundation trust deed to be held by them on the trusts of the foundation trust deed.' Although the words are apparently words of outright gift they are essentially words of gift on trust.[19]

In effect the settlor made a gift of the intended trust property to himself in his capacity as trustee, which had the effect of constituting the trust. The trust was enforceable even though the trust property had only been vested in one of the trustees. Since it is somewhat artificial to regard the settlor as having made a gift to himself, as there was no need for any transfer of the assets concerned, it might be better to treat the settlor as having declared himself a trustee of the assets which were already his.[20] Thus, words of gift by the settlor to himself on trust should be regarded in substance as a declaration of self as trustee.

(d) Declaration by conduct

It seems an effective declaration of trust may also be inferred from conduct, even though no words approximating to such a declaration are actually used. In *Re Vandervell's Trust (No 2)*,[21] the Vandervell Trust Company held a share option on trust for Mr Vandervell. The option was exercised using £5,000 that the trust company held on separate trusts for Vandervell's children. Thereafter, the trustees wrote to the Inland Revenue, saying that the shares would be held on trust for the children's settlement, and dividends arising from the shares were henceforth paid into the children's settlement. Given that this was all done with the full assent of Mr Vandervell, the Court of Appeal held that the evidence of the intention to declare a trust was clear and manifest and that the trustee company held the shares on trust for the children. Unless the trustees can be treated as acting as agents for Mr Vandervell in declaring the trust, the reasoning in this case is unconvincing, as passive assent by Mr Vandervell does not suggest a clear and present irrevocable declaration of trust or, indeed, unequivocal conduct suggesting such a declaration.[22] This aspect of effective declaration of a trust should, therefore, be treated with caution.

(e) Overarching intention to create a trust

In *Don King Productions Inc v Warren (No 1)*,[23] Lightman J was faced with the task of interpreting two multi-million pound contracts between the leading boxing promoters in the UK and the USA. The judge remarked that 'the drafting of the first agreement is

[19] [2001] 1 WLR 1 at 11–12.

[20] See Ricketts, 'Completely Constituting an Inter Vivos Trust: Property Rules?' [2001] Conv 515, where it is suggested that this was not a novel set of facts at all, and should have been considered as a transfer of property to trustees, given that title was being transferred to third parties.

[21] [1974] Ch 269.

[22] See also Battersby, 'Formalities for the Disposition of Equitable Interests under a Trust' [1979] Conv 17.

[23] [1998] 2 All ER 608.

somewhat primitive for a transaction of this size and importance for the parties'.[24] By the agreements, Frank Warren, the UK boxing promoter, purported to assign his promotion, management, and associated contracts ('PMA contracts') to a partnership with Don King, the 'larger than life' American promoter. The contracts related to personal services, so no assignment could take place. However, Lightman J held that the benefit of the PMA contracts had been subjected to a trust in favour of the partnership since this had been the overriding intention of the parties:

> the clear intent of the parties manifested in the first and second agreements was that the promotion management and associated agreements should be held by the partnership or by the partners for the benefit of the partnership absolutely, and that this intent should be given the fullest possible effect. The agreements have accordingly at all times been held by the partners as trustees for the partnership.[25]

5 Constituting the trust by transfer

(1) Requirements for effective transfer

Where a settlor wishes to create a trust of which a third party is the trustee, the trust will only be constituted if the trust property is vested in the trustee by means of an effective transfer of his legal or beneficial title. In *Choithram (T) International SA v Pagarani*, the Privy Council held that where the settlor intends to establish a trust with a body of trustees it will be sufficient to constitute the trust if the property is transferred to at least one of the intended trustees, since that recipient will be bound by the trust and must give effect to it by transferring the trust property into the name of all the trustees.[26] The requirements for an effective transfer of the settlor's title vary, depending on the type of property that has to be transferred.

(a) Land

By s 52 of the Law of Property Act 1925, all conveyances of land, or of interests in land, are void unless made by deed. With some exceptions for short leases, the transfer of the legal title to land must also be perfected by the registration of the transferee as the 'registered proprietor' at the Land Registry.[27] An attempted oral transfer of land, a transfer by mere writing, or even granting the trustees physical possession of the land will thus be insufficient to create a constituted trust. In *Richards v Delbridge*,[28] a grandfather attempted to create a trust of a leasehold interest for his grandson by assigning the lease to the boy's mother. Although the assignment was in writing, it was not made by deed. There was, therefore, no effective transfer of the lease and the trust remained incompletely constituted.

(b) Shares

The way in which individuals own shares is changing. Shares are owned at law by the person who is registered as the owner on the 'share register' of the company to which they relate. Historically a share certificate was issued to the person registered and this is evidence of ownership. A transfer requires a share transfer form to be completed and signed by the owner, and forwarded with the share certificate to the company registrar for registration,

[24] [1998] 2 All ER 608 at 615. [25] [1998] 2 All ER 608 at 635.

[26] [2001] 2 All ER 492 at 502. See also *Re Ralli's Will Trust* [1964] Ch 288, considered later in the chapter.

[27] See Land Registration Act 2002; *Mascall v Mascall* (1984) 50 P & CR 119, CA.

[28] [1874] LR 18 Eq 11.

sometimes subject to restrictions such as the consent of a private company.[29] This is cumbersome and slow, so increasingly shares in companies quoted on the stock exchange are held in dematerialized form in one of two ways. An investor can register for direct electronic legal ownership through the CREST system,[30] or, more commonly, can buy shares through a stockbroker registered with CREST who holds them as a trustee on behalf of individual investors in a nominee account. The stockbroker executes transactions on behalf of the investor on receipt of instructions from the investor, which may be given electronically.

For a trust to be constituted, the transfer of the shares must follow the rules for transfer appropriate to the form in which they are held. In the leading case, *Milroy v Lord*,[31] Thomas Medley attempted to create a trust of 50 shares in the Bank of Louisiana in favour of the plaintiffs by transferring them on trust to Samuel Lord. By the constitution of the bank, the shares were only transferable in the books of the company. Although Medley had executed a deed of assignment and delivered the share certificates to Lord, the view of the court was that title had not been effectively transferred and the trust remained incompletely constituted.

(c) Copyrights

By s 1 of the Copyright, Designs and Patents Act 1988, a copyright must be transferred in writing.

(d) Chattels

Title to chattels, i.e. tangible personal property, may be effectively transferred by means either of a deed or gift, or delivery of possession of the chattel to the intended transferee.

(e) Cheques and bills of exchange

A cheque is an instruction by a customer to a bank authorizing a payment, and must be signed by the customer or customers in accordance with the terms of the account. As a form of mandate, if made by way of gift, it is valid only during the lifetime of the account holder.[32] If a payee wishes to transfer an existing cheque to a third party, this requires endorsement, namely by the payee writing the name of the person to whom the cheque is transferred and signing to confirm the transfer. Mere physical delivery to the intended trustee is not sufficient. This was evident in *Jones v Lock*,[33] where the mere fact that the father had handed his cheque to his infant son was insufficient to transfer title to the son.

The same rules apply to bills of exchange, which are often used to finance commercial transactions.

(f) Equitable interests

If the intended trust property is an equitable interest enjoyed in property by the settlor, it can only be transferred to the trustee by writing, as required by s 53(1)(c) of the Law of Property Act 1925, which provides:

> a disposition of an equitable interest or trust subsisting at the time of the disposition, must be in writing signed by the person disposing of the same, or by his agent thereunto lawfully authorised in writing or by will.

[29] Companies Act 2006, ss 770–1; Stock Transfer Act 1963, s 1.

[30] See 'CREST Revealed. From Paper to Automation' BISS Research, 2016. Where an individual is a personal member of CREST, the membership must be sponsored by a stockbroker.

[31] [1862] 4 De GF & J 264.

[32] *Hewitt v Kaye* [1868] LR 6 Eq 198; *Curnock v Inland Revenue Commissioners* [2003] UKSC SPC00365. If the cheque has been drawn to pay a debt, it remains valid after the death of the account holder, since in those circumstances the mandate is irrevocable.

[33] [1865] LR 1 Ch App 25.

(2) Transfers where registration is required

The legal title to some forms of property such as shares or land can only be transferred by registration of the transferee as the new legal owner. What is the position where the relevant transfer documents have been completed, but registration has not been applied for, or has not taken place? In some instances equity will treat the transfer as if it had been fully completed.

(a) Transfer is past the point of no return

It is well established that even where registration is needed fully to complete a transfer, equity will treat the transfer as complete from the moment that the transferor has done 'everything within his power' to achieve the transfer of the property.[34] This principle emerged in *Re Rose (Decd)*,[35] where Eric Rose had transferred 10,000 shares to his wife. The share transfer form was completed on 30 March 1943 and forwarded to the company. The transfer was registered in the books of the company on 30 June. Estate duty was due unless the transfer was completed prior to 10 April. The Court of Appeal held that the transfer had in fact been completed on 30 March, since at that time the transferor had done everything within his power to divest himself of his interest in the shares (see Figure 6.2).

The concept of the transferor having done 'everything within his power' to transfer legal title to his property does not allow a transfer to be treated as complete where the transferor was, for instance, physically unable to sign a transfer form. The question is rather whether the donor has gone 'beyond the point of no return' so that he is no longer

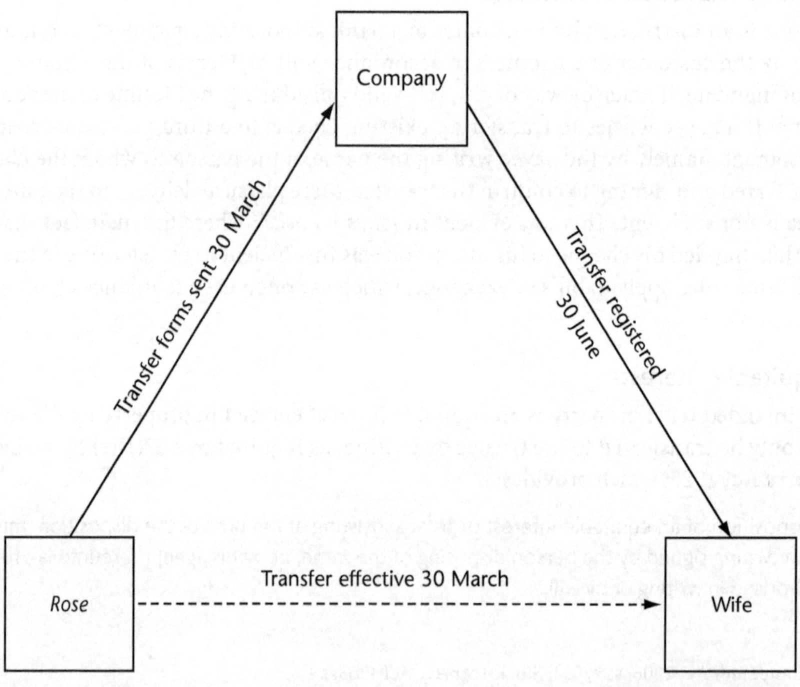

Figure 6.2 The settlor has done everything within his power to transfer the property: *Re Rose*

[34] See Lowrie & Todd, 'Re Rose Revisited' [1998] CLJ 46. See also *Hunter v Moss* [1994] 3 All ER 215, 220; *Re Harvard Securities Ltd (In Liquidation)* [1997] 2 BCLC 369, 375. [35] [1952] Ch 499.

able to prevent the transfer being completed, and any outstanding steps can be taken by others. The principle was explained by Jenkins LJ:

> [Rose] had done all in his power to divest himself of and to transfer to the transferees the whole of his right, title and interest, legal and equitable, in the shares in question . . . [He] had thus done all he could, in appropriate form, to transfer the whole of his interest, but so far as the legal title was concerned, it was not in his power himself to effect the actual transfer of that, inasmuch as it could only be conferred on the transferees in its perfect form by registration of the transfers.[36]

The rule did not operate in *Re Fry*[37] where the requirements were applied remarkably strictly. The owner of shares in an English company, who was domiciled in America, had executed a share transfer form and sent it to England to be registered. Under wartime legislation in force, the company was prohibited from registering the transfer without the consent of the Treasury. Although the transferee had obtained, completed, and returned the appropriate forms seeking such consent, he had died before it was given. In these circumstances, Romer J held that he had not done everything within his power to transfer title to the shares, and that they, therefore, remained his at the date of his death:

> Now I should have thought it was difficult to say that the testator had done everything that was required to be done by him at the time of his death, for it was necessary for him to obtain permission from the Treasury for the assignment and he had not obtained it. Moreover the Treasury might in any case have required further information of the kind referred to in the questionnaire which was submitted to him, or answers supplemental to those which he had given in reply to it.[38]

In *Zeital v Kaye*,[39] a donor was held not to have met the strictures of the rule in *Re Rose*, when he handed the donee an incomplete but signed share transfer form, but not the share certificate.[40]

The rule in *Re Rose* was applied to a transfer of registered land in *Mascall v Mascall*.[41] William Mascall wanted to transfer his house to his son. He filled in all the relevant parts of the Land Registry transfer form and handed it to his son. The son completed those parts that the intended transferee was required to complete and sent the form to the Stamp Office, a necessary step prior to sending the form for registration. He then had a row with his father, who sought a declaration that the transfer was void. The transfer form had not yet been sent to the Land Registry. The Court of Appeal held that the transfer was completed when the father completed his part of the form and handed it to his son. Although it had not yet been sent to the Land Registry, this was the responsibility of his son as transferee, and, therefore, the father had done everything within his power, or more precisely everything that was necessary by him, to transfer the title. All that remained were the acts of third parties, the son sending the form to the Land Registry and their registering him as the proprietor, which were out of the father's control. Browne-Wilkinson LJ explained:

> A gift is complete as soon as the settlor or donor has done everything that the donor has to do, that is to say, as soon as the donee has within his control all those things necessary to enable him, the donee, to complete his title.[42]

Re Rose[43] and *Mascall v Mascall*[44] concerned absolute transfers of property by way of outright gift, but the rule would equally operate in favour of a transferee who was intended to acquire the legal title as a trustee. In such a case, the trust would be completely constituted

[36] [1952] Ch 499 at 515. [37] [1946] Ch 312. [38] [1946] Ch 312 at 317–18.
[39] [2010] EWCA Civ 159. [40] [2010] EWCA Civ 159 at 43. [41] [1984] 50 P & CR 119.
[42] [1984] 50 P & CR 119 at 126. [43] [1952] Ch 499. [44] [1984] 50 P & CR 119.

from the very moment that the settlor had done everything within his power to transfer title. Technically, this is not an exception to the rule that 'equity will not assist a volunteer', because there is no need for the court to intervene and order the trust to be constituted on behalf of the beneficiaries. Nevertheless, in practical terms, the rule in *Re Rose*[45] does indirectly operate to assist volunteers by widening the circumstances in which equity will regard a trust as having come into existence.

(b) **Recalling the gift would be unconscionable**

It used to be considered that an attempted transfer of shares would only be regarded as complete if the strict requirements of the rule in *Re Rose* were satisfied. However, in *Pennington v Waine*,[46] the Court of Appeal held that, in appropriate circumstances, the execution of a share transfer form might in itself be sufficient to give rise to an equitable assignment of the beneficial interest in the shares. The result would be that the transferor would hold the shares on trust for the transferee, even though the completed form has not been delivered to the transferee or the company's registrar. The facts are important.

In September 1998, Ada Crampton executed a share transfer form in favour of her nephew, Harold Crampton, in respect of 400 shares in a family company. The share transfer form had been drawn up for her by a partner in the company's auditors. She returned the form to him and it was placed on the company's file. Ada also wanted Harold to become a director of the company, and the auditor wrote to him enclosing instructions to complete the prescribed form of consent to act as a director (form 288A), and also stating that Ada had instructed him to arrange the transfer to him of 400 shares in the company, adding that this did not require any action on his part. The auditor took no further action to transfer the shares prior to Ada's death in November 1998. It was clear that Ada had not done everything in her power to effect transfer of the shares, because the transfer form had not been delivered to Harold or submitted to the company for registration. Nevertheless, the Court of Appeal held that the gift of the shares was effective in equity. Arden LJ, with whom Schiemann LJ agreed, held that the gift was complete because Ada had intended to make an immediate gift and it would have been unconscionable for her to recall the gift.[47] Clarke LJ instead held that the execution of the share transfer form could be taken as a complete assignment of her equitable interest in the shares, thus generating a trust under which she could have been compelled to procure the registration of the shares in Harold's name.[48]

In the view of the majority, the crucial element that renders a transfer complete in equity is that it would be unconscionable for the transferor to recall the gift. Arden LJ identified the circumstances which she considered had made it unconscionable for Ada to recall the gift:

> There can be no comprehensive list of factors which makes it unconscionable for the donor to change his or her mind: it must depend on the court's evaluation of all the relevant considerations. What then are the relevant facts here? Ada made the gift of her own free will: there is no finding that she was not competent to do this. She not only told Harold about the gift and signed a form of transfer which she delivered to Mr Pennington for him to secure registration; her agent also told Harold that he need take no action. In addition Harold agreed to become a director of the Company without limit of time, which he could not do without shares being transferred to him. If Ada had changed her mind on (say) 10 November 1998, in my judgment the court could properly have concluded that it was too late for her to do this as by that date Harold signed the form 288A.[49]

[45] [1952] Ch 499. [46] [2002] 1 WLR 2075. [47] [2002] 1 WLR 2075 at 66.

[48] [2002] 1 WLR 2075 at 110. It is submitted that this seems to directly contravene *Re Rose* itself, where no such trust was found, and is, therefore, dubious reasoning. [49] [2002] 1 WLR 2075 at 64.

It is submitted that this case dangerously undermines the established principles that equity will not act to perfect an imperfect gift nor assist a volunteer. A finding that a donor intended to make an immediate gift does not mean that an immediate gift was made. The established equitable principles enable a transferor to change his or her mind whether to make a gift even after they have completed many of the steps necessary to effect a transfer. While it might have been clear on the particular facts in *Pennington v Waine* that Ada had not changed her mind about the intended transfer, in other cases, the evidence will be more equivocal. The effectiveness of alleged transfers of property should not be determined by the vagaries of whether the court considers that it would be 'unconscionable' for the transferee to change his or her mind.[50]

Arden LJ said that if she had been wrong to hold that the delivery of the share transfers to the company or donee was not required, then the case could have been decided the same way by finding that Ada and the company auditor had become agents for Harold for the purpose of submitting the share transfer to the company.[51] This reasoning involves stretching the concept of agency beyond its normal limits.[52] Alternatively, it might have been argued that Harold had provided valuable consideration by agreeing to become a director of the company without limit of time in return for the gift of shares, thus entitling equity to act on his behalf.

It may be significant that there have been few decisions since *Pennington v Waine* which have adopted a similarly benevolent view of when an incomplete transfer will be treated as effective[53]. In *Deslauriers v Guardian Asset Management Ltd*,[54] the Privy Council refused to follow a 'benovelent construction' of an arrangement to construe it as a trust. As part of a commercial loan arrangement, the respondents had successfully obtained an order for a sale of land, which the appellant claimed was subject to a trust for her son and daughter following a deed of settlement in 2009. It was clear, on construction of the deed, that it had been intended to create a trust by transfer of the land to trustees, which had never taken place. Hence, the trust was incompletely constituted and unenforceable. The argument on appeal was that, following *Pennington v Waine*, the failed transfer should be instead construed as the appellant holding the property on trustee of the property until such time as the land was vested in the third party trustees. The Privy Council did not feel this was a justifiable construction of the deed, for the two reasons that the appellant showed no immediate intention to deprive herself of the beneficial interest in the land[55] and the language of the deed clearly demonstrated that the property was to held on trust by third party trustees.[56]

(c) Reinterpreting unsconscionability

The potentially unruly approach of unconscionability in *Pennington v Waine* was considered at first instance by Biggs J in *Curtis v Pullbrook*.[57] Biggs J found that, despite Mr Pullbrook having done 'his incompetent best'[58] as the managing director of a private company to transfer legal title in some shares to his wife and daughter, the power to

[50] See further Halliwell, 'Perfecting Imperfect Gifts and Trusts: Have We Reached the End of the Chancellor's Foot?' [2003] Conv 192; Delaney & Ryan 'Unconscionability: a unifying theme in equity' [2008] Conv 401. Cf Garton, 'The Role of the Trust Mechanism in the Rule in *Re Rose*' [2003] Conv 364, who favours the flexibility and conceptual clarity that an approach based on unconscionability might bring over the existing equitable principles.

[51] [2002] 1 WLR 2075 at 67.

[52] See Halliwell, 'Perfecting Imperfect Gifts and Trusts: Have We Reached the End of the Chancellor's Foot?' [2003] Conv 192.

[53] For an interesting analysis, see Sutherland 'Defying easy explanations – the case of *Pennington v Waine* 18 years on' (2020) Trusts & Trustees 404.

[54] [2017] UKPC 34.

[55] [2017] UKPC 34 at [40]–[43].

[56] [2017] UKPC 34 at [44]–[45].

[57] [2011] EWHC 167 (Ch).

[58] [2011] EWHC 167 (Ch) at 42.

issue and record share transfers was a power of the company board which had not been delegated to Mr Pullbrook. Mr Pullbrook had not satisfied the requirements of *Re Rose*, as he had not done all he could do to transfer the shares, as he had not deposited the share transfer forms with the company solicitors. In considering the question whether it would be unconscionable to resile from the gift, Biggs J treated the question as a matter of detrimental reliance.[59] Hence, where there is detrimental reliance by the donee, that may bind the conscience of the donor to justify the imposition of a constructive trust. In the present case, there was no evidence of any reliance, detrimental or otherwise, by the wife or daughter on Mr Pullman's purported gift of the shares. This interpretation of *Pennington v Waine* was adopted by Carr J in *Winkler v Shamoon*.[60]

In explicitly linking the question of unconscionability to detrimental reliance by the donee, this potentially has the benefit of qualifying when it will be unconscionable for the donor to recall a gift and make the *Pennington v Waine* principle less unruly.[61] It does at least bring the rule in line with other areas where equity imposes a constructive trust on another.[62] This line of reasoning appears to have been followed in *Nosnehpetsj Ltd (in liquidation) v Watersheds Capital Partners Ltd*.[63] Here, in a case concerning an ineffective voluntary transfer of shares, Chief Insolvency and Companies Court Judge Nicolas Biggs made no substantive reference to the rule in *Re Rose*. It was clear that no physical executed share transfer form could actually be found, it was presumed that a share transfer form likely existed (on the basis of the professional experience of the parties involved) and there was a clear intention, inferred from the facts, to transfer ownership in the shares. This was held to be an effective equitable assignment of the shares, applying *Pennington v Waine*, as it would have been unconscionable for the transferor to deny the transfer of the shares, and, importantly, detrimental reliance had been shown as the transfer had been relied upon by the HMRC in assessing tax liabilities.[64] The fact that the case involved insolvency proceedings, and that the settlor was seeking to use formalities to disown a gift in the face of involvency, may have added weight to the court finding that a valid gift had been made.[65]

However, it is still difficult to see what advantages even this reinterpreted approach to upholding an imperfect gift, if followed, adds to the certainty and predictability of the rule in *Re Rose*,[66] and a decision of a higher court[67] is still awaited to determine conclusively the fate of unconscionability.[68]

(3) **Constitution through coincidental receipt by the trustee**

In most cases, a trust will only be fully constituted if the trust property is transferred to the trustee by the deliberate act of the settlor. However, in some very rare cases, a trust

[59] [2011] EWHC 167 (Ch) at 43. [60] [2016] EWHC 217 (Ch) at 141.

[61] See further Luxton, 'In Search of Perfection: the *Re Rose* Rationale' [2012] Conv 70, who opines that this is an example of proprietary estoppel. This remedy is considered in the context of the family home in Chapter 14.

[62] Constructive trusts are considered in Chapter 10.

[63] [2020] EWHC 1938 (Ch). [64] [2020] EWHC 1938 (Ch) at [41].

[65] See also Morris 'No Longer Waning – *Pennington* Revived?' (2021) 35(1) TLI 50, who argues that the decision could easily have been reached on grounds of prevention of fraud.

[66] *Nosnehpetsj Ltd* is an example of an approach which could, if Untrammelled, undermine the need to follow statutory formalities, though, as noted, the particular context of that decision suggests that it will not always be easy to create a gift.

[67] The Privy Council decision in *Deslauriers v Guardian Asset Management Ltd* [2017] UKPC 34 does not engage directly with unconscionability, and in *Zeital v Kaye* [2010] EWCA Civ 159 the Court of Appeal sidestepped the issue by applying *Re Rose*.

[68] It is worth noting that Biggs J in *Curtis v Pullbrook* did not feel there was any clear rationale or objective for equitable intervention to perfect imperfect gifts of shares (at 47), suggesting he was also dismissive of the rule in *Re Rose*.

will be fully constituted if the trustee received the legal title to the trust property by coincidence. In *Re Ralli's Will Trusts*,[69] a number of trusts were created by the members of a family (see Figure 6.3). The patriarch, Ambrose Ralli, died in 1899. Under his will, his residuary estate was to be held on trust for his widow for life, and on her death, it would pass to his daughters, Helen and Irene, in equal shares. In 1924 Helen executed a marriage settlement, under which she promised to settle any after-acquired property for the benefit of the beneficiaries of the settlement. This would include the remainder interest in her father's estate to which she would become entitled on the death of her mother. The beneficiaries under the marriage settlement were her sister Irene's children. Helen died in 1956, and the testator's widow in 1961. The plaintiff, who had been appointed a trustee of Ambrose Ralli's will in 1946, was at that date the sole surviving trustee of the trusts established under the will. He was, coincidentally, also the sole surviving trustee of Helen's marriage settlement. On Ambrose's widow's death, the remainder interest in his residuary estate was vested in him as trustee under the will. The central question was whether he held Helen's half-share as part of Helen's estate, in which case it would pass under her will, or whether he held it under the terms of her marriage settlement, in which case it would pass to Irene's children. Although there had been no intentional transfer of the property to the plaintiff in his capacity as trustee of the marriage settlement, Buckley J held that the fact that he had received it in his capacity as the trustee of the will was sufficient to constitute the trust, and the property was, therefore, held on the terms of the

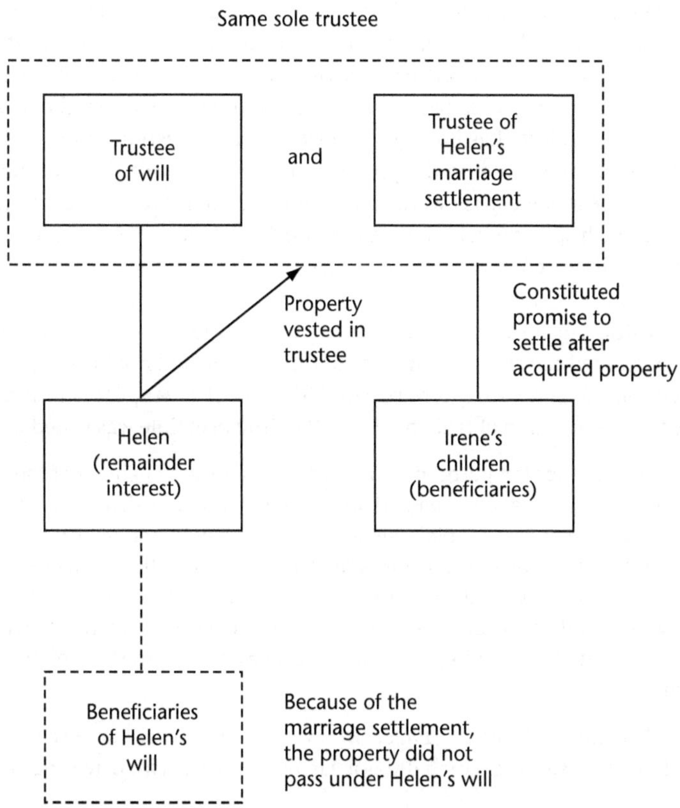

Figure 6.3 *Re Ralli's Will Trusts*

[69] [1964] Ch 288.

marriage settlement. He concluded that it did not matter how the trustee had come to receive the legal title to the trust property, it was sufficient that the title had vested in him:

> In my judgment the circumstance that the plaintiff holds the fund because he was appointed a trustee of the will is irrelevant. He is at law the owner of the fund, and the means by which he became so have no effect on the quality of his legal ownership. The question is: For whom, if anyone, does he hold the fund in equity?[70]

In the circumstances that transpired, it was a fortuitous coincidence that the plaintiff had enjoyed a double capacity as trustee of both the will and of the marriage settlement. It meant that Helen could not claim the property from him without breaking her promise to give it to him on trust. On a narrow reading of the case, this was an essential part of the decision. On a wider reading, the case supports the view that it is not essential for a trustee to obtain the legal title to the trust property by way of a deliberate transfer from the settlor.

As with the principle in *Re Rose*[71] examined earlier, *Re Ralli's Will Trusts*[72] does not provide an example of equity assisting a volunteer. The trust is completely constituted, so there is no need for equity to assist the beneficiaries. Again, the practical effect of the principle is to broaden the circumstances in which equity will regard a trust as having been constituted, which indirectly assists the position of volunteers.

6 Ineffective transfers and declaration

It has been seen that a fully constituted trust may be created either by an effective declaration of self as trustee or by an effective transfer of the property to the trustee on trust. If there was an intention by the settlor to create a trust in favour of the beneficiaries by transferring the trust property to trustees, but an attempt to constitute the trust was ineffective because the property has not been transferred, the question arises whether equity should treat the settlor as holding the property on trust. This would have the advantage of ensuring that the beneficiaries were able to enforce their equitable entitlement to the trust property, which seems to have been the settlor's intention. However, in such circumstances, equity will not construe an ineffective transfer as a declaration of trust by the settlor. This was made clear in *Milroy v Lord*,[73] where, as was noted earlier, the settlor who intended to create a trust of shares had failed to transfer title to the intended trust, because he had merely handed the share certificates to him and he had not been registered as the owner thereof on the company share register. The Court of Appeal held that there had been no effective declaration of trust by the settlor. The principle was stated by Turner LJ:

> it is plain that it was not the purpose of this settlement, or the intention of the settlor, to constitute himself a trustee of the bank shares. The intention was that the trust should be vested in . . . Samuel Lord, and I think therefore that we should not be justified in holding that by the settlement, or by any parol declaration made by the settlor, he himself became a trustee of these shares for the purposes of the settlement. By doing so we should be converting the settlement or the parol declaration to a purpose wholly different from that which was intended to be created by it, and, as I have said, creating a perfect trust out of the imperfect transaction.[74]

In *Choithram (T) International SA v Pagarani*,[75] which was also discussed earlier, the Privy Council dealt with a situation which did not easily fit into the two categories identified in

[70] [1964] Ch 288 at 301. [71] [1952] Ch 499. [72] [1964] Ch 288.
[73] [1862] 4 De GF & J 264. See also *Winkler v Shamoon* [2016] EWHC 217 (Ch).
[74] [1862] 4 De GF & J 264 at 275. [75] [2001] 1 WLR 1.

Milroy v Lord. The decision does not, however, undermine the traditional principle that a failed transfer will not be construed as a declaration of trust.[76] Instead it is submitted that the highly unusual situation of a settlor's words of gift to himself should be construed benevolently in substance as a declaration of trust.[77]

7 Enforcing a trust

(1) Enforcing fully constituted trusts

Where a trust has been fully constituted, whether in consequence of a settlor's declaration or through an effective transfer of the intended trust property to trustees, the beneficiaries are immediately entitled to the equitable interest in the property held on trust for them. They can seek the aid of equity to compel the trustees to perform the trust obligations by virtue of their interest as beneficiaries, irrespective of whether they were volunteers or whether they had provided consideration to the settlor in return for the creation of the trust. Once the trust has been created, the settlor cannot change his mind.[78]

This can be seen from the following two cases. *Paul v Paul*[79] concerned a marriage settlement executed by parties who had since separated. Under the terms of the settlement, as husband and wife, they were entitled to enjoy the income derived from the trust property for life, with the remainder interest passing on their deaths to the children of the marriage. If there were no children, the property was to go to the couple's next of kin, subject to a general testamentary power of appointment exercisable by the wife. As there were no children, the husband and wife applied to have the capital of the trust paid over to themselves, arguing that the only other persons with any interest in it were the next of kin, who were volunteers. The Court of Appeal held that although the next of kin were volunteers, they enjoyed an immediate equitable interest in the capital because the trust was fully constituted and they were beneficiaries under it. As such, the trust could not be brought to an end without their consent. In *Re Bowden*,[80] Catherine Bowden agreed to settle any property to which she might become entitled under her father's will on trust. Her father died in 1869, and between 1871 and 1874, the property to which she was entitled under his will was transferred to the trustees. In 1935 she requested that the trustees transfer the trust funds to her absolutely. Bennett J held that she was not entitled to the transfer because the property had become impressed with the trust the moment that it had been received by the trustees.

(2) Enforcing incompletely constituted trusts

Where a settlor has not evinced any intention to create a trust, then there can be no trust, and, therefore, there are no beneficiaries with rights which they can enforce. But what if a settlor has declared a trust, but failed to transfer the property to the trustees? What are the rights of the beneficiaries in this situation? Although, as we have seen earlier, the trust could be described as incompletely constituted, in reality no trust exists. The settlor remains the owner of the property. The intended beneficiaries enjoy no entitlement to the

[76] See *Deslauriers v Guardian Asset Management Ltd* [2017] UKPC 34 (ineffective transfer to create a trust was not to be construed as a declaration of trust).

[77] See *Pennington v Waine* [2002] 1 WLR 2075 at 60.

[78] See *Jefferys v Jefferys* [1841] Cr & Ph 138; *Bentley v Mackay* [1851] 15 Beav 12; *Kekewich v Manning* [1851] 1 De GM & G 176; *Milroy v Lord* [1862] 4 De GF & J 264; *Richardson v Richardson* [1867] LR 3 Eq 686; *Henry v Armstrong* [1881] 18 Ch D 668.

[79] [1882] 20 Ch D 742, CA.

[80] [1936] Ch 71.

putative trust property, nor can they enforce the trust obligations against the intended trustees, because there is no trust. In substance, the intended beneficiaries are the victims of the settlor's unfulfilled intention to create a trust in their favour. Is there any way by which the intended beneficiaries can compel the settlor to carry out his intention or promise to subject the property to a trust in their favour? The basic principle is that if the intended beneficiaries have provided valuable consideration in return for the settlor's promise to create a trust in their favour, then equity will compel the settlor to constitute the trust. However, if they are volunteers, the rule that 'equity will not assist a volunteer' operates to prevent them compelling the settlor to constitute the trust.

(a) Beneficiaries who have given valuable consideration

Where the potential beneficiaries have given valuable consideration, equity will come to their assistance and compel the settlor to constitute the trust.[81] Equity does not take the same view of consideration as the common law and will not enforce a promise made in return for merely nominal consideration or a promise made by deed without any other consideration. Instead, equity requires 'valuable consideration'. 'Valuable consideration' is a technical term requiring either 'money or money's worth'[82] or marriage consideration.[83] The ability of equity to compel the creation of trusts which are not completely constituted on behalf of those who have provided valuable consideration can be illustrated from the context of marriage settlements. In *Pullan v Koe*,[84] a wife covenanted as part of a marriage settlement to settle after-acquired property of a value greater than £100 on the marriage settlement trusts. She subsequently received a gift of £285 from her mother, which she failed to transfer to the trustees and which was instead invested in bonds. On the death of her husband, the bonds were in the possession of his executors. Swinfen Eady J held that the trustees were entitled to enforce the trust on behalf of her children because they were within the scope of the marriage consideration and not mere volunteers. (It may be a surprising concept nowadays, but it is well accepted that a contract made in expectation of marriage can be enforced by the parties to the marriage and any of their children.) The bonds were held on the terms of the marriage settlement, even though they had not been transferred to the trustees.

(b) Volunteer beneficiaries of an incompletely constituted trust

In contrast, where the beneficiaries of an incompletely constituted trust are volunteers who have provided no valuable consideration in return for the settlor's promise to create a trust, equity will not compel the constitution of the trust.[85] This is an application of a more general principle that equity will not act to complete an imperfect gift, which was explained by Page-Wood V-C in *Donaldson v Donaldson*:

> [Where there is an imperfect gift] which requires some other act to complete it on the part of the assignor or donor, the court will not interfere to require anything else to be done by him.[86]

[81] See *Donaldson v Donaldson* [1854] Kay 711; *Lee v Lee* [1876] 4 Ch D 175.

[82] If value was given, it is irrelevant whether the consideration was adequate: *Bassett v Nosworthy* [1673] Cas temp Finch 102.

[83] Marriage consideration exists where gifts are made in contemplation of, or at the time of, marriage of the potential beneficiaries. Only the husband, wife, and direct issue (children) of the marriage are within the marriage consideration: *De Mestre v West* [1891] AC 264; *A-G v Jacobs-Smith* [1895] 2 QB 341, CA; *Rennell v IRC* [1962] Ch 329; *Re Cook's Settlement's Trusts* [1965] Ch 902.

[84] [1913] 1 Ch 9.

[85] See *Jefferys v Jefferys* [1841] Cr & Ph 138; *Dening v Ware* [1856] 22 Beav 184; *Re D'Angibau* [1880] LR 15 Ch D 228; *Harding v Harding* [1886] 17 QBD 442; *Re Earl of Lucan* [1890] 45 Ch D 470.

[86] [1854] Kay 711 at 718.

This limitation prevented the enforcement of a trust in *Re Plumptre's Marriage Settlement*,[87] which, like *Pullan v Koe* (see earlier), also concerned a wife's covenant in her marriage settlement to transfer any after-acquired property to the trustees. She was subsequently given certain stocks by her husband, but they were never transferred to the trustees of the marriage settlement. On her death her next of kin sought to enforce the trust. It was held that they were unable to do so because (since they were not children or other issue) they were outside of the scope of the marriage consideration and volunteers in equity. The stocks, therefore, remained free of the marriage settlement trusts and formed part of her estate. Similarly, in *Re Cook's Settlement Trusts*,[88] it was held that volunteer beneficiaries were not entitled to enforce a settlor's promise to create a trust, even though other beneficiaries had given consideration. Sir Francis Cook had covenanted by deed that he would settle the proceeds of sale of any picture he had received from his father, and which he sold in his lifetime, on trust for members of his family. The beneficiaries provided no consideration for this covenant. During his lifetime he gave Rembrandt's 'Titus' to his wife, which she wished to sell. The trustees sought the opinion of the court as to the steps they should take if the picture was sold and the proceeds were not paid over to them. Buckley J held that since the potential beneficiaries were volunteers, equity would not enforce the trust if it was not completely constituted by the promised transfer of the proceeds of sale.[89]

(c) Indirect enforcement

Even if a volunteer beneficiary cannot compel the constitution of a trust, that beneficiary will nevertheless benefit if the trust is constituted at the behest of a beneficiary who had given consideration. There is another way in which indirect enforcement may occur. In *Beswick v Beswick*,[90] Peter Beswick contracted to transfer his business to his nephew, John, in return for his promise to pay an annuity of £5 per week to his wife. The business was transferred, but after Peter died John refused to pay the annuity. The House of Lords held that Mrs Beswick, although a volunteer who was not privy to the contract, was entitled to an order of specific performance to compel the nephew to pay the annuity. She was not, however, entitled to this remedy in her own right, but rather, because she stood in the shoes of her husband, as she was the administrator of his estate. It was, therefore, as if Peter Beswick himself were seeking the remedy. *Beswick v Beswick* did not in fact involve a trust, but if the nephew had agreed to settle property on Mrs Beswick, she would have been similarly able, as administratrix, to obtain an order of specific performance, enforcing the trust. Her status as administratrix meant she was able to obtain indirectly what she was not entitled to obtain directly.

8 Exceptions to the rule that 'equity will not assist a volunteer'

(1) Importance of the exceptions

In limited circumstances equity is prepared to assist a volunteer transferee of property where a transferor has failed effectively to transfer the legal title to him. These exceptions to the rule that 'equity will not assist a volunteer' operate whether the ineffective transfer was intended as an absolute gift or whether the property was intended to be held by the transferee on trust for third party beneficiaries. If the transferee was intended to hold the

87 [1910] 1 Ch 609.

88 [1965] Ch 902.

89 The abrogation of the doctrine of privity of contract by the Contracts (Rights of Third Parties) Act 1999 would probably enable the beneficiaries to obtain common law damages for breach of contract in such a situation, but this does not enable them to obtain specific performance.

90 [1968] AC 58.

property as trustee, the effect of equity compelling the perfection of the imperfect transfer is to constitute the trust.

(2) The rule in *Strong v Bird*

If a donor makes an imperfect gift during his lifetime, so that the donee does not receive the legal title to the property, the rule in *Strong v Bird*[91] can operate to perfect the gift if the donee is appointed the donor's executor, or becomes the donor's administrator on intestacy. The gift is perfected because the donee receives legal title to all the donor's property in his capacity as executor or administrator, including the property that was the intended subject matter of the gift. This has the effect of completing the imperfect transfer, by vesting the necessary legal title in the trustee.[92] Although the rule in *Strong v Bird*[93] is commonly cited as an example of an exception to the rule that equity will not assist a volunteer, it is questionable whether this is genuinely the case. Instead, like the principles identified in *Re Rose*[94] and *Re Ralli's Will Trusts*,[95] it may be viewed as an example of widened circumstances in which equity is willing to find that a transfer has in fact been completed.

Strong v Bird[96] concerned an incomplete release of a debt. Strong had borrowed £1,100 from his stepmother, who lived in his house and paid board to him. It was initially agreed that he would repay the sum to her by means of a deduction of £100 from the board she paid quarterly. After two quarters where the deduction was made, she told him that she did not want the money returned, and reverted to paying full board. This was not effective as a release of the debt at common law, which required a deed, and Strong had not provided any consideration for the release. Four years later, the step-mother died. Strong was appointed sole executor in her will. The court held that his appointment operated to perfect the imperfect release of the debt, so that Strong was not liable to repay the loan to the estate. The principle was stated by Jessel MR:

> it appears to me that there being a continuing intention to give, and there being a legal act which transferred the ownership or released the obligation—for it is the same thing—the transaction is perfected, and he does not want the aid of a court of equity to carry it out, or to make it complete, because it is complete already, and there is no equity against him to take the property away from him.[97]

This principle was applied to complete the gift of a house in *Re James*.[98] Sarah James, who had been told she would be given the house after acting as an unpaid housekeeper for James for nineteen years, was given the title deeds by James' son John, who had inherited the property on James' death. John later died intestate, and Sarah was granted letters of administration. Farwell J held that this had the effect of perfecting the gift of the house, which was imperfect because there had been no conveyance to her. He held that:

> by her appointment as one of the administratrixes she got the legal estate vested in her . . . she needs no assistance from equity to complete her title.[99]

Similarly, in *Day v Harris*,[100] Sir Malcolm Arnold gave a letter gifting manuscripts deposited at the Royal College of Music to his carer for twenty-two years, Anthony Day. The gift was imperfect since it required physical delivery of the manuscripts, but the Court of Appeal held that the gift was perfected when Anthony Day was appointed Sir Malcolm's executor.

[91] [1874] LR 18 Eq 315; Kodilinye, 'A Fresh Look at the Rule in *Strong v Bird*' [1982] Conv 14.
[92] See *Re Ralli's Will Trusts* [1964] Ch 288. [93] [1874] LR 18 Eq 315. [94] [1952] Ch 499.
[95] [1964] Ch 288. [96] [1874] LR 18 Eq 315. [97] [1874] LR 18 Eq 315 at 319.
[98] [1935] Ch 449. [99] [1935] Ch 449 at 451. [100] [2013] EWCA Civ 191 at 110 and 116.

A number of conditions must be satisfied before the rule in *Strong v Bird* will operate to perfect an imperfect gift.

(a) The donor must have intended to make an inter vivos gift

The rule will only apply if an immediate inter vivos gift of the property had been intended by the donor, which failed because the transfer was ineffective given the nature of the property. The rule has no application where the donor did not intend to make a gift[101] or only intended a gift which would take effect on his death, since this requires a will.

(b) The donor's intention must have continued until his death

The donor's intention to make a gift must be a 'continuing intention' to make the gift at the time of his death. This was emphasized in *Strong v Bird*[102] and also in *Re James*,[103] where Farwell J concluded that he was 'completely satisfied that there was a continuing intention in the donor up to the time of his death to give the property to the defendant'.[104] In contrast, in *Re Gonin*,[105] it was held that the donor had no continuing intention, and the rule could not operate. The plaintiff, Lucy Gonin, had returned home in 1944 to look after her parents. They promised that in return she should have their house when they died. Because Lucy had been born illegitimate, her mother mistakenly believed that she could not leave the property to her by will. In 1962 she drew a cheque for £33,000 in Lucy's favour, which she left in an envelope that was discovered after her death. Lucy claimed that in these circumstances the imperfect gift of the house was perfected when she was granted letters of administration over her mother's estate. Walton J held that the rule in *Strong v Bird* could not apply because her mother had not had a continuing intention to make a gift of the house at the time of her death:

> so far as the land is concerned no such continuing intention can be found . . . I think that the intention changed by the latest in 1962 when the deceased drew her cheque in favour of her daughter. I find it impossible to think that from then on what she really had in mind was anything other than that the plaintiff would inherit the cheque on the deceased's death—no immediate gift, and no gift of land.[106]

(c) The donee must have been granted administration

It is the vesting of legal ownership in the donee by a grant of probate or administration that enables the rule in *Strong v Bird* to operate. It is irrelevant whether the donee is a sole executor, or one of several joint executors.[107] Some doubts were expressed in *Re Gonin*[108] as to whether the rule should apply to administrators, because 'it is often a matter of pure chance which of many persons equally entitled to a grant of letters of administration finally takes them out'.[109] However, Walton J was unwilling to determine the issue and noted that the rule was applied to an administrator in *Re James*,[110] which had been cited without dissent by Buckley J in *Re Ralli's Will Trusts*.[111]

(d) The property must have survived the death of the donor

Most property, whether tangible or intangible, is capable of enduring past the death of its owner. However, a gift made by a cheque which has not been endorsed by the payee

[101] *Bourne v Lloyds TSB Bank Plc* [2015] EWCA Civ 881.

[102] [1874] Lr 18 Eq 315. [103] [1935] Ch 449.

[104] See also *Re Freeland* [1952] Ch 110; *Re Wale* [1956] 1 WLR 1346; *Choithram (T) International SA v Pagarani* [2001] 2 All ER 492.

[105] [1979] Ch 16; [1977] 93 LQR 488. [106] [1979] Ch 16 at 35. [107] *Re Stewart* [1908] 2 Ch 251.

[108] [1979] Ch 16. [109] [1979] Ch 16 at 35. [110] [1935] Ch 449. [111] [1964] Ch 288 at 301.

constitutes nothing more than a revocable mandate of the customer on whose account it was drawn, to his bank, requesting them as his agents to make payment to the payee. On the death of the customer, this mandate is automatically terminated. It follows that a cheque given as a gift which remains uncashed at the date of death of the drawer will be incapable of passing title to the money instructed to be transferred, even if the payee is appointed the executor or administrator of the estate. Thus, in *Re Gonin*,[112] the daughter had no entitlement to the £33,000 cheque her mother had left for her.

(3) Donatio mortis causa (gift on account of death)

The donatio mortis causa (sometimes referred to as a 'deathbed' gift), or in brief a DMC, provides a genuine exception to the principle that equity will not assist a volunteer. It operates where an owner wants to make a gift of property to the donee that is only intended to take effect if he dies. If, in such circumstances, the donor failed to make an effective transfer of the property to the donee during his lifetime, equity will act to compel his executors, or administrators, to perfect the donee's imperfect title. It does not matter that the donee is a volunteer. If the donee was intended to receive the property as a trustee, the operation of the donatio mortis causa will have the effect of constituting the trust.

In its simplest form, a DMC is merely a gift which is conditional upon death. Where the intended subject matter of a gift is personal property, a straightforward gift (such as a birthday present) is normally made by handing the property to the recipient with the intention to make a gift. The intention will normally be unconditional. However, it is possible for the intention to be subject to some condition being satisfied. For instance, a doting father might lend a car to his daughter, telling the daughter that she can keep it if she passes her examinations. If the daughter does pass, then the gift is completed. Where the condition which has to be satisfied is the death of the donor, the gift could be described as a donatio mortis causa. In extended forms of the DMC the gift may go beyond the simple characteristics of such a conditional gift, as will be seen from the cases described below. The objection to donationes mortis causa[113] is that they allow a gift to take effect on death. That normally requires a will, with all the formalites described in Chapter 17. The DMC is, therefore, seen as an anomaly.

(a) Requirements for a donatio mortis causa

The requirements for a valid donatio mortis causa were set out by the Court of Appeal in *King v Dubrey*.[114] Jackson LJ identified three 'proper bounds':

(i) Contemplation of imminent death

Most cases involving DMCs involve deathbed gifts, and the Court of Appeal in *King v Dubrey* considered that, although DMCs were not confined to that situation, the donor 'should be contemplating death in the near future for a specific reason': the donor 'must have good reason to anticipate death in the near future from an identified cause'.[115] A person suffering from advanced terminal cancer[116] or about to have a surgical operation with a significant risk of mortality[117] would meet this requirement, but the ordinary risks of commercial air travel are not sufficient.[118] The Court considered that *Vallee v*

[112] [1979] Ch 16.

[113] Because donatio mortis causa is a Latin phrase, its plural follows the Latin form. It translates as 'gift on account of death'.

[114] [2016] Ch 221. Cumber, 'Donationes mortis causa; a doctrine on its deathbed?' [2016] Conv 56. See also *Davey v Bailey* [2021] EWHC 445 (Ch), where on a strict application of the three criteria, no valid DMC was found on the facts.

[115] *King v Dubrey* [2016] Ch 221 at 55.

[116] *Sen v Headley* [1991] Ch 425.

[117] *Re Craven's Estate* [1937] 1 Ch 423.

[118] *Thompson v Mechan* [1958] OR 357.

Birchwood,[119] in which there was no specific reason for contemplating death in the near future, was wrongly decided, even though the donor was elderly, in poor health, and died within six months.

It is not necessary for death to be inevitable, or for the death to occur from the anticipated cause. In *Wilkes v Allington*,[120] the donor was diagnosed as suffering from cancer in 1922. Although he continued to farm, he considered himself under a sentence of death. He, therefore, made several incomplete gifts to his nieces. In January 1928, after coming home in a bus from Worcester market, he caught a chill and died of pneumonia. Lord Tomlin held that there was a valid DMC, despite the cause of death being different to that contemplated.

It was held when suicide was a crime that a gift made in contemplation of suicide will not operate as a valid DMC.[121] That may no longer be the case since suicide was decriminalized by the Suicide Act 1961. In addition, the Irish case *Mills v Shields*[122] held that a gift in contemplation of death by natural causes was a valid DMC even though the donor subsequently committed suicide.

(ii) Conditional and revocable

As the description of the nature of a DMC indicates, it is a form of conditional gift, and will, therefore, only take effect in the event that the donor dies. As Jackson LJ says, 'It comes to an end if [the donor] fails to succumb to the death which was anticipated when he made the DMC[123] . . . It will only take effect if his contemplated death occurs.'[124] This is because, as a form of conditional gift, the condition has to be satisfied for the gift to be effective. Otherwise, the gift is simply an ineffective inter vivos transfer. There will be no effective DMC if the donor intended the donee to have the property at all events. As Wynn-Parry J said in *Re Lillingston*:

> The gift should be conditional, ie, on the terms that, if the donor should not die, he should be entitled to resume complete dominion of the property the subject matter of the gift.[125]

Similarly, as the gift must take effect upon death, not simply be conditional upon it, this requirement was not satisfied where a couple's intention was not to transfer property to the intended beneficiary on the wife's death but for her husband to incorporate those wishes to transfer the property into a new will after her death.[126]

A DMC will not be invalid merely because the donor knows that he will not recover, and in such cases, the intention to make a revocable gift is implied.[127] Where the DMC has been made in contemplation of death from an illness, the gift is automatically revoked by the donor's recovery.[128] The donor may also revoke the gift at any time during his lifetime, for example, by retaking dominion over the property,[129] or giving the donee notice of revocation.[130] However, he cannot revoke the gift by will, since his death completes the gift.[131]

119 [2014] Ch 271. 120 [1931] 2 Ch 104.

121 *Agnew v Belfast Banking Co* [1896] 2 IR 204, CA; *Re Dudman* [1925] Ch 553. 122 [1948] IR 367.

123 As *Wilkes v Allington*, cited with approval in *King v Dubrey*, shows, the death does not have to be from the anticipated cause.

124 *King v Dubrey* [2016] Ch 221 at 57–8. Jackson LJ treated this as an aspect of the first requirement.

125 [1952] 2 All ER 184 at 187.

126 See *Davey and Jones v Bailey and Others* [2021] EWHC 445 (Ch) at [27]–[29].

127 *Wilkes v Allington* [1931] 2 Ch 104; see also *Sen v Headley* [1991] Ch 425, where the donor knew there was no practical possibility of his ever returning home from hospital.

128 *Gardner v Parker* [1818] 3 Madd 184; *Staniland v Willott* [1852] 3 Mac & G 664; *Keys v Hore* [1879] 13 ILT 58.

129 *Bunn v Markham* [1816] 7 Taunt 224; *Staniland v Willott* [1852] 3 Mac & G 664.

130 *Bunn v Markham* [1816] 7 Taunt 224. 131 *Jones v Selby* [1710] Prec Ch 300.

(iii) Delivery of dominion

Jackson LJ admitted to some difficulty in understanding this requirement, that the donor should deliver 'dominion' over the subject matter, and concluded:

> that 'dominion' means physical possession[132] of (a) the subject matter or (b) some means of accessing the subject matter (such as the key to a box) or (c) documents evidencing entitlement to possession of the subject matter.

With respect, Jackson LJ should not have had this degree of difficulty. Seen as a conditional gift, a DMC in principle requires all the elements of a gift to have been completed, subject only to the intention to give being conditional on death. What gives rise to the concept being 'slippery' is that some cases have gone beyond this simple analysis.

The simplest case of DMC involves chattels, where gifts require the delivery of possession coupled with an intention to give. No other formalities are required. A DMC can, therefore, take place if the donor had delivered the property to the donee before his death.[133] Applying *Cain v Moon*,[134] delivery could take place before the intention to make a gift has been expressed. For small items, delivery can usually be achieved by handing physical possession of the property to the donee.[135] However, some chattels cannot be physically handed over in the same way, and by extension, handing over the means of access to chattels can be seen as giving 'dominion'. A car, for instance, would be delivered by giving the donee the keys, as in *Woodard v Woodard*.[136] Giving the donee the key to a locked box in which the property is kept has been held to deliver dominion.[137] In *Re Lillingston*,[138] the donor gave the donee the key to a trunk, which contained the key to a safe deposit at Harrods, which in turn contained the key to a safe deposit at the National Safe Deposit and Trustee Co. It was held that there was a valid DMC of the jewellery in the trunk and the contents of the two safe deposit boxes. It is unclear whether handing over a key will be sufficient if the donor retains another, because in such a case the donor retains a personal level of control.[139] In *Vallee v Birchwood* Deputy Judge Jonathan Gaunt thought that this was not a problem and commented that:

> There seems to be no reason why acts of continued enjoyment [by the donor] of his own property should be regarded as incompatible with his intention to make an effective gift on his death.[140]

However, the case has been overruled on other grounds, and the case is unlikely to be a convincing authority on this point.

The most problematic aspect of dominion relates to property which cannot be transferred simply by delivery of possession. A relatively easily explicable example concerns a shareholding in a public company. *Staniland v Willott*[141] suggests that handing the donee an executed share transfer form is sufficient for a valid DMC of the shares, even though the formal transfer of such rights requires the transfer to be sent to the company registrar and registered. The principle in *Re Rose* would have allowed the outstanding steps to be completed if it had been an inter vivos gift. Where the difficulty arises is that some cases have held that a DMC can occur when the donor has delivered the 'essential indicia or evidence of title'[142] to the donee, or has given the means of access to these indicia. For money

[132] The ancient Roman concept of dominion is best expressed in English law by the concept of possession.

[133] *Ward v Turner* [1752] 2 Ves Sen 431.

[134] [1896] 2 QB 283.

[135] *Miller v Miller* [1735] 3 P Wms 356.

[136] [1991] Fam Law 470.

[137] See *Re Wasserberg* [1915] 1 Ch 195; *Re Cole (A Bankrupt)* [1964] Ch 175; *Sen v Headley* [1991] Ch 425, CA.

[138] [1952] 2 All ER 184.

[139] See *Reddel v Dobree* [1839] 59 ER 607.

[140] [2013] EWHC 1449 (Ch) at 27.

[141] [1852] 3 Mac & G 664.

[142] *Birch v Treasury Solicitor* [1951] Ch 298, CA.

held in a bank deposit account,[143] post office saving account,[144] or national saving certificates,[145] the relevant pass-book or certificates have been found to be the necessary indicia. In *Sen v Headley*,[146] the Court of Appeal held that in the case of unregistered land the deeds were the essential indicia of title, and that the passing of dominion over the deeds effected a valid DMC of the unregistered land. That decision was not questioned in *King v Dubrey*.[147] The problem in such a case is that money in a bank account cannot be transferred by giving someone the pass-book (which is no more than a statement of account), nor can ownership of a house be transferred by giving someone the deeds. In both cases there has to be a transfer in the required form—a deed of conveyance or transfer in the case of land.[148] For a DMC to operate where the required formalities have not been met, the court has to intervene and order them to be completed by the donor's personal representatives. That is not permitted in any other context. If the doctrine of donatio mortis causa is an anomaly to be treated narrowly, then there may need to be a reconsideration of those cases which hold that transferring indicia of title without the necessary form of assignment for that kind of property is sufficient for a DMC.

(b) Property which cannot be subject to a donatio mortis causa

Even where the other conditions for a DMC are satisfied, it has been held that some types of property are not capable of forming the subject matter of a valid DMC. A cheque payable to the donor is capable of forming the subject matter of a DMC,[149] but a cheque written by the donor cannot,[150] because it is merely a revocable mandate to his bank which automatically terminates on death. For a similar reason, the donor's promissory note is incapable of forming the subject matter of a DMC.[151] There is conflicting English and international authority on whether giving the donee a share certificate will be sufficient for a DMC.[152] Some cases adopt the view that shares cannot be the subject of a valid donatio,[153] but other cases have held that there could be a valid DMC of shares in a public company.[154]

Following dicta of Lord Eldon in *Duffield v Elwes*,[155] land was traditionally regarded as incapable of forming the subject matter of a valid DMC because it was not thought possible to grant dominion to the donee. In *Sen v Headley*,[156] the Court of Appeal held that it was possible to part with dominion over the essential indicia of title of unregistered land, namely the title deeds, and that to refuse to permit a DMC of land would create an anomalous exception.[157] Mrs Sen had lived with Mr Hewitt for ten years and had remained very close to him after this. When he was dying he told her that his house, title to which was unregistered, was hers, and he gave her the keys to a steel box which contained the deeds. It was held that in these circumstances, a valid DMC had been made in her favour, and she was, therefore, entitled to compel the administrator of his estate to transfer the legal title of the house into her name.

143 *Re Dillon* [1890] 44 Ch D 76; *Birch v Treasury Solicitor* [1951] Ch 298.

144 *Re Thompson's Estate* [1928] IR 606; *Re Weston* [1902] 1 Ch 680.

145 *Darlow v Sparks* [1938] 2 All ER 235. 146 [1991] Ch 425. 147 [2016] Ch 221.

148 In *Davey and Jones v Bailey and Others* [2021] EWHC 445 (Ch), it was confirmed that provision of pre-registration deeds was not sufficient to demonstrate delivery of dominion of registered land.

149 *Re Mead* [1880] LR 15 Ch D 651; *Re Mulroy* [1924] 1 IR 98.

150 *Re Beaumont* [1902] 1 Ch 886; *Tate v Hilbert* [1793] 2 Ves 111.

151 *Tate v Hilbert* [1793] 2 Ves 111; *Re Leaper* [1916] 1 Ch 579.

152 See also Samuels 'Donatio Mortis Causa of a Share Certificate' [1966] 30 Conv 189.

153 *Ward v Turner* [1752] 2 Ves Sen 431 (South Sea annuities); *Moore v Moore* [1874] LR 18 Eq 474 (railway stock); *Re Weston* [1902] 1 Ch 680 (building society shares); *Mills v Shields (No 2)* [1950] IR 21.

154 *Staniland v Willott* [1852] 3 Mac & G 664; *Dufficy v Mollica* [1968] 3 NSWR 751 (Australia).

155 [1823] 1 Sim & St 239. See also *Wilkes v Allington* [1931] 2 Ch 104.

156 [1991] Ch 425. 157 [1991] Ch 425 at 440, per Nourse LJ.

Increasingly property like registered land and shares are held in dematerialized form, so that there are no indicia of title, but only an electronically accessible register of ownership. In such cases it is hard to see how DMC can operate unless the donor has completed an appropriate form of transfer where this is still possible in documentary form.[158]

(c) Critique

Jackson LJ in *King v Dubrey*[159] thought that 'the doctrine of DMC in the context of English law is an anomaly' because it allowed property to be transferred on death without complying with the Wills Act or the need for a deed to transfer ownership of land, the formalities required for the transfer of land: 'Thus the doctrine paves the way for all of the abuses which those statutes are intended to prevent.' He added:

> I must confess to some mystification as to why the common law has adopted the doctrine of DMC at all. The doctrine obviously served a useful purpose in the social conditions prevailing under the later Roman Empire. But it serves little useful purpose today, save possibly as a means of validating death bed gifts. Even then considerable caution is required . . . The court should resist the temptation to extend the doctrine to an ever wider range of situations.[160]

He suggested that the doctrine only served a useful social purpose in deathbed situations where the donor had no time to make a formal will.[161] With respect, this goes too far. Caution about extending the doctrine where the court has to order missing steps to be completed is justified. So is concern about being sure about the donor's intentions where they are expressed informally, but this is already sufficiently addressed since, as Patten LJ said, 'the court will require clear and unequivocal evidence of the gift and will subject that evidence to the strictest scrutiny.'[162] The case of a claimant who relied upon contradictory, ambiguous, and uncorroborated statements was described in a later decision as 'hopeless'.[163] However, there should not be the same hesitation about recognizing the validity of conditional gifts where no assistance is required from the court to complete missing formalities. Moreover, the view that only testamentary wishes expressed in a formal manner should be effective looks rather old fashioned when the Law Commission has consulted on 'enabling the court to dispense with the formalities for a will where it's clear what the deceased wanted'.[164]

The Law Commission has consulted over whether the DMC doctrine should be abolished and, in its consultation paper, has looked at some of the arguments for and against doing so.[165] In its consultation summary[166] the Law Commission observed:

> While some commentators have suggested that the doctrine be abolished, the doctrine does have the virtue of giving effect to a dying person's wishes. Furthermore, we are not aware of any evidence of widespread problems caused by DMC in practice. In short, any assessment of the doctrine must weigh up its beneficial effects against the need for clarity and certainty in the law. We ask whether consultees believe that the doctrine should be abolished.

[158] See further Roberts, 'Donatio mortis causa in a dematerialised world' [2012] Conv 113.

[159] [2016] Ch 221 at 51.

[160] [2016] Ch 221 at [53–54].

[161] Briggs, 'DMC: not quite dead?' [2015] 165 NLJ 16 infers that DMC can only operate where the donor has no time to make a will. It is doubtful whether this conclusion is justified.

[162] [2016] Ch 221 at [91].

[163] *Re Exler (Deceased)* [2017] EWHC 1189 (Ch).

[164] Law Commission Consultation Paper 231: 'Making a will' [2017] online introduction. See para 5 of the main report.

[165] Ibid main report paras 13.43 to 13.50.

[166] 'Making a will' Consultation summary para 1.86.

9 Common law remedies for incompletely constituted trusts

(1) Significance of common law remedies

The limitation that equity will not assist a volunteer does not apply at common law. A volunteer named as a beneficiary in an incompletely constituted trust declared by deed may be entitled to sue the settlor at common law and recover compensatory damages for the failure to constitute the trust. This is because the common law will enforce contracts made by deed (generally described as covenants) even if they are not supported by consideration, and will recognize purely nominal consideration as sufficient to found a legally binding contract. Where damages at common law are available, the measure recoverable will be the quantum of loss suffered in consequence of the settlor's failure to constitute the trust, which will generally be the value of the beneficiary's share of the promised trust property. The ability of volunteer beneficiaries to obtain a remedy at common law has been significantly widened by the Contracts (Rights of Third Parties) Act 1999. This is especially significant where a settlor has covenanted or contracted to create a trust with the intended trustees but not the beneficiaries. The regime applies to contracts entered into on or after 11 May 2000.[167]

It is important to realize that the beneficiaries' entitlement to claim damages at common law is not a means by which they can constitute the trust, thus circumventing the rule that equity will not assist a volunteer. Any damages recovered are compensation for the fact that no trust was ever created in their favour, and they will receive such damages absolutely and free from any trust. By contrast, where a beneficiary who has given consideration recognized by equity brings a suit, the remedy will normally be to compel the constitution of the trust which will, of course, also work to the advantage of the beneficiaries who have provided no consideration. Whether beneficiaries are in fact able to recover damages for the settlor's breach of covenant will depend on the circumstances of the case. All of the situations examined are based on the settlor having entered into a legally binding contract recognized at common law.

(2) Settlor contracted with the beneficiary

Where a settlor has contracted directly with a beneficiary, either by way of deed or for consideration, even nominal, the beneficiary will be entitled to sue to recover damages at common law if the settlor fails to fulfil his promise to constitute the trust. The beneficiary is a party to the covenant or contract, so there is no difficulty of privity. In *Cannon v Hartley*,[168] Bernard Hartley executed a covenant on his separation from his wife, to which his wife and daughter were parties. He agreed that he would settle any money or property worth more than £1,000 which he subsequently received on the death of his parents on trust for his daughter. When his parents died, he received a substantial amount of money but refused to transfer it to the trustees. Romer J held that although the daughter was a volunteer, and therefore unable to enforce the incompletely constituted trust in equity, she was entitled to receive damages for breach of covenant:

> The plaintiff, although a volunteer, is not only a party to the deed of separation but is also a direct covenantee under the very covenant upon which she is suing. She does not require the assistance of the court to enforce the covenant for she has a legal right herself to enforce it. She is not asking for equitable relief but for damages at common law for breach of covenant.[169]

[167] Contracts (Rights of Third Parties Act) 1999, s 10(2).

[168] [1949] Ch 213.

[169] [1949] Ch 213 at 223.

Cases like this will be rare, as most settlors do not enter into contracts with beneficiaries to create trusts.

(3) **Settlor covenanted or contracted only with the trustee**

(a) Contracts from 11 May 2000

The Contracts (Rights of Third Parties) Act 1999, s 1(1) provides that a third party is entitled to enforce a term of a contract if it expressly provides that he may, or if it purports to confer a benefit on him. Where a settlor enters into a covenant[170] or contract to create a trust with the intended trustee, the beneficiary will be entitled to sue to recover damages at common law if the settlor fails to fulfil his promise, unless the contract made clear that it was not intended to be enforceable by the beneficiary.[171] Although s 1(5) provides that a third party is entitled to obtain any remedy that would have been available to him in an action for breach of contract if he had been a party to the contract, the better view appears to be that this does not mean that the beneficiary can obtain specific performance, as the rule that equity will not assist a volunteer has not been abrogated.[172]

(b) Contracts before 11 May 2000

The Contracts (Rights of Third Parties) Act 1999 does not apply to covenants or contracts made prior to 11 May 2000. The rights of the beneficiaries to enforce such a covenant will continue to be determined by the older rules. The beneficiary cannot sue the settlor for breach in his own right, as he has no privity of contract to do so. Unless the intended trustees hold the benefit of the covenant on trust for him,[173] he similarly cannot compel them to bring an action for breach against the settlor. The central question in these cases is, therefore, whether the intended trustee is able to sue the settlor if he so wishes and, if so, as to the quantum of damages recoverable.

(4) **Actions by the trustee**

(a) Directions by the court

It was well established before the Contracts (Rights of Third Parties) Act 1999 that where a trustee who is party to the settlor's covenant seeks the court's direction whether he should sue, he will be directed not to take proceedings to enforce the covenant. In *Re Pryce*,[174] Eve J directed the trustees of a marriage settlement to take no proceedings to enforce a covenant to settle after-acquired property. In *Re Kay's Settlement Trusts*,[175] Simonds J followed the decision in *Re Pryce* and held that where a spinster had failed to perform her voluntary covenant to settle after-acquired property, the trustees should be directed not to take any proceedings to enforce the covenant by an action for damages for breach. These authorities were approved in *Re Cook's Settlement Trusts*,[176] where Buckley J held that volunteer beneficiaries could not compel the trustees to sue on the settlor's covenant to settle the proceeds of sale of certain paintings, even though other beneficiaries had given consideration. The rationale underlying these decisions is that to allow trustees to recover under the settlor's deed at common law would indirectly assist volunteers who are not entitled to the direct assistance of the court in equity.[177] This logic would not apply

[170] s 7(3). [171] s 1(2).

[172] See Andrews, 'Strangers to Justice No Longer: The Reversal of the Privity Rule under the Contracts (Rights of Third Parties) Act 1999' [2001] 60 CLJ 353.

[173] This is referred to as a 'trust of a promise' and is discussed later in this chapter.

[174] [1917] 1 Ch 234. [175] [1939] Ch 329.

[176] [1965] Ch 902. [177] See *Re Pryce* [1917] 1 Ch 234 at 241, per Eve J.

since the Contracts (Rights of Third Parties) Act 1999 in situations where the beneficiaries have a direct cause of action.

(b) Actions at the trustees' initiative

If an intended trustee were to decide to sue the settlor on their own initiative, rather than asking the court for a direction, it is debatable whether they would be entitled to recover substantial damages. One view, supported by the Canadian decision of *Re Cavendish Browne's Settlement Trusts*,[178] is that the trustee in such circumstances should be entitled to recover damages equivalent to the value of the property that was to be settled on trust, and hold those damages on trust for the beneficiaries.[179] The case concerned a covenant entered into with the intended trustees to settle land on beneficiaries who were volunteers, and the court held that the trustees were entitled to damages to the value of the land, to be held on trust for the intended beneficiaries.[180]

In the English cases, it has been argued that, as a matter of principle, a covenantee is only entitled to recover damages as compensation for his own personal loss[181] resulting from breach of the covenant to which he was a party. It follows that, as a trustee derives no personal gain from a trust, the personal loss suffered is negligible, so the intended trustee would be entitled to recover only nominal damages from the settlor. Furthermore, even if a trustee were held entitled to recover substantial damages, it has been suggested that he should hold them on a resulting trust for the settlor, rather than for the volunteer beneficiaries.[182]

These arguments would have little force in situations where, since the Contracts (Rights of Third Parties) Act 1999, beneficiaries have a direct cause of action, but they might apply even more forcefully where the contract makes it clear that the beneficiaries are not entitled to enforce it.[183] The current law remains to be resolved.

(5) Trusts of a promise

A contractually binding promise is a 'chose in action' which is capable of being held on trust. A contractually binding promise to create a trust is, therefore, itself property which can be held on trust. If such a covenant is held on a completely constituted trust, then the beneficiaries of the trust can compel the trustees to enforce it, and if necessary can take direct action to enforce the covenant, joining the trustees as claimants or defendants.

The concept of a 'trust of the benefit of a covenant', which enables a beneficiary to enforce a settlor's covenant with the trustees, was accepted by Wigram V-C in the mid-nineteenth-century case, *Fletcher v Fletcher*:

> One question made in argument has been whether there can be a trust of a covenant the benefit of which shall belong to a third party; but I cannot think there is any difficulty in that . . . The proposition, therefore, that in no case can there be a trust of a covenant is clearly too large, and the real question is whether the relation of trustee and [beneficiary] is established in the present case.[184]

[178] [1916] WN 341.

[179] See Barton 'Trusts and Covenants' [1975] 91 LQR 236; Friend 'Trusts of voluntary covenants: an alternative approach' [1982] Conv 280.

[180] However, *Re Cavendish Browne's Settlement Trusts* is distinguishable from *Re Pryce*, *Re Kay* and *Re Cook* as it involved a covenant to settle identified specific property rather than after-acquired property.

[181] *Woodar Investment Developments Ltd v Wimpey Construction UK Ltd* [1980] 1 WLR 277; *Panatown Ltd v Alfred McAlpine Construction Ltd* [2000] 4 All ER 97.

[182] Lee 'Public Policy of *Re Cook's Settlement Trusts*' [1969] 85 LQR 213.

[183] Although *Panatown Ltd v Alfred McAlpine Construction Ltd* [2000] 4 All ER 97 could be taken to suggest the contrary.

[184] [1844] 4 Hare 67.

Ellis Fletcher had executed a voluntary covenant to settle £60,000 on trust for his illegitimate sons, John and Jacob, if they survived him. He retained the deed and did not make known its existence either to the trustees with whom it was made or to his sons. The deed was found among his papers after his death. Jacob, who had survived his father and attained the age of twenty-one, sued the executors of his father's estate for £60,000. Wigram V-C held that although Jacob was not a party to the deed himself he was entitled to recover the £60,000 from the executors because the trustees held the benefit of the covenant on trust for him.

The legitimacy of the concept of a 'trust of a promise' has been confirmed by the courts in a large number of cases;[185] including *Don King Productions v Warren*,[186] where Lightman J cited the dicta of Lord Shaw in *Lord Strathcona Steamship Co Ltd v Dominion Coal Co Ltd*:

> The scope of the trusts recognised in equity is unlimited. There can be a trust of a chattel, or of a right or obligation under an ordinary legal contract, just as much as a trust of land.[187]

However, while *Fletcher v Fletcher*[188] clearly establishes that the benefit of a covenant may form the subject matter of a trust, such trusts are not commonplace. There is great difficulty is establishing that such a trust has come into existence. There is a marked reluctance to find that such trusts have been created because they are capable of undermining the doctrine of privity of contract. *Fletcher v Fletcher* is open to criticism in that there was no evidence on the facts of an intention to create a trust of the benefit of the covenant. There was no evidence that Fletcher intended to create such a trust, and the trustees and beneficiaries were unaware of the existence of the covenant. How could the trustees be said to be holding the benefit of a covenant, the existence of which they were unaware of, on trust for beneficiaries for whom they did not know they were trustees? In subsequent cases the courts have held that a trust of a covenant will only be created by clear express intention. In *Vandepitte v Preferred Accident Insurance Corpn of New York*,[189] the Privy Council held that to establish a trust of the benefit of an insurance contract 'the intention to constitute the trust must be affirmatively proved', and that such an intention could not necessarily be inferred from the words of the policy. There was, therefore, no intention that the policy-holder had any intention to create a trust in favour of the plaintiff. Similarly, in *Re Schebsman*,[190] Lord Greene MR held that it was 'not legitimate to import into the contract the idea of a trust when the parties have given no indication that such was their intention'.[191] These cases suggest that a trust of the benefit of a promise will not be implied merely from the fact that a promise has been made between two parties for the benefit of a third. Such a trust will only arise if there is clear evidence of an intention on the part of the parties to the promise to create such a trust.[192] It clearly cannot arise if the contract contains a term prohibiting such a declaration.[193]

One further anomalous restriction on the scope of the concept of a trust of the benefit of a covenant is that it has been held that a covenant to settle future property is incapable of forming the subject matter of a trust. In *Re Cook's Settlement Trusts*,[194] Sir Francis Cook covenanted to settle the proceeds of sale of certain pictures sold during his lifetime. This covenant did not create a property right that would have been capable of being the

[185] See *Lloyd's v Harper* [1880] 16 Ch D 290, CA; *Vandepitte v Preferred Accident Assurance Corpn of New York* [1933] AC 70, PC; *Re Schebsman (Decd)* [1944] Ch 83, CA; *Re Cook's Settlement Trusts* [1965] Ch 902; *Swain v Law Society* [1983] 1 AC 598, HL.

[186] [1998] 2 All ER 608. [187] [1926] AC 108 at 124. [188] [1844] 4 Hare 67.

[189] [1933] AC 70. [190] [1944] Ch 83. [191] [1944] Ch 83 at 89.

[192] *Swain v Law Society* [1983] 1 AC 598.

[193] *Don King Productions v Warren* [1998] 2 All ER 608 at 632–3. [194] [1965] Ch 902.

subject matter of an immediate trust, so Buckley J held that no trust of the covenant could have been created:

> this covenant upon its true construction is . . . an executory contract to settle a particular fund or particular funds of money which at the date of the covenant did not exist and which might never come into existence. It is analogous to a covenant to settle an expectation or to settle after-acquired property. The case, in my judgment, involves the law of contract, not the law of trusts.[195]

This limitation has been severely criticized,[196] since although the covenant concerns future property, which could not itself form the subject matter of an immediate trust, it is no less a valid chose in action than a covenant to settle existing property. The promise itself is the subject matter of a trust of the benefit of a covenant, not the property to which the promise relates.

The mechanism of a trust of a promise may become of increasingly marginal utility given the requirement of a clearly demonstrated intention to create a trust, which is not something a settlor is often likely to do, and the impact of the Contracts (Rights of Third Parties) Act 1999.

[195] [1965] Ch 902 at 914.

[196] See, for example, Jones 'The Enforcement of Settlements in Equity by Volunteers' [1965] 24 CLJ 46; Feltham 'Intention to Create a Trust of a Promise to Settle Property' [1982] 98 LQR 17.

7

Formalities

1 Introduction

There are some situations where the creation of a valid trust requires special formalities, such as a requirement of being made or evidenced in writing. In *Taylor v Taylor*[1] a father and a son entered into an informal partnership, buying and renovating property. A question arose as to the beneficial ownership of a property acquired in both of their names. The son's case depended in part upon a declaration made in the document transferring legal ownership, which stated that the property was held on trust for the father and the son as beneficial joint tenants. The judge held that, even though the father and the son had not signed the form, because it was signed by the seller, it complied with the legal requirement that a trust of land had to be evidenced in writing by a person able to declare it.

2 Inter vivos declarations of trust

(1) Trusts of land

(a) Formalities required

Section 53(1)(b) of the Law of Property Act 1925[2] provides:

> a declaration of a trust respecting any land or any interest therein must be manifested and proved by some writing signed by some person who is able to declare such a trust or by his will.

Formalities are required for declarations of trusts of land to prevent the disputes and inconvenience which would result if purely oral declarations were allowed. In essence s 53(1)(b) imposes an evidential safeguard. It is important to note that a purported oral declaration of a trust of land is not void, but only unenforceable.[3] The requirement of writing applies whether the trust is created by the land owner declaring himself trustee or transferring the land to trustees. It is not necessary that the actual declaration of the trust be made in writing, nor need the writing which evidences the declaration be contemporaneous with the declaration of the trust:[4] it could, for instance, be a written severance of a joint tenancy.[5] However, the written evidence must contain all the material terms of the trust, namely the beneficiaries, the trust property, and the nature of the trust.[6] Unlike the parallel provision s 53(1)(c), s 53(1)(b) will not be satisfied if the writing was signed by an agent. However, if the land is transferred subject to a trust, the transferee of the land

1 [2017] EWHC 1080 (Ch). 2 Re-enacting the Statute of Frauds 1677, s 7.

3 *Gardner v Rowe* [1828] 5 Russ 258; *Gissing v Gissing* [1969] 2 Ch 85 at 99; *Cowcher v Cowcher* [1972] 1 WLR 425 at 430–1; *Midland Bank plc v Dobson* [1986] 1 FLR 171 at 175.

4 *Forster v Hale* [1798] 3 Ves 696; *Rochefoucauld v Boustead* [1897] 1 Ch 196.

5 *Taylor v Taylor* [2017] EWHC 1080 (Ch) at 50.

6 *Smith v Matthews* [1861] 3 De GF & J 139; *Rochefoucauld v Boustead* [1897] 1 Ch 196.

may sign the written evidence of the declaration.[7] In *Taylor v Taylor*[8] it was held that the signature of the transferor on the standard land registry transfer form would also be sufficient, even if the form was not signed by the purchaser.[9]

(b) The rule in *Rochefoucauld v Boustead*

Although s 53(1)(b) renders an orally declared trust of land unenforceable in the absence of substantiating writing, this requirement is not always strictly enforced.[10] The courts have held that where insistence upon writing would allow the statute to be used as 'an instrument of fraud' the trust will be enforced, irrespective of the lack of writing. A fraud arises if a person to whom land was conveyed, subject to an oral understanding that it was to be held on trust, seeks to deny the trust, and claims to be absolutely entitled to the land because the requisite formalities are lacking. In *Rochefoucauld v Boustead*[11] the Comtesse de la Rochefoucauld owned the Delmar Estates in Ceylon, subject to a mortgage of £25,000. The land was sold by the mortgagee to the defendant, who was intended to take as trustee for the Comtesse. He subsequently mortgaged the land for a further £70,000 without her consent. The Comtesse sought a declaration that the defendant had acquired the land subject to a trust in her favour. The defendant claimed that the alleged trust had not been proved by any writing signed by him, as required by the Statute of Frauds 1677, s 7.[12] The Court of Appeal held that, despite the lack of formalities compliant with the statutory provision, evidence other than writing signed by the defendant would be admitted to prove the trust, since otherwise the defendant would be committing a fraud against the Comtesse. The principle was stated by Lindley LJ:

> the Statute of Frauds does not prevent the proof of a fraud; and it is a fraud on the part of a person to whom land is conveyed as a trustee, and who knows it was so conveyed, to deny the trust and claim the land himself. Consequently, notwithstanding the statute, it is competent for a person claiming land conveyed to another to prove by parol evidence that it was so conveyed upon trust for the claimant, and that the grantee, knowing the facts, is denying the trust and relying upon the form and conveyance and the statute, in order to keep the land himself.[13]

This can be understood as an instance of equity striving to do justice and refusing to allow formalities to defeat fair outcomes in disputes between litigating parties. That is clear from *Archibald v Alexander*.[14] In the case, a mother had arranged that a house in Bromley in Kent should be bought with only the mother and one of the children—named Patsy—named as joint tenants. It was the mother's orally expressed intention that upon her death, the property was to be divided between the surviving children. Patsy, although fully aware of the arrangement, claimed upon her mother's death that she owned the house outright rather than subject to a trust, so reneging on her mother's wishes. While there was no evidence of the family arrangement in writing, it would have been inequitable for Patsy to keep the house and exclude her siblings. The judge applied *Rochefoucauld v Boustead*, finding that 'equity will not allow the transferee to rely on the absence of a

[7] *Gardner v Rowe* [1828] 5 Russ 258; *Smith v Matthews* [1861] 3 De GF & J 139.

[8] [2017] EWHC 1080 (Ch).

[9] A different conclusion was reached in *Insol Funding Company Ltd v Cowlam* [2017] EWHC 1822 (Ch), where it does not appear to have been argued that the transferor had authority to sign on behalf of the transferees.

[10] See Youdan, 'Formalities for Trusts of Land, and the Doctrine in *Rochefoucauld v Boustead*' [1984] CLJ 306; McFarlane, 'Constructive Trusts Arising on a Receipt of Property *Sub Conditione*' [2004] 120 LQR 667.

[11] [1897] 1 Ch 196.

[12] Predecessor of s 53(1)(b) of the Law of Property Act 1925.

[13] [1897] 1 Ch 196 at 206.

[14] [2020] EWHC 1621 (Ch).

formal deed of trust and keep the property for herself...'[15] In a contemporary example of equity doing justice, a trust was found to carry through the mother's intention.[16]

The resolution to this unfortunate family dispute shows that the principle adopted in *Rochefoucauld v Boustead* has the merit of equity. But it is not easy to explain through ordinary statutory intepretation. The problem, from the perspective of a hard-headed lawyer, is that if an express trust is thought to govern the transaction, then that finding runs contrary to the clear wording of the statute which insists on conveyance in writing.

For this reason, certain cases have tended to treat the principle as an example of where a constructive trust is imposed, so that the intended trustee cannot rely on the absence of writing to deny the trust because he is already a constructive trustee of the land for the intended beneficiary.[17] In *Bannister v Bannister*, for example, Scott LJ described the principle as:

> the equitable principle on which a constructive trust is raised against a person who insists on the absolute character of a conveyance to himself for the purpose of defeating a beneficial interest.[18]

This constructive trust analysis of the rule in *Rochefoucauld v Boustead* has the attraction of not seeming to contradict the wording of s 53(1)(b) of the Law of Property Act 1925, as s 53(2) provides that formalities are not required for the creation of 'resulting, implied or constructive trusts'. Therefore, if a constructive trust of the land can be found, the court will not be seen to be enforcing a trust that the clear words of s 53(1)(b) render unenforceable. However, in *Rochefoucauld v Boustead*[19] itself, the Court of Appeal was of the view that an express trust was being enforced, despite the lack of statutory formalities. Lindley LJ stated that 'the trust which the plaintiff has established is clearly an express trust'. Given this, it seems more satisfactory to regard *Rochefoucauld v Boustead* as authority for the proposition that the court will enforce an express trust of land, despite an absence of writing, where to do otherwise would be to allow the statute to facilitate a fraud.

(c) Conflict between the transferor and third party beneficiaries

The simplest circumstance in which the rule in *Rochefoucauld v Boustead*[20] is of relevance is where A transfers land on trust to B without satisfying the s 53(1)(b) formalities. In that scenario, B is prevented from taking outright through a fraud. This is a straightforward legal circumstance because the judge will only have to consider the interests of two competing parties.

However, the case might be less straightforward. A might transfer to B to hold for the benefit of C. This creates a circumstance in which the court is confronted with the interests of third party beneficiaries.[21] This more complex issue came to court for the first time in *Solomon v McCarthy*.[22] There, a father had attempted to transfer a property named 'Morden' to his then partner. It was accepted that this transfer had been intended for the benefit of three children.[23] The couple were estranged and the ownership of the property was in dispute. Resolving the property dispute between the former partners, the judge did not find that property was held on trust for the benefit of the children. Instead, he found that there was a resulting trust for the benefit of the transferring father on the basis that

[15] *Archibald v Alexander* [2020] EWHC 1621 (Ch) at [28]. [16] [2020] EWHC 1621 (Ch) at [32].

[17] *Bannister v Bannister* [1948] 2 All ER 133; *Neale v Willis* [1968] 19 P & CR 836; *Re Densham (A Bankrupt)* [1975] 1 WLR 1519.

[18] [1948] 2 All ER 133. [19] [1897] 1 Ch 196. [20] [1897] 1 Ch 196.

[21] See, Atkins, 'Solomon v McCarthy: unwritten trusts of land' (2020) 26 Trusts and Trustees 372.

[22] [2020] 1 WLUK 130. [23] [2020] 1 WLUK 130, [45].

the intended transfer for the children had failed for want of compliance with the s 53(1)(b) formalities.[24]

(2) **Trusts of personal property**

Section 53(1)(b) has no application to declarations of trusts of personal property. An absolute owner may orally declare himself the trustee of such property without the need for any further formalities.[25]

(3) **Declaration of a sub-trust**

Where property is already held on trust, the beneficiary enjoys an immediate proprietary interest in the trust property. Since equitable proprietary interests are themselves capable of forming the subject matter of a trust, the beneficiary is entitled to declare himself a trustee of his interest under the trust, creating a sub-trust. If the property held under the head trust is land, any declaration of a sub-trust will only be enforceable by the sub-beneficiary if it is evidenced in writing in compliance with s 53(1)(b), since the trust property consists of an 'interest in land'. If the property held under the head trust is personalty, formalities will only be required to create the sub-trust if s 53(1)(c) applies. This section stipulates that dispositions of subsisting equitable interests can only be made in writing. The central question is whether a declaration of a sub-trust is to be characterized

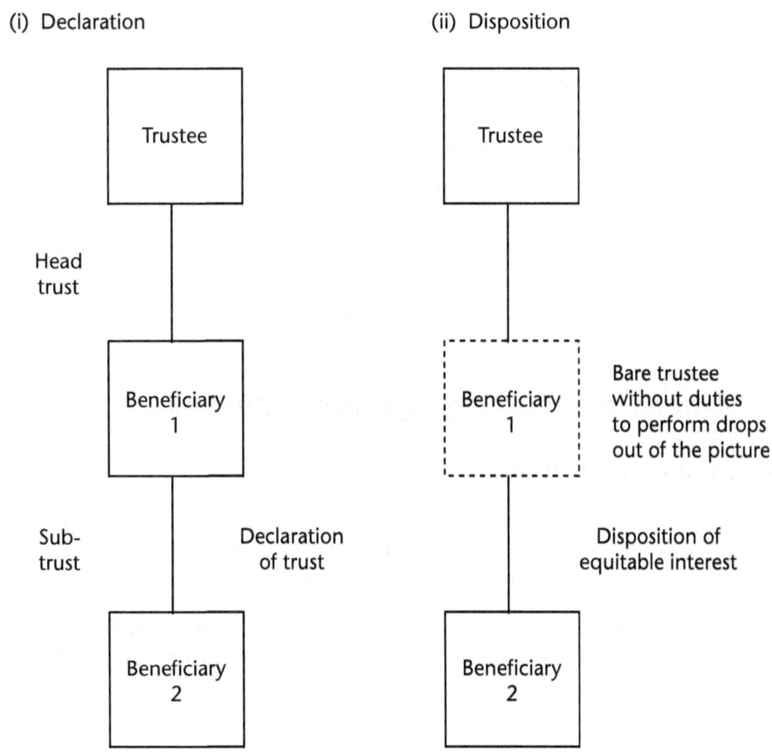

Figure 7.1 The declaration of a 'sub-trust'

[24] [2020] 1 WLUK 130, [45].

[25] See, for example, *Re Kayford Ltd* [1975] 1 WLR 279; *Paul v Constance* [1977] 1 WLR 527, CA.

as effecting a 'disposition' of the original beneficiary's equitable interest under the head trust. If so, any purported declaration which is not effected in writing will be of no effect. In addressing this question, it seems that the courts have drawn a distinction between genuine declarations of a sub-trust, and transactions which, though in the form of a declaration of sub-trust, are in substance a disposition of the beneficiary's equitable interest. If the sub-trust declared is a bare trust, so that the sub-trustee has no active duties to perform because the sub-beneficiary's entitlement to the trust property is identical to his own, he will be regarded as having effected a disposition of his interest. The sub-trust would merely amount to a duplication of the head-trustee's duties, so the sub-trustee is said to drop out of the picture and the head trustee holds the property on trust for the newly declared beneficiary (see Figure 7.1). This principle was recognized in *Grainge v Wilberforce*.[26] More significantly, it was accepted in *Grey v IRC*,[27] where Upjohn J used the language of a sub-trustee 'disappearing from the picture'[28] when a sub-trust is declared. Where a beneficiary who declares a sub-trust 'drops out of the picture' in this manner, the reality of the transaction is that he has effected a disposition of his equitable interest under the trust to the intended sub-beneficiary, and therefore the transaction will be ineffective unless the declaration is effected in writing.

In contrast, if an intended sub-trustee has active duties to perform under the sub-trust, he does not drop out of the picture and there is no disposition. Instead, a genuine sub-trust arises. This would be the case, for example, if a beneficiary created a life-interest of his interest under the trust in favour of a sub-beneficiary. Provided that the trust property is not land, in such circumstances there is no need for the declaration to be made in writing under s 53(1)(c). A purely oral declaration of the sub-trust will be sufficient.[29]

3 Declarations of trusts by will

A valid declaration of trust can be made by will for any property, whether land or personalty.[30] The requirements of a valid will are set out in s 9 of the Wills Act 1837. A will is only valid if it is made in writing,[31] which is signed by the testator (or by some other person acting at his direction in his presence)[32] in the presence of two witnesses, who themselves attest and sign the will (or acknowledge their signature) in the presence of the testator.[33] The formalities for wills are explored in more detail in Chapter 17.

4 Dispositions of subsisting equitable interests

(1) The requirement of writing

It has already been noted in the context of the difficulties associated with the declaration of sub-trusts that a different formality requirement applies to dispositions of existing equitable interests. Section 53(1)(c) of the Law of Property Act 1925 provides that:

> a disposition of an equitable interest or trust subsisting at the time of the disposition must be in writing signed by the person disposing of the same, or by his agent thereunto lawfully authorised in writing or by will.

[26] [1889] 5 TLR 436. See also: *Re Lashmar* [1891] 1 Ch 258, CA; *Trustees' Powers and Duties* (Law Com No 260, 1999), para 5.4, fn 3.

[27] [1958] Ch 375.

[28] [1958] Ch 375 at 382, per Upjohn J.

[29] Green, '*Grey, Oughtred* and *Vandervell*—A Contextual Reappraisal' [1984] 47 MLR 385.

[30] s 53(1)(b) and (c).

[31] s 9(a).

[32] s 9(a).

[33] s 9(c) and (d).

This section applies whenever the beneficiary of a trust attempts to transfer his equitable interest in the trust property to someone else. In *Vandervell v IRC*, Lord Upjohn provided an explanation of why formalities are required to effect such dispositions of a beneficiary's interest under a trust:

> the object of the section, as was the object of the old Statute of Frauds, is to prevent hidden oral transactions in equitable interests in fraud of those truly entitled, and making it difficult, if not impossible, for the trustees to ascertain who are in truth his beneficiaries.[34]

It is questionable whether it is truly correct that the requirement of writing prevents hidden transactions, as there is no obligation on the part of the transferor or transferee to bring the transfer to the attention of the trustees.[35] Writing is required because, as in the case of other forms of intangible property such as copyrights, there is no other means of effecting a transfer, as the property cannot be physically possessed or delivered. Unlike s 53(1)(b), where the effect of a lack of written evidence is merely to render an oral declaration of a trust of land unenforceable, a failure to comply with s 53(1)(c) renders the purported disposition void.[36] As such, the transferee-beneficiary will have failed to divest himself of his equitable interest in the trust property.

The following aspects of the requirement deserve attention.

(a) Meaning of 'disposition'

Section 53(1)(c) only applies to dispositions of subsisting equitable interests. It, therefore, has no application to declarations of trust, otherwise s 53(1)(b) would be redundant in requiring a declaration of a trust of land to be evidenced in writing. It is clear that an assignment of a subsisting equitable interest must be made in writing, as was held in *Re Danish Bacon Co Ltd Staff Pension Fund Trusts*.[37] Nevertheless, the meaning of the term 'disposition' has been the subject of much debate, as beneficiaries have sought to avoid compliance with the requirement of writing for tax reasons. The tax in question in many of the cases before the courts was ad valorem stamp duty. This tax is calculated as a percentage of the consideration given for the transfer and is payable when the transfer is made using a stock transfer form. It used to be the case that the tax could be avoided if the transfer did not require writing, but that loophole has been closed by the introduction of stamp duty reserve tax (SDRT), which is payable on paperless (including private 'off-market') transactions. Until the introduction of SDRT, ingenious methods were devised to effect transfers of shares without them being classed as 'dispositions' required to be in writing and subject to tax. The change in the tax laws makes it much less likely that new cases about what constitutes a disposition will arise.

The scope of a 'disposition' was considered by the House of Lords in *Grey v IRC* (see Figure 7.2),[38] where it was held that it should be given its 'natural meaning'.[39] The appellants held 18,000 shares on a bare trust as nominees for Mr Hunter. On 18 February 1955, Hunter orally directed them to henceforth hold the shares under six trusts, of 3,000 shares each, in favour of his grandchildren. On 25 March, the trustees executed a declaration of trust to that effect. The central question was whether the oral direction of 18 February was effective to transfer the equitable interest in the shares to the grandchildren. The Revenue argued that without writing, the oral direction was void and ineffective to

[34] [1967] 2 AC 291 at 311. [35] See Harris [1975] 38 MLR 557.

[36] See *Grey v IRC* [1960] AC 1; *Oughtred v IRC* [1960] AC 206. [37] [1971] 1 WLR 248.

[38] [1960] AC 1; [1960] CLJ 31 (Thornely); see also *Re Danish Bacon Co Ltd Staff Pension Fund Trusts* [1971] 1 WLR 248 at 254, per Megarry J; *Halley v The Law Society* [2003] WTLR 845.

[39] [1960] AC 1 at 13, 15, per Lord Simmonds.

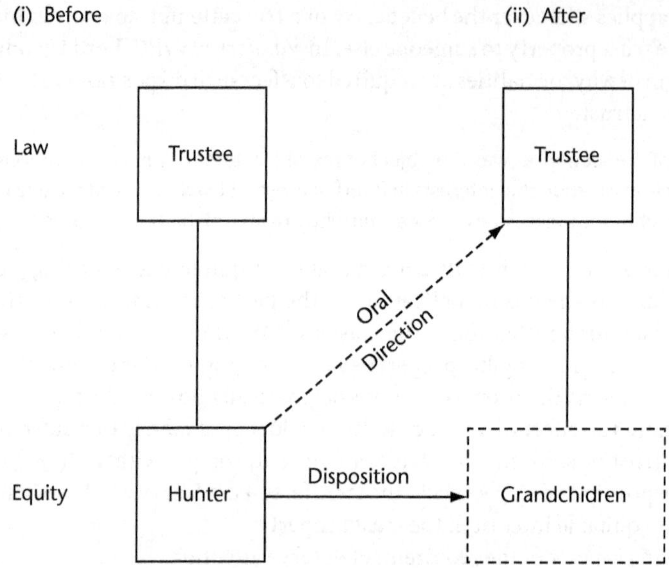

Figure 7.2 *Grey v IRC*

transfer the equitable interest in the shares. The trustees responded that the transaction did not require a written instrument because there had been no 'disposition' within the meaning of s 53(1)(c). They alleged that the Law of Property Act 1925 was merely a consolidating act, and that the word 'disposition' should be given no wider meaning than that accorded to the words 'grants and assignments' in the Statute of Frauds.[40] The House of Lords rejected this argument and held that the word 'disposition' should be given its natural meaning, in which case the oral direction to the trustees had been a disposition and was void and ineffective to transfer the equitable interest in the shares to the children. Lord Radcliffe stated:

> if there is nothing more in this appeal than the short question whether the oral direction that Mr Hunter gave to his trustees on February 18th 1955 amounted in any ordinary sense to a 'disposition of an equitable interest or trust subsisting at the time of the disposition', I do not feel any doubt as to my answer. I think that it did. Whether we describe what happened in technical or in more general terms the full equitable interest in the 18,000 shares concerned, which at that time was his, was . . . diverted by his direction from his ownership into the beneficial ownership of [his grandchildren] . . .[41]

As the oral directions of 18 February were ineffective because of the absence of writing, the transfer of the equitable interest in the shares had only been effected by the deed executed on 25 March. This written declaration was instead the disposition, and therefore liable to ad valorem stamp duty. It is worth considering how far the decision in this case was influenced by the fact that it involved a tax avoidance scheme.

A disclaimer of an equitable interest will not be regarded as a 'disposition' requiring writing,[42] whereas a surrender of an equitable interest is a disposition and will fall within the ambit of s 53(1)(c).[43]

[40] Statute of Frauds 1677, s 9. [41] [1960] AC 1 at 15.

[42] *Re Paradise Motor Co Ltd* [1968] 1 WLR 1125.

[43] See *Newlon Housing Trust v Al-Sulaimen* [1999] 1 AC 313 in the context of Matrimonial Causes Act 1973, s 37.

(b) 'An equitable interest... subsisting at the time of the disposition'

Section 53(1)(c) only applies to beneficial interests which actually exist at the date of the disposition. In *Re Danish Bacon Co Ltd*,[44] an employee had nominated someone to receive pension benefits if he died in pensionable service. Megarry J suggested that in these circumstances, s 53(1)(c) did not apply because the employee had been dealing with something that could never be his. He had no subsisting equitable interest in the benefits he was allocating.

(c) 'In writing'

Unlike s 53(1)(b), which only requires that a declaration of trust be evidenced in writing, s 53(1)(c) requires that a disposition actually be made in writing. This writing must obviously be contemporaneous with the intended disposition, although the disposition may be found in two or more separate documents, provided they are sufficiently connected.[45] The requirements of writing and signing may be satisfied by an electronic document.[46] This will be important where, for example, shares are held in trust and are traded electronically.

(d) 'Signed by the person disposing of the same or his agent'

Again, in contrast to s 53(1)(b), the written instrument effecting a disposition need not be personally signed by the beneficiary or other person disposing of the equitable interest. It will be effective if signed by his lawfully authorized agent (such as the trustees in *Grey v IRC*).

(e) 'Or by will'

A disposition of a subsisting equitable interest may be effected by will. The requirements of a valid will are considered in Chapter 17.

(2) Exceptions to the need for writing

Although the requirement of writing under s 53(1)(c) appears comprehensive, in a number of situations the courts have concluded that writing was not required to effect a transaction which was in substance a disposition of an equitable interest. These cases have largely arisen in the context of taxation, where, as we have seen, transferees have in the past sought to avoid stamp duty by effecting transfers of their equitable interest without using a written instrument that will attract duty. The cases suggest that writing will not be required to effect a transfer of a subsisting beneficial interest in the following circumstances.

(a) Direction by the beneficiary of a bare trust

In *Vandervell v IRC*,[47] the House of Lords held that s 53(1)(c) did not have to be satisfied where a beneficiary with a subsisting equitable interest under a bare trust directed the trustees to transfer the legal title to a third party and the transaction was completed (see Figure 7.3). The facts are complicated but important. Mr Vandervell was the sole beneficiary of a bare trust of shares in his company, Vandervell Products Ltd, of which

[44] [1971] 1 WLR 248.

[45] *Re Danish Bacon Co Ltd Staff Pension Fund Trusts* [1971] 1 WLR 248 at 254–5.

[46] See Electronic Communications Act 2000, s 8; Pt 3 of the Advice from the Law Commission, *Electronic Commerce: Formal Requirements in Commercial Transactions* (Law Com, 3 December 2001).

[47] [1967] 2 AC 291; [1966] 24 CLJ 19 (Jones); [1967] 31 Conv (NS) 175 (Spencer); [1967] 30 MLR 461 (Strauss); [1975] 38 MLR 557 (Harris). Nolan has argued that the decision can be explained on the basis of overreaching: '*Vandervell v IRC*; A Case of Overreaching' [2002] 61 CLJ 169.

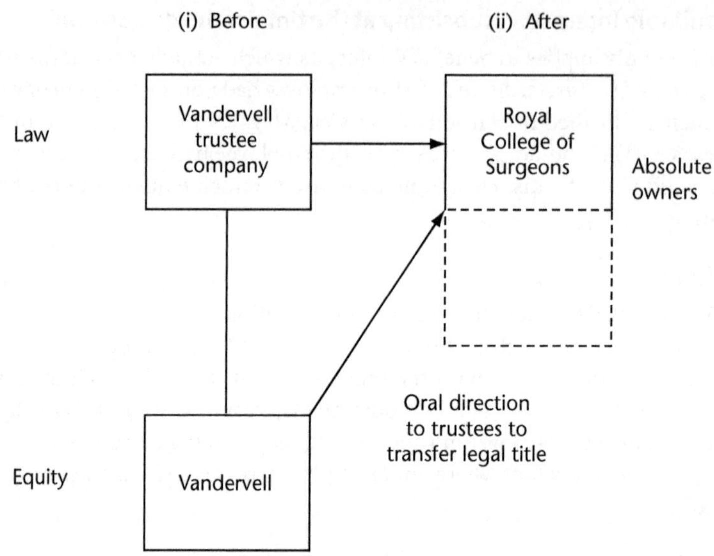

Figure 7.3 *Vandervell v IRC*

Vandervell Trustees Ltd was the trustee. He decided to endow a chair of pharmacology at the Royal College of Surgeons. At the time income tax (surtax) rates were very high (the top combined rate in 1965–66 was 96.25 per cent), and there was no tax relief for gifts to charity. Mr Vandervell wished to save tax on his gift. His scheme was to transfer shares in his company to the Royal College of Surgeons, and to fund the new professorship by declaring a sufficiently large dividend on the shares. He, therefore, directed the trustee company to execute a share transfer form for the shares and to pass it to him, leaving the name of the transferee blank. The trustees duly completed the transfer form and handed it to Mr Vandervell, who entered the name of the Royal College of Surgeons as transferee. The College was then registered as the owner of the shares on the company share register. In return for the transfer of the shares, the college granted the trustees an option to repurchase the shares for £5,000. Dividends of some £250,000 were subsequently declared on the shares to provide the endowment for the chair. The Revenue claimed that Mr Vandervell was liable to pay surtax on these dividends, arguing that the transaction amounted to a settlement of property in which the settlor had not absolutely divested himself of his interest in the property.[48] One ground of the Revenue's case was that Vandervell had failed to divest himself of his equitable interest in the shares, because the disposition had not been effected in writing.

Addressing this argument, the House of Lords held that, in the circumstances, writing had not been necessary to effect a transfer of Vandervell's equitable interest in the shares to the college. As the beneficiary of a bare trust he was entitled to direct the trustee to transfer the legal title to the trust property, and there was no need for a separate disposition to transfer the equitable title. The rationale was explained by Lord Upjohn:

> I cannot agree . . . that prima facie a transfer of the legal estate carries with it the absolute beneficial interest in the property transferred; this plainly is not so, e.g., the transfer may be on a change of trustee; it is a matter of intention in each case. But if the intention of the beneficial owner in directing the trustee to transfer the legal estate to X is that X should be the beneficial owner I can see no reason for any further document or further words in the

[48] Income Tax Act 1952, Pt XVIII.

> document assigning the legal estate also expressly transferring the beneficial interest; the greater includes the less. X may be wise to secure some evidence that the beneficial owner intended him to take the beneficial interest in case his beneficial title is challenged at a later date but it certainly cannot, in my opinion, be a statutory requirement that to effect its passing there must be some writing under section 53(1)(c).[49]

He also held that a transfer without writing in such circumstances would not offend against the policy underlying the formality requirement noted earlier, namely to prevent hidden oral transactions in equitable interests in fraud of those truly entitled and which might make it difficult or impossible for the trustees to ascertain their beneficiaries:

> when the beneficial owner owns the whole beneficial estate and is in a position to give directions to his bare trustee with regard to the legal as well as the equitable estate there can be no possible ground for invoking the section where the beneficial owner wants to deal with the legal estate as well as the equitable estate.[50]

This does make perfect sense, as in this situation, the trust itself is coming to an end, as both Vandervell and his trustees dropped out of the picture. Had it not been for the option to repurchase the shares, Vandervell would have had no rights to recover any interest in the shares, as the Royal College of Surgeons were the outright owners in law and equity of the shares. This dealt with the issue of formalities under s 53(1)(c). Nevertheless, while Vandervell was able to avoid ad valorem stamp duty on the transfer of his equitable interest in the shares, the majority of the House of Lords went on to find Vandervell liable to surtax on the dividends declared. They held that the option to repurchase the shares granted by the College to the trustee company was, in the absence of an express declaration of trust, held on an automatic resulting trust for Vandervell himself.[51] Since he was the beneficiary of the option he had failed to fully divest himself of all interest in the shares, thus attracting liability to surtax.

(b) A specifically enforceable contract

Where a beneficiary enters a specifically enforceable contract to transfer a subsisting equitable interest under a trust, that interest passes to the intended transferee immediately on the making of the contract by means of a constructive trust. Since the transferee obtains the equitable interest by means of the constructive trust arising from the contract, there is no need for further writing under s 53(1)(c). In *Oughtred v IRC*,[52] shares in a private company were held on trust for Mrs Oughtred for life with remainder to her son, Peter (see Figure 7.4). On 18 June, they entered an oral contract in which Peter agreed to release his interest in the shares subject to the settlement, so that his mother would be absolutely entitled to them, in return for which she would transfer 72,700 shares, of which she was already the absolute owner, to nominees for him. A deed of release was executed on 26 June. The central question before the House of Lords was whether ad valorem stamp duty was payable on this deed, which depended on whether the deed was a 'transfer on sale' within the provisions of the tax legislation then in force. The Oughtreds argued that the deed was not a 'transfer on sale' because the equitable remainder interest in the shares had passed to Mrs Oughtred by virtue of the contract to transfer, since, from the moment of the agreement, Peter held his interest on constructive trust. The majority of the House of Lords[53] held that irrespective of any constructive trust the deed of 26 June was a 'transfer on sale' for the purposes of the Stamp Act, and that stamp duty was therefore payable.[54]

[49] [1967] 2 AC 291 at 311. [50] [1967] 2 AC 291 at 311.

[51] For a discussion of automatic resulting trusts, see Chapter 9. [52] [1960] AC 206.

[53] With the exception of Lord Denning.

[54] Per Lords Keith, Denning, and Jenkins; Lords Radcliffe and Cohen dissenting.

However, Upjohn J at first instance, and Lord Radcliffe in the House of Lords, took the view that the oral contract had given rise to a constructive trust which effected a transfer of the remainder interest in the shares to Mrs Oughtred without the need for further writing. Lord Radcliffe explained:

> The reasoning of the whole matter, as I see it, is as follows: On June 18 1956 the son owned an equitable reversionary interest in the settled shares: by his oral agreement of that date he created in his mother an equitable interest in his reversion, since the subject-matter of the agreement was property of which specific performance would normally be decreed by the court. He thus became a trustee for her of that interest sub modo: having regard to subsection (2) of section 53 Law of Property Act 1925, subsection (1) of that section did not operate to prevent that trusteeship arising by operation of law . . .[55]

There has been some question whether Lord Radcliffe's comments establish that a specifically enforceable contract to transfer a subsisting equitable interest passes the interest by way of a constructive trust without the need for further writing, because the other members of the House of Lords did not express an opinion. However, his approach seems to have been adopted as correct in subsequent cases. It was accepted by Megarry J in *Re Holt's Settlement*[56] and by the Court of Appeal in *Neville v Wilson*.[57] This case concerned

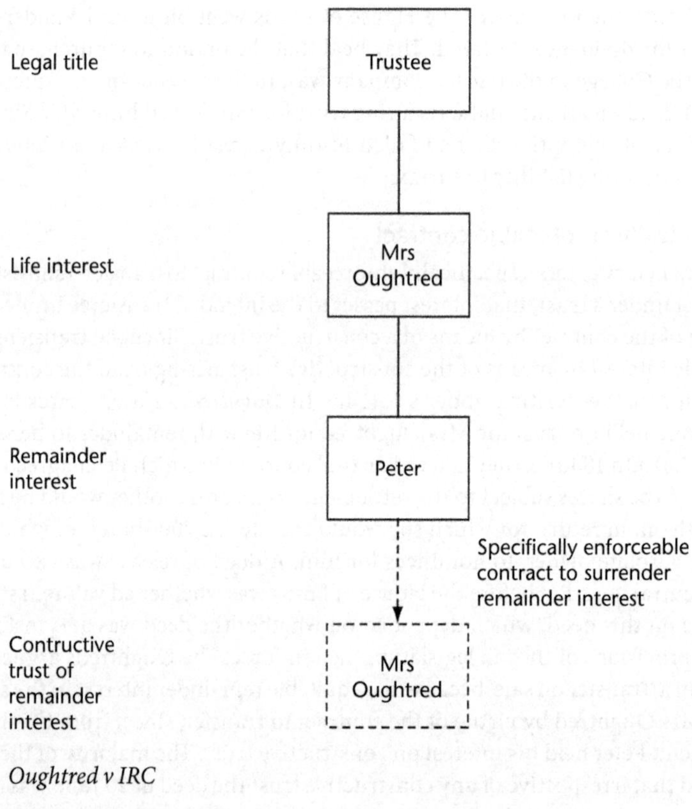

Figure 7.4 *Oughtred v IRC*

[55] [1960] AC 206 at 227.

[56] [1969] 1 Ch 100. See *DHN Food Distributors Ltd v London Borough of Tower Hamlets* [1976] 3 All ER 462 [1977] 93 LQR 170 (Sugarman and Webb); *Chinn v Collins (Inspector of Taxes)* [1981] 1 All ER 189, HL.

[57] [1997] Ch 144; [1996] 55 CLJ 436 (Nolan); [1996] Conv 368 (Thompson); [1997] 113 LQR 213 (Milne). See also *Bishop Square Ltd v IRC* [1999] 78 P & CR 169, where the Court of Appeal applied *Oughtred v IRC* to a very similar fact situation.

a trust of 120 shares in a company (U Ltd), which were held by the directors of the company as nominees for a separate family company (J Ltd). In 1969 J Ltd had been struck off the register because it had become defunct. It was claimed that in 1969 an oral agreement had been reached between the shareholders of J Ltd that the assets of the company should be divided among the shareholders rateably. The central question was whether this oral agreement gave rise to a constructive trust of the 120 shares in favour of the shareholders of J Ltd or whether it was void for failure to comply with the requirements of s 53(1)(c). If no such constructive trust had arisen, the shares would pass to the Crown as bona vacantia. The Court of Appeal held that the oral agreement of the shareholders had produced a constructive trust of the shares, so that they were held by the directors of U Ltd on behalf of the shareholders of J Ltd Nourse LJ explained:

> The simple view of the present case is that the effect of each individual agreement was to constitute the shareholder an implied or constructive trustee for the other shareholders, so that the requirement for writing contained in sub-s (1)(c) of s 53 was dispensed with by sub-s (2). That was the view taken by Upjohn J at first instance and by Lord Radcliffe in the House of Lords in *Oughtred v IRC* . . . So far as it is material to the present case, what sub-s (2) says is that subs-s (1)(c) does not affect the creation or operation of implied or constructive trusts. Just as in *Oughtred v IRC* the son's oral agreement created a constructive trust in favour of the mother, so here each shareholder's oral or implied agreement created an implied or constructive trust in favour of the other shareholders. Why then should sub-s (2) not apply? No convincing reason was suggested in argument and none has occurred to us since. Moreover, to deny its application in this case would be to restrict the effect of the general words when no restriction is called for, and to lay the ground for fine distinctions in the future. With all the respect which is due to those who have thought to the contrary, we hold that sub-s (2) applies to an agreement such as we have in this case.

Following *Neville v Wilson*, it seems clear that there is a general principle that where a subsisting equitable interest is the subject of an oral contract to transfer which gives rise to a constructive trust, there is no need for further writing in satisfaction of s 53(1)(c) because the constructive trust itself effects the disposition of the subsisting equitable interest to the transferee. However, in practice this possibility will be of relatively limited scope. It will only apply to oral contracts which are specifically enforceable. While contracts to transfer interests in land are specifically enforceable, giving rise to a constructive trust, there is no possibility of an oral contract to transfer a subsisting equitable interest under a trust of land avoiding formality provisions altogether, because the contract itself must be in writing.[58] In the case of personal property, contracts are not specifically enforceable unless the subject matter of the contract is unique because no market substitute is available. For example, a contract to transfer shares in a public company is not usually thought to give rise to a constructive trust.[59] In *Oughtred v IRC*,[60] the contract was specifically enforceable because the shares were in a private company and were not freely available in the market.

(c) Extinguishing a resulting trust

It further seems that there is no need for writing in satisfaction of s 53(1)(c) if the act of a third party has the effect of extinguishing a subsisting equitable interest which has arisen under an automatic resulting trust. It has already been seen how, in *Vandervell v IRC*,[61] Mr Vandervell failed to divest himself absolutely of his interest in shares transferred to

[58] Law of Property (Miscellaneous Provisions) Act 1989, s 2.

[59] See, however, *Chinn v Collins (Inspector of Taxes)* [1981] AC 533, which provides some authority that even in the case of shares in a public company a constructive trust will arise.

[60] [1960] AC 206.

[61] [1967] 2 AC 291.

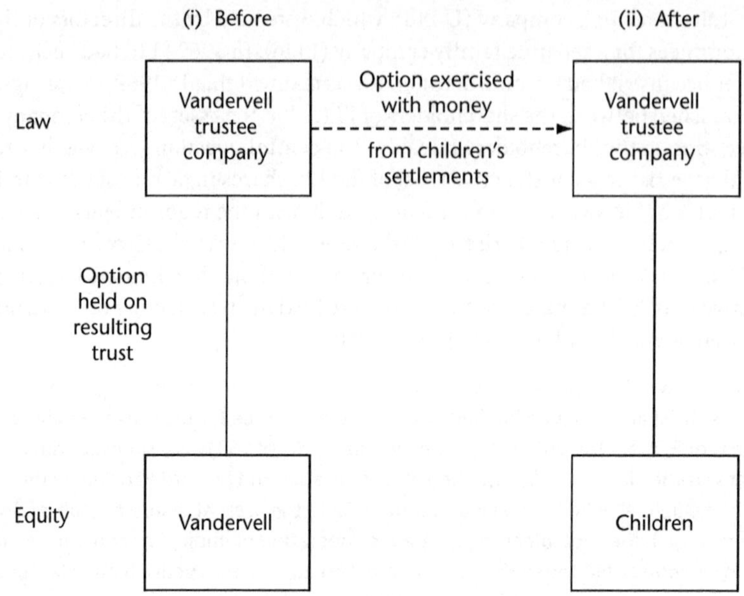

Figure 7.5 *Re Vandervell's Trusts (No 2)*

the Royal College of Surgeons because the option to repurchase was held on resulting trust for him by the Vandervell Trustee Company. The trustee company subsequently exercised this option, using money they held on other trusts for Vandervell's children. They then informed the Revenue that they held the re-acquired shares on trust for the children, and all dividends deriving from those shares were paid to the children's settlement. In *Re Vandervell's Trusts (No 2)* (see Figure 7.5),[62] the Revenue claimed that Vandervell was liable to pay surtax on these dividends as well, on the grounds that he had still not divested himself absolutely of his interest in the shares. Their argument that there had been no effective declaration of trust in favour of the children was accepted by Megarry J, at first instance, but rejected by the Court of Appeal, which held that the conduct of the trustees was sufficient to amount to a declaration of trust in favour of the children. The Revenue further argued that Vandervell had never effectually disposed of his equitable interest under the resulting trust of the option, because he had never done so in writing as required by s 53(1)(c). The Court of Appeal also rejected this argument, holding that there had been no need of a written instrument to extinguish Vandervell's resulting trust interest. Lord Denning MR based his conclusion on the nature and function of the resulting trust:

> A resulting trust for the settlor is born and dies without any writing at all. It comes into existence whenever there is a gap in the beneficial ownership. It ceases to exist whenever that gap is filled by someone becoming beneficially entitled. As soon as the gap is filled by the creation or declaration of a valid trust, the resulting trust comes to an end. In this case, before the option was exercised, there was a gap in the beneficial ownership. So there was a resulting trust for Mr Vandervell. But as soon as the option was exercised and the shares registered in the trustee's name, there was created a valid trust of the shares in favour of the children's settlement . . .[63]

[62] [1974] Ch 269; [1975] 38 MLR 557 (Harris). [63] [1974] Ch 269 at 320.

Lawton LJ took the view that the declaration of the trust of the shares in favour of the children's settlement had the effect of extinguishing Vandervell's interest under the resulting trust of the option. An extinction was not a 'disposition', and, therefore, writing was not required:

> The exercise of the option and the transfer of the shares to the trustee company necessarily put an end to the resulting trust of the option. There could not be a resulting trust of a chose in action which was no more. The only reason why there ever had been a resulting trust of the option was the rule that the beneficial interest in property must be held for someone if the legal owner is not entitled to it. The legal but not the beneficial interest in the option had vested in the trustee company. The beneficial interest had to be held for someone and as the trustee company had declared no trusts of the option, the only possible beneficiary was Mr Vandervell. Once the trustee company took a transfer of the shares the position was very different. The legal title to them was vested in the trustee company and by reason of the facts and circumstances to which I have already referred it held the beneficial interest for the trusts of the children's settlement. There was no gap between the legal and beneficial interests and in consequence no need for a resulting trust in favour of Mr Vandervell to fill it. Neither the extinction of the resulting trust of the option resulting from its exercise nor the creation of a beneficial interest in the shares by the declaration of trust amounted to a disposition of an equitable interest or trust within the meaning of sections 53(1)(c) and 205(1)(ii) of the Law of Property Act 1925.[64]

The precise impact of the decision in *Re Vandervell's Trusts (No 2)*[65] is open to question, as is the reasoning within it. It is doubtful whether, in reality, the acts of the trustee company were of themselves sufficient to divest Vandervell of his resulting trust of the option. As Megarry J had commented at first instance:

> That issue is, in essence, whether trustees who hold an option on trust for X will hold the shares obtained by exercising that option on trust for Y merely because they used Y's money in exercising the option. Authority apart, my answer would be an unhesitating no. The option belongs to X beneficially, and the money merely exercises rights which belong to X. Let the shares be worth £50,000 so then an option to purchase those shares for £5,000 is worth £45,000, and it will be at once seen what a monstrous result would be produced by allowing trustees to divert from their beneficiary X the benefits of what they hold for him merely because they used Y's money instead of X's.

More significantly, it is questionable whether the mere fact that the beneficial interest in the option arose under a resulting trust should provide a justification for the inapplicability of s 53(1)(c). There is no conceptual imperative for treating a disposition of a subsisting equitable interest which has arisen by way of a resulting trust any differently from a disposition of an interest arising under an express trust. The court's reasoning that the resulting trust is somehow eliminated by the act of the trustee identifying new beneficiaries is spurious. While it is true that the original resulting trust arose because Vandervell had failed to specify who was to be the beneficial owner of the option, the trust is only a 'resulting trust' to the extent that it was not expressly created, and this characterization should not colour its nature for the whole of its existence. The prime duty of a trustee, whether of a bare or active trust, is to preserve the trust fund for the beneficiary. The beneficiary's interest cannot be transferred to different beneficiaries by the mere act of the trustees without assignment by the beneficiary, otherwise the trustee would be able to dispose of the beneficial interests under the trust without reference to the beneficiary. For example, if two friends (X and Y) contributed equally to the purchase of shares valued

[64] [1974] Ch 269 at 326. [65] [1974] Ch 269.

at £100,000 acquired in the name of X alone, surely X should not be able to eliminate Y's beneficial half-interest under a resulting trust merely by declaring that henceforward he regards himself as holding the shares on trust for Z. To conclude that interests subsisting behind resulting trusts can be disposed of without writing would also provide an easy means of evading the ruling in *Grey v IRC*, which concerned an equitable interest subsisting under an express bare trust. If a settlor were to transfer property to a nominee, without specifying a beneficiary and thus giving rise to a resulting trust in his favour, he could then transfer the equitable interest to new beneficiaries by merely orally directing the trustees to declare new trusts.

If any general principle can be construed from *Re Vandervell's Trusts (No 2)* it would, therefore, seem that it should be limited to a case where the extinction of the equitable interest arising under a resulting trust is the act of a third party, and not of the person who enjoys the interest. It was only because the declaration of trust was made by the trustees that there was no need for writing. If Vandervell himself had sought to transfer his equitable interest under the resulting trust, writing would surely have been required in satisfaction of s 53(1)(c).

5 Resulting and constructive trusts

The formality requirements of s 53(1) only apply in respect of declarations of express trusts and dispositions of existing equitable interests. As will be evident in the following chapters, they have no application to resulting or constructive trusts. This is the effect of s 53(2), which provides:

> This section does not affect the creation or operation of resulting, implied or constructive trusts.

8

Policy limits

1 Introduction

Although a prime purpose of the law of equity is to enable owners to deal with their property as they wish, there are certain policy-motivated limits which constrain their freedom. The rule against perpetuities prevents owners tying their property up outside of the market for too long a period of time. Conditional and determinable interests, where the conditions are designed to influence the beneficiaries' behaviour in a way that is contrary to public policy, are also restricted. Legislation also provides that trusts may be set aside if they are established with the object of defrauding the creditors of the settlor.

2 The rule against perpetuities

The rule against perpetuities has been modernized as a result of recommendations by by the Law Commission, which proposed significant legislative reform.[1] The new scheme, which was finally enacted[2] on 12 November 2009 as the Perpetuities and Accumulations Act 2009, only has prospective effect,[3] so that trusts executed before the new legislation came into force on 6 April 2010 will continue to be administered under the old scheme.[4] The continuing existence of separate schemes complicates the law, but it is part of the price paid for simplification over the longer course.[5]

(1) The perpetuity rules

(a) Remoteness of vesting

The law requires that gifts of property will certainly vest within a certain period of time, the perpetuity period. This complex rule is also the most doctrinally important of the perpetuity schemes. It is best illustrated by way of an example from the case law. In *Re Peel's Release*,[6] a settlor provided land for the use of a school. He also stated in the trust that if the school were to cease to operate in accordance with his plans for it, then his

[1] *The Rules Against Perpetuities and Excessive Accumulations* (Law Com No 251, 1998).

[2] The Law Commission's recommendations were accepted by the government in 2001, but no time was found to implement them. In 2008, the Bill was proposed as the first in the trial of the new House of Lords' procedure for Law Commission Bills (HL Paper 63, *1st Report of Session 2007–08: Law Commission Bills*), which, in essence, is a streamlined procedure for enacting uncontroversial Law Commission Bills that allows them to be taken in Committee, off the floor of the House.

[3] Perpetuities and Accumulations Act 2009, s 15 and Perpetuities and Accumulations Act 2009 (Commencement) Order 2010, SI 2010/37.

[4] There are limited opt-in opportunities for existing trusts, so that they may be administered under the statutory scheme—see Perpetuities and Accumulations Act 2009, s 12.

[5] For a critique, see Gallanis, 'The Rule Against Perpetuities and the Law Commission's Flawed Philosophy' [2000] 59 CLJ 284.

[6] *Re Peel's Release* [1921] Ch 218.

heirs should instead receive the school land. This contingency fell foul of the common law remoteness rule. It was not certain when the land would vest in the heirs.

In consequence of Law Commission reforms, there are now two statutory regimes governing this aspect of the perpetuity rules: those for trusts created before 6 April 2010, and those for trusts created after this date. Before looking at these regimes, two other perpetuity rules need to be noted as all three schemes interrelate.

(b) Excessive accumulations

An accumulation involves adding trust income to the capital. This process of addition causes the capital to build up over time. If permitted over a long period, it ties up the accumulating property and so renders it useless. With the passing of the Accumulations Act 1800, a complicated statutory rule was introduced which created a rule against 'excessive accumulations' of income.[7]

The old statutory code, though repealed, forms the basis of the six permitted periods of accumulation of income under what is now s 164 of the Law of Property Act 1925.[8] Yet s 164 will be of diminishing importance over time. It applies only to trusts created before the commencement date of the Perpetuities and Accumulations Act 2009 (6 April 2010). Insofar as it applies, the effect of s 164 is that no person may settle or dispose of property for accumulation for a period longer than:

(i) the life of the grantor or settlor; or

(ii) a term of twenty-one years from the death of the grantor, settlor, or testator; or

(iii) the duration of the minority (or respective minorities) of any person living or en ventre sa mère at the death of the grantor, settlor testator; or

(iv) the duration of the minority (or respective minorities) of any person who under the limitation of the trust or will if of full age would be entitled to the income directed to be accumulated; or

(v) twenty-one years from the making of the disposition;[9] or

(vi) the minority (or respective minorities) of any person in being at the date of the disposition.

For accumulations after the commencement date of the Perpetuities and Accumulations Act 2009, the law has been greatly simplified. For those trusts, there is no specified duration of accumulation.[10] This means that income can be accumulated for 125 years in line with new rules on remoteness of vesting. [11]

(c) Rule against inalienability

In addition to the other two rules, the law does not allow trust property to be tied up and, hence, to become inalienable,[12] for ever. In common with property that is left accumulating over time, 'locked up', inalienable property, is at risk of being rendered useless.

[7] The Act was a direct, Parliamentary response to the decision in *Thellusson v Woodford* [1799] 4 Ves 227; 11 Ves 112. See, further, Polden, 'Panic or Prudence? The Thellusson Act 1800 and Trusts for Accumulation' [1994] 45 NILQ 13.

[8] As amended by the Perpetuities and Accumulations Act 1964, s 13.

[9] These last two periods were inserted by the 1964 Act, s 13.

[10] Except in the case of perpetual charitable trusts. Unless the Court or Charity Commission provide otherwise, charitable accumulations can only last for twenty-one years in consequence of the Perpetuities and Accumulations Act, s14(4). For leading analysis of charitiable accumulations, see Murray, *Charity Law and Accumulation: Maintaining an Intergenerational Balance* (CUP 2021).

[11] Perpetuities and Accumulations Act, s 5. See later sections.

[12] This means that the property cannot be transferred or sold (alienated) and enter the general property market.

The most likely application of the rule against inalienability arises in the context of non-charitable purpose trusts, such as an attempted trust to maintain a non-charitable personal monument or grave over a long period. That scheme would fall foul of the rule against inalienability.[13]

The Perpetuities and Accumulations Act 1964 did not affect the rule against inalienability (or 'the rule against perpetual trusts', as it is sometimes known), nor did the Law Commission consider the rule as part of its reform. It is an area which might benefit from its own careful review in the future. Thus, the rule is unaffected by the new statutory schemes.[14] The common law period of life in being plus twenty-one years continues to apply to non-charitable purpose trusts.

(2) Remoteness of vesting rules

(a) Perpetuity rules before 6 April 2010

At common law, if the property might vest outside of the perpetuity period, the gift would be void. The relevant perpetuity period was a life in being plus twenty-one years. This meant that the gift must not vest outside of a period of twenty-one years after the lifetime of a human person living at the date of the creation of the interest. Out of context, the rule seems odd and arcane. It should be kept in mind that it arose in the testamentary setting. So, a gift in a will might be made to the first of A's children to attain the age of twenty-one after A's death. In that legal 'home', a logical shape can be discerned.

The common law rule preventing remoteness of vesting was reformed by the Perpetuities and Accumulations Act 1964.[15] Under s 1, a settlor could specify the relevant perpetuity period in the trust instrument instead of a perpetuity period of a life in being plus twenty-one years, up to a period of eighty years. This was obviously simpler than the requirement of a life in being and was a more attractive option than the 'royal lives' clauses previously regularly used in trust instruments.[16] Where no perpetuity period was specified under s 1 and the trust would have been invalid under the common law rule because it might have vested outside of the perpetuity period,[17] s 3 provided a 'wait and see' procedure. The trust would only be void if it does not in fact vest within the perpetuity period.[18] Section 3 provided its own list of statutory lives by which the perpetuity period is to be measured.

(b) Perpetuity rules on or after 6 April 2010

The Law Commission recommended that the rule against remoteness of vesting be retained but reformed. Two key components of the reform of the rule are:

(1) Under s 5 of the 2009 Act a single perpetuity period of 125 years is adopted, and it applies whether or not adopted in the express wording of the trust instrument.

(2) Under s 7 of the 2009 Act, a 'wait and see' principle operates, regardless of the wording of the instrument,[19] so that a trust will only be void if it does not vest, as a matter of fact, within the perpetutity period.

[13] *Re Filshie* [1939] NZLR 91. Charitable trusts are exempt from this requirement and may be perpetual. See *Re Faraker* [1912] 2 Ch 488.

[14] Perpetuities and Accumulations Act 2009, s 18.

[15] This Act has not been repealed, as it applies to trusts arising before the commencement of the Perpetuities and Accumulations Act 2009, although, by s 16 of the 2009 Act, the 1964 Act has no application to trusts falling under the new statutory perpetuity regime.

[16] These clauses defined the perpetuity period by reference to the lives of the living descendants of a member of the royal family such as Queen Victoria.

[17] It will be invalid, even though it may be highly likely in fact to vest within the perpetuity period.

[18] In other words, it is not sufficient to invalidate the gift that it might not vest within the perpetuity period; it must actually fail to vest.

[19] Perpetuities and Accumulations Act 2009, s 7(4)(a).

There is a possibility, in limited circumstances, for a private trust created before 6 April 2010 to be partially brought within the scheme. Section 12 of the 2009 Act gives trustees of an existing trust a fiduciary power[20] to adopt by deed a perpetuity period of one hundred years (and no other period) *if* the trust contains an express perpetuity period of lives in being plus twenty-one years *and* they believe that it is difficult or impracticable to ascertain the existence or whereabouts of the measuring lives.

(3) Complexity

While the 2009 Act is a welcome simplification and modernization of the law, the fact that many existing trusts fall outside the scheme means that students and practitioners alike will have to struggle with three different sets of perpetuity rules and periods (two different schemes for remoteness of vesting and accumulations, plus a different time period for the inalienability rule) for some time into the future.

3 Conditional and determinable interests

(1) Ways of qualifying a gift

Owners may choose not to make absolute gifts to others, but instead to make gifts that are subject to conditions. There are three ways of doing this:

(i) to impose a condition which has to be satisfied before a person qualifies as a beneficiary (a condition precedent);

(ii) to impose a condition which means that the beneficiary will be disqualified if a certain event occurs (a condition subsequent);

(iii) to define the gift in such a way that it last only for so long as a certain state of affairs continues (a determinable interest).

Suppose that Terrance created a trust in his will and left '(i) £10,000 to my niece Mary if she graduates from university with first class honours; (ii) Blackacre to my close friend Joyce for life, on condition that she does not marry; and (iii) £10,000 per year to my daughter Louise, so long as she remains married to her husband Ralph.' Each of these three gifts would match one of the ways of qualifying a gift by condition precedent, condition subsequent, and determining event respectively.

Imposing conditions can be a very powerful method of controlling a donee's behaviour. However, if the condition is illegal, or one that would constrain the donee's behaviour in a way contrary to public policy, it will be void. The effect of this will depend upon the type of gift, and will be considered later.

(2) Conditions void for uncertainty

If the condition or determining event is uncertain, then it will be void. Lord Cranworth stated the principle in *Clavering v Ellison*[21] that the court must be able to 'see from the beginning, precisely and distinctly, upon the happening of what event it was that [the gift] was to determine'.[22] Conditions which have been held void for uncertainty include: a requirement that the donee 'conform to' the Church of England;[23] not marry a person

[20] Hence, the trustees are under a duty to consider whether to opt in to the new statutory regime. The duties of donees of fiduciary powers are discussed further in Chapter 35.

[21] [1859] 7 HL Cas 707. [22] [1859] 7 HL Cas 707 at 725. [23] *Re Tegg* [1936] 2 All ER 878.

'not of Jewish parentage';[24] not have a 'social or other relationship with a named person';[25] 'continue to reside in Canada';[26] or 'take up permanent residence in England'.[27]

Where the condition is a condition precedent, the courts take a more relaxed view of certainty. In *Re Barlow's Will Trust*;[28] the testatrix provided that 'any friends of mine' could buy a painting from her estate for considerably below its open market value. Browne-Wilkinson J held that this was sufficiently certain. In his view, 'anyone who can prove that by any reasonable test he or she must have been a friend of the testatrix is entitled to exercise the option.'[29] This would not be sufficient for a condition subsequent. A good reason for making this distinction is that a higher level of certainty should be required to deprive a person of a benefit than it is to grant them one.

(3) **Conditions void as contrary to public policy**

Certain types of condition have also been held to be void because they offend against public policy.

(a) **Conditions restricting alienation**

If a condition attached to a gift is tantamount to a complete restriction on alienation or transfer of the property, it will be void as contrary to public policy.[30] In *Re Brown*[31] a father bequeathed his freehold properties to his four sons in equal shares, with a condition that they were not to alienate their shares other than to each other. Harman J held that this amounted to a general prohibition on alienation because they were a small and diminishing class, and the condition was void.[32]

(b) **Conditions restraining marriage**

Marriage was traditionally viewed as the fundamental building block of society, and conditions which seek to undermine marriage are void as contrary to public policy.[33] Conditions that completely restrain the donee's freedom to marry are void.[34] Similarly, conditions that encourage separation or divorce of husband and wife are void.[35] Thus, in *Re Johnson's Will Trusts*[36] a donor established a trust in favour of his daughter which would pay her £50 per year as long as she continued to be married to her husband, but would pay her the full income from the fund if she were divorced or separated. Buckley J held that the condition was void as it amounted to an incentive to the break-up of the marriage.[37]

[24] *Clayton v Ramsden* [1943] AC 320, HL. [25] *Re Jones* [1953] Ch 125.

[26] *Sifton v Sifton* [1938] AC 656. [27] *Re Gape* [1952] Ch 743.

[28] [1979] 1 WLR 278. See also *Re Allen* [1953] 1 Ch 810 *and Re Abrahams' Will Trusts* [1967] 1 Ch 463.

[29] Ibid at 282.

[30] *Muschamp v Bluet* [1617] J Bridge 132; *Hood v Oglander* [1865] 34 Beav 513; *Re Rosher* [1884] 26 Ch D 801; *Corbett v Corbett* [1888] 14 PD 7; *Re Dugdale* [1888] LR 38 Ch D 176; *Re Cockerill* [1929] 2 Ch 131.

[31] [1954] Ch 39.

[32] Contrast *Re Macleay* [1875] LR 20 Eq 186, where a restriction to alienation within 'the family' was upheld. Harman J considered that this was a large and indeterminable group of people that may increase.

[33] See *Long v Dennis* [1767] 4 Burr 2052 at 2059, per Lord Mansfield: 'conditions in restraint of marriage are odious . . .'.

[34] *Low v Peers* [1770] Wilm 364 at 372: an absolute restraint on marriage 'tends to evil and the promoting of licentiousness; it tends to depopulation, the greatest of all political sins . . .'.

[35] *Wren v Bradley* [1848] 2 De G & Sm 49; *Re Moore* [1888] 39 Ch D 116; *Re Caborne* [1943] Ch 224; *Re Johnson's Will Trusts* [1967] Ch 387; *Re Hepplewhite Will Trust* [1977] CLY 2710.

[36] [1967] Ch 387. [37] [1967] Ch 387 at 396.

On the other hand, conditions that restrain marriage to particular individuals[38] or classes have been held valid. In *Jenner v Turner*,[39] a testatrix left property to her brother on condition that he did not marry a 'domestic servant'. This was held to be a valid condition by Bacon V-C. Similarly, conditions that restrain the donee's freedom to *remarry* have in the past been upheld.[40]

(c) Conditions restraining religion

Although the position may have changed because of human rights legislation, at common law, conditions restricting the choice of religion of a beneficiary were never regarded as void because they offend against public policy.[41] In *Blathwayt v Baron Cawley*,[42] a condition that a beneficiary forfeit his interest if he 'be or become a Roman Catholic' was upheld by the House of Lords. It was neither uncertain nor contrary to public policy. Lord Wilberforce explained that:

> to introduce for the first time a rule of law which would go far beyond the mere avoidance of discrimination on religious grounds... would bring about a substantial reduction of another freedom, firmly rooted in our law, namely that of testamentary disposition. Discrimination is not the same thing as choice: it operates over a larger and less personal area, and neither by express provision nor by implication has private selection yet become a matter of public policy.[43]

However, if the condition restrictive of religion is uncertain it will not be binding. In *Clayton v Ramsden*,[44] a provision forfeiting the beneficiary's interest on marriage to a person 'not of Jewish parentage' was held void for uncertainty.[45]

(d) Conditions affecting parental duties

Conditions which seek to separate parent from child are void as contrary to public policy.[46] In *Re Sandbrook*[47] the condition that a gift of the income of a fund was to be forfeited if children lived with their father was held void. Such a condition is void even if the parents are divorced.[48] Some cases have suggested that conditions that interfere with the exercise of parental duties are void. In *Re Borwick*[49] a condition that a minor forfeit an interest if she 'become a Roman Catholic or not be openly or avowedly Protestant' was held void as it operated to interfere with the exercise of a parent's duty in the religious instruction of his children.[50] In *Blathwayt v Baron Cawley*,[51] the House of Lords limited the range of this principle, holding that:

> To say that any condition which in any way might affect or influence the way in which a child is to be brought up, or in which parental duties are exercised, is void seems to me to state far too wide a rule.[52]

[38] *Re Bathe* [1925] Ch 377; *Re Hanlon* [1933] Ch 254: a gift by testator to her daughter subject to the condition that she does not 'intermarry with AB' upheld by Eve J.

[39] [1880] 16 Ch D 188.

[40] *Jordan v Holkham* [1753] Amb 209: provision of testator's will that his wife would forfeit her interest if she remarried was upheld. Contrast the Irish case of *Duddy v Gresham* [1878] 2 LR Ir 442, where a condition in the testator's will that his wife not remarry but enter a convent of her choice was held void.

[41] The boundary between race and religion is uncertain. In *Mandla v Dowell Lee* [1983] 2 AC 548, Sikhs were held to be a racial group, and in *King-Ansell v Police* [1979] 2 NZLR 531, Jews were also held to be a racial group. However, the distinction is of no practical importance for the law of trusts, since conditions on grounds of neither religion nor race are invalid.

[42] [1976] AC 397, HL.

[43] [1976] AC 397, HL at 426.

[44] [1943] AC 320, HL.

[45] See also *Re Tegg* [1936] 2 All ER 878, where a condition 'to conform' to the Church of England was held void for uncertainty.

[46] See *Re Morgan* [1910] 26 TLR 398; *Re Boulter* [1922] 1 Ch 75.

[47] [1912] 2 Ch 471.

[48] *Re Piper* [1946] 2 All ER 503, which concerned a gift by will to children provided they do not live with their father before attaining the age of thirty. Mother had divorced father before the date of the will.

[49] [1933] Ch 657.

[50] The condition was also held void on the grounds of uncertainty.

[51] [1976] AC 397.

[52] [1976] AC 397 at 426, per Lord Wilberforce.

(e) Impact of legislation and changes in social attitudes

Many of the decisions on public policy date from the nineteenth century. There have been significant changes in social views since then, and especially since the late twentieth century, reflected in legislation, notably the Equality Act 2010 (replacing earlier legislation with narrower scope), which generally prohibits discrimination on the grounds of religion, race, sex, and other protected characteristics,[53] and the Human Rights Act 1998, incorporating the European Convention on Human Rights and Fundamental Freedoms 1950 (the ECHR) into British law. It is likely that this change in societal attitudes and the legislative framework will be reflected in judicial decisions. The Equality Act 2010 does not apply to private trusts, and most aspects of the ECHR do not directly impact relationships between private citizens.[54] However, they do influence public policy. Conditions which aim to restrain marriage to particular individuals, or encourage divorce, could be characterized as an interference with the right to respect for private and family life under Article 8 ECHR, or the right to marry under Article 9, and would reinforce the current approach of the courts to such clauses. In *Duggan v Kelly*,[55] a condition not to marry a 'Papist' was upheld, as was a condition not to marry a 'Scotchman' in *Perrin v Lyon*.[56] Whilst the court could take the view that such discrimination is permissible if clearly imposed by private parties and not compounded or created by the court,[57] it is hard to believe that it would not be influenced by the distaste for such kinds of discrimination some one and a half or two centuries later.

(4) Effect of an invalid condition

The exact consequences of a condition being found to be void will depend on whether the gift was made subject to a condition or was a determinable interest.

(a) Conditions precedent

If a condition precedent is too uncertain, then the gift to which it applies fails because no one can prove that they satisfy the condition. If the condition is void for public policy reasons, the same should apply. However, in the Australian case of *Re St George (deceased)*,[58] Jacobs J was prepared to delete a condition precedent to a gift in a will and treat the gift as absolute because this did no violence to the intention of the testator by changing the whole nature of the gift. Whether such an approach could be applied more broadly is uncertain. Another approach is to treat the condition as a condition subsequent, if this interpretation is possible, since in that case, if the condition is void, the gift becomes absolute. There is judicial support for this:

> Where it is doubtful whether a condition be precedent or subsequent the court prima facie treats it as being subsequent.[59]

(b) Conditions subsequent

If the gift is subject to a condition subsequent and the condition is uncertain or unlawful, the gift is not void and the condition is merely struck out. The gift will thus become absolute.[60] In *Re Beard*[61] a testator made a gift of his estates to his nephew, Herbert, 'provided that he does not enter into the naval or military services of the country'. As the condition

[53] Equality Act 2010, s 4 lists the protected characteristics.
[54] *Re Erskine 1948 Trust* [2012] EWHC 732 (Ch).
[55] [1848] 10 I Eq R 473.
[56] [1807] 9 East 170.
[57] See *Re Erskine 1948 Trust* [2012] EWHC 732 (Ch) at 25.
[58] [1964] NSWR 587.
[59] *Sifton v Sifton* [1938] AC 656 at 676.
[60] See *Re Croxon* [1904] 1 Ch 252; *Re Turton* [1926] Ch 96.
[61] [1908] 1 Ch 383.

was held contrary to public policy,[62] it was struck out and the nephew took an absolute interest in the estates.

(c) Determinable interests

If the gift is characterized as 'determinable' and the determining event is uncertain or unlawful for reasons of public policy, the gift will fail and the property reverts to the original owner. Thus, in *Re Moore*,[63] a trust to pay a weekly sum to a woman 'whilst . . . . living apart from her husband' was held to be a determinable interest and the gift was void.

(5) Distinguishing conditional and determinable gifts

Gifts subject to conditions subsequent or determining events are treated differently when the condition or event is uncertain or unlawful, making it critically important to distinguish between them. The distinction is notoriously difficult to pin-point and has been described as 'little short of disgraceful to our jurisprudence'.[64] The essence of the distinction is that a determinable gift is defined as lasting only for the duration of a certain state of affairs, whilst a conditional gift is one which may be cut short if a given event occurs. For instance, a gift to Myfanwy 'whilst she remains a widow' would be a determinable gift; on the other hand, a gift to Myfanwy 'provided that she does not remarry' would be a gift subject to a condition subsequent.

Put another way, in a determinable gift, the gift is never contemplated as being absolute, but only as lasting until the determining event occurs.[65] Thus, a gift to George 'until he becomes a brain surgeon' will be a determinable gift. If the determining event occurs, the gift will automatically revert to the original donor. In a conditional gift, the gift is contemplated as being absolute from the very beginning, but the occurrence of the condition brings it to an end. A gift to George 'unless he becomes a brain surgeon' would be a conditional gift. In cases concerning conditional gifts of land, it has been held that a gift does not end automatically when the condition occurs, but that the donor or his successor in title must 're-enter' by taking steps to terminate the interest.[66] This dogma has no application to a conditional gift by way of trust, where the condition represents a direction to trustees that they will carry out without any further intervention by the original donor.

[62] [1908] 1 Ch 383 at 387, per Swinfen Eady J: 'there can be few, if any, provisions more against public good and the welfare of the State than one tending to deter persons from entering the naval or military service of the country'.

[63] [1888] 39 Ch D 116.

[64] Porter MR in *Re King's Trusts* [1892] 29 LR Ir 401 at 410.

[65] If the determining event becomes impossible in fact, the gift automatically becomes absolute: *Re Leach* [1912] 2 Ch 422.

[66] See Challis's *Real Property* (3rd edn, Butterworth 1911), pp 219, 261.

PART III

Resulting and Constructive Trusts

9. Resulting trusts ... 195
10. Constructive trusts ... 238

9

Resulting trusts

1 Introduction

Trusts are sometimes created by the deliberate intention and act of the settlor. Such trusts are known as 'express trusts'. However, in some situations, property will be regarded as subject to a trust despite the absence of any express intention on the part of the settlor. The English word 'resulting' derives from the Latin verb *resultare*, meaning to 'jump back'. In English law, such 'resulting trusts' are one of the two main categories of such informal trusts, the other being that of 'constructive trusts' (considered in the Chapter 10). In general, resulting trusts arise to fill gaps in beneficial ownership or to give effect to the implied intention of the owner of property that someone else should not enjoy the benefit of it. The application of resulting trusts is also considered in the context of acquiring rights in the family home in Chapter 12.

2 What are resulting trusts?

The circumstances in which property will become subject to a resulting trust were examined by the House of Lords in *Westdeutsche Landesbank Girozentrale v Islington London Borough Council*.[1] Lord Browne-Wilkinson identified two circumstances in which a resulting trust would arise:

> Under existing law a resulting trust arises in two sets of circumstances: (A) where A makes a voluntary payment to B or pays (wholly or in part) for the purchase of property which is vested either in B alone or in the joint names of A and B, there is a presumption that A did not intend to make a gift to B; the money or property is held on trust for A (if he is the sole provider of the money) or in the case of a joint purchaser by A and B in shares proportionate to their contributions. It is important to stress that this is only a *presumption*, which presumption is easily rebutted either by the counter presumption of advancement or by direct evidence of A's intention to make an outright transfer . . . (B) Where A transfers property to B *on express trusts*, but the trusts declared do not exhaust the whole beneficial interest.[2]

These two different types of resulting trust were described by Megarry J in *Re Vandervell's Trusts (No 2)* as 'presumed' and 'automatic' resulting trusts, respectively,[3] and these, more descriptive, labels are the most commonly used. Although there is some overlap between the two categories, they are useful for the purposes of exegesis and analysis.

[1] [1996] AC 669. See Birks, 'Trusts Raised to Avoid Unjust Enrichment: The *Westdeutsche* Case' [1996] RLR 3.

[2] [1996] AC 669 at 708. See Chambers, *Resulting Trusts* (Clarendon Press 1997); Swadling, 'Explaining Resulting Trusts' [2008] LQR 72.

[3] [1974] Ch 269 at 289 and 294–6.

3 Distinguishing resulting trusts

(1) Trusts resulting in operation

The relationship between resulting trusts, constructive trusts, and express trusts is an awkward one, and it has not been made easier by some recent decisions. In one sense a resulting trust is just a description of a situation in which beneficial ownership results (in the sense of coming back) to the original owner of the property or of the funds used to acquire it.

(2) Why do trusts result?

That does not, though, explain *why* the trust arises. Answering the question 'why' is challenging, partly because the labels 'resulting', 'constructive', and 'express' are fluid. For instance, there are some cases in which the House of Lords seem to have used 'resulting' and 'constructive' trusts as interchangeable terms,[4] suggesting that it is not necessary to distinguish between them. However, most case law supports the view that resulting, constructive, and express trusts operate differently.

Constructive trusts[5] are imposed by the court as a consequence of the conduct of the party who becomes a trustee. Automatic resulting trusts are used to explain gaps in beneficial ownership. Presumed resulting trusts are not imposed as a response to the conduct of the trustee, but to give effect to the implied or inferred intentions of the owner. Express trusts arise to give effect to the actual intention of the owner.

(3) The importance of intention

In *Marr v Collie*,[6] the Privy Council was concerned with the ownership of a number of items which had been acquired by Terry Marr and Bryant Collie, who had been in a personal relationship which had broken down. Some of the property had been acquired in Marr's name, and some jointly. Marr had the higher income and had funded most of the purchases, and he, therefore, claimed to be entitled to the property on the basis of a resulting trust. Collie claimed that under the constructive trust principles which apply to the family home (discussed in Chapter 12), the property should be shared. The Privy Council considered that neither argument was the correct starting-point. The starting-point should be what the parties' intentions were:

> In this, as in so many areas of law, context counts for, if not everything, a lot. Context here is set by the parties' common intention—or by the lack of it. If it is the unambiguous mutual wish of the parties, contributing in unequal shares to the purchase of property, that the joint beneficial ownership should reflect their joint legal ownership, then effect should be given to that wish. If, on the other hand, that is not their wish, or if they have not formed any intention as to beneficial ownership but had, for instance, accepted advice that the property be acquired in joint names, without considering or being aware of the possible consequences of that, the resulting trust solution may provide the answer.[7]

Unfortunately for the parties in that case, the Privy Council did not think that there was enough evidence of the parties' actual intentions, and the case was remitted to a lower court for further hearing.

[4] For example, *Gissing v Gissing* [1971] AC 886 at 905, per Lord Diplock; *Tinsley v Milligan* [1993] 3 All ER 65 at 86–7, per Lord Browne-Wilkinson.

[5] See Chapter 10. [6] [2017] UKPC 17.

[7] At 54. A similar approach was taken by Henderson J in *Haque v Raja* [2016] EWHC 1950 (Ch), which is not discussed in *Marr v Collie*.

(4) No evidence of intention

Where there is no evidence of the parties' actual intentions, the task of the court becomes more difficult. There cannot be an express trust, because that requires certainty of intention. How should the court proceed? That is a question to which we shall have to return later in this chapter, but it is important, as the Court of Appeal decision in *Oxley v Hiscock*[8] shows. Ms Oxley had contributed 22 per cent of the cost of acquiring the family home, and this is the share of ownership she would have acquired on classic resulting trust analysis, but the Court of Appeal held that on the basis of a constructive trust she was entitled to a 40 per cent share of the value of the home even though there had never been any discussion about what share she should have. One of the questions which we address in Chapter 12 is whether there is a special regime applying to the family home. In other cases, the court attempts to find the subjective intention of the parties, but may resort to finding a resulting trust, either because by inference from all the circumstances the parties intended it,[9] or as a last resort.[10]

(5) Constructive rather than resulting trust?

The seminal cases of *Stack v Dowden*[11] and *Jones v Kernott*[12] (discussed in Chapter 12) have suggested that there is no, or only a limited role, for resulting trusts in identifying shares in the family home, and Professor John Mee, using arguments described below, has suggested that all presumed resulting trusts are better explained as constructive trusts. *Prest v Petrodel Resources Ltd*[13] shows that it is premature to reject entirely the role of resulting trusts. The case itself concerned divorce proceedings concerning assets worth in excess of £17.5 million. Many of the assets were homes held by overseas companies controlled by the husband, Mr Prest. These properties had come into corporate ownership through a variety of methods, either by the husband providing the purchase money to the company to purchase the property or by the husband transferring ownership to the companies for nominal consideration. It is important to note that these arrangements had been put in place before any difficulties in the marriage had arisen, so had not been done simply to try and make the assets unavailable to the wife, Mrs Prest, in divorce proceedings. At first instance, the properties were ordered to be transferred to the wife as part of the divorce settlement, despite being under corporate ownership. On appeal, the Court of Appeal reversed this decision, on the basis that the properties in question belonged to each of the relevant companies, not its shareholders or directors, and so were not part of the Mr Prest's assets. The Supreme Court overruled this decision and concluded that the relevant companies held the property on trust for Mr Prest, meaning that the properties were available as part of his assets for the divorce settlement. The Court reached this conclusion, not by piercing or setting aside the corporate veil, nor by giving any special dispensation to family matters to look behind the corporate structure under the powers given to settle property on divorce under the Matrimonial Causes Act 1973, but by applying the principles of resulting trusts to the facts of the case. They found that the companies held the properties as bare trustees on trust for Mr Prest in equity, on the basis that the factual situations of the purchase meant that, on resulting trust principles, Mr Prest had provided the purchase money either directly or by selling the properties to the

[8] [2004] EWCA Civ 546. The case was referred to with approval by the Supreme Court in *Stack v Dowden* [2007] 2 AC 437 (HL) and *Jones v Kernott* [2012] 1 AC 776.

[9] *Cooper v Fanmailuk.Com Ltd* [2009] EWCA Civ 1368; *Gallarotti v Sebastianelli* [2012] EWCA Civ 865.

[10] *NRC Holding Ltd v Danilitskiy* [2017] EWHC 1431 (Ch) at 41–44 quoting *Stockholm Finance Limited v Garden Holdings Inc* (unreported, 26 October 1995).

[11] [2008] EWCA Civ 645 at 27. [12] [2012] 1 AC 776. [13] [2013] UKSC 34.

companies at an undervalue. The properties had not been purchased using profits from the relevant company's trading activities or in the course of normal company business.

4 Rationale of resulting trusts

There are a number of different explanatory theories for the resulting trust, and individual judges and academics have interpreted the concept of the resulting trust in considerably different ways over time.

(1) Presumed intention of the parties

In *Westdeutsche Landesbank Girozentrale v Islington London Borough Council*,[14] Lord Browne-Wilkinson stated that resulting trusts arise to fulfil the implied intentions of the parties:

> Both types of resulting trust are traditionally regarded as examples of trusts giving effect to the common intentions of the parties. A resulting trust is not imposed by law against the intentions of the trustee (as is a constructive trust), but gives effect to his presumed intention.[15]

However, this formulation is open to question. While it is certainly the case that a presumed resulting trust arises in consequence of the presumed intention of the transferor of the trust property (or contributor to its purchase, as the case may be), it is not necessarily the case that the trustee who received the legal title intended the property to be held on trust. In many cases, a resulting trust has been found in circumstances where the transferee of the legal title anticipated that a gift had been made divesting the transferor of his entire interest in the property. This can be seen from the fact that many cases involve a dispute as to whether a presumption of resulting trust has been rebutted. As Lord Browne-Wilkinson himself observed, a resulting trust of the first type arises because 'there is a presumption that A did not intend to make a gift to B'.[16] A resulting trust will arise in favour of A in such circumstances even though B anticipated that he was the beneficiary of an absolute gift, and in this sense B will be required to hold the property on resulting trust against his intentions. More significantly, a resulting trust may even arise where the transferee of property was unaware that the transfer had occurred.[17]

(2) Intention of the transferor

There are flaws in the theory that a resulting trust is based on the mutual intention of the parties. An alternative theory is that only the intention of the transferor matters. As Lord Reid observed in *Vandervell v IRC*:

> where it appears to have been the intention of the donor that the donee should not take beneficially, there will be a resulting trust in favour of the donor.[18]

The problem with this is that there will frequently be no evidence of the intention of the transferor.

(3) Lack of intention to make a gift

A variant on the last theory is, therefore, that a resulting trust should arise whenever a transferee (or contributor) cannot be shown to have possessed the intention to make a

[14] [1996] AC 669. [15] [1996] AC 669 at 708. [16] [1996] AC 669 at 708.
[17] As, for example, in *Re Vinogradoff* [1935] WN 68. [18] [1967] 2 AC 291, HL.

gift. Lord Goff stated in the *Westdeutsche* case that a presumed resulting trust arises when there is a voluntary transfer and:

> where there is no presumption of advancement or evidence of intention to make an out-and-out gift.[19]

The justification for this view is that gifts require an intention to make a gift; such intention should not be presumed, therefore the question of the effect of an 'ambiguous transfer'[20] should be resolved by finding it not to be a gift. Professor John Mee argues that the idea that a transferor does not intend a gift is an outdated concept. Whilst it may have been the case when presumed resulting trusts first developed that a transferor making a voluntary transfer intended to make the recipient a trustee, that is no longer the case. In his view, although there is still a role for resulting trusts which fill a gap in ownership,[21] presumed resulting trusts no longer have any justification, and any resulting trust of this kind would be better explained as a constructive trust.[22]

(4) **Retention of ownership**

A related argument is that a resulting trust arises because an original owner who makes an incomplete gift fails to part with the whole of ownership and, therefore, retains beneficial ownership, a view supported by James Penner.[23] Mee points out that this is doctrinally incorrect since, prior to the resulting trust arising, there is no separation of legal and beneficial ownership.[24] He differs from Penner, who sees this as 'very theoretical.' Mee asserts that, without some normative justification, there is no basis for departing from the strict legal position.

(5) **Unjust enrichment**

A theory which has gained little traction and which has been soundly rejected by Professor John Mee[25] is the idea that resulting trusts are explained by the principles of unjust enrichment.[26] Under the principles of unjust enrichment, where (i) one person gains a benefit (ii) at the expense of another and (iii) unjustly (sometimes explained as without juristic justification), then (iv), subject to any defences, the recipient is under an obligation to make restitution to the person at whose expense the benefit was gained.[27] For instance, where a local authority was given a loan as part of a complex financial transaction which was beyond its powers, it could not refuse to restore the funds it received, because otherwise it would have been unjustly enriched.[28] Whilst there is potentially an

[19] [1996] AC 669 at 689; *Revenue and Customs v The Investment Trust Companies* [2017] UKSC 29; *High Commissioner for Pakistan in the United Kingdom v Prince Mukkaram Jah, His Exalted Highness the 8th Nizam of Hyderabad* [2016] EWHC 1465 (Ch) at 129.

[20] Swadling, 'Explaining resulting trusts' [2008] 124 LQR 72 at 86.

[21] See also, Mee, '"Automatic" resulting trusts: retention, restitution, or reposing trusts?' in Mitchell (ed), *Constructive and Resulting Trusts* (Hart 2010).

[22] Mee, 'The Past, Present, and Future of Resulting Trusts' (2017) 70 CLP 189.

[23] See Penner, 'Resulting Trusts and Unjust Enrichment: Three Controversies' in Mitchell (ed), *Constructive and Resulting Trusts* (Hart 2010).

[24] Citing Lord Browne-Wilkinson in *Westdeutsche Landesbank Girozentrale v Islington London Borough Council* [1996] AC 669.

[25] Mee, 'The Past, Present, and Future of Resulting Trusts' [2017] 70 CLP 189.

[26] This is the case even in Canada, where unjust enrichment operates over a wider field than in England and Wales: Chambers, 'The Presumption of Resulting Trust' [2014] 51 Alberta Law Rev 667.

[27] *Banque Financière de la Cité v Parc (Battersea) Ltd* [1999] 1 AC 221 at 227; *Benedetti v Sawiris* [2013] UKSC 50, [2014] AC 938.

[28] *Westdeutsche Landesbank Girozentrale v Islington LBC* [1996] AC 669.

overlap between the resulting trust doctrine and unjust enrichment principles,[29] the latter do not add to an understanding of resulting trusts. Elements which are common to both resulting trusts and unjust enrichment are that the recipient must have an ostensible benefit which has arisen at the expense of the claimant. The question is whether that benefit or enrichment is unjust because 'the claimant's consent to the defendant's enrichment was impaired, qualified or absent'.[30] The answer to that question will be the same whether it is asked in the context of resulting trust or of unjust enrichment.[31] Unjust enrichment is considered further at the end of this chapter.

(6) **Automatic resulting trusts**

Automatic resulting trusts explain what happens to the beneficial ownership where a trust fails. Suppose that a settlor creates a trust in which, after various other provisions, the capital is to go to such of his children as reach the age of eighteen, but they all die before this age in a car crash. On these facts, unless the settlement makes alternative provision, the capital will be held on a resulting trust for the settlor. The alternative would be for the property to be treated as ownerless, in which case it could be claimed by the Crown as bona vacantia (goods without an owner). Megarry J in *Re Vandervell's Trusts (No 2)*[32] said that 'automatic' resulting trusts arise by operation of law, and not on the basis of any presumed intention on the part of the original owner of the property. As he observed:

> What a man fails effectually to dispose of remains automatically vested in him, and no question of a mere presumption can arise.[33]

Lord Browne-Wilkinson in *Westdeutsche Landesbank Girozentrale v Islington London Borough Council*[34] disagreed with this, and argued that automatic resulting trusts, like presumed resulting trusts, were based on intention:

> Megarry J in *Re Vandervell's Trusts (No 2)* suggests that a resulting trust of type (B) [an automatic resulting trust] does not depend on intention but operates automatically. I am not convinced that this is right. If the settlor has expressly, or by necessary implication, abandoned any beneficial interest in the trust property, there is in my view no resulting trust: the undisposed of equitable interest vests in the Crown as bona vacantia.[35]

While these comments rightly indicate that an automatic resulting trust is not an inevitable result whenever an express trust fails, it is unlikely that Megarry J ever meant what Lord Browne-Wilkinson says. Whilst it is true that a resulting trust would not arise where there is an intention to relinquish all claim to property, Lord Browne-Wilkinson's reliance on intention is forced, as is illustrated by a case like Mr Vandervell's. On Mr Vandervell's instructions, shares which he controlled had been given to the Royal College of Surgeons as part of a legitimate tax-avoidance scheme, but subject to an option, held by the trustees,

[29] See *Bank of Cyprus UK Ltd v Menelaou* [2016] AC 176 for an action framed in unjust enrichment but which shares many characteristics of resulting trust.

[30] *Lowick Rose LLP v Swynson Ltd* [2017] UKSC 32 at 22, quoting Burrows, *A Restatement of the English Law of Unjust Enrichment* (OUP 2012).

[31] Chambers, 'The Presumption of Resulting Trust' [2014] 51 Alberta Law Rev 667 at 675.

[32] [1974] Ch 269. [33] [1974] Ch 269 at 289.

[34] [1996] AC 669. See Birks, 'Trusts Raised to Avoid Unjust Enrichment: The *Westdeutsche* Case' [1996] RLR 3; Cape, 'Compound Interest and Restitution' (1996) 112 LQR 521; Jones, 'Ultra Vires Swaps: The Common Law and Equitable Fall-Out' [1996] CLJ 432; Stevens, 'Simple Interest Only? Autonomous Unjust Enrichment and the Relationship between Equity and Common Law' [1997] LMCLQ 441.

[35] [1996] AC 669, per Lord Goff at 708.

to repurchase them. Unfortunately for Mr Vandervell, no indication was given as to who were the beneficiaries of this option. Lord Wilberforce said, in *Vandervell v IRC*:

> the option was vested in the trustee company as a trustee on trusts, not defined at the time, possibly to be defined later. But the equitable, or beneficial interest, cannot remain in the air: the consequence in law must be that it remains in the settlor . . .[36]

The consequence of finding that he had not entirely parted with the beneficial interest in the shares was that he faced a huge tax bill. Had he been asked whether this was what he intended, he would certainly have denied it.

The role which is played by intention is probably best expressed by Lord Millett in *Air Jamaica Ltd v Charlton*:[37]

> Like a constructive trust, a resulting trust arises by operation of law, though unlike a constructive trust it gives effect to intention. But it does arise whether or not the transferor intended to retain a beneficial interest—he almost always does not—since it responds to the absence of any intention on his part to pass a beneficial interest to the recipient. It may arise even where the transferor positively wished to part with the beneficial interest, as in *Vandervell v IRC* . . . The House of Lords affirmed the principle that a resulting trust is not defeated by evidence that the transferor intended to part with the beneficial interest if he has not in fact succeeded in doing so.[38]

Cases where it can be shown that a settlor has expressly, or by necessary implication, abandoned any beneficial interest in the trust property will be quite exceptional,[39] for instance, where small donations have been made anonymously in a collection box.

5 Presumed resulting trusts

Presumed resulting trusts arise where the transferor of property did not intend to dispose of his entire ownership interest in the property transferred. The classic resulting trust presumption[40] is that an ambiguous transfer is not intended to be a gift. Unless the transferee can show that it was meant as a gift, the transferee will hold it on resulting trust for the donor. However, in some circumstances, the nature of the relationship between the transferor and the transferee gives rise to an opposite presumption, namely that the transferor did intend to benefit the transferee, in which case unless the presumption of a gift is rebutted there will be no resulting trust. This counter-presumption is known as the 'presumption of advancement'. The rules have been applied differently where the parties are in a close personal relationship, and we explore this in Chapter 12. The development of the jurisprudence relating to the family home may now be affecting the operation of the classic resulting trust presumption.

(1) The classic resulting trust presumption

English law adopts two basic presumptions about the intentions of property owners, both of which are rebuttable by evidence of a contrary intention.

[36] [1967] 2 AC 291 at 329. [37] [1999] 1 WLR 1399. [38] [1999] 1 WLR 1399 at 1412.

[39] See *Simpson v Gowers* [1981] 32 OR (2d) 385; *Dennis v North Western Nat Bank* 81 NW 2d 254 [1957] (cases involving chattels).

[40] A phrase used in *Jones v Kernott* [2011] UKSC 53; [2012] 1 AC 776 at 31.

(a) A presumption against gifts

First, it is presumed that, outside of certain relationships, voluntary transfers are not intended to be a gift. If an owner voluntarily transfers the legal title of his property to a third party without receiving any consideration in return, he is presumed to have intended to retain the equitable interest for himself. The transferee will, therefore, hold the property on resulting trust for him. This presumption was invented by equity to defeat the misappropriation of property as a consequence of potentially fraudulent or improvident transactions.[41]

(b) The provider of purchase money

By extension of this first presumption, it is also presumed that a person who provides the money required to purchase property intends to obtain the equitable interest in the property acquired. Therefore, when the property is purchased in the name of someone who did not provide the purchase money, he will be presumed to hold the legal title on trust for the provider thereof. This presumption is long established and was recognized in *Dyer v Dyer*, where Eyre CB stated:

> the trust of a legal estate . . . whether taken in the names of the purchasers and others jointly, or in the names of others without that of the purchaser; whether in one name or several; whether jointly or successive, results to the man who advances the purchase-money.[42]

Where a person has only contributed a part of the purchase price of property, a resulting trust will be presumed in his favour of an equivalent proportion of the equitable interest.[43] *Tinsley v Milligan*[44] (see Figure 9.2) provides an example.

(c) Acquisition in joint names

The equitable presumption developed without regard to whether a purchase or transfer was made in the sole name of a third party (although this was usually the case) or in the joint names of the original owner or provider of funds and a third party. However, at least in relation to the family home, the Supreme Court has indicated that where a cohabiting couple acquire a family home in joint names, the starting-point for evaluating beneficial ownership is that the property should be treated as owned jointly, in the absence of any other evidence, rather than in proportion to the parties' financial contributions.[45] It has been in doubt whether the same principle applies in situations other than the family home. *Marr v Collie*,[46] a decision of the Privy Council, suggests that it does. Marr and Collie were in a close personal relationship, which ultimately broke down. They disputed who owned various assets, including the home in which they had lived together and some investment assets to which they had made unequal financial contributions. Some of the investments had been acquired in joint names, with funds mainly provided by Marr. The Privy Council said that it was simplistic to assume that the principle that a conveyance into joint names indicates legal and beneficial joint tenancy unless the contrary is proved applied only in the domestic consumer context. In this case, 'an intense examination is warranted of why the properties . . . were purchased in joint names'.[47] The Privy Council remitted the case to a lower court for an examination of the parties' actual intentions. Unfortunately, the decision fails to indicate what outcome should be reached if there was no, or only inconclusive,

[41] *Lynch v Burke* [1995] 2 IR 159, per O'Flaherty J.

[42] [1788] 2 Cox Eq Cas 92 at 93.

[43] *Midland Bank plc v Cooke* [1995] 4 All ER 562; *Drake v Whipp* [1996] 1 FLR 826.

[44] [1993] 3All ER 65.

[45] *Jones v Kernott* [2011] UKSC 53; [2012] 1 AC 776; *Stack v Dowden* [2007] 2 AC 432.

[46] *Marr v Collie (Bahamas)* [2017] UKPC 17.

[47] [2017] UKPC 17 at 55.

evidence of intention. However, it strongly suggests that the purchase in joint names should be treated as part of the evidence of an intention to enjoy the beneficial interest jointly; how far the close personal relationship of Marr and Collie is relevant is left wholly unclear.

(2) **Voluntary transfers of personal property**

The classic resulting trust presumption is well illustrated by *Re Vinogradoff* (see Figure 9.1).[48] Mrs Vindogradoff transferred £800 of War Loan stock into the joint names of herself and her infant granddaughter. It was a voluntary transfer, so made without Mrs Vindogradoff receiving any consideration. Farwell J held that the stock was held on resulting trust for her,[49] and that, therefore, on her death, it belonged in equity to her estate. A similar case is *Thavorn v Bank of Credit and Commerce International SA*.[50] In 1981 Mrs Thavorn opened an account with some £20,000 in her young nephew's name. She directed the bank that she alone was to operate the account. Lloyd J held that in these circumstances there was no evidence to rebut the presumption of a resulting trust:

> There was not the slightest evidence on which I could hold that, by opening the account in his name, she intended to transfer any beneficial interest to him during her lifetime.[51]

The bank was, therefore, liable to pay damages when they paid the money into his current account. A presumption of resulting trust will also arise where a person transfers money into a bank account in joint names. In *Aroso v Coutts*,[52] it was held that the presumption of resulting trusts operated when Sr Aroso transferred money into a joint account opened in the names of himself and his nephew, although the presumption was held to have been rebutted by evidence that a gift had been intended.[53] In some cases involving joint accounts, there may be an intention to pass ownership of the property on the transferor's death. What happens then is considered later in this chapter.

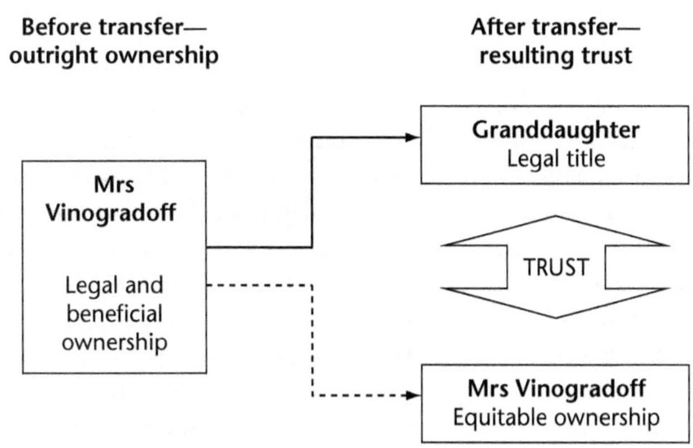

Figure 9.1 *Re Vinogradoff*

[48] [1935] WN 68. See also *Re Muller* [1953] NZLR 879.

[49] The granddaughter was held to be a trustee of the resulting trust despite her minority. See Law of Property Act 1925, s 20.

[50] [1985] 1 Lloyd's Rep 259. Compare also *Re Howes* [1905] 21 TLR 501.

[51] [1985] 1 Lloyd's Rep 259 at 263.

[52] [2002] 1 All ER (Comm) 241.

[53] See also *Re Northall (Deceased)* [2010] EWHC 1448 (Ch) which has similar facts, but there was no evidence of a gift.

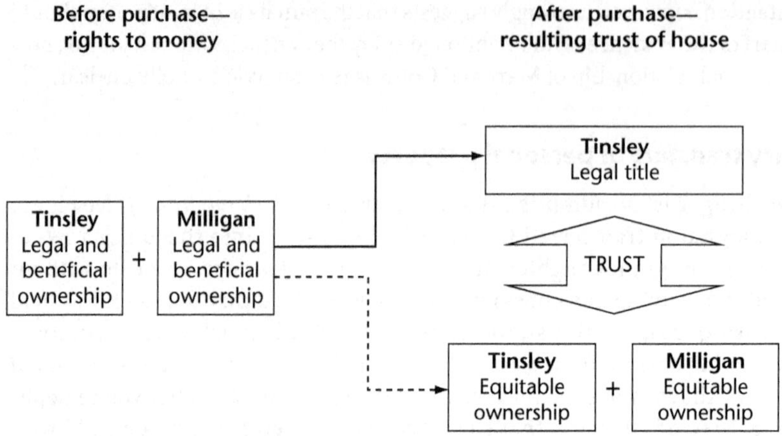

Figure 9.2 *Tinsley v Milligan*

(3) **Voluntary transfers of land**

While the presumption of resulting trust clearly operates in respect of voluntary transfers of personal property, a more difficult question is whether the presumption against gifts applies to voluntary transfers of land. Section 60(3) of the Law of Property Act 1925 provides:

> In a voluntary conveyance a resulting trust for the grantor shall not be implied merely by reason that the property is not expressed to be conveyed for the use or benefit of the grantee.

There has been much debate as to whether this provision was enacted to remove the presumption of resulting trust where land is conveyed voluntarily,[54] or whether it was merely intended to remove a conveyancing inconvenience. Prior to the enactment of s 60(3), it was the normal practice to declare in a voluntary conveyance that land was granted 'unto and to the use of' the grantee. It has, therefore, been argued that s 60(3) was intended as a word-saving provision, while leaving the operation of the presumption intact.[55] The true effect of s 60(3) has not fallen for a convincing determination by the higher courts. In *Tinsley v Milligan*,[56] Lord Browne-Wilkinson commented that it was 'arguable that the position has been altered by the 1925 property legislation'.[57] This would support the view that the presumption had been abolished. Similarly, in the first instance decision in *Lohia v Lohia*,[58] Nicholas Strauss QC held that although both proposed interpretations of s 60(3) could reasonably be adopted by the court, on a 'plain reading' the presumption of resulting trust had been abolished in respect of a voluntary conveyance of land. He thought that there had to be some additional factor, such as that the parties are strangers. In the light of this interpretation, he held that no resulting trust had arisen where a son had conveyed his share in the family home to his father. The mere fact that there was no evidence of any sensible reason why he had so conveyed his share in the house to his father, and that he

[54] Chambers, *Resulting Trusts* (Clarendon Press 1997), pp 18–19.

[55] See Cheshire and Burn, *Modern Law of Real Property* (15th edn, Lexis 1994), p 161. Mee, 'Resulting trusts and voluntary conveyances of land' [2012] Conv 307 suggests that there may have been no presumption of resulting trust before 1926.

[56] [1993] 3 All ER 65, HL.

[57] See also *Hodgson v Marks* [1971] Ch 892, where Russell LJ described the proposition that s 60(3) has put an end to the presumption, resulting trusts of land as 'debatable'.

[58] [2001] WTLR 101.

had continued to share mortgage payments and rental income, was not sufficient to lead to the inference of a resulting trust. Unfortunately from a perspective concerned with legal clarity, on appeal in *Lohia v Lohia*,[59] the Court of Appeal agreed with the finding of a resulting trust on the facts, but were more cautious as to the survival of the presumption of resulting trust. Mummery LJ refused to pronounce on the matter 'without having heard very extensive argument',[60] and Sir Christopher Slade acknowledged that it was a 'knotty issue'[61] but similarly refused to give an opinion. Nevertheless, in the subsequent decision of the Court of Appeal in *Ali v Khan*,[62] Morritt V-C followed the view of Nicholas Strauss QC that the presumption of resulting trust had been abolished on voluntary conveyances of land and could only be established by additional evidence. However, as Mee argues, it does not appear that Morrit V-C was aware of the approach of the Court of Appeal in *Lohia*, which weakens the strength of the authority.[63]

By contrast, it is also possible to evidence the view that the presumption has been maintained. In *Prest v Petrodel Resources Ltd*,[64] the Supreme Court held that properties transferred for the nominal sum of £1 were held on 'an ordinary resulting trust', although the importance of this holding is weakened by the fact that the relevance of s 60(3) was not discussed. More recently, a direct consideration of the issue can be found by the High Court in *National Crime Agency v Dong*,[65] where Chief Master Marsh said that the presumption of a resulting trust for voluntary transfers of land was not abolished by the statute. The judge thought it unlikely that the presumption should have been abolished for land but not for chattels.[66] Finally, in *Ali v Dinc*,[67] Deputy High Court Judge Sarah Worthington QC stated obiter, following a review of academic and learned commentary, that while the issue was, 'finely balanced',[68] she agreed with the view in *Dong*.

Where does that leave the law? The presumption of a resulting trust does not operate or is not needed where there is evidence showing that a gift was or was not intended.[69] The presumption is only needed where there is no reliable evidence. It is submitted that in such cases, Chief Master Marsh has taken the correct view in *National Crime Agency v Dong*, and the presumption has remained. It is doubtful whether the differences between land and personalty, and between methods of making apparent gifts, provide meaningful bases for distinction,[70] and in the absence of evidence of a motive for making a gift, the presumption that no gift was intended is not unreasonable. Of course, to avoid any doubt, it would be desirable in any voluntary transfer, if it is made explicit whether or not a gift is intended.

(4) **Purchase money resulting trusts**

The presumption of a resulting trust in favour of a contributor to the purchase price of property applies to both personal property and land. This is based in the same legal logic as the presumption against gifts. It is assumed that someone who parts with property, in this case as contributions to a purchase price, does not intend to lose their beneficial interest.

[59] [2001] EWCA Civ 1691. [60] [2001] EWCA Civ 1691 at 24. [61] [2001] EWCA Civ 1691 at 34.
[62] [2002] EWCA Civ 774. [63] See Mee [2012] Conv 307. [64] [2013] UKSC 34 at 49.
[65] [2017] EWHC 3116 (Ch). For analysis, see, Mee, 'Voluntary conveyances of land: the presumption of resulting trust redux? *National Crime Agency v Dong* [2017] EWHC 3116 (Ch)' (2018) 2 Conv 184.
[66] See also, *M v M* [2013] EWHC 2534 (Fam), where King J proceeded on the basis that the presumption had not been abolished.
[67] [2020] EWHC 3055 (Ch). [68] Ibid [277].
[69] *Ali v Khan* [2002] EWCA Civ 974 at 24; *Marr v Collie* [2017] UKPC 17 at 54.
[70] Cf Mee [2012] Conv 307 who argues (at 325–6) that there is a justifiable difference between land and personalty, and that the coherence of the law is better served by the removal of the presumption.

(a) Purchase of personal property

The presumption of a resulting trust of personal property was raised in *Fowkes v Pascoe*.[71] John Pascoe was the grandson of Sarah Baker. Over a period of some five years, Sarah Baker purchased annuities totalling £7,000 in the joint names of herself and John Pascoe. The Court of Appeal accepted that there was thus a presumption of a resulting trust in favour of Sarah Baker, but held the evidence rebutted this presumption and demonstrated that a gift had been intended. In *The Venture*,[72] a resulting trust was held to have arisen in favour of a contributor to the purchase price of a yacht. In *Abrahams v Trustee in Bankruptcy of Abrahams*,[73] it was held that a presumption of resulting trust operated where a wife, who was separated from her husband, contributed to a syndicate purchasing National Lottery tickets in the name of her husband. Since the presumption was not rebutted the husband held his share of the winnings, some £242,000, on resulting trust for his wife.

(b) Payment of instalments

The important case of *Foskett v McKeown*[74] concerned the question whether a contributor to the premiums of a life insurance policy thereby gained a proportionate share of the proceeds of the policy. Mr Murphy had taken out a life insurance policy in 1986 that would provide a death benefit of £1 million. He paid the annual premiums for the first two years using his own money, but paid subsequent premiums using misappropriated trust money. He committed suicide in 1991, at which point at least 40 per cent of the premiums had been paid using trust money. The question was whether the beneficiaries were entitled to a proportionate share of the proceeds of the policy. The Court of Appeal (Morritt LJ dissenting) held that there was no resulting trust because the trust funds had not been used to make periodic payments from the start of the policy, and they had not served to increase the sum payable on death. The majority of the House of Lords approved the dissenting judgment of Morritt LJ, and held that the beneficiaries were entitled to a proportionate share of the proceeds of the policy. Contribution to the premiums required under an insurance policy will, therefore, entitle the contributor to a proportionate share of the proceeds.

However, *Foskett v McKeown*[75] also illustrates the potential problems of determining the exact extent of an interest acquired by resulting trust where contributions have been made to a purchase by instalments. Lords Hoffman and Browne-Wilkinson held that the extent of the interest in the proceeds of the policy should be proportionate to the contributions the parties had made to the premiums. Lord Millett considered that, since the policy was unit-linked in nature, the appropriate division was in proportion to the number of units that were acquired by the respective premiums.

(c) Purchase of land

In the context of the acquisition of land it is clear that a presumed resulting trust will arise in favour of a contributor to the initial purchase price. The general principle was stated by Lord Reid in *Pettitt v Pettitt*:

> in the absence of evidence to the contrary effect, a contributor to the purchase-price will acquire a beneficial interest in the property.[76]

This was reiterated by Lord Pearson in *Gissing v Gissing*, where the issue was whether a wife was entitled to a share of the ownership of her matrimonial home, which had been purchased in the sole name of her husband:

71 [1875] 10 Ch App 343. 72 [1908] P 218. 73 [1999] BPIR 637.
74 [2001] 1 AC 102. 75 [2001] 1 AC 102. 76 [1970] AC 777 at 794.

> If [the wife] did make a contribution of a substantial amount towards the purchase of the house, there would be a resulting trust in her favour . . . The presumption is a rebuttable presumption: it can be rebutted by evidence showing some other intention . . .[77]

Those statements of general principle remain valid, although different principles are now used to resolve issues about the ownership of the family home, as we will see in Chapter 12.

(d) Nature of contributions

Whilst a different principle applies to constructive trusts, considered in Chapter 10, in regard to resulting trusts, it is almost certainly the case that only 'direct' contributions to the purchase price will give rise to a presumption of resulting trust in favour of the contributor. The judge at first instance in *Drake v Whipp* thought that this could include the costs of renovation or improvement (in that case of converting a barn), but the Court of Appeal dealt with the case on a different basis and did not need to resolve the issue.[78] Contributing to the household expenses[79] or working for a low wage[80] will not be sufficient. Providing finance through a loan is, in principle, no different from providing finance from savings, but contributing to mortgage payments on a mortgage in another person's name has caused considerable difficulties. Mortgage instalments are technically not payments to the purchase price, but the servicing and reduction of a debt. There would also be practical difficulties in quantifying the beneficial share from mortgage repayments,[81] especially since the main element in most mortgage payments is the interest charge rather than a reduction of the loan. Whilst the matter is not completely free from doubt, unless there is a repayment agreement made before the mortgage was entered into, payment of the mortgage instalments on a property will not give rise to the presumption of resulting trust.[82]

(e) Size of beneficial share

The logic of a presumed resulting trust is that the share of beneficial ownership acquired through a purchase money resulting trust is directly proportional to the contribution to the purchase. That principle was muddied in some cases involving the family home, but *Jones v Kernott*[83] shows that these cases should now be resolved using constructive trust principles.

(5) Rebutting the presumption of resulting trust

Presumptions, such as the presumption in favour of a resulting trust, are only important where the evidence is ambiguous. Where there is evidence of contrary intention, the presumption is rebutted. The Privy Council in *Marr v Collie*[84] emphasized the primacy of the intention of the parties. In *Pettitt v Pettitt* Lord Diplock observed that the presumptions of resulting trust and advancement are:

> no more than a consensus of judicial opinion disclosed by reported cases as to the most likely inference of fact to be drawn in the absence of any evidence to the contrary.[85]

It, therefore, follows that they can be rebutted by evidence that in a specific situation the 'most likely inference' was not, in fact, intended. The strength of the evidence required to

[77] [1971] AC 886. [78] *Drake v Whipp* [1996] 1 FLR 826. [79] *Burns v Burns* [1984] Ch 317.
[80] *Ivin v Blake* [1994] 67 P & CR 263 (no resulting trust where daughter worked in her mother's pub).
[81] See *Marsh v Von Sternberg* [1986] 1 FLR 526.
[82] *Curley v Parkes* [2004] EWCA Civ 1515. See also *Barrett v Barrett* [2008] EWHC 1061 (Ch) at 24.
[83] [2012] 1 AC 776 at 51–52. [84] [2017] UKPC 17 at 54–55. [85] [1970] AC 777 at 823.

rebut the presumption of a resulting trust will depend upon the strength of the presumption, which will in turn depend upon the facts and circumstances which gave rise to it.[86] The parties' actual intentions may, of course, be an intention to share in proportion to the contributions made by each party.[87] For instance in *Gallarotti v Sebastianelli*,[88] where two close friends bought a flat together, the Court of Appeal found that 'the inference to be made from the parties' course of conduct was that they intended that their financial contributions should be taken into account but not that there should be any precise accounting.'

(a) **Alternatives to a resulting trust**

(i) Evidence a gift was intended

It was noted earlier that in *Fowkes v Pascoe*,[89] a presumption of a resulting trust was raised when Sarah Baker purchased annuities in the joint names of herself and John Pascoe. However, this presumption was rebutted by evidence indicating that a gift had been intended. Two initial purchases of stock were made by Sarah, one of £250 in the joint names of herself and John Pascoe, and another of £250 in the joint names of herself and her companion. She also held large quantities of the same stock in her own name, besides other property. The court considered this 'absolutely conclusive' that a gift was intended. As James LJ said:

> Is it possible to reconcile with mental sanity the theory that she put £250 into the names of herself and her companion, and £250 into the names of herself and [John Pascoe], as trustees upon trust for herself? What . . . object is there conceivable in doing this?[90]

In *Re Young*[91] it was similarly held that the presumption of a resulting trust had been rebutted. Colonel and Mrs Young had a joint bank account, which contained money derived from Mrs Young's separate income. The account was used to pay for household expenses, and Colonel Young, with his wife's consent, withdrew money to purchase investments in his own name. Pearson J held that the evidence showed that the money in the account was intended to be joint, and that the investments purchased in his own name were his own property, and were not held on resulting trust for his wife.

In *Aroso v Coutts & Co*[92] Collins J held that the presumption of resulting trust was rebutted where a wealthy Portuguese gentleman had transferred money into a joint account in the names of himself and his nephew. The evidence, primarily the mandate establishing the account that clearly stated that the beneficial interest was to be held jointly and the evidence of the bank client relationship officer who had explained the effect of the account, established that he had intended the nephew to take the property beneficially. The Privy Council held by a majority in *Whitlock v Moree*[93] that if the document opening a joint account, on its proper construction, identified how the beneficial interests were to be held, that would be conclusive and would accordingly exclude any possibility of a resulting trust.

(ii) Gift to take effect on death

It appears that a presumption of resulting trust may be rebutted even where money has been paid into a joint bank account with the intention that the transferee is not allowed to draw on the account until the death of the transferor. This approach was adopted in *Russell v Scott*,[94] where an aunt had opened a joint account in the names of herself and

[86] *Vajpeyi v Yijsaf* [2003] EWHC 2339, per Peter Prescott QC at 71.
[87] *Wodzicki v Wodzicki* [2017] EWCA Civ 95. [88] [2012] EWCA Civ 865 at 25.
[89] [1875] LR 10 Ch App 343. [90] [1875] LR 10 Ch App 343 at 349. [91] [1885] 28 Ch D 705.
[92] [2002] 1 All ER (Comm) 241. [93] [2017] UKPC 44. [94] [1936] 55 CLR 440.

her nephew, but did not intend her nephew to benefit during her lifetime. The Australian High Court held that she had nevertheless conferred an immediate beneficial interest on him that would only fall into possession on her death through the operation of the right of survivorship. Because of her control over the account, the interest that she conferred on him remained revocable by her during her lifetime. This decision was followed in England in *Young v Sealey*.[95] In contrast, in Ireland, it was held in *Owens v Greene*[96] that the presumption of resulting trust could not be rebutted in such cases because the transferor's intention amounted to an intention to make a testamentary gift, and that evidence of this intention was not admissible, since otherwise the requirements for making a will would be avoided. However, as many commentators have observed,[97] rebutting the presumption of resulting trust in such circumstances is no more offensive to the policy of the Wills Act than the recognition of secret trusts. *Owens v Greene* has since been overruled by the Irish Supreme Court in *Lynch v Burke*.[98] In *Aroso v Coutts & Co*,[99] Collins J indicated that he would have followed *Russell v Scott* and *Young v Sealey*, but the point did not arise for decision.

In *Drakeford v Cotton*,[100] Morgan J applied the principles explained in previous paragraphs to hold that where a mother had transferred a building society account into the joint names of herself and her daughter, initially on trust for herself, but later changed her mind and indicated that she wished the daughter to become sole owner on the mother's death, this constituted a new declaration of trust which changed the beneficial interests, was not a testamentary disposition, and did not need to be in writing since it was not the disposition of an existing equitable interest.[101]

(iii) Evidence a loan was intended

The presumption of a resulting trust will be rebutted where evidence shows that money was advanced by way of a loan. In *Re Sharpe (a bankrupt)*[102] Mr and Mrs Sharpe lived in a maisonette with Mr Sharpe's eighty-two-year-old aunt, Mrs Johnson. The property had been purchased in the name of Mr Sharpe for £17,000. Mrs Johnson had contributed £12,000 towards the purchase price, while the remainder was raised by way of a mortgage. Mr and Mrs Sharpe were subsequently declared bankrupt, and Mrs Johnson claimed to be entitled to a proprietary interest in the maisonette by means of a resulting trust presumed from her contribution to the purchase price. Browne-Wilkinson J held that the money had in fact been advanced by way of a loan, with the intention that it would be repaid. She was not, therefore, entitled to any share of the equitable interest of the property. A presumption of a resulting trust was also rebutted by evidence that a loan was intended in *Vajpeyi v Yijaf*.[103] In this case, the claimant provided the defendant, who was her lover, with £10,000 to enable him to purchase a house in his sole name. At the time of the purchase in 1980, the defendant was a young man of limited means. The claimant alleged that by virtue of this payment she was entitled to a 33.89 per cent share of the equitable ownership of the property on the basis of a presumed resulting trust, whereas the defendant claimed that the money had been advanced by way of a loan, which he had repaid. Peter Prescott QC held that the following factors had rebutted the presumption of a resulting trust in favour of a loan: the fact that the defendant had been a young man of

95 [1949] Ch 278. 96 [1932] IR 225.

97 See Delaney, *Equity and Trusts in the Republic of Ireland* (Round Hall 1995), p 133.

98 [1995] 2 IR 159. See [1996] ILSI Gazette March, p 70 (Mee).

99 [2002] 1 All ER (Comm) 241. 100 [2012] 3 All ER 1138.

101 If it was a disposition of an existing equitable interest, Law of Property Act 1925 s 53(1)(c) would have required the disposition to be in writing.

102 [1980] 1 WLR 219. See also *Blue Sky One Ltd v Blue Airways LLC* [2009] EWHC 3314 (Comm) at 255–7.

103 [2003] EWHC 2339.

limited means who was anxious to get on the property ladder, whereas the claimant was a lady who was already on the property ladder when the money was advanced; the fact that the claimant had tolerated the defendant collecting rents from the property and keeping them for himself for some twenty-one years; the fact that the claimant had failed to propound her claim to an interest for twenty-one years, and the fact that she had never said anything about her alleged interest in the house when it was mortgaged by the defendant to enable him to purchase her matrimonial home some years previously.

(b) Quality of evidence

Fowkes v Pascoe[104] makes clear that the quality of evidence required to rebut a presumption of a resulting trust will vary depending on the circumstances in question, because the presumption of resulting trust will be given varying weight depending upon the context. As Mellish LJ stated:

> the presumption must . . . be of very different weight in different cases. In some cases it would be very strong indeed. If, for instance, a man invested a sum of stock in the name of himself and his solicitor, the inference would be very strong indeed that it was intended solely for the purpose of a trust, and the court would require very strong evidence on the part of the solicitor to prove that it was intended as a gift; and certainly his own evidence would not be sufficient. On the other hand, a man may make an investment of stock in the name of himself and some person, although not a child or wife,[105] yet in such a position to him as to make it extremely probable that the investment was intended as a gift. In such a case, although the rule of law, if there was no evidence at all, would compel the Court to say that the presumption of trust must prevail, even if the court might not believe that the fact was in accordance with the presumption, yet, if there is evidence to rebut the presumption, then, in my opinion, the court must go into the actual facts.[106]

Henderson J, in *Hamilton v Hamilton*,[107] thought that the failure by the defendant in *Prest v Petrodel*[108] to give evidence to rebut the presumption of a resulting trust enabled adverse inferences to be drawn against him. In *Hamilton* a transfer to a Liechtenstein foundation (which served similar purposes to a trust) was effective as an outright transfer.

(c) Admissibility of evidence

In litigation over whether there is a resulting trust, any acts or declarations by the parties forming part of the transaction to which the presumption of a resulting trust relates will be admissible in favour of, or against, the parties performing them. However, in *Shephard v Cartwright*,[109] the House of Lords held, in the context of the rebuttal of a presumption of advancement, that subsequent acts to the transaction and declarations are admissible only as evidence against the party who made them, and not in his favour. This prevents the party from being incentivized to manufacture later evidence. Lord Simmonds approved a summary of the law in Snell's *Equity*:

> The acts and declarations of the parties before or at the time of the purchase, or so immediately after it as to constitute a part of the transaction, are admissible in evidence either for or against the party who did the act or made the declaration . . . But subsequent declarations are admissible as evidence only against the party who made them, and not in his favour.[110]

In 1929 Philip Shephard subscribed for shares in the name of his children. In 1934 the shares were sold to a company promoted by him, and the children signed the requisite

[104] [1875] LR 10 Ch App 343. [105] Where the presumption of advancement would apply.
[106] [1875] LR 10 Ch App 343 at 352–3. [107] [2016] EWHC 1132 (Ch) at 190.
[108] [2013] 2 AC 415. [109] [1955] AC 431.
[110] [1955] AC 431 at 445; Snell, *Principles of Equity* (24th edn, Sweet & Maxwell 1990), p 153.

documents at his request without knowing what they were doing. The proceeds of sale were paid into separate deposit accounts in the children's names. They later signed documents, unaware of their contents, authorizing him to withdraw money from the accounts, whereupon he withdrew money from them without their knowledge. In an action by the children against his executors, the central issue was whether the presumption of advancement had been rebutted. The House of Lords held that evidence of the father's acts after the transaction of 1929 were not admissible to prove the rebuttal of the presumption of advancement, as they did not form part of the original transaction.[111]

It is questionable whether justice will be served by a hard and fast rule. Subsequent decisions are not wholly consistent, but they have suggested a more relaxed attitude to post-acquisition evidence. Lord Phillips MR in *Lavelle v Lavelle* said that *Shephard v Cartwright* had lost much of its force in modern times, and that it was unsatisfactory to apply a rigid rule.

> Plainly, self-serving statements or conduct of a transferor, who may long after the transaction be regretting earlier generosity, carry little or no weight. But words or conduct more proximate to the transaction itself should be given the significance that they naturally bear as part of the overall picture.[112]

In *M v M*[113] King J accepted the argument of counsel 'that the rule *Shephard v Cartwright* set out as long ago as 1955 has been overtaken by the modern approach that relevant evidence is admissible and the issue for the court is as to the weight such evidence should carry.' However, in *Antoni v Antoni*,[114] the Privy Council applied the rule.

(6) Illegal purposes

(a) The problem

'No court will lend its aid to a man who founds his cause of action upon an immoral or an illegal act.'[115] So, what happens where property is transferred to someone else or purchased in someone else's name as part of an illegal transaction? This is a question to which the answer is found in the decision of the Supreme Court in *Patel v Mirza*.[116] Patel had insider information about an anticipated government announcement which would significantly affect the price of shares in the Royal Bank of Scotland. He gave Mirza £620,000 for the latter to bet on the price of the shares. The bet was never made because the expectation of a government announcement was mistaken. Mirza failed to repay the money to Patel. Had the bets been made, this would have been a criminal offence. Despite this, Patel was able to recover the money on the basis of unjust enrichment. The Supreme Court was agreed that a claimant should not be debarred from enforcing a claim of this kind simply because he was seeking to recover money paid pursuant to an agreement to carry out an illegal activity.

(b) A multi-factorial approach

The majority of the Supreme Court[117] in *Patel v Mirza* considered that there was no rigid rule preventing recovery where an illegal act or purpose was involved. Under the new approach, in deciding whether or not to deny a claimant a remedy, the court openly and

[111] Similarly, evidence of the children's acts in signing the documents at their father's request was not admissible against them, because they had been unaware of the contents.

[112] [2004] EWCA Civ 223 at 19.

[113] *M v M* [2013] EWHC 2534 (Fam).

[114] [2007] UKPC 10.

[115] Lord Mansfield in *Holman v Johnson* (1775) 1 Cowp 341 at 343.

[116] [2017] AC 467. Grabiner (2017) 76 CLJ 18; Burrows, 'Illegality after *Patel v Mirza*' (2017) 70 CLP 55.

[117] Lords Toulson, Kerr, Hale, Wilson, and Hodge.

explicitly assesses the policy consequences of that possible denial. The court also asks whether denying a remedy would have a disproportionately negative impact on claimants. It was said that there are two key concerns which the law in this area needed to address:

> One is that a person should not be allowed to profit from his own wrongdoing. The other, linked, consideration is that the law should be coherent and not self-defeating, condoning illegality by giving with the left hand what it takes with the right hand.[118]

There were some cases where there was an explicit statutory rule allowing or prohibiting claims. In other cases, there was a 'trio of necessary considerations' which judges should apply in deciding whether or not to deny a remedy to the claimant:

> one cannot judge whether allowing a claim which is in some way tainted by illegality would be contrary to the public interest, because it would be harmful to the integrity of the legal system, without a) considering the underlying purpose of the prohibition which has been transgressed, b) considering conversely any other relevant public policies which may be rendered ineffective or less effective by denial of the claim, and c) keeping in mind the possibility of overkill unless the law is applied with a due sense of proportionality.[119]

In deciding on the proportionality of refusing a claim, it was inappropriate to lay down a prescriptive or definitive list, but:

> Potentially relevant factors include the seriousness of the conduct, its centrality to the contract, whether it was intentional and whether there was marked disparity in the parties' respective culpability.[120]

It is striking that a very similar conclusion was reached by the Irish Supreme Court in *Quinn v Irish Bank Resolution Corporation Ltd (In Special Liquidation).*[121] *Quinn* contains a much longer list of relevant criteria which might prove of value in future cases.[122]

(c) A majority decision

The decision was not unanimous in *Patel v Mirza*. The view of the majority in the Supreme Court was that the earlier cases on illegality were inconsistent and that the law was at a crossroads where a choice needed to be made between the application of a rigid rule (the reliance rule) with a range of exceptions, and the use of the flexible approach which the majority preferred. The view of the minority of the court[123] was that the court was changing the law in an unjustified way which would lead to making value judgments 'by reference to a widely spread mélange of ingredients'[124] and that it would produce 'complexity, uncertainty, arbitrariness and lack of transparency'.[125] The minority would have applied the old rules, but would have reached the same conclusion as to the outcome on the facts.

(d) Impact on the old reliance rule

The former reliance rule permitted claimants to enforce equitable interests, only if those claimants did not have to rely on their illegality in court in order to make a case. The claimant was not able to plead or lead evidence of the legality to prove the equitable interest.

[118] [2017] AC 467 at 99.

[119] [2017] AC 467 at 101. This is a case which does not appear to have been opened to the UK Supreme Court.

[120] [2017] AC 467 at 107. The majority also referred with approval to a list of factors set out by Burrows in his *Restatement of the English Law of Contract* (Oxford University Press, 2016) pp 229–30: [2017] AC 467 at 93.

[121] [2015] IESC 29.

[122] See the summary at para 8.55.

[123] Lords Sumption, Mance, and Clarke.

[124] Lord Mance at 206.

[125] Lord Clarke at 217.

On a strict understanding of the rule, if they had to do so, then they would be denied a remedy. *Patel v Mirza* overrules the reliance rule laid down in *Tinsley v Milligan*, which is a resulting trusts case.[126] In that case a house had been purchased in the sole name of Tinsley, using money which both Tinsley and Milligan, a cohabiting lesbian couple, had raised from the sale of a previous property, augmented by a mortgage loan. The reason for this was to enable Milligan to appear to be a mere lodger in the property, rather than a co-owner, so that she could make false claims for various state social welfare benefits. After the breakdown of their relationship, Milligan claimed that Tinsley held the house on trust for them in equal shares. The House of Lords held that Milligan's contribution to the cost of acquiring the property had given rise to a resulting trust of a half share in her favour. She was entitled to enforce this resulting trust, notwithstanding the illegality involved in the transaction, because she did not need to rely on the illegality to make her claim. That reasoning would have led to different conclusions depending upon whether a claimant relied on resulting trust or constructive trust[127] (where the purpose of the transaction would have to be brought into evidence), and on whether there was a presumption of resulting trust[128] or a presumption of advancement.[129]

The old reliance rule had already been weakened. The rigour of the reliance rule was modified by allowing a person to rely upon an illegal purpose if that purpose has not been carried into effect. In *Tribe v Tribe*,[130] the father, fearful that he might face a substantial claim for repairs in respect of two leases, transferred the shares in his company to his son in order to protect them. When the anticipated liability failed to materialize, his son refused to retransfer the shares. The Court of Appeal held that because no creditors had actually been defrauded, the father could rely on his illegality to recover the shares. There was uncertainty about whether this 'locus poenitentiae' (space to recant) modification of the reliance rule applied only where there was genuine repentance and/or the illegal purpose had not been carried into effect at all. The minority in *Patel v Mirza* would have extended the locus poenitentiae to include all cases where the illegal purpose had not been fully carried out for whatever reason. That extension became redundant in the light of the majority view, although Lord Neuberger would have combined both approaches.

(e) Contextualizing the change

The Law Commission recommended the abandonment of the 'reliance principle' adopted in *Tinsley v Milligan* in favour of granting the court a discretion,[131] and that recommendation has now effectively been judicially adopted by the explicit rejection of the reliance rule in *Patel v Mirza*. It should, though, be noted that the factors enumerated by the majority in the Supreme Court are not the same as those listed by the Law Commission. Notably, the Commission took the view that the degree of 'guilt' or 'innocence' of the claimant should be key to any illegality defence.[132] Yet culpability is not at the centre of

[126] [1994] 1 AC 340.

[127] The dilemma created by such a distinction was finessed by the Court of Appeal in *O'Kelly v Davies* [2014] EWCA Civ 1606; [2015] 1 WLR 2725.

[128] *Silverwood v Silverwood* (1997) 74 P & CR 453; *Lowson v Coombes*[1999] Ch 373; *Zabihi v Janzemini & Ors* [2008] EWHC 2910 at [286].

[129] *Collier v Collier* [2002] EWCA 1095 (daughter did not hold lease granted by her father on a resulting trust because the father would need to rely on his illegal purpose of deceiving creditors to rebut the presumption of advancement).

[130] [1995] 4 All ER 236; [1996] 112 LQR 386 (Rose); [1996] CLJ 23 (Virgo); [1997] 60 MLR 102 (Creighton). See also (1995) 111 LQR 135 (Enonchong); [1996] RLR 78 (Enonchong).

[131] *The Illegality Defence* (Law Com No 320, 2010), following *Illegal Transactions: The Effect of Illegality on Contracts and Trusts* (Law Com CP No 154, 1999).

[132] *The Illegality Defence* (Law Com No 320, 2010), 2.64.

the ratio in *Patel v Mirza*. Regardless of this change in the law, the outcome in *Tinsley v Milligan*, however, would still be the same under the new approach in *Patel v Mirza* because the Supreme Court has confirmed that ownership can be acquired or passed through an illegal transaction,[133] and on the facts of *Tinsley v Milligan*, it would have been disproportionate to have prevented Milligan from enforcing her equitable interest.[134]

(f) A focus on policy considerations

Patel v Mirza is a multi-factor approach, designed to apply across a range of different contexts.[135] Even so, *Patel v Mirza* undoubtedly brings policy considerations right to the fore of judicial decision-making. This is evident from the Supreme Court case, *Stoffel & Co v Grondona*.[136] Ms Grondona raised a mortgage to buy a flat in London. She was involved in a fraud with the vendor of the flat, who was her business associate. The vendor was passing on the flat to Ms Grondona for a fraction of price he had paid three months earlier. Using her name on the mortgage loan application enabled him to access capital that he could not acquire under his own name on the ordinary loan market.

Ms Grondona instructed Stoffel & Co, a law firm, in the purchase of the flat. Negligently, the firm failed make the requisite legal filings with the Land Registry so legal title of the flat did not pass to Ms Grondona. The vendor remained the legal owner and an already-existing charge on the property remained in place. Ms Grondona defaulted on her mortgage and was sued by the mortgage lender. In turn, Ms Grondona sought to pass the claim onto Stoffel & Co, on the basis that the law firm had been negligent in failing to make the correct legal filings. Stoffel & Co claimed that Ms Grondona should be denied a remedy on the basis of illegality. Despite her fraud, the Supreme Court found for Ms Grondona and allowed her to pass on the claim to the negligent law firm.

Policy considerations sit right at the centre of the Supreme Court's reasoning in *Stoffel & Co*. There is a clear principle in the case that negligence on the part of solicitors should not be encouraged, and that where such negligence does occur, clients should be able to seek a remedy. The case is concerned not to let negligent solicitors off the hook even in circumstances where their clients are involved in a fraud.

(g) Special cases

People who have engaged in a criminal activity cannot expect to be treated in the same way as those who have kept within the law. In *R v Ahmad*[137] (decided before *Patel v Mirza*) the Supreme Court held that where the courts made a confiscation order under the Proceeds of Crime Act 2002 against more than one defendant in relation to a joint criminal enterprise, each defendant would be liable for the whole of the benefit obtained through the crime, but with a condition that the state may not recover the sum twice by enforcing the order in full against more than one defendant. This would not be treated as joint and several liability, with the consequence that if the debt were enforced against just one of the defendants, that defendant would be unable to seek contribution from the others. Lord Neuberger observed:

> This approach may appear to risk producing inequity between criminal conspirators, on the basis that some of them may well obtain a 'windfall' because the amount of the confiscation order will be paid by another. However, that is an inherent feature of joint criminality. If the

[133] [2017] AC 467 at 110, following *Singh v Ali* [1960] AC 167, 176; and *Sharma v Simposh Ltd* [2013] Ch 2.

[134] *Patel v Mirza* [2017] AC 467 at 112.

[135] See, *Subhani v Sultan* [2017] EWHC 1686 (Ch) involving the fraudulent avoidance of a charging order; *Singularis Holdings Ltd v Daiwa Capital Markets Europe Ltd* [2019] UKSC 50 involving breach of contract and negligence.

[136] *Stoffel and Co v Grondona* [2020] UKSC 42.

[137] [2014] 4 All ER 767.

victim of a fraud were to sue the conspirators and to obtain judgments against them, he would be entitled to enforce against whichever defendant he most easily could. The losses must lie where they fall, and there is nothing surprising, let alone wrong, in the criminal courts adopting that approach.[138]

(7) The presumption of advancement

(a) Nature of the presumption

In some circumstances where a person voluntarily transfers property into the name of another, or contributes to its purchase, the law presumes that a gift was intended and that the transferor/contributor did not intend to retain any interest in the property concerned. This presumption, known as the 'presumption of advancement', displaces the presumption of resulting trust. The presumption of advancement arises as a consequence of a pre-existing relationship between the parties to the transfer or acquisition, where the transferor/contributor is regarded as morally obliged to provide for the person benefiting. As Lord Eldon stated in *Murless v Franklin*:

> The general rule that on a purchase by one man in the name of another, the nominee is a trustee for the purchaser, is subject to exception where the purchaser is under a species of natural obligation to provide for the nominee.[139]

The range of relationships where equity recognizes a presumption of advancement reflects a nineteenth-century understanding of family responsibility, and it is clear that, today, the strengths of the presumptions vary to reflect differing social circumstances. However, the state of the law in this area remains far from satisfactory.

(b) Pending abolition of the presumption

The presumption of advancement may at some time be relegated to legal history. Section 199 of the Equality Act 2010[140] would abolish the presumption of advancement with prospective effect.[141] The reason for the abolition of the presumption is motivated not by the concern that the presumption is seen as antiquated and outmoded in the modern day, but by the suggestion that it is in breach of Article 5 of Protocol 7 of the European Convention on Human Rights and Fundamental Freedoms 1950.

The need for the provision has been questioned,[142] and there has also been such a long delay in implementing this (and some other provisions of the Act) that it is an open question when, if ever, it will come into force. At the time of writing, this section is not yet in force and is still awaiting an order of the Lord Chancellor to commence it.[143] The fact that the provision is on the statute book, even though not in force, may have some relevance to judges' approach. Mostyn J said in *Bhura v Bhura*[144] that the presumption 'can be regarded as being on its death-bed given that it is abolished by s199 Equality Act 2010, which is awaiting implementation'. The hiatus in implementation has also created some confusion. In *Bank of Scotland plc v Forrester*,[145] the section was incorrectly treated as

[138] [2014] 4 All ER 767 at 73. [139] [1818] 1 Swan 13 at 17.

[140] This section is part of a package of provisions relating to family property, located in Part 15 of the Act.

[141] See s 199(2) relating to property transfers undertaken before the commencement of the section (s 199(2)(a)) or acts done in pursuance of an obligation arising under a pre-existing obligation under the presumption of advancement (s 199(2)(b)).

[142] See further Glister, 'Section 199 of the Equality Act 2010: How Not To Abolish The Presumption of Advancement' (2010) 73 MLR 807; where is it is argued that the presumption does not breach Article 5 of Protocol 7, and at any rate, the drafting of s 199 (particularly s 199(2)(a)) means that abolition will not have this effect and should only be enacted in part, if at all. [143] The time of writing is January 2022.

[144] [2014] EWHC 727 (Fam) at 8. [145] [2014] EWHC 2036 (Ch).

already in force, but the decision in that case that a father had not made an advancement to his son was justified on the basis of evidence of an express agreement. In *Anglo Financial v Goldberg*,[146] Roth J included the abolition of the presumption by s 199 in his summary of the legal rules, but considered it inapplicable because the purchase involved had been made before the section came into force.

(c) When the presumption applies

(i) Father and child

Traditionally, the presumption of advancement applied only in a very narrow and archetypically paternalistic way. There was a strong presumption of advancement between a father and his child.[147] In *Re Roberts (Decd)*,[148] Evershed J held that the presumption of advancement applied where a father had made payments on a policy of assurance taken out on his son's life. He said that:

> It is well established that a father making payments on behalf of his son prima facie, and in the absence of contrary evidence, is to be taken to be making and intending an advance in favour of the son and for his benefit.[149]

In *B v B*[150] a Canadian court held that the presumption of advancement applied where a father had purchased a winning lottery ticket in the name of his twelve-year-old daughter. She was, therefore, entitled to the winnings absolutely. The rationale for the presumption of advancement between a father and child is that a father, by the very nature of his position, is under a duty to provide for his child.[151]

(ii) Persons standing in loco parentis

A presumption of advancement also arises between a child and a person standing in loco parentis.[152] The rationale for this extension of the presumption was stated by Jessel MR in *Bennet v Bennet*:

> as regards a child, a person not the father of the child may put himself in the position of loco parentis to the child, and so incur the obligation to make provision for the child . . .[153]

(iii) Husband and wife

The presumption of advancement also arises between a husband in favour of his wife (but not vice versa). The principle was stated in *Re Eykyn's Trusts*, by Malins V-C:

> The law of this court is perfectly settled that when a husband transfers money or other property into the name of his wife only, then the presumption is, that it is intended as a gift or advancement to the wife absolutely at once, subject to such marital control as he may

[146] [2014] EWHC 3192 (Ch) at 71.

[147] See *Shephard v Cartwright* [1955] AC 431. In *Oliveri v Oliveri* (1995) 38 NSWLR 665, Powell J suggested that a presumption of advancement could operate between a stepfather and stepchild.

[148] [1946] Ch 1.

[149] [1946] Ch 1 at 5. See also, in more recent times, *Antoni v Antoni* [2007] UKPC 10, which concerned the transfer of company shares between father and child.

[150] [1976] 65 DLR (3d) 460.

[151] *Bennet v Bennet* [1879] LR 10 Ch D 474 at 476, per Jessel MR. This has led some other jurisdictions to hold the presumption of advancement inapplicable to children of adult age, as they are not in need of support—see Glister, 'The Presumption of Advancement to Adult Children' [2007] Conv 370; Low, 'Apparent Gifts: Re-Examining The Equitable Presumption' [2008] 124 LQR 369.

[152] *Hepworth v Hepworth* [1870] LR 11 Eq 10; *Re Orme* (1883) 50 LT 51; *Shephard v Cartwright* [1955] AC 431; *Re Paradise Motor Co Ltd* [1968] 1 WLR 1125, CA.

[153] [1879] LR 10 Ch D 474.

> exercise. And if a husband invests in money, stocks, or otherwise, in the names of himself and his wife, then also it is an advancement for the benefit of the wife absolutely if she survives her husband . . .[154]

The operation of the presumption in this context reflects a nineteenth-century social understanding of a husband's obligation to provide for his wife. The presumption of advancement has also been applied between a man and his fiancée,[155] even though it is even harder to find a present-day justification for doing so.

(d) When the presumption does not apply

(i) Mother and child

No presumption of advancement arises between a mother and her child,[156] and therefore if a mother transfers property voluntarily to her child, the counter-presumption of resulting trust will apply.[157] In *Bennet v Bennet*,[158] Jessel MR explained the absence of the presumption on the basis that:

> there is no moral legal obligation . . . no obligation according to the rules of equity—on a mother to provide for her child.[159]

Again, such reasoning reflects nineteenth-century concepts of the family, and in modern social conditions mothers almost invariably share the responsibility to provide for their children.[160] Despite the socially archaic rationale, more modern cases have confirmed that there continues to be no presumption of advancement between a mother and child.[161] The presumption of resulting trust was applied by the Court of Appeal in *Gross v French*,[162] and by Hoffmann J in *Sekhon v Alissa*.[163] In the latter case, a mother had provided £22,500 to help her daughter purchase a house. In the absence of sufficient evidence to rebut the presumption of a resulting trust, the mother was held entitled to an interest in the property.

In *Nelson v Nelson*,[164] the Australian High Court has held that a presumption of advancement should operate between a mother and child.[165] In England the decision in *Re Cameron (Decd)*[166] suggests a possible avenue by which it might be found that the presumption should operate between a mother and child. Lindsay J held that, in the light of the difference between Victorian and modern attitudes to the ownership and ability to dispose of property, it would be appropriate nowadays to take both parents to be in loco parentis for the purposes of the succession rule against double portions unless the contrary is proved.[167]

[154] [1877] 6 Ch D 115 at 118.

[155] *Moate v Moate* [1948] 2 All ER 486; *Silver v Silver* [1958] 1 WLR 259; *Tinker v Tinker (No 1)* [1970] P 136; *Mossop v Mossop* [1989] Fam 77.

[156] See Dowling, 'The Presumption of Advancement between Mother And Child' [1996] Conv 274.

[157] *Re De Visme* [1863] 2 De GJ & Sm 17; *Bennet v Bennet* [1878–79] LR 10 Ch D 474. See also: *Sayre v Hughes* [1867–68] LR 5 Eq 376; *Gore-Grimes v Grimes* [1937] IR 470.

[158] [1879] LR 10 Ch D 474. [159] [1879] LR 10 Ch D 474 at 478.

[160] Compare *Dullow v Dullow* [1985] 3 NSWLR 531.

[161] See, however, *Close Invoice Company Ltd v Abowa* [2010] EWHC 1920 (QB), where Deputy Judge Mr Simon Picken QC felt that, as in Australian law, the presumption of advancement should apply between mother and child.

[162] [1975] 238 Estates Gazette 39. [163] [1989] 2 FLR 94. [164] [1995] 132 ALR 133.

[165] In *Re Dreger Estate* [1994] 97 Man R (2d) 39 it was held that in modern conditions the presumption of advancement ought to be applicable between mother and child.

[166] [1999] 2 All ER 924. [167] [1999] 2 All ER 924 at 939.

(ii) Wife and husband

Similarly, no presumption of advancement operates between a wife and her husband, so that in orthodox theory if a wife voluntarily transfers property into the name of her husband, or contributes to the purchase of property in his name, a presumption of resulting trust arises. Thus, in *Re Curtis*,[168] in the absence of evidence that a gift was intended, a wife was presumed to enjoy the equitable interest in shares, which she had voluntarily transferred into the name of her husband, by way of a resulting trust.[169] The absence of the presumption seems to have been accepted in *Mossop v Mossop*,[170] and it led to the presumption of a resulting trust in *Abrahams v Trustee in Bankruptcy of Abrahams*,[171] where a wife contributed to a syndicate purchasing National Lottery tickets in the name of her husband.

The absence of the presumption of advancement between a wife and her husband yet again reflects nineteenth-century social circumstances.

(iii) Same-sex marriages

There is no case dealing with the application of the presumption of advancement to same-sex marriages, but it is inconceivable that any presumption could apply.

(iv) Cohabiting partners

There is no presumption of advancement between cohabiting couples (whether heterosexual or homosexual),[172] nor between a man and his mistress.[173]

(v) Other family relationships

There is traditionally no presumption of advancement in the case of family relationships other than father and son. No presumption of advancement, therefore, applies between siblings,[174] in favour of a son-in-law,[175] or of a nephew.[176]

(e) Strength of presumption of advancement

Even in those situations where they may be applicable, presumptions of advancement carry very little weight and can be displaced by evidence of the parties' actual intentions. In *Pettitt v Pettitt*,[177] the House of Lords acknowledged that the presumption between husband and wife had reduced in significance.[178] Lord Reid suggested that the only reasonable basis for the presumption had been the economic dependence of wives on their husbands, and that given the changes in social circumstances 'the strength of the presumption must have much diminished'.[179] Lord Diplock considered that it was not appropriate that transactions between married couples should be governed by presumptions

[168] [1885] 52 LT 244.

[169] See also *Mercier v Mercier* [1903] 2 Ch 98; *Pearson v Pearson* [1965] *The Times*, 30 November; *Pettitt v Pettitt* [1970] AC 777; *Heseltine v Heseltine* [1971] 1 WLR 342; *Northern Bank Ltd v Henry* [1981] IR 1; *Allied Irish Banks Ltd v McWilliams* [1982] NI 156.

[170] [1988] 2 All ER 202 at 206, where Lawton LJ cited the relevant principles from Snell, *Principles of Equity* (28th edn, Sweet & Maxwell 1982), p 183.

[171] [1999] BPIR 637.

[172] *Rider v Kidder* [1805] 10 Ves 360; *Soar v Foster* [1858] 4 K & J 152; *Allen v Snyder* [1977] 2 NSWLR 685; *Calverly v Green* [1984] 56 ALR 483.

[173] *Diwell v Farnes* [1959] 1 WLR 624.

[174] *Noack v Noack* [1959] VR 137; *Gorog v Kiss* (1977) 78 DLR (3d) 690.

[175] *Knight v Biss* [1954] NZLR 55.

[176] *Dury v Dury* [1675] 75 SS 205; *Russell v Scott* [1936] 55 CLR 440.

[177] [1970] AC 777 at 815, per Lord Upjohn.

[178] See *Silver v Silver* [1958] 1 All ER 523 at 525, per Evershed MR. The presumption of advancement between husband and wife also applies in Ireland and Australia: *Heavey v Heavey* [1971] 111 ILTR 1; *M v M* [1980] 114 ILTR 46; *Doohan v Nelson* [1973] 2 NSWLR 320; *Napier v Public Trustee (Western Australia)* (1980) 32 ALR 153.

[179] [1970] AC 777 at 792.

'based upon inferences of fact which an earlier generation of judges drew as to the most likely intentions of earlier generations of spouses belonging to the propertied classes of a different social era'.[180] Nourse LJ, in *McGrath v Wallis*,[181] described the presumption of advancement as a 'last resort' in cases involving a property acquired for joint occupation, and, indeed, since *Stack v Dowden*[182] and *Jones v Kernott*,[183] the 'starting-point' when such a property is acquired in joint names is that the beneficial ownership is to be shared, regardless of who contributed the finance.[184]

(f) Inferences of intention

Since the presumption of advancement is readily displaced by evidence of the parties' actual intentions, it is possible for judges to rely on the circumstances of a transaction to find an explanation that does not require the use of any presumption, and the relationship of the parties is one of those circumstances.[185] For instance, in *Bennet v Bennet*, Jessel MR observed:

> We arrive then at this conclusion, that in the case of a mother . . . it is easier to prove a gift than in the case of a stranger: in the case of a mother, very little evidence beyond the relationship is wanted, there being very little additional motive required to induce a mother to make a gift to her child.[186]

Because the presumption of advancement is 'no more than a circumstance of evidence'[187] based on social conditions when the presumptions were established, it would be possible for the presumption to be sidestepped or modified by an inference based on what would now be considered the most appropriate explanation of an ambiguous transaction. For instance, in *Lavelle v Lavelle*[188] Lord Phillips MR explained the presumptions as based upon the existence of a close relationship:

> Normally there will be evidence of the intention with which a transfer is made. Where there is not, the law applies presumptions. Where there is no close relationship between A and B, there will be a presumption that A does not intend to part with the beneficial interest in the property and B will take the legal title under a resultant trust for A. Where, however, there is a close relationship between A and B, such as father and child, a presumption of advancement will apply. The implication will be that A intended to give the beneficial interest in the property to B and the transaction will take effect accordingly.

His reference to a close relationship could be no more than a shorthand describing the very specific situations in which a presumption of advancement has traditionally arisen. It could equally be a suggestion that the inference that a gift was intended could be found upon the balance of probabilities on the basis of close relationships which do not fall within those traditional categories.[189]

(g) Alternative explanations

A presumption of advancement will be rebutted by evidence that the transferor (or contributor) did not intend to make a gift but wished to retain an interest in the property transferred or acquired. In *Re Gooch*[190] Sir Daniel Gooch transferred shares into the

[180] Ibid. [181] [1995] 2 FLR 114 at 115. [182] [2008] EWCA Civ 645 at 27.

[183] [2012] 1 AC 776.

[184] *Gibson v Revenue and Customs Prosecution Office* [2008] EWCA Civ 645 at 27.

[185] See *Marr v Collie* at 49.

[186] [1879] 10 Ch D 474 at 480. See, however, *Sekhon v Alissa* [1989] 2 FLR 94, where Hoffmann J held that the evidence was inconsistent with there being a gift.

[187] Per Lord Upjohn in *Pettitt v Pettitt* [1970] AC 777 at 814. [188] [2004] 2 FCR 418 at 14.

[189] Compare *Chaudhary v Chaudhary* [2013] EWCA Civ 758 at 35 (rebuttal of presumption of advancement). [190] [1890] 62 LT 384.

name of his eldest son. The son paid the dividends from the shares to his father, who also retained the share certificates. Kay J held that the presumption of advancement was rebutted by evidence that the shares had been transferred to qualify the son to become a director of the company, and that no gift had been intended. In *Warren v Gurney*,[191] a father purchased a house in the name of his daughter prior to her wedding. He retained the title deeds until his death. The Court of Appeal held that the presumption of advancement was rebutted by evidence that at the time of the transaction, the father had intended her husband to repay the money. The retention of the title deeds was considered a very significant fact, as 'one would have expected the father to have handed them over either to [his daughter] or her husband, if he had intended the gift'.[192] In *McGrath v Wallis*,[193] a house was acquired for joint occupancy by a father and son in the sole name of the son. The purchase price was provided partly by the proceeds of sale of the father's previous house and partly by means of a mortgage. The Court of Appeal held that the presumption of advancement was rebutted by evidence that the father had intended to retain an interest in the ownership of the house, including an unsigned declaration of trust which would have shared the beneficial ownership in the proportions represented by the deposit and mortgage, respectively.

The mere fact that any rents and profits generated from the property concerned are returned to the purchaser or transferor will not conclusively rebut a presumption of advancement. In *Stamp Duties Comrs v Byrnes*,[194] a father had purchased property in Australia in the name of his sons. They paid over to him the rents received from the properties, and he paid for rates and repairs. The Privy Council held that as it was not unusual for a father to transfer property to a son while continuing to receive any rents and profits during his lifetime, the presumption of advancement had not been rebutted:

> Having regard to the state of the family and the relations subsisting between Mr Byrnes and his two sons who were living at home, it seems very natural that the sons receiving advances should yet feel a delicacy in taking the fruits during their father's lifetime. They had all they wanted as things were, and if they were unduly favoured it might possibly have created some feeling of jealousy among the rest.[195]

Although the opening of a bank account by a husband in the joint names of himself and his wife will lead to the presumption of a joint tenancy of the money therein,[196] the presumption of advancement operating between them may be rebutted. In the nineteenth-century case of *Marshal v Crutwell*,[197] it was held that the presumption of advancement was rebutted where a husband had transferred his bank account into the joint names of himself and his wife. The court held that the transfer was merely for convenience, since the husband was in ill-health and could not draw cheques himself. His wife was not therefore entitled to the balance in the account on his death. In *Anson v Anson*,[198] the presumption of advancement was rebutted where a husband had entered a guarantee of an overdraft on a bank account in his wife's name. After their divorce he was called to pay £500 to the bank under the guarantee, and demanded repayment from his wife. Pearson J held that the intention was that the debt would remain her debt, and the guarantee to the bank was not intended to relieve her of her obligation but merely to solve her immediate banking emergency.

[191] [1944] 2 All ER 472. See also *Webb v Webb* [1992] 1 All ER 17; refd [1994] 3 All ER 911.
[192] [1944] 2 All ER 472 at 473, per Morton LJ. [193] [1995] 2 FLR 114. [194] [1911] AC 386.
[195] [1911] AC 386 at 392. [196] See *Re Bishop* [1965] Ch 450; *Re Figgis* [1969] 1 Ch 123.
[197] (1875) LR 20 Eq 328. [198] [1953] 1 QB 636.

(h) Evidence of an illegal purpose

When the reliance rule set out in *Tinsley v Milligan*[199] (but now overruled) applied, there could be problems where a claimant needed to rely on evidence of an illegal purpose in order to rebut the presumption of advancement. Some of the cases involve attempts to shield property from creditors by a husband transferring property to his wife. Millett LJ said of this in *Tribe v Tribe*:

> The only way in which a man can protect his property from his creditors is by divesting himself of all beneficial interest in it. Evidence that he transferred the property in order to protect it from his creditors, therefore, does nothing by itself to rebut the presumption of advancement; it reinforces it. To rebut the presumption it is necessary to show that he intended to retain a beneficial interest and conceal it from his creditors.[200]

Concealing property in this way is unlawful, and on the basis of the reliance rule, the property would not be recoverable. In *Gascoigne v Gascoigne*,[201] a husband took a lease of land in his wife's name in order to evade any claims by his creditors. The Court of Appeal held that he was not entitled to rebut the presumption of advancement by raising evidence of the illegal purpose underlying the transaction.[202]

Similarly, in *Tinker v Tinker (No 1)*,[203] a husband had purchased a house in the name of his wife, on the advice of his solicitor, again with the intention of preventing the house being seized by creditors if his business failed. On the breakdown of the marriage, it was held that he could not rebut the presumption of advancement. We have already noted how the reliance rule was mitigated by the concept of a locus poenitentiae (space to recant), helping to make the effect of illegality similar whether there was a presumption of a resulting trust or a presumption of advancement. The effect of *Patel v Mirza*[204] (discussed in relation to the presumption of a resulting trust) is that, in both situations, the approach is now the same. The existence of an illegal purpose, or the need to prove it in order to make a claim, is not an automatic bar to success.

(i) Admissibility of evidence

As in the case of the rebuttal of presumptions of a resulting trust, evidence of the claimant's acts and declarations contemporaneous with the transaction carry the greatest weight and there is a view, which may no longer apply, that subsequent evidence cannot be used to support a claimant's case.

6 Resulting trusts operating to reverse unjust enrichment?

(1) Restitutionary resulting trusts?

At the beginning of this chapter it was noted that there are two categories of resulting trusts recognized in English law, historically differentiated as 'presumed' and 'automatic' resulting trusts. However, there has been considerable debate about the role of unjust enrichment principles. It has been argued that not only can unjust enrichment explain resulting trusts, but it could justify the recognition of a third type of resulting trust, namely, a restitutionary resulting trust, which arises for the purpose of reversing unjust enrichment.

199 [1993] 3 All ER 65. 200 [1995] 4 All ER 236 at 259. 201 [1918] 1 KB 223.

202 [1918] 1 KB 223 at 226. Cases involving different types of illegality, but with a similar outcome, are *Re Emery's Investments Trusts* [1959] Ch 410 (avoidance of taxes) and *Chettiar v Chettiar* [1962] 1 All ER 494 (restrictions on land ownership).

203 [1970] P 136. 204 [2017] AC 467.

(2) Unjust enrichment an autonomous cause of action

Although English law did not historically recognize a right to restitution founded on a general principle against unjust enrichment, in *Likpin Gorman v Karpnale Ltd*,[205] the House of Lords held that 'unjust enrichment' should be recognized as a valid autonomous cause of action. This recognition has been reiterated in many subsequent decisions[206] and is now beyond doubt. The scope of the action for unjust enrichment is yet to be fully settled. As Lord Sumption said in *Lowick Rose LLP v Swynson Ltd*: 'English law does not have a universal theory to explain all the cases in which restitution is available.'[207] The underlying principle is that a claimant will be entitled to restitution whenever (i) he can demonstrate that the defendant was (ii) enriched, (iii) at his expense, (iv) unjustly, and (v) where there are no available defences.[208] Unjust enrichment has been used to justify decisions in a wide range of situations, the principal ones being where a payment has been made in mistake[209] or a mutual expectation has been defeated by a defective transaction.[210]

(3) Remedy for unjust enrichment

Where a claimant can demonstrate an entitlement to receive restitution from the defendant on the basis of unjust enrichment, the question arises as to the nature of the remedy available to him to effect such restitution. The claimant will generally be entitled to a personal remedy, requiring the defendant to pay over to him an amount equivalent to the enrichment that had been received, but this remedy will be of little use if the defendant is insolvent. If, however, it can be shown that property constituting the enrichment received by the defendant was subjected to a trust, the plaintiff will be able to assert a proprietary claim to any assets remaining in the defendant's hands which are the traceable proceeds of the enrichment received. In a significant article, Professor Birks argued that a resulting trust should arise whenever a defendant receives an unjust enrichment conferred by mistake or under a contract the consideration for which wholly fails.[211] If such a resulting trust were to arise from the mere fact of enrichment in such cases the claimant would be entitled to a proprietary remedy.

(4) Resulting trust rejected

Professor Birk's resulting trust thesis was considered in *Westdeutsche Landesbank Girozentrale v Islington London Borough Council*,[212] where it was comprehensively rejected by the House of Lords, which preferred the critical approach of William Swadling.[213] The

[205] [1991] 2 AC 548. See Birks, 'English Recognition of Unjust Enrichment' [1991] LMCLQ 473.

[206] See *Woolwich Equitable Building Society v IRC* [1993] AC 70; *Westdeutsche Landesbank Girozentrale v Islington London Borough Council* [1996] AC 669; *Kleinwort Benson Ltd v Glasgow City Council* [1999] 1 AC 153, HL.

[207] [2017] UKSC 32 at 22.

[208] *Banque Financière de la Cité v Parc (Battersea) Ltd* [1999] 1 AC 221, 227; *Benedetti v Sawiris* [2013] UKSC 50 at 50.

[209] Other instances are profits made from the infringement of a patent or confidential information: *Design & Display Ltd v Abbott* [2016] EWCA Civ 95 and subrogation to a vendor's lien against a property purchase made with an ineffective mortgage: *Menelaou v Bank of Cyprus UK Ltd* [2015] UKSC 66.

[210] *Lowick Rose LLP v Swynson Ltd* [2017] UKSC 32 at 30; *Cheltenham & Gloucester plc v Appleyard* [2004] EWCA Civ 291.

[211] Birks, 'Restitution and Resulting Trusts', in Goldstein (ed), *Equity and Contemporary Legal Development* (Hebrew University of Jerusalem 1992). See also Chambers, *Resulting Trusts* (Clarendon Press 1997), pp 93–219.

[212] [1996] AC 669; (1996) 112 LQR 521 (Cape); [1996] CLJ 432 (Jones); [1997] LMCLQ 441 (Stevens).

[213] [1996] 16 LS 133. See also the rejection of the theory in Mee, 'The Past, Present, and Future of Resulting Trusts' (2017) 70 CLP 189.

case involved a payment made by the bank as part of a complex financial arrangement which was beyond the powers of the local authority and, therefore, void.[214] The bank sought restitution of the balance of the payment it had made, less the repayments the authority had already made, together with interest. In the House of Lords the sole remaining question was as to the nature of the interest payable on the award of restitution. If the bank was only entitled to restitution at common law, then the court had no jurisdiction to award compound interest. However, the bank alleged that the payment had been received subject to a resulting trust, because the contract under which it was made was void, thus rooting their claim in equity and entitling the court to award compound interest. Lord Browne-Wilkinson explained that the circumstances of the payment could not have given rise to a resulting trust if conventional principles were applied: at the time when the bank made its payment to the Council, it was 'the intention that the moneys so paid should become the absolute property of the local authority'.[215] He further elucidated three reasons for rejecting Professor Birks' thesis that the concept of the resulting trust should be extended to provide a plaintiff with a proprietary remedy whenever he had transferred value to a defendant under a mistake or subject to a condition which is not subsequently satisfied. First, he held that trust interests could not arise in relation to the restitutionary concept of 'value transferred' but only in relation to defined property. Second, he considered that a trust would only arise at the moment that a defendant received a payment if he was aware of the circumstances alleged to give rise to the trust. Since a recipient of a payment subsequently found void for mistake or failure of consideration will not have been aware of the circumstances rendering it void at the date of receipt, his conscience cannot have been affected so as to generate a trust. Third, he noted that the thesis was flawed by the need to artificially exclude cases of partial failure to perform a contract, despite the fact that the wider concept logically led to a resulting trust in such cases.

Alongside these conceptual objections to the recognition of restitutionary resulting trusts, the House of Lords considered that the consequential expansion in proprietary entitlements would have unacceptable practical consequences for third parties.[216] For example, if money paid under a void contract was subject to a resulting trust, third parties who entered into transactions with the recipient of the payment might be affected by the trust interest of the payor, even though no one knew that the contract was void, so that they could not have been aware of the supposed trust. In the light of these considerations Lord Browne-Wilkinson concluded:

> If adopted, Professor Birks' wider concepts would give rise to all the practical consequences and injustice to which I have referred. I do not think it right to make an unprincipled alteration to the law of property (ie the law of trusts) so as to produce in the law of unjust enrichment the injustices to third parties . . . and the consequential commercial uncertainty which any extension of proprietary interests in personal property is bound to produce.[217]

(5) **Institutional resulting trust**

The result of the House of Lords decision is that a resulting trust cannot be used as a remedy. Instead, resulting trusts are institutional: that means they arise as a direct consequence of the circumstances rather than being imposed at the discretion of the judge.

[214] As a result of the decision of the House of Lords in *Hazell v Hammersmith and Fulham London Borough Council* [1992] 2 AC 1.

[215] [1996] AC 669 at 708.

[216] See Burrows, 'Swaps and Friction between Common Law and Equity' [1995] RLR 15 for a fuller consideration of the practical implications of the adoption of restitutionary resulting trusts.

[217] [1996] AC 669 at 709.

This fits with unjust enrichment being a part of the law of obligations (like contract and torts) rather than part of the law of property.[218] As will be seen in Chapter 10, there has been a similar debate about remedial constructive trusts. Lord Browne-Wilkinson suggested that:

> Although the resulting trust is an unsuitable basis for developing proprietary restitutionary remedies, the remedial constructive trust, if introduced into English law, may provide a more satisfactory road forward.[219]

(6) **Relationship between resulting trusts and unjust enrichment**

The same facts could give rise to both a resulting trust and an example of unjust enrichment. Suppose that a scheming lodger persuades his landlady to transfer her house to him on the basis of a promise that her rights to the property will not change. This could be seen as an express declaration of trust, but it would be unenforceable without proof in writing. However, the situation fits the requirements for unjust enrichment: he would (i) be enriched (ii) at her expense and (iii) unjustly. But this is also a description of the facts in *Hodgson v Marks*,[220] where the Court of Appeal held that because this was a voluntary transfer not intended as a gift, there was a resulting trust.

The relationship between trusts and unjust enrichment is also illustrated by *Davis (As Trustee In Bankruptcy of Jackson) v Jackson*.[221] Mr and Mrs Jackson, a married couple who were estranged and living apart, acquired a property as a home for Mrs Jackson and their children, initially in Mrs Jackson's name with an express declaration of trust in favour of them both in equal shares. The property was later registered in both their names with an express statement that they held on trust for themselves as joint tenants. Mr Jackson failed to make any of the mortgage payments which had been anticipated, so that all of the mortgage payments were made by Mrs Jackson. When he was declared bankrupt, the question arose as to what share he had in the property. Mrs Jackson claimed a higher share because she had made all the mortgage payments. This might have been arguable on the basis of resulting trust, but Snowden J held that the express declaration of trust and the absence of any countervailing considerations excluded the possibility of a resulting trust, so that as a matter of property law, the property was owned jointly. However, Mrs Jackson should be given credit for the mortgage repayments on the basis of equitable accounting.[222] An alternative claim was made on the basis of unjust enrichment. Snowden J held that this also failed to strip Mr Jackson of any gain he made as a result of an increase in the value of the property because:

> the law of unjust enrichment's essential concern is not with the disgorgement of gains made by defendants, nor with the compensation of losses sustained by claimants, but with the reversal of transfers of value between claimants and defendants.[223]

On this basis, also, Mrs Jackson was limited to claiming the value of the mortgage payments which Mrs Jackson effectively made on behalf of Mr Jackson.

[218] *Revenue and Customs v The Investment Trust Companies* [2017] UKSC 29 at 39; *Banque Financière de la Cité v Parc (Battersea) Ltd* [1999] 1 AC 221 at 227.

[219] [1996] AC 669 at 716.

[220] [1971] Ch 892.

[221] [2017] EWHC 698 (Ch).

[222] When assessing compensation, equity takes account of expensed incurred in achieving benefits.

[223] [2017] EWHC 698 (Ch) at 87, quoting a statement from Mitchell, Mitchell, and Watterson, *Goff and Jones: The Law of Unjust Enrichment* (9th ed, Sweet & Maxwell 2016) para 6–01, and endorsed by Lord Clarke in *Menelaou v Bank of Cyprus* [2016] AC 176 at 23.

7 Automatic resulting trusts

We have already noted that resulting trusts fall into two categories, presumed resulting trusts and automatic resulting trusts. Presumed resulting trusts help to interpret ambiguous transactions. Automatic resulting trusts serve a different role. They help to explain who owns property when there appears to be a gap in beneficial ownership. Professor John Mee has called them 'gap-filling' resulting trusts.[224] What happens, for instance, if an express trust made by Philip leaves property on trust for Elizabeth for life, and on her death, on trust for her children, but she dies childless? Initially this will depend upon the interpretation of the trust instrument, which may give an answer. Failing this, there will be a resulting trust in favour of Philip: in creating the trust, he failed to dispose of the whole beneficial ownership in the property; therefore, what was not given away remains, returns, or results to him.

(1) Gaps in beneficial ownership

A gap in beneficial ownership can arise for a variety of reasons.

(a) Non-existent beneficiary

An attempt to create a trust in favour of, or to make a gift to, a person who does not exist, cannot operate as an effective disposition, and beneficial ownership will therefore remain in the donor. In *Omojole v HSBC Bank Plc*[225] a Nigerian company paid £3m into the account of a company with which it was associated without being aware that the company had been struck off for failing to file its returns. It was held that the money was held on resulting trust for the company which made the payment. In some instances an attempted transfer to a non-existent entity will be completely void: a resulting trust arises only where legal ownership has passed (in *Omojole* it had passed to the bank).

(b) Failure to declare beneficial interests

If property is transferred to trustees upon trust but the settlor makes no effective declaration of the beneficial interests, so that the trustees do not know who they are to hold the property for, they will hold the property transferred on a resulting trust for the settlor, or if he is dead, for his successors in title.[226] The option retained by the trustees in *Vandervell v IRC* is an example.[227] It was clear that the trustees were not beneficial owners of the option, but there was no other identified beneficiary.

(c) Declared beneficial interests fail

If a valid trust is created but subsequently fails for some reason, any trust property that remains in the hands of the trustees will be held on resulting trust for the settlor unless some other destination of the beneficial interest can be found in the trust instrument. For example, in *Re Ames' Settlement*,[228] Louis Ames created a marriage settlement of £10,000 on the marriage of his son in 1908. The marriage was declared 'absolutely null and void' in 1927 by the Supreme Court of Kenya, on the grounds of the husband's incapacity to consummate the marriage.[229] Vaisey J concluded that, since the marriage had been void

[224] Mee, 'The Past, Present, and Future of Resulting Trusts' (2017) 70 CLP 189.

[225] [2012] EWHC 3102 (QB).

[226] See *Johnson v Ball* (1851) 5 De G & Sm 85; *Re Keen* [1937] 1 All ER 452 and *Re Boyes* (1884) 26 Ch D 531, where there were ineffective attempts to create secret trusts.

[227] [1967] 2 AC 291. For the facts see section 4(6) of this chapter.

[228] [1946] Ch 217.

[229] See *Re d'Altroy's Will Trusts* [1968] 1 WLR 120; *Re Rodwell* [1970] Ch 726.

ab initio, there was a total failure of the consideration for the marriage settlement and the property should result back to the father's estate (in other words a resulting trust arises). A resulting trust would also arise if a settlement was created in contemplation of a marriage which never took place.[230]

A resulting trust will also arise where there is a partial failure of the beneficial interest. In *Re Cochrane*[231] a marriage settlement was created in favour of a wife 'so long as she shall continue to reside with' her husband. They separated and the income was (incorrectly, in view of the terms of the trust) paid to the husband, who then predeceased her. It was held that the income should be held on resulting trust for the settlors in proportion to the contributions they had made to the fund.

(d) Essential requirements of trust not satisfied

Where a trust is void because it fails to comply with all the requirements necessary for the creation of a valid trust, the trust property will again be held on a resulting trust for the settlor or his estate. In *Chichester Diocesan Fund and Board of Finance Inc v Simpson*,[232] Caleb Diplock created a discretionary trust in favour of charity. However, because the trust included some non-charitable objects, it was invalid for uncertainty and the property resulted back to his estate. In *Re Astor's Settlement Trusts*[233] a trust created in 1945 for the promotion of 'good understanding between the nations' and the 'preservation of the independence and integrity of newspapers' was held void because it contravened the beneficiary principle. The property was, therefore, held on resulting trust.

(e) Specific charitable purpose which fails

Where property has been given for a specific charitable purpose which has failed, it may similarly result to the settlors or donors if there was no intention to make an outright charitable gift. For example, in *Re Ulverston and District New Hospital Building Trusts*,[234] a fund had been created for the purpose of building a new hospital. The fund consisted of contributions from named donors, anonymous donors, street collections, and the proceeds of entertainments. The purpose became impossible, and it was held that the fund should be held on resulting trust for its donors because the donations had been made for only this purpose. If the donors' intentions had been more generally to support medical care, the gift property could have been applied to other charitable purposes under the cy-près doctrine, considered in Chapter 22.

(f) Trust fund has not been exhausted

Where a trust has been established for a specific purpose, any surplus funds that have not been exhausted on the completion of the purpose should in most cases be returned to the original contributors by way of a resulting trust in proportion to their contributions. The principle was stated by Harman J in *Re Gillingham Bus Disaster Fund*:

> The general principle must be that where money is held upon trust and the trusts declared do not exhaust the fund it will revert to the donor under what is called a resulting trust.[235]

(2) Interpreting gifts to individuals for purposes

A problem which can arise in the context of automatic resulting trusts is making sense of gifts to individuals for defined purposes. In *Re Abbott Fund Trusts*,[236] a fund was collected

[230] *Essery v Cowlard* (1884) 26 Ch D 191; *Bond v Walford* [1886] 32 Ch D 238. [231] [1955] Ch 309.
[232] [1944] AC 341. [233] [1952] Ch 534. [234] [1956] Ch 622.
[235] [1958] Ch 300 at 310. [236] [1900] 2 Ch 326.

and established in 1890 for the support of two deaf and dumb ladies. On their death in 1899, a surplus remained in the fund. The court held that the surplus should be held for the benefit of those who had subscribed to the fund. Central to the decision was the finding by Stirling J that the fund was never 'intended to become the absolute property of the ladies'.[237] However, in subsequent cases, the courts have construed gifts for beneficiaries with a description of purposes as if they were outright gifts, thereby excluding any possibility of a resulting trust to the contributors. In *Re Andrew's Trust*,[238] the friends of a deceased clergyman subscribed to a fund for the education of his children. After all the children had completed their education, there was a surplus of some £460 remaining in the fund. Kekewich J held that there should not be a resulting trust to the subscribers because the gift was to be construed as an absolute gift to the children, with the purpose being merely a motive for the gift. He took the view that the court always[239] construed such gifts in this way.[240] *Re Andrew's Trust*[241] was followed in *Re Osoba (Decd)*,[242] which concerned a trust established by a testator 'for the training of my daughter Abiola up to university grade and for the maintenance of my aged mother'. His mother had died and the daughter had completed her university education, leaving a surplus in the fund. The Court of Appeal held that the gift was an absolute gift and the reference to the purpose 'merely a statement of the testator's motive in making the gift'.[243] It is difficult to reconcile[244] *Re Abbott Fund Trusts*[245] with *Re Andrew's Trust*.[246] Ultimately, as was recognized by the Court of Appeal in *Re Osoba*,[247] each turns on its own facts, and it is of perhaps crucial importance that in *Re Abbott Fund Trusts*,[248] the beneficiaries of the fund were deceased, and could derive no further benefit from it.[249] There are two other factors which may be relevant: a gift for a purpose which benefits an individual is tantamount to a gift directly to that individual;[250] and since, with only a few exceptions, the law does not recognize purpose trusts, there may be a predisposition to interpret trusts for the benefit of ascertainable beneficiaries as outright gifts. This is an approach which has also been taken in regard to gifts to unincorporated associations.[251]

(3) 'Out and out' transfers

It is possible for a person to renounce all claim to property so that they cannot benefit from a resulting trust. This most obviously happens when a person pays for a benefit, but it can also happen with unconditional gifts. Imagine that there is a project to build a new village hall in Warmington-on-Sea, which has to be abandoned because insufficient money has been raised. Most of the funds would be returnable to the donors on the basis

[237] [1900] 2 Ch 326 at 330. [238] [1905] 2 Ch 48.

[239] See *Re Sanderson's Will Trust* [1857] 3 K & J 497; *Barlow v Grant* [1684] 1 Vern 255; *Webb v Kelly* [1839] 9 Sim 469; *Lewes v Lewes* [1848] 16 Sim 266; *Presant and Presant v Goodwin* [1860] 1 Sw & Tr 544.

[240] [1905] 2 Ch 48 at 52–3: 'If a gross sum be given, or if the whole income of the property be given, and a special purpose be assigned for that gift, this court always regards the gift as absolute and holds the purpose merely as the motive of the gift and, therefore, holds that the gift takes effect as to the whole sum or the whole income, as the case may be.' [241] [1905] 2 Ch 48.

[242] [1979] 1 WLR 247; [1978] CLJ 219 (Rickett). See also *Re Lipinski's Will Trusts* [1976] Ch 235.

[243] [1979] 1 WLR 247 at 257, per Buckley LJ.

[244] See the judgment of Megarry V-C at first instance in *Re Osoba* [1978] 1 WLR 791.

[245] [1900] 2 Ch 326. [246] [1905] 2 Ch 48.

[247] [1979] 1 WLR 247 at 251. [248] [1900] 2 Ch 326.

[249] This was pointed out by Kekewich J in *Re Andrew's Trust* [1905] 2 Ch 48 at 52.

[250] Compare *Re Bowes* [1896] 1 Ch 507; gift to landowner to plant trees could be used in any way the landowner wished.

[251] *Re Lipinski's Will Trusts* [1976] Ch 235 discussed in relation to clubs and societies in Chapter 16.

of an automatic resulting trust. However, there would be at least two classes of contributor who would be unlikely to be able to make a claim (even if they could provide proof of their contribution). People who had paid to attend a music concert or who had bought afternoon tea at a fundraiser would have no claim, because they would have received all they had bargained for.[252] People who had put small sums into a collecting tin could also be considered to have intended to part with all claim because segregating their contribution from the general mass would be impossible or impracticable. In both of those instances, the sums (if any remained) would be treated as bona vacantia, although case law on the latter point is inconsistent. In *Re Gillingham Bus Disaster Fund*,[253] a fund had been established in the aftermath of an accident in which twenty-four Royal Marine cadets had been killed, to defray the funeral expenses of the dead and care for the disabled. Some £9,000 was raised, largely by anonymous contributors to street collections. After providing for the funerals and care, there was a large surplus of the fund remaining, and the question before the court was whether that surplus should be returned to the donors on the basis of a resulting trust, be applied cy-près to other charitable purposes, or pass as bona vacantia to the Crown. Harman J held that as the objects of the fund were not exclusively charitable, there could be no application cy-près, and the surplus should be held on resulting trust for the contributors. He recognized the tremendous practical difficulty of this solution that many of those who had contributed were unknown, but concluded that this did not make a resulting trust unworkable, because the trustees could pay the money into court.[254] However, this appears to be an inappropriate solution. The individual donors surely intended to part with their money when they contributed it to the fund. As such, they should have ceased to enjoy any interest in it, even the possibility of reverter by way of a resulting trust. This more realistic approach was adopted by Goff J in *Re West Sussex Constabulary's Widows, Children and Benevolent (1930) Fund Trusts*,[255] in the context of an unincorporated association. He declined to follow the judgment of Harman J in *Re Gillingham Bus Disaster Fund*,[256] but followed the earlier cases of *Re Welsh Hospital (Netley) Fund*[257] and *Re Hillier*,[258] which held that persons contributing to a fund through street collections parted with their money 'out-and-out'[259] and retained no interest in it. As P O Lawrence J had observed in *Re Welsh Hospital*:

> It is inconceivable that any person placing a coin in a collecting-box presented to him in the street should have intended that any part of the money so contributed should be returned to him. To draw such an inference would be absurd.[260]

In the light of this analysis it should perhaps be questioned whether a resulting trust should have arisen in favour of the donors in *Re Abbott Fund Trusts*.[261]

While the resulting trust analysis in such cases appears inappropriate, the alternative, whereby the surplus passes as bona vacantia to the Crown, is equally unattractive as an option. The contributors to the *Gillingham Bus Disaster Fund* surely would not have wanted the surplus to pass to the Crown, thus making an involuntary contribution to government funds. The central problem with such cases is that they concerned

252 A phrase used in this context by Scott J in *Davis v Richards & Wallington Industries Ltd* [1990] 1 WLR 1511.

253 [1958] Ch 300.

254 [1958] Ch 300 at 314. In 1993 it was announced that the money was to be paid out and used for a memorial to the victims. See Hanbury and Martin, *Modern Equity* (18th edn, Sweet & Maxwell 2009), p 247.

255 [1971] Ch 1.

256 [1959] Ch 62.

257 [1921] 1 Ch 655.

258 [1954] 1 WLR 9; on appeal [1954] 1 WLR 700, CA.

259 *Re Hillier* [1954] 1 WLR 9 at 21–2, per Upjohn J; [1954] 1 WLR 700 at 714, per Denning LJ.

260 [1921] 1 Ch 655 at 660.

261 [1900] 2 Ch 326.

non-charitable purpose trusts, and that there is no equivalent principle to that of cy-près by which any surplus can be applied to similar purposes.[262] If the donors to such purpose trusts are taken to have given their property out-and-out, it is right that a resulting trust should not be implied, but equity should provide a mechanism permitting the application of any such surplus by the trustees in a manner consistent with the original objectives of the trust.

(4) **Resulting trust for whom?**

If a provision in a trust fails, the property does not automatically result back to the settlor. The first task is one of interpretation. There may be a provision in the trust instrument that indicates what happens if a provision fails. For instance, if a gap arises because a power has not been exercised, there may be an express or implied trust in favour of the class of objects.[263] The second task is again one of interpretation: was the gift that failed 'grafted' on another gift, so that the earlier gift stands unencumbered if the failed provision is excised? For instance, a house is gifted 'to my daughter Emily provided that she allows my wife, Mary, to live in the house rent-free for so long as she wants', but Mary chooses not to live in the house, the effect will be that the gift to Emily becomes unconditional. Finally, once all other options within the terms of the trust have been eliminated, there will be a resulting trust in favour of the settlor or donors. Deciding who they are can be complicated. In *Re St Andrew's (Cheam) Lawn Tennis Club Trust*,[264] Arnold J, having held that a trust of land for use as a tennis club failed because it was for mixed charitable and non-charitable purposes, held that the land was held on resulting trust for the previous owner (Mr Tweddle), despite significant contributions by other parties, because 'Mr Tweddle appears to have been the largest single donor, and the donations made by the smaller donors were predicated upon Mr Tweddle's donation.'

(5) **Pension fund surplus**

Particular problems have arisen concerning the applicability of a resulting trust analysis to a surplus under a pension scheme trust.[265] There is only one kind of pension scheme where this can arise: where the scheme is paid from a fund into which the member and/or his employer have made contributions, and the pension is defined independently of the value of the investments. This type of pension is described as a funded defined benefit scheme. Most funded pension schemes pay a pension based on the value of the investments which are attributed to an individual member. By definition these cannot be in surplus. With a defined benefit scheme it is possible for there to be either a shortfall or a surplus. Falling investment returns and increased longevity have meant that few defined benefit pension schemes now have a surplus, but pension scheme surpluses were common in the 1990s, and may still arise where a well-funded scheme is wound up. A variety of solutions have been adopted which demonstrate the unclear relationship between trust and contract.[266]

[262] If *Re Gillingham Bus Disaster Fund* had concerned a charitable trust, the surplus remaining after the purposes had been satisfied would have been applied cy-près: *Re Wokingham Fire Brigade Trusts* [1951] Ch 373; *Re Ulverston and District New Hospital Building Trusts* [1956] Ch 622.

[263] See Chapter 26 on powers of appointment.

[264] [2012] EWHC 1040.

[265] See Pollard, 'Pensions Law and Surpluses: A Fair Balance between Employer and Members?' (2003) TLI 2.

[266] As Megarry J observed in *Re Sick and Funeral Society of St John's Sunday School, Golcar* [1973] Ch 51, many of the difficulties arise because of the confusion of property with contract.

8 *Quistclose* trusts

(1) Trust of unused loan funds

A situation which has proved hard to categorize is the trust which can arise where money has been lent for a specific purpose that has failed. On the failure of the purpose, the borrower may hold the money lent on trust for the lender. Because the trust is for the person providing the money, this looks like a resulting trust, although there is much debate as to whether it should be so described. Such a trust is extremely significant if the borrower becomes insolvent, since the lender will be entitled to assert an equitable proprietary claim to the money lent and it will not form part of the assets of the creditor. The lender will not, therefore, merely rank among the general creditors of the borrower, which would have been his position in the absence of a trust because he would only have been entitled to a contractual claim for the repayment of the debt. It is not surprising that the principle originally evolved in cases where lenders were willing to make last-ditch loans to companies in extreme financial peril, since the added security of the resulting trust encourages them to make what would otherwise be extremely risky investments.

(2) Loan normally excludes a trust

One of the idiosyncracies of the trust in this situation is that it appears to defy the normal rules. Because when a person makes a loan they normally intend to give the whole legal and beneficial ownership in the money lent to the borrower, receiving in return a contractual obligation to repay an equivalent sum, the existence of a loan normally excludes the possibility of a trust.

(3) The *Quistclose* case

The kind of trust we are considering was first recognized by the House of Lords in *Barclays Bank Ltd v Quistclose Investments Ltd*,[267] the case which has given its name to this type of trust. A company, Rolls Razor Ltd, was in severe financial difficulties. The company obtained a loan from Quistclose on the agreed condition that it would only be used to pay the dividend to shareholders, and for that purpose the money was to be kept in a separate bank account with Barclays Bank. Before the dividend could be paid, Rolls Razor went into voluntary liquidation. The House of Lords held that, because of the exclusive purpose for which the loan was made, the money was received by Rolls Razor in the fiduciary character of a trust to pay the dividend. Since that purpose had failed, there was a resulting trust in favour of the lenders. The principle was explained by Lord Wilberforce:

> There is surely no difficulty in recognising the co-existence in one transaction of legal and equitable rights and remedies: when the money is advanced, the lender acquires an equitable right to see that it is applied for the primary designated purpose: when the purpose has been carried out . . . the lender has his remedy against the borrower in debt: if the primary purpose cannot be carried out, the question arises if a secondary purpose (ie repayment to the lender) has been agreed, expressly or by implication: if it has, the remedies of equity may be invoked to give effect to it . . .[268]

[267] [1970] AC 567. See also Mitchell, 'Subrogation, Tracing and the *Quistclose* Principle' [1995] LMCLQ 451; Matthews, 'The New Trust: Obligations without Rights' in Oakley, *Trends in Contemporary Trust Law* (Clarendon Press 1997), p 16.

[268] [1970] AC 567 at 581.

This principle has been developed and applied in subsequent cases,[269] and the House of Lords again considered whether such a trust was operative in *Twinsectra Ltd v Yardley*.[270] In this case, a finance company agreed to lend £1 million to the prospective purchaser of residential land. The money was paid into the client account of the purchaser's solicitor, subject to an express undertaking that the money be utilized 'solely for the acquisition of property on behalf of our client and for no other purpose'. Contrary to the terms of this undertaking, £358,000 of the money was used for other purposes. One question was whether the arrangement had given rise to a trust of the money, a crucial prerequisite to the claim of dishonest assistance in a breach of trust that was being maintained by the finance company. The House of Lords held that the money was subject to a trust because it had been paid subject to an undertaking that it would only be used for a specific purpose.

(4) **What is the nature of the trust?**

While these cases establish that a trust will arise where money is lent for a specific purpose that fails, the exact nature of such a trust has been a matter of academic controversy. In particular it has been difficult to determine when the trust comes into existence, to identify the beneficiary, and to reconcile the existence of the trust with the beneficiary principle, since as it was described in the *Quistclose* case it appears to require the existence of a primary trust under the terms of which money is held for the carrying out of a purpose. These theoretical problems were not explored by the House of Lords in *Quistclose* itself. There are several possibilities, none of which is free from difficulty.[271]

(a) **Primary trust for intended recipients**

First, a loan for a specific purpose may be regarded as creating a primary trust in favour of the persons intended to receive payment, for example specific creditors or shareholders, which gives rise to a resulting trust when the purpose fails. This approach seems to have been adopted by Megarry V-C in *Re Northern Developments (Holdings) Ltd*[272] However, this analysis can be criticized[273] on the grounds that such loans are made to benefit the borrower, and not for the benefit of the creditors or shareholders as such, and that it cannot explain cases where the loan was made for an abstract purpose.[274]

(b) **Primary trust for a purpose**

The Supreme Court referred to 'a special purpose (or *Quistclose*) trust' in *Bailey & Anor v Angove's PTY Ltd*[275] This may simply have been a description of the circumstances in which it arises rather than an explanation of how it operates. If the latter, the loan might create a primary trust to use the money for a purpose, with a resulting trust arising only when the purpose, and hence the primary trust, fails. Under this approach, which was

[269] *Carreras Rothmans Ltd v Freeman Mathews Treasure Ltd* [1985] Ch 207 at 222, per Peter Gibson J, who explained the trust as arising from the principle 'that equity fastens on the conscience of the person who receives from another property transferred for a specific purpose only and not therefore for the recipient's own purposes, so that such person will not be permitted to treat the property as his own or use it for other than the stated purpose'. See also *Re EVTR* [1987] BCLC 646.

[270] [2002] 2 AC 164; [2002] 2 All ER 377. See [2002] RLR 111 (Ricketts); [2002] Con 387 (Thompson); (2002) 16 TLI 165 (Penner); (2002) 16 TLI 223 (Glister); (2003) 119 LQR 8 (Yeo and Tijo); (2004) 63 CLJ 632 (Glister).

[271] See Hedlund and Rhodes, 'Loan or commercial trust? The continuing mischief of the Quistclose trust' [2017] Conv 254.

[272] 6 October 1978, unreported.

[273] *Twinsectra Ltd v Yardley* [2002] 2 All ER 377 at 85–9.

[274] For example, as in *Re EVTR* [1987] BCLC 646.

[275] [2016] UKSC 47 at 21.

advocated by the Court of Appeal in *Twinsectra Ltd v Yardley*,[276] the equitable interest in the money might be regarded as being 'in suspense' until the stated purpose is carried out, so that neither the lender nor the borrower is, strictly speaking, the beneficiary. However, it has the difficulty of appearing to offend the beneficiary principle, and was subjected to criticism in the House of Lords on the grounds that it is unorthodox, fails to have regard to the role which resulting trusts play in equity, and fails to explain why the money is not simply held on resulting trust for the lender from the outset.[277]

(c) No primary trust

Third, Chambers has argued that the loan does not create a primary trust at all. Rather, the borrower receives the entire beneficial ownership in the money lent, subject only to a contractual right in the lender to prevent the money being used otherwise than for the stated purpose, and a resulting trust springs into being only if the purpose fails.[278] This view has been criticized because it cannot explain cases of non-contractual payments, and it is inconsistent with the judgments in *Quistclose* that describe the borrower as under a fiduciary duty.[279]

(d) Resulting trust throughout

Finally, the money lent for a specific purpose may be regarded as being held on resulting trust by the borrower for the lender from the very beginning, the resulting trust arising from the fact that the lender did not intend the borrower to enjoy the beneficial ownership in the money lent. Instead, it has been suggested, the borrower has the power to spend the money for the agreed purpose.[280] This analysis has been advocated extrajudicially by Lord Millett,[281] and was, therefore, unsurprisingly, adopted by him in *Twinsectra Ltd v Yardley*.[282] He explained what he considered to be the nature of the *Quistclose* trust:

> As Sherlock Holmes reminded Dr Watson, when you have eliminated the impossible, whatever remains, however improbable, must be the truth. I would reject all the alternative analyses, which I find unconvincing and hold the Quistclose trust to be an entirely orthodox example of the kind of default trust known as a resulting trust. The lender pays the money to the borrower by way of loan, but he does not part with the entire beneficial interest in the money, and in so far as he does not it is held on a resulting trust for the lender from the outset . . . When the purpose fails, the money is returnable to the lender, not under some new trust in his favour which only comes into being on the failure of the purpose, but because the resulting trust in his favour is no longer subject to any power on the part of the borrower to make use of the money.[283]

While this analysis has the merit of simplicity, and of avoiding any problem of any conflict with the beneficiary principle, it is submitted that it is somewhat artificial to regard a resulting trust as subsisting from the very moment that the loan is made, prior to the failure of the purpose, unless the resulting trust is essentially an express trust based on the intentions of the parties. It is also unclear whether Lord Millett's analysis was

[276] [1999] Lloyd's Rep Bank 438. Green J referred to a '*Quistclose* purpose trust' in *Schenk v Cook* [2017] EWHC 144 (QB) at 85.

[277] *Twinsectra Ltd v Yardley* [2002] 2 All ER 377 at [90], per Lord Millett.

[278] Chambers, *Resulting Trusts* (Clarendon Press 1997), pp 68–89.

[279] Ho and Smart, 'Reinterpreting the *Quistclose* Trust: A Critique of Chambers' Analysis' (2001) 21 OJLS 267. See also *Twinsectra Ltd v Yardley* [2002] 2 All ER 377 at 95, per Lord Millett.

[280] *Bellis v Challinor* [2015] EWCA Civ 59 at 63.

[281] Sir Peter Millett, 'The *Quistclose* Trust: Who Can Enforce It?' (1985) 101 LQR 269.

[282] [2002] 2 All ER 377.

[283] [2002] 2 All ER 377 at 403.

supported by the majority of the House of Lords. Lord Hoffmann agreed that there was a trust, but did not specifically refer to the *Quistclose* case, and he appears to have regarded the arrangement as more akin to an express trust created by the undertaking. Lord Slynn agreed with Lord Hoffmann. Lord Hutton agreed with both Lords Hoffmann and Lord Millett that the money was subject to a trust, but did not comment further on their reasoning. Lord Steyn simply agreed with both Lords Hoffmann and Hutton. The basis of the decision is therefore open to debate, but it was described at first instance in *Challinor v Juliet Bellis & Co* as the characterization which 'probably holds sway',[284] and by the Court of Appeal in the same case as a compelling and authoritative resolution of the issue.[285]

(e) Mandate?

Another similar option is to view the arrangement in contractual terms. On this analysis, the bargain between the parties gives the borrower a mandate to use the loan for a particular purpose only, but unless and until the loan is used in this way, the money lent remains the property of the lender. Hildyard J, in *Challinor v Juliet Bellis & Co (A Firm)*,[286] described such a contractual arrangement as an escrow agreement, but thought that it might differ in some respects from a *Quistclose* trust since the latter does not depend upon the existence of a contract (although the two would usually coexist). The rationale is almost identical to Lord Millett's, but expressed in the language of contract rather than of trust. This analysis is supported by comments of Norris J approved on appeal by the Court of Appeal in *Bieber v Teathers Ltd*[287] and is the solution which was adopted in another context by the Court of Appeal in *Conservative Central Office v Burrell.*[288] It is also mirrored by the rules applying to the lien which a solicitor has for unpaid fees. The normal rule is that the firm will have a professional lien allowing it to retain any deed, paper, chattel, or money belonging to the client until the fees have been paid. The lien does not apply to any funds held by the solicitor subject to a trust for a particular purpose,[289] nor to funds subject to a court order which does not impose a trust, but which does restrict their use.[290]

(f) Express trust

Because the cases emphasize the need to find the objective intention of the parties, it would be possible to characterize *Quistclose* trusts as express, as is the case in Australia, although doing so adds little if anything to treating them as resulting trusts.[291]

(g) Sui generis situation?

If there is no better justification, it might be better to acknowledge the essentially anomalous and sui generis nature of the *Quistclose* trust, rather than to search for the 'truth' as to its nature by fitting it within 'orthodox' categories. As Potter LJ suggested in the Court of Appeal, the *Quisclose*-type trust 'is in truth a "quasi-trust"'.[292]

[284] *Challinor v Juliet Bellis & Co* [2013] EWHC 347 (Ch) at 543.

[285] *Bellis v Challinor* [2015] EWCA Civ 59 at 544–3. The analysis was again adopted by the Court of Appeal in *PK Airfinance SARL v Alpstream AG* [2015] EWCA Civ 1318 at 136.

[286] [2011] EWHC 3249 (Ch). (Application for reverse summary judgment. The main judgment is referred to later.)

[287] [2012] EWCA Civ 1466 at 14.

[288] [1982] 1 WLR 522. The context was that of an unincorporated organization which was not an unincorporated association. See Chapter 16.

[289] *Stumore v Campbell & Co* [1892] 1 QB 314.

[290] *Withers LLP v Langbar* [2012] 2 All ER 616.

[291] See Hedlund and Rhodes, 'Loan or commercial trust? The continuing mischief of the Quistclose trust' [2017] Conv 254.

[292] [1999] Lloyd's Rep Bank 438 at 76.

(5) Criteria needed for *Quistclose* trusts

The essence of a *Quistclose* trust is that the terms of the arrangement are such that ownership of the money concerned does not pass to the recipient, but that the recipient is authorized to use it only in a defined way. *Bieber v Teathers Ltd*[293] contains a distillation of the criteria drawn from the *Quistclose* and *Twinsectra* cases, that has been adopted in other cases both in the United Kingdom[294] and Ireland.[295] The key criteria are also restated rather more succinctly in *Bellis v Challinor*.[296]

(a) Money advanced for a specific purpose

A *Quistclose* resulting trust will only arise if the loan or other payment[297] (such as money to be invested by the recipient[298]) was made exclusively[299] for an agreed specific purpose.[300] In *Quistclose*, the purpose was the payment of a share dividend. In *Carreras Rothmans Ltd v Freeman Mathews Treasure Ltd (in liquidation)*,[301] a resulting trust was held to arise where a loan had been made by Rothmans to their advertising agency, who were in financial difficulty, for the purpose of paying third parties with whom Rothmans' adverts had been placed. In *Re EVTR*[302] a resulting trust was found where a loan had been made to a company in financial difficulties for the purchase of new machinery.

(b) Money not at free disposal of recipient

It is not enough that it is intended the money should be used in a particular way. The terms of the transfer must be such that the money is not at the free disposal of the recipient.[303] In *First City Monument Bank Plc v Zumax Nigeria Ltd*,[304] Zumax paid money into a bank account with the purpose of transferring funds to Nigeria. The transfers did not in fact occur but Zumax was still unable to establish that there was a trust. The problem for Zumax was that bank had free disposal. The basic relationship between customer and bank is creditor and debtor. When money is paid into an account the bank can normally do as it pleases with that specific capital. Another way of putting this is that the money must be advanced on such terms or in such circumstances that it was made objectively clear 'that the funds transferred should not be part of the general assets of the recipient but should be used *exclusively* to effect particular identified payments'.[305] The recipient must be party to this agreement or understanding.[306] If the funds are at the free disposal of the recipient, there cannot be a *Quistclose* trust.[307] The effect of this requirement is

[293] [2012] EWCA Civ 1466 at 14 and 15. The criteria are drawn from the first instance judgment of Norris J.

[294] *Gore v Mishcon de Reya* [2015] EWHC 164 (Ch); *Challinor v Juliet Bellis & Co* [2013] EWHC 347 (Ch); *Eleftheriou v Costi* [2013] EWHC 2168 (Ch); *Brown v Innovatorone Plc* [2012] EWHC 1321 (Comm).

[295] *Harlequin Property (SVG) Ltd v O'Halloran* [2013] IEHC 362.

[296] [2015] EWCA Civ 59 at 56 and following.

[297] In *Patel v Mirza* [2013] EWHC 1892 (Ch) at 40 (bet to be placed on behalf of principal); *G v A* [2009] EWHC 11 (Fam) (moneys payable for a particular purpose by way of financial provision on divorce).

[298] *Wise v Jimenez* [2014] WTLR 163 and *Brown v Innovatorone Plc* [2012] EWHC 1321 (Comm) (trust established); *Bieber v Teathers Ltd* [2012] EWCA Civ 1466 (trust not established).

[299] See *Gabriel v Little* [2013] EWCA Civ 1513 at 20 and 41; *Soutzos v Asombang* [2010] EWHC 842 (Ch) at 144.

[300] There does not have to be a contractual agreement between the parties. See *Patel v Barlow's Solicitors and others* [2020] 2753 (Ch) in which a third party advanced monies to a firm of solicitors which negligently passed them on. In those circumstances the monies were still found to be subject to a *Quistclose* trust.

[301] [1985] Ch 207. [302] [1987] BCLC 646.

[303] *Bellis v Challinor* [2015] EWCA Civ 59 at 63.

[304] *First City Monument Bank Plc v Zumax Nigeria Ltd* [2019] EWCA Civ 294.

[305] *Bieber v Teathers Ltd* [2012] EWCA Civ 1466 at 14 and 15.

[306] *Challinor v Juliet Bellis & Co* [2013] EWHC 347 (Ch) at 552.

[307] *Re Goldcorp Exchange* [1995] 1 AC 74.

that the words or circumstances show an objective intention to create a trust because it demonstrates that the transfer was not meant to give the recipient the whole legal and beneficial interest.[308]

(c) High level of certainty

It is also necessary that the particular purpose must be specified in terms which enable a court to say whether a given application of the money does or does not fall within its terms.[309] This is important to enable it to be identified whether the recipient has acted within the mandate or power and at what point the trust ceases. However, in *Twinsectra Ltd v Yardley*, the purpose was expressed in relatively vague terms, namely, that the money was only to be used for the 'acquisition of property',[310] without specifying the particular property to be acquired. Carnwath J at first instance thought this too uncertain. In the House of Lords, Lord Millett held that the undertaking was stated with sufficient certainty:

> Provided that the power is stated with sufficient clarity for the court to be able to determine whether it is still capable of being carried out or whether the money has been misapplied, it is sufficiently certain to be enforced. If it is uncertain, however, then the borrower has no authority to make any use of the trust money at all and must return it to the lender under the resulting trust.[311]

(d) Unused funds to be returned

It is a corollary of the requirement that the funds can be used only for a specified purpose that they should be returned to the extent that they have not been used in that way. If only part of the money is properly applied, a resulting trust will apply to the remaining balance.[312] If all the funds have been properly applied, any trust comes to an end.

It is possible for there to be a contractual obligation to refund any excess payment even if there is no *Quistclose* trust.[313] For instance, a security deposit payable to a car hire company is returnable under the terms of the contract even though there is no question of any trust being involved.

(e) Existence of trust must be compatible with terms of business

No *Quistclose* trust can arise if it is excluded by the terms of business between the parties. For instance, in *Bieber v Teathers Ltd*,[314] the agreement between the parties was that the funds allegedly subject to a *Quistclose* trust were to be held as partnership assets. That was incompatible with there being a resulting trust.

> Once the partnership was in existence and their subscriptions had been paid into the partnership account . . . each investor's beneficial ownership of his or her individual subscription ceased and was replaced with a right to participate in the profits of the partnership and in its net assets on dissolution.

In *Bellis v Challinor*[315] the Court of Appeal held that no *Quistclose* trust arose where solicitors received funds into their client account, because under the terms of the arrangement, they did so as agents for a third party.

[308] *Bellis v Challinor* [2015] EWCA Civ 59 at 60–65.

[309] *Twinsectra Ltd v Yardley* [2002] 2 All ER 377 at 16; *Bieber v Teathers Ltd* [2012] EWCA Civ 1466 at 14.

[310] [2002] 2 All ER 377.

[311] [2002] 2 All ER 377 at 101.

[312] *Latimer v Commissioner of Inland Revenue* [2004] 2 AC 164.

[313] *Carman v Bucci* [2013] EWHC 2371 (Ch) per Warren J at 94.

[314] [2012] EWCA Civ 1466 at 59.

[315] *Challinor v Juliet Bellis & Co* [2015] EWCA Civ 59. See Hedlund and Rhodes, 'Loan or commercial trust? The continuing mischief of the Quistclose trust' [2017] Conv 254.

(f) Money kept in a separate bank account?

In both *Quistclose* and *Carreras Rothmans*, the money lent was kept in a separate bank account.[316] However, while this is obviously extremely clear evidence that the money is intended for the specified purpose only,[317] it is not essential. In *Re EVTR*,[318] *Twinsectra Ltd v Yardley*,[319] and *Re Lehman Bros International (Europe)*,[320] a trust was found even though the money was held in a general account rather than a separate account. Conversely, in *First Personnel Services Ltd v Halfords Ltd*,[321] Jeremy Cousins QC declined to find a *Quistclose* trust under which certain payments for agency staff were returnable to Halfords because of:

> the complete absence of any provision for reconciliations as to sums now said to have been due to Halfords, and the absence of any prohibition upon FPS concerning the mixing of funds which it was entitled to treat as its own with those funds, which on Halfords' case, beneficially belonged to Halfords.[322]

Without a requirement for the money concerned to be segregated from the recipient's general funds, it is likely to be harder to establish the obligation to return them if they are not used for the specified purpose.[323] An unperformed obligation to segregate funds may provide evidence of a trust obligation. In the *Lehman* case, the firm had ignored the statutory rules for protecting client funds on a 'truly spectacular scale',[324] involving several billion pounds, and over a very considerable period. These rules required client funds to be segregated, and then to be subject to a statutory trust. No segregation took place, but a trust was still imposed on the funds. In some cases the lack of segregation may make it impossible to trace the funds subject to the trust.[325]

(g) The purpose has failed?

In cases prior to *Twinsectra Ltd v Yardley*, it was held that the resulting trust in favour of the lender only arises where the purpose, and, thereby, the primary trust, fails. In *Quistclose* and *Carreras Rothmans* this was when the borrower went into liquidation. The meaning of 'failure' was further considered by the Court of Appeal in *Re EVTR*.[326] If the explanation of the *Quistclose* trust adopted by Lord Millett in *Twinsectra Ltd v Yardley* is accepted, then it would be better to say that the trust subsists for as long as the purpose has not been carried out rather than arising only on failure of the purpose, since the resulting trust will simply remain in effect until the money is properly applied.

(6) Finding *Quistclose* trusts

Quistclose trusts are relatively rare because the requirements are seldom met in ordinary business transactions. The commonest instance where trusts of this kind are found is in relation to house purchases. When a solicitor or licensed conveyancer acts for a bank lending on mortgage, the bank normally provides the funds to the solicitor in advance of the date for completion, but with an express provision that the funds are to be held on trust for the lender until completion, released only upon completion, and returned if

[316] *Quistclose* trusts, arising in commercial contexts, tend to be trusts of money. However, in *Ali v Dinc* [2020] EWHC 3055 (Ch), [244], a *Quistclose* trust of real estate was found.

[317] See *Challinor v Juliet Bellis & Co* [2013] EWHC 347 (Ch) at 559–72 where payment into a solicitor's client account was held to be a very strong indication that it was held on trust.

[318] [1987] BCLC 646.

[319] [2002] 2 All ER 377.

[320] [2012] 3 All ER 1.

[321] [2016] EWHC 3220 (Ch) at 235.

[322] A similar decision was reached in *Gabriel v Little* [2013] EWCA Civ 1513 at 43.

[323] *Eleftheriou v Costi* [2013] EWHC 2168 (Ch) at 71.

[324] [2012] 3 All ER 1 at 48.

[325] [2012] 3 All ER 1 at 2. See Chapter 5.

[326] [1987] BCLC 646.

completion does not take place or is delayed.[327] Most cases treat this as an express trust, or do not characterize the trust at all,[328] but some have held that this creates a trust of a *Quistclose* type.[329] Even if express, the trust exhibits all the characteristics of a *Quistclose* trust.

9 Charitable trusts

The existence of special rules for charities—the cy-près doctrine—has already been briefly referred to. It is possible for a gift to charity to survive the failure of a specific application if the gift was made with a general or overriding charitable intent. The scope of this doctrine is considered in the Chapter 22.

10 Exhaustion of a fund

Clearly, the operation of a resulting trust requires that there is property to result. Where a trust has been completely performed (for instance, because the property has been transferred to the beneficiaries), the trust is brought to to an end. This does not prevent actions being taken against the trustees if they have committed any breaches of trust which have occasioned loss to the beneficiaries.

[327] These are found in the standard terms of the Council of Mortgage Lenders, used by most banks.

[328] *AIB Group (UK) Plc v Mark Redler & Co Solicitors* [2014] UKSC 58, *Target Holdings v Redfern* [1995] UKHL 10; *Bristol and West BS v Mothew* [1998] Ch 1; *Lloyds TSB Bank Plc v Markandan & Uddin (A Firm)* [2012] EWCA Civ 65; *Davisons Solicitors (a firm) v Nationwide Building Society* [2012] EWCA Civ 1626; *Santander UK Plc v R.A. Legal Solicitors* [2014] EWCA Civ 183.

[329] *LSC Finance Ltd v Abensons Law Ltd* [2015] EWHC 1163 (Ch); *Global Marine Drillships Ltd v Landmark Solicitors LLP* [2011] EWHC 2685 (Ch) at 23; *Twinsectra Limited v Yardley* [2002] UKHL 12.

10

Constructive trusts

1 Introduction

(1) When are constructive trusts used?

Two neighbours are interested in a plot of land which is coming up for sale by auction. They agree between themselves that, rather than bid against each other in the auction, only one of them will participate in the auction sale, and, if successful, they will subsequently divide the land between themselves. The neighbour who goes to bid wins the property but then refuses to divide the land. Can he get away with this behaviour?

Harman J, in *Pallant v Morgan*,[1] held that, although the arrangement was insufficiently certain to amount to a contract, the defendant had conducted himself in such a way that equity would intervene by imposing a constructive trust requiring him to give effect to the understanding.

This is just one of the situations in which constructive trusts are used to prevent unconscionable behaviour.

In some jurisdictions the imposition of a trust is seen as a form of remedy. However, English law recognizes only institutional constructive trusts: those which arise automatically as a consequence of the behaviour of the parties. The way in which they are used to allocate interests in a family home will be explored in Chapter 12. This chapter is concerned with the general principles and with other situations.

(2) What are constructive trusts?

A major obstacle to any analysis of the English doctrine of constructive trusts is the wide number of circumstances described by the term 'constructive trust'. This has led Sir Peter Millett to comment that 'the use of the language of constructive trust has become such a fertile source of confusion that it would be better if it were abandoned'.[2] It has been used to describe a range of situations as diverse as the remedy available against a fiduciary who has made an unauthorized profit in breach of his duty, to the creation of a trust where parties make mutual wills. At its simplest, the term 'constructive trust' describes the circumstances in which property is subjected to a trust by operation of law. Unlike an expressly declared trust, a constructive trust does not come into being solely in consequence of the express intention of a settlor. Unlike automatic resulting trusts, it does not fill gaps in beneficial ownership. Like presumed resulting trusts, intention can form an important element in its genesis. In *Westdeutsche Landesbank Girozentrale v Islington London Borough Council*,[3] Lord Browne-Wilkinson identified

[1] [1953] Ch 43.
[2] McKendrick, *Commercial Aspects of Trusts and Fiduciary Obligations* (Clarendon Press 1992), p 3.
[3] [1996] AC 669; [1996] 112 LQR 521 (Cape); [1996] CLJ 432 (Jones); [1997] LMCLQ 441 (Stevens).

a constructive trust as a trust 'which the law imposed on [the trustee] by reason of his unconscionable conduct'.[4]

(3) Institutional or remedial?

Although the terminology of 'constructive trust' is used throughout common law jurisdictions, it does not describe identical concepts. Different jurisdictions have developed widely differing views as to the nature of constructive trusts and the circumstances in which they come into existence. One of the most significant conceptual distinctions is between what are described as 'institutional' and 'remedial' constructive trusts.

(a) The 'institutional' constructive trust

An institutional constructive trust is a trust that is brought into being on the occurrence of specified events, without the need for the intervention of the court. The trust comes into being if the facts that are necessary to give rise to it are proved to have occurred. It exists from the time that the relevant events occurred.[5] For example, where a fiduciary receives a bribe, so breaching fiduciary duty, the bribe is subject to a constructive trust. The fiduciary receiving the bribe is treated as though he received it for the benefit of his principal. This is true by operation of law.[6] The court does not impose the trust based in discretion, but rather, recognizes that the beneficiary enjoys a pre-existing proprietary interest in the trust property. Since an institutional constructive trust does not arise from the judgment of the court, it is capable of gaining priority over any interests acquired by third parties in the trust property during the period between the creation of the trust and its recognition by the court.

(b) The 'remedial' constructive trust

In contrast to the 'institutional' constructive trust, some other jurisdictions have come to regard constructive trusts as one of a range of remedies to facilitate restitution where a defendant has been unjustly enriched at the expense of a plaintiff. Having found that there has been an unjust enrichment, the court can, in its discretion, impose a constructive trust over assets representing any remaining enrichment in the hands of the defendant if appropriate, or alternatively award a monetary remedy. A remedial constructive trust is imposed by the court, which does not merely recognize a pre-existing proprietary right. The trust arises from the date of the court's judgment and it will not therefore gain automatic priority over the rights of third parties. These characteristics of a 'remedial' constructive trust were recognized in *Metall and Rohstoff AG v Donaldson Lufkin & Jenerette Inc*,[7] where Slade LJ stated:

> the court imposes a constructive trust *de novo* on assets which are not subject to any pre-existing trust as a means of granting equitable relief in a case where it considers it just that restitution should be made.[8]

[4] [1996] AC 669 at 705. See also *Paragon Finance plc v D B Thakerar & Co* [1999] 1 All ER 400, 409, where Millett LJ stated that a 'constructive trust arises by operation of law whenever the circumstances are such that it would be unconscionable for the owner of property (usually but not necessarily the legal estate) to assert his beneficial interest in the property'.

[5] *Re Sharpe* [1980] 1 All ER 198 at 203, per Browne-Wilkinson J; *Zumax Nigeria Ltd v First City Monument Bank Plc* [2017] EWHC 2804 (Ch) at 82 (Barling J).

[6] *FHR European Ventures LLP v Cedar Partners LLC* [2014] UKSC 45, [47].

[7] [1990] 1 QB 391.

[8] [1990] 1 QB 391 at 478. See also *Re Polly Peck (No 2)* [1998] 3 All ER 812 at 831, where Nourse LJ defined a remedial constructive trust as 'an order of the court granting, by way of remedy, a proprietary right to someone who, beforehand, had no proprietary right'.

At present, despite some dicta in cases to the contrary,[9] English law only recognizes the 'institutional' constructive trust and has not been willing to adopt the remedial constructive trust,[10] although the phrase has been used to describe the personal liability of a person 'required by equity to account as if they were trustees or fiduciaries, although they are not'.[11] Other jurisdictions, in particular Canada, have adopted an unjust enrichment analysis to explain the availability of constructive trusts, and the operation of the remedial constructive trust will be examined in detail at the end of this chapter.

(4) **The search for a coherent theory**

Given that the terminology of constructive trusts is utilized in so many different contexts, it is difficult to provide any coherent unifying theory that will adequately explain their incidence. English law has tended to take the view that constructive trusts arise in a range of relatively well circumscribed conditions in which the trustee's conduct is considered unconscionable. The focus is normally on the conduct of the party who is required to hold property subject to the constructive trust. Constructive trusts are imposed by equity in order to satisfy the demands of justice and good conscience,[12] and where it would be unjust to allow the trustee to assert an absolute entitlement to property. As Lord Denning MR observed in *Binions v Evans*,[13] quoting the words of an American judge:

> A constructive trust is the formula through which the conscience of equity finds expression. When property has been acquired in such circumstances that the holder of the legal title may not in good conscience retain the beneficial interest, equity converts him into a trustee.[14]

The concept of 'justice and good conscience' is too broad to be of direct practical value. The Privy Council in *Bailey v Angove's Pty Ltd*[15] dealt with the question of whether an agent permitted to receive funds on behalf of its principal, but with only a contractual obligation to account for them, would become a constructive trustee if, at the time it received any payment, it was aware that by reason of insolvency, it might not be able to pay the principal all that was due. It rejected the notion that 'good conscience' was enough to create a trust.

> Property rights are fixed and ascertainable rights. Whether they exist in a given case depends on settled principles, even in equity. Good conscience therefore involves more than a judgment of the relative moral merits of the parties.

It is, therefore, necessary, working from precedent, to identify the circumstances in which English law will find that a constructive trust has been created.

2 The role of constructive trusts

Constructive trusts play a significant role in a wide range of situations. Later in this chapter we will be looking at the use of constructive trusts to prevent a person benefiting from a crime, to give effect to implied or imputed common intentions, and to enforce bargains.

[9] See, particularly, *Thorner v Major* [2007] 2 AC 432; *Clarke v Meadus* [2010] EWHC 3117 (Ch).

[10] *Bailey v Angove's Pty Ltd* [2016] UKSC 47 at [27]. See also *Metall und Rohstoff AG v Donaldson Lufkin & Jenrette Inc* [1990] 1 QB 391; *Westdeutsche Landesbank Girozentrale v Islington London Borough Council* [1996] AC 669; *Re Polly Peck (No 2)* [1998] 3 All ER 812; *Safe Business Solutions Ltd v Cohen* [2017] EWHC 145 (Ch) at 24.

[11] *Williams v Central Bank of Nigeria* [2014] UKSC 10 at 9; *High Commissioner for Pakistan in the United Kingdom v Prince Mukkaram Jah* [2016] EWHC 1465 (Ch) at 125.

[12] *Carl-Zeiss-Stiftung v Herbert Smith & Co (No 2)* [1969] 2 Ch 276 at 301, per Edmund Davies LJ.

[13] [1972] Ch 359 at 386.

[14] *Beatty v Guggenheim Exploration Co* 225 NY 380 [1919] at 386 per Cardozo J.

[15] [2016] UKSC 47.

It is worth noting here, though, the way in which constructive trusts are used in other contexts more fully explored in other chapters.

(1) Allocation of beneficial interests

As we explore in the next chapter, the so-called common intention constructive trusts are now the primary means for allocating interests in domestic property acquired through joint endeavours, whether by a married couple or by those in a cohabiting or other family relationship. They are also used where an intention to create a trust is ineffective because it is not expressed in compliance with the appropriate statutory formalities[16] (see Chapter 7), and in some instances where an intended transfer is incomplete[17] (see Chapter 6).

Secret trusts (trusts imposed on the recipient of property under a will) are usually explained as a special form of constructive trust. They are discussed in Chapter 18.

(2) Preservation of pre-existing equitable interests

Constructive trusts operate to preserve the interest of the beneficiaries of an existing trust, however created, if the legal title to the trust property is wrongly transferred by the trustee. We look in Chapter 38 at how it is possible to trace trust property into the hands of a third party. A person who receives misappropriated trust property in its original or substituted form will hold it on a constructive trust unless they are a bona fide purchaser for value without notice.

(3) Misappropriated property

Constructive trusts are imposed on those who acquire property by fraud or who have misappropriated it in breach of fiduciary duty[18] (see Chapter 35). In *Westdeutsche Landesbank Girozentrale v Islington London Borough Council*,[19] Lord Browne-Wilkinson said that a thief would hold the money he had stolen on constructive trust for the victim.[20]

(4) Receipt of an unauthorized profit by a fiduciary

A constructive trust arises when a fiduciary receives an unauthorized profit in breach of the duty of loyalty that is owed to his principal.[21] This is examined in Chapter 35.

(5) Personal liability to account

In Chapter 37 we look at the liability of strangers to a trust who have dishonestly assisted in a breach of trust or received trust property in circumstances where it would be unconscionable for them not to account for the benefit they have received. This is personal liability, often described as a liability to account as a constructive trustee. In *Paragon Finance plc v D B Thakerar & Co*,[22] Millett LJ considered that the terminology of constructive trusts was inappropriate to describe such liability. He distinguished between two

16 *Rochefoucauld v Boustead* [1897] 1 Ch 196; *Matchmove Ltd v Dowding* [2016] EWCA Civ 1233.

17 *Re Rose (Deceased)* [1952] Ch 499.

18 *Bannister v Bannister* [1948] 2 All ER 133.

19 [1996] AC 669.

20 [1996] AC 669 at 716. See *Twentieth Century Fox Film Corp v Harris* [2013] EWHC 159 (Ch), where it was held that while copyright materials (in this case, films and related media) could be the subject matter of a constructive trust, there was no proprietary right to the proceeds of infringement of copyright materials, as such a right was not akin to theft of property.

21 *FHR European Ventures LLP v Mankarious* [2014] UKSC 45.

22 [1999] 1 All ER 400.

categories of constructive trusts. The first category was those situations in which a person had assumed the duties of a trustee even though he had not been expressly appointed as such. The second was circumstances in which the defendant was implicated in a fraud. In respect to this second category of cases, he considered that the language of constructive trusts was inappropriate:

> The second class of case is different. It arises when the defendant is implicated in a fraud. Equity has always given relief against fraud by making any person sufficiently implicated in the fraud accountable in equity. In such a case he is traditionally though I think unfortunately described as a constructive trustee and said to be 'liable to account as a constructive trustee'. Such a person is not in fact a trustee at all, even though he may be liable to account as if he were. He never assumes the position of a trustee, and if he receives the trust property at all it is adversely to the plaintiff by an unlawful transaction which is impugned by the plaintiff. In such a case the expressions 'constructive trust' and 'constructive trustee' are misleading, for there is no trust and usually no possibility of a proprietary remedy; they are 'nothing more than a formula for equitable relief': *Selangor United Rubber Estates Ltd v Craddock (No 3)*.[23]

This call to abandon the description of constructive trust has not been followed, but the distinction between the two types of constructive trust was acknowledged by the Supreme Court in *Williams v Central Bank of Nigeria*,[24] which considered that Class 1 constructive trusts (in which the defendant held trust property) and Class 2 constructive trusts (in which ancillary liability was imposed on the defendant for dishonest assistance in breach of trust or unconscionable receipt of trust property) were governed by different rules relating to limitation of actions.

3 Preventing benefit from crime

(1) The principle that no criminal may benefit from his crime

It is a basic principle of English law that no criminal should be entitled to retain a material benefit derived from his crime.[25] As Fry LJ said in *Cleaver v Mutual Reserve Fund Life Association*:

> no system of jurisprudence can with reason include among the rights which it enforces rights directly resulting to the person asserting them from the crime of that person . . . This principle of public policy, like all such principles, must be applied to all cases to which it can be applied without reference to the particular character of the right asserted or the form of its assertion.[26]

The principle operates to prevent property coming into the hands of a criminal as a result of his crime, and instead deflects it to others who would be entitled in his place by forfeiting his entitlement. The potentially harsh operation of the rule was illustrated in *Re D W S (Decd)*,[27] where a person killed both his parents, neither of whom left a will. Following the forfeiture rule, the Court of Appeal decided that not only the killer, but also his son, was excluded from inheriting. The inheritance went instead to the couple's other relatives. The outcome of this case led the Law Commission to recommend that the rule be reformed,[28]

[23] [1999] 1 All ER 400 at 409. [24] [2014] UKSC 10.

[25] See Oakley, *Constructive Trusts* (3rd edn, Sweet & Maxwell 1996), pp 46–53; Goff and Jones, *The Law of Restitution* (5th edn, Sweet & Maxwell 1998), pp 802–14; Youdan, 'Acquisition of Property by Killing' [1973] 89 LQR 235; Earnshaw and Pace, 'Let the Hand Receiving It Be Ever So Chaste' [1974] 37 MLR 481.

[26] [1892] 1 QB 147 at 156. [27] [2001] Ch 568.

[28] *The Forfeiture Rule and the Law of Succession* (Law Com No 295, 2005), paras 1.14–1.15.

and these suggestions have subsequently been enacted in the Estates of Deceased Persons (Forfeiture Rule and Law of Succession) Act 2011.[29]

Where, however, a criminal has already received property into his hands in consequence of his crime, it will be subjected to a constructive trust in favour of those who would have been entitled to it in his place. Suppose, for example, a man kills his wife and subsequently inherits property that she bequeathed to him in her will. If it is later discovered that she was murdered, he will hold what remains of the property, or its traceable proceeds, on constructive trust. The imposition of this constructive trust has the effect of depriving him of the beneficial interest in the property, although he will continue to hold the legal title as trustee.

The principle that a criminal cannot benefit from his crime could have application in two main circumstances; first, where a person receives property by theft, and second, where a person acquires property (whether by succession or survivorship) from someone who has died in consequence of a crime committed by that person.

(2) Property obtained by theft

The principle has little practical application to the area of theft because a thief does not normally acquire legal title to the property that he steals.[30] Under s 28 of the Theft Act 1968, the court has power to order a person convicted of theft to return the property to its owner. The equitable rules of tracing may be helpful in following the property into the hands of a third party where the thief has disposed of it.[31] The process of tracing is considered in Chapter 38.

(3) Property acquired by a crime causing death

A person who unlawfully kills another will not be entitled to retain property received as a result of his victim's death, whether under the victim's will, on intestacy, or through the operation of survivorship in the context of jointly owned property. Similarly, an unlawful killer will not be able to recover under an insurance policy covering the consequences of the death of the unlawfully killed person. In each of these cases, the courts intervene to prevent the criminal obtaining a benefit. Alongside a long-established common law principle, s 1 of the Forfeiture Act 1982 also precludes 'a person who has unlawfully killed another from acquiring a benefit in consequence of the killing.'

(a) Must violence be used or threatened?

The principle of forfeiture by imposition of a constructive trust will apply where a person has received property from a victim he has unlawfully killed. Unlawful killing obviously includes murder, but forfeiture will not operate against a killer found innocent on the grounds of insanity, because such a verdict constitutes an acquittal.[32] It has been less clear whether forfeiture applies where a killer has committed manslaughter, which:

> [Is] a crime which varies infinitely in its seriousness. It may come very near to murder or amount to little more than inadvertence, although in the latter class of case the jury only rarely convicts.[33]

[29] This is discussed later in this chapter.

[30] A purchaser from a thief will obtain good title in only a few cases. See Bradgate, *Commercial Law* (3rd edn, Oxford University Press 2000).

[31] See *Westdeutche Landesbank v Islington Borough Council* [1996] AC 669.

[32] Criminal Procedure (Insanity) Act 1964, s 1. This is different from a sentence of detention for treatment of a mental disorder under the Mental Health Act 1983, which is consistent with a finding of guilt.

[33] *Gray v Barr* [1971] 2 QB 554 at 581 per Salmon LJ.

Rather than distinguish between cases of 'voluntary manslaughter' and 'involuntary manslaughter',[34] the law instead considered that the forfeiture rule would be applicable in manslaughter cases only where the killer used violence, or threats of violence, against his victim, even if the death was accidental.[35]

In *Gray v Barr*,[36] Mr Barr confronted Mr Gray believing that his wife, with whom Mr Gray had been having an affair, was present. He involuntarily shot Mr Gray after falling backwards while threatening him with a loaded shotgun. The Court of Appeal held that in these circumstances the principle of forfeiture should apply.

At first instance, Geoffrey Lane J had held that the forfeiture rule should apply if a person was 'guilty of deliberate, intentional and unlawful violence or threats of violence'. The Court of Appeal agreed.[37] This test was cited with approval and applied by Vinelott J in *Re K*,[38] where a wife had intended to threaten her husband with a loaded shotgun following domestic violence, but had accidentally shot and killed him when she removed the safety catch.

However, in *Dunbar v Plant*,[39] the Court of Appeal rejected the view that forfeiture only operates where deliberate violence, or threats of violence, have been used and concluded that it applied where a woman had aided and abetted the suicide of her fiancé. The facts of the case were tragic. Miss Plant, who was facing a trial for theft from her employers, decided to commit suicide rather than face the prospect of jail. Mr Dunbar, her fiancé, said that he could not contemplate life without her, so they agreed that they would commit suicide together. An initial attempt to gas themselves in a car failed, as did an attempt to hang themselves with cable. On a further attempt to hang themselves with sheets, Dunbar was successful but Plant survived. Further suicide attempts, including cutting her throat and jumping out of a window, were also unsuccessful. The case concerned the question whether forfeiture should operate to prevent her obtaining the benefit of Dunbar's life insurance policy, of which she was the beneficiary. Counsel for Plant argued that the forfeiture rule should not apply at all because she had not used or threatened violence against Dunbar. This was rejected unanimously by the Court of Appeal, which held that the forfeiture rule prima facie applied. Mummery LJ explained:

> In my judgment . . . the presence of acts or threats of violence is not necessary for the application of the forfeiture rule. It is sufficient that a serious crime has been committed deliberately and intentionally. The references to acts or threats of violence in the cases are explicable by the facts of those cases. But in none of those cases were the courts legislating a principle couched in specific statutory language. The essence of the principle of public policy is that (a) no person shall take a benefit resulting from a crime committed by him or her resulting in the death of the victim and (b) the nature of the crime determines the application of the principle. On that view, the important point is that the crime that had fatal consequences was committed with a guilty mind (deliberately and intentionally). The particular means used to commit the crime (whether violent or non-violent) are not a necessary ingredient of the rule.[40]

[34] Voluntary manslaughter is where what would otherwise be murder is reduced to manslaughter by provocation or diminished responsibility, or because the death occurred in pursuance of a suicide pact. Involuntary manslaughter is where an unlawful killing is reduced to manslaughter because there was no intent to kill or to do grievous bodily harm—see *Re K* [1985] Ch 85 at 98.

[35] There was some earlier evidence that forfeiture might be inapplicable to manslaughter in death through reckless driving cases, as drivers were held able to claim on insurance policies—see *Tinline v White Cross Insurance Association Ltd* [1921] 3 KB 327; *James v British General Insurance Co Ltd* [1927] 2 KB 311. However, in such cases of 'motor manslaughter', the forfeiture rule has applied if the driver's conduct had been wilful—see *Hardy v Motor Insurers' Bureau* [1964] 2 QB 745.

[36] [1971] 2 QB 554. [37] [1971] 2 QB 554 at 581 per Salmon LJ.

[38] [1985] 2 WLR 262 at 276. [39] [1998] Ch 412.

[40] [1997] 4 All ER 289 at 300. Mummery LJ cited the Canadian case *Whitelaw v Wilson* [1934] OR 415, where it had been held that the forfeiture rule applied to the survivor of a suicide pact in which a husband and wife both drank poison.

Given that violence was not required, it was held that the forfeiture rule operated where the offence of aiding and abetting suicide contrary to s 2(1) of the Suicide Act 1961 had been committed in the context of a suicide pact. Miss Plant had encouraged Dunbar to commit suicide, thus committing the offence and attracting the operation of the forfeiture rule. In *Dalton v Latham*,[41] Patten J held that *Dunbar v Plant*:

> must now be taken to be a binding statement of the law as to the application of the rule of public policy. It applies to all cases of unlawful killing, including manslaughter by reason of diminished responsibility or by reason of provocation. The only possible exception is where the defendant is found to be criminally insane, which leads to an acquittal . . .[42]

The forfeiture rule applied in *Dalton v Latham*, where the claimant was acquitted of murder on the grounds of diminished responsibility but pleaded guilty to manslaughter. It was also applied in *Land v Land*[43] to a man, assessed as probably having a developmental disorder, who had pleaded guilty to manslaughter after failing to call for medical assistance to aid his domineering mother, who was terminally ill and bedridden with breast cancer.

It is not necessary that there should have been a trial and conviction. The forfeiture rule was thought to apply, although it was not ultimately enforced, in *Re Ninian*,[44] where a widow who was the beneficiary of her husband's estate, had assisted the suicide of her husband. He was 80 years old and had an incurable progressive disease. She accompanied him to Dignitas in Switzerland, helping with the administration of his death through the provision of a birth certificate and passport. The forfeiture rule was *prima facie* applicable even though the Crown Prosecution Service decided not to prosecute, meaning that the widow had no conviction.[45] It might also be the case that no conviction is possible because the person who committed the crime has committed suicide.[46] In *Gray v Barr*,[47] the Court of Appeal held that the forfeiture rule should apply even though Mr Barr had been acquitted at trial of both murder and manslaughter. In the civil trial, the lower evidential standard of the 'balance of probabilities' applied. For this reason, Lord Denning MR was able to conclude: 'there is no doubt, to my mind, that Mr Barr was guilty of manslaughter'.[48]

(b) Forfeiture of entitlement under the victim's will

Where the forfeiture rule applies, a criminal will not, *prima face*, be permitted to derive any benefit under the will of his victim.[49] This can be illustrated by the sad and dramatic facts of *Re Amos*,[50] where a married couple had set off by car to attend a funeral in Canterbury. After driving for around 10 hours, the wife did not brake when approaching traffic. She became unconscious upon collision but her husband was killed. She could not remember why she had not braked. In these distressing circumstances, the wife accepted that she had caused death by careless driving, which is a criminal offence.[51] In that context the forfeiture rule applied, prima facie preventing her from benefiting from the transfer of the matrimonial home under her husband's will.[52] The case was the first time that forfeiture had been considered in the context of careless driving and it seems likely that the decision will be of significance in years to come.

41 [2003] EWHC 796.

42 [2003] EWHC 796 at 9. Applied in *Chadwick v Collinson* [2014] EWHC 3055 (Ch) at 25.

43 [2006] EWHC 2069.

44 [2019] EWHC 297 (Ch).

45 The widow did not forfeit the estate even while it held the rule was held to be applicable. The court permitted her relief under section 2(1) of the Forfeiture Act 1982.

46 See *Re Sigsworth* [1935] Ch 89.

47 [1971] 2 QB 554.

48 [1971] 2 QB 554 at 568.

49 *Re Sigworth* [1935] Ch 89. See also *Re Callaway* [1956] Ch 559; *Re Peacock* [1957] Ch 310.

50 [2020] EWHC 1063 (Ch).

51 Section 2B of the Road Traffic Act 2006. Inserted by s 20, Road Safety Act 2006.

52 On the basis that it would be unjust for the rule to apply, the court permitted relief under s 2(1) of the Forfeiture Act 1982 and so the widow inherited under the will.

(c) Forfeiture of entitlement on the victim's intestacy

Similarly, the forfeiture rule operates to preclude the criminal receiving any property to which he would ordinarily have been entitled on the intestacy of the deceased. In *Re Crippen*,[53] Harvey Crippen was executed following his conviction for the murder of his wife, Cora. She had left no will. Before his execution he made a will leaving all his property to his mistress, Ethel Le Neve. The court held that Le Neve was not entitled to receive the property to which Crippen would have been entitled from his wife's estate under the rules of intestacy. The principle was again stated by Clauson J in *Re Sigsworth*:

> the principle of public policy which precludes a murderer from claiming a benefit conferred on him by his victims will preclude him from claiming a benefit conferred on him, in case of his victim's intestacy, by statute.[54]

(d) Forfeiture of entitlement by survivorship

Where property is held by co-owners as joint tenants, the principle of survivorship (the ius accrescendi) operates, so that the property vests automatically in the surviving joint tenant or tenants. This will apply whether the joint tenancy is of the legal or the equitable title to property. Therefore, if Harry and Joan are the joint tenants of a house in law and in equity, and Harry dies, the title will vest automatically in Joan. It will make no difference if he had left all his property by will to charity, as the operation of survivorship takes precedence over the disposition by will. However, if Joan unlawfully killed Harry and survivorship were allowed to operate, she would benefit from her crime. Therefore, the forfeiture rule is applied and the principle of survivorship will not operate between the joint tenants.[55] In *Re K*,[56] Vinelott J held that the principle of forfeiture applied so that a wife who was guilty of the manslaughter of her husband was not entitled to their jointly owned matrimonial home by the operation of survivorship between them. Instead, she held the house on trust for herself and her husband's next of kin in equal shares as tenants-in-common.[57] Similarly, in *Dunbar v Plant*,[58] the forfeiture rule prima facie excluded the operation of survivorship in respect of a jointly owned house.

(e) Rights under pre-existing trusts

Forfeiture does not apply to interests under a trust, constituted before the death, of which the killer was a beneficiary, even in respect of allocations made after the death. The killer's interest does not arise or result from the death.[59] It would probably be different if the interest is created or enlarged by the death.

(4) The court's jurisdiction to grant relief from forfeiture

Although the forfeiture rule prima facie applies where a person has died in consequence of a crime, under the Forfeiture Act 1982, the court has the discretion to grant relief from the effects of the rule. Section 2(1) provides that where the forfeiture rule has precluded a person who has unlawfully killed another from acquiring any interest in property: 'the

[53] [1911] P 108. [54] [1935] Ch 89 at 92.

[55] It should be noted that the rule does not deprive the killer of his or her own presumptive share under the joint tenancy. [56] [1985] Ch 85.

[57] See also *Schobelt v Barber* (1966) 60 DLR (2d) 519; *Re Pechar* [1969] NZLR 574. Although the forfeiture rule operates simply where there are only two joint tenants, it is much more complicated where there are three or more and one joint tenant kills another. See *Rasmanis v Jurewitsch* [1970] 70 SRNSW 407.

[58] [1997] 4 All ER 289. [59] *Henderson v Wilcox* [2015] EWHC 3469 (Ch).

court may make an order . . . modifying the effect of that rule'. This jurisdiction applies to property in the form of beneficial interests under the deceased's will, intestacy, a donatio mortis causa, or under a trust. The section has no application to persons convicted of murder.[60] Under s 2(2) the court may only exercise its jurisdiction to grant relief if satisfied that:

> having regard to the conduct of the offender and of the deceased and to such other circumstances as appear to the court to be material, the justice of the case requires the effect of the rule to be modified in that case.

The jurisdiction was exercised in *Re K*.[61] Vinelott J held that the discretion conferred by the Act requires the court to investigate the moral culpability of the killing, and he concluded that, because of the tragic circumstances of the case, and the fact that a loyal wife had suffered grave violence at the hands of her husband, it was appropriate for the court to grant relief so that she would not be deprived of the provision which her husband had made for her under his will or of the matrimonial home under the operation of survivorship. He also considered that it was relevant to take into account the relative financial position of persons claiming relief under the Act and those who would be entitled if the forfeiture rule was applied.

In *Dunbar v Plant*,[62] the Court of Appeal also held that Miss Plant should be granted relief against forfeiture of the proceeds of Dunbar's life insurance policy, even though this was contested by his father. It was unanimously held that the approach of the first instance judge, who had sought to 'do justice between the parties', was an inappropriate approach to the exercise of the jurisdiction. The majority went on to conclude that, in the case of suicide pacts which were the result of irrational depression or desperation, total relief from forfeiture would be appropriate. Phillips LJ, with whom Hirst LJ agreed, concluded that there was nothing in the circumstances to require a different approach:

> The desperation that led Miss Plant to decide to kill herself, and which led to the suicide pact, was an irrational and tragic reaction to her predicament. I do not consider that the nature of Miss Plant's conduct alters what I have indicated should be the normal approach when dealing with a suicide pact—that there should be full relief against forfeiture. The assets with which this case is concerned were in no way derived from Mr Dunbar's family. They are the fruits of insurance taken out by Mr Dunbar for the benefit of Miss Plant.[63]

In *Land v Land*,[64] judge Alastair Norris QC mitigated the impact of forfeiture by making an order for the claimant under the Inheritance (Provision for Family and Dependants) Act 1975 as envisaged by s 3(1) of the Forfeiture Act 1982.

Relief against forfeiture is not automatic, and has been refused in cases involving brutal assaults or stabbings, even when the perpetrator has been provoked (as in *Mack v Lockwood*[65]), or was suffering from a mental illness which justified detention in a medium secure mental hospital (as in *Chadwick v Collinson*[66] and *Henderson v Wilcox*[67]). Relevant factors, in addition to the conduct and culpability of the offender, are the wishes of the deceased (if known), the value and source of the property in issue, and the financial position of the offender and the moral claims and wishes of those will acquire the property if the forfeiture rule is applied.[68]

[60] s 5. [61] [1985] Ch 85, Vinelott J; affd [1986] Ch 180, CA. [62] [1997] 4 All ER 289.
[63] [1997] 4 All ER 289 at 313. [64] [2006] EWHC 2069. [65] [2009] EWHC 1524.
[66] [2014] EWHC 3055 (Ch). [67] [2015] EWHC 3469 (Ch).
[68] *Dunbar v Plant* [1997] 4 All ER 289; *Chadwick v Collinson* [2014] EWHC 3055 (Ch).

(5) Reform of the forfeiture rule

Where the forfeiture rule operates, *Re DWS (Decd)*[69] established that neither the perpetrator of the offence nor anyone claiming through him can benefit under the will or intestacy. In this case a son had murdered his parents, who had died intestate. Clearly the son was disqualified from inheriting their estates. The Court of Appeal held that his illegitimate son was also unable to inherit his grandparents' estate because the rules of intestacy state that 'no issue shall take whose parent is living at the date of the intestate'.[70] Their estates passed to more distant relatives. This harsh consequence led the Law Commission to recommend that the rule be reformed. The Commission suggested that the forfeiture rule be replaced by a 'deemed predecease' rule,[71] so that the property of the intestate would be distributed as if the killer had died immediately before the deceased. The rule would also extend to situations where the deceased had made a will and the potential beneficiary is excluded because he or she claims through the person who killed the deceased.[72] The Estates of Deceased Persons (Forfeiture Rule and Law of Succession) Act 2011, which came into force on 1 February 2012, implements these recommendations by inserting a new s 46A into the Administration of Estates Act 1925 and a new s 33A into the Wills Act 1837. Neither of these provisions affects the operation of the survivorship rule in joint tenancies.[73]

4 Common intention constructive trusts

(1) Ambit of common intention trusts

One of the most significant areas of operation of the doctrine of constructive trusts in the past sixty years has been in the context of land ownership, and especially the ownership of the family home.[74] This is explored more fully in the next chapter, but it is worth noting here that it is in this context that an important form of constructive trust, called the common intention constructive trust, has developed. The trust is imposed on a landowner:

> if by his words or conduct he has induced the [beneficiary] to act to his own detriment in the reasonable belief that by so acting he was acquiring a beneficial interest in the land.[75]

This form of constructive trust has developed from the 'twin peaks'[76] of *Pettitt v Pettitt*[77] and *Gissing v Gissing*,[78] through *Lloyds Bank v Rosset*,[79] to the current leading cases of *Stack v Dowden*[80] and *Jones v Kernott*.[81] As we will see in the next chapter, this type of trust is largely a response to the problem of dealing with the allocation of beneficial interests in property acquired as a home through the joint efforts of cohabiting couples, and there is an argument that this kind of trust should be confined to that kind of situation. However, the statements of principle explaining common intention constructive trusts have not been expressed in terms confined to the family home, and there are cases in which common intention constructive trust analysis has been applied to commercial or investment property.[82]

[69] [2001] Ch 568. [70] Administration of Estates Act 1925, s 47(1)(i).

[71] *The Forfeiture Rule and the Law of Succession* (Law Com No 295, 2005), paras 1.14–1.15.

[72] *The Forfeiture Rule and the Law of Succession* (Law Com No 295, 2005), para 1.16.

[73] *The Forfeiture Rule and the Law of Succession* (Law Com No 295, 2005), para 2.29.

[74] See, generally, Stevens and Pearce, *Land Law* (5th edn, Sweet & Maxwell 2013) Ch 11, pp 322–56.

[75] *Gissing v Gissing* [1971] AC 886 at 905 (Lord Diplock).

[76] A description used in *Grant v Edwards* [1986] Ch 638. [77] [1970] AC 777.

[78] *Gissing v Gissing* [1971] AC 886. [79] [1991] 1 AC 107.

[80] [2007] 2 AC 432. [81] [2012] 2 AC 776.

[82] *Marr v Collie* [2017] UKPC 17 being a notable example. See also *Bhushan v Chand* [2015] EWHC 1298 (Ch).

(2) **Underlying theory**

The theory underlying common intention constructive trusts is that they arise to give effect to the mutual intention of the parties where it would be unconscionable for the defendant not to recognize rights which both parties intended to confer on the claimant. The same principle underlies the trust imposed in cases like *Lyus v Prowsa Developments*,[83] discussed later, in which the bargain is to confer rights on a third party. The *Pallant v Morgan* equity, which is also discussed later, has been considered by the House of Lords to be a form of common intention constructive trust.

In practice, in many common intention constructive trust cases, the defendant may never have intended to confer rights on the claimant, but acted in such a way as to encourage that belief on the part of the claimant. In that respect, they may be seen as trusts giving effect to reasonable and legitimate expectations which the defendant has induced or encouraged, much like the rights generated by proprietary estoppel, a doctrine with which common intention constructive trusts have an uncertain relationship. It has even been suggested that common intention constructive trusts could be entirely subsumed by proprietary estoppel,[84] an argument which is unlikely to find favour. The main distinction between the two concepts is that proprietary estoppel usually gives effect to promises to create rights in the future; common intention constructive trusts recognize rights which the parties intend to arise immediately.

(3) **Examples**

It is unsurprising that most cases involving common intention constructive trusts arise in a family context, because this is a context in which parties are more likely to make informal arrangements. Most of the recorded cases involve the family home, and those will be examined in the next chapter. However, common intention constructive trusts have been considered in relation to other property.

In *Rehman v Ali*[85] it was argued that a privately acquired property was held on a common intention constructive trust to be used as a mosque. The argument was rejected because there was no evidence of such an intention at the time the property was acquired, or subsequently. Similarly, in *Shield v Shield*,[86] a claim that a father held shares in the family company on trust for his son failed for lack of evidence of this intention. A successful claim was made in *Bhushan v Chand*.[87] Five brothers ran a number of businesses over a period of over forty years before falling out. They had acquired several commercial and residential properties, sometimes in the name of one brother, sometimes in the name of another. The understanding between them, never formally recorded as a contract or as a partnership, was that these assets were acquired for their joint benefit. HHJ David Cooke, sitting as a High Court judge, held that because the brothers had acted on this common understanding by working in the businesses without any formal right to a reward, the assets would be shared equally between them in accordance with their understanding, irrespective of the brother whose name was on the legal title. The judge expressly rejected the need to look at whether the brothers could have succeeded in claims based on proprietary estoppel or the *Pallant v Morgan* equity. The Court of Appeal held in *Matchmove Ltd v Dowding*[88] that an agreement between former friends relating to the acquisition of a plot of land was enforceable through a common intention constructive trust, despite not complying with the formalities required for a binding contract.

[83] [1982] 1 WLR 1044.
[84] Liew, 'The Secondary-Rights Approach to the "Common Intention Constructive Trust"' (2015) Conv 210.
[85] [2015] EWHC 4056 (Ch).
[86] [2014] EWCA Civ 1136.
[87] [2015] EWHC 1298 (Ch).
[88] [2016] EWCA Civ 1233.

5 Enforcing bargains

Constructive trusts are sometimes used to support the enforcement of bargains either because the bargain is inchoate and, therefore, falls short of being contractually enforceable or because common law remedies are inadequate.

(1) Specifically enforceable contract to sell property

From the very moment that a vendor enters a specifically enforceable contract to sell property, he holds it on constructive trust for the purchaser. The reason for the imposition of the trust in these circumstances is that the contract of sale renders the vendor subject to an obligation to transfer the property to the purchaser that will be enforced in equity by means of the remedy of specific performance. By applying the maxim that 'equity treats as done that which ought to be done', the constructive trust ensures that the purchaser is entitled to the equitable interest immediately, even though he will not become the full absolute owner until the vendor transfers the legal title in fulfilment of the contract. The operation of such constructive trusts was explained in *Lysaght v Edwards*[89] by Jessel MR:

> the moment you have a valid contract for sale the vendor becomes in equity a trustee for the purchaser of the estate sold, and the beneficial ownership passes to the purchaser . . .[90]

As seen in Chapter 4, such constructive trusts will most commonly arise in the context of contracts for the purchase of land, as the majority of contracts for the purchase of personal property are not specifically enforceable because the subject matter is not unique. However, if specific performance would be available, a constructive trust will arise. Such a constructive trust was found to have arisen in *Oughtred v IRC*,[91] for example, which involved a contract for the sale of shares in a private company. This decision was reaffirmed by the Court of Appeal in *Neville v Wilson*.[92]

From the moment of contract, a genuine trust relationship is created, so that the vendor holds the title of the property on trust for the purchaser. His duties are not the same as those of an ordinary trustee,[93] for example, he is entitled to retain profits arising from the property before completion of the contract.[94] However, he is under a duty to 'use reasonable care to preserve the property in a reasonable state of preservation'.[95]

The advantage of a contract for the sale of land creating an immediate equitable interest in the purchaser is that, subject to requirements of registration, the purchaser has rights which bind the property if it is transferred to a third party. The contract is, therefore, enforceable beyond the normal limits of privity of contract.

(2) Promise involving a third party

The rules relating to land law protect purchasers for value from certain rights affecting the land that have not been protected by registration. However, it has been held that if

[89] [1876] 2 Ch D 499; see also *Haywood v Cope* (1858) 25 Beav 140.

[90] Compare *Rayner v Preston* [1880–81] LR 18 Ch D 1, CA, where Brett LJ held that a trust did not arise; *KLDE Pty Ltd v Stamp Duties Comr (Queensland)* [1984] 155 CLR 288.

[91] [1960] AC 206. See also *Re Holt's Settlement* [1969] 1 Ch 100.

[92] [1996] 3 All ER 171; [1996] 55 CLJ 436 (Nolan); [1996] Conv 368 (Thompson).

[93] *Shaw v Foster* [1872] LR 5 HL 321; *Earl of Egmont v Smith* [1877] 6 Ch D 469; *Royal Bristol Permanent Building Society v Bomash* [1887] LR 35 Ch D 390; *Cumberland Consolidated Holdings Ltd v Ireland* [1946] KB 264; *Engelwood Properties v Patel* [2005] 3 All ER 307.

[94] *Cuddon v Tite* [1858] 1 Giff 395.

[95] *Clarke v Ramuz* [1891] 2 QB 456 at 459–60, per Lord Coleridge CJ. See also *Royal Bristol Permanent Building Society v Bomash* [1887] LR 35 Ch D 390; *Phillips v Lamdin* [1949] 2 KB 33; *Lucie-Smith v Gorman* [1981] CLY 2866.

a transferee of the land expressly agrees that he will honour the rights of a third party, he will be bound by those rights under a constructive trust even though it had not been properly protected on the register. This constructive trust prevents the purchaser taking advantage of his strict rights under the land law legislation. Such a constructive trust was held to have arisen in *Lyus v Prowsa Developments*.[96] Mr and Mrs Lyus entered a contract to purchase a house that was to be built on a new estate. The developers subsequently went into liquidation, and the bank that held a mortgage of the land sold it to another developer. This second developer agreed in the contract to take the land 'subject to, but with the benefit of the contract made with Mr and Mrs Lyus'. This developer subsequently sold the land to a third, who agreed to the same terms. The contract entered between the first developer and Mr and Mrs Lyus was protected by an entry on the register affecting sales by the developer, but this was not effective against the bank or a purchaser from it. Nevertheless, Dillon J held that the developers who had purchased the land were bound by the contract. They had expressly agreed to take subject to the interest and therefore a constructive trust was raised to 'counter unconscionable conduct or fraud'.[97] Dillon J stressed that the agreement was not a general agreement to take the land subject to possible encumbrances but a positive stipulation in favour of a particular identified interest.

The operation of such a constructive trust was further considered in *Ashburn Anstalt v Arnold*.[98] The Court of Appeal addressed, obiter, the question whether a purchaser could be bound by a constructive trust when he had expressly agreed to acquire land subject to a third party's contractual licence. The court accepted that a constructive trust could arise in such circumstances, but stated that 'the court will not impose a constructive trust unless it is satisfied that the conscience of the estate owner is affected'.[99] The mere fact that land was expressly said to be conveyed 'subject to' a contractual right would not suffice alone:

> We do not think it is desirable that constructive trusts of land should be imposed in reliance on inference from slender materials.[100]

It was suggested that other factors would be necessary to justify the imposition of a constructive trust, for example evidence that the purchaser paid a lower price for the land as a consequence of the express agreement to take subject to the interest. The essence of the constructive trust is the purchaser's voluntary acceptance of obligations in favour of the third party.[101] The appropriate test, following the Court of Appeal decision in *Lloyd v Dugdale*, is whether the purchaser has:

> undertaken a new obligation, not otherwise existing, to give effect to the relevant encumbrance or prior interest. If, but only if, he has undertaken such a new obligation will a constructive trust be imposed.[102]

In *Chaudhary v Yavuz*,[103] Lloyd LJ described the conditions which he thought needed to be met. First, he made clear that general words, such as that the transfer states that it is 'subject to' any rights of third parties, even if coupled with an indemnity clause, would be insufficient because these are standard terms in a contract of sale, often intended simply

[96] [1982] 1 WLR 1044. This case deals with registered title. The reasoning would be equally applicable to unregistered title—see further Stevens and Pearce, *Land Law* (5th edn, Sweet & Maxwell 2013), pp 118–19.

[97] [1982] 1 WLR 1044 at 1052.

[98] [1989] Ch 1; [1988] Conv 201 (Thompson); [1988] 51 MLR 226 (Hill); [1988] 104 LQR 175 (Sparkes).

[99] [1989] Ch 1 at 25.

[100] [1989] Ch 1 at 25 and 26.

[101] There is a clear analogy with cases such as *Bannister v Bannister* [1948] 2 All ER 133 and *Binions v Evans* [1972] Ch 359. See also McFarlane, 'Constructive Trusts Arising on a Receipt of Property *Sub Conditione*' [2004] 120 LQR 667.

[102] [2002] 2 P & CR 13 at 52, per Slade LJ.

[103] [2011] EWHC Civ 1314.

to protect the seller.[104] Second, Lloyd LJ said that he was unaware of any English precedent in which *Lyus v Prowsa* had been successfully argued to make binding on a purchaser of land an interest which could have been, but was not, protected by registration.[105] He felt that a party's failure to protect a registerable interest by registration could raise the threshold for proving a constructive trust. For this reason, he believed that what would be needed was 'express reference in the contract to the rights asserted by the claimant and an express provision requiring the purchaser to take the property subject to those rights.'[106]

In *Groveholt v Hughes*,[107] Richards J cited the dicta of Lloyd LJ in *Chaudhary* on the operation of constructive trusts, and concluded that *Lyus v Prowsa* 'must be regarded as being on the outer edge of circumstances in which a constructive trust will be found to exist'.[108] On the facts, Richards J did not need to consider whether to apply the criteria set out by Lloyd LJ because, even apart from this, there was an insufficient basis for finding an intention to impose the obligation alleged.

Whilst the juridical basis of a *Lyus v Prowsa* constructive trust is sound, the need for the trust is much diminished by the Contracts (Rights of Third Parties) Act 1999 which, subject to certain conditions, gives third parties a direct cause of action in respect of contractual stipulations made in their favour in contracts made by others.

(3) **Mutual wills**

It is a fundamental principle that a man is entitled to make a will leaving his property to whomsoever he chooses. Any will he makes remains revocable until his death. However, if two persons enter into a contract to execute wills containing agreed provisions, and the survivor subsequently changes their will, the court will impose a constructive trust on the property in the hands of the executors of the survivor in favour of the beneficiaries of the mutual wills. The doctrine of mutual wills is considered in Chapter 17.

(4) **The *Pallant v Morgan* equity**

Pallant v Morgan,[109] the facts of which were given in the introduction to this chapter, has given its name to a line of cases in which the courts have intervened to enforce informal agreements. They are sometimes called 'joint venture trusts' as they arise in the context of business relationships where arrangements between partners have not been formalized into contract. The decision has been followed and applied on a number of occasions, most notably in *Banner Homes Group plc v Luff Developments Ltd*,[110] a decision which was endorsed by the House of Lords in *Yeoman's Row Management Ltd v Cobbe*.[111]

In *Banner Homes* two companies (Banner and Luff) informally agreed to purchase a development site using a joint venture company established for that purpose, sharing the costs and profits equally. Heads of agreement were drawn up, but a formal contract was never signed. Luff decided to go ahead on its own, but did not inform Banner. The Court of Appeal decided that Luff held half of the shares in the joint venture company on constructive trust for Banner. Chadwick LJ referred to *Pallant v Morgan* and similar cases and concluded that 'what may be called the *Pallant v Morgan* equity' would arise where:

[104] See *Ridgewood Properties Group Ltd v Valero Energy Ltd* [2013] EWHC 98 (Ch).

[105] [2011] EWHC Civ 1314 at 61. McFarlane, 'Eastenders, Neighbours and Upstairs Downstairs: *Chaudhary v Yavuz*' [2013] Conv 74. See, however, *Bahr v Nicolay (No 2)* [1988] 78 ALR 1, where the Australian High Court found a constructive trust to arise in similar circumstances to *Lyus v Prowsa*.

[106] [2011] EWHC Civ 1314 at 69.

[107] [2012] EWHC 3351. Referred to in *Lictor Anstalt v Mir Steel UK Ltd* [2014] EWHC 3316 (Ch) at 286.

[108] [2012] EWHC 335 at 17. [109] [1953] Ch 43. [110] [2000] Ch 372. [111] [2008] UKHL 55.

(i) there is a pre-acquisition arrangement or understanding (which need not, and usually will not, be contractually enforceable[112]); (ii) the arrangement contemplates that one party will take steps to acquire a property on the basis that the other will also acquire an interest in it (and the acquiring party has not informed the other that it does not intend to honour the agreement); (iii) the non-acquiring party has, because of the arrangement, refrained from taking an action (such as bidding for the property itself) which is either detrimental to it or which gives the acquiring party an advantage.[113] Where these conditions were satisfied, 'it would be inequitable or unconscionable to allow the acquiring party to retain the property for himself, in a manner inconsistent with the arrangement or understanding which enabled him to acquire it.' Those conditions were met in *Banner Homes*. Banner had acted to its detriment in reliance on the arrangement with Luff by staying out of the market and without having been told by Luff that it was withdrawing from the arrangement.

The underpinning rationale for the equity remains in question in the courts. Most cases, including *Yeoman's Row* treat the *Pallant v Morgan* equity as a form of common intention constructive trust. The majority of the Court of Appeal in *Crossco No 4 Unlimited v Jolan Ltd*[114] (McFarlane and Arden LJJ) felt that the Court of Appeal was obliged to adopt this interpretation,[115] but Etherton LJ considered that it could not survive strong indications in *Stack v Dowden*[116] and *Jones v Kernott*[117] that the common intention constructive trust was to 'be seen clearly in retrospect as a specific jurisprudential response to the problem of a presumption of resulting trust and the absence of legislation for resolving disputes over property ownership where a married or unmarried couple have purchased property for their joint occupation as a family home'.[118] He preferred to view the *Pallant v Morgan* equity as being based upon a breach of fiduciary duty. Later cases have also provided support for the rationale that breach of fiduciary duty might be at the heart of the authorities, but have not been prepared to explicitly challenge the common intention reasoning in other cases.[119] A future shift in focus to a fiduciary underpinning might be thought to be a means to limit the applicability of the *Pallant v Morgan* equity. This is because people in business relationships often interact as competitors free from duties and obligations towards each other. With this in view, business people might best be encouraged to draft a clear contract in order to crystallize their shared intentions in a legally enforceable form. In *Crossco*, Arden LJ expressed this point by saying:

> For the law in general to provide scope for claims in respect of unsuccessful negotiations that do not result in legally enforceable contracts would, in my judgment, be likely to inhibit the efficient pursuit of commercial negotiations, which is a necessary part of proper entrepreneurial activity.[120]

(5) **Alternatives to constructive trusts**

Finding a constructive trust is not the only way in which the courts can enforce joint ventures. Chadwick LJ noted in *Banner Homes* that where a concluded contract has been made, specific performance might provide a similar remedy to the *Pallant v Morgan*

[112] See the discussion of this point in *Generator Developments LLP v Lidl (UK) GmbH* [2016] EWHC 816 (Ch).

[113] [2000] Ch 372 at 35–6. A shorter statement of requirements is given by Lord Scott in *Yeomans Row* [2008] UKHL 55 at 30. See also *Chong v Alexander* [2016] EWHC 735 (Ch) at 156, where two different formulations of the criteria can be found.

[114] [2011] EWCA Civ 1619.

[115] [2011] EWACA Civ 1619 at 120–22 and 128–30.

[116] [2007] 2 AC 432 at 40–6.

[117] [2011] UKSC 53 at 25, 56, 57, 61 and 78.

[118] [2011] EWCA Civ 1619 at 85.

[119] *Farrar v Miller* [2018] EWCA Civ 172, [32]; *Generator Developments Ltd v Lidl Gmbh* [2018] EWCA Civ 396, [72].

[120] [2011] EWCA Civ 1619, [133].

equity.[121] Likewise, he suggested that in some cases (for instance where a property had been acquired before the arrangement) a remedy might be available in proprietary estoppel.[122] Where one party to an informal joint venture 'freezes out' another, but the agreement does not relate to the joint acquisition or improvement of property, there may be a remedy based on unjust enrichment or *quantum meruit*.[123] Unjust enrichment was the basis for a remedy in the Malaysian failed joint venture case *Dream Property Sdn Bhd v Atlas Housing Sdn Bhd*.[124] There are differences between the approaches. In enforcing a contract, the measure of the remedy is based upon what the parties agreed; similarly, in cases of common intention constructive trust or the *Pallant v Morgan* equity, the starting-point, as indicated by *Banner Homes*, is what the parties informally agreed. The case law (some cases involving family homes notwithstanding) does not suggest that the intention can be modified in relation to what a court considers fair. On the other hand, in proprietary estoppel, the remedy the court awards is not necessarily what was promised, but what the court considers proportionate. Finally, with unjust enrichment, the award is normally based upon the market value of the benefit conferred rather than any higher figure the parties may have had in mind.[125]

6 The 'remedial constructive trust'

(1) Defining the 'remedial constructive trust'

It is generally accepted that English law recognizes only institutional constructive trusts under which the court recognizes (but does not create) an equitable interest generated by the conduct of the parties. There is little scope for flexibility, other than by manipulation of the criteria that must be satisfied for the creation of a constructive trust, and the nature of the claim predetermines the remedial outcome.[126]

In other jurisdictions, an entirely different approach towards constructive trusts has emerged. An equitable proprietary right is regarded as one possible remedial response to effect restitution where a defendant has been unjustly enriched. Restitution may be effected either by a personal remedy requiring the enriched defendant to pay a monetary sum equivalent to the value of the enrichment he received to the plaintiff or by the award of a proprietary remedy over any assets representing the enrichment in the defendant's hands. The essence of the 'remedial' constructive trust[127] is that the court enjoys the discretion to determine whether or not a proprietary remedy should be awarded. If the court exercises its discretion to award a constructive trust, the resulting beneficial entitlement can be said to have been 'imposed' by the court, which does not merely recognize a pre-existing proprietary interest. The plaintiff's equitable proprietary interest does not therefore arise from the facts per se, which establish a cause of action in unjust enrichment, but from the exercise of the court's discretion to award such a remedy.

121 He suggested *Chattock v Muller* [1878] 8 ChD 177 might be best explained this way.

122 He suggested that *Holiday Inns Inc v Broadhead* [1974] 232 EG 951 was an example.

123 *Benedetti v Sawiris* [2013] UKSC 50.

124 [2015] 2 CLJ 453; See, 'Restitution for the mistaken improver of land' [2016] Conv 61.

125 *Benedetti v Sawiris* [2013] UKSC 50. Although it was not necessary for the decision, a majority of the Supreme Court suggested that in some circumstances where the benefit was worth less to the defendant, an award might be for less than the market value of the services.

126 We explore in the next chapter how true this remains of constructive trusts of a family home.

127 See Birks (ed), *The Frontiers of Liability* (Oxford University Press 1994) Vol 2, pp 163–223; (1998) 114 LQR 399 (Sir Peter Millett).

(2) Development of the remedial constructive trust

The Commonwealth approaches to resolving issues concerning the ownership of the family home suggest a movement away from the institutional approach to constructive trusts, towards a more remedial understanding. The courts of Canada seem to have taken the greatest steps towards the recognition and acceptance of a general remedial constructive trust in both familial and commercial contexts, even in instances where the English courts would find an institutional constructive trust.[128] The best description of how the remedial nature of the constructive trust came to be recognized in Canada is found in the judgment of Dickson CJC in *Hunter Engineering Co Inc v Syncrude Canada Ltd*:

> The constructive trust has existed for over two hundred years as an equitable remedy for certain forms of unjust enrichment. In its earliest form, the constructive trust was used to provide a remedy to claimants alleging that others had made profits at their expense. Where the claimant could show the existence of a fiduciary relationship between the claimant and the person taking advantage of the claimant, the courts were receptive . . . Equity would not countenance the abuse of the trust and confidence inherent in a fiduciary relationship and imposed trust obligations on those who profited from abusing their position of loyalty. The doctrine was gradually extended to apply to situations where other persons who were not in a fiduciary relationship with the claimant acted in concert with the fiduciary or knew of the fiduciary obligations. Until the decision of this court in *Pettkus v Becker*, the constructive trust was viewed largely in terms of the law of trusts, hence the need for the existence of a fiduciary relationship. In *Pettkus v Becker* the court moved to an approach more in line with restitutionary principles by explicitly recognising a constructive trust as one of the remedies for unjust enrichment. In finding unjust enrichment the court . . . invoked three criteria: namely (1) an enrichment (2) a corresponding deprivation, and (3) absence of any juristic reason for the enrichment. The court then found that in the circumstances of the case a constructive trust was the appropriate remedy to redress the unjust enrichment.[129]

Several key points of this restatement of principle require examination.

(a) A restitutionary cause of action

The remedial constructive trust was first recognized in Canada as a means of dealing with property disputes concerning the family home.[130] It has been developed as a remedy for unjust enrichment.[131] It follows that, in the absence of an unjust enrichment, a constructive trust would not be imposed. For this reason a constructive trust was not imposed in *Hunter Engineering Co v Syncrude Canada Ltd*.[132] Syncrude ordered some specialist gearboxes from Hunter Canada Ltd, a company which fraudulently misrepresented that it acted on behalf of an American company, Hunter US. Hunter Canada placed a contract for the gearboxes with a subcontractor, Alco Sales and Engineering. When Hunter US discovered the circumstances they immediately alerted Syncrude and began an action against Hunter Canada for 'passing off'. Syncrude immediately terminated the contract with Hunter Canada, and paid the contract price into a trust fund from which Alco was paid directly. Hunter US argued that there was a constructive trust in its favour of the balance. This claim was rejected by the majority of the Supreme Court on the basis that, in view of the termination of its contract, Hunter Canada was not entitled to payment. There was therefore no enrichment which Hunter US could claim.

[128] *Soulos v Korkontzilas* [1997] 2 SCR 217, 1997 CanLII 346 (SCC); *Sun Indalex Finance, LLC v United Steelworkers* [2013] 1 SCR 271, 2013 SCC 6 (CanLII).

[129] [1989] 57 DLR (4th) 321 at 348.

[130] *Pettkus v Becker* [1980] 2 SCR 834.

[131] *Kerr v Baranow* [2011] 1 RCS 269; *Garland v Consumers' Gas Co* [2004] 1 SCR 629.

[132] [1989] 57 DLR (4th) 321.

(b) A range of remedial responses

Once liability has been established by demonstrating an unjust enrichment which calls for restitution, the court is entitled to select the appropriate remedy to effect restitution. It may conclude that a proprietary remedy is appropriate. Alternatively, a purely personal monetary award may be made. This flexibility was recognized by the Supreme Court in *Sorochan v Sorochan*, where Dickson CJC stated:

> The constructive trust constitutes one important judicial means of remedying unjust enrichment. Other remedies, such as monetary damages, may also be available to rectify situations of unjust enrichment. We must, therefore, ask when and under what circumstances it is appropriate for a court to impose a constructive trust . . .[133]

This remedial flexibility was similarly adopted in *Rawluk v Rawluk*.[134] McLachlin J explained:

> The significance of the remedial nature of the constructive trust is not that it cannot confer a property interest, but that the conferring of such an interest is discretionary and dependant on the inadequacy of other remedies for the unjust enrichment in question.[135]

This discretionary aspect of the remedial constructive trust was restated in *LAC Minerals Ltd v International Corona Resources Ltd*[136] Corona owned the mining rights over land, and approached LAC with a view to negotiating a joint venture to exploit mineral deposits. In the course of these negotiations Corona revealed results from their exploratory drilling, from which it was clear that adjacent land was also likely to contain mineral deposits. Corona sought to purchase the neighbouring land but were defeated by a competing bid by LAC, which proceeded to exploit the deposits alone. The court held that in these circumstances, LAC had been unjustly enriched by misuse of the confidential information they had received from Corona. The central question was as to the nature of the remedy. The Supreme Court of Canada emphasized that as the plaintiff's right to restitution had been established it possessed a remedial discretion:

> The court can award either a proprietary remedy, namely that LAC hand over the [land], or award a personal remedy, namely a monetary award. The constructive trust does not lie at the heart of the law of restitution. It is but one remedy, and will only be imposed in appropriate circumstances.[137]

The majority of the court held that, in the circumstances, a constructive trust was appropriate, and that LAC should hold the land on trust for Corona.

(3) Beyond unjust enrichment

The Supreme Court of Canada has recognized by a majority in *Soulos v Korkontzilas*[138] that remedial constructive trusts can arise in other circumstances, even if there has been no enrichment. In the case, an agent bought land in the name of his wife, despite undertaking to buy it for his principal. There was not enrichment in the case for the straightforward reason that the value of the land had fallen.[139] Nevertheless, the Supreme Court of Canada imposed a constructive trust. In coming to that decision, the majority identified four criteria. Despite the attempt to define the circumstances in which a remedial

133 [1986] 29 DLR (4th) 1. 134 [1990] 65 DLR (4th) 161. 135 [1990] 65 DLR (4th) 161 at 185–6.

136 [1989] 61 DLR (4th) 14. 137 [1989] 61 DLR (4th) 14 at 48, per La Forest J.

138 [1997] 2 SCR 217, [1997] 146 DLR (4th) 214.

139 For analysis of the case in context, see Chambers, 'Constructive Trusts in Canada' (1999) 37 Alberta LRev 173, 174.

constructive trust will arise, it can be seen that some of the factors remain discretionary. They are: (i) the breach of an equitable obligation by the defendant; (ii) assets in the defendant's hands resulting from that breach; (iii) a legitimate reason for the plaintiff seeking a proprietary remedy; (iv) no factors making a constructive trust unjust.[140] The case is a Canadian example of the imposition of a remedial constructive trust in response to the breach of duty of loyalty.

(4) **Difficulties**

(a) **No single coherent theory**

If remedial constructive trusts were limited to cases of unjust enrichment, this might seem to provide a single coherent theory justifying them. The Canadian courts' recognition of remedial constructive trusts required by good conscience affects this argument by showing the desirability of using constructive trusts to address a wider range of situations.[141]

(b) **Uncertainty as to the cause of action**

The use of a remedial constructive trust to address unjust enrichment and 'good conscience' requires a well-developed and well-defined concept both of what constitutes enrichment and when it will be unjust and of what is required by good conscience. Without this, the remedial constructive trust would evolve into the 'palm tree justice' that the courts have been so keen to avoid, and which was the prime reason for the rejection of Lord Denning's new model constructive trust. The Privy Council has rejected the test of good conscience as open to the objection of lacking clarity (although possibly appropriate in the context of a remedial discretion).[142]

(c) **Uncertainty as to the remedy**

Even once a case of unjust enrichment or breach of good conscience has been established, it is for the court to determine the appropriate remedy.[143] This creates an additional layer of uncertainty. In an analysis of the development of the remedial constructive trust in common law jurisdictions, Ying Khai Liew detects a 'minimum equity' approach.[144] This means that personal remedies must be considered to be inadequate before a constructive trust is awarded.[145] However, such an approach will be inherently discretionary. In *LAC Minerals v International Corona Resources Ltd*, the court was aware of the problems of uncertainty attendant on the remedial constructive trust. La Forest J observed that:

> There is no unanimous agreement on the circumstances in which a constructive trust will be imposed.[146]

The approach advocated by Goff and Jones, who had argued that a restitutionary proprietary remedy should be awarded when it is 'just, in the particular circumstances of the case, to impose a constructive trust',[147] was rejected unless further guidance could be given as to what those circumstances might be.[148] However, some guidelines were

[140] See also, *Sun Indalex Finance, LLC v United Steelworkers* [2013] 1 SCR 271, 2013 SCC 6 (CanLII).

[141] See Delaney and Ryan, 'Unconscionability: A Unifying Theme in Equity' (2008) Conv 401.

[142] *Bailey v Angove's PTY Ltd* [2016] UKSC 47 at 28.

[143] It appears that upon their imposition, courts treat them as having a retrospective effect: *Rawluk v Rawluk* [1990] 1 SCR 70, 92.

[144] Liew, 'Reanalysing Institutional and Remedial Constructive Trusts' (2016) 75 Cambridge LJ 528, 547.

[145] *Rawluk v Rawluk* [1990] 1 SCR 70, 107; *Peter v Beblow* [1993] 1 SCR 980, 988.

[146] [1989] 61 DLR (4th) 14 at 49.

[147] Goff and Jones, *The Law of Restitution* (3rd edn, Sweet & Maxwell 1986), p 78.

[148] [1989] 61 DLR (4th) 14 at 51.

suggested, and it was held that there was no need to demonstrate a special relationship between the parties as a prerequisite of a constructive trust, nor that there must have been a pre-existing property right. La Forest J suggested that 'a constructive trust should only be awarded if there is reason to grant the plaintiff the additional rights that flow from the recognition of a right of property'.[149] A number of factors were identified which may be relevant in determining whether to award a proprietary remedy:

> Amongst the most important of these will be that it is appropriate that the plaintiff receive the priority accorded to the holder of a right of property in a bankruptcy. More important in this case is the right of a property owner to have changes in value accrue to his account rather than to the account of the wrongdoer . . . The moral quality of the defendant's acts may also be another consideration in determining whether a proprietary remedy is appropriate. Allowing the defendant to retain a specific asset when it was obtained through conscious wrongdoing may so offend a court that it would deny to the defendant the right to retain the property.

Having considered these factors, La Forest J, with whom the majority concurred, concluded that a constructive trust should be imposed:

> [the constructive trust] is but one remedy, and will only be imposed in appropriate circumstances. Where it could be more appropriate than in the present case, however, it is difficult to see.[150]

However, the absolute certainty of the rightness of a proprietary remedy in this statement only serves to emphasize the presence of uncertainty, for whilst La Forest J and the majority considered that the facts provided the clearest possible case for a proprietary remedy, Sopinka J and McIntyre J dissented and held that a personal monetary award of restitution was sufficient to reverse the unjust enrichment.[151] This leads to the wider question of whether the law should tolerate this high level of judicial discretion. Bridging the academic impasse, Liew argues that the question might be reframed. For the author, the key issue might not be whether judges should be permitted remedial discretion but rather how such discretion might be constrained.[152] Looking at the Canadian approach, it would be wrong to say the judges have an entirely free hand. They have attempted to lay down rules and the doctrine of precedent restrains the law's development. From the perspective of legal certainty, it is perhaps an open question whether or not that is sufficient restraint.[153]

(5) **The rise and fall of the 'new model' constructive trust**

During the 1970s, Lord Denning MR advocated a novel approach whereby a constructive trust should be imposed simply to achieve perceived justice between cohabitants in the family home in acquiring an interest in land. He described this principle as a 'new model' constructive trust.[154] In *Hussey v Palmer* he expounded the nature and operation of such a trust:

> it is a trust imposed by law whenever justice and good conscience require it. It is a liberal process, founded on large principles of equity, to be applied in cases where the defendant cannot

149 [1989] 61 DLR (4th) 14. 150 [1989] 61 DLR (4th) 14 at 48.

151 See also Tang, 'Confidence and the Constructive Trust' (2003) 23 LS 135, who argues that a constructive trust should not have been imposed.

152 Liew, 'Reanalysing Institutional and Remedial Constructive Trusts' (2016) 75 Cambridge LJ 528, 549.

153 For further insightful analysis in favour of a flexible half-way house between the institutional and remedial constructive trust, see Virgo, 'The genetically modified constructive trust' (2016) 2 CJCCL 579.

154 *Eves v Eves* [1975] 1 WLR 1338 at 1341. See also *Binions v Evans* [1972] Ch 359; *Cooke v Head (No 1)* [1972] 1 WLR 518; *Hussey v Palmer* [1972] 1 WLR 1286.

> conscientiously keep the property for himself alone, but ought to allow another to have the property or a share in it. The trust may arise at the outset when the property is acquired, or later on, as the circumstances may require. It is an equitable remedy by which the court can enable an aggrieved party to obtain restitution.[155]

In essence, the 'new model' constructive trust was a trust imposed to prevent the legal owner of land being unjustly enriched by refusing to acknowledge that the beneficiary was entitled to an interest. The 'new model' constructive trust was derived from the American model of constructive trusts, as stated in the Restatement of Restitution:

> Where a person holding title to property is subject to an equitable duty to convey it to another on the ground that he would be unjustly enriched if he were permitted to retain it, a constructive trust arises.[156]

Lord Denning even claimed that in advocating the 'new model' constructive trust he was merely extending the concept that had been approved by the House of Lords in *Gissing v Gissing*.[157] In *Eves v Eves* he stated:

> Equity is not past the age of child bearing. One of her latest progeny is a constructive trust of a new model. Lord Diplock brought it into the world[158] and we have nourished it . . .[159]

However, on careful reading, his citation of Lord Diplock's comments was extremely selective and the House of Lords did not, as he claimed, suggest anything approximating to the 'new model' constructive trust. What Lord Denning was advocating was a form of remedial constructive trust, which arises as a remedy to correct a wrong, rather than an institutional constructive trust which arises on a particular set of legal principles.

The 'new model' constructive trust has been comprehensively rejected by the English courts. The main objection has been the absence of a coherent principle by which it can be decided whether the imposition of a constructive trust is warranted in any particular situation, which would lead to uncertainty and unpredictability in proprietary rights. After Lord Denning had retired, the Court of Appeal held in a number of cases that, whilst the actual decisions where he had advocated the 'new model' constructive trust could be justified on other grounds, Lord Denning's reasoning was inconsistent with earlier authorities. For example, in *Grant v Edwards*,[160] Nourse LJ suggested that Lord Denning's decision in *Eves v Eves*[161] had been 'at variance with the principles stated in *Gissing v Gissing*'.[162]

The main objection raised against the new model constructive trust was the fear that such an approach to proprietary entitlements would create uncertainty, and that decisions would depend on the personal moral feelings of the individual judge. This danger was clearly expressed by Bagnall J in *Cowcher v Cowcher*,[163] where he considered the argument that injustice could result from the narrow criteria required for a constructive trust by the House of Lords in *Pettitt v Pettitt*[164] and *Gissing v Gissing*:[165]

> In any individual case the application of these propositions may produce a result which appears unfair. So be it; in my view, that is not an injustice. I am convinced that in determining rights, particularly property rights, the only justice that can be attained by mortals, who are fallible and are not omniscient, is justice according to law; the justice which flows from the application of sure and settled principles to proved or admitted facts. So in the field of equity

155 *Hussey v Palmer* [1972] 3 All ER 744 at 747; [1973] 37 Conv (Hayton); [1973] 89 LQR 2; [1973] 32 CLJ 41 (Fairest); [1973] 36 MLR 426 (Ridley); [1973] 26 CLP 17 (Oakley); [1978] 8 Sydney LR 578 (Davies).

156 Para 16.

157 [1971] AC 886.

158 In *Gissing v Gissing* [1971] AC 886.

159 [1975] 1 WLR 1338 at 1342.

160 [1986] Ch 638 at 647.

161 [1975] 1 WLR 1338.

162 [1971] AC 886.

163 [1972] 1 WLR 425 at 430.

164 [1970] AC 777.

165 [1971] AC 886.

> the length of the Chancellor's foot has been measured or is capable of measurement. This does not mean that equity is past the age of child bearing: simply that its progeny must be legitimate—by precedent out of principle. It is well that this should be so; otherwise no lawyer could safely advise on his client's title and every quarrel would lead to a law suit.

This attitude was echoed in *Springette v Defoe*,[166] where Dillon LJ proclaimed:

> The court does not as yet sit, as under a palm tree, to exercise a general discretion to do what the man in the street, on a general overview of the case, might regard as fair.

The new model constructive trust was also initially rejected by some Commonwealth jurisdictions on similar grounds of uncertainty and lack of principle. In Australia, *Allen v Snyder*[167] doubted whether the new model constructive trust could be supported from *Gissing v Gissing*,[168] and the High Court rejected it in *Muschinski v Dodds*.[169] In New Zealand the 'new model' constructive trust was described in *Carly v Farrelly*[170] by Mahon J as:

> a supposed rule of equity which is not only vague in its outline but which must disqualify itself from acceptance as a valid principle of jurisprudence by its total uncertainty of application and result.

It is somewhat ironic that, as we have seen, these jurisdictions have subsequently adopted forms of constructive trust which are imposed as remedies to prevent 'unjust enrichment' similar to the new model constructive trust as Lord Denning described it.

(6) **Prospects for the remedial constructive trust in England**

(a) **Judicial attitudes**

The remedial constructive trust has yet to find a place in English law, although from time to time there are judicial statements which suggest that it might, one day, do so.[171] In *Westdeutsche Landesbank Girozentrale v Islington London Borough Council*,[172] Lord Browne-Wilkinson took the opportunity of rejecting an argument by Professor Birks that the rule of resulting trusts should be extended to suggest that English law may yet decide to adopt the remedial constructive trust:

> Although the resulting trust is an unsuitable basis for developing proprietary restitutionary remedies, the remedial constructive trust, if introduced into English law, may provide a more satisfactory road forward. The court by way of remedy might impose a constructive trust on a defendant who knowingly retains property of which the plaintiff has been unjustly deprived. Since the remedy can be tailored to the circumstances of the particular case, innocent third parties would not be prejudiced and restitutionary defences, such as change of position, are capable of being given effect. However, whether English law should follow the United States and Canada by adopting the remedial constructive trust will have to be decided in some future case when the point is directly in issue.[173]

However, in subsequent cases the courts have rejected any suggestion that English law should introduce the remedial constructive trust. In *Halifax Building Society v Thomas*,[174]

166 [1992] 2 FLR 388 at 393. 167 [1977] 2 NSWLR 685.

168 [1971] AC 886. 169 [1985] 160 CLR 583, 62 ALR 429 at 452.

170 [1975] 1 NZLR 356; (1978) 94 LQR 347 (Samuels). See also *Avondale Printers & Stationers Ltd v Haggie* [1979] 2 NZLR 124.

171 The possible existence of the remedial constructive trust was left open by the Privy Council in *Re Goldcorp Exchange Ltd (In Receivership)* [1995] 1 AC 74.

172 [1996] AC 669; (1996) 112 LQR 521 (Cape); [1996] CLJ 432 (Jones); [1996] LMCLQ 441 (Stevens). See [1996] RLR 3 (Birks).

173 [1996] AC 669 at 716. 174 [1996] Ch 217.

Peter Gibson LJ refused to impose a constructive trust where a defendant had obtained a profit by purchasing a house, which had subsequently risen in value, using a fraudulently obtained mortgage. An even stronger refutation was made in *Re Polly Peck (No 2)*.[175] The applicants, who were the owners of land in Cyprus, applied for leave, pursuant to s 11(3)(d) of the Insolvency Act 1986, to commence proceedings by writ against the administrators of Polly Peck International. They claimed that they were entitled to a remedial constructive trust of the profits which Polly Peck had obtained by wrongful exploitation of their land after it had been misappropriated by the Turkish Republic of Northern Cyprus. As Polly Peck was in administration, the grant of such a proprietary remedy would enable them to gain priority over other creditors. The Court of Appeal held that there was no prospect that the court would grant the order requested. To do so would impose a retrospective proprietary interest on the assets of the insolvent company, excluding those assets from distribution amongst the general creditors, thereby modifying the statutory scheme for the distribution of the company's assets under the Insolvency Act. Nourse LJ held that the remedial constructive trust could only be introduced into English law by an Act of Parliament.[176] He said of Lord Browne-Wilkinson's suggestion in *Westdeutsche Landesbank Girozentrale v Islington London Borough Council* that the remedial constructive trust may become part of English law:

> such observations, being both obiter and tentative, can only be of limited assistance when the question has to be decided, as it does here. There being no earlier decision, we must turn to principle. In doing so, we must recognise that the remedial constructive trust gives the court a discretion to vary proprietary rights. You cannot grant a proprietary right to A, who has not had one beforehand, without taking some proprietary right away from B. No English court has ever had the power to do that, except with the authority of Parliament . . . It is not that you need an Act of Parliament to prohibit a variation of proprietary rights. You need one to permit it.[177]

(b) The controversy revived?

In the light of these cases, some commentators have suggested that there is no prospect that the remedial constructive trust will be introduced in England.[178] However, the prospect has never completely disappeared. Lord Scott, using a technique reminiscent of Lord Denning, laid down a 'marker' in *Thorner v Major*,[179] which could enable courts in the future to adopt the remedial constructive trust. The House of Lords applied the doctrine of proprietary estoppel to compel a farmer to honour his promise to leave his farm to a cousin who had provided unpaid assistance for many years. Giving his opinion, Lord Scott, whilst concurring in that view, expressed his preference for using a 'remedial constructive trust'. He said:

> The possibility of a remedial constructive trust over property, created by the common intention or understanding of the parties regarding the property on the basis of which the claimant has acted to his detriment, has been recognized at least since *Gissing v Gissing*.[180]
>
> (see particularly Lord Diplock at p 905).[181]

[175] [1998] 3 All ER 812.

[176] This almost certainly underestimates the power of the House of Lords, and now the Supreme Court, to develop the law. No such statutory authority was required in Canada.

[177] [1998] 3 All ER 812 at 831. Nourse LJ placed particular reliance on the judgment of Lord Simmond LC in *Chapman v Chapman* [1954] AC 429.

[178] Birks, 'The End of the Remedial Constructive Trust?' (1998) 12 TLI 202; Wright, 'Professor Birks and the Demise of the Remedial Constructive Trust' [1999] RLR 128.

[179] [2009] UKHL 18. [180] [1971] AC 886. [181] [2009] UKHL 18 at 20.

This view is open to challenge on a number of counts. First, he has taken a view about proprietary estoppel that is not shared by his peers.[182] Second, he adopts a highly idiosyncratic view of Lord Diplock's comments, since the passage to which he refers has always been taken to relate to an institutional rather than a remedial constructive trust. Third, if Lord Scott is merely renaming the common intention constructive trust, then it is confusing and unnecessary. Finally, since none of the other Law Lords passed comment on this view, it cannot be taken to represent the view of the court.

Lord Scott's comments in relation to the possible existence of a remedial constructive trust in English law have been endorsed by the summary judgment of Warren J in *Clarke v Meadus*.[183] This case concerned a claim, through either proprietary estoppel or a constructive trust, to a beneficial interest in property arising after such interests had already been declared in an earlier, express trust. In holding that an express declaration of trust did not preclude a claim through proprietary estoppel arising as a result of promises and representations made after the deeds of trust were executed, Warren J noted that the constructive trust argument in this case relied on 'a *remedial* constructive trust, a juridical beast which English case law has set its face against'.[184] Nevertheless, he felt Lord Scott's dicta in *Thorner* lent 'support to the view that such a remedy should be available in cases of this sort'[185] and that:

> Proprietary estoppel and remedial constructive trust are simply different routes to the same result which is to give Mrs Clarke an interest in the property going beyond the half share which she already has . . . the authorities, in particular *Stack v Dowden*,[186] do not in my view preclude a remedial constructive trust once Mrs Clarke has jumped the hurdle of establishing the availability of such a remedy as a matter of English law.[187]

On the other hand, in *Cook v Thomas*[188] (an appeal on findings of fact concerning an estoppel claim), Lloyd LJ suggested that Lord Scott was 'on his own' in his view.

(c) The changing environment

There are changes in the legal environment which might open the door to the possible acceptance of a remedial style of constructive trust in the future. First, since the decision of the House of Lords in *Lipkin Gorman v Karpnale Ltd*[189] English law has recognized the existence of an autonomous cause of action in unjust enrichment, which has been consistently affirmed in subsequent decisions. The criteria for a finding of unjust enrichment are 'now well-established'.[190] A gateway for extending the remedies (currently only personal) to align with the Canadian approach has therefore been opened.

Another factor is that English law has stood against the recognition of a remedial constructive trust because historically certainty has been prioritized over discretion. There are signs that this is shifting. For instance, the development of the common intention constructive trust of the family home in *Stack v Dowden*[191] and *Jones v Kernott*[192] (discussed in Chapter 12) confers, under the guise of judgment, a discretion in many cases to do what the courts consider to be fair. Writing extrajudicially, Etherton LJ has suggested that the decision in *Stack v Dowden*[193] has introduced a remedial constructive trust in the family

[182] See the comments made by Lord Walker in *Thorner v Major* [2009] UKHL 18 at 67, on Lord Scott's observations about proprietary estoppel in *Yeoman's Row Management Ltd v Cobbe* [2008] UKHL 55.

[183] [2010] EWHC 3117 (Ch).

[184] [2010] EWHC 3117 (Ch) at 82 (the emphasis on the word 'remedial' is contained in the text of the judgment and has not been added).

[185] [2010] EWHC 3117 (Ch). [186] [2007] 2 AC 432. [187] [2010] EWHC 3117 (Ch) at 83.

[188] [2010] EWCA Civ 227 at 105. [189] [1991] 2 AC 548.

[190] *Benedetti v Sawiris* [2013] UKSC 50 at 10. [191] [2007] 2 AC 432.

[192] [2012] 2 AC 776. [193] [2007] 2 AC 432.

home by introducing a new method of acquiring a proprietary interest without the need for detrimental reliance, a change 'driven by social policy rather than strict adherence to precedent'.[194] Cynics might also suggest that there is no material difference between a remedial constructive trust and an 'ambulatory' institutional constructive trust where the shares of the beneficial owners remain uncertain and in flux until a decision of the court implying or imputing those shares.[195]

It should be emphasized that, despite these occasional expressions of judicial sympathy for the remedial constructive trust and the changing legal environment, the introduction of remedial constructive trusts would, for most judges, be a step too far. In an extrajudicial capacity, Lord Neuberger has expressed the view that the judicial acceptance of the remedial constructive trust would be to usurp the role of the legislature.[196] In his judicial capacity, Lord Neuberger rejected the development of the remedial constructive trust in the Supreme Court in *FHR European Ventures LLP v Cedar Partners LLC*,[197] where it has already been seen that the court developed the rule that bribes received by a fiduciary were to be held on an institutional trust. The current consensus is, as Lord Sumption said, on behalf of the Judicial Committee of the Privy Council in *Bailey v Angove's PTY Ltd*:[198]

> English law is generally averse to the discretionary adjustment of property rights, and has not recognized the remedial constructive trust favoured in some other jurisdictions, notably the United States and Canada.

[194] Etherton, 'Constructive Trusts and Proprietary Estoppel: The Search for Clarity and Principle' [2009] Conv 104.

[195] See the discussion of *Jones v Kernott* in Chapter 12.

[196] Lord Neuberger, 'The Remedial Constructive Trust: Fact or Fiction' presented on 10 August 2014 to the Banking Services and Finance Law Association Conference, Queenstown New Zealand, [6].

[197] [2014] UKSC 45, [47].

[198] [2016] UKSC 47 at 27.

PART IV

Equity in Action: The Family Home

11. The family home in context ... 267
12. Determining interests in the family home through trusts ... 273
13. The evolution of rights in the family home ... 297
14. Proprietary estoppel ... 316
15. Family homes: Postscript ... 344

11

The family home in context

1 Introduction

In this section, we turn to a very real demonstration of the contribution of equity in modern times, showcasing that the flexibility of equity remains and can grow new approaches from existing principles to meet novel circumstances.[1]

When a family is living happily together, there are unlikely to be disputes about the ownership of the family home. However, where the relationship fails, or one of the parties dies, then the division of assets—including the family home—can be a deeply divisive issue. Where a couple are married, their dispute can often be resolved through the divorce legislation. Even then, equity may have a part to play, for instance, as in *Prest v Petrodel Resources Ltd*,[2] in resolving whether assets held in the name of a company can be treated as family assets or as belonging to one of the parties. When the parties are not married or in a civil partnership, the problem over ownership of the assets becomes even more of an issue, because there is no legislative mechanism for dividing assets between the parties on the basis of what is fair, just, or appropriate. Instead, the courts have to find another means of deciding who is entitled to what. Amongst the mechanisms that may be used are express, implied, resulting and constructive trusts, and the doctrine of proprietary estoppel (see Figure 11.1). The law has had to adapt to significant social and economic changes, and in adjusting to the new environment, there have been a number of step changes in the approach of the courts and, as we shall see, the results remain unsatisfactory both in the sense of doctrinal coherence and in the outcome for many claimants.

In this chapter we start by outlining some of the changes in society that have driven the development of the law.

2 The social and legal context

(1) The family home

The family home is much more than a financial asset, though it remains the key property asset that most family members will own in their lifetimes.[3] Individuals tend to have an emotive relationship with the place in which they live their own lives, and raise any children—it 'means more than just a roof over one's head.'[4] Similarly, it has often been the

[1] There are limits: see *Western Fish Products v Penwith DC* [1981] 2 All ER 204 at 218 per Megaw LJ: 'As Hardman LJ pointed out in *Campbell Discount Co Ltd v Bridge* the system of equity has become a very precise one. The creation of new rights and remedies is a matter for Parliament, not for the judges.'

[2] [2013] 2 AC 415.

[3] See O'Mahoney, *Conceptualising Home: Theories, Law and Policies* (Hart Publishing 2007).

[4] *Gandesha v Gandesha* [2020] EWHC 1743 (QB) per Andrews J at [60].

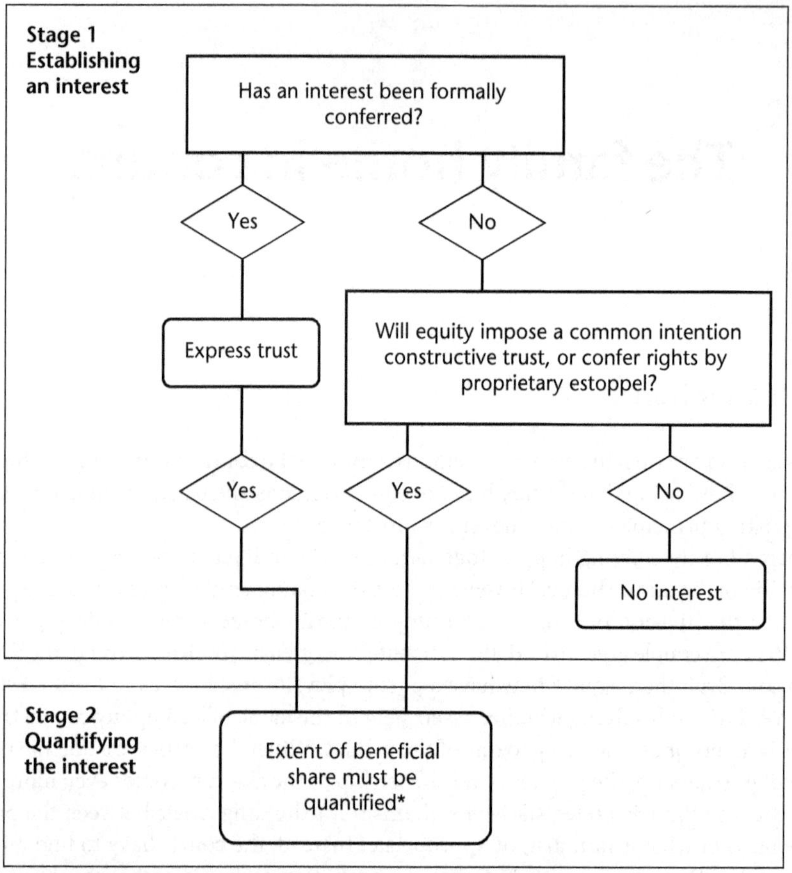

Figure 11.1 Acquiring an interest in the family home

case that people who live together in the household have not given appropriate thought to whether or how the home is owned between them. This may only become a reality when a relationship comes to an end, and one or both parties to the relationship want to leave the property or have the home sold.

For the purposes of discussion in this and the other chapters in this section, we will primarily consider cohabiting couples, in situations where the home (the property) is being shared by two people in an intimate relationship and the cohabitants regard the home as the family home. Other parties may have an interest in the home, as the rising cost of home ownership means that adult children may now live with parents or elderly relatives might live in the family home. Both may make contributions to the costs of running the home, and may be entitled to rights in it. The focus of this treatment remains the two adult partners in the relationship, but, as we shall see, some of the reported cases deal with these differing relationships but the applicable principles remain the same.

Similarly, one of the questions we need to consider is whether the same principles apply where property is bought by a couple as an investment, or whether the rules that have developed in the family home are applicable in the absence of a family relationship.

(2) **Ownership of the family home**

Before the Second World War, most people in Britain rented the house in which they lived. Nowadays, most people aspire to live in homes that are owned by at least one of the persons living there,[5] as evidenced by the 2014 British Social Attitudes survey which found that, given a free choice, 86 per cent of those surveyed would prefer to buy their own home rather than rent. However, while ownership remains the tenure of choice, in practice home ownership has been declining from the 2003 peak of 71 per cent[6] to 65 per cent in 2020.[7] The cost of home ownership is rising, which acts as a barrier; as of September 2021, the average house price in the UK was £270,000.[8]

(3) **The emancipation of women**

It is hard to overestimate the change in the status of women since the middle Victorian era. Before the Married Women's Property Act 1882, a wife did not have a separate legal existence to her husband, and, in consequence, property vested in the husband alone. During the first half of the twentieth century, the majority of matrimonial homes were purchased in the sole name of the husband, who generally worked to provide the family income while the wife brought up their children and took care of the domestic needs of the family. Divorce was less common than it is now, and it was often unnecessary to determine whether the wife had any independent interest in the property. The increasing recognition of the equal place of women, their growing economic contribution to marriage through their participation in the labour market, and especially the growth in divorce, made it essential to determine when a wife enjoyed a share of the ownership of her matrimonial home.[9] Under early divorce laws, the court possessed no jurisdiction to divide the matrimonial property between the parties. If the husband was the sole owner of the matrimonial home, it would remain his on divorce. Since the Matrimonial Causes Act 1973, divorce laws do now contain provisions for the allocation of assets between married couples on the dissolution of marriage, and there is also special protection for marital relationships on the death of one of the parties.[10] Spousal rights have been enhanced by other matrimonial legislation, including a statutory right of occupation in the family home[11] and division of property entitlements on death for spouses and family.[12]

Marriage still remains the dominant legal form for couples occupying the home, with some 12.985 million families[13] out of 19.4 million families in the UK being married or registered civil partners.[14]

[5] See Law Commission, *Cohabitation: The Financial Consequences of Relationship Breakdown* (Law Com No 208, 2007) Part I & II.

[6] English Housing Survey Headline Report, 2015–16.

[7] Wilson et al, *Extending home ownership: Government Initiatives* (HC Briefing Paper 036668, 30 March 2021).

[8] Office of National Statistics, *UK House Price Index: September 2021*, November 2021.

[9] See Cretney, *Family Law in the Twentieth Century* (Oxford University Press 2005).

[10] A discussion of such legislation is outside the scope of this book—see further Lamont, *Family Law* (2nd edn, OUP 2022) Chs 3 and 4.

[11] Family Law Act 1996, s 30(1).

[12] Inheritance (Provision for Family and Dependents) Act 1975.

[13] Office for National Statistics Statistical Bulletin, *Families and Households in the UK: 2020*. Note: this data is estimated due to the impact of the Covid-19 pandemic.

[14] Civil partnerships, originally open to same-sex couples who were unable to marry but now also open to heterosexual couples, are considered below.

(4) Non-marital relationships: cohabitants

There has been significant growth in the number of people living together as a couple without marrying. Over the twenty years to 2017, the number of cohabiting families more than doubled to 3.3 million families,[15] and as of 2020, this had increased to around 6.4 million unmarried cohabitants.[16]

(5) Same-sex relationships

The introduction of civil partnership[17] and marriage[18] for same-sex couples has enabled them to formalize their relationship with similar protections on the breakdown of the relationship or on death as married heterosexual couples. A higher proportion of same-sex couples live in unmarried relationships, and, on 2020 figures, 120,000 unmarried cohabitants identified as same-sex couples. The legal issues are the same whether a same-sex or opposite-sex relationship is involved.[19]

(6) Legal issues

The divorce legislation applies only at the end of a marriage. Questions as to the ownership of the family home can arise even where a couple are happily married, for instance, if the family home has been bought, as was traditional, in the husband's name, he has mortgaged it to secure a business loan, and his business has failed. The question may then arise whether the wife has a proprietary interest in the home, and whether it has priority on the bank. The divorce legislation does not apply to unmarried couples and there is no legal concept of 'common law marriage',[20] despite a sustained and mistaken belief of a large proportion of the population that such relationships are given special recognition.[21] There is currently no other legislation similar to the divorce legislation in such circumstances. A Cohabitation Rights Bill was introduced to the House of Lords in June 2016, with the purpose of enabling financial settlement orders to be made in respect of cohabiting couples, as well as for provision on death. This attempt, like earlier attempts, to change the law failed. This, and previous proposals have been controversial. The Law Commission proposed in 2011 that certain cohabitants should have entitlements similar to those of married couples when one of the cohabitants dies intestate. This proposal was not implemented. The Law Commission noted when making its proposal:

> There is no overwhelming consensus in favour of reform, and that is perhaps to be expected. For some people, the granting of legal rights to the survivor of an unmarried couple is simply unacceptable, notwithstanding that many cohabitants already inherit when a partner dies

[15] Office for National Statistics Statistical Bulletin, *Families and Households: 2017.*

[16] Office for National Statistics Statistical Bulletin, *Families and Households in the UK: 2020.*

[17] Civil Partnerships Act 2004.

[18] Marriage (Same Sex Couples) Act 2013.

[19] Although it should be noted that s 65 of the Civil Partnerships Act 2004 expressly provides that a civil partner who contributes in money or money's worth to the improvement of property will be entitled to a share, or an increased share, of the beneficial ownership of the property, either on the basis of what may have been agreed between the parties or in default of such agreement on the basis of what may seem just to the court in all the circumstances.

[20] Probert, 'Why Couples Still Believe in Common-Law Marriage' (2007) 37 Fam Law 403.

[21] The British Social Attitudes survey in 2006 found that 51 per cent of respondents believed that an unmarried couple who live together for some time 'definitely' or 'probably' have a 'common law marriage' which gives them the same legal rights as married couples: see Barlow, Burgoyne, Clery, and Smithson, 'Cohabitation and the Law: Myths, Money and the Media', in Park, Curtice, Thomson, Phillips, Johnson, and Clery (eds), *British Social Attitudes: The 24th Report* (British Social Attitudes Survey Series, Sage 2008) pp 40–2.

> intestate, through a claim for family provision. For many who take this view, the concern is that greater legal equivalence between marriages and civil partnerships on the one hand, and cohabiting relationships on the other, risks undermining the institution of marriage. We appreciate those concerns but do not share them.[22]

Without the intervention of equitable principles of unmarried cohabitants, normal rules of property law apply. Hence, if only one person appears on the legal title to the home, that person is considered the owner of the home, to do with what they like. The other cohabitant will have no rights or entitlements to the home at common law, even if they have lived together for a long time and made a substantial, financial contribution in making a home together and/or raising children in the home.[23]

The nature of home sharing also means that even when both cohabitants appear on the legal title to the property, so that they are both co-owners at common law, there can still be dispute as to their respective entitlements in the home. Indeed, as we shall see, many of the cases that have reached the courts have not been about whether a non-legal owner is entitled to a right in the family home, but instead the nature and extent of that interest.

3 The legal response

There are two principal ways in which the courts can respond to disputes about ownership of the family home. One is to apply the same legal principles in the same way, whether a dispute involves a cohabiting couple, other family members, or complete strangers (a property-based approach). The other is to treat the family home as a special situation which merits the application of special rules (a relationship-based approach). The justification for doing this is that family members are bound by ties which run much deeper than those between strangers; they are much less likely than strangers to assert independent claims to 'family assets' whilst their relationship continues; relationships and agreements between family members, particularly between cohabiting couples, are much more likely than other relationships to be formalized; the relationship is enduring and is likely to evolve over time. This is an area where 'the unattainable precision of property law collides with the casual inarticulacy of home sharing'.[24]

As a broad generalization, the way in which the courts have approached this issue was initially to apply the same rules to all types of property dispute, but now to recognize that the special characteristics of family relationships can justify a different approach. Like all generalizations, this is not wholly accurate, since family relationships have always been given special treatment in equity, as is evidenced by the presumptions of advancement in resulting trusts[25] and the way in which issue were treated as having provided consideration in a marriage settlement.[26]

The adoption by the courts of a relationship-based approach is not without some drawbacks. It raises the question of whether the courts have encroached on the legislative function of law-making. It also creates a boundary problem: if there are special rules which apply to the family home, do these rules apply to other property acquired by a cohabiting couple, for instance as a holiday home or as an investment? These are questions to which we will return throughout this section, but particularly in Chapter 15.

[22] *Intestacy and Family Provisions Claims on Death* (Law Com No 331, 2011) at para 8.36.

[23] If cohabiting couples have children, there is a duty to maintain those children and a property adjustment order can be made under the Children Act 1989—this is a matter of family law. See, for example, Lamont, *Family Law* (2nd edn, OUP 2022) Ch 6.

[24] Briggs, 'Co-ownership and an Equitable Non Sequitur' (2012) 128 LQR 183.

[25] See Chapter 9. [26] See Chapter 6.

4 Avoiding the need for judicial intervention

Most disputes about ownership of the family home would be resolved if the parties had formally recorded their understanding or agreement about ownership. This would not, of course, displace the jurisdiction of the courts to vary the arrangements on divorce or death, but it would avoid most of the difficulties that arise in other situations. The agreement would usually need to take the form of an express trust, since even where the legal ownership of the property is vested in the parties jointly, this does not automatically exclude the possibility of the beneficial interests being held in some other way or in unequal shares. In a surprisingly high proportion of cases, the arrangements concerning rights to the family home are not formally recorded, either through inadvertence or through ignorance.[27]

[27] See *Cohabitation: The Financial Consequences of Relationship Breakdown* (Law Com No 207, 2007); Cooke, 'Cohabitants, Common Intention and Contributions (Again)' [2005] Conv 555.

12

Determining interests in the family home through trusts

1 The current approach

In this chapter, we consider the current state of the law in the family home utilizing the trust mechanisms. Although the chapter can be read on its own, it is better to read it in conjunction with Chapter 13, which examines how the law in this area has evolved. This is not only because that evolution helps to explain the current approach but also because some aspects of the previous regime (such as whether mortgage payments are treated as equivalent to direct financial contributions to the purchase of the home) have been carried through to the current regime.

(1) Equity fills the gap

In the absence of legislative provisions dealing with some of the situations where disputes can arise, and, in particular, in assessing which of an unmarried cohabiting couple owns what, the courts have had to deal with the problems to which this gives rise. Equity has filled the gap. Equity has taken on this task because it is the best suited vehicle for addressing informal arrangements.

(2) The common intention constructive trust

(a) The leading cases

After using a number of other approaches (which will be considered in Chapter 13) to address this issue, the English courts have now adopted the common intention constructive trust as the mechanism of choice for resolving disputes relating to the family home. The starting-point for current analysis is the House of Lords decision in *Stack v Dowden*[1] and the subsequent Supreme Court decision in *Jones v Kernott*.[2] These cases have formed the foundation for a new approach which contains a much greater degree of flexibility than the previous approach. There have been enough decisions since the introduction of the new approach to confirm that it has become the new orthodoxy, although there remain a number of unanswered questions.

(b) Stack v Dowden

In *Stack v Dowden*, a couple had lived together for twenty-five years, and had four children. The original family house had been purchased by Ms Dowden alone, using £8,000

[1] [2007] 2 AC 432. [2] [2011] UKSC 53.

savings and a mortgage of £22,000. Ms Dowden paid all the mortgage repayments, and Mr Stack helped with improvements. On sale, title to the new house was registered in both names. The purchase was funded 65 per cent from Ms Dowden (proceeds of sale and savings), and the remainder from an endowment mortgage loan. Mr Stack paid the interest on the loan. Capital was repaid by lump sums, of which Mr Stack contributed £27,000, and Ms Dowden the remaining £38,000. The parties kept their financial affairs entirely separate throughout their relationship together. On the breakdown of the relationship, Mr Stack sought an order for sale and equal division of any proceeds of sale. The Court of Appeal had divided the proceeds of sale 65 per cent to Ms Dowden, 35 per cent to Mr Stack as representing a fair share of the course of dealings between the parties, with which the House of Lords agreed.

Baroness Hale concluded that this was an unusual case and that Ms Dowden had successfully rebutted the strong presumption of joint beneficial ownership created by the fact that title to the family home was in joint names. The couple kept their affairs 'rigidly separate',[3] and Ms Dowden had contributed much more to the financial acquisition of the property than Mr Stack had done:[4]

> This is not a case in which it can be said that the parties pooled their separate resources, even notionally, for the common good . . . they undertook separate responsibility for that part of the expenditure which each had agreed to pay.[5]

Mr Stack had not agreed to pay for 'consumables and child minding' so it was not 'possible to deduce some sort of commitment that each would do what they could'.[6]

(c) Jones v Kernott

In *Jones v Kernott*,[7] Ms Jones and Mr Kernott started living together in 1983, initially living together in a mobile home which Ms Jones had bought in her own name two years earlier. In 1985 the mobile home was sold, and the proceeds of sale were used as a deposit for a house in Thundersley, Essex, which was bought in their joint names. Whilst Ms Jones paid the mortgage (which was in joint names) Mr Kernott met most of the cost of an extension which significantly increased the value of the house. He also made a significant contribution towards the family's household expenses. The couple (who by now had two children) separated in 1993. Mr Kernott made no further contribution towards the house or household expenses (nor very much towards the support of the children). An attempt was made to sell the Thundersley house, and when this proved unsuccessful, the parties cashed in an insurance policy, and Mr Kernott used his share of the proceeds as the down-payment of another home of his own in Benfleet. There was no discussion about how the parties' affairs should be resolved until Mr Kernott in 2008 claimed a half-share of the Thundersley property.

There had been some difficulty in the lower courts in applying the principles set out in *Stack v Dowden*. The trial judge, and on appeal, the High Court judge, had concluded that Mr Kernott should have only a 10 per cent share of the Thundersley house. Although it might initially have been the parties' intention to share it equally, Mr Kernott had effectively turned his back on it for over fourteen years, during which the majority of the increase in value had occurred, and he had benefited from being able to buy another property of his own. In those circumstances the parties could not have intended the original shares to remain the same. The High Court judge agreed with the trial judge that 'in the absence of any indication by words or conduct as to how they should be altered, the appropriate

[3] [2007] 2 AC 432 at 92. [4] [2007] 2 AC 432 at 89. [5] [2007] 2 AC 432 at 90–1.
[6] [2007] 2 AC 432 at 91. [7] [2011] UKSC 53.

criterion was what he considered to be fair and just.'[8] The Court of Appeal disagreed, the majority holding that there was nothing to indicate that the parties had substituted an agreement to share otherwise than equally, and such an intention could not be imputed.

Lord Walker and Lady Hale concluded that it was a reasonable inference from the aborted decision to sell the Thundersley house that the parties had intended their shares to crystallize at that date. 'Insofar as the judge did not in so many words infer that this was their intention, it is clearly the intention which reasonable people would have had had they thought about it at the time.'[9] In short, in cases where no inference is possible, an imputation of intention is permissible. This was the view of the majority of the court. The outcome if the parties' shares had been crystallized in 1993 was so close to the outcome reached by the judge that it would be inappropriate to change it.

(3) **A significant change**

The House of Lords and Supreme Court in the two leading cases only implicitly acknowledged that the new approach constitutes a significant change of direction. Etherton LJ has been more explicit. In his words:

> [The] line of cases on the common intention constructive trust can be seen clearly in retrospect as a specific jurisprudential response to the problem of a presumption of resulting trust and the absence of legislation for resolving disputes over property ownership where a married or unmarried couple have purchased property for their joint occupation as a family home.[10]

Legal commentators have similarly seen the new jurisprudence as an approach which is hard to explain using conventional principles of property law. As Dixon succinctly puts it:

> If we look for an explanation of the role and impact of [recent] cases within the jurisprudence of property law, we will not find it . . . [perhaps] what we now have, is a reasonably structured judicial discretion to vary the property rights of cohabitants and other property sharers that is not based on property law at all. It is something else: call it family law, call it an exercise of the court's inherent equitable jurisdiction, but, maybe, do not call it property law.[11]

Justifications can be found for the new approach. The status of the family home is more than simply another part of an individual's property portfolio; there is an emotional connection and investment in the home that is not captured in traditional property-based thinking.[12] The use of the property is also shared in a way which is untypical of most other assets. Legislative change was introduced to Scotland by the Family Law (Scotland) Act 2006, although this was in the context of abolishing the Scots law concept of common law marriage by cohabitation with habit and repute.[13] Lade Hale, speaking judicially, in *Gow v Grant* (a case involving the interpretation of the Scottish law), regretted the introduction of similar rules in England:

> There is some reason to think that a family law remedy such as that proposed by the Law Commission would be less costly and more productive of settlements as well as achieving fairer results than the present law.[14]

On the other hand, successive governments have chosen not to change the law in England and Wales, even when proposed by the Law Commission.[15] Whether the new

[8] Nicholas Strauss QC sitting as a Deputy Judge [2009] EWHC 1713 at [49].

[9] [2011] UKSC 53 at 48. [10] [2011] EWCA Civ 1619 at 85. [11] [2012] Conv 1 (Editorial), 2–3.

[12] See, generally, O'Mahoney, *Conceptualising Home: Theories, Laws and Policies* (Hart 2007).

[13] A much more limited concept than most cohabiting couples may have thought: see the observations of Lord Hope in *Gow v Grant* [2012] UKSC 29.

[14] [2012] UKSC 29 at 47.

[15] *Cohabitation: The Financial Consequences of Relationship Breakdown* (Law Com No 307, 2007).

judicial approach is an illegitimate intrusion by the courts into the domain of law reform that is the responsibility of Parliament, and the demotion of the status of marriage in regulating domestic relationships, is a question to which we shall return in Chapter 15.

2 Features of the current approach

(1) Focus on the family home

Divorce legislation allows a court to take into account all of the wealth to which a married couple have access, even assets to which they may have no current legal entitlement, such as the right to a prospective inheritance[16] or the possibility of receiving a distribution through a discretionary trust.[17] The common intention constructive trust has a focus on assets acquired through joint efforts, and in particular on the family home.

(2) Acquisition and quantification

The current approach distinguishes two stages to the creation of an interest in the family home. These are (1) the acquisition of an interest in the family home, and (2) the quantification of the interest granted, in terms of the size or nature of the interest granted. The distinction is not always clear, but it provides a useful analytical structure and is reflected in many cases. The two stages of acquisition and quantification were recognized and adopted by the Court of Appeal in *Geary v Rankine*[18] and *Capehorn v Harris*.[19] The leading cases of *Stack* v *Dowden*[20] and *Jones v Kernott*[21] are both cases in which there was no question of acquisition of interests as both parties were express co-owners of the legal title; the decisions strictly concerned the question of quantification. One of the challenges for the application of these decisions is how far the approach they adopted applies also the acquisition of an interest. Another challenge is how far the principles in the cases can be used to vary an express arrangement.

(3) The intention of the parties

As the name of the common intention constructive trust suggests, it is at least notionally based upon the intention of the parties. One of the keys to understanding the new approach is to appreciate that intention can be identified in a number of different ways. Before *Stack v Dowden* and *Jones v Kernott*, the courts looked for express intention (as with an express trust, or where there has been an explicit agreement), implied intention (derived from an understanding between the parties that may not have been expressed in clear language), inferred intention (based upon a necessary deduction from the parties' conduct or actions), and presumed intention (which we have explored in the context of resulting trusts in Chapter 9). After the two cases, the courts could also take into account imputed intention, which is the intention which parties would have had if they had given thought to the matter.

[16] *Alireza v Radwan* [2017] EWCA Civ 1545. [17] *Hart v Hart* [2017] EWCA Civ 1306.
[18] [2012] EWCA Civ 55 (CA) per Lewison LJ at 19 and 20.
[19] [2015] EWCA Civ 955. [20] [2007] 2 AC 432. [21] [2011] UKSC 53.

3 Express trusts

The most straightforward way for a cohabitant to acquire an interest in the family home is by means of a formally created express trust. These rules are tolerably clear and relatively inexpensive to operate in practice. An express trust arises where the parties have agreed on their shares in the property, and have recorded this agreement. This trust might be created at the time the family home is acquired, or subsequently. Given the trust relates to land, it must be declared or evidenced in writing[22] and it must also comply with the general rules that apply to the creation of any express trust.[23]

(1) When an express trust can be created

The most common form of express trust will be where there are joint legal owners, and an express declaration is made at the time of the purchase stating what their interests are. It is equally possible for a sole legal owner to create an express trust in favour of himself or herself and their partner or spouse, again declaring their interests. The creation of an express trust relating to the family home is now encouraged in relation to registered land. For current transactions in registered land, the form requesting a change of registration on transfer (form TR1) provides a box for the transferees to declare the trusts on which they wish to hold the property.[24] If this express declaration were made in every situation, the scope for dispute would be much diminished, a point made forcibly by Lady Hale in *Stack v Dowden* in relation to the role played by legal advisers.[25] A declaration of trusts remains optional through either the TI or JO forms, so that a legal adviser cannot insist that trusts are declared.[26] It is also not necessary for the transferees to sign the form, and although the signature of the transferor alone is sufficient compliance with the formality requirement in Law of Property Act 1925 s 53(1)(b),[27] there can then be an issue as to whether the declaration has been signed with the transferees' authority.[28] Hopefully the ease with which trusts can now be declared will lead to the creation of more express trusts. Prevention is much better than cure.

Although less common, there is nothing to prevent an express trust being declared after the purchase has been completed.[29] There is no special provision in the land registration system to encourage or facilitate this, but a person entitled to the benefit of an express trust can protect their rights by registering a restriction in the register.[30]

(2) Functions of an express trust

An express trust usually serves two functions: it both establishes the existence of an equitable interest (fulfilling the acquisition stage of creation of the beneficial interests), and simultaneously quantifies that interest. A beneficial interest in the family home is

22 Law of Property Act 1925, s 53(1)(b).

23 The property must be vested in the trustee, there must be a clear intention to create a trust, and the terms of the trust must be clear. See Chapter 5.

24 This new section on the form was introduced following *Stack v Dowden*. The information can also be provided on a separate form, form JO.

25 [2007] 2 AC 432 at 48.

26 See further Moran, 'Anything to Declare? Express Declarations of Trust on Land Registry Form TR1: The Doubts Raised in *Stack v Dowden*' [2007] 71 Conv 364.

27 *Taylor v Taylor* [2017] EWHC 1080 (Ch).

28 See *Insol Funding Company Ltd v Cowlam* [2017] EWHC 1822 (Ch) at 50.

29 An example is *Arif v Anwar* [2015] EWHC 124 (Fam) at 6.

30 Land Registration Act 2002, ss 40–47.

an interest in land, and is therefore a proprietary interest.[31] The nature of the beneficial shares in land will depend on the method of co-ownership declared under an express trust. There are two possibilities in equity, that the beneficiaries hold under either a joint tenancy or a tenancy in common.[32] Where the trust creates an equitable joint tenancy, there is no division of ownership as both joint tenants are seen as together owning the whole of the property; the whole of the ownership passes to the survivor or survivors when a joint tenant dies.[33] On the dissolution of any relationship between the parties during their lifetime, the presumption of equal shares applies in relation to the parties' respective entitlements in the home. It is only where there is a validly created tenancy in common that the beneficial co-owners can have a declared and separate share in the property.[34] This can be in equal or defined unequal shares.

(3) **Express trust declaring beneficial interests**

Where the claimant is a party to the expressly declared trust, the terms of the trust will normally be conclusive of the interest[35] which that party has unless it is set aside or rectified on the basis of fraud,[36] mistake, or undue influence, or varied by subsequent agreement.[37] The effect of an express declaration was explained by Slade LJ in *Goodman v Gallant*:

> If, however, the relevant conveyance contains an express declaration of trust which comprehensively declares the beneficial interests in the property or its proceeds of sale, there is no room for the application of the doctrine of resulting implied or constructive trusts unless and until the conveyance is set aside or rectified; until that event the declaration contained in the document speaks for itself.[38]

(4) **Subsequent variation of shares**

Comments in *Stack v Dowden*,[39] repeated in *Jones v Kernott*,[40] suggest that the shares of the parties may not remain the same throughout their relationship, producing what Lord Hoffman described during argument as an 'ambulatory trust'. Lord Neuberger suggested that, where it was argued that the intention of the parties had changed since a property was acquired, compelling evidence would be needed, involving:

> [D]iscussions, statements or actions, subsequent to the acquisition, from which an agreement or common understanding as to such a change could properly be inferred.[41]

31 See Chapter 1 for the distinction between proprietary and personal interests. In English law, all ownership rights are expressed as 'estates', which describe bundles of rights exercised over the relevant areas of land (described as 'parcels' of land). See Bevan, *Land Law* (2nd edn, OUP 2020) Ch 1.

32 There can only ever be a joint tenancy at law, simply as a process to allow land to be easily bought and sold—see, e.g. Bevan, *Land Law* (2nd edn, OUP 2020) Ch 5.

33 This is known as the right of survivorship. See, e.g. *AG Securities v Vaughan* [1990] 1 AC 417 (HL).

34 A tenant in common's shares are considered 'undivided' shares, as they are shares of the value of the home, not of particular rooms or areas in the home.

35 See *Pankhania v Chandegra* [2012] EWCA Civ 1438; applied in *Taylor v Taylor* [2017] EWHC 1080 (Ch).

36 See *S v J and Others* [2016] EWHC 559 (Fam), where the wife's signature on a purported written document that the four properties concerned in the dispute were shared was found to have been forged and was therefore set aside.

37 This variation would normally have to comply with s 53(1)(b) of the Law of Property Act 1925.

38 [1986] Fam 106 at 110–11. See also *Clarke v Harlowe* [2005] EWHC 3062.

39 [2007] 2 AC 432 at 62 and 138.

40 [2011] UKSC 53 at 14, 47–51, and 68.

41 [2007] 2 AC 432 at 475 [138] per Lord Neuberger, who was in dissent, but is unlikely to be doubted on this issue. See also *Bedson v Bedson* [1965] 3 All ER 307 at 316 per Davies LJ.

It is easier to envisage an ambulatory trust where the parties have not made any agreement than it is when they have made and recorded an express trust. The normal rule, as we have already seen in Chapter 7, is that variations of an existing trust need to be made in writing since they involve the disposition of an existing equitable interest. Whilst this requirement does not apply to constructive trusts, the drawback of allowing an ambulatory trust to vary the interests declared by an express trust is that it upsets the settled rule, referred to and accepted by Lady Hale in *Stack v Dowden*[42] that an express declaration of trust is binding in the absence of fraud or mistake; it is inconsistent with the statement by Lord Upjohn in *Pettitt v Pettitt*[43] that an express declaration concludes the question of beneficial title 'for all time'; it also reintroduces the uncertainty which the express declaration is intended to avoid.

Subsequent decisions do not provide a conclusive way forward. In *Pankhania v Chandegra*, for example, in dealing with an express declaration of trust, Patten LJ emphasized the orthodox approach that alteration of the beneficial interests required a deed of variation and the suggestion that a contrary intention could be inferred or imputed 'was misplaced'.[44]

In *Clarke v Meadus*,[45] the parties were mother and daughter, and the daughter claimed entitlement through proprietary estoppel[46] to the whole beneficial interest in the home of which she was already a half-owner under an express trust on the basis of detrimental reliance on assurances made by her mother. In holding that Master Bragg at first instance had been wrong to strike out the estoppel claim, Warren J opined:

> [E]xpress trusts . . . are capable of being overridden by a proprietary estoppel . . . as a result of promises and representations . . . It cannot, in my judgment, sensibly be argued that once beneficial interests have been declared in a formal document, those interests become immutable and incapable of being affected by a proprietary estoppel.[47]

It remains to be seen whether this decision will be followed in later cases[48] or extended to common intention constructive trusts, but since proprietary estoppel permits the creation of new rights, it is suggested that on this point Warren J is correct, and his view is supported by some comments of Lady Hale in *Stack v Dowden*.[49] Judge Cooke, in *Gaspar v Zaleski*,[50] thought that an express trust could be varied by a subsequent common intention constructive trust.

It can be seen that whether a change in circumstances after an acquisition can change the shares of parties under an express trust remains uncertain. If such a change is not possible, a claimant who has followed legal advice and agreed their share through an express trust could be prejudiced where subsequent events make this formal allocation of rights unfair.

(5) **Express trust not declaring beneficial interests**

It is possible for the parties buying a home to declare that they are joint legal owners and that they hold the property on trust, without defining the nature or extent of their beneficial interests. In that case, quite obviously, the declaration of trust is not conclusive about the quantification of the beneficial interests of the parties, since this is a matter on which it is silent.

42 *Stack v Dowden* [2007] 2 AC 432 (HL) at 49.

43 [1970] AC 777 at 813.

44 [2012] EWCA Civ 1438 at 28 (Mummery LJ). The leading speech in that case was delivered by Patten LJ, with whom Mummery LJ agreed.

45 [2010] EWHC 3117 (Ch). See also *Davis (As Trustee In Bankruptcy of Jackson) v Jackson* [2017] EWHC 698 (Ch) at 18 (no evidence to support a variation).

46 The requirements to establish a valid claim to an interest through proprietary estoppel are discussed in Chapter 14.

47 [2010] EWHC 3117 (Ch).

48 See Pawlowski, 'Informal variation of express trusts' [2011] Conv 245.

49 [2007] 2 AC 432 at 49.

50 [2017] EWHC 1770 (Ch) at 28.

4 Applying the current approach

(1) Resulting trusts

(a) Resulting trust analysis rejected

Before *Stack v Dowden*, resulting trusts had played a part in ascertaining both whether ownership of the family home was shared, and in quantifying that share. In *Stack v Dowden*,[51] the majority of the House of Lords dismissed this approach.[52] Lord Walker was emphatic:

> In a case about beneficial ownership of a matrimonial or quasi-matrimonial home (whether registered in the names of one or two legal owners) the resulting trust should not in my opinion operate as a legal presumption, although it may (in an updated form which takes account of all significant contributions, direct or indirect, in cash or kind) happen to be reflected in the parties' common intention.[53]

Lord Neuberger was alone in *Stack v Dowden* in considering that there was a continuing role for resulting trusts in relation to the family home.[54] He agreed with the conclusion of the majority in *Stack*, but dissented on the reasoning; he felt that the resulting trust approach was to be favoured as part of the process of determining the rights of parties acquiring a family home.

The abandonment of resulting trust principles drew some criticism, not least because it was, in Swadling's words, 'made with the benefit of almost no reasoning',[55] but it appeared to have been confirmed in *Jones v Kernott*,[56] where at least some analysis of the legal position was undertaken.[57] In that case, Lord Walker and Lady Hale make it quite explicit that there is no place for resulting trusts to determine beneficial interests:

> in the case of the purchase of a house or flat in joint names for joint occupation by a married or unmarried couple, where both are responsible for any mortgage.[58]

Later in the same speech, they repeat the point for clarity:

> The assumptions as to human motivation, which led the courts to impute particular intentions by way of the resulting trust, are not appropriate to the ascertainment of beneficial interests in a family home.[59]

Nevertheless, the judiciary has shown itself unwilling to give up on the resulting trust as a concept.

(b) A continuing role for resulting trusts?

A common feature of both *Stack* and *Kernott* is that they were not concerned with the acquisition of an interest by the parties. Property had been purchased in joint names in both cases, showing that ownership was shared. The question was only about the size of

[51] [2007] 2 AC 432.

[52] [2007] 2 AC 432 at 60 per Baroness Hale, citing with approval Lord Walker's discussion at 19–31. See also *Fowler v Barron* [2008] EWCA Civ 377 (CA), where Arden LJ agreed at least in relation to cases of joint legal ownership. Lord Walker's comments go further.

[53] [2007] 2 AC 432 at 31.

[54] Although his view has been supported in Singapore: *Chan Yuen Lan v See Fong Mun* [2014] 3 SLR 1048, discussed by Wu [2015] Conv 169.

[55] Swadling 'The Common Intention Constructive Trust in the House of Lords: An Opportunity Missed' [2007] LQR 511 at 518.

[56] [2012] 1 AC 776 per Lord Walker and Lady Hale at 15 and 51.

[57] [2012] 1 AC 776 per Lord Walker and Lady Hale at [23]–[24]; suggesting that the constructive trust was the better approach.

[58] [2012] 1 AC 776 at 25. [59] [2012] EWCA Civ 555 at 53.

the respective beneficial interests. This, and since in neither case was the earlier decision of *Gissing v Gissing*[60] overruled, might have suggested that resulting trusts still have a role to play in the family home, for instance in reaching a conclusion on the acquisition stage. This view has not often found favour in subsequent cases.[61] In *Rowlands v Blade*,[62] the court held that a second home was held to be equally shared between two parties to the relationship, on the basis of joint purchase in their joint names While noting that the result would have been different if the resulting trust analysis had been applied, 'whatever I may think about the fairness of the result is irrelevant; *Stack v Dowden* and *Jones v Kernott* marked a decisive break and move away from the presumed resulting trust in this context'.[63]

Moreover, since the financial contributions the parties make to acquiring the family home are evidence of their intentions, and the presumptions of advancement are so attenuated as to have no practical impact, the common intention constructive trust has essentially subsumed the resulting trust within it.[64]

(c) Property other than the family home

Stack and *Kernott* do not reject the use of resulting trusts in contexts other than the family home, but the limits to the area in which resulting trusts should not be used are as yet not fully demarcated. As Moylan J said, in a different context (financial orders on divorce):

> It is, perhaps, worth reflecting that the concept of property being either matrimonial or non-matrimonial property is a legal construct. Moreover, it is a construct which is not always capable of clear identification.[65]

We have already looked, in Chapter 9, at the uncertain boundary of situations where resulting trusts can be used. The family home is an undefined concept, and there is an enormous range of different domestic arrangements, meaning that situations will not always fall neatly into one category or another.[66] A property acquired as an investment might later be used as a family home and vice versa. Domestic accommodation may and (because of housing costs) frequently is, shared by strangers. Parties may cohabit sporadically, or even not at all (for instance where a house is purchased for convenience in the location of the workplace of one cohabitant, which is many miles away from where the parties actually live in rented accommodation). Should the *Stack/Kernott* approach be used in all these situations?

In *Laskar v Laskar*,[67] property was bought by a mother and her daughter primarily as an investment, not as a home in which to live together. According to Lord Neuberger (sitting as a Lord Justice of Appeal in the Court of Appeal), the correct approach to determine the beneficial ownership of the investment asset on the breakdown of the relationship is to apply the presumption of resulting trust.[68]

None of the judges in *Jones v Kernott* cast doubt on this. Lady Hale and Lord Walker were content to say that while resulting trusts were not appropriate to the family home '[w]hether they remain appropriate in other contexts is not the issue in this case.'[69]

60 [1971] AC 886.

61 See, for example, *Aspden v Elvy* [2012] EWHC 1387; *Thompson v Hurst* [2012] EWCA Civ 1752.

62 [2021] EWHC 426 (Ch). 63 [2021] EWHC 426 (Ch) at [145].

64 Bailey-Harris, 'Property' [2004] Fam Law 569. See *Krawczynska v Rozuk* [2020] 1 WLUK at [62], where, in the Property Chamber First-Tier Tribunal, Land Registration Division, McAllister J suggested that resulting and constructive trusts achieved the same result where there had been a monetary contribution 'where the intention held the parties was that [the claimant] should have an interest commensurate with that contribution'.

65 *Hart v Hart* [2017] EWCA Civ 1306 at 85.

66 *Haque v Raja* [2016] EWHC 1950 (Ch) at 29; *Rowlands v Blade* [2021] EWHC 426 (Ch).

67 [2008] EWCA Civ 347. Applied in *Erlam v Rahman* [2016] EWHC 111 (Ch).

68 [2008] EWCA Civ 347 at 17. 69 [2012] 1 AC 776 at 53.

There are several cases after *Stack* and *Kernott* in which resulting trusts have been used for property other than the family home. In *Geary v Rankine*,[70] Mrs Geary claimed an interest in the guest house which had been purchased by Mr Rankine in his sole name and with his own funds as a business venture. The couple had been cohabiting elsewhere, but had taken up residence in the guest house following the departure of an unsuccessful manager, and Mrs Geary had helped run the business. Her claim failed. In reaching judgment, Lewison LJ opined that the burden of establishing a constructive trust was 'all the more difficult to discharge where, as here, the property was bought as an investment rather than as a home' and that the presumption of a resulting trust 'may arise where the partners are business partners as well as domestic partners'.[71]

Favor Easy Management Ltd v Wu[72] also proceeded on the basis that a resulting trust was applicable to property purchased as an investment between cohabitants and that the constructive trust was properly applied where the property was purchased as their home.[73] Again, in *Wodzicki v Wodzicki*,[74] the Court of Appeal considered that a resulting trust was more appropriate than a constructive trust for resolving a property dispute between an estranged stepmother and her stepdaughter about the home in which the stepdaughter was living, but which had never been used by the stepmother.

Conversely, the Privy Council in *Marr v Collie*,[75] suggests that a single approach should be used in respect of assets acquired by a couple in a very close personal relationship, whether the properties were acquired for use as their home or as an investment. It was, according to Lord Kerr, all a matter of context.[76] The facts were atypical and concerned a number of properties owned jointly between Mr Marr and Mr Collie, as well as collection of other items of property, including a boat and an art collection. Subsequent cases have occasionally resorted to a resulting trust analysis, but have often been at pains to explain that the situation was not one where a common intention constructive trust could be argued.[77]

(d) The fate of resulting trusts in the family home

So, where does that leave the resulting trust in relation to the family home? Overtly, the answer is very clear. Barring some intervention by the Supreme Court, the resulting trust is, now of historical interest only in the acquisition of interests;[78] or exists only in disguise, clothed in the language of the constructive trust, since financial contributions are one source from which intentions can be inferred or imputed. It is only where there is a commercial context to the purchase of the home, as where the property is bought for investment purposes, that the resulting trust still has more than a spark of life.

There remains good reason to suggest that a resulting trust, free of the shackles of constructive trust language, should continue to exist, not least Lord Neuberger's intelligent,

[70] [2012] EWCA Civ 555. [71] [2012] EWCA Civ 555 at 18.

[72] [2012] EWCA Civ 1464 (CA (Civ Div)).

[73] Yip and Lee suggest that Chinese cultural aspects of the relationship made the case more difficult: 'Less than straightforward people, facts and trusts: reflections on context: *Favor Easy Management Ltd v Wu*' [2013] Conv 431 at 433.

[74] [2017] EWCA Civ 95.

[75] [2017] UKPC 17. See George and Sloan 'Presuming Too Little About Resulting and Constructive Trusts?' [2017] *The Conveyancer and Property Lawyer* 303.

[76] [2017] UKPC 17, at [54]. It is worth noting that the parties in this case where already joint legal owners.

[77] See, for example, *Soloman v McCarthy* [2020] 1 P&CR 22 (used to resolve declarations of beneficial ownership, *Stack* distinguished); *Tahir v Faizi* [2019] EWHC 1627 (QB) (title held on resulting trust for other party, but this was not a case of acquisition of the home).

[78] See *Rowlands v Blade* [2021] EWHC 426 (Ch), the court did not consider that the second property in question (both parties had their own, separate homes) fell within the investment approach and refused to apply a resulting trust analysis.

compelling, and overlooked dissenting reasoning in *Stack*, which permits both the arithmetical calculation and the ability to look to other factors to rebut the arithmetical formula when it is necessary to take a wider range of circumstances into account. What appears to be more likely is that the resulting trust will be subsumed by the constructive trust as part of a trend in which growing judicial discretion overtakes and replaces the certainty of property concepts such as the resulting trust.

(2) The starting-point

(a) Express trust

We have already seen that where the parties make an express trust declaring their beneficial interests, this is conclusive in the absence of a vitiating factor such as fraud or mistake. However, this may be only the starting-point for assessing beneficial interests because those beneficial interests can be changed by an express variation of trust. It is possible, also, that the beneficial interests can be changed by subsequent conduct or informal agreement.

(b) Joint legal ownership

Stack v Dowden[79] and *Jones v Kernott*[80] were both cases where the family home had been purchased in joint names but no express trust had been declared as to the respective shares of beneficial ownership. It was made very clear that in this situation, on the basis that equity follows the law, the starting-point for analysis was that the parties are joint beneficial owners:

> At its simplest the principle in *Stack v Dowden* is that a 'common intention' trust, for the cohabitants' home to belong to them jointly in equity as well as on the proprietorship register, is the default option in joint names cases. The trust can be classified as a constructive trust, but it is not at odds with the parties' legal ownership. Beneficial ownership mirrors legal ownership.[81]

This modern presumption (or assumption[82]) is likely in most cases to provide an accurate means of ascertaining the parties' intention at the time of acquisition. The initial presumption of joint ownership can, however, be displaced by evidence of a different common intention as to ownership.

(c) Sole legal ownership

Since equity follows the law, the starting-point or default position is that beneficial ownership is vested exclusively in the sole legal owner where only one of the cohabiting partners has legal title to the family home.[83] This initial presumption can be rebutted.

(3) Rebutting the presumptions

(a) Express trust

An express trust declaring the beneficial shares is conclusive, in the absence of a vitiating factor, of the shares at the time the declaration was made, even if those shares can subsequently be varied. The same does not apply if the trust does not declare the shares; in this case the starting-point is the relevant presumption which arises from joint legal title or sole legal title. This presumption can be rebutted.

[79] [2007] 2 AC 432. [80] [2011] UKSC 53.

[81] *Jones v Kernott* at [15], per Lord Walker and Lady Hale. [82] *Jones v Kernott* at [17].

[83] This is true whether the property was acquired by the legal owner before the relationship began, or during the relationship—see, for example, *Graham York v York* [2015] EWCA Civ 72.

(b) Joint legal title

Where there is joint legal title, the presumption of joint equitable ownership both overcomes the question as to whether ownership is shared (the acquisition stage) and answers the quantification stage (it indicates that the parties have joint beneficial ownership). Whilst the initial presumption of joint ownership is very strong, and not to be displaced lightly,[84] it is nevertheless capable of being displaced, and this became the central issue on the facts of both *Stack* and *Kernott*. This is discussed under quantification, later, and the approach is represented in Figure 12.2.

(c) Sole legal title: the original approach[85]

The starting presumption in a case of sole legal title is that the person who is not on the legal title has no beneficial interest. Baroness Hale indicated in *Stack v Dowden*, in cases of sole ownership 'the claimant had first to surmount the hurdle of showing that she had any beneficial interest at all, before showing exactly what that interest was.'[86]

In some instances of sole legal title, the legal owner concedes that the other party has a beneficial interest, meaning that the court can proceed directly to quantification; sometimes the court has to decide whether the first hurdle has been cleared. According to the leading House of Lords decision, *Lloyds Bank v Rosset*,[87] to do this the person alleging an interest had to show a common intention that there was some express agreement or understanding, or inferred from the conduct of the parties alone. In either case, to acquire an interest, the non-legal owner has to show that they had acted to their detriment on the common intention to acquire an interest, as otherwise the common intention would simply amount to a promise which is unenforceable in English law.[88] Where the common intention is demonstrated through an agreement, a change of position on the basis of the agreement will be sufficient and there is no requirement that the claimant made a financial contribution to the purchase price. In cases were a common intention was inferred from conduct, only something in the nature of a financial contribution to the purchase of the family home would demonstrate detriment by the non-legal owner.

(d) Sole legal ownership: the revised approach

Following *Stack v Dowden* and *Jones v Kernott*, the case law demonstrates that the courts now feel able to infer a common intention, in the absence of an express agreement or direct monetary contribution, to displace the presumption that sole beneficial ownership follows sole legal ownership. It now appears clear that these pathways to an interest require both establishing the common intention and an element of detriment on the part of the claimant cohabitant on the basis of that common intention.

This needs further explanation. The question had arisen should it be possible to simply infer or even impute a common intention where the parties have cohabited, on the basis that the home is shared and so the property rights should be shared also? This would have been a very important development of the law for non-legal owner cohabitants. Effectively, their right to own the family home would be imputed from the fact they had shared a home with the legal owner, and could have removed the requirement to demonstrate an agreement or detriment such as a financial contribution.

This issue is still not beyond doubt, though a definitive answer is emerging. The primacy of *Rosset* remains, as neither *Stack* nor *Kernott* sought to overrule the decision, and they were both decisions concerning the entitlements of cohabitants who were already

[84] *Jones v Kernott* [2012] 1 AC 773 at [15], [23], and [51].

[85] Explored in detail in Chapter 13. [86] [2007] 2 AC 432 at 61. [87] [1991] 1 AC 107.

[88] See *Amin v Amin* [2020] EWHC 2767 (Ch); *O'Neill v Holland* [2020] EWCA Civ 1583.

joint legal owners of the family home. Lady Hale and Lord Walker, who together gave the leading speech, noted that 'sole legal owner cases have a different starting point . . . because the claimant . . . has the burden of establishing some sort of implied trust . . .'[89] Having outlined the factors applicable to determining the size of a beneficial share, they also said of single owner cases:

> The first issue is whether it was intended that the other party have any beneficial interest in the property at all. If he does, the second issue is what that interest is. There is no presumption of joint beneficial ownership. But their common intention has once again to be deduced objectively from their conduct.[90]

Read together, these statements suggest that the impact of the Supreme Court decision to sole legal owner in the family home does not extend or alter the principles upon which an entitlement to an interest in the home is acquired. The two-stage approach of establishing a beneficial interest under a trust either by express agreement, or by financial contribution by the non-legal owner set out in *Lloyds Bank v Rosset*, still applies. This strict interpretation of the law was followed in some subsequent cases, such as *Geary v Rankine*:[91]

> Whether the beneficial interests are to be shared at all is still a question of a party's actual shared intentions. An imputed intention only arises where the court is satisfied that the parties' actual common intention, express or inferred, was that the beneficial interest would be shared, but cannot make a finding about proportions in which they were to be shared.

Similarly, in *Capehorn v Harris*[92] the Court of Appeal clearly stated that it was not open in sole legal owner cases for the court to impute an intention to acquire an interest, and because the trial judge had done just that when no agreement was evident between the parties, Mr Harris was deprived of an interest behind a constructive trust.[93]

This approach maintains a role for certainty and predictability in the property entitlements of parties, and, viewed from this perspective:

> Problems of uncertainty might well abound if a more holistic approach were taken to the acquisition question, and the answer to the fundamental question whether a legal non-owner does or does not have an interest in a given piece of property could become extremely difficult to predict before litigation.[94]

Not all decisions have been so consistent and other judges felt that the law should embrace a simpler approach to establishing an interest in the family home.[95] In *Bhura v Bhura*,[96] Mostyn J simply asked: what are the parties' beneficial shares? There was no distinction made between acquiring an interest and quantifying it, once acquired. The Privy Council in *Abbott v Abbott*[97] expressly disapproved of the approach in *Rosset* and found that the approach of inference of a common intention should be enough to allow joint division of assets on the facts of that case.

The most significant issue with inference was whether there was any role for detrimental reliance by the non-legal owner to gain an interest in the home. Nothing was said about this in either *Stack v Dowden* or *Jones v Kernott*, but, of course, in those cases the

[89] [2011] UKSC 53, at [17]. [90] [2011] UKSC 53, at [52].

[91] [2012] EWHC 1387, at [19] (Lewison J). See also *Aspden v Elvy* [2012] EWHC 1387; *Capehorn v Harris* [2015] EWCA Civ 955 (CA); *Barnes v Philips* [2015] EWCA Civ 1056 (CA).

[92] [2015] EWCA Civ 955 (CA). [93] See *Barnes v Philips* [2015] EWCA Civ 1056 (CA).

[94] Sloan 'Keeping Up With the Jones Case: Establishing Constructive Trusts in "Sole Legal Owner" Scenarios' (2015) 35 *Legal Studies* 226.

[95] See Gardner 'Heresy—or Not?—in Family Property?' (2015) 79 *The Conveyancer and Property Lawyer* 332.

[96] [2014] EWHC 727 (Fam). [97] [2012] EWHC 1387.

cohabitant was already entitled to some interest in equity by being named on the legal title of the property. Without detriment, a sole legal owner of the family home would be deprived of their beneficial entitlement to the home when a cohabitant moved in, without any express statement acknowledging this by the sole legal owner, or any financial contributions or other acts of detriment made by the claimant cohabitant. That would have represented a sea change in the law, with property rights in the home being determined by the nature of the familial relationship rather than any sense of property or trust law principles.

Nonetheless, it is arguable that imputing an intention to share ownership of the property when the parties are living together, irrespective of the names on the legal title, is a more realistic reflection of the relationship and the nature of family life, even if it gives rise to uncertainty of ownership in some cases.

Recent case law appears to balance these concerns, albeit imperfectly, by suggesting that another element has been added to the approach in *Rossett*, that in the absence of either an express agreement or a financial contribution to the purchase price to demonstrate a common intention, the court may infer such a common intention to share the home from the conduct of the parties.[98] While it is tempting to classify this approach as 'new third way', it is, in essence, a response to the fact that cases following *Rosset* took a very restrictive approach of conduct by tying it to direct financial contributions to the family home.[99]

In all these cases, the claimant cohabitant has had to demonstrate that they have acted to their detriment on the basis of the common intention to acquire a beneficial interest.[100] In *Archibald v Alexander*,[101] the need for detrimental reliance was emphasized, as without this necessary change of position, the common intention amounted to a promise which would be unenforceable in English law. In *Amin v Amin*,[102] Nugee LJ confirmed that, in his view, the court could objectively infer a common intention to share the beneficial interests in the home in cases where one party was the sole legal owner to displace the presumption that the sole legal owner was the sole beneficiary. He noted that detrimental reliance, while necessary, had to be considered in the light of the common intention objectively found to exist between the parties, so that the payment of mortgage repayments could be inferred to be detriment where there was a common intention to share the home.[103] Henderson LJ in *O'Neill v Holland*,[104] made it clear that the claimant must demonstrate detrimental reliance on the common intention to gain an interest. The mere fact that it may be unconscionable on the facts for the sole legal owner to claim the full beneficial title would not assist the claimant in the absence of her having acted to the detriment.

So, it would appear on the weight of authority, without a fresh decision of the Supreme Court to the contrary, the approach to common intention constructive trusts allows a common intention to be objectively inferred from the conduct of the parties in the absence of an express agreement, but there must still be detrimental reliance on that common intention for the courts to displace the presumption in sole legal owner cases that the sole legal owner is also entitled to the whole of the beneficial ownership of the home. There is still a difference between sole and joint legal ownership cases, as there remains a need

[98] See *Pilmoor v Miah* [2019] EWHC 3696 (Ch); *Kanval v Kanval* [2021] EWHC 853 (Ch) at [16]–[18], emphasizing that it was not open to the court to impute an intention.

[99] Explored in Chapter 13.

[100] See *Dobson v Griffey* [2018] EWHC 1117 (Ch), where HHJ Paul Matthews [20]–[23] suggested there were three stages to finding a constructive trust (i) whether there was an express or inferred common intention; (ii) whether there was detrimental reliance on that common intention; and (iii) quantification of the parties' beneficial shares in the home.

[101] [2020] EWHC 1621 (Ch) at [32].

[102] [2020] EWHC 2675 (Ch) at [32].

[103] [2020] EWHC 2675 (Ch) at [53].

[104] [2020] EWHC 3533 (Ch). See also *Kanval v Kanval* [2021] EWHC 853 at [1670].

to demonstrate that an interest has been acquired. Few commentators would doubt the direction of travel, which is that, as noted by Judge Mithan QC in *Miah v Miah*, 'the courts will be more willing to find a constructive trust proved that it might have been willing to do so when *Rosset* was decided'.[105] The difference, in practice, between sole and joint ownership cases is increasingly less important, as in both cases the constructive trust arises because it would be inequitable to allow the legal owner to deny that their partner is entitled to a share of the home (in sole legal owner cases) or for one partner to take a larger share than the other (in joint legal ownership cases).

(e) Acquisition in sole legal owner cases: express agreement

The search is supposed to be for the actual common intentions that the parties have manifested or would have manifested had they considered it directly, not a common intention created for them by the courts. In the words of Lord Morris of Borth-y-Guest in *Gissing v Gissing*,[106] cited with approval by Lord Bridge:[107]

> The courts cannot devise agreements which the parties never made. The court cannot ascribe intentions which the parties in fact never had.

When considering whether the common intention arises from an express agreement, the court says it is 'discovering' an agreement either from the words used or including the conduct of the parties. Where the court now feels able to infer a common intention in the absence of an express agreement, objectively from the conduct of the parties in the home, that common intention is one which the parties would recognize if they had been forced to sit down and articulate how they thought the home would be owned between them.[108] By requiring consideration of whether a common intention can be established, it is not the court imposing a view of what it considers fair in the circumstances of a particular case by giving the cohabitant without legal title an interest in the home. There has been some inconsistency, however. In *Iranian Offshore Engineering and Construction Co v Zavari*,[109] it was suggested that in sole legal owner cases it was possible to impute a common intention to the parties. Imputation differs from inference, in that it is based on what the court considers to be fair between the parties, not what the parties would have agreed between themselves had they put their minds to it. This, with respect, goes too far in sole legal owner cases.

The nature of an express agreement is explored in Chapter 13, but, in effect, the court is not looking for an agreement in the sense of a consensus ad idem, but instead for a representation or assurance by the sole legal owner, on which the cohabitant can act to their detriment.[110]

In terms of detriment, this need not involve the expenditure of money, but there must be some link between the act claimed as detrimental reliance and the common intention to share in the beneficial ownership of the home. In *Oberman v Collins*,[111] unusually the claim through a constructive trust was to a portfolio of forty-one properties. There was no need, according to Deputy Judge Tom Leach QC, to prove detriment to each and every property comprised in the portfolio. On the facts the person making financial

[105] [2020] EWHC 3374 (Ch) at [64]. [106] [1971] AC 886, 898.

[107] Numerous other judges have cited this passage with approval, including Lady Hale in *Stack v Dowden*.

[108] See *Amin v Amin* [2020] EWHC 2675 (Ch); *Dobson v Griffey* [2018] EWHC 1117 (Ch); *Pilmoor v Miah* [2019] EWHC 3696 (Ch).

[109] [2020] EWHC 2497, at [47].

[110] See *Morris v Morris* [2008] EWCA Civ 257 (no representation, so no common intention). See also *James v Thomas* [2007] EWCA Civ 1212 (express agreement could not be *imputed* from conduct); *Re Ali* [2012] EWHC 2302 (no credible evidence given of representations on which to found a common intention); *Pilmoor v Miah* [2019] EWHC 3696 (Ch) (burden of proof likes on the claimant).

[111] [2020] EWHC 3533 (Ch).

contributions, working unpaid and giving their partner day-to-day control of the portfolio, whilst providing bank guarantees and assuming financial liabilities, was sufficient to amount to detriment on the basis of the common intention to share the portfolio. More recently, in *O'Neill v Holland*,[112] Henderson LJ stressed that it was important for the claimant to clearly set out the acts of detriment in the pleadings. Nonetheless, the court could characterize acts as detriment from the facts before it, and it was an 'objective set of affairs which leaves the claimant in a substantially worse position'. On the facts of that case, the fact that the claimant had relied on a misrepresentation as to why her name did not appear on the legal title was sufficient detriment, as otherwise she would have been a joint legal and beneficial owner of the home.

(f) Acquisition in sole legal owner cases: inferred from conduct

This element of the legal framework established in *Rosset* drew considerable criticism, even though Lord Bridge was clear that more than a change of position was needed for appropriate detriment to be demonstrated in the absence of an express agreement. The strictness of this approach led to results that were difficult to defend.[113]

Following *Stack v Dowden* and *Jones v Kernott* the position has changed. The courts, in the absence of a direct payment, now feel able to consider the whole course of dealings between the parties to infer a common intention to share the beneficial interest.[114] This allows the courts to consider a broad range of factors to objectively find a common intention which the parties would have reached, had they put their minds to it. In *Pilmoor v Miah*,[115] it was suggested that such inference of a common intention would only take place where the circumstances were 'exceptional',[116] so that simply purchasing the home as a property to house the family, taking part in any business of the sole legal owner or carrying out remedial or improvement works on the property would ordinarily be insufficient to raise this common intention.[117] The need to find exceptional circumstances is not a consideration that, to date, has attracted widespread support.[118] The common intention to be found in sole legal owner cases is simply that the beneficial interests in the property were intended to be shared, thereby displacing the presumption that beneficial title follows the legal title. Hence, in *Amin v Amin*,[119] the presumption of sole legal ownership was displaced by the fact the claimant had made mortgage repayments, whereas the sole legal owner had made no contribution. The trial judge had also been influenced by the fact the grant of legal title had appeared to be almost accidental, as the relevant family had a history of transferring titles to property between their extended family.

The factors the courts may examine to infer an intention are the same as those considered by the courts in quantifying the size of the beneficial share of the property, which are extensive and are explored later in this chapter.

Detrimental reliance by the claimant on the common intention remains a feature where that common intention is inferred objectively from the conduct of the parties in their dealings with the family home. It would appear that a change of position is sufficient and that this need not involve financial contributions,[120] so that the approach is similar to where

[112] [2020] EWCA Civ 1583 at [62]–[63]. [113] See Chapter 13.

[114] *Amin v Amin* [2020] EWHC 2675 (Ch) at [32]. [115] [2019] EWHC 3696 (Ch).

[116] [2019] EWHC 3696 (Ch) at [27]. [117] [2020] EWCA Civ 1583.

[118] See *Miah v Miah* [2020] EWHC 3374 (Ch); *Oberman v Collins* [2020] EWHC 3533 (Ch), where there was no substantive discussion of the applicable legal rules, yet the court felt able to find a common intention constructive trust over an £8 million property portfolio.

[119] [2020] EWHC 2675 (Ch).

[120] *O'Neill v Holland* [2020] EWCA Civ 1583 (CA), where the court held there had been sufficient detriment demonstrated where the claimant had been induced by a misrepresentation as to mortgage finance not to appear on the legal title to the property.

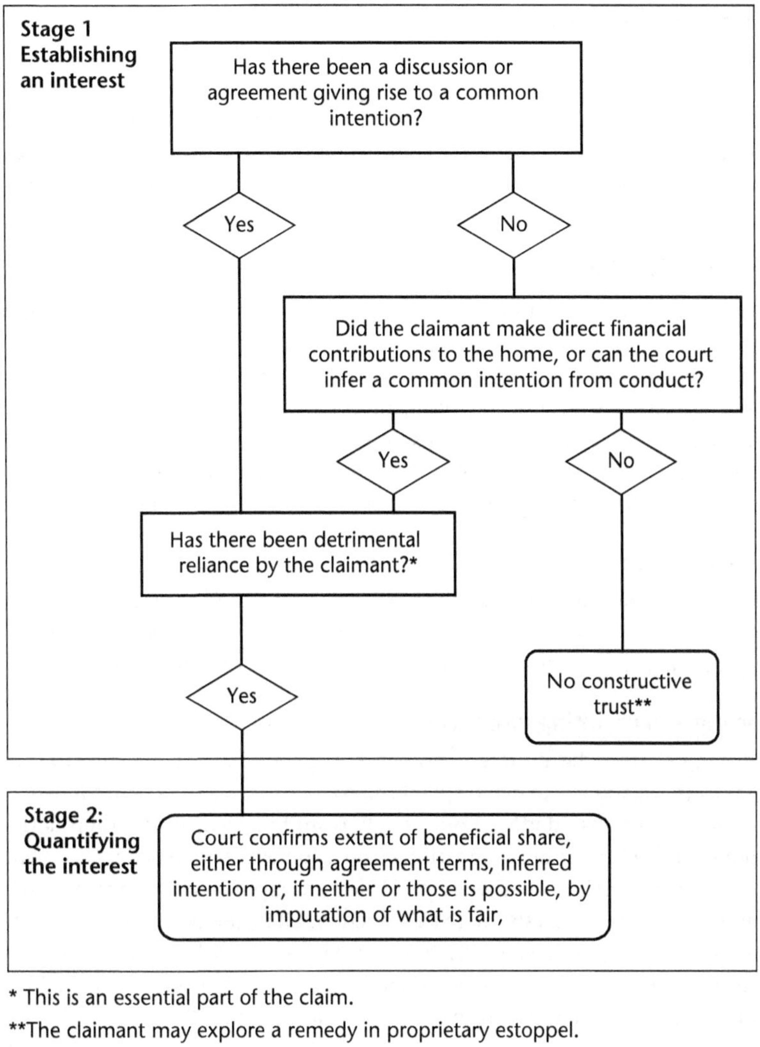

Figure 12.1 Constructive trusts of the family home: sole legal owner

the common intention arises from an express agreement.[121] Indeed, the acts claimed as detriment may be explained by the common intention itself as they provide a context for the actions of the claimant.[122] The requirements are summarized in Figure 12.1.

(g) Cultural factors

In some cases, cultural factors may be relevant in identifying a common intention, for instance the possibility that a Hindu or Sikh family intend to acquire property subject to Mitakshara, under which, through a form of coparceny (a term which describes a form of joint heirship), the property belongs jointly to the male members of that family down to the third generation from a common male ancestor.[123]

[121] Financial contributions may still provide strong evidence of detrimental reliance, as in *Oberman v Collins* [2020] EWHC 3533 (Ch), where assuming financial liabilities in relation to the property portfolio was held to be sufficient in that case (though not every property within the portfolio).

[122] *Amin v Amin* [2020] EWHC 2675 (Ch), where mortgage payments were viewed as detrimental reliance because they were advanced by the claimant in the belief that the property partially belonged to them. See also *Barrett v Barrett* [2008] EWHC 1061 (Ch) at [24].

[123] *Singh v Singh* [2014] EWHC 1060 (Ch).

(h) Ownership by a company or third party

Where title to the family home is vested in a company, the normal implication will be that the beneficial interest lies with the company, but the evidence may show that the acquisition or transfer to the company was on trust for one or both of the occupiers.[124] The fact that the acquisition was financed by the occupiers of the property will point strongly to there being a trust in their favour, but that is not necessarily the only conclusion.[125]

(4) Quantifying shares

Once the threshold for acquisition has been crossed, the next stage is the quantification of the parties' shares. Where there is an express trust quantifying shares the declaration of trust answers both whether the parties share ownership, and what shares they each enjoy. In joint name and single legal owner cases, quantification of the shares is a separate exercise. This may be based upon the same evidence as acquisition, but at the second stage a different approach is taken: 'the task . . . is to ascertain the parties' common intentions as to what their shares in the property would be, in the light of their whole course of conduct in relation to it.'[126]

(a) Express intention

Where there the evidence shows that the parties discussed and agreed what shares (if any) they should have, the court cannot go behind their agreement,[127] even if the result is that one party has no beneficial share because, having asked for it, the other party refuses.[128]

(b) Inferring and imputing intention

In quantifying shares where there is no express agreement, the courts will look at the whole of the circumstances to decide what the parties intended. Where there is evidence of the parties' intentions, 'deduced objectively from their words and their actions', it is (again) not the role of the court to substitute a decision which it considers to be fair.[129] The court is therefore inferring an agreement. However, imputation is permitted 'where it is clear that the beneficial interests are to be shared, but it is impossible to divine a common intention as to the proportions in which they are to be shared'.[130] In these situations, the court may have no alternative but to ask what the parties' intentions as reasonable and just people would have been had they thought about it at the time.[131]

(c) Basis of quantification

Where the court is obliged to impute an intention, it cannot do so by reference to the parties' actual intentions. So how, instead, should the shares be determined? In *Stack v Dowden*, Lady Hale had expressed agreement with the approach adopted in *Oxley v Hiscock*.[132] There, Chadwick LJ had said that where the evidence did not permit the court to identify the parties' actual intentions, they were entitled to 'that share which

[124] *Prest v Petrodel Resources Ltd* [2013] UKSC 34.

[125] See *O'Donnell v Governor & Company of the Bank of Ireland* [2014] IESC 77.

[126] Lord Walker and Lady Hale at 13.

[127] *Wodzicki v Wodzicki* [2017] EWCA Civ 95 at 24. See also *Ball v De* Marzo [2019] EWHC 1587 (Ch), where quantification was based on the express agreement, even though the agreement was a result of a forged will and the act of detrimental reliance was tainted with fraud.

[128] *Curran v Collins* [2015] EWCA Civ 404 at 3.

[129] [1991] 1 AC 107 at 46.

[130] [2011] UKSC 53 at 31. Hayward, 'Common intention constructive trusts and the role of imputation in theory and practice' [2016] Conv 233 argues that *Barnes v Phillips* [2015] EWCA Civ 1056 shows that the courts resort too readily to imputation.

[131] [2011] UKSC 53 at 47.

[132] [2005] Fam 211.

the court considers fair having regard to the whole course of dealing between them in relation to the property.' The Supreme Court in *Jones v Kernott*[133] adopted the same approach. This resolves some of the uncertainty that was left by *Stack v Dowden* since in that case, despite Baroness Hale's approval of Chadwick LJ's approach, some of her remarks suggested that she did not agree that this meant that the search was for 'fair shares'. The 'fair shares' approach has been adopted in subsequent cases. An early example is *Abbott v Abbott*,[134] a Privy Council case decided after *Stack* but before *Kernott*. Here the husband had acquired a building plot in his sole name by gift from his mother. The construction costs were paid by the husband and wife taking out a bridging loan and then a mortgage, and the husband's mother also contributed. The wife made herself jointly and severally liable for the repayment of principal and interest on the mortgage. The couple had a joint bank account and all payments were made from it. The wife did not work for a period of nearly nine years. The parties ultimately divorced, and the question before the court was to consider the extent of the wife's beneficial interest. In deciding that the parties shared the beneficial ownership equally, the Privy Council disapproved the *Rosset* approach and said that the parties' whole course of conduct in relation to the property had to be taken into account in determining their shared intentions as to its ownership, as with *Stack v Dowden*. Equal division was the correct inference (without more) from the fact that the gift by the husband's mother was intended for both of them, and that was backed up by the conduct of the couple throughout their marriage, as they arranged their finances jointly and undertook joint liability on the mortgage.

(d) Factors to take into account

As Roberts J said in *S v J*:

> If I am satisfied that it was the parties' common intention that the beneficial interest in any or all of the properties was to be shared in some proportion or another, the court can give effect to that common intention by determining what, in all the circumstances, represents a fair share to apportion to each.[135]

When the court is assessing the shares of the parties, it is entitled to take into account the whole course of the parties' dealings with respect to the property, and where there is no evidence of actual intention, to reach the conclusion from this as to shares which is fair between the parties. There is, in this respect, a degree of paradox. Fairness is the guiding factor where the parties have had no discussions about ownership, but it is irrelevant if there is evidence of actual intention. In *Curran v Collins* Toulson LJ, on the application for leave to appeal, said that 'the appellant has in truth been treated unfairly',[136] but at trial, in the face of evidence that her partner had refused to put a property in which they lived in joint names, she was declined an order for any beneficial share.[137] Even where there is no evidence of agreement, a woman in an abusive relationship is less likely to receive a share in a family home than one in a warmer relationship. Tomlinson LJ in *Graham-York v York* said:

> It is essential, in my judgment, to bear in mind that, in deciding in such a case what shares are fair, the court is not concerned with some form of redistributive justice. Thus it is irrelevant that it may be thought a 'fair' outcome for a woman who has endured years of abusive conduct by her partner to be allotted a substantial interest in his property on his death. The plight of Miss Graham-York attracts sympathy, but it does not enable the court to redistribute property interests in a manner which right-minded people might think amounts to appropriate compensation.[138]

133 [2011] UKSC 53. 134 [2008] Fam Law 215 (PC).

135 [2016] EWHC 586 (Fam) at 48. 136 [2013] EWCA Civ 382 at 13. 137 [2015] EWCA Civ 404.

138 *Graham-York v York* [2015] EWCA Civ 72 at [22]. See Greer and Pawlowski, 'Imputation, fairness and the family home' [2015] Conv 512.

In *Stack v Dowden*,[139] Baroness Hale said that in determining the size of a beneficial share in the property, the court should have recourse to the following indicative list of factors:

> any advice or discussions at the time of transfer which cast light on their intentions then; the reasons why the home was acquired in their joint names; the reasons why (if it be the case) the survivor was authorised to give a receipt for the capital moneys; the purpose for which the home was acquired; the nature of the parties' relationship; whether they had children for whom they both had responsibility to provide a home; how the purchase was financed, both initially and subsequently; how the parties arranged their finances, whether separately or together or a bit of both; how they discharged their outgoings on the property and their other household expenses.[140]

These were not intended to be exhaustive, just useful guidelines. Factors which cases have been taken into account in subsequent cases include financial contributions, direct and indirect;[141] the liability to pay a mortgage, even if few contributions have actually been made;[142] the extent to which the parties have kept their financial affairs separate or treated them as merged, pooled or common resources;[143] the length of cohabitation;[144] assistance in caring for children.[145] Cultural or religious views about family property may also, in an appropriate case, be relevant.[146]

In fact, despite the supposed clarity of this approach to quantification, the courts have continued to have difficulty in practice. Judges have struggled with factors introduced in inference and imputation[147] and have instead tended to fall back on financial contributions, rather than deal with the 'messier' issues of the nature of the relationship or the character of the parties in imputing an intention as to what is a 'fair' award between the parties.

Graham-York v York[148] provides a good illustration of the issues.[149] Miss Graham-York contested a finding that she was entitled to a 50 per cent beneficial interest in the family home behind a constructive trust. It was beyond argument that the sole legal owner of the home, Mr Norton York, had been abusive and controlling in his dealings with his partner, and that she had lived with him for 33 years until his death. Nevertheless, the Court of Appeal found that, on the basis of her financial contributions to the property and joint contributions to household expenditure and bringing up the couple's daughter, Miss Graham-York was entitled to a 25 per cent share of the beneficial ownership of the home.

It is unclear, however, from the judgment just exactly what factors, beyond the financial, made up the share. Tomlinson LJ noted that Miss Graham-York had made as much of a financial contribution as she possibly could. This is a return to focusing on financial matters, while placing non-financial factors in the background.[150]

139 [2007] 2 AC 432.
140 [2007] 2 AC 432 at 69 and 70.
141 *CPS v Piper* [2011] EWHC 3570 (Admin).
142 *Fowler v Barron* [2008] EWCA Civ 377.
143 *CPS v Piper* [2011] EWHC 3570 (Admin); *S v J* [2016] EWHC 586 (Fam).
144 *O'Kelly v Davies* [2014] EWCA Civ 1606; *Graham-York v York* [2015] EWCA Civ 72.
145 *Barnes v Phillips* [2015] EWCA Civ 1056 at 39–41; *O'Kelly v Davies* [2014] EWCA Civ 1606; *Graham-York v York* [2015] EWCA Civ 72.
146 *Singh v Singh* [2014] EWHC 1060 (Ch).
147 See *Aspden v Elvy* [2012] EWHC 3570 (arbitrary figure reached); *S v J and Others* [2016] EWHC 559 (Fam) (mixed up inference and imputation); *O'Neill v Holland* [2020] EWCA Civ 1583 (50% interest granted on the basis that there was an intention that the home be shared).
148 [2015] EWCA Civ 7.
149 See also *Sandhu v Sandhu* [2016] EWCA Civ 1050.
150 Greer and Pawlowski, 'Imputation, Fairness and the Family Home' [2015] Conv 512, 521.

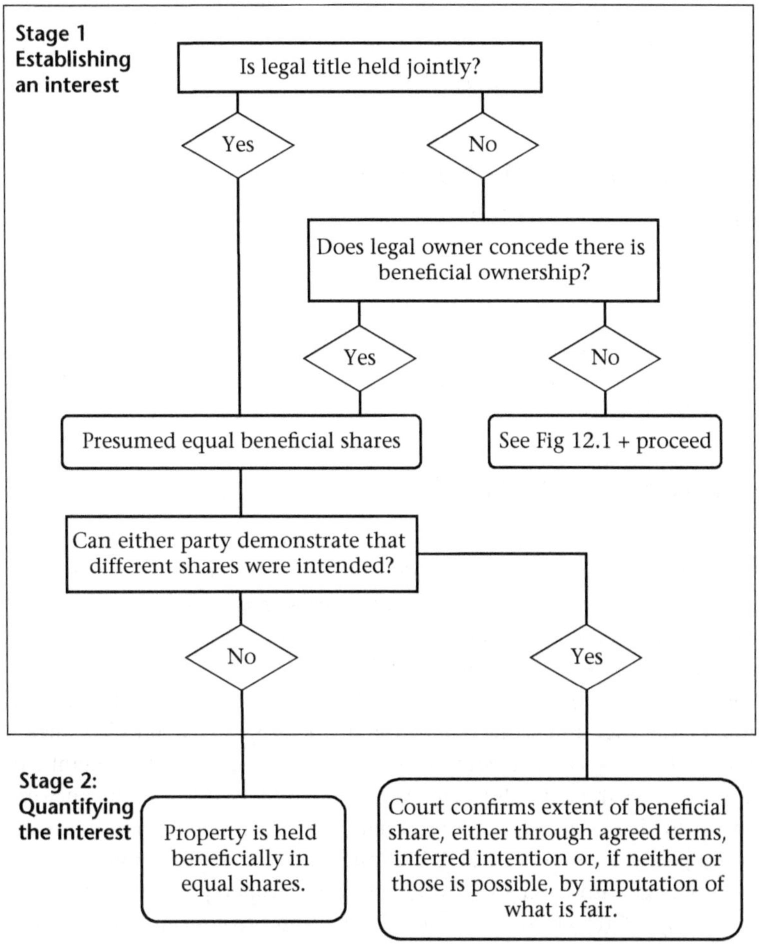

Figure 12.2 Constructive trusts of the family home: joint ownership cases

(e) Comparison with divorce

There are some similarities between the approach of the courts to the family home and the way in which they approach financial provision on divorce.[151] There are also some significant differences. In statutory matrimonial proceedings, three strands are relevant: the financial needs of the parties; compensation; and the equal-sharing principle in relation to matrimonial property. The first two strands have no application to the judge-made rules relating to the ownership of the family home (although they could have a part to play if a different approach were adopted, such as reliance on the principles of unjust enrichment). In relation to the sharing principle, once it has been established that a cohabiting couple intended to share ownership, the assessment of shares follows much the same course, whether statutory[152] or judge-made rules apply. In particular the reliance on fairness, the regard to the integration of the parties' finances, and the duration of the relationship, are

[151] For the statutory rules see Matrimonial Causes Act 1973, s 25; *Sharp v Sharp* [2017] 4 All ER 1046.

[152] *White v White* [2001] 1 All ER 1; *Miller v Miller* [2006] 3 All ER 1.

factors shared in both approaches. However, because in the judge-made regime the search is ostensibly for the parties' intention, a clearly expressed intention cannot be overridden by fairness; that is possible under the statutory rules.

5 The practical impact of proprietary rights in the family home

Until now, this chapter has focused on the acquisition and quantification of an interest in the family home, through either an express trust or a constructive trust of common intention. There is another dimension which concerns the entitlements that arise from having an interest in the land. This is traditionally considered in land law textbooks, but has far reaching implications for the claimant so is worth considering here.

(1) Rights of the cohabitant before sale

Whether the interest of the cohabitant would bind a third party on sale is also relevant, but that is a matter for land law texts as it depends on a variety of factors and whether title to the family home is part of the unregistered or registered land system. At the very least, where property is sold, the equitable owner will be entitled to a share of the proceeds of sale proportionate to the size of their equitable interest.[153]

An express (or implied) trust of the family home will be classed as a trust of land, which is a statutory construct under the Trust of Land and Appointment of Trustees Act 1996 (TOLATA).[154] If the legal owner wants to sell the property, can the cohabitant with a beneficial interest under the trust stop sale, or remain in the property? The answer to these questions is provided by an analysis of the rights of each cohabitee and then by applying the rules and principles set out in TOLATA and the Land Registration Act 2002. Under TOLATA, a person with a beneficial interest in the property has a right of occupation which can be regulated by the courts, and can also apply to court to prevent a sale taking place under s 14. In making a decision on, say, the question of sale, the court has regard to various factors set out in s 15(1).

In the domestic context, it would be difficult to argue that the 'purpose' of the trust continues through a relationship breakdown, and the court would normally order sale in such circumstances. Decisions are not always consistent, so in *Holman v Kingston Howes*,[155] the purchase of the property as a home for one of the beneficiaries led to the court postponing sale. The fact that the family home may be required to house any children of a relationship is not a sufficient reason for the court to refuse an order for sale, unless there is a real threat of harm to the children.[156]

More problematic is the situation where it is not the other party in the relationship seeking sale, and a mortgagee or other secured creditor is asking that the home be sold to pay off existing debts. Here, it appears that the use and occupation of land by the home-owners is not protected. In the absence of hardship to children as a factor to be taken into consideration, it seems from the case law that the rights of mortgagees and other creditors will be given precedence, and at best sale will only be postponed to allow for alternative arrangements for accommodation to be made. In *Mortgage Corporation v Shaire*,[157] for example, sale was not immediately ordered, but the creditor mortgagee was entitled to

153 See, generally, Dixon, *Modern Land Law* (10th edn, Routledge 2016).

154 s 36(1).

155 [2005] EWHC 2824 (Ch).

156 See *First National Bank plc v Achampong* [2003] EWCA Civ 487.

157 [2000] 1 FLR 273.

be paid interest as the price of not making an order for sale. The order was postponed, not suspended for all time. Nevertheless, it remains true that a party granted a beneficial interest under a trust of land is still better off than someone unable to establish a proprietary interest in the home, as no such discussion even arises in relation to personal interests such as a licence to occupy the home.

(2) Cohabitants' rights on sale

Let us take a case where the sole legal owner of property holds it on a constructive trust to give effect to a proprietary interest in favour of his partner. Suppose, for instance, that Darby and Joan purchase a house together, having agreed that they will both enjoy an interest in it. They both contribute to the purchase, and they do not require a mortgage. For some reason the house is purchased in the name of Joan alone. Joan will almost certainly hold the property on constructive trust for herself and Darby in the shares they have agreed. If Joan later mortgages or sells the house without Darby's knowledge or approval, can Darby's rights be enforced against the bank or purchaser? The answer is relatively complicated. It depends upon whether the land was unregistered or registered, and whether there is a single legal owner, or there are joint legal owners.

(a) Sole legal owner of unregistered land

In the now relatively rare situation where the land is not registered (because the property was purchased some time ago),[158] Darby will be protected against subsequent mortgages and sales by the equitable doctrine of notice. This means that any subsequent purchaser (a word which includes a mortgagee)[159] will have to respect Darby's rights if they had actual, constructive, or imputed notice of them. In other words, Darby's rights are protected against later sales and mortgages if the buyer or the bank knew of his rights or could have discovered them. One of the ways in which Darby's rights could be discovered is by inspecting the land. If Darby is living there, the buyer or the bank (acting usually through a surveyor) is expected to have discovered this and to have asked Darby to confirm whether or not he has any rights. If Darby's rights have arisen, not by virtue of a constructive trust, but through proprietary estoppel, it is unclear whether they will be binding on a subsequent purchaser.[160] Technically, the interest granted through estoppel is crystallized by court order, so that in many cases it will postdate the creation of competing interests in the land. Despite this, there is some authority that suggests that rights arising by proprietary estoppel can be enforced against purchasers of the land. Although there is little authority, it has also been argued that proprietary estoppel might give rise to a continuing personal liability even after the land or property to which it relates has been sold.[161]

(b) Sole legal owner of registered land

The position is different if land is registered. A sale or mortgage is treated as a registered disposition. A registered disposition takes effect in precedence or priority to all earlier rights unless they have been recorded or protected on the register, or those rights constitute an overriding interest. Darby could protect his rights by registering a restriction

[158] Unregistered title is of diminishing importance, as the triggers requiring land to be registered have been greatly extended under ss 4–5 of the Land Registration Act 2002.

[159] See the definition of a purchaser in s 205(1)(xxi) of the Law of Property Act 1925 and s 11 of the Land Charges Act 1972. In registered land, a mortgage is classed as a registered disposition under s 27 of the Land Registration Act 2002 (the definition includes transfer and other purchases of estates in land).

[160] *Sledmore v Dalby* (1996) 72 P & CR 196.

[161] Bright and McFarlane, 'Personal Liability in Proprietary Estoppel' [2005] Conv 14.

on the register, preventing any sale taking place without his consent.[162] If he does not do this, then he will only be protected if his rights constitute an overriding interest.[163] The most relevant category of such rights are the rights of a person 'in actual occupation' of the land. That includes a person who is living at the property unless the 'occupation would not have been obvious on a reasonably careful inspection of the land at the time of the disposition'.[164] The protection extends to include rights arising by proprietary estoppel.[165]

(c) Joint legal owners

Where legal title is vested in two or more legal owners, the land legislation permits trust interests to be overreached. This is a process in which, after a sale, the equitable beneficial interests which were previously enforceable against the land instead can be enforced only against the proceeds of the sale. For overreaching to apply, the sale (or mortgage) must be agreed by all the legal owners, and any restrictions on the register (when the title is registered) must be complied with.[166] Since in most jointly owned family home cases the cohabitants are registered as legal owners, this means that their rights cannot be converted by overreaching without their knowledge and approval. In the fairly rare circumstances where legal title is held by joint legal owners but equitable beneficial interests are held by other people as well (for instance, where a married couple are registered as legal owners, but their parents have kept an equitable interest in return for helping to finance the purchase), it is possible for overreaching to take place without the knowledge and approval of all the beneficial owners. The way in which the beneficial owners can protect themselves against this possibility is by registering a restriction requiring their consent to any registered disposition.

162 For the operation of restrictions, see Land Registration Act 2002, Part IV, ss 40–47.

163 Land Registration Act 2002, ss 29 and 30.

164 Land Registration Act 2002, Sch 3. The rights of a person in actual occupation are protected even if their occupation is not obvious if the rights are known to the purchaser.

165 Land Registration Act 2002, s 116.

166 An overreaching sale requires the capital purchase money or the sum raised by the mortgage to be paid to or by the direction of two trustees.

13

The evolution of rights in the family home

1 Introduction

We saw in Chapter 12 how interests in the family home are governed by a special regime established by the twin decisions of *Stack v Dowden*[1] and *Jones v Kernott*.[2] The problem of how to resolve disputes about the family home goes back much further than these two cases. It is both interesting and informative to see how the law has developed; in addition, because the *Stack/Kernott* regime is based upon an evolutionary development from previous cases, significant aspects of the old rules remain relevant. There are also some instances where cases prior to *Stack* and *Kernott* provide answers to questions which have not been addressed since the introduction of the current regime.

2 The deserted wife's equity

The deserted wife's equity was one of the first attempts to provide an answer to a dispute about the family home. In *National Provincial Bank v Ainsworth*,[3] a wife who had been deserted by her husband and remained living in the family home claimed that she had a right to remain living there, even when a bank, which had secured a loan to the husband after he had left the house, sought to enforce its right to possession. Her claim failed because the right she claimed was personal rather than proprietary and, therefore, could not be enforced against third parties.

Several aspects of the claim are particularly worth noting. The first is that the arrangement showed what was then a stereotypical situation, where the matrimonial home had been acquired in the husband's name alone. Joint ownership was much less common then than it is now. The second is that the wife made no claim to a proprietary interest. A reason for both is that in the years immediately after the Second World War there was frequently only one 'breadwinner'. Many fewer married women worked—a bar on married women working in the civil service was not lifted until 1946. The third is that the right claimed is not one which would be available to a cohabiting but unmarried couple. Finally, the right encapsulated concepts of marital fault, and required 'good behaviour' by the wife.

[1] [2007] 2 AC 432. [2] [2011] UKSC 53. [3] [1965] AC 1175.

3 A proprietary interest in the home

It was not long following *National Provincial Bank v Ainsworth* before a claim to a proprietary interest in the matrimonial home reached the House of Lords in *Pettitt v Pettitt*.[4] Interestingly in this case the claim was by a husband. The wife had inherited a house from her mother. The husband had spent £800—then a significant sum—on repairs and redecoration. The wife sold that house and bought another—again in her sole name. The husband bought a car with the money left over, and later spent more money on improvements to the new house. The House of Lords rejected the husband's claim to have a proprietary interest. It held that it had the power to declare the rights of the spouses, but not the power to vary them. Lord Reid explained that the money the husband had spent could be explained as indulging 'in what is now a popular hobby' of do-it-yourself and to make the house a pleasanter place to live 'while the wife does the shopping, cooks the family dinner or baths the children'.

A year later another case, *Gissing v Gissing*,[5] reached the House of Lords. This was a claim by a wife to a half-share in a house purchased in her husband's name using a small deposit, an unsecured loan, and a mortgage for the balance. The husband paid the loan and mortgage instalments, and the wife funded the purchase of furniture, a cooker, refrigerator, and improvements to the lawn. The House of Lords rejected her claim: her spending on depreciating assets was insufficient to infer a common intention that she was to have a share in the house.

There is little doubt that both cases would be decided differently today, although some aspects of the decisions still resonate: there was a presumption that beneficial ownership followed legal title; expenditure (or the lack of it) on the acquisition of the property was a relevant factor; there was reference to the owner behaving in a way which induced the other to believe that they would have a beneficial interest; there was reference to identifying the common intention of the parties; and there was reference in *Gissing* to how the parties kept their finances separate. It is on some of these strands that the present law has been built.

4 Resulting trusts

(1) The original acquisition method

We saw in Chapter 12 that the Supreme Court has rejected the use of resulting trusts in deciding the ownership of the family home where the dispute is between a cohabiting couple. This has not always been the approach. Resulting trusts were, at one time, the primary means for identifying interests in the family home, as *Gissing v Gissing*, in particular, shows. Resulting trusts can still be used to help in identifying beneficial ownership of assets other than the family home; they may also be relevant where the dispute involves parties in addition to, or other than, the cohabiting couple, for instance, where legal title to a family home is held by another family member[6] or a company,[7] rather than by one or both of the cohabitants. Finally, even in common intention constructive trust analysis, financial contributions are a significant factor in inferring or imputing intention. There may be very little practical difference between resulting trust and constructive trust analysis where the main evidence is the financial history.

4 [1970] AC 777. 5 [1971] AC 886.

6 *Sandhu v Sandhu* [2016] EWCA Civ 1050 (resulting trust principles used in a constructive trust analysis).

7 *Prest v Petrodel Resources Ltd* [2013] UKSC 34; *NR v AB* [2016] EWHC 277 (Fam).

(2) General principles

We have already seen in Chapter 9 how the purchase money resulting trust leads to a presumption that the person who pays for an asset is the beneficial owner of it. It is based on a presumption that the purchaser would not have financed the transaction without wishing to retain a share of the beneficial ownership. The general principle was stated by Lord Reid in *Pettitt v Pettitt*:

> in the absence of evidence to the contrary effect, a contributor to the purchase-price will acquire a beneficial interest in the property.[8]

(3) Contribution to the purchase price

(a) Direct contributions

A major area of controversy concerned the nature of the 'contributions' sufficient to give rise to the presumption. While 'indirect' contributions may constitute sufficient detriment to support claims based on constructive trust or proprietary estoppel, only 'direct' contributions to the purchase price have been held to give rise to a presumption of resulting trust in favour of the contributor.

(b) Contribution to mortgage repayments

In the majority of cases land is not purchased outright, but with the help of a mortgage. In such circumstances it might be thought that a person who contributes to the mortgage repayments should be treated as having contributed to the purchase price, thus raising a presumption of resulting trust in his or her favour in proportion to his contributions. However, the principle traditionally taken as a starting point is that the amount paid through mortgage is treated in the same way as a cash contribution by the person taking out the mortgage, since that person has a legal liability to repay it.[9] That principle can be modified if there is an agreement at the time the mortgage is taken out that the sum raised by mortgage will be treated as a joint contribution to the purchase price. In this case the payment of mortgage instalments will be taken to give rise to a resulting trust. This was explained in *Cowcher v Cowcher*, where Bagnall J considered the consequences of a conveyance of a house to A for £24,000, where A had provided £8,000 of his own money and the remainder was provided by a mortgage taken out in the name of B:

> suppose that at the time A says that as between himself and B he, A, will be responsible for half the mortgage repayments... Though as between A and B and the vendor A has provided £8,000 and B £16,000, as between A and B themselves A had provided £8,000 and made himself liable for the repayment of half the £16,000 mortgage namely a further £8,000, a total of £16,000; the resulting trust will therefore be as to two-thirds for A and one-third for B.[10]

Applying this principle, Bagnall J held that a resulting trust was presumed in favour of a wife who had made some of the repayments on a mortgage taken out by her husband. Similarly in *Tinsley v Milligan*[11] the House of Lords held that there was evidence to support finding a resulting trust where the parties had agreed that the mortgage repayments would be made from an account containing the proceeds of their joint business operation, even though this was in the sole name of Tinsley. In *Gallarotti v Sebastianelli*[12] (decided

[8] [1970] AC 777 at 794. See also *Gissing v Gissing* [1971] AC 886.

[9] This view still has judicial support—see *Barrett v Barrett [2008]* EWHC 1061 (Ch) at 6–7 and 24 per David Richards J.

[10] [1972] 1 WLR 425. [11] [1994] 1 AC 340. [12] [2012] EWCA Civ 865.

after *Jones v Kernott*) two single men acquired a flat together. The trial judge found that they had an express agreement 'that their ultimate shares in the Flat should, broadly speaking, represent their contributions to it [in repaying the mortgage]'.

(c) Mortgage contributions not referable to agreement

Curley v Parkes[13] was a case in which there was no pre-purchase agreement about mortgage contributions. Mr Curley and Miss Parkes were living together. A house was purchased in 2001 in the sole name of Parkes. The purchase was funded exclusively by the proceeds of sale of her previous solely owned house, cash she provided and a mortgage of £138,000, which was taken out in her sole name. Curley subsequently paid some £9,000 into Park's bank account, from which the mortgage instalments were paid, as a way of assisting her with the huge commitments she was taking on. Curley claimed that these payments entitled him to an 8.5 per cent share of the equitable ownership of the house by way of a resulting trust. The Court of Appeal rejected his claim to an interest on this basis, holding that the payments could not be regarded as a contribution to the purchase price. Peter Gibson LJ explained the relevant principles:

> The relevant principle is that the resulting trust of a property purchased in the name of another, in the absence of contrary intention, arises once and for all at the date on which the property is acquired. Because of the liability assumed by the mortgagor in a case where monies are borrowed by the mortgagor to be used on the purchase, the mortgagor is treated as having provided the proportion of the purchase price attributable to the monies so borrowed. Subsequent payment of the mortgage instalments are not part of the purchase price already paid to the vendor, but are sums paid for discharging the mortgagor's obligations under the mortgage.[14]

Since it will frequently be the case that there is no direct evidence of an agreement to treat mortgage payments as a joint contribution to the cost of acquiring a property, it may be possible for the payments themselves to be treated as evidence from which such an agreement can be inferred. Lord Neuberger, in his dissenting speech in *Stack v Dowden*, suggested that it might be possible to classify mortgage repayments as direct contributions, particularly where property is bought almost exclusively by means of a mortgage as:

> repayments of mortgage capital may be seen as retrospective contributions towards the cost of acquisition, or as payments which increase the value of the equity of redemption.[15]

(d) Impact of excluding mortgage contributions

The importance of resulting trusts in determining the ownership of the family home was very much diminished by the decision to exclude payments subsequent to the date of purchase, except where these can be referred back to an agreement at the date of purchase. On the other hand, it avoided the need for difficult calculations to determine the proportion of the ownership of property acquired by way of subsequent contributions to mortgage payments, a difficulty which was acknowledged by the House of Lords in *Gissing v Gissing*, and for which no easy solution had been found.[16] However, even though such contributions may have been insufficient to gain an interest by way of a resulting trust, they may be relevant for the purposes of a constructive trust.

(e) Contribution by discount against purchase price

If a property is purchased at a discounted price, the amount of the discount is regarded as a contribution to the purchase price.[17] Therefore, the person who qualified for the

[13] [2004] EWCA Civ 1515. [14] [2004] EWCA Civ 1515 at 14. [15] [2007] 2 AC 431 at 117.
[16] [1971] AC 886 at 987, per Lord Reid. [17] *Thompson v Hurst* [2012] EWCA Civ 1752.

discount will be presumed to be the beneficiary of a resulting trust to that extent in the property. In *Marsh v Von Sternberg*,[18] Bush J held that a discount gained on the market value of a long lease because one of the parties was a sitting tenant was to be treated as a contribution to the purchase price in assessing their respective interests under a resulting trust. In *Springette v Defoe*,[19] a discount of 41 per cent of the market value of a council flat obtained because the plaintiff had been a tenant for more than eleven years was counted as a contribution to the purchase price by the Court of Appeal.

(f) Contributions to the cost of repairs or renovation

Where, contemporaneously with the purchase, the property is repaired or renovated, and its value is thereby increased, a person who contributes towards the cost of such repairs or renovations will be entitled to an interest in the land by way of a resulting trust proportionate to the extent to which the increase was attributable to their contribution.[20] Improvements made much later than the date of purchase may give rise to a constructive trust.

(g) Contributions to general household expenses

In contrast to indirect contributions to the purchase price of land, contributions made to general household expenses were unlikely to give rise to a presumption of resulting trust in favour of the contributor because they are not sufficiently referable to the purchase price. In *Burns v Burns*,[21] Mr and Mrs Burns began living together as man and wife in 1961. In 1963 a house was purchased in the sole name of Mr Burns, who financed the purchase by way of a mortgage. Mrs Burns began to work in 1975. She used part of her earnings to pay the rates and telephone bills and to buy various domestic chattels for the house. When they split up in 1980, she claimed to be entitled to an equitable interest in the house by reason of her contributions. The Court of Appeal held that she was not entitled to an interest by way of resulting trust because she had 'made no direct contribution to the purchase price'.[22] It should be noted that although such contributions to family expenses will not give rise to a presumption of resulting trust, they may, if substantial, constitute sufficient detriment to lead to the imposition of a constructive trust.

(h) Contributions to incidental expenses

In *Curley v Parkes*,[23] the Court of Appeal held that neither the payment of solicitor's fees and expenses, nor the payment of removal costs, were capable of giving rise to a resulting trust. Although such costs might be substantial, they do not form any part of the purchase price of the property itself, and hence do not give rise to a presumption of resulting trust. The same reasoning was used in *FHR European Ventures LLP v Mankarious*.[24] An agent had received unauthorized commission on the acquisition of the Monte Carlo Grand Hotel. The Supreme Court held that this commission was held on constructive trust for the principal. Part of the commission was used to pay the stamp duty and legal costs on the purchase of a house. It was held that the principal could not claim any part of the beneficial ownership of the house relating to these expenses.

(i) Contributions otherwise explained as loans

Even where there is a direct contribution towards the cost of acquiring a property which would normally lead to a resulting trust, the presumption of a resulting trust will be rebutted where the money was advanced by way of a loan.[25] In *Re Sharpe (a bankrupt)*[26]

[18] [1986] 1 FLR 526. [19] [1992] 2 FLR 388. [20] *Drake v Whipp* [1996] 1 FLR 826.
[21] [1984] Ch 317. [22] [1984] Ch 317 at 326, per Fox LJ. [23] [2004] EWCA Civ 1515.
[24] [2016] EWHC 359 (Ch). [25] *NR v AB* [2016] EWHC 277 (Fam). [26] [1980] 1 WLR 219.

Mr and Mrs Sharpe lived in a maisonette with Mr Sharpe's eighty-two-year-old aunt, Mrs Johnson. The property had been purchased in the name of Mr Sharpe for £17,000. Mrs Johnson had contributed £12,000 towards the purchase price, while the remainder was raised by way of a mortgage. Mr and Mrs Sharpe were subsequently declared bankrupt and Mrs Johnson claimed to be entitled to a proprietary interest in the maisonette by means of a resulting trust presumed from her contribution to the purchase price. Browne-Wilkinson J held that the money had in fact been advanced by way of a loan, with the intention that it would be repaid. She was not, therefore, entitled to any share of the equitable interest of the property. A presumption of a resulting trust was also rebutted by evidence that a loan was intended in *Vajpeyi v Yijaf*.[27] In this case the claimant provided the defendant, who was her lover, with £10,000 to enable him to purchase a house in his sole name. At the time of the purchase in 1980, the defendant was a young man of limited means. The claimant alleged that by virtue of this payment she was entitled to a 33.89 per cent share of the equitable ownership of the property on the basis of a presumed resulting trust, whereas the defendant claimed that the money had been advanced by way of a loan, which he had repaid. Peter Prescott QC held that the following factors had rebutted the presumption of a resulting trust in favour of a loan: the defendant had been a young man of limited means who was anxious to get on the property ladder, whereas the claimant was a woman who was already on the property ladder when the money was advanced; the claimant had tolerated the defendant collecting rents from the property and keeping them for himself for some twenty-one years; the claimant had failed to propound her claim to an interest for twenty-one years; and she had never said anything about her alleged interest in the house when it was mortgaged by the defendant to enable him to purchase her matrimonial home some years previously.

(j) Contributions otherwise explained as gifts

The normal presumption that a contribution to the purchase price of property creates a resulting trust will also be rebutted by evidence that the payment was made by way of gift. The presumption of advancement (described in Chapter 9) where a husband makes a transfer to, or contributes towards the cost of purchase in the name of, his wife is unlikely to support this because any such presumption is extremely weak,[28] and was described by Lord Diplock in *Pettitt v Pettitt* as a judicial instrument of last resort.[29] Indeed, even stronger doubt has come in later cases,[30] and Arden LJ confirmed in *Gibson v Revenue and Customs Prosecution Office*, that the presumption of advancement, like the presumption of resulting trust, is displaced by the presumption that that beneficial ownership follows legal ownership.[31]

(4) Quantifying the interest

The normal method of quantifying an interest arising out of a resulting trust is an arithmetical calculation, so that the share of the beneficial ownership attained is proportionate to the share of the purchase price contributed. This was one of the weaknesses of the resulting trust approach when compared to the common intention constructive trust,

[27] [2003] EWHC 2339.

[28] The high point was Lord Denning's use of the presumption in *Tinker v Tinker* [1970] 2 WLR 331 to frustrate a husband who had conveyed property into his wife's name to shield the family assets from his creditors, and later wished to claim the property back.

[29] [1970] AC 777.

[30] *Stack v Dowden* [2007] 2 AC 432 at 16 per Lord Walker; [101] per Lord Neuberger.

[31] [2008] EWCA Civ 645 at 27. Confirmed in *Jones v Kernott* [2012] 1 AC 776.

which has always allowed a wider range of factors to be considered in determining a share of the beneficial interest. Even before *Stack* and *Kernott*, there were some instances where different approaches to quantification were adopted.

(a) Utilizing constructive trust analysis

In *Midland Bank v Cooke*,[32] the Court of Appeal found that the circumstances that established a resulting trust also sufficed to establish a constructive trust.[33] Moving quantification to a constructive trust allowed for a more holistic approach to considering the factors applicable to determining the size of the beneficial share:

> [T]o determine (in the absence of express evidence of intention) what proportions the parties must be assumed to have intended for their beneficial ownership, the duty of the judge is to undertake a survey of the whole course of dealing between the parties relevant to their ownership and occupation of the property and their sharing its burdens and advantages. That scrutiny will not confine itself to a limited range of acts of direct contribution of the sort that are needed to found a beneficial interest in the first place. It will take into consideration all conduct which throws light on the question what shares were intended.[34]

On the facts of that case, Mrs Cooke was entitled to a 50 per cent share of the property, though her direct contribution to the purchase price would have entitled her only to a 6.74 per cent share. Subsequent decisions confirmed that the only way for a cohabitant to enjoy an interest greater than the exact mathematical equivalent of the contribution was to demonstrate that the land was held on constructive trust,[35] and the approach, which may be termed 'the assumed intention approach' gathered favour.[36] This approach reached its apex in the Court of Appeal decision in *Oxley v Hiscock*.[37] Chadwick LJ adopted a new broad principle that the beneficial interests of the parties should be determined by the court on the basis of what seemed 'fair' in the light of all the circumstances:

> It must now be accepted (at least in this Court and below) the answer is that each is entitled to that share which the court considered fair having regard to the whole course of dealing between them in relation to the property. And, in that context, the 'whole course of dealing between them in relation to the property' includes the arrangements which they make from time to time in order to meet the outgoings (for example, mortgage contributions, council tax and utilities, repairs, insurance and housekeeping) which have to be met if they are to live in the property as their home.[38]

On the facts, Ms Oxley, who had contributed 22 per cent of the purchase price, was awarded a 40 per cent share to reflect the fact that Mr Hiscock had contributed nearly twice as much to the purchase price of the home and that the parties' conduct was:

> consistent with an intention to share the burden of the property (by which she must, I think, have meant the outgoings referable to ownership and cohabitation), it would be fair to treat them as having made approximately equal contributions to the balance of the purchase price (£30,000).[39]

This form of what may be termed 'judicial discretion' was applied in subsequent cases, *Cox v Jones*[40] and *Pinfield v Eagles*.[41] It was rejected in relation to the *inference* of a

[32] [1995] 4 All ER 562; (1995) 27 HLR 733; (1997) 60 MLR 420 (O'Hagan); [1997] Conv 66 (Dixon). See also *McHardy and Sons (A firm) v Warren* [1994] 2 FLR 338.

[33] Supported by comments of Lord Bridge in *Lloyds Bank v Rosset* [1991] 1 AC 107 at 133 (discussed later).

[34] (1995) 27 HLR 733 at 745.

[35] See *Drake v Whipp* [1996] 1 FLR 826.

[36] See, for example, *Le Foe v Le Foe* [2001] 2 FLR 970.

[37] [2005] Fam 211.

[38] [2005] Fam 211 at 69.

[39] [2005] Fam 211 at 74.

[40] [2004] EWHC 1486; Probert, 'Land, Law and Ex-Lovers' [2005] Conv 168.

[41] [2005] EWHC 447.

common intention between the parties when quantifying an interest.[42] It has, however, been explicitly adopted by the Supreme Court in *Jones v Kernott*,[43] in relation to *imputing* a common intention to decide on the size of the beneficial share in a common intention constructive trust where no objective common intention between them can be inferred. Although the Court of Appeal did not confine its remarks in *Oxley v Hiscock* to the family home, it is almost certainly the case that the approach it espoused should be confined to that situation, as is confirmed by the treatment of the decision in *Stack* and *Kernott*.

(b) Constructive trusts subsuming resulting trusts

The approach in *Oxley v Hiscock* was taken one step further by *Stack* and *Kernott*, which decided that the constructive trust analysis should entirely replace resulting trusts in relation to questions between cohabitants about the ownership of the family home, as explored in Chapter 12. A summary of the traditional requirements of resulting trusts is provided in Figure 13.1.

5 Common intention constructive trusts

We have seen how limitations in resulting trust analysis led to the use of common intention constructive trust principles when dealing with ownership of the family home. This form of constructive trust finds its origins in *Pettitt v Pettitt*,[44] where Lord Diplock said

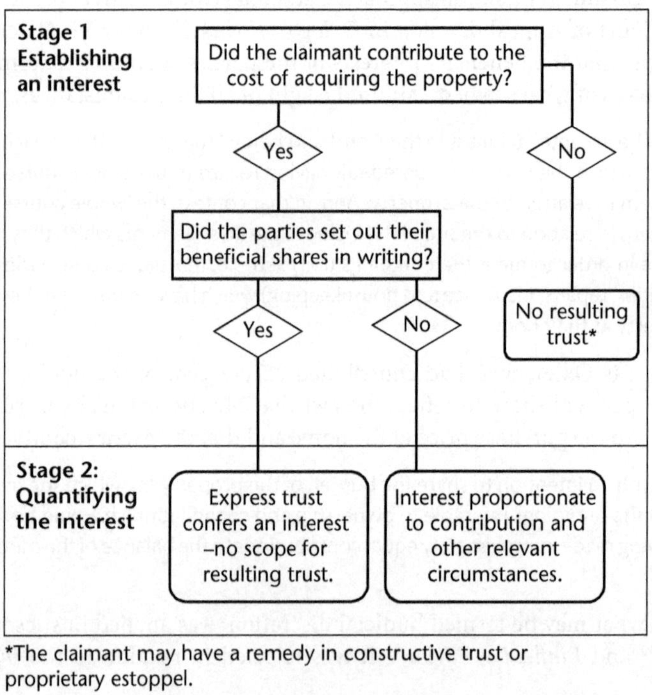

Figure 13.1 Resulting trust of the family home: the traditional approach

[42] See *Stack v Dowden* [2007] 2 AC 432 at 127 per Lord Neuberger, affirming the view expressed by Lady Hale at 61; *Jones v Kernott* [2012] 1 AC 776 at 51 per Lady Hale and Lord Walker.

[43] [2012] 1 AC 776 at 51–2.

[44] [1970] AC 777.

that the approach to be adopted in cases involving the family home should be based upon seeking the common intention of the parties. This form of constructive trust has the advantage of greater flexibility than resulting trusts with the ability to resolve issues about ownership both at the time of acquisition of the family home and later.

(1) **Development of the common intention trust**

(a) **The traditional use of constructive trusts**

Although the House of Lords held in *Gissing v Gissing*[45] that a constructive trust should be imposed whenever it is 'inequitable' for a legal owner to deny the beneficiary an equitable interest in land, the circumstances in which this test would be met were closely defined. Lord Diplock emphasized that a legal owner would only have acted so as to justify the imposition of a constructive trust:

> if by his words or conduct he has induced the [beneficiary] to act to his own detriment in the reasonable belief that by so acting he was acquiring a beneficial interest in the land.[46]

This formulation captures the essential elements of the constructive trust, namely that the court is acting to fulfil the reasonable expectations of the beneficiary, who is entitled to have his expectation fulfilled because he has acted to his detriment in the belief that they would be fulfilled. The legal owner cannot be allowed knowingly to enjoy the benefit conferred by the beneficiary's detrimental reliance without also allowing him to enjoy the expected interest.

(b) **The criteria developed**

The principles set out in *Gissing v Gissing* were traditional and represented a strict property-based approach which was more concerned with the nature of the parties' contributions to the property rather than to the nature of their relationship. Under this approach, contributions to family life which could not be related to ownership of a house, such as child-rearing or the performance of the usual domestic tasks that partners ordinarily have to do around the home, would not be sufficient to gain an interest in the property. Some judges preferred a less limiting approach to the determination of constructive trust interests. Lord Denning in particular was responsible for attempting to introduce a radically different approach—the 'new model' constructive trust—by giving the court a wide discretion to determine on the facts of any given case whether a person should be entitled to an interest by way of a constructive trust. On his approach the chief criterion was that of 'justice', and not the type of contribution that had been made. The death of Lord Denning's new model constructive trust has already been explored in the Chapter 10.

(c) **The *Rosset* reformulation**

For many years the classic statement of the criteria, following the death of the 'new model constructive trust' was contained in the speech of Lord Bridge in *Lloyds Bank plc v Rosset*.[47] Lord Bridge, with the agreement of the rest of the House of Lords, rationalized the case law up until that point. He stated that to displace the presumption that beneficial ownership follows legal title (so that a sole legal owner would enjoy the whole of the beneficial interest in the property), the parties had to demonstrate a common intention for a constructive trust to give effect to these intentions. The House of Lords drew a sharp distinction between two different methods through which this common intention could be demonstrated.

[45] [1971] AC 886. [46] [1971] AC 886 at 905. [47] [1991] 1 AC 107.

(i) Express common intention

The first *Rosset* category of circumstances in which a constructive trust could arise is where there was an express common intention between the parties that they were to share the ownership of the land. The establishment of such an express intention is a matter of evidence of what the parties said to each other at the time that the property was purchased and thereafter:

> The first and fundamental question which must always be resolved is whether . . . there has at any time prior to the acquisition, or exceptionally at any later date, been any agreement, arrangement or understanding reached between them that the property is to be shared beneficially. The finding of an agreement or arrangement to share in this sense can only, I think, be based on evidence of express discussions between the partners, however imperfectly remembered and however imprecise their terms may have been.[48]

(ii) Common intention inferred from conduct

Although Lord Bridge stated that a common intention could be inferred, he also made it clear that this would be difficult without a direct contribution to the purchase price:

> In sharp contrast [to the case where there is an express common intention] is the very different one where there is no evidence to support a finding of an agreement or arrangement to share, however reasonable it might have been for the parties to reach such an arrangement if they had applied their minds to the question, and where the court must rely entirely on the conduct of the parties both as the basis from which to infer a common intention to share the property beneficially and as the conduct relied on to give rise to a constructive trust. In this situation direct contributions to the purchase price by the partner who is not the legal owner, whether initially or by payment of the mortgage instalments, will readily justify the inference necessary to the creation of a constructive trust. But, as I read the authorities, it is at least extremely doubtful whether anything less will do.[49]

(iii) Detrimental reliance

Once a common intention was demonstrated, the claimant would then need to show 'that he or she has acted to his or her detriment or significantly altered his or her position in reliance on the agreement in order to give rise to a constructive trust or a proprietary estoppel'.[50] In situations where a common intention was inferred from a direct contribution to the purchase prices, detriment was not a major issue, as in paying the money the contributor would clearly have acted to his detriment sufficiently to justify a constructive trust.

(iv) Quantification

Once this had been done, the court would then quantify the interest by reference to the express or inferred common intention, which, as we have seen under the treatment of resulting trusts, allowed for a greater share of the property than the value of any financial contributions made to the purchase or upkeep of the property.

(v) Impact of dual approach

This dual approach of express or inferred common intention supported by detrimental reliance, dominated analysis of the rights of cohabitants in the absence of an express declaration of trust and the development of the law for some sixteen years. No distinction was drawn between those situations where a property had been purchased in the sole name of one of the parties, or in joint names.

48 [1991] 1 AC 107 at 132.

49 [1991] 1 AC 107 at 132–3.

50 [1991] 1 AC 107 at 132–3.

(d) Application beyond the family home

The criteria set out in *Rosset* were neither explicitly not implicitly limited to cases involving cohabiting couples or the family home, and we have seen in Chapter 10 how they have been applied to commercial arrangements.

(2) Common intention

In *Lloyds Bank plc v Rosset*,[51] the central issue was whether the wife had acquired an interest in her matrimonial home by way of a constructive trust that was capable of gaining priority over a legal mortgage of the house that the husband had granted to a bank. Mr and Mrs Rosset were married in 1972. In 1982 Mr Rosset became entitled to a substantial sum of money under a trust fund established by his grandmother in Switzerland. They found a house that required complete renovation. It was purchased for £57,500 in the sole name of Mr Rosset because the Swiss trustee had refused to advance the money for a purchase in joint names. The cost of the renovation work was also provided by Mr Rosset alone, so that his wife made no direct financial contribution to the purchase. Mrs Rosset had, however, helped with the renovation work. She had decorated some bedrooms and prepared others for decoration. She had also supervised the work of builders who were carrying out the renovation work. In the light of this she claimed to be entitled to a share of the ownership by way of a constructive trust. The House of Lords held that no common intention to share beneficial ownership could be inferred from the work she had done, and that, in the absence of an express common intention, no constructive trust had arisen in her favour, Consequently Mrs Rosset had no proprietary interest that could take priority over the rights of the mortgagee bank.

(a) Examples of 'common intention'

Lord Bridge in *Rosset* considered that the earlier cases of *Eves v Eves*[52] and *Grant v Edwards*[53] were 'outstanding examples'[54] of constructive trusts created through an express common intention. In *Eves v Eves*,[55] an unmarried couple, Janet and Stuart Eves,[56] moved to a new house. It was purchased solely in the name of Stuart, who told Janet that it was to be their house, and a home for themselves and their children. He also told her that the purchase could not be completed in their joint names because she was under twenty-one, but that if she had been of age it would have been purchased in their joint names. In *Grant v Edwards*,[57] a man purchased a house in his name alone to provide a home for himself and his lover. He told her that he had not purchased it in their joint names because that would prejudice her divorce proceedings.

However, in both of these cases the supposed 'common intention' was in reality merely an appearance of common intention. Neither of the male parties genuinely wished their partners to enjoy a share of the ownership of their respective houses. It is worth noting that if either case came before the courts today in the post *Stack* and *Kernott* regime, the result would likely be the same, but the courts would simply infer that a common intention had been reached from the conduct of the parties.[58] A more convincing example of a true common intention can be found in *HSBC Bank plc v Dyche*.[59] Here, when

[51] [1991] 1 AC 107. [52] [1975] 1 WLR 1338. [53] [1986] Ch 638.

[54] [1991] 1 AC 107 at 133. See also *Hammond v Mitchell* [1992] 2 All ER 109. [55] [1975] 1 WLR 1338.

[56] Although they shared the same name, they were unmarried. She had changed her name to his by deed poll.

[57] [1986] Ch 638. [58] See *O'Neill v Holland* [2020] EWCA Civ 1583, where such an inference was made.

[59] [2009] EWHC 2954 (Ch).

Mr Collelldevall had been made bankrupt, he had (with the consent of his trustee in bankruptcy) transferred his jointly owned family home to his daughter and son-in-law (Mr and Mrs Dyche) for much less than its open market value. The Collelldevalls remained in the house, and alleged that an agreement had been reached that the property would be held by the Dyches for them and that it would be transferred back when a loan taken out to finance the transfer had been repaid. Judge Purle QC (sitting as a High Court judge) found an agreement on the evidence which gave rise to a common intention constructive trust. The claimant had agreed to transfer the property upon faith of a clear agreement or understanding that it would thereafter be held for him and his wife (who had since died). That agreement had been acted upon by his transferring the property, at a price that bore no relationship to its true value, to his daughter and son-in-law and by making repayments to his son corresponding broadly to the sums falling due under the mortgage. The requisite common intention was to be inferred also from the simple fact that the claimant had continued to have sole beneficial use of the property as his home.

(b) The agreement must be operative

The agreement to share ownership must, of course, be operative at the relevant date. In *Clarke v Corless*,[60] three landowners had made an express agreement to acquire a strip of land that provided an access to their properties. Two of them later acquired parts each in their own right, and the third objected to one of these purchases. Proudman J held that there was no constructive trust because at the time of the purchase the agreement had been abandoned, and also had not been relied upon by the claimants.

(c) Agreement on shares is not essential

In *Drake v Whipp*,[61] the Court of Appeal stressed that the principles identified in *Lloyds Bank plc v Rosset* did not require the parties to have reached a common intention 'as to the respective shares to be taken by the beneficial owners'.[62] Peter Gibson LJ stated:

> All that is required for the creation of a constructive trust is that there should be a common intention that the party who is not the legal owner should have a beneficial interest and that that party should act to his or her detriment in reliance thereon.[63]

(d) Express agreement amounts to a declaration of trust

Where a genuine express agreement to share the ownership of land is found, in substance the legal owner has expressly declared, or agreed to declare, a trust in favour of the claimant. However, such a declaration would be merely oral and therefore ineffective to create an enforceable trust due to the absence of compliance with the formality requirements of s 53(1)(b) of the Law of Property Act 1925.[64] Although there is no enforceable express declaration of trust, a constructive trust will be imposed if the claimant acted to their detriment on the basis of the express agreement, as it would be inequitable to allow the legal owner to deny a trust which would give effect to his intentions.

(e) Agreement is not imputed

While the evidence needed to support a finding of a 'common intention' falls short of that needed to support the finding that there was a legally binding contract,[65] the courts were originally clear that they were not imputing an agreement to the parties.

60 [2009] EWHC 1636 (Ch).

61 [1996] 1 FLR 826.

62 [1996] 1 FLR 826 at 830, per Peter Gibson LJ.

63 [1971] AC 886 at 898.

64 Law of Property Act 1925.

65 *Clarke v Corless* [2009] EWHC 1636 (Ch) at 22.

This aspect of the common intention constructive trust has not entirely survived the changes in approach introduced by *Stack* and *Kernott*, as we have seen in Chapter 12. It is now possible to infer, not impute a common intention at the acquisition stage where a common intention cannot otherwise be discovered. Imputation, however, is not permissible at the acquisition stage, and the few cases that do so do not represent the current state of the law. At the second stage of acquiring an interest, the imputation stage, there is a clear role for imputing the size of an interest based on fairness, where the comment intention cannot be discovered from the agreement reached between the parties or easily be inferred from the facts of the case.

(3) **Inference from conduct**

(a) Direct contribution to the purchase price

In *Lloyds Bank plc v Rosset*, the House of Lords significantly concluded that a common intention should only be inferred where a claimant had made direct contributions to the purchase price of the property concerned. A common intention, in other words, would only be inferred in circumstances where a presumption of resulting trust might have arisen.

(b) Contributions after the date of purchase

A difference between resulting trusts and the common intention constructive trust was that a common intention can be inferred from a contribution referable to the acquisition or improvement of the family home made after the date of its purchase. For instance, in *Aspden v Elvy* a substantial contribution to the renovation of a property in the expectation of being able to live there and to have a share in it was held by Judge Behrens to be enough to justify implying a common intention.[66]

However, relatively insignificant improvements will not be sufficient to give rise to an inference of a common intention. In *Lloyds Bank plc v Rosset* itself, the House of Lords held that Mrs Rosset's assistance with the decoration of the house 'could not possibly justify' the inference of a common intention that she was to gain a share of the ownership thereof:

> Mrs Rosset was extremely anxious that the new matrimonial home should be ready for occupation before Christmas if possible. In these circumstances it would seem the most natural thing in the world for any wife, in the absence of her husband abroad, to spend all the time she could spare and to employ any skills she might have, such as the ability to decorate a room, in doing all she could to accelerate progress of the work quite irrespective of any expectation she might have of enjoying a beneficial interest in the property.[67]

The monetary value of her work, in the light of a total purchase price exceeding £70,000, was also said to have been 'so trifling as to be almost de minimis'.[68]

(c) Indirect contributions

Some cases have stretched the concept of what constitutes a direct contribution to acquisition. In *Gissing v Gissing*,[69] Lord Diplock suggested that it might be corroborative of a common intention if the wife's 'payments of other household expenses were intended by both spouses to be treated as including a contribution by the wife to the purchase price of

[66] [2012] EWHC 1387 at 123 to 124.

[67] [1991] 1 AC 107 at 131.

[68] Contrast, however, *Midland Bank plc v Cooke* [1995] 4 All ER 562, where a small contribution to the purchase price of property derived from a joint gift was sufficient to establish a common intention.

[69] *Gissing v Gissing* [1970] UKHL 3.

the matrimonial home'. He may have had in mind evidence of a wife acting to her detriment, but it suggests a way in which one party can be treated as making a financial contribution to acquisition. In *Le Foe v Le Foe*,[70] Nicholas Mostyn QC held that the financial contributions of a couple to the acquisition of their home should be viewed as a whole, so that a wife's contributions towards the household expenses could be regarded as an indirect contribution to the purchase price of the property:

> Although I am sure that H earned more than W . . . I have no doubt that the family economy depended for its function on W's earnings. It was an arbitrary allocation of responsibility that he paid the mortgage, service charge and outgoings, whereas W paid for day-to-day domestic expenditure. I have clearly concluded that W contributed indirectly to the mortgage repayments, the principal of which furnished part of the consideration of the initial purchased price.[71]

Thus contributions to the purchase price that are, strictly speaking, indirect, may still be capable of leading to the inference of a common intention if they enabled the other party to make a direct contribution. Not every financial commitment will be treated in this way. In *Driver v Yorke*,[72] it was held that a person who had acted as a guarantor of the mortgage on behalf of the purchaser of a flat had not made any contribution to the purchase price because he had not shown any intention of being liable for the mortgage instalments.

(d) Contributions towards mortgage payments

The question of how contributions to the repayment of a mortgage can be treated has already been considered in relation to resulting trusts. The choice is essentially between treating them as deferred or indirect contributions towards acquiring a property, or treating them simply as the discharge of a debt. *Curley v Parkes*[73] held that contributions made toward the payment of mortgage instalments subsequent to the acquisition of a property are simply sums paid to discharge the mortgagor's obligations under the mortgage, and do not, therefore, give rise to a share by way of resulting trust. Similarly, in *Driver v Yorke*,[74] it was held that occasional contributions to the mortgage instalments made by the two sons of the purchaser of a flat would not give rise to an inference of a common intention, because the payments did not have sufficient connection with the purchase to be treated as a contribution to the purchase price. If the dicta in *Curley v Parkes* are strictly applied, a claimant who moved in with an owner of a mortgaged property and then contributed to the mortgage instalments—even paying them all—would not be able to establish an inferred common intention to share the ownership from the payments alone, and so would only be able to maintain a constructive trust if the payments were made on the basis of an express common intention to share the ownership. Since this is one of the most common scenarios in which cohabitation may occur without the parties giving any express consideration to their respective property rights, such an application would severely reduce the ability of home sharers to establish an interest by way of a constructive trust. In *Lightfoot v Lightfoot-Browne*,[75] the Court of Appeal accepted the view of the trial judge that, although payment of regular mortgage payments did not give rise to an inference of a common intention, a substantial capital payment to reduce the mortgage debt was 'harder to explain' and could (although it did not on the facts) give rise to an expectation of benefit.

[70] [2001] 2 FLR 970. [71] [2001] 2 FLR 970 at 973. [72] [2003] 2 P & CR 210.
[73] [2004] EWCA Civ 1515. [74] [2003] 2 P & CR 210.
[75] *Lightfoot v Lightfoot-Browne* [2005] EWCA Civ 201.

(e) Financial contribution alone insufficient

The mere fact that a financial contribution has been made towards the purchase price or improvement of a property did not in itself guarantee that a common intention would be inferred. No constructive trust will arise if the contribution is made in circumstances that demonstrate that there was no intention on the part of the contributor to obtain an interest in the property, for example, because the contribution was by way of a loan or gift.[76] Similarly, a common intention will not be inferred if the parties have merely done what spouses or partners would ordinarily do. In *Burns v Burns* May LJ said:

> The court is only entitled to look at the financial contributions or their real and substantial equivalent to the acquisition of the house; that the husband may spend this weekend redecorating or laying a patio is neither here nor there, nor is the fact that the woman has spent so much of her time looking after the house, doing the cooking and bringing up the family.[77]

Going beyond the ordinary is better evidence of a common intention. In *Eves v Eves*,[78] Lord Denning had considered that Janet had done 'a great deal of work to the house and garden . . . much more than many wives would do',[79] including stripping the hall of wallpaper, painting the woodwork in the lounge and kitchen, painting the kitchen cabinets, painting the brickwork, breaking up concrete in the front garden, and demolishing a shed. In *Grant v Edwards*,[80] Linda Grant had made a substantial contribution to housekeeping expenses. However, Lord Bridge, in *Rosset*, concluded that the conduct of neither of the respective claimants had been sufficient to infer a common intention. The constructive trusts in each case were only justifiable on the basis of an express common intention. In *Morris v Morris*,[81] the Court of Appeal held that the courts should be slow to interpret the conduct of spouses or cohabitants as meaning that a beneficial interest of some sort should be acquired. The respondent and his mother were joint owners of a farmhouse that was part of the family farm. The claimant married and moved in with the respondent and contributed without remuneration to the family farming business. She also provided the money to purchase an enclosure and started her own riding school funded partly by a free loan made by the respondent and his mother. The conduct was not exceptional, as required in post-acquisition cases, partly because she had received benefits towards her own business.[82]

(f) Knowledge of both parties

Actions which are unknown to the legal owner cannot give rise to a common intention. In *Lightfoot v Lightfoot-Browne*, a claimant who had made a payment of £41,000 towards discharging the mortgage of a property without the knowledge of the sole legal owner was, therefore, held unable to establish a common intention by inference from the payment.[83]

(4) Reliance or detriment

We have already seen that a 'common intention' will not alone give rise to a constructive trust. The criteria as set out by Lord Bridge in *Lloyds Bank v Rosset*,[84] following a similar requirement described in *Gissing v Gissing*,[85] is that a constructive trust will only arise in favour of a person who acted to his detriment, or substantially changed his position in reliance on the common intention.

[76] See *Re Sharpe (A Bankrupt)* [1980] 1 WLR 219.

[77] *Burns v Burns* [1984] Ch 317 at 344. Similar observations were made by Lod Diplock in *Pettitt v Pettitt* [1970] AC 777 at 826.

[78] [1975] 1 WLR 1338.

[79] [1975] 1 WLR 1338 at 1340.

[80] [1986] Ch 638.

[81] [2008] EWCA Civ 257.

[82] [2008] EWCA Civ 257.

[83] [2005] EWCA Civ 201.

[84] [1991] 1 AC 107.

[85] [1971] AC 886.

(a) Rationale

The constructive trust arises because it would be inequitable to allow the legal owner to refuse to give effect to the intention when the claimant has acted in a personally detrimental manner. It is absolutely essential to grasp that the standard of conduct sufficient to establish detrimental reliance is different from the standard of conduct required to justify an inference of a common intention. While only a direct contribution to the purchase price will justify the inference of a common intention, a much wider range of conduct will constitute sufficient detriment to lead to the imposition of a constructive trust if there was an express common intention.

(b) Where there is an express common intention

Lord Bridge in *Rosset* summarized what was required in the way of detriment to establish a constructive trust founded upon an express common intention to share the ownership of the property:

> it will only be necessary for the partner asserting a claim to a beneficial interest against the partner entitled to the legal estate to show that he or she has acted to his or her detriment or significantly altered his or her position in reliance on the agreement in order to give rise to a trust . . .[86]

This clearly adopts a much lower standard than the restrictive threshold of conduct from which it is possible to infer a common intention. There is no need for a direct contribution to the purchase price of the property. *Grant v Edwards*[87] shows that Grant demonstrated sufficient detrimental reliance by making a substantial contribution from her own wages to the housekeeping and bringing up the children.

(c) Must the conduct relate to the expected interest?

A difference of opinion appears in the judgments in *Grant v Edwards* as to whether the conduct alleged to represent reliance or detriment needed to be directly linked to the interest claimed. Nourse LJ addressed the question as to the nature of conduct required and concluded:

> In my judgment it must be conduct on which the woman could not reasonably have been expected to embark unless she was to have an interest in the house.[88]

He held that Grant's contribution to the housekeeping amounted to an indirect contribution to the mortgage instalments, as it enabled Edwards to pay them from his own wages. This was conduct that could not have been reasonably expected unless she was to have an interest in the house. Sir Nicholas Browne-Wilkinson V-C took a more liberal view:

> Once it has been shown that there was a common intention that the claimant should have an interest in the house, any act done by her to her detriment relating to the joint lives of the parties is, in my judgment, sufficient detriment to qualify. The acts do not have to be referable to the house.[89]

He emphasized the practical difficulties attendant on a test that required the court to find that the claimant's conduct could only be explained on the basis that a beneficial interest in the property would be thereby acquired:

> In many cases of the present sort, it is impossible to say whether or not the claimant would have done the acts relied on as a detriment even if she thought she had no interest in the

86 [1971] AC 886 at 132. 87 [1986] Ch 638. 88 [1986] Ch 638 at 648.

89 [1986] Ch 638 at 657. Compare the similar debate on part performance in *Steadman v Steadman* [1976] AC 536.

> house. Setting up house together, having a baby, making payments to general housekeeping expenses (not strictly necessary to enable the mortgage to be paid) may all be referable to the mutual love and affection of the parties and not specifically referable to the claimant's belief that she has an interest in the house.[90]

Given that Lord Bridge indicated in *Lloyds Bank plc v Rosset*[91] that 'a significant change of position by the claimant' was sufficient detriment to support a constructive trust in fulfilment of an express common intention, it seems that the more liberal approach of Browne-Wilkinson V-C is to be preferred. This also follows from the growing recognition that the detriment required in the case of a constructive trust based on an express common intention is analogous to that required to sustain a claim to a remedy under the principles of proprietary estoppel.[92]

(d) Where a common intention is inferred

Where there was no express common intention but the criteria are satisfied to entitle the court to infer a common intention, the element of detriment used to present much less difficulty. Given that the court could originally only infer a common intention from conduct constituting a direct contribution to the purchase price of the property,[93] the contributor would clearly have acted to his detriment sufficiently to justify a constructive trust. Indeed, it is this essential fact which demonstrates how resulting trusts can be clothed in the language and trappings of common intention, as the necessary payment to the purchase price which gives rise to the presumption of resulting trust provides both the intention and necessary detriment to support the finding that there is a constructive trust. The nature of the detriment will, however, be crucial to the determination of the extent of the beneficial interest thereby acquired and it was here that the attractiveness of arguing an inferred common intention rather than resulting trust manifests itself.

It is worth remembering that, following the new regime in *Stack*, it is now possible to infer a common intention in the absence of a direct payment to the purchase price, and that a similar approach is taken as to detriment based on an express agreement between the parties.

(5) Quantifying the beneficial interest

(a) The need for quantification

Where the evidence establishes that the parties had reached an express agreement as to the ownership of the property, the constructive trust will operate to fulfil that agreement. However, where there is no express common intention as to the respective shares of the parties in the property, either because they had an express common intention to share the ownership of the property but had not discussed the specific proportions in which the ownership was to be shared[94] or because the common intention to share has had to be inferred from a contribution to the purchase price, the extent of the equitable interest arising under the constructive trust will have to be determined by the court.

[90] [1986] Ch 638 at 657. [91] [1991] 1 AC 107.

[92] *Lloyds Bank plc v Rosset* [1991] 1 AC 107 at 132. See also *Grant v Edwards* [1986] Ch 638 at 656, where Browne-Wilkinson V-C thought that 'useful guidance may in future be obtained from the principles underlying the law of proprietary estoppel which in my judgment are closely akin to those laid down in *Gissing v Gissing*'.

[93] *Lloyds Bank plc v Rosset* [1991] 1 AC 107 at 133.

[94] As in *Cox v Jones* [2004] EWHC 1486 and *Pinfield v Eagles* [2005] EWHC 477.

(b) Method of quantification

The starting point for analysis is the basic principle that constructive trusts arise to fulfil the intentions of the parties, so as Browne-Wilkinson V-C stated in *Grant v Edwards*,[95] 'prima facie the interest of the claimant will be that which the parties intended'. Unlike the principles of resulting trusts, the size of the parties' contributions are not the determinative factor, nor, unlike proprietary estoppel, is the extent of any detriment the main guide. The Court of Appeal very rapidly departed from conferring an interest which equated only with the value of the parties' respective financial contributions. In *Midland Bank plc v Cooke*,[96] it held that, for a variety of reasons, including the fact that the parties had entered into the commitment of marriage, a wife who had contributed less than 10 per cent of the cost of acquiring the family home was, nevertheless, entitled to a half beneficial share as the assumed intention of the parties. In *Oxley v Hiscock*,[97] the Court of Appeal indicated that the exercise in which the court needed to engage was one of ascertaining, where there was no agreement, what the court adjudged to be a fair share in all the circumstances of the case. Chadwick LJ, with more than a nod to the approach in proprietary estoppel,[98] stated the principle thus:

> It must now be accepted (at least in this Court and below) the answer is that each is entitled to that share which the court considers fair having regard to the whole course of dealing between them in relation to the property. And, in that context, the 'whole course of dealing between them in relation to the property' includes the arrangements which they make from time to time in order to meet the outgoings (for example, mortgage contributions, council tax and utilities, repairs, insurance and housekeeping) which have to be met if they are to live in the property as their home.[99]

There is a divergence between the 'assumed intention' approach adopted by the Court of Appeal in *Midland Bank v Cooke* and the seeming 'judicial discretion' approach adopted in *Oxley v Hiscock*. These decisions were both subject to academic and judicial criticism, not least that the determination of the beneficial interest arising under a constructive trust will ultimately turn on subjective value judgements rather than legal principles. The approach adopted in *Oxley v Hiscock* has, though, now been endorsed by the Supreme Court in *Jones v Kernott*,[100] with an honest acknowledgment that it involves the imputation of an intention that may not exist.

(6) Deficiencies in the *Rosset* approach

(a) Invented agreement

One of the major criticisms of the *Rosset* formulation of the common intention constructive trust is that, whether intentionally or otherwise, the court is often devising an agreement from scraps of conversation between the parties and construing their words out of context.[101] Indeed, a cynic might suggest that the criteria encouraged claimants to invent recollections of conversations about sharing ownership which may never actually have taken place.

95 [1986] Ch 638 at 657.
96 [1986] Ch 638; O'Hagan, 'Quantifying Interests under Resulting Trusts' (1997) 60 MLR 420.
97 [2005] Fam 211.
98 In particular he relied on *Yaxley v Gotts* [2000] Ch.162. See [2004] EWCA Civ 546 at 70.
99 [2004] EWCA Civ 546 at 69.
100 [2011] UKSC 53.
101 See, for example, Clarke, 'The Family Home: Intention and Agreement' [1992] Fam Law 72.

(b) Assurance rather than common intention?

Even more compelling, particularly when considering that an excuse to exclude a partner from the legal title was construed as an express common intention to grant an interest in *Grant v Edwards*,[102] is the suggestion that what the court is really looking for is a representation or assurance from the legal owner, or a reasonable expectation on the part of the claimant, even if the other party never meant what they said. That certainly appears to have been the case in *Eves v Eves*[103] and *Grant v Edwards*.[104] The vagueness of what can suffice as a common intention is illustrated by the Northern Irish case of *Bank of Scotland v Brogan*.[105] The wife gave evidence that the husband had repeated a number of times 'that what was hers was his and his hers', not least, as Deeny J said 'in the context of [the husband] obtaining cash from her before going out for an evening'.[106] This, accompanied by a range of other circumstances, was enough to support her claim to shared ownership of the farm owned in his name.

(c) Limited basis for inferring intention

In the absence of an expression of an intention to share beneficial ownership, the *Rosset* approach only allowed an intention to share to be inferred from direct financial contributions to the acquisition of the property. This has been changed by cases following *Stack* or *Kernott* where a property has been acquired in the name of one cohabiting party only.

The issues that still exist with the constructive trust, even within the new regime, are explored in Chapter 15.

[102] [1986] Ch 638.
[103] [1975] 1 WLR 1338.
[104] [1986] Ch 638.
[105] [2012] NICh 21.
[106] At 31.

14

Proprietary estoppel

1 Introduction

A domineering father, a farmer, repeatedly tells his son that if the son continues to help on the farm without pay, he will eventually inherit the farm. The son gives up opportunities of working elsewhere, but then finds that the father has left the farm to charity. Does the son have a remedy? The arrangement was never formalized in writing (a requirement for contracts to grant interests in land), and is unlikely because of its lack of specificity and the family context to be contractually enforceable. It cannot be treated as a resulting trust, because the son has made no financial contribution to the purchase of the farm. It is unlike a common intention constructive trust, because it involves the promise of a future benefit. Despite all this, the son may have a remedy through proprietary estoppel.[1]

2 The nature of proprietary estoppel

(1) What is it?

Proprietary estoppel can confer proprietary rights despite the lack of a formal grant or transfer.[2] It can be used in three situations: where a person mistakenly believes that they have an existing right in land and the real owner acquiesces in this belief; where a person is encouraged by the owner to believe that they have an existing right in land; and where a person is led by the owner to believe that they will have a right in the future if they act in a particular way.[3] It has much in common with common intention constructive trusts, but is capable of operating in different circumstances. Most cases involve rights in land, but the doctrine is not confined to this kind of property.[4]

(2) Overlap with constructive trusts

There is a substantial overlap between constructive trusts and proprietary estoppel. This means that the same facts might give rise either to the recognition of a constructive trust or to the award of an estoppel remedy.[5] The overlap has in the past led the judiciary to enquire whether there is any substantive difference between the two.[6] Nevertheless, it is

[1] See Bevan, *Land Law* (3rd edn, OUP 2022) Ch 8.

[2] (1984) 100 LQR 376 at 381. [3] See *Tyrell v Bowden* [2018] EWHC 106 (Ch) at 65–6.

[4] *Motivate Publishing FZ LLC v Hello Ltd* [2015] EWHC 1554 (Ch) (licence to publish *Hello!* magazine); Shaw-Mellors, 'Proprietary estoppel and the enforcement of promises' [2015] Conv 529.

[5] *Patrick v McKinley* [2017] EWCA Civ 2068 at 10; *Matchmove Ltd v Dowding* [2016] EWCA Civ 1233 at 23.

[6] See, for example, the obiter statements of Chadwick LJ in *Oxley v Hiscock* [2005] Fam 211 at 66: 'it may be more satisfactory to accept that there is no difference, in cases of this nature, between constructive trust and proprietary estoppel'; see also the comments of McAllister J in *Krawczynska v Rozuk* [2020] 1 ELUK 473 at [12].

not unusual for a claimant to have two alternative bases of claim on the same facts.[7] In some cases, such as *Liden v Burton*,[8] where a man assured a woman helping to pay the mortgage that he would look after her for ever and make provision in his will, the facts may be better aligned to proprietary estoppel than even the broad brush common intention constructive trust following *Stack v Dowden*.

(3) **Distinguishing constructive trusts and proprietary estoppel**

Even though there are circumstances in which both mechanisms operate, Lord Hope in *Stack v Dowden*, correctly identified that the two doctrines are different in both approach and outcome:

> Proprietary estoppel typically consists of asserting an equitable claim against the conscience of the 'true' owner. The claim is a 'mere equity'. It is to be satisfied by the minimum award necessary to do justice . . . which may sometimes lead to no more than a monetary award. A 'common intention' constructive trust, by contrast, is identifying the true beneficial owner or owners, and the size of their beneficial interests.[9]

In some cases, as we shall see, the court has felt that it is appropriate to award the claimant the full fee simple ownership of the land concerned. In other cases a lesser interest, such as a right to occupy, has been granted. The only available remedy with a constructive trust is a finding of a share of beneficial ownership. Thirdly, whereas a constructive trust arises at the moment when the common intention is acted upon, which means that it may bind third parties acquiring interests in the land after that time but before the court has recognized the entitlement, any interest by way of proprietary estoppel may only arise after it has been awarded by the court.

3 Establishing the equity

(1) **The essence of proprietary estoppel**

The essence of proprietary estoppel is that if the legal owner of property has so conducted himself (whether by encouragement or representations) that the claimant believes that he has, or will obtain, some rights in respect of the land, and he has acted to his detriment on the basis of his induced belief, it would be unconscionable for the legal owner to assert his strict legal entitlement to the property, and equity will, therefore, intervene to prevent this. The remedy granted in satisfaction of the estoppel equity is, therefore, awarded because the claimant has experienced a 'frustrated expectation'.[10]

(2) **Based on unconscionable conduct**

Although the principle of proprietary estoppel has a long historical pedigree, dating from before the nineteenth century,[11] it was only towards the end of the twentieth century that the full scope of the doctrine was recognized and that the courts formulated the key requirements in a general way. The most important question is to identify the circumstances in

[7] For instance, a person injured by a defective product may have both a claim for breach of contract and a claim for negligence.

[8] [2016] EWCA 275.

[9] [2007] 2 AC 432 at 448, 37.

[10] Gray, *Elements of Land Law* (2nd edn, Butterworths 1993), p 356.

[11] See *Bridges v Kilburne* (1792) (referred to in *Jackson v Cator* [1800] 5 Ves 688); *Dillwyn v Llewelyn* [1862] 4 De G F & J 517; *Ramsden v Dyson* [1866] LR 1 HL 129.

which a legal owner's conduct can be regarded as 'unconscionable', thus calling for the court to provide the claimant with a remedy and preventing him from asserting his legal rights.

(a) Strict criteria: the 'five probanda'

In the late nineteenth century, the courts held that there were strict and rigid criteria that must be met before an estoppel equity was raised. Despite earlier and broader statements of principle in *Ramsden v Dyson*,[12] in *Willmott v Barber*, Fry J stipulated five essential elements which had to be established before the court would restrain a defendant from asserting his legal rights over property:

> A man is not to be deprived of his legal rights unless he has acted in such a way as would make it fraudulent for him to set up those rights. What, then are the elements or requisites necessary to constitute fraud of that description? In the first place the plaintiff must have made some mistake as to his legal rights. Second, the plaintiff must have expended some money or must have done some act (not necessarily upon the defendant's land) on the faith of his mistaken belief. Thirdly, the defendant, the possessor of the legal right, must know of the existence of his own right which is inconsistent with the right claimed by the plaintiff. If he does not know of it he is in the same position as the plaintiff, and the doctrine of acquiescence is founded upon conduct with a knowledge of your legal rights. Fourthly, the defendant, the possessor of the legal right, must know of the plaintiff's mistaken belief of his rights. If he does not, there is nothing which calls upon him to assert his own rights. Lastly, the defendant, the possessor of the legal right, must have encouraged the plaintiff in his expenditure of money or in the other acts which he has done, either directly or by abstaining from asserting his legal right. Where all these elements exist, there is fraud of such a nature as will entitle the court to restrain the possessor of the legal title from exercising it, but, in my judgment, nothing short of this will do.[13]

These five 'probanda' came to be regarded as essential requirements of estoppel, and claims failed where it was not possible to establish all five.[14] In *Crabb v Arun District Council*,[15] Scarman LJ considered that the five requirements were 'a valuable guide as to the matters of fact which have to be established in order that a plaintiff may establish this particular equity' and they became entrenched within the law.

(b) A broader understanding

The restrictive approach of *Willmott v Barber*[16] has given way to a much broader understanding of proprietary estoppel.[17] In *Taylor Fashions Ltd v Liverpool Victoria Trustees Co Ltd*,[18] Oliver J restated the requirements of proprietary estoppel:

> the recent cases indicate,[19] in my judgment, that the application of the *Ramsden v Dyson* principle—whether you call it proprietary estoppel, estoppel by acquiescence or estoppel

[12] [1866] LR 1 HL 129 at 152 (Lord Cranworth LC) and at 170 (Lord Kingsdown).

[13] [1880] 15 Ch D 96 at 105–6.

[14] See *Kammins Ballroom Co Ltd v Zenith Instruments (Torquay) Ltd* [1971] AC 850 at 884; *E and L Berg Homes Ltd v Grey* [1979] 253 *Estates Gazette* 473.

[15] [1976] Ch 179.

[16] [1880] 15 Ch D 96.

[17] However, in *Taylor v Dickens* [1998] 1 FLR 806, Judge Weeks QC rejected the notion of a broad doctrine of estoppel founded on the principle of 'unconscionability' and said that the existence of such a doctrine would mean that 'you might as well forget the law of contract and issue every judge with a portable palm tree'. His comments appear to be inconsistent with the majority of modern cases and have been severely criticized: [1998] Conv 213 (Thompson).

[18] [1982] QB 133; *McMahon v Kerry County Council* [1981] ILRM 419; [1985] 79 ILSI Gaz 179 (Pearce).

[19] See *Inwards v Baker* [1965] 2 QB 29; *ER Ives Investment Ltd v High* [1967] 2 QB 379; *Crabb v Arun District Council* [1976] Ch 179; *Moorgate Mercantile Credit Co Ltd v Twitchings* [1976] QB 225, CA; *Shaw v Applegate* [1977] 1 WLR 970, CA.

> by encouragement is really immaterial—requires a very much broader approach which is directed rather at ascertaining whether, in particular individual circumstances, it would be unconscionable for a party to be permitted to deny that which, knowingly or unknowingly, he has allowed or encouraged another to assume to his detriment than to inquiring whether the circumstances can be fitted within the confines of some preconceived formula serving as a universal yardstick for every form of unconscionable behaviour.[20]

Therefore, rather than determining whether an equity had been established by application of a rigid list of requirements which must be satisfied, he held that the appropriate inquiry was simply whether the defendant's conduct had been, in all the circumstances of the case, 'unconscionable'.[21]

In *Gillett v Holt*, Robert Walker LJ similarly emphasized that the prevention of 'unconscionability' is the essence of proprietary estoppel:

> Moreover, the fundamental principle that equity is concerned to prevent unconscionable conduct permeates all the elements of the doctrine. In the end the court must look at the matter in the round.[22]

(c) Three requirements

Although the approach taken in *Taylor Fashions*[23] explains the doctrine of proprietary estoppel on the general principle of 'unconscionability', to establish an equity the courts have held that the three key elements of 'assurance', 'reliance', and 'detriment or change of position' must be present.[24] Although these elements can be separated for analytical purposes, in *Gillett v Holt*,[25] Robert Walker LJ suggested that in practice they are often interrelated because 'the quality of the relevant assurances may influence the issue of reliance' and that 'reliance and detriment are often intertwined'.[26] There must also be no bar, such as unconscionable conduct on the part of the claimant, to the grant of a remedy.

(3) Assurance

No estoppel 'equity' will arise unless the claimant can establish that the legal owner of land created or encouraged an expectation on the claimant's part (whatever the legal owner's real intention)[27] that he was presently entitled, or would become entitled,[28] to an interest in the land. This assurance may be given 'actively' through the acts of the legal owner, or 'passively' through his silence and failure to disabuse the claimant of his belief that he is entitled to an interest in the land.[29] To be valid, the assurance must be:

> unambiguous and must appear to have been intended to be taken seriously. Taken in its context, it must have been a promise which one might reasonably expect to be relied upon by the person to whom it was made.[30]

[20] See also *Amalgamated Investment and Property Co Ltd (in liquidation) v Texas Commerce International Bank Ltd* [1982] QB 84.

[21] [1982] QB 84 at 155.

[22] [2000] 2 All ER 289 at 301. See also *Guest v Guest* [2020] EWCA Civ 387.

[23] [1982] QB 133n.

[24] See *A-G of Hong Kong v Humphreys Estate (Queen's Gardens) Ltd* [1987] AC 114, PC; *Gillies v Keogh* [1989] 2 NZLR 327 at 346, per Richardson J.

[25] [2000] 2 All ER 289 at 301.

[26] These sentiments were repeated in *Davies v Davies* [2016] EWCA 463 at 38. See also *Jennings v Rice* [2003] 1 P & CR 8 and *Henry v Henry* [2010] 1 All ER 998 at 55.

[27] See *Tyrell v Bowden* [2018] EWHC 106 (Ch) at 68.

[28] *Re Basham (Decd)* [1987] 1 All ER 405.

[29] *Warnes v Headley* (31 January 1984, unreported), CA.

[30] [2009] UKHL 18 at 56 per Lord Walker, approving the words of Hoffmann LJ in *Walton v Walton* (unreported).

In some cases the assurance may take the form of an actual agreement between the parties. In others there may be a promise that falls short of an agreement, and in others again there may be no more than an understanding or even a course of dealing that shows that a particular state of affairs was assumed or accepted.

(a) Active assurance

In *Pascoe v Turner*,[31] the plaintiff made an active assurance to the defendant, a woman with whom he was living. The defendant had left the house when he started an affair with another woman, but the evidence showed that he had visited the defendant and had declared to her that she had nothing to worry about, as the house was hers and everything in it. The Court of Appeal held that the evidence established an assurance sufficient to found an estoppel equity, and since she had acted to her detriment in reliance upon it she was entitled to a remedy by way of proprietary estoppel. In *Inwards v Baker*,[32] Mr Baker's son, Jack, was intending to build a bungalow. He was persuaded by his father to build the bungalow on his land, which he subsequently did. The Court of Appeal held that this amounted to a sufficient inducement or encouragement to give rise to an estoppel. In *Griffiths v Williams*,[33] the Court of Appeal held that an estoppel equity was established where a mother had assured her daughter that she would be entitled to live in her house for the whole of her life. An active assurance will certainly have been given if the legal owner of property promised that the claimant was, or would become, entitled to some interest in it.[34]

(b) Precision of assurance

For nearly thirty years, David Thorner (the claimant in *Thorner v Major*[35]) worked without pay on the farm of his father's cousin, Peter. Although no express promise had been made, the clear understanding between David and Peter was that David would inherit the farm on Peter's death. In the event, Peter died without making a will. The House of Lords held that David's reasonable belief that he would inherit the farm should be fulfilled, since he had acted on that belief by forgoing other opportunities. The view of the majority was that this was in most respects a straightforward instance of proprietary estoppel.[36] There had been a number of acquisitions and disposals of parcels of land over the thirty-year period in which David had worked without payment on the farm. It was argued that consequently the property had not been established with sufficient certainty. Their Lordships, while noting the requirement of certainty, felt that the fluidity of the farm holding did not stop it being identified as the proprietary subject of the assurance.

Lord Walker and Lord Neuberger both indicated that the assurance or understanding on which a claimant relied did not need to be expressed with precise and exact definition.[37] Lord Neuberger opined that:

> It would represent a regrettable and substantial emasculation of the beneficial principle of proprietary estoppel if it were to be artificially fettered so as to require the precise extent of the subject of the alleged estoppel to be strictly defined in every case focusing on technicalities can lead to a degree of strictness–inconsistent with the fundamental aims of equity.[38]

[31] [1979] 1 WLR 431. [32] [1965] 2 QB 29. [33] [1977] 248 *Estates Gazette* 947.

[34] *Wayling v Jones* [1993] 69 P & CR 170. [35] [2009] UKHL 18.

[36] Lord Scott agreed, but would have liked to use a remedial constructive trust: [2009] UKHL 18 at 14.

[37] See, for example, [2009] UKHL 18 at 98. [38] [2009] UKHL 18 at 98.

His Lordship was responding, in part, to the contention in the earlier speech of Lord Scott in *Yeoman's Row v Cobbe*,[39] which suggested that a contractual level of certainty as to assets identified was required in estoppel claims. Lord Walker, in a postscript, expressed his difficulty with Lord Scott's alignment in *Yeoman's Row* of proprietary estoppel with the requirements of promissory estoppel (including the requirement of a 'clear and unambiguous' representation). In *Thompson v Foy*,[40] Lewison J followed the guidance of Lords Walker and Scott in *Thorner v Major*. In this case, the relevant assurance related to the building of an extension to the family home by Mrs Foy. Lewison J, held that, despite there being no evidence of specific conversations between Mrs Thompson and Mrs Foy, it was 'clear enough'[41] that there was a 'mutual understanding'[42] that the extension would belong to Mrs Foy. The more flexible approach has been cited recently with approval in a number of first instance decisions. In *Clarke v Corless*, Proudman J held that:

> there must be a clear agreement on the basic details of the arrangement without difference of principle.[43]

Similarly, in *Gill v Woodall*, Deputy Judge James Allen QC stated:

> The relevant assurance must be clear enough but what amounts to sufficient clarity in a case of this kind is hugely dependent upon context. A representation can be sufficient to found proprietary estoppel even if it is not made expressly. It may be made in oblique and allusive terms providing it was reasonable for the person to whom it was made, given his knowledge of the maker and background circumstances, to have understood the maker not merely that his present intention was to leave the property to the other but that he would definitely do so.[44]

(c) **Assurance relating to specific assets?**

In *Layton v Martin*,[45] a man had given a woman who had moved in with him a general assurance that he would provide her with 'financial security'. It was held that this assurance was too amorphous and insufficiently connected with specific property to give rise to an estoppel equity. The real issue is probably one of clarity. In *Re Basham (Decd)*[46] it was held that a plaintiff was able to claim a right by way of proprietary estoppel to the residuary estate of the defendant, on the basis that the assurance had extended to the 'the whole of A's estate',[47] rendering it clearly identifiable.

(d) **Resolving ambiguity in an assurance**

The House of Lords indicated in *Thorner v Major*,[48] that the requirement of clarity must not be used to defeat otherwise meritorious claims. Lord Neuberger, exploring this issue in detail,[49] opined that any assurance needs to be adjudged according to three separate (though related) criteria: (1) in context,[50] (2) without rigidity,[51] and (3) that any ambiguity, such as where the assurance has more than one possible meaning, should be taken into account in quantifying the estoppel interest, rather than to negative the assurance.

39 [2008] UKHL 55. 40 [2009] EWHC 1076 (Ch). 41 [2009] EWHC 1076 (Ch) at 90.
42 [2009] EWHC 1076 (Ch) at 92. 43 [2009] EWHC 1636 at 23.
44 [2009] EWHC 834 at 51. See also *Whittaker v Kinnear* [2011] EWHC 1479 (QB) at 30 per Bean J.
45 [1986] 2 FLR 227. 46 [1986] 1 WLR 1498. 47 [1986] 1 WLR 1498 at 1510.
48 [2009] UKHL 18. 49 [2009] UKHL 18 at 84–6.
50 See *Cook v Thomas* [2010] EWCA Civ 227 at 99.
51 [2010] EWCA Civ 227 at 85: 'The court should not search for ambiguity or uncertainty, but should assess the question of clarity and certainty practically and sensibly, as well as contextually.'

(e) Passive assurance

Assurance may occur by conduct, for example, if a legal owner stands by while the claimant acts to his detriment, in the belief that he is entitled to an interest in the land, this will constitute a sufficient assurance to give rise to an estoppel equity.[52] Although it is not strictly essential[53] that the owner knew of the claimant's action and mistaken belief, and of his own rights to intervene,[54] these are relevant issues, and it will be easier to establish an equity where they are present. It will also be difficult to establish a claim to the grant of a future right where the legal owner is unaware of the claimant's expectation.[55] In *St Pancras and Humanist Housing Association Ltd v Leonard*,[56] Mr Leonard (described by the judge as a seasoned squatter) had, for over twelve years, been in exclusive possession of a garage close to a group of houses that had been acquired from Camden Council by a cooperative of which he was a member. He attended a meeting of the cooperative in which the decision was taken to seek a lease of land, including the garage from the Council, for the benefit of all the members. He raised no objection. The trial judge, upheld by the Court of Appeal, held that Mr Leonard was later estopped from asserting his claim to exclusive rights to the garage, even though he was not aware at the time of the meeting that his adverse possession gave him a right to claim title. He did believe at the time that he had the right to prevent other cooperative members from using the garage, and his failure to assert this was enough to make his silence at the meeting an acceptance that the garage would become a communal asset.

(f) Assurance relating to a grant of future rights

An estoppel equity can arise when an assurance is made concerning the future grant of rights in specific property, something which has been described as the 'promise principle'.[57] This will most commonly occur where an owner had made assurances that he will leave property to the claimant in his will. For example, an estoppel equity was established in *Wayling v Jones*,[58] where the owner of a hotel had promised his partner that he would leave it to him by will on his death. *Thorner v Major*[59] is another example.

However, in *Taylor v Dickens*,[60] it was held that there was no claim by way of proprietary estoppel where an elderly lady had said that she would leave her estate to her gardener, but changed her mind without telling him after he had stopped charging her for his help. Judge Weeks QC held that, in light of the inherent revocability of testamentary dispositions, such an assurance would only give rise to an estoppel equity if it created or encouraged the claimant to believe that the owner would not exercise her right to change her will. This decision was subjected to severe academic criticism,[61] which was accepted by the Court of Appeal in *Gillett v Holt*.[62] In this case Gillett had worked for Holt, who was

[52] *Ramsden v Dyson* (1866) LR 1 HL 129.

[53] *Shaw v Applegate* [1978] 1 All ER 123, CA; *Taylor Fashions Ltd v Liverpool Victoria Trustees Co Ltd* [1982] QB 133; *Thorner v Major* [2009] UKHL 18.

[54] Compare *Armstrong v Sheppard & Short Ltd* [1959] 2 QB 384, CA.

[55] *Hoyl Group Ltd v Cromer Town Council* [2015] EWCA Civ 782; *Tyrell v Bowden* [2018] EWHC 106 (Ch) at 78.

[56] [2008] EWCA Civ 1442.

[57] Shaw-Mellors, 'Proprietary estoppel and the enforcement of promises' [2015] Conv 529.

[58] (1993) 69 P & CR 170. See also *Gillett v Holt* [1998] 3 All ER 917, where it was held that an assurance that the defendant would leave his estate to the plaintiff was capable of founding an entitlement by way of proprietary estoppel. However, in the event Carnwath J held that a claim failed because the defendant had only expressed a mere intention to leave his estate by will to the plaintiff, and not an irrevocable promise that he would inherit regardless of any changes in circumstances.

[59] [2009] UKHL 18. [60] [1998] 3 FCR 455.

[61] Thompson, 'Emasculating Estoppel' [1998] Conv 220; Swadling, 'Case Note on *Taylor v Dickens*' [1998] RLR 455.

[62] [2000] 2 All ER 289.

a gentleman farmer, for nearly forty years. On seven separate occasions, Holt had assured him that he would leave his entire estate to him, and that he and his family could, therefore, be sure of a secure future. Robert Walker LJ explained that these assurances were sufficient to give rise to an estoppel equity, even though they did not include an explicit assurance that the owner would not alter his will:

> But the inherent revocability of testamentary dispositions (even if well understood by the parties, as Mr Gillett candidly accepted that it was by him) is irrelevant to a promise or assurance that 'all this will be yours'. . . Even when the promise of assurance is in terms linked to the making of a will . . . the circumstances may make clear that the assurance is more than a mere statement of present (revocable) intention, and is tantamount to a promise.[63]

The Court of Appeal addressed the same issue in *Bradbury v Taylor*.[64] Bill Taylor had encouraged his nephew, Roger, and his partner and children to move into his house on the basis of oral promises that he would leave the house to them after his death. Some years later relations soured and Bill changed his mind. The Court of Appeal upheld the decision of the trial judge that Roger and his family's expectation of inheriting the property were enforceable through proprietary estoppel.[65]

(g) Assurance not required to have been intended to be acted upon

It is not necessary for the party making the assurance to intend that the assurance be acted upon. This was confirmed by Lord Scott in *Thorner v Major*:

> If it is reasonable for a representee to whom representations have been made to take the representations at their face value and rely on them, it would not in general be open to the representor to say that he or she had not intended the representee to rely on them.[66]

(h) Assurances and false representations

As befits a doctrine based on the equitable concept of unconscionability, it is clear that it is not possible to rely on an assurance which has been obtained by dishonest conduct and through false representations. In *Murphy v Rayner*,[67] Mrs Murphy had been Mr Rayner's carer for many years and had all her expenses paid by him. Mr Rayner had given gifts and provided food and other necessities to Mrs Murphy. He frequently told her that he intended to give her his property and a percentage of his investments after death. Mrs Murphy had falsely represented that an adult family relative was her daughter, and Mr Raynor had made payments for her education in India and assisted in the purchase of property for her. Mr Rayner's family became suspicious, and following an investigation which revealed that there was no daughter, Mrs Murphy was dismissed. Mrs Murphy claimed that she was entitled to live in the property during Mr Rayner's lifetime and to have it transferred to her on his death by means of estoppel, as well as to a share of the investments. Jeremy Cousins QC held that in light of her dishonest conduct, Mrs Murphy could not rely on the assurances that had been induced on the basis of false representations of fact.[68]

[63] [2000] 2 All ER 289 at 304. Pawlowski and Brown argue that an estoppel equity would also arise where a testator promises to create a secret trust and then subsequently changes his will so that the property is not left to the secret trustee: 'Constituting a Secret Trust by Estoppel' [2004] Conv 388.

[64] [2012] EWCA Civ 1208.

[65] For a trenchant criticism of the validity of the oral assurance in this case, see Mee, 'Proprietary estoppel and influence: enough is enough?' [2013] Conv 280.

[66] [2009] UKHL 18 at 17. [67] [2011] EWHC 1 (Ch).

[68] The same would not appear to true with innocent misrepresentations of fact, which are to be treated as one of the factors in considering all aspects of whether a valid estoppel claim has been made out—see *Qayyum v Hameed* [2009] EWCA Civ 352.

In a similar vein, it will be more difficult for an interest to be acquired through proprietary estoppel where the claimant is a trustee under a family trust and the right alleged is being acquired in breach of duty against beneficiaries who are said to have acquiesced.[69]

(i) Assurances and common intention

There is significant overlap between the requirements necessary to demonstrate an express common intention to acquire an interest by means of a constructive trust and a representation or assurance to found a claim through proprietary estoppel. Neither requires a contractual style of agreement in the family homes context and both require that the understanding or assurance relates to a right in particular property. An important distinction is that in proprietary estoppel the courts are focusing on finding an assurance or representation by the representor; in the constructive trusts context the courts are supposedly seeking the common intention of the parties. That distinction may be narrower than appears at first blush since analysis of the case law on common intention suggests that the courts are in fact concerned only with a representation from the legal owner which the claimant relies upon. It would be rare for circumstances which give rise to the finding of an express common intention to not also give rise to an assurance in proprietary estoppel.[70]

(j) Assurance by agreement

An assurance may be made as part of a bargain which is potentially contractually enforceable. However, contracts relating to the grant of an interest in land,[71] and dispositions of an equitable interest must be made in writing.[72] Can proprietary estoppel avoid these requirements? In *Yaxley v Gotts*,[73] a builder had entered into an oral agreement with the owner to refurbish and convert a house into flats in return for his acquiring the ground-floor flats. The Court of Appeal held that, although this agreement was unenforceable as a contract for lack of formalities, it could give rise to a claim by way of proprietary estoppel. Lord Scott suggested in *Yeoman's Row v Cobbe*[74] that 'proprietary estoppel cannot be prayed in aid in order to render enforceable an agreement that statute has declared to be void',[75] such as a contract to grant an interest in land which has not been made in writing. At face value, this would have robbed proprietary estoppel of any real utility in cases involving land such as the family home,[76] although Lord Neuberger emphatically pointed out in *Thorner v Major* that Lord Scott's comments can have no relevance in a case with no contractual connection.[77] It is also relevant that *Yeoman's Row v Cobbe* was a commercial case where the sophisticated and legally aware parties would have known they were taking risks by acting without a binding contract. In addition, the expectation of the parties was that they would enter into a binding agreement, some of the provisions of which had not been agreed. This was Lord Scott's principal reason for rejecting proprietary estoppel as a basis for a remedy,[78] because a right to a contract falls short of an expectation of an interest in property. Lord Walker explicitly suggested in his judgment that a distinction should be drawn between commercial cases involving individuals who are aware of their rights and who may well have taken legal advice, and domestic cases where the

[69] See *Sinclair v Sinclair* [2009] EWHC 926 (Ch) at 71.

[70] Dixon, 'Invalid Contracts, Estoppel and Constructive Trusts' [2005] Conv 247. See *Patrick v McKinley* [2017] EWCA Civ 2068.

[71] Law of Property (Miscellaneous Provisions) Act 1989, s 2.

[72] Law of Property Act 1925, s 53.

[73] [2000] 1 All ER 711.

[74] [2008] UKHL 55.

[75] [2008] UKHL 55 at 29.

[76] Etherton 'Constructive Trusts and Proprietary Estoppels: The Search for Clarity and Principle' [2009] Conv 104 at 120.

[77] [2009] UKHL 18 at 96–8, per Lord Neuberger.

[78] The claimant did not go without a remedy. It was held that he was entitled to reasonable remuneration for the time and effort which he had spent on a quantum meruit basis.

claimant is much less likely to be legally advised and where expectations and understandings might be much less clearly formulated.[79] It is likely that this view will prevail, but an easier route to enforcing an agreement often lies in constructive trust, which is expressly excepted from the need for writing by the relevant statutory provisions. In *Matchmove Ltd v Dowding*,[80] Francis, who considered his word to be his bond, agreed to sell a meadow to Dowding. He later declined to perform this agreement. The judge enforced the agreement, despite the lack of writing, on the basis of both constructive trust and proprietary estoppel. On appeal to the Court of Appeal Dowding defended the decision on the basis of constructive trust alone in order to avoid the issue of whether the claim in proprietary estoppel was barred by the lack of writing.

(k) Assurance by whom?

The assurance will usually be made directly by the legal owner. It may also be made by an agent where the agent has the principal's authority to make the representation.[81] It has been held that trustees can be subject to estoppels even though they do not have the beneficial interest.[82]

(l) Interpreting assurances

Whether an assurance has been made is a question of fact for the trial judge. The difficulties of making an assessment are illustrated by *James v James*[83] where the judge believed that Sam, a farmer's son, had convinced himself that his father had promised him the farm on the father's death, and interpreted all events and comments in this light. In fact, the judge believed that, while the father had included Sam in the farm partnership, he had never promised him the land: there was no clear assurance to that effect; there had been some statements about the father's will, but as deputy Judge Matthews observed, 'a statement of *current intentions* as to future conduct is not a *promise* of that conduct, let alone a promise intended to be acted upon.'[84] The judge added: 'Sam's eagerness to inherit the farmland from his father has caused him to persuade himself that he was being promised something when he was not.'[85] In a commercial context, it is less likely that the courts will treat discussions as creating an assurance than in a domestic context because the parties should be aware that they are assuming a commercial risk if the discussions do not result in a formal agreement.[86]

(4) Reliance

(a) Requirement of reliance

An essential element of proprietary estoppel is that the claimant must have acted in reliance upon the assurance in relation to which the claim is being made.[87] It is not unconscionable to make an assurance if it is not acted upon.

[79] [2008] UKHL 55 at 68, 81, and 87. Dixon differs on the basis that unconscionability is the only issue, but may more easily be shown in the domestic context: 'Developments in estoppel and trusts of land' [2015] Conv 469.

[80] *Matchmove Ltd v Dowding* [2016] EWCA Civ 1233. See also *Ghazaani v Rowshan* [2015] EWHC 1922 (Ch).

[81] *Preedy v Dunne* [2016] EWCA Civ 805.

[82] *Forester Maurice Labrouche v Frey* [2016] EWHC 268 (Ch) at 160.

[83] [2018] EWHC 43 (Ch); *Fielden v Christie-Miller* [2015] EWHC 87 (Ch) at [38]–[39]; *Catchpole v Trustees of the Alitalia Airlines Pension Scheme* [2010] PLR 387 at 54.

[84] [2018] EWHC 43 (Ch) at 24. [85] [2018] EWHC 43 (Ch) at 35.

[86] *Baird Textile Holdings Ltd v Marks & Spencer Plc* [2001] EWCA Civ 274 at 94; *Motivate Publishing FZ LLC v Hello Ltd* [2015] EWHC 1554 (Ch) at 74–5; Shaw-Mellors [2015] Conv 529.

[87] See further Robertson, 'The Reliance Basis of Proprietary Estoppel Remedies' [2008] Conv 295.

(b) Reliance as a causal connection

Reliance connects the assurance with the detriment. It demonstrates that the assurance caused the claimant to act to his detriment. As Balcombe LJ stated in *Wayling v Jones*:

> There must be a sufficient link between the promises relied upon and the conduct which constitutes the detriment.[88]

(c) Burden of proving reliance

In order to establish an estoppel equity a claimant must demonstrate[89] not merely that an assurance was made by the legal owner of land, but also that he relied upon the assurance made. In *A-G of Hong Kong v Humphreys Estate (Queen's Gardens) Ltd*[90] the Privy Council stated that it was necessary for the claimants to 'show' that they had relied on an expectation that had been encouraged by the landowner. In *Lim Teng Huan v Ang Swee Chuan*[91] the Privy Council held that the requisite reliance could be established by an 'inevitable'[92] inference drawn from the facts. In *Wayling v Jones* Balcombe LJ held:

> Once it has been established that promises were made, and that there has been conduct by the plaintiff of such a nature that inducement may be inferred then the burden of proof shifts to the defendant to establish that he did not rely on the promises.[93]

(d) Establishing reliance

A claimant will fail to establish an estoppel equity if it can be shown that he acted as he did for reasons other than the assurance. In *Coombes v Smith*,[94] Mrs Coombes had an unhappy marriage and fell in love with Mr Smith. He bought a house where it was intended they should live together. She became pregnant by him, and moved into the house. Mr Smith never moved in with her, but visited regularly. The house was sold and another purchased, which Mrs Coombes decorated. After their relationship had broken down, Mrs Coombes claimed an interest in the house by way of proprietary estoppel. Jonathon Parker QC held that even if an assurance had been made, Mrs Coombes had not acted in reliance on it. As to her becoming pregnant, he considered:

> it would be wholly unreal, to put it mildly, to find on the evidence adduced before me that the plaintiff allowed herself to become pregnant by the defendant in reliance on some mistaken belief as to her legal rights. She allowed herself to become pregnant because she wished to live with the defendant and bear his child.[95]

Likewise, leaving her husband was not because of any assurance that Mr Smith had made but because 'she preferred to have a relationship with . . . the defendant rather than continuing to live with her husband . . . There is no evidence that she left her husband in reliance on the defendant's assurance that he would provide for her if and when their relationship came to an end.' Even the decorating she carried out failed to demonstrate reliance, since it was done 'by the plaintiff as occupier of the property, as the defendant's mistress, and as [the child's] mother, in the context of a continuing relationship with the defendant'.[96]

[88] [1993] 69 P & CR 170 at 173. See also *Eves v Eves* [1975] 1 WLR 1338 at 1345, per Brightman J; *Grant v Edwards* [1986] Ch 638 at 648–9, 655–7, per Nourse LJ and per Browne-Wilkinson V-C; *Gillett v Holt* [2000] 2 All ER 289, 306.

[89] See *Greasley v Cooke* [1980] 1 WLR 1306, where Lord Denning MR considered that there is a presumption of reliance once a representation has been established.

[90] [1987] AC 114. [91] [1992] 1 WLR 113. [92] [1992] 1 WLR 113 at 118.

[93] [1993] 69 P & CR 170 at 173. [94] [1986] 1 WLR 808. [95] [1986] 1 WLR 808 at 820.

[96] Compare the House of Lords' views of the wife's activities in *Lloyds Bank plc v Rosset* [1991] 1 AC 107. For similar reasoning, see also *Stilwell v Simpson* [1983] 133 NLJ 894; *Layton v Martin* [1986] 2 FLR 227.

However, it may be that *Coombes v Smith* adopts an unduly restrictive approach to the concept of reliance and an over-optimistic confidence in the ability of the court to determine the true rationale for the claimant's actions. Motives are invariably mixed rather than pure, and it would not be unreasonable to suggest that Mrs Coombes' actions were at least partially influenced by the assurances she had received from her lover. Only with the promise of security was she prepared to continue her relationship and have a child. Subsequent cases have tended to take a more generous attitude towards questions of reliance. In *Matharu v Matharu*,[97] a wife returned to live with her husband on the mistaken basis that the matrimonial home was as much hers as his. She later discovered that it was in fact owned by his father. She subsequently acted to her detriment by installing a new kitchen. The Court of Appeal held that this indicated that she had acted in reliance upon an assurance by her father-in-law, through his conduct, that he would abstain from asserting his legal rights to the house, even though the expenditure had been incurred after she was aware of her mistaken assumption as to the ownership of the property.

Similarly, in *Wayling v Jones*,[98] the plaintiff and deceased defendant had cohabited in a homosexual relationship. The defendant ran a hotel business in which he was helped by the plaintiff, who acted as his companion and chauffeur in return for pocket money and the promise that the defendant would leave the business to him on his death. When the defendant died he had left the plaintiff only a motor car valued at £375. The Court of Appeal held that sufficient reliance was demonstrated and could be established by inference from the plaintiff's conduct. Balcombe LJ stated the principle:

> The promises relied upon do not have to be the sole inducement for the conduct: it is sufficient if they are an inducement.[99]

Nevertheless, in *James v Thomas*,[100] the reasoning is as restrictive as in *Coombes*. Peter Thomas had acquired a cottage, previously owned by his parents, by buying out the shares of his brother and sister in 1986. In 1989, he developed a relationship with Sharon James, and she moved to live with him. Sharon worked without pay in Peter's business. She also helped with the manual work involved in carrying out improvements. Peter told Sharon that these actions 'will benefit us both' and he told her he would ensure that she was provided for if he died. The relationship broke down in 2005 and Sharon claimed an interest in the cottage. Sir John Chadwick, in the Court of Appeal, held that the trial judge was correct to form the conclusion that Peter had not given any assurance that Sharon would acquire an interest in the cottage. He added:

> for completeness, I should add that the factors which lead to the conclusion that the assurances were not intended or understood as a promise of some property interest lead, also, to the conclusion that it would be unreal to think that Miss James did what she did in reliance on such a promise. The true position, as it seems to me, is that she worked in the business, and contributed her labour to the improvements to the property, because she and Mr Thomas were making their life together as man and wife. The Cottage was their home: the business was their livelihood. It is a mistake to think that the motives which lead parties in such a relationship to act as they do are necessarily attributable to pecuniary self-interest.[101]

Whether there has been reliance will therefore be very much a question of fact in every case, and it is relatively easy to find apparent inconsistencies in the approach of individual members of the judiciary.

[97] [1994] 68 P & CR 93.

[98] [1994] 68 P & CR 93; Cooke, 'Reliance and Estoppel' [1995] 111 LQR 389; Davis, 'Estoppel—Reliance and Remedy' [1995] Conv 409.

[99] [1995] 69 P & CR 170 at 173.

[100] [2007] EWCA Civ 1212.

[101] [2007] EWCA Civ 1212 at 36.

(e) Reasonableness of reliance

The reliance on the assurance must be reasonable on a holistic appraisal of all the facts, not just those known at the time of the reliance:

> Past events provide context and background for the interpretation of subsequent events and subsequent events throw retrospective light upon the meaning of past events. The owl of Minerva spreads its wings only with the falling of dusk. The finding was that [the appellant] reasonably relied upon the assurance from 1990, even if it required later events to confirm that it was reasonable for him to have done so.[102]

(5) Detriment or change of position

(a) Requirement of detriment or change of position

An estoppel equity calling for a remedy will only be established if a claimant can show that he acted to his detriment in reliance upon the assurance.[103] This final element of detriment renders it unconscionable for the legal owner to assert his strict rights.[104] If the owner had created an expectation on the part of the claimant, but the claimant had done nothing in response, there would be no reason why he should not be entitled to assert his rights. The courts have often expressed the requirement of detriment in terms of 'change of position'.[105]

(b) Detriment and unconscionability

In *Gillett v Holt*, Robert Walker LJ summarized what detriment requires:

> The overwhelming weight of authority shows that detriment is required. But the authorities also show that it is not a narrow or technical concept. The detriment need not consist of the expenditure of money or other quantifiable financial detriment as long as it is something substantial. The requirement must be approached as part of a broad inquiry as to whether repudiation of an assurance is or is not unconscionable in all the circumstances. The issue of detriment must be judged at the moment when the person who has given the assurance seeks to go back on it. Whether the detriment is sufficiently substantial is to be tested by whether it would be unjust or inequitable to allow the assurance to be disregarded–that is, again, the essential test of unconscionability.[106]

Thus detriment must be considered together with the question of unconscionability: a change of position will only be sufficiently substantial if it means it would be unjust or inequitable to withdraw the assurance or expectation. This has been criticized by Wells, on the basis that it is destroying existing categories and principles of detriment and thereby creating uncertainty.[107] Nevertheless, Robert Walker LJ's words have been affirmed directly in *Campbell v Griffin*,[108] *Parker v Parker*,[109] and tacitly by the House of Lords in *Thorner v Major*.[110] In *Suggitt v Suggitt*, Arden LJ, whilst affirming the need for detriment, emphasized that it did not need to be proportional to the expectation, although proportionality was relevant to the nature of the relief granted.[111]

[102] *Thorner v Major* [2009] UKHL 18 at 8, per Lord Hoffmann.

[103] Detriment may not be necessary in promissory estoppel: *MWB Business Exchange Centres Ltd v Rock Advertising Ltd* [2016] EWCA Civ 553 at 54.

[104] See *Grundt v Great Boulder Pty Gold Mine Ltd* (1937) 59 CLR 641.

[105] See *ER Ives Investment Ltd v High* [1967] 2 QB 379, CA; *Bhimji v Salih* (4 February 1981, unreported), CA; *Re Basham (Decd)* [1986] 1 WLR 1498 at 1504; *Lloyds Bank v Rosset* [1991] AC 107 at 132.

[106] [2000] 2 All ER 289 at 308.

[107] 'The Element of Detriment in Proprietary Estoppel' [2001] Conv 13.

[108] [2001] WTLR 981.

[109] [2003] EWHC 1846.

[110] [2009] UKHL 18.

[111] [2012] EWCA Civ at 44. Ironically, the apparent lack of detriment on the facts in what was a successful estoppel claim has drawn considerable criticism—see Mee, 'Proprietary Estoppel and Influence: Enough Is Enough?' [2013] Conv 280.

(c) Types of detriment

The cases show that a wide range of conduct is sufficient 'detriment' to give rise to an equity. They also show that 'the categories of detriment [are] not closed'.[112]

(i) Improvement of the legal owner's land

Sufficient detriment will be demonstrated if the claimant had expended money improving the land in respect of which an assurance was given.[113] For example, in *Inwards v Baker*,[114] it was held that a son had acted to his detriment by building a bungalow on his father's land in reliance on an assurance he had received. In *Pascoe v Turner*,[115] an equity was raised where the claimant had spent money on redecoration, improvements, and repairs to a house that was owned by her former lover, while he passively assured by his acquiescence that she had an interest in the house. In *Matharu v Matharu*,[116] it was held that a wife had acted to her detriment when she installed a new kitchen in a house owned by her father-in-law in reliance upon an assurance that it belonged to her husband and that she would have an interest in it. In *Gillett v Holt*,[117] one of the ways in which the claimant had acted to his detriment was by incurring substantial expenditure improving the farmhouse he occupied. In *Thompson v Foy*,[118] the claimant had acted to her detriment by building and paying for an extension to the family home. Incurring liability to repay a mortgage has been held as sufficient detriment where a claimant was promised a half share in the property in *Qayyum v Hameed*.[119]

(ii) Improvement of the claimant's own land

A claimant will also be held to have acted to his detriment if he improved his own land in reliance upon an assurance that he is to enjoy a right over the land of the legal owner. In *Rochdale Canal Co v King*,[120] a mill-owner built a mill on his own land after having applied to the canal company to take water from the canal to operate his steam engines. The company did not refuse the application, and pipes were laid in the presence of their engineers. The court held that, due to their acquiescence, they were not entitled to an injunction restraining the mill owner from drawing water from the canal.[121]

(iii) Acquisition of new land by the claimant

In *Salvation Army Trustees Co Ltd v West Yorkshire Metropolitan County Council*,[122] the council informed the Salvation Army that the site of their hall would be required for a proposed road-widening scheme. Although there was no contract for the sale of the hall to the council, the Salvation Army acquired a new site and built a new hall. The council subsequently informed them that the proposed scheme would not be adopted for some years and that they would not, therefore, be acquiring the old site. Woolf J held that the Salvation Army was entitled to a claim on the basis of proprietary estoppel. He held that the principle of proprietary estoppel was:

> capable of extending to the disposal of an interest in land where that disposal is closely linked by an arrangement that also involves the acquiring of an interest in land.[123]

[112] *Watts v Storey* [1983] 134 NLJ 631.
[113] See *Voyce v Voyce* [1991] 62 P & CR 290, CA. [114] [1965] 2 QB 29. [115] [1979] 1 WLR 431.
[116] [1994] 68 P & CR 93. [117] [2000] 2 All ER 289 at 309–10. [118] [2009] EWHC 1076 (Ch).
[119] [2009] EWCA Civ 352. [120] (1853) 16 Beav 630.
[121] See also *Cotching v Bassett* (1862) 32 Beav 101.
[122] (1980) 41 P & CR 179. [123] [1980] 41 P & CR 179 at 192.

(iv) Working without adequate remuneration

In *Wayling v Jones*,[124] it was held that an estoppel equity was established where the claimant had helped his homosexual partner to run a cafe and hotel in reliance upon the assurance that it would be left to him by will. The fact that he received 'little more than pocket money' as remuneration for his work was sufficient to constitute the necessary element of detriment. Similarly, in *Thorner v Major*,[125] the House of Lords held that the claimant had acted to his detriment by doing substantial farm work for thirty years without pay, for most of that time in reliance on an assurance that he would inherit the farm. Along similar lines, giving up a job and moving to a new area has been held to be a sufficient change of position.[126]

(v) Personal disadvantage

A claim may arise by way of proprietary estoppel even if the claimant did not act to his detriment financially by incurring the expenditure of money. In a number of cases, purely personal disadvantage, such as being 'deprived of the opportunity of a better life elsewhere',[127] has been held sufficient to give rise to an equity. A classic example is *Greasley v Cooke*.[128] Doris Cooke moved into the house of Arthur Greasley as a maidservant in 1938. She lived with one of his sons, Kenneth, from 1946. Throughout that time she looked after the son and his mentally disabled sister, Clarice. When Kenneth died in 1975, the members of the family who had inherited the house asked her to leave. The trial judge found that she 'reasonably believed and was encouraged by members of the family to believe that she could regard the property as her home for the rest of her life', but held that she had not acted to her detriment. The Court of Appeal allowed her appeal. Lord Denning MR stated that it was not necessary that the change of position take the form of expenditure of money. He held that:

> It is sufficient if the party, to whom the assurance is given, acts on the faith of it in such circumstances that it would be unjust and inequitable for the party making the assurance to go back on it.[129]

The importance of cumulative detriment was emphasized in *Re Basham (decd)*,[130] in which acts such as refraining from taking a job outside the area, paying legal expenses for boundary disputes, and spending time and money on the upkeep of the property, while individually not particularly significant, collectively demonstrated acts beyond 'normal love and affection' that supported a finding of detrimental reliance as the claimants had 'subordinated their own interests to the wishes of the deceased'.[131] Similar evidence of personal detriment was approved to support financial detriment by the Court of Appeal in *Gillett v Holt*,[132] including the claimant and his wife performing tasks beyond the normal scope of an employee's duties and subordinating their wishes to those of *Holt*, such as the decision as to the school their son would attend.

(d) **Equivocal actions**

Detriment is closely allied to reliance: this can help to answer the question whether the acts relied upon constitute a sufficient change of position. This was addressed by Browne-Wilkinson V-C in *Grant v Edwards*.[133] The case concerned a common intention constructive

[124] [1993] 69 P & CR 170. See also *Gillett v Holt* [1998] 3 All ER 917, where Carnwath J accepted that a 'lower salary than would otherwise have been appropriate would have been sufficient detriment to establish a claim by way of proprietary estoppel'. However, there was no evidence to prove that the plaintiff had received a lower salary and the claim, therefore, failed.

[125] [2009] UKHL 18.

[126] See *Jones v Jones* [1977] 1 WLR 438.

[127] *Henry v Henry* [2010] UKPC 3 at 61.

[128] [1980] 1 WLR 1306.

[129] [1980] 1 WLR 1306 at 1311.

[130] [1986] 1 WLR 1498.

[131] [1970] AC 777.

[132] [2000] 2 All ER 289 at 309–10.

[133] [1986] Ch 638; Hayton, 'Equity and the Quasi-Matrimonial Home' [1986] CLJ 394; Warburton, 'Interested or Not?' [1986] Conv 291.

trust,[134] but he considered that 'useful guidance may be obtained from the principles underlying the law of proprietary estoppel'. On the question of detriment he stated:

> In many cases of the present sort, it is impossible to say whether or not the claimant would have done the acts relied on as a detriment even if she thought she had no interest in the house. Setting up house together, having a baby, making payments to general housekeeping expenses (not strictly necessary to enable the mortgage to be paid) may all be referable to the mutual love and affection of the parties and not specifically referable to the claimant's belief that she has an interest in the house. As at present advised, once it has been shown that there was a common intention that the claimant should have an interest in the house, any act done by her to her detriment relating to the joint lives of the parties is, in my judgment, sufficient detriment to qualify.[135]

Applying the test of 'any act done by her relating to the joint lives of the parties' to proprietary estoppel claims,[136] a whole range of non-monetary detriment would be sufficient to raise an equity. Not all cases support this view. In particular, in *Coombes v Smith*,[137] Jonathan Parker QC held that a woman who had left her husband to live with her lover, became pregnant by him, gave birth to their child, and looked after the shared property and their daughter, had not 'acted to her detriment' in reliance on an assurance that she was entitled to an interest in the house.[138] These cases would now be decided within the *Stack/Kernott* framework.

(e) Weighing detriment against any benefits derived

Whether there has, in fact, been a detriment depends upon a balance in which the courts weigh any benefits gained in acting on an assurance against the claimed detriment. If the balance is a detriment overall, then a claim may succeed. In *Watts v Storey*,[139] the claimant was persuaded by his grandmother to give up a tenancy of a house in Leeds and move into her home, Apple House, in Nottinghamshire, following her move to the Isle of Wight. He gave up his prospects of finding employment in Leeds. Although the Court of Appeal found that there was an assurance that Apple House would be left to him by will, it held that there was insufficient detriment to found a claim by way of proprietary estoppel:

> when the benefits derived by him from his rent-free occupation . . . are set against any detriments suffered by him as a result of making the move from his protected flat in Leeds, he has not on balance suffered any detriment in financial or material terms.

In *Powell v Benney*,[140] a couple befriended a man who died relatively young. He allowed them to use two houses he owned for their music lesson business and he promised them the houses when he died. The couple appealed against the trial judge's decision to award only a relatively small cash sum rather than the freehold of the properties. In dismissing the appeal, Sir Peter Gibson factored in the use of the premises during lifetime and found that '[i]t would offend common sense to leave out of account a benefit received in connection with a detriment when considering the detriment for the purpose of proprietary estoppel.'

[134] See Chapter 13. [135] [1986] Ch 638 at 657.

[136] Although Browne-Wilkinson J did not rest his judgment on the analogy between common intention constructive trusts and proprietary estoppel because the point had not been fully argued.

[137] [1986] 1 WLR 808.

[138] In the Australian case *W v G* [1996] 20 Fam LR 49, the NSW Supreme Court held that a lesbian partner had acted to her detriment where she had agreed to have a child by way of artificial insemination on the basis of an assurance that her partner would assist in the upbringing of the child. The court did not, however, find that having a child per se was a detriment: see Bailey-Harris, 'Equity Still Childbearing in Australia?' (1997) 113 LQR 227.

[139] [1983] 134 NLJ 631. [140] [2008] 1 P & CR DG 12.

In *Henry v Henry*,[141] the claimant had been living and cultivating land in St Lucia for over thirty years. It was his case that Mrs Henry had promised to leave him the land on her death and that he had acted to his detriment by working on the land, and taking care of Mrs Henry until she died. The claim had been dismissed at first instance, on the basis that rather than suffer a detriment, he had positively benefited from living there and reaping its produce. Sir Jonathan Parker upheld the claim by estoppel. It was clear from the evidence that, by remaining on the land, Mr Henry had deprived himself of the opportunity of a better life elsewhere. That detriment had not been outweighed by the advantages he enjoyed as a result of remaining on the land.[142]

(f) Knowledge of legal owner

The legal owner will normally be aware of the acts of reliance, but 'although some formulations of the rule speak of the party estopped having knowledge of the acts of detrimental reliance, this is not a requirement that is rigidly insisted on in cases of encouragement.'[143] The legal owner's knowledge of the detrimental reliance is an essential element in cases of acquiescence.[144]

4 Satisfying the equity

(1) A range of remedial responses

Once a claimant has established an estoppel equity by demonstrating the elements of assurance, reliance, and detriment, the question arises as to his remedial entitlement. The mere fact that he has established an equity does not entitle him to any particular remedy, or even to a remedy at all. It is for the court to determine, in its discretion, whether the estoppel equity requires the award of a remedy, and if so, the type of remedy that would be appropriate to achieve justice between the parties. This process of determining the appropriate remedial response is described as 'satisfying the equity'. This terminology is long established, as in *Plimmer v Wellington Corpn* the Privy Council stated that:

> the court must look at the circumstances in each case to decide in what way the equity can be satisfied.[145]

(2) Types of award

Where an estoppel equity has been established, the courts have awarded a wide range of remedies in satisfaction. The right granted may be lesser or greater than the parties expected or might have wished.

(a) Transfer of the legal ownership of land

The most powerful remedy by which the court may satisfy an estoppel equity is to order the legal owner to transfer his land to the claimant. In *Dillwyn v Llewelyn*[146] and *Pascoe v Turner*,[147] the legal owner was ordered to convey the fee simple in his house to the claimant.[148]

[141] [2010] UKPC 3 (PC). [142] [2010] UKPC 3 (PC) at 61.

[143] *Hoyl Group Ltd v Cromer Town Council* [2015] EWCA Civ 782 at 54; *Joyce* v *Epsom & Ewell Borough Council* [2012] EWCA Civ 1398.

[144] *Republic Bank Ltd v Lochan* [2015] UKPC 26 at [25].

[145] [1883–4] LR 9 App Cas 699 at 714. [146] [1862] 4 De GF & J 517. [147] [1979] 1 WLR 431.

[148] See also *Thomas v Thomas* [1956] NZLR 785; *Cameron v Murdoch* [1983] WAR 321; *Riches v Hogben* [1986] 1 Qd R 315; *Re Basham (Decd)* [1987] 1 All ER 405; *Voyce v Voyce* (1991) 62 P & CR 290, CA; *Durant v Heritage and Hamilton* [1994] NPC 117; *Walton v Walton* (20 July 1994, unreported), Ch Div.

In *Gillett v Holt*,[149] the court ordered Holt to transfer the freehold of the farm they occupied to the claimant in part satisfaction of his estoppel interest. The court may also be able to award a conditional or determinable fee simple, specifying the conditions on which the right will come to an end. In *Williams v Staite*,[150] Goff LJ stated that:

> the court might hold in any proper case, that the equity is in its nature for a limited period only or determinable upon a condition certain. In such a case the courts must then see whether, in the events which have happened, it has determined or it has expired or been determined by the happening of that condition.[151]

In *Thompson v Foy*,[152] Lewison J granted Mrs Foy ownership of an extension she had built, rather than a licence to occupy it, which, it was argued by Mrs Foy's mother, was the minimum equity to do justice between the parties. This was in line with what his Lordship considered the underlying expectation between the parties.

(b) **Transfer of an undivided share in the land**

Where land is held on trust, the court may order one joint tenant to transfer his undivided share in the land to another in satisfaction of an estoppel equity. In *Lim Teng Huan v Ang Swee Chuan*,[153] the plaintiff and the defendant were the equitable joint tenants of land in Brunei. The defendant built a house on the land believing (wrongly) that a contract had been entered between himself and the plaintiff. The Privy Council held that the plaintiff was, therefore, estopped from claiming his title to the land, and that the land should belong outright to the defendant, subject to him paying compensation for the value of the land.

(c) **Grant of a lease**

In some cases the court has awarded a leasehold estate in satisfaction of proprietary estoppel, as, for example, in *Siew Soon Wah v Yong Tong Hong*.[154] In *Grant v Williams*,[155] a daughter who had lived for most of her life in her mother's house and had cared for her and incurred expenditure improving the property on the basis of a representation that she would be entitled to live in it for the rest of her life was granted a long lease at a nominal rent, determinable on death, in satisfaction of her estoppel equity. In *Yaxley v Gotts*,[156] the Court of Appeal upheld the grant of a long lease in satisfaction of an estoppel equity where a builder had refurbished and converted a house into flats in reliance upon an assurance from the owner that he would, thereby, acquire the ground-floor flats.

(d) **Right of occupancy**

In the majority of cases, the courts have stopped short of awarding a claimant full ownership of the property and have granted some form of a right of occupancy. For example, in *Greasley v Cooke*,[157] the Court of Appeal held that the claimant should be entitled to remain in the house rent-free for as long as she wished. Similarly, in *Inwards v Baker*,[158] the son, who had built his bungalow on his father's land, was held entitled to remain there as long as he wanted. In *Matharu v Matharu*,[159] the Court of Appeal held that a claimant was entitled to 'a licence . . . to remain in this house for her life or such shorter period as she may decide'.[160] Such rights of occupation virtually amount to the grant of

[149] [2001] Ch 210. [150] [1979] Ch 291. [151] [1979] Ch 291 at 300.
[152] [2009] EWHC 1076 (Ch). [153] [1992] 1 WLR 113. [154] [1973] AC 836.
[155] [1977] 248 *Estates Gazette* 947. [156] [2000] 1 All ER 711.
[157] [1980] 1 WLR 1306. [158] [1965] 2 QB 29. [159] [1994] 68 P & CR 93.
[160] [1994] 68 P & CR 93 at 103.

a 'life interest'. Prior to the introduction of trusts of land under the Trusts of Land and Appointment of Trustees Act 1996, such a right would have tended to create a strict settlement under the provisions of the Settled Land Act 1925.[161] The grant of a lease in *Griffiths v Williams*[162] was a means of avoiding the unsatisfactory consequences of a strict settlement. With the introduction of the trust of land, the courts may become more willing to utilize the equitable life interest as a means of satisfaction of an estoppel equity. Unlike the Irish courts, the English courts have not recognized rights of residence not conferring exclusive possession as proprietary interests in land.

(e) Financial compensation

In some other cases, the courts have awarded a claimant only financial reimbursement in satisfaction of his estoppel equity. In *Dodsworth v Dodsworth*,[163] the legal owner of a bungalow allowed the claimants, her brother and his wife, to live in it on their return from Australia. They spent £700 on improvements in the expectation that they would be able to remain in the bungalow as long as they wished. After a breakdown in the relationship between the parties, the Court of Appeal held that the claimants were not entitled to occupy rent-free for life, but were entitled to be repaid their outlay on improvements. In *Davies v Davies*,[164] a case explored further below, the court awarded £500,000 as compensation for work done on the farm over a number of years and the expectation of at least an interest in the farm.[165] The court may award the claimant a lien or a charge over the property to the value of the improvements made.[166] In *Wayling v Jones*,[167] the Court of Appeal held that the claimant should be entitled to recover the proceeds of sale of the hotel that his partner had promised to leave him by will. In *Jennings v Rice*,[168] the Court of Appeal held that a gardener who had acted to his detriment by looking after an elderly lady in reliance upon her assurance that she would 'see to it' that he would be all right in her will should receive £200,000 from her estate.

(f) Grant of easement

Where appropriate, the courts have held that a claimant is entitled to the grant of an easement over the land of the person estopped, as, for example, in *ER Ives Investment Ltd v High*[169] and *Crabb v Arun District Council*.[170] The loss of an easement is also possible, as in *Lester v Woodgate*.[171]

(g) Composite remedy

On occasion, the court has awarded a composite remedy. For example, in *Re Sharpe (a bankrupt)*,[172] Dorothy Johnson moved into a house, with her nephew Thomas Sharpe, which had been purchased in his name. She provided £12,000 of the purchase price of £17,000 by way of a loan to him. Browne-Wilkinson J held that since the payment was made by way of loan, there was no possibility of a resulting trust, but that she was entitled

[161] See *Dodsworth v Dodsworth* (1973) 228 *Estates Gazette* 1115; *Ungurian v Lesnoff* [1990] Ch 206; *Costello v Costello* [1994] 70 P & CR 297.

[162] [1977] 248 *Estates Gazette* 947.

[163] [1973] 228 *Estates Gazette* 1115.

[164] [2016] EWCA Civ 463 (CA).

[165] Many of the reported cases in recent years have also involved disputes over farms (often testamentary disputes) and financial awards—see Dixon, 'Proprietary Estoppel: The Law of Farms and Families' [2019] Conv 89.

[166] *Unity Joint Stock Mutual Banking Association v King* (1858) 25 Beav 72; *Taylor v Taylor* [1956] NZLR 99.

[167] [1995] 69 P & CR 170.

[168] [2002] NPC 28.

[169] [1967] 2 QB 379, CA.

[170] [1976] Ch 179, CA.

[171] [2010] EWCA Civ 199 (acquiescence in blocking of right of way).

[172] [1980] 1 WLR 219.

to an interest under the principles of proprietary estoppel. He held that she should have the right to live in the house until her loan was repaid.[173] As has been seen, in *Gillett v Holt*,[174] the Court of Appeal awarded the claimant the freehold of the farm he occupied. In addition he was also awarded a sum of £100,000 to compensate him for his exclusion from the rest of the farming business carried on by Holt.

(h) Imposition of a constructive trust

Although the courts have not yet awarded an interest by way of a constructive trust in satisfaction of an estoppel equity, there appears to be no reason in principle why this would not be possible. The effect would be similar to an order to transfer the legal ownership of land, in that the claimant would receive an ownership interest in the property, only in the form of a share of the beneficial ownership behind a trust of land. There are indications in dicta that a constructive trust may be awarded as a remedy. Originally, these came from Lord Denning MR in *Hussey v Palmer*,[175] in which his Lordship suggested his now discredited new model constructive trust. However, in *Re Basham (Decd)*,[176] Edward Nugee QC also took the view that a constructive trust was an appropriate remedy for cases of proprietary estoppel 'at all events where the belief is that A is going to be given a right in the future'.[177] In *Matharu v Matharu*[178] the first instance judge held that the claimant was entitled to a share of the beneficial ownership of her matrimonial home by way of proprietary estoppel. This could only take effect by means of a trust.

If the court does possess the jurisdiction to award an equitable interest by way of a constructive trust in satisfaction of an estoppel equity, such a constructive trust would be radically different to the 'institutional' common intention constructive trust. A constructive trust imposed by the court by way of proprietary estoppel would be akin to the remedial constructive trust adopted in other jurisdictions, since the claimant's equitable interest would only arise at the date of judgment, and not at the date of the assurance, reliance, and detriment.[179] We have already seen that in some recent cases, the courts have considered that estoppel and trusts are interchangeable methods of quantifying an interest. Indeed, in the House of Lords' decision in *Thorner v Major*,[180] Lord Scott talked in terms of the overlap between constructive trusts and estoppel, and suggested that a set of facts which he agreed gave rise to a proprietary estoppel could also give rise to a 'remedial constructive trust'.[181] Any suggestion that the principles of constructive trusts and proprietary estoppel have melded to create a remedial trust should be treated with extreme caution, as this does not yet reflect the orthodox view.[182]

(i) No remedy

In some cases the courts may find that a claimant does not require the award of any remedy at all in order to satisfy an estoppel equity because he has already received advantages which have fully satisfied his claim. In *Sledmore v Dalby*,[183] Mr Dalby had lived in a

[173] See also *Dodsworth v Dodsworth* [1973] 228 *Estates Gazette* 1115, CA; *Stratulatos v Stratulatos* [1988] 2 NZLR 424.

[174] [2001] Ch 210. [175] [1972] 3 All ER 744. [176] [1986] 1 WLR 1498.

[177] [1986] 1 WLR 1498 at 1503–4. [178] [1994] 68 P & CR 93.

[179] If an equitable proprietary interest was created as an automatic consequence of the assurance, reliance and detriment, the constructive trust would similarly arise automatically and would be recognized, rather than created, by the court.

[180] [2009] UKHL 18. [181] [2009] UKHL 18 at 18.

[182] See *Cook v Thomas* [2010] EWCA Civ 229 at 105.

[183] [1996] 72 P & CR 196; Pawlowski, 'Proprietary Estoppel—Satisfying the Equity' (1997) 113 LQR 232.

house owned by his parents-in-law since 1965. Initially, he and his wife paid rent, but in 1976, they ceased to do so because his wife became seriously ill. He subsequently substantially improved the property, having been encouraged to do so by Mr and Mrs Sledmore. Following the death of his wife, he continued to live in the house, which was then owned by Mrs Sledmore alone, rent-free. In 1990 she gave him notice to quit. At first instance Mr Dalby was held entitled to a non-assignable licence to occupy the house for life on the grounds of proprietary estoppel, but the Court of Appeal held that, although he was entitled to an estoppel equity, it had been fully met. Although he had spent money on the property, he had enjoyed the benefits of that expenditure through more than fifteen years' rent-free occupation. Roch LJ also took account of the parties' respective situations, weighing the fact that Mrs Sledmore was a widow dependent upon benefit, who urgently wanted to sell the house, against the fact that Mr Dalby was employed and currently making minimal use of the house because he enjoyed accommodation elsewhere.

(3) Determining the appropriate remedy

(a) Principles governing the award

As is clear from the preceding section, the courts have awarded a wide range of remedies in satisfaction of estoppel equities.[184] In deciding what award to make, 'the court has to exercise a broad judgmental discretion.'[185] Lewison LJ observed in *Davies v Davies* that:

> There is a lively controversy about the essential aim of the exercise of this broad judgmental discretion. One line of authority takes the view that the essential aim of the discretion is to give effect to the claimant's expectation unless it would be disproportionate to do so. The other takes the view that essential aim of the discretion is to ensure that the claimant's reliance interest is protected, so that she is compensated for such detriment as she has suffered. The two approaches, in their starkest form, are fundamentally different . . . Others argue that the outcome will reflect both the expectation and the reliance interest and that it will normally be somewhere between the two.[186]

The Court of Appeal indicated a preference for the second approach, but did not think it necessary to resolve this controversy on the appeal it was considering. In the earlier case of *Jennings v Rice*,[187] the Court of Appeal had favoured a composite approach which would ensure that there was proportionality between the remedy awarded and the detriment experienced.

(b) Fulfilment of the claimant's 'reasonable expectation'

Many cases before the start of the century suggested that when the court satisfies an estoppel equity, it selects the remedy which as far as possible fulfils the reasonable expectations of the claimant.[188] This analysis has the attraction of aligning the approach in proprietary estoppel with that in the common intention constructive trust.

[184] See especially Gardner, 'The Remedial Discretion in Proprietary Estoppel' [1999] 115 LQR 438; Bright and McFarlane, 'Proprietary Estoppel and Property Rights' [2005] 64 CLJ 449; Gardner, 'The Remedial Discretion in Proprietary Estoppel—Again' [2006] LQR 492; McFarlane and Sales, 'Promises, Detriment, and Liability: Lessons from Proprietary Estoppel' [2015] LQR 610.

[185] *Jennings v Rice* [2002] EWCA Civ 159 at 51, quoted in *Davies v Davies* [2016] EWCA Civ 463 at 38.

[186] *Davies v Davies* [2016] EWCA Civ 463 at 39.

[187] 2002 WL 45443, [2002] NPC 28.

[188] See [1984] 100 LQR 376 (Moriarty); [1997] 17 LS 258 (Cooke).

(i) What was promised?

The fulfilment of expectation analysis explains the apparent conflict in outcome between *Dillwyn v Llewelyn*[189] and *Pascoe v Turner*,[190] where the court ordered the transfer of the fee simple to the claimant, and *Inwards v Baker*[191] and *Williams v Staite*,[192] where only a lesser right of occupancy was awarded. The crucial distinguishing feature is said to be the nature of the claimant's expectation raised by the assurance of the legal owner. In *Pascoe v Turner*,[193] the assurance given to Mrs Turner was that 'the house is yours and everything in it'. Therefore, her reasonable expectation was that she owned the house, and, having acted to her detriment in reliance on that assurance, the court acted to fulfil her expectation. In contrast, in *Inwards v Baker*,[194] the father's representation to his son was simply 'Why not put the bungalow on my land and make the bungalow a little bigger?' Although this amounted to a clear indication that the son would be entitled to remain on the land, it cannot be taken as an assurance that the son would own the land. The award of a right to occupy for as long as he wished, therefore, fulfilled the reasonable expectation raised by the assurance he received. Similarly, in *Williams v Staite*,[195] the representation was merely that 'you can live here as long as you like', and on the basis of such a representation there could be no reasonable expectation of ownership.

(ii) How can financial remedies be explained?

Slightly more difficult to analyze on this 'expectation model' are cases where the claimant was awarded merely monetary compensation for detriment suffered, as, for example, in *Dodsworth v Dodsworth*.[196] However, in these cases, financial compensation seems to operate as a default remedy when the circumstances prevent the fulfilment of the claimant's legitimate expectation. In *Dodsworth*[197] the plaintiff's brother and sister-in-law moved into her bungalow with her on their return from Australia, and spent £700 on improvements in reliance on the assurance by the plaintiff that they would be able to remain in the bungalow as their home for as long as they wished. Obviously, this representation is comparable to that made in *Williams v Staite*,[198] and a similar remedy of a right of occupancy would be expected. However, the court awarded the defendants only monetary compensation for their improvements. The explanation may well be that it was impossible to fulfil the claimants' reasonable expectation, namely the right to reside in the bungalow with the plaintiff, because the relationship between them had broken down.[199] As Russell LJ observed, the consequence of awarding the defendants a right of occupancy would be that the plaintiff:

> would have to continue sharing her home for the rest of her life with the defendants with whom she was, or thought she was, at loggerheads.

The award of monetary compensation is, therefore, a default remedy given where a reasonable expectation of shared occupation is no longer a realistic possibility. This analysis is also capable of explaining the award of monetary compensation in *Hussey v Palmer*,[200]

[189] [1862] 4 De GF & J 517.
[190] [1979] 1 WLR 431, CA.
[191] [1965] 2 QB 29, CA.
[192] [1979] Ch 291, CA.
[193] [1979] 1 WLR 431, CA.
[194] [1965] 2 QB 29, CA.
[195] [1979] Ch 291, CA.
[196] [1973] 228 *Estates Gazette* 1115: see also *Taylor v Taylor* [1956] NZLR 99; *Re Sharpe* [1980] 1 WLR 219.
[197] [1973] 228 *Estates Gazette* 1115.
[198] [1979] Ch 291, CA.
[199] See *Thompson v Park* [1944] KB 408.
[200] [1972] 1 WLR 1286, CA. Although the plaintiff was only claiming monetary compensation, there had been a breakdown of the sharing relationship between the mother-in-law and son-in-law.

Re Sharpe,[201] and *Burrows and Burrows v Sharp*.[202] Moriarty summarizes the argument as follows:

> The remedies granted [for proprietary estoppel] are not the product of an unpredictable discretion; but are selected in accordance with well-established principles of English property law. Normally, therefore, a remedy will be chosen which gives the party precisely what he has been led to expect, but occasionally, where joint rights to land have been represented, he may get money instead.[203]

(iii) Criticism of expectation analysis

Although the 'fulfilment of the reasonable expectation' analysis has the attractive merit of certainty, a number of criticisms may be made. First, it ignores a large number of judicial statements that emphasize the court's flexibility in determining the appropriate remedy.[204] Second, it assumes that it is possible to correctly identify the reasonable expectations of the claimant, whereas the reality is often that the assurance, and, therefore, the derived expectation are ambiguous. Undue emphasis may be put on the actual words used in a case like *Inwards v Baker*[205] rather than on what the claimant understood. As Lord Westbury LC said in *Dillwyn v Llewelyn*:

> No one builds a house for his own life only, and it is absurd to suppose that it was intended by either party that the house at the death of the son, should become the property of the father.[206]

Moriarty's claim that 'we can get quite some way towards explaining the court's intuitive choice of remedy by merely paying closer attention to the precise content of the representation'[207] is an overstatement. Determining the claimant's expectation is not an exact science, not helped by expectations potentially shifting and changing with time and circumstances.

(c) Redressing detriment

In *Sledmore v Dalby*,[208] Hoffmann LJ adopted the view that there must be 'proportionality' between the detriment experienced and the remedy awarded, so that the claimant's expectations will not be fulfilled if to do so would be disproportionate to the amount of detriment he had experienced.[209] In *Davies v Davies*, Lewison LJ said that 'logically, there is much to be said' for the view that the objective of the remedy was to redress any detriment:

> Since the essence of proprietary estoppel is the combination of expectation and detriment, if either is absent the claim must fail. If, therefore, the detriment can be fairly quantified and a claimant receives full compensation for that detriment, that compensation ought, in principle, to remove the foundation of the claim.[210]

[201] [1980] 1 WLR 219. Although the sharing relationship between aunt and nephew had not broken down, it was the nephew's trustee in bankruptcy who was seeking to evict the aunt.

[202] [1991] Fam Law 67; [1992] Conv 54.

[203] [1984] 100 LQR 376 at 412.

[204] See *Plimmer v Wellington Corpn* [1883–4] LR 9 App Cas 699; *Crabb v Arun District Council* [1976] Ch 179, CA; *Griffiths v Williams* (1977) 248 *Estates Gazette* 947; *Denny v Jensen* [1977] 1 NZLR 635; *Greasley v Cooke* [1980] 1 WLR 1306, CA; *Morris v Morris* [1982] 1 NSWLR 61.

[205] [1965] 2 QB 29.

[206] [1862] 4 De GF & J 517 at 522.

[207] [1984] 100 LQR 376 at 383.

[208] [1996] 72 P & CR 196. See [1997] 113 LQR 232 (Pawlowski) and [1998] Conv 213 (Thompson).

[209] Robertson, 'The Reliance Basis of Proprietary Estoppel Remedies' [2008] Conv 295.

[210] *Davies v Davies* [2016] EWCA Civ 463 at 39.

Against this view, we have already seen how difficult it can be to identify detriment, let alone to quantify it where the change of position does not involve the expenditure of money, but instead comprises a loss of other opportunities. It demotes expectation to a degree which is not justified by most judicial statements. It also creates a sharp contrast with the approach in common intention constructive trusts—where the trust gives effect to the understanding of the parties.

(d) Composite approach

The Court of Appeal held in *Jennings v Rice*[211] that a pure 'fulfilment of expectations' approach was not the appropriate means of determining the remedy to satisfy an estoppel equity. The case concerned a gardener who had taken care of an elderly lady without remuneration, relying upon her assurance that she would 'see to it' that he was alright, and her statements to him that her house would 'all be yours one day'. At first instance Judge Weeks held that he was entitled to a claim by way of proprietary estoppel, but that he should receive a sum of £200,000 rather than the freehold of the house and its furniture, which was worth considerably more. On appeal it was argued that he should have been entitled to the house and furniture on the grounds that an estoppel equity should be satisfied by making good the expectation of the claimant. The Court of Appeal held that while the nature of the expectation was a relevant consideration, it did not alone determine the appropriate remedy. The court was rather required to do justice by ensuring that there was proportionality between the remedy and the detriment. The importance of proportionality was emphasized in *Malik v Kalyan*,[212] *Henry v Henry*,[213] and *Gow v Grant*.[214]

(e) Untrammelled discretion

Some judicial statements are expressed in a way which suggests that the court has an unfettered discretion.[215] In *Plimmer v Wellington Corpn*,[216] Sir Arthur Hobhouse stated that 'the court must look at the circumstances in each case to decide in what way the equity can be satisfied'. In *Crabb v Arun District Council*,[217] Lord Denning MR emphasized that in answering the question how an established equity should be satisfied, 'equity is displayed at its most flexible'. He also restated the principle in *Greasley v Cooke*:

> The equity having thus been raised . . . it is for the courts of equity to decide in what way that equity should be satisfied.[218]

Such flexibility was also emphasized in *Griffiths v Williams*,[219] where Goff LJ answered the question 'What is the relief appropriate to satisfy the equity?' in this way:

> the next question is one upon which the court has to exercise a discretion. If it finds that there is an equity, then it must determine the nature of it, and then, guided by that nature and exercising discretion in all the circumstances, it has to determine what is the fair order to make between the parties for the protection of the claimant.[220]

211 [2002] WL 45443, [2002] NPC 28. 212 [2010] EWCA Civ 113.

213 [2010] UKPC 3 at 65. 214 [2012] UKSC 29 (Scotland).

215 See Thompson, 'Estoppel and Clean Hands' [1986] Conv 406; Dewar, 'Licences and Land Law: An Alternative View' (1986) 49 MLR 741.

216 [1883–4] LR 9 App Cas 699 at 714. 217 [1976] Ch 179 at 189.

218 [1980] 1 WLR 1306 at 1312. 219 [1977] 248 *Estates Gazette* 947.

220 See also *Williams v Staite* [1979] Ch 291 at 298, where Goff LJ said: 'In the normal type of case . . . whether there is an equity and its extent will depend . . . simply upon the initial conduct said to give rise to the equity, although the court may have to decide how, having regard to supervening circumstances, the equity can best be satisfied.'

The wide discretion of the court was also stressed in New Zealand in *Stratulatos v Stratulatos*,[221] where McGehan J said that 'the range of available remedies should not be cluttered by arbitrary rules'.

The key criticism of this approach is that of uncertainty.[222] If the remedy is entirely within the choice of the courts, without any defined criteria as to how that choice will be made, it will not be possible to advise accurately on the likely remedy, which could range from a transfer of the fee simple to mere monetary compensation. The Court of Appeal rejected a purely discretionary approach in *Jennings v Rice*.[223] While it was accepted that equity acts flexibly to do justice by preventing unconscionability, Robert Walker LJ rejected any notion of an unfettered discretion:

> It cannot be doubted that in this as in every other area of the law, the court must take a principled approach, and cannot exercise a completely unfettered discretion according to the individual judge's notion of what is fair in any particular case.

(f) Multifactorial approach

Jennings v Rice[224] and *Davies v Davies*,[225] show that the current approach of the Court of Appeal is to take into account a range of factors, of which fulfilling expectation and redressing detriment are the main ones. These are not, though, the only factors.

(i) Quasi-bargains

As is described in both of those cases, some situations[226] can be described as quasi-bargains which, although falling short of creating a contract, have a consensual character in which 'both the claimant's expectations and the element of detriment will have been defined with reasonable clarity'.[227] In this kind of case, provided that the claimant has performed his part of the quasi-bargain, the court is likely to vindicate the claimant's expectations.

(ii) Unspecific assurances

At the other end of the spectrum, an assurance can only be divined from the conduct of the parties because no clear promise has been made, or it has only been made in the most general of terms. It is then likely that redressing detriment is the best guide to the appropriate remedy.

(iii) Excessive expectations

One of the classes of case identified by Robert Walker LJ in *Jennings v Rice* was:

> if the court, although satisfied that the claimant has a genuine claim, is not satisfied that the high level of the claimant's expectations is fairly derived from his deceased patron's assurances, which may have justified only a lower level of expectation. In such cases the court may still take the claimant's expectations (or the upper end of any range of expectations) as a starting point, but unless constrained by authority I would regard it as no more than a starting point.[228]

221 [1988] 2 NZLR 424.

222 *Re Sharpe* [1980] 1 WLR 219 at 226. See also *Cowcher v Cowcher* [1972] 1 WLR 425 at 430, where Bagnall J said: '[justice] flows from the application of sure and settled principle for proved or admitted facts'; *Taylor v Dickens* [1998] 1 FLR 806; [1998] Conv 210 (Thompson).

223 [2003] 1 P & CR 8. 224 [2003] 1 P & CR 8. 225 [2016] EWCA Civ 463 at 39.

226 As, for example, in *Yaxley v Gotts* [2000] Ch 162. 227 *Jennings v Rice* [2003] 1 P & CR 8 at 45.

228 [2003] 1 P & CR 8 at 47.

Lewison LJ, in *Davies v Davies*, noted that this passage gave no guidance as to where the court should proceed from this starting-point, but accepted as a useful working hypothesis the suggestion of counsel:

> that there might be a sliding scale by which the clearer the expectation, the greater the detriment and the longer the passage of time during which the expectation was reasonably held, the greater would be the weight that should be given to the expectation.

This working hypothesis is likely to be influential in a wider context than just where expectations are disproportionate to any detriment.

(iv) Proportionality

Robert Walker LJ stated the underlying principle as follows:

> The task of the court is to do justice. The most essential requirement is that there must be proportionality between the expectation and the detriment.[229]

In cases of quasi-bargains, the 'consensual element of what has happened suggests that the claimant and the benefactor probably regarded the expected benefit and the accepted detriment as being (in a general, imprecise way) equivalent, or at any rate not obviously disproportionate'.[230] An illustration is given by *Suggitt v Suggitt*.[231] Arden LJ supported as not disproportionate the findings of a trial judge to award property (a farm and farmhouse worth some £3.3m) on the basis of questionable detrimental reliance of some work done on the farm, 'for lower wages than he might have expected had he been an agricultural worker'.[232] In Arden LJ's view:

> Since the promise was that [the claimant] should have the farmland unconditionally, I do not consider that to grant him the farmland . . . could be said to be out of all proportion.[233]

By contrast, as Robert Walker LJ said in *Jennings v Rice*:

> if the claimant's expectations are uncertain, or extravagant, or out of all proportion to the detriment which the claimant has suffered, the court can and should recognise that the claimant's equity should be satisfied in another (and generally more limited) way.[234]

Proportionality does not work in the opposite direction. If no expectation has been created by an assurance by a father who treats 'money as God' and who is 'reluctant to make commitments'[235] that his son would inherit a farm, 'fairness' would be insufficient to confer an equity on the son who has convinced himself against the evidence that he was promised the farm even if there had been detrimental reliance.[236]

(v) Other factors

In *Gillett v Holt*,[237] Robert Walker LJ noted that in deciding on a remedy the court should look at all the circumstances, including the need to achieve a 'clean break' between the parties and to avoid or minimize future friction. In *Jennings v Rice*, without trying to create an exhaustive list, he stated that factors to consider in identifying an appropriate remedy included: the misconduct of the claimant, particularly oppressive conduct on the part of the defendant, the court's recognition that it cannot compel people who have fallen

[229] *Jennings v Rice* [2003] 1 P & CR 8 at 36. [230] [2003] 1 P & CR 8 at 45.
[231] [2012] EWCA Civ 1140. [232] [2012] EWCA Civ 1140 at 22.
[233] [2012] EWCA Civ 1140 at 45. [234] [2003] 1 P & CR 8 at 50.
[235] *James v James* [2018] EWHC 43 (Ch) at 24 and 34.
[236] In *James v James*, the judge held that there was no detrimental reliance.
[237] [2000] 2 All ER 289.

out to live peaceably together,[238] alterations in the benefactor's assets and circumstances, the likely effects of taxation, and (to a limited degree) the other claims (legal or moral) on the benefactor or his or her estate.[239] The Court of Appeal concluded that the first instance judge had exercised his discretion correctly in awarding the claimant £200,000 rather than ownership of the benefactor's house and its furniture. He had been unaware of the extent of her wealth, the actual value of her estate was out of all proportion to what he might reasonably have charged for the services he had provided free, and the nature of the house was such that it was unsuitable for him to reside in on his own.

Individual cases may raise other considerations. A good example is *Parker v Parker*,[240] where the court had to consider the right of Lord Macclesfield to live in Shirburn Castle. There had been a representation by the company owning the castle that it would negotiate and agree terms for Lord Macclesfield's occupation of the castle, in reliance on which Lord Macclesfield gave up the tenancy of a farm. By the time of the action, relationships between the parties had broken down to such an extent that the court felt ordering them to live together would have been inadvisable. Instead, they held that Lord Macclesfield was entitled to occupation until given at least two years' notice to quit, to allow his Lordship the time necessary, from the evidence, to catalogue and remove his chattels and find alternative accommodation.

In *Davies v Davies*, a daughter claimed that she was entitled to receive her parents' farm when they died because of assurances they had made over a number of years in return for her helping out on the farm for less than a full wage. Her claim was made before their death, after the family relationship broke down. At first instance, the daughter was awarded £1.3 million pounds to satisfy her equity, though her parents had offered £350,000 in compensation for her work on the farm, not the farm itself. On appeal, the Court of Appeal confirmed that only monetary compensation was payable, and reduced the award to £500,000. Lewison LJ thought that the daughter's expectation of inheriting could not be justified on the basis of what she had been told. It was also relevant that there was 'a series of different (and sometimes mutually incompatible) expectations', rather than an unambiguous assurance made publicly over a number of years. He also took into account the extent to which any change of position could be reversed, and how monetary compensation could purchase alternative performance: how paying off a mortgage on her own property would give her the rent-free accommodation for life, which had been one of her expectations if she acquired the farmhouse. This was a forensic analysis of the financial contributions to the farm discounting the other factors, but it has been argued that it lead to an inequitable result. As noted by Tattersall:

> The stark reality of the Court of Appeal's judgment is that Eirian Davies suffered detriment; such detriment was acknowledged by the courts and then thereafter worsened. Eirian's sisters, the unwitting beneficiaries, have prospered by having their 33% share of the estate increased to 50%. Subsequently, Eirian's detriment is worsened further by having to pay substantial legal fees. The facts of the case lead one to question whether it is good law for a claimant in a proprietary estoppel claim to have their injustice recognised by the courts and then made worse – such an approach would seem to represent the antithesis of equity's role within the English legal system.[241]

In *Guest v Guest*,[242] on similar facts to *Davies*, another monetary award had made by the trial to claimant son in this case of 50 per cent of the farming business and 40 per cent of

[238] A principle applied in *Burrows and Burrows v Sharp* [1991] Fam Law 67, where financial compensation was ordered rather than requiring a grandmother to allow the plaintiff and her family to live in her house after the relationship had broken down.

[239] [2003] 1 P & CR 8 at 51. [240] [2003] EWHC 1846.

[241] Tattersall, 'A Portable Palm Tree: Proprietary Estoppel in *Davies v Davies*' (2006) 30 TLI 237, 242.

[242] See, for example, *Moore v Moore* [2018] EWCA Civ 3196 (Ch); *Guest v Guest* [2019] EWHC 869 (Ch).

the farm property, in line with the son's expectations. The parents made an appeal that the remedy should achieve a more proportionate result, as had happened in *Davies*. The Court of Appeal refused, but, interestingly, leave was granted to appeal the decision to the Supreme Court on 15 December 2020 and was heard on 2 December 2021. The results may provide a definitive statement of the appropriate approach to be taken to quantify an estoppel interest.

5 Bars to a remedy

It follows from the fact that proprietary estoppel is an equitable remedy, based on the conscience of the parties, that there must be no bar in any given case to the claimant seeking to rely on an estoppel to found an interest (see Figure 14.1). Hence, the claimant must 'come with clean hands', so that if the original representation was procured through any falsehood on the part of the claimant, no claim to an interest by estoppel will be supported by the courts. Similarly, unreasonable delay in bringing an action under estoppel may bar a claim to a remedy.[243]

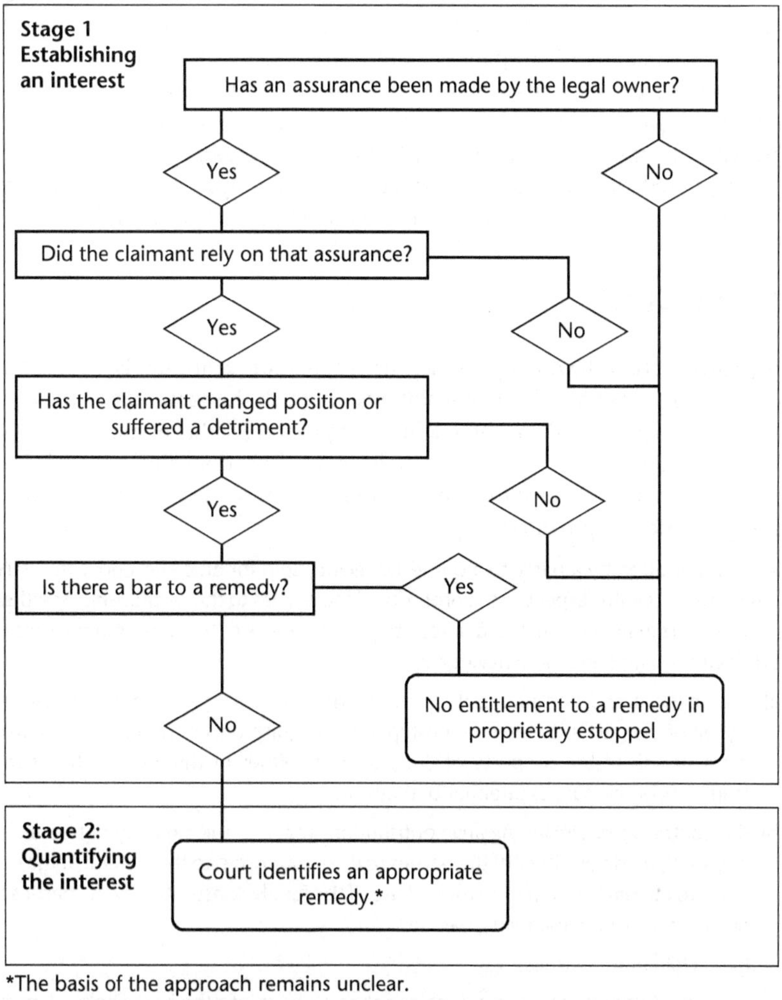

Figure 14.1 Proprietary estoppel

[243] See, e.g., *Voyce v Voyce* (1991) 62 P & CR 290, where, on the facts, there was no unreasonable delay.

15

Family homes: Postscript

1 Introduction

In this chapter, we reflect on the different mechanisms used to give entitlements in the family home, either to those who would otherwise not appear on the legal title or to those who wish to move away from the rule that equality is equity. The use of constructive trusts of common intention (replacing resulting trusts) and the later use of proprietary estoppel claims, represent a pragmatic response to a real problem, but it is not a perfect solution, and it can be criticized on a number of grounds, quite apart from the issue as to whether it constitutes a usurpation of a legislative function. This chapter will also consider whether the approach we have now has moved away from traditional assertion of property principles to a sense of redistributive justice more familiar to family lawyers. It begins, though, with a brief consideration of why a legislative solution had not been found.

2 Attempts at reform

Other legal jurisdictions have adopted a legislative solution, granting the courts a discretion to adjust the property rights of cohabitants, in much the same way as the courts in England have been granted the right to adjust the property rights of married couples on divorce. For example, the New South Wales Property (Relationships) Act 1984 granted the court the discretion to adjust the property rights of those who are party to a domestic relationship.[1] Section 20 provides:

(1) On an application by a party to a domestic relationship for an order under this Part to adjust interests with respect to the property of the parties to the relationship or either of them, a court may make such order adjusting the interests of the parties in the property as it seems just and equitable having regard to:

(a) the financial and non-financial contributions made directly or indirectly by or on behalf of the parties to the relationship to the acquisition, conservation or improvement of any of the property of the parties or either of them or to the financial resources of the parties or either of them, and

(b) the contributions, including any contributions made in the capacity of homemaker or parent, made by either of the parties to the relationship to the welfare of the other party to the relationship or to the welfare of the family constituted by the parties and one or more of the following, namely:

(i) a child of the parties,

(ii) a child accepted by the parties or either of them into the household of the parties, whether or not the child is a child of either of the parties.

[1] Other examples include: Victoria Property Law (Amendment Act) 1987; Northern Territory De Facto Relationships Act 1991; ACT Domestic Relationships Act 1994.

One problem with such legislative solutions is the difficulty of formulating an adequate definition of a 'domestic' or 'de facto' relationship. Thus in New South Wales a 'de facto relationship' is defined as a relationship between two adult persons, who live together as a couple, and who are not married to one another or related by family. To determine whether two persons are in a de facto relationship, all the circumstances of the relationship are to be taken into account, including: the duration of the relationship; the nature and extent of common residence; whether or not a sexual relationship exists; the degree of financial dependence or interdependence; any arrangements for financial support between the parties; the ownership, use, and acquisition of property; the degree of mutual commitment to a shared life; the care and support of children; the performance of household duties; and the reputation and public aspects of the relationship.[2]

The lack of a legislative solution in England and Wales has not been for the want of effort. The Law Commission has expended considerable time, and public monies, on numerous, elaborate proposals for automatic joint ownership of the matrimonial home during marriage.[3] They failed to gain support, as many suggested that this was an issue that could be addressed in practical terms, rather than through legislative intervention. Conveyancing practice could allow joint legal ownership, as we have seen, and many felt that the existing equitable rules, through implied trusts, were sufficient to deal with the situation.

In 1995, the Law Commission began an expansive project to review the law with the aim to develop a scheme applicable to all home-sharers, whether sexual partners or friends. The Commission was unable to propose any scheme to cover all relationships, and, again met with resistance in consultation, on the basis that such proposals undermined the sanctity of marriage, which Parliament had seen fit to protect separately from unmarried cohabitation. The *Sharing Homes* project was not a success, and the final report contained no legislative suggestions for reform, but provided the basis for debate for that reform.[4]

The last attempt at reform by the Commission was to suggest a statutory scheme for cohabiting couples that would allow for the determination of the property rights of cohabitants on a similar basis to married couples and registered civil partners.[5] This proposed a scheme which would apply to cohabitants who either had children or met a minimum qualifying period of cohabitation in the home and who had made some sort of lasting contribution to the family. The scheme was to be voluntary, in that it could be excluded by a written agreement between the parties. If it applied, on relationship breakdown, the court could make a property adjustment award, which reflects not only the contributions of the parties during the relationship but also the financial needs and resources the parties could call upon in the future and the welfare of any children living with, or expected to live, with either party.

This scheme would represent a vast improvement on the current position available through the intervention of equity. Unfortunately, though a similar scheme now exists in Scotland under the Family Law (Scotland) Act 2006, there is no indication that it will ever be enacted in England and Wales. In September 2011, the then government announced

[2] Section 4. See also s 5, where a 'domestic relationship' is defined as a de facto relationship, or a close personal relationship (other than a marriage or a de facto relationship) between two adult persons, whether or not related by family, who are living together, one or each of whom provides the other with domestic support and personal care.

[3] See Law Commission reports: Law Com No. 5, 1973; Law Com No. 86, 1978; Law Com No. 115, 1982; and Law Com No. 175, 1988.

[4] See Law Commission, *Sharing Homes* (Law Com No. 278, 2002); Law Commission, *Cohabitation: The Financial Consequences of Relationship Breakdown* (Law Com No. 179, 2006).

[5] Law Commission, *Cohabitation: The Financial Consequences of Relationship Breakdown* (Law Com No. 179, 2006).

that it did not plan to implement the Law Commission's proposals during the session. Nothing has happened since.

Despite this, calls for reform have also come from the judiciary, including Lord Wilson in *Jones v Kernott*, and Lady Hale in *Gow v Grant*.[6] In June 2014, Lord Mark introduced a Private Members Bill, the Cohabitation Rights Bill, which sought to provide basic protections for cohabitants and for the provision of their property upon death. Under the Bill, the court would have been able to make a financial settlement order where there was a 'retained benefit' or an 'economic disadvantage' dependent on any 'qualifying contributions' made—either financial or other. It was similar to, but not the same as, the Commissions Bill. It has proved unsuccessful.

The plight of cohabitants remains in the hands of the judiciary and their equity-based solutions.

3 Criticism of the current law

(1) Concerns with the current approach

The approach to the acquisition and quantification of interests under a common intention constructive trust raises significant issues and criticisms are rife.[7] The focus is on the family home rather than the overall wealth of the parties, and on the conduct of the parties in relation to the family home, rather than more generally, meaning that the court is much more limited in doing justice between the parties than when the statutory provisions under the Matrimonial Causes Act 1973 are available. Under s 25 of the 1973 Act, making adjustment orders ostensibly equal division is the norm, but, in practice, in using their powers, the courts focus on the immediate housing needs of the parent with care of dependent children.[8] The factors listed when quantifying a beneficial interest held on constructive trust do not go so far, and the needs of the parties are only one factor considered, and, as we have seen, are often not given the same value or weight as financial considerations. A couple who live in rented accommodation and hold their wealth in other assets are likely to fall outside the new regime. It has been argued that the economic difficulties following relationship breakdown 'cannot be solved without express reference to the nature, or effects of, the relationship between the parties and an express policy aimed at dealing specifically with the problems encountered in such relationships'.[9] Proprietary estoppel does not provide a positive way forward, as all the equitable mechanisms look to ascertain how the parties intended to divide the assets concerned between themselves, even where the starting point for that enquiry is a presumption or set of presumptions. The evidence at which the courts look is generally designed to ascertain what the parties themselves intended or, particularly with estoppel claims, what the claimant could reasonably be expected to understand or believe. The courts are not seeking to redistribute the family assets on the basis of need, length of relationship, whether there are children, or other considerations. As Stephen Cretney has said:

> The general principles of law and equity do not in the main operate as a means of resource distribution, i.e. they do not transfer entitlement from one party to another in

[6] [2012] UKSC 29, at [47].

[7] See, for example, Mee, *The Property Rights of Cohabitees* (Hart Publishing, 1999) pp 173–4, who described the then state of the law as 'stubbornly half baked. Clearly, this ill-conceived doctrine should find no place in the law of England.'

[8] Hitchings, 'Everyday Cases in the Post-*White* Era' [2008] *Family Law* 873, 877.

[9] Miles, 'Property Law v Family Law: Resolving the Problems of Family Property' (2003) 23 *Legal Studies* 624, 648.

> order to achieve a just result. Thus their very nature and origins render these doctrines imperfect vehicles for achieving social justice in the context in which they are now commonly invoked, namely the resolution of property disputes on the breakdown of unmarried relationships.[10]

The uncertain limits of the new regime, and the rejection of resulting trust analysis, even as a route to a decision, have left judges with a degree of discretion in imputing intention masked by the description of this function as an exercise in judgment.

(2) **Common intention–an artificial exercise?**

Although the common intention approach to constructive trusts adopted in *Stack* and *Kernott* has antecedents stretching back to before *Lloyds Bank plc v Rosset*,[11] it has been subjected to extensive criticism.[12] The major objection is that the whole process of finding, and then enforcing, the 'common intention' of the parties, is highly artificial. Thus, whereas Lord Bridge in *Rosset* described *Eves v Eves*[13] and *Grant v Edwards*[14] as 'outstanding' examples of express common intention, the facts would suggest that there was no real agreement between the parties to share the ownership of the property concerned. In both cases the men concerned had no real intention that their partners should enjoy an interest in the property. Stuart Eves refused to put Janet on the title of the house, using the excuse that she was under twenty-one. Grant would not put Edwards on the title because he said that it would prejudice her forthcoming matrimonial proceedings. Both of these excuses covered the real intention of the men that their partners were not to receive any proprietary interest in the house. They were to remain the owners and to enjoy the power and control that are necessarily commensurate with such ownership. If the relationship broke down, they wanted to be able to remove their erstwhile partner and not to be encumbered by their presence in the house. To describe the parties in these cases as enjoying a 'common intention' to share the ownership is nothing short of a fiction. The inference of common intention is similarly fraught with the danger that the court is merely inventing a justification for imposing a constructive trust.

Where there is no express common intention the process of inferring an intention is even less authentic, under the fiction that it is what the parties would have understood to be an agreed position, had they put their minds to it.

The court is at best engaged in a process of creative assessment of the parties' desires and it is simply false to suggest that the court is in any way responding to what they would have wanted, or thought they would have wanted. This is even less so where the court identifies what is fair having regard to the circumstances. In many of the cases, the dispute has only reached court because one of the parties is behaving unfairly, and may have been doing so throughout the relationship.

In proprietary estoppel cases, the express embracing of unconscionability as the reason for intervention might seem to be more intellectually honest, but the circumstances in which an estoppel claim could be made out and a constructive trust of common intention found are so similar that, as we have seen, they are often conflated together.

[10] *Family Law in the Twentieth Century: A History* (OUP 2005), p 113.

[11] [1991] 1 AC 107.

[12] Gardner, 'Rethinking Family Property' [1993] 109 LQR 263; Riniker, 'The Fiction of Common Intention and Detriment' [1998] Conv 202.

[13] [1975] 1 WLR 1338.

[14] [1986] Ch 638.

(3) Gender imbalance?

It has also been argued that women are denied fair shares in property, due to the traditional sexual division of labour, the lack of financial value accorded to housework and childcare, unequal access to capital, and pay inequalities. Some have suggested that a gendered basis for intervention is needed, giving women special treatment as:

> If women continue to suffer structural social and economic disadvantage at the hands of men, then the removal of a gendered basis for intervention can place them at a legal disadvantage too.[15]

By contrast, it has been argued that the current system, which allows for parties to declare their legal interests or find a common intention is preferable to any gendered intervention, as although it relies on knowledge, it attributes autonomy rather than stereotyping familial roles and appropriate behaviour.[16]

(4) Away from property law?

The rights in favour of cohabitants generated by the common intention constructive trust appear in many cases to have more affinity to the rights of spouses when a financial adjustment order is made on divorce than to conventional property rights. A cynic might even see recent developments as a revival of Lord Denning's once discredited new model constructive trust. Perhaps the time has come to stop trying to subject the trust of the family home to any form of property law analysis:

> To put it another way, one reason why *Stack* and *Kernott* raise so many property law questions, and fail to answer them, could be that the cases are not really about property law at all. Not any more. If we look for an explanation of the role and impact of these cases within the jurisprudence of property law, we will not find it.[17]

The courts have often insisted that they have not developed new or special rules for acquiring an interest in the family home, and that they have simply applied existing property rules to new situations. It is, however, possible to say one thing and in practice do another. The width of the factors considered when quantifying an interest, and an approach which allows inference and, if necessary imputation of intention to decide on the size of the beneficial share, could be viewed as further evidence of a willingness to engage with the social justice of the situation between the parties, rather than simply to determine property rights and entitlements.

Against that, property law seeks to provide some certainty in process and outcome. In most negotiations, it is helpful to have a clear starting point. Clarity is also important when dealing with proprietary interests, because of their capacity to bind third parties.[18] In providing an institutional set of methods to provide for cohabitants seeking an interest in the family home, English law is involved in a search for fairness balanced by clarity, however flawed that search may be. If the balance swings too far in favour of fairness, there is not only a problem in deciding what factors are relevant and what weight they should carry, there is also a problem of lack of clarity and certainty, particularly when strangers to the relationship are involved. It can be argued that if English law is to continue to develop a process that promotes social justice through adjustments in property

[15] Auchmuty, 'Unfair Share for Women: The Rhetoric of Equality and the Reality of Inequality' in Lim and Bottomley *Feminist Perspectives on Land Law* (Routledge-Cavendish 2007), p 180.

[16] Bottomley, 'Women and Trust(s): Portraying the Family in the Gallery of Law' in Bright and Dewar, *Land Law: Themes and Perspectives* (OUP 1998), p 221.

[17] Dixon [2012] Conv 1 (Editorial) 2 at 3.

[18] *National Provincial Bank v Ainsworth* [1965] AC 1175.

rights, or through an enlarged jurisdiction to take account of a wide range of factors in 'discovering' entitlements to property, it should do so by adopting a remedial rather than institutional approach. If this argument is correct, then the observations of Lord Scott in *Thorner v Major and others*[19] about a 'remedial constructive trust' have merit. Those observations, have not yet, however, received majority support.

(5) Judicial legislation?

We saw at the start of this chapter that successive governments have declined to introduce legislation to address the rights of cohabitants on the breakdown of their relationship, and this has left a gap which the courts have filled. The way in which the gap has been filled has been through a mechanism which explicitly recognizes characteristics based upon the relationship between the parties rather than strict property law issues. It is true that the rules can apply to married couples in situations which fall outside the provisions in the Matrimonial Causes Act 1973 for financial provision orders, for instance, where a confiscation order is made against one party, or where a bank is seeking to enforce a mortgage. Nevertheless, the judicial approach has narrowed—but not eliminated—the difference between married and unmarried couples. It is as clear an example of judicial law-making as can be found, and addresses social and political issues that some might consider to trespass upon the legislative function, but which will be thought of by others as too small a step in giving equality to all relationships regardless of gender or marital status.

4 A clash of legal cultures: property and family law

Ownership of the family home lies at the intersection of two areas of legal analysis: property law and family law. Family law and property law adopt different approaches on the issues associated with property division on relationship breakdown. Property law is traditionally concerned with identifying and protecting competing property rights between different rights holders. Family law, by contrast, is often discretion based and concerned about familial status, and the consequences of relationship breakdown.[20] Lord Neuberger, in the approach of lawyers to cohabitation issues, said:

> Chancery law—in particular, company and property law—and family law—in particular, financial remedies—are not happy cohabitants either. Indeed, some might say that property lawyers and family lawyers have something of an oil-and-vinegar quality.[21]

Seen through the lens of a property lawyer, particularly in the sole legal owner cases, equity is being used to give a cohabitant an interest in the home, by depriving the legal owner of what is otherwise his or her interest alone. It is as much about deprivation of property for one cohabitant, as it is about the creation of an interest for the non-legal owner. Hence, particularly in sole legal owner cases, it must be demonstrated that this person is entitled because of a combination of the words and deeds of the legal owning partner, on which the cohabitant had acted to his or her detriment. This approach is not expressly concerned with balancing the contributions to family life which could not be

[19] [1970] AC 777.

[20] Miles 'Property Law v Family Law: Resolving the Problems of Family Property' (2003) 23 *Legal Studies* 624, 627.

[21] Lord Neuberger, 'The Plight of the Unmarried', Keynote Speech for 'At a Glance' Conference 2017, 21 June 2017, at [2].

related to ownership of a house, such as child-rearing or the performance of the usual domestic tasks that partners ordinarily undertake in the home. These are valuable contributions, but property law, which is about managing people's competing interests in and over property, is designed to promote certainty, to allow decisions to be predicted. To stray too far into situations which depend almost exclusively on their facts, as would be necessary to do real justice between individual parties in the family home, would increase disputes and litigation.

Family law, by contrast, would prefer to treat the issue of entitlements to the family home in terms of a 'materially communal relationship'.[22] The lack of a regime giving discretion to the court to adjust the property rights of individuals, instead of declaring how the property is held, means that the trust concept will never be an entirely satisfactory vehicle for the resolution of disputes.[23] The trust is a method of managing wealth, and often of providing tax advantages to the owner of property by manipulation of the separation of ownership and control of assets.[24] It is not a mechanism which lends itself easily to determining entitlements in the family home, beyond allowing some simple sharing of the home as an asset.

The current legal approaches satisfy neither side of the equation.

5 Concluding thoughts

It is patent that traditional trusts principles have been strained to provide solutions in this difficult area. The issues with which the courts are dealing are complex, so it is not surprising that there have been some false starts, and that there has been, and will continue to be, some uncertainty or inconsistency in applying the law. Whether we are moving to a future where the constructive trust is simply a vehicle for doing justice between family members remains to be seen. The fact that, in sole legal owner cases, there remains a need to acquire an interest and to demonstrate some form of detriment to do so, means we have not reached that point yet. With proprietary estoppel cases, the uncertainty about the basis of the remedy granted to feed an estoppel, and the increasing judicial trend to see a financial award as the most appropriate remedy,[25] means that, to claimants, it does not provide a more satisfactory alternative to constructive trusts.

It is to be remembered that equity exists, both historically and in the modern days, to ameliorate the impact of the common law, but must do so by evolving existing rules, not creating entirely new ones. This is where our treatment of the family homes started in Chapter 11. To move forward positively, it should be recognized that trusts are not the mechanism to achieve fairness between unmarried cohabitants. Such issues would be better addressed through legislative intervention.

However, as legislative intervention has proved impossible to this point, the plight of cohabitants remains in the hands of the judiciary and their equity-based solutions, and will doubtless remain a fertile area of litigation.

[22] Gardner 'Family Property Today' (2008) 124 LQR 422.

[23] See Cretney, *Family Law in the Twentieth Century: A History* (OUP 2003) 113.

[24] For criticism of the trust concept, see, e.g. Knobel, 'Trusts: Weapons of Mass Injustice?' (2013) *Tax Justice Network*. Available at: https://taxjustice.net/reports/trusts-weapons-of-mass-injustice/, (accessed August 2021).

[25] Dixon, 'Proprietary Estoppel: The Law of Farms and Families' [2019] Conv 89.

PART V

Equity in Society

16. Clubs and societies 353
17. Wills and intestate succession 369
18. Secret trusts 401

16

Clubs and societies

1 Introduction

Few people would give the issues about how clubs and societies can hold and manage property much thought. However, since some forms of club do not have a legal personality as such, there is a real issue about how they can deal with property, whether this concerns everyday management, the receipt of gifts, or who is entitled to the club's property if the club is dissolved. Trusts play a role in providing an explanation. The legal analysis of clubs also affects what happens should a club or society cease to exist. (In one leading case, the last surviving member of a society set up to prevent the use of animals in performances was held to be personally entitled to all the society's assets, worth over £2 million.)

2 Types of clubs and societies

Clubs and societies can take a number of different legal forms.

(1) **Proprietary clubs**

A proprietary club is privately owned by an individual or company. The owner permits members to use the facilities in return for membership and other fees. A hotel with leisure facilities that permits members of the public to use the swimming pool and exercise rooms in return for an annual fee, describing those subscribing in terms such as members of the 'Park Hotel Health Club', would be a club of this kind. Since all the club assets belong to the owner,[1] there are no special considerations for the involvement of equity.

(2) **Incorporated clubs and societies**

A variant of the proprietary club is where the proprietor that owns the club assets is a company and its shareholders are also the members of the club. In such a case, each member of the club may be required to acquire a share in the company owning the club assets at the time of being admitted as a member. On leaving membership, the member may then be required to surrender the share. In this way, only members of the club are shareholders, and through their shareholdings, they own and control the club assets, although it is the company that will be treated as owner for such legal purposes as bringing and defending legal actions. On the dissolution of the club, any club assets will be distributed in accordance with company law.

[1] *Rehman v Ali* [2015] EWHC 4056 (Ch) at 55 (privately owned mosque).

(3) Members' club

Another type of club is a members' club. Clubs and societies belonging to this category are generally described as unincorporated associations. They are a group of individuals, bound together by the club rules, but without having acquired separate legal personality for the group by incorporation.[2] It is in this situation that the issue arises of who owns and controls the club assets, and, in this chapter, we look mainly at this type of organization.

(4) Societies that are not unincorporated associations

After we have considered the theory upon which unincorporated associations legally own and manage property, we shall see that there is, in fact, a further type of association or society which cannot fit within the ordinary principles created by equity, and a further set of extraordinary principles have had to be developed to cover this situation.

3 The problem of asset holding and management

The absence of an independent legal personality for an unincorporated association creates a theoretical problem of asset holding and management.[3] At its most basic, before it is seen through a legal prism, an unincorporated association is just a group of people and a set of club rules. Most clubs and societies get along perfectly well, raising funds by subscriptions from members and by fundraising events such as cake sales, car boot sales, and other activities. They will find little difficulty in opening a bank or building society account. A problem can arise when someone leaves a legacy by will to an unincorporated association, and the next of kin or residuary beneficiary challenges the validity of the legacy; or when the association is being wound up and there is a dispute between the members; or in some similar situation.

The courts have been prevented by precedent and English legal tradition from saying that an unincorporated association, as such, is capable of owning property. Yet were the courts to say that the association is incapable of enjoying or managing property, they would be flying in the face of reality. The courts have, therefore, had to invent or construct[4] a solution to the 'problem' in order to justify the fact that in practice unincorporated associations can enjoy and manage, and receive by subscription or gift (sometimes substantial) funds and assets.

(1) The purpose trust theory

English law does not permit the creation of a trust that has no beneficiaries, with the exception of a few narrowly defined categories. One such exception used to apply to gifts to unincorporated associations[5] which were considered valid as gifts for the purposes

[2] For examples of the effect of this on litigation see *Bohm v Secretary of State for Communities and Local Government* [2017] EWHC 3217; *Rostron v Guildford Borough Council* [2017] EWHC 3141 (Admin); *The Official Receiver v Brown* [2017] EWHC 2728 (Ch) at 14; and *Malik v Trump* [2016] EWHC 2011 (QB). Unincorporated associations are recognized as entities for certain purposes: see, for instance, the Friendly Societies Acts 1974 and 1992; the Co-operative and Community Benefit Societies Act 2014; and the Serious Crime Act 2007, s 32 (which authorizes a serious crime prevention order in the name of an unincorporated association).

[3] See Warburton, *Unincorporated Associations: Law and Practice* (2nd edn, Sweet and Maxwell 1992), Ch 5.

[4] See Hackney, *Understanding Equity and Trusts* (Fontana Press, 1987), pp 75–82.

[5] See *Re Endacott* [1960] Ch 232.

of the association provided that the association was free to dispose of its assets at any time.[6] If the terms of the gift, or the rules of the association to which it was made, did not permit the association to be wound up and its assets disposed of within a period of lives in being, plus up to a further twenty-one years, then the disposition would be invalid for infringing the rule against perpetual trusts, otherwise known as the rule against inalienability.[7] In *Leahy v A-G of New South Wales*,[8] Viscount Simonds expressed the firm opinion that a gift upon trust for the purposes of an unincorporated association would be invalid for want of beneficiaries. In consequence of legal developments flowing from that case, a different theory is now normally used to explain how unincorporated associations hold property. However, even accepting this general shift away from a 'purpose-based' understanding of unincorporated associations, the law is not entirely clear cut on the issue. In *Re Denley's Trust Deed*,[9] where there was a gift of land for a sports ground to be used primarily for the employees of a company and as a secondary purpose, for the use of people that the trustees approved, Goff J controversially suggested that a gift for such non-charitable purposes would not fall foul of the beneficiary principle if the purposes were directly or indirectly for the benefit of an individual or individuals. It might be thought to flow from this reasoning that, subject to the gift being confined to the perpetuity period, a gift for the purposes of an unincorporated association that benefits the members of that association can be valid notwithstanding Viscount Simonds' observations.

(2) Gift to members

The theory that Lord Simonds adopted in *Leahy* was that the law treated a gift to an association as valid if the gift could be treated as to the present members rather than upon trust for the purposes of the society. That case concerned a gift by will of a homestead and land upon trust to whatever order of Roman Catholic nuns or Christian Brothers his executors might select. The gift could not be treated as wholly charitable, because his executors were at liberty to select a purely contemplative order of nuns.[10] The Privy Council advised that it could not be treated as a valid private trust either. The gift could not be valid as a private purpose trust. It could, therefore, be upheld only if it were a gift to the members of the chosen order. In the opinion of the Privy Council, a gift to an unincorporated association was to be treated prima facie as a gift to the individual members of that association at the time of the gift so that they could together dispose of it as they thought fit. On that footing, a gift to an unincorporated association would be valid. But that interpretation of the gift was not possible in this case, and the gift was invalid. The testator had not made a gift to the members of a selected order, but upon trust for the order itself; the order could be numerically very large and spread over the whole world, and although the homestead had twenty rooms, and there were 730 acres of land, it was unrealistic to expect this to be shared beneficially by the members of a religious order. The Privy Council believed that:

> . . . however little the testator understood the effect in law of a gift to an unincorporated body of persons by their society name, his intention was to create a trust not merely for the benefit of the existing members of the selected order but for its benefit as a continuing society and for the furtherance of its work.[11]

[6] *Re Drummond* [1914] 2 Ch 90; *Re Clarke* [1901] 2 Ch 110; *Re Taylor* [1940] Ch 481; *Re Price* [1943] Ch 422.

[7] *Carne v Long* [1860] 2 De GF & J 75; *Re Macaulay's Estate* [1943] Ch 435.

[8] [1959] AC 457. [9] [1969] 1 Ch 373.

[10] The necessary element of demonstrable public benefit for the advancement of religion was lacking: see Chapter 21.

[11] [1959] AC 457 at 486.

To give effect to this, the gift would have to include future, as well as present, members of the order. It would then fail for perpetuity.

The inadequacy of this theory is obvious. The court was obliged to frustrate the intentions of the testator because of the lack of an adequate theory to explain how a contemplative order of nuns could receive, hold, and manage assets. Yet there are contemplative orders with substantial property interests.

There are other problems. If a gift to a club or society is treated as a gift to the individual members beneficially, it enables them to deal with it collectively however they wish. But if they are all entitled to a share, any one or more of them could call for their share to be separated and paid to them. That is not how clubs work. Again, the theory does not explain what happens to the share of each member when new members join or existing members resign.

(3) **Mutual contract theory**

In *Neville Estates Ltd v Madden*,[12] Cross J put forward a refined version of the *Leahy* theory that goes some way to meet the objections. The essence of his view is that the gift is made subject to the rules of the association. He said that a gift could be construed as:

> . . . a gift to the existing members not as joint tenants, but subject to their respective contractual rights and liabilities towards one another as members of the association. In such a case a member cannot sever his share. It will accrue to the other members on his death or resignation, even though such members include persons who became members after the gift took effect. If this is the effect of the gift, it will not now be open to objection on the ground of perpetuity or uncertainty unless there is something in its terms or circumstances or in the rules of the association which precludes the members at any given time from dividing the subject of the gift between them on the footing that they are solely entitled to it in equity.[13]

Cross J did not need to apply the analysis to the case before him, since he was concerned with a charitable association in relation to which it is clear that property may validly be held upon trust for the purposes of the association. The analysis was, however, adopted by Brightman J in *Re Recher's Will Trusts*,[14] the case with which this theory is most frequently associated. In that case, Brightman J held that a gift by will to the London and Provincial Anti-Vivisection Society would have been valid on this interpretation if the society had still been in existence at the date of the testatrix's death. Other cases subsequently have adopted the same analysis and it is now generally accepted as the proper way in which to explain how unincorporated associations receive gifts, hold their assets, and distribute them on the winding-up of the association. As Walton J said in *Re Bucks Constabulary Fund (No 2)*:[15]

> I can see no reason for thinking that this analysis is any different whether the purpose for which the members of the association associate are a social club, a sporting club, to establish a widows' and orphans' fund, to obtain a separate Parliament for Cornwall, or to further the advance of alchemy. It matters not. All the assets of the association are held in trust for its members (of course subject to the contractual claims of anybody having a valid contract with the association) save and except to the extent to which valid trusts have otherwise been declared of its property.

The theory allows the club or society to own assets by deeming them to be vested beneficially in the members, although legal title will normally be held by some trustee, such as

[12] [1962] Ch 832. [13] [1962] Ch 832 at 849. [14] [1972] Ch 526. [15] [1979] 1 All ER 623.

the secretary,[16] who will hold the assets upon trust to deal with them in accordance with the rules of the association[17] and the instructions of the committee of management[18] and ultimately the members; but it prevents members from withdrawing their share of the assets from the society by treating the rules of the society as paramount,[19] which members have mutually agreed by contract to observe.[20]

In *Hanchett-Stamford v Attorney-General*,[21] Lewison J affirmed this analysis in dealing with the proprietary entitlements of the sole survivor of an unincorporated association established for the purpose of securing a ban on the use of performing animals in films or on stage. In holding that all property vested in the sole surviving member under the rules of survivorship of a joint tenancy, he held:

> It is true that this is not a joint tenancy according to the classical model; but since any collective ownership of property must be a species of joint tenancy or tenancy in common, this kind of collective ownership must, in my judgment, be a subspecies of joint tenancy, albeit taking effect subject to any contractual restrictions applicable as between members. In some cases . . . those contractual restrictions may be such as to exclude any possibility of a future claim. In others they may not. The cases are united in saying that on a dissolution the members of a dissolved association have a beneficial interest in its assets . . . I cannot see why the legal principle should be any different if the reason for the dissolution is the permanent cessation of the association's activities or the fall in its membership to below two. The same principle ought also to hold if the contractual restrictions are abrogated or varied by agreement of the members.[22]

(4) Limits to the mutual contract theory

(a) Restriction on dissolving the society

The mutual contract theory explained in *Neville Estates Ltd v Madden* and *Re Recher's Will Trusts* can only apply, as Cross J explained, where there is nothing in the terms of the gift or in the rules of the society that will prevent the distribution of the association's assets. If there is, then even under this analysis, any gift will fail under the rule against perpetual trusts. In *Carne v Long*,[23] a testator had made a gift of his house to the trustees of the Penzance Public Library, a subscription library. The rules of the library provided that it could not be broken up as long as ten members remained. The House of Lords held that, under the rules, the library was intended to be a perpetual institution, so that the gift could not be upheld.

[16] See *Mitchell v Watkinson* [2014] EWCA Civ 1472.

[17] For the principles applying to the interpretation of the rules see *Evangelou v McNicol* [2016] EWCA Civ 817.

[18] It is desirable that a gift by will to an unincorporated association should provide that the receipt of the treasurer or other officer is a sufficient discharge, for if this is not provided for by the rules of the society, the administrators of the estate should technically obtain the discharge by way of receipt from every member.

[19] In *Hanchett-Stamford v Attorney-General* [2009] Ch 173, Lewison J rejected any suggestion that members of unincorporated associations held under any specialized form of co-ownership: 'Megarry & Wade, *The Law of Real Property* (6th edn, 2000), Sweet and Maxwell, London, para 9–95, accuses the courts of having developed "a new form of property holding by unincorporated associations" in order to escape from technical difficulties of the classic models of joint tenancies and tenancies in common. I do not think that the courts have purported to do so . . . the "ownership" of assets by an unincorporated association must, somehow, fit into accepted structures of property ownership' (at 31).

[20] As in *Clarke v Earl of Dunraven and Mount-Earl* [1897] AC 59. See *Foster v McNicol* [2016] EWHC 1966 (enforcing the rules of the Labour Party).

[21] [2009] Ch 173. Cited with approval by the Court of Appeal in *Mitchell v Watkinson* [2014] EWCA Civ 1472.

[22] [2009] Ch 173 at 188.

[23] [1860] 2 De GF & J 75.

(b) Members do not have control of the assets

In the leading case of *Re Grant's Will Trusts*,[24] a testator left property 'to the Labour Party Property Committee for the benefit of the Chertsey Headquarters of the Chertsey and Walton Constituency Labour Party'. Under the rules of the Constituency Labour Party, its constitution could not be altered without the consent of the National Labour Party, to which it was subordinate. Vinelott J held that the element of control by an outside body meant that the gift infringed the rule against perpetual trusts, since the Constituency Party was not at liberty to dissolve itself.[25] This reasoning was distinguished by Lawrence Collins J in *Re Horley Town Football Club*.[26] In that case, the club constitution, owing to an amendment made in the year 2000, allowed other clubs, known as 'associate members', voting rights at its annual general meeting. This constitutional arrangement might appear to clash with *Re Grant's Will Trusts* because outside organizations had an influence over the club's constitutional affairs. Be that as it may, the judge in the case, Lawrence Collins J, did not take the view that the earlier case applied. Instead, he found that the members of the club could hold the property on mutual contracts. A key deciding factor for the judge appeared to be the fact that the associate members did not have any great influence at the club. He said:

> I do not consider that it matters that the Rules were changed in 2000 to confer a right to vote on a body which is not itself a member, namely the club of which Associate Members are members. This is far from the case of *Re Grant's Will Trusts*, where Vinelott J held that the influence of a body (not itself a member) on the rules and the destination of Club property was fatal to the argument that a gift should be analysed as one within [mutual contract theory] . . .[27]

(c) Assets held for mixed purposes

In *Re St Andrew's (Cheam) Lawn Tennis Club Trust*,[28] land had been acquired by trustees on trusts which included the provision of land for a tennis or sports ground, and charitable purposes. Arnold J held that the land could not be treated as belonging to the members of the club because the trust was for mixed charitable and non-charitable purposes. It could not be treated as a purely charitable trust because this would defeat the primary purpose of providing a tennis ground which was a non-charitable purpose. The trust deed was an attempt to achieve the legally impossible: a perpetual trust for a non-charitable purpose, namely to enable the members of the club to play tennis. In consequence of this impossibility, the trust failed, and the property had to go on a resulting trust.

(d) Lack of identifiable membership

The theory can only apply where there is an identifiable membership, who are capable (in theory) of being beneficial owners subject to the rules of membership. This presented a problem in *Conservative and Unionist Central Office v Burrell*.[29] The political party at the

[24] [1980] 1 WLR 360.

[25] Compare *News Group Newspapers Ltd v Society of Graphical and Allied Trades* [1986] ICR 716, CA, where, although the local branch of a trade union was subordinate to the national union, it was in theory possible for the local branch to secede from the union and dissolve itself. It may be that even where there is no provision under the rules of an association for amendment and dissolution, this would be permitted by the unanimous agreement of the members: see *Universe Tankships Inc of Monrovia v International Transport Workers Federation* [1983] 1 AC 366, HL.

[26] [2006] EWHC 2386 (Ch).

[27] [2006] EWHC 2386 (Ch) at 117. See further, in support, Luxton, 'Gifts to Clubs: Contract-Holding Is Trumps' [2007] Conv 274.

[28] [2012] EWHC 1040 (Ch).

[29] [1982] 1 WLR 522.

centre of the case was considered by the Court of Appeal to be a combination of a number of elements that could not be considered an unincorporated association, because of the lack of a body of mutual rights and duties binding those elements together.

(e) Conditions attached to gifts to unincorporated associations

There may be something in the terms of a gift rather than in the rules of an association that makes the mutual contract theory inapplicable. The theory cannot apply if the terms of the gift exclude the possibility of the members of the association taking beneficially. This was considered by Oliver J in *Re Lipinski's Will Trusts*.[30] Harry Lipinski had left his residuary estate to an unincorporated association, the Hull Judeans (Maccabi) Association, 'in memory of my late wife to be used solely in the work of constructing new buildings for the association and/or improvements to the said buildings'. Counsel for the next-of-kin argued that the terms of the gift meant that the members of the association could not take beneficially, since the money had to be used for a particular purpose and because there was an intention to create a permanent endowment. Oliver J rejected the argument that the words of the gift showed an intention to create a permanent endowment: the whole of the money could be spent immediately. Nor did he think that the direction of Harry Lipinski as to how the money should be spent was binding on the association. The association was free within its rules to alter its constitution and to divide the whole of its assets between the members.[31] Oliver J, therefore, believed that there was nothing to prevent the application of the mutual contract theory. As an alternative, he considered that, even if the association was bound to apply the money for a particular purpose, on the authority of *Re Denley's Trust Deed*, 'a trust which, though expressed as a purpose, was directly or indirectly for the benefit of an individual or individuals was valid provided that those individuals were ascertainable at any one time and the trust was not otherwise void for uncertainty'.[32]

The latter analysis might ensure that Harry Lipinski's bounty was used as he intended, although even in this case, some of Oliver J's remarks suggest that the members of the association would be free as both trustees and beneficiaries of the gift to treat it as an absolute one.[33] In order to sustain the validity of Harry Lipinski's gift, Oliver J is thus permitting the association to disregard his directions. One wonders if Harry Lipinski would have turned in his grave at the suggestion that the members of the association would be free to divide the legacy among themselves, rather than building as he requested. If he intended an absolute gift to the members, why did he seek to impose a direction as to how it was to be used?

There might be situations in which the addition of a direction in a gift to an unincorporated association could not be overcome in one of the ways suggested by Oliver J in *Re Lipinski's Will Trusts*.[34] If a gift to an unincorporated association imposes in clear terms a trust to use that gift in a way which is neither directly nor indirectly for the benefit

[30] [1976] Ch 235.

[31] [1976] Ch 235 at 248, per Oliver J. He drew an analogy with *Re Bowes* [1896] 1 Ch 507, where it was held that a gift by will to be used for planting trees on the Wemmergill Estate could be used in any way which the landowner chose.

[32] This analysis of the gift appears to represent a return to the purpose trust theory that was rejected in *Leahy v A-G for New South Wales*. Some doubt about the decision in *Re Denley* was expressed by Lawrence Collins J in *Re Horley Town Football Club* [2006] EWHC 2386 (Ch) at 99 and 131 because 'there are difficulties with regard to termination of such a trust which make it an unsafe basis for decision.'

[33] By analogy with *Re Turkington* [1937] 4 All ER 501. This appears to be an application of the rule in *Saunders v Vautier* (1841) 10 LJ Ch 354.

[34] [1976] Ch 235.

of the members, it would be rather more difficult to treat the gift as an absolute one to the members of the association subject to its rules, since the members would not also be beneficiaries. This is one way in which *Re St Andrew's (Cheam) Lawn Tennis Club Trust*[35] could be viewed. Even in this case, however, if the purposes of the trust were within the purposes of the society (which was not so in the *St Andrew's* case), it might be possible to take the view that the direction to hold upon trust was otiose and could, therefore, be disregarded. There is persuasive authority that in the case of benevolent associations established for altruistic purposes the mutual contract analysis is the one which prima facie applies to the assets of the association.[36]

(f) Charitable unincorporated associations

It is possible for a charity to be established via the mechanism of an unincorporated association. In this case, the assets of the association are dedicated to charitable purposes and are not available to the members individually.

(5) Associations without mutual contract status

Mention has already been made of *Conservative and Unionist Central Office v Burrell*,[37] a case that involved the tax status of the Conservative Party. If it was an unincorporated association, then the treasurer would have been liable to pay corporation tax on behalf of the association. The Court of Appeal held that the Conservative Party was not an unincorporated association because, although it was an association of individuals, it lacked a set of rules regulating its affairs and binding its members together by means of mutually enforceable rights and obligations.[38] Since the existence of such a body of rules is essential to the mutual contract analysis of property-holding by clubs and societies, the court felt obliged to offer a solution as to how the Conservative Party was legally entitled to manage its finances. In the High Court,[39] Vinelott J put forward the suggestion that a person making a donation to the party entered into a contract with the treasurer under which the latter would be in breach of contract if he failed to apply the sums received for the purposes of the party, and that the treasurer might also be under some special equitable obligation akin to that of an executor. Without commenting on these possibilities, Brightman LJ, in the Court of Appeal, put forward another possibility. He suggested that the contributor would confer an irrevocable mandate on the party treasurer[40] to add the donation or subscription to the general funds of the party. The contributor would have the right to prevent a misapplication of the general funds, or to have a misapplication remedied, until on ordinary accounting principles no part of the contributor's donation is represented in the general funds.[41]

[35] [2012] EWHC 1040 (Ch).

[36] *Re Bucks Constabulary Widows' and Orphans' Fund Friendly Society (No 2)* [1979] 1 All ER 623, where Walton J believed that nothing turned upon the status of the benevolent fund as a friendly society in deciding how its property was held for the purpose of distribution on its dissolution.

[37] [1982] 1 WLR 522, CA.

[38] The Court of Appeal also suggested that an unincorporated association required a defined date upon which it had come into existence, and that members should be free to join or to leave at will. The necessity for these requirements may be doubted. The party was described as an unincorporated association in *Story v McLoughlin* [2017] EWHC 3350 (Edis J).

[39] [1980] 3 All ER 42.

[40] The effect of the mandate would be to make the treasurer the contributor's agent in relation to the funds transferred.

[41] There are parallels between this analysis and *Quistclose* trusts, discussed in Chapter 9.

Brightman LJ acknowledged that the mandate theory could not easily support donations by will, since mandate and agency relationships can subsist only during the lifetime of the principal.[42] It would, however, be possible for a testator to authorize his personal representatives to enter into a mandate on his behalf.

The potential of the mandate theory to explain and justify gifts where there is no obvious beneficiary has yet to be fully explored or exploited. For instance, there is no reason why mandate or agency theory could not equally apply to gifts to unincorporated associations with clear rules as it does to less formally constituted groups. The mandate theory could also make a gift for purposes effective even without any ascertainable human beneficiaries. The willingness of the court to put the theory forward in the *Conservative Central Office* case, even though any such theory is unlikely to have been in the mind of many Conservative Party members, is an indication of how the courts will stretch legal theory to solve a problem which legal theory has itself created.

4 Dissolution of clubs and societies

(1) Incorporated bodies

An incorporated body is wound up in accordance with the principles which apply to that type of body. For instance a limited company can be wound up in accordance with the Companies Act 2006, and a charitable incorporated organization established under the Charities Act 2011 can be wound up or dissolved in accordance with the procedures set out in that Act.

(2) Unincorporated associations

Unincorporated associations as groups of individuals bound together by mutual agreement can be wound up in accordance with the rules which form the contractual bond making the individuals into an association, and if the rules make no provision for dissolution, by unanimous agreement of all members.[43] Hogan J held in *Dunne v Mahon*[44] that, even in the absence of specific provision in the rules of a club permitting dissolution, it was to be implied that the club could dissolve on the basis of a majority decision. He considered that it was reasonable to imply a term that changes to the rules of a society could be agreed by a majority, except so far as this affected the vested rights of existing members.[45] The association also ceases to exist if all its members die or leave, or if the number of members is reduced to one.[46] An unincorporated association is not dissolved spontaneously merely by inactivity. In *Trustees of the Graphic Reproduction Federation v Wellcom London Ltd*,[47] it was held that a printing trade association which had engaged in no significant activity for twenty-seven years was still in being: 'But inactivity may be so prolonged or so circumstanced that the only reasonable inference is that the club has become dissolved.'[48] This is likely to be the case where a club has become incapable

[42] See *Re Wilson* [1908] 1 Ch 839. There might also be difficulty where a new treasurer took office, since the relationship between principal and agent is essentially a personal one.

[43] *Re William Denby & Sons Ltd Sick and Benevolent Fund* [1971] 1 WLR 973 at 978–9.

[44] [2012] IEHC 412.

[45] This restriction invalidated a purported rule change requiring any surplus funds on disbanding the club to be donated to charity.

[46] *Hanchett-Stamford v Attorney-General* [2009] Ch 173.

[47] [2014] EWHC 134 (Ch).

[48] *Re GKN Bolts and Nuts Sports and Social Club* [1982] 2 All ER 855 at 779 (Sir Robert Megarry V-C).

of carrying out any of its objects. It is possible, although likely to be rare, that a court can infer a mutual agreement between the members to regard a club as having ceased to exist.[49]

In addition to winding up by the members in accordance with the rules, the court has an inherent equitable jurisdiction to wind up an unincorporated association.[50] This jurisdiction was exercised in *Re Enniskillen Trust*[51] to wind up an insolvent charitable unincorporated association. The jurisdiction can be exercised even when it is still open to the members to wind up by mutual agreement, but in fairness this should be on terms which are no less favourable to the members than if they had wound up voluntarily, and the court should not disturb the existing property rights of members.[52]

5 Surplus funds on dissolution

(1) Incorporated or proprietary clubs

Where an incorporated club dissolves, any surplus assets will be distributed in accordance with company law. As *Rehman v Ali*[53] makes clear, if a proprietary club (in that case, a privately owned mosque) dissolves, any surplus assets belong to the proprietor.

(2) Unincorporated associations

(a) Resulting trust

Before the adoption of the theory that assets held by unincorporated associations belong to the members beneficially, subject to the club rules, it was not clear what should happen to surplus assets if the association wound up. Some cases decided that any surplus funds would be held on a resulting trust for those who had contributed,[54] a concept easy to describe, but hard to apply. This is illustrated by *Re West Sussex Constabulary's Widows, Children and Benevolent (1930) Fund Trusts*.[55] A fund to provide benefits to the widows of members of the West Sussex police force was wound up when the force was amalgamated with others, leaving a surplus of £35,000. The club's revenue was derived from: (a) members' subscriptions; (b) legacies and donations from outsiders; and (c) proceeds of entertainments and collecting-boxes. The question arose as to how the surplus should be distributed. Goff J dealt separately with each type of revenue (see Figure 16.1).

(i) Members' subscriptions

Goff J held that the members were not entitled to take any share of the surplus on the basis of resulting trusts because they had made their contributions on the basis of contract and

[49] *Re GKN Bolts and Nuts Sports and Social Club* [1982] 2 All ER 855 at 782 (Sir Robert Megarry V-C). See also *Boyle v Collins* [2004] EWHC 271 (Ch) and *Sanderson v Hi Peak Property Ltd* [2014] EWHC 4918 (Ch).

[50] *Re William Denby & Sons Ltd Sick and Benevolent Fund* [1971] 1 WLR 973; *Butts Park Ventures (Coventry) Ltd v Bryant Homes Central Ltd* [2003] EWHC 2487 (Ch) at 18. There is a power to appoint a liquidator.

[51] [2013] NI Ch 10.

[52] *Trustees of the Graphic Reproduction Federation v Wellcom London Ltd* [2014] EWHC 134 (Ch).

[53] [2015] EWHC 4056 (Ch) at 56.

[54] *Re Printers and Transferrers Amalgamated Trades Protection Society* [1899] 2 Ch 184; *Re Lead Co's Workmen's Fund Society* [1904] 2 Ch 196; *Tierney v Tough* [1914] 1 IR 142; *Re Hobourn Aero Components Air Raid Distress Fund* [1946] Ch 86.

[55] [1971] Ch 1.

(i) *Re West Sussex*

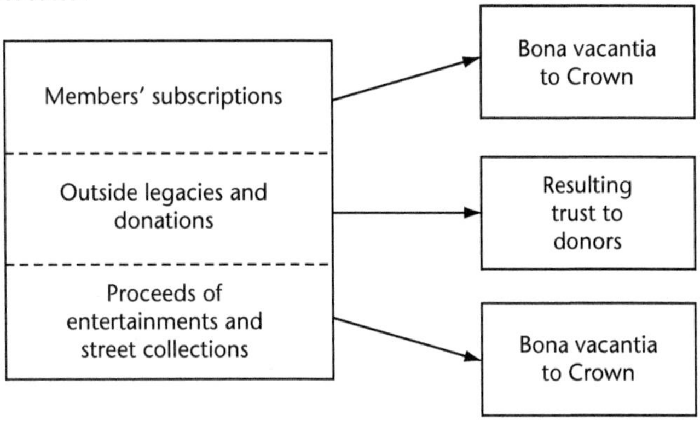

(ii) *Re Bucks Constabulary*

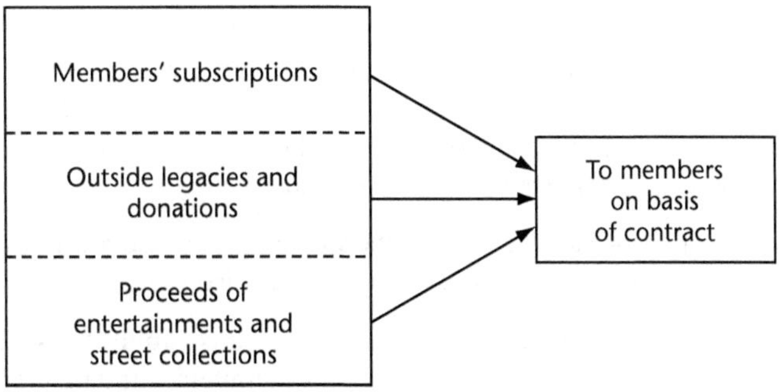

Figure 16.1 Distribution of assets on the dissolution of an unincorporated association

not trust.[56] They had received all that they had bargained for from their membership of the club. Therefore, this property went bona vacantia to the Crown.

(ii) Outside legacies and donations

Since these were not given on the basis of contract, Goff J held there should be a resulting trust in favour of those who had contributed, in so far as the surplus was attributable to their contributions.[57] He considered that this aspect of the case was indistinguishable from *Re Abbott Fund Trusts*.[58] In that earlier case, money had been raised for the support of two 'deaf and dumb' sisters. On the death of the sisters, the left-over funds had resulted to the subscribers.

(iii) Proceeds of entertainments and collecting-boxes

Because the donors of these funds could not be identified, Goff J held that there could be no resulting trust of the surplus attributable to revenue from these sources, and they thus passed bona vacantia to the Crown.[59]

[56] Following *Cunnack v Edwards* [1896] 2 Ch 679; *Re Gillingham Bus Disaster Fund* [1958] Ch 300.
[57] [1971] Ch 1 at 14–16. [58] [1900] 2 Ch 326. [59] [1971] Ch 1 at 11–14.

The result of this decision is that the majority of the surplus passed bona vacantia to the Crown, with the surviving members receiving nothing for their contributions. There was no argument that the members had any contractual rights to the surplus. Goff J observed in his judgment:

> The surviving members . . . may well have a right in contract on the ground of frustration or total failure of consideration, and that right may embrace contributions made by past members, though I do not see how it could apply to moneys raised from outside sources. I have not, however, heard any argument based on contract . . .[60]

If Goff J was right in his analysis that most of the association's funds had no owner on the association's dissolution, it would have followed as a matter of logic that there was no owner immediately before the association's dissolution. If that was indeed the case, it is hard to see how any of the association's purposes could have been achieved.

(b) The current approach

The approach in *West Sussex* would not now be adopted. There were very similar facts in the later case of *Re Bucks Constabulary Fund (No 2)*.[61] The case concerned a society registered under the Friendly Societies Act 1896, which was wound up because of the amalgamation of the Buckinghamshire Constabulary, leaving a surplus. Given that an unincorporated association derives its existence from an 'implied contract between all the members inter se governed by the rules of the society',[62] Walton J held that this contract should govern the distribution of the surplus:

> as on dissolution there were members of the society . . . in existence, its assets are held on trust for such members to the total exclusion of any claim on behalf of the Crown.

This is entirely consistent with the reasoning that unincorporated associations hold their property on the basis of the contract between the members,[63] and that they must be able to alter the rules of the association so as to put the assets into their own pockets.[64] Since this shows that 'the money was theirs all the time',[65] they should be entitled to what is theirs on the winding-up of the association. This reasoning excludes any possibility of a resulting trust, either of the members' own contributions or of the donations of outsiders,[66] and provides the members with a basis for entitlement to the surplus which was not found in *Re West Sussex Constabulary's Widows, Children and Benevolent (1930) Fund Trusts*.[67] Therefore, none of the assets of the association, whatever their source, should pass under a resulting trust or as bona vacantia.[68] This is also shown in Figure 16.1.

60 [1971] Ch 1 at 10: this did not prevent the property being paid over as bona vacantia, as the Crown had offered a full indemnity to the trustees.

61 [1979] 1 WLR 936. 62 [1979] 1 WLR 936 at 943.

63 *Re Sick and Funeral Society of St John's Sunday School, Golcar* [1973] Ch 51 at 60, per Megarry J: 'membership of a club or association is primarily a matter of contract. The members make their payments, and in return they become entitled to the benefits of membership in accordance with the rules. The sums they pay cease to be their individual property, and so cease to be subject to any concept of resulting trust. Instead, they become the property, through the trustees of the club or association, of all the members for the time being, including themselves.'

64 See *Re Lipinski* [1976] Ch 235; *Re Grant's Will Trusts* [1980] 1 WLR 360.

65 *Re Bucks Constabulary Widows' and Orphans' Fund Friendly Society (No 2)* [1979] 1 WLR 936 at 951; *Dunne v Mahon* [2012] IEHC 412.

66 Since these too are held by the association on the basis of the contract for the members absolutely. See *Re Lipinski's Will Trusts* [1976] Ch 235, where Mr Lipinski's gift to the association was held to be a gift to the members subject to their contract inter se, which they could decide to distribute among themselves.

67 [1971] Ch 1.

68 Walton J suggested ([1979] 1 WLR 936 at 943) that bona vacantia might apply where an association ceased to exist because there was only one surviving member, but even this possibility was rejected in *Hanchett-Stamford v A-G* [2008] EWHC 330 (Ch).

(3) **Who are the members?**

The members of an unincorporated association for the purpose of any distribution of assets are those who are (or were) members at the time of the dissolution. The identity of the members at that date will be governed by the rules of the association, as indeed will the extent of their shares (discussed later). Thus honorary or associate members may participate differently, or not at all, compared with full members.[69]

A person who was a member of the association, even for many years, but who had ceased to be a member at the date of dissolution, will not be entitled to a share. In the case of corporate members, corporations which themselves have dissolved before the dissolution of the association will not be entitled to a share of the assets: 'Entitlement goes with membership. If membership goes, entitlement to any funds goes.'[70]

(4) **The members' contractual rights**

The exact entitlement of each surviving member on a distribution of the surplus assets of an association depends on its rules. In the absence of express rules providing for dissolution, distribution will be on the basis of an implied term, which, in the absence of countervailing considerations, will be that distribution should be in equal shares.[71] This was the conclusion reached by Walton J in *Re Bucks Constabulary Fund (No 2)*.[72] However, the rules of the society may expressly or impliedly indicate that something other than equal division was intended. In *Re Sick and Funeral Society of St John's Sunday School, Golcar*[73] a society existed to provide members with sickness allowances and death benefits. Members aged five to twelve paid half-contributions and were only entitled to half-benefits. Megarry J held that since this inequality was written into the rules, dividing the members into different classes, it should be applied to the surplus funds on dissolution. Those paying half-contributions were only entitled to half-shares in the surplus.[74] Similarly, in *Re North Harrow Tennis Club* there was a provision that distribution was to be according to length of membership. Although this did not apply in the exact circumstances of the dissolution of the club, it was used as the basis for implying a term as to the basis for distribution.

(5) **Last surviving member of an association**

Hanchett-Stamford v A-G[75] concerned the assets of the Performing and Captive Animals Defence League, which had been established in 1914 to seek to prevent animals being used in performances. Lewison J held that the League was not charitable, because it was campaigning to change the law. The question was what should happen to its assets, worth over

[69] See *Re Horley Town Football Club* [2006] EWHC 2386 (Ch), in which Lawrence Collins J, in considering the entitlement of members to land settled on trust to provide a permanent ground for Horley FC, applied the contractual theory to find that property was settled on a bare trust for the full-time members on a per capita basis, to the exclusion of associate and temporary members.

[70] *Trustees of the Graphic Reproduction Federation v Wellcom London Ltd* [2014] EWHC 134 (Ch) at 30.

[71] See *Re North Harrow Tennis Club* [2017] EWHC 2476 (Ch), where Edward Pepperall QC analyzes a range of cases, including *Re Printers and Transferrers Amalgamated Trades Protection Society* [1899] 2 Ch 184; *Re Lead Co's Workmen's Fund Society* [1904] 2 Ch 196; *Tierney v Tough* [1914] 1 IR 142; *Brown v Dale* (1878) 9 Ch D 78; *Feeny and Shannon v MacManus* [1937] IR 23; *Re Blue Albion Cattle Society* [1966] CLY 1274; *Re St Andrew's Allotments Association's Trusts* [1969] 1 WLR 229.

[72] [1979] 1 WLR 936 at 951–5.

[73] [1973] Ch 51.

[74] See also *Re St Andrew's Allotments Association's Trusts* [1969] 1 WLR 229 and *Re Horley Town Football Club* [2006] EWHC 2386 (Ch).

[75] [2008] EWHC 330 (Ch).

£2.44 million. Although at one time there had been 250 members, when Mr Hanchett-Stamford (one of two trustees for the League) died, the only traceable member was Mrs Hanchett-Stamford. Who was entitled to the assets? If Mrs Hanchett-Stamford was entitled to the funds, she intended to follow her late husband's wishes and to apply the funds to another animal charity, the Born Free Foundation. Lewison J accepted that where no express restriction had been placed on the funds of an association, 'the members for the time being of an unincorporated association are beneficially entitled to "its" assets, subject to the contractual arrangements between them'.[76] Lewison J saw no basis for restricting this principle to cases only where there were two members or more. It would breach human rights law to deprive the surviving member of the assets on the death of the last but-one member. The League was still active up to the death of Mr Hanchett-Stamford. In the view of Lewison J:

> I consider that the League ceased to exist upon his death in January 2006, when its membership fell below two. Since Mrs Hanchett-Stamford is the sole surviving member of the League, she is, in my judgment, entitled to its assets. She is therefore entitled to be registered as proprietor of Sid Abbey [one of the assets] and as shareholder of the shares now held in the League's name. Her entitlement is free from any restrictions imposed by the rules of the League, which must have ceased to bind on the death of her husband. It follows that she is free, if she so chooses, to give all the former assets of the League to the Born Free Foundation.[77]

(5) **Special cases**

The solution of dividing the assets of a dissolved unincorporated association between its members at the time of dissolution can apply only where the members could claim a beneficial entitlement immediately before that date. It could not apply, therefore, in a case like *Re St Andrew's (Cheam) Lawn Tennis Club Trust*,[78] where the land on which the club played tennis was held on trusts for purposes which excluded any claim by the members to have full ownership. Where a charitable unincorporated association is dissolved, the assets of the association are not available for distribution between the members because of the principle that assets dedicated to charitable purposes are dedicated to charity in perpetuity. The assets will instead be applied to another charity in accordance with the rules of the association or a scheme approved by the Charity Commission or the court.[79]

(6) **Mutual contract theory doubted?**

In *Davis v Richards and Wallington Industries Ltd*,[80] Scott J had to decide what happened to surplus funds in a pension scheme to which employees had made contributions in return for defined retirement and other benefits, and the employer made additional payments. On the termination of the scheme there was a surplus of £3 million, after allowing for the payment of all contractually due payments. Although this situation was similar to that involving the police benevolent funds, and counsel had argued that a pension fund should be treated as similar to an unincorporated association (but without it seems arguing for the mutual contract theory), Scott J applied a resulting trust analysis which

[76] [2008] EWHC 330 (Ch) at 31.

[77] [2008] EWHC 330 (Ch) at 50. See Griffiths, '*Hanchett-Stamford v Attorney General*: Another Twist in the Tale—Unincorporated Associations and the Distribution of Surplus Funds' [2009] 73 Conv 428; Panesar, 'Surplus Funds and Unincorporated Associations' (2008) *Trusts and Trustees* 698.

[78] [2012] EWHC 1040 (Ch). [79] See Chapter 22. [80] [1991] 2 All ER 563.

ignored *Re Bucks Constabulary Fund (No 2)*,[81] even though the case had been cited in argument, and instead referred with approval to *Re West Sussex Constabulary's Widows, Children and Benevolent (1930) Fund Trusts*.[82] Scott J held that because, in his view, the surplus had been generated primarily by employer contributions (since the employer was only required to contribute to top-up the fund if the employee contributions were insufficient), the employer had the first claim. Even if the employees could show that their contributions had created or contributed to the surplus, they should still have no claim to it both because no workable method could be identified for distributing funds between members with greatly differing contractual rights, and because benefits payable to pension scheme members are limited by Inland Revenue rules. This part of the surplus would therefore go to the Crown as bona vacantia. Scott J's reasoning was rejected by the Privy Council in *Air Jamaica Ltd v Charlton*,[83] but the Privy Council still adopted a resulting trust analysis and held that the surplus on a winding up of a pension scheme, in so far as it was attributable to contributions made by members, should be returned to them pro rata and in proportion to the amounts they had contributed to the scheme. Payments should include the estates of deceased and surviving members, and should take no account of any benefits received. This scheme of payment was clearly very different from the payments which would be made under the mutual contract theory.

There are considerations which apply to pension funds which may not apply to some clubs and societies, but pension fund schemes do not differ markedly from some benevolent societies such as the one in *Re Sick and Funeral Society of St John's Sunday School, Golcar*.[84] The very different treatment of such associations from pension schemes highlights the artificiality of the reasoning which the courts are obliged to employ to resolve issues about property ownership.

6 Critique

Most people joining a club do so because they wish to engage in the activities which the club supports. Unless they have studied this branch of the law they would probably be surprised to discover that by joining the club they have acquired a share of the club's assets. Members who supported the club in its early years, but who have left because they have moved from the area or for any other reason would probably be equally surprised to discover that their successors could close the club and share all the assets. The windfall gains are potentially very large. The sale of the RAC rescue service division in 1998 produced in the order of £30,000 for each of the Club's members; the assets held by the Performing and Captive Animals Defence League when it ceased to exist were worth more than £2 million.

Windfall gains are all the more surprising where an association provides social amenities. If that private association had instead been formed as a charity, then a very different set of rules would apply to it. Where a charity dissolves, its assets would have to be applied to other similar purposes rather than be shared by the members. It is tempting to argue that the same should happen in the case of non-charitable unincorporated associations,[85] which have been the focus of this chapter. *Gibbons v Smith*[86] shows that the present law can lead to the loss of socially valuable assets. An association with a clubhouse and land

[81] [1979] 1 WLR 936. [82] [1971] Ch 1. [83] [1999] 1 WLR 1399. [84] [1973] Ch 51.

[85] See Tribe, 'Deploying Communitarianism Bankruptcy Theory to Rescue Charities and Maintain Charitable Purposes' in Picton & Sigafoos (eds), *Debates in Charity Law* (Hart 2020) p 81, which argues that incorporated and non-incorporated charities should be treated alike upon their dissolution.

[86] [2020] EWHC 1727 (Ch).

for the use of British Railway workers had sought to achieve charitable status. It appears that, despite not being open to the general public, the organization had sporting and welfare functions.[87] The trustees had, at one point, applied to register as charity but had been refused. That decision of Charity Commission had far-reaching consequences. After the death of the last trustee, Roth J held that the value of significant areas of land should be distributed amongst the final membership.

The loss of a social amenity, as in *Gibbons v Smith*, seems unfortunate. Yet keeping the assets of dissolved unincorporated associations applied to social purposes rather than passing their value to the final members would be challenging from an administrative perspective. In the Charity Commission, there is a special body to oversee the task of distributing left-over charitable funds,[88] but the same is not true for non-charitable property. There is no machinery in place. Nor, in the light of the unique character of many associations, is it obvious as to the particular social purposes to which the assets should be directed.

If keeping the assets applied to social purposes appears potentially problematic, then returning the funds to the original contributors would be even more challenging. There might be a very large of number of original contributors to the club and some of them could even be anonymous. The sizes of their contributions might also vary greatly. For small contributors it might not be worth the time or effort to apply for the money back. If there is no-one to claim the surplus, a judge who declared that surplus should be returned to the donors might be demanding an impossibility. In the light of this, dividing the assets between the final members so that they get a windfall, as the current law does, may be the most straightforward solution. It is a least worst option.

[87] *Gibbons v Smith* [2020] EWHC 1727 (Ch), [18].

[88] See Picton, 'Donor Intention and Dialectic Policy Frames' in Harding (ed), *Research Handbook on Not-For-Profit Law* (Edward Elgar 2018) 199.

17

Wills and intestate succession

1 Introduction

It is a simple truth that a man cannot take his property with him when he dies. 'We brought nothing into the world, and we can take nothing out of it.'[1] We may, however, want to decide to whom our property should pass on our death.

When a person dies, some of their property rights die with them. A person's retirement annuity pension payments normally end on their death, and if they had the right under a trust to live in a house during their lifetime, the use of the house will pass on their death to the next person entitled.[2] Similarly, the property rights of a joint tenant end on their death.[3] However, most of a person's property endures beyond their death, and although we cannot enjoy our worldly goods from our graves, as owners of property, we can influence (even if not fully control) who will be entitled to our property after our death. This chapter is concerned with the arrangements which people can make to choose who will benefit from their property after their death.

It has been said that only two things are certain in life: death and taxes. The two are linked in another way, because death is an occasion on which the state levies taxes, primarily through inheritance tax. The tax treatment of inheritance arrangements is important and has considerable influence on the way in which people arrange their affairs, but it is a specialist subject not covered in this book.[4] The Law Commission has consulted on some wide-ranging changes to the rules governing wills, on the basis that the law needs to be updated to improve clarity, bring it up to date and make it 'workable'.[5] Reference will be made, where appropriate, to the Law Commission's proposals for reform.[6]

2 Methods of making provision after death

There are several ways in which a person can choose who will benefit from their property after their death.

[1] St Paul, First Letter to Timothy, Ch 6, v 7.

[2] This used to happen under a strict settlement, regulated under the Settled Land Act 1925. Since the introduction of the Trust of Land and Appointment of Trustees Act 1996, it is no longer possible to create new strict settlements, and the legal structure used to pass successive interests in the 'trust of land'—see ss 1 and 2. See, generally, Thompson and George, *Modern Land Law* (6th edn, Oxford University Press 2017) Ch 8.

[3] Their interest passes under the right of survivorship to any remaining joint tenants, discussed below. See, generally, Thompson and George, *Modern Land Law* (6th edn, Oxford University Press 2017) Ch 10.

[4] See, generally, Sloan, *Borkowski's Law of Succession* (3rd edn, Oxford University Press 2017).

[5] *Making a Will* (Law Commission CP 231, 2017), para 1.3.

[6] *Making a Will* (Law Commission CP 231, 2017).

(1) Lifetime gift

The owner of property can make a gift of property during his lifetime. The effect of this is to pass ownership immediately to the beneficiary. If the gift is complete, the donor cannot change his mind and ask for the property back, even if his circumstances change. So if Andy transfers his farm to his daughter, Belinda, but then the two of them fall out, or if Andy needs expensive drug therapy which is not available on the NHS, Belinda cannot be compelled to return the farm or to sell it to support her father.

(2) Donatio mortis causa

It is possible to make a gift which is made in expectation of death and which is conditional upon the donor dying. Such gifts are instances where equity will complete an imperfect gift and are discussed in Chapter 6.[7]

(3) Lifetime trust

The owner of property can also create a lifetime trust and transfer funds to it. In this case, like a gift, provided the trust is complete, there is nothing the settlor can do to change the terms of the trust or to revoke it, unless the power to do so has been expressly reserved as a term of the trust.[8] Life insurance policies are sometimes 'written in trust', so that the policyholder declares who is to benefit from the payment when the policy matures.

(4) Joint tenancy

Where property is vested jointly in the deceased and another person or persons, and one of the joint tenants dies, the rights to that property pass automatically to the survivors. It is possible for most forms of property to be enjoyed through a joint tenancy. In the case of land a trust is required;[9] in the case of most other property (including bank accounts), it is possible for a joint tenancy to be created directly. However, a joint tenancy will not always operate to confer a beneficial interest on the survivor. In *Re Vinogradoff*,[10] an aunt had transferred government stock into the names of herself and her young granddaughter. It would not be unreasonable to assume that the purpose was to permit her granddaughter to acquire the property by survivorship on her death, but because there was no evidence of an intention to make a gift, it was held that there was a resulting trust in favour of the grandmother. In *Young v Sealey*[11] and in *Aroso v Coutt*,[12] the method succeeded in similar circumstances because there was sufficient evidence of an intention to make a gift. Romer J, in *Young v Sealey*, rejected the argument that this method of giving was invalid because it attempted to circumvent the rules relating to making wills.

(5) Nominations and expressions of wishes

Some pension fund and life assurance schemes provide for the payment of a death benefit when a member of the scheme dies. Some of these schemes allow the member to nominate the person who is to receive the payment on the member's death. This enables the

[7] The Law Commission, has 'not formed a definite view as to whether [the doctrine] should be abolished', and has consulted on whether it should be abolished or retained—*Making a Will* (Law Commission CP 231, 2017), Ch 13, Consultation Question 63.

[8] *Paul v Paul* (1882) 20 Ch D 742, CA.

[9] Law of Property Act 1925, ss 1(3), 53(1)(b); Trusts of Land and Appointment of Trustees Act 1996, s 1.

[10] [1935] WN 68. [11] [1949] Ch 278. [12] [2002] 1 All ER (Comm) 241.

payment to be made without the need for probate. A similar method, which may have tax advantages, is where the trustees of the scheme have discretion as to whom to make the payment, but where they will take into account a non-binding expression of wishes by the member.

(6) **Will and testament**

The most obvious way in which a person can control their property beyond the grave is through making a will. A person making a will is known as either a testator or testatrix (if male or female, respectively), and is said to die testate. When a testator dies, the will must be proved (i.e. checked and registered) by the Probate Registry (part of the Family Division of the High Court). It is then available for public inspection. For this reason it was possible for reporters to discover the exact details of the will of Diana, Princess of Wales. There is no requirement in England and Wales for a will to be registered prior to a testator's death. It is thought that around 40 per cent of adults in England and Wales have not made a will,[13] and, as we shall see, there are good reasons for doing so to avoid the costs of the intestacy regime.

(7) **Intestacy**

Where a person does not make a will, then any property to which they are entitled on their death passes to their next of kin under statutory intestacy wills. A person who dies without a will is said to die intestate.

(8) **Partial intestacy**

If a person has made a will, but this does not deal with the whole of that person's property, the person is said to die partially testate. The rules which then apply are a combination of the rules relating to wills and the intestacy rules.

(9) **Provision for family and dependants**

In some jurisdictions (for instance, in France and in the Republic of Ireland), a person is not free to dispose of all his or her property on death. Instead, close family members (in France children, and in Ireland a surviving spouse) are automatically entitled to a share of the estate (this is called the legal right share in Ireland). A testator is free to dispose of the balance of the estate. The rule in England and Wales is different. A testator is free to cut his family out of his estate entirely. However, under the Inheritance (Provision for Family and Dependants) Act 1975, as amended by the Inheritance and Trustees' Powers Act 2014,[14] a surviving spouse or civil partner, or a child, or a person who was dependent upon the deceased, may apply to court to have an order made requiring reasonable provision to be made for them out of the estate. The Act also allows an application where a cohabitant has been living with the deceased 'as husband and wife' for at least two years at his death. So, in *Baker v Baker*,[15] a man who was dying from liver cancer made a will shortly before his death. He left everything to the woman with whom he was living. His daughter successfully challenged the will on the basis that her father did not have mental

[13] See *Making a Will* (Law Commission CP 231, 2017), para 1.2, citing a variety of sources for this estimated percentage figure.

[14] s 6, implementing the substantive changes in Sch 2 to the 2014 Act.

[15] [2008] EWHC 937 (Ch).

capacity at the time. The court, however, ordered that his domestic partner should have a life interest in his house. In view of her limited means, reasonable provision for her required the provision of a home for her lifetime.

The operation of the 1975 Act was reviewed by the Supreme Court in the atypical[16] case of *Ilott v The Blue Cross*,[17] which concerned a claim of a financially independent adult daughter[18] to a net estate worth £486,000, which her mother had left in its entirety to three animal charities.[19] The claimant, Heather Ilott, had been aware that her mother, Melita Jackson, intended her to inherit nothing, having written to her to that effect after executing her will. The two had never reconciled following a rift caused by Heather moving out of the family home, aged seventeen, to live with a man her mother entirely disapproved of. At the time of her mother's death, Mrs Ilott, aged forty-four, was living in property rented from a Housing Association with her husband and children, and the family were dependent on state benefits for the home and other living expenses.

The legal saga of Heather Ilott and the contested gift to the three charities lasted for almost a decade. At first instance, on the basis that Melita Jackson had not made reasonable financial provision for her daughter, a sum of £50,000 was awarded.[20] On appeal, the Court of Appeal had awarded a sum of £143,000 to Heather Ilott, with an option to access some £30,000 more if needed, a figure arrived at to allow her to buy the property she rented and to supplement her state benefits.[21] In reaching this conclusion, the Court of Appeal asserted not only that the judge at first instance had erred in his application of the rules on reasonable financial provision but also that charities, having had no particular connection with Melita Jackson during her life, would not be prejudiced by the higher award to Heather Ilott, as effectively they were receiving a windfall. It was this aspect that attracted significant media attention, given both the significance of testamentary gifts to charities,[22] and the concern that gifts to charities would now be open to a slew of challenges under the Inheritance (Provision for Family and Dependants) Act 1975.[23] The charities brought an appeal to the Supreme Court.[24] In restoring the original £50,000 award on the basis that the Deputy Judge at first instance had committed no legal errors, the Supreme Court recognized the importance charities placed on testamentary bequests and that, as they were the chosen beneficiaries of the deceased, they did not have to justify a claim on the basis of need.[25] The decision has generally been welcomed by charities, and those who feel that testamentary freedom should be respected unless there is very good reason to depart from it.[26] This was the first time the operation of the 1975 Act had come before the highest court, and the decision does little to clarify the operation of the

[16] See Conway, 'Case Comment: Testamentary freedom, family obligation and the Illott legacy—*Ilott v The Blue Cross* [2017] UKSC 17', [2017] Conv 372; Sloan, 'Case Comment: Testamentary freedom reaffirmed in the Supreme Court' (2017) CLJ 499.

[17] [2017] UKSC 17.

[18] Children who are not financially dependent on their parents have often been treated differently than those who are financially dependent by the courts—see Conway, 'Do Parents Really Know Best? Family Provision and the Adult Child' in Barr (ed), *Modern Studies in Property Law: Volume 8*, (Hart 2015), Ch7.

[19] The charities concerned were the Royal Society for the Protection of Cruelty to Animals, the Royal Society for the Protection of Birds, and the Blue Cross.

[20] *Ilott v Mitson* [2009] EWHV 3114.

[21] *Ilott v Mitson* [2014] EQHC 542 (Fam).

[22] See, for example, Davies and Walsh, 'Case Comment: A Fatal Flaw?' [2016] NLJ 17.

[23] See Picton, 'Supreme Court Legacy Ruling: Leaving a Gift to Charity Can Be Egoistic as Well as Altruistic' *The Conversation* (15 March 2017).

[24] Hence, the change of name in the parties.

[25] [2017] UKSC 17 at 46, per Lord Hughes.

[26] See, for example, Conway, 'Rights versus Responsibilities: Adult Children, Parental Wealth and Contested Wills' (2017) JSWFL 494.

legislation or the factors that will be considered when operating it.[27] Indeed, the Supreme Court emphasized that in cases under s 3 of the 1975 Act, judges make a value judgment.[28] Hence, different judges will reach different conclusions on the same set of facts. This offers cold comfort to those advising people making wills or those who may contest them.[29]

3 Probate

None of the property to which a deceased is entitled passes automatically to those entitled on the death by virtue of a will or intestacy. Instead, the assets of the deceased vest in personal representatives whose function it is to ascertain if there is a will; to dispose of the deceased's remains (for instance, by organizing a funeral and burial or cremation); to collect together all the assets; to pay all the debts including any taxes due, including inheritance tax; and then, only if there are sums remaining, to distribute them amongst those entitled. The personal representatives are either executors (if they are named in the deceased's will) or administrators, but there is no difference in their function. The personal representatives derive their authority from a grant of representation made by the Probate Registry. The grant of representation may also be called a grant of Probate (where executors prove that there is a valid will) or a grant of Letters of Administration with will attached (where a will is proved by representatives who are not named in the will) or Letters of Administration (where there is no will).

4 Intestacy

The modern rules of intestate inheritance—the circumstance where the deceased has left no relevant will—were first introduced by the Administration of Estates Act 1925, s 46, and have been modified a number of times. The Law Commission has kept this area under review.[30] The Commission's recommendations in its 2011 report *Intestacy and Family Provision Claims on Death* largely became law,[31] feeding into the Inheritance and Trustees' Powers Act 2014 which amended the previous rules. The law of intestacy is underpinned by a key principle: it is supposed to give effect to the wishes of the deceased.[32] However desirable this might be, it is only an aspiration. The creation of a statutory system which genuinely reflects the large mass of individual intentions of intestates is self-evidently impossible. Each intestate is different and will have lived a life in a network of variable family relationships. In such circumstances, all the law can do is set out a backstop scheme which resembles, or attempts to resemble, the wishes of the average deceased person. It reflects only presumed intention and it can only do so imperfectly.

(1) **The intestacy rules**

The first rule of any intestacy must be to check that there really is no will. It is essential that the personal representatives search the deceased's home; contact solicitors who

[27] See Probert, 'Case Comment: Family and Other Animals' [2017] LQR 550.
[28] Ibid at 24 and 66.
[29] See *Lewis v Warner* [2017] EWCA Civ 2182.
[30] See, *Family Law: Distribution on Intestacy* (Law Commission No 187, 1989).
[31] Intestacy and Family Provision Claims on Death (Law Commission No 331, 2011).
[32] See, Sloan, 'Testamentary Freedom and Caring Adult Offspring in England & Wales and Ireland' in Boeli-Woelki, Miles, and Sherpe (eds) *The Future of Family Property in Europe* (Intersentia 2011) p 253.

might have drafted a will; place adverts;[33] and search registries where the will might have been lodged. Where the personal representatives make an appropriate search, they will likely be relieved of liability for wrongfully distributing the estate if a will is discovered at a later date.[34]

(a) Principles of inheritance

Upon an intestacy, the personal representatives (the persons acting to share out the estate) will hold the estate subject to a statutory trust under which they have a power to sell the assets.[35] Under the rules for the distribution of a person's estate where there is no will, or an existing will fails to distribute property,[36] any surviving spouse or civil partner has the first claim on the assets. The extent of that claim depends upon whether the deceased is survived by issue (which includes children, grandchildren, and any other direct lineal descendants). Only if there is neither spouse (or civil partner) nor issue do other relatives inherit. The relatives who can then inherit are set out in an ordered list. Although these rules seem complicated, there is a guiding principle in play—closer relatives are preferred to more distant relatives. If there are no surviving relatives in any of the categories enumerated, then the estate goes to the Crown in default of heirs or successors. Only blood relatives inherit (although adopted children are treated as if they were natural children of their adoptive parents). No distinction is made between children born in wedlock and children whose parents are not married.

(b) Surviving spouse or civil partner inherits personal chattels

Under section 46 of the Administration of Estates Act 1925 a surviving spouse or civil partner always inherits all the personal chattels which belonged to the deceased absolutely. This has proved difficult to define. Prior to the Law Commission's recommendation simplifying the law, s 55(1)(x) of the Administration of Estates Act 1925 defined 'personal chattels' primarily by reference to a list of examples (e.g. 'linen, china, glass, books, pictures. . .'). This was unfortunate, as specific lists will inevitably generate a mass of case aw turning on disputes as to whether any given item falls under the definition. So, for example, although jewellery was explicitly listed in the subsection, in *Re Whitby*,[37] there was litigation over whether uncut diamonds might be classified as such. On the facts of the particular case, it was held that uncut diamonds came within the definition of subsection, and that the term 'jewellery' extended beyond items that could be worn. Lists lead to litigation.[38]

These problems have to a large extent been met by the new definition contained in an amended s 55(1)(x).[39] Now the 'personal chattels' are defined as the deceased's 'tangible movable property', with three exceptions. First, personal chattels do not include money and securities for money. Second, they do not include property of the deceased used solely or mainly for business purposes. Third, they do not include property held solely as an investment. While this definition, comprising a broad category subject to exceptions, is much more satisfactory in legal terms than its predecessor, it is not entirely without difficulty. In a context where litigation between relatives is inevitable, the definition of the exceptions is itself likely to be the subject of future legal disputes.

33 This will also help protect them from liability from the claims of creditors over the estate. See Trustee Act 1925, s 27.

34 Trustee Act 1925, s 61.

35 Administration of Estates Act 1925, s 33.

36 *Re Skeats* [1936] Ch 683.

37 [1944] Ch 210.

38 See also, *Re Hutchinson* [1925] Ch 255, defining the word 'horses' as including racehorses; *Re Chaplin* [1950] Ch 507 holding that the phrase 'items of personal use' included a yacht.

39 Amended by Inheritance and Trustees' Powers Act (2014), s 3(1)(x).

(c) Spouse or civil partner survives with no issue

Under s 46 of the Administration of Estates Act 1925 if the deceased has a surviving spouse or civil partner, but leaves no surviving issue (i.e. lineal descendants including adopted children), then the whole of the estate goes to the surviving spouse or civil partner. A partner who has not married or entered into a civil partnership with the deceased has no claim under the intestacy rules.[40] Providing that there is no question as to whether the marriage or civil partnership is void,[41] this is a legally uncomplex scenario in most of cases. Yet even straightforward legal concepts might run into definitional problems in difficult cases. One such example is polygamous marriages, which cannot be made in the United Kingdom. Despite this, the contemporary legal approach is to recognize polygamous marriages lawfully made abroad.[42] There is an example of this acceptance in the context of intestacy: in *Official Solicitor to the Senior Courts v Yemoh*,[43] the deceased was survived by eight wives in Ghana. The marriages were validly celebrated, but he died intestate in Ghana, leaving property in England. The court found that the wives were collectively 'the surviving spouse' for the purposes of the Administration of Estates Act 1925.

(d) Issue and no spouse or civil partner

If there are surviving issue, but no surviving spouse or civil partner, then the issue take the whole estate. Very often, the estate will be divided between issue. Section 47(1)(i) of the Administration of Estates Act 1925 directs the nature of that division. Unsurprisingly, in the absence of a spouse or civil partner, the children of the deceased are prioritized. If all the descendant's children are living, they will take in equal shares. Where one or more of the descendant's children have themselves died prior to the deceased, then the percentage of the property due to the deceased issue will be sub-divided per stirpes ('through the stems'). The per stirpes principle is intuitive. It means that the property flows down the lineal branches of the relations, dividing equally between each of the people at each stem.

There is another aspect which the rules must cover—i.e. the circumstance where children of the deceased, or more remote issue, have not reached the age of 18. Unless they are married or in a civil partnership, then the property will be held on a trust, subject to power for capital and income to be distributed for their benefit,[44] until the issue reaches the age of 18 and can take free from the trust.

(e) Division between spouse and issue

A more complex, but very common, circumstance arises where a deceased is survived by both a surviving spouse or civil partner and also by issue. In that case, the estate is shared between the spouse/civil partner and the issue. The division is not equal. The spouse or civil partner receives the better treatment under the intestacy rules. It has already been seen that the spouse or civil partner inherits all the personal chattels. Alongside those chattels, the spouse or civil partner will receive a statutory legacy before any division of the estate is made.[45] As of 6 February 2020, the statutory legacy is worth £270,000. This sum might be larger than the entire estate, in which case, the issue will receive nothing.[46]

[40] For leading cross-jurisdictional analysis of the succession rules as they relate to cohabitants, see Sloan, 'The Concept of Coupledom in Succession Law' (2017) 70 CLJ 623.

[41] Matrimonial Causes Act 1973, s 11; Civil Partnership Act 2004, s 49.

[42] See, *Re Sehota (deceased)* [1978] All ER 385, applying the Inheritance (Provision for Family and Dependants) Act 1975 to a polygamous spouse.

[43] [2010] EWHC 3727 (Ch).

[44] Trustee Act 1925, ss 31–32.

[45] Administration of Estates Act 1924, s 46(1)(i).

[46] Subject to Sch 1A of the Administration of Estates Act 1925, in order to prevent the value of the legacy received by spouses and civil partners reducing in different cases over time, Lord Chancellor has the power to raise the value of this legacy accounting for the consumer price index.

If the value of the estate is more than the statutory legacy of £270,000, then the surviving spouse or civil partner will share the residue with the issue. This was not always the case. Prior to the Law Commission's 2011 recommendations,[47] which led to the enactment of the Inheritance and Trustees' Powers Act 2014, the spouse or civil partner received only a life interest in the residue, so giving them a right to income rather than capital. This was to the advantage of the surviving children who would receive the other half of the estate when the life interest came to an end. The disadvantage suffered by the surviving spouse or civil partner was mitigated by the fact that the value of the life interest could be capitalized, within 12 months of the grant of representation, and paid as a lump sum to the spouse or civil partner.[48] If this option was taken, the remainder of the value would then be paid to the issue of the deceased. Nevertheless, in a reform which both removes legal complexity and improves the position of the surviving spouse or civil partner, since 1 October 2014, the spouse or civil partner now straightforwardly receives a half share free from any life interest. The other half then goes to the descendants in equal shares by line of descent (per stirpes).

The matrimonial or civil partnership home will inevitably be of very great importance upon an intestacy. It will not always be in question. If the deceased and the surviving spouse or civil partner were joint tenants (i.e. where there is a right of survivorship) then the home will not be a part of the estate. In other circumstances where there is a 'competition' between the potential inheritors, the law favours surviving spouses and civil partners above the issue of the deceased. Schedule 2 of the Intestates' Estate Act 1952 permits a surviving spouse or civil partner with an interest in a dwelling house in which they were resident at the intestate's death to appropriate that interest. In the case of expensive properties, where the value of the house exceeds the spouse or civil partner's interests upon the intestacy (including the statutory legacy), it is possible for the surviving spouse or civil partner to pay off the difference and still appropriate.[49] This scenario depends upon the surviving spouse or civil partner being able to raise sufficient capital to make a payment to the personal representatives.

(f) Order of inheritance amongst remoter relatives

Where there are no lineal descendants, spouse or civil partner, s 46(1) of the Administration of Estates 1925 sets out an order in which remoter relatives inherit. The order is: parents; full blood brothers and sisters (brothers and sisters who share both parents); half-blood brothers and sisters (brothers and sisters who share just one parent); grandparents; uncles and aunts by full blood (full blood brothers or sisters of a parent of the deceased); half-aunts and half-uncles (a half-brother or half-sister of a parent of the deceased). Relatives only inherit if they are still living when the deceased died (even if they have died subsequently before receiving their share). Where brothers and sisters or aunts and uncles have died before the deceased, then any share which they would have received if they survived would be taken instead by their living descendants, taking by line of descent.

(2) Partial intestacy

The rules set out above apply to a partial intestacy (i.e. the circumstance where only a part of the property is left undisposed of). It used to be the case that in some circumstances a complex and little admired doctrine called 'hotchpot' applied, and allowance had to be made for any gift received by will against any sums which would be payable on intestacy. That rule was abolished in relation to partial intestacy by the Law Reform (Succession) Act 1995.

[47] Intestacy and Family Provision Claims on Death (Law Commission No 331, 2011), para 2.62.

[48] Administration of Estates Act 1925, s 47A.

[49] Intestates' Estate Act 1952, Sch 2 para 5(2).

(3) **Problems raised by including only blood relations**

The restriction of next of kin on intestacy to blood relations is, in many ways, understandable, and has the advantage of certainty. However, it can in some circumstances cause problems. For instance, if a couple, who both have children from a previous relationship, marry or remarry, on the death of the first to die intestate the surviving spouse will inherit a substantial part of the estate, or the whole of a smaller estate. When the surviving spouse then dies, only the blood relations of that person will inherit on intestacy. The children from the first marriage of the first deceased will receive nothing under the intestacy rules. This underlines the importance of making wills, but even then there can be problems, because even if the wills made by a remarrying couple make provision for each other's children, the rules relating to wills permit the survivor to make a new will excluding the children of their spouse. For this reason, some remarrying couples may choose to make mutual wills which contain an agreement not to revoke the provision in favour of each other's children.[50] Mutual wills are considered later in this chapter.

(4) **Bona vacantia**

Where the deceased leaves no relatives listed in the intestacy rules, the property will be bona vacantia (i.e. ownerless property). In that case, the estate will normally go to the Crown. For intestates in the County Palatine of Lancaster, property will pass to the Duchy of Lancaster. For intestates in Cornwall, property will pass to the Duke of Cornwall.[51] The treatment of property which is bona vacantia is a little obscure, as it is difficult to find detailed evidence of its ultimate destination. The Law Commission investigated the bona vacantia processes as a part of a consultation paper.[52] It reported that in modern times, following advertisements for entitled relatives, and discretionary payments to relatives that might reasonably have expected to have been provided for, the Crown ultimately pays the net proceeds over to general government expenditure. By contrast, the County Palatine of Lancaster and in Cornwall, the surplus is paid into charitable funds.

5 Wills

A will is an expression of a person's wishes intended to take effect on their death. Whilst we normally associate wills with the disposition of property, they may also deal with matters such as the wishes of the deceased concerning their funeral, or the custody and care of their children or pets. Most of the requirements relating to wills are set out in the Wills Act 1837, as amended. As an exception to the normal requirements, it is possible for a soldier in actual military service, members of the naval or marine forces in actual military service, and any mariner or seaman at sea to make a will without complying with the normal rules. Indeed, a privileged will can be made, with the necessary intention and capacity, by an oral statement.[53] The Law Commission has recommended that the status of privileged wills be rationalized by confining the scope of the rule only to those serving in the British armed forces or civilians who are subject to service discipline.[54]

[50] See, as an example, *Fry v Densham-Smith* [2010] EWCA Civ 1410.

[51] Administration of Estates Act 1925, s 46(1)(vi).

[52] Intestacy and Family Provision Claims on Death (Law Commission CP 191, 2009), para 6.69.

[53] Wills Act 1837, s 11, as explained and extended by Wills (Soldiers and Sailors) Act 1918.

[54] *Making a Will* (Law Commission CP 231, 2017), Ch 5, paras 5.75–5.80 and Consultation Question 26. Service discipline has a meaning within the Armed Forces Act 2006, Sch 15.

This would, in the Commission's view, link the privilege with the Armed Services Covenant, and remove it for those, such as merchant seaman, who do not serve in the armed forces.

(1) Capacity to make wills

(a) Age

Under the Wills Act 1837, s 7, a person must be an adult (have attained the age of eighteen) in order to make a normal will (this requirement does not apply to privileged wills).[55] The Law Commission has suggested that the age of testamentary capacity may need to be re-examined, as there may be good reason for children to want, and be able, to make wills.[56] One example given is where a child has received significant assets and has become estranged from a parent who would otherwise become entitled to the child's property under the intestacy rules.[57] Another relates to the ability of a child to have their wishes as to the ultimate disposal of their mortal remains respected, without interference from either parent.[58] The Commission provisionally proposed two options—either that the age of capacity be lowered to sixteen years of age and/or that the courts should have a discretionary power to authorize underage testators to make wills.

(b) General test for capacity

The testator must also have testamentary capacity. Where a person does not have testamentary capacity any will they make has no effect,[59] but the loss of mental capacity after a will has been made does not affect it. The test for testamentary capacity was set out in *Banks v Goodfellow*.[60] Lord Cockburn CJ said:

> It is essential to the exercise of such a power that a testator shall understand the nature of the act and its effects; shall understand the extent of the property of which he is disposing; shall be able to comprehend and appreciate the claims to which he ought to give effect; and with a view to the latter object, that no disorder of the mind shall poison his affections, pervert his sense of right, or prevent the exercise of his natural faculties–that no insane delusion shall influence his will in disposing of his property and bring about a disposal of it which, if the mind had been sound, would not have been made.

The requirement can be summarized by saying that the testator must be 'of sound mind, memory and understanding'.[61] There are four elements:

(1) the testator must know that he is making a document that will deal with his property on his death;[62]

(2) the testator must have a general awareness of the extent of his property;

[55] Wills (Soldiers and Sailors) Act 1918, s 1. The provision was enacted to allay any doubts about the validity of informal wills made by young soldiers in the Great War.

[56] *Making a Will* (Law Commission CP 231, 2017), Ch 8. In Scotland, for example, the age of testamentary capacity is twelve years—Age of Legal Capacity (Scotland) Act 1991, s 2.

[57] *Making a Will* (Law Commission CP 231, 2017), paras 8.14–8.16, 8.39–8.44.

[58] The Commission cited *Re JS* [2016] EWHC 2859 (Fam), where a fourteen-year-old girl wanted her body cryogenically frozen, having fully researched the idea, but a complicated legal intervention was necessary to stop her father, as co-executor of her estate, from stopping this happening.

[59] *Bunter v Coke* [1707] 91 ER 210.

[60] [1869–70] LR 5 QB 549.

[61] See *Mortimer on Probate, Law and Practice* (1st edn, Sweet & Maxwell 1911), p 42 (quoted regularly in the courts, for instance in *Perrins v Holland* [2010] EWCA Civ 840 at 13).

[62] See *Simon v Byford* [2014] EWCA Civ 280, where the testatrix understood the gifts of shares she was making to her children and so the will was held valid, even though she did not appreciate that the collateral effect would be to create voting deadlock amongst the shareholders.

(3) the testator must understand and recall those who have a moral claim to his estate, even if he does not intend to make provision for them in the will;

(4) the testator must not be suffering from any illness or condition which may impair his judgement in regard to disposing of his property.

There is no fixed standard of testamentary capacity. Where the testator's affairs are simple, a lower standard will apply than where his affairs are complex and more complex provision is made (or is required) in the will.[63] It is also possible for a person to execute a will during a lucid interval, even if they periodically lack capacity.[64]

The black letter rules attempt to bring legal objectivity to a type of litigation which is likely to be extraordinarily personal. So, in *Re Clitheroe*,[65] a mother's two wills were set aside. One of the adult children opposed the wills because the mother did not have capacity. The judge analysed a painful family history. Amongst other things, it transpired that the mother had not accepted that the disinherited adult child had been abused by her former husband, and so blamed her for breaking up her marriage.

(c) Presumption of capacity

Testamentary capacity does not have affirmatively to be proved unless there is something in the circumstances to question it.[66] So if the testator had general mental capacity at the time the will was made, and the will is rational, capacity will be presumed. This common law position is confirmed by the Mental Capacity Act 2005, s 1, which states that a person is assumed to have capacity unless it is established that he lacks capacity. The test applied is still the common law test.[67]

(d) Will can be perverse

A testator is not required to make a rational will: 'The law does not say that a man is incapacitated from making a will if he proposes to make a disposition of his property moved by capricious, frivolous, mean, or even bad motives.'[68] However, the fact that the will appears irrational is likely to mean that proof of capacity will be required.[69]

(e) Reform of capacity

The Law Commission has proposed that the rules on capacity be reformed,[70] primarily on the basis that the language of the common law test is outdated and should instead be governed, as with other areas of law, by the capacity test[71] as set out in the Mental Capacity Act 2005.[72] The principles which underline that test are that:

(1) a person must be assumed to have capacity unless it is established that he or she lacks capacity;

(2) a person is not to be treated as unable to make a decision unless all practicable steps to help him or her to do so have been taken without success; and

(3) a person is not to be treated as unable to make a decision merely because he or she makes an unwise decision.[73]

[63] *In the Estate of Park* [1954] P 112.

[64] *In the Estate of Walker* [1912] 28 TLR 466.

[65] [2021] EWHC 1102 (Ch).

[66] *Symes v Green* 164 ER 785.

[67] See *Re Walker* [2014] EWHC 71 (Ch).

[68] *Boughton v Knight* [1872–75] LR 3 P & D 64.

[69] See *The Vegetarian Society v Scott* [2013] EWHC 4097 (Ch), where a schizophrenic testator's gift of his whole estate to the Vegetarian Society was held valid, even though he had no links to the society (and was not vegetarian), but could be shown to have capacity to make a will and did not feel any affection for his family.

[70] *Making a Will* (Law Commission CP 231, 2017), Ch 2.

[71] Ibid, paras 2.43–2.58.

[72] Mental Capacity Act 2005, ss 1–3.

[73] *Mental Capacity and Deprivation of Liberty* (Law Com No 372, 2017), Ch 3.

The Commission acknowledges that the differences in the outcome of applying the statutory test and the common law test in *Banks v Goodfellow* may be limited in practice, but nonetheless suggests that the test under the Mental Capacity Act 2005 reflects more modern understandings of the factors that can influence (in)capacity.[74]

The Commission also proposes, as an alternative, on the basis that many stakeholders feel that the common law test is well established, that it be put on a statutory footing to clarify issues[75] alongside a statutory presumption of capacity.[76] It will be interesting to see in the forthcoming Report, what the ultimate recommendations from the Law Commission will be.

(f) The 'golden rule'

In circumstances where the testator's mental capacity is in doubt, perhaps because of the onset of dementia, or because an elderly person has suffered a serious illness,[77] it is wise to follow a 'golden if tactless rule'[78] that the will 'ought to be witnessed or approved by a medical practitioner who satisfied himself of the capacity and understanding of the testator, and records and preserves his examination and finding.'[79] Whilst this is not the only way of ensuring that the testator's capacity can be proved, it will provide strong supporting (but not conclusive) evidence.[80] The Law Commission has sensibly suggested reform of the golden rule, as it 'lacks the nuance necessary to recognise the modern understanding of mental capacity and to deal with the diverse range of situations in which questions about capacity might arise.'[81] The Commission proposes separating the questions of when and by whom capacity should be assessed through a code of practice on testamentary capacity.[82]

(g) Undue influence or fraud

A will which has been procured through fraud or undue influence will be set aside.[83] *Schrader v Schrader*[84] sets out the principles which apply when deciding whether undue influence has been applied to a person making a will. The Law Commission is of the view that these principles are inadequate in testamentary cases, as they do not adequately protect vulnerable testators from financial abuse and are construed too narrowly as there is no presumption of undue influence available to claimants, who have to prove that undue influence took place.[85] It proposes the creation of a statutory doctrine of testamentary undue influence, attuned to the testamentary context, where a presumption is raised which must be rebutted by the proponent of the will. Two competing approaches are suggested for consultation: either a structured approach based on the doctrine as it applies to lifetime gifts[86] or a discretionary approach where the court has the power to presume undue influence where it is satisfied it is just to do so in all the circumstances of the case.[87]

[74] *Making a Will* (Law Commission CP 231, 2017), paras 2.66–2.73; Consultation Question 3.

[75] Ibid, Consultation Questions 4 and 5.

[76] Ibid, Consultation Question 6.

[77] Other reasons might include impaired capacity through the effects of medication to address a chronic or short-term illness, or a learning disability—see Frost, Lawson, and Jacoby, *Testamentary Capacity: Law, Practice and Medicine* (Oxford University Press 2015).

[78] *Kenward v Adams*, *The Times*, 29 November 1975.

[79] *Re Simpson (Decd)* [1977] 121 SJ 224 (Templeman J).

[80] *Perrins v Holland* [2009] EWHC 2558 (Ch) at 10; *Re Watson (Probate)* [2008] EWHC 2582 (Ch).

[81] *Making a Will* (Law Commission CP 231, 2017), para 2.99.

[82] Ibid, Consultation Questions 8, 9, and 10.

[83] See Ch 7.

[84] [2013] EWHC 466 (Ch).

[85] *Making a Will* (Law Commission CP 231, 2017), Ch 7.

[86] Ibid, paras 7.111–7.127.

[87] Ibid, paras 7.128–7.129.

(2) Execution of wills

(a) Statement of rules

The rules for the execution of a will are found in the Wills Act 1837, s 9, as substituted by the Administration of Justice Act 1982, s 17:

> No will shall be valid unless–
>
> (a) it is in writing, and signed by the testator, or by some other person in his presence and by his direction; and
> (b) it appears that the testator intended by his signature to give effect to the will; and
> (c) the signature is made or acknowledged by the testator in the presence of two or more witnesses present at the same time; and
> (d) each witness either–
>
> (i) attests and signs the will; or
>
> (ii) acknowledges his signature, in the presence of the testator (but not necessarily in the presence of any other witness), but no form of attestation shall be necessary.

(b) 'In writing'

With the exception of privileged wills, all wills must be in writing. There is no general requirement that it should be dated, but it is good practice to date a will because where a testator has made more than one will it helps to identify which is the most recent. The Law Commission has asked for views as part of its consultation process as to whether to allow electronic wills, having identified that there are two significant challenges in implementing electronic creation of wills: security and infrastructure.[88] The purpose of allowing electronic wills would be significant benefits in cost savings and convenience to encourage an upturn in will-making.[89]

(c) 'Signed by the testator'

The testator may sign personally. Any mark intended as a signature will suffice. It is also possible for the will to be signed on the testator's behalf. Where someone signs on the testator's behalf, it is essential that there is something which constitutes a 'direction' to do so. In *Barrett v Bem*,[90] the hand of the testator, who was seriously ill in hospital, was shaking too much for him to sign a will which had been prepared for him by his niece, Hanora. Although what happened then was not easy to know, the judge concluded that Hanora's mother Anne, the only beneficiary in the will, and the sister of the testator, took the pen and completed the signature. The Court of Appeal held that the absence of any instruction to do this meant that Anne did not sign on his behalf 'and by his direction'. 'The testator must make some positive communication of his desire that someone else should sign the will on his behalf.'[91]

The Law Commission provisionally propose that e-signatures should not be capable of fulfilling the requirement of a signature of a will,[92] unless and until a full system of electronic will-making is introduced. This is designed to bring clarity to the current law, as the Commission believes that electronic signatures are too easily copied and, therefore, do not protect testators from fraud.[93] They also propose that restrictions should be placed on those who can sign a will on behalf of the testator, to protect testators from fraud.[94]

[88] Ibid, Ch 6, paras 6.33–6.43. [89] Ibid, paras 6.9–6.14. [90] [2012] EWCA Civ 524.

[91] [2012] EWCA Civ 524 at 24 and 36.

[92] *Making a Will* (Law Commission CP 231, 2017), Ch 6, Consultation Question 31. The same is true for the signature of witnesses to the will (discussed later in this chapter).

[93] Ibid, paras 6.73–6.87. [94] Ibid, Ch 5.

They provisionally propose that, at the very least, a person who signs a will on behalf of the testator should not benefit from any gift under the will in question.[95]

(d) 'Intended. . . to give effect to the will'

The testator must know that what is being signed is a document containing instructions for the disposition of the testator's property on death, and must also be aware of the instructions contained in the will.[96] Normally, this can be assumed, but if the testator is illiterate or blind, evidence may be required to prove that the testator was aware of the contents. This could have been done through the will being read to him. It is wise to include a statement to this effect as part of the attestation (the description alongside the signatures). Evidence that the testator was aware of the contents of the will and intended to approve them would also be necessary where the will was prepared by someone who benefits from it or there are other factors which 'excite the suspicion of the court'.[97]

It used to be a requirement that the signature appear 'at the foot or end of the will', but that requirement no longer applies, it being sufficient, wherever the signature appears, that it is intended to give effect to the will.

(e) An interesting problem

In *Marley v Rawlings*,[98] a husband and wife had made almost identical wills, differing only in the references to each other. By mistake each signed the other's will and this only came to light after their deaths. The Court of Appeal held that their signatures did not give effect to the relative wills because 'Mr Rawlings did not authenticate the document as his will and he did not intend it to operate as his will.'[99] In a victory for common sense, the Supreme Court held that the documents were valid wills because they had been signed with the intention that they should be the parties' wills. The contents of the will concerned could be rectified since the solicitor involved had candidly admitted that he had made a 'silly mistake' in giving the husband and wife the wrong wills to sign. This constituted a clerical error which the court was permitted to correct.[100]

(f) Witnesses

There must be two witnesses who are both present physically and mentally[101] when the testator signs or acknowledges his signature. The witnesses do not have to be present together when they, in turn, sign the will, but they must each sign in the presence of the testator. The witnesses must have been in a position to see the testator sign or to have seen his signature if he is acknowledging it, but they do not need to have taken advantage of that opportunity or even to know that the signature was on a will.[102] Because of the requirement of being able to see the signature, a blind person cannot act as a witness.[103]

It is possible for the testator to acknowledge to the witnesses a signature which he has already made. Similarly, it is possible for the witnesses to acknowledge to the testator a signature which has been made in his absence, but the order of events is still important because the witnesses' function is to verify that the signature of the testator is indeed his

[95] Ibid, paras 5.51–5.55 and Consultation Question 17.

[96] *Cleare v Cleare* [1865–9] LR 1 P&D 655.

[97] *Sherrington v Sherrington* [2005] EWCA Civ 326 at 69.

[98] [2012] EWCA Civ 61, [2013] Ch 271; on appeal [2014] UKSC 2.

[99] [2012] EWCA Civ 61 at 105 (Thomas LJ).

[100] On the impact of this decision on the extent of rectification of wills and the everyday nature of mistake, see Drummond, 'Case Comment: Whose will is it anyway?' [2014] Conv 357.

[101] *Hudson v Parker* [1844] 163 ER 948.

[102] *Smith & Smith v Smith* [1869] LR 1 P&D 143; *Cooke v Henry* [1932] IR 574; *Kavanagh v Feegan* [1932] IR 566.

[103] *Re Gibson* [1949] P 434.

or one which he acknowledges as his. An acknowledgment can be in either words or conduct; for instance, in *Weatherhill v Pearce*,[104] Mrs Weatherhill handed the two witnesses a will which she had already signed and asked them to witness it. The judge said:

> It is plain that a signature which has already been written can be acknowledged in many ways and no set form is required. It is sufficient to proffer a document which all concerned know is a will for the witnesses to sign, and no express declaration is necessary.

(g) Who can be a witness?

There is no age requirement for a person to act as a witness, but since the witnesses 'attest' the will, that is they validate and bear witness to the testator's signature,[105] they must have the capacity and understanding to know that this is what they are doing.

A beneficiary is not, as such, prevented from acting as a witness, but the consequence of a person being a witness is that they and any spouse or civil partner is disqualified from receiving a benefit under the will.[106] The Law Commission proposes that this disqualification should be extended to include any cohabitant of the signing witness,[107] and have asked consultees whether it should also include the parent or sibling of a witness, or perhaps even family members more generally.[108]

An exception to the disqualification is that a person signing, not as a witness, but only to confirm that they are content with the provisions of the will may still be a beneficiary. The effect of this used to be limited because, even if there were at least two other witnesses, it was presumed that any person signing at the end of a will was doing so as a witness.[109] The Wills Act 1968 modified the exception so that provided that there are at least two witnesses who are not also beneficiaries, the attestation of a will by a person who is also a beneficiary can be disregarded.

(h) Attestation

There is no statutory requirement for a will to contain an attestation clause—that is to contain a statement alongside the signatures of the testator and witnesses explaining how and why they were signing the will. However, a description to this effect can help in providing evidence that the requirements of the Wills Act have been met, and so it is common and good practice to use an attestation clause such as:

> Signed by the said testatrix [name] in the presence of us both present at the same time who at her request in her presence and in the presence of each other have subscribed our names as witnesses.[110]

In the absence of any evidence to the contrary (which may come from the will itself, or from extrinsic evidence), there is a strong presumption that a will that contains an attestation clause has been properly executed.[111] Without an attestation clause, affidavit evidence of compliance with the Wills Act 1837 requirements may be needed before a will is accepted by the Probate Registry. The Law Commission is not convinced that the requirement of attestation by witnesses is necessary, and it suggests either the abolition or reform of the requirement to make the purpose of it clearer and to apply it in all cases.[112]

104 [1995] 1 WLR 592. 105 *Sherrington v Sherrington* [2005] EWCA Civ 326 at 38.

106 Wills Act 1837, s 15.

107 Law Commission CP 231, *Making a Will* (July 2017), paras 5.56–5.59 and Consultation Question 20.

108 Ibid, Consultation Question 21. 109 *In the Estate of Bravda* [1968] 1 WLR 479.

110 This was substantially the form of the clause used in *Weatherhill v Pearce* [1995] 1 WLR 592.

111 *Sherrington v Sherrington* [2005] EWCA Civ 326 at 63.

112 *Making a Will* (Law Commission CP 231, 2017), paras 5.62–5.66 and Consultation Questions 23 and 24.

(3) Incorporation

It is possible for a will to include supplementary documents where these are appropriately referred to in the main will. These supplementary documents do not themselves have to be signed and witnessed if they are 'incorporated by reference'. Where a document is effectively incorporated into the will, it 'becomes part of the will'.[113] As such, the incorporated document must also be admitted to probate, and, thereby, it becomes a public document in the same way as the will itself.

A document will only be incorporated by reference into a will if the conditions stated by Gorell-Barnes P in *Re Smart's Goods*[114] are met. HH Judge Russen QC noted in *Re Wippell* that, 'all three conditions are interlinked'.[115] This is a matter of common sense. A document can only be clearly identified in a will and referred to in a will if, at the time the will was written, it was in existence.

(a) Incorporated document was in existence at the date of the will

Only a document that was in existence at the date the will was executed can be incorporated by reference, thus becoming part of the will.[116] A document may be incorporated if it was written after the will was executed, provided that a subsequent properly executed codicil is added confirming that it is to be incorporated.

(b) Incorporated document is referred to in the will

To be incorporated into a will a document must not only exist at the date of the will, but it must also be referred to in the will as existing at that date. In *Re Smart's Goods*,[117] the testatrix, Caroline Smart, executed a will in 1895 leaving her property to the friends she might designate in a book or memorandum. At the time that the will was executed no such book or memorandum existed. A book was written between 1898 and 1899, and in 1900, a codicil was added to the will. However, although this book was in existence at the date of the execution of the codicil, it was held that it was not incorporated into the will because the codicil made no reference to it as existing at the date that it was executed. The will continued to refer to the book as a future document.[118]

(c) Incorporated document must be clearly identified in the will

A document will only be incorporated by reference if it is clearly identified in the will.[119]

(4) Alterations

Alterations made to a will before it has been executed will be validated by the execution of the will. Since it may not always be evident when alterations have been made, it is good practice to make a note of the alterations, confirming that they were made prior to execution, alongside the attestation clause. Without this, extrinsic evidence may be needed to confirm when the alterations were made. There are three ways in which alterations can be made to a will after it has been executed.

113 *Re Smart's Goods* [1902] P 238 at 240.

114 [1902] P 238.

115 *Re Wippell* [2018] EWHC 730 (Ch).

116 *Singleton v Tomlinson* [1878] 3 App Cas 404, HL.

117 [1902] P 238.

118 See also *University College of North Wales v Taylor* [1908] P 140; *Re Bateman's Will Trusts* [1970] 3 All ER 817.

119 See *Croker v Marquis of Hertford* [1844] 8 Jur 863; *Re Balmes' Goods* [1897] P 261; *Re Saxton's Estate* [1939] 2 All ER 418; *Re Mardon's Estate* [1944] P 109.

(a) New will or codicil

The provisions of an existing will can be amended or modified by a new will. The second will must comply with the same rules as to formal validity as apply to an original will under the Wills Act 1837. Where the second will acts simply as a supplement to a previous will, it is called a codicil.

(b) Alterations on the will itself

It is possible for textual amendments to be made to the original will, but under the Wills Act 1837, s 21, these all need to comply with the same formalities as for an original will.

(c) Obliteration of words in the will

A limited form of alteration can be made in accordance with the Wills Act 1837, s 21, where words in a will are obliterated to such an extent that 'the words or effect of the will before such alteration shall not be apparent'. Scientific methods now make it much easier to decipher obliterated text than when the Wills Act 1837 was enacted, but according to Sir Francis Jeune P in *Ffinch v Combe*:[120]

> The result of the authorities, therefore, appears to be that the words beneath obliterations, erasures, or alterations on a testamentary document are 'apparent' within the meaning of the Wills Act, if experts, using magnifying-glasses, when necessary, can decipher them and satisfy the court that they have done so; but that it is not allowable to resort to any physical interference with the document, so as to render clearer what may have been written upon it.

Applying these principles, in *Re Itter (No 2)*,[121] it was held that words had been obliterated where a testatrix had tried to increase the sums of various gifts by sticking slips of paper containing new amounts over the original amounts. The gifts were only saved from failing altogether because the judge held that a deletion was only effective if it was made with the intention to revoke that particular gift. In the circumstances, it could be inferred that the testatrix intended to revoke the part of the bequest covered by the slips only if new bequests were effectually substituted. The substitution was not effective because it had not been signed and witnessed, as required for an alteration.

(5) Interpretation

(a) Will 'speaks from death'

The Wills Act 1837, s 24, provides that a will 'shall be construed, with reference to the real estate and personal estate comprised in it, to speak and take effect as if it had been executed immediately before the death of the testator, unless a contrary intention shall appear by the will'. This means that the will can apply to property acquired by the testator between the date of the will and his death, and not just property owned by the testator when he made the will.

(b) Principles of interpretation

The Supreme Court held in *Marley v Rawlings*[122] that wills should be interpreted using the same canons of construction as other documents: 'Whether the document in question is a commercial contract or a will, the aim is to identify the intention of the party or parties

[120] [1894] P 191 at 199. See also *Re Adams (Deceased)* [1990] Ch 601.
[121] [1950] P 130.
[122] [2014] UKSC 2 at 20.

to the document by interpreting the words used in their documentary, factual and commercial context.' This means that:

> the court is concerned to find the intention of the party or parties, and it does this by identifying the meaning of the relevant words, (a) in the light of (i) the natural and ordinary meaning of those words, (ii) the overall purpose of the document, (iii) any other provisions of the document, (iv) the facts known or assumed by the parties at the time that the document was executed, and (v) common sense, but (b) ignoring subjective evidence of any party's intentions.[123]

(c) Evidence of intention

The Administration of Justice Act 1982, s 21, contains some general rules relating to the evidence which can be admitted to aid in the interpretation of wills. These go further than the general rules of interpretation by allowing evidence of the testator's intention to be admitted to assist in the interpretation of a will where any part of a will is meaningless, the language used in the will is ambiguous, or there is evidence (other than evidence of the testator's intention) which 'shows that the language used in any part of it is ambiguous in the light of surrounding circumstances.' The Law Commission has consulted on whether there is a need for any new interpretative provisions in the law of wills, and has asked consultees to provide examples of why such provisions would be necessary in practice.[124]

(d) Lapse

The ordinary rule is that if a beneficiary named in a will does not survive the testator, the gift lapses, that is, it does not take effect.[125] This rule about lapse will not apply where a contrary intention appears, nor does it apply where a testator makes a gift to one of his own children or other issue who have predeceased him, but have left issue of their own who have survived the testator.[126] Suppose Bill makes a will in 2001 leaving '£100,000 to each of my children', but one of his children, Pat, dies shortly after giving birth to her son Robbie in 2005. If Bill dies in 2014, Pat's £100,000 will go to Robbie (who will share it with any other of Pat's children). Had the gift been made to Bill's housekeeper, who died before him, the gift would lapse.

(e) Rectification

Under the Administration of Justice Act 1982, s 20, the courts may rectify a will if it is satisfied that the will is so expressed that it fails to carry out the testator's intentions in consequence of a clerical error or of a failure to understand his instructions. This jurisdiction was invoked by the Supreme Court in *Marley v Rawlings*,[127] described earlier. The Supreme Court took the view that the expression 'clerical error' should be given a broad interpretation to cover mistakes such as that involved in *Marley v Rawlings*, as well as the correction of typographical errors. There is, as noted by the Law Commission in their consultation on wills, a degree of overlap between rectification and interpretation, on the basis that 'interpretation is an unavoidable part of the process of rectification.'[128] Consultees have also been asked if there is any purpose in widening the powers of rectification.[129]

[123] [2014] UKSC 2 at 19.

[124] *Making a Will* (Law Commission CP 231, 2017), paras 9.48–9.55 and Consultation Question 48.

[125] *Elliott v Davenport* [1705] 1 P Wms 83; *Mabank v Brooks* [1780] 1 Bro CC 84.

[126] Wills Act 1837, s 33.

[127] [2014] UKSC 2.

[128] *Making a Will* (Law Commission CP 231, 2017), paras 9.20–9.27. See also the example cited of *Guthrie v Morei* [2015] EWHC 3172 (Ch), where the court interpreted a will in a way which allowed the correction of a mistake about the house number of the testator's property without resort to rectification.

[129] *Making a Will* (Law Commission CP 231, 2017), paras 9.56–9.62 and Consultation Question 50.

(6) A dispensing power?

The Law Commission believe that the formalities on the creation of wills are too rigid, in that non-compliance renders a will void. In addition to the proposed changes already outlined, they have proposed the creation of a dispensing power.[130] This would allow the court to recognize a will as valid if there had been some minor failure to comply with formalities, as, for example, where a witness did not sign the will in the presence of the testator. The basis for the exercise of this power is the ordinary civil standard of proof (balance of probabilities), and the Commission believe it would avoid small errors from frustrating testator's legitimate intentions to direct the application of their property after death. It will be interesting to see if consultees agree that such a power is necessary.

(7) Revocation

(a) Revocability of wills

It is a cardinal rule relating to wills that they can be changed or revoked by the testator at any time up to his death. As was said in *Vynior's case*:

> If a man makes his testament and last will irrevocably, yet he may revoke it; for his acts or his words cannot alter the judgement of the law, to make that irrevocable which, of its own nature, is revocable.[131]

Even if a will states that the testator cannot amend or revoke it, this will not prevent subsequent changes or revocation. Similarly, even if a testator enters into what would otherwise be a legally binding contract not to change his will, he cannot be prevented from doing so. However, this rule can be circumvented in a number of ways. Firstly, a contract not to change a will could give rise to liability in damages. Secondly, the rules relating to mutual wills (to be considered shortly) may impose a trust on some or all of the testator's assets.[132] Thirdly, the doctrine of proprietary estoppel may bind a testator's estate where a promise has been made in relation to his assets, and it would be inequitable for the promise not to be honoured. In some instances, more than one ground of claim may be possible.[133]

(b) How wills can be revoked

There are four ways in which a will can be revoked.

(i) Marriage

Where a testator who has made a will marries or enters into a civil partnership, the effect is to revoke any earlier will except for one which has been made in contemplation of the particular marriage or civil partnership concerned.[134] It must appear from the will itself that the testator was expecting to be married to a particular person, and that is the marriage which took place. The Law Commission has consulted on whether there is public awareness of the rule, and whether it should be abolished.[135] They take no definite view, noting that the arguments for and against the abolition of the rule are finely balanced.[136]

[130] Ibid, paras 5.81–5.105 and Consultation Questions 27 and 28.

[131] [1610] 8 Co Rep 80a.

[132] *Shovelar v Lane* [2011] EWCA Civ 802 makes it clear at 44 that a claim based on mutual wills is a trusts, not a probate, issue.

[133] *Fox v Jewell* [2013] EWCA Civ 1152 (claim made on the basis of both mutual will and proprietary estoppel).

[134] Wills Act 1837, s 18.

[135] *Making a Will* (Law Commission CP 231, 2017), Ch 11, Consultation Question 59.

[136] Ibid, para 11.52.

(ii) Divorce

The dissolution or annulment of a marriage does not revoke the whole of a will, but it does have the effect of revoking any gift in a will by treating the gift as if the spouse or concerned had predeceased the testator, unless a contrary intention appears in the will.[137]

(iii) New will or document in the form of a will

Under the Wills Act 1837, s 20, an existing will is revoked by a new will or codicil made in proper form. If the new will contains a clause expressly revoking all previous wills, then that will have effect, otherwise any existing will is revoked to the extent that it is inconsistent with the later will or codicil. The same section permits a declaration revoking a will to be made in the same form (i.e. complying with the requirements of the Wills Act 1837, s 9) without the need to substitute any new will.

(iv) Destruction

A will can also be revoked in accordance with the Wills Act 1837, s 20, by 'the burning, tearing, or otherwise destroying the same by the testator, or by some person in his presence and by his direction, with the intention of revoking the same.'

It will be seen that two elements are required: the destruction and an intention to revoke. In *Cheese v Lovejoy*,[138] the testator had written 'This is revoked' across his will and thrown it into a pile of scrap papers. It was retrieved by a housemaid and kept for several years until his death. It was held that the will had not been revoked. James LJ adopted the argument of counsel: 'All the destroying in the world without intention will not revoke a will, nor all the intention in the world without destroying: there must be the two.'

(c) Revival of a revoked will

A revoked will can only be revived by being re-executed as if it were a new will, or by a new will or codicil declaring that it is revived.[139]

(8) Liability of draftsman for negligence

Where a legal professional offers support in the preparation of a will, that person can be liable to a disappointed beneficiary in negligence if through a lack of care the will is invalid or for some other reason an intended gift cannot take effect. This is a duty which applies as much to a will-writing business[140] as it does to solicitors.[141] Liability has been imposed for failing to ensure that a will was properly executed,[142] failing to ensure that a beneficiary's husband was not a witness,[143] and failing to advise a client that a joint tenancy should be severed in order to dispose of a share in jointly held property.[144] It might well have been the case that the solicitor in *Marley v Rawlings*[145] could have been held liable to the disappointed beneficiary for his admitted mistake in giving the husband and wife the wrong wills to sign, had the will not been rectified.

137 Wills Act 1837, s 18A. 138 [1877] 2 PD 251. 139 Wills Act 1837, s 22.

140 *Esterhuizen v Allied Dunbar Assurance Plc* [1998] 2 FLR 668.

141 *Ross v Caunters* [1980] Ch 297; *White v Jones* [1995] 2 AC 207.

142 *Esterhuizen v Allied Dunbar Assurance Plc* [1998] 2 FLR 668.

143 *Ross v Caunters* [1980] Ch 297. 144 *Carr-Glynn v Frearsons (A Firm)* [1999] Ch 326.

145 [2014] UKSC 2.

6 Mutual wills

(1) The practical problem

The potential revocability of a will presents a significant obstacle if an owner wishes to leave property to one person absolutely, subject to a requirement that the recipient bequeaths it to an agreed third person. For example, if a husband and wife have one child, the husband may want his wife to enjoy all his property if he predeceases her, but also to ensure that it is ultimately left to their daughter. If he simply executes a will leaving his property to his wife, it will become her absolute property on his death, and she will be free to execute her own will leaving the property to whomsoever she chooses, perhaps to the children of a second marriage or to some charitable object. To try to avoid such difficulties, they may decide to execute wills with identical terms, leaving their property to each other in the event that they predecease, but to their daughter if they survive. However, even where identical wills (often referred to as 'mirror' wills) have been executed, the survivor will remain free to revoke the former will and leave the property to others.

While these difficulties can be avoided by bequeathing property directly to the intended ultimate beneficiaries, or through the use of a life interest that will ensure that the survivor is only entitled to use the income derived from the property but not the capital, in reality these are often impracticable solutions. Where the testators do not possess great wealth, the survivor may need to make use of the property bequeathed to them, for example, to provide retirement income or to pay for nursing care if needed, and solutions which do not enable them to do so are inadequate to fulfil their intentions.[146] What is required is a mechanism which enables the survivor to enjoy the property inherited from the first to die, if necessary, but which prevents the survivor from making an effective bequest of any of that property remaining at the date of their death to anyone other than the agreed beneficiary. Equity provides such a mechanism through the doctrine of 'mutual wills'.

(2) The doctrine of mutual wills

The essence of the doctrine of mutual wills was stated by Morritt J in *Re Dale (Decd)*:

> The doctrine of mutual wills is to the effect that where two individuals have agreed as to the disposal of their property and have executed mutual wills in pursuance of the agreement, on the death of the first (T1) the property of the survivor (T2), the subject matter of the agreement is held on an implied trust for the beneficiary named in the wills. The survivor may thereafter alter his will, because a will is inherently revocable, but if he does his personal representatives will take the property subject to the trust.[147]

Where mutual wills have been executed, equity does not prevent the survivor from changing his will.[148] Instead, the executors of the new will hold any property that was intended to be left to the beneficiary of the mutual wills on constructive trust. By means of this trust the property will be held for the beneficiary named in the original mutual wills, and will not pass to those named in the new will. As the Privy Council stated in *Gray v Perpetual Trustee Co Ltd*:

> If two persons simultaneously make wills to the same effect, and in that sense mutually, a second will be [*sic*] made by one of them after succeeding to the other's estate under the originally made will is precluded from being treated as effective to interfere in equity with the existing disposition.[149]

[146] See Stevens, 'Avoiding Disinheritance' [1996] NLJ 961. [147] [1993] 4 All ER 129 at 132.
[148] See *Re Hey's Estate* [1914] P 192. [149] [1928] AC 391 at 399.

In *Re Cleaver*,[150] it was held that wills executed by Arthur and his wife were 'mutual wills', so that the equitable doctrine applied and a constructive trust had come into existence. The widow's executors therefore held the property she had received under her husband's will on constructive trust for the Cleavers' three children in equal shares, so she was unable to leave property on the terms of her own will to provide for only one of the children.

(3) Rationale for the imposition of a constructive trust

A constructive trust will be imposed if the testators executed mutual wills on the basis of an agreement not to revoke. The rationale for imposing a constructive trust in such circumstances is that equity will not permit the survivor to commit a fraud by going back on his agreement. Since the property he received on the death of the first testator had only been bequeathed to him on the basis of the agreement not to revoke his own will, it would be a fraud for him to take the benefit while failing to observe the agreement, and equity intervenes to prevent this fraud.[151] This rationale is evident from the judgment of Lord Cottenham LC in the early case of *Dufour v Pereira*, where there was an express reference to fraud as the basis for equity's intervention.[152]

In *Re Dale (Decd)*, Morritt J reiterated the fraud justification for the imposition of a constructive trust:

> There is a contract between the testators which on the death of T1 is carried into effect by him, that T1 dies with the promise of T2 that the agreement will stand and that it would be a fraud on T1 to allow T2 to disregard the contract which became irrevocable on the death of T1.[153]

The reasoning in *Re Dale (Decd)* was cited with approval by the Court of Appeal in *Olins v Walters*.[154]

Given that the mutual wills operate to prevent the survivor acting fraudulently, the question has arisen whether the doctrine of mutual wills operates if the surviving testator gains no personal benefit under the will of the first testator who predeceases him. In the majority of cases, this question will not arise because the mutual wills provide that the survivor is to inherit the estate of the predeceasing party absolutely, or to receive a life interest in it. However, the problem did arise in *Re Dale (Decd)*.[155] Norman and Monica Dale executed mutual wills in September 1988. They had two children, a son Alan and a daughter Joan. Under the terms of the mutual wills, all of their property, real and personal, was to be divided equally between their children. They left nothing to each other. Norman died in November 1988, and his estate was worth about £18,500. Monica died in 1990, having made a new will earlier that year leaving £300 to Joan and everything else to Alan. Her estate was valued at £19,000. Joan claimed that the doctrine of mutual wills applied so that Alan, as executor, held Monica's estate on constructive trust in accordance with the terms of the mutual wills. Alan argued that the doctrine could not operate because Monica had derived no personal benefit under Norman's will. After reviewing the authorities, Morritt J concluded that the doctrine of mutual wills could operate even where the surviving testator received no benefit under the first testator's will:

> As all the cases show the doctrine applies when T2 benefits under the will of T1. But I am unable to see why it should be any the less a fraud on T1 if the agreement was that each testator should leave his or her property to particular beneficiaries, for example their children,

[150] [1981] 2 All ER 1018.

[151] See *Re Dale (Decd)* [1993] 4 All ER 129 at 142, per Morritt J.

[152] (1769) 2 Hargreave's Juridical Arguments 304. The key passage was cited by Morritt J in *Re Dale (Decd)* [1993] 4 All ER 129 at 135–6.

[153] [1993] 4 All ER 129 at 136; Brierley 'Mutual Wills—Blackpool Illuminations' [1995] 58 MLR 95.

[154] [2009] Ch 212 at 221, 37.

[155] [1993] 4 All ER 129; O'Hagan, 'Mutual Wills' [1994] NLJ 1272.

> rather than to each other. It should be assumed that they had good reason for doing so and in any event that is what the parties bargained for. In each case there is the binding contract. In each case it has been performed by T1 on the faith of the promise of T2 and in each case T2 would have deceived T1 to the detriment of T1 if he, T2, were permitted to go back on his agreement. I see no reason why the doctrine should be confined to cases where T2 benefits when the aim of the principle is to prevent T1 from being defrauded.[156]

(4) **Establishing mutual wills**

(a) Necessity of a contract

The doctrine of mutual wills will only operate if the testators had agreed that their wills would not be revoked. In the absence of such an agreement there will be no fraud if the surviving testator revokes his will. As Lord Loughborough LC indicated in *Walpole v Lord Orford*,[157] the principal difficulty in establishing that wills were intended to be mutual is determining whether the testators had entered a legally binding obligation not to revoke their wills rather than a mere 'honourable engagement'. In *Re Cleaver* Nourse J stated:

> I would emphasise that the agreement or understanding must be such as to impose on the donee a legally binding obligation to deal with the property in the particular way.[158]

More recent cases have held that this agreement between the parties must take the form of a valid contract. In *Re Dale (Decd)*,[159] Morritt J held that 'there is no doubt that for the doctrine to apply there must be a contract at law.' The requirement of a contract was reiterated in *Goodchild v Goodchild*,[160] where it had been argued that a contract should not be required because it was not an essential element of the establishment of a constructive trust. The Court of Appeal rejected the purported analogy between the operation of mutual wills and secret trusts and concluded that a contract was required. Morritt LJ stated:

> As Leggatt LJ has pointed out, a consistent line of authority requires that for the doctrine of mutual wills to apply there must be a contract between the two testators. In delivering the advice of the Privy Council in *Gray v Perpetual Trustee Co Ltd*[161] such requirement was made abundantly clear by Viscount Haldane. Counsel . . . suggests that this test is too high. He does so by reference to the requirements for a secret trust or for the imposition of a constructive trust. I do not accept that there is any justification to be found in those areas of equity such as would justify departing from the clear statement of Viscount Haldane.[162]

While critics have suggested that Morritt LJ misrepresented the earlier cases cited in support of his conclusion that a contract is required,[163] and argued that the doctrine of mutual wills should operate whenever testators have reached an agreement or understanding not to revoke their wills,[164] subsequent decisions make clear that a contract

[156] [1993] 4 All ER 129 at 142. In the Canadian case *Lynch Estate v Lynch Estate* (1993) 8 Alta LR (3d) 291, it was held that a 'disposition agreement' was generally only enforceable against someone who had taken a benefit under it.

[157] [1797] 3 Ves JR 402 at 419. Cited by Nourse J in *Re Cleaver* [1981] 2 All ER 1018 at 1024.

[158] [1981] 2 All ER 1018 at 1024.

[159] [1993] 4 All ER 129 at 133.

[160] [1997] 3 All ER 63; Grattan, 'Mutual Wills and Remarriage' [1997] Conv 153.

[161] [1928] AC 391 at 400.

[162] [1997] 3 All ER 63 at 75.

[163] *Dufour v Pereira* [1769] 1 Dick 419; *Walpole v Lord Orford* [1797] 3 Ves JR 402; *Gray v Perpetual Trustee Co Ltd* [1928] AC 391; *Birmingham v Renfrew* [1937] CLR 666; *Re Cleaver* [1981] 2 All ER 1018.

[164] Harper, 'A Retreat from Equitable Mutuality?' [1997] Conv 182; Grattan, 'Mutual Wills and Remarriage' [1997] Conv 153.

(or in one case 'what amounts to a contract'[165]) will be required.[166] The courts have enjoyed ample opportunity to adopt a lower threshold but have pointedly, and repeatedly, chosen not to do so. For example, in *Olins v Waters*,[167] Mummery LJ reiterated that it 'is a legally *necessary* condition of mutual wills that there is clear and satisfactory evidence of a contract between two testators'.[168] This decision must in principle be correct. The effect of a finding that there are mutual wills is to impose a binding legal obligation in respect of the property affected. To give rise to this, even if a contract is not required, there must be an agreement intended to have legal effect. The difference between such an agreement and a contract is no more than semantic.

(b) Necessity of consideration

In order to establish that the testators had entered into a binding contract not to revoke their wills, it is necessary to show that consideration was provided. In *Re Dale (Decd)*,[169] the defendants argued that consideration was only given for the promise not to revoke if the first testator to die had provided a benefit to the survivor other than his promise not to revoke his own will. Morritt J rejected this submission and held that a testator has acted sufficiently to his detriment to constitute consideration where he has performed his promise by executing the mutual will, and not subsequently taken advantage of his legal right to revoke it.

(c) Absence of any contract

In the absence of a contract the testators' wills will not be mutual, and a constructive trust cannot arise.[170] In *Re Oldham*,[171] Mr and Mrs Weldon executed similar wills in 1907. In 1914 the husband died. As a result his estate passed to his wife absolutely. In 1921 she married Mr Oldham, who was some thirty-five years her junior, and altered her will to grant him a life interest in a large portion of her estate. She died in 1922, leaving some £108,000, all but £10,000 of which had come from her first husband's estate. Astbury J held that there was no evidence of an agreement that the 'mutual' wills should be irrevocable, and therefore, there was no trust raised in favour of the beneficiaries named in them.

In *Healey v Brown*,[172] a question arose about the effect of s 2 of the Law of Property (Miscellaneous Provisions) Act 1989 (which requires contracts relating to interests in land to be made in writing). Thomas and Mary Theresa Brown, in accordance with an oral agreement, had made identical mutual wills under which, on the death of the survivor, the flat which they jointly owned was to go to Mary's niece, Jacqueline. David Donaldson QC, sitting as a deputy High Court judge, held that Jacqueline's claim based on the mutual wills was precluded by the fact that there was no written contract signed by both Thomas and Mary. In his view if there was no enforceable contract, the mutual wills doctrine could not apply. He was, however, prepared to hold that the half-share in the flat which Thomas had acquired from Mary on her death was subject to a constructive trust—akin to either a secret trust or a common intention constructive trust. With respect, this decision is mistaken for two reasons. First, s 2 of the 1989 Act applies only to contracts 'for the sale or other disposition of an interest in land'. A mutual wills contract does not dispose

[165] *Charles v Fraser* [2010] EWHC 2154 (Ch) at 59.

[166] See also *Birch v Curtis* [2002] FLR 1158. In New Zealand it was held that the doctrine of mutual wills may be founded on the basis of either contract or restitution: *Re Newey* [1994] 2 NZLR 590.

[167] [2009] Ch 212 at 221, 36.

[168] Oddly, in *Fry v Densham-Smith* [2010] EWCA Civ 1410, Mummery LJ did not refer expressly to the need for a contract, but referred to the need for an 'express agreement' 'to become irrevocable on the death of the first to die' (at 4) and later to a 'bilateral agreement' (at 35). It is hard to see how a bilateral agreement which is intended to be irrevocable is anything other than a contract.

[169] [1994] Ch 31.

[170] *Birch v Curtis* [2002] FLR 1158.

[171] [1925] Ch 75.

[172] [2002] EWHC 1405 (Ch).

of an interest in land, but has a freezing effect on the terms of the agreed wills.[173] Secondly, s 2 of the 1989 Act preserves the effect of implied, constructive, or resulting trusts. Since mutual wills agreements are enforced as constructive trusts of the property subject to the agreement, they should not be rendered unenforceable merely by the absence of a single document signed by both parties. This is an issue which would merit reconsideration by a higher court.

(d) Breach of contract by revocation

As mutual wills are executed on the basis of a contract not to revoke, a testator who unilaterally revokes his will before either has died will have acted in breach of his contractual obligations. As such, he will be prima facie liable to pay damages to his fellow testator, and if he has died, his estate will be liable to the survivor.[174] There will be no liability for breach if the revocation occurred by operation of law, for example where the testator married or divorced, but the relevant property may still be subject to a constructive trust.

(e) The standard of proof

In *Re Cleaver*[175] Nourse J held that the agreement not to revoke the mutual wills can only be established by 'clear and satisfactory evidence', and that the burden of proof is the ordinary civil standard of the balance of probabilities.

(f) Mere fact of identical wills

In *Dufour v Pereira*,[176] Lord Cottenham LC had suggested that, where identical wills had been executed, it was possible to infer that the parties had agreed that they should not be revoked because 'the instrument itself is the evidence of the agreement'. However, it is clear from more recent cases a contract cannot be implied from the testators having simultaneously executed identical wills. In *Gray v Perpetual Trustee Co Ltd*,[177] the Privy Council concluded that:

> the mere simultaneity of the wills and the similarity of their terms do not appear, taken by themselves, to have been looked on as more than some evidence of an agreement not to revoke. The agreement . . . was a fact which had in itself to be established by evidence, and in such cases the whole of the evidence must be looked at.[178]

This statement of principle was approved by Nourse J in *Re Cleaver*.[179] For this reason, no constructive trust was established in *Re Oldham*,[180] the facts of which were noted earlier. The only evidence of an agreement came from the fact that identical wills had been executed, and Astbury J held that this was insufficient. He regretted his conclusion, because he was sure that the testator would have made a different will if he had foreseen that after his death, his wife 'would marry a young man and leave the whole of her first husband's property to that young man and her own relatives'.[181] He added that a mutual will agreement was not the only possible interpretation of what happened:

> Each may have thought it quite safe to trust the other, and to believe that, having regard to their ages, nothing was likely to occur in the future substantially to diminish the property taken by the survivor, who could be trusted to give effect to the other's obvious wishes. But that is a very different thing from saying that they bound themselves by a trust that should be operative in all circumstances and in all cases.[182]

[173] Compare *Yeates v Line* [2012] EWHC 3085 (Ch).
[174] *Robinson v Ommanney* (1883) 23 Ch D 285. [175] [1981] 2 All ER 1018 at 1024.
[176] [1769] 1 Dick 419; see also *Walpole v Lord Orford* (1797) 3 Ves JR 402.
[177] [1928] AC 391 at 400. [178] [1928] AC 391 at 400. [179] [1981] 2 All ER 1018 at 1022.
[180] [1925] Ch 25. [181] [1925] Ch 25 at 87. [182] [1925] Ch 25 at 88–9.

Although the mere fact of the execution of mutual wills is not alone sufficient to prove the necessary contract, it may provide a strong indication that a contract had been concluded between the testators.[183] This was recognized even in *Re Oldham*.[184]

(g) Additional evidence of agreement

Since a contract will not be inferred from the mere execution of identical wills, additional evidence will have to be provided to demonstrate that the testators had concluded a contract not to revoke. A constructive trust will be established if the mutual wills themselves contain a statement that they have been executed on the basis of an agreement, as was the case in *Re Hagger*.[185] Written evidence outside of the wills, for example, a memorandum stating the testators' intentions, will also support the establishment of a mutual wills constructive trust. In *Olins v Walters*,[186] a statement in the wills that they were intended to be mutual wills was supported by an attendance note from the testators' solicitor (who was also their grandson and a beneficiary), and by his oral evidence.

It is possible for a mutual wills agreement to be established by oral evidence, but this will be no easy task. Factors which may help to establish the agreement are similarities in the wills, particularly where they are unusually detailed, and evidence of family conversations[187] or statements to friends.[188] There will be particular difficulty about establishing the essential agreement not to revoke,[189] but the conduct of the survivor may help to establish this.[190] In *Re Cleaver*,[191] Nourse J held that his conclusion was helped by the attitude of Mrs Cleaver after her husband's death, which seemed to suggest that she was aware that she was under an obligation to dispose of her estate in accordance with the terms of their mutual wills, and not merely an honourable engagement.[192] It was only later that she adopted the attitude that she did not have to worry about promises made to her husband, because he was dead and could do nothing about it.[193] Contradictory evidence, particularly from the attending solicitor, will carry some weight. In *Goodchild v Goodchild*,[194] family members and friends gave evidence that the wills were intended to be mutually binding.[195] However, this body of anecdotal evidence was weighed against the evidence of the family solicitor who had drawn up the wills in question. He claimed that it was not his normal practice to draw up mutually binding wills, but rather to grant a life interest to the survivor. He claimed to have discussed the matter with them and that they clearly intended the survivor to be free to deal with the property during his or her lifetime. Faced with this conflict of evidence, Carnwath J placed greater weight on the evidence of the solicitor. He concluded that in the circumstances, no agreement had been proved. The Court of Appeal upheld his conclusion that there was insufficient evidence to establish anything beyond a mere moral obligation.

It should be noted that the overriding difference between the evidence presented in the cases of *Re Cleaver* and *Goodchild v Goodchild* was the evidence of the respective solicitors. In *Re Cleaver* the solicitor's evidence was relatively weak.[196] In contrast, in

[183] [1925] Ch 25 at 88–9 at 87, where Astbury J said: 'Of course it is a strong thing that these two parties came together, agreed to make their wills in identical terms and in fact so made them. But that does not go nearly far enough.' The approach of Astbury J was approved by the Privy Council in *Gray v Perpetual Trustee Co Ltd* [1928] AC 391 at 400.

[184] [1925] Ch 75. [185] [1930] 2 Ch 190. [186] [2009] Ch 212.

[187] *Re Cleaver* [1981] 2 All ER 1018. [188] *Charles v Fraser* [2010] EWHC 2154 (Ch).

[189] *Charles v Fraser* [2010] EWHC 2154 (Ch) at 70.

[190] *Charles v Fraser* [2010] EWHC 2154 (Ch) at 69.

[191] [1981] 2 All ER 1018. [192] [1981] 2 All ER 1018 at 1027. [193] [1981] 2 All ER 1018 at 1027–8.

[194] [1997] 3 All ER 63. [195] [1997] 3 All ER 63 at 679.

[196] As it was in *Charles v Fraser* [2010] EWHC 2154 (Ch), another case in which a mutual wills agreement was established on the basis of oral evidence.

Goodchild, the solicitor was adamant that no agreement had been intended, and that he had expressly outlined to the testators the various options as to how they could ensure that the estate passed to the son, and that they had decided to opt for the identical, but not mutual, wills, which he had explained would mean that the survivor was still free to dispose of the property freely as they chose.

(h) Certainty of subject and objects

In *Re Cleaver*,[197] Nourse J also emphasized that there must be certainty of subject matter and of objects for a constructive trust to arise on the basis of mutual wills. He considered that these requirements 'are as essential to this species of trust as they are to any other'. It is not necessary, however, that the mutual wills agreement should deal with every eventuality. In *Olins v Walters*,[198] counsel argued that there was no binding mutual wills agreement because there were some unanswered questions, such as the extent to which the survivor could use any property they inherited for their own purposes. This argument about insufficiency of terms was roundly rejected by Mummery LJ, who said:

> Possible, and as yet unexplored, legal consequences of the application of the equitable principles do not negative the existence of the foundation contract or prevent a constructive trust from arising by operation of law on the death of the Deceased.[199]

(5) The operation of mutual wills

While English law clearly accepts the doctrine of mutual wills, there are many theoretical and practical difficulties concerning the nature of the trust interest they establish.[200] In *Goodchild v Goodchild*,[201] Morritt LJ emphasized that 'the doctrine of mutual wills is anomalous',[202] and for this reason uncertainties and inconsistencies are tolerated which would render a more conventional trust void.

(a) Date of creation of the constructive trust

When it is established that wills were intended to be mutual, it has been seen that a constructive trust will arise to prevent the survivor disposing of his property in contravention of his contractual agreement not to vary his will. While it is clear that equity imposes a constructive trust, it is less clear when the trust arises.[203] A number of alternatives present themselves.

(b) Date the mutual wills are executed

As a matter of logic, this cannot be the date at which the constructive trust arises. The parties remain free to revoke their wills by agreement at any time before the death of the first testator.[204] It may even be that a revocation without agreement will prevent a constructive trust arising. Sir Gorell Barnes P held in *Stone v Hoskins*[205] that the survivor has no claim to a constructive trust where the testator who has died revoked his mutual will and executed another in a different form.

[197] [1981] 2 All ER 1018. [198] [2009] Ch 212. [199] [2009] Ch 212 at 221, 41.

[200] For an excellent critique of the operation of mutual wills see Hudson and Sloan, 'Testamentary Freedom: Mutual Wills Might Let You Down' in Barr (ed), *Modern Studies in Property Law: Volume 8* (Hart 2015).

[201] [1997] 3 All ER 63. [202] [1997] 3 All ER 63 at 76.

[203] See [1951] 14 MLR 137 (Mitchell).

[204] However, if the testator revokes his will before death, he will have committed a breach of contract and his estate will be liable to the survivor in damages: see *Robinson v Ommanney* (1883) LR 23 Ch D 285.

[205] [1905] P 194.

(c) Date of the first testator's death

There is authority for the view that a constructive trust imposed on the basis of the doctrine of mutual wills arises on the date of the death of the first of the testators who executed them. In *Thomas and Agnes Carvel Foundation v Carvel*,[206] Thomas and Agnes Carvel made mutual, identical wills, each leaving their estate on trust to the other for life, with the remainder on trust for the claimant, an American corporation. By a reciprocal will agreement they agreed not to alter the provisions of their wills without the consent of the other, and that the survivor would not make any alterations. Following the death of Thomas in America, Agnes made two further wills, the last of which revoked all previous wills. When Agnes died in England, the claimant instituted proceedings in the United States of America to enforce the reciprocal will agreement. By the time the case reached the English High Court, the main issue before the court was the potential removal of Agnes's personal representative for failing to administer the estate as required by the mutual will. Lewison J had to determine whether the claimant foundation had any interest under the will, to determine whether the personal representative was acting improperly. He concluded that the mutual will arose on the time of the first testator's death, therefore, binding Agnes from that point. In his view:

> The essential point, to my mind, is that the trust does not arise under the will of the surviving testator. Nor does it arise under any previous will of the surviving testator. It arises out of the agreement between the two testators not to revoke their wills, and the trust arises when the first of the two dies without having revoked his will. In so far as there is an 'operative will', it seems to me that it is the will of the first testator (and his death with that will unrevoked) which brings the trust into effect.[207]

This view that the trust arises on the death of the first testator is reinforced by *Re Hagger*.[208] In that case John and Emma Hagger executed mutual wills leaving one-sixth interests in their estates to Edward Adams, Eleanor Palmer, and Alice Young. All three survived Emma's death in 1904, but predeceased John, who died in 1928. Clauson J held that their respective interests had not failed because the trust took effect from the date of the wife's death. The trust arose before the death of the survivor and so the mutual will was successful.

(d) An alternative view

This is not an area in which even core principles have been firmly settled. There is contrary authority to the effect that the constructive trust arises on the death of the survivor. In *Legg v Burton*,[209] HHJ Paul Matthews gave judgment in circumstances where a surviving wife had changed her will after the death of the first testator. This was to the detriment of the claimants who had significantly lost out in consequence of the changes. The will in question expressly stated that the wife was to receive the estate free from any trust obligation. HHJ Paul Matthews took the view that because any relevant trust arose outside the will, the wording of the will was not conclusive as to the existence or otherwise of that trust. He went further and held that there was no trust arising on the death of the first testator. For the judge, at the point of death of the first testator, there was a binding promise upon the wife as, 'the clock of her testamentary freedom had stopped with the death of her husband'.[210] Her testamentary freedom was limited by equitable obligation but, 'there [was] no trust imposed on the death of the first to die. . .'[211] The judge stated the law as being that under the mutual wills doctrine, the trust would arise on the death of the second testator.[212] This reasoning is difficult to reconcile with *Thomas and Agnes*

206 [2008] Ch 395. 207 [2008] Ch 395 at 404, 27. 208 [1930] 2 Ch 190.
209 [2017] EWHC 2088 (Ch). 210 *Legg v Burton* [2017] EWHC 2088 (Ch), [71].
211 *Legg v Burton* [2017] EWHC 2088 (Ch), [70]. 212 *Legg v Burton* [2017] EWHC 2088 (Ch), [21].

Carvel Foundation v Carvel. From a perspective concerned with conceptual certainty, it is evident that this is an area in need of oversight from the higher courts.

(6) The beneficial interest under the constructive trust

(a) What property is subject to the trust?

Although it seems that a constructive trust arises on the death of the first testator, it is more difficult to identify the precise nature and extent of the beneficial interest subsisting under the trust. There are two questions here, the first being what property is subject to the trust; the second, how the trust affects that property. On the first question the only logical answer is that it depends on the agreement of the testators,[213] although some cases seem to make assumptions. In *Re Hagger*[214] Clauson J held that a mutual will trust applied only to the property received by the survivor after the death of the first testator. However, in *Goodchild v Goodchild*,[215] the Court of Appeal treated a trust affecting all the testator's property as the normal mutual wills arrangement. There is no reason in principle why, if it is based on the agreement of the parties, the trust should not encompass property acquired by the survivor after the death of the first testator, for example, through receipt of a windfall profit such as gambling winnings.[216]

(b) How does the trust affect the property?

This second question is more difficult. It would defeat the intentions of most testators if the effect of mutual wills is to make the survivor an immediate bare trustee for the ultimate beneficiaries and with no personal interest in the property. If this was what was intended, the will of the first to die could have made the gifts to the ultimate beneficiaries directly, and the ultimate beneficiaries would be able to call for the property to be transferred to them immediately. An alternative is that the survivor has only a life interest in the property affected. This was the view of Clauson J in *Re Hagger*.[217] That interpretation is more plausible in the case of a trust affecting only the interest of the first to die, but less plausible where it affects the whole of the property of the survivor, whether inherited from the first to die or not. Having a life interest only gives no right to the capital. What if the survivor faces expensive medical bills which are not covered by the NHS, or needs constant care and attention in a nursing home? Could capital be used for this purpose?

The practical reality is that, in most cases, the underlying intention of the mutual wills is to allow the survivor to use the property inherited, including the capital, for his or her own support and maintenance during their lifetime, but that the residue remaining at their death will be bequeathed to the agreed beneficiaries, rather than to others. As Nourse J observed in *Re Cleaver*,[218] Mr Cleaver wanted Mrs Cleaver to enjoy 'the security after his death which a free power of disposal over his estate would give her' and at the same time 'to ensure that anything which was left at her death should go back to his side of the family'.

(c) What are the rights of the beneficiaries?

If the survivor has the use of capital, and only the residue goes to the ultimate beneficiaries, then this suggests that the property rights of the beneficiaries of the mutual wills cannot crystallize until the date of the death of the survivor. If the trust were to fix

213 *Re Cleaver* [1981] 2 All ER 1018. 214 [1930] 2 Ch 190. 215 [1997] 3 All ER 63.

216 The issue was raised in *Olins v Walters* [2009] Ch 212, but had not been pleaded on the facts, so neither the trial judge nor the Court of Appeal expressed any binding view on the matter.

217 [1930] 2 Ch 190. 218 [1981] 2 All ER 1018 at 1029.

unconditionally on the death of the first testator, ludicrous and unintended results could follow. Although the issue was not considered in *Re Dale (Decd)*,[219] the facts of that case can be used as an illustration. If the beneficiaries' interests had crystallized as absolute rights at the date of their father's death, their mother would have held all her property, which was the subject matter of the trust, on trust for the children in equal shares, and she would in effect have no longer owned anything at all. Alternatively, if they crystallized then, but the mother retained a life interest, she would have no right to use any capital for her own needs.

An alternative model is, therefore, required to explain the nature of the entitlement of the beneficiaries of a constructive trust arising under mutual wills. The cases which have explored this problem have suggested that the property in the hands of the survivor affected by the mutual wills is rendered subject to a floating trust which arises at the date of death of the first testator, but which does not crystallize in favour of the beneficiaries until the death of the survivor. The possibility of such a 'floating trust' was raised by Dixon J in the Australian case *Birmingham v Renfrew*:

> The purpose of an arrangement for corresponding wills must often be, as in this case, to enable the survivor during his life to deal as absolute owner with the property passing under the will of the party first dying. That is to say, the object of the transaction is to put the survivor in a position to enjoy for his own benefit the full ownership so that, for instance, he may convert it and expend the proceeds if he chooses. But when he dies he is to bequeath what is left in the manner agreed upon. It is only by the special doctrines of equity that such a floating obligation, suspended, so to speak, during the lifetime of the survivor can descend upon the assets at his death and crystallise into a trust.[220]

The concept of such a 'floating', uncrystallized trust was raised in England in *Ottaway v Norman*[221] in the context of a fully secret trust.[222] Harry Ottaway left his bungalow by will to Eva Hodges, a woman he had been living with, having communicated his intention that on death she should leave it to his son, William. Although argued and decided on the basis that a fully secret trust had been created, this does not easily accord with the facts. It was not the intention of Harry that Eva should hold the bungalow on trust for William from the moment of his death. Nor were there mutual wills. Despite an expectation that Eva would leave the bungalow by will to William, she made no simultaneous will alongside Harry. Having held that a secret trust had arisen, Brightman J considered the nature of the beneficiary's rights during the lifetime of Eva, the trustee:

> I am content to assume for present purposes but without so deciding that if property is given to the primary donee on the understanding that the primary donee will dispose by his will of such assets, if any, as he may have at his command at his death in favour of the secondary donee, a valid trust is created in favour of the secondary donee which is in suspense during the lifetime of the primary donee, but attaches to the estate of the primary donee at the moment of the latter's death.[223]

It therefore seems best to regard mutual wills as creating some type of floating trust, which allows the survivor to dispose of the property subject to it if necessary but crystallizing over whatever remains at his death[224] or on any asset subject to an unauthorized voluntary disposition prior to death.[225] This approach was also assumed by Astbury J in *Re Oldham*.[226] Most significantly, in *Goodchild v Goodchild*,[227] Leggatt LJ assumed that

[219] [1994] Ch 31. [220] [1937] CLR 666. [221] [1972] Ch 698. [222] See Chapter 18.

[223] [1972] Ch 698 at 713.

[224] As has been seen in Chapter 5, a number of cases hold that such a trust, if created expressly, would fail for lack of certainty. [225] *Healey v Brown* [2002] EWHC 1405 (Ch) at 13.

[226] [1925] Ch 25 at 88. [227] [1997] 3 All ER 63.

mutual wills operated to create a floating trust. In the course of his comments concerning the need for a contractual agreement between the testators, he stated:

> The fact that each expected that the other would leave them to him is not sufficient to impress the arrangement with a floating trust.[228]

(d) Use of the property subject to the 'floating' trust by the survivor

Where the doctrine of mutual wills operates so that property in the hands of the surviving testator is subject to a floating constructive trust, the question arises as to duties of the survivor as trustee. The doctrine of mutual wills clearly operates to prevent the survivor disposing of the trust property by will in a manner inconsistent with the mutual wills, but the more significant issue is whether he is prevented from disposing of it during his lifetime. In *Re Oldham*[229] Astbury J was of the opinion that the survivor could dispose of the property inter vivos. However, it is clear that there must be limits to the power of the survivor to dispose of the property subject to the trust, otherwise the entire purpose of the arrangement could easily be defeated. This difficulty was recognized by Dixon J in *Birmingham v Renfrew*:

> No doubt gifts and settlements, inter vivos, if calculated to defeat the intention of the compact, could not be made by the survivor and his right of disposition, inter vivos, is, therefore, not unqualified. But, substantially, the purpose of the arrangement will often be to allow full enjoyment for the survivor's own benefit and advantage upon condition that at his death the residue shall pass as arranged.[230]

Adopting this analysis, the position would be very similar to a floating charge over the assets of a company.[231] So long as the survivor continued to behave in an ordinary way that was in accordance with his means and circumstances, he would continue to have freedom of disposition over the assets subject to the inchoate trust. The trust would, however, crystallize and settle on the assets upon his death, and even during his lifetime he could be called upon to account for any extraordinary transaction inappropriate to his circumstances. If a purported extraordinary transaction was identified in time, a beneficiary affected by it could presumably take steps to restrain it. If the transaction has already taken place, the recipient could be held subject to a constructive trust. For instance, in *Healey v Brown*,[232] Thomas Brown put into joint names with his son a flat which Thomas had agreed with his wife to leave to her niece (the claimant) on his death. The deputy High Court judge took the view that, if a mutual wills agreement had been established, Thomas's son would have held the flat on constructive trust for the niece. The judge, David Donaldson QC, observed:

> Had Mr Brown sold the flat and used the proceeds to fund a place in a nursing home, there would have been no basis for complaint. But to give away the flat to his son—with immediate effect as to a 50% undivided share, and with effect on death as to the remainder by operation of the doctrine of survivorship—could scarcely run more directly and fully counter to the intention of the mutual will compact that the flat should pass to his deceased's wife's niece on his own death. Subject therefore to the impact of the 1989 Act [the need for a contract disposing of land to be in writing] I have no doubt that the mutual wills doctrine would apply in the present case so as to impose in favour of the Claimant a constructive trust attaching to the flat.[233]

[228] [1997] 3 All ER 63 at 71. [229] [1925] Ch 25 at 88. [230] [1937] CLR 666.
[231] *Re Panama, New Zealand and Australian Royal Mail Co* [1870] 5 Ch App 318.
[232] [2002] EWHC 1405 (Ch). [233] [2002] EWHC 1405 (Ch) at 14–15.

The Law Commission has considered mutual wills as part of the consultation exercise on making wills, and did not propose that the doctrine be abolished.[234] However, one significant issue raised by Hudson and Sloan is that the operation of the doctrine means that funds subject to a mutual will agreement are not available for an award under the Inheritance (Provision for Family and Dependants) Act 1975.[235] The Commission has proposed an amendment to the 1975 Act to cover property passing under a mutual will.[236]

234 *Making a Will* (Law Commission CP 231, 2017), Ch 12.

235 Hudson and Sloan, 'Testamentary Freedom: Mutual Wills Might Let You Down' in Barr (ed), *Modern Studies in Property Law: Volume 8* (Hart 2015). The operation of the 1975 Act is considered towards the beginning of this chapter.

236 *Making a Will* (Law Commission CP 231, 2017), para 12.42 and Consultation Question 62.

18

Secret trusts

1 Introduction to secret trusts

Secret trusts arise where the recipient of a gift (usually by will) agrees to use that gift in a particular way, but the terms of that arrangement are not contained in the will. Exactly how secret trusts should be categorized is a matter on which there are different views. The most widely held theory is that they are forms of lifetime trusts set up outside a will, but depending upon the will for their operation. Some of the cases suggest that they are a mechanism for making provision via a will for illegitimate children or mistresses which avoids the publicity of describing the gift in the will,[1] but there are more secure and effective means of concealing the identity of a beneficiary by making lifetime gifts or creating lifetime trusts. More often than not, secret trusts are used to provide for a beneficiary who has been forgotten, and in some cases because the testator was unsure as to who should be the ultimate beneficiary when he made his will. What is secret about a secret trust is not that no one knows about it—there would be problems relating to enforcement if that were the case—but that the existence or the terms of the trust are not disclosed in the will. An excellent example of secret trusts is provided by *Rawstron & Anor (Executrices of the Estate of Lucian Freud) v Freud*.[2] During his life, Freud was an unconventional figure and very famous painter. He left not only a legacy of artwork, at least fourteen children by several partners but also an estate worth £96 million. The will contained a number of clauses and bequests, and the one which caused the litigation related to the residue of the estate, £42 million:

> I give all the residue of my estate (out of which shall be paid my funeral and testamentary expenses and my debts) and any property over which I have a general power of appointment to the said Diana Mary Rawstron and the said Rose Pearce jointly.

In fact, this gift to the two women was subject to a secret promise that they would distribute it to a number of undisclosed recipients (including some of his many children). One of the children contested the will. It, therefore, fell to the court to interpret Lucian Freud's will to determine whether the trust created over the residuary estate was in fact a fully secret trust (whose existence would not be made public at all) or half-secret trust (whose existence is known but whose details are not). In applying the normal rules of interpretation in *Marley v Rawlings* and the ordinary and natural meaning of the words, Deputy Judge Spearman found that an absolute gift had been created for the two women, who were then free to carry out the terms of the promise they had made with Freud. One reason a half-secret trust was not found to have existed was that an earlier will contained

[1] Eg, *Re Boyes* [1884] LR 26 Ch D 531; *Blackwell v Blackwell* [1929] AC 318.

[2] [2014] EWHC 2577 (Ch).

a version of the same clause, differently worded and clearly intended to create a half-secret trust, which had been revoked.

2 Types of secret trust

English law recognizes, as we have seen, two categories of secret trust, namely 'fully secret trusts' and 'half-secret trusts'. The central difference between these categories is the extent to which the testator's will discloses that the person named as the recipient of a bequest is intended to take the property as a trustee rather than for himself. While the difference might appear slight, for a long period of time, it was held that only fully secret trusts should be recognized as valid, and even though half-secret trusts are now accepted, the rules governing their creation are somewhat more restrictive.

(1) **Fully secret trusts**

A fully secret trust is created when a testator leaves property to a specified person in his will who has agreed that he will hold the property left to him on trust for a third party. In a fully secret trust, neither the fact of the trust nor the identity of the beneficiary under the trust are revealed in the will. For example, imagine that George wants to leave something to his first wife, Henrietta, without his second wife discovering her existence. He, therefore, leaves £50,000 in his will to his close friend, Ian, who has agreed that he will ensure that Henrietta receives the money. On the face of George's will, it appears that Ian is the absolute beneficiary of the bequest, whereas in fact, behind the scenes, Henrietta is intended to benefit. This arrangement would give rise to a fully secret trust. On the death of George, Ian will receive the money under the terms of the will, but he will be required to hold it as trustee for Henrietta. Ian is, therefore, the trustee of the secret trust, and Henrietta the beneficiary. There are a number of ways in which the secret trust could be proved. Ian might willingly accept the obligation (in which there is no need for proof); there might be witnesses who can testify to the discussion between Ian and George; or Ian's agreement might have been recorded in an exchange of letters or e-mails. The trust is only secret in not being disclosed by will: that does not mean it has to be covert in the sense that no one knows about it.

(2) **Half-secret trusts**

The performance of a fully secret trust is to some extent dependent on the integrity of the beneficiary who has agreed to act as the secret trustee. There is always a danger that the secret trustee will ignore the trust and take the property as his own. This danger can be avoided by confirming the instructions in writing, asking the trustee to sign this, and giving a copy to the intended beneficiary. Alternatively, if the testator indicates in his will that the recipient of the bequest is intended to take the property as a trustee it is impossible for the trustee recipient to deny the existence of a trust. The identity of the beneficiary can be disclosed separately. Amending the example used above, if George were to leave £50,000 to Ian in his will 'on trust', without disclosing that Henrietta was the ultimate beneficiary, a half-secret trust would have been created. The trust is described as 'half-secret' because the fact that the property is subject to a trust obligation appears on the face of the will, but the identity of the true beneficiary is not disclosed by the will. It may not be secret in any other sense, because the terms of the trust may have been recorded in writing, and might have been discussed widely within the family.

(3) Secret trusts arising on intestacy

Although secret trusts generally arise in the context of a testamentary disposition, a secret trust may arise in a case of intestacy,[3] provided that the person entitled to the deceased's estate on his intestacy had agreed that he would receive the specified property as a trustee and not for himself absolutely. As Romer J stated in *Re Gardner (No 2)*:

> The principle has been applied . . . where the owner of property refrains from making a will and so allows the property to pass to the donee as on an intestacy.[4]

Therefore, if, under the rules of intestacy, Ian was entitled to receive a share of George's estate, George could ask him to hold that share for the benefit of Henrietta. Provided that Ian agreed, and George died without making a will, Ian would hold whatever he received from the administration of George's estate on trust for Henrietta.

(4) Secret trust arising on transfer by survivorship in joint tenancy

A secret trust can probably also arise where a person acquires an enlarged interest in property through survivorship to a joint tenancy. In *Healey v Brown*[5] David Donaldson QC (sitting as a Deputy High Court Judge) held that a constructive trust applied to the half-interest in a flat to which Mr Brown had succeeded as a joint tenant on the death of his wife, after he had promised to leave the flat to a named beneficiary on his own death. David Donaldson observed that 'the present case differs from the ordinary case of secret trusts, since the property passed outside the will and by operation of law rather than pursuant to a bequest. But to my mind that is a matter of form without substantive significance.'[6]

3 Requirements for the creation of secret trusts

The essential requirements of 'intention, communication and acceptance' must be satisfied to create a valid fully secret, or half-secret, trust. It has been questioned whether the creation of a secret trust requires a contract between the testator and the intended trustee, whereby the trustee agrees to hold the property bequeathed to him on trust for the indicated beneficiary. In *Re Goodchild (Decd)*,[7] Morritt LJ suggested that the 'principles applicable to cases of a fully secret trust do, in substance, require the proof of a contract,' although he accepted that they do not 'require exactly the same degree of agreement as does a contract at law'.[8] While many of the authorities elucidating the meaning of these requirements are applicable to both categories of secret trust, it should be noted in advance that there are significant differences regarding the application of the requirement of communication to half-secret trusts.

4 Fully secret trusts

The leading authority stating the requirements of a fully secret trust is *Ottaway v Norman*.[9] Harry Ottaway cohabited with Miss Hodges in his house, 'Ashcroft'. On his death, 'Ashcroft' was left to Miss Hodges in his will, and she left it in her will to Mr and

[3] *Stickland v Aldridge* [1804] 9 Ves 516.
[4] [1923] 2 Ch 230 at 233.
[5] [2002] EWHC Ch 1405.
[6] [2002] EWHC Ch 1405 at 29. While this remark referred to secret trusts, most of the judgment concerns mutual wills—see earlier.
[7] [1997] 3 All ER 63.
[8] [1997] 3 All ER 63 at 75.
[9] [1972] Ch 698; [1972] 36 Conv 129.

Mrs Norman. Harry's son, William, claimed that the house had been left to Miss Hodges on the understanding that she would leave it to him on her death. He claimed that a secret trust had been created in his favour, so that Miss Hodges held the house on trust for him and that it had not, therefore, formed part of her estate. Although the case is open to criticism on the grounds that it did not really involve a secret trust, as Miss Hodges was not subjected to an immediate obligation to hold the house on trust for William on the death of Harry, it was argued and decided on the basis that the existence of a secret trust was in issue. Having examined the facts, Brightman J concluded that a fully secret trust had been created. In the course of his judgment he referred to the secret trustee as the 'primary donee' (who would take the property under the will) and the secret beneficiary as the 'secondary donee'.[10] He held that subjection of property to a fully secret trust required the three elements of intention, communication, and acceptance.

(1) **Intention**

Brightman J stated that a secret trust would not be created unless it was 'the intention of the testator to subject the primary donee to an obligation in favour of the secondary donee'.[11] This requirement is no different from the requirement that conventional express trusts must demonstrate sufficient 'certainty of intention' to create a trust.[12] It must be shown that the testator intended to subject the secret trustee to a mandatory obligation to hold the property for the benefit of the secret beneficiary. An intention to impose a purely moral obligation is insufficient, as can be seen in *Re Snowden (Decd)*,[13] where an elderly testatrix left her entire residuary estate to her older brother because she was uncertain as to how she should leave her property among her relatives, and she said that her brother would 'know what to do'. She died without changing her will, and six days later, her brother also died, leaving all his property to his only son. The question was whether the brother had taken Mrs Snowden's residuary estate on secret trust for her nephews and nieces equally. Megarry V-C concluded that she had not possessed the necessary intention to impose a trust on her brother, but that she had merely intended to impose on him a 'moral obligation' to do what he thought best. As a result no secret trust was established, and the brother's son was entitled to the entire residue absolutely.

(2) **Communication**

The mere fact that a testator intends to create a secret trust is insufficient on its own to subject the recipient of the trust property under his will to an enforceable secret trust. As Brightman J stated in *Ottaway v Norman*, creation of a valid secret trust requires 'communication of that intention to the primary donee'.[14] The conscience of a beneficiary under the will is only affected, so as to justify the imposition of a trust, if the testator made him aware that he was to receive the property bequeathed as a trustee.

Communication will only be effective to create a fully secret trust if it satisfies the following criteria.

(a) **Communication of both the fact of the trust and the terms of the trust**

A fully secret trust will only arise if the testator makes the intended trustee aware of both the fact that he is to hold the property bequeathed to him on trust, and the identity (or the

[10] [1972] Ch 698, [1972] 36 Conv 129 at 711. [11] [1972] Ch 698, [1972] 36 Conv 129.

[12] See Chapter 5.

[13] [1979] 2 All ER 172. Similar cases are *Taylor v HMRC* [2008] STC (SCD) 1159 and *Davies v HMRC* [2009] UKFTT 138 (TC).

[14] *Ottaway v Norman* [1972] Ch 698 at 711.

means of discovering the identity) of the intended trust beneficiary. Where either of these elements is missing, the property will not be held on trust. For example, in *Re Boyes*,[15] George Boyes left his entire estate by will to his solicitor, Frederick Carritt. Prior to his death Boyes had informed Carritt that he was to hold the property on trust, the terms of which he said he would communicate to him by letter. No communication of the terms of the trust was made during the testator's lifetime, but after his death, papers were discovered directing Carritt to hold the property for his mistress and illegitimate child. Kay J held that in these circumstances a secret trust had not been established in favour of the mistress and child. However, as the solicitor had admitted that he had agreed to receive the property left to him as a trustee, he was not entitled to take it absolutely for himself, and therefore he held it on a resulting trust for Boyes' next of kin.

While a complete failure to communicate the terms of the trust before the testator's death prevents the creation of a valid secret trust, communication of the terms of the trust by means of a sealed envelope, given to the trustee during the testator's lifetime with the stipulation that it was not to be opened until after his death, will be sufficient to create a secret trust. This was accepted by the Court of Appeal in *Re Keen*,[16] where Lord Wright MR considered such communication analogous with that of a ship sailing under sealed orders, which he considered is 'sailing under orders though the exact terms are not ascertained by the captain till later'.

(b) Communication of the extent of the trust

A secret trust will only affect property bequeathed to the intended trustees to the extent that effective communication had been made. In *Re Cooper*[17] a testator left £5,000 by will to two trustees. He had previously communicated the terms of the trust to them both. He subsequently added a codicil to his will, increasing the amount of the gift to £10,000, but without communicating this alteration to the trustees. The Court of Appeal held that only £5,000 of the money bequeathed to the trustees was subject to the secret trust.[18]

(c) Communication must be made before the death of the testator

A valid fully secret trust will be created provided that effective communication was made to the trustee at any time prior to the death of the testator. It has already been seen how failure to communicate the terms of the intended trust before the testator's death prevented the finding of a secret trust in *Re Boyes*.[19] In *Wallgrave v Tebbs*,[20] William Coles left property by will to the defendants. From a letter he had written it appeared that he had intended that it should be applied by them for the charitable purpose of endowing a church. However, as this intention had not been communicated to them during his lifetime, Page-Wood V-C held that no trust had been created, and that the defendants were entitled to take the property bequeathed to them absolutely.

(d) Communication to joint trustees

Particular difficulties of communication emerge if a testator intends to subject property to a secret trust bequeathed to two or more persons jointly in his will. The question arises whether the joint beneficiaries under the will are bound by the secret trust if communication had been made to only some of them. In answering this dilemma the

[15] (1884) LR 26 Ch D 531.

[16] [1937] Ch 236. See also *Re Boyes* [1884] LR 26 Ch D 531 at 536; *Re Bateman's Will Trusts* [1970] 1 WLR 1463.

[17] [1939] Ch 811.

[18] As it was a half-secret trust, the remaining £5,000 was held on resulting trust for the testator's residuary legatees. If it had been an attempted fully secret trust, the intended trustees would have been entitled to the remaining £5,000 absolutely.

[19] [1884] LR 26 Ch D 531.

[20] [1855] 2 K & J 313.

law distinguishes between bequests made to the intended trustees as joint tenants, and bequests made to them as tenants-in-common. The principles were stated by Farwell J in *Re Stead*.[21] Where the intended trust property is bequeathed to two or more persons as tenants-in-common, a secret trust will only bind the respective shares of those tenants-in-common to whom the testator had communicated the terms of the trust. Those to whom the trust had not been communicated are entitled to receive their respective shares of the bequeathed property absolutely.[22] In *Re Stead*, Mrs Stead had left property to Mrs Witham and Mrs Andrews as tenants-in-common. She informed Mrs Witham that £2,000 was to be held on trust for John Collett, but made no communication to Mrs Andrews. It was held that Mrs Andrews took her share of the property free from any trust. Where the intended trust property is bequeathed to joint tenants, a further distinction is made on the grounds of the timing of any communication of the trust. Farwell J held that if a testator made effective communication to any one of the joint tenants before executing the will, they would all be bound by the secret trust.[23] However, he held that where communication occurred after the will had been executed, only those to whom communication had been made would be bound by the trust, and that, therefore, those tenants-in-common to whom no communication had been made would be entitled to take their respective shares of the bequeathed property absolutely.[24] Although clearly representing the present law, it has been persuasively argued that the rules expounded in *Re Stead*[25] are incorrect because Farwell J developed his reasoning from a misunderstanding of earlier cases cited as authority.[26] It is suggested that, rather than distinguishing between joint tenants and tenants-in-common (and in the latter case, also between communication before and after the execution of the will), the question in each case should be whether the testator was induced to make the joint bequest only because of the promise of some of those entitled that the property would be held on trust.[27] Clearly, it will be more difficult to show that the gift was so induced if it was made to tenants-in-common, or if the promise was only made after the will had been executed.

(3) **Acceptance**

A secret trust is not imposed on property left to an intended secret trustee merely because the testator effectively communicated his intention that it should be held on trust. The property will only be subject to a secret trust if the intended trustee accepted that he would hold it on trust. As Brightman J said in *Ottaway v Norman*,[28] the third essential element for the creation of a fully secret trust is 'the acceptance of that obligation by the primary donee either expressly or by acquiescence'. Such acceptance does not need to be active. It has been held that if the terms of the trust have been communicated to the intended trustee, his silence will be taken to be an acceptance of the trust. In *Moss v Cooper*,[29] John Hill left property in his will to James Gawthorn, William Sedman, and James Owen. He communicated his intention to all three that the property should be used for the benefit of certain charities. The trust was accepted by Gawthron and Sedman. However, Owen remained silent. Page-Wood V-C held that, having learned of the testator's intention,

[21] [1900] 1 Ch 237.

[22] See *Tee v Ferris* [1856] 2 K & J 357; *Rowbotham v Dunnett* [1878] LR 8 Ch D 430; *Re Young (Decd)* [1951] Ch 344. Compare also *Geddis v Semple* [1903] 1 IR 73.

[23] *Russell v Jackson* [1852] 10 Hare 204; *Jones v Badley* [1868] 3 Ch App 362.

[24] *Burney v Macdonald* [1845] 15 Sim 6; *Moss v Cooper* [1861] 1 John & H 352.

[25] [1900] 1 Ch 237.

[26] Perrins, 'Can You Keep Half a Secret?' [1972] 88 LQR 225.

[27] Applying the principle of *Huguenin v Baseley* [1807] 14 Ves 273 that: 'No man may profit by the fraud of another.'

[28] [1972] Ch 698 at 711.

[29] [1861] 1 John & H 352.

such silence amounted to an acceptance of the trust. He justified this conclusion on the grounds that 'the legatees, as soon as they learned the intention of the testator, would be bound to elect whether they would undertake the trust or not.'

5 Half-secret trusts

The creation of a valid half-secret trust is dependent upon satisfaction of the same three elements of intention, communication, and acceptance. However, there are significant differences concerning the application of the requirement of communication. The leading case stipulating the requirements for half-secret trusts is *Blackwell v Blackwell*,[30] where Lord Sumner stated that the essential criteria were 'intention, communication and acquiescence'.[31] As the criteria of intention and acceptance are identical to those required for a valid fully secret trust, which have been discussed earlier, only the element of communication will be examined.

(1) Communication must be made before the execution of the will

It has already been seen that property bequeathed to an intended trustee will be subject to a fully secret trust if the testator made effective communication of the trust at any time before his death. In contrast, in the case of half-secret trusts, it has been held that the testator must make communication to the intended trustee before his will is executed. Communication subsequent to the execution of the will, even though prior to the testator's death, will not subject the bequeathed property to an enforceable half-secret trust. This follows from the judgment of Lord Sumner in *Blackwell v Blackwell*,[32] who stated:

> A testator cannot reserve to himself a power of making future unwitnessed dispositions by merely naming a trustee and leaving the purposes of the trust to be supplied afterwards . . .

His comments in this respect were strictly obiter, because the trust in question had been communicated to the intended trustee before the testator's will was executed. However, the limitation was accepted by the Court of Appeal in *Re Keen*,[33] and followed in *Re Bateman's Will Trusts*.[34] It is hard to see the logic for this differentiation between fully and half-secret trusts.[35] In *Gold v Hill*,[36] a man who had separated from his wife nominated a solicitor as the beneficiary of a life insurance policy, having communicated to him that the proceeds were to be held on trust for his partner and her children. This nomination and communication had taken place after the execution of his will, which had left his estate to his wife. Carnwath J held that the situation was analogous to that of a half-secret trust, but held that any doubts as to the effectiveness of communication after the execution of a will were derived from the particular rules applying to wills and should not create difficulties for nominations. Even in the case of wills it is hard to see a convincing justification. It may be that the insistence on communication before the execution of the will arises by analogy between the doctrine of half-secret trusts and the principle of incorporation by reference. As was explained earlier, a document can only be incorporated into a will if it was in existence when the will was executed. It is submitted that this analogy is false, and that there is no reason for maintaining a distinction between the rules of communication applicable to fully and half-secret trusts. A document incorporated by reference becomes part of the will itself, whereas according to the prevailing theory a secret trust, whether

[30] [1929] AC 318, HL. [31] [1929] AC 318, HL at 334. [32] [1929] AC 318, HL at 339.
[33] [1937] Ch 236. [34] [1970] 1 WLR 1463. [35] Holdworth 'Secret Trusts' [1937] 53 LQR 501.
[36] [1999] 1 FLR 54.

fully or half-secret, arises wholly outside of the terms of the will.[37] It may yet be open to the Supreme Court to find that a half-secret trust can be validly created by communication at any time before the death of the testator, and other jurisdictions have rejected the distinction and held that the same rule applies to both fully and half-secret trusts.[38] In the Irish case *Riordan v Banon*,[39] Chatterton V-C seems to have suggested that a valid half-secret trust can be created by communication after the date of the will but before the testator's death, and this has been supported by later cases.[40]

(2) **Communication must be consistent with the will**

Even if a testator communicates the trust to the intended trustee of a half-secret trust before executing his will, evidence of such communication will not be admitted to establish the trust if it is inconsistent with the face of the will. Therefore, evidence of a communication inconsistent with the manner in which the will stated that communication would be made will not be admissible to prove the existence of a half-secret trust. The application of this rule had the effect of preventing the creation of a half-secret trust in *Re Keen*.[41] While the terms of the trust had in fact been communicated to the trustee before the execution of the will, by means of a sealed envelope, the Court of Appeal held that evidence of the communication was inadmissible because clause 56 of the will anticipated that communication would only be made after the will had been executed. Therefore, evidence of the prior communication was inconsistent with the face of the will. In *Re Spence*[42] a testator had communicated the trust to some of the four trustees to whom he had jointly bequeathed the intended property. While such communication would have been sufficient to establish a fully secret trust, it was held that evidence of the communication was inadmissible to establish a half-secret trust. It was inconsistent with the terms of the will, which stated that communication had been made to them all.

The validity of this restriction should also be questioned. It is inconsistent with the approach applied to fully secret trusts, where parol evidence of communication is admissible to prove the secret trust, despite the fact that it is always inconsistent with the face of the will, which suggests that an absolute gift has been made. The inconsistency should only be material where it casts significant doubt upon whether the testator had intended the communication to be an effective expression of his wishes.

6 The burden of proof required to establish a secret trust

The level of proof necessary to establish a secret trust has been a matter of some debate. Traditionally, secret trusts were thought to be imposed by the court to prevent the secret trustee committing a fraud by denying the existence of the trust. In *McCormick v Grogan*,[43] Lord Westbury, therefore, held that an extremely high burden of proof must be discharged before the court would impose a secret trust:

> Now, being a jurisdiction founded on personal fraud, it is incumbent on the court to see that a fraud, a malus animus, is proved by the clearest and most indisputable evidence . . . You are obliged, therefore, to show most clearly and distinctly that the person you wish to convert

[37] See the discussion later in the chapter.

[38] See Scott, *Law of Trusts* (4th edn, Aspen Law & Business 1988), para 55.8.

[39] [1876] 10 IrR Eq 469.

[40] See *Re King's Estate* [1888] 21 LR Ir 273; *Re Browne* [1944] IrR 90; *Re Prendeville* (5 December 1990, unreported) (Irish High Court). See [1992] Conv 202 (Mee).

[41] [1937] Ch 236. [42] [1949] WN 237. [43] [1869] LR 4 HL 82.

> into a trustee acted mala animo. You must show distinctly that the testator or the intestate was beguiled and deceived by his conduct . . .

As will be seen later, this view of secret trusts imposed to prevent personal fraud has been rejected by more modern cases in favour of the theory that they are inter vivos trusts arising wholly outside of the testator's will. It is therefore illogical to require the same special standard of proof as that which applies to an allegation of fraud. In *Ottaway v Norman*,[44] Brightman J suggested that what was required was a standard of proof 'analogous to that required before the court would rectify a written instrument'. This is higher than the usual civil law standard of proof on the balance of probabilities. However, in *Re Snowden*,[45] Megarry V-C considered that even this was inappropriate, since it demanded a higher threshold than the ordinary civil standard of proof, and it was founded upon a false analogy between rectification of documents and the operation of secret trusts. He concluded that the standard of proof required to establish a secret trust was simply the 'ordinary standard of evidence required to establish a trust'.[46] The higher standard appropriate for fraud would only need to be satisfied in circumstances where the secret trust could only be established by holding the legatee guilty of fraud. It is possible that in some cases, despite an intention to create a secret trust, there is no evidence of it. However, in many (if not most) cases, there will be evidence from the records of solicitors, witnesses who were present when the terms of the secret trust were discussed, or written correspondence. Where the evidence is contradictory, the judge will have to resolve that inconsistency using normal forensic principles about the credibility and weight of the evidence.

7 Failure of secret trusts

Where a testator has left property in his will intending that it should be subject to a secret trust, but has failed to satisfy the requisite criteria, the ultimate location of the ownership of the intended trust property will depend upon whether the trust was fully or half-secret.

(1) Failure of a fully secret trust

If a testator fails to establish a valid fully secret trust, the intended secret trustee will be entitled to take the property for himself absolutely. This is nothing other than his entitlement under the will because the fact of the trust does not appear from the face of the will.[47] The intended trustee will only be required to hold the property on resulting trust for the testator's residuary legatees or next of kin[48] if he admits that he was intended to receive the property as a trustee.

(2) Failure of a half-secret trust

Unlike a fully secret trust, a half-secret trust is evident from the face of the will. If the trust fails for any reason the trustee will, therefore, be prevented from retaining the property bequeathed to him by the will. Instead, he will hold it on resulting trust, either for the residuary legatees under the will or, if the bequest is of the residuary estate, for the testator's next of kin.[49]

[44] [1972] Ch 698 at 699. [45] [1979] 2 All ER 172. [46] [1979] 2 All ER 172 at 178.

[47] E.g. *Wallgrave v Tebbs* [1855] 2 K & J 313; *Jones v Badley* [1868] 3 Ch App 362; *McCormick v Grogan* [1869] LR 4 HL 82; *Re Pitt Rivers* [1902] 1 Ch 403.

[48] *Re Boyes* [1884] LR 26 Ch D 531. [49] See *Re Cooper* [1939] Ch 811, CA.

8 Death or disclaimer of the secret trustee

A secret trust does not come into existence until the death of the testator who has bequeathed the trust property in his will to the intended secret trustee. Inevitably there is, therefore, a period of time, which in some cases may be substantial, between the communication and acceptance of the trust and the death of the testator. This time interval will give rise to practical difficulties if the intended secret trustee predeceases the testator, or disclaims the trust on the death of the testator. In either event, the question will arise whether the intended trust property is subject to a valid trust on the death of the testator. The answer will be determined primarily by the nature of the secret trust concerned.

(1) Secret trustee predeceases the testator

(a) Fully secret trust

Under the law of succession, a bequest lapses and fails if the beneficiary predeceases the testator. As a matter of logic, the predeceasing of a trustee of a fully secret trust should therefore cause the trust to fail. This was accepted in *Re Maddock*,[50] where Cozens-Hardy LJ stated that a fully secret trust will fail if the trustee dies during the lifetime of the testator. This is consistent with the modern explanation of the operation of secret trusts discussed later, namely, that a secret trust is an expressly declared inter vivos trust which remains unconstituted until the testator's will operates to transfer the legal title to the trust property to the trustee. Since the predecease of the trustee causes the gift to lapse, the testator's will fails to effect a constitution of the trust.

(b) Half-secret trusts

In the case of a fully secret trust, the existence of the intention to subject the property bequeathed to a trust is entirely absent from the face of the will. In contrast, where the trust is half-secret, the fact that the property bequeathed was intended to be subject to a trust is apparent from the will itself. It is, therefore, clear that the legatee was never intended to enjoy the property left to him absolutely. If the intended trustee of a half-secret trust predeceases the testator, equity will not allow the trust to fail for want of a trustee. The testator's personal representative will act as trustee in his place.[51] Provided that it is still possible to identify the terms of the half-secret trust, it will not fail.

(2) Secret trustee dies after the testator

If the trustee of a secret trust, whether half- or fully secret, dies after the testator, the trust will not fail. In both cases the testator's will operates according to its terms to transfer the legal title of the property bequeathed to the secret trustee at the moment of the testator's death, thus constituting the trust. As the trust is fully constituted from the death of the testator, it will not fail for want of a trustee. However, if the death of the secret trustee renders it impossible to identify the beneficiary of the trust, the property will pass by resulting trust to the testator's residuary legatees or next of kin.

(3) Secret trustee disclaims the trust

(a) Revocation of acceptance before the death of the testator

It has been seen that a secret trust will only be established if the intended trustee accepts that he will hold the property bequeathed to him on trust. His acceptance, however,

[50] [1902] 2 Ch 220 at 231.

[51] See *Mallott v Wilson* [1903] 2 Ch 494.

is not irrevocable. A secret trustee is entitled to revoke a previous acceptance of the trust at any time before the death of the testator. If the trust was fully secret, a trustee who has revoked the trust will be entitled to take the property bequeathed to him in the will absolutely for his own benefit. In contrast, if the trust was half-secret, the intended trust property will be held on resulting trust for the testator's residuary legatees or next of kin. To be effective, the trustee must communicate his change of mind to the testator. He will otherwise be estopped from asserting his revocation of the agreement to hold upon trust.

(b) Disclaimer after the death of the testator

While a secret trustee may revoke his acceptance of the secret trust at any time before the death of the testator, in principle, disclaimer after the will has taken effect should not invalidate the trust. Despite dicta to the contrary by Cozens-Hardy LJ in *Re Maddock*,[52] dicta of Lord Buckmaster and Lord Warrington in *Blackwell v Blackwell*[53] suggest that a secret trust will not fail if the trustee disclaims the trust subsequent to the testator's death. This is logical because the trust is constituted by the operation of the testator's will, thus crystallizing the secret beneficiary's equitable entitlement to the trust property. Since the trust has come into existence, it should not be allowed to fail for want of a trustee.

9 Can a secret trustee benefit from a secret trust?

In some cases, the trustee of a secret trust will enjoy no personal entitlement to the trust property and will hold it entirely for others. However, in others, the testator may also wish to grant the trustee some entitlement to the trust property, either as a joint beneficiary of the secret trust or by way of a right to retain any surplus funds remaining after the beneficiaries have been allocated their interests. In *Irvine v Sullivan*,[54] it was held that the trustee of a fully secret trust was entitled to retain the surplus of the trust property remaining after the trusts had been carried out. In contrast, in *Re Rees' Will Trusts*,[55] the Court of Appeal held that the trustee of a half-secret trust was not entitled to assert any entitlement to such a surplus because this would be inconsistent with the terms of the will, which suggested that all the property bequeathed to him was subject to the trust. This decision was doubted by Pennycuick J in *Re Tyler's Fund Trusts*,[56] and there is no logical justification for maintaining this differentiation between fully secret and half-secret trusts.[57] It may be significant that in *Re Rees' Will Trusts* the trustee was the testator's solicitor and a beneficial gift was, therefore, inherently less likely.[58]

10 Justifying the enforcement of secret trusts

While it is easy to appreciate the practical advantages that have contributed to the evolution of secret trusts as mechanisms for allocating property on death, it is less easy to provide an adequate explanation of the legal principles justifying their enforcement. They appear to operate in contradiction of the clear policy of the Wills Act since such enforcement appears to permit a testamentary disposition (i.e. a disposition intended to take effect only on death) without satisfaction of the requisite formalities. Equity's effort to provide an adequate explanation for the enforcement of secret trusts is an ex post facto

[52] [1902] 2 Ch 220. [53] [1929] AC 318 at 328, 341. [54] [1869] LR 8 Eq 673.
[55] [1950] Ch 204. [56] [1967] 1 WLR 1269.
[57] See Oakley, *Constructive Trusts* (3rd edn, Sweet & Maxwell 1997), p 259.
[58] See [1950] Ch 204 at 211, per Lord Evershed MR.

rationalization of a mechanism that had already developed. It has already been noted that historically, equity enforced secret trusts on the grounds that to fail to do so would allow the Wills Act to be used as an instrument of fraud. This historic explanation has been eclipsed by a more fashionable alternative. Cases after the decision of the House of Lords in *Blackwell v Blackwell*[59] have held that they are enforced as valid inter vivos trusts arising outside (dehors) the will. The advantage of this explanation is that it does not predicate a conflict between the enforcement of secret trusts and the requirements of the Wills Act 1837, s 9. However, even this theory is not wholly satisfactory.

(1) **Secret trusts enforced to prevent fraud**

In the nineteenth century, equity accepted that secret trusts were enforced in order to prevent fraud. The secret trustee had induced the testator to leave property to him on the understanding that he would apply it for the benefit of the secret beneficiary. If the secret trustee were permitted to deny the trust, because of a lack of testamentary formalities, and to assert a personal entitlement to the property bequeathed to him in the testator's will, he would be using the Wills Act as an instrument of fraud. To prevent such a fraud, equity would allow the admission of parol evidence on behalf of the beneficiary to prove that the bequest had been subject to a trust. This rationale was accepted by the House of Lords in *McCormick v Grogan*,[60] where Lord Hatherley LC described the enforcement of secret trusts as:

> a doctrine which involves a wide departure from the policy of. . . the [Wills Act] and it is only in clear cases of fraud that this doctrine has been applied—cases in which the court has been persuaded that there has been a fraudulent inducement held out on the part of the apparent beneficiary in order to lead the testator to confide to him the duty which he so understood to perform.[61]

Lord Westbury also emphasized that the enforcement of secret trusts was 'founded altogether on personal fraud'.[62] However, despite the early acceptance of the fraud explanation by the House of Lords, it came to be thought that the fraud theory was inadequate as a justification for the enforcement of secret trusts.[63] A number of defects were identified. First, the fraud theory accepts that the enforcement of secret trusts is in direct conflict with the provisions and policy of the Wills Act. Although such conflict has been tolerated in other areas, for example, where the principle of *Rochefoucauld v Boustead*[64] operates to enforce an oral declaration of a trust of land despite the lack of writing, the courts today are reluctant to adopt an analysis so directly opposed to the terms of legislation. Second, a major defect of the fraud theory was that it did not provide an adequate justification for the enforcement of half-secret trusts. In the case of a half-secret trust, the fact of the trust is evident from the face of the will, so that there is no possibility of fraud. The secret trustee cannot take the property absolutely for himself. Fraud would easily be avoided by the secret trustee holding any property received under the will on resulting trust for the residuary legatees or the testator's next of kin. Third, it is questionable whether the fraud theory is also capable of explaining why a fully secret trust should be enforced in favour of the secret beneficiary. While it might justify the refusal to allow the secret trustee to take the property bequeathed to him by the testator absolutely, it is less easy to see why

59 [1929] AC 318. 60 [1869] LR 4 HL 82. 61 [1869] LR 4 HL 82 at 89.

62 [1869] LR 4 HL 82 at 99.

63 See Hodge, 'Secret Trusts: the Fraud Theory Revisited' [1980] Conv 341.

64 [1897] 1 Ch 196, CA.

the possibility of fraud justifies enforcement of the trust in favour of the secret beneficiary. Any fraud could equally be prevented if the trustee was required to hold the property on resulting trust for the residuary legatees under the will or the testator's next of kin. This would prevent the trustee benefiting by his fraud, but would not contradict the provisions of the Wills Act. Fourth, as has been noted earlier, adoption of the fraud theory had the effect that an unduly high burden of proof needed to be discharged if a beneficiary was to establish that property was held on secret trust. In consequence of these inadequacies, the fraud analysis has been rejected in more modern cases.

However, the fraud theory continues to enjoy the support of some academics. Critchley has argued that the modern theory that secret trusts arise outside of the will is implausible, and argues that secret trusts are upheld to prevent fraud where this is demanded by legal policy.[65] Such enforcement will only be justified where there is a combination of personal wrongdoing on the part of the trustee, and harm would be caused to beneficiary and/or testator if the trust were not enforced. The requisite element of personal wrongdoing would only be satisfied if 'the trustee was fully aware that the property was only to be transferred to him on trust, but that he took no steps to deny this understanding until the transfer was completed beyond the recall of the testator'.[66] However, this argument does not address all of the problems identified earlier. Critchley concludes that while the fraud maxim might justify the enforcement of a fully secret trustee where the trustee actively seeks to deny the trust, it is 'less overwhelmingly supportive' of justifying the enforcement of other fully and half-secret trusts. She, therefore, suggests that these other secret trusts must be allowed to tag along in the wake of those which can be justified on the basis of fraud, since otherwise further problems, such as the increase of opportunities for fraud, or of litigation over the construction of the will, seem likely, if not bound, to emerge.[67] It is submitted that this concedes that the fraud theory, even articulated in a more sophisticated form, is incapable of adequately justifying the enforcement of secret trusts.

(2) **Secret trusts arise outside of the testator's will**

The modern justification of the enforcement of secret trusts was neatly summarized by Megarry V-C in *Re Snowden*:[68]

> the whole basis of secret trusts, as I understand it, is that they operate outside the will, changing nothing that is written in it, and allowing it to operate according to its tenor, but then fastening a trust on to the property in the hands of the recipient.

This explanation evolved from the decision of the House of Lords in *Cullen v A-G for Ireland*, where Lord Westbury said:

> I think it very material to point out that where there is a secret trust . . . the title of the party claiming under the secret trust . . . is a title dehors the will, and which cannot be correctly termed testamentary.[69]

It was utilized and developed by the House of Lords in *Blackwell v Blackwell*[70] to justify the enforceability of half-secret trusts. Its overwhelming advantage is that it does not presuppose a contradiction between the enforcement of secret trusts and the Wills Act.[71]

[65] Critchley, 'Instruments of Fraud, Testamentary Dispositions, and the Doctrine of Secret Trusts' [1999] 115 LQR 631.

[66] Ibid at 647. [67] Ibid at 653. [68] [1979] 2 All ER 172 at 177.

[69] [1866] LR 1 HL 190 at 196. [70] [1929] AC 318. [71] [1929] AC 318 at 340.

The essence of this modern justification for the enforcement of secret trusts is that they come into existence entirely outside of the operation of the will to which they relate, so that the equitable interest enjoyed by the secret beneficiary is not a species of testamentary disposition. The modern theory postulates two distinguishable stages in the creation of a valid secret trust. First, the testator communicates to the secret trustee his intention to subject the property bequeathed to a trust, at which point the secret trustee accepts the trust obligation. However, at this point the secret trust has not yet come into existence. The intended subject matter of the trust remains the absolute property of the testator, and the legal title to it has not been transferred to the trustee. In effect the testator and trustee have agreed that the property will be subject to a trust when it comes into the hands of the trustee, but at present the trust remains incompletely constituted. Second, when the testator dies, his will operates according to its terms to transfer the legal title to the secret trustee. His receipt of the property in this way has the effect of constituting the incompletely constituted trust.[72] He, henceforth, holds the property on trust for the secret beneficiary (see Figure 18.1). The secret trust does not, therefore, arise completely independently of the testator's will. As Kincaid has commented:

> A secret trust relies on the death of the settlor to constitute the trust and the terms of the will or the rules of intestate succession to vest the property in the hands of the secret trustee or legatee. The trust can be revoked until the death of the settlor and therefore it does not stand alone until it is properly constituted either *inter vivos* or on the death of the settlor.[73]

This explanation appears to involve no element of conflict between the enforcement of a secret trust and the provisions of the Wills Act. The testator's will operates according to its terms, transferring ownership of the bequeathed property to the legatee. The trust is enforced not under the will, but because the legatee has previously agreed that he will observe the terms of the trust which were communicated to him by the testator. In a sense the secret trust is constituted by a mechanism similar to the rule in *Strong v Bird*[74] examined in Chapter 6.

The practical operation of the modern theory for the enforcement of secret trusts is clearly seen in *Re Young (Decd)*.[75] Roger Young left his entire estate to his wife, Eveleen. Prior to his death, he informed her of his intention that his chauffeur, Thomas Cobb, should receive a legacy of £2,000. This prima facie established a fully secret trust in Cobb's favour. However, Cobb was coincidentally one of the witnesses to Roger's will. By the Wills Act 1837, s 15, a legacy to a person attesting a will is forfeit. The central question was, therefore, whether Cobb's entitlement to the £2,000 subject to the secret trust should be characterized as a legacy under the will, in which case it would be void. Danckwerts J held that the chauffeur was entitled to receive the money because his entitlement was by way of a secret trust which had arisen wholly outside of the will:

> The whole theory of the formulation of a secret trust is that the Wills Act has nothing to do with the matter because the forms required by the Wills Act are entirely disregarded, since the persons do not take by virtue of the gift in the will, but by virtue of the secret trusts imposed upon the beneficiary, who does in fact take under the will.[76]

[72] Critchley, however, argues that this analysis is 'implausible': [1999] 115 LQR 631 at 634.

[73] Kincaid, 'The Tangled Web: The Relationship between a Secret Trust and the Will' [2000] Conv 420 at 442.

[74] [1874] LR 18 Eq 315. [75] [1951] Ch 344. [76] [1951] Ch 344 at 350.

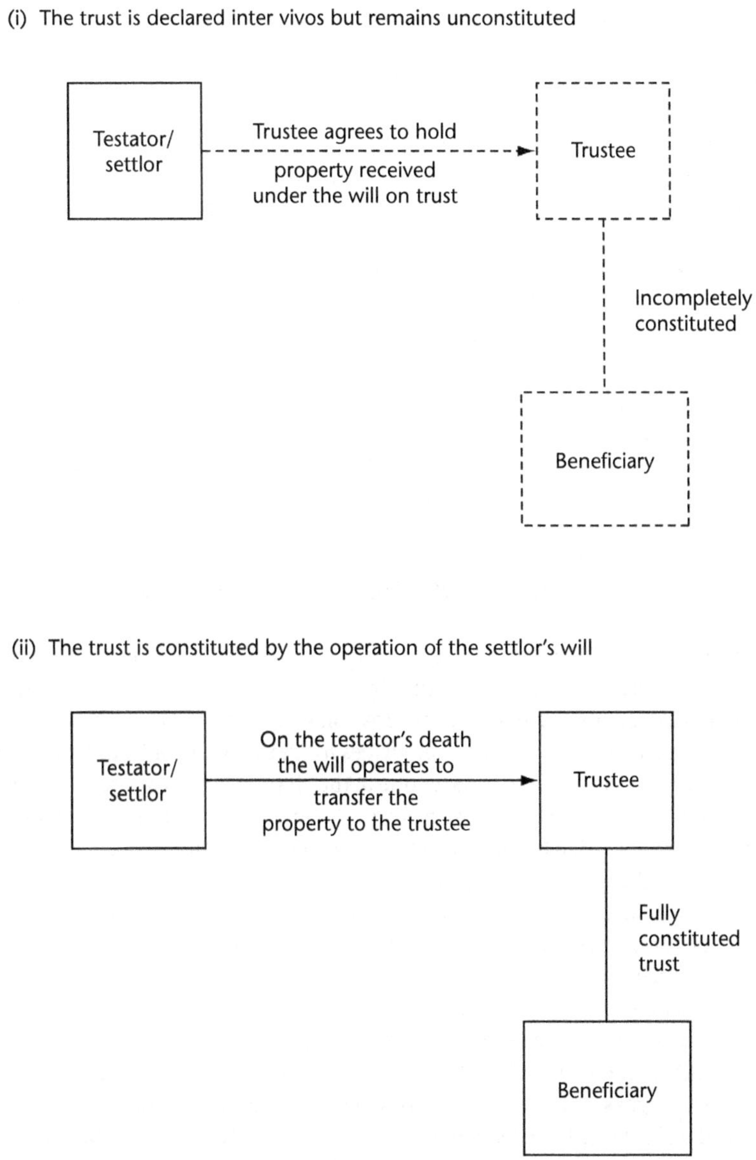

Figure 18.1 The operation of secret trusts

11 Date of accrual of the beneficial interest under a secret trust

A further practical problem that has arisen relates to the time at which the beneficiary of a secret trust acquires the property subject to the trust. In principle, because a secret trust is only fully constituted when the testator's will operates to transfer the bequeathed property to the trustee, a secret beneficiary should not be entitled to any interest in the putative trust property until the death of the testator. Prior to his death, the testator retains the right to change his will, enabling him to subvert the trust by bequeathing the property to someone other than the secret trustee, thus ensuring that the trust is never constituted.[77] The logic of this argument was not, however, followed in *Re Gardner (No 2)*.[78] A testatrix made a will leaving all her property to her husband for life, with the remainder subject to a secret trust in favour of her two nieces and nephew. At the date of the testatrix's death, she had been predeceased by one of her nieces. The court was required to decide whether the personal representative of the niece was entitled to a one-third share of the remainder interest by way of the secret trust. Romer J held that, as a secret beneficiary, the niece had been entitled to her share of the trust property from the moment that the husband had accepted the terms of the trust. Her one-third share was, therefore, held on trust for her personal representative, notwithstanding that she had predeceased the testator. This case is open to the criticism that the niece cannot have gained an interest in the testatrix's estate until her death, since a secret trust remains unconstituted until the will operates to transfer the trust property to the trustee.[79] Prior to the testator's death, the trust does not exist. It is, therefore, submitted that the decision in *Re Gardner (No 2)* is incorrect and that a secret beneficiary enjoys no entitlement to the putative trust property until the trust is fully constituted through the operation of the testator's will.[80]

12 Problems associated with the modern theory

The currently fashionable theory for explaining secret trusts is less elegant than it may seem and has attracted academic criticism. There appears to be no reason why the testator should not change his mind about the creation of the trust prior to his death, either by informing the trustee that he no longer wishes to create a trust or by an amendment to his will. The secret trust, therefore, shares one of the characteristics of a testamentary gift, namely, that it is revocable at any time prior to the testator's death. Furthermore, secret trusts are clearly intended to become operative only on the testator's death, so that they do not in any way inhibit the testator's power to deal as he wishes with his property during his lifetime. This is also a characteristic of a testamentary gift. Finally, in *Re Maddock*,[81] a gift by way of a secret trust was treated as if it had been made by will in a case where the estate was insufficient to meet all the specific gifts made by the testator. The case for treating gifts under a half-secret trust in this way would be even stronger.

Critchley has, therefore, argued that the dehors (outside) the will theory cannot justify the enforcement of secret trusts.[82] She submits that secret trusts are testamentary dispositions because they possess the characteristics of being ambulatory and revocable, in that they do not take effect until the death of the testator, and the testator can change his mind:

> the *dehors* theory seems to be fatally flawed. In essence the mistake is to confuse 'outside the will' with 'outside the Wills Act'. The *dehors* theory needs—and fails—to demonstrate the trust of the latter and too often ends up resting merely upon the former, which is wholly inadequate as a justificatory argument.[83]

[77] Pawlowski and Brown argue, however, that an estoppel equity may arise from the moment that the testator departs from his promise to benefit the secret beneficiary and changes his will: 'Constituting a Secret Trust by Estoppel' [2004] Conv 388.

[78] [1923] 2 Ch 230.

[79] See Pawlowski and Brown, 'Constituting a Secret Trust by Estoppel' [2004] Conv 388.

[80] Glister, 'Disclaimer and Secret Trusts' [2014] Conv 11.

[81] [1902] 2 Ch 220.

[82] Critchley, 'Instruments of Fraud, Testamentary Dispositions, and the Doctrine of Secret Trusts' [1999] 115 LQR 631.

[83] Ibid at 641.

It would be possible to treat secret trusts as well-established anomalies which do not fit easily with any justification. It is also possible to argue that as unjustifiable anomalies, they should no longer be recognized.[84] Aside from these extremes, whilst the fashionable modern theory explaining their operation is imperfect, it has the merit of pragmatism and it is certainly the explanation that commands the support of the authorities.

Evans[85] has argued that the clandestine nature of half-secret trusts (and perhaps even fully secret trusts) can be undermined by the obligation of a solicitor attending the drafting and execution of a will to provide a statement, which according to Buckley LJ in *Larke v Nugus*[86] should:

> extend to all matters surrounding the making of a disputed will which are relevant to the questions in the action and, in my view, should consequently extend to the circumstances leading up to the preparation and making of the will.[87]

Evans suggests that this may import an obligation to disclose the terms of any secret or half-secret trust if the solicitor was involved in drafting them as part of the process of making a will. In making this argument, Evans is probably mistaken. Firstly, not all secret trusts are clandestine. Secondly, although Evans cites *Schmidt v Rosewood Trust Ltd* as confirming a trend towards openness and transparency, he does not observe that the case also establishes that in ordering the disclosure of information about a trust the court must perform a balancing act to protect confidential information, and that disclosure in that case was ordered only subject to safeguards to prevent the claimants seeing information in which they had no legitimate interest. If the order in *Larke v Negus* seems to be in more absolute terms, this can be explained because there was not in that instance any competing consideration of preserving confidence.

13 The juridical nature of secret trusts

The accepted modern justification for enforcement of secret trusts is that they arise inter vivos outside of the will. However, the acceptance of this theory does not of itself answer the question whether secret trusts should be characterized as express or constructive trusts. This is not an entirely esoteric academic question. If secret trusts are characterized as express in nature, practical difficulties arise where the intended trust property is land or an interest in land, as s 53(1)(b) of the Law of Property Act 1925 renders an oral declaration of a trust of land unenforceable without substantiating evidence in writing. In contrast, if they are characterized as constructive in nature, a secret trust of land will be enforceable without the need for further formalities as s 53(2) exempts all constructive trusts from the need of writing.

(1) Secret trusts characterized as express trusts

The modern theory that secret trusts arise inter vivos outside of the testator's will would logically suggest that they are express in nature. The acceptance of the trust by the secret trustee amounts to an express inter vivos declaration of trust. This view has been favoured

[84] Emma Challinor has argued that no logical rationale for the enforcement of secret trusts may be discerned, and that they are covert devices by which the courts avoid the statutory formalities of the Wills Act 1837, thus subverting the policy of the Wills Act: 'Debunking the Myth of Secret Trusts?' [2005] Conv 493. She, therefore, proposes abolition or fundamental revision of the law relating to secret trusts.

[85] Evans, 'Should Professionally Drafted Half-Secret Trusts Be Extinct after *Larke v Nugus*?' [2014] Conv 229.

[86] [2000] WTLR 1033.

[87] Ibid at 1047B.

in the past by most academic writers.[88] However, such a characterization could produce the unsatisfactory implication of rendering an oral agreement to hold land subject to a secret trust unenforceable through the absence of writing, as required by s 53(1)(b) of the Law of Property Act 1925.[89] Thus, in *Re Baillie*,[90] North J held a secret trust of land unenforceable because the Statute of Frauds applied and the trust had not been indicated in writing. In other cases, for example, *Ottaway v Norman*,[91] orally declared secret trusts of land have been enforced without question. Of itself the enforcement of the trusts in such cases fails to prove the point, since a trust will not fail for lack of formalities unless the absence of writing is specifically pleaded as a ground of invalidity.[92] However, even if secret trusts are characterized as express trusts, it is submitted that an orally declared secret trust of land should not fail merely because of the lack of writing. The court should invoke the well-established doctrine of *Rochefoucauld v Boustead*,[93] namely, that equity will not allow the statute requiring trusts of land to be evidenced in writing to be used as an instrument of fraud, to prevent the secret trustee denying the trust because of the absence of writing. This would not mark a reversion to the fraud explanation of the enforcement of secret trusts in conflict with the terms of the Wills Act, as the rule in *Rochefoucauld v Boustead* would only be employed to prevent the use of s 53(1)(b) of the Law of Property Act as an instrument of fraud.

(2) **Secret trusts characterized as constructive trusts**

Despite traditional academic consensus that secret trusts are express in nature, in *Re Cleaver*,[94] Nourse J characterized them as constructive trusts. As the case concerned the doctrine of mutual wills, his expression of opinion is strictly obiter. A number of commentators have adopted the view that secret trusts are gratuitous promises enforced as constructive trusts on the grounds of fraud or unconscionability.[95]

[88] See Snell, *Principles of Equity* (30th edn, Sweet & Maxwell 2000), pp 132–6; Pettit, *Equity and the Law of Trusts* (12th edn, Oxford University Press 2009); Oakley, *Constructive Trusts* (3rd edn, Sweet & Maxwell 1997), p 263; [1991] 5 Tru LI 69 (Caughlon). See also Sheridan, 'English and Irish Secret Trusts' [1951] 67 LQR 314—where half-secret trusts are held to be express, but fully secret trusts to be constructive.

[89] See Chapter 6. [90] [1886] 2 TLR 660. [91] [1972] Ch 698.

[92] *North v Loomes* [1919] 1 Ch 378. [93] [1897] 1 Ch 196, CA.

[94] [1981] 1 WLR 939.

[95] McFarlane, 'Constructive Trusts Arising on a Receipt of Property Sub Conditione' [2004] 120 LQR 667.

PART VI

Charitable Trusts

19. The role and status of charities 421
20. Charitable purposes 432
21. Public benefit 471
22. Cy-près: redistributing funds and changing purposes 493
23. Regulation and control of charitable trusts 510

19

The role and status of charities

1 Introduction

Except for some anomalous exceptions, gifts for purposes will fail by virtue of the 'beneficiary principle'. The most significant exception to this is the area of charitable giving, where the law upholds and encourages giving to purposes that are regarded in law as charitable. Charity has a legal meaning, well beyond the everyday concept of helping the underprivileged in society. Charities can take a variety of forms, which include but are not limited to, charitable trusts. Charities receive financial benefits from the state in the form of tax exemptions, and also legal advantages over trusts set up for private beneficiaries.

This chapter considers the nature and benefits of an organization gaining charitable status. Chapters 20 and 21 provide an in-depth look at the legal requirements to be granted charitable status, charitable purposes, and the public benefit requirement respectively. Schemes for dealing with surplus property for charities are detailed in Chapter 22, and the regulation and control of charitable activity is considered in the final chapter of this part, Chapter 23.

2 Charities in society

(1) The influence of charities

Charity, in the sense of doing good for one's fellow man, is often linked with philanthropy, which is the desire to promote the welfare of others. However, the legal definition of charity is one that is carefully controlled, owing to the advantages that organizations which are classed as charities at law enjoy. Nevertheless, it includes a variety of purposes which impact the everyday lives of citizens. The word 'charity' conjures up images of either Dickensian levels of poverty or malnourished children in far-flung countries, such is the impact of visual media in our everyday lives. While the relief of poverty and famine relief overseas would be considered charitable purposes under the law, the reach of charities as part of the fabric of society is such that, as noted by the House of Lords Select Committee on the future of charities:

> Charities are the eyes, ears and conscience of society. They mobilise, they provide, they inspire, they advocate and they unite. From small local organisations run entirely by volunteers to major global organisations with turnover in the hundreds of millions, their work touches almost every facet of British civic life.[1]

It follows that many people in England and Wales have real, if unknowing, contact with the law of charitable trusts, whether they are putting a small donation into collection boxes or envelopes, putting something into a collection at church, signing a Gift Aid

[1] House of Lords Select Committee on Charities *Stronger Charities for a Stronger Society* HL Paper 133 (March 2017), p 3.

declaration on admission to National Trust properties, contributing regularly through payroll giving schemes, or responding to major disaster appeals.

(2) The extent of the charity sector

There is such variance in the nature, variety, and size of charities in England and Wales that it is often difficult to treat them as one, complete sector. The charitable organizations themselves can be, at one end of the scale, a small group of enthusiastic volunteers, very much rooted in pursuing social good in a particular locale in England and Wales, to huge, multinational organizations such as Oxfam, who operate across the whole of the UK and overseas.

Charities form a very significant part of a wider civil society,[2] which includes 'not for profit', voluntary and community sector, social enterprise, and mutual societies or organizations, cooperatives, and non-governmental organizations, all working independently of direct governmental direction.

In 2020, the Charity Commission reported that there were 168,033 registered charities,[3] with an annual income of over £81 billion.[4] In the year 2019–20, the Charity Commission received an average of 23 applications for the register a day, although it removed 6,046.[5] There is a trend that sees the number of registered charities grow rather than contract year on year.[6] There are inefficiencies in having too many organizations dealing with the same issues, and it is true that there is much duplication of effort across charities which can lead to fragmentation in pursuing charitable purposes.[7]

(3) Charity finance

A high proportion of total charity funds are held by a small number of very large charities, such as the famous Wellcome Trust, with investments generating a net income of £2.23 billion in 2019, spending £1.1 billion, mostly on scientific research.[8] At the other end of the scale, there are charities with very small funds, or even no investments at all. Large charities will have a board of trustees with professional backgrounds. In the case of Wellcome Trust, they will occasionally break the sector norm and pay their trustees. By contrast, at small charities the trustees are almost exclusively volunteers.[9]

One significant source of income for charities comes from public donations, either from individuals or corporate donations. Charities such as 'Comic Relief' or 'Children in Need' have high-profile fundraising campaigns on television and social media and raise significant sums in the millions from events running alongside the main telethons, but the importance attached to charities more generally is demonstrated by the fact that,

[2] See Garton, *The Regulation of Organised Civil Society* (Hart 2009).

[3] Not all charities are required to be registered, so the actual number of charities in England and Wales will be slightly higher than the figure presented here. Definitive figures are difficult to find, but in 2012, a report from the National Audit Office estimated that there may be as many as 191,000 unregistered charities with an income close to £58bn—*Regulating charities: a landscape review* (July 2012).

[4] Charity Commission Annual Report and Accounts 2019–20.

[5] Ibid, p 25.

[6] 2007 was a statistical high for charities, with 169,297 on the register. The fact remains that numbers have been growing rather than contracting over the last few years.

[7] This has drawn attention and criticism—see, for example, Warburton and Barr, 'Charity mergers—property problems' [2002] Conv 531, 531.

[8] Wellcome Trust Annual Report and Financial Statements 2019.

[9] For an analysis of the impact of the size of a charity on effective regulation, see, Sigafoos and Picton,'Charity Law and Policy: Looking Forward' in Picton and Sigafoos (eds), *Debates in Charity Law* (Hart 2020) p 301.

in 2018, the value of charitable donations from individuals was estimated to be approximately £10.1 billion.[10] This includes legacies (gifts by will). Charities are also increasingly financed by income from commercial activity (such as charity shops), contracts or commission from central government, and Lotto (National Lottery) funding.[11] According to the NCVO UK Civil Society Almanac, these sources of funding outstrip donations and legacies.

(4) **People and charities**

The other impact on society is the opportunities charities offer to the public. Charities are for people, but also depend on people. Charities are often overseen and controlled by trustees. These can range from highly skilled professionals, dedicating their time and experience to facilitate the operations of their chosen charity, to local residents, passionate about the cause that a charity pursues in their area. In line with the general principle that the office of trustee is voluntary, such trustees are generally unpaid.[12] The voluntary principle of trusteeship is a contentious one in the charity sector, as for many it sits at odds with attracting the best people to run charitable organizations, who may feel the need to be paid something for their time and skill, while others feel that the voluntary nature of trusteeship is a key element of the effectiveness of the sector.[13] Most charity trustees are motivated by altruism, but they benefit from the training and opportunities available from working in some organizations. This helps explain why there were 940,000 trustees of registered charities in the year 2019–20.[14]

It is estimated that charities provide employment for over 900,000 people[15] in the UK. Volunteers who give up their free time unpaid to further the work of charities are often referred to as the lifeblood of the sector, and without the input of over 19 million volunteers[16] many charities would simply be unable to carry out their purposes.

(5) **A brief history of charities**

Charity has a long history.[17] Originally, provision for the poor was the purview of the Church, but, by the reign of Elizabeth I, the establishment of a wealthy merchant class, as well as a decline in the influence of the Church in society, saw a move to private philanthropy and to purposes such as education or poor relief. During Tudor times, vast economic change meant that the state could no longer ignore poverty. Alongside statutory provision of the poor, the Court of Chancery recognized and enforced charitable uses, which, as they grew in popularity, became the legal mechanism of choice to dispense charitable activity. In time, as with all uses, these become charitable trusts, and they were

[10] This is a UK figure, so not limited to England and Wales. See Charities Aid Foundation, *UK Giving 2019* (May 2019) p 11.

[11] In the year ending March 2020, health, education, environment, and charitable causes received 40 per cent of Lotto funding of a sum of £1,853 million.

[12] Payment of trustees must be distinguished from reimbursement of expenses, which are permissible—see Chapter 35.

[13] See, for example, the House of Lords Select Committee report (n 1), where the voluntary principle is stressed, though commentators have suggested this was something of a missed opportunity—Morris and Barr, 'Will the Lords Report on Charities Be Helpful?' 13 April 2017, *Third Sector* (https://www.thirdsector.co.uk/debra%20morris%20warren%20barr%20will%20lords%20report%20charities%20helpful/policy%20and%20politics/article/1430505).

[14] Charity Commission Annual Report and Accounts 2019–20.

[15] NCVO Civil Society Almanac 2020. [16] Ibid.

[17] See, for example, Jones, *History of the Law of Charity 1532–1827* (Cambridge University Press 1969); Weiner, 'Social Control in Nineteenth Century Britain' (1978) V 12 *Journal of Social History* 314.

enforced by the Attorney-General, in the absence of private individuals who benefitted from these purpose trusts. By 1601, a series of statutory poor laws had been enacted,[18] alongside the Statute of Charitable Uses 1601, which gave powers to investigate abuse of charitable trusts.[19]

The next major development in charity law came with the sweeping impact of the industrial revolution across England and Wales in the eighteenth and nineteenth centuries. Alongside state provision for the poor, which included the provision of workhouses,[20] private philanthropy sought to alleviate poverty for those in need. Alongside these developments, many of the institutions now recognizable as part of society, such as hospitals for the relief of suffering, were established. Charity law developed apace, and the recognition of legal and fiscal privileges to charities, the basic shape of regulation through Charity Commissioners and the defining approach to recognizing charitable purposes for the public benefit were all established by end of the nineteenth century.[21]

The twentieth century saw the emergence of the modern welfare state, so that the state became the major provider of welfare, taking over hospitals, schools, housing, and provision for the impoverished. This was consolidated in the 1940s in the aftermath of the Second World War, which saw the implementation of the National Health Service,[22] free education for children in primary and secondary schools,[23] and the abolition of the poor law system, replaced by a system of social security payments for those out of work.[24]

The charity sector did not disappear during this period, but instead reconfigured to fill gaps in state provision, or to establish new provision, such as hospice provision for the terminally ill. Two major reports in this era, the Nathan Report[25] and the Wolfenden Report,[26] both concluded that charities still had a valuable role to play in society. These included acting as a critic of state provision and campaigning for change. In the 1960s and 70s, economic decline hit public expenditure on social welfare, and this led to the establishment of some instantly recognizable charities, such as Shelter,[27] to deal with the impact of economic uncertainty. Slowly, through the 1980s and 90s, the welfare state moved from the position of the provider of services to the public to the commissioner of services, from either the private or voluntary and charitable sectors.[28] Charities were seen as a key part of this provision (as evidenced by the Deakin report commissioned by the National Council for Voluntary Organizations),[29] and continued to grow in this period.

[18] Poor relief could take many forms, including payment of rent, food, goods, and money for that individual and his family. The system included punishment for the 'idle' poor—those who were deemed able to work but chose not to. These punishments could be horrific, such as whipping in the streets or ear-boring, and such invididuals could also be imprisoned. See, for example, Charlesworth, 'The Poor Law: A Modern Legal Analysis' [1999] 6(2) *Journal of Social Security Law* 79.

[19] The legacy of the 1601 statute lies, however, in the preamble, which listed certain charitable uses and became the foundation of the present-day legal definition of charity.

[20] Conditions in workhouses were dreadful, and their establishment continued the concept that poverty was a social evil brought upon those in need by idleness in all but the most vulnerable and needy, rather than an issue which required proper treatment. See, for example, Green, 'Pauper Protests: Power and Resistance in Early Nineteenth-Century London Workhouses' [2006] *Social History* 137.

[21] See *Income Tax Special Purposes Comrs v Pemsel* [1891] AC 531, itself following the pivotal decision in *Morice v Bishop of Durham* [1804] 9 Ves 399.

[22] National Health Service Act 1946.

[23] Education Act 1944.

[24] National Assistance Act 1948.

[25] *Report of the Committee on the Law and Practice Relating to Charitable Trusts* (Cmd 8710, 1952).

[26] Wolfenden Committee, *The Future of Voluntary Organisations* [1978].

[27] Established 1966, principally to deal with the issue of homelessness.

[28] For an interesting treatment, see Johnson, *Reconstructing the Welfare State: A Decade of Change 1980–1990* (Harvester 1990). See also Lewis, 'Reviewing the Relationship Between the Voluntary Sector and the State in Britain in the 1990s' [1999] 3 *Voluntas* 255.

[29] *Meeting the Challenge of Change: Voluntary Action into the 21st Century* (NCVO Publications 1996).

(6) The continuing importance of charities

Charities remain as relevant today as they were in the past. The move towards looking to charities to provide welfare services has continued into the twenty-first century. Charities are viewed as an essential component of social provision,[30] as they encourage and create 'new services ... [which plug] gaps in delivery ... and often focus on meeting the needs of the disadvantaged and socially excluded'.[31]

The success of charitable organizations in carrying out their purposes has led to a view that charities (and other voluntary organizations) should be utilized in providing front-line public services, such as social housing, rather than simply providing additional or complementary services to those for which the state has responsibility. This initiative, originally referred to as 'the Third Way', and then 'Big Society',[32] is an extension of state commission of welfare services, and it seeks to make charities enablers and providers of public services. In an important registration decision,[33] the Charity Commission confirmed that charities should be free to undertake public services of whatever nature, provided the normal characteristics of a charity are present and that the charity remains independent.

However, the desirability of this sort of initiative has been questioned, both in terms of the charity sector's capacity to do what is asked of it against a backdrop of huge public service cuts[34] and at a more theoretical level, as freedom to critique the welfare provision of the state (a vital role of charities) and independence in running charity affairs are potential costs of such close alignment of charities and state.[35]

Charity law has seen major development in the twenty-first century, both in terms of statutory enactments and in terms of regulatory change, and interest has never been greater in the impact of charities than it is today. The rise of other not-for-profit organizations, as well as social enterprises (companies with a social conscience), mean that charities operate in an increasingly complex, multi-plural society. In 2017, the House of Lords Select Committee on the future of charity law, whilst concluding that charities are vital in a changing world, in a final report of 150 pages, came up with over one hundred conclusions, including forty-two recommendations.[36] Many of these are about charities adapting to the world in which they operate to make themselves as effective as possible,[37] whereas others call for governmental backing. The government response to this report, while broadly supportive in tone, stops far short of any legislative or other substantive change in policy or regulation.[38] Civil Society Futures has launched an ambitious

[30] See HM Treasury, *Exploring the Third Sector In Public Service Delivery and Reform: A Discussion Document* [2005], Ch 1.

[31] FCO, 'Implementing the Cross Cutting Review on "The Role of the Voluntary and Community Sector in Service Delivery"' [2004].

[32] Cabinet Office, *Building The Big Society* (May 2010); Holt 'The Big Idea' [2011] *Solicitor's Journal*, Charity & Appeals Supplement, February.

[33] Charity Commission, Decisions of the Charity Commission for England and Wales, Applications for Registration (i) Trafford Community Leisure Trust; and (ii) Wigan Leisure and Culture Trust, April 2004.

[34] See Morris, 'Charities and the Big Society: A Doomed Coalition?' [2012] *Legal Studies* 132; and in a narrower context of social housing, Barr, 'The Big Society and Social Housing: Never the Twain Shall Meet?' in Hopkins (ed), *Modern Studies in Property Law: Volume 7*, [2013], Ch 3.

[35] See Glover-Thomas and Barr, 'Enabling or Disabling? Increasing Involvement of Charities in Social Housing' [2009] Conv 209.

[36] *Stronger Charities for a Stronger Society* (HL Paper 133, March 2017).

[37] Having a strong digital media presence, by way of example, given the importance of social media to inform and inspire in the modern world.

[38] Department for Culture, Media & Sport, *Response to 'Stronger Charities for a Stronger Society' the Report of the House of Lords Committee on Charities*, December 2017. This has drawn criticism from Baroness Pitkeathly (who chaired the HL Committee), including the tardiness of the reply—see https://www.thirdsector.co.uk/baroness-pitkeathley-criticises-government-disappointing-response-lords-report/policy-and-politics/article/1454727.

two-year project that involves a national conversation to consider the future of charities as part of wider civil society.[39] This may well lead to substantive change. Such major projects and reports continue to underline the vitality and importance of charities to contemporary life.

3 Mechanisms for charitable giving

Owners of property may decide to apply it for the furtherance of charitable purposes in a variety of ways. Charities are not limited in form to charitable trusts, though it is charitable trusts and the equitable rules that surround them that are the focus of this part of the textbook.[40]

(1) Outright gifts to charitable organizations

An owner may make a gift to an organization which enjoys charitable status, whether an unincorporated association or a charitable corporation. Charitable corporations may be established by royal charter (as is the case with many of the older universities); as a company limited by guarantee; by virtue of specific legislation (as is the case with further education corporations); or, following the Charities Act 2006 (consolidated in the Charities Act 2011 Part 11), as a charitable incorporated organization (CIO) registered as such by the Charity Commission.[41] The organization will receive the property, and apply it to its charitable purposes. A gift to Cancer Research UK, Oxfam GB (both companies limited by guarantee), or to a particular educational establishment would be such a gift.

(2) Trusts in favour of defined charitable objects

Alternatively, an owner may transfer property to trustees to be used for specified charitable purposes. In such a case, the trustees will be subject to a duty to apply the funds to those purposes only. A gift by will to trustees to be applied for the education of the testator's poor relations would be an example.

(3) Discretionary trusts in favour of charitable objects

An owner may alternatively transfer the property to trustees, granting them discretion as to the charitable purposes to which the fund may be applied. This may be a wide discretion, for example a gift of '£100,000 to trustees to be applied for such charitable purposes as they see fit', or the owner may place limits on the width of the discretion, for example, 'for such educational charities as they see fit'.

[39] See https://civilsocietyfutures.org/.

[40] For a brief introduction to the different forms of charity, see *Technical Issues in Charity Law* (Law Com No 375 September 2017), Ch 2: The Different Types of Charity. See, generally, Picarda QC, *The Law and Practice Relating to Charities* (4th edn, Bloomsbury 2010); Charity Commission, *Charity Types: How to Choose a Structure (CC22a)* (updated 4 November 2014).

[41] The operation, regulation, and potential benefits of the CIO are beyond the scope of this text, but in essence, the structure seeks to provide the advantages of a corporate structure (including limited liability) without the burden of regulation under company law. CIOs are an increasingly popular model, and in 2016–17 accounted for 3,684 of the 6,045 charities registered in that year—Charity Commission, *Annual Reports & Accounts 2016–17* (July 2017). Their popularity is likely to grow, as it is now possible, from 1 January 2018, for existing incorporated charities and community interest companies to convert to CIOs—see The Charitable Incorporated Organisations (Conversions) Regulations 2017.

(4) **All charitable institutions are treated similarly**

Whether a charity exists as an incorporated or unincorporated body or as a trust, it is governed by essentially similar rules.[42]

4 The unity of charity

Although there are numerous charitable organizations, and distinct charitable purposes covering wide ranges of human activity, in some senses, the law regards all property dedicated to charity as comprising a single fund, a 'common pot'. This is evident in the way that a gift 'to charity' will be upheld, despite the absence of any indication of the giver's intention as to how it should be used. In such circumstances, the Crown disposes of the property to charitable purposes by sign manual. Similarly, if a charity fails, or a charitable purpose comes to an end, any property dedicated to that charity or purpose will be applied to other similar charitable purposes under the principle of cy-près.[43] The property, once dedicated to charity, is seen as placed into the 'common pot', and cannot be removed from it, but will be applied to other purposes. Hence, it is not possible for an organization that has become a charity to voluntarily cease operating as a charity, taking with it its assets, as the property is held for charitable purposes.

5 Regulation and control of charities

Given both the quantity of money concerned and the dangers of abuse and misuse, the area of charities is regulated by the government. The Attorney-General enforces charitable trusts in the name of the Crown, but they are regulated and overseen by the Charity Commission,[44] which plays the predominant role in the supervision and regulation of charities. This regulation and supervision will be examined in Chapter 23. The law concerning the regulation of charities was consolidated through a variety of acts, culminating in the Charities Act 2011, as amended by the Charities (Protection and Social Investment) Act 2016. Regulation provides an important public validation of charitable organizations, and a safeguard for those contributing to worthy causes. It is a truism that 'trust is the voluntary sector exchange rate',[45] so that an effective charity 'is accountable to the public and other stakeholders in a way that is transparent and understandable'.[46] There have, unfortunately, been many high-profile charity scandals in the media over the last decade, which have eroded this trust—some of these are discussed in Chapter 23.[47]

Most charities are required to be registered,[48] and the Charity Commission also undertakes the process of registration and the maintenance of the register.

[42] This treatment is concerned with charitable trusts, though many of the rules also apply to charitable corporations. Charitable companies are also subject to the rules of company law, which means that they are subject to two regulatory regimes.

[43] Discussed in Chapter 22.

[44] Prior to the Charities Act 2006 that constituted the Charity Commission as an incorporated body, the functions of the Commission were vested in the Charity Commissioners.

[45] NCVO, 'Blurred vision' in *Research Quarterly* Issue 1, January 1998.

[46] Charity Commission, CC10, *The Hallmarks of an Effective Charity* (July 2008), p 11.

[47] Scandals in early 2018 included reports that aid was offered in return for sex by Oxfam workers in Haiti, and alleged sexual harassment at an all-male charity dinner of the 'Presidents Club'.

[48] Each registered charity is given a unique registration number. The register is open to public inspection, and is now computerized.

6 Negative perceptions of charity

While the social importance of charities has been explored, the concept of 'charity' is not without difficulty. Few, if any, recipients[49] of charitable endeavours would like to be referred to as 'objects of charity', as there are negative connotations in that status. Similarly, research undertaken for the Charity Commission suggests that public trust and confidence in the charity sector has fallen significantly in recent years.[50] The reasons for this are multifarious and include fears that charities might be used to facilitate money-laundering or be misused to raise funds for terrorist activity,[51] the concern that charitable organizations are using intrusive fundraising methods;[52] concerns as to how donations to charities were actually being spent and how much of the money raised was reaching the end cause;[53] distrust of the ways in which some charitable organizations carry out their functions; and a view that charities should not be using public money to pay for a service that the public purse was already financing, as there was a duty on the government to provide the service directly through public sector organizations. Altruism alone no longer fuels private donations to charities by individuals. There is also a widely held view that there are too many charities.[54]

The Charities Act 2006, now consolidated in the 2011 Act, brought some significant changes to the regulation of charities and to the promotion of the work that they do, and seeks to address some of the negative aspects of the charity 'brand'.[55] The Charity Commission's first statutory objective, as regulator of the sector, is to increase public trust and confidence in charities.[56] This trend might not be permanent. Despite the gloom in the sector concerning public perceptions and trust, there is evidence that matters might be improving. Recently, the Charity Commission has stated that, while reported levels of trust remains lower than in the past, there has been a small uptick in trust and confidence in the sector.[57]

7 Privileges enjoyed by charitable trusts

Charities and charitable trusts are granted various privileges that are not enjoyed by other private trusts. In *Dingle v Turner*,[58] Lord Cross observed that the privileges enjoyed by charitable trusts were of 'two quite different sorts', namely privileges as to their

[49] The choice of language is important. Charitable trusts are for purposes, so do not have named beneficiaries, as they must benefit (a sufficient cross-section of) the public to be classed as charitable.

[50] Charity Commission, *Public Trust and Confidence in Charities 2016* (June 2016).

[51] See, for example, Knobel, 'Trusts: Weapons of Mass Injustice?' *Tax Justice Network*, February 2017.

[52] The Olive Cooke saga, which saw a pensioner harried to her eventual suicide by over-zealous charity appeals, is one of the high-profile and damaging scandals, discussed in Chapter 23. This has led to sharp changes in allowable fundraising practice (see the Charities (Protection and Social Investment) Act 2016, s 13) and the creation of a Fundraising Regulator.

[53] This was the strongest reason not to trust one charity over another—Charity Commission, *Public Trust and Confidence in Charities 2016* (June 2016), p 30.

[54] See, for example, Buzzacott and Third Sector, *Major Issues Facing Charities in 2000* (75 per cent of businesses responding felt that charities with similar purposes should merge). The latest intelligence suggests that charity mergers remain rare, with only 142 organizations undertaking seventy mergers in the year 2016–17—Bidgood, *Good Merger Index 2016–17* (Eastside Primetimers, 2017).

[55] The Act is concerned with the modernization of both the regulatory framework for charities and, to a lesser extent, the rationalization of the legal principles underpinning charity law. The Act has a chequered history, explored further later, but in essence it arose following a process of review undertaken by the Charity Commissioners and, more significantly, a report of the Cabinet Office Strategy Unit, *Private Action, Public Benefit, A Review of Charities and the Wider Not-For-Profit Sector* (2002). Challenges to the charity brand are considered alongside regulation of charities in Chapter 23.

[56] Charities Act 2011, s 14.

[57] Charity Commission Annual Report and Accounts 2019–20.

[58] [1972] AC 601.

essential validity, and financial privileges through exemption from some forms of taxation. Underlying this privileged status of charitable trusts is public policy, which seeks to encourage benevolent giving to purposes that are in the public interest.

(1) Privileges as to essential validity

Charitable trusts enjoy exemption from various requirements that would render a non-charitable trust invalid.

(a) Purpose trusts

It is a trite proposition that private non-charitable trusts must be for the benefit of persons and not purposes.[59] Charitable trusts are thus the major exception to this 'beneficiary principle'. However, since a mechanism for the enforcement of charitable trusts is provided by the state rather than individual beneficiaries litigating in pursuit of their own interests, the chief objection to purpose trusts (that there is nobody in whose favour the court can decree performance of the trust)[60] does not apply. Charitable trusts are enforced by the Charity Commission or by the Attorney-General in the name of the Crown.

(b) Certainty of objects

While non-charitable trusts must have objects that are certain, gifts made exclusively for charitable purposes are valid even though the exact purposes have not been identified with certainty. Thus, a gift to trustees 'for charity' will be valid. Sometimes the courts have gone very far indeed to find a valid gift even where the charitable objects of the donor are not certain. To take one example, in *Re Davis*,[61] a testamentary donor left a gift to the 'Home for the Homeless, 27, Red Lion Square, London'. The organization did not exist. Although it is difficult to think of a clearer example of an uncertain object, Buckley J found that the gift was valid because the donor had a general charitable intention.[62] This liberal legal attitude to chartable certainty flows from the fact that the law regards 'charity' as if it were a single common pot, and since the gift was certainly intended for that common pot, it will be upheld. If the exact charitable purposes to which the owner of the property intends to give are uncertain, the Charity Commission[63] and the court have jurisdiction to draw up a scheme to apply the funds.

(c) Perpetuity

Charitable trusts are valid even though they may last for an indefinite period of time. They are exempt from the rule against inalienability, by which trusts requiring capital to be retained for a period longer than the perpetuity period of a life in being plus twenty-one years are invalid. However, the rule against remoteness of vesting applies to gifts to charities as to other gifts. This rule requires that all property given to the trust must vest during the perpetuity period of 125 years laid down by the Perpetuities and Accumulations Act 2009 (see Chapter 8). There is a special exception for charities where there is a gift over from one charity to another charity. The gift to the second charity will be valid even though it takes place outside of the perpetuity period.[64] The exception was used in *Re Tyler*[65] to give effect indirectly to a non-charitable purpose. Sir James Tyler left

[59] There are a small number of anomalous exceptions.

[60] *Morice v Bishop of Durham* [1804] 9 Ves 399.

[61] [1902] 1 Ch 876. The gift was saved for charity under the cy-près doctrine.

[62] See also *Re Constable* [1971] VR 742. For analysis of the testamentary rules in this area, see Picton, 'Reconstructing Charitable Intention' (2013) 15 *Charity Law and Practice Review* 125.

[63] Charities Act 2011, Pt 6.

[64] *Re Hanbey's Will Trusts* [1956] Ch 364 (Ch).

[65] [1891] 3 Ch 252, CA.

£42,000 of stock to the London Missionary Society, with the condition that they were to maintain his family vault. If the condition was broken, there was a gift over in favour of the Blue Coat School. The gift over did not render the gift void for perpetuity, even though it could conceivably have vested outside of the perpetuity period. Although the London Missionary Society could not be compelled to maintain the vault, they would have had a strong financial incentive to do so.

(2) **Financial privileges**

Charities and charitable trusts enjoy tremendous financial advantages over private trusts. It is difficult to be certain of the precise value of these privileges, but HM Revenue and Customs estimated that in the year 2018–19, the value of tax relief for charities was around £3.8 billion.[66] This is likely to be a conservative estimate, and it does not include the value of tax advantages (excluding Gift Aid) that are provided to donors to promote donation to charity, either corporate or as private individuals.[67] Charities are exempt from tax on income and capital gains from most sources, and may be exempt from tax on certain trading activities, such as running a charity shop.[68] Gifts to charities are exempt from inheritance tax.[69] Charities also benefit from Gift Aid donations, whereby the charity can reclaim the basic rate of tax on the gift.[70] There is an 80 per cent exemption from non-domestic rates on properties they occupy.[71] Charities are not exempt from VAT. These financial privileges amount to a massive state subsidy of charitable trusts. Some charities may even enjoy exceptional financial privileges. For example, in *Scott v National Trust*,[72] Robert Walker J observed that the trust, which was established by statute, is a charity 'whose special place in the affairs of the nation has been recognized by tax exemptions and reliefs (especially in connection with capital taxation) going well beyond those accorded to charities generally'.[73]

(3) **Are the privileges afforded to charities justified?**

It is clear that charitable trusts enjoy tremendous advantages over non-charitable trusts through their enjoyment of these privileges. The justification for such advantageous treatment is that charitable purposes are of sufficient importance to the community at large that they deserve both to be upheld and encouraged. It is for this reason that the definition of charity focuses on the notion of 'public benefit', for only those purposes that can be said to be of benefit to the public as a whole can be considered worthy of such special treatment. However, it is questionable whether all charities and charitable trusts need be treated alike. At the moment, every charitable trust enjoys not only the privileges as to

[66] HMRC, *UK Charity Tax Relief Statistics 1990–91 to 2018–19*.

[67] These include, for private individuals, employer payroll deduction schemes, whereby employees can obtain tax relief for donations to charity deducted from their wages (see Income Tax (Earning and Pensions) Act 2003, ss 713–15). Corporate donations may be deductible from taxable profits for the purposes of corporation tax, for example, through Gift Aid (Income and Corporations Tax Act 1988, s 339).

[68] See HMRC guidance note at www.hmrc.gov.uk/charities/guidance-notes/annex1/annex_i.htm.

[69] Inheritance Tax Act 1984, ss 23 and 76.

[70] Total donations from individuals and companies in the United Kingdom on which Gift Aid was reclaimed in 2015/16 were £5.05 bn. See Income Tax Act 2007, ss 413–30 and 520–2 (individuals); Corporation Tax Act 2010 ss 191–202 (corporations). On 21 November 2013, the National Audit Office published a report, *Gift Aid and Reliefs on Donations*, finding that the HMRC was not able to prove that the scheme had met its objective of encouraging charitable giving.

[71] Local Government Finance Act 1988, s 43(5); under s 47, the rating authority has discretion to relieve up to the whole amount payable.

[72] [1998] 2 All ER 705. [73] [1998] 2 All ER 705 at 710.

essential validity but also the financial privileges. There is no necessary reason why every charitable trust should automatically enjoy the financial privileges, a conclusion that Lord Cross described in *Dingle v Turner*[74] as 'unfortunate'. Obviously, all must receive the privileges as to validity; otherwise, most would fail under the beneficiary principle. The proposal that only some charities should enjoy financial privileges was made by the Radcliffe Commission in 1956,[75] and, as many charities begin to act more like companies, operating in a commercial manner, running what are often multimillion pound trading operations, and paying salaries to their senior staff which many would see as excessive, it is perhaps time that the question of universal financial privilege was re-examined. The financial privileges available to public schools such as Eton and Harrow are a particularly contentious issue, and were the subject of extensive debate in the progress of the Charities Act 2006 through Parliament.

It is also an open question whether the availability of financial privilege is a factor to be taken into account when the court is considering if a trust is charitable. In *Dingle v Turner*,[76] Lord Cross took the view that, in considering whether a trust was for the benefit of the 'public', regard should be had to the availability of fiscal privileges. However, the other four members of the House expressed doubts as to its relevance. The issue is not resolved by the Charities Act 2011.

74 [1972] AC 601, HL.

75 *Royal Commission on Taxation of Profits and Income* (Cmd 9474, 1955), Ch 7.

76 [1972] AC 601, HL.

20

Charitable purposes

1 Introduction

Charities must follow purposes recognized as such in law, and are also required to demonstrate that they carry out their activities to the benefit of the public at large. These purposes are the focus of this chapter.

2 Defining charitable trusts

(1) When is a trust charitable?

There are other requirements. For a trust to be charitable in law, it must be of a charitable character: it must be for a purpose that is considered in law to be charitable. That purpose must be carried out in way which is for the benefit of the public, rather than for a small group of individuals. Finally, it must not be possible for funds to be applied by the charity in ways that are not considered to be charitable. If so, this will prevent the whole trust from being considered to be charitable, even if parts, taken alone, could have been held charitable. This is often referred to as the requirement that the activities must be 'exclusively charitable'. Only where the non-charitable purposes are so minor relative to the main activities that they can be disregarded may the gift be saved as charitable. The requirements of public benefit is considered in Chapter 21.

(2) Statutory definition of 'charity'

The Charities Act 2006, introduced the first statutory definition of charity (apart from the descriptive list contained in preamble to the Statute of Charitable Uses 1601). Until then the meaning of 'charity' as a legal concept was determined by reference to judicial precedents and the registration decisions of the Charity Commission. The statutory definition of charity is now contained in ss 1 to 5 of the Charities Act 2011.

Section 1 of the Charities Act 2011 states that, '"charity" means an institution which . . . is established for charitable purposes only.' Section 2 in turn says that a charitable purpose is one which is described in s 3 and is for the public benefit. Section 3 then sets out a list of charitable purposes. The definition essentially consolidates the previous law by reclassifying existing recognized purposes with almost no change. It preserves the flexibility that was a fundamental feature of the previous categorization of charitable purposes. The main drawback with the list is that, because it incorporates a reference to the old law, it is necessary to have regard to most of the case law and registration decisions prior to its enactment.[1]

[1] See also Parachin, 'Regulating Charitable Activities through the Requirement of Charitable Purposes: Square Peg Meets Round Hole' in Picton and Sigafoos (eds), *Debates in Charity Law* (Bloomsbury Hart 2020) Ch 7, who argues that 'charitable purposes' should be replaced by 'charitable activities'.

(a) Relevance of previous law

The Charities Act 2011, s 3, provides a list of purposes which are prima facie considered to be charitable, but then states that any purposes which do not fall within the specific categories in the list shall be recognized as charitable if they are 'recognised as "charitable purposes" under the old law', meaning 'the law relating to charities in England and Wales as in force immediately before 1 April 2008', the date on which the Charities Act 2006 came into force.[2] The statutory definition adds to rather than replaces existing law.

(b) List is not closed

The Charities Act retains the dynamism of the previous concept of charitable purposes. The old law recognized the possibility of development by analogy or because of changes in society and public attitudes. For example, in *Scottish Burial Reform and Cremation Society v Glasgow City Corpn*,[3] a trust to promote cremation as a method of disposal of the dead was held charitable by the House of Lords, as it was analogous to earlier cases in which it had been held that trusts for the maintenance of graveyards were charitable. Development was possible even where previous case law suggested that a purpose would not, in the past, have been considered to be charitable. For instance in *Funnell v Stewart*,[4] Hazel Williamson QC held that faith healing had 'become a recognised activity of public benefit' so as to be charitable, even though an earlier decision had held that a trust to promote faith healing was non-charitable.[5] Preservation of this ability to develop charitable purposes is essential, as, in the words of Viscount Simonds in *IRC v Baddeley*, 'there is no limit to the number and diversity of the ways in which man will seek to benefit his fellow man.'[6] The concept of development by analogy (and by analogy upon analogy) is recognized by s 3(1)(m) of the Charities Act 2011.

The only change effected by the statutory definition is that the list of purposes which it contains can be changed only by legislation: under the previous law, it was possible for a purpose which was once considered to be charitable to cease to be charitable because of changing social conditions. As Lord Wilberforce observed in *Scottish Burial Reform and Cremation Society v Glasgow City Corpn*,[7] 'the law of charity is a moving subject' which evolves over time. This flexibility to take into account changes in society and in public attitudes by restricting the range of charitable purposes can now only be exercised by legislative change or through the application of the public benefit requirement, unless it can be shown to fall within s 3(1)(m) as an 'analogous' purpose.

(3) The categories of charitable purpose

The original three sources from which charity law was drawn can still be discerned in the statutory list.

(a) The Charitable Uses Act 1601

The Charitable Uses Act 1601[8] did not set out to define charity, but rather, to correct abuses in the administration of charitable trusts. However, the preamble to the Act contained a list of the objects that the law regarded as charitable in 1601, which became a guide to which the courts referred to determine whether purposes were charitable. Although the preamble was repealed in 1960,[9] it continued to provide guidance in defining charity, until the changes made by the Charities Act 2006 as consolidated in the 2011 Act.

[2] Charities Act 2006, s 2(2)(m) and s 2(4). [3] [1968] AC 138. [4] [1996] 1 WLR 288.
[5] *Re Hummeltenberg* [1923] 1 Ch 237. [6] [1955] AC 572. [7] [1968] AC 138.
[8] 43 Eliz, c 4. This is often referred to as the 'Statute of Elizabeth' in shorthand.
[9] Charities Act 1960, s 38(1).

(b) Income Tax Special Purposes Comrs v Pemsel

In *Income Tax Special Purposes Comrs v Pemsel*,[10] Lord Macnaghten provided an organizing classification of charitable purposes. He identified four 'heads' of charity:

> Charity in its legal sense comprises four principal divisions; trusts for the relief of poverty; trusts for the advancement of education; trusts for the advancement of religion; and trusts for other purposes beneficial to the community, not falling under any of the preceding heads.

This classification was not an exhaustive definition of the law of charity, but a convenient grouping of the cases into areas of benefit that the law regards as charitable, with the exception of the fourth division, which is obviously a 'catch-all' category. The categories themselves did not provide the answers as to whether a particular purpose was indeed charitable,[11] but defined the approach to considering charitable purposes up to the enactment of a statutory list of purposes in the Charities Act 2006 (now the Charities Act 2011).

(c) The role of the Charity Commission in defining 'charity'

The Charity Commission plays an increasingly important role in shaping the development of the definition of charitable purposes. The Commission has a legal obligation to keep a register of institutions that are charitable.[12] The Commission has the power to recognize a new purpose as charitable in circumstances where it believes that the courts of law would do so, and it, therefore, has in practice (even if not in law) similar powers as a court to take into account changing social and economic circumstances in determining whether an organization is charitable or not.

The Commission had recognized a number of new charitable purposes (such as the promotion of urban and rural regeneration in areas of social and economic deprivation and the conservation of the environment) that have now been included in the list contained in the Charities Act 2011.

The role of the Commission in determining whether a purpose is charitable confers on it the ability to develop the law, subject to the possibility of its decisions being challenged through the tribunal system[13] and ultimately the courts. For instance, using reasoning by analogy, the Commissioners decided in 2003–04 that the promotion of restorative justice was charitable, as it:

> was analogous to the charitable purposes of the preservation of public order and the prevention of breaches of the peace, the protection of life and property and the promotion of the sound administration of the law, and as such was for the public benefit.[14]

The Commission has been prepared to make decisions in some potentially contentious areas. For instance, it registered religious charities that do not involve belief in a deity, before there was judicial (and now legislative[15]) recognition that this was possible, even

[10] [1891] AC 531. See Mummery, '*The Commissioners for Special Purposes of Income Tax v Pemsel*' [2013] 16 CLPR 1.

[11] See, for example, *Scottish Burial Reform and Cremation v Glasgow City Corpn* [1968] AC 138, 233 where Lord Wilberforce cautioned against giving the classification 'the force of statute'.

[12] Charities Act 1993, s 3. Under s 4(1) of the Act, the register is deemed conclusive of the charitable nature of an organization. Certain charities are not required to be registered. These include exempt charities (see s 3A(2)(a) and Sch 2), which are organizations that are subject to another form of regulatory or supervisory control, e.g. universities, national galleries, and museums. Small charities, defined as having a total income of less than £5,000 a year, are also not required to register (s 3A(2)(d)) but may choose to do so. See further Lloyd, *Charities—The New Law 2006: A Practical Guide To The Charities Acts* (Jordan 2007), Ch 3.

[13] The Tribunal system is considered in Chapter 23.

[14] *Annual Report of the Charity Commissioners for England and Wales 2003–2004*, p 11.

[15] Charities Act 2011, s 3(2).

though belief in a deity had been stated as a requirement in the previous case law. While it can be argued that the authority given to the Charity Commission does not enable it to change the law, since any guidance issued or decisions made on registration only have effect unless and until they are tested in the courts, it is nevertheless the case that many registration decisions will not be appealed immediately or at all.[16] In consequence, there is often little choice for organizations seeking registration other than to follow existing Commission decisions in contentious areas.

(4) **The new list of charitable purposes**

The list is essentially an extended formulation of the classification provided in *Pemsel*, even to the extent of including the first three substantive categories, and after an additional group of substantive categories, a 'catch-all' category. This catch-all category includes any other purposes currently considered to be charitable, but which are not included in the previous paragraphs, as well as any other purposes which could on the basis of analogy (and by analogy from analogy) be considered to be charitable. The new list is no more than a classification, but, being statutory, it is authoritative.

The list of charitable purposes is set out in s 3 of the Charities Act 2011 as follows:

(a) the prevention or relief of poverty;
(b) the advancement of education;
(c) the advancement of religion;
(d) the advancement of health or the saving of lives;
(e) the advancement of citizenship or community development;
(f) the advancement of the arts, culture, heritage or science;
(g) the advancement of amateur sport;
(h) the advancement of human rights, conflict resolution or reconciliation or the promotion of religious or racial harmony or equality and diversity;
(i) the advancement of environmental protection or improvement;
(j) the relief of those in need because of youth, age, ill-health, disability, financial hardship or other disadvantage;
(k) the advancement of animal welfare;
(l) the promotion of the efficiency of the armed forces of the Crown or of the efficiency of the police, fire and rescue services or ambulance services;
(m) any other purposes [recognized under the old law, or development by analogy from it], or recognized as recreational trusts under s 5 of the Act.

The Act states that where the list contains a term which 'has a particular meaning under the law relating to charities in England and Wales, the term is to be taken as having the same meaning where it appears in that provision'.[17] Even where this is not the case, previous case law is a guide to the scope and effect of some of the categories. In one of the first reported cases involving the Act, a case involving an animal welfare charity, Lewison J observed, 'I do not regard this as amounting to any change in the substance of the law.'[18]

The requirements to create a valid charitable trust are summarized in Figure 20.1.

[16] The cost of an appeal in time and money, whether to the High Court, or (following the introduction of the Tribunal service) to the First Tier Tribunal (Charity), means that few organizations seeking charitable status are likely to have the will or resources to mount such an appeal.

[17] Charities Act 2011, s 2(3).

[18] *Hanchett-Stamford v Attorney-General* [2009] Ch 173 at [14] & [23].

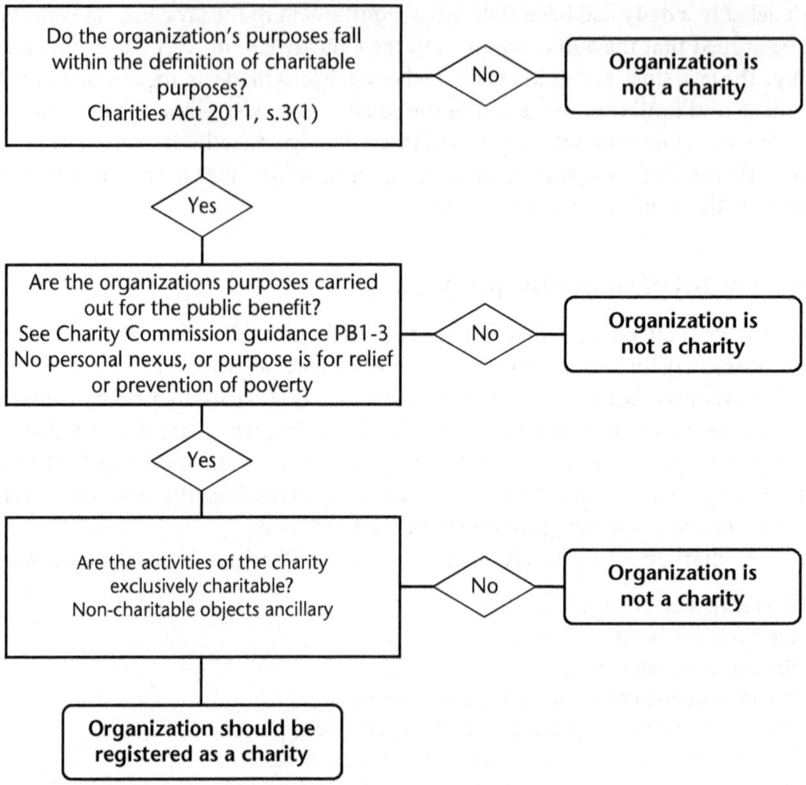

Figure 20.1 Requirements of charitable trusts

3 Charitable purposes

(1) Trusts for the prevention or relief of poverty

The first general head of charitable purposes identified in *Pemsel* and repeated in the list in the Charities Act 2011 was that of the 'relief of poverty', a description now extended to include the prevention of poverty. In a social era when there was no welfare state and little other state provision for those at the bottom of society, it was obviously 'beneficial' for private individuals to provide for them. Thus, the law has always regarded the relief of poverty as a charitable purpose to be encouraged.

The preamble to the Statute of Charitable Uses 1601 referred to the relief of poverty in a wider context, including the 'relief of aged, impotent [i.e. infirm or disabled] and poor people'. As a result, trusts dealing with the relief of problems arising from age or infirmity were recognized as charitable. Trusts for these purposes are now covered by separate categories in the statutory list.

(a) The meaning of 'poverty'

Poverty is neither defined nor explained in the Charities Act 2011. Case law prior to 2006 indicated that it is a relative concept, and that what a society regards as 'poor' will vary with changes in social circumstance and what is regarded as a 'normal' level of income and ownership of consumer products. Charity law treats poverty as a relative, rather than an absolute, concept.

It is clear that 'poverty' is not synonymous with destitution:

> It is quite clearly established that poverty does not mean destitution; it is a word of wide and somewhat indefinite import; it may not unfairly be paraphrased for present purposes as meaning persons who have to 'go short' in the ordinary sense of that term, due regard being had to their status in life.[19]

Poverty is not to be understood as something experienced only by those at the very bottom of society, and the concept of 'going short'[20] will mean different things to people at different social levels. Those who are middle class yet have fallen on hard times may well fall within this understanding of poverty, since they 'go short' compared to their social peers, although there may be others with similar financial circumstances who are not regarded as poor, because in the light of their social and economic background they do not 'go short'. Thus, gifts in favour of 'distressed gentlefolk'[21] or persons of 'moderate means'[22] have been held to fall within this understanding of 'poor'. In *Re Segelman (Decd)*,[23] Chadwick J suggested that future considerations might be appropriate, as people may 'need a helping hand from time to time in order to overcome an unforeseen crisis'.[24]

One of the issues in *Cawdron v Merchant Taylors' School*[25] was whether a trust was for the relief of poverty. Funds were available to pay for the education of sons of Old Merchant Taylors (a public school which charges substantial fees) who had been killed or injured in the First World War and to provide assistance to the dependent relatives of such killed or injured Merchant Taylors. Blackburne J held that (even though those eligible were likely to have relatively privileged backgrounds), the references to assistance and dependency showed that relief could only be given to those who were in financial need, or in other words those who would otherwise 'go short'.[26] Improving the position of those who would otherwise 'go short' is permissible.[27]

In contrast, in *Re Gwyon*,[28] a gift for the provision of clothing for children was held not charitable, since the terms of the gift did not exclude children who were from affluent backgrounds. Similarly, in *Re Sanders' Will Trusts*,[29] money was given to provide dwellings for 'the working classes and their families'. Harman J held this was not charitable, since the term 'the working classes' did not indicate poor persons.[30]

Two simple propositions can be drawn from the cases. First, that the legal concept of poverty is a relative one, and that poverty is to be judged in relation to whether a person is suffering hardship having regard to their social and economic position and other circumstances. Second, that to be a valid gift for the relief of poverty, the gift must be exclusively for the benefit of those who are experiencing hardship.

In its guidance, the Charity Commission recognizes the contextual meaning of poverty:

> There can be no absolute definition of what 'poverty' might mean since the problems giving rise to poverty are multi-dimensional and cumulative. It can affect individuals and whole communities. It might be experienced on a long or short-term basis . . . Generally speaking, it

[19] *Re Coulthurst* [1951] Ch 661, CA per Sir Raymond Evershed MR.

[20] This term was approved by Lightman J in *IRC v Oldham Training and Enterprise Council* [1996] STC 1218 at 1233.

[21] *Re Young* [1951] Ch 344. [22] *Re Clarke* [1923] 2 Ch 407. [23] [1995] 3 All ER 676.

[24] [1995] 3 All ER 676 at 690. [25] [2009] EWHC 1722 (Ch).

[26] [2009] EWHC 1722 (Ch) at [33]. See also *Independent Schools Council v Charity Commission for England and Wales* [2011] UKUT 421 (TCC), where the Upper Tribunal restated the position that 'poor' does not mean 'destitute' but can cover persons of modest means in certain cases and persons of 'some means' in others.

[27] See *IRC v Oldham Training and Enterprise Council* [1996] STC 1218 at 1233 per Lightman J.

[28] [1930] 1 Ch 255. [29] [1954] Ch 265.

[30] Cf *Re Niyazi's Will Trusts* [1978] 1 WLR 910 (gift was charitable to 'working men's hostel', as 'hostel' connotes modest, temporary accommodation for those with a relatively low income).

> is likely to be charitable to relieve either the poverty or the financial hardship of anyone who does not have the resources to provide themselves, either on a short or long-term basis, with the normal things of life which most people take for granted.[31]

It gives some examples of what may constitute the relief of poverty: it includes grants of money; provision of items (either on loan or outright) such as clothing or furniture; payment for services such as essential house decoration, repairs, meals on wheels; and the provision of facilities such as books, fees for examination or instruction, travelling expenses to help people earn a living and funds for recreational pursuits.[32]

The latest guidance also notes that not everyone in financial hardship is necessarily poor, but it may still be charitable to relieve that financial hardship under one of the other statutory recognized purposes, Charities Act 2011, s 3(j) which includes 'the relief of those in need because . . . of financial hardship'.[33]

(b) **The meaning of 'relief' or 'prevention'**

Under the first category, a gift is not charitable merely because it is for the benefit of the poor. It must also relieve a need that they have as a result of their condition of poverty or must operate to prevent poverty. The concept of relief has been well explored in the courts, but the concept of prevention has been added by the Charities Act. The requirement of relief is best explained in a wider context than that of the relief of poverty. In *Joseph Rowntree Memorial Trust Housing Association Ltd v A-G*,[34] the housing association wished to build small dwellings for elderly people, who would be able to purchase them on long leases. The elderly would pay 70 per cent of the purchase price of the premises, with the remainder being paid by the housing association. To be charitable, Peter Gibson J emphasized that:

> there must be a need which is to be relieved by the . . . gift, such need being attributable to the aged . . . condition of the person to be benefited.

Therefore, as counsel for the Attorney-General had argued, a gift for the 'aged millionaires of Mayfair' would not be charitable, as it would not relieve a need that such millionaires experienced as aged people. The fact that the housing association was providing a specialist type of accommodation for the elderly meant that a need was being relieved and the purpose was charitable.

In *Densham v Charity Commission*,[35] the First-tier Tribunal (Charity) upheld that the provision of 'allotments for the labouring poor' was considered appropriate relief of poverty to be the subject matter of a charitable trusts.[36] Relief was provided merely by proving the labouring poor with the opportunity to have a stake in the soil, which, without the allotments, they would not have had.[37]

In the Charity Commission's view, the relief and prevention of poverty are generally interchangeable terms and '[i]n most cases the commission will treat the relief of poverty and the relief of financial hardship the same'[38] but, where a charity is set up purely for the prevention of poverty, it will 'tend to take a very specific approach to poverty, which usually involves tackling its root causes'.[39] Nevertheless, this will be the exception, as 'many

[31] Charity Commission, *Guidance: Charitable Purposes, Pt 3* (16 September 2013).

[32] Ibid. [33] Ibid. [34] [1983] Ch 159. [35] CA/2015/0011 and CA/2017/002.

[36] The case concerned the legality of a scheme in relation to allotment gardens in Hughenden, Buckinghamshire, created under the Inclosure Act 1845. The Charity Commission scheme was upheld, but it was key to the decision whether the allotments where charitable or not.

[37] Rent was payable on the allotments, but this did not stop the creation of charitable trusts as any residue was to be paid to the parish overseers of the poor to relieve poverty in the location.

[38] Charity Commission, *Guidance: Charitable Purposes, Pt 3* (16 September 2013). [39] Ibid.

charities that are concerned with preventing or relieving poverty will do so by addressing both the causes (prevention) and the consequences (relief) of poverty'.[40]

Examples of purposes for the prevention of poverty are thus providing money management training or debt counselling advice to someone at actual risk of being in poverty[41] There would seem to be considerable sense in this approach, and it is unlikely that the courts would take issue with this guidance.

(2) Trusts for the advancement of education

(a) A broad concept of 'education'

Under the second head of the classification of charity, gifts for the advancement of education will be charitable. In *IRC v McMullen*, Lord Hailsham spoke of the education of the young as:

> a balanced and systematic process of instruction, training and practice containing . . . both spiritual, moral, mental and physical elements.[42]

Education thus covers skills and understanding, as well as knowledge, and is not confined to teaching in schools and colleges.[43]

This wide concept of education has been reflected in the cases that have held that not only gifts to advance academic study but also for research, culture, and sport may be charitable. The Charities Act 2011 now contains separate heads that cover some of these areas.

(b) Teaching

The advancement of school and tertiary level teaching and of institutions that provide such teaching is clearly charitable. Charitable gifts have included: the founding of a professorial chair (*A-G v Margaret and Regius Professors in Cambridge*[44]); the endowments of schools and colleges (*Abbey Malvern Wells Ltd v Ministry of Local Government and Planning*);[45] and the payment of teachers and administrative staff of an institution (*Case of Christ's College Cambridge*).[46] In *Customs and Excise Comrs v Bell Concord Educational Trust Ltd*,[47] it was held that trusts endowing fee-paying schools are charitable, provided that the school is non-profit-making or uses its profits for school purposes only. Purposes ancillary to teaching institutions may also be charitable, as for example in *A-G v Ross*,[48] where the students' union was held charitable as it furthered the educational function of the institution.

(c) Industrial training and professional bodies

The advancement of industrial and technical training has also been held charitable (*Re Koettgen's Will Trusts*[49] and *Construction Industry Training Board v A-G*).[50] In *IRC v White*,[51] an association with the purpose of encouraging craftsmanship and maintaining the standards of the modern and ancient crafts was held to be charitable. The Royal College of Surgeons, which exists to promote the study and practice of the art of surgery,

[40] Ibid. [41] Ibid. [42] [1981] AC 1, HL.

[43] See, for example, Decision of the Charity Commissioners For England and Wales, *Application for Registration of Millennium College UK Limited*, 27 April 2004, where a purpose to advance education by using information technology to 'cultivate a multi-disciplinary approach to certain areas of study and include people hitherto excluded from formal education' was held charitable.

[44] [1682] 1 Vern 55. [45] [1951] Ch 728. [46] [1757] 1 Wm Bl 90.

[47] [1990] 1 QB 1040, CA. See also *Independent Schools Council v Charity Commission for England and Wales* [2011] UKUT 421 (TCC). [48] [1986] 1 WLR 252.

[49] [1954] Ch 252. [50] [1973] Ch 173, CA. [51] [1980] TR 155.

has been held charitable,[52] as has the Royal College of Nursing, whose objects are the better education and training of nurses and to promote nursing as a profession.[53] In contrast, the General Nursing Council, which was established by statute to regulate the nursing profession, has been held not charitable[54] since its objects included the enhancement of the status of nurses, which is analogous to the objectives of trade unions to advance the interests of their members.

(d) Research

The advancement of education extends beyond mere teaching to include research activity.[55] But not all research will be charitable. The courts have sought to distinguish research which is of truly educational value and worthy of charitable status, from that which is not. Research that is of no educational value, or of purely esoteric value to the researcher, will not be charitable.[56] The three criteria laid down by Slade J in *Re Besterman's Will Trusts*[57] summarize the present state of the law. For a trust for research to be charitable:

(1) the subject matter of the research must be a useful subject of study;
(2) the knowledge acquired by the research must be disseminated to others; and
(3) the trust must be for the benefit of the public, or a sufficiently important section of the public.

The case concerned a trust for research into the works of Voltaire and Rousseau, and since the three criteria were met it was held to be charitable.

Propaganda—the promotion of a single viewpoint or a set of singular views—masquerading as research will not be charitable. The educational value of research comes from the presentation of a balanced argument, reaching conclusions through analysis of evidence, and considering competing arguments.[58]

This does not mean that research cannot be value-driven, provided that it does not amount to campaigning for a particular view. Hence, in *The Countryside Alliance* registration decision,[59] a purpose to 'educate the public in subjects pertaining to the conservation, protection and enjoyment of the countryside' could be charitable even though it proceeded from the generally accepted position that the countryside is beneficial.[60] Contrast this with *Re Hopkinson*,[61] where a proposed trust for educating adults in the

[52] *Royal College of Surgeons of England v National Provincial Bank Ltd* [1952] AC 631, HL.

[53] *Royal College of Nursing v St Marylebone Corpn* [1959] 1 WLR 1077, CA.

[54] *General Nursing Council for England and Wales v St Marylebone Borough Council* [1959] AC 540, HL.

[55] The case law on this purpose now overlaps to some degree with the distinct purpose of the advancement of arts, culture, heritage, or science under the Charities Act 2011, s 3(1)(f).

[56] See, for example, the registration of the Theosophical Society in England as a charity (Charity Commission, *Annual Reports and Accounts 2016–2017*, pp 41–2), whose purposes include to encourage the secular study of comparative religion, philosophy, and science, was held to be charitable both on the purposes of advancing education and promoting moral and ethical improvement.

[57] [1980] *The Times*, 21 January. See also *Re Hopkins' Will Trusts* [1965] Ch 669, where a gift to the Francis Bacon Society to be used to find manuscripts proving that the plays of Shakespeare were written by Francis Bacon was held charitable.

[58] See, for example, Decision of the Charity Commissioners For England and Wales, *Application for Registration of Living in Radiance*, 24 August 2005, where an organization which argued that study of 'The Radiance Technique', which included meditation and peace education, was held not sufficiently educational, on the basis that the organization's activities were more about promotion and raising awareness of the technique, rather than research or instruction into its benefits.

[59] Decision of the Charity Commissioners For England and Wales, *Application for Registration of The Countryside Alliance Foundation*, 23 March 2017, para 13.

[60] See *Hipkiss v The Charity Commission* [2018] 8 WLUK 229 (research into cryogenics has charitable status, even though cryopreservation of organs for later human transplant was not possible at the current time).

[61] [1949] 1 All ER 346.

views of a single political party was not held charitable.[62] The issue often overlaps with the promotion of political purposes or campaigning, which is discussed later in the chapter.

In summary, it is essential that the subject of proposed research must be of some usefulness. This requires a value judgement on the part of the court or the Charity Commission. The results of the research must also enter the public domain, usually by publication, and if the information is kept purely for the benefit of the researcher alone it will not be charitable, as there is no advancement of education in non-disseminated work. Similarly, research carried out by companies and intended for their exclusive commercial use will not be charitable, as it is not publicly available. Nor will it be charitable for a university to conduct research on behalf of a corporation if the results of the research cannot enter the public domain. It is worth noting that the requirement of research being in the public domain in this context means that the research must be available to the public, not in the technical sense understood in copyright law of it being free of author's copyright or freely accessible to the public (without payment).

(e) Advancement

It is clear from the preceeding discussion that, however broad a view is taken of what is understood as 'education', it will only be charitable if the proposed charitable activities actually *advance* education. In the words of guidance issued by the Charity Commission this means 'to promote, sustain and increase' individual and collective knowledge and understanding of specific areas of study, skills, and expertise.[63] The Commission also provides a list of example purposes that they would consider to be charitable,[64] which draw upon the legal decisions reached in the previously discussed cases.

(3) The advancement of religion

Trusts for the advancement of religion fall into the third category of *Pemsel* that has been retained by the Charities Act 2011. The law assumes that any religious activity, provided it is carried on in the public domain,[65] is charitable. There is no need at this first stage of the test as to whether a purpose is charitable for the particular religion in issue to prove its value, or for the court to weigh the validity of its beliefs. This was emphasized by Lord Reid, who stated in *Gilmour v Coats*, that:

> A religion can be regarded as beneficial without it being necessary to assume that all its beliefs are true, and a religious service can be regarded as beneficial to all those who attend it without it being necessary to determine the spiritual efficacy of that service or to accept any particular belief about it.[66]

Thus, in *Funnell v Stewart*,[67] a gift to further the work of a small group of faith healers was not denied charitable status merely because there was no evidence that anyone had ever been healed. Even a religious sect which holds beliefs which contain 'elements of detriment' can be charitable in law. The Charity Commission reported in January 2014 that, despite considerable controversy, and evidence which 'suggests that "there

[62] See *Re Shaw* [1957] 1 WLR 729, where Harman J held that the will by George Bernard Shaw to fund research into a forty-letter alphabet, and translation of one of his plays into it, was not charitable, on the basis that the gift was for the promotion of an alternative alphabet, not really to research the benefits of the Shaw alphabet as compared to the existing Roman system.

[63] Charity Commission, *The Advancement of Education for the Public Benefit* (2008, amended December 2011). This guidance is currently under review.

[64] Charity Commission, *Advancement of Education for the Public Benefit* (2008, amended December 2011), Annex A, pp 23–4. See also Charity Commission, *Guidance: Charitable Purposes, Pt 4* (16 September 2013).

[65] See *Gilmour v Coats* [1949] AC 426.

[66] [1949] AC 426 at 862.

[67] [1996] 1 WLR 288.

were elements of detriment and harm" associated with the doctrines and practices of the Plymouth Brethren Christian Church, especially its disciplinary practices, which include socially isolating members who have not complied with strict codes of behaviour', it had agreed to register the Preston Down Trust, which supported a Plymouth Brethren meeting hall.[68]

(a) The meaning of 'religion'

The courts originally defined religion so as to require belief in a divine being.[69] That view changed over time, and nowadays, reflecting a society in which differences are increasingly to be respected and cherished, a new definition can be found in the Charities Act 2011, which states that:

> 'religion' includes–
>
> (i) a religion which involves belief in more than one god, and
> (ii) a religion which does not involve belief in a god;[70]

This confirms the practice which the Charity Commission had already adopted of registering Hindu and Buddhist trusts.[71]

In 1999 the Charity Commission rejected the application of the Church of Scientology for registration as a charity.[72] It held that a body would only be charitable for the advancement of religion if it engaged in the *worship* of a divine being.[73] While it was accepted that the Church of Scientology believed in the existence of a divine being, its activities did not exhibit the defining characteristics of worship, namely, the 'reverence or veneration for that supreme being'. The activities of Scientology consisted of 'auditing', which was found to be very much akin to counselling, and 'training', which involved the detailed study of the works of L Ron Hubbard.

In *R (on the application of Hodkin) v Registrar General of Births, Deaths and Marriages*,[74] the Supreme Court held unanimously that a Church of Scientology chapel was 'a place of meeting for religious worship'. The decision arose in a different context from charity law, but will nevertheless be influential. The court considered that there has never been a universal legal definition of religion in English law, given the variety of world religions, changes in society, and the different legal contexts in which the issues arise. Belief in deity or a supreme being was not an essential requirement. Lord Toulson said that religion could be described in summary as:

> a spiritual or non-secular belief system, held by a group of adherents, which claims to explain mankind's place in the universe and relationship with the infinite, and to teach its adherents how they are to live their lives in conformity with the spiritual understanding associated with the belief system.[75]

[68] Decision of the Charity Commissioners For England and Wales, *Application for Registration of The Preston Down Trust*, 3 January 2014. See also Chapter 21.

[69] See, for example, *Bowman v Secular Society* [1917] AC 406, HL; *Re South Place Ethical Society* [1980] 1 WLR 1565.

[70] s 2(3)(a).

[71] See, for instance, *Varsani v Jesani* [1998] EWCA Civ 630. A search of the register of charities discloses many more examples.

[72] For interesting commentaries on the Charity Commission's decision from the perspective of human rights, see Quint et al, 'Religion, *Charity Law and* Human Rights' [1999] *Charity Law and Practice Review* 153; Harding, 'Trusts for Religious Purposes and the Question of Public Benefit' [2008] MLR 159.

[73] Decision of the Charity Commissioners for England and Wales made on 17 November 1999. See also *R v Registrar General, ex p Segerdal* [1970] 2 QB 697.

[74] [2013] UKSC 77.

[75] [2013] UKSC 77 at 57.

He added that in his view, 'spiritual or non-secular':

> means a belief system which goes beyond that which can be perceived by the senses or ascertained by the application of science . . . Such a belief system may or may not involve belief in a supreme being, but it does involve a belief that there is more to be understood about mankind's nature and relationship to the universe than can be gained from the senses or from science.

With this approach to religion, Scientology was clearly a religion for the purpose under consideration.[76] It does not follow that it will now similarly be recognized in charity law, because the test for charity requires a consideration of public benefit.[77] However, the view of the Supreme Court is likely to have an impact on the approach of any court or of the Charity Commission should the question arise again. It is also relevant that Charity Commission guidance recognizes that worship is not an essential element in the recognition of a religion. It states that a religion which does not involve worship could be recognized where it instils a sense of 'connectedness' with the spiritual belief system or the force or power extending beyond the self, particularly where this 'might motivate or be expressed through the quality of life led by adherents, especially activity which involves helping others and inspiring others to do likewise'.[78] The Commission cites Jainism as an example, where there is no worship of a supreme being, but the teaching of a supreme being or entity serves to inspire followers to lead better lives. This appears to be a correct view since public worship is just one way of demonstrating public engagement and benefit which lies at the foundation of the recognition of religion in charity law.

To the dismay of many fans of the Star Wars franchise, the Commission has held that 'Jediism' is not a religion within charity law.[79] Although adherents could follow it as a secular belief system, it lacked the necessary spiritual or non-secular belief essential to religious belief and cohesion, as individuals had the ability to follow their own experiential philosophy within the loose framework provided by the Jedi doctrine and belief in the Force as a 'ubiquitous and metaphysical power'.

(b) Equal treatment of different religions

Given that the benefit the court assumes to derive from a trust for the advancement of religion is the benefit of an improved life through religious belief, it follows that the precise nature of the religious belief is not important, and the law does not discriminate between different faiths and traditions. This was expressed by Cross J in *Neville Estates Ltd v Madden*:

> as between different religions the law stands neutral, but it assumes that any religion is at least likely to be better than none.

The promotion of the Christian religion in all its denominational forms is clearly charitable, and despite little direct authority it seems that the mainstream non-Christian religions will be treated similarly.[80] In contrast to their willingness to attempt to assess the

[76] [2013] UKSC 77 at 60. In Australia Scientology has been held to be a religion and entitled to charitable status and tax exemptions: *Church of the New Faith v Comr of Pay-Roll Tax* [1983] 49 ALR 65.

[77] See Chapter 21.

[78] Charity Commission, *The Advancement of Religion for the Public Benefit* (2008, amended December 2011), Annex A, p 23.

[79] Decision of the Charity Commissioners For England and Wales, *Application for Registration of The Temple of the Jedi Order*, 19 December 2016. This decision is considered further in Chapter 21.

[80] See the discussion earlier in relation to Buddhism and Hinduism. See, for example, *Neville Estates Ltd v Madden* [1962] Ch 832 for the promotion of Judaism. The Charity Commission has also registered organizations or trusts for the promotion of Islam.

value of research or supposed art, the courts have not in the past weighed the merits of religious belief. Thus, in *Re Watson*,[81] a trust to promote the works of H G Hobbs, the leader of a small group of non-denominational Christians comprising only members of his family, was held charitable despite the unanimous conclusion of expert evidence that they were of no value.

If past authority is followed, it seems that sects and cults will be charitable provided that they are not destructive to the whole concept of religion, or contrary to the foundations of society, no matter how obscure or foolish their beliefs. In *Thornton v Howe*,[82] a trust to promote the publication of the works of Johanna Southcote, who claimed that she was the mother of the second messiah, was held charitable. The Unification Church (commonly known as the 'Moonies') has been registered as a charity.

(c) Purposes ancillary to religion

Purposes ancillary to the advancement of religion will also be charitable. The construction or maintenance[83] of religious buildings, and even the provision of bells,[84] have been held charitable. Provision for the benefit of religious ministers, retired missionaries,[85] and the church choir[86] have also been held charitable.

(d) Gifts to religious leaders

Gifts made to religious leaders in their capacity as such will be considered charitable gifts for the advancement of religion, provided that the gifts are exclusively for the spiritual work of the leader.[87] Hence, in *Farley v Westminster Bank*,[88] a gift to a vicar for his 'work in the parish' was held charitable, but in *Re Simson*,[89] a gift to a vicar for his 'parish work' was held not to be charitable, since as a matter of construction it was held that his 'parish work' may include work which was not exclusively charitable. This distinction is tenuous, if not spurious.

(e) Advancement, not merely belief

A purpose will not be charitable simply because it involves belief in a religion. It must be for the *advancement* of religion. The activities involved must in some way promote, maintain, or practise the religion or encourage or increase belief in the faith concerned.[90] In *United Grand Lodge of Ancient Free and Accepted Masons of England v Holborn Borough Council*,[91] freemasonry was held not to be charitable because it did not advance religion as such, but merely encouraged its members to lead a good moral life. Current examples of purposes that advance religion can be found in Annex B to the Charity Commission guidance, *The Advancement of Education for the Public Benefit*.[92]

(4) Advancement of health or the saving of lives

(a) Medical and healthcare charities

This is the first of the new categories of charitable purpose added by the Charities Act 2006. It does not represent an entirely new category, but simply a subdivision of the

[81] [1973] 1 WLR 1472. [82] [1862] 31 Beav 125.

[83] *Re Hooper* [1932] 1 Ch 38—trust to upkeep a tablet and a window in a church. See also *Mount Pleasant Islamic Trust v Skykes (Valuation Officer)* [2019] 5 WLUK 697.

[84] *Re Pardoe* [1906] 2 Ch 184. [85] *Re Mylne* [1941] Ch 204. [86] *Re Royce* [1940] Ch 514.

[87] *Re Flinn* [1948] Ch 241. [88] [1939] AC 430, HL. [89] [1946] Ch 299.

[90] Charity Commission, *The Advancement of Religion for the Public Benefit* (2008, amended December 2011), p 8. See also Charity Commission, *Guidance: Charitable Purposes, Pt 5* (16 September 2013).

[91] [1957] 1 WLR 1080. [92] (2008, as amended December 2011) at pp 24–6.

Pemsel category of 'other purposes beneficial to the community'. The preamble to the Statute of Charitable Uses referred to the relief of the 'aged, impotent and poor'. The word 'impotent' in this context does not have its modern meaning relating to sexual function, but was used in a more general but now archaic sense to refer to incapacity, infirmity, or illness. In *Joseph Rowntree Memorial Trust Housing Association Ltd v A-G*,[93] it was held that the words of the preamble were to be read disjunctively, so, for four centuries, the provision of medical care has been recognized as a charitable purpose.[94]

The provision of healthcare is not confined to conventional treatment. In *Funnell v Stewart*,[95] the court held that a trust to further the work of a group offering faith healing was charitable. The view of the Charity Commission is that the promotion of alternative and complementary therapies can be charitable, but evidence is required of its efficacy:

> Assessing the efficacy of different therapies will depend upon what benefits are claimed for it (ie whether it is diagnostic, curative, therapeutic and/or palliative) and whether it is offered as a complement to conventional medicine or as an alternative. Each case is considered on its merits, but the Report on complementary and alternative medicine provides a useful guide.[96]

The Charity Commission launched a consultation on complementary and alternative medicines on 13 March 2017,[97] with the purpose of working out the level of evidence the Commission should accept when making assessments of charitable status. That report has since been published.[98]

It also seems clear that this category of charitable purpose extends beyond formal healthcare to include services to ease the suffering of the sick, disabled, or infirm.[99] A hospice providing palliative care for the terminally ill would, therefore, fall within this category.

(b) Imposition of fees or charges for treatment

Hospitals which charge fees for the treatment they provide can be charitable, even if as a result their services are only available to those who are capable of paying or have insurance.[100] In *Re Resch's Will Trusts*,[101] a gift of $8m was made to the St Vincent's Private Hospital. The Privy Council held that this was a valid charitable gift, and that there was sufficient benefit to the community resulting from:

> the beds and medical staff of the general hospital, the availability of a particular type of nursing and treatment which supplements that provided by the general hospital and the benefit to the standard of medical care in the general hospital which arises from the juxtaposition of the two institutions.[102]

It was emphasized that if the hospital was carried on as a commercial venture, with a view to making profits for individuals, then it would not be charitable.[103] This means that the majority of privately owned and run nursing homes and old people's homes will not be charitable. This is sensible, since profit-making ventures do not warrant the tax privileges

[93] [1983] Ch 159.

[94] See also *Re Smith's Will Trusts* [1962] 2 All ER 563, where the Court of Appeal found a testamentary gift for the provision of hospitals was charitable.

[95] [1996] 1 WLR 288.

[96] Charity Commission Guidance on the advancement of health or the saving of lives. The Report referred to is the 6th Report of the House of Lords Report Select Committee on Science and Technology (Session 1999–2000). See also Charity Commission, *Guidance: Charitable Purposes, Pt 6* (16 September 2013).

[97] The consultation closed on 19 May 2017.

[98] Charity Commission *Complementary and alternative medicine: outcome report* (11 December 2018).

[99] Charity Commission, *Guidance: Charitable Purposes, Pt 5* (16 September 2013). There is thus likely to be some overlap between this category and the relief of those in need in s 2(2)(j) of the Charities Act 2006.

[100] See also the discussion in Chapter 21 on the impact of fees upon public benefit.

[101] [1969] 1 AC 514.

[102] [1969] 1 AC 514 at 540, per Lord Wilberforce.

[103] [1969] 1 AC 514.

granted to charities. This approach was followed by the Charity Commission in *Odstock Private Care Ltd.*[104] The organization provided private care by entering into agreements with patients and insurers and then contracting with unused staffed NHS facilities. *Re Resh* was distinguished on the basis that this case concerned private financing, which not all those in the affected community would have been able to afford, and, in providing NHS facilities and staff rather than private facilities as in *Re Resh*, the potential benefits of attracting a higher calibre staff were not present.

(c) Saving lives (and property)

Trusts for the protection of human life and property have been held to be charitable as falling within the 'spirit and intendment' of the preamble. For example, in *Re Wokingham Fire Brigade Trusts*[105] the provision of a voluntary fire brigade was held charitable. The Royal National Lifeboat Institution is also charitable.[106] Clearly, such services must not exist to make profits for individuals, which would rule out commercial organizations offering emergency services such as most (or all) motoring assistance agencies. The Charity Commission considers that a trust for the provision of emergency services or services assisting the emergency services, or for the provision of life-saving or self-defence classes, could be considered charitable purposes under this head.[107]

(d) Analogous and ancillary purposes

The Charities Act 2011 makes it clear that the advancement of health is to be given an expansive meaning. It states that it 'includes the prevention or relief of sickness, disease or human suffering'.[108] As with trusts for the advancement of education and religion, purposes ancillary to the provision of medical care are charitable, so in *Re Bernstein's Will Trusts*,[109] a surgeon's gift of part of his residuary estate to provide extra comforts at Christmas for the nurses of a specified hospital was held charitable. In *London Hospital Medical College v IRC*,[110] a students' union at a medical school was held charitable as being a practical necessity to the efficient functioning of the school. The Charity Commission has also decided that the General Medical Council should be registered as a charity on the grounds that it was established for the charitable propose of 'the protection, promotion and maintenance of the health and safety if the community' by ensuring proper standards in the practice of medicine.[111]

(5) Advancement of citizenship or community development

The Charity Commission considers that this head of charity covers a broad range of purposes 'directed towards support for social and community infrastructure which is focused on the community rather than the individual'.[112]

(a) Rural or urban regeneration

Section 3(2)(c) of the Charities Act 2011 states that this head of charitable purpose 'includes rural or urban regeneration'. This is a category of charity recognized by the Charity Commission[113] before the passing of the 2006 Act, and is an area of activity

[104] Decision of the Charity Commissioners For England and Wales, *Application for Registration of Odstock Private Care Ltd*, 25 September 2007.

[105] [1951] Ch 373. [106] *Re David* [1889] 43 Ch D 27.

[107] Charity Commission, *Guidance: Charitable Purposes, Pt 6* (16 September 2013).

[108] s 3(2)(b). [109] [1971] 115 Sol Jo 808. [110] [1976] 1 WLR 613.

[111] Decision of the Charity Commissioners, 2 April 2001.

[112] Charity Commission, *Guidance: Charitable Purposes, Pt 7* (16 September 2013).

[113] See *Charity Commission Annual Report 2003–2004*, p 8.

on which the Commission has issued guidance.[114] In order to attain charitable status, an organization must seek to maintain or improve 'the physical, social and economic infrastructure' and assist people 'who are at a disadvantage because of their social and economic circumstances'. Such purposes might include: providing financial assistance to people who are poor; providing or improving housing standards; helping people find employment; providing education, training, and retraining; providing assistance to businesses, including land and buildings on favourable terms; providing and maintaining roads and transport; providing, maintaining, and improving recreational facilities; preserving historic buildings in the area; and providing public amenities.[115]

(b) Promotion of community capacity-building

The Charity Commission has decided that the promotion of community capacity-building in relation to communities that are socially or economically disadvantaged should be recognized as charitable.[116] Community capacity-building means 'developing the capacity and skills of the members of a community in such a way that they are better able to identify, and help meet, their needs and to participate more fully in society'.[117] This might involve: equipping people with skills and competencies; realizing existing skills and developing potential; promoting people's increased self-confidence; promoting people's ability to take responsibility for identifying and meeting their own, and other people's, needs; and encouraging people to become involved in their community and wider society in a fuller way.[118]

(c) Civic responsibility and good citizenship

Organizations such as the Guides and Scouts would be considered charitable under this category.[119] Another example, reported by the Charity Commission in their Annual Report for 2004–2005 is 'Funky Dragon', the Welsh youth parliament.

(d) Promoting ethical standards in business and corporate responsibility

Despite the extensiveness of the list of charitable purposes set out in the Charities Act 2011, there are many examples of charitable activity that are hard to classify. For instance, even though there was no direct judicial authority, the Charity Commission has decided to recognize as charitable organizations which promote the incorporation of ethics into business practice, and which advise and protect vulnerable employees faced with ethical dilemmas in the course of their work. In the light of this, the Commission considered that the objects of the Centre of Corporate Accountability, which sought to promote safety by encouraging corporate accountability for breaches of health and safety laws, were capable of being charitable, although the organization itself was held not to be charitable because its objects were also political.[120]

(e) Volunteering and the voluntary sector

Volunteering consists of engaging in action which is not compulsory, for which financial reward is not the primary motivation, and which benefits others or society.[121] According

[114] RR2—*Promotion of Urban and Rural Regeneration* [1999].

[115] RR2—*Promotion of Urban and Rural Regeneration* [1999], para 7.

[116] RR5—*The Promotion of Community Capacity Building* (November 2000).

[117] Ibid, para 7. [118] Ibid, para 13.

[119] The promotion of civic responsibility is specifically included within this head by the Charities Act 2011, s 3(2)(c)(ii).

[120] Decision of the Charity Commission for England and Wales, *Application for Registration of the Centre for Corporate Accountability*, 24 August 2001.

[121] RR13—*The Promotion of the Voluntary Sector for the Benefit of the Public* (September 2004), para 3.

to the Home Office Citizenship Survey in 2003, more than 50 per cent of the adult population volunteers.[122] Volunteering makes a very substantial contribution to many areas of life, including culture and the arts, sport and recreation, conservation and regeneration, health and care, and politics. Section 3(2)(c)(ii) of the Charities Act 2011 includes the promotion of volunteering and the voluntary sector in this head of charity.

(f) Promoting the efficiency of charities

Promoting the effectiveness or efficiency of charities is included in the list of charitable purposes under this head by s 3(2)(c)(ii)of the Charities Act 2011. While this is a slightly unusual categorization, there could be little doubt that trusts seeking to enhance the effectiveness of charities would be recognized as beneficial to the public, since they could only be encouraging the better performance of functions which have already been held, themselves, to be charitable.

One such charity registered as a charity for the purpose of promoting the voluntary sector is Guidestar UK,[123] which maintains a publicly available and comprehensive database about the activities and finances of UK charities. The Charity Commission felt the activities of the organization were capable of providing tools to both monitor the effectiveness and efficiency of charities and to encourage donors to make donations to effective charities.

(g) Charities concerned with social investment

The Charities (Protection and Social Investment) Act 2016, which came into force on 31 July 2016, introduces a new statutory power for charities to make social investments.[124] This arose from a Law Commission consultation paper[125] and subsequent final report.[126] A financial investment is an investment made solely for the purpose of achieving a financial return for the charity, and will not classify as a social investment. Instead, a 'social investment' means a 'relevant act' of a charity which is carried out 'with a view to both directly furthering the charity's purposes and achieving a financial return for the charity'.[127] A relevant act is simply the application of funds or other property by the charity to the investment purposes, or by using the same for a guarantee.[128]

A good example of a social investment would be where a homelessness charity purchases empty properties to renovate and let out at a low rent to homeless people. This would qualify as a social investment, as the charity achieves its purposes in providing housing for the homeless,[129] and obtains a financial return through the rental income and any increase in the value of the property.[130] A social investment is thus linked to the other charitable purposes by definition, but an organization would be charitable if it were set up to with the sole purpose of making such social investments.

[122] Russell Commission Report 2005, p 19.

[123] Decision of the Charity Commissioners For England and Wales, *Application for Registration of Guidestar UK*, 7 March 2003.

[124] Charities (Protection and Social Investment) Act 2016, s 15 which inserted s 292A into the Charities Act 2011.

[125] *Social Investment by Charities* (Law Com CP No 216, 2014).

[126] *Social Investment by Charities: The Law Commission's Recommendations* (Law Com, September 2014).

[127] Charities Act 2011, s 292A. [128] Charities Act 2011, s 292A(4).

[129] Charities Act 2011, s 3(1)(j).

[130] See *Social Investment by Charities* (Law Com CP No 216, 2014), Ch 2, p 13.

(6) Advancement of the arts, culture, heritage, or science

(a) Art, culture, and education

Trusts which promote an appreciation of the arts and other cultural activities have long been held to be charitable. Previously, they would have been considered as extensions of trust for the advancement of education under the *Pemsel* classification. As noted by Lord Greene MR in *Royal Choral Society v IRC*,[131] 'the education of artistic taste is one of the most important things in the development of a civilized human being'. Hence, a trust for the promotion of the musical works of the composer, Fredrick Delius, has been held charitable,[132] as has a trust to promote the works of William Shakespeare,[133] and similarly a trust to hold exhibitions of Egyptian archaeological finds.[134] In *IRC v White*[135] the Clerkenwell Green Association of Craftsmen, which existed to further crafts and craftsmanship, was held charitable.

Purposes that are too vague and uncertain will not be held charitable. So in *Associated Artists Ltd v IRC*[136] the promotion of 'artistic dramatic works' was not considered charitable.

(b) Monuments

A trust to erect a public statue of Earl Mountbatten of Burma was considered charitable by the Charity Commissioners.[137] The chief consideration was that the person to be commemorated could be considered a figure of historical importance. The benefit of such a statue was that it would foster patriotism and good citizenship, and act as an incentive to heroic and noble deeds. Memorials to private individuals of no such historical importance will not be charitable.[138] The Charity Commission accepted in 2003 that an appeal to provide a new statue in Banbury to celebrate the nursery rhyme 'Ride a cock horse to Banbury Cross, to see a fine lady upon a white horse' was charitable on the grounds of a trust for the enhancement of a locality and raising artistic taste, even though it was not accepted that the associated activities proposed in the application for registration were of educational value.[139] It is suggested that this decision might now be explained as an example of the preservation of heritage,[140] as an activity 'concerned with preserving or maintaining a particular tradition where the benefit to the public in preserving it can be shown'.[141]

(c) A requirement of merit

Despite the desire to uphold gifts that genuinely advance artistic and cultural appreciation, the Charity Commission and the courts are astute to ensure that gifts that promote purposes of no artistic merit are not held charitable. The very nature of art makes it difficult for the courts to exercise objective judgments as to what is artistically valuable, and what is not. One man's masterpiece is another man's rubbish. In *Re Delius*[142] it was suggested that the subjective nature of such a judgment would mean that the court would have no option but to hold charitable a trust to promote the work of even an inadequate

[131] [1943] 2 All ER 101. [132] *Re Delius (Decd)* [1957] Ch 299.

[133] *Re Shakespeare Memorial Trust* [1923] 2 Ch 398.

[134] *Re British School of Egyptian Archaeology* [1954] 1 WLR 546.

[135] [1980] TR 155. [136] [1956] 1 WLR 752.

[137] Report of the Charity Commissioners for England and Wales 1981, paras 68–70.

[138] See *Re Endacott* [1960] Ch 232, CA.

[139] Decision of the Charity Commissioners for England and Wales, *Application for Registration of The Fine Lady Upon A White Horse Appeal*, 29 September 2003.

[140] See Charity Commission RR9, *Preservation and Conservation* (February 2001).

[141] Charity Commission, *Guidance: Charitable Purposes, Pt 8* (16 September 2013).

[142] [1957] Ch 299.

composer. On the facts, the issue did not arise because the high standard of Delius's work was not challenged.

It is now clear that the court will take expert advice as to the value of work of supposed artistic merit, and if the expert advice is unanimous that it is of no value, then the courts will not find that there is a charity for the advancement of education.[143] In *Re Pinion (Decd)*[144] Harry Pinion had been a prolific collector of paintings, furniture, china, glass, and other objets d'art. On his death he left his residuary estate to trustees to open his studio as a museum housing the collection. Expert witnesses considered the merits of the collection, and were unanimous in their conclusion that it was of no value. Indeed, one expert expressed his surprise that such a voracious collector had not even managed to pick up a single meritorious piece by accident. In the light of this evidence the Court of Appeal held that the trust was not charitable. Harman LJ concluded: 'I can conceive of no useful object to be served in foisting upon the public this mass of junk.'

(d) Can the vernacular and the popular have merit?

There is an increasing interest in the study of the vernacular, and of the need to preserve historical evidence of the way of life of ordinary people in the past. The National Trust, for instance, has preserved an ordinary terraced house in the north of England, using it to reflect a comparatively recently bygone way of life.[145] Industrial and folk museums have developed substantially over recent decades. No doubt all of these could be considered charitable, even though they reflect 'ordinary' rather than 'high' culture.

(7) Advancement of amateur sport

(a) The evolution of the promotion of sport

It was originally considered that trusts encouraging the playing of sport would not in themselves be considered charitable.[146] Some other factor was required to justify a conclusion that the playing of sport was a charitable purpose. Hence, sport could be regarded as for the advancement of education, as in *IRC v McMullen*,[147] where a trust for the promotion of football and other games and sports in schools and universities was held charitable by the House of Lords.[148] Similarly, the gift of a prize for chess to boys and young men resident in Portsmouth was held charitable in *Re Dupree's Deed Trusts*,[149] expanding the definition of 'sport' to include intellectually stimulating games.

In November 2002 the Charity Commissioners decided that Community Amateur Sports Clubs (CASCs) should be recognized as charitable, as they encourage community participation in healthy sports, owing to 'the enormous public interest in sport as a means of promoting health and the vital role that sport plays in improving the health of the nation.'[150] The test the Commission applied was one of 'healthy recreation', so that

[143] This is reflected in the Charity Commission's review of the register, which sets out the selection requirements of such experts—Charity Commission, RR10 *Museums and Art Galleries* (August 2002), paras A12–A17. See also *R (Preservation and Promotion of the Arts Ltd) v Greater Manchester Magistrates Court* [2020] EWHC 2435.

[144] [1965] Ch 85.

[145] 20 Forthlin Road, Liverpool (the former council house home of the Beatle Sir Paul McCartney) has been opened to the public by the National Trust.

[146] See *Re Nottage* [1895] 2 Ch 649, CA.

[147] [1981] AC 1. See also *Re Mariette* [1915] 2 Ch 284 (gift to provide fives and squash courts at a specific school).

[148] Contrast this with the failure of Birchfield Harriers, a leading athletic club, to be registered as a charity, on the basis that there was insufficient evidence of education in their activities—Report of the Charity Commissioners for England and Wales 1989, para 52.

[149] [1945] Ch 16.

[150] RR11—*Charitable Status and Sport* (April 2003), para 5.

it included sports 'which, if practised with reasonable frequency, will tend to make the participant healthier, that is, fitter and less susceptible to disease'.[151]

(b) Statutory extension of the promotion of sport

The Charities Act 2011 extends the category of sporting activity that can be held to be charitable. By s 3(1)(g) the promotion of amateur sport is a charitable purpose. Only sports that involve 'physical or mental skill and exertion' are charitable under this head.[152] It is unlikely that promoting the playing of darts or snooker would be considered to be charitable under this head. On a similar basis, target shooting is not charitable under this head.[153] More difficulty might be experienced with a game such as croquet, where the extent of exertion required is modest. A bridge club has been held charitable: even though this card game involves minimal physical skill, it presents considerable mental challenge.[154]

(c) Not all amateur sports clubs are charitable

It does not follow that because it is possible for an amateur sports club to be charitable, all clubs will satisfy the requirements to be charitable. This might be because the benefits are confined to a small, private, group of members, as may be the case with some golf clubs. It might be because the sport does not satisfy the test of promoting health or involving physical exertion and skill. It might be because the sport is insufficiently inclusive. Sports such as polo and motor racing may be considered to be 'elite' sports which fail to satisfy the test of public benefit, unless a trust to promote these sports includes measures which enable participation by people who, without the support offered by the trust, could not afford to acquire the expensive equipment needed.[155] Certain amateur sports clubs[156] can register with HM Revenue & Customs (HMRC) as Community Amateur Sports Clubs (CASC) in order to gain tax-exempt status,[157] but it is not possible, following the Charities Act 2011, for a club to be both registered in this way and to be a registered charity, even if the club was established for charitable purposes.[158]

(8) Advancement of human rights, conflict resolution, and equality

(a) A broad category

This new head of charity contained in the Charities Act 2011 has the longest description. It comprises 'the advancement of human rights, conflict resolution or reconciliation or the promotion of religious or racial harmony or equality and diversity'. This is a category of charitable purpose that, perhaps more than any other, reflects changes in society and social attitudes. The category is clearly of considerable scope.

[151] RR11—*Charitable Status and Sport* (April 2003), paras 8 and 9.

[152] Charities Act 2011, s 3(2)(d).

[153] See *Cambridgeshire Target Shooting Association (CTSA) v Charity Commission* Appeal No CA\2015\0002.

[154] See *English Bridge Union Ltd v Revenue and Customs Commissioners* [2015] UKUT 0401 (TCC). This was an appeal from an earlier decision of the First-tier Tribunal (Charities) ([2014] UKFTT 181 (TC)).

[155] RR11—*Charitable Status and Sport* (April 2003), para 26.

[156] The current rules mean that to be eligible for registration as a CASC with HMRC, an organization must not only provide facilities for eligible sports and encourage people to take part, but at least 50 per cent of the members must take part. For detailed requirements, see https://www.gov.uk/government/publications/community-amateur-sports-clubs-detailed-guidance-notes (accessed November 2021).

[157] Finance Act 2002, Sch 18, c 23. The range of tax reliefs includes Gift Aid. Note, though, that for VAT purposes, a CASC cannot be a charity under the Finance Act 2010: *Eynsham Cricket Club v HMRC* [2021] EWCA Civ 225.

[158] Charities Act 2011, s 6.

(b) Advancement of human rights

The advancement of human rights was seen as being charitable by analogy with other charitable purposes,[159] a position confirmed by the Charities Act 2011. The problem is that the promotion of human rights may often require advocating a change in the law, and advocating such a change has been held to be a political purpose that cannot, therefore, be charitable.[160]

By adopting a less cautionary view of what is permissible in relation to political campaigning, the Charity Commission has enabled human rights charities to be registered, even if seeking to influence government policy or to change the law may be activities that the charity will undertake. The Commission has provided what it considers an example set of objects for a human rights charity.[161] This sets out a range of ways in which human rights can be promoted without engaging in political activity, and then adds:

> In furtherance of that object but not otherwise, the trustees shall have power to engage in political activity provided that the trustees are satisfied that the proposed activities will further the purposes of the charity to an extent justified by the resources committed and the activity is not the dominant means by which the charity carries out its objects.

This tension with political purposes was precisely the issue that faced the Commission when considering the Human Dignity Trust, an organization established to carry out or support litigation in foreign states in support those seeking to challenge domestic law which criminalizes sexual conduct in the LGBTI community contrary to human rights obligations. The stated purposes of the organization were the advancement of human rights and the sound administration of the law. The Commission refused to register the organization as a charity, on the basis that the purposes were not exclusively charitable, as seeking change in the law in foreign states was a political purpose. On appeal to the Tribunal,[162] the purposes of the trust were found to be charitable, on the basis that the Human Dignity Trust was promoting and protecting human rights as set out in Universal Declaration on Human Rights and subsequent United Nations conventions and declarations. It was upholding the law, not campaigning to change it, given the supremacy of constitutional or international obligations.[163]

(c) Advancement of conflict resolution or reconciliation

This description would include a trust seeking to resolve national or international conflicts, and also a trust promoting restorative justice 'where all the parties with a stake in a particular conflict or offence come together to resolve collectively how to deal with its aftermath and its implications for the future'.[164]

(d) The promotion of religious or racial harmony or equality and diversity

The Charity Commission has indicated that this purpose will include a broad range of charitable activities, including enabling people to understand the religious beliefs of others, promoting equality and diversity by eliminating discrimination on the grounds of

[159] RR12—*The Promotion of Human Rights* (January 2005), para 8.

[160] Charities and political purposes are considered further in the chapter.

[161] Charity Commission RR12—*The Promotion of Human Rights* (January 2005), para 37.

[162] *Human Dignity Trust (HDT) v The Charity Commission* Appeal number CA/2013/0013.

[163] Ibid, paras 43–4 on the transnational nature of human rights obligations.

[164] The promotion of restorative justice was recognized as a charitable purpose by the Charity Commission in 2003: Decision of the Charity Commissioners For England and Wales, *Application for Registration of Restorative Justice Consortium Limited*, 15 January 2003. See also Decision of the Charity Commissioners For England and Wales, *Application for Registration of Concordis International Trust*, 23 July 2004.

age, race,[165] sex,[166] or sexual orientation,[167] as well as the promotion of good relations between different groups.[168]

The promotion of religious harmony was first accepted as charitable by the Charity Commission in 2002 when it registered the Friends of Three Faiths Forum, an organization intended to promote religious harmony by enabling people of one faith to understand the religious beliefs of others. The three faiths concerned were Christianity, Judaism, and Islam. The Commissioners considered that the purposes were charitable by virtue of the analogy 'to the existing purposes of promoting equality of women with men, promoting racial harmony and promoting the moral or spiritual welfare or improvement of the community'.[169]

(9) **Advancement of environmental protection or improvement**

The preservation of national heritage and conservation of the environment are charitable purposes under the 2011 Act. The National Trust is charitable,[170] since its objects of 'promoting the permanent preservation for the benefit of the nation of lands and tenements (including buildings) of beauty or historic interest and as regards lands for the preservation since of their natural aspect features and animal and plant life',[171] are for the public benefit. Charities concerned with the conservation of a particular species of animal or plant will be charitable,[172] including the provision of zoological gardens.

Where the organization is set up to maintain a particular building, site, or habitat, the element of public benefit will normally only be satisfied if the public have access. However, if there are valid reasons for limiting or excluding such access the public benefit element may be satisfied if the organization puts in place alternative means of informing the public about its activities.[173]

In 2001, the Charity Commission recognized the conservation of the environment as a charitable purpose in its own right, including organizations that conserve the environment by promoting biodiversity.[174] In April 2002 the Charity Commission decided that Recycling in Ottery, a company which sought to 'protect and safeguard the environment particularly through the promotion of re-use and recycling and the provision of recycling facilities', and which ran a scrap yard where members of the public could bring items for recycling, was charitable.[175] Conservation was held to extend to sustainable

[165] See *Re Strakosch (Decd)* [1949] Ch 529, CA, where a gift to appease racial feelings in a community was held not to be charitable on the basis it has very wide objects. This did not stop the Commission recognizing racial harmony as a charitable purpose—see Report of the Charity Commissioners for England and Wales 1983, paras 18–20.

[166] See *Halpin v Steear* (27 February 1976, unreported), which concerned the promotion of equality between men and women.

[167] See Decision of the Charity Commissioners For England and Wales, *LGB Alliance—Full Decision*, 20 April 2021 (purposes are to promote equality and diversity and human rights for lesbian, gay and bisexual people and those who face discrimination on the grounds of sexual orientation).

[168] Charity Commission, *Guidance: Charitable Purposes, Pt 10* (16 September 2013).

[169] *Charity Commission Annual Report 2002–2003*, p 22.

[170] *Re Verrall* [1916] 1 Ch 100. [171] National Trust Act 1907, s 4(1).

[172] See, however, Decision of the Charity Commissioners For England and Wales, *Application for Registration of The Wolf Trust*, 9 May 2003; where a trust for the conversation of wolves was not charitable on the basis that the real purpose was to re-introduce wolves into Scotland to influence public opinion about predators.

[173] RR9—*Preservation and Conservation* (Feb 2001), paras A18–A20.

[174] RR1—*The Review of the Register of Charities* [2001], para B9.

[175] Decision of the Charity Commissioners for England and Wales, *Application for Registration of Recycling in Ottery*, April 2002.

development.[176] However, environmental campaign groups that have primarily political purposes will not enjoy charitable status.

(10) Relief of need

It has already been seen that the Statute of Charitable Uses recognized that charitable purposes included the relief of poverty, infirmity, and illness. The Charities Act 2011 states that it is a charitable purpose to provide relief for those in need 'by reason of youth, age, ill-health, disability, financial hardship or other disadvantage'.[177] This 'includes relief given by the provision of accommodation or care to the persons mentioned in that paragraph'.[178]

(a) Examples of the relief of need

There is clearly considerable overlap between this head of charity and the head relating to the relief of poverty and the advancement of health, and many trusts that are charitable under those heads would also be charitable within this category. The provision of social housing is expressly included in the category. In *Joseph Rowntree Memorial Trust Housing Association Ltd v A-G*,[179] the Housing Association, which wished to build small dwellings for sale to the elderly, was considered charitable even though those who would benefit by purchasing the dwellings would not fall within the definition of 'poor'. Other forms of assistance to disadvantaged groups would also be charitable, including the relief of unemployment. As part of its review of the Register, the Charity Commission decided in 1999 that an organization for the relief of unemployment would be charitable per se if it can be demonstrated that it was tackling unemployment, either generally or for a significant section of the community. Acceptable activities include the provision of: advice and training to unemployed individuals; practical support for unemployed people by way of accommodation, child care facilities, or assistance with travel; land, and buildings at below market or subsidized rents to businesses starting up; capital grants or equipment to new businesses; and payments to an existing commercial business to take on additional staff.[180]

It is not necessary that the needs relieved relate only to the UK. The Charity Commission has held the promotion of trading fairly is a charitable purpose. Thus in 1995 it registered as a charity an organization which would award a 'Fair Trade mark' on the packaging of goods sold in supermarkets, which would have the effect of relieving the conditions of life of third-world workers.[181]

(b) Provision of recreational facilities

Until the position was changed by the Recreational Charities Act 1958, the provision of recreational facilities was not, in itself, charitable, even if those facilities are provided to the public at large. This position was established by three decisions of the House of Lords in the mid-twentieth century.[182] In *IRC v Baddeley*,[183] a gift of land was made to a Methodist Mission, including an area laid out as a playing field complete with a pavilion and groundsman's bungalow. The purposes of the gift included 'the provision of facilities for religious services and instruction and for the social and physical training and recreation' of persons resident in West Ham and Leyton. The House of Lords held that this

[176] Decision of the Charity Commissioners For England and Wales, *Application for Registration of Environment Foundation*, 24 January 2003.

[177] Charities Act 2011, s 3(1)(j). [178] s 3(2)(e).

[179] [1983] Ch 159. [180] RR3—*Charities for the Relief of Unemployment* [1999].

[181] RR1—*The Review of the Register of Charities* [2001], para B17.

[182] RR1—*The Review of the Register of Charities* [2001], para B17.

[183] RR1—*The Review of the Register of Charities* [2001], para B17.

was not a gift made exclusively for charitable purposes, following the earlier decision of *Williams' Trustees v IRC*.[184]

A number of cases have held that gifts for the provision of public recreation grounds can be charitable, for example in *Re Hadden*,[185] where a gift was made for the provision of playing fields, parks, and gymnasiums in Vancouver, and in *Re Morgan*,[186] where a gift for the provision of a public recreation ground for a particular parish was held charitable. In *Brisbane City Council v A-G for Queensland*,[187] a trust to provide an area for 'a park and recreation purposes' was also held charitable. Viscount Simmonds in *IRC v Baddeley* was careful to stress that the provision of recreation grounds would still be charitable.[188]

The decision in *IRC v Baddeley* gave rise to concern that Women's Institutes and similar organizations, previously considered to be charitable, would no longer qualify for that status. To eliminate any uncertainty, the Recreational Charities Act 1958 (now consolidated in the Charities Act 2011, s 5) was enacted. This Act was not intended to enlarge the definition of charity, but instead to give statutory confirmation of purposes already recognized as charitable. The statute covered the provision of 'facilities for recreation or other leisure-time occupation' and specific mention is made of facilities at 'village halls, community centres and women's institutes'. The key provision of the Act was that the facilities must be provided in the 'interests of social welfare'. This requirement could not be met unless the facilities provided have the object of 'improving the conditions of life for the persons for whom the facilities are primarily intended' and those persons must fall within either of the two groups specified:

(1) persons needing such facilities because of their youth, age, infirmity or disability, poverty or social and economic circumstances;
(2) the public at large or the male[189] or female members of the public.

Thus, private clubs, such as golf clubs, which provide facilities only for their members and which, therefore, lack altruism,[190] will not attract charitable status and the consequent tax privileges. A club confined to a single sport may also be less likely to be considered charitable.[191] The statute did not exactly define 'social welfare',[192] stating instead the essential elements that must be present. The approach now taken is that of Lord Keith in *Guild v IRC*,[193] and does not require deprivation but that 'persons in all walks of life and all sorts of social circumstances may have their conditions of life improved by the provision of recreational facilities of a suitable character'.[194]

(11) **Advancement of animal welfare**

Gifts to specific animals may be upheld as valid unenforceable purpose trusts since they are recognized as anomalous exceptions to the beneficiary principle.[195] In contrast, trusts

[184] [1947] AC 477. [185] [1932] 1 Ch 133. [186] [1955] 1 WLR 738.
[187] [1979] AC 411, PC. [188] [1955] AC 572 at 559.
[189] Male members of the public were included by the Charities Act 2006, s 5(2) (now the Charities Act 2011, s 5(3)). Prior to this, benefits could be confined to female members of the public, but not to male members of the public.
[190] A characteristic considered necessary by the Charity Commission: see RR4—*The Recreational Charities Act 1958* [2000], paras A13–A14 and A34–A35.
[191] RR4—*The Recreational Charities Act 1958* [2000], paras A24–A25.
[192] See *Valuation Comr for Northern Ireland v Lurgan Borough Council* [1968] NI 104 at 126–7, per Lord MacDermott LCJ.
[193] [1992] 2 AC 310, approving an earlier interpretation of Bridge LJ in *IRC v Mullen* [1979] 1 WLR 130. That interpretation had been followed by the Charity Commission—*Report of the Charity Commissioners for England and Wales 1989*, para 55.
[194] [1992] 2 AC 310. [195] See Chapter 19.

that promote the welfare of animals in general are charitable. This was recognized before the 2006 Act, which according to Lewison J in *Hanchett-Stamford v Attorney-General*,[196] has not effected 'any change in the substance of the law'.[197] In *Re Wedgwood*[198] Frances Wedgwood left property to her brother on secret trust for the protection and benefit of animals. She had discussed with him the possible use of the money to forward the movement for humane slaughtering of animals, which the Court of Appeal held to be a valid charitable object. The necessary element of public benefit was not found in any benefits to the animals themselves, but in the beneficial effects that the relief of cruelty to animals was expected to have on public morality. This was emphasized by all the members of the Court of Appeal.[199]

This reasoning was accepted without question by Nourse J in *Re Green's Will Trusts*.[200] In *Re Moss*[201] the welfare of cats and kittens was held charitable, as was a home for lost dogs.[202] In *Tatham v Drummond*,[203] the RSPCA was held charitable, and more recently in *Re Green's Will Trusts*[204] a trust for the rescue, maintenance, and benefit of cruelly treated animals was held charitable. Gifts for animal sanctuaries have been held charitable, as in *Re Murawski's Will Trusts*,[205] where a gift was made to the Bleakholt Animal Sanctuary, whose constitution adopted the objects of 'the provision of care and shelter for stray, neglected and unwanted animals of all kinds and the protection of animals from ill-usage, cruelty and suffering'. However, it seems that the sanctuary must either relieve cruelty or provide access to the public to view the animals, if it is to be regarded as for the benefit of the public. Thus, in *Re Grove-Grady*,[206] the Court of Appeal considered that a gift to found the 'Beaumont Animal Benevolent Society' was not charitable. Its purposes were to provide a refuge where animal life of all types might be completely undisturbed by man. The court held that the public derived no benefit from such a refuge, since the purpose was not the reduction of pain or cruelty to the animals and the public could be excluded from entering the area or even looking into it. Russell LJ considered that there was no public benefit when:

> all that the public need know about the matter would be that one or more areas existed in which all animals (whether good or bad from man's point of view) were allowed to live free from any risk of being molested or killed by man; though liable to be molested and killed by other denizens of the area.[207]

It is questionable whether this attitude would still prevail, given greater awareness and concern about environmental and conservation issues (a specific category of charity following the Charities Act 2006) and of the desirability of maintaining genetic diversity. It is artificial to justify animal welfare charities on the unproven and far from self-evident basis that they 'elevate the human race'. It would be rather better to accept them as charitable simply because they benefit the animals themselves, the approach taken in Ireland,[208] and suggested by the statutory recognition of the welfare of animals as a free-standing charitable purpose.[209]

An organization promoting the welfare of animals will not be a charity if its principal purpose is to campaign for a change in the law. In *Hanchett-Stamford v Attorney-General*,[210] Lewison J held that the Performing and Captive Animals Defence League was not charitable because the achievement of its purposes required a change in the law.

[196] [2009] Ch 173. [197] See, for example, Swinfen Eday LJ [2009] Ch 173 at 22.
[198] [1915] 1 Ch 113. [199] [1915] 1 Ch 113 at 122. [200] [1985] 3 All ER 455 at 458.
[201] [1949] 1 All ER 495. [202] *Re Douglas* [1887] 35 Ch D 472. [203] [1864] 4 De GJ & Sm 484.
[204] [1985] 3 All ER 455. [205] [1971] 1 WLR 707. [206] [1929] 1 Ch 557.
[207] [1929] 1 Ch 557 at 586. [208] *Armstrong v Reeves* [1890] 25 LR Ir 325.
[209] See, for example, the wording of the latest Charity Commission guidance, which suggests it includes 'any purpose directed towards the prevention or suppression of cruelty to animals or the prevention or relief of suffering by animals'—Charity Commission, *Guidance: Charitable Purposes, Pt 13* (16 September 2013).
[210] [2009] Ch 173.

(12) Promotion of the efficiency of the defence and rescue services

Gifts that promote the efficiency of the armed forces had long been held charitable under the fourth head. This was held to follow from the 'spirit and intendment' of the preamble, which mentioned the 'setting out of soldiers'. By analogy, it has been held that gifts which promote the efficiency of the police force will also be charitable.[211] The statutory list includes the armed forces, and the police, fire, and ambulance services.[212]

Some of the older cases need to be followed with caution. In *Re Good*[213] a gift of plate for an officers' mess was held charitable, and in *Re Gray*,[214] a gift for the promotion of shooting, fishing, cricket, football, and polo for a regiment was held charitable, as it promoted the physical efficiency of the army.[215] The more recent cases suggest that the *prime* object of the purposes must be to promote efficiency, if a gift is to be charitable. In *IRC v City of Glasgow Police Athletic Association*,[216] a gift to promote sport and athletic pastimes in the police force was held not charitable because, although similar to the facts of *Re Gray*,[217] the promotion of efficiency was only incidental to the promotion of sport.[218] The Charity Commission's guidance suggests that charitable activities would include providing equipment or services, or encouraging recruitment to the services.[219] The provision of RAF playgroups and of ex-servicemen's associations has been recognized as charitable.[220]

(13) Other purposes beneficial to the community

Notwithstanding the length of the list contained in the Charities Act 2011, there are many instances of charity which do not fall under any of these categories, but which will remain charitable because of the preservation of the current law by s 3(1)(m).[221] For instance, a number of cases hold that the promotion of trade and industry can be charitable.[222] The promotion of agriculture and horticulture has also been held charitable,[223] as was the provision of a 'showground'[224] that would encourage agriculture. These include, according to the latest Charity Commission guidance, the provision of public works and services and the provision of public amenities, the preservation of public order and the promotion of ethical standards of conduct and compliance with the law in the public and private sectors.[225]

However, the promotion of the interests of individuals rather than industry in general will not be charitable. In *Hadaway v Hadaway*,[226] a trust to 'assist planters and agriculturists' by the provision of loans at favourable rates of interest was held non-charitable by the Privy Council because it was directed at conferring private benefits. Similarly, in *IRC v Oldham Training and Enterprise Council*,[227] Lightman J held that a trust to promote 'trade

[211] *IRC v City of Glasgow Police Athletic Association* [1953] AC 380.

[212] Fire and rescue services are as defined in Pt 2 of the Fire and Rescue Services Act 2004.

[213] [1905] 2 Ch 60. [214] [1925] Ch 362. [215] [1925] Ch 362 at 365, per Romer J.

[216] [1953] AC 380. [217] [1925] Ch 362.

[218] Essentially, the gift was not exclusively charitable. This requirement is considered later in this chapter.

[219] Charity Commission, *Guidance: Charitable Purposes, Pt 14* (16 September 2013).

[220] Charity Commission for England and Wales, *Annual Report 1997*, para 90.

[221] See also Charity Commission, RR1a *Recognising New Charitable Purposes* (1 October 2001), particularly Appendices A and B, which summarize the court's and Charity Commission's approach, respectively.

[222] See *Construction Industry Training Board v A-G* [1971] 1 WLR 1303 (training for those employed in the construction industry); *Crystal Palace Trustees v Minister of Town and Country Planning* [1951] Ch 132 (promotion of industry commerce and art).

[223] See *IRC v Yorkshire Agricultural Society* [1928] 1 KB 611.

[224] *Brisbane City Council v A-G for Queensland* [1979] AC 411.

[225] Charity Commission, *Guidance: Charitable Purposes, Pt 15* (16 September 2013).

[226] [1955] 1 WLR 16. [227] [1996] STC 1218.

commerce and enterprise' in the Oldham area by providing 'support services and advice to and for new businesses' was not exclusively charitable because of the private benefits. The purposes would enable the TEC to 'promote the interests of individuals engaged in trade commerce or enterprise and provide benefits and services to them'.[228]

Other charitable purposes which cannot easily be located in any other category include establishing and running a Cyber Café in a socially deprived area,[229] and operating an internet content rating service.[230]

4 Recognizing new charitable purposes

Since the list of charitable purposes is not closed, a question arises as to how new charitable purposes will be recognized. The Charities Act 2011, s 3(1)(m), allows the recognition not only of those charitable purposes which are listed in the Act and those recognized under the old law before the Charities Act 2006 but also of any purposes 'analogous to or within the spirit of' those purposes or any new recognized purposes.

(1) The 'spirit and intendment' of the Statute of 1601

The Charities Act appears to exclude a method of reasoning which has been extensively used in the past. Traditionally, the 'spirit and intendment' of the preamble to the Statute of 1601 has acted as the benchmark to determine which purposes benefit the public in ways which are charitable. In *Williams' Trustees v IRC*,[231] where the House of Lords held that a trust for promoting Welsh interests in London was not charitable, Lord Simmonds said that:

> it is still the general law that a trust is not charitable and entitled to the privileges which charity confers, unless it is within the spirit and intendment of the preamble to the Statute of Elizabeth.[232]

However, the preamble cannot possibly anticipate the needs of society in the twenty-first century, and is an inadequate vehicle for determining charitable status. As Lord Upjohn commented in *Scottish Burial Reform and Cremation Society Ltd v Glasgow City Corpn*,[233] 'the authorities show that the spirit and intendment of the preamble to the Statute of Elizabeth have been stretched almost to breaking point.'

(2) Development by analogy

The practice of development by analogy, incorporated in the Charities Act, has become the predominant means of ascertaining whether a new purpose can be considered charitable. Lord Wilberforce, in the *Scottish Burial Reform* case, examined how the principle of the spirit and intendment had been applied in practice:

> the courts appear to have proceeded first by seeking some analogy between an object mentioned in the preamble and the object with regard to which they had to reach a decision. And

[228] [1996] STC 1218 at 1235.

[229] Decision of the Charity Commissioners For England and Wales, *Application for Registration* of *Community Server*, September 2003.

[230] Decision of the Charity Commissioners For England and Wales, *Application for Registration of Internet Rating Association*, September 2002.

[231] [1947] AC 447. [232] See also *A-G of the Cayman Islands v Wahr-Hansen* [2001] 1 AC 75, PC.

[233] [1968] AC 138 at 153.

> then they appear to have gone further and to have been satisfied if they could find an analogy between an object already held to be charitable.[234]

The Goodman Committee in 1976 recommended that the preamble should be replaced by a modern list of purposes deemed charitable to serve as a new benchmark for further development.[235] It took thirty years for the Committee's recommendations to be implemented.

An example of the difficulties demonstrated in reasoning by analogy can be found in the appeal to First Tier Tribunal (Charity) by the Independent Press Regulation Trust.[236] The organization sought to 'promote for the public benefit high standards of ethical conduct and best practice in journalism and the editing and publication of news in the print and other media' by funding and supporting an independent press regulator. It has been refused registration as a charity by the Charity Commission on the grounds that, while the organization's purposes could be considered analogous either to promoting the ethical or moral improvement of the community or to promoting compliance with the law, the regulation of the industry was too big a jump from reasoning by analogy for the purpose to be held charitable. The First Tier Tribunal upheld the appeal, as, in their view, the purpose was analogous to ethical or moral improvement,[237] and charitable on the basis it was for the public benefit, as demonstrated by the recommendation of the Leveson Inquiry.[238] This latter evidence had not been available to the Commission at the time it made the initial decision not to register the Trust.

(3) **Purposes without an analogy**

A new situation will occasionally arise in which, although there appears to be a public benefit, there is no obvious analogy. The problem may then arise as to whether this can be considered charitable. In *Williams' Trustees v IRC*, Lord Simmonds said, 'it is not enough to say that the trust in question is for public purposes beneficial to the community or for the public welfare; you must show it to be a charitable trust.'[239] How is this to be done in the absence of any analogy? An approach which has been suggested is that trusts which are for purposes manifestly for the public benefit should be prima facie charitable, unless there are any reasons why they should not be. In *Incorporated Council of Law Reporting for England and Wales v A-G*,[240] Russell LJ recognized the inadequacies of the 'spirit and intendment' principle and proposed instead that purposes which 'cannot be thought otherwise than beneficial to the community and of general public utility' should be charitable in law 'unless there are any grounds for holding it to be outside of the equity of the Statute [of 1601]'. This proposal was embraced by Sachs and Buckley LJJ. Applying this principle, it was held that the Incorporated Council of Law Reporting was registrable as a charity since its object of the production of law reports was clearly of general public utility and there were no grounds on which it should not be held charitable.

This approach has much to commend it, as the Privy Council indicated in *A-G of the Cayman Islands v Wahr-Hansen*.[241] It provides the capability to embrace new charitable purposes justified by changing social conditions. However, in *Barralet v A-G*, Dillon J expressed doubt whether it is consistent with the decision of the House of Lords in *Williams' Trustees v IRC*,[242] and concluded:

234 [1968] AC 138 at 147.

235 Report of the Goodman Committee: *Charity Law and Voluntary Organisations* [1976], para 32.

236 *Vernor-Miles and Ors v Charity Commission* Appeal number: CA/2014/0022 (12 May 2015).

237 Ibid at para 36.

238 See Leveson Inquiry, *Report into the Culture, Practices and Ethics of the Press* Volumes 1–4, (29 November 2012).

239 [1947] AC 447. 240 [1972] Ch 73, CA. 241 [2001] 1 AC 75. 242 [1947] AC 447.

> it seems to me that the approach to be adopted in considering whether something is within the fourth category is the approach of analogy from what is stated in the preamble to the Statute of Elizabeth or from what has already been held to be charitable within the fourth category.[243]

The Court of Appeal in *Helena Partnerships v HMRC*[244] also thought that reasoning by analogy or by reference to the spirit of the preamble was essential, and that the decision in the *Incorporated Council of Law Reporting* case did not depart from that view, given the reference by Russell LJ to the 'equity of the Statute'. The language of s 3(1)(m) of the Charities Act 2011 does not help since it is capable of being interpreted to include both reasoning by analogy and 'any other purposes recognised as charitable purposes . . . under the old law' by whatever means of reasoning.

5 Charitable purposes overseas

A trust is not denied charitable status merely because any benefit from its execution will be experienced abroad rather than within the jurisdiction. Examples of charities with an international dimension include: a gift to the German government for the benefit of soldiers disabled in the Great War;[245] a trust for aid to churches, hospitals, and schools and for the assistance of the poor and aged in Cephalonia;[246] a trust for planting a grove of olive trees in Israel;[247] and a trust for a working men's hostel in Cyprus.[248]

The approach to benefits outside the UK has evolved. In their *Annual Report* for 1963 the Charity Commissioners had no doubt that the advancement of religion, the advancement of education, and the relief of poverty are charitable in any part of the world.[249] For charities within Lord Macnaghten's fourth head of 'other purposes beneficial to the community', however, they said that there must be some benefit to the community of the UK and not merely to the foreign country, reflecting a dictum of Lord Evershed MR in *Camille and Henry Dreyfus Foundation Inc v IRC*.[250] The Commissioners suggested that this might be more easily found in benefits to a Commonwealth country.[251] In their report for 1990, the Commissioners noted the trend toward a European and international dimension in new charities, illustrated by the registration of the Gdansk Hospice Fund, the Nairobi Hospice Trust, and the USSR Support Charity.[252]

In their *Annual Report* of 1992, the Charity Commissioners went further and rejected the complex concepts of tangible and intangible benefit to the community of the UK. In future, the Commissioners indicated that a charity of any type operating abroad will be presumed charitable in the same way as if its operations were confined to the UK.[253] This presumption will be rebutted if it would be contrary to public policy to recognize the charity.[254] There is nothing in the Charities Act 2011 that challenges this practice.

[243] [1980] 3 All ER 918. [244] [2012] EWCA Civ 569 at 61–3.

[245] *Re Robinson* [1931] 2 Ch 122. [246] *Re Vagliano* [1905] WN 179.

[247] *Re Jacobs* [1970] 114 Sol Jo 515. [248] *Re Niyazi's Will Trusts* [1978] 1 WLR 910.

[249] *Report of the Charity Commissioners for England and Wales 1963*, para 72.

[250] [1954] Ch 672 at 684.

[251] *Report of the Charity Commissioners for England and Wales 1963*, para 72.

[252] *Report of the Charity Commissioners for England and Wales 1990*, paras 32 and 33.

[253] The Commissioners adopted an approach which had already been adopted in some Commonwealth jurisdictions. See *Re Lowin* [1967] 2 NSWR 140, CA; *Re Stone* [1970] 91 WNNSW 704 (SC); *Lander v Whitbread* [1982] 2 NSWLR 530; *Re Levy Estate* [1989] 58 DLR (4th) 375.

[254] *Report of the Charity Commissioners for England and Wales 1992*, para 76.

6 Trusts with political objects

The fundamental principle behind the definition of charity is that purposes that are charitable must be for the public benefit. However, even if a purpose falls within one of the previously discussed categories, and is, therefore, considered as beneficial, it will not be charitable if it is for political purposes. Lord Parker, in *Bowman v Secular Society*,[255] stated that equity had always refused to recognize as charitable 'purely political objects'. This restriction was applied by Slade J in *McGovern v A-G*.[256] Amnesty International wanted to set up a trust with four main objects:

(1) the relief of needy relatives and dependants of prisoners of conscience;
(2) attempting to secure the release of prisoners of conscience;
(3) procuring the abolition of torture or inhuman or degrading treatment or punishment;
(4) undertaking, and disseminating the results of research into the observance of human rights.

The Charity Commissioners had refused to register the trust as a charity, and their decision was affirmed by Slade J, who held that the main purpose was political.

(1) Meaning of 'political objects'

In the course of his judgment Slade J identified the circumstances in which a court would regard a trust as political. The tests he proposed were later approved (although in a different context) by the Court of Appeal in *R v Radio Authority, ex p Bull*.[257] According to Slade J, a trust will be regarded as political if it has as a direct or principal purpose supporting a political party, changing the law, or changing government policy.

(a) To further the interests of a political party

In *Re Ogden*[258] a trust to promote 'Liberal principles' in politics was held not to be charitable.[259] The Charity Commissioners refused to register 'Youth Training' as a charity, since its purpose was to assist the Workers' Revolutionary Party.[260]

(b) To procure changes in the laws of this country

A ground for the decision of the House of Lords in *National Anti-Vivisection Society v IRC*[261] was that the society's object of the abolition of vivisection would necessitate a change in the law of the land.[262] This, it was held, would not be charitable. Summarizing the law and the rationale for this principle, Slade J said:

> the court will not regard as charitable a trust of which the main object is to procure an alteration of the law of the United Kingdom for one of two or both of two reasons; first, the court will ordinarily have no sufficient means of judging as a matter of evidence whether the proposed

[255] [1917] AC 406.

[256] [1982] Ch 321. See Dunn, '*McGovern v Attorney-General*' [2013] 16 CLPR 105; Walton, '*McGovern v Attorney General*: constraints on judicial assessment of charitable benefit' [2014] Conv 317.

[257] [1998] QB 294.

[258] [1933] Ch 678.

[259] See also *Bonar Law Memorial Trust v IRC* [1933] 49 TLR 220.

[260] Charity Commissioners for England and Wales, *Annual Report 1982*, paras 451–651.

[261] [1948] AC 31.

[262] *IRC v Temperance Council of Christian Churches of England and Wales* [1926] 10 TC 748; *National Anti-Vivisection Society v IRC* [1948] AC 31.

change will or will not be for the public benefit.[263] Secondly, even if the evidence suffices to enable it to form a prima facie opinion that a change in the law is desirable, it must still decide the case on the principle that the law is right as it stands since to do otherwise would usurp the functions of the legislature.

The promotion of the present status quo by maintaining the existing law or policy is equally a political purpose,[264] unless the effect of the law or policy concerned is to promote a charitable purpose.[265]

(c) To procure changes in the law of a foreign country

Although there is no obligation on the court to assume that foreign law is right as it stands, Slade J considered that it was still impossible to judge whether a change in foreign law would be beneficial to the community, and, therefore, such purposes are not charitable.

(d) To procure a reversal of government policy or of particular decisions of governmental authorities in this country

The courts are also unwilling to encroach on the functions of the executive. Therefore, and because it is impossible to determine whether any changes would result in a public benefit, Slade J held that such purposes would not be charitable.

(e) To procure a reversal of government policy or of particular decisions of governmental authorities in a foreign country

Similarly, the court has no satisfactory means of judging whether there is any public benefit from such a reversal.

(2) Application of the restriction

Whatever the category of charitable purpose, if a trust or organization has political purposes, it cannot be recognized as charitable. In *Re Hopkinson*[266] a gift was made for the advancement of adult education on the lines of a Labour Party memorandum. Vaisey J held that the purpose was 'political propaganda masquerading as education' and, therefore, not charitable.[267] In *Re Bushnell*[268] a trust for the promotion of socialized medicine through the publishing and distribution of books was held to be political, rather than for the provision of medical care. In contrast, in *Re Koeppler Will Trusts*,[269] a gift to Wilton Park, an institution which was not party political and sought to promote greater cooperation in Europe, was held charitable. The Court of Appeal emphasized that the discussions it organized were neither party political nor propagandist. The Charity Commission has decided that the Centre for Corporate Accountability was not exclusively charitable because, although it was established for the charitable purpose of promoting public safety, it sought to do so by advocating changes to the law of corporate killing and influencing the prosecutions and investigations policy of the Crown Prosecution Service and the Health and Safety Executive.[270] Charities have been held not to be entitled to

[263] See *Bowman v Secular Society* [1917] AC 406 at 443, per Lord Parker of Waddington: 'a trust for the attainment of political objects has always been held invalid, not because it is illegal . . . but because the court has no means of judging whether a proposed change in the law will or will not be for the public benefit'.

[264] *Re Hopkinson* [1949] 1 All ER 346; *Re Koeppler Will Trusts* [1984] Ch 243.

[265] *Re Vallance* [1876] 2 *Seton's Judgments* (7th edn) 1304; *Re Herrick* [1918] 52 ILT 213.

[266] [1949] 1 All ER 346.

[267] However, in *Re Trust of Arthur McDougall Fund* [1956] 3 All ER 867 it was held that a trust for the education of the public in forms of government and in political matters generally was charitable.

[268] [1975] 1 WLR 1596. [269] [1986] Ch 423.

[270] Decision of the Charity Commissioners for England and Wales, *Application for Registration of the Centre for Corporate Accountability* (24 August 2001).

engage in public campaigning on political issues unrelated to their charitable objects. In *Baldry v Feintuck*,[271] a student union was held to have applied money to a non-charitable object when it supported a campaign against the government policy of ending free milk in schools. Similarly, in *Webb v O'Doherty*,[272] support by a student union of a campaign against the Gulf War was held non-charitable. In *R v Radio Authority, ex p Bull*,[273] Lord Woolf pointed out that an activity that was not in itself political could be considered to become political if it had the objective of promoting a political purpose. 'It takes its nature from the principal objective.'[274]

In *Hanchett-Stamford v Attorney-General*,[275] a society was established to prevent cruelty to animals by prohibiting their use for performances on stage or in films. The association had been denied the benefits of charitable status in the past, on the basis that it was campaigning for a change in the law. Lewison J held that the:

> Charities Act 2006 has not changed the fundamental principle that if one of the objects or purposes of an organisation is to change the law, it cannot be charitable.[276]

(3) **Ancillary political activities**

Slade J's decision in *McGovern v A-G*[277] initially gave many charities cause for concern. Amnesty International had taken professional advice in drawing up their trust deed. It affected not just Amnesty International, but also other charities, like Oxfam or Shelter, which, in addition to fulfilling their main purpose of providing relief or care services, would also seek to influence government opinion in favour of the causes which they espoused. Slade J had recognized that a limited degree of political activity was permissible, provided that it was not a main purpose of the trust. He said:

> Trust purposes of an otherwise charitable nature do not lose it merely because the trustees, by way of furtherance of such purposes, have incidental powers to carry on activities which are not themselves charitable ... If all the main objects of the trust are exclusively charitable, the mere fact that the trustees may have incidental powers to employ political means for their furtherance will not deprive them of their charitable status.[278]

In *R v Radio Authority, ex p Bull*, Brooke LJ commented on the impact of this exception:

> Many charitable trusts today—national charities concerned with children, or the physically or mentally disabled, or with housing the homeless, for example—are prominent in their espousal of political means to attain their ends.[279]

(4) **Legitimate political activity by charities**

It is obviously correct that purposes of a truly political nature should not receive the state subsidy in effect granted to charities through tax privileges. However, it is also the case that many well-established charities engage in political activity of some type, whether campaigning, lobbying Parliament, or advocating changes in the law. For example, the housing charity Shelter may challenge government housing policy, and relief agencies may demand a different attitude by government towards the Third World. A fine balance must be drawn between legitimate political activity by charities, and political activism that is incompatible with the retention of charitable status—any political activity must

[271] [1972] 2 All ER 81. [272] [1991] *The Times*, 11 February. [273] [1997] 2 All ER 561.
[274] [1997] 2 All ER 561 at 572. [275] [2009] Ch 173. [276] [2009] Ch 173 at 181.
[277] [1982] Ch 321. [278] [1981] 3 All ER 493 at 509 and 511. [279] [1997] 2 All ER 561 at 580.

be purely ancillary to their main charitable objects. The Charity Commission sought to clarify the impact of the *McGovern* decision in their 1981 report, which was quite directive in explaining what a charity could or could not do, and was cautionary in tone. This approach has evolved over time into their latest guidance,[280] which instead of telling charity trustees what they are or are not permitted to do, is more general, leaving the ultimate decision on appropriateness of any given activity to the organization itself.

The Commission acknowledges that, while an organization can never be a charity if it is established solely for political purposes, so long as a charity is 'engaging in campaigning or political activity solely in order to further or support its charitable purposes, and there is a reasonable likelihood of it being effective, it may carry out campaigning and political activity'.[281] Charity trustees must consider that the methods used are lawful and an effective use of charity resources,[282] and be satisfied that the activities are permitted under the governing document of the charity.[283] A charity may seek to influence government.[284] It may provide and publish comments on possible or proposed changes in the law or government policy,[285] and advocate a change in the law or public policy, provided that these activities do not become the dominant means by which it carries out its purposes.[286] The evaluation of risk is a key feature of the guidance,[287] as when considering campaigning and political activity charity trustees must carefully weigh up the possible benefits against the costs and risks in deciding whether the campaign is likely to be an effective way of furthering or supporting the charity's purposes.[288] Similarly, the decision whether to use emotive or controversial material is a value judgement for the trustees, taking into account whether it is justifiable in the context of the campaign and has a legitimate evidence base to support the claims made.[289]

Additionally, although charities may not support a political party, they may support specific policies advocated by political parties if the policy would help them achieve their charitable purpose.[290] Moreover, it appears that a charity may focus most or all of its resources on political activity for a period, if this is the best way to support the charity's purposes and does not become the reason for the charity's existence.[291]

The interpretation given by the Charity Commission of what political activities are permitted go significantly beyond the limits set out by Slade J in *McGovern v A-G*,[292] even as subsequently glossed in *Re Koeppler's Will Trusts*.[293]

The new interpretation has yet to come before the courts, but political purposes have been considered through the Tribunal system. The Charity Commission refused to register Crocels Community Media Group as a charity. The proposed objects were to improve fraternity between nations,[294] advancing understanding and promoting the cause of peace, and innovating for the abolition and reduction of standing armies were political purposes, and not for the public benefit. An appeal to the First Tribunal (Charity) was dismissed,[295] and leave to appeal to the Upper Tribunal was denied.[296] The fact that the organization sought to carry out its purposes by utilizing recognized charitable purposes

[280] CC9—*Speaking Out: Guidance on Political Activities and Campaigning by Charities* (March 2008).

[281] CC9—*Speaking Out: Guidance on Political Activities and Campaigning by Charities* (March 2008), para D1.

[282] Ibid, para G2. [283] Ibid, paras D1 and D4. [284] Ibid, para D9.

[285] Ibid, para D7. [286] Ibid, paras D3 and D7.

[287] See further Atkinson, 'Charities and Political Campaigning: The Impact of Risk-based Regulation' [2008] *Liverpool Law Review* 143.

[288] CC9—*Speaking Out* [2008], para F1. [289] Ibid, para G4. [290] Ibid, para D5.

[291] Ibid, para D8. [292] [1982] Ch 321. [293] [1986] Ch 423.

[294] Promoting international friendship or understanding is not a charitable purpose: *Anglo Swedish Society v IRC* [1931] 47 TLR 29. The legal position had not altered with the passing of the Charities Act 2006 or 2011.

[295] *Bishop v Charity Commission* CA/2015/0009. [296] *Bishop v Charity Commission* UT/2016/0149.

(e.g. promoting the cause of peace through the advancement of education) did not make them charitable. The organization was seeking to change government policy by promoting a cause and thus fell squarely within the meaning of a political purpose as outlined by Slade J in *McGovern*.[297]

Charities, and often established and well-resourced organizations, can still fall foul of the political purposes rule.[298] Oxfam found itself the subject of a Charity Commission compliance case[299] in relation to a tweet as part of a campaign on poverty in Britain. The communication in question was part of a social media campaign advertising a report into food poverty in Britain.[300] The tweet listed a number of policy areas of the then government, with text that suggested they were leading Britain into poverty and an image of a mock film poster, 'the perfect storm'. The Commission found that while Oxfam was motivated by a desire to draw attention to problems of those living in poverty in Britain, it should have done more to avoid a perception of political bias. It was also felt that the link to the report was not as obvious as it might have been. These factors combined meant that the tweet could be misconstrued by some as party-political campaigning.

(5) **Lobbying before a General Election**

The general ability of charities to undertake legitimate political activity is curtailed under special election-time rules. These rules restrict campaigning on policy platforms that are intended to procure the electoral success of a particular party or candidate, If charities do want to campaign on policy platforms associated with political parties, there are particular election-time rules about how much money they can spend and they must be registered to do so. These rules were first introduced with the coming into force of the UK Transparency of Lobbying, Non-Party Campaigning and Trade Union Administration Act 2014. This was an electoral law reform, but the operation of these rules, and their impact on charities, was brought into sharp relief by the General Election of 2015, followed by the unexpected General Election less than two years later, in 2017. In the word of Morris, they have had a 'chilling effect' on political lobbying by charities,[301] and the Charity Commission has produced two reports detailing investigations and actions it has undertaken in the sector in relation to both the 2015 and 2017 elections.[302] The chilling effect has continued,[303] even though actions taken by the Commission were proportionate[304] and the reports are intended to be educative, not punitive in nature, and guidance for charities has been updated.

[297] *Bishop v Charity Commission* CA/2015/0009 paras 19 and 20.

[298] See Morris, 'Legal Limits on Political Campaigning by Charities: Drawing the Line' [2016] *Voluntary Sector Review* 109.

[299] Charity Commission, *Operational Case Report: Oxfam (202918)* (Charity Commission, 2014). This power to conduct investigations is one of the regulatory powers explored in Chapter 23.

[300] Cooper, Purcell, and Jackson, *Below the Breadline: The Relentless Rise of Food Poverty in Britain* (Oxfam GB and Trussell Trust, 2014).

[301] Morris, 'Legal Limits on Political Campaigning by Charities: Drawing the Line' [2016] *Voluntary Sector Review* 109; Morris, 'Charities and Political Activity in England and Wales: Mixed Messages' [2016] *Charity Law & Practice Review* 109.

[302] See *Campaigning and Political Issues Arising in the Run-Up to the 2015 General Election: Case Report* (17 December 2015) (seventeen cases); *Campaigning and political issues arising in the run-up to the 2017 General Election: Case Report* (17 July 2017) (forty-one cases).

[303] See, for example, https://www.civilsociety.co.uk/news/lobbying-rules-continue-to-have-chilling-effect-despite-better-guidance-charities-tell-mps.html.

[304] See Picton, 'Why Charities Should Be Allowed to Campaign Freely at Election Time', *The Conversation* (May 31 2017), who comments on the intervention on the Shacklewell Lane Mosque, a charity which was seen to be supporting an anti-UKIP candidate by daubing his name on the outside of the mosque. The Commission imposed no sanctions, but visited the premises to make sure the trustees were aware of the law and removed the offending markings.

(6) Critique of the political purposes test

A larger question than the limits on political campaigning is whether the judicial aversion to political trusts is well founded.[305] Slade J, in *McGovern v A-G*,[306] spoke of the difficulty of judges in identifying whether a change in the law is for the public benefit and of the danger of usurping the functions of the legislature. The objection that Slade J gives to party political purposes is that:

> Since their nature would ex hypothesi be very controversial, the court could be faced with even greater difficulties in determining whether the objects of the trust would be for the public benefit; correspondingly, it would be at even greater risk of encroaching on the functions of the legislature and prejudicing its reputation for political impartiality, if it were to promote such objects by enforcing the trust.[307]

Slade J gave almost identical reasons for objecting to trusts that sought to achieve their objective through influencing opinion. There would again be no way of telling whether a reversal of government policy was for the public benefit 'and in any event [the court] could not properly encroach on the functions of the executive, acting intra vires, by holding that it should be acting in some other manner'.[308]

The objections that Slade J sets out are almost certainly overstated. His aversion to comment on whether the changes in the law are for the public benefit does not seem to have prevented the judges shaping the law through the development of new rules and principles,[309] nor has it prevented them, on occasions, from making suggestions for law reform in their judgments. Judges have also taken a leading role in law reform through chairmanship of the Law Commission. Lord Woolf, in *R v Radio Authority, ex p Bull*,[310] acknowledged that a campaign to seek a change in the law would be political, even though it could also be commendable. Fine distinctions have also been made. Slade J had no difficulty in reconciling *Jackson v Phillips*[311] with his view of political purposes. There the Massachusetts Supreme Court had upheld as a charitable trust to campaign against slavery, before slavery was prohibited in the United States. Slade J took the view that 'the pressure was to be directed by the trustees against individual persons, rather than governments with a view to obtaining the "voluntary manumission" of the slaves belonging to such individuals'.[312]

Much of the objection to the court 'taking sides' would be overcome if the court adopted the policy of accepting purposes as being for the public benefit if they are not immoral, illegal, or subversive and are adopted by a significant proportion of the public. It would then be possible for opposing views both to be capable of being considered charitable. It may also be that a distinction needs to be made between propagandist trusts and those which seek to influence public and governmental opinion, and perhaps even influence changes in laws, not through any pre-ordained view of what is right and wrong (which is the position taken in many 'political' activities), but only after careful and considered debate. After all, why should a trust to promote the work of the Law Commission not be held charitable, even though the whole purpose of the Commission is to change the law?

Strong support for the view that such a distinction should be made can be found in *Re Koeppler's Will Trusts*.[313] The testator had left a substantial gift to support the work of Wilton Park in making 'a British contribution to the formation of an informed international public opinion and to the promotion of greater co-operation in Europe and the

[305] See Walton, '*McGovern v Attorney General*: Constraints on Judicial Assessment of Charitable Benefit' [2014] Conv 317, who criticizes the basis of the rule, and queries whether it is fit for purpose in the modern era.

[306] [1982] Ch 321. [307] [1981] 3 All ER 493 at 507. [308] [1981] 3 All ER 493 at 508.

[309] See the discussion in Chapter 1. [310] [1997] 2 All ER 561 at 571.

[311] 96 Mass 539 [1867]. [312] [1981] 3 All ER 493 at 514. [313] [1986] Ch 423.

West in general'. The organization worked by bringing together in conferences a broad range of politicians, academics, civil servants, industrialists, and journalists to exchange views on political, economic, and social views of common interest. Peter Gibson J, at first instance, having considered the *McGovern* case, held that:

> trusts aimed at securing better international relations, including co-operation in a particular part of the world, can properly be called political causes . . . Whether there should be better relations and co-operation and, if so, how it should be achieved and with whom are matters for government decision, not for the court.[314]

This view was overruled by the Court of Appeal. The judgment of the court was given by Slade LJ (who had now been promoted to the Court of Appeal). He distinguished the case from his previous decision in *McGovern*:

> In the present case the activities of Wilton Park are not of a party political nature. Nor, as far as the evidence shows, are they designed to procure changes in the laws or governmental policy of this or any other country: even when they touch on political matters, they constitute, so far as I can see, no more than genuine attempts in an objective manner to ascertain and disseminate the truth. In these circumstances I think that no objections to the trust arise on a political score . . . the court is entitled to presume that the trustees will only act in a lawful and proper manner appropriate to the trustees of a charity and not, for example, by the propagation of tendentious political opinions.[315]

For Slade LJ to say in this case that there was no intention to change laws or governmental policy seems rather disingenuous. A large part of the reason for bringing together distinguished conference participants capable of influencing opinion in Europe and the West must surely have been to act as a driver for cooperation between states and governments. If that is not 'political' at an international level, it is hard to see what could be. The major significance of this judgment must, therefore, be the recognition that a distinction can be drawn between 'the propagation of tendentious political opinions' which the court will not consider to be charitable, and 'genuine attempts objectively to ascertain and disseminate the truth', even in a political context, which can be charitable. Applying this test, a trust to promote the work of the Law Commission could be charitable, even if a trust to reform the rule against perpetuities would not.

In the words of Picton:

> A bolder path would be to accept that all charity is straightforwardly and unambiguously political. Charities are mostly run by people motivated to change the world. They have political campaigning missions and it will benefit everyone if they can speak out freely.[316]

7 Interpreting charitable gifts

(1) **Purposes must be exclusively charitable**

For a trust to be upheld as a valid charitable trust it must be for exclusively charitable purposes. None of the trust property must be applicable to non-charitable objects. Similarly, a corporation or unincorporated association will only be a charity if its purposes are exclusively charitable. If there is a combination of purposes, some charitable and others not, then it will not be charitable and will not enjoy the privileges outlined earlier. Thus, in *IRC v Oldham Training and Enterprise Council*,[317] Lightman J held that an organization

[314] [1984] 2 All ER 111 at 124. [315] [1985] 2 All ER 869 at 878.

[316] Picton, 'Why Charities Should Be Allowed to Campaign Freely at Election Time', *The Conversation* (31 May 2017). [317] [1996] STC 1218.

to support business development was not a charitable body because its objects included some non-charitable elements, including the promotion of the interests of individuals rather than of the community in general. Similarly, in *McGovern v A-G*,[318] the trust established by Amnesty International included some charitable objects, but also some non-charitable political purposes, and was not held charitable. In *Williams' Trustees v IRC*,[319] the objects included many that were charitable, but also the promotion of social activities that are not. In *IRC v Baddeley*,[320] the promotion of Methodism was a charitable purpose, but the promotion of sport and recreation were not.

(2) **Ordinary rules of construction**

The starting point for construing a charity's governing documents is that ordinary principles of construction apply. According to Lord Hoffman in *Attorney General of Belize v Belize Telecom Ltd*:[321]

> It is the meaning which the instrument would convey to a reasonable person having all the background knowledge which would reasonably be available to the audience to whom the instrument is addressed.

(3) **Benignant construction in cases of ambiguity**

There are some circumstances where the court may take a generous approach and give a disposition a 'benignant construction'.[322] This means that, where there is an ambiguity such that a gift is capable of two constructions, one of which would make it void and the other effectual, the court will uphold it. This approach was confirmed by the House of Lords in *Guild v IRC*.[323] The precise scope of the principle permitting a benignant construction was considered by Hazel Williamson QC in *Funnell v Stewart*.[324] She indicated that it would not save a 'dual purpose gift' where one identifiable object was clearly present but plainly not charitable, as the court could not simply ignore the non-charitable element of the trust. However, it would enable the court to save a gift which had a single purpose which was capable of being carried into effect in two different ways, one of which would be charitable and the other of which would not.[325]

(4) **Statutory amendment**

Where a charitable instrument limits benefits to persons defined by colour, then under the Equality Act 2010, s 193(4),[326] the instrument will operate as if there had been no reference to skin colour. This provision was applied in *Re Harding*.[327] A dying nun made a will leaving her property to be held 'in trust for the black community of Hackney, Haringey, Islington and Tower Hamlets'. Lewison J held that the gift was charitable in character as a gift for the benefit of a local area, and that, applying the statutory provision, the restriction to the black community should be removed. Since there was no specific scheme for the use of the funds, this could be resolved by the approval of a scheme by the Charity Commission.[328]

[318] [1982] Ch 321. [319] [1947] AC 447. [320] [1955] AC 572.

[321] [2009] UKPC 10 at 16. Although this was a case involving the interpretation of a written contract, the principles are considered to be of general application. See also *Investors Compensation Scheme Ltd v West Bromwich Building Society* [1998] 1 WLR 896 for a statement of canons of interpretation.

[322] *IRC v McMullen* [1981] AC 1 at 14, per Lord Hailsham LC; *Weir v Crum-Brown* [1908] AC 162 at 167, per Lord Loreburn LC. [323] [1992] 2 AC 310 at 322.

[324] [1996] 1 WLR 288 at 296–7. [325] See also *Re Hetherington* [1990] Ch 1.

[326] Replacing Race Relations Act 1976, s 34. [327] [2008] Ch 235. [328] [2008] Ch 235 at 27.

(5) **Conjunctions**

Where a trust lists a variety of purposes, the conjunctions used may determine whether the gift is to be construed as exclusively for charitable purposes. The word 'or' is usually given a disjunctive construction, so that 'charitable or benevolent' purposes are not exclusively charitable. In contrast, the word 'and' is usually given a conjunctive construction, so that 'charitable and benevolent' purposes would be exclusively charitable. Although providing a strong prima facie indication, these are not binding rules of construction and each case must be examined in the light of the surrounding circumstances.

(a) **'And'**

In *Re Sutton*[329] a gift to 'charitable and deserving' objects was held exclusively charitable. The word 'and' was given a conjunctive interpretation so that only deserving objects which were also charitable were contemplated. In *Re Best*[330] a gift to 'charitable and benevolent' institutions was similarly held exclusively charitable. The conjunctive construction is only a prima facie guide that may be displaced. In *A-G of the Bahamas v Royal Trust Co*,[331] a gift for purposes connected with the 'education and welfare' of Bahamian children was, in the light of all the circumstances, construed disjunctively and the gift, therefore, failed since it permitted the application of funds for educational purposes alternatively for welfare purposes, which need not necessarily be educational.[332]

(b) **'Or'**

In *Blair v Duncan*,[333] a testatrix gave her trustee discretion to apply part of her residuary estate to 'charitable or public purposes'. The House of Lords held that this was to be read disjunctively, so that the gift included 'public purposes', which may fall outside the scope of charity. The gift, therefore, failed. A similar result was reached in *Houston v Burns*,[334] where a gift was made for 'public, benevolent or charitable purposes'. In *Chichester Diocesan Fund and Board of Finance v Simpson*,[335] a gift in favour of 'charitable or benevolent objects'[336] was reluctantly held not to be exclusively charitable. The House of Lords could not find a more favourable interpretation than that the purposes were to be considered disjunctively.[337] Subsequently, in *A-G of the Cayman Islands v Wahr-Hansen*,[338] the Privy Council advised that a trust established for the benefit of 'any one or more religious, charitable or educational institution or instructions or any organizations or institutions operating for the public good' was not exclusively charitable.

In some circumstances, on the construction of a gift as a whole, the word 'or' may not be read in this disjunctive way. In *Re Bennett*,[339] a gift to educational purposes and 'other objects of charity, or any other public objects in the parish of Farringdon' was held to be exclusively charitable. Taken as a whole, and especially noting the word 'other', Eve J held that it was not to be construed disjunctively but to mean other public purposes that are also charitable.

[329] [1885] 28 Ch D 464. [330] [1904] 2 Ch 354. [331] [1986] 1 WLR 1001.

[332] See also *Re Eades* [1920] 2 Ch 353, 'religious, charitable and philanthropic objects' held not exclusively charitable.

[333] [1902] AC 37. [334] [1918] AC 337. [335] [1944] AC 341, HL.

[336] See also *Oxford Group v IRC* [1949] 2 All ER 537, CA.

[337] See also *Re Macduff* [1896] 2 Ch 451, where a gift to charitable or philanthropic purposes was held not exclusively charitable.

[338] [2001] 1 AC 75. [339] [1920] 1 Ch 305.

(6) **Charitable Trusts (Validation) Act 1954**

This Act mitigates the impact of *Chichester Diocesan Fund v Simpson*[340] by treating similar cases as if the trust had been exclusively charitable. It retrospectively validates trusts coming into effect prior to 16 December 1952. The Act has no application to trusts coming into effect after 15 December 1952. Equally, the Act does not apply where the primary purpose of a trust is to provide non-charitable benefits. In *Re St Andrew's (Cheam) Lawn Tennis Club Trust*,[341] land was held on trust for a range of purposes including both providing premises for a tennis club associated with the local church, and also for the benefit of the church. Arnold J held that the trust could not be treated as wholly charitable by the 1954 Act since it would have deprived the club of the benefit it was intended to receive. He approved the test set out by Hart J in *Ulrich v Treasury Solicitor*,[342] that the Act did not apply where it 'would flout either the intention of the settlor or the legitimate expectations of those interested under the non-charitable objects' for the trust to be confined to those purposes which were charitable.

Apart from the 1954 Act, there is no legislation in England allowing a gift which is partly charitable and partly non-charitable to be upheld in so far as it is charitable.[343]

(7) **Trusts for the benefit of a locality**

For reasons which have now become obscure, the courts have adopted a benevolent construction towards gifts made in general terms for the benefit of a named locality or its inhabitants. Such gifts are construed to be impliedly limited to charitable purposes in the specified community. Thus a gift to a particular parish,[344] or for the good of a particular country,[345] such as a gift for 'the benefit and advantage of Great Britain',[346] will be upheld as a valid charitable trust. However, in *A-G of the Cayman Islands v Wahr-Hansen*,[347] the Privy Council advised that this generous rule of construction should not be extended to encompass all cases where there are general statements of benevolent or philanthropic objects.

340 [1944] AC 341, HL. 341 [2012] EWHC 1040 (Ch). 342 [2005] EWHC 67 (Ch).

343 There is legislation to this effect in the Republic of Ireland: Charities Act 1960, s 49. See also *Leahy v A-G for New South Wales* [1959] AC 457, where similar Australian legislation was applied.

344 *West v Knight* [1669] 1 Cas in Ch 134.

345 *A-G v Earl of Lonsdale* [1827] 1 Sim 105; *Re Smith* [1932] 1 Ch 153.

346 *Nightingale v Goulburn* [1847] 5 Hare 484. 347 [2001] 1 AC 75.

21

Public benefit

It is not enough for a charity to pursue a legally recognized charitable purpose. It must also pursue that purpose in a way which is demonstrably for the public benefit. This principle suffuses the whole of charity law.[1] Legal validity under the Charities Act 2011 requires public benefit in two respects. First and most intuitively, the nature of the general purpose must be beneficial. At its most basic this means that a charitable organization cannot be set up to create public harms. Second, the purpose must be carried through in such a way as to benefit a sufficiently numerous and broad group of beneficiaries to constitute public rather than private benefit. The charity cannot be established to create private profits, or in the service of a small group of people. In addition, once a gift, trust, or organization has been recognized as charitable, it must continue to operate in a way which is charitable. That requires ongoing benefits to be conferred on the public. This multi-faceted requirement of public benefit has been the case for many years (even if not always clearly articulated), but that requirement has been given statutory force by the Charities Act 2011, ss 2(1)(b) and 4. There is no new statutory definition, so public benefit is defined as having the same meaning as under the previous law.[2]

1 Practical impact of public benefit

The public benefit requirement can be understood as a regulatory tool. It is a standard which allows the Charity Commission and the courts to keep a watchful eye on the charity sector. All charities must operate for the public benefit and if they fall foul of the standard then they risk losing their charitable status.

(a) When does the public benefit test apply?

The public benefit test applies to new organizations or trusts seeking to be registered as a charity. It also applies to existing charities, which must continue to satisfy the public benefit test and must demonstrate that they do so. Charities are now required to report on public benefit as part of the Trustees' *Annual Report*.[3] This information must be set in the context of the charity's aims, and must demonstrate how in practice each purpose of the charity has been carried out for the public benefit. The focus, of course, is upon a charity's continuing operations, rather than in reiterating the information which is necessary to establish whether a charity meets the criteria for registration.

[1] See Warburton, 'Charities and Public Benefit—From Confusion to Light?' [2008] *Charity Law and Practice Review* 1.

[2] Charities Act 2011, s 4(3).

[3] Charities (Accounts and Reports) Regulations 2008, SI 2008/629, Annex A.

(b) Where does the public benefit test apply?

A small charitable organization will normally operate on a single site. For example, a local homeless charity might provide welfare and counselling advice, alongside food and shelter in one building. By contrast, large charities will be spread across multiple sites. This raises the question as to whether each particular site must be used for the public benefit. In *Nuffield Health v London Borough of Merton*,[4] a large charity, known for running hospitals and medical centres, also ran one of a chain of gyms in Merton as a commercial venture, feeding earnings back into the charity. The particular gym did not have an intuitively charitable character.

By a majority,[5] the Court of Appeal reasoned that while the activities on the particular site might not have been for the public benefit, the organization as a whole was a registered charity. In turn, Nuffield did not have to pay local business rates.[6] Taken as a broad principle, this means that activities at a particular location do not have to be for the public benefit.[7]

(c) Charity Commission guidance

To assist trustees, the Charity Commission, as it was required to do under s 4 of the Charities Act 2006 (now s 17 of the Charities Act 2011), published guidance. The content of this guidance was challenged by the Independent Schools Council. The dispute went to the Upper Tribunal which, in a landmark decision, concluded that material aspects of the guidance were incorrect in law or obscure,[8] and that parts of the guidance should be withdrawn.[9] The significance of the Commission guidance is that 'the charity trustees of a charity must have regard to any such guidance when exercising any powers or duties to which the guidance is relevant'.[10] Trustees are also obliged to report as to whether they have complied with the duty to have due regard to the guidance.[11]

New general guidance was issued in September 2013. It comprises three sections or guides explaining public benefit in three different contexts: the requirement as it applies to the recognition of charities;[12] the requirement as it applies to the operation of a charity;[13] and a guide to reporting on a charity's work.[14] This guidance has clear and close regard to the decision of the Upper Tribunal in the *Independent Schools* case. This guidance was further supplemented by an introductory guide, issued in February 2014.[15]

The Charity Commission has produced guides on a number of specific charitable purposes, but some of these, issued before the *Independent Schools* case, no longer form part of its statutory guidance to which trustees must have regard. They comprise the three guides covering the substantive *Pemsel* categories of charitable purpose: *The Prevention*

[4] [2021] EWCA Civ 826.

[5] Richards LJ dissenting, as on his interpretation of the Finance Act 1988, s 43(6)(a), the gym should carry out public benefit activities at the particular hereditament.

[6] Relief was attached to the relevant hereditament, subject to the Finance Act 1988, s 43(6)(a).

[7] See also, *Oxfam v Birmingham City Council* [1976] AC 126, 139 in which the head office of Oxfam was held to qualify for ratings relief. The premises directly facilitated the carrying out of the charitable purposes.

[8] *The Independent Schools Council v The Charity Commission* [2011] UKUT 421 (TCC) (13 October 2011).

[9] *Independent Schools Council v HMRC* [2011] UKUT B27 (TCC) (2 December 2011).

[10] Charities Act 2006, s 4(6). Now the Charities Act 2011, s 17(5).

[11] Charities (Accounts and Reports) Regulations 2008, SI 2008/629.

[12] Charity Commission, *Public Benefit: The Public Benefit Requirement* (PB1) (September 2013).

[13] Charity Commission, *Public Benefit: Running a Charity* (PB2) (September 2013).

[14] Charity Commission, *Public Benefit: Reporting* (PB3) (September 2013).

[15] Charity Commission, *Introductory Guide: Public Benefit: Rules for Charities* (14 February 2014).

or Relief of Poverty for the Public Benefit,[16] *The Advancement of Education for the Public Benefit*,[17] and *The Advancement of Religion for the Public Benefit*.[18]

(d) **Consequences of failing the public benefit test**

Where a proposed charity does not meet the public benefit test, it will not be a charity and will not enjoy the benefits and advantages of that status. It may be possible for the objectives or purposes of the trust or organization to be amended to satisfy the test.

Where an existing charity fails to satisfy the public benefit test, the trust or organization will have essentially one of three choices. It could challenge the Charity Commission's interpretation of the requirements of public benefit. It may amend its purposes and modify its activities in order to comply with the Charity Commission guidance, and may be required to do this by the Charity Commission. Finally, if it is not possible to make such changes, it could cease to be a registered charity. The impact of the last course of action could be catastrophic for the entity concerned. Once assets have irrevocably been devoted to charitable purposes, they cannot be used for any non-charitable purposes, but must, in the event of an organization ceasing to be charitable, be applied to other charitable purposes. Thus, if a public school lost its charitable status, and wished to operate as a private-sector school, it would not be able to transfer its assets to the new non-charitable entity. The new entity would either have to purchase the assets or acquire new premises and facilities. That would inevitably have a dramatic and negative impact upon the level of fees that the new entity would need to charge, or upon the quality of the provision which it could offer.

2 What is 'public benefit'?

What constitutes public benefit is very much dependent upon the context, and it is not easy to describe criteria which are of general application.[19] It is not enough to make the obvious point that public benefit has two dimensions: whether the proposed charity provides benefits (the 'benefit' aspect); and whether those benefits are conferred upon the public (the 'public' aspect). The concept needs more refinement. It used to be thought that there was a presumption of public benefit in relation to purposes which fell within the first three of the *Pemsel* categories, namely the advancement of education, the relief of poverty, and the advancement of religion.[20] However, according to the *Independent Schools* case,[21] establishing whether there is a benefit is a question of fact in every case. That will be a decision which must be based upon the evidence presented to the Charity Commission, tribunal, or court, although there may be some cases (for instance, mainstream education available to all free of charge) where the answer as to whether there is a benefit is self-evident and is a matter on which a judge can take judicial notice. This may well be the case where the purpose is to relieve or prevent poverty, in relation to which it is not normally necessary to demonstrate the 'public' aspect of public benefit.[22]

[16] December 2008. [17] December 2008. [18] December 2008.

[19] See Synge, *The 'New' Public Benefit Requirement Making Sense of Charity Law?* (Hart 2015); Garton, *Public Benefit in Charity Law* (Oxford University Press 2013).

[20] See Charity Commission, *Public Benefit: Analysis of the Law Relating to Public Benefit* (September 2013), para 12.

[21] *The Independent Schools Council v The Charity Commission* [2011] UKUT 421 (TCC) (13 October 2011) at 70.

[22] Charity Commission, *Public Benefit: The Public Benefit Requirement* (PB1), Annex A (September 2013).

(a) The benefit aspect

It does not follow that because a proposed purpose falls within one of the recognized categories of charitable purpose, the specific way in which that purpose will be implemented (or is being implemented) is charitable.[23] It could be argued that a trust to provide training to the Islamic State (ISIS) in making explosive devices is 'educational', but it is hardly a charitable purpose to train terrorists. There would be no public benefit from the particular form of education proposed.[24]

(i) Form of benefit may be practical or intangible

The public benefit may consist of practical assistance, as in most cases involving the relief of need, for instance, through the provision of housing to the homeless, financial assistance to the poor, or advocacy for those who lack the mental capacity to represent themselves. However, not all charitable activity is 'hands on'. A great number of charitable organizations provide abstract public goods which have only an intangible benefit. For example, a charity might say in its annual report that it is seeking to promote cultural and artistic developments. The production of these abstract public goods cannot easily be understood as 'tangible', but they are often recognized by the law. A good example of this is found in the judicial reasoning on the public benefit in animal welfare charities.[25] In *Re Wedgwood*, Lord Cozens-Hardy MR reasoned that a gift for the protection of animals would, 'promote public morality by checking the innate tendency to cruelty.'[26] For the judge, the public benefit in animal welfare came from a broad uplifting of moral behaviour. According to the reasoning of the judge, this is a general public good which is difficult to understand in tangible terms.

(ii) Benefit may be direct or indirect

It is possible for indirect benefits to be taken into account in deciding whether there is public benefit.[27] A hospice providing care for the terminally ill confers benefits not only on the patients who may receive care more closely aligned to their needs than would otherwise be the case; it also relieves the burden which the National Health Service would need to carry, and it provides assistance to the family of the patient, who might find it difficult to cope in providing the level of intensive support which a patient needs. All of these factors can be weighed in the balance in deciding whether there is a benefit to the public. The Upper Tribunal provided an explanation in *R (Independent Schools Council) v Charity Commission*:

> (1) Direct benefits: benefits to persons whose needs it is a purpose of the charity to relieve which are received by such persons as recipients of the main service which the charity provides. (2) Indirect benefits: benefits to persons whose needs it is a purpose of the charity to relieve which are received by such persons otherwise than as recipients of the main service which the charity provides.[28]

[23] For the use of the term 'beneficial in nature' see *Attorney-General v Charity Commission (The Poverty Reference)* [2012] WTLR 977 at 32.

[24] See *R (Independent Schools Council) v Charity Commission* [2012] Ch 214 and *Attorney General v Charity Commission (The Poverty Reference)* [2012] WTLR 977 at 66–7, where the examples of non-charitable purposes are a school for pickpockets and a library of pornography. The examples are drawn from observations in *Re Macduff* [1896] 2 Ch 451 at 474 (Rigby LJ), and in *Re Pinion* [1965] Ch 85 at 106 (Harman LJ).

[25] See, e.g., *Re Grove-Grady* [1929] 1 Ch 557; *Re Green's Will Trusts* [1985] 3 All ER 455.

[26] [1915] 1 Ch 113, 118.

[27] See Garton, *Public Benefit in Charity Law* (Oxford University Press 2013) p 88.

[28] *R (Independent Schools Council) v Charity Commission* [2011] UKUT 421 (TCC) at 37; *Helena Partnerships Ltd v HMRC* [2012] EWCA Civ 569 at 78.

An example of an indirect benefit being accepted as charitable is found in *Incorporated Council of Law Reporting for England and Wales v A-G*,[29] where the preparation of law reports was held to be for the public benefit. The court did not find that the organization produced only a private benefit for the members of the legal profession that purchased its reports. Instead, it found a broad and general benefit for the entire community. There was an indirect benefit to all from the fact that the reports communicated to the wider world. Or as Russell LJ put the point, the fact that professionals use the reports does not, 'detract from the benefit that accrues to the community from the fact that the law does not remain locked in the bosom of the judiciary.'[30]

The approach taken in *Incorporated Council of Law Reporting for England and Wales v A-G* cannot necessarily be transferred across to other contexts. There are some cases where indirect benefits will be insufficient to carry the day because they are outweighed by direct non-charitable benefits to individuals.[31] Thus in a case involving a housing association established 'for the benefit of the community', the Court of Appeal held that the general public interest in the provision of good quality housing was insufficient to make the purposes of a housing association charitable; it would be necessary for the objects of the association to confine provision to those who had some special need, for instance by reason of disability or other disadvantage.[32]

(iii) Benefit must be recognized as charitable

It is so obvious that it hardly needs saying that for a benefit to be recognized by law, it must be of a kind which promotes a purpose which has been recognized by law as charitable. Acting illegally cannot be considered to be beneficial. In *Re Shaw*, Harman J illustrated the point by saying that a college for pickpockets would not be validly charitable.[33] In that hypothetical and somewhat tongue-in-cheek example, while the pickpocket college would have an educational purpose, that educational purpose, in training pickpockets, would be carried out in a way which that it is harmful. In the historic case, *Attorney General v Vint*,[34] an attempt to provide inmates of a workhouse aged over 60 with porter, the alcoholic drink, was said to be unlawful under the Poor Law and so the trust on those terms was not successful. This is because whatever the attempted purpose, if it is illegal, it will not be charitable. For example, in modern times, a proposed trust to provide illegal drugs to chronic sufferers of arthritis would not be charitable, even if it could be proved that the drug would improve the condition of life of those receiving the treatment. Nor will the law allow private profits, so a trust to build a private (for profit) hospital would not be charitable because even if it could be considered as for the advancement of health, doing so for profit is not considered to be charitable.

(iv) Benefit must relate to the aims of the charity

Although benefits can be indirect, they must be sufficiently related to the primary activities or purposes of the organization or trust. In *IRC v Oldham Training and Enterprise Council*,[35] an organization established to provide 'support services and advice to and for new businesses' in the Oldham area was principally directed as raising the profitability of local businesses. However, this would indirectly improve employment prospects in the area. Lightman J held that these indirect 'benefits to the community conferred by such

[29] [1972] Ch 73, CA.

[30] *Incorporated Council of Law Reporting for England and Wales v A-G* [1972] Ch 73, 86.

[31] *Helena Partnerships Ltd v HMRC* [2012] EWCA Civ 569 at 108.

[32] *Helena Partnerships Ltd v HMRC* [2012] EWCA Civ 569. See also *Inland Revenue Commissioners v Oldham Training and Enterprise Council* [1996] STC 1218, where a similar conclusion was reached.

[33] *Re Shaw* [1957] 1 WLR 729, 737.

[34] (1850) 3 De G & Sm 704.

[35] [1996] STC 1218.

activities are too remote'.[36] This may just be another way of saying that the private benefits outweigh the public benefit.[37]

(b) Assessing benefit

Different views can be taken about what constitutes a benefit. For example, some members of the community may think that public health would be improved by campaigning to promote vegetarianism, but others may think that advocating the eating of red meat would be in the public interest for similar reasons. How can the Charity Commission or the court determine whether there is a public benefit without simply making a value judgement?

(i) Assessment of benefit can be controversial

The assessment of benefit is not free from controversy. A particularly contentious issue concerns the charitable status of public schools. Following the enactment of the then Charities Act 2006, the Charity Commission, which anticipated the possibility of challenge,[38] published its initial views, following considerable consultation, in December 2008 in three separate reports, *Public Benefit and Fee-Charging*, an *Analysis of the Law Underpinning Public Benefit and Fee Charging*, and *The Advancement of Education for the Public Benefit*. It published its first public benefit assessments of some independent schools in 2009. This is an issue on which feelings can sometimes run high. Aspects of the Charity Commission guidance were found to be unlawful in a successful challenge by the Independent Schools Council.[39]

In the light of this controversy, it is important to keep an open mind on whether or not the concept of 'public benefit' is up to the task of regulating the entire charity sector. It will be seen as this chapter progresses that the cases defining public benefit have developed piecemeal over time. Sometimes, while the reasoning of judges makes perfect sense in a particular context, the rule cannot easily be abstracted and applied to the enormously diverse range of existing charities operating in England and Wales. Alison Dunn argues that public benefit has been developed as a loose standard in equity.[40] For example, even amongst one limited class of charities, such as charities for the advancement of religion, it might mean a variety of different things. The benefit might be said to come from public preaching, from good works in the community, or through the development of moral character. When the range of different purposes are considered, any unifying idea of benefit becomes very difficult to theorize. This means that it is at least arguable that the Charity Commission is using the 'wrong policy tool' in order to regulate the sector. Whether or not it is possible to devise a better tool or regulatory standard is however also an open question.

(ii) The view of the public

What benefits the public could be judged by public opinion—an 'ask the audience' approach. This is not the approach used in the UK. Public opinion is not easy to measure, and it can change frequently.

[36] [1996] STC 1218 at 1235.

[37] This was how Lloyd LJ interpreted the decision in *Helena Partnerships Ltd v HMRC* [2012] EWCA Civ 569.

[38] *Public Benefit—The Charity Commission's Position on How Public Benefit Is Treated in the Charities Act* (July 2005).

[39] See Synge, *The 'New' Public Benefit Requirement: Making Sense of Charity Law?* (Hart 2015) p 57.

[40] Dunn, 'Using the Wrong Policy Tools: Education, Charity, and Public Benefit' (2012) 39 JLS 491, 508.

This does not mean public views are irrelevant. Lord Wright, in *National Anti-Vivisection Society v IRC*,[41] said that whether there was a benefit could be judged on the basis of 'approval by the common understanding of enlightened opinion for the time being' that there is benefit to the public, and, in *Funnell v Stewart*,[42] it was held that a trust to advance the practice of faith healing was charitable on the grounds that it had become 'a recognised activity of public benefit'. This suggests that the attitude of the public cannot be disregarded in determining whether an activity should be characterized as for the public benefit, but the way in which wider opinion is referred to leaves a subjective value judgement to be made by the court.

(iii) An objective assessment of benefit

In *National Anti-Vivisection Society v IRC*,[43] the House of Lords adopted an objective approach to the question of public benefit. Lord Simmonds stated:

> Where on the evidence before it the court concludes that, however well-intentioned the donor, the achievement of his object will be greatly to the public disadvantage, there can be no justification for saying that it is a charitable object.[44]

The House was faced by the decision of fact of the Special Commissioners for Income Tax that any benefit 'was far outweighed by the detriment to medical science and research and consequently to the public health which would result if the society succeeded in achieving its objects'.[45]

The *National Anti-Vivisection Society* decision suggests that the underpinning requirement for all kinds of public benefit is that the benefit must be capable of proof. The classic formulation of this requirement can be found in the judgment of Slade J in *McGovern v AG*:

> The question whether a purpose will or may operate for the public benefit is to be answered by the court forming an opinion on the evidence before it . . . No doubt in some cases a purpose may be so manifestly beneficial to the public that it would be absurd to call evidence on this point.[46] In many other instances, however, the element of public benefit may be much more debatable. Indeed, in some cases the courts will regard this element [as] being incapable of proof one way or the other and thus will inevitably decline to recognise the trust as being of a charitable nature.[47]

(iv) Balance of benefit and detriment

For an activity to be charitable, it is not necessary for there to be unqualified benefits. It is sufficient if, on balance, the benefits sufficiently outweigh the disadvantages. The balancing process is well illustrated in *National Anti-Vivisection Society v IRC*,[48] where the evidence before the House of Lords was that the benefits achievable through medical research from experimentation on animals far outweighed the moral benefits in preventing vivisection of animals. It has been said judicially that there will be a predisposition to discount alleged disadvantages arising from what would otherwise be a beneficial purpose unless those disadvantages have been clearly demonstrated.[49]

(v) Can benefit always be measured objectively?

The objective approach adopted in the *National Anti-Vivisection* case assumes that the court is competent to make judgements of what is in the public interest. This is

41 [1948] AC 31 at 49. 42 [1996] 1 WLR 288.
43 [1948] AC 31. 44 [1948] AC 31 at 65–6. 45 [1948] AC 31 at 65–6.
46 See an identical observation by Vaisey J in *Re Shaw's Will Trusts* [1952] Ch 163 at 169.
47 [1981] 3 All ER 493 at 504. 48 [1948] AC 31.
49 *R (Independent Schools Council) v Charity Commission* [2012] Ch 214 at 106.

questionable, since there are many instances where the issue of whether there is a benefit to the public is a matter of opinion. This is especially the case if fine moral issues over which there is a real divergence of opinion in society are involved, and at best the court can only give its own value judgement on the issue. There are also some very interesting examples of activities held to be charitable despite no evidence having been provided to demonstrate public benefit. These include religious organizations engaged in public worship and societies promoting the humane treatment of animals. In both of these instances the courts have been prepared to assume public benefit without any form of proof of benefit being offered. In both cases, quantification or measurement of the benefits (if they exist) would be difficult or impossible.

(vi) Is a hybrid approach preferable?

The subjective approach, with objective limitations, might provide a more attractive alternative than a purportedly purely objective approach. This was suggested in the Irish case of *Re Cranston*,[50] which concerned a gift to a vegetarian society. Fitzgibbon LJ took the view that it would be charitable provided the purpose was one which the founder of the society believed to be to public advantage, and that his belief 'be at least rational and not contrary either to the general law of the land or to the principles of morality'. The key factor is the subjective belief of the donor, within certain objective limits, that the purpose is beneficial. There is no need for the court—or the Charity Commission—to make its own value judgements about relative merits. Is it not possible that both a trust for the prevention of animal experimentation and a trust for the promotion of medical research could be considered charitable, although their objects are to some extent in conflict? Similarly, could not a trust for exploring the health benefits of vegetarianism be charitable alongside a trust for the exploration of the health benefits of eating meat? All that is really needed is a test that will eliminate those purposes that are in no sense in the public interest or are of benefit only to small and obscure groups and sects. A test which upholds purposes that a substantial body of public opinion regards as beneficial would be adequate for this purpose, and more honest than a spurious claim to make all judgements objectively.

(c) Assessing benefit in the light of modern conditions

There is not the slightest doubt that the concept of what constitutes a public benefit has changed over the years, and that this is reflected in the decisions of the courts and of the Charity Commission. Views relating to the conservation of the built and natural heritage have changed. There is now, for instance, a belief that the protection of biodiversity could in itself be of value, without needing to establish immediate practical benefits.[51]

Changes in social conditions and emerging scientific findings can change the view of what will be considered to be a public benefit. The Charity Commission gave an example in its 2008 analysis of the law:

> for a long time in the earlier part of the 20th century, the supply of cigarettes to sick people in hospital was regarded as charitable. During the First World War, major charities, in carrying out such a charitable aim, would provide cigarettes as 'useful sedatives for sick or wounded men'... Today, we would not regard the provision of cigarettes to hospital patients as being charitable for the public benefit. Any apparent benefits from the cigarettes acting as a sedative would be more than outweighed by the very real and considerable detriment caused to the patients and others by cigarette smoke.[52]

[50] [1898] 1 IR 431. [51] RR1—*The Review of the Register of Charities* [2001], para B9.

[52] *Charities and Public Benefit* (January 2008), para D6.

Another example of changed social attitudes about benefit reflected through decisions concerning charitable validity can be found in relation to gun and rifle clubs. There is a court case directly on point, albeit one which now seems old fashioned. In *Re Stephens*,[53] a gift was made to the National Rifle Association. The gift had a very striking purpose, being the teaching of shooting at moving objects so as to prevent a military loss similar to that at Majuba Hill in the Boer War. Kekewich J held the gift to be charitable on the basis that it would help to promote the efficiency of the armed forces. In the contemporary legal era, despite the authority of that case, views on the benefits of shooting have changed considerably. Generally, it is no longer thought that a population trained in shooting will be beneficial for the defence of the realm. This leaves the benefit of gun clubs open to question and the Charity Commission is now at least reluctant to register them.[54] In a sign of this shift in attitude, the First-tier Tribunal denied the Cambridgeshire Target Shooting Association charitable status. It did so on the basis that the organization could not show itself to be beneficial. Shooting was found not to be of any particular health benefit, either physical or mental.[55] Despite this, the Tribunal was not of the view that there is any blanket ban on the registration of gun clubs. It indicated that there are some circumstances where the purposes of a gun club might be sufficiently beneficial to achieve charitable status. It suggested that if the club set out its purposes as the promotion of education about shooting, or set out its purposes as the inclusive participation of disabled people in the sport, then it might be charitable and so registrable.[56]

(d) **The public aspect**

In most cases, it might seem fairly obvious as to whether there is a benefit to the public, but in some cases it is hard to determine whether benefits are genuinely public. For instance, the provision of a park in Lampeter is unlikely to be of much value to the residents of Birmingham, Liverpool, or Worcester. Does it, therefore, confer benefits on the public? If a trust provides advice and guidance to people suffering from a rare disease, can that be considered to be providing benefits to the public? The answer in both cases is likely to be that the activities concerned are for the public benefit, but they are clearly not for the benefit of the whole of the public, if by that we mean the whole population of England and Wales, or of the UK. Benefits can be public even if they are available only to part of the public, but how can we determine whether those benefits are to the public or merely to a group of private individuals? The cases on public benefit raise complex issues and are not always easy to reconcile. Nevertheless, there are some recurrent themes and common principles. These include what is known as the 'personal nexus' rule, and the need for a class of beneficiaries which is sufficiently large.

(i) **A sufficiently large group**

For a class or group to constitute a section of the public it must not be 'numerically negligible'.[57] This rule is not applied to trusts for the relief of poverty. In *Re Duffy*[58] Roth J held that a trust to provide amenity benefits for the residents and staff of a single residential care home, even if a beneficial purpose, could not be charitable because a gift for the benefit of no more than thirty-three residents at a particular care home could not be

[53] (1892) 8 TLR 792.

[54] See Luxton, *Making Law?: Parliament v The Charity Commission* (Politeia 2009) p 14. See generally, Clarke, 'The charitable status of rifle clubs: out with a bang?' (1992–3) 1 CLPR 137.

[55] *Cambridgeshire Target Shooting Association (CTSA) v Charity Commission* Appeal No CA\2015\0002, [51].

[56] *Cambridgeshire Target Shooting Association (CTSA) v Charity Commission* Appeal No CA\2015\0002, [75].

[57] *Oppenheim v Tobacco Securities Trust Co Ltd* [1951] AC 297.

[58] [2013] EWHC 2395 (Ch).

regarded as a gift to a sufficient section or class of the community as to meet the public benefit requirement. This decision must be considered good law but it is not without controversy. In an analysis of the authority, Mary Synge argues that no consideration in the case was given to the fact that a care home is necessarily limited in size.[59] The charitable gift was attempted by a resident of the home who had intended to share his wealth with those around him. The consequence of the decision was that his two nephews shared a legacy of around a quarter of a million pounds. It is a peculiarity of the case that the court did not consider whether or not the gift should have been kept in charity and applied to another similar organizsation (see Chapter 22). There is no evidence that the nephews had a particularly strong relationship with the care home resident. In the light of this, it must be hoped that the rule is not relied upon by the Charity Commission in its regulatory decision-making. In effect, it means that gifts for ordinarily sized care homes are not valid as charitable bequests.

(ii) The 'personal nexus' rule

It is rather more difficult than it might seem to distinguish between public and private benefits. There is, of course, no difficulty at the extremes. Funding research into a cure for cancer on terms that the research is to be made publicly available is obviously for the public benefit. Conversely, a trust for a named individual will be considered to confer only private benefits, even if the gift will transform the life of a person who is in poor health, badly housed, badly educated, and impecunious. One test to distinguish public from private benefits is the 'personal nexus' test, but it will be seen that this test has drawbacks.

(iii) Meaning of the personal nexus rule

This test has its foundation in the decision of the House of Lords in *Oppenheim v Tobacco Securities Trust Co Ltd*[60] John Phillips was a large shareholder in British American Tobacco (BAT), and on his death he left property on trust to use the income for the education of the children of the employees or ex-employees of BAT. The House of Lords took the view that this group was not a section of the public but a private class, and that the trust was, therefore, non-charitable. The principle was stated by Lord Simmonds, who identified two characteristics that would render a class of beneficiaries a 'section of the public'. First (as has just been considered), such a class would have to be 'not numerically negligible'. Second, the identity of the members of the class could not be defined by means of a personal nexus. He explained that:

> the quality which distinguishes [the potential beneficiaries] from other members of the community, so that they form by themselves a section of it, must be a quality which does not depend on their relationship to a particular individual.[61]

Thus, although the employees and ex-employees formed a class of some 110,000 persons, they were not a section of the public because they were identified by their personal contractual relationship with BAT. As Lord Simmonds said:

> A group of persons may be numerous but, if the nexus between them is their personal relationship to a single propositus or to several propositi, they are neither the community nor a section of the community for charitable purposes.[62]

(iv) Impact of the personal nexus rule

Lord Simmonds did not qualify or seek to limit the 'personal nexus' rule. If the identifying feature of the class is the members' nexus or relationship to a particular individual or

[59] Synge, 'Charitable status: not a negligible matter' (2016) 132 LQR 303, 315.
[60] [1951] AC 297.
[61] [1951] AC 297 at 306.
[62] [1951] AC 297.

group of individuals, they cannot constitute a section of the public. So, the employees of a company would not constitute a section of the public, nor would the relatives of an individual[63] or the members of a trade union.[64] A strict application of the test might mean that the patients of a particular general medical practice, the clients of a firm of solicitors, and the members of a university and other similar classes would all be considered to be private groups. The rule can apply even if the class of beneficiaries is identified in a way which does not require specific reference to a single 'propositus'. In *IRC v Educational Grants Association Ltd*,[65] Metal Box Ltd established and funded the EGA, which had the object of advancing education by providing grants for individuals to attend university or private schools. Between 76 per cent and 85 per cent of the grants made by the EGA were made to children of employees of Metal Box, although Metal Box was not mentioned in the memorandum of association of the EGA. The Court of Appeal held that in practice there was a personal nexus, and that the EGA was not exclusively charitable. In *Re Koettgen's Will Trusts*,[66] an educational trust was open to the public at large, subject to a direction that the trustees were to give preference to the families of employees, up to a maximum of 75 per cent of the income. This was held to be valid, although Pennycuick J, in *IRC v Educational Grants Association*, expressed considerable difficulty with it. In *Caffoor v Income Tax Comr for Columbo*,[67] it was held that a preference for the grantor's family made an educational trust non-charitable. This seems to be the better view, although it must be a question of degree in each case whether the extent of a preference is sufficient to deprive an otherwise charitable trust of its charitable status.

(v) Criticism of the personal nexus test

The rationale behind the personal nexus test is understandable, namely that purely private groups should not receive the tax privileges enjoyed by charities. If BAT had attempted to set up a similar trust in favour of its own employees, charitable status should not have been granted, as the company would have been seeking to provide its employees with a tax-free benefit. This was, in effect, what had been done in the *Metal Box* case. However, the facts of *Oppenheim* were essentially different. The trust was established by a man whose only interest in the company was that he owned a substantial shareholding,[68] and in no sense was there an attempt by the company to give their employees a tax-free perk. In such circumstances, where the gift was made by an outside donor to a substantial class, there is less justification for refusing charitable status.

The philosophy of providing rigid tests for public benefit is also questionable, since it is impossible to devise a rule that will cover all circumstances and not lead to anomalous results. For this reason, Lord MacDermott dissented from the decision of the other members of the House of Lords in *Oppenheim*, and rejected the personal nexus test.[69] He pointed out that far from proving conclusive, the 'personal nexus' test would produce unacceptable anomalies.[70]

(vi) Continued relevance of the personal nexus test

Despite these criticisms, the personal nexus test has continued to be applied and is contained (without qualification) in the Charity Commission guidance on public benefit.[71]

[63] See *Re Compton* [1945] Ch 123, where the Court of Appeal held that a trust for the education of the descendants of three named persons was not charitable.

[64] *Re Mead's Trust Deed* [1961] 1 WLR 1244.

[65] [1967] Ch 993. [66] [1954] Ch 252. [67] [1961] AC 584.

[68] See [1951] AC 297 at 299, where it is recorded that 'no evidence was given of any connection of the grantors with the company except that John Phillips was a large stockholder'.

[69] [1951] AC 297 at 314. [70] [1951] AC 297 at 318.

[71] Charity Commission, *Public Benefit; The Public Benefit Requirement (PB1)* [2013] Pt 5: Benefiting the public or a sufficient section of the public.

However, in the Commission's legal analysis of public benefit, in 2005 and 2008,[72] the Commission indicated that the rule should be applied with caution and flexibility, and in its 2013 analysis, it suggests, citing *Dingle v Turner*,[73] that the rule has been 'assumed' by the House of Lords to apply to trusts in the *Pemsel* fourth category only.

(vii) The scope of the personal nexus rule

The personal nexus test has not been applied to all categories of charity. *Oppenheim v Tobacco Securities Trust Co Ltd* and *IRC v Educational Grants Association* (the *Metal Box* case) both concerned trusts for the advancement of education. It was also applied to charities within the fourth head identified in *Pemsel* of 'other purposes beneficial to the community'.[74] It was not applied to trusts for the advancement of religion, provided that the religiously affected people lived their lives among the community at large (an illustration of the acceptance of indirect benefits). Most significantly, it did not apply to charities that fell under the head of relief of poverty. Thus, as Chadwick J observed in *Re Segelman (Decd)*:

> a gift for the relief of poverty is no less charitable because those whose poverty is to be relieved are confined to a particular class limited by ties of blood or employment.[75]

This exception enjoyed an insurmountable historical pedigree. The special treatment of trusts for the relief of poverty does not seem to apply to trusts relieving needs of other types. Thus, in *Re Mead's Trust Deed*,[76] a trust to provide a home for aged members of a trade union and to provide a sanatorium for members suffering from tuberculosis was held not to be charitable because the members of a trade union are not a section of the public. In *Attorney General v Charity Commission (The Charity Commission Poverty Reference)*,[77] the Upper Tribunal accepted that different tests for public benefit could apply to different types of charity.

(viii) Poor relations

In *Re Compton*,[78] where the personal nexus test was first suggested, Lord Greene MR referred to a series of cases where gifts to the 'poor relations' of an individual had been held charitable.[79] He concluded that although these cases would fail under the personal nexus test, they were to be regarded as 'anomalous'[80] exceptions to the principle. In *Oppenheim*, Lord Simmonds was similarly unwilling to 'harmonize' and overturn the 'poor relations' cases.[81] It might be thought that members of a family are just the type of class that is private rather than public, and, therefore, not deserving of charitable status. The exception can only be justified on public policy grounds that the relief of poverty is such an important object to society that any gift that seeks to relieve it will be encouraged and upheld[82] or that the relief of poverty, even for a very small number of individuals,

[72] Charity Commission, *Public Benefit—The Legal Principles* (January 2005), para 23; *Analysis of the Law Relating to Public Benefit* (September 2013), para 71. See also the Law Commission document, *Analysis of the Law Underpinning Charities and Public Benefit* [2008] v 1.1.1, para 3.45.

[73] *Dingle v Turner* [1972] AC 601 at 625D.

[74] See *Re Drummond* [1914] 2 Ch 90, where a gift to provide the holiday expenses of the workpeople of a spinning company was held not charitable, since it was not for general public purposes.

[75] [1996] Ch 171, [1995] 3 All ER 676 at 687.

[76] [1961] 1 WLR 1244. [77] [2012] WTLR 977 at 34. [78] [1945] Ch 123.

[79] *Isaac v DeFriez* [1754] Amb 595; *A-G v Price* [1810] 17 Ves 371; *Bernal v Bernal* [1838] 3 My & Cr 559; *Browne v Whalley* [1866] WN 386; *Gillam v Taylor* [1873] LR 16 Eq 581; *A-G v Duke of Northumberland* [1877] 7 Ch D 745.

[80] [1945] Ch 123 at 139. [81] [1951] AC 297 at 308.

[82] See *Re Scarisbrick* [1951] Ch 622 at 639, per Evershed MR: 'The "poor relations" cases may be justified on the basis that the relief of poverty is of so altruistic a character that the public element may necessarily be inferred thereby, or they may be accepted as a hallowed, if illogical, exception.'

provides significant indirect benefit to the public as a whole.[83] Thus, in *Re Scarisbrick's Will Trusts*,[84] Bertha Scarisbrick left her residuary estate to trustees upon trust for her relations 'in needy circumstances'. The Court of Appeal held that this was a valid charitable trust. In *Dingle v Turner*,[85] this exception was confirmed by the House of Lords. Frank Dingle left his residuary estate to trustees, the income to be used to pay pensions to the 'poor employees' of E Dingle & Co, a company that he jointly owned. The House of Lords held unanimously that the personal nexus rule had no application to trusts for the relief of poverty.[86] The exemption was re-affirmed in *Re Segelman*,[87] where a testator left property in his will to be used for a period of twenty-one years for the benefit of the poor and needy members of his family. A schedule was drawn up in which he named six members of his extended family and the issue of five of them as comprising the class of beneficiaries. Chadwick J held that this created a valid charitable gift, falling within the scope of the exception, because it was 'a gift to particular poor persons, the relief of poverty among them being the motive for the gift'.[88]

It might have been thought that the anomalous treatment of poverty could not survive the abolition of the presumption of public benefit in the Charities Acts 2006 and 2011. Nevertheless, in *Attorney General v Charity Commission (The Charity Commission Poverty Reference)*,[89] the Upper Tribunal came to the firm and clearly expressed view that there was no requirement for a trust for the relief of poverty to satisfy the public benefit requirement by benefiting a sufficiently large and appropriately described part of the community or public; it was sufficient if the trust met the test of being charitable in nature.[90] The Tribunal did not consider it necessary to decide whether poverty charities were anomalous or whether, as a question of fact, the indirect public benefit of relieving poverty, even for small groups, was sufficient. The Upper Tribunal decision is consistent with *Cawdron v Merchant Taylors' School*,[91] decided after the 2006 Act, where Blackburne J saw no objection to holding charitable a gift to provide assistance (including scholarships) for the sons and other dependent relatives of Old Merchant Taylors killed or disabled in the First World War—a class defined by reference to a single propositus.

(ix) Prevention of poverty

The Upper Tribunal in the *Charity Commission Poverty Reference* case considered that logic and coherence would normally require the same principles to be applied to trusts for the prevention of poverty as to those for the relief of poverty. The two objects would often be combined, and it would likely be illogical to apply different public benefit rules to a charity established purely for the prevention of poverty. However, there might be some (undefined) circumstances in which a different rule might be logical and appropriate.[92]

(e) An alternative approach to public benefit

In contrast to the strict approach to questions of public benefit in the personal nexus test outlined earlier, others have advocated a more flexible response, arguing that strict tests

[83] See *Gibson v South American Stores (Gath & Chaves) Ltd* [1949] Ch 572 at 576.

[84] [1951] Ch 622. [85] [1972] AC 601.

[86] [1972] AC 601 at 623, per Lord Cross: 'it must be accepted that whatever else it may hold sway the *Compton* rule has no application in the field of trusts for the relief of poverty'.

[87] [1996] Ch 171, [1995] 3 All ER 676; Histed, 'Rectification of Wills and Charitable Trusts for Poor Relations: Broadening the Boundaries' [1996] Conv 379.

[88] [1995] 3 All ER 676 at 688. [89] [2012] WTLR 977.

[90] [2012] WTLR 977 at 64. [91] [2009] EWHC 1722 (Ch).

[92] *Attorney General v Charity Commission (The Poverty Reference)* [2012] WTLR 977 at 69–82. This is also clear from the latest Commission guidance on public benefit, which treats the relief and prevention of poverty separately from other types of charitable purpose—see Charity Commission *Public benefit: the public benefit requirement (PB1)* (September 2013).

are unworkable in practice and lead to anomalous results. They consider that each situation should be considered on its own facts, with a variety of circumstances being taken into account before an impressionistic judgement is made whether a class constitutes a section of the public or not.

As was noted earlier, in *Oppenheim v Tobacco Securities Trust Co Ltd*, Lord MacDermott dissented from the decision of the majority and held that the personal nexus rule should not alone govern the question of public benefit. He considered that to separate the attributes dividing human beings into classes of those purely personal and those purely impersonal was a task 'no less baffling and elusive than the problem to which it is directed, namely, the determination of what is and what is not a section of the public'.[93] He also pointed out the anomalous results that would follow from such a rigid approach, so that a trust framed to provide for the education of children of those employed in the tobacco industry in a named town would be charitable, even though the class of potential beneficiaries may have been appreciably smaller than that under the trust in question. He advocated a flexible approach whereby the court would 'regard the facts of each case and . . . treat the matter very much as one of degree', with a process of 'reaching a conclusion on a general survey of the circumstances and considerations regarded as relevant rather than of making a single, conclusive test'.[94] On such an approach he would have held the trust charitable, taking into account the numerical size of the class and the fact that it was not limited to present employees but also ex-employees. The intention of the donor was to 'advance the interest of the class described as a class rather than as a collection or succession of particular individuals'.[95]

In *Dingle v Turner*,[96] Lord Cross, who delivered the leading judgment, expressed his dissatisfaction with the strict approach taken in *Oppenheim*. He accepted the force of the criticisms of Lord MacDermott, and acknowledged that he himself would 'prefer to approach the problem on much broader lines'.[97] He considered that the distinction between personal and impersonal relationships was unsatisfactory, and concluded that 'at the end of the day one is left where one started with the bare contrast between "public" and "private".'[98] Like Lord MacDermott, he accepted that the question whether a trust was for the benefit of the public was a question of degree[99] and that a variety of factors would be taken into account. He suggested that a number of factors were significant.

(i) The size of the class

Obviously, the larger the class of potential beneficiaries the more likely it is that they will constitute a section of the public.[100] Thus, the employees of a fairly small firm are less likely to be a section of the public than the employees of large companies like ICI and GEC, which employ many thousands of men and women who are largely unknown to each other.[101]

(ii) The purpose of the trust

The objects of the trust will exert a major influence on whether it should be regarded as charitable. Lord Cross explained that there was an intrinsic relationship between the size of the class and the objects of the trust:

> It may well be that, on the one hand, a trust to promote some purpose, prima facie charitable, will constitute a charity even though the class of potential beneficiaries might fairly be called a private class and that, on the other hand, a trust to promote another purpose, also prima

[93] [1951] AC 297 at 317. [94] [1951] AC 297 at 314. [95] [1951] AC 297 at 315.
[96] [1972] AC 601. [97] [1972] AC 601 at 623. [98] [1972] AC 601 at 623.
[99] [1972] AC 601 at 624. [100] See *Re Duffy* [2013] EWHC 2395 (Ch). [101] [1972] AC 601 at 624.

> facie charitable, will not constitute a charity even though the class of potential beneficiaries might seem to some people fairly describable as a section of the public.[102]

Unfortunately, he did not give any illustration of how this principle might apply in practice.

(iii) The fiscal privileges of charitable status

Lord Cross further indicated that the question of charitable status cannot be determined in isolation from the benefits that such status will bring, so that regard to the fiscal privileges attendant upon charitable status cannot be avoided. He was of the view that the decisions in *Re Compton* and *Oppenheim* were influenced by the 'consideration that if such trusts as were there in question were held valid they would enjoy an undeserved fiscal immunity'.[103] However, Lord MacDermott expressed doubt whether fiscal privilege was a factor to be taken into account in determining whether a class constitutes a section of the public, and Viscount Dilhorne and Lord Hodson concurred with his reservation.

(f) The unsatisfactory state of the current law

While the judgment of Lord Cross in *Dingle v Turner*[104] highlights the deficiencies of the *Oppenheim* test, it sadly fails to eliminate the difficulties the test causes.[105] Its status is in doubt. Although all the members of the House of Lords expressly concurred with the opinion of Lord Cross, their comments vis-à-vis the *Oppenheim* test were purely obiter because the trust in question fell within the 'poverty' exception to the personal nexus rule. It is unfortunate that the law is in such a state of uncertainty, and an early resolution of the issue, although unlikely, would be desirable. Given the arbitrary character of the strict 'personal nexus' approach advocated by Lord Simmonds, the 'impressionistic' approach advocated by Lord MacDermott and Lord Cross, which takes into account a wide range of factors, is preferable. There is no reason why fiscal privilege should not be considered as a factor, since the very reason why the law insists that a charity must benefit the public or a section of the public is that private groups should not be entitled to massive state subsidy at the expense of the taxpayer.

(g) Impact of conditions or restrictions on benefit

(i) Assumption that benefits will be available to all in need

Even where a group or class may prima facie constitute a section of the public, there may be conditions, restrictions, or aspects of the disposition or association which deprive it of charitable status. The starting point for this is that, once it has been determined that a purpose is in its nature charitable, there is an assumption that the benefits should be available to all those in need, and that it would be illogical to restrict the benefits in an arbitrary way.

(ii) Some restrictions may be justified

It is not inconsistent with charitable status for limits to be provided on access to benefits, provided that these limits are not irrational or unreasonable, and they can be justified by reason of the nature of the charity. It is inevitable that many charitable purposes are not available to every single member of the public. Trusts for the benefit of the blind or the disabled are not available to every member of the community because not every member

[102] [1972] AC 601 at 624. [103] [1972] AC 601 at 625. [104] [1972] AC 601.

[105] Jones, 'Charitable Trusts. What is Public Benefit?' [1974] 33 CLJ 63.

of the community is blind or disabled. Trusts to provide for sea defences are not of direct benefit to members of the public living inland.[106]

There can also legitimately be limits that are not dictated simply by the nature of the benefit conferred. The provision of almshouses or sheltered accommodation could reasonably be confined to residents of a geographical area, since this is a rational way of allocating a limited provision. Participation in an orchestra might be confined to those who reach a satisfactory musical standard, since otherwise the quality of the musical experience might be affected.

(iii) Equality Act 2010

Charitable gifts flow from the values and views of donors. Unfortunately, if those donors have unacceptable or discriminatory views, then they might attempt to create a charity which is harmful rather than beneficial. A clear example is found in *Re Lysaght*,[107] where a donor attempted to establish charitable scholarships at the Royal College of Surgeons. To her otherwise beneficial gift, she attached a harmful condition. She stated that only British born subjects who were men and not of the Jewish or Roman Catholic faiths could benefit. When the case was decided in 1966, this type of discriminatory gift was not unlawful. The key reason that the donor was frustrated was that the Royal College of Surgeons refused to accept the gift unless the religious discrimination was removed. Fortunately, in modern times, the gift would not be lawful to effect. The Equality Act 2010 prohibits discrimination by reference to a protected characteristic, namely age, disability, gender reassignment, marriage and civil partnership, pregnancy and maternity, race, religion or belief, sex, or sexual orientation.[108] There is an exception for charities which by their constitution are permitted to provide benefits only to a group sharing a protected characteristic, and either the object of the trust is to tackle a disadvantage relating to that characteristic or there is some other legitimate aim which the charity is addressing in a proportionate way. The Charity Commission may approve a change in the governing instrument of a charity to permit discrimination by reference to a protected characteristic, but it refused to do so for the Catholic Care charity, which offered an adoption service for 'hard to place' children, but was willing to do so only for heterosexual couples. For mainly religious reasons, the charity was not prepared to place children for adoption with homosexual couples. The charity failed in its appeals from the Charity Commission since it did not succeed in showing that there were sufficiently weighty reasons to justify the discrimination it proposed to engage in.[109]

(iv) Arbitrary restrictions are not permitted

Even apart from the Equality Act 2010 restrictions that operate arbitrarily are not permitted. The bar on arbitrary restrictions is illustrated by *IRC v Baddeley*.[110] In this case a gift to a Methodist Mission in London for the promotion of the 'religious, social and physical training' of persons resident in West Ham and Leyton 'who were or were likely to become members of the Methodist Church' was held non-charitable because of the inclusion of social and recreational purposes. However, the House of Lords also held that the class of potential beneficiaries did not constitute a section of the public, so that there was insufficient 'public benefit'. There is no doubt that the residents of a particular area will be regarded as constituting a section of the public, but Viscount Simmonds drew a

[106] See *IRC v Baddeley* [1955] AC 572. [107] [1966] Ch 191 (Ch).

[108] For an analysis of the impact of the legislation on all areas of a charity, see Morris, Sigafoos et al, *The Impact of the Equality Act on Charities* (Charity Law & Policy Unit 2013).

[109] *Catholic Care (Diocese of Leeds) v Charity Commission* [2012] UKUT 395 (TCC); *Catholic Care (Diocese of Leeds) v Charity Commission* [2010] EWHC 520 (Ch). [110] [1955] AC 572.

distinction between 'a form of relief extended to the whole community yet by its very nature advantageous only to the few and a form of relief accorded to a selected few out of a larger number equally willing and able to take advantage of it'.[111] He said that it would be charitable to provide a bridge, available to the public at large, but only used by a very small number. However, it would be different for 'a bridge to be crossed only by impecunious Methodists'. He held that the proposed gift fell within the second category because it was not available to all the residents of West Ham and Leyton but only those who were, or were likely to become, members of the Methodist Church. The principle has sometimes been described as a prohibition on having 'a class within a class'. Its scope is uncertain.

(v) A 'class within a class' is not permitted?

The description of the principle as preventing the creation of a 'class within a class' goes too far, since there are many cases where a charitable trust operates despite a double limitation on eligibility. For instance, a trust for poor widows in Rotherhithe was charitable despite there being three conditions for eligibility.[112] The real objection, it is submitted, is the introduction of an arbitrary restriction on eligibility. There is no objection to funding a church for the use of Methodists, or a synagogue for the use of Jews. But to limit the use of a bridge to Methodists (even poor Methodists) is an arbitrary and capricious restriction in the use of a facility that should be made available to all.

(vi) Excluding the less well-off

There are many cases that demonstrate that it is not inimical to charitable status for charges to be made by a charity for the services which it provides. It has already been seen earlier that this has been held to be the case for a housing charity, a healthcare charity, for a sports centre, and for educational charities. Nevertheless, there is continuing disquiet in some circles about charities such as public schools or private hospitals that impose charges for their services, with the result that benefits are only available to those who can afford to pay for these services. The fact that these organizations make no private profit, or that any profit that they do make is ploughed back into the further enhancement of their provision, does not silence their critics. In *Re Resch's Will Trusts*,[113] it was made clear that the assessment of public benefit in the case of a fee-charging organization need not be confined to an assessment of the benefits to the direct recipients of the services. Indirect benefits to the public can also be taken into account. However, if an organization excludes the less well-off from both direct and indirect benefits, this is likely to affect its charitable status. In *R (Independent Schools Council) v Charity Commission*,[114] the Upper Tribunal considered a challenge by independent schools to the Law Commissions somewhat prescriptive guidance on public benefit. The Upper Tribunal, chaired by Warren J, after a careful review of the case law, considered that the activities of independent schools were of a character that they would be charitable if provided by a free school open to all. The essential question was, therefore, whether the fact that the schools charged fees affected their charitable status. This was a question as to whether the application of the charitable purposes conferred sufficient public benefit.[115] The tribunal considered the hypothetical case of a school which had the sole object of advancing the education of children whose families can afford to pay fees representing the cost of the provision of their education. The tribunal's view was that such a school would not have purposes which provide that element of public benefit necessary to qualify as a charity.[116] The reason for this is that 'a trust which excludes the poor from benefit cannot be a charity'.[117] Few schools were likely

[111] [1955] AC 572 at 592. Lord Reid dissented on this point and Lords Tucker and Porter expressed no opinion: [1955] AC 572 at 612, 614, and 593.

[112] *Re Faraker* [1912] 2 Ch 488.

[113] [1969] 1 AC 514.

[114] [2012] Ch 214.

[115] At 112.

[116] At 177.

[117] At 178.

to have constitutions which excluded the poor, so defined, but they were also required to operate in a way which did not exclude the poor.[118] It was not, however, an objection that a trust charges fees which equate to the full cost of the provision of its services; the problem arose only where the level of fees was such that only the richer members of the public could afford to pay them.[119] The test in such a case would be whether the fees were affordable to the 'not very well off.'

Provided that a school was not established with a restriction on benefits excluding the poor, and the poor were not de facto excluded, there were a number of ways in which public benefit could be demonstrated by a school with fees higher than those which people of modest means could afford:[120]

(1) through the provision of scholarships and bursaries enabling children from poorer families to attend, whether funded from the school's own resources, or from associated or independent trusts or other grant making bodies;[121]
(2) through arrangements under which students from local state schools can attend classes in subjects not otherwise readily available to them;
(3) by sharing of teachers or teaching facilities with local state schools;
(4) by making available (whether on the internet or otherwise) teaching materials used in the school;
(5) by making available to students of local state schools other facilities such as playing fields, sports halls, swimming pools, or sports grounds.

Taking children out of the state sector who would otherwise have to be educated at public expense might be a minor benefit, but was not in itself sufficient public benefit.[122] Overall, in order to demonstrate public benefit, fee-charging schools needed to demonstrate that they were doing enough for those who cannot afford fees. This required at least that the school admitted a non-token number of children from less well-off families,[123] but also that it engaged in such other activities in the interests of the community as a whole (such as those just described) as were appropriate to its own individual circumstances:[124]

> It is for the charity trustees of the school concerned to address and assess how their obligations might best be fulfilled in the context of their own particular circumstances . . . It is not for the Charity Commission or the Tribunal or the court to impose on trustees of a school their own idea of what is, and what is not, reasonable.[125]

The nature and extent of the benefits which needed to be provided to the wider community would be greater where a school provided facilities and services at the luxury end of the spectrum than in the case of a school with more modest provision.[126]

(h) **Non-charitable benefits must be incidental**

(i) The 'exclusively charitable' rule

It has already been seen that a trust that combines both charitable and non-charitable objects will not be considered to be charitable. The same principle applies to the way in which the charity operates and the benefits which it confers. By definition, a charity exists for the public benefit. A trust which confers only private benefits cannot be a charitable trust, nor can a trust which provides a mixture of both public and private benefits,

[118] At 215. [119] At 179. [120] At 196–205. [121] At 184.
[122] At 205–7. [123] At 215. [124] At 215–16. [125] At 217 and 220.
[126] At 219. See, now, Charity Commission, *Charging for Services: Benefits for the Poor* (16 September 2013).

unless the private benefits can be seen as being no more than ancillary or subordinate to the public benefits. There can, therefore, be issues relating to the relative balance of benefits, particularly in the case of membership organizations or trusts that confer benefits on a narrow range of beneficiaries. The essential test with a membership organization is whether the organization has an altruistic purpose with a membership structure adopted as an effective way of delivering charitable benefits or for administrative convenience, or whether the purpose is primarily self-help.[127] Hence, the Countryside Alliance was unable to prove that promoting the production of game to eat was exclusively charitable. While public benefits could arise fron the activity, such as health benefits in eating game and in the conservation of the land needed as habitat to raise game, these benefits were incidental to the commercial (private) benefits of raising game.[128]

(ii) Incidental private or non-charitable benefits

Although as a general rule a trust will only be charitable if its objects are exclusively charitable, the courts have held that there is an element of leeway such that a trust is not invalidated merely because it contains some non-charitable objects that are subsidiary or ancillary to the main charitable purposes. Thus, in *IRC v City of Glasgow Police Athletic Association*,[129] Lord Cohen posed the question whether 'the main purpose of the body . . . is charitable and the only elements in its constitution and operation which are non-charitable are merely incidental to that purpose'.[130] The House of Lords held that, in the circumstances, the promotion of sport was not purely ancillary to the purpose of promoting the efficiency of the police force. The decision would have been different if the non-charitable benefits had been only incidental. It is, for instance, possible for universities as charitable bodies to pay their teaching and support staff, even though this confers private benefits, provided that the payments made represent a fair payment for services rendered.

In *London Hospital Medical College v IRC*,[131] a students' union[132] that provided social, cultural, and athletic activities for the students of a London teaching hospital was held charitable. Brightman J considered that the prime object of the union was the furtherance of the purposes of the medical college and not the private and personal benefit of the students, which was ancillary.[133] Similarly, in *Re South Place Ethical Society*,[134] Dillon J regarded the organization of social activities by the society as purely ancillary to the society's main object of the promotion of ethical principles.[135]

In *Funnell v Stewart*,[136] the testatrix had left a substantial sum of money to a faith-healing group which held private religious services but which saw its *raison d'être* as 'the healing work it did for members of the community'.[137] Hazel Williamson QC held that despite the non-charitable nature of the private services, the trust as a whole was charitable because the private services were 'clearly ancillary or subsidiary to the public faith healing part of the group's work, which was its predominant function'.[138] A similar distinction between primary and ancillary purposes was made in *Longridge on the Thames v Revenue and Customs Commissioners*[139] (a tax tribunal decision), where it was held that making charges below commercial cost was ancillary to the primary educational purposes of a youth training centre in water-based activities.

[127] Charity Commission, *Public Benefit: Analysis of the Law Relating to Public Benefit* [2013] para 72; see also *Charities and Public Benefit* (January 2008), para F12.

[128] *Decision of the Charity Commissioners for Registration of the Countryside Alliance* (23 March 2017).

[129] [1953] AC 380. [130] [1953] AC 380 at 405. [131] [1976] 1 WLR 613.

[132] See also *A-G v Ross* [1986] 1 WLR 252, where the students' union of North London Polytechnic was held charitable despite some non-charitable activities which were regarded as ancillary.

[133] [1976] 1 WLR 613 at 623. See also *Re Coxen* [1948] Ch 747 a charitable trust was upheld despite the presence of some non-charitable elements.

[134] [1980] 1 WLR 1565. [135] [1980] 1 WLR 1565 at 1569. [136] [1996] 1 WLR 288.

[137] [1996] 1 WLR 288 at 296. [138] [1996] 1 WLR 288 at 296. [139] [2013] UKFTT 158 (TC).

(iii) Severance of non-charitable elements

In some cases it will be possible to sever the non-charitable or private elements in a trust. Where a gift is made in favour of some charitable and other non-charitable purposes, the court may sever the good from the bad. In *Salusbury v Denton*,[140] a gift to the testator's widow was to be applied partly toward charitable objects and the rest to his relatives. The widow died without making any appointments, and the court held that there could be a division of the fund between the charitable and non-charitable objects. Page-Wood V-C applied the maxim 'equality is equity' and divided the fund into two equal shares. However, where severance is possible, equal division may not always be the most appropriate solution. In *Re Coxen*[141] Jenkins J held that if he had not been able to find that the object of providing a dinner for the aldermen attending a meeting of trustees was charitable, he would have been prepared to divide the fund unequally so as to sever the charitable from the non-charitable objects.

3 Public benefit in particular circumstances

(a) Public benefit can be self-evident

The Upper Tribunal has rejected the view that prior to the Charities Act 2006 there were any presumptions about public benefit in relation to education[142] or to poverty.[143] It has taken the view that a decision is taken in each case on the basis of the evidence, although there are some cases (such as in relation to the provision of mainstream education open to all without the payment of a fee) where it is so obvious that there is a public benefit that evidence may not be required. As Vaisey J said in *Re Shaw's Will Trusts*:

> there are many cases on this question of whether a bequest is 'charitable' or 'non-charitable' where the purpose is so obviously beneficial to the community that to ask for evidence would really be quite absurd.[144]

(b) Public benefit in relieving poverty

Trusts for the relief of poverty are treated more favourably in applying the public benefit requirement than other trusts. It has been seen that this is either because they are anomalous or because there is such a substantial and self-evident indirect public benefit in relieving poverty that there is no need to demonstrate direct benefit to a class which is not numerically insignificant and which constitutes a section of the community. If the latter is the case, this proposition appears to have been established without any need for formal proof.

(c) The public benefit of religion

There is undoubtedly a requirement for trusts for the advancement of religion to demonstrate public benefit in order to be charitable.[145] The Charities Acts 2006 and 2011 will not have changed this position. Despite this, the case law does not always distinguish

140 [1857] 3 K & J 529. 141 [1948] Ch 747.

142 *R (Independent Schools Council) v Charity Commission* [2012] Ch 214.

143 *Attorney General v Charity Commission (The Poverty Reference)* [2012] WTLR 977.

144 [1952] Ch 163 at 169.

145 *Gilmour v Coats* [1949] AC 426 and *Neville Estates Ltd v Madden* [1962] Ch 832.

between the need for a purpose to be beneficial in nature and for it to be beneficial in operation. In *Neville Estates v Madden*,[146] Cross J famously said that 'as between different religions the law stands neutral, but it assumes that any religion is at least likely to be better than none' and in *Re Watson*,[147] a trust to promote Christian spiritual works which experts unanimously considered to be worthless was held to be charitable. From this it might be thought that the public benefit requirement applies only to the operation of the charity and the law will not question its nature. However, the Charity Commission has refused to register some alleged religions on the basis that they 'must tend directly or indirectly to the moral or spiritual improvement of the public' and have 'an identifiable positive, beneficial, moral or ethical framework', conditions which were not met in the case of Gnosticism and Druidry.[148] Whilst these requirements may be sensible, they are not directly supported by the later Supreme Court decision in *R (on the application of Hodkin) v Registrar General of Births, Deaths and Marriages*,[149] and it has been argued that they are not justified in law.[150] There is a difficulty for the law in recognizing new religions or religious sects because it can involve examining matters of spiritual belief which according to the Court of Appeal in *Shergill v Khaira*[151] are non-justiciable because they are not matters of law at all, but subjective inward matters incapable of proof by direct evidence or by inference. According to the court it is, therefore, inappropriate for a court to pronounce on matters of religious doctrine and practice, although there may be rare occasions on which they have to foray into such matters to resolve issues of property rights.

Where the courts search for public benefit in the operation of a religion they look for forensic proof of that benefit. Contemplative religious orders that are cloistered and have no contact with the community at large have been held not to be charitable. In *Gilmour v Coats*,[152] a gift of £500 was made to a priory of Carmelite nuns, who were cloistered and devoted their lives to prayer. The House of Lords held that they were not a charity because there was not the necessary element of benefit to the public. There was no interaction between the nuns and the community, and Lord Simmonds rejected as 'too vague and intangible' any claimed edification of the public through the example of their spiritual lives and sacrifice. He also rejected the alleged benefit to the community of their intercessory prayer according to Roman Catholic doctrine, as evidenced by an affidavit of the Archbishop of Westminster. This alleged benefit was dismissed as 'manifestly not susceptible of proof', and he stated that the court does not accept as fact whatever a particular religion believes. In *Leahy v A-G of New South Wales*,[153] a gift to religious orders which could have included contemplative orders would have been held invalid by the Privy Council as not being exclusively for charitable purposes if it had not been saved by the New South Wales Conveyancing Act 1919–54.

By contrast, the courts have consistently taken the view that public religious worship will provide sufficient public benefit. This may well be capable of forensic proof, but it is not self-evident to many atheists and agnostics, nor is it a matter on which the courts have ever expected evidence to be presented. In *Neville Estates Ltd v Madden*, this attitude was reflected by Cross J, who said:

> the court is . . . entitled to assume that some benefit accrues to the public from the attendance at places of worship of persons who live in this world and mix with their fellow citizens.[154]

[146] [1962] Ch 832 at 853. [147] [1973] 1 WLR 1472.

[148] See Luxton and Evans, 'Cogent and Cohesive? Two Recent Charity Commission Decisions on the Advancement of Religion' [2011] 75 Conv 144. [149] [2013] UKSC 77.

[150] See Luxton and Evans, 'Cogent and Cohesive? Two Recent Charity Commission Decisions on the Advancement of Religion' [2011] 75 Conv 144. [151] [2012] EWCA Civ 983 at 69–70.

[152] [1949] AC 426. [153] [1959] AC 457. [154] [1962] Ch 832.

This was echoed by Sir Nicholas Browne-Wilkinson V-C in *Re Hetherington (Decd)*:

> The celebration of a religious rite in public does confer a sufficient public benefit because of the edifying and improving effect of such a celebration on the members of the public who attend.[155]

He, therefore, held that the saying of masses for the dead was prima facie charitable, since the invariable practice is that they are said in public, 'which provides a sufficient element of public benefit'. No evidence was presented as to the nature of the benefit either to the dead or to the living.

An interesting test-case for these principles and an illustration of a degree of uncertainty in their application is the Charity Commission's decision not to register the Temple of the Jedi Order. It is important to keep in mind that it is the Commission and not the courts which has immediate responsibility over the Register.[156] The circumstances of the decision are striking. While people who have truly adopted the Jedi faith, as derived from the popular Star Wars films, might be small in number, they do exist as a genuine group of believers, mostly as an online community. In relation to the Temple, the Commission applied a strict standard, finding that the organization was not for the public benefit.[157] This finding was a part of its reason for refusing to register the Temple. The Commission took its task as being a search for benefit in the nature of the faith as well as its operation. Taking a direct stance on the nature of the religion, the Commission found that Jediism as promoted by the Temple was insufficiently formal, as believers are able to opt in and out of its core tenets. Taking an equally direct stance on the operation of the religion it found that, despite the fact the Temple had live online sermons, the organization lacked public benefit on the basis that the Temple did not reach out into the community sufficiently. This appears to mark the application of a stricter standard than suggested by the case law which, as it has been seen, generally holds that public worship is beneficial by itself.

It is necessary to be cautious before saying that the Commission got the law wrong in taking this strict approach. This is an area where the law is uncertain and in need of clarification. It is also important to re-emphasize that this decision was not a court case. It is a regulatory decision without precedential force. The decision is also not just about public benefit. The Commission rejected the Temple's application on multiple grounds, notably a view that the faith lacked cogency, cohesion, and seriousness, a standard not found in ordinary charity law cases.[158] Despite all this, the working through of public benefit criteria in relation to the Temple of the Jedi Order should still be taken seriously. It shows that the public benefit requirement, at least as it might be interpreted by the Commission, has a potential blocking effect on the registration of new faiths.

[155] [1990] Ch 1. [156] Charities Act 2011, s 29.

[157] Decision of the Charity Commissioners For England and Wales, *Application for Registration of The Temple of the Jedi Order*, 19 December 2016, [31]–[35].

[158] Decision of the Charity Commissioners For England and Wales, *Application for Registration of The Temple of the Jedi Order*, 19 December 2016, [21].

22

Cy-près: redistributing funds and changing purposes

1 Introduction

(1) Reform of charitable trust purposes

Cy-près is the body of case law and statutory rules which allows for the purposes of charitable trusts to be changed. The alteration of charitable purposes always means recharacterizing charitable funds by changing the terms on which they are applied. The change of purpose means that different projects and activities will benefit. Cy-près is an ancient, Norman French, legal phrase which is said to mean 'as near as possible'.[1] At one point, this translation was important because there was a general rule that whenever the purposes of a trust were changed, the new objects should be very similar to the old ones. To understand cy-près in this way in now misleading.[2] It will be seen in this chapter that the new purposes no longer have to be as near as possible to the old ones. Equally, while the expression maintains a link with legal history, it is also misleading because it suggests that the process of trust reform is somehow old fashioned or steeped with the traditions of Chancery. This is not the case. Although courts have jurisdiction to reform trusts,[3] in modern times, cy-près has become a largely bureaucratic process, undertaken by the Charity Commission. Much of the decision-making is taken by administrators following online guidance.[4]

There are two broad circumstances where cy-près will be desirable. The first is where a donor attempts a gift by will, but the trust has somehow failed and so needs modification. Cy-près in the wills context is a 'rescue' process that requires an alteration of the purposes of the testator's gift so that it can be carried through without problems. So for example, a charitable organization specified by the donor might have closed down, leaving it unable to receive the gift. In this context, cy-près has a special role. It can be used to save the gift and direct it to an alternative charitable purpose. This change of purpose 'saves the gift for charity'. If the will were not altered, there would be a resulting trust for the benefit of the testator's next-of-kin. The gift would lapse. Where these rescue cases do come to court in modern times, rather than just being decided by administrators at the Commission, it is normally because the next-of-kin are attempting to argue that the testamentary gift should indeed result to them.[5]

[1] Sheridan and Delaney, *The Cy-près Doctrine* (Sweet & Maxwell 1959) p 1.

[2] Sherman, *The Uses of the Dead the Early Modern Development of Cy-Près Doctrine* (Catholic University of America Press 2018) p 4.

[3] Charities Act 2011, s 69.

[4] See Crumley and Picton, 'Still Standing? *Cy-près* and Charitable Service Users in the First-tier Tribunal (Charity)' (2018) 82 Conv 262, 272.

[5] The Charity Commission is unable to determine title. Where there is a dispute the case should go to court. See Charities Act 2011, s 70.

The second circumstance in which cy-près applies is outside of the will context. Sometimes the purposes of a charity which has been established for a number of years will fail. For example, it might serve a group of historic veterans, who have died away over the decades. That circumstance is an uambiguous failure of the gift, paralleling the testamentary circumstance where a gift is made to an organization which does not exist. However, charitable trustees might want to reform their purposes even if there has been no failure. The charitable purposes might simply need changing because they have become out of date. Even if they are strictly possible, social change might have rendered the purposes less useful than they once were. For example, there is very little point in a charity supplying affordable coal in a local area in modern times.[6] The fund could be better spent in other more useful ways.

The modern cy-près rules therefore cover a wide range of functions, including failure of gifts in wills, failure of established charities, and the circumstance where there is no failure in an established charity but the trustees wish to update its purposes anyway.

(2) **Different types of failure**

In cases where there is a failure of the purposes, the principles determining whether the property will be applied cy-près operate differently, depending upon whether the failure was 'initial' or 'subsequent' to the vesting of the gift.

(a) **Subsequent failure**

Subsequent failure occurs where funds have already been devoted to a charitable purpose which then fails, for instance if an established organization is wound up because the class of people it serves has become very small.[7] In the wills context, subsequent failure can also arise where a charitable gift is made by will to an organization in existence at the date of a testator's death, but which is wound up before the personal representatives are able to transfer the gift.[8] If the organization exists at the point of death, even for a short period, then failure is still subsequent. The gift was at one point possible and so there is no failure.[9]

(b) **Initial failure**

There can also be problems with 'initial' failure, where a charitable purpose is from the outset incapable of achievement. This could apply where a testator makes a gift by will to a charity that has already ceased to exist before the testator died, or a gift is too small to achieve the desired result. The line between initial and subsequent failure is normally clear, but difficult cases do sometimes trouble the courts.[10] In *Attorney General v Zedra Fiduciary Services Ltd (UK)*,[11] Zacaroli J was faced with a £512.2 million charitable fund designed to accumulate through investments over time and so pay off the national debt. The trust had been established after the First World War. By the time of the case, the national debt was valued at £2,004 billion and so it had become clear that the charity fund would never accumulate sufficiently to pay it off. A question for the judge was whether the scheme had always been impossible and so an initial failure, or whether the capital had successfully been applied to charitable purposes for many years, only to

[6] *Re Monk* [1927] 2 Ch 197. [7] *Peggs v Lamb* [1994] Ch 172.

[8] See, for example, *Phillips v The Royal Society for the Protection of Birds* [2012] EWHC 618 (Ch).

[9] *Re Slevin* [1891] 2 Ch 236.

[10] See *Kings v Bultitude* [2010] EWHC 1795 (Ch); Picton, '*Kings v Bultitude*—a gift lost to charity' [2011] Conv 69. [11] [2020] EWHC 2988 (Ch).

fail after a period of time. Zacaroli J found that there was a subsequent failure. This is a complex conceptual issue, in regard to which, other judges might reasonably have fallen on the other side of the line.[12]

(c) General charitable intent

The main difference between the treatment of initial failure and of subsequent failure is that since, in the latter, funds have already been devoted to charity, they remain devoted to charity in perpetuity. In the case of initial failure, there is a legal possibility that the gift will be lost to charity, so that the gift will lapse into private hands. It will be seen that, in this testamentary context, this outcome can still be prevented if the judge or Charity Commission take the view that there is a general charitable intention—i.e. an intention to give to broad purposes despite the fact that specific purposes were set out by the testator in his will.[13]

(d) Problems of interpretation

It is not uncommon for a testator to misdescribe a charity. This can happen for a variety of reasons. The charity may have a formal name, but be known by some less formal description. Equally, a testator may simply have guessed at the name, and guessed wrongly. If it is impossible to tell what charity a testator meant to support, the gift may still be capable of surviving where there is a general charitable intent, but it is sometimes possible to escape this problem by using extrinsic evidence to make good any uncertainty in the will.[14]

(3) Changing purposes

Outside of the will context, trustees of an established charity might seek to change its purposes whether or not there is a failure. The recognized charitable purposes considered in Chapter 20 are often referred to as the objects of a charity. An established charity may wish to change their objects in their governing document, as part of the good administration of the charity. This could arise where a charity wishes, for example, to follow funding opportunities that were unavailable to the organization when it was formed, or change its purposes to meet new needs that have arisen in the locale since the existing charity forms. A scheme is a cy-près scheme as opposed to an administrative scheme if it involves an alteration of the charities purposes.

The legal structure that a charity has adopted has a direct bearing on how easily it may amend its objects. This chapter is concerned with charitable trusts, which are referred to as unincorporated charities.[15] In the absence of an express power in the trust instrument,[16] charitable trusts can only alter their purposes if they can use a cy-près scheme.

[12] See Picton, 'Equity Favours Charity' (2021) 136 LQR 363–368.

[13] *Re Wilson* [1913] 1 Ch 314.

[14] See *Marren v Masonic Havens Ltd* [2011] IEHC 525 (applying the slightly different rules as to interpretation of wills in the Republic of Ireland).

[15] For an excellent summary of the powers and processes for charities formed as companies limited by guarantee or charitable incorporated organizations, see *Technical Issues in Charity Law* (Law Com No 375, 2017), Ch 4, paras 4.4–4.13.

[16] There are extremely limited statutory powers contained in the Charities Act 2011, ss 275 and 280, for certain small charities and for administrative provisions, respectively. See Picarda QC, *The Law and Practice relating to Charities* (4th edn, Bloomsbury 2010) Part III Schemes.

2 Circumstances triggering cy-près application

(1) The historic triggers

Prior to legislative change, property would only be applied cy-près if a charitable purpose had become 'impossible' or 'impracticable'. Strictly understood, these triggers for a change of purpose required something near total failure before an alteration cy-près was possible. For example, in *A-G v London Corpn*,[17] a trust for 'the propagation of the Christian religion among the infidels of Virginia' was found to have become impossible, as Lord Thurlow LC held that there were no infidels left in Virginia. Similarly, in *Ironmongers' Co v A-G*,[18] a trust for the redemption of British slaves in Turkey was impossible because there were no such British slaves remaining to be redeemed. In *Re Robinson*,[19] a trust had been established to endow an Evangelical church in Bournemouth, subject to a condition that the preacher always wear a black gown. Since this was alienating the congregation, PO Lawrence J held that this rendered the purpose impracticable,[20] and sanctioned a scheme dispensing with the condition.[21]

The shift towards making charitable reform easier can be seen as a long process. In more modern times, even in cases where the courts have not directly considered or applied the permissive contemporary statute, judges can be seen to be pushing the boundaries, making it easier to reform gifts. In order to extend the scope of this narrow jurisdiction, the courts did not insist strictly upon impossibility or impracticality.[22] In *Re Dominion Students Hall Trust*,[23] a charity maintained a hostel for male students from the British Empire, but only those of European origin. The charity sought to remove the restriction. Evershed J held that 'the word "impossible" should be given a wide significance'[24] and that in the circumstances the 'colour bar' did render the charity impossible since it would undermine its main objects. He approved a scheme removing the bar. In *Re Lysaght (Decd)*,[25] a bar on awarding medical studentships to Jews or Roman Catholics was removed because the trustee named in the will, the Royal College of Surgeons (RCS), refused to accept the gift with the restrictions, making the trust 'impossible'.[26] In *Re JW Laing Trust*,[27] a trust of shares in favour of a variety of evangelical Christian purposes required all the funds to be disbursed within ten years of the settlor's death. On his death in 1978, the trust was worth some £24 million. The court held that although the cy-près jurisdiction was not available, the court had an inherent jurisdiction to delete the time requirement, and should do so because the types of organization that the trust had been supporting were unsuited to receiving large sums of capital.

(2) Charities Act 2011, s 62

Given the historically restrictive scope of the cy-près jurisdiction, the Nathan Committee recommended in 1952 that the requirements of 'impossibility' and 'impracticability' be relaxed.[28] It was recommended that cy-près should be possible even without failure. A wider jurisdiction was thus introduced in s 13 of the Charities Act 1960, which has been

[17] [1790] 3 Bro CC 171. [18] [1844] 10 Cl & Fin 908.

[19] [1921] 2 Ch 332. See also *Re Campden Charities* [1881] 18 Ch D 310, CA.

[20] See also *Re Weir Hospital* [1910] 2 Ch 124.

[21] In essence, he held that the paramount intention was to endow a church, and not to enforce the wearing of a black robe, and that the paramount intention would be rendered impossible by the condition. See *Re Lysaght* [1966] Ch 191 at 208. [22] See *Re Weir Hospital* [1910] 2 Ch 124.

[23] [1947] Ch 183. [24] Ibid at 186. [25] [1966] Ch 191.

[26] See also *Re Woodhams* [1981] 1 WLR 493. [27] [1984] Ch 143.

[28] *Report of the Committee on the Law and Practice relating to Charitable Trusts* (1952) (Cmd 8710), para 365.

re-enacted as s 62 of the Charities Act 2011. This section substantially broadens the occasions on which property can be applied cy-près to include situations where the original purposes have not just failed in whole or in part, but also where the funds could more effectively be used in other ways. Section 62 of the statute has been regularly applied in the context of established charities.[29] While there is nothing in the language of the statute to prevent it from being applied in the testamentary context, there has been no court to this date which has done so.[30] In testamentary cases, the courts have been much more likely to look for a true failure.[31] This means that in consequence of s 62 two different approaches have emerged. In wills cases, at least as a matter of practice if not law, something reasonably close to true failure is normally still required. By contrast, in the context of established charities, it is possible for trustees to seek a reform of their charitable objects even if the purposes of the charity remain strictly workable. They will rely on the statute to do so. It is correct that it should be more difficult to reform a gift in a will than an established charity. Where a testator has left a gift by will, to alter it immediately without good cause would be interfere with his testamentary freedom. The same policy problem does not occur in relation to established charities which will have been carrying through the wishes of their donors for a period of time.[32]

Regard is to be had to a number of factors, including changes in local boundaries, the suitability of restrictions in the gift, and especially, 'the spirit of the gift', and changed social and economic circumstances. Section 62(1)(a)–(e) provides for five circumstances in which property given to charitable purposes which have not strictly failed can be applied cy-près:

(a) where the original purposes, in whole or in part–
  (i) have been as far as may be fulfilled, or
  (ii) cannot be carried out, or not according to the directions given and to the spirit of the gift; or
(b) where the original purposes provide a use for part only of the property available by virtue of the gift; or
(c) where the property available by virtue of the gift and other property applicable for similar purposes can be more effectively used in conjunction, and to that end can suitably, regard being had to *the appropriate considerations*, be made applicable to common purposes; or
(d) where the original purposes were laid down by reference to an area which then was but has since ceased to be a unit for some other purpose, or by reference to a class of persons or to an area which has for any reason since ceased to be suitable, regard being had to *the appropriate considerations*, or to be practical in administering the gift; or
(e) where the original purposes, in whole or in part, have, since they were laid down–
  (i) been adequately provided for by other means, or
  (ii) ceased, as being useless or harmful to the community or for other reasons, to be in law charitable, or
  (iii) ceased in any other way to provide a suitable and effective method of using the property available by virtue of the gift, regard being had to *the appropriate considerations*.

[29] For analysis of the cases, see Mulheron, *The Modern Cy-près Doctrine: Applications and Implications* (UCL 2006) p 91.

[30] It was assumed by counsel in *Re JW Laing Trust* [1984] Ch 143 that a predecessor to the current statute could be applied in the testamentary context but the case was decided on other grounds.

[31] *Re Woodhams* [1981] 1 WLR 493; *Re Spence* [1979] Ch 483; *Kings v Bultitude* [2010] EWHC 1795 (Ch).

[32] Hobhouse, *The Dead Hand: Addresses on the Subject of Endowments and Settlements of Property* (Chatto & Windus 1880).

The Charities Act 2006 introduced the italicized words above, in place of the original phrase 'the spirit of the gift'. This change further extends the circumstances in which cy-près will be possible. Section 62(2) defines what is meant by 'appropriate considerations':

(a) (on the one hand) the spirit of the gift concerned, and
(b) (on the other) the social and economic circumstances prevailing at the time of the proposed alteration of the original purposes.

This amendment facilitates a cy-près application where, for instance, a trust specified the award of an annual prize which over the years has fallen in value because of the effect of inflation, but which otherwise could still be awarded. It was held in *White v Williams* that 'the spirit of the gift, for the purposes of [this provision] is to be ascertained more broadly than by a slavish application of the language of the relevant trust deed.'[33] In that case it was held that, although individual church buildings had been acquired by a single church organization and were vested in a single group of trustees, the spirit in which those buildings had been acquired was to provide facilities for worship by local congregations. The consequence of a schism was that the existing arrangements inhibited that purpose being implemented.

A number of cases have shown how the statutory amendments have widened the cy-près jurisdiction. There is no need for true failure under statute. In *Re Lepton's Charity*,[34] a trust established in 1716 provided for the payment of £3 per annum from the income generated by a piece of land to the minister of a dissenting church, with the remainder distributed among the poor. In 1716 the income was £5, but at the date of the case, it was some £800. Pennycuick V-C held that, although the purpose of the trust had not failed, the circumstances fell within the new statutory jurisdiction and directed that £100 per annum be paid to the minister. In *Varsani v Jesani*,[35] the Court of Appeal used the statutory rules in order to deal with the assets of a religious charity that had suffered an irretrievable schism. Chadwick LJ said that under the law as it stood before the statutory changes, the court could not direct a scheme:

> This is because it would still be possible to carry out the original purposes of the charity through the use of its property by the group who . . . had been found to be the adherents to the true faith; and any application of any part of the property for use by the other group would be open to attack as a breach of trust.[36]

Because the original purposes 'are no longer a suitable and effective method of using the property',[37] the court ordered a scheme under the new rules for the division of the funds between the two groups.

Conversely, it is possible that reference to the spirit of a gift may exclude cy-près application. When Sir Edward Heath, the former British Prime Minister, died, he left his home, Arundells, and his personal papers on charitable trusts. The trustees made a loss in opening Arundells to the public, and sought a scheme to allow its sale. The Charity Commission decided that the spirit of the gift was not simply the memorialization of Sir Edward Heath. Arundells was a house of genuine historical and architectural merit, containing works of art and decorative features of worth, both intrinsically and culturally. Arundells was an essential and integral part of the trust's purposes, and since ways of making its opening to the public more viable had not been explored, it was inappropriate to approve a scheme to allow its sale.[38]

[33] *White v Williams* [2010] EWHC 940 (Ch) at 20. [34] [1972] Ch 276.
[35] [1999] Ch 219. [36] [1999] Ch 219 at 237.
[37] [1999] Ch 219 at 238. [38] *Re Sir Edward Heath Charitable Trust* [2012] WTLR 1469.

(3) **Ongoing reform**

The process of reform to the cy-près triggers is not over. At the time of writing, the Charities Bill 2021–22 was making its way through Parliament. Following a recommendation by the Law Commission,[39] the Bill contained a power for unincorporated charities, including trusts, to amend their governing documents, so long as they are satisfied that the amendment is expedient in the interests of the charity.[40] This can be achieved by a vote passed by 75 per cent of the trustees.[41] This means, in effect, that charitable purposes can prima facie be altered without there being a 'trigger' to justify that alteration. While this is a potentially far-reaching power in the hands of trustees, the Charity Commission will still have a power to remove consent before changes are permitted.[42] The Charities Act 2022 came into force on 24th February 2022.

(4) **Administrative schemes**

Sometimes there is no need for a cy-près scheme because no change in purposes is required. In *Oldham Borough Council v A-G*,[43] a council owned a piece of land 'upon trust to preserve and manage the same at all times hereafter as playing fields . . . for the benefit and enjoyment' of local inhabitants. The council wished to sell the land to developers and use the proceeds to purchase a different piece of land with better facilities. The Court of Appeal held that the planned sale and reinvestment for exactly the same purposes did not involve an alternation of the 'original purposes' of the charitable gift. The court could authorize the sale under its statutory or common law power relating to charities.

The same inherent powers were used in *Re JW Laing Trust*,[44] referred to earlier, where a stipulation that all the property of the trust be distributed within ten years of the settlor's death was removed. Similarly, in *Varsani v Jesani*,[45] the court held that, even if both groups remained true to the faith as prescribed in the original gift, the court had power under the inherent jurisdiction to authorize an administrative scheme 'for no alteration of the purpose of the Charity would arise'.

3 Subsequent failure of charitable gifts in wills

Where a testator leaves property to a charity in his will which fails after his death but before the administration of the estate is complete, it will be applied cy-près to other charitable purposes rather than resulting to the residuary legatees, even though it was never in fact received by the charity. This is because the property was fully dedicated to charity from the very moment that the testator died. There is no requirement of a general charitable intent because, unless the gift was restricted, it is presumed that there was an outright and perpetual dedication to charitable purposes.[46] A number of cases illustrate the operation of cy-près in the context of subsequent failure. In *Re Slevin*[47] a testator left a gift of £200 to St Dominic's Orphanage, Newcastle. The orphanage closed after his death but before the legacy had been paid over. The Court of Appeal held that

[39] *Technical Issues in Charity Law* (Law Com No 375, 2017), Ch 4.

[40] Charities Bill 2021–22, Clause 3(2), inserting section 280(A) into the Charities Act 2011.

[41] Charities Bill 2021–22, Clause 3(2), inserting subsection 280(A)(6) into the Charities Act 2011. If the charity has members, then only a majority of the trustees need vote in favour, but 75 per cent of the members must vote for the change (s 280A(5)).

[42] Charities Bill 2021–22, Clause 3(2), inserting subsection 280(A)(7) into the Charities Act 2011.

[43] [1993] 2 All ER 432.

[44] [1984] Ch 143.

[45] [1998] 3 All ER 273 at 285, per Morritt LJ.

[46] See *Re North Devon and West Somerset Relief Fund Trusts* [1953] 2 All ER 1032; *Re Cooper's Conveyance Trusts* [1956] 1 WLR 1096.

[47] [1891] 2 Ch 236.

the property should be applied cy-près, as it had become the property of the charity from the date of the testator's death. The same result was reached in *Phillips v The Royal Society for the Protection of Birds*,[48] where a bird sanctuary, established as a company, had ceased operations before the death of the testatrix, but was only dissolved a few days after her death.[49]

Property will also be applied cy-près without the need to show a general charitable intention if it was given to accomplish a charitable purpose but the purpose has been completed without the exhaustion of the property given. In *Re King*[50] property worth £1,500 was bequeathed to install a window in a church, the cost of which could not possibly exhaust that sum. Romer J held that the surplus should be applied cy-près.[51]

4 Initial failure of charitable gifts in wills

A charitable gift will fail initially if the charity has ceased to exist before it receives any interest in the property donated. In contemporary cases, the most common example of this is where a testator bequeaths property to a charity that ceases to exist before the date of his death. For example, in *Re Spence*,[52] a testatrix left part of her estate to 'The Old Folk's Home at Hillworth Lodge Keighley', in a will that was executed in 1968. She died in 1972, but the Old People's Home had closed down in 1971. In cases of initial failure the testator could have changed his will to take account of the failure of the charity but has not done so, perhaps because of his health, or through lack of knowledge that the charity has ceased to exist. The question arises whether the property should be applied cy-près to other charitable purposes or whether it should pass by resulting trust to his residuary legatees. Since the testator cannot be consulted, the law seeks to 'second-guess' what he would have wanted to happen to the property. If it can be shown that he had a 'general charitable intention' when he made the gift in his will, the property will be applied cy-près. Such an intention indicates that the testator would have preferred the property to be applied to another charity rather than result back under his will. If there is no general charitable intention, then it is presumed that the testator intended to benefit only the specific charity that has failed, and that in the event of the failure, he would have preferred his property to result back to the residuary legatees rather than pass to a replacement charity.

In *Kings v Bultitude*,[53] the testatrix made a gift to a schismatic independent catholic church group[54] of which she was such an important member that it ceased to meet following her death. Proudman J held that this was a case of initial failure because on an interpretation of the will it was only intended to take effect if the group continued in existence after the death of the testatrix. The gift was not saved by a paramount or general charitable intent.[55]

48 [2012] EWHC 618 (Ch).

49 See also *Re Wright* [1954] Ch 347; *Re Moon's Will Trust* [1948] 64 TLR 123; *Re Tacon* [1958] Ch 447.

50 [1923] 1 Ch 243.

51 See, however, *Re Stanford* [1924] 1 Ch 73, where Eve J held that a similar surplus should pass by way of a resulting trust to the residuary legatees.

52 [1979] Ch 483. 53 [2010] EWHC 1795 (Ch).

54 It was a church which refused to recognize the modernization of the Roman Catholic Church.

55 See Picton, '*Kings v Bultitude*—a gift lost to charity' [2011] Conv 69. It is worth noting that two bank accounts, held by the testatrix in the name of the Church and separate from her personal bank accounts, were validly applied to charity cy-près. There was nothing to rebut the presumption that the testatrix held the accounts for charitable purposes, not beneficially, and they were held unconditionally for the church at a time when it was still functioning.

(1) Has the charity actually failed?

In the testamentary context, application cy-près will normally only be necessary if the charity to which a gift was made has actually failed. Yet it is said the court leans in favour of charity, and so in some cases where it appears that a charity has failed, the court has found a way of saving the gift by holding that the charity has in some way continued. Instead of finding a failure of the testamentary gift, it is said that the gift is 'successful'. If this is the case there is no need to apply the property cy-près, and it will be applied to the charitable purposes in their continuing form. By treating the gift as successful rather than failed there is no possibility of lapse. The gift will be kept in charity.

(a) Amalgamation with other charities

A process to save gifts for charity has emerged where a bequest is left to an organization that has merged with another. On the face of things this might be thought to be a failure because the original nominated organization has ceased to exist as a result of the merger. However, in modern times, such gifts are likely to be saved. The Charities Act 2011, s 311, contains provision for gifts to charities which have merged to be treated as gifts to the new organization. This applies both to direct gifts and to gifts on trust.[56] Even before this provision, the courts took a similar view, on the basis that a merged charity has not ceased to exist, but continues in a different form. In *Re Faraker*[57] a testatrix left £200 to Hannah Bayly's Charity. Hannah Bayly's Charity had been founded in 1756 for the benefit of the poor widows of Rotherhithe, but had ceased to exist as a separate entity in 1905, when it was amalgamated with other charities for the benefit of the poor of Rotherhithe. The Court of Appeal held that there had been no failure because Hannah Bayly's Charity had not ceased to exist but continued in the form of the amalgamated charity, which encompassed its objects. The principle was applied in *Re Lucas*,[58] where a testatrix, who died in 1942, left £550 to 'the Crippled Children's Home, Lindley Moor, Huddersfield'. The 'Huddersfield Home for Crippled Children' had been founded in 1916, but was closed in 1941. However, its assets were applied to a new charity, 'The Huddersfield Charity for Crippled Children', under a scheme made by the Charity Commissioners. The Court of Appeal applied *Re Faraker*[59] and held that, rather than there being an initial failure, the legacy should pass to the new charity.[60] A more modern example might be the merger between the Imperial Cancer Research Fund and the Cancer Research Campaign to form Cancer Research UK.

The principle of *Re Faraker*[61] was not applied in *Re Roberts*.[62] Jane Roberts, who died in 1961, left a share of her residuary estate to the 'Sheffield Boys' Working Home'. The home had closed in 1945, at which point the trustees had transferred the majority of the assets to the 'Sheffield Town Trust', retaining only nominal funds themselves. Wilberforce J held that the property could not be applied to the Sheffield Town Trust on the basis of the principle of *Re Faraker*,[63] as the original charity was still in existence, although lacking the machinery to administer the legacy. It was, therefore, to be applied to the trustees of the home, and then applied cy-près.

Any funds received by the trustees of the amalgamated charity can be used for the general purposes of the charity. They are not limited to the specific purposes contemplated by

[56] *Berry v IBS-STL Ltd* [2012] EWHC 666 (Ch).

[57] [1912] 2 Ch 488. Expenditure is not confined to the purposes of the original charity.

[58] [1948] Ch 175; revsd [1948] Ch 24, CA. [59] [1912] 2 Ch 488.

[60] See also *Re Lucas* [1948] Ch 175; revsd [1948] Ch 242, CA; *Re Bagshaw* [1954] 1 All ER 227; *Re Slatter's Will Trusts* [1964] Ch 512; *Re Stemson's Will Trusts* [1970] Ch 16.

[61] [1912] 2 Ch 488. [62] [1963] 1 WLR 406. [63] [1912] 2 Ch 488.

the testator. It might therefore have surprised the testatrix in *Re Faraker* that not a penny of the funds she left need be spent on widows.

(b) Unincorporated charities

Saving gifts to merged organizations are not the only example of the courts leaning in favour of charity. Importantly, where a bequest is left to a unincorporated charity that ceased to exist before the death of the testator, the courts have held that the gift does not fail, because it should be construed as a gift to the continuing purposes of the charity and not to the specific unincorporated organization as an entity. A gift for purposes will likely be successful because even if an organization has shut its doors it can be said that the purposes that it used to serve can be carried on. The rationale for this principle was considered by Buckley J in *Re Vernon's Will Trusts*:

> Every gift to an unincorporated charity by name without more must take effect as a gift for a charitable purpose. No individual or aggregate of individuals could claim to take such a bequest beneficially.[64] If the gift is to take effect at all, it must be as a bequest for a purpose, viz, that charitable purpose which the named charity exists to serve. A bequest which is in terms made for a charitable purpose will not fail for lack of a trust purpose.[65]

This is a technical legal logic which cannot be thought to reflect anything that might be in the mind of the testamentary donor. It relies on the fact that an unincorporated charity has no independent legal personality, the gift can be construed as a gift to the purposes of the unincorporated charity, and those purposes continue even though the particular organization has ceased to exist.[66] Expressed differently, the idea is that because there is no 'person' to receive the gift, then the gift must be made for the purposes of the organization. The gift will only fail if the testator's intention to make the gift was dependent upon the character of the named organization to apply the gift.[67]

(c) Incorporated charities

The courts have been less generous to incorporated charities than unincorporated charities. Where a bequest is left to a charitable corporation, it will be construed as a gift to that particular body, which has legal personality, and if the corporation has ceased to exist the gift fails, and the property will only be applied cy-près if a general charitable intention can be shown.[68] These principles were applied in *Re Finger's Will Trusts*.[69] Georgia Finger left a share of her residuary estate to a number of charitable organizations, including the National Radium Commission (NRC), an unincorporated charity, and the National Council for Maternity and Child Welfare (NCMCW), a corporate body. Both had ceased to exist before the death of the testator. Goff J held that since the gift to the NRC was a gift to an unincorporated charity, the gift should be construed as a gift to the purposes of the Commission, which had not failed. The gift to the NCMCW had failed, but the property was applied cy-près because there was a general charitable intention.

It is noteworthy that Australian courts have rejected any difference of construction of gifts made to charitable corporate and unincorporated bodies, and have held that there

[64] Although the usual interpretation of gifts to unincorporated associations is that the members take beneficially (see Chapter 16), this interpretation is excluded in the case of charities, since it is inconsistent with charitable status for the members of the charity to take a beneficial interest.

[65] [1972] Ch 300. See also *Re Morrison* (1967) 111 Sol Jo 758.

[66] This construction was approved by the Court of Appeal in *Re Koeppler Will Trusts* [1986] Ch 423 at 434, per Slade LJ.

[67] E.g. *Re Spence* [1979] Ch 483.

[68] *Re Ovey* [1885] 29 Ch D 560; *Liverpool and District Hospital for Diseases of the Heart v A-G* [1981] Ch 193.

[69] [1972] Ch 286; (1972) 36 Conv 198 (Cotterell); (1974) 38 Conv 187 (Martin).

is a presumption that the gift is made for the purposes of the body in either case.[70] This removes the artificiality of the distinction.

(d) Charitable company becomes insolvent

There is no cause for an application cy-près where a testator leaves property to a charitable company that has become insolvent and entered into liquidation before the date of his death, provided that it has not been dissolved. In *Re ARMS (Multiple Sclerosis Research) Ltd*,[71] testators had left property to a charity that sought to promote research into a cure for multiple sclerosis, which had gone into liquidation before their deaths, with debts of just under £1.5 million. Neuberger J held that although the testators would not have wanted their gifts to take effect if they had known that the company was in liquidation at the date of their deaths, their gifts took effect because the company was still in existence, even if insolvent. Their bequests were, therefore, available to pay creditors, and were not able to be applied cy-près to other similar charitable purposes.

(2) Application cy-près where the charity has failed

It might be that none of the rules apply that would make it possible to save the gift for charity. The court might not be able to find that the gift is successful. This is most obviously true with gifts to incorporated charities where, as it has been seen, the rules point the decision-maker towards finding a failure. Yet even where an initial charitable bequest fails, it is possible that the testator's will provides for what is to happen, for instance, by a gift over to another charity.[72] Where even this does not assist, a gift which suffers initial failure will only be applied cy-près if it can be shown that the testator had a 'general charitable intention'. 'General charitable intention' has a technical meaning, which encapsulates the idea that the testator was not so committed to the particular charity nominated in his will that, in the event of its failure, he would have preferred his gift to result back to the residuary legatees under his will rather than to be applied to similar charitable purposes. The principle was outlined by Sir Robert Megarry V-C in *Re Spence*:

> the essence of the distinction is in the difference between particularity and generality. If a particular institution or purpose is specified, then it is that institution or purpose, and no other, that is to be the object of the benefaction. It is difficult to envisage a testator as being suffused with a general glow of broad charity when he is labouring, and labouring successfully, to identify some particular specified institution or purpose as the object of his bounty. The specific displaces the general. It is otherwise where the testator has been unable to specify any particular charitable institution or practicable purpose, and so, although his intention of charity can be seen, he has failed to provide any way of giving effect to it. There, the absence of the specific leaves the general undisturbed success.[73]

This makes clear that whether a gift is made with general charitable intention or not is a matter of degree, and there is no single factor which will determine whether a gift falls on the 'particular' or 'general' side of the line. This will be determined in the light of all the circumstances of the gift. In assessing whether a gift was made with 'general charitable intention' the courts have taken account of the following factors.

[70] *Sir Moses Montefiore Jewish Home v Howell & Co (No 7) Pty Ltd* [1984] 2 NSWLR 406.
[71] [1997] 1 WLR 877.
[72] As in *Games v Attorney-General* (2012) 14 ITELR 792 (Isle of Man).
[73] [1979] Ch 483 at 493.

(a) Gifts to specific institutions or bodies

Where a gift is made to a specific charitable institution or body, this is likely to indicate the absence of any general charitable intention. In *Re Rymer*[74] Horatio Rymer bequeathed a legacy of £5,000 to 'St Thomas' Seminary' in Westminster. The seminary had closed before his death, and the students had transferred to a seminary near Birmingham. The Court of Appeal held that there was no general charitable intention because the gift was a gift to a specific seminary.[75] In *Re Spence*[76] Beatrice Spence left half her residuary estate to the 'Old Folk's Home at Hillworth Lodge Keighley'. She died in 1972, and the home had closed in 1971. Megarry V-C held that this was a gift to a specific institution alone, and that there was no general charitable intention.

(b) Gifts with an underlying general charitable intention

Even when a gift is made to a specific institution, if the court can see a 'clear general intention underlying the particular mode' of carrying the charitable purpose out[77] they will find a general charitable intention and apply the property cy-près. Thus, in *Biscoe v Jackson*,[78] a gift was made by will for the establishment of a soup kitchen and cottage hospital in Shoreditch. This had become impossible, but Kay J held that the testator had a general charitable intention in that the underlying purpose of the gift was to benefit the poor of Shoreditch through the establishment of the soup kitchen and hospital. In *Re Woodhams (Decd)*,[79] the court held that a testator who had left money for the musical education of boys from specific children's homes was held to have a paramount intention to benefit musical education. It does not follow that because someone sponsors a charitable purpose, they have a charitable intent.[80] In *Re Spence*[81] Megarry V-C was unable to find an underlying general intention because the purpose was to benefit the specific patients of the specific home, and not the aged in general.

(c) 'Charity by association'

Even though a gift is made to a specific institution, the court may find a general charitable intention if the gift is one of a number of charitable bequests, and it is clear that the testator intended all of the property so bequeathed to go to 'charity'.[82] In *Re Knox*[83] Dorothy Knox left her residuary estate to three hospitals and to Dr Barnardo's Homes in equal shares. One hospital, the 'Newcastle-upon-Tyne Nursing Home', did not exist, and Luxmore J held that the quarter-share of the residuary estate should be applied cy-près. He found a general charitable intention in the context of the will, drawing from the fact that the residuary estate was divided among four beneficiaries, three of whom were undoubtedly charitable.[84] Similarly, in *Re Satterthwaite's Will Trusts*,[85] a testatrix who hated all human beings left her residuary estate to be divided among nine specifically named animal charities, including the 'Animal Welfare Service'. There was no such charity. Russell LJ held that a general charitable intention could be discerned from the

[74] [1895] 1 Ch 19. [75] See *Fisk v A-G* [1867] LR 4 Eq 521; *Clark v Taylor* [1853] 1 Drew 642.

[76] [1979] Ch 483. [77] *Re Spence* [1979] Ch 483 at 495, per Megarry V-C.

[78] [1887] 35 Ch D 460. See also *A-G v Boultbee* [1794] 2 Ves 380; *Cherry v Mott* [1836] 1 My & Cr 123.

[79] [1981] 1 All ER 202.

[80] See *Rehman v Ali* [2015] EWHC 4056 at 61 (privately owned mosque). [81] [1979] Ch 483.

[82] The categorization of these cases by Megarry V-C in *Re Spence* [1979] Ch 483 at 494.

[83] [1937] Ch 109.

[84] Although the case could equally be explained on the principle of *Re Harwood* [1936] Ch 285, it was not cited, and the judge reached his conclusion by looking to the other charitable gifts in the context of the will.

[85] [1966] 1 WLR 277.

fact that the other eight-ninths of her estate was left to animal charities.[86] The principle of charity by association only applies where a charitable gift fails for lack of certainty or non-existence and has no application where one gift among a number of charitable gifts fails because it is non-charitable.

(d) Specific charities that had never existed

It has been held that it is easier to find a general charitable intention where a gift is made to a specific charity that has never existed than to a charity that has ceased to exist.[87] In *Re Harwood*[88] a testatrix left bequests to a long list of charitable societies, including those devoted to peace. Among these were a gift to the 'Wisbech Peace Society', which had ceased to exist before the testator's death, and the 'Peace Society of Belfast', which the evidence suggested had never existed. Farwell J held that the gift to the Wisbech society failed, and that as it was a gift to a specific institution the testatrix had no general charitable intention. In contrast, he held that because the Belfast society had never existed, she had demonstrated a general charitable intention for the purposes of peace in Belfast, and the gift was applied cy-près. The rationale behind this analysis is probably that, as the testatrix did not check whether a particular charity existed, she must have assumed that it did, and that her intention was, therefore, to benefit the purposes that the invented name suggested were being pursued.[89]

A gift to an organization which never existed will likely still fail where the name of the organization suggests that it has a narrow and specific purpose.[90] By contrast, in *Knipe v British Racing Drivers' Motor Sport Charity*,[91] a gift was left to the 'Cancer Research Fund'. At the time of death no such organization existed. Despite the fact that the testamentary donor had used capital letters in her will, HHJ Paul Matthews took the view that the phrase referred to a general purpose. On this basis, it was possible to save the gift for charity.

(3) Criticism of the testamentary rules

When these testamentary rules, which determine whether or not a gift has failed, are presented in a neat, tabulated form it can give the impression that they are clear and coherent. Yet, the rules can be criticized for internal artificiality.

It is not clear what the reasoned basis for the rules might be at the level of judicial principle. It cannot be said that all the rules are attempting to carry out the wishes of the donor. Notably, the rule that a gift to a closed unincorporated charity will be treated as a

[86] However, as Megarry V-C noted in *Re Spence*, *Re Satterthwaite's Will Trusts* is not such strong authority as *Re Knox* because Harman LJ had 'the gravest doubts' whether there was general charitable intention, and Diplock LJ agreed with both other judgments.

[87] *Loscombe v Wintringham* [1850] 13 Beav 87; *Re Clergy Society* [1856] 2 K & J 615; *Re Maguire* [1870] LR 9 Eq 632; *Re Rymer* [1895] 1 Ch 19; *Re Davis* [1902] 1 Ch 876; *Re Harwood* [1936] Ch 285: This construction was rejected by the Court of Appeal of New South Wales in *A-G for New South Wales v Public Trustee* [1987] 8 NSWLR 550, where the court held that there is no rule or principle that it is more difficult to conclude that a testator had a general charitable intention where there is a gift to a named charity which existed at the date of the will but which has ceased to exist before death than in the case where the named charity never existed at all.

[88] [1936] Ch 285.

[89] Two difficulties arise with regard to the decision in *Re Harwood*. First, it was doubted in *Re Koeppler Will Trusts* [1984] 2 All ER 111 whether the purposes of a peace society are charitable because of their political nature. Second, in holding that there was no general charitable intention with regard to the gift to the Wisbech society, the judge did not consider whether in the context of the will, and the large number of charitable bequests, there was a general charitable intention through the principle of 'charity by association'.

[90] *Re Jordan* [2014] IEHC 678.

[91] *Knipe v British Racing Drivers' Motor Sport Charity* [2020] EWHC 3295.

successful gift for the purposes of that closed organization seems to have very little to do with intention.[92] Although it can be rebutted,[93] it is at heart a rule of construction flowing from the nature of the constitution of the closed charity, not the donor's real-world intention.

It is because the rules do not always reflect the intention of the donor that their impact can be arbitrary. While unincorporated charities are favoured by the precedents, gifts to incorporated charities are left without a special mechanism to save them.[94] In cases of gifts to closed incorporated charities, the judge will look for a general charitable intention and do nothing else, as in these circumstances, that is the only tool available in the judicial tool-box. The consequence is that gifts to incorporated charities are more likely to be lost to charity than gifts to unincorporated charities.

Yet no ordinary donor will understand these rules in advance. It is unlikely whether he will know whether or not his intended charity is incorporated or unincorporated. His intention is filtered through an artificial body of case law.

5 Cy-près schemes

After cy-près is successfully triggered, it becomes necessary to choose new purposes for the charity. This final stage in the process is called 'making a scheme'. As a practical matter, scheme-making is almost always undertaken by the Charity Commission rather than by judges. Where a trust in a will has failed, the Commission is very unlikely to make radical alterations out of respect for the wishes of the testamentary donor.[95] Yet the reasonably broad wording of the relevant legislation does allow far-reaching schemes in the context of established charities.

(1) Choosing the new purposes

The point at which new purposes are chosen by the Charity Commission marks the moment at which funds are effectively redistributed so that they can be lawfully devoted to fresh charitable objectives. Where charity assets are applicable cy-près, the Charity Commission (or much more rarely, the court) may make or approve a cy-près scheme (see Figure 22.1).

Under subsection 67(3) of the Charities Act 2011, there are key criteria to be followed in deciding how funds should be applied. In making a scheme, the court or the Charity Commission is required to have regard to:

(a) the spirit of the original gift,
(b) the desirability of securing that the property is applied for charitable purposes which are close to the original purposes, and
(c) the need for the relevant charity to have purposes which are suitable and effective in the light of current social and economic circumstances.

92 See Picton, 'Donor Intention and Dialectic Legal Policy Frames' in Harding (ed), *Research Handbook on Not-For-Profit Law* (Edgar Elgar 2018) 189, 201.

93 *Kings v Bultitude* [2010] EWHC 1795 (Ch), [45]. See Picton, '*Kings v. Bultitude* – A Gift Lost To Charity' (2011) 1 Conv 269–274.

94 *Re Finger's Will Trusts* [1972] Ch 286 (Ch).

95 Taxonomically, certain of the testamentary rules preventing failure (e.g .the rule that a gift to a closed unincorporated organisation presumptively will not lapse) are not 'cy-près', and so as a matter of logic, the cy-près legislation will not apply to them at all. This leaves judges and the Charity Commission operating outside of the statute.

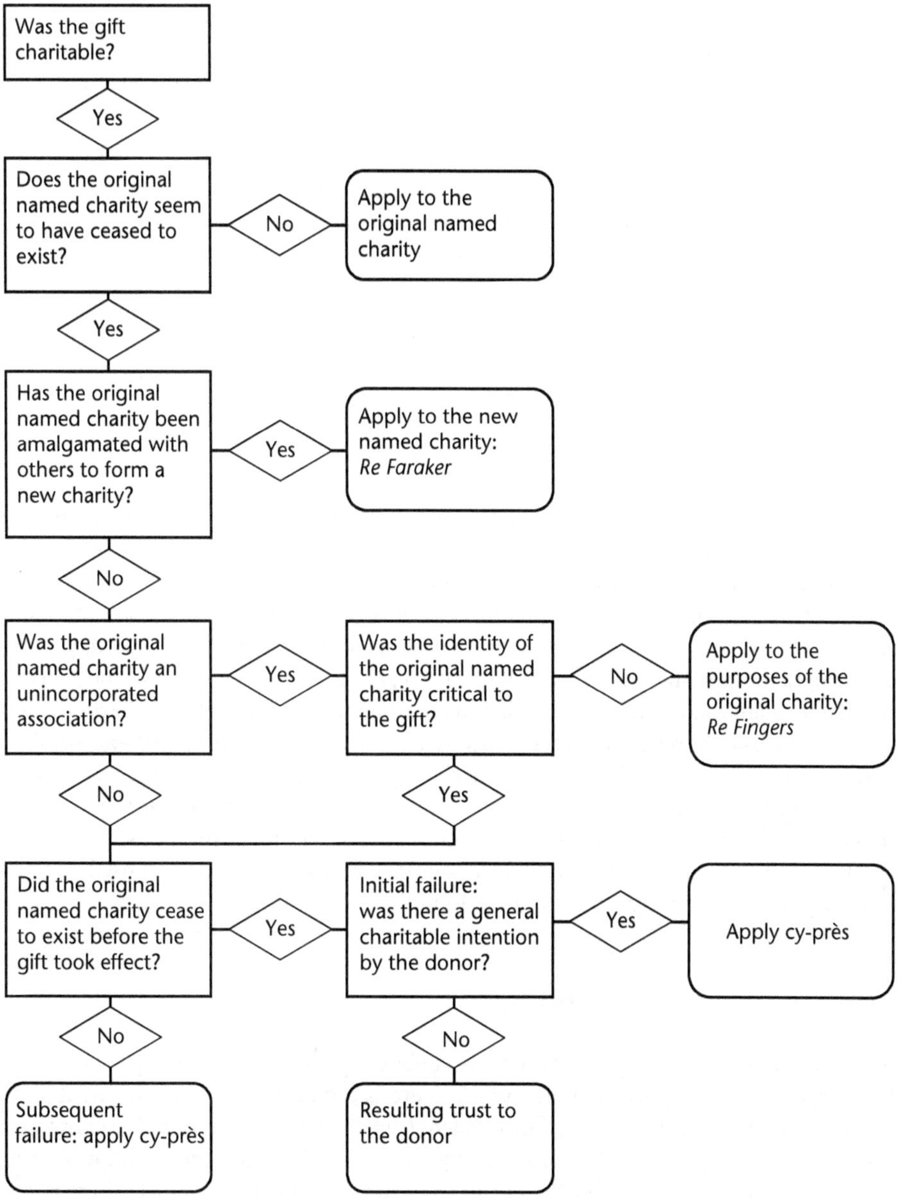

Figure 22.1 The operation of cy-près

Importantly, these statutory principles do not point towards choosing new purposes 'as near as possible' to the old ones. For this reason, calling the process 'cy-près' is somewhat old fashioned, as it refers to the case law standards before the passing of legislation.[96]

The modern criteria are also closely intertwined with the criteria for deciding whether a cy-près application is justified in the first place. In *White v William*,[97] the statutory provisions were used to make a scheme separating individual churches to enable them

[96] See, e.g., *Philpott v St George's Hospital* (1859) 27 Beav 107, 112; 54 ER 42; *Attorney General v The Governors of Sherborne Grammar School* (1854) 18 Beav 256; *Re Prison Charities* (1873) LR 16 Eq 129; *Re Avenon's Charity* [1913] 2 Ch 261 (Ch).

[97] [2010] EWHC 940 (Ch) at 20.

to be used by congregations which had split owing to a schism in their mother organization.[98] That was the only way of giving effect to the spirit in which the buildings had been acquired, namely, to provide facilities for worship available to the local congregations. The Charity Commission have made it clear that in guidance that:

> [The Commission] should be flexible and imaginative in applying the cy-près doctrine, balancing usefulness and practicality with respect for the existing purposes and beneficiaries. The purpose of making a cy-près scheme is to enable a charity to continue being effective, useful and relevant to its beneficiaries' needs in modern society, where without our intervention it would not be. We should, however, exercise caution where a proposed change might be a significant departure from the founder's intentions or might exclude existing beneficiaries (unless, for example, the problem is that the existing beneficial class has ceased to exist). We should always take account of the trustees' views when deciding how to amend a charity's objects.[99]

(2) **Ongoing reform**

It was seen earlier in this chapter,[100] that the Charities Bill 2021–22 will give trustees a power to change the charity purposes by a vote. In the light of Law Commission recommendations,[101] the Bill also proposes to alter the scheme-making stage.

The Charity Commission will continue to have a power to give or refuse consent to the scheme. The grounds for consent are not greatly changed from those already existing in the current legislation.[102] The Commission will have regard to: (a) the purposes of the charity when it was established, if and so far as they are reasonably ascertainable; (b) the desirability of securing that the purposes of the charity are, so far as reasonably practicable, similar to the purposes being altered; and (c) the need for the charity to have purposes which are suitable and effective in the light of current social and economic circumstances.[103]

Differences can be teased out in relation to the existing statutory provisions.[104] Notably the 'spirit of the original gift' terminology has been abandoned. Yet the proposed reform at this stage is plainly incremental rather than radical.

6 Failure of charitable appeals

Special statutory rules[105] apply where there is a public appeal for funds for a specific charitable purpose but that purpose fails. Again, there is a distinction between initial and subsequent failure here. In the latter, insufficient funds will have been raised to carry out the purposes of the appeal, whereas a subsequent failure describes the situation where there is a surplus remaining after the purposes of the appeal have been met. There is no need for special rules in relation to cases of surplus as there is no requirement for a general charitable intention in subsequent failure cases. It follows that the surplus of a charitable appeal could therefore be applied cy-près as with any other surplus fund.[106]

[98] The judge followed a similar course of action which had been taken in *Varsani v Jesani* [1999] Ch 219.

[99] Charity Commission, *OG2 Application of Property Cy-près* (March 2012), para 3.2.

[100] At 2(3).

[101] *Technical Issues in Charity Law* (Law Com No 375, 2017), para 4.139, Recommendation 4.

[102] Charities Act 2011, s 67(3), detailed in 5(1) of this chapter.

[103] Charities Bill 2021–22, Clause 3(2), inserting subsection 280A(10) in the Charities Act 2011.

[104] Charities Act 2011, s 67(3), detailed in 5(1) of this chapter.

[105] Charities Act 2011, ss 63–6 and Charities (Failed Appeals) Regulations 2008.

[106] This may not always be the case, as gifts might be conditional via donation—see Henderson and Fowles, *Tudor on Charities* (10th edn, Sweet & Maxwell 2015) paras 10-70–10-80.

In cases of initial failure, the default position is that donations must be returned to the identified donors, as the nature of donation means that it often impossible to find a 'general charitable intention' on which to apply the funds cy-près to a related charitable purpose. An appeal can contain an express statement that donations may be applied to alternative purposes in the event that the principal purposes cannot be achieved, in which case the fund can be applied to those stated purposes. Otherwise, funds may be applied cy-près only if one of five cases set out in what is now the Charities Act 2011 is identified. The first of these is where donors cannot be identified or found after advertisements and inquiries,[107] and the donor has not responded within a three-month period.[108] The second and third cases concern the donor disclaiming the right to have funds returned, either expressly[109] or under a statutory scheme which allows that a donor will be treated as disclaiming the gift unless a declaration is made to have it returned.[110] Donors via collecting boxes or similar fundraising methods are conclusively treated as unidentifiable without the need for advertisement.[111] Finally, it would be possible to apply funds cy-près where either the court or Charity Commission would consider the return of the donations to be unreasonable.[112] There are various statutory factors to be taken into account, but the Commission has stated in guidance that if the funds raised are less than £1,000, the trustees may make a scheme without court approval.[113] None of these principles apply where an appeal is for non-charitable purposes, as was the case in *Re Gillingham Bus Disaster Fund*.[114]

The Charities Bill 2021–22. will also bring about reform in this area, based on recommendations from the Law Commission recommending alterations to the principles applicable on the failure of charitable appeals,[115] on the basis that the use of cy-près in such situations is unnecessarily complex.[116] In summary, where there has been an initial failure of a charitable appeal, it is proposed that the trustees can be applied cy-près, provided the donations are small, meaning no more than £120 across a year.[117] In other cases, the requirements of advertising are to be simplified so that the trustees would agree a course of action to locate the donors with the Charity Commission.[118] Where proceeds from the fundraising are applicable cy-près, whether through initial or subsequent failure, it is proposed that a trustee resolution would be sufficient to direct the fund to new purposes.[119] There would be no need for Charity Commission oversight where the funds are small, which is proposed to be equal to or less than £1,000.[120] There is no doubt that these changes would simplify the treatment of appeals by charities, but it remains to be seen whether these recommendations, and the draft amending Bill that details them, will see legislative enactment.

[107] Charities Act 2011, s 63(1)(a); Charities (Failed Appeals) Regulations 2008, regs 3–5 and Schs 1 and 2 for requirements around advertisements.

[108] Charities Act 2011, s 63(2); Charities (Failed Appeals) Regulations 2008, reg 2.

[109] Charities Act 2011, s 63(1)(b); Charities (Failed Appeals) Regulations 2008, reg 8 and Sch 4 (form of disclaimer).

[110] Charities Act 2011, s 65. [111] Charities Act 2011, s 64(1). [112] Charities Act 2011, s 64(2).

[113] Charity Commission, *OG53 Charitable appeals: avoiding and dealing with failure* (November 2014). This also follows a recommendation of Lord Hodgson that failed appeal funds should go to charitable purposes, unless their return was expressly requested—see *Trusted and Independent: Giving Charity Back to Charities—Review of the Charities Act 2006* (July 2012), Appendix A, para 4. [114] [1958] Ch 300.

[115] *Technical Issues in Charity Law* (Law Com No 375, 2017), Ch 6. [116] Ibid, para 6.23.

[117] Ibid, para 6.46, Recommendation 11. This would insert s 63A(3) into the Charities Act 2011—Appendix 3: Draft Charities Bill, cl 6.

[118] Ibid, para 6.65, Recommendation 12. This would insert s 63A into the Charities Act 2011—Appendix 3: Draft Charities Bill, cl 6.

[119] Ibid, para 6.80, Recommendation 13. This would insert s 67A into the Charities Act 2011—Appendix 3: Draft Charities Bill, cl 7.

[120] This is in line with the existing guidance of the Charity Commission, and would simply put the current practice into law.

23

Regulation and control of charitable trusts

1 Introduction

Just as the trustees of a private trust have the potential to breach their duty and act in their own interests rather than in the interests of their beneficiaries, the trustees of charitable trusts have the opportunity to defraud both the charity for which they act as trustee and the public at large who make donations. It is essential to protect against spurious charities and to ensure that the funds of genuine charities are properly applied. Charities also trade on public trust and confidence, which in turn fuels donations to charities and motivates people to give of their time in volunteering activities. It is important that this public trust and confidence is maintained, and it is for this reason, alongside ensuring that public monies are properly spent through the tax reliefs afforded to charities, that the sector requires independent regulation. In the last few years, high-profile scandals in the media have done considerable damage to the reputation of charities, leaving the charity brand tarnished. Examples include the excessive targeting of older donors by charity fundraisers, such as the poppy-seller, Olive Cooke, who committed suicide because of the pressure.[1] In early 2018, reports emerged concerning one of the oldest and most trusted aid charities, Oxfam, suggesting that the charity had supressed details of the use of prostitutes by senior staff during the relief effort that followed the 2010 Haiti earthquake. In consequence the Charity Commission instituted a formal inquiry into the organization.[2] Few people will not have heard of the high profile collapse of Kids Company, which went into insolvent liquidation in 2015 following much media attention surrounding the trustee board, and the former CEO, Ms Batmanghelidjh and her alleged failures of governance within the organization.[3] The impact of these and other scandals on the reputation of the sector as a whole, and the consequential changes in regulation policy and practice, will be discussed later in this chapter.

In the case of private trusts the primary task of supervising the trustees and ensuring that they do not abuse their position falls to the beneficiaries. Charitable trusts do not have beneficiaries as such since, by their very nature, they are purpose trusts[4] and an exception to the beneficiary principle, although there may obviously be persons who are interested in seeing that assets held on trust for charity are properly applied, for example,

[1] See Fundraising Standards Board, FRSB Investigation into Charity Fundraising Practices Instigated by Mrs Olive Cooke's Case (20 January 2016).

[2] See Charity Commission, Press Release 'Charity Commission opens statutory inquiry into Oxfam and sets out steps to improve safeguarding in the charity sector' (12 February 2018).

[3] This led to costly litigation (estimated at some £8 m) as to whether Ms Batmanghelidjh, and the board of trustees who supervised her actions as CEO, could be the subject of a disqualifaction order—*Re Keeping Kids Company* [2021] EWHC 175 (Ch). No disqualification order was warranted on the facts. See Tribe, 'Charities and Directors' Disqualification' [2021] 137 LQR 542.

[4] See Chapter 20.

donors. Historically, charities were supervised and controlled by the Attorney-General acting on behalf of the Crown. However, his function has largely been replaced by a regulatory system with a statutory footing. The law was revised by the Charities Acts 1993 and 2006, and is further revised by the consolidating Charities Act 2011.

2 Features of the regulatory system

(1) The Charity Commission

The main feature of the regulatory mechanism for charities is the role of the Charity Commission, which is now a body corporate.[5] The Charity Commission has the task of overseeing charities in general and investigating abuses. It is obliged to maintain a register of charities. The legislation provides that some persons (for instance, undischarged bankrupts) are disqualified from holding office as trustees and requires charity trustees to maintain accounts and to submit an annual report of the charity's activities and an annual statement of accounts to the Commission. The report and accounting requirements enable the Commission to supervise the conduct of charities, and they are also open to public inspection. Some charities which used to be exempt charities,[6] are now regulated by another principal regulator; in the case of universities, the Higher Education Funding Council for England.[7]

The Charities Act 2011, incorporating changes made by the Charities Act 2006, extended the role of the Charity Commission in the regulation of charities, conferring on it extended powers to suspend or remove trustees,[8] to give specific directions for the protection of charity,[9] and to direct the application of charity property.[10] These powers have been bolstered by a raft of additional powers granted by the Charities (Protection and Social Investment) Act 2016, including a power to issue official warnings to charities. There is, however, an obligation on the Charity Commission to have regard to the principles of best regulatory practice, 'including the principles under which regulatory activities should be proportionate, accountable, consistent, transparent and targeted only at cases in which action is needed'.[11] The role of the Charity Commission is considered in detail later.

(2) The Crown

The Crown is parens patriae of charity[12] and, therefore, protector of charity in general.[13] However, this function is exercised on behalf of the Crown by the Attorney-General.

(3) The Attorney-General

Historically, the main mechanism for the supervision and control of charitable trusts was the Attorney-General, acting on behalf of the Crown. As Hoffmann J stated in *Bradshaw*

[5] Charities Act 2011, Pt 2, s 13. While the functions of the Commission are to be exercised on behalf of the Crown, s 13(4) makes clear that it shall not be subject to control by a government department or any Minister of the Crown.

[6] Charities Act 2011, s 22 and Sch 3.

[7] Charities Act 2011, Pt 3, ss 25–8, describe the duties and powers of the principal regulator. Universities in Wales are no longer exempt.

[8] Charities Act 2011, s 83.

[9] Charities Act 2011, s 84.

[10] Charities Act 2011, s 85.

[11] Charities Act 2011, s 16(4).

[12] *Wallis v Solicitor-General for New Zealand* [1903] AC 173 at 181–2.

[13] *Moggridge v Thackwell* [1803] 7 Ves 36; *National Anti-Vivisection Society v IRC* [1948] AC 31, HL; *Hauxwell v Barton-upon-Humber UDC* [1974] Ch 432.

v University College of Wales, Aberystwyth: 'So far as the enforcement of the trust is a matter of public interest, the guardian of that interest is the Attorney-General.'[14]

Prior to the Charities Act 1993, the Attorney-General was generally a necessary party to charity proceedings[15] because he represented the beneficial interest,[16] in other words, the charitable purposes of the trust. As Lord Simmonds observed in *National Anti-Vivisection Society v IRC*,[17] it is the right and duty of the Attorney-General to inform the courts if the trustees of a charity fall short of their duty,[18] and to help the court formulate schemes for the execution of charitable trusts.[19]

Hence, only the Attorney-General was entitled to bring an action to determine whether a trust was charitable. However, what is now s 144 of the Charities Act 2011[20] grants the Charity Commission the same powers as the Attorney-General to take legal proceedings with reference to charities, or the property affairs of charities, and to compromise claims to avoid or end proceedings. This emphasizes that the primary responsibility for controlling and enforcing charitable trusts falls today to the Commission.

(4) The court

(a) The jurisdiction of the court

The court possesses a general inherent jurisdiction[21] over charitable trusts. It has the power to draw up schemes for the administration of a charity,[22] particularly where there is a need to administer a fund cy-près,[23] and it remedies breaches of trust by charity trustees. This jurisdiction derives from the court's general jurisdiction over trusts. If a gift has been made to charity in general, or simply to one of the heads of charity, for example, 'the poor', the court has the jurisdiction to draw up a scheme for the application of the property if a trust was intended, but if no trust was intended the Crown applies the property under the sign manual.[24] The court has no jurisdiction in the case of a charity founded by Royal Charter[25] or over a charity completely regulated by statute.[26] However, the court does have jurisdiction to ensure that the terms of the charter or statute are properly kept. The court retains an inherent jurisdiction over corporate charities, even though, in the strict sense, a company required to apply its assets for charitable purposes does not hold those assets on trust.[27]

An example of the exercise of the court's supervisory jurisdiction over charitable trusts is provided by *Royal Society for the Prevention of Cruelty to Animals v A-G*.[28] The Society sought to exclude members and applicants for membership who had joined for

14 [1987] 3 All ER 200 at 203.

15 See *Wellbeloved v Jones* [1822] 1 Sim & St 40; *National Anti-Vivisection Society v IRC* [1948] AC 31, HL; *Hauxwell v Barton-upon-Humber UDC* [1974] Ch 432.

16 *Ware v Cumberlege* [1855] 20 Beav 503; *Re King* [1917] 2 Ch 420.

17 [1948] AC 31 at 62.

18 *A-G v Brown* [1818] 1 Swan 265; *National Anti-Vivisection Society v IRC* [1948] AC 31.

19 *National Anti-Vivisection Society v IRC* [1948] AC 31; *Re Harpur's Will Trusts* [1962] Ch 78, CA.

20 Originally Charities Act 1993, s 32.

21 *Mills v Farmer* [1815] 1 Mer 55; *A-G v Sherborne Grammar Schools Governors* [1854] 18 Beav 256.

22 See *A-G v Coopers' Co* [1812] 19 Ves 187; *A-G v St Olave's Grammar School* [1837] Coop Pr Cas 267; *A-G v Dedham School* [1857] 23 Beav 350.

23 See Chapter 22.

24 *Moggridge v Thackwell* [1803] 7 Ves 36; *Re White* [1893] 2 Ch 41, CA; *Re Bennett* [1960] Ch 18.

25 *A-G v Smart* [1748] 1 Ves Sen 72; *A-G v Middleton* [1751] 2 Ves Sen 327; *A-G v Governors of the Foundling Hospital* [1793] 2 Ves 42. If the charity was granted a Royal Charter subsequent to its foundation to provide an incorporated trustee, the court retains its inherent jurisdiction: *A-G v Dedham School* [1857] 23 Beav 350.

26 *Re Shrewsbury Grammar School* [1849] 1 Mac & G 324.

27 *Liverpool and District Hospital for Diseases of the Heart v A-G* [1981] 1 All ER 994.

28 [2001] 3 All ER 530.

the ulterior purpose of changing its anti-hunting policy. Members and applicants who fell within defined categories would be treated as conclusively proved deserving of exclusion, without the need to consider the merits of their individual cases. Lightman J held that whilst the policy of exclusion did not contravene the Human Rights Act, the Society should not operate its chosen method of implementing its membership policy. He considered that it was 'arbitrary and unattractive' and that it was not necessary to exclude from membership persons to whom no conceivable objection could be taken if the full facts were allowed to be taken into account. Given that emergency action was not required, the 'plight of the innocent' needed to be given greater weight. He also considered that the 'public image and reputation' of the Society had not been sufficiently taken into account in adopting such a draconian policy.

(b) Concurrent jurisdiction of the Charity Commission

The primacy of the role of the Charity Commission in the supervision and control of charitable trusts is also evident, in that the Commission enjoys concurrent jurisdiction alongside that of the court. It is thus able to exercise many of the functions formerly the exclusive preserve of the court. By s 69(1) and (2) of the Charities Act 2011, the Charity Commission enjoys the same jurisdiction and powers that are exercisable by the High Court in charity proceedings for the purposes of:

(a) establishing a scheme for the administration of a charity;
(b) appointing, discharging, or removing a charity trustee or trustee for a charity, or removing an officer or employee;
(c) vesting or transferring property, or requiring or entitling any person to call for or make any transfer of property or any payment.

(c) Charity proceedings

The effectiveness of the supervision of charitable trusts by the court depends on those who might have some interest being able to start an action. Other than the Attorney-General and the Charity Commission, s 115(1) of the Charities Act 2011 provides that:

> Charity proceedings may be taken with reference to a charity either by—
>
> (a) the charity,
> (b) any of the charity trustees,
> (c) any person interested in the charity, or
> (d) if it is a local charity, any two more inhabitants of the area of the charity,
>
> but not by any other person.

They do not include proceedings by or against a charity for debt, contractual disputes, negligence or property issues. Hence, in *Watts v Stewart*,[29] a case which concerned the legal status and protection of residents in a charitable almshouse under land law, the Court of Appeal held that possession proceedings to evict residents were not 'charity proceedings' and were not to do with the 'internal administration' of the charity.

(i) Any person interested in the charity

The definition of this phrase has been considered in a number of cases. *Re Hampton Fuel Allotment Charity*[30] concerned a charity relieving hardship and distress amongst residents of Hampton. The charity sought to sell land that it owned to a supermarket for £8 million. A minority of the trustees felt that the sale was at a gross undervalue, and that

[29] [2016] EWCA Civ 1247. [30] [1989] Ch 484.

the real value was some £14 million. They started an action seeking orders concerning the administration of the charity along with Richmond Council, which had the power to appoint three of the trustees and in whose borough the charity operated. At first instance the council was struck out as not being a person 'interested in the charity'. However, the Court of Appeal held that it did enjoy sufficient interest to maintain an action. It was unwilling to attempt a comprehensive definition of 'any person interested in the charity' but stated that:

> If a person has an interest in securing the due administration of a trust materially greater than, or different from, that possessed by ordinary members of the public . . . that interest may, depending on the circumstances, qualify him as a 'person interested' . . .[31]

The council had an interest greater than that of the ordinary public because it had a functional role with regard to the charity, in that it appointed three of the eleven trustees, and it was the local authority of the area benefited by the carrying out of the purposes. The Court of Appeal referred to *Haslemere Estates Ltd v Baker*,[32] where Megarry V-C had held that enjoyment of an adverse interest against a charity did not necessarily equate with having a good reason for seeking to enforce the trust. Thus, he suggested that not even tenants of charity land, or those with easements, profits, mortgages, or restrictive covenants, or those who had contracted to repair or decorate charity houses or had agreed to buy or sell goods to the charity, would have sufficient interest. It seems that a donor to a charity may have sufficient interest,[33] but not the executors of a donor.[34]

Haslemere Estates Ltd v Baker, which concerned a claim by a property developer against the trustees of Dulwich College, was distinguished by Robert Walker J in *Scott v National Trust*[35] on the grounds that it concerned a wholly commercial dispute which had no real connection with the internal or functional administration of charitable trusts.[36] In contrast, he held that the hunts and tenant farmers affected by a decision of the National Trust not to allow the hunting of deer with hounds on its land in Devon and Somerset were sufficiently interested in the charity to bring proceedings. He pointed out that they had been hunting there since long before the land had belonged to the Trust, and that they had been partners with the National Trust in the management of its land.[37]

The ambit of s 115(1) was considered in *Royal Society for the Prevention of Cruelty to Animals v A-G*.[38] The RSPCA sought to change its membership rules so as to exclude members who had been campaigning to persuade the Society to change its anti-hunting stance and prevent applicants becoming members who shared this objective. Lightman J held that an existing member of the Society did have sufficient interest in the charity to commence charity proceedings challenging the propriety of the Society's actions, but that a mere applicant for membership did not:

> But I do not think that a disappointed applicant for membership has any such sufficient interest. Any member of the public is free to apply for membership; the exercise of that liberty cannot elevate the status of a non-member into that of a person interested. To extend the right of suit to any such applicant would be to cast the net too wide.[39]

In *Rosenzweig v NMC Recordings Ltd*,[40] Norris J held that a British composer who had applied to have his work recorded by a charity and had been rejected was a 'person interested in' charity proceedings. The objects of the charity included the promotion of British

[31] [1989] Ch 484 at 494. [32] [1982] 1 WLR 1109. [33] *Brooks v Richardson* [1986] 1 WLR 385.
[34] *Bradshaw v University College of Wales, Aberystwyth* [1988] 1 WLR 190.
[35] [1998] 2 All ER 705. Note, the section was then the Charities Act 1993, s 33(1).
[36] [1998] 2 All ER 705 at 715. [37] [1998] 2 All ER 705. [38] [2001] 3 All ER 530.
[39] [2001] 3 All ER 530 at 21. [40] [2013] EWHC 3792 (Ch).

composers, but that was not enough to make Mr Rosenzweig a person interested under s 115(1), as that would describe too large a section of the public. Instead, he had standing because of the threefold facts that he had applied to the charity for inclusion of his works in musical CDs they produced; that he had some benchmark achievements suggesting he was a composer of note, and that the charity had recognized him by including him in a publication of a 'Musical Map' of twentieth century composers.[41]

(ii) Consent of the Charity Commission

Section 115(2) provides that no proceedings shall be taken in any court without the authorization of the Charity Commission. The Commission is not to authorize proceedings if the case could be dealt with under their own powers.[42] The reason for these limitations is to prevent pointless actions which would simply waste the charity's money. It is now clear from *Park v Cho and others*[43] that 'taking of proceedings' relates not only to commencing proceedings but also to the taking of steps within existing proceedings. It also meant that the Charity Commission could, in certain circumstances, give retrospective authorization to proceedings which had not been properly commenced.

(iii) Court's jurisdiction

The court has the discretion to authorize (and to disallow) proceedings, even where the Charity Commission has not done so. Hence, in *Rosenzweig v NMC Recordings Ltd*,[44] Norris J, citing *Haslemere Estates Ltd v Baker*, that it was important to 'avoid charities being vexed with frivolous and ill founded claims',[45] refused Mr Rosenzweig permission to commence proceedings on the basis that their purpose was not for any public benefit, but for his personal benefit only.

In *Singh v Charity Commission and others*,[46] the charity proceedings arose from a dispute over the validity of a contested election of members of the charity management committee. The Charity Commission had ruled the election invalid, but proceedings had been commenced by members of the committee, without the Commission's consent, to overturn that decision. Before the proceedings were heard, it became clear that the claimants were operating a separate bank account, which had been kept secret from the trustees and the Commission. The claimants sought to discontinue the proceedings. The High Court refused permission to discontinue the proceedings on the basis of concerns over the administration of the charity, and the abuse of process in having a secret bank account.

(5) **Other regulators**

In addition to regulation as described above, certain charities may be subject to additional regulation. Hence, charities that are set up as charitable companies are subject to regulation under the companies legislation, including registering with Companies House and filing an annual report on finance and activities.[47] Similarly, charities that provide housing as charitable providers of social houses, are also regulated by the Regulator of Social Housing,[48] a statutory committee of Homes England.[49] They are required to register as a provider of social housing.

[41] Norris J was less impressed by a claim of benchmarks of the standard and influence of his work, though it did play a part in the decision.

[42] s 115(3). [43] [2014] EWHC 55 (Ch).

[44] [2013] EWHC 3792 (Ch). [45] [1982] 1 WLR 1109 at 494A. [46] [2016] EWHC B33.

[47] Companies Act 2006, s 193; Charities Act 2011, s 351(3). In relation to accounting requirements, see Companies Act 2006, Pt 15.

[48] See Housing and Regeneration Act 2008.

[49] This body replaced the Homes and Communities Agency in January 2018.

The increased demands of serving more than one regulator is an important factor that could influence organizations seeking to register as charities, in terms of either the structure they adopt or, indeed, whether they wish to seek charitable status at all.[50] It also remains a common complaint, especially for smaller charities, that the increased bureaucracy of dealing with at least two separate regulators can be time-consuming and expensive.

3 The Charity Commission

(1) Structure

The Charity Commissioners were first appointed under the Charitable Trusts Act 1853. Their position was modernized by the Charities Act 1960, which implemented the recommendations of the Nathan Committee Report.[51] It was enshrined in the Charities Act 1993, which followed the Woodfield Report,[52] was further amended by the Charities Act 2006, and is now consolidated in the Charities Act 2011.[53] The Charity Commission is a body corporate with a membership and structure specified in Sch 1 to the Charities Act 2011, and with specified objectives:[54]

(1) The public confidence objective is to increase public trust and confidence in charities.

(2) The public benefit objective is to promote awareness and understanding of the operation of the public benefit requirement.

(3) The compliance objective is to promote compliance by charity trustees with their legal obligations in exercising control and management of the administration of their charities.

(4) The charitable resources objective is to promote the effective use of charitable resources.

(5) The accountability objective is to enhance the accountability of charities to donors, beneficiaries, and the general public.

The functions of the Charity Commission underline the importance of the Charity Commission in applying charity law, regulating charities, disseminating information, and providing information and advice.

(2) Challenges in regulation

The Charity Commission has undertaken several reviews of its activities and is still under considerable pressure. This is due to a twofold issue of the approach of the Commission as regulator, shaped to a large extent by scandals that have challenged public trust and confidence in the sector and the threat of charities being used as vehicles for criminal activity (e.g. terrorist funding), and a loss in real terms of funding for the Commission's activities.

[50] Guidance on the advantages and disadvantages of different structures for charities can be found in Charity Commission CC22a (30 May 2014).

[51] The Committee on the Law and Practice relating to Charitable Trusts, Cmnd 8710 of 1952.

[52] *Efficiency Scrutiny of the Supervision of Charities*, 1987; National Audit Office Report, House of Commons Paper 380, 1986–87; Annual Report 1987.

[53] This consolidating Act came into force on 14 March 2012, and replaces the Charities Act 1992, 1993, 2006 and the Recreational Charities Act 1958.

[54] Charities Act 2011, s 14.

(a) The Commission and charity scandals

The trustworthiness of charities and their independence from external influences have been questioned by numerous high-profile scandals. These include the 'Cup Trust' saga, in which a charity was used as an elaborate tax avoidance scheme worth some £46 million in fraudulent Gift Aid claims,[55] the high media profile collapse of the children's charity, Kids Company, through extremely poor governance,[56] and the Olive Cooke case, in which, as noted above, charities were accused by the media of driving an elderly supporter to suicide through excessive fundraising requests.[57] Major shockwaves were caused by Oxfam's apparent complicity in covering up a sexual scandal involving aid workers in Haiti in 2010.[58] There have been others,[59] but the Cup Trust saga provides an effective example of the damage that can be done both to the sector and to the Charity Commission as an effective regulator. It is also a scandal which has helped shape the approach of the Charity Commission as regulator, and the actions taken to redress the Oxfam situation demonstrate this new approach.

The 'Cup Trust' was established on 10 March 2009, and registered by the Commission as a charity on 7 April 2009. The trust was run by a sole corporate trustee, Mountstar (PTC) Limited, which was registered in the British Virgin Islands. The trust was established as a general grant-making charity with the intention of giving grants to small or start-up charities that aim to improve the lives of children and young adults. This purpose was, however, a cover for an elaborate tax avoidance scheme,[60] and the Cup Trust submitted claims for £46 million Gift Aid on more than £176 million in private donations, but gave just £152,292 to charitable causes over two years. HMRC did not pay the Gift Aid claims. The Commission eventually opened an inquiry in April 2013, acting on evidence from HMRC and its own concerns about the charity. In June 2013, the House of Commons Public Accounts Committee published a critical report on the Charity Commission's handling of the Cup Trust.[61] In its report, the Public Accounts Committee concluded that the Cup Trust was set up as a tax avoidance scheme, and expressed dismay at the Commission's handling of the whole affair.[62] The Committee asked the National Audit Office to review the Commission's effectiveness as a regulator, which it did,[63] and

[55] House of Commons Committee of Public Accounts. Charity Commission: The Cup Trust and Tax Avoidance (Seventh Report of Session 2013–14, HC 138, 4 June 2013).

[56] House of Commons Public Administration and Constitutional Affairs Committee, The Collapse of Kids Company: Lessons for Charity Trustees, Professional Firms, the Charity Commission, and Whitehall (Fourth Report of Session 2015–16, HC 433, 1 February 2016).

[57] House of Commons Public Administration and Constitutional Affairs Committee, The 2015 Charity Fundraising Controversy: Lessons for Trustees, the Charity Commission, and Regulators (Third Report of Session 2015–16, HC 431, 25 January 2016). The impact of this scandal led to the establishment of a new fundraising regulator for charities, discussed at the end of this chapter.

[58] This led to affirmative action by the Charity Commission, first a statutory inquiry in February 2018, followed by an inequiry report which introduced statutory supervision measures which were lifted in February 2021—see Charity Commission, *Charity inquiry follow-up: Oxfam GB progress on safeguarding* (25 February 2021).

[59] See, for example, the commercial arrangements of Age UK, which was accused of recommending expensive E.ON energy tariffs as part of a commercial deal with the energy company to aged (and often vulnerable) people, from which it netted £6m in profit—Charity Commission, Age UK: Charity Commission Case Report (19 April 2016).

[60] For details of the operation of the scheme, see HC 814 National Audit Office, 'Charity Commission: The Cup Trust' (4 December 2013), paras 1.5–1.7.

[61] HC 138, 'Charity Commission: the Cup Trust and Tax Avoidance' (4 June 2013) p 3.

[62] It is worth noting that the Charity Commission was required to register the charity, on the basis that it met the tests for recognition as a charity in English law. The criticism was that it did not act sooner in investigating whether the Cup Trust was actually carrying out those purposes.

[63] HC 814 National Audit Office, 'Charity Commission: The Cup Trust' (4 December 2013), paras 1.5–1.7.

concluded that the Commission had 'not regulated charities effectively'.[64] This led to a hearing and further highly critical report from the Public Accounts Committee,[65] who felt that the Charity Commission was not using its resources well to deal with potentially serious abuse of charitable status:

> In the last 3 years, the Commission has not removed any trustees, it has only suspended a trustee twice and it has only restricted charities from entering into specific transactions 17 times when it is responsible for overseeing 165,000 charities . . . and, when faced with clear cases of abuse, it has failed to act promptly and robustly, or use the full range of powers to intervene that it has available.[66]

It was clear that the approach of the Commission had to change, and the Commission has requested, and been granted, new powers to help it carry out its regulatory functions more effectively.[67] The damage that this single scandal did to the sector was well expressed by Sir Stuart Etherington, chief executive of the National Council for Voluntary Organisations, who said that the Commission's handling of the affair 'has brought damage and disrepute to the sector as a whole, putting [it] at serious risk of losing the trust and confidence of the public'.[68] The end of this particular saga only came in late 2017, with the removal in May 2017 of the Cup Trust from the register of charities and, on 14 June, the disqualification of Mountstar from being a charity trustee for a period of fifteen years.[69]

Following initial criticism of the Commission's approach to dealing with the Oxfam scandal, a full Charity Commission inquiry into safeguarding practices was launched,[70] which found that the charity's governance and culture with regard to safeguarding had repeatedly fallen below expected standards, and that the charity had tolerated poor behaviour.[71] The Charity Commission issued Oxfam (GB) with both an official warning[72] and a legal direction (under Charities Act 2011, s 84) to implement actions and recommendations to improve internal governance and the approach to safeguarding, as set out in an independent review commissioned by the charity. This contained some 100 actions, and these Commission has since been monitoring their implementation, including overseeing an independent assessment of progress. In February 2021, the Commission concluded that this period of statutory supervision should be brought to an end and the charity reverted the Commission's standard, regulatory oversight provisions.[73]

(b) The threat from terrorist financing and money laundering

Another challenge the Commission continues to face is the threat of misuse of the charity sector for terrorist financing.[74] The simple fact that charities have been highly valued

[64] Ibid, para 24.

[65] HC 792, 'The Charity Commission: Forty-Second Report of Session 2013–14' (29 January 2014).

[66] HC 792, 'The Charity Commission: Forty-Second Report of Session 2013–2014' (29 January 2014), p 5.

[67] Charities (Protection and Social Investment) Act 2016.

[68] See www.thirdsector.co.uk/charity-commission-brought-sector-disrepute-says-ncvo-chief/governance/article/1181487.

[69] See Charity Commission, Press Release: 'Update on Cup Trust Inquiry' (14 June 2017). This was one of the first uses of a new disqualification power, granted under the Charities (Protection and Social Investment) Act 2016. This power is discussed below.

[70] See Charity Commission, Press Release 'Charity Commission opens statutory inquiry into Oxfam and sets out steps to improve safeguarding in the charity sector' (12 February 2018).

[71] Charity Commission, *Oxfam GB: Statement of the results of an Inquiry*, 11 June 2019.

[72] This was another of the powers conferred by the Charities Act (Protection and Social Investment) Act 2016.

[73] Charity Commission, *Charity inquiry follow-up: Oxfam GB progress on safeguarding*, 25 February 2021.

[74] See, generally, Barr, 'Shell Charities and Terrorist Financing: A Sledgehammer to Crack a Shell?' [2018] TLI 202.

in society can make them attractive targets for criminal abuse and the financing of acts of terrorism. Charities often work in conflict zones, where terrorists are operating, and they may provide an attractive and efficient way to raise and/or channel funds.[75] Terrorist financing is the raising, moving, storing, and using of financial resources for the purposes of terrorism. There is a marked overlap between money laundering[76] and terrorist financing.[77] Criminals and terrorists both use similar methods to store and move funds, but the motives for generating and moving funds differ. Money laundering is about hiding illicit profits, and terrorist financing is ultimately used to plan and carry out terrorist attacks.

This potential threat has not gone unnoticed, either nationally or internationally. Starting with the international perspective, the Financial Action Task Force (FATF) is an inter-governmental body[78] that, through a set of forty Recommendations, provides a set of global anti-money laundering and counter-terrorist financing standards that members should strive to achieve. They are non-binding (soft law) tools, and the principles that they promote are open to interpretation by nation states as to how best to implement them into their national law. The Recommendation which involves charities in particular is Recommendation 8, which relates to non-profit organizations.[79] Both the UK and the EU are members of FATF, and charities in England and Wales are now under new obligations to maintain and provide information about their beneficiaries under the Money Laundering, Terrorist Financing and Transfer of Funds (Information on the Payer) Regulations 2017,[80] which is in response to FATF recommendations.

Domestically, the Charity Commission has tried to maintain the difficult balance between effective regulation and over-regulation. While the Commission acknowledges that charities are vulnerable to terrorist or other criminal abuse, it is clear that 'proven instances of terrorist involvement in the charitable sector are rare in comparison to the size of the sector'.[81] It makes clear that any such activity is 'completely unacceptable'.[82] It has published a whole suite of guidance.[83] Nonetheless, increasing terrorist activity has meant that this aspect of regulatory practice has been under intense scrutiny. Following the killing (and near beheading) of the soldier Lee Rigby, the Prime Minister's extremism taskforce noted that some extremist groups target charities.[84] The Home Affairs Committee on Counter Terrorism also noted the threat in 2014, and suggested that the Charity Commission be given extra resources and new legal powers to deal with potential abuse of charities by terrorists.[85] As we shall see, they got the latter, not the former.

[75] Ibid.

[76] Money laundering is the process of turning the proceeds of crime into property or money that can be accessed legitimately without arousing suspicion. The term 'laundering' is used because criminals turn 'dirty' money into 'clean' funds which can then be integrated into the legitimate economy as though they have been acquired lawfully. In England and Wales, and internationally, money laundering is a crime, and the relevant offences are set out in the Proceeds of Crime Act 2002.

[77] Terrorist financing is a crime, and the offences are set out in ss 15–18 of the Terrorism Act 2000.

[78] The organization has a mandate for its existence, which runs in eight-year cycles. The current mandate continues until the end of December 2020—FATF, Financial Action Task Force Mandate 2012–2020, 20 April 2012.

[79] For a critique of FATF and its impact on charities, see Shillito, 'Countering Terrorist Financing via Non-Profit Organisations: Assessing Why Few States Comply with the International Recommendations' [2015] Nonprofit Policy Forum.

[80] SI 2017/692. These came into force on 26 June 2017, and implement the Fourth Money Laundering Directive (2015/849/EU) into UK law.

[81] Charity Commission, Compliance toolkit: Module 3 at pp 1–2. [82] Ibid.

[83] See, for example, Charity Commission, Compliance Toolkit: Chapters 1–5 (September 2013). Chapter 1 was updated 11 June 2021.

[84] HM Government, *Tackling Extremism in the UK* (December 2013), para 2.1.

[85] Home Affairs Committee, HC 231 Counter-Terrorism (9 May 2014), para 134.

(c) Funding the Charity Commission

Over the period of the significant regulatory challenges outlined, the operating budget of the Commission has sharply declined. This started in 2012, with a 33 per cent cut to funding over four years as a result of the public spending squeeze following the impact of the global recession.[86] By 2015–16, the Commission's budget had seen a reduction of 48 per cent in real terms since 2007–08,[87] yet the number of charities it was responsible for had not seen a corresponding decrease in numbers, and demand for its services as regulator had increased. In an attempt to make its functions sustainable against this reduction in funding from government, the Commission negotiated an £8 million 'Transform Programme' with HM Treasury to redesign its operating model and business process to make it more efficient. In 2020–21, the regulators revenue budget was £28.3 million with £2.2 million capital budget, but additional operational and capital funding has been secured in the Autumn 2021 budget which will see finding rise on revenue and capital to £29.8 million and £2.7 million respectively in 2022–23.[88]

It is clear that an effective regulator needs effective funding and it is equally clear, bar a significant change of Treasury policy, that increased funding will not come from government. A potential levy on charities to fund the regulator has been mooted, but this has yet to materialize and is a divisive issue within the sector.[89]

(d) Changing regulatory approaches

The combination of scandals, terrorist threats, and a shrinking budget has seen the regulatory approach of the Charity Commission transform. The first Strategic Review of its activities happened in 2011 following the first significant loss of budget, and saw the Commission enter a period of consultation with key members of the charity sector and its advisors. This process resulted in the publication of its Strategic Plan 2012–2015, which indicated that the Commission's priorities would be developing the compliance and accountability of the sector and developing the self-reliance of the sector.

The significant shift from previous approaches was that the Charity Commission would be concentrating on its role as independent regulator of the sector, rather than champion of the sector, leaving other charitable organizations (such as the National Council for Voluntary Organisations) to fill the gap on highlighting and sharing good practice and providing individual advice. Hence, the removal of a dedicated, personalized advice service to charities and its replacement with internet advice publications to address its guidance functions.[90]

During this period, the Commission adopted a risk-based approach in order to concentrate its engagement with charities where it was most needed and which takes account of the risk involved to the charity and its beneficiaries, and the capacity of the charity to

[86] The review was prompted by a 33 per cent cut to funding over four years as a result of the public spending squeeze: see http://charitycommissionreview.blogspot.com for details.

[87] National Audit Office, The Regulatory Effectiveness of the Charity Commission, 4 December 2013, HC 813 2013–14, para 1.12.

[88] HC 822, Autumn Budget and Spending Review 2021, October 2021, HM Treasury, This has nonetheless drawn criticism, that this is a scant increase for the demands on charities coping with the ongoing Covid-19 pandemic.

[89] See Hogg, 'What Regulation, Who Pays? Public Attitudes to Charity Regulation in England and Wales' [2017] Nonprofit and Voluntary Sector Quarterly 1, who tentatively concludes that the public in England and Wales might be amenable to charities using some of their resources to fund a regulator, at least where that funding led to an improved and more transparent regulation.

[90] The negative impact of this change of advice function, against the backdrop of changes to advice for charities (and those helped by charities) by the removal of funding by the Legal Aid, Sentencing and Punishment of Offenders Act 2012, is considered in D Morris and W Barr, 'The Impact of Cuts on Legal Aid Funding in Charities' [2013] 35 JSWFL 79.

comply. This was coupled with a move towards resolving most compliance issues through guidance and supervision, on the basis that '[p]revention is invariably better than cure'.[91] However, in the wake of the Cup Trust affair and the intense pressure noted from the reports undertaken by government departments, this approach was no longer sustainable. The then Chairman of the Charity Commission responded to these criticisms, suggesting that the Commission was 'making rapid, visible progress'[92] towards improving regulation on the basis of the National Audit Report recommendations.[93]

In October 2018, the Commission published a new strategy[94] which sets out a revised approach to regulation under which the Commission has set out five key strategic objectives as well as a plan to develop those objectives over the duration of the strategy. Those priorities are: (a) holding charities to account; (b) dealing with wrongdoing and harm; (c) informing public choice; (d) giving charities the understanding and the tools they need to succeed; and (e) keeping charity relevant for today's world. The Commission has stepped up the use of its power of intervention to ensure good governance and to deal with wrongdoing and harm, and reports the use of such powers through various media, including the Comission's website. The speed with which it acted in relation to the Oxfam crisis, for example, is further evidence of the Commission being seen to be acting quickly and decisively to scandals, in marked contrast to the approach to the Cup Trust saga. Nevertheless, media appetite for charity scandals has not diminished, and the challenges and critique of the Commission as regulator continue.[95]

(3) Duties and powers

(a) Annual report

The Commission has the duty under Sch 1, para 11 of the Charities Act 2011 to make an annual report, which must be laid before Parliament. These reports provide a review of the administration of charities and bring attention to any particular problems. The Commission also provides precedents for purposes that it has registered as charitable, and any changes in their requirements, as well as providing legal updates for charities on key cases or developments in which it has been involved, including the use of its powers and functions as regulator.

(b) Power to institute inquiries

By s 46(1) of the Act, the Commission has the power to 'institute inquiries with regard to charities, or a particular charity or class of charities'.[96] In connection with this power it has wide-ranging ancillary powers to obtain relevant information. It may order any person to furnish accounts and statements and to return answers in writing to any questions or inquiries,[97] to furnish copies of documents under his control,[98] and to give evidence,[99] which may be taken under oath.[100] By s 60 of the Act, it is a criminal offence knowingly

[91] Annual Report 2008–2009, p 2.

[92] See www.charitycommission.gov.uk/news/charity-commission-rebuts-pac-criticism/.

[93] HC 814 National Audit Office, 'Charity Commission: The Cup Trust' (4 December 2013), paras 1.5–1.7.

[94] Charity Commission Statement of Strategic Intent 2018–2023 (4 October 2018).

[95] For a recent critique of the regulator, see Hogg, 'Licking their Own Lollipops: What do Charities and the Public Think about the Regulation of Charitable Activities?' in Picton and Sigafoos (eds) Debates in Charity Law (Hart Bloomsbury 2020), Ch 10; see also, more broadly, Harding, 'Indpendence and Accountaility in the Charity Sector', Ch 2 in the same volume.

[96] This power did not extend to exempt charities, but this was modified by the Charities Act 2006, meaning that the Commission can investigate at the request of the principal regulator of the exempt charity (s 46(2)).

[97] s 47(2)(a). [98] s 47(2)(b). [99] s 47(3)(b). [100] s 47(3)(a).

or recklessly to provide the Commission with false or misleading information, or to wilfully alter, suppress, conceal, or destroy any document required to be produced to the Commission. The Commission may obtain a warrant to search premises.[101]

(c) Power to act for the protection of charities

Section 76 grants the Commission wide-ranging powers to take action where it has instituted an inquiry under s 46 and is satisfied:

(a) that there is or has been any misconduct or mismanagement in the administration of the charity; or
(b) that it is necessary or desirable to act for the purpose of–
  (i) protecting the property of the charity or,
  (ii) securing a proper application for the purposes of the charity of that property or of property coming to the charity.[102]

The action the Commission may take includes: the suspension of any trustee pending consideration of his removal;[103] appointing additional trustees;[104] vesting the property of the charity in the Official Custodian;[105] restraining persons who hold property on behalf of the charity from parting with it without their approval;[106] restricting the transactions and payments that may be entered or made without approval;[107] and appointing a receiver and manager.[108] In addition, where the Commission is satisfied that both criteria (a) and (b) above are met, it has the power to: (i) remove any trustee, charity trustee, officer, agent, or employee of the charity who has been responsible for or privy to the misconduct or mismanagement or has by his conduct contributed to it or facilitated it;[109] (ii) by order, establish a scheme for the administration of the charity.[110]

Additional powers were conferred on the Charity Commission by the Charities Act 2006, including the power to give specific directions for the protection of charity and to direct the application of charity property.[111] Following the impact of the National Audit Office and Public Accounts Committees' damning reports into the effectiveness of the Charity Commission as regulator, the Commission argued for, and received, an extension to the regulatory powers available to deal with charities.[112] These were granted in the Charities (Protection and Social Investment) Act 2016. Most are amendments and clarifications to the existing powers provided under s 76 of the Charities Act 2011, but three major revisions are worthy of particular note.[113] The first is a power to suspend and disqualify a trustee if their behaviour has been such that it could damage public trust in the charity.[114] It does not require that the trustee knew or ought to have known about misconduct or mismanagement of the charity. Second, the Commission now has

[101] Charities Act 2011, s 48.

[102] s 76(1), as amended by Charities (Protection and Social Investment) Act 2016, s 2. See also s 761A, as added by the 2016 Act.

[103] s 76(3)(a). [104] s 76(3)(b). [105] s 76(3)(c).

[106] s 76(3)(d). [107] s 76(3)(e). [108] s 76(3)(g).

[109] s 79, as substituted by s 4 of the Charities (Protection and Social Investment) Act 2016.

[110] s 79. [111] See now Charities Act 2011, ss 84 and 85.

[112] For a fascinating commentary on the passage of the Act, and the influence of academic commentary on legislative change, see Morgan and Morris, 'Strengthening Charity Regulation in England and Wales? The Charities (Protection and Social Investment) Act 2016 and the Impact of Academic Witnesses' [2017] Voluntary Sector Review 89.

[113] The 2016 Act also introduces some new rules in relation to automatic disqualification of persons who may act as charity trustees, which are discussed later in this chapter.

[114] Charities (Protection and Social Investment) Act 2016, s 10, inserting s 181A(7A): Disqualification Orders into the Charities Act 2011.

the power, under the Charities Act 2011, s 84A,[115] to direct that specified action should not be taken by a charity or its trustees. The final provision is an entirely new power to issue official warnings to trustees or charities, granted by the introduction of s 75A into the Charities Act 2011.[116] This wide-ranging power allows the Commission to issue a warning where it considers there has been a breach of trust, misconduct, or other mismanagement. Controversially, charities are unable to appeal such a warning to the Tribunal, and concerns were expressed over how the Commission might exercise this power, and the impact such a warning might have on public trust and confidence in the affected charity. The Commission entered into a consultation exercise about how it intended to use the power,[117] and has, on the basis of responses, published official guidance in the form of a Q&A.[118] It also clarified that charities would have twenty-eight days' notice within which to act before an official warning was issued. The official warning specifies the action that the Commission expects the charity trustee to take to rectify the situation. If the charity trustees fail to do so, this could trigger a formal statutory inquiry and enable the Commission to use its full arsenal of protective powers.

On 3 July 2017, the Charity Commission published its first official warning to the National Hereditary Breast Cancer Helpline, following an inquiry into the organization.[119] The official warning set out the action the Commission expected the charity trustees to take to rectify the breaches of trust or duty, or misconduct or mismanagement in the administration of the charity, identified by the regulator as grounds for issuing it. There have been numerous warnings since, but it appears that the Commission is following its published guidance carefully, and is seeking only to issue warnings where there has been serious and continued failures of governance within charities.

The powers conferred by the 2016 Act have been the subject of criticism, as it has been argued that the issue was not, as the Commission has claimed, that it lacked the powers to regulate charities, but that it was not using its existing powers effectively.[120] Nevertheless, there had been an intense period of pre-legislative scrutiny of the Bill that became the 2016 Act, and there had been broad support for bolstering the Commission's powers.[121]

(d) Duty to maintain a register of charities

Section 29 of the Charities Act 2011 requires the Charity Commission to maintain a register of all charities. The scope and purpose of this register is considered later.

(e) Duty to inform the Charity Commission of the desirability of bringing legal proceedings

Section 115(2) place the trustees under a duty to inform the Charity Commission if it is desirable to take legal proceedings with reference to any charity. The Charity Commission will inform the Attorney-General if it feels legal proceedings are desirable under s 115(7).

(f) Power to give advice to charity trustees

Section 110 empowers the Commission to give its opinion or advice to a charity trustee on any matter affecting the performance of his duties as such or the proper administration

[115] Inserted by the Charities (Protection and Social Investment) Act 2016, s 6.

[116] Charities (Protection and Social Investment) Act 2016, s 1.

[117] Charity Commission, *Consultation on Official Warnings to Charities and Trustees* (1 July 2016).

[118] Charity Commission, *Official Warnings to Charities and Trustees: Q and A* (December 2016).

[119] Charity Commission, *National Hereditary Breast Cancer Helpline: Official Warning* (3 July 2017).

[120] Morgan and Morris, 'Strengthening Charity Regulation in England and Wales? The Charities (Protection and Social Investment) Act 2016 and the Impact of Academic Witnesses' [2017] Voluntary Sector Review 89, pp 94 and 97.

[121] Ibid, pp 91–3.

of the trust. A charity trustee who acts in accordance with such advice is deemed 'to have acted in accordance with his trust',[122] unless he knew or had reasonable cause to suspect that the advice had been given in ignorance of material facts,[123] or a decision of the First Tier-Tribunal (Charity) is pending or has been obtained on the matter in question.[124]

(g) The Official Custodian

By s 21(3) of the Charities Act 2011 the Charity Commission is required to designate a person to act as the Official Custodian for charitable trusts, so that charity trustees can vest charity property in him as custodian trustee, thereby obviating the need for property (and, in particular, land) to be transferred to the new trustees every time the trustees of a charity change.[125]

(4) The Charities Register

A scheme of general registration of charities was first introduced by the Charities Act 1960. It is now the duty of the Commission to maintain the register, which by s 29(2) of the Charities Act 2011 shall contain the name of the charity and such other particulars or any other information the Commission thinks fit. Some charities are not required to register, namely: the 'exempt' charities;[126] charities which are excepted by order or regulations and which have a gross income of less than £100,000 per annum;[127] charities with a low income (less than £5,000 gross per annum).[128] All other charities are required to register[129] and are required to provide a copy of their trusts when they apply for registration.[130] The register, including the copies of the charities' trust instruments, is open to public inspection at all reasonable times.[131] The register can be inspected online. On 22 September 2020, the Commission launched a new and improved online version of the register of charities to increase public transparency, by displaying a wider range of information about registered charities[132] alongside a more effective search tool.[133]

It was formerly the case that exempt charities were exempt not only from the requirement to register but also from many of the regulatory provisions contained in the Charities Acts. This was because they were drawn from sectors which had alternative forms of regulation. The Charities Act 2006, which has now been consolidated within the 2011 Act, significantly altered that position. It made some changes (now s 22 and Sch 3 of the 2011 Act) to the categories of institution with exempt charity status. The law now requires a 'principal regulator' to be appointed for all exempt charities.[134] The principal regulator is charged to 'promote compliance by the charity trustees with their legal obligations in exercising control and management of the administration of the charity'.[135] The Charities Act 2011 gives the Charity Commission, as we have seen, the power to institute inquiries. This was an increase in regulation first introduced by the Charities Act 2006. This power to institute an inquiry can only be exercised at the request of the principal regulator.[136]

[122] s 110(2). [123] s 110(3)(a). [124] s 110(3)(b).

[125] Provisions relating to the powers and duties of the Official Custodian are contained in Sch 2 to the Act.

[126] s 30(2). The definition of exempt charities is contained in s 22 and Sch 3.

[127] s 30(2)(b) (orders); s 30(2)(c) (regulations).

[128] s 30(2)(d). [129] s 30(1). [130] ss 35(1) and (2). [131] s 38(1).

[132] This includes employee salaries, income from government contracts and grants, and payments to trustees.

[133] CharityCommissionBlog(https://charitycommission.blog.gov.uk/2020/09/03/the-online-register-of-charities-new-and-improving/).

[134] s 25. [135] s 26(1). [136] s 46(2).

Universities are exempt charities, and as such are not required to register with the Charity Commission. Universities were already subject to detailed scrutiny by the Higher Education Funding Councils in England and Wales, and in England (but not in Wales), the Funding Council is now the principal regulator for this group of exempt charities. Universities in Wales will be regulated directly by the Charity Commission in regard to charity matters.

The Charity Commission has the power, under s 34 of the Charities Act 2011, to remove a charity from the register, either because the organization has ceased to exist or operate as a charity[137] or because the Commission no longer considers it to be a charity.[138] In *The 1 Click Charitable Trust*,[139] the Charity Commission had registered the named charity in 2010 on the basis of assurances that it would meet the minimum income threshold of £5,000 under the Charities Act 2011, s 30. The organization's income never reached this threshold, and the Commission removed it on the basis that it had ceased to operate as charity under s 34(1)(b) of the Charities Act 2011. The organization appealed the decision to the First-Tier Tribunal (Charity), who upheld the removal on the basis that it was unable to provide sufficient evidence that it was operating as a charity, in the sense of generating sustainable funds to carry out its activities, not on the basis that annual income was below the £5,000 threshold.

(5) **The First-Tier Tribunal (Charity)**

A number of cases have been cited in this and previous chapters, which are decisions of the First-Tier Tribunal (Charity). The Charities Act 2006 established a new body, the Charity Tribunal.[140] On 1 September 2009, the Charity Tribunal was abolished and its jurisdiction passed to the First-Tier Tribunal (Charity), following the Transfer of Functions of the Charity Tribunal Order 2009/1834. The First-Tier Tribunal (Charity) is administered by the unified Tribunals Service, an executive agency of the Ministry of Justice.[141] Before the establishment of any tribunal service for charity appeals, a person who was unhappy with a decision of the Charity Commission, for instance because of a refusal to register a body or a trust as a charity, could ask the Commission to review the decision using its own internal review processes and, if still unhappy, could appeal to the High Court. There is now in many cases a right of appeal to the First-Tier Tribunal (Charity) following a final decision, direction, or order of the Charity Commission.[142]

There is then a further right of appeal to the Upper-Tier Tribunal and then the High Court, but only on points of law. The Upper-Tier Tribunal, established under the wholesale reform of the Tribunal system under the Tribunals, Courts and Enforcement Act 2007, is established as a court of superior record with the power to bind itself and the Lower-Tier Tribunals on matters within its remit.[143] The Attorney-General has the right to refer certain matters to the Tribunal,[144] and is given the power to intervene in proceedings before the Tribunal, to which he is not a party.[145]

137 s 34(1)(b). 138 s 34(1)(a). 139 CA/2016/0001.

140 See now Charities Act 2011, Pt 17, ss 315–30 and Sch 6.

141 The First-Tier Tribunal is regulated by the Tribunal Procedure (First-Tier Tribunal) (General Regulatory Chamber) Rules 2009 (UK), SI 2009/1976 (as amended). The Upper-Tier Tribunal is regulated by the Tribunal Procedure (Upper Tribunal) Rules 2008 (UK), SI 2008/2698.

142 s 319 and Sch 6, col 1.

143 Indeed, under s 25 of the Tribunals, Courts and Enforcement Act 2007 it has the same powers as the High Court for matters within its remit. See further McKenna, 'Transforming Tribunals: The Reform of the Charity Tribunal by the Tribunals, Courts and Enforcement Act 1997' [2009] 11 CLPR 1.

144 s 326. 145 s 318.

The sorts of matter over which the First-Tier Tribunal (Charity) has jurisdiction are appeals against decisions to register or to refuse to register an institution as a charity, to institute an inquiry with regard to a particular institution or group of institutions, a decision to appoint or remove a charity trustee, and many other decisions listed in Sch 6 to the 2011 Act. It was anticipated that the flexible Tribunal procedure would allow matters of law to be 'fast-tracked' directly to the Upper-Tier Tribunal, and, if necessary, remitted to the First-Tier Tribunal. This would promote a particular saving in terms of cost to charities. This was certainly the wish of the then President[146] of the original Charity Tribunal[147] (now principal judge of the First-Tier Tribunal (Charity)). It is fair to say that the operation of the Tribunal is not without its critics,[148] but it has nonetheless heard numerous cases and, as noted in Chapter 21, has provided some key guidance on issues such as measuring public benefit.

Before the introduction of the Tribunal system for charities, disputed decisions made by the Charity Commission did not get any further than the internal review process, owing to the high expense of an appeal action in the High Court. The Tribunal system was intended to offer a cheaper and speedier alternative, which should increase the number of Charity Commission decisions that are appealed. Despite the introduction of the original Charity Tribunal, there was still major criticism of the way in which the service operated. Namely, it was considered that the legal costs of accessing the Charity Tribunal were too high for most charities, the lack of formal rules led to lengthy procedural arguments, and a combination of an adversarial atmosphere and a feeling that it was an uneven playing field for the parties weakened the effectiveness of the system.[149] Despite 'bedding in' to the wider Tribunal structure, there is still concern. The difference in quality of the legal advice that a charity might call upon compared to the Commission helps produce a perception of unfairness.[150] Some of the decisions reached by the First-Tier Tribunal, and the Upper Tribunal have also provoked robust, critical comment.[151] Principal Judge McKenna, writing extra-judicially on the operation of the First-Tier Tribunal (Charity),[152] noted that approximately three to six cases a year receive a full hearing at the Tribunal, which was too few to influence procedure of the Tribunal service more generally.

Suggestions for reform to the operation of the Tribunal service came from Lord Hogdson's review of the Charity Act 2006, which was published in July 2012,[153] which included streamlining the procedure and reducing the cost and time of action. The government responded positively to most of this report, and the Law Commission published a consultation paper as part of its work on reform of charity law in 2014, which led to a series of recommendations in the 2017 report on *Technical Issues in Charity Law*.[154] The Law Commission's recommendations were limited in scope, but important. Two

[146] This person now serves as a judge of the First-Tier Tribunal and as a Deputy Judge of the Upper Tribunal—The Transfer of Functions of the Charity Tribunal Order 2009/1834, art 3.

[147] McKenna, 'Transforming Tribunals: The Reform of the Charity Tribunal by the Tribunals, Courts and Enforcement Act 1997' [2009] 11 CLPR 1, 10.

[148] See, for example, Morris, 'The First-tier Tribunal (Charity): Enhanced Access to Justice for Charities or a Case of David versus Goliath?' [2010] 29 CJQ 89.

[149] Third Sector, 'Teething Problems for the Charity Tribunal' (23 June 2008).

[150] Morris, 'The First-tier Tribunal (Charity): Enhanced Access to Justice for Charities or a Case of David versus Goliath?' [2010] 29 CJQ 89.

[151] See, for example, Luxton, 'Opening Pandora's Box: the Upper Tribunal's Decision on Public Benefit and Independent Schools' [2012] CLPR 15.

[152] McKenna, 'Should the Charity Tribunal Be Reformed?' [2012] CLPR 1.

[153] 'Trusted and Independent: Giving Charity Back to Charities', Review of the Charities Act 2006 (TSO, 2012). This was carried out pursuant to s 73 of the Charities Act 2006, which required the review to take place. See also the current government's response—Cmnd 8700 (TSO, September 2013).

[154] Technical Issues in Charity Law (Law Com No 375, 2017).

aspects relate to costs. The first is to remove the potential conflict of interest in seeking the Charity Commission's consent to take 'charity proceedings' against a decision of the Commission, by giving charities the option to get authorization from the court instead.[155] The second is to give the Tribunal a power to make 'authorized cost orders' so that trustees can obtain advanced assurance that any costs they incur can be paid from the funds of the charity.[156] The remaining recommendations related to process to simplify the process for the Charity Commission to make references to the Tribunal,[157] and a recommended change of practice that the Commission should delay the date on which its decisions take effect to allow a time for a challenge 'where the decision is likely to be controversial and not time-sensitive'.[158] These changes remove barriers to cases being brought before the Tribunal. Following a government response,[159] the Law Commission were forced to drop all but the recommendation relating to authorized cost orders.[160] The revised proposals were formally introduced as the Charities Bill 2021–22,[161] which was enacted on 24 February as the Charities Act 2022.

It is important that an effective and efficient service is available to charities. In particular, the powers and remit of the Upper-Tier Tribunal are likely to mean that, where a point of law is involved, fewer cases will be dealt with by the courts. It is important for the sector as a whole that the Tribunal works as effectively as it can, and that charities feel able to bring cases before it.

(6) **Control of charity trustees**

The legislative framework recognizes the importance of the role of the trustees of charities, and that they enjoy major opportunities for abuse. Some persons are disqualified from serving as charity trustees, whilst those who can occupy such positions are subject to onerous duties.

(a) **Disqualification**

The Charities Act 2011 disqualifies certain individuals from acting as charity trustees. The main circumstances in which a person will be so disqualified were:[162] (i) previous conviction of any offence involving dishonesty or deception; (ii) undischarged bankruptcy; (iii) previous removal from the office of a charity trustee by an order of the Commission; and (iv) previous disqualification from serving as a company director under the Company Directors' Disqualification Act 1986. Any person who serves as a charity trustee while disqualified commits a criminal offence.[163] The Charity Commission now has a power, in limited circumstances, to waive the disqualification.[164]

Effective from 1 August 2018, changes to the automatic disqualification rules for charity trustees under s 9 of the Charities (Protection and Social Investment) Act 2016 mean that there are now more restrictions on who can run a charity.[165] The new grounds include

155 Ibid, paras 15.5–15.18, Recommendation 40; Charities Bill, cl 38.

156 Ibid, paras 15.28–15.47, Recommendation 41; Charities Bill, cl 39.

157 This would remove the need to get consent from the Attorney General, and instead institute a notice procedure—ibid, paras 15.59–15.67, Recommendation 43; Charities Bill, cl 40.

158 Ibid, paras 15.49–15.58, Recommendation 42.

159 Government response to the Law Commission report 'Technical Issues in Charity Law' (22 March 2021).

160 Technically, the government suggested that Rec 42 (delay the date on which its decisions take effect to allow a time for a challenge) was a matter for the Charity Commission, which the Charity Commission has indicated it is minded to accept.

161 Charities Bill 2021–22, Part 6 cl 36.

162 s 178(1). There are two other cases listed in the statute. 163 s 183. 164 s 181.

165 This section made a series of amendments to the Charities Act 2011, Pt 9, ss 178–84.

being on the sex offenders register, and certain unspent convictions, such as for terrorism or money laundering offences. In addition, people who are disqualified from acting as a trustee are also disqualified from holding certain senior manager positions at a charity. These include both Chief Executive (or equivalent) positions and Chief Finance Officer (or equivalent) positions. Persons already in post who fall within these new grounds will be automatically disqualified on 1 August 2018, unless they apply for a waiver of disqualification of their disqualification before the rules change.[166]

(b) Duties of charity trustees

The trustees of most charities are under a duty to keep proper financial records and to provide an annual report to the Charity Commission. Under the Charities (Accounts and Reports) Regulations 1995[167] a new framework was introduced for charity accounting requiring charities to produce annual accounts and a trustee report, the Statement of Recommended Practice (SORP).[168] The presentation of this information is required to be uniform, thus allowing people to see more clearly how charities are spending their money and to compare different charities. A system of thresholds seeks to ensure that the heaviest burden falls to the larger charities, where a stricter regime of external scrutiny will apply. Smaller charities are subject to less demanding requirements.[169] The reporting requirements for charities are now consolidated in Pt 8 of the Charities Act 2011.[170] The annual report and charity accounts are open to public inspection.[171] The trustees of exempt charities are merely under a duty to keep proper books of account that must be preserved for six years.[172] Where the charity is a company the trustees are exempt from the accounting requirements of the Charities Act 2011,[173] but must comply with the company law provisions relating to accounts.[174]

(i) Duty to apply for registration

Under s 35(1) of the Charities Act 2011, the trustees of a charity which is not registered and is not exempted or excepted from the requirement to be registered are under a duty to apply for it to be registered.

(ii) Duty to keep accounts

Charity trustees are under a duty to keep accounting records that are sufficient to show and explain all the charity's transactions, and which must be retained for at least six years.[175]

(iii) Duty to prepare annual accounts

They are also under a duty to prepare an annual statement of accounts in accordance with the regulations made by the Secretary of State.[176]

[166] They were able to do so from 1 February 2018, and their disqualification under the new rules would not take effect until they have received a decision or any appeal of that decision has been decided.

[167] SI 1995/2724.

[168] The SORP has undergone many revisions since its inception. The last SORP, Charities SORP (FRS 102) 2nd edn, was released in October 2019, following a series of update bulletins.

[169] Charities Act 2011, s 133.

[170] ss 130–75. This is split into five chapters, with Chapters 1 and 2 dealing with individual and group accounts; Chapter 3 with audit requirements; and the remaining chapters with annual reports and powers to set financial thresholds.

[171] s 170. [172] s 136. [173] s 135. [174] Companies Act 2006, Pt 15.

[175] ss 130 (accounts) and 131 (preservation).

[176] s 132. These statements must also be retained for the next six years.

(iv) Duty to have an annual audit

If the annual income of the charity exceeds a specified limit the accounts must be audited, but if it does not exceed that amount they can be examined by an independent examiner. If an audit is not carried out the Commission may order an audit at the expense of the charity or the charity trustees.[177]

(v) Duty to prepare an annual report

The trustees of a charity are under a duty to prepare an annual report for each financial year containing a report on the activities of the charity during the past year and other information, as may be prescribed by regulation.[178] The annual report must be transmitted to the Charity Commission and have attached the statement of accounts[179] and, where appropriate, the auditor or independent examiner's report.[180] The annual report is to be kept open to public inspection by the Commission.[181]

(7) **Local authorities and local charities**

Although the Charity Commission operates a national scheme for the registration and supervision of charities, the Charities Act 2011 also makes provision for localized schemes. Under s 294, county and district councils, London borough councils, and the Common Council of the City of London may maintain an index of local charities, from which they may publish information, summaries, or extracts, and which is to be open to public inspection. They are entitled to receive from the Commission copies of entries on the register which are relevant for the index.

(8) **Judicial review of decisions taken by charities**

In *Scott v National Trust*,[182] Robert Walker J considered the question whether a decision of the National Trust to ban deer hunting with hounds on its land was amenable to judicial review. He noted that charitable trusts involved a public element and that the charity enjoyed powers and discretions which might affect different sections of the public directly or indirectly. Whilst he was unwilling to consider whether any charity, or even any charity specially established by statute is subject to judicial review, he stated his opinion that the National Trust would be susceptible:

> the National Trust is a charity of exceptional importance to the nation, regulated by its own special Acts of Parliament. Its purposes and functions are of high public importance, as is reflected by the special statutory provisions (in the fields of taxation and compulsory acquisition) to which I have already referred. It seems to me to have all the characteristics of a public body which is, prima facie, amenable to judicial review, and to have been exercising its statutory public functions in making the decision which is challenged.[183]

However, he held that the availability of judicial monitoring through charity proceedings in the Chancery Division meant that judicial review would not be appropriate in all but the most exceptional cases, which he suggested might include where a local authority held land on charitable trusts and questions about its dealings with that land were caught up with other questions about its dealings with land which it owned beneficially.[184]

In contrast, in *Royal Society for the Prevention of Cruelty to Animals v A-G*,[185] Lightman J held that disappointed applicants for membership of the Society were not entitled to seek judicial review. He held that, whilst the Society was a very important charity and its

[177] s 146. [178] s 162. [179] With the exception of charities which are companies: s 164(3).
[180] s 164(1). [181] s 170. [182] [1998] 2 All ER 705. [183] [1998] 2 All ER 705 at 716.
[184] [1998] 2 All ER 705 at 717–18. [185] [2001] 3 All ER 530.

activities were of great value to society, it could be distinguished from the National Trust on the grounds that it had no statutory or public law role. Thus, although it is the largest non-governmental law enforcement agency in England and Wales, in carrying out these activities it is in no different position from that of any citizen or other organization.

The Court of Appeal, in *R (Weaver) v London and Quadrant Housing*,[186] held that a registered social landlord was a 'public body' for the purposes of judicial review in carrying out allocation or management of housing stock. The claimant, an assured tenant, contended that the trust was in breach of a legitimate expectation in failing to pursue all reasonable alternatives before resorting to a mandatory ground for possession and that the decision was in breach of, inter alia, article 8 of the European Convention on Human Rights, guaranteeing respect for home life. Although the claim was dismissed, Richards LJ held that the functions a social landlord carried out were of a public nature. The nature and level of public subsidy and state control of such bodies were essential factors in finding that a social landlord was a public authority. The fact that eviction may be considered a private act was not sufficient to withdraw the public character of the action.

This has since been applied in *R (McIntyre) v Gentoo Group Ltd*[187] Judicial review was not approved on the facts, as the tenants had other options open to them, where it was confirmed that the decision in *R v London and Quadrant Housing* extended beyond acts relating to termination of a tenancy, and would allow for review of other management functions of a social landlord in relation to stock—the case concerned a mutual exchange of tenancies.

The impact of the decision in *R v London and Quadrant Housing* for other charities has yet to be felt, but it suggests that a restrictive approach is no longer tenable.

(9) **Human Rights Act**

Those charities which are public authorities are subject to the provisions of the Human Rights Act 1998. The Charity Commission is a public authority and thus subject to the provisions of the Act. Most charities, however, as *RSPCA v A-G*[188] shows, will not be considered to be public authorities. It is now clear that registered social landlords in discharging at least some of their functions will be classified as 'public authorities' for the purposes of s 6(3)(b) of the Human Rights Act 1998, and decisions relating to management and allocation of stock must adhere to human rights principles or can be challenged in court.

(10) **Good governance: self-support**

Much has been said in this chapter about the need for effective regulation, through provision of legal powers and an effective regulatory regime, to support and maintain public trust and confidence in charities. Charities, as organizations, individually and collectively also bear responsibility for putting in place effective governance procedures and dealing proactively with issues before they arise. It makes sense, therefore, to conclude the treatment of charities with a brief overview of some of the initiatives undertaken by the charity sector to try and make it more effectively self-governing.

(a) **The Fundraising Regulator**

The Olive Cook scandal, considered in this chapter, lead to widespread public and media concern about how charities contact potential donors. Over the summer of 2015, Sir

[186] [2009] EWCA Civ 587. See Alderson, '*R (Weaver) v London and Quadrant Housing Trust*' [2013] 16 CLPR 129.

[187] [2010] EWHC 5.

[188] [2001] 3 All ER 530.

Stuart Etherington, Chief Executive of the National Council for Voluntary Organisations, led a government-commissioned review into the self-regulation of charity fundraising. The review took evidence from stakeholders, including charities, as to how to rebuild trust in fundraising activities by charities. The Fundraising Regulator holds the Code of Fundraising Practice for the UK.

The voluntary aspect, which engages the sector, is that the Fundraising Regulator is funded through a voluntary levy on charities spending £100,000 or more each year on fundraising. The amount of the levy is variable, up to £15,000 a year to cover the costs of the regulator. The Fundraising Regulator also invites charities spending less than £100,000 a year on fundraising to register with it to demonstrate commitment to the fundraising standards set out within the Code of Fundraising Practice and Fundraising Rulebooks. Registration in these circumstances attracts an annual fee of £50.

Uptake has been increasing, with the year 2019–20 demonstrating the highest payment rate of the voluntary levy since inception and the highest number of voluntary registrations (up from 1,668 to 2,262 organizations)[189]

(b) The Charity Governance Code

The new Charity Governance Code was launched on 13 July 2017, and was refreshed at the end of 2020.[190] It sets out principles and recommended standards of governance best practice for all charities in England and Wales and their charity trustees to aspire to. It is a significantly updated version of the previous Code of Governance, devised by a cross-sector steering group. The Code, which is voluntary, seeks to strength governance and accountability in the charity sector. The Code was devised by a cross-sector steering group and has been endorsed by the Charity Commission, who have withdrawn the publication *Hallmarks of an Effective Charity (CC10)* to encourage charities to use the Code. This highlights that the Charity Commission is very well aware of the need for governance to come from the ground up, from charities themselves, rather than simply top down, from themselves as regulator.

There are two versions of the Code which share common principles and outcomes—one for smaller charities,[191] and one for larger charities whose accounts are audited.[192] All charity practitioners will be interested in the new Code, which is a valuable tool for charity trustee training and induction courses, as well as for conducting governance reviews. It is based on a core set of seven principles, all built on the foundation that a charity is already meeting its legal and regulatory responsibilities. The seven principles are (i) organizational purpose; (ii) leadership; (iii) integrity; (iv) decision-making, risk, and control; (v) board effectiveness; (vi) equality, diversity, and inclusion[193]; and (vii) openness and accountability.

Amongst the significant recommendations, this new Code suggests that every governing board should review its own internal performance every year, and larger charities should undergo external reviews every three years. The Code promotes more openness on the appointment and removal and trustees, and suggests a limit of nine years on how long trustees may serve with charities, unless there is a good reason to extend the term beyond that period.

This Code is a significant and essential step in raising the profile of good governance as an essential element of all aspects of charity regulation.

189 Fundraising Regulator, Annual Report for 2019/20, (4 February 2021). Only twenty charities refused to pay the levy.

190 This followed a consultation exercise on the operation of the Code—see Charity Governance Code, Refreshing the Charity Governance Code: Summary of consultation responses (August 2020).

191 Good Governance Steering Group, Charity Governance Code for smaller charities (2020).

192 Good Governance Steering Group, Charity Governance Code for larger charities (2020).

193 Originally simply 'diversity', but changed as part of the 2020 refresh.

PART VII

Allocation of Benefit

24. Choosing who benefits 535
25. Fixed trusts 550
26. Powers of appointment 560
27. Discretionary trusts 581
28. Powers of maintenance and advancement 594
29. Variation of beneficial interests 603

24

Choosing who benefits

1 Introduction

Zebedee is making his will, but has three children: Quentin, Rebecca, and Stuart. Zebedee wants to leave his estate to St Anthea's Hospice (a registered charity), but he also wants to ensure all of his children have enough money to pay the deposit on the purchase of their first home. The equitable mechanisms of fixed and discretionary trusts and powers of appointment allow a settlor like Zebedee to achieve these ends (if he has enough money) by choosing who benefits from a trust fund, or by delegating the power to choose. Each of these mechanisms will be examined in detail in the following chapters. This chapter will sketch some of the recurrent themes that run through the area.

2 Certainty

We have already seen (in Chapter 5) that because trusts and powers are subject to the control of the courts, they must be created in terms which are sufficiently certain for the courts to understand what obligations are imposed and what the limits are to any obligations or authorities.

3 Beneficial entitlement and ownership

A second recurrent theme is the question of the nature of the rights in the fund enjoyed by the potential objects of allocation. This has been explored in Chapter 2, but to recap, this will depend on the exact nature of the equitable mechanism that has been created, and will range from a subsisting property interest in a share of the fund, to no property right at all in the fund. There can be cases where no one is entitled to beneficial ownership for a time. To explore this, we can start by looking at the rights of the parties if Zebedee made a will to achieve the aims described above, and left an estate worth £850,000 to Tristan and Una as trustees.

(1) Fixed trust

At one end of the scale is the fixed trust.[1] The beneficiaries here are entitled to a fixed amount or to a fixed proportion of a fund. That would be the case if Zebedee specified in his will that each of his children were to have £150,000 to use as the deposit on a house purchase. The gift to the children could be subject to a condition, such as requiring

[1] See Figure 2.1, which shows the scale of equitable obligations.

them to survive to a particular age. In that case the gift would be contingent until the condition is satisfied, at which point it becomes unconditional or vested. Once a fixed interest becomes vested, then the beneficiaries have an immediate proprietary interest in the fund. They would each be the owners in equity of the part of the fund allocated to them, and, under the rule in *Saunders v Vautier*,[2] can call upon the trustees to pay them immediately.

(2) Power of appointment

At the other end of the scale is the power of appointment. If Zebedee, instead of giving the children a fixed sum, stated that they were to receive such sum as Tristan and Una saw fit, then the children would have no immediate proprietary interest in the fund at all.[3] None of them has any interest in the fund unless and until Tristan and Una exercise their power to make an appointment in favour of all or some of them.[4] Because Tristan and Una are trustees, it is likely that they will hold any such power subject to fiduciary obligations. It is also unlikely that Zebedee would want to give only a power of appointment since, if he did, Tristan and Una would not be obliged to implement his wishes.

(3) Discretionary trust

Between the two extremes of the fixed trust and the power of appointment lies the discretionary trust. The beneficiaries do not have immediate proprietary rights to specific shares of the fund, but, depending on how the trust is worded, they may not be without any proprietary right in the fund as a whole. Suppose Zebedee had allocated half of his estate for Tristan and Una to 'distribute among my children for the purpose of enabling them to buy a home as they in their discretion think fit'. As a class, the children have proprietary rights to this fund of half of the estate, but as individuals they could not identify any particular share of the fund as their own, unless and until it was allocated to them by the trustees. They can, if they all come together, call for the transfer of the legal title under the rule in *Saunders v Vautier*,[5] as was done in *Re Smith*.[6] In practice, this would be almost impossible if the class were a large group, for example in the case of a discretionary trust for the benefit of 'all the employees and ex-employees' of a company. The position taken in *Gartside v IRC*[7] and *Sainsbury v IRC*[8] was that the potential beneficiary of a discretionary trust has no actual proprietary interest in the fund unless a selection in their favour has been made. Instead, they merely have a right to be considered as a beneficiary by the trustees. This means that under some types of discretionary trust the beneficial interest in the property is held 'in the air' without a specific group who have proprietary rights in the fund, until allocations are made by the trustee.

(4) Unidentified beneficiaries

It is possible to have a trust in favour of beneficiaries who, although defined with certainty, cannot yet be identified. Thus it is possible to make a trust in favour of as yet unborn grandchildren, or a trust for 'the first woman to land on the moon'. There are restrictions, known as perpetuity rules, as to how long a gift can be tied up in favour of unidentified beneficiaries. While a beneficiary remains unidentified, ownership of the property remains in abeyance.

[2] [1841] 4 Beav 115. [3] *Vestey v IRC* [1980] AC 1148, HL.
[4] *Re Brookes' Settlement Trusts* [1939] Ch 993 at 997. [5] [1841] 4 Beav 115. [6] [1928] Ch 915.
[7] [1968] AC 553. [8] [1970] Ch 712.

(5) Divestment

It is possible to have a vested interest under a fixed trust which is subject to the possibility of all or part of the gift being taken away (or divested) if a power of appointment in favour of another person is exercised. St Anthea's Hospice would be in that position if Zebedee's will had given the whole of his estate to the hospice, subject to a power of appointment to make gifts to his children.

4 Purpose trusts

Although there can, as has just been seen, be some situations where beneficial ownership may be in abeyance, the normal situation is that a trust does have beneficiaries who are capable of owning property and enforcing the trust. Without such beneficiaries, who can apply to the court if a trust is not performed according to its terms? For this reason, the law insists that trusts must be for the benefit of legal persons[9] and not merely for the object of carrying out purposes. This limitation is not, however, absolute.[10] By far the most significant exception to this rule is the area of charity, already covered in Chapter 24, where purpose trusts are upheld as valid and a mechanism to supervise and enforce them is provided by the state for reasons of public policy. There are also several minor exceptions that are considered later in the chapter.

(1) The beneficiary principle

The rule against purpose trusts is long established. In *Morice v Bishop of Durham*, Sir William Grant MR stated that:

> Every . . . trust must have a definite object. There must be somebody, in whose favour the court can decree specific performance.[11]

Similarly, in *Bowman v Secular Society*,[12] Lord Parker of Waddington said that 'for a trust to be valid it must be for the benefit of individuals'.[13]

(a) Rationale for the beneficiary principle

There are three main problems with the validity of purpose trusts that have led to the adoption of the beneficiary principle.

(i) Without beneficiaries there is no owner

In its simplest form, a trust makes the beneficiaries into equitable owners. However, as has been seen, the principle that a trust fund 'belongs' to the beneficiaries is not absolute. There are many cases where property may—at least for a time—have no owner in equity. For instance, a trust in favour of Sandra's grandchildren will have no ascertained beneficiaries before at least one grandchild has been born. Similarly, a trust to invest and accumulate a fund for the first woman to land on the moon has no owner in equity until the condition has been satisfied. A discretionary trust in favour of a large class defined in a conceptually certain way, but too large to list, has no identifiable owner. Yet again, it

[9] See Naffine, 'Who are Law's Persons? From Cheshire Cats to Responsible Subjects' (2003) 66 MLR 346.

[10] See Matthews, 'The New Trust: Obligations without Rights?' in Oakley, *Trends in Contemporary Trust Law* (Oxford University Press 1997).

[11] (1804) 9 Ves Jr 399 at 405.

[12] [1917] AC 406 at 441.

[13] See also *Leahy v A-G for New South Wales* [1959] AC 457, per Viscount Simmonds: 'a trust may be created for the benefit of persons as cestui que trust but not as a purpose or object unless the purpose or object be charitable'.

has been held that there is no beneficial owner of the estate of a deceased person until the completion of the administration of the estate.[14] The concept of property being subject to enforceable obligations but having no immediate beneficial owner is thus well established. This should not be an objection to purpose trusts.

(ii) The trust cannot be enforced by the court

The supervision of trusts relies first and foremost on the beneficiaries, as the persons most interested in the proper administration of the trust, bringing abuses to the attention of the court.[15] Where a trust is created to carry out a purpose there is no person with locus standi to apply to the court to ensure that the terms of the trust are being carried out and that the trustees do not act in breach of trust, for example by misappropriating the trust property for themselves.

(iii) The trust will violate the rule against perpetuity

The law has always been reluctant to allow property to become subject to restrictions that would unduly prevent its free marketability. The terms of a trust may prevent its most efficient use. For this reason the law provides that property may not be subject to a trust for an excessive period of time. This rule is known as the rule against inalienability. A private trust (as opposed to a charitable trust) must not exceed the perpetuity period, which has been defined to last for up to twenty-one years longer than the life of any human life connected to the gifts in the trust and in being at the date that the trust was established. Trusts for purposes will frequently have the potential to last longer than this, and might even be perpetual. If a trust offends against the perpetuity period it is void ab initio.[16]

(b) Application of the beneficiary principle

The beneficiary principle was applied so as to invalidate the trust in *Re Astor's Settlement Trusts*.[17] A settlement was made by Viscount Astor of all the issued shares of the *Observer* newspaper. The terms of the trust were that the income was to be applied for the 'maintenance of good understanding between nations' and 'the preservation of the independence and integrity of the newspapers', purposes which were considered at the time not to be charitable. Roxburgh J held that the trust was invalid on two grounds: first, that it offended against the beneficiary principle, and second, that the purposes were uncertain. He examined the beneficiary principle laid down by Lord Parker in *Bowman v Secular Society*[18] and concluded that it was not susceptible to attack from a base of principle, and that it was well established in authority. Since the purposes did not fall within any of the exceptions to the beneficiary principle, the trust was void.

In *Re Shaw*[19] George Bernard Shaw left his residuary estate to trustees to apply the income to purposes including research into a proposed forty-letter alphabet, and the transliteration of one of his plays into such an alphabet. These were held not to be charitable purposes, and they failed as purpose trusts. Harman J indicated some dissatisfaction with the 'beneficiary principle',[20] but felt himself bound by the higher authority of the

[14] *Stamp Duties Comr (Queensland) v Livingston* [1965] AC 694.

[15] See also *Re Astor's Settlement Trusts* [1952] Ch 534 at 549; *Re Shaw* [1957] 1 WLR 729 at 744–6.

[16] The more relaxed rules to be found in either the Perpetuities and Accumulations Act 1964 (for trusts arising before 6 April 2010) or the Perpetuities and Accumulations Act 2009 (for trusts arising on or after 6 April 2010) only apply to the rule against remoteness of vesting and accumulation, not to the rule against perpetual trusts.

[17] [1952] Ch 534.

[18] [1917] AC 406. He also drew support from *Re Wood* [1949] Ch 498 at 501 (Harman J).

[19] [1957] 1 WLR 729.

[20] [1957] 1 WLR 729 at 745.

House of Lords and Court of Appeal.[21] In *Re Endacott*[22] Harman LJ in the Court of Appeal applied the beneficiary principle to a gift by Albert Endacott to the North Tawton Devon Parish Council 'for the purposes of providing some useful memorial to myself'. He did not indicate any of the doubts he had mentioned in *Re Shaw*[23] but instead applauded the 'orthodox sentiments expressed by Roxburgh J in the *Astor* case'.[24] The Court of Appeal held that the gift was a non-charitable purpose trust that did not fall within any of the exceptions to the beneficiary principle.

(2) Exceptions to the beneficiary principle

Whilst the cases cited earlier confirm the existence of the 'beneficiary principle' rendering non-charitable purpose trusts void, English law recognizes a number of exceptions where pure non-charitable purpose trusts will be upheld despite the lack of beneficiaries. There is no logical rationale for these exceptions, and in this sense, they are said to be anomalous. In *Re Astor's Settlement Trusts*, Roxburgh J reviewed the exceptions and commented that they were 'anomalous and exceptional concessions to human weakness or sentiment'.[25] In *Re Endacott*[26] Harman LJ confirmed their anomalous nature, and indicated that the number of exceptions should not be increased. They are decisions:

> which are not really to be satisfactorily classified, but are perhaps merely occasions where Homer has nodded, at any rate these cases stand by themselves and ought not to be increased in number, nor indeed followed, except where the one is exactly like the other.[27]

Even where a trust falls within the ambit of one of the anomalous exceptions, it will be void if it offends the rule against perpetual trusts because it might exceed the perpetuity period. Opinion differs as to the exact juridical status of the exceptions but they are probably best regarded as valid unenforceable trusts ('trusts of imperfect obligation').[28] As such, they are not void, but the trustees cannot be required to carry out the trust, though the court will prevent them from misapplying the trust property. In that respect, they operate rather like powers of appointment.

(a) Care of particular animals

A trust for the welfare of animals in general, or of a particular class of animals, will be charitable. A trust for the maintenance of a specific animal is not charitable but may be upheld as an anomalous exception to the beneficiary principle, provided that it does not offend against the perpetuity period. In *Pettingall v Pettingall*,[29] a gift by a testator of £50 per annum for the upkeep of his favourite black mare was upheld. In *Mitford v Reynolds*,[30] a gift for the upkeep of the testator's horses was upheld. In *Re Dean*[31] William Dean left his eight horses and his hounds to his trustees, and charged his freehold estates with an annuity of £750 per year for fifty years, if they should live that long, to be paid to the trustees for their upkeep. North J held that this was a valid non-charitable trust. However, he seemed to reject the 'beneficiary principle' entirely, stating that he did not assent to the view that a trust is not valid if there is no cestui que trust to enforce it.[32] Although *Re Dean*

[21] *Bowman v Secular Society* [1917] AC 406; *Re Diplock* [1941] Ch 253 at 259; *IRC v Broadway Cottages Trust* [1955] Ch 20, CA.

[22] [1960] Ch 232. [23] [1957] 1 WLR 729. [24] *Re Endacott* [1960] Ch 232 at 250.

[25] [1952] Ch 534 at 547. [26] [1960] Ch 232, CA. [27] [1960] Ch 232, CA at 250–1.

[28] See [1953] 17 Conv (NS) 46 (Sheridan); [1953] 6 CLP 151 (Marshall); [1970] 34 Conv (NS) 77 (Lovell); [1973] 37 Conv (NS) 420 (McKay); [1971] 87 LQR 31 (Harris); [1970] 40 MLR 397 (Gravells); [1977] 41 Conv (NS) 179 (Widdows).

[29] (1842) 11 LJ Ch 176 at 177. [30] [1848] 16 Sim 105. [31] [1889] 41 Ch D 552.

[32] [1889] 41 Ch D 552 at 556–7.

has been taken as authority for the upholding of trusts for the maintenance of particular animals, the reasoning is incompatible with the beneficiary principle.

Another difficulty with *Re Dean*[33] is that it seems to offend against the perpetuity period. A non-charitable trust must not last beyond the period of lives in being plus twenty-one years. In *Re Dean* the gift to the horses and hounds was for a maximum of fifty years, which exceeds the perpetuity period. One possible solution would be to measure the perpetuity period by reference to an animal life, but this was rejected by Meredith J in *Re Kelly*,[34] who said 'there can be no doubt that "lives" means lives of human beings, not of animals or trees in California'. In some cases the courts have taken judicial notice that an animal's lifespan is less than twenty-one years,[35] or that the particular animal has less than twenty-one years to live. Again, this approach was questioned in *Re Kelly*.[36] It would still leave problems with animals that clearly have a life expectancy beyond twenty-one years.

The most common circumstance in which a trust will be established for a particular animal is where a testator leaves property for the benefit of his favourite pet.[37] It should not be forgotten in such circumstances that the animal also constitutes property and ownership of it will also devolve on the testator's death. The new owner will have the prime responsibility to care for the animal, and failure of the trust does not necessarily mean that there is no one to care for the animal.

It must not be forgotten, either, that a gift to an individual with a statement that it is to be used for a particular purpose will often be treated as an absolute gift. The expression of the purpose is considered to be no more than the motive for the gift, imposing a moral obligation rather than a legally binding trust obligation.

(b) Maintenance of specific graves and monuments

Trusts to provide for the maintenance of specific graves and monuments have been upheld as valid and unenforceable despite the lack of a beneficiary who can enforce them.[38] In *Mitford v Reynolds*,[39] a gift for the erection of a monument was upheld as valid. In *Pirbright v Salwey*,[40] a gift of £800 for the upkeep of the burial enclosure of a child in a churchyard for 'as long as the law permitted' was upheld for at least twenty-one years from the testator's death. In *Re Hooper*[41] a testator left £1,000 to his executors to use the income for the upkeep of various family graves and monuments for 'so long as they legally can do so'. Following *Pirbright v Salwey*[42] Maugham J held that the trust was valid for twenty-one years from the testator's death. If the purpose exceeds the perpetuity period, the trust will be void. In *Mussett v Bingle*[43] a testator gave £300 for the erection of a monument and £200 to provide income for its upkeep. This second gift was held void for perpetuity.[44]

[33] [1889] 41 Ch D 552. [34] [1932] IR 255 at 260–1.

[35] See *Re Haines* [1952] *The Times*, 7 November, where Danckwerts J took judicial notice that a cat would not live for more than twenty-one years and upheld the gift.

[36] Meredith J: 'It was suggested that the last of the dogs could in fact not outlive the testator by more than twenty-one years. I know nothing of that. The court does not enter into the question of a dog's expectation of life. In point of fact neighbours' dogs and cats are unpleasantly long lived . . . '.

[37] See Brown, 'What Are We To Do with Testamentary Trusts of Imperfect Obligation?' [2007] Conv 148, where a survey of probate practitioners demonstrated that such trusts are still common, along with testamentary trusts for the maintenance of specific graves or monuments.

[38] See *Trimmer v Danby* (1856) 25 LJ Ch 424 (testator gave £1,000 to his executors to erect a monument to himself in St Paul's Cathedral).

[39] (1848) 16 Sim 105. [40] [1896] WN 86. [41] [1932] 1 Ch 38. [42] [1896] WN 86.

[43] [1876] WN 170.

[44] By s 1 of the Parish Councils and Burial Authorities (Miscellaneous Provisions) Act 1970, a burial authority may agree, for the payment of a sum, to maintain a grave or monument for a period not exceeding ninety-nine years.

This exception did not apply in *Re Endacott*, because no specific memorial was identified: 'some useful memorial' was too vague. Even though suitable projects like a bus shelter, a park bench, or public conveniences might come to mind, there was insufficient guidance to enable the trustees to direct the property to a specific project.

(c) Saying masses for the dead

According to Catholic theology, on death, the soul does not go direct to heaven but to purgatory, a place of punishment where unforgiven sins must be paid for before the soul can go to heaven. The saying of masses for the dead soul may reduce the length of time that must be spent in purgatory. Thus, testators may seek to leave money to provide for the saying of masses for the benefit of their own souls, or those of their relatives. The saying of masses for the dead was held to be a charitable activity for the advancement of religion in *Re Hetherington (Decd)*,[45] provided they are celebrated in public. Thus, a trust for the saying of masses may be valid as a charity. However, it is possible that a gift for the saying of masses in private will be a valid, unenforceable purpose trust even though it is not charitable. Such an approach is suggested by the decision of the House of Lords in *Bourne v Keane*.[46] Again, the duration of the gift must not exceed the perpetuity period.

The exception may also extend to the provision of other non-charitable rites. In *Re Khoo Cheng Teow*,[47] a gift for the performance of ceremonies called Sin Chew to perpetuate the testator's memory during the perpetuity period was upheld by the Supreme Court of the Straits settlement.

(3) Policy limitations on purpose trusts

Even if a purpose trust falls within the anomalous exceptions, it appears that it will be invalid if it is for capricious or useless purposes. In *Brown v Burdett*,[48] a trust to block up all the rooms of a house for twenty years was held void. The Scottish courts have been astute to hold that trusts for useless purposes are invalid on grounds of public policy. In *M'Caig v University of Glasgow*,[49] a trust to erect statues of the testator and 'artistic towers' on his estates was set aside. In *M'Caig's Trustees v Kirk-Session of United Free Church of Lismore*,[50] a trust to erect bronze statues of the testatrix's parents and their children was void on grounds of public policy, since it involved 'a sheer waste of money'.[51]

(4) Purposes that benefit an identifiable class

Whilst a non-charitable purpose trust will generally be void unless it falls within the limited categories of the anomalous exceptions, a trust will not be void merely because it is expressed to be for the carrying out of a purpose if it will in fact benefit identifiable individuals who possess sufficient locus standi to enforce it. For instance, it is unquestioned that a trust to pay for a child's education is valid. The central question is whether the carrying out of the specified purpose directly or indirectly benefits an ascertainable and certain group of individuals.

[45] [1990] Ch 1. [46] [1919] AC 815; see also *Re Hetherington (Decd)* [1989] 2 All ER 129 at 132.
[47] [1932] Straits Settlements LR 226. [48] (1882) 21 Ch D 667. [49] 1907 SC 231.
[50] 1915 SC 426.
[51] Per Lord Salvesen. Other cases include *Aitken's Trustees v Aitken* 1927 SC 374 (erection of a massive bronze equestrian statue); *Lindsay's Executor v Forsyth* 1940 SC 568 (£1,000 on trust to provide weekly supply of flowers to own and mother's graves).

(a) The rule in *Re Denley's Trust Deed*

In *Re Denley's Trust Deed*,[52] the court upheld a gift that appeared to establish a purpose trust. Charles Denley had transferred land to trustees to be maintained and used as a sports field for the employees of a company. Goff J took the view that, although the trust was expressed to be for a purpose, it was in fact for the benefit of individuals (the employees of the company) because they would benefit, directly or indirectly, from the carrying out of the purpose. As such, it was outside the mischief of the beneficiary principle.[53] Since the employees were an ascertainable and certain class, they had locus standi to apply to the court to enforce the trust. He emphasized that the employees gained a direct benefit from the carrying out of the purposes, and warned that if the benefit was not so direct or intangible, the beneficiary principle would invalidate the trust.[54] The trust was, therefore, upheld because the court could act to enforce it at the suit of the beneficiaries, either negatively by restraining any improper disposition or use of the land or positively by ordering the trustees to allow the employees to use the land for recreation.[55]

Although the decision prevents the trust falling foul of the beneficiary principle by finding that the employees can enforce the trust, it does not answer the problem of the beneficial ownership of the land. Do the trustees hold the land on trust for the employees? If so, the employees could together demand the transfer of the land to them under the principle of *Saunders v Vautier*,[56] for example, if they wanted to sell it to a supermarket for a lucrative development. If that were the case, it would defeat the settlor's intention in establishing the trust. The only other logical conclusion from the decision is that the beneficial interest is suspended for the duration of the trust, which must be limited to the perpetuity period.

(b) Application of the principle to an unincorporated association

Re Denley's Trust Deed was applied in slightly different circumstances by Oliver J in *Re Lipinski's Will Trusts*.[57] Harry Lipinski left his residuary estate to the Hull Judeans (Maccabi) Association in memory of his wife, to be used solely in constructing new buildings for the association. As the gift was made to an unincorporated association, it would normally be treated as a gift to the individual members of the association.[58] However, it would be difficult to construe a gift for a purpose as a gift to the individual members. Oliver J adopted *Re Denley's Trust Deed* with approval, and concluded that although this gift was expressed as a gift for a purpose (the new buildings), it was directly for the benefit of the members of the association and could be construed as a gift to them as individuals. He summarized the principle of the case:

> A trust which, though expressed as a purpose, was directly or indirectly for the benefit of an individual or individuals was valid provided those individuals were ascertainable at any one time and the trust was not otherwise void for uncertainty.[59]

In conclusion, this means that although a gift may be expressed as a gift to a purpose, the court can find that it is really a gift for the benefit of individuals if there is a certain and ascertainable class who will benefit sufficiently directly from its performance. Provided it is not void for perpetuity, it will be upheld.

[52] [1969] 1 Ch 373. For comment on Re Denley's Trust Deed see Jaconelli, 'Independent Schools, Purpose Trusts and Human Rights' [1996] Conv 24; Matthews, 'The New Trust: Obligations without Rights' in Oakley, Trends in Contemporary Trust Law (Oxford University Press 1997), pp 13–15.

[53] [1969] 1 Ch 373 at 383–4. [54] [1969] 1 Ch 373 at 383. [55] [1969] 1 Ch 373 at 388.

[56] [1841] 4 Beav 115. [57] [1976] Ch 235. [58] See Chapter 16. [59] [1976] Ch 235 at 248.

(c) Administratively unworkable class

The principle in *Re Denley's Trust Deed* will not apply if the class of beneficiaries is administratively unworkable through being too wide to form anything like a class. In *R v District Auditor, ex p West Yorkshire Metropolitan County Council*,[60] a trust was established to assist economic development, youth, and community projects and encourage ethnic and minority groups for 'the benefit of all or any or some of the inhabitants of West Yorkshire'. It was held invalid as a private purpose trust, and it could not be upheld on the basis of the *Denley* principle. This is because there were no 'ascertained or ascertainable beneficiaries', as the court had also held that with some 2.5 million potential beneficiaries, the trust was administratively unworkable.[61]

(5) Criticism of the beneficiary principle

The central reason for the beneficiary principle is that if a trust does not have beneficiaries then the court will not be able to enforce and supervise it. As Roxburgh J said in *Re Astor's Settlement Trusts*:

> a court of equity does not recognise as valid a trust which it cannot both enforce and control.[62]

Where there is no beneficiary, there is no one in whose favour the court can order performance. There is also no one who is interested in the performance of the trust to apply to the court if the obligation is not being appropriately performed. The court relies on the self-interest of beneficiaries to police trusts and bring any wrongdoing on the part of the trustees to their attention.

However, the force of these objections may have been overstated.[63] Where a trust is made for a purpose, there is always someone who will be entitled to the property in default if the purpose is not carried out,[64] whether the residuary legatee under a will or the owner of the property himself under a resulting trust. Such a person would have sufficient interest to apply to the court if the property were being misapplied by the trustee. This would provide a potential mechanism for control and enforcement.[65] Roxburgh J noted in *Re Astor's Settlement Trusts* that in many of the cases of exceptions to the beneficiary principle there was a residuary legatee who would be able to ensure that the purpose was carried out.[66] Such a mechanism for enforcement seems to have been applied in *Re Thompson*.[67] The testator bequeathed £1,000 to his friend, George Lloyd, to be applied for the promotion of fox hunting.[68] The residuary legatee under the will was Trinity Hall, University of Cambridge. Clauson J ordered that the executors pay the money to Lloyd, on his giving an undertaking that he would so apply the money. Trinity Hall would be at liberty to apply to the court if the property was misapplied. Although this seems to offer a way of avoiding

60 [1986] RVR 24.

61 See Harpum, 'Administrative Unworkability and Purpose Trusts' [1986] 45 CLJ 391.

62 [1952] Ch 534 at 549.

63 See Hayton, 'Developing the Obligation Characteristic of the Trust' [2001] 117 LQR 96.

64 Although that person will not always be immediately ascertainable, as where the residuary beneficiary is whoever happens to be the Vice-Chancellor of the University of Buckingham twenty-one years from the death of the testator.

65 See Brown, 'What are We to Do with Testamentary Trusts of Imperfect Obligation?' [2007] Conv 148 at 159–60.

66 *Pettingall v Pettingall* [1842] 11 LJ Ch 176; *Mitford v Reynolds* [1848] 16 Sim 105; *Re Dean* [1889] 41 Ch D 552; *Re Hooper* [1932] 1 Ch 38; *Pirbright v Salwey* [1896] WN 86. See also *Re Astor's Settlement Trusts* [1952] Ch 534 at 542–5.

67 [1934] Ch 342.

68 Such a gift could no longer be upheld, as fox hunting with hounds is now illegal, following the Hunting Act 2004.

the beneficiary principle, the case is of limited value. The case was uncontested, and both parties wanted to see the gift upheld. The court only granted the order that they together requested. The result would have been different if the residuary legatee had not wanted to see the purpose performed, but had wanted to see the gift fail so that they would receive the £1,000 as part of the residue.

The problem with this mechanism for enforcement is that in most cases the residuary legatees are the very people who will benefit if the purpose is not carried out and, therefore, have no incentive to ensure that the testator's wishes are followed. In fact, in most cases they are actively challenging the validity of the purpose trust because they will be entitled to the property in default. This mechanism for enforcement would only be able to ensure that the property was not misapplied, but would not be able to ensure that the trustee carried out his duty to perform the trust.

In the light of these difficulties, other jurisdictions have introduced statutory schemes that facilitate the enforcement of non-charitable purposes trusts.[69] The essence of many such schemes is the introduction of a third party 'enforcer' who is empowered to act to ensure that the trustees carry out their duties. For example, under the Cayman Islands Special Trusts (Alternative Regime) Law 1997,[70] the 'enforcer' of a trust, who may not himself enjoy any interest in the trust property, is granted 'the same personal and proprietary remedies against the trustee and against third parties as a beneficiary of an ordinary trust'.[71] The enforcer therefore performs a similar function to that of the Crown in relation to the oversight and enforcement of charitable trusts. Whilst such regimes have been adopted in many offshore jurisdictions,[72] no equivalent has yet been adopted in England.[73]

(6) **The beneficiary principle and certainty of objects**

There is a very close relationship between the beneficiary principle and the requirement that the objects of a trust must be certain. In both cases, the requirement follows from the fact that the court must be able to supervise and enforce the operation of the trust. It is possible to re-analyse the cases that have offended against the beneficiary principle as cases of uncertainty. Where the purpose is so uncertain that the court could not properly supervise or enforce its execution, then it will not be valid. If the purpose is sufficiently certain and its performance is capable of judicial scrutiny, then it should be valid and upheld.

In *Re Thompson*[74] Clauson J emphasized that the purpose was 'defined with sufficient clearness and is of a nature to which effect can be given'.[75] Similarly, the anomalous exceptions that have been recognized are all sufficiently certain to enable a court to determine whether the property is being applied to the purpose specified. The court can objectively assess whether specified graves are being maintained, animals cared for, or masses said. In contrast, *Re Astor's Settlement Trusts*,[76] *Re Shaw*,[77] and *Re Endacott*[78] are all explicable on

[69] For example, Jersey, Bermuda, Isle of Man, Cayman Islands, and British Virgin Islands.

[70] See Duckworth, STAR Trusts (1998).

[71] s 7(1).

[72] Note also that the Ontario Perpetuities Act 1966 enacts that trusts for non-charitable purposes should be construed as powers, thus overcoming the beneficiary principle, and that the US Uniform Trust Code permits purpose trusts for twenty-one years.

[73] See Pawlowski and Summers, 'Private Purpose Trusts—A Reform Proposal' [2007] Conv 440, advocating proposals for statutory reform of private purpose trusts along similar lines to those found in the offshore jurisdictions listed.

[74] [1934] Ch 342. [75] [1934] Ch 342 at 344. [76] [1952] Ch 534.

[77] [1957] 1 WLR 729. [78] [1960] Ch 232.

the basis of uncertainty. It would have been impossible for the court to scrutinize whether the trust property was being applied to the 'maintenance of good understanding between nations', or 'the preservation of the independence and the integrity of newspapers', because these concepts are themselves uncertain.[79] Similarly, a trust to provide 'some useful memorial to myself' is unenforceable because it is uncertain.[80] How would the court be able to decide whether the terms of the trust had been carried out?

Although this analysis on the basis of certainty is attractive, and would eliminate the beneficiary principle as an independent requirement, it is not supported by present authority. Uncertainty was a secondary ground for the decision in *Re Astor's Settlement Trusts*[81] and the objection that there were no beneficiaries was treated separately. In *Re Endacott* Lord Evershed MR made absolutely clear that there was a separate 'beneficiary principle':

> No principle perhaps has greater sanction or authority behind it than the general proposition that a trust by English law, not being a charitable trust, in order to be effective must have ascertained or ascertainable beneficiaries.[82]

(7) 'Red Cross' Trusts

Whatever the position in England, certain offshore jurisdictions have pushed the link between certainty and the beneficiary principle to the very limts.[83] Lionel Smith criticizes a type of trust existing in other jurisdictions which contains only 'massively discretionary' powers and a so-called 'residuary beneficiary', which will be charity.[84] It is because they have a charity as the residuary beneficiary, that they are sometimes called 'Red Cross' Trusts. In the arrangement, the charitable residuary beneficiary would receive the trust property only in the unlikely circumstance that the objects of the power were to die. It is clear that such a trust challenges the traditional understanding of legal certainty and the beneficiary principle. There is no certain private beneficiary at all, just a charitable organization, serving broad charitable purposes, that has only limited rights to the trust property.

Smith suggests that the motivation behind creating this type of massively discretionary arrangement is perhaps to make it difficult to tax the trust property.[85] If it is not clear how the powers are to be exercised, then taxable ownership is difficult to establish. Similarly, the arrangement, being built around discretionary powers, makes it difficult to divide property between cohabiting couples who separate. Again, this is because it is not certain who owns the trust property. Whatever the financial motivations behind them, these trusts cannot be thought to be conceptually satisfactory. Within the arrangement, there might be no single beneficiary with a strict legal right to benefit from, or to enforce, the massively discretionary trust at all. By design, they are a way to sidestep the beneficiary principle.

5 Charitable and benevolent giving

Although purpose trusts are not as a general rule valid, it is often the case that owners wish to allocate their property to purposes rather than to specific individuals. This is particularly so when owners want to support causes that they consider to be worthy. The law

[79] See [1952] Ch 534 at 548.

[80] [1960] Ch 232 at 247, per Lord Evershed MR: 'though this trust is specific, in the sense that it indicates a purpose capable of expression, yet it is of far too wide and uncertain a nature . . . '.

[81] [1952] Ch 534. [82] [1960] Ch 232 at 246.

[83] See *Tasarruf Mevduati Sigorta Fonu v Merrill Lynch Bank and Trust Company (Cayman) Ltd* [2011] UKPC 17.

[84] Smith, 'Massively Discretionary Trusts' (2019) 25 Trusts and Trustees 397.

[85] Ibid 408.

provides that certain purposes are charitable and gifts and trusts for these purposes are valid, even though there are no beneficiaries as such. The purposes considered charitable are those that have come to be recognized as for the 'public good', and which are now listed in s 3 of the Charities Act 2011.

Charitable trusts not only are valid but also enjoy extensive financial support through government grants and tax exemptions, as explored in Chapter 19. The state provides a mechanism by which they can be enforced and supervised, thus preventing their invalidity under the beneficiary principle. They are enforced by the Attorney General or Charity Commission in the name of the Crown. The general administration of charities is supervised by the Charity Commission. All this state support of purpose trusts is provided in the interests of encouraging giving to worthy causes.

6 The duty to act even-handedly

(1) A general duty

Where a trust has been created for the benefit of multiple beneficiaries, the trustees who have the task of allocating the property have a duty to act even-handedly between them, so that they are all treated impartially and no favouritism is shown to one beneficiary or category of beneficiaries. In *Lloyds Bank plc v Duker*,[86] John Mowbray QC stated that there was a general principle that:

> trustees are bound to hold an even hand among their beneficiaries and not to favour one as against another.[87]

This clearly means that a trustee must not be partisan to the interests of one beneficiary at the expense of others.[88] The Law Reform Committee in its 23rd Report[89] recommended that trustees be under a statutory duty to hold a fair balance between beneficiaries.[90]

The need to maintain even-handedness between beneficiaries is a fiduciary duty which operates particularly acutely in two contexts: first, in the context of discretionary trusts where the trustee is entitled to decide how the trust property should be allocated among the class of beneficiaries; and, second, where a trust creates successive interests so that a life tenant is to enjoy the income generated by the trust property for his lifetime, but the person entitled to the remainder interest will receive the capital of the fund on his death.

(2) The duty to act even-handedly and discretionary trusts

The trustees' duty to act even-handedly in the context of a discretionary trust was examined by the Court of Appeal in *Edge v Pensions Ombudsman*.[91] The case concerned a decision by the trustees of a pension scheme to increase the benefits payable to members in service on a particular date. Pensioners who had been in service prior to this date complained to the ombudsman that the changes in the rules introduced were unjust. At first instance, Scott V-C concluded that the trustees were under a duty to act impartially between the different beneficiaries, and that they had acted with 'undue partiality' towards those preferred by the rule change. He rejected any notion of a general duty to act impartially in the context of a discretionary trust, as the very essence of the trust is that the trustees select some to benefit from the wider class of potential beneficiaries. Instead,

[86] [1987] 1 WLR 1324.
[87] [1987] 1 WLR 1324 at 1330–1, citing *Snell's Principles of Equity* (28th edn, Sweet & Maxwell 1982), p 225.
[88] See *Simpson v Bathurst* [1869] 5 Ch App 193 at 202. [89] Cmnd 8733.
[90] Cmnd 8733 at para 3.36. [91] [2000] Ch 602.

he held that the trustees were under a duty not to take into account irrelevant, irrational, or improper factors. Chadwick LJ, delivering the opinion of the Court of Appeal, cited Scott V-C's words with approval and agreed that the trustees had properly exercised their discretion and had in fact considered the position of those pensioners who would not benefit. The Pensions Ombudsman and the court had no right to interfere in the proper exercise of a discretionary trust. He concluded:

> Properly understood, the so-called duty to act impartially . . . is no more than the ordinary duty which the law imposes on a person who is entrusted with the exercise of a discretionary power: that he exercises the power for the purpose for which it is given, giving proper consideration to the matters which are relevant and excluding from consideration matters which are irrelevant. If pension fund trustees do that, they cannot be criticised if they reach a decision which appears to prefer the claims of one interest—whether that of employers, current employees or pensioners—over others. The preference will be the result of a proper exercise of the discretionary power.[92]

(3) The duty to act even-handedly and successive interests

Where property is subject to a life interest behind a trust it is important to ensure that both the life tenant and those entitled to the remainder receive a fair share of the fruits of the trust fund, and that the fund is not invested and allocated in such a way that income is generated at the expense of the preservation of the capital, or that the capital is preserved but no income is generated. Equity has tackled this problem by means of rules designed to ensure that the trust fund is invested in such investments as by their very nature will operate fairly in producing income whilst preserving capital. These rules have become known as rules of apportionment and have been subject to considerable reform through the enactment of the Trusts (Capital and Income) Act 2013. It is still important to appreciate the existing equitable rules, as they apply to trusts already in existence before the passing of the 2013 Act, and may survive the legislative reforms by express incorporation of the rules into the trust instrument in trusts arising after the 2013 Act.

(a) The duty to convert investments

As will be seen in Chapter 31, the trustees may be under a duty to convert unauthorized investments (i.e. to sell and reinvest the property). This duty may be expressly imposed in the trust instrument[93] or, in the case of a residuary bequest in a will in a trust arising before 1 October 2013,[94] implied[95] under the rule in *Howe v Earl of Dartmouth*.[96] This rule, which was abolished for new trusts by the Trusts (Capital and Income) Act 2013,[97] required trustees to sell unauthorized investments and reinvest the proceeds. This rule could operate to balance the interests of beneficiaries. For example, if the trust fund consistsed of wasting assets, for example copyrights,[98] the consequence of retaining them would be that they would generate a large income for the life tenant, but would be of rapidly depreciating capital value, leaving perhaps little or nothing for the remainderman. Even if the rule in *Howe v Lord Dartmouth* had not been abolished, the introduction by

[92] [2000] Ch 602 at 627. [93] Trusts (Capital and Income) Act 2013, s 1(4).

[94] The commencement date of the Trusts (Capital and Income) Act 2013.

[95] Unless it is excluded by contrary intention of the testator: *Hinves v Hinves* [1844] 3 Hare 609; *Re Pitcairn* [1896] 2 Ch 199.

[96] [1802] 7 Ves Jr 137.

[97] Implementing a recommendation of the Law Commission: Capital and Income in Trusts: Classification and Apportionment (Law Com No 315, 2009), para 6.65.

[98] *Re Sullivan* [1930] 1 Ch 84.

the Trustee Act 2000 of a general power of trustees to invest as if absolutely entitled to the assets of the trust would have significantly restricted the operation of the rule.[99]

(b) Apportionment between income and capital

If trust funds are properly invested, the life tenant receives the income, and the capital is retained for the remainderman. If the trustees are subject to a duty to convert the trust property, any delay in making the conversion of a non-income-producing asset might deprive the life tenant of some of the income, or the remainderman of some of the capital in the converse situation. For this reason, equity used to intervene to apportion the price received for an unauthorized investment between income and capital. Those rules no longer apply to trusts created after 1 October 2013, so-called 'new trusts', unless they are expressly incorporated into the trust instrument.

The exact application of the equitable rules depended upon the type of property that was converted. The basic position at equity was that when unauthorized investments were converted, the life tenant was entitled to receive the income that he would have received if they had been authorized investments all along. Rules emerged to define the level of income, and the date on which the property was to be valued.[100]

The equitable rules governing apportionment were criticized on the grounds that they were rigid, technical, and outdated.[101] They were generally excluded in professionally drafted trust instruments and required very complex calculations affecting small amounts of money. The rate of interest used to calculate the respective allocations to income or capital would now be seen as arbitrary. The Law Commission recommended the abolition of all existing equitable rules of apportionment in all new trusts, subject to any contrary provision in the trust instrument.[102] This has since been enacted,[103] and the sale and reinvestment of trust property now forms part of a trustee's general investment duties under the Trustee Act 2000.

(c) Corporate receipts received as a 'windfall' by the trust

Problems of allocation between the life tenant and remainderman may arise if the trust receives a 'windfall' because of the assets held. This is particularly the case when the trust holds shares in a company which either makes cash payments to shareholders as a 'capital profits dividend', capitalizes its profits, and issues bonus or scrip dividend shares to the existing shareholders, or demerges and gives shares in the new company to the original shareholders.[104] The question arises whether these payments or shares should be allocated to capital or income. Whether a sum received by trustees constitutes capital or income for the purpose of distribution between beneficiaries is not necessarily the same as what constitutes capital or income for tax purposes. For instance a scrip dividend (payment of a dividend by means of the allocation of new shares) could be taxable as deemed income under the relevant tax legislation, even if it is treated as capital for trust purposes.[105] The trust instrument may expressly confer on trustees a discretion as to how they are to apportion receipts between capital and income, but there are some 'rules of thumb' where there is no such discretion. For instance, in the event of a company liquidation, all payments to the trustees who hold shares are regarded as capital.[106]

[99] Capital and Income in Trusts: Classification and Apportionment (Law Com CP No 175, 2004), para 3.8.

[100] For further information about these, see previous editions of this book.

[101] Capital and Income in Trusts: Classification and Apportionment (Law Com No 315, 2009), para A.6.

[102] Ibid, paras 6.54–6.65 and cl 1(2)(a)–(2b) (*Howe v Earl of Dartmouth* rules) and cl 1(3) (*Re Earl of Chesterfield's Trusts* rule).

[103] Trusts (Capital and Income) Act 2013, s 1(1) (removing general equitable rules), s 1(2)(b) (removing the rule in *Re Earl of Chesterfield's Trusts*).

[104] See *Sinclair v Lee* [1993] Ch 497.

[105] *Gilchrist v HMRC* [2014] 4 All ER 943 (UT).

[106] *Re Armitage* [1893] 3 Ch 337; *IRC v Burrell* [1924] 2 KB 52.

(i) Cash payments

If a company decided to distribute some form of cash bonuses to shareholders, any payments received by trustees who hold shares as part of trust assets are to be regarded as income and, therefore, allocated to the life tenant. In *Re Bates*[107] a company distributed cash bonuses to shareholders after selling some vessels at prices exceeding their value in the company balance sheets. Eve J held that the life tenant of a trust holding shares in the company was entitled to receive the entire payment as income.[108]

(ii) Bonus shares

If the company decides to capitalize its profits and issue bonus shares to the present shareholders and they are received by the trustees, then they are to hold them as part of the capital of the trust. This was so held by the House of Lords in *Bouch v Sproule*,[109] where it was emphasized that the decision whether to distribute cash or to capitalize was for the company alone. The result would no doubt be different if the trustees were entitled to elect to take a dividend either in cash or in the form of additional shares.[110]

(iii) Demergers

A demerger is a process of company restructuring, where an enterprise is split into different components. The allocation between capital and income where a company demerges is complex, and a distinction may be drawn between a direct and an indirect demerger. A direct demerger occurs where the original company allocates the shares in the new company to its shareholders. In such cases the HMRC views the shares distributed as income. An indirect demerger occurs where the new company allocates its own shares to the shareholders of the original company. In *Sinclair v Lee*,[111] it was held that new shares were to be treated as capital assets.

(iv) Reform of the allocation of corporate receipts

The distinction between indirect and direct demergers is of considerable artificiality, and on that basis the state of the case law is open to criticism. Cases of substantive importance ought not to turn on fine distinctions. For this reason, the Law Commission also sought to address this issue. It considered that the law regarding the classification of corporate receipts as capital or income did not rest on principle, and failed to deliver either certainty or fairness. The Law Commission would have liked to propose an abolition of the existing rules and the introduction of a more appropriate regime allowing more flexible treatment of trust receipts, but it felt it was constrained from doing so by the tax implications of these changes.[112] It therefore proposed only that the distinction between direct and indirect demergers should be abolished, a measure which would be tax-neutral. This has been adopted, so that income from either set of demerger is now classed as capital under s 2(1) of the Trusts (Capital and Income) Act 2013 in all trusts, whether created before or after the commencement of the Act.[113] Like the other reforms under this Act, the original equitable rules may be expressly incorporated within the trust instrument.[114] The Act also provides the trustees with the power to make a compensatory payment out of the capital where a beneficiary has been prejudicially affected by the classification of the income as a capital sum.[115]

[107] [1928] Ch 682. [108] See also *Re Whitehead's Will Trusts* [1959] Ch 579.

[109] [1887] 12 App Cas 385.

[110] For the treatment of scrip dividend shares, see *Pierce v Wood* [2009] EWHC 3225 (Ch).

[111] [1993] Ch 497.

[112] Capital and Income in Trusts: Classification and Apportionment (Law Com No 315, 2009), para 5.83.

[113] Trusts (Capital and Income) Act 2013, s 2(5). [114] Ibid, s 2(2). [115] Ibid, s 3.

25
Fixed trusts

1 Introduction

In Chapter 24, we noted that the equitable mechanisms of fixed and discretionary trusts and powers of appointment allow a settlor to choose who benefits from a trust fund, or to delegate the power to choose. This chapter looks in detail at the first of these mechanisms, the fixed trust.

2 Nature of a fixed trust

In a fixed trust the interests of the beneficiaries have already been defined by the settlor. The trustee must carry out those terms and distribute the fund as has been specified.

(1) Example of fixed trusts

If Dae leaves 10,000 shares in a public company to Eui on trust for his three children, Jade, Feng, and Hiromi, in equal shares, Eui has no discretion as to how the fund is to be allocated as the beneficial interests of the three children have already been defined by Dae. They will each have an immediate beneficial entitlement to a third of the fund (see Figure 25.1). It is Eui's duty to allocate them their respective shares. If Dae provides that the children should take in unequal proportions, for example, that Jade should be entitled to 5,000 shares, and the others 2,500 each, Eui would have to allocate in those defined shares.

(2) Fixed trusts in favour of a class

The interests granted under a fixed trust may also be specified by means of a class definition rather than by listing each individual who is intended to benefit. Instead of naming Jade, Feng, and Hiromi as beneficiaries, Dae could have left the shares to Eui 'on trust for such of my children who survive me', or alternatively 'to all the present employees at the date of my death' of a particular company. The presumption would be that the members of the class would take the property in equal shares. If such a class definition is used, the trust will only be valid if the objects of the trust are sufficiently certain to enable the trustee, or if necessary, the court, to carry out the trust. The trust must, in addition, be administratively workable.

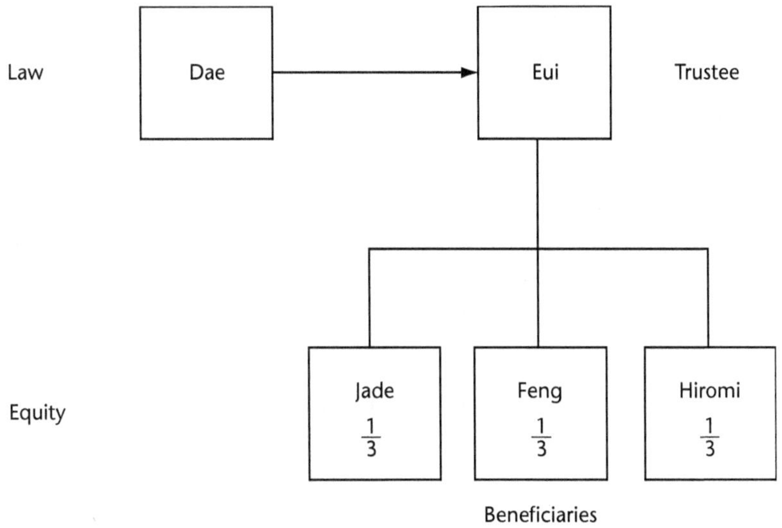

Figure 25.1 Example of fixed trusts

3 Uses of fixed trusts

(1) Bare trusts

A bare trust is a form of fixed trust 'where property is vested in one person on trust for another where there are no active duties arising from the status of trustee'.[1]

The trustee acts exclusively at the direction of the beneficiary, who is able to demand the legal title to be conveyed to him at any time under the principle of *Saunders v Vautier*.[2] The trustee is, in effect, the nominee of the beneficiary and acts at his direction. For example, in *Vandervell v IRC*[3] the National Provincial Bank held stock in Vandervell Products Ltd for Mr Vandervell. This was a bare trust, and the bank was acting as his nominee. It was obliged to follow his directions, and thus when he asked them to complete a share transfer form to enable him to transfer the shares to the Royal College of Surgeons, they acted at his request.

In many cases the trust will be little more than a 'front' for the real beneficial owner,[4] as in *Prest v Petrodel Resources Ltd*.[5] In this case the Supreme Court held that although a company was the legal owner of a number of houses, it held these on resulting trust for the oil trader who had financed their purchase or transferred the houses to the companies. The case is very important in the context of company law because it allows the court to look beyond the face of the transaction at the reality without having to invoke the contentious doctrine of lifting the corporate veil.[6] In *Hardoon v Belilios*,[7] shares were acquired by a firm of stockbrokers in the name of one of their employees. The same result can arise even if the parties are unaware that their arrangement has created a trust. In *Pennington*

[1] *Clutterbuck v Al Amoudi* [2014] EWHC 383 (Ch) at 458 (Asplin J).

[2] [1841] 4 Beav 115.

[3] [1967] 2 AC 291, HL.

[4] See *Young v Young* [2013] EWHC 3637 (Fam) at 24.

[5] [2013] UKSC 34.

[6] See *Antonio Gramsci Shipping v Lembergs* [2013] EWCA (Civ) 730.

[7] [1901] AC 118. See also *Sainsbury Plc v O'Connor (Inspector of Taxes)* [1991] 1 WLR 963 at 969; *Arrow Nomineees Inc v Blackledge* [2000] 1 BCLC 709.

v Waine (No 1),[8] the Court of Appeal held that a completed share transfer form, although never submitted to the company for registration, was nevertheless effective as an equitable assignment under which the transferor became a bare trustee for the transferee. Another illustration is provided by *Pleshakov v Sky Stream*,[9] where the Privy Council reinstated the first instance decision of Bannister J in the British Virgin Islands that beneficial ownership of shares in a company (Sky Stream) was held on bare trust for Mr Pleshakov. The company has been incorporated for the purpose of receiving a 19.9 per cent share in a Russian airline. Though no express trust had been declared, Bannister J had reached his conclusion by drawing inferences from the conduct of the respondents both at the time of the company's formation and conduct subsequent to formation that a trust had been intended. The Court of Appeal had reversed that decision, principally on the basis that there was no oral contract agreed between the respondants and Mr Pleshakov to hold the shares on trust. Lord Sales confirmed that all that was needed for a valid trust of shares was the three certainties, and there was no need for an oral contract to create a trust, as certainty of intention could be inferred from conduct.[10]

(2) **Nominee trusts**

A bare trust works by the legal title being vested in a trustee, but with the beneficiary being entitled to beneficial ownership. As just explained, this means that the name of the beneficiary can be kept concealed behind the trust. This type of trust is often called a nominee trust or a holding trust.

Nominee trusts have proved useful for share ownership. One of the methods allowing shares to be held in dematerialized form is for the shares to be held by a trustee as a nominee. The purchaser becomes the beneficial owner of the shares, but the trustee is registered in the company share register as a nominee for the beneficiary. Dealings with the shares are conducted by the nominee on the footing of directions given by the beneficiary (also called the principal). The appointment of nominees by trustees is expressly sanctioned by the Trustee Act 2000.[11]

The obligations of the nominee trustee will depend upon what was agreed when the relationship was established and as recorded in the trust instrument. In the usual case, the obligation of the nominees will be to act upon the instructions of the principal: the nominees, therefore, have no independent right to deal with the property, for instance, by sale and reinvestment, and 'failure to deal with the property in the way instructed amounts to a breach of trust.'[12] As legal owners the nominees must execute any dealings with the legal title and will also normally be entitled to receive any income generated by the trust property. This does not mean, however, that the nominees are free to deal with the proceeds of the assets in any way they choose. The nominees hold the property on behalf of the principal, and must, therefore, deal with it for the principal's benefit. They must account to the principal both for the original property and for any income or capital derived from it. Nominees, therefore, like Janus,[13] face two ways. As between themselves and the principal, it would not be misleading to describe the principal as the owner. It is he who will benefit from any gain (or bear any loss) in the value of the property. It is he who is entitled to the capital value of the assets, and to any income or revenue they

[8] [2002] EWCA Civ 227, [2002] 1 WLR 2075. [9] [2021] UKPC 15.

[10] [2021] UKPC 15 at [47]–[48]. [11] Trustee Act 2000, s 16(1).

[12] *Clutterbuck v Al Amoudi* [2014] EWHC 383 (Ch) at 458 (Asplin J). However, trustees cannot be required to act in a way which would be unlawful:, for instance in breach of the terms of a lease which they hold on bare trust: *Clarence House Ltd v National Westminster Bank plc* [2009] EWCA Civ 1311 at 45.

[13] Janus was the god of Gates in Ancient Greek mythology. He is usually depicated as having two faces, to show transitioning between what was and what is yet to come.

produce. He may also transfer or otherwise deal with his equitable interest. This is, however, only one face of the nominees. As between the nominees and the outside world, it is the nominees who are, to most intents and purposes, the owners.

In some exceptional cases, the beneficiaries may be able to bring actions directly. Under Part 22 of the Companies Act 2006, companies have rights to seek information about interests in shares held by a nominee, and, with the approval of the court, to impose restrictions on the transfer or use of those shares. In *Eclairs Group Ltd v JKX Oil & Gas plc*,[14] the Court of Appeal held that the beneficial owner of shares held by a nominee had locus standi to apply to court to prevent a company exercising similar powers granted by the articles of association, and which did not require a court order to permit the imposition of restrictions on the shares.

(3) **Custodian trusts**

A special form of holding trust displaying greater complexity than a nominee arrangement is a custodian trust. Whereas with a nominee arrangement the nominee normally holds a single asset or a single class of assets, the function of custodian trustees is to hold all the assets of the trust. The effect is to separate the legal ownership and custody of the trust assets from the function of managing those assets. The *custodian trustees* hold the assets to the order of other *management trustees* who have the powers of management (see Figure 25.2). The custodian trustees hold the legal title to the trust assets, but the management trustees make all the decisions relating to the administration of the trusts. This structure is used for the administration of unit trusts and many pension schemes.[15]

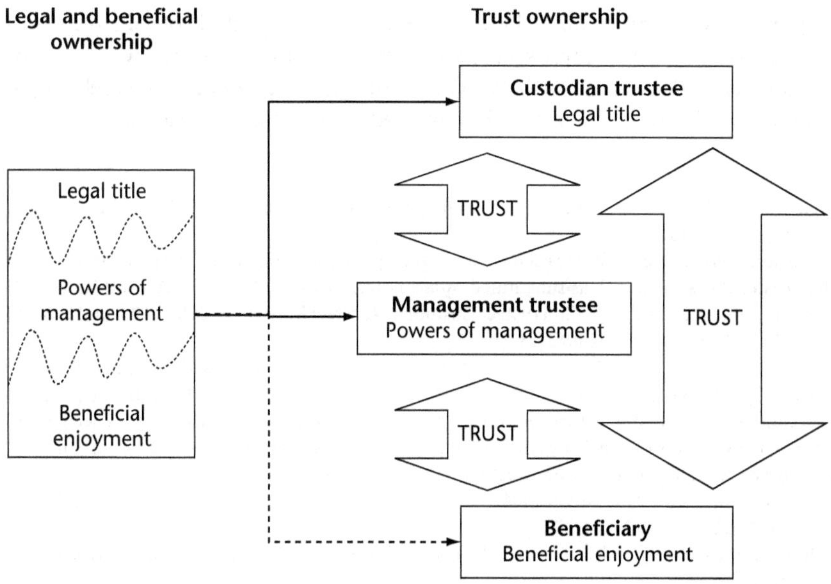

Figure 25.2 Separating management and custody by a trust

[14] [2014] 4 All ER 463.

[15] See, for instance, *British Airways Pension Trustees Ltd v British Airways Plc* [2001] EWHC Ch 13, where Lloyd J was asked in litigation between the custodian trustees and the management trustees to resolve doubts and disagreements concerning the construction of the Airways Pension Scheme.

One advantage of a custodian trust is that the management trustees can be changed without the need to transfer all the trust property from the old trustees to the new.[16] Only the Public Trustee, the Official Custodian for Charities, and trust corporations[17] are authorized by statute to act as custodian trustees,[18] but there is no reason why a custodian trust should not be established where this is expressly permitted by the terms of the documents establishing a trust.[19] A sports club, for instance, may have taken the lease of a sports field and clubhouse in the names of up to four trustees. The trustees can hold that land upon trust to deal with in accordance with the directions of the club committee. There is no need to change the trustees every time the composition of the committee changes.

Trustees appointed as custodian trustees under the statutory scheme[20] are obliged to follow the instructions of the management trustees, except where to do so would amount to concurring in a breach of trust.[21] Bare trustees may not even have this freedom, for the terms of their appointment might require them to act upon any instruction of the principal.[22] Trustees appointed as custodian trustees without using the statutory scheme will not enjoy the statutory protection afforded to statutory custodian trustees, and they must use their own judgement in deciding whether to follow instructions given to them.[23] Where, however, the terms of the trust are so tightly drawn as to leave no scope for the exercise by them of their own judgement, it will not be a breach of trust for the trustees to follow binding instructions, even if the transaction would otherwise have been imprudent and so a breach of trust.[24]

(4) **Non-trustee custodians**

The Trustee Act 2000 permits the appointment of custodians by trustees.[25] Their function is to undertake safe (physical) custody of trust assets or any documents or records concerning trust assets. This could include, for instance, taking custody of valuable works of art belonging to the trust, bearer securities[26] (which must be deposited with a custodian),[27] or important documents such as share certificates or title documents relating to land. Custodians in this sense should not be confused with custodian trustees.

16 See Maurice, 'The Office of Custodian Trustee' [1960] 24 Conv (NS) 196; Pearce, 'Directing the Trustee' (1972) 36 Conv (NS) 260 at 260–1.

17 Trust corporations are companies specially authorized by statute to undertake trust business.

18 Public Trustee Rules 1912, r 30, as substituted by the Public Trustee (Custodian Trustee) Rules 1975 (SI 1975/1189) and amended by the Public Trustee (Custodian Trustee) Rules 1976, 1981, 1984, and 1985 (SI 1976/836; SI 1981/358; SI 1984/109; SI 1985/132).

19 See *Cadogan v Earl of Essex* (1854) 2 Drew 227 (trustees subject to directions as to investments). Before the enactment of the Companies Acts permitting companies to be incorporated through a registration procedure, a commonly adopted structure for joint stock companies was one in which, under a deed of settlement, the company's assets were held by trustees on trust for the investors in the company, with the firm being managed by a separate committee of directors.

20 Established by the Public Trustee Act 1906.

21 See *Brook v Brook Bond* [1963] Ch 357.

22 See *IRC v Silverts Ltd* [1951] Ch 521, where the Court of Appeal distinguished custodian trusts from bare trusts on this ground.

23 *Beauclerk v Ashburnham* [1845] 8 Beav 322; *Re Hart's Will Trusts* [1943] 2 All ER 557 (trustees required to be satisfied that a directed investment was purchased at a fair price).

24 *Re Hurst* [1890] 63 LT 665. See, generally, Pearce, 'Directing the Trustees' [1972] 36 Conv (NS) 260.

25 Trustee Act 2000, s 17(1).

26 For example, securities such as investments in a company that are repayable to the person presenting the security document, unlike most investments, which are repayable to the person in whose name the investment is made.

27 Trustee Act 2000, s 18(1).

(5) Concurrent interests

The fixed trust can be used to allocate concurrent interests in the same assets. Often the property comprised in a fund is physically indivisible, and the only way that more than one person can enjoy shares in it is through the allocation of the beneficial interest. For example, it is not possible for people to enjoy shared ownership of land other than behind a trust. If Akeen wanted to leave his house to his sons, Saleem and Tariq, in equal shares, it is unlikely to be possible for the house to be physically divided between them. Instead, he can leave it to them on trust as tenants-in-common in equity in equal shares. From the moment that the trust comes into being, they enjoy equal shares of the equitable interest in the house under a trust of land.[28]

(6) Consecutive interests

Fixed trusts also enable interests in the property to be divided by time, so that one person may enjoy the use of the property for the present, but another has an interest for the future. Rashid could leave his estate by will on trust for his wife Fatima for life, and on her death, to be divided equally between his grandchildren, born or yet to be born. Fatima would have a life interest to in the estate, which gives her an immediate interest in the property for her lifetime only, which will entitle her to the income from it. Rashid's grandchildren do not have any immediate entitlement to the capital of the fund so they cannot demand that the trustees transfer the legal title to them now, but they enjoy a remainder interest in the fund and will be entitled to the capital in equal shares on the death of Fatima. This is a proprietary right that they can sell or assign to others, and if they die, it will pass to their own heirs. The task of the trustees is to obey the terms of the trust by investing the fund and by paying the income to Fatima, and when she dies, by allocating it equally between the children. If they fail to do so, they have committed a breach of trust.

4 Beneficial entitlement to defined interests

(1) Ascertainable immediately or in the future

The beneficiaries under a fixed trust may be either immediately ascertainable or ascertainable only in the future. In the example just given, Rashid identified Fatima by name, but his grandchildren only by description. Those grandchildren already born would be identifiable from the description, but there may also be some who are not yet ascertainable since they have not yet been born.

(2) Vested or contingent

Beneficiaries under a fixed trust may also have vested or contingent interests. They have vested interests where they are immediately ascertainable, and do not have to satisfy any conditions in order to benefit. An interest can be vested even if enjoyment is postponed to a future date. For instance, in Rashid's trust, any grandchildren already born will have vested interests, even though they will only get the capital of the fund when Fatima dies. If they die before Fatima, they may not be able to enjoy their capital share personally, but it will form part of their estate to be dealt with by will or intestacy. Even though they have vested interests, their interest will be divested to the extent necessary if new grandchildren are born and are, therefore, entitled to share the fund.

[28] Trusts of Land and Appointment of Trustees Act 1996, s 1.

A contingent interest, by contrast, is one where, even though a beneficiary is immediately ascertainable, some further condition has to be satisfied. For instance, if Rashid provided in his will for his estate to be divided equally between those of his grandchildren who are living when Fatima dies, even grandchildren already born do not have a vested interest. They have to satisfy the condition of being alive at Fatima's death.

(3) Applying the *Saunders v Vautier* principle

Immediately ascertainable beneficiaries with a vested interest under a fixed trust have immediate proprietary interests in the assets of the fund. If they are of full age, mentally competent, and entitled to the whole beneficial interest in the property, they can require the trustee to transfer the legal title to them or at their direction under the principle of *Saunders v Vautier*.[29] If the beneficiaries are not immediately entitled but have a vested or contingent future interest, they will have to wait until they have an immediate entitlement before they can exercise this right. Thus, a remainder interest behind a life interest in the trust fund does not entitle the beneficiary to call for the legal title. However, when the life tenant dies, he becomes the sole beneficiary and can demand the conveyance of the legal title.

5 Certainty of objects

It has already been explained in Chapter 5 that a valid trust requires certainty of intention, certainty of subject matter, and certainty of objects. It is also a cardinal principle that the court must be able to carry out the trust if the trustee is unable and unwilling to do so. This reflects the mandatory nature of the trust obligation. If the objects of the trust are not sufficiently certain, it is impossible for the trustee to carry out his duty of allocation, nor can the court carry out the trust in the event of his default if necessary.

6 Execution and performance

A fixed trust will continue for so long as the trustees hold the trust assets for the beneficiaries. Some trusts may be set up for a limited time. In the case of Rashid's trust, the obligation of the trustees is to divide the capital value of estate between the grandchildren on Fatima's death. When they do this, the trustees will have fully performed their duties, and the trust will be said to be executed (in other words, fully carried out).[30]

Even before this, by way of agreement between all of the beneficiaries and the trustees or, in the absence of agreement, under the rule in *Saunders v Vautier*,[31] the beneficiaries can call for the trustees to transfer the whole of the trust property to them or to a third party or to deal with it in some other way. This again will normally bring the trust to an end. For instance, in *Vandervell v IRC*,[32] when Mr Vandervell asked the National Provincial Bank, as his nominees, to transfer the shares to the Royal College of Surgeons, the House of Lords held that the transfer of the shares to the Royal College of Surgeons was effective to give them both the legal title to the shares held by the bank, and Mr

[29] [1841] 4 Beav 115.

[30] Note that a trust can also be described as executed rather than executory because the precise rights of the beneficiaries have already been identified, even though legal ownership has not yet been transferred to the beneficiaries.

[31] [1841] 4 Beav 115. [32] [1967] 1 All ER 1, HL.

Vandervell's equitable beneficial interest. Whether the equitable beneficial interest passed on the transfer depended upon the intention of Mr Vandervell as the person entitled to the beneficial interest. There was no need for some separate transfer of Mr Vandervell's equitable rights. Mr Vandervell had not, therefore, retained an equitable interest in the shares.[33]

7 Dealing with the equitable interest

It is possible for the principal or beneficiary under a bare or fixed trust to deal with his equitable interest without terminating the trust. Equity treats the beneficiary under a bare or fixed trust as having a beneficial proprietary interest, and not merely personal rights enforceable against the trustee.[34] That proprietary interest may be sold or given away, used as security for a loan, or itself held upon trust. The alienability of an equitable interest has many times been emphasized. According to Romer LJ in *Timpson's Executors v Yerbury (Inspector of Taxes)*,[35] an equitable interest in property in the hands of a trustee can be disposed of by the person entitled to it in favour of a third party in any one of four different ways:

The person entitled to it:

(1) can assign it to the third party directly;

(2) can direct the trustees to hold the property in trust for the third party;

(3) can contract for valuable consideration to assign the equitable interest to him; or

(4) can declare himself to be a trustee for him of such interest.

(1) Direct assignment

The Law of Property Act 1925, s 136, permits the assignment of choses in action. There is some authority that the section applies to equitable rights, including interests under a trust,[36] although the matter is not entirely free from doubt.[37] For the section to operate, the assignment must be an absolute assignment of the whole interest and not an assignment of part only of the interest or a charge extending only to part of the interest.[38] It must also be made in writing and signed by the assignor, and express notice in writing must be given to the trustee.[39]

[33] This was not enough, however, to enable Mr Vandervell to avoid the taxes. Because the Royal College of Surgeons had given the trustees of a Vandervell family trust an option to repurchase the shares, and there had been no declaration of who was to be the beneficiary of this option, the House of Lords considered that the trustees held the option on Mr Vandervell's behalf until he named some other beneficiary. Because Mr Vandervell, therefore, retained a power to control who would benefit from the shares once the option was exercised, he had sufficient power of disposition of beneficial entitlement to the shares to subject him to liability to tax.

[34] *Baker v Archer-Shee* [1927] AC 844. For an analysis of the debate as to whether equitable rights are properly characterized as in rem or in personam, see Waters, 'The Nature of the Trust Beneficiary's Interest' [1967] 45 Can BR 219.

[35] [1936] 1 KB 645 at 664. The statement was approved in *Sheffield v Sheffield* [2013] EWHC 3927 (Ch) at 80.

[36] *King v Victoria Insurance Co Ltd* [1896] AC 250 at 254; *Torkington v Magee* [1902] 2 KB 427 at 430–1, per Channell J (reversed on facts [1903] 1 KB 644); *Re Pain, Gustavson v Haviland* [1919] 1 Ch 38 at 44–5, per Younger J.

[37] *Snell's Principles of Equity* (30th edn, Sweet & Maxwell 2000), pp 84–6.

[38] *Durham Bros v Robertson* [1898] 1 QB 765, CA. A charge operating by way of a mortgage by assignment of the entire interest, with a proviso for reassignment on the discharge of the loan, is, however, within this section: *Tancred v Delagoa Bay and East Africa Rly Co* (1889) 23 QBD 239.

[39] *Campania Colombiana de Seguros v Pacific Steam Navigation Co* [1965] 1 QB 101; [1964] 1 All ER 216 (notice too late if served after commencement of action against debtor).

Where an assignment fails to comply with the statutory provisions, it may, nevertheless, be effective as an assignment in equity. An equitable assignment does not need to be in any particular form, or to use any particular set of words or language.[40] It is enough if a clear intention is manifested, by words or conduct, to transfer the benefit of a clearly identified right from the assignor to the assignee.[41] The equitable assignment need not be communicated to the trustee,[42] although if the trustee has notice of the assignment it completes the transaction as to third parties, establishes priority on the part of the assignee, and protects the assignee against any fraudulent receipt by the assignor.[43]

(2) Directions to the trustees to hold on trust

The alienation may take the form of instructions to the trustee to hold the property upon trust for some other person, as in *Tierney v Wood*.[44] Wood, the principal under a bare trust of property held by his nominee, Tierney, gave directions to his nominee by letter to hold the property upon trust for Wood's wife and daughters.[45] Where the directions impose upon the trustee an obligation more onerous than that required by the original terms of the trust, then it may be necessary for the trustee to agree to perform these obligations,[46] but the alienation is valid even if no consideration has been given, provided that the beneficiary has demonstrated an unconditional intention to make an outright transfer.[47] The alienation may also be of part only of the equitable interest in the property,[48] or be in some other way less than an outright transfer.[49]

(3) Contract to assign

Under the principle that 'equity treats as done that which ought to be done', a contract to transfer property, if specifically enforceable, will normally be effective to pass title in equity to the beneficiary of the contract.[50] Once any conditions which relate to the transfer have been satisfied, such as the identification of the property concerned, equity treats the transfer as if it had already been made.[51] In *Collyer v Isaacs*, for instance, Jessel MR said:

> A man can contract to assign property which is to come into existence in the future, and when it has come into existence, equity, treating as done that which ought to be done, fastens upon that property, and the contract to assign thus becomes a complete assignment.[52]

[40] *William Brandt's Sons & Co v Dunlop Rubber Co* [1905] AC 454 at 462, per Lord MacNaghten.

[41] *Voyle v Hughes* [1854] 2 Sm & G 18. See also *Pennington v Waine* [2002] 1 WLR 2075, where it was held that a share transfer form was capable of operating as an equitable assignment because it demonstrated an immediate and unconditional intention to transfer ownership.

[42] *Kekewich v Manning* [1851] 1 De GM & G 176; *Voyle v Hughes* [1854] 2 Sm & G 18.

[43] *Kekewich v Manning* [1851] 1 De GM & G 176.

[44] [1854] 19 Beav 330.

[45] Similar cases to the same effect are *Rycroft v Christy* [1840] 3 Beav 238; *Bentley v Mackay* [1851] 15 Beav 12; and *Paterson v Murphy* [1853] 11 Hare 88.

[46] *Rycroft v Christy* [1840] 3 Beav 238.

[47] *Bentley v Mackay* [1851] 15 Beav 12; *Re Chrimes* [1917] 1 Ch 30.

[48] *Rycroft v Christy* [1840] 3 Beav 238.

[49] *Tierney v Wood* [1854] 19 Beav 330 (life interest followed by entailed interest in land created out of an interest in fee).

[50] *Wright v Wright* [1750] 1 Ves Sen 409, 412 (Lord Hardwicke); *Legard v Hodges* [1792] 1 Ves 477 (Lord Thurlow LC).

[51] *Tailby v Official Receiver* [1888] 13 App Cas 523; *Stephens v Green* [1895] 2 Ch 148, CA.

[52] [1881] 19 Ch D 342 at 351.

Where the contract is for the immediate transfer of existing and identifiable property, equity does not, therefore, distinguish between an equitable assignment and a contract to assign.[53]

The equitable maxim treating a contract to assign as an actual assignment applies only to contracts for value. It cannot be relied upon by volunteers who have not themselves provided any consideration,[54] possibly even if there may have been someone else who has provided consideration but who does not seek to support the assignment.[55]

(4) **Declaration of subsidiary trust**

Although there may originally have been some doubt as to whether a trust could be created to fasten upon a beneficial interest under an existing trust,[56] it very soon became established that there was no objection to the imposition of such a trust.[57]

As with any trust, however, the trust will come into effect only if there is a clear intention to create an irrevocable trust, and an ineffective attempt to transfer the property will not be construed as a declaration of trust.[58] As Turner LJ observed in *Milroy v Lord*:[59]

> If it [a gift] is intended to take effect by transfer, the Court will not hold the intended transfer to operate as a declaration of trust, for then every imperfect instrument would be made effectual by being converted into a perfect trust.[60]

Where a sub-trust has been created, the trustees of the head trust will be acting properly if they deal with the sub-trustees, but if the trust is a bare trust, they can also deal directly with the ultimate beneficiary.[61]

[53] *Heap v Tonge* [1851] 9 Hare 90 at 104.

[54] *Re Anstis* [1886] 31 Ch D 596; *Re D'Angibau* [1879] 15 Ch D 228 at 242; *Re Plumptre's Marriage Settlement* [1910] 1 Ch 609 at 616.

[55] *Re Cook's Settlement Trusts* [1965] Ch 902. This case involved a promise to create a trust of the proceeds of sale of certain paintings should they ever be sold, rather than a contract to transfer an existing equitable interest. The judge held that such a promise did not create an existing proprietary interest capable of being held upon trust. The position concerning the assignment of an existing beneficial interest under a trust is, therefore, distinguishable.

[56] See the discussion in Simpson, *An Introduction to the History of the Land Law* (Clarendon Press 1961), pp 189–92.

[57] *Kekewich v Manning* [1851] 1 De GM & G 176. See also *Pulvertoft v Pulvertoft* [1811] 18 Ves 84 at 99, per Lord Eldon LC; *Meek v Kettlewell* [1842] 1 Hare 464 at 470–1, per Wigram V-C.

[58] *Edwards v Jones* [1835] 1 My & Cr 226; *Antrobus v Smith* [1805] 12 Ves 39; *Searle v Law* [1846] 15 Sim 95; *Jones v Lock* [1865] 1 Ch App 25.

[59] [1862] 4 De GF & J 264 at 274.

[60] See further the discussion concerning the constitution of trusts in Chapter 6.

[61] *Sheffield v Sheffield* [2013] EWHC 3927 (Ch) at 82–6.

26

Powers of appointment

1 Introduction

Given that the equitable mechanisms of trusts and powers lie on a continuum, it might seem logical that, after looking at fixed trusts, we should next look at discretionary trusts. There is a practical reason, however, for looking next at powers of appointment: it means that we look at the ends of the range, and this will make it easier to make sense of the intermediate points.

2 Nature of powers of appointment

Powers of appointment confer on a person who does not own property the authority to choose who shall become the owner. The key feature of a power of appointment is that it is discretionary in character. The donee of a power is under no enforceable obligation to make any appointments of the fund at all. Even if the donee were never to make any appointments at all, he would not be in breach of a duty owed either to the donor or to the potential objects of the power. The court will not step in to compel the exercise of the power, but it will exercise a supervisory jurisdiction to ensure that, if the donee does decide to exercise the power, he does so properly. Powers of appointment are commonly used as a mechanism to determine the allocation of the surplus remaining in a trust fund after the beneficiaries have received their defined interests. Many older cases concern family trusts where the property of a testator was left on trust for a spouse for life, with a power of appointment granted over the remainder interest (see Figure 26.1).[1] This allows the donee of the power to decide how the capital of the fund should be allocated on the death of the life tenant. The discretionary nature of the power means that the testator does not have to predetermine how the remainder interest should be distributed, and allows the donee of the power to take account of changing circumstances between the death of the testator and the death of the life tenant. Some later cases concern pension funds, where the donee was given a power of appointment over any surplus that remained after the contributors have received their contractual entitlements.[2] Although the position has now changed, with many pension funds operating in deficit, in the 1990s some pension funds had assets exceeding their liabilities. The power to allocate the surplus by exercise of a power of appointment, whether to the pensioners or the company, was, therefore, an extremely valuable right.

[1] *Re Weekes' Settlement* [1897] 1 Ch 289.

[2] *Hillsdown Holdings plc v Pensions Ombudsman* [1997] 1 All ER 862; *Edge v Pensions Ombudsman* [1998] 2 All ER 547.

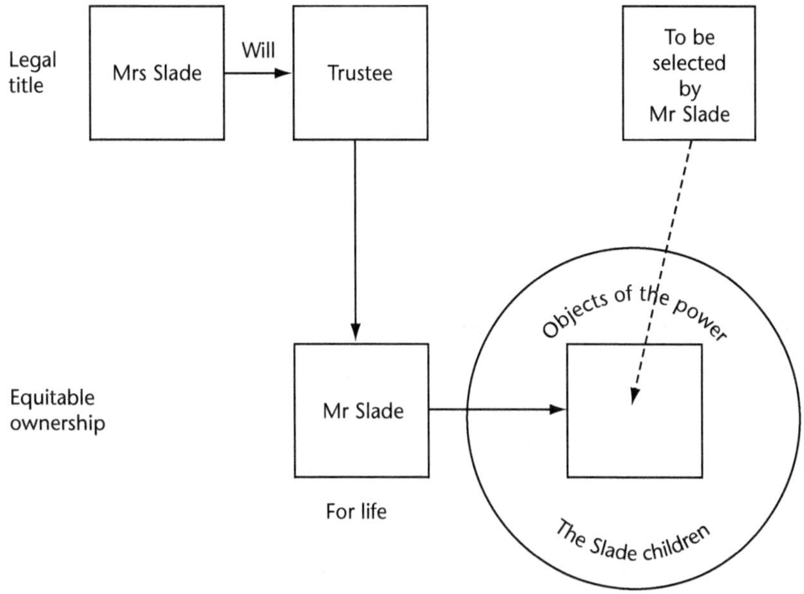

Figure 26.1 An example of powers of appointment: *Re Weekes' Settlement*

(1) Classification by the nature of the class

It is possible to classify powers in three ways: by the nature of the class of objects; by the duties of the done; or by the way the power can be exercised. Looking first at different classes of objects, powers can be general, special, or hybrid.

(a) General powers

Under a general power of appointment, the donee enjoys the right to allocate the property by appointment to anyone he wishes. The donee may even appoint the property to himself. This extremely wide power is tantamount to absolute ownership by the donee.[3]

(b) Special powers

Where the donor of a power has specified that it should only be exercised in favour of a class of people, it is said to be a special power. Any appointments made must be to persons within the specified class. In *Re Weekes' Settlement*,[4] Mrs Slade granted a life interest of her estate to her husband and gave him a power of appointment over the reversionary interest in favour of their children (see Figure 26.1). This created a special power in favour of the class of their eight surviving children. Mr Slade had discretion whether or not to make any appointments, but he could only make appointments to those who fell within the class of potential objects (see Figure 26.1).

[3] See *TMSF v Merril Lynch Bank* [2011] UKPC 17 at [41–43]; at *Webb v Webb* [2020] UKPC 22 at [77].

[4] [1897] 1 Ch 289. See also *Re Gestetner Settlement* [1953] Ch 672 (wide class including named persons, named charitable bodies, and employees and ex-employees of the settlor's company); *Re Sayer* [1957] Ch 423 (class in favour of employees, ex-employees, and widows and infant children of Sayers Confectionary Ltd).

(c) Hybrid powers

A hybrid,[5] or intermediate,[6] power is the inverse of a special power. The donee is entitled to make appointments in favour of anyone except the members of a specified class. In *Re Byron's Settlement*,[7] a power of appointment was given by the testatrix to her daughter in favour of anyone except 'her present husband or any friend or relative of his'. In *Re Lawrence's Will Trusts*,[8] Mr Lawrence granted his wife a power of appointment over his residuary estate in favour of anyone except her relatives.[9] Restrictions on the exercise of powers excluding the settlor from receiving any benefit under a trust are often used for tax reasons.

(2) Classification by donee's duties

Powers may also be divided into those where the donee owes no duty of a fiduciary nature to the potential objects of the power, and those where some fiduciary duties are owed. Although, in both cases, the power remains essentially discretionary, there is a slight difference in the duties owed. This difference normally arises because the donee is also a trustee.

(a) Bare or mere powers

If the donee of the power does not hold the power in a fiduciary capacity, then he owes no duties to the objects concerning its exercise. He is under no duty to exercise it, and need not even consider whether he should exercise the power. He can completely forget that he has it, and never apply his mind to the question whether he should exercise it. This type of power is known as a bare or mere power.

(b) Fiduciary powers

If the donee holds the power of appointment in a fiduciary capacity, most commonly because it is a power which arises under a trust of which he is the trustee, then he owes limited fiduciary duties to the potential objects of the powers.[10] He must periodically consider whether to exercise the power, although it remains entirely discretionary and he is under no enforceable obligation to make appointments.[11] If he does decide to exercise the power, he must first survey the range of potential objects before making particular appointments. In some instances, the donee may even be under an obligation to exercise the power.[12] The fact that the donee has fiduciary obligations does not mean that he is a trustee. Although there is a wide spectrum of fiduciary duties, some of which are analogous to or akin to the duties of a trustee,[13] there can be 'considerable differences between the office or the capacity of a trustee and the position of a donee of a fiduciary power'.[14]

[5] See *Re Lawrence's Will Trusts* [1972] Ch 418 at 423.

[6] See *Re Manisty's Settlement* [1974] Ch 17, where Templeman J described a power to appoint anyone in the world except the settlor, his wife and other excepted persons as an 'intermediate power'.

[7] [1891] 3 Ch 474. [8] [1972] Ch 418.

[9] See also *Re Park* [1932] 1 Ch 580; *Re Abrahams' Will Trusts* [1969] 1 Ch 463; *Re Manisty's Settlement* [1974] Ch 17.

[10] See *Re Hay's Settlement Trusts* [1982] 1 WLR 202.

[11] See *Re Allen-Meyrick's Will Trusts* [1966] 1 WLR 499, where the court refused to intervene to compel trustees to exercise a power that they held over a fund in favour of the settlor's husband. Cf the exceptional case of *Lehtimäki v Cooper* [2020] UKSC 33 where the court directed a member of a charitable company to exercise their discretionary powers to vote in favour of a proposed distribution of assets. This is explored below.

[12] *Bridge Trustees Ltd v Noel Penny (Turbines) Ltd* [2008] EWHC 2054 (Ch) at [18].

[13] See *Gomez and others v Gomez-Monche Vives and others* [2008] EWCA Civ 1065, [2009] Ch 245 (CA) at [94].

[14] Ibid [2009] Ch 245 (CA).

(3) Classification by mode of exercise

The instrument creating a power may prescribe how the power should be exercised. The instrument may require the power to be exercised by deed, by will, or without any specific formality. A power exercisable by will can be described as a testamentary power of appointment.[15] Where one mode of exercise is prescribed, the power cannot be exercised by another mode.

3 Rights of the objects of powers

Beneficiaries with a vested interest in possession in a fixed trust have an immediate proprietary interest in the share of the fund which is earmarked for them, and, if of age and legally competent, they can demand that the trustees transfer the property to them.[16] The potential objects of a power of appointment have no immediate proprietary interest in the property over which the donee has power.[17] An object only gains a proprietary interest in any property which is allocated to him by the donee. In *Re Brooks' Settlement Trusts*, Farwell J said of the position of a son who was a potential object of a special power under his mother's marriage settlement:

> It is ... impossible to say that until an appointment has been made in favour of this son that the son had any interest under his mother's settlement other than an interest as one of the people entitled in default of appointment.[18]

4 The validity of powers of appointment

(1) Certainty of objects

Chapter 5 explored the requirements of certainty for trusts and powers and explained how they are based on the role of the court in enforcing them. In the case of a special power, the court must be able to determine whether any person selected by the donee was within the class, and, therefore, entitled to enjoy the benefit of the exercise. As Lord Upjohn observed in *Re Gulbenkian's Settlement*:

> those entitled to the fund in default [of appointment] must clearly be entitled to restrain the trustees from exercising it save amongst those within the power. So the trustees, or the court, must be able to say with certainty who is within and who without the power.[19]

If an appointment is made to a person who is outside the class of objects, then the exercise is excessive and void.

(2) Capriciousness

Even if a special power of appointment is sufficiently certain, it will be invalid (at least if it is a fiduciary power) if it is capricious in nature. The principle of capriciousness was considered applicable to special powers in *Re Manisty's Settlement*,[20] where Templeman J suggested that a special power in favour of the 'residents of Greater London' would be

[15] As in *De Bruyne v De Bruyne* [2010] EWCA Civ 519 at 6. The phrase 'testamentary power' is sometimes also used to describe testamentary capacity, or the capacity to make a will.

[16] *Saunders v Vautier* [1841] 4 Beav 115. [17] *Vestey v IRC* [1980] AC 1148, HL.

[18] [1939] Ch 993 at 997. [19] [1970] AC 508 at 525. [20] [1974] Ch 17.

capricious 'because the terms of the power negated any sensible intention on the part of the settlor'.[21] Capriciousness does not invalidate a power merely because of the width of the power, as a general power is valid even though the donee has the discretion to make appointments to anyone in the whole world. Instead, it invalidates a special power because there is no rational reason why the donor selected the specified class, and consequently the donee has no rational basis on which he can exercise his discretion.[22] 'Residents of Greater London' would be capricious, because the class was 'an accidental agglomeration of persons who have no discernible link with the settlor or with any institution'.[23] If there were a link between the donor of the power and the class of potential objects, the power would not be open to the charge of capriciousness. In *Re Hay's Settlement Trusts*,[24] Megarry V-C suggested that a power in favour of 'the residents of Greater London' would not be capricious if the donor were a former chairman of the Greater London Council. In *R v District Auditor, ex p West Yorkshire Metropolitan County Council*,[25] it was held that a discretionary trust created by the council for the benefit of the residents of West Yorkshire was not capricious.[26]

Where a power is found to be capricious, it will be rendered void. Capriciousness will only invalidate a special power, and the principle has no application to a general power, or a hybrid power.[27] Both *Re Manisty's Settlement* and *Re Hay's Settlement Trusts* concerned fiduciary powers. In this context the need for a rational basis for decision-making is explicable since the donee has a duty to consider how the power should be exercised. It is hard to see the rationale for applying the same principle to bare powers where the donee is under no such obligation.

(3) **Administrative unworkability**

In *McPhail v Doulton*,[28] Lord Wilberforce suggested that a discretionary trust which is not void for uncertainty may yet be void for 'administrative unworkability'[29] if the class is 'too wide to form anything like a class'.[30] In *Re Hay's Settlement Trusts*,[31] Sir Robert Megarry V-C considered that the principle of 'administrative unworkability' was directed only towards discretionary trusts and had no application to fiduciary powers. It would not, therefore, apply to mere powers.

5 Exercise of powers of appointment

(1) **Formalities**

As a general rule, no special formalities are required for the valid exercise of a power of appointment. However, the donee of the power must intend to allocate the fund or part of the fund to an object of the power. Where the power is granted in relation to land an

[21] [1974] Ch 17 at 27.

[22] [1974] Ch 17. 'A capricious power negatives a sensible consideration by the trustees of the exercise of the power.'

[23] [1974] Ch 17. [24] [1982] 1 WLR 202. [25] [1986] RVR 24.

[26] It was, however, found to be 'administratively unworkable', demonstrating that 'capriciousness' and 'administrative unworkability' are distinct concepts.

[27] See *Re Manisty's Settlement* [1974] Ch 17 at 27; *Re Hay's Settlement Trusts* [1982] 1 WLR 202 at 212.

[28] [1971] AC 424.

[29] [1971] AC 424 at 444. See Gardner, 'Fiduciary Powers in Toytown' [1991] 107 LQR 214.

[30] [1971] AC 424 at 457. [31] [1982] 1 WLR 202.

appointment must be evidenced in writing signed by the donee, in accordance with s 51(1)(b) of the Law of Property Act 1925. In some circumstances additional formalities may be required.

(a) Formalities required by the terms of the power

The terms of the power may require it to be exercised in a particular form, for example, by deed. If so, the power can only be exercised in that form. Where it is stipulated that a power must be exercised by deed, a purported exercise by will be ineffective.[32] Similarly, a power which can only be exercised by will cannot be exercised inter vivos.[33]

(b) Limitations on additional formalities

Although the terms of the power may specify additional formalities, legislation has limited the range of stipulations which must be observed to effect a valid exercise. Under s 159(1) of the Law of Property Act 1925, where a power is exercised inter vivos, the exercise will be valid if executed by a valid deed,[34] even though the terms of the power required some 'additional or other form of execution or attestation or solemnity'. This does not exclude the necessity for the donee to comply with any terms of the power requiring him to gain the consent of another individual, or performing an act not relating to the mode of executing the deed.[35] In the case of a will, s 10 of the Wills Act 1837 provides that the exercise of a power by a valid will is effective notwithstanding the absence of any additional formalities required by the terms of the power.[36]

(2) Protectors

A trust instrument may provide that a power can be exercised only with the consent of a named individual. The person whose consent is required is frequently described as a protector.[37] The role of the protector may be more extensive and can include adding beneficiaries[38] or giving directions to the donee of the power.[39]

(3) Defective exercise

In general, a defective exercise of a power is void, and the purported appointment of the fund does not take place. However, equity may validate a defective exercise if the donee 'in discharge of moral or natural obligations shows an intention to execute [a] power'.[40] This will only apply in favour of purchasers for value, creditors, charities, and persons to whom the donee is under a natural or moral obligation to provide. Some key elements must be proved if the defective exercise is to be upheld:

> the intention to pass the property . . . the persons to be benefited . . . the amount of the benefit . . . good consideration.[41]

32 *Re Phillips* [1889] LR 41 Ch D 417.

33 *Re Evered* [1910] 2 Ch 147 at 156, per Cozens-Hardy MR.

34 Executed in the presence of and attested by two or more witnesses (Law of Property (Miscellaneous Provisions) Act 1989, s 1).

35 Law of Property Act 1925, s 159(2).

36 See also Wills Act 1963, s 2.

37 *Schmidt v Rosewood Trust Ltd (Isle of Man)* [2003] UKPC 26 at 1.

38 *Z v Z* [2016] EWHC 911 (Fam) at 18.

39 See, for example, *Walbrook Trustees (Jersey) Ltd v Fattal & Ors* [2007] EWHC 2808 (Ch) at [49]; *JSC Mezhdunarodniy Promyshlenniy Bank v Pugachev* [2016] EWHC 248 (Ch) at [10] (protector to discretionary trust).

40 *Farwell on Powers* (3rd edn, London 1916), p 378; *Chapman v Gibson* [1791] 3 Bro CC 229.

41 *Farwell on Powers* (3rd edn, London 1916), p 379.

(4) Contracts to exercise

A contract to exercise a power of appointment will operate in equity as a valid exercise of the power, provided that the contract is specifically enforceable. This is an application of the maxim that 'equity treats as done that which ought to be done'. Since a contract to exercise a testamentary power is not specifically enforceable,[42] it does not operate as an effective exercise of the power, and the only remedy available to the disappointed object is an action for damages for breach of contract against the estate.

(5) Excessive exercise

The exercise of the power will be excessive if the donee makes an appointment to a person outside of the potential objects of the power. In the case of a special power, appointments can only be made to members of the specified class, while in the case of a hybrid power, appointments must not be made to members of the excluded class. Any such excessive appointments are void and of no effect.[43]

If an appointment is made which is partly good and partly bad, the court will sever the good from the bad if possible. In *Re Kerr's Will Trusts*,[44] Maria Young had a special power of appointment over a fund in favour of the children of her marriage. By will, she appointed the fund to two of her children, Charlotte and Catherine. Catherine was a child of the marriage and within the power, but Charlotte was an illegitimate child of Maria before she married. The exercise was thus excessive, but the court applied severance, and Catherine took the share of the fund appointed to her. The remainder of the fund was divided equally among those entitled in default of appointment. In *Re Holland*[45] an appointment was made with attached conditions which rendered the exercise excessive. The conditions were severed from the appointment, and it was upheld as a valid exercise.[46] If it is impossible to sever the condition from the appointment, the exercise will be excessive and void.[47]

(6) Effect of valid exercise

The effect of a valid exercise of the power is to allocate the share of the fund appointed to the person in whose favour the donee has exercised the power. The appointee will then (depending upon the terms of the exercise) be entitled to an immediate proprietary interest in the share of the fund which has been allocated.[48] In *Churchill v Churchill*,[49] Lord Romilly MR held that the effect of an appointment by Sir Orford Gordon under a special power of a fund to his three daughters in equal shares was to vest in them absolute interests in the appointed fund. Even after the exercise of a power which vests an interest in a beneficiary, the power may remain exercisable, in which case the exercise of the power will have a divesting effect.

[42] *Re Bradshaw* [1902] 1 Ch 436; *Re Cooke* [1922] 1 Ch 292.

[43] See the discussion of *Pitt v Holt* [2013] UKSC 26 in Chapter 33.

[44] [1877] 4 Ch D 600.

[45] [1914] 2 Ch 595.

[46] See also *Churchill v Churchill* [1866–67] LR 5 Eq 44; *Price v William-Wynn* [2006] EWHC 788 (Ch) (a clause inserted into deeds of appointment and revocation, which was held to exceed the powers given to trustees under a settlement, was therefore severed from each of the affected deeds so that they could validly be read without the offending clause).

[47] *Re Cohen* [1911] 1 Ch 37.

[48] See *Vestey v IRC* [1980] AC 1148, HL.

[49] [1866–67] LR 5 Eq 44.

6 Duties of the donee of a mere power of appointment

(1) No duty to exercise the power

The donee of a mere power of appointment is under no duty to exercise the power and make appointments in favour of the potential objects. He has complete discretion and the court will not compel him to exercise the power, nor even to consider periodically whether he should exercise the power. If he fails to make any appointments at all he is not in breach of any duty owed either to the donor of the power or to the potential objects, and they in turn have no legal cause for complaint against him.

(2) No duty to consider the width of the field

If the donee of the mere power does decide to exercise it, he has no duty to survey and consider the range of potential objects of the power before exercising his discretion in favour of any one object. He may appoint to whomsoever he wishes, provided they are within the class, without having to take account of others who could benefit if he were to exercise his discretion in their favour. If it is within the scope of the power, the donee may appoint the fund entirely to himself without even considering the other potential objects. Thus, in *Re Penrose*,[50] an exercise of a special power of appointment by the donee in favour of himself, where he was an object, was upheld.

(3) Duty not to delegate the exercise of the power

The donee must not delegate the power of appointment to others except in so far as this is authorized by the terms of the grant: delegatus non potest delegare (a delegate has no power to delegate).

(4) Duty not to exercise the power excessively

The donee of the power is under a duty to make appointments only to those who are objects of the power. As has been seen, any appointments which are excessive will be void.

(5) Duty not to exercise the power fraudulently

Even if the donee exercises the power and makes appointments which appear to be within the scope of the power, they will be void if the exercise amounts to a 'fraud on the power'. The power must be exercised honestly, and the court will look to the motives and intentions of the donor of the power to ensure that they are not improper. As Lord Parker of Waddington observed in *Vatcher v Paull*:

> The term fraud in connection with frauds on a power does not necessarily denote any conduct on the part of the appointor amounting to fraud in the common law meaning of the term or any conduct which could be properly termed dishonest or immoral. It merely means that the power has been exercised for a purpose or with an intention, beyond the scope of or not justified by the instrument creating the fraud . . .[51]

Thus, in *Hillsdown Holdings plc v Pensions Ombudsman*,[52] an exercise of a power was held to constitute a 'fraud', despite the fact that the donee and all parties had acted honestly

[50] [1933] Ch 793. [51] [1915] AC 372 at 378. [52] [1997] 1 All ER 862.

and with good intentions. In *Edge v Pensions Ombudsman*,[53] Scott V-C held that pension trustees were required to 'exercise their discretionary power honestly and for the purpose for which the power was given and not so as to accomplish any ulterior purpose'.

Where the exercise of a power is held invalid on the grounds of fraud, the court acts to protect the interests of those who would be entitled to the fund if no appointments are made. They are the victims of the fraud if appointments are made with improper motives, since they are thereby divested of an interest in the fund to which they would otherwise have become entitled.[54] The effect of fraud is to render the exercise of the power void, not merely voidable.[55]

In *Vatcher v Paull*,[56] Lord Parker indicated three circumstances in which the exercise of a power would amount to a fraud. The essence of each is that the benefit is not exclusively conferred upon objects of the power.[57] Clearly, these limitations apply only to special powers and not to general powers, since in the case of a general power there are no persons outside of the scope of the power, and the donee may even appoint in his own favour.

The obligation not to exercise a power for an improper purpose applies to administrative as well as to dispositive powers. In *Dalriada Trustees v Faulds*,[58] Bean J held that even if a power of investment allowed for money to be advanced on unsecured personal loans, it did not permit six HMRC-registered pension funds[59] to make reciprocal loans to the members of the other schemes in order to circumvent the fiscal rules of HMRC barring members of pension schemes from obtaining access to their pension capital prior to retirement. The loans were beyond the scope of the pension fund trustees' powers, and 'the fact that everyone involved with the transactions wished to validate [the] loans does not prevent the loans from being a fraud on the trustees' powers.'[60]

(a) Bargain with the appointee

If an appointment is made on the basis of a prior agreement between the donee/appointor and the appointee as to how the appointed share of the fund should be used, the appointment is void. The purpose of the bargain may be for the donee to gain some benefit for himself, or for a non-object of the power. The objection to such a bargain is 'that the power is used not with the single purpose of benefiting its proper objects'.[61] In *Hillsdown Holdings plc v Pensions Ombudsman*,[62] Hillsdown plc participated in a pension scheme (the FMC scheme) which had accumulated an actuarial surplus of some £20 million. The scheme contained no power allowing the trustees to repay any surplus to employers participating in the scheme, and the scheme could not be amended to confer such a power. After an agreement had been negotiated between Hillsdown and the FMC trustees to augment the benefits of FMC pensioners and to transfer to the company £11 million of the surplus, the trustees exercised a power under the scheme to transfer the entire fund to another scheme (the HF scheme), the rules of which were changed to allow the surplus to be paid to Hillsdown. Knox J held that the FMC trustees' exercise of the power, transferring the assets to HF was a fraud on the power as it amounted to 'an improper use of the power for a collateral purpose'[63] of paying the surplus to Hillsdown.

There is no objection to an appointment made on the basis of a bargain with those who are entitled in default of any appointment being made.[64] Where an appointment is a fraud

[53] [1998] 2 All ER 547 at 569. [54] *Re Brooks' Settlement Trusts* [1939] Ch 993.

[55] *Cloutte v Storey* [1911] 1 Ch 18, CA. This is a decision which 'may have to be revisited one day': *Pitt v Holt* [2013] UKSC 26 at 62.

[56] [1915] AC 372 at 378. [57] See *Re Merton* [1953] 1 WLR 1096.

[58] [2012] 2 All ER 734. [59] Her Majesty's Revenue and Customs. [60] At 72.

[61] *Vatcher v Paull* [1915] AC 372 at 379. [62] [1997] 1 All ER 862. [63] [1997] 1 All ER 862 at 883.

[64] [1915] AC 372 at 379.

because it was made on the basis of such a bargain, the court may sever the good from the bad provided that it:

> can clearly distinguish between the quantum of the benefit bona fide intended to be conferred on the appointee and the quantum of benefit intended to be derived by the appointor or to be conferred on a stranger.[65]

(b) Appointor intends to secure a personal benefit

The exercise of a power will constitute a fraud if the purpose of the appointment was to enable the appointor to receive a benefit. *Lord Hinchinbroke v Seymour*[66] is an example. A father appointed £10,000 in favour of his daughter, who was 14 and dying of consumption. The intention of the appointment was that the father would take the money as administrator of the child. It was 'as plain a case of gross fraud on a power as can well be imagined', and 'it was quite obvious what the motive was. It could not have been for the benefit of the child, because she was already provided for.'[67] An appointment made to a child who is healthy is not a fraud, even though the appointor stands to gain if the child subsequently dies.[68]

(c) Benefit for a person who is not an object of the power

An appointment in favour of an object of the power will be fraudulent if the real intention of the donee/appointor was to benefit a non-object. In *Re Dick*,[69] Mrs Sherman was the donee of a special power of appointment over property left on trust by her father in favour of her brothers or sisters and their issue. She exercised the power by will in favour of her sister, Miss Dick, but contemporaneously with the will executed a formal memorandum desiring her sister provide an annuity of £800 per annum for her gardener Mr Claydon, who was not an object. The memorandum expressly stated that it did not impose a 'trust or legal obligation' on Miss Dick, so that there was no bargain between the appointor and appointee. Nevertheless, the Court of Appeal held that this amounted to an excessive exercise of the power. Evershed MR stated that the central question was:

> whether the right inference is that what Mrs Sherman intended to do, her real deliberate purpose which she wanted and set out by all means that were possible to achieve, was to benefit the Claydons via her relations . . . or whether her purpose was really to benefit her relations subject only to this, that she had indicated to them that she hoped . . . they would so something for the Claydons on the lines she had suggested.[70]

The court held that in all the circumstances the real intention was to benefit the non-object. This case suggests that the court will weigh the appointor's motives and intentions from all the available evidence, a principle that was established by Cohen LJ in *Re Crawshay (Decd) (No 2)*.[71] This is notoriously difficult, as evidenced by the large number of indications and counter-indications considered by the Court of Appeal in *Re Dick*.

7 Failure to exercise a mere power

Since a mere power of appointment is purely discretionary in nature, a donee is under no obligation to exercise it, and the objects have no rights to the fund unless it is appointed to them. If the power is not exercised, the fund passes to those entitled in default. Usually this will occur where a donee has been granted a power but has died without making any valid appointments, either inter vivos or by will (see Figure 26.2).

65 [1915] AC 372 at 378.

66 [1784] 1 Bro CC 395. 67 *Henty v Wrey* [1882] LR 21 Ch D 332 at 342, per Jessel MR.

68 [1882] LR 21 Ch D 332. See also *Smith v Michelmore Trust Corporation* [2021] EWHC 1425 (Ch), a case involving a discretionary trust, where the exercise of a power of appointment was considered to be a fraud on a power as it would not benefit the recipient but instead his creditors—see [58]–[59].

69 [1953] Ch 343. 70 [1953] Ch 343 at 363. 71 [1948] Ch 123.

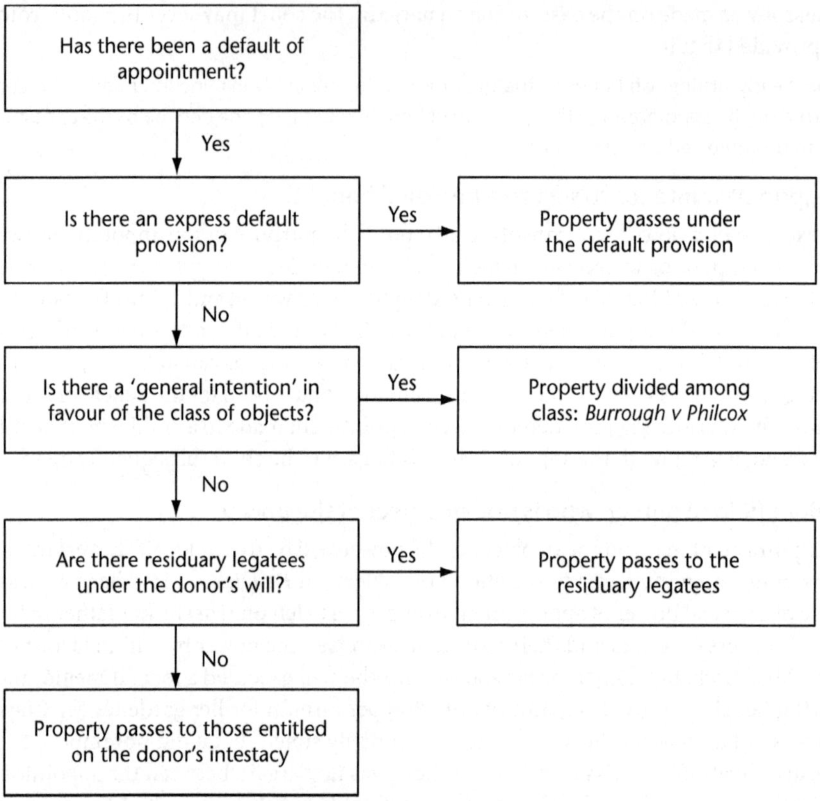

Figure 26.2 Effect of default of appointment

(1) Express gift over in default of appointment

The power of appointment may itself contain an express stipulation of who is to receive the fund if no appointments are made. Such an express provision will determine how the fund should be distributed.

(2) No express gift over in default

If the power does not contain an express gift over in default, the fund will fall to be distributed according to the general principles governing the distribution of surplus funds. If the fund was created by will, the property passes to those entitled to the residuary estate under the will. If the fund was created by an inter vivos settlement, it will result back to the settlor, or his heirs, by a resulting trust. There may, however, be an implied trust producing a different result.

(3) An implied trust in default

In some circumstances, even though no appointment has been made, the court may hold that the fund should be divided among the objects rather than passing to the residuary legatees or by resulting trust. This will only be possible if the court can find that there was a 'general intention' by the donee of the power to benefit a class. The leading case is *Burrough v Philcox*.[72] John Walton granted his surviving daughter, Ann, a power of

[72] [1840] 5 My & Cr 72.

appointment over his property in favour of his nephews and nieces. The power contained no express gift over in default and Ann died without making any appointments. Under the rules of succession, the testator's next of kin would be entitled to the fund. However, Lord Cottenham LC held that the effect of the arrangement was to create a trust in favour of the nephews and nieces subject to Ann's power of selection, so that when Ann died without having made any appointments, they each took an equal share in the fund. The principle was stated by Lord Cottenham:

> where there appears a general intention in favour of a class, and a particular intention in favour of individuals of a class to be selected by another person, and the particular intention fails, from that selection not being made, the court will carry into effect the general intention in favour of the class.[73]

The key element is the finding of a general intention in favour of the class. In effect, the court is concluding from the circumstances of the creation of the power that if it has not been exercised the donor would have wanted the fund to go to the objects. In this sense the operation of the implied trust in default is somewhat similar to an application cy-près, where a charitable gift has failed initially on the grounds that the donor had an overriding charitable intention.[74]

(a) Demonstrating a general intention

An implied trust in default will only arise if it can be shown that the donor of the power possessed a general intention to benefit the objects as a group. If the power contained an express gift in default, then the court cannot conclude that there was a general intention in favour of the class of objects because the donee had already expressed his intention vis-à-vis the fund in default of any appointments.[75] It is not inevitable that the absence of an express gift over in default will lead to the finding of a general intention in favour of the objects. In *Re Weekes' Settlement*,[76] Mrs Slade granted her husband a power of appointment over a fund established under her marriage settlement. Mr Slade died without making any appointments, and the children of the marriage claimed to be equally entitled to the fund. Romer J held that there was no general intention in favour of the class, and the fund, therefore, passed to the eldest son, who was Mrs Slade's heir at law. He stated:

> The authorities do not show . . . that there is a hard and fast rule that a gift to A for life with a power to appoint among a class and nothing more must, if there is no gift over in the will, be held a gift by implication to the class in default of the power being exercised . . . you must find in the will an indication that the testatrix did intend the class or some of the class to take—intended in fact that the power should be regarded in the nature of a trust.[77]

No general intention in favour of the class was found in *Re Combe*[78] or *Re Perowne (Decd)*.[79] Such a general intention is only likely to be found where the power is in favour of a small and well-defined class, especially a close family group.

(b) Juridical nature of the implied trust in default

There remains confusion as to the basis under which the fund subject to a power is distributed to the objects under the rule in *Burrough v Philcox*. One analysis is that the power is in fact a discretionary trust under which the donee is under an obligation to make an

[73] [1840] 5 My & Cr 72 at 92. [74] See Chapter 22. [75] *Re Mills* [1930] 1 Ch 654.
[76] [1897] 1 Ch 289. [77] [1897] 1 Ch 289 at 292. [78] [1925] Ch 210. [79] [1951] Ch 785.

appointment. Thus, in *Burrough v Philcox*, Lord Cottenham LC cited the dictum of Lord Eldon in *Brown v Higgs*[80] that the power is given so as to:

> make it the duty of the donee to exercise it; and, in such case, the court will not permit the objects of the power to suffer by the negligence or conduct of the donee, but fastens upon the property a trust for their benefit.[81]

Similarly, in *Re Weekes' Settlement*,[82] Romer J considered that if there had been a general intention in favour of the class this would have rendered the power in the nature of a trust.

A second analysis is that the general intention in favour of the class creates a fixed trust in favour of the whole class, so that from the very beginning the objects/beneficiaries enjoy equal shares in the fund, but that the donor of the power is entitled to divest them of their interests by the exercise of the power.

A third analysis is that the trust in favour of the whole class applies only in default of appointment, just as would be the case if the trust had contained an express gift over in default of appointment. In this situation the beneficiaries of the trust in default of appointment do not have vested, but only contingent, interests which depend for their vesting and fulfilment on the power not being exercised.

The confusion has arisen because the rule only comes into play after there has been a failure on the part of the donee to exercise the power. If appointments had been made, no difficulties would arise. It is better to regard the court as acting ex post facto, and implying a trust in favour of the objects of power in the event of no appointment being made, rather than to construe a trust in their favour from the beginning. This was the approach taken by Buckley J in *Re Wills' Trust Deeds*.[83] He considered that a trust in favour of the objects only arose in the event of default:

> A perusal of these cases . . . leads to the conclusion that they really turn on the question whether on the particular facts of each case it was proper to infer that there was a trust in default of appointment for the objects of the power. The court did not, and I think, could not compel the donee personally to exercise the power but carried what it conceived to be the settlor's intention into effect by executing an implied trust in default of appointment.[84]

It, therefore, seems that the best analysis is that a power is given to the donee, which he is under no duty to exercise, but that in the event of there being no exercise the court implies a trust in favour of the class on the basis of a general intention in their favour on the part of the donor. The objects thus have no beneficial entitlement to the fund until the trust is implied and the donee of the power has no enforceable duties and is not in breach by failing to make appointments.

8 When is a power fiduciary?

If a power of appointment is held by the donee in a fiduciary capacity, the power is a 'fiduciary power'. This will normally occur because the donee is also a trustee of the property subject to the power. In *Re Hay's Settlement Trusts*,[85] David Greig and Colin Oliver were the trustees of a settlement made by Lady Hay. As part of the settlement, they enjoyed a general power of appointment over the property subject to the trust. As they were trustees, they held their power in a fiduciary capacity.[86] In *Mettoy Pension Trustees Ltd v*

80 [1803] 8 Ves 561.
81 [1840] 5 My & Cr 72 at 92.
82 [1897] 1 Ch 289.
83 [1964] Ch 219.
84 [1964] Ch 219 at 230.
85 [1982] 1 WLR 202.
86 See also *Breadner v Granville-Grossman* [2001] Ch 523.

Evans,[87] Warner J described such an obligation as a 'fiduciary power in the full sense',[88] which he defined as:

> comprising any power conferred on the trustees of the property or any other person as a trustee of the power itself.

The case concerned the pension fund of a company, Mettoy plc, which had gone into liquidation. After the fund had met the fixed entitlements of pensioners, there was a surplus of some £9 million remaining in the fund. Rule 13(5) of the fund's rules granted a power of appointment over any surplus, which could be exercised to increase the entitlements of the pensioners. This power was held by the company and not by the separate trustee of the fund. If the power was not exercised, an undistributed surplus would pass to the company itself (see Figure 26.3). In these circumstances Warner J concluded that the power was a fiduciary power, even though the trustee was not the donee.[89] He relied on two main factors to reach this conclusion. First, he considered that if the power were a mere power and not a fiduciary power, any supposed discretion by the company to appoint increased entitlements to the pensioners would be 'illusory', since the company would in effect only be making ex gratia gifts from property which they owned absolutely.[90] Second, the objects of the power were not volunteers, as the fund surplus had arisen partially from their own pension contributions and not from successful investment or over-contribution by the company alone.[91]

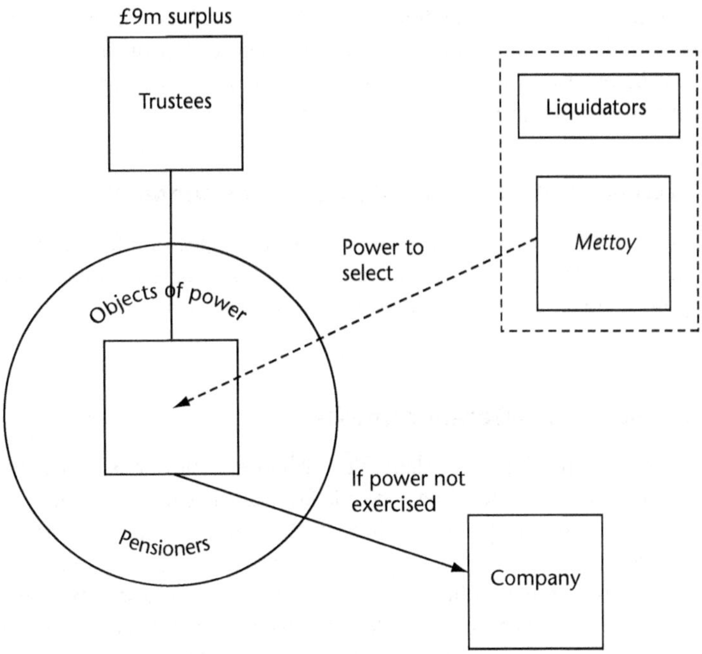

Figure 26.3 Fiduciary powers: *Mettoy Pension Trustees v Evans*

[87] [1990] 1 WLR 1587. See Gardner, 'Fiduciary Powers in Toytown' [1991] 107 LQR 214. The reasoning as it relates to the setting aside of decisions by trustees (the rule in *Re Hastings Bass*) was restricted by *Pitt v Holt* [2013] UKSC 26, but the case remains relevant on the points cited.

[88] Using the language of Chitty J in *Re Somes* [1896] 1 Ch 250.

[89] This finding of a fiduciary duty has been subject to criticism—see Barkley, 'The Content of the Trust: What Must a Trustee Be Obliged to Do with the Property?' [2013] Trusts & Trustees 452.

[90] Ibid at 547. [91] [1993] OPLR 171.

9 Duties of the donee of fiduciary powers

The key difference between a 'fiduciary power' and a 'mere power' is that the donee of a fiduciary power owes limited duties to the objects. In *Re Hay's Settlement Trusts*,[92] Sir Robert Megarry V-C held that there were three additional duties owed by the donee to the objects of a fiduciary power.

(1) Considering whether to exercise the power

Unlike a mere power, which the donee need never consider whether or not to exercise, Megarry V-C held that the donee of a fiduciary power cannot 'simply fold his hands and ignore it, for normally he must from time to time consider whether or not to exercise the power'.[93] This duty is enforceable by the court, which may direct the donee to consider whether he should exercise the power.[94]

(2) Duty to consider the range of objects

The fiduciary nature of the position of the donee also affects the manner in which a donee makes appointments. Following the decision of the House of Lords in *McPhail v Doulton*,[95] which concerned the duties of trustees of a discretionary trust, Megarry V-C held that the donee of a fiduciary power must 'make such a survey of the range of objects' as will enable him to carry out his fiduciary duty.[96] This does not mean that he has to identify every single member of the class of objects before making any allocations of the fund, but that he must find out 'the permissible area of selection'. He cannot make an appointment to the first object who comes to mind.

(3) Duty to consider the appropriateness of appointments

Having considered the range of potential objects, the donee of a fiduciary power must 'then consider responsibly, in individual cases, whether a contemplated beneficiary was within the power and whether, in relation to other possible claimants, a particular grant was appropriate'.[97]

(4) Different duties in different contexts

There is a degree of circularity in identifying whether a power is fiduciary and what duties are imposed on the donee. The power is fiduciary because the donee is subject to duties; but it follows that if the power is fiduciary, the donee is subject to duties. Sir Robert Megarry's analysis in *Re Hay's Settlement Trusts*[98] of the duties of a donee of a fiduciary power tends to assume that all fiduciary powers involve the same duties. The decision of the Court of Appeal in *Gomez v Gomez-Monche Vives*[99] accepts that there is a wide range of fiduciary duties, some analogous to those of a trustee, and some less so. This means that a more sophisticated analysis of fiduciary powers is required: a power will be fiduciary if

[92] [1982] 1 WLR 202. [93] [1982] 1 WLR 202 at 209. [94] [1982] 1 WLR 202.

[95] [1971] AC 424.

[96] Per Lord Wilberforce, quoted by Sir Robert Megarry V-C in *Re Hay's Settlement Trusts* [1982] 1 WLR 202 at 209.

[97] *McPhail v Doulton* [1971] AC 424 at 457, quoted by Sir Robert Megarry in *Re Hay's Settlement Trusts* [1982] 1 WLR 202 at 209.

[98] [1982] 1 WLR 202. [99] [2008] EWCA Civ 1065; [2009] Ch 245 (CA).

the donee is subject to duties, but the nature of those duties will depend upon an analysis of the instrument creating the power and any other relevant circumstances. The power may even be one which the donee is bound to exercise.[100] One such situation, which demonstrates that importance of context, is in relation to members of charitable companies. In *Lehtimäki v Cooper*,[101] the Supreme Court directed a member of a charitable company, Dr Lehtimäki, to vote in favour of a proposed distribution of charity assets to another charitable company. The Children's Investment Fund was a company limited by guarantee and a registered charity set up for the purpose of improving children's health in the developing world. As a result of governance difficulties caused by the breakdown of the spousal relationship between two of the eight charity directors (and trustees), a scheme was agreed to set up a new charity, run by the estranged wife, who would resign from the existing charity. A transfer of $360m from the existing charity to the new charity had been agreed, which required both court and Charity Commission approval. Dr Lehtimäki, one of the three charity members (alongside the estranged spouses) but not also a director, had the right to vote whether this distribution was in the best interests of the charity under s 217 of the Companies Act 2006. The Supreme Court found that Dr Lëhtimaki, as a charity member, was a fiduciary and was bound to consider whether the resolution should be passed solely by considering the best interests of the object of the charity. This was in common with the findings of the judges at first instance and the Court of Appeal, but the point of variance from the Court of Appeal concerned whether the court could require Dr Lehtimäki to exercise his direction in a particular way. While noting that normally the court would not interfere in the exercise of a discretionary power unless it was exercised improperly or unreasonably, Lady Arden noted that 'the present case is a rare exception to that principle' and:

> The trustees of CIFF have surrendered their discretion to the court and the court's priority is to see that fiduciaries for the charity perform their duties in the way most likely to achieve its continued existence notwithstanding what has been held to be in effect an existential threat to the proper governance of the charity. I also consider that the court has jurisdiction to give a direction to Dr Lehtimäki to vote in favour of the section 217 resolution.[102]

10 Supervision by the court of fiduciary powers

Since the donee of a fiduciary power owes duties to the objects, the court will ensure that these duties are properly performed.

(1) Appointments made without due consideration

If appointments are made by the donee without proper consideration of the range of objects and the appropriateness of the particular appointments being made, then such appointments will be an invalid exercise of the power. In *Turner v Turner*,[103] the trustees

[100] *Bridge Trustees Ltd v Noel Penny (Turbines) Ltd* [2008] EWHC 2054 (Ch) at 18.

[101] [2020] UKSC 33. See Picton, '*Lehtimäki v Cooper*: Duty and Jurisdiction in Charity Law' (2020) 84 MLR 383.

[102] [2020] UKSC 33 at [201]. Note, however, that Lord Briggs (with whom Lord Wilson and Lord Kitchin agreed), did not think an exception was needed, as once the court had determined what was in the best interests of the charity, it would be a breach of duty for the member to vote against that, so the court could intervene to stop the breach. This was the approach taken by the High Court: *The Children's Investment Fund Foundation (UK) v Att-Gen* [2017] EWHC 1379 (Ch).

[103] [1983] 2 All ER 745.

of a settlement made appointments by deed under a power of appointment they held in their capacity as trustees. They had executed the deeds at the request of the solicitors acting for the settlor without reading or understanding what they were signing, and without making a decision to appoint. Mervyn Davies J held that these appointments should be set aside because they had been made 'in breach of their duty, in that it was their duty to "consider" before appointing, and this they did not do'.[104] If the exercise of the power is, on the face, within the powers of the done, then the improper exercise will be voidable rather than void.[105]

(2) **Failure to exercise the power**

Where the donee of a fiduciary power has failed to make any appointments, the question arises whether the court can intervene to compel them to carry out their duties. In *Re Hay's Settlement Trusts*,[106] Sir Robert Megarry V-C indicated that the courts would compel the donee of a fiduciary power to consider exercising it.[107] However, the courts have been reluctant to suggest that they would compel the donee to *exercise* the power, as this is inconsistent with its discretionary character. In *McPhail v Doulton*[108] Lord Wilberforce cited the judgment of Lord Upjohn in *Re Gulbenkian's Settlement*[109] and stated:

> although the trustees may . . . be under a fiduciary duty to consider whether or in what way they should exercise their power the court will not normally compel its exercise.[110]

However, in the *Mettoy*[111] case, Warner J considered that in some circumstances the court might be willing to step in and compel the exercise of a fiduciary power. On the facts of *Mettoy*, the company donee was incapable of exercising the power itself, and it was held by the liquidators. They would be unable to exercise it because of a conflict between their duty to give proper consideration to exercising it in favour of the pensioners and their duty to the company's creditors, which would require them to exercise the power to enable the company to take the surplus in default. Warner J held that, since there was no one remaining who could exercise the power, the court should step in. He held that in such circumstances the court could exercise the fiduciary power in the same way that it was entitled to intervene if the trustees of a discretionary trust were failing to carry out their duties.

It is suggested that caution is needed. The traditional distinction between trusts, which the court will enforce, and powers, which it will not, would be all but abolished if the courts are willing to enforce fiduciary powers in exactly the same way that they will enforce discretionary trusts. The limitation seems to be the recognition that this procedure is only available in the limited exceptional circumstances where the power cannot be exercised because there is no donee able to make any appointments, or where the nature of the obligation is such that the donee is obliged to exercise the power.[112]

A different problem arises where the donee of a fiduciary power has failed to make any appointments because he has not fulfilled his duty to consider whether or not to exercise the power. In *Breadner v Granville-Grossman*,[113] the two trustees of a discretionary trust were granted a power of appointment in 1976. Under the terms of the trust, this power

[104] [1983] 2 All ER 745 at 752.

[105] Pitt v Holt [2013] UKSC 26, resolving earlier uncertainty on this point.

[106] [1982] 1 WLR 202. [107] [1982] 1 WLR 202 at 209. [108] [1971] AC 424.

[109] [1970] AC 508. [110] [1971] AC 424 at 456–7. [111] [1990] 1 WLR 1587.

[112] This explains the situation, outlined above, in *Lehtimäki v Cooper* [2020] UKSC 33.

[113] [2000] 4 All ER 705.

had to be exercised before a specified date, namely, 2 August 1989. At a late stage, one of the trustees prepared a deed appointing the entire beneficial interest to one beneficiary, which he only explained to his co-trustee on the day that the deed was executed, which was 2 August 1989; in other words, after the last day for exercising the 1976 power. The beneficiary claimed that the appointment was still effective in equity, on the grounds that the trustees had failed to comply with their duty to consider exercising it. Park J held that, while the trustees had failed to perform their duty to consider exercising the power, the court could not intervene because the power had ceased to be exercisable, even though they would have made the appointment if they had performed their duty.

11 Effect of failure to exercise a fiduciary power

Unless the court is prepared to intervene to compel the exercise of a fiduciary power, the effect of its non-exercise is identical to the failure to exercise a mere power.

12 Release of powers

The donor of a power of appointment, whether a bare power or a fiduciary power, may wish to release it. As a consequence of release he will cease to be able to make any appointments. This has the same effect on the ownership of the property subject to the power as if the power had not been exercised. Therefore, on release, those entitled in default will automatically become entitled to the property previously held subject to the power. Sometimes a power may be released to remove persons from the class of potential recipients of the property if the possibility of their receiving a benefit would result in tax disadvantages. For example, it may be advantageous to exclude the settlor from the class of objects of a power to avoid inheritance tax under the 'reservation of benefit' rules. Similarly, a settlement may be liable to income tax if the settlor or his wife may benefit from the exercise of a power of appointment in their favour. In *Muir v IRC*,[114] the Court of Appeal held that the trustees had released their power to pay income from the trust towards the payment of premiums of insurance policies held by persons including the settlor, and that, therefore, the settlor had no interest in the income from the settlement and was not liable to surtax. In *Re Wills' Trust Deeds*,[115] property was held on trust for such of the issue of the testator or charitable institutions as the trustees should appoint. The trustees sought to release the power in favour of the testator's issue so that the trust would be for exclusively charitable objects.

(1) The consequences of release

If property is gifted to persons subject to a power of appointment which may divest them of their interest, on the release of the power their interests will become indefeasible. This was seen in *Re Mills*,[116] which concerned the will of Algernon Mills. His residuary estate was to be held for the benefit of such of his father's children and remoter issue that his brother should appoint or, in default of any such appointment, for his brother absolutely. The brother made a number of appointments and then released the power by deed. The Court of Appeal held that this was a valid release, and the consequence was that the brother became absolutely entitled to the property under the default provision.

[114] [1966] 1 WLR 1269. [115] [1964] Ch 219. [116] [1930] 1 Ch 654, CA.

Not every power is capable of being released by the donee. The leading authority concerning the circumstances in which a power may be released is the judgment of Buckley J in *Re Wills' Trust Deeds*.[117] Generally, a donee will only be able to release a power which he is under no obligation to exercise or to consider exercising.

(a) Mere powers

In the case of a bare or mere power, which is not held in any fiduciary capacity and where there is no express or implied trust in favour of the objects in default of appointment, the donee may release the power. As Buckley J said:

> Where a power is conferred on someone who is not a trustee of the property to which the power relates or, if he is such a trustee, is not conferred on him in that capacity, then in the absence of a trust in favour of the objects of the power in default of appointment, the donee is, at any rate prima facie, not under any duty recognisable by the court to exercise a power such as to disenable him from releasing the power.[118]

Mere powers fall within the ambit of s 155 of the Law of Property Act 1925, which provides:

> A person to whom any power, whether coupled with an interest or not, is given, may by deed release, or contract not to exercise, the power.[119]

(b) Mere powers with a trust in default of appointment

Where there is a trust in default of appointment under the power, according to Buckley J, the donee is not entitled to release the power so as to defeat the trust. This will be so whether the trust in default is express or implied under the rule in *Burrough v Philcox*.[120] This was explained by Buckley J:

> if a power is granted to appoint among a class of objects and in default of appointment there is a trust, express or implied, in favour of the members of that class, the donee of the power cannot by failure to appoint or by purporting to bind himself not to appoint or, which comes to the same thing, by purporting to release his power, defeat the interests of the members of the class of objects. This proposition really needs only to be stated to be accepted. The problem in such cases, where there is no express trust in default of appointment, is whether such a trust should be inferred . . . [A] power of the kind just mentioned cannot be released, for the donee is under a duty to exercise it, notwithstanding that the court may not be able to compel him personally to perform that duty, and can remedy his default only be executing the trust in default of appointment.[121]

Buckley J's view that a power cannot be released in this situation is based on the assumption that the trust in favour of the members of the class arises from an obligation to exercise the power. As has already been explained, this may not be the best interpretation of *Burrough v Philcox*. Despite his view to the contrary, the logic of his statement that the power cannot be released also cannot apply to an express trust by way of gift over in default in favour of the class of objects. Such release will accelerate the gift in favour of the class. In *Re Radcliffe*[122] a father held a power of appointment in favour of the class of objects of his children, with an express trust in favour of them equally in default of appointment. One of the three children had died in infancy, and the father was entitled as his administrator. The father released the power of appointment by deed and demanded that the trustees pay a third of the trust property to him. The Court of Appeal, following

[117] [1964] Ch 219. [118] [1964] Ch 219 at 237.

[119] Law of Property Act 1925, s 160 provides that s 155 applies to 'powers created or arising either before or after the commencement' of the Act.

[120] [1840] 5 My & Cr 72. [121] [1964] Ch 219 at 236. [122] [1892] 1 Ch 27.

the earlier case of *Smith v Houblon*,[123] held that there had been a valid release and that, subject to the father surrendering his life-interest over the trust, he was entitled to the third to be transferred to him.

(c) Fiduciary powers

(i) Fiduciary powers with no authorization to release

Where a power is held in a fiduciary capacity, whether by a trustee or other fiduciary, the donee may not release it unless release is authorized by the instrument creating the power, although Warren J permitted a release as part of a variation of trust approved by the court since it was strongly arguable that the variation was for the benefit of the objects.[124] When the predecessor to s 155 of the Law of Property Act 1925 was enacted in 1881,[125] the courts held that it did not apply to trusts held in a fiduciary capacity.[126] This was followed by the Court of Appeal in *Re Mills*[127] and in *Re Wills' Trust Deeds*, where Buckley J said:

> [W]here a power is conferred on trustees virtute officii in relation to their trust property, they cannot release it or bind themselves not to exercise it . . . [T]he same is true if the power is conferred on persons who are in fact trustees of the settlement but is conferred on them by name and not by reference to their office, if on the true view of the facts they were selected as donees of the power because they were the trustees.[128]

This principle was applied by Millett J in *Re Courage Group's Pension Schemes*,[129] where he held that a committee of management of a pension scheme could not release their powers or discretion so as to deprive their successors of the right to exercise them as they were vested in the committee in a fiduciary capacity. This restriction will also apply where the power is held in a fiduciary capacity, even though the donees are not trustees, as in *Mettoy Pension Trustees v Evans*,[130] the company, although not a trustee of the fund, held a power of appointment in a fiduciary capacity and could not release it.

(ii) Fiduciary powers with authorization to release

The donee of a fiduciary power will be entitled to release it if the instrument creating the power gives him the authority to do so. The principle was stated by Harman LJ in *Muir v IRC*,[131] where he commented on the judgment of Buckley J in *Re Wills' Trusts Deeds*:[132]

> I would agree that, if a power is conferred on trustees virtute officii, that is to say, if it be a [fiduciary] power which the trustees have the duty to exercise, they cannot release it in the absence of words in the trust deed authorising them to do so . . .[133]

On the facts he found that the trust instrument did authorize a release.[134]

(d) Discretionary trusts

Owing to the evolutionary development of concepts and terminology, some early cases referring to 'trust powers' would today be recognized as 'discretionary trusts'. Clearly, these cannot be released because the obligation is in the nature of a trust, and the court will compel its exercise.

123 [1859] 26 Beav 482. 124 *A v B* [2016] EWHC 340 (Ch). 125 Conveyancing Act 1881, s 52.

126 See *Weller v Kerr* [1866] LR 1 Sc & Div 11; *Re Eyre* [1883] 49 LT 259; *Saul v Pattinson* [1886] 55 LJ Ch 831.

127 [1930] 1 Ch 654. 128 [1964] Ch 219. 129 [1987] 1 WLR 495. 130 [1991] 2 All ER 513.

131 [1990] 1 WLR 1587. 132 [1964] Ch 219. 133 [1966] 1 WLR 1269 at 1283.

134 See also *Blausten v IRC* [1972] Ch 256, CA.

(2) Means of release

It seems clear that a purely oral release will be ineffective to release a power.[135] However, if a donee of a power of appointment possesses the jurisdiction to release the power, he may do so by deed, as provided in s 155 of the Law of Property Act 1925. Alternatively, a power may be released by the donee entering into a contract not to exercise the power, as also provided in s 155. A power may be released as part of a variation of trust approved by the court.[136] It seems that a power will also be released where there has been any dealing with the property subject to it which is inconsistent with the exercise of the power. In *Foakes v Jackson*,[137] a power was held jointly by a husband and wife, and the survivor had a separate power. A deed was executed in 1886 by the husband, wife, and those beneficially entitled to the property assigning it to one of the objects. In 1899, after the wife's death, the husband purported to appoint the property to a different object. Farwell J held that the earlier deed which, with the intention of the donees and the parties entitled in default, had the effect of passing the property absolutely to the object operated as a release of the power. Similarly, in *Re Courtauld's Settlement*,[138] Plowman J held that where there had been an application to vary a settlement so that a power was extinguished, there was no need to execute a separate deed of release. Trustees may surrender their trusts and powers by paying the trust property into court, as provided in s 63 of the Trustee Act 1925. The application of proprietary estoppel may also have the effect of operating as a release of a power.[139]

(3) Release and fraud on a power

The equitable doctrine that will invalidate the fraudulent exercise of a power has no application to the release of a power of appointment, and, therefore, a donee may release a power even though he thereby derives a personal benefit. In *Re Somes*[140] a father held a power of appointment over property held on his marriage settlement. In default, his daughter was absolutely entitled. He was suffering financial difficulties and, therefore, released the power, and he and his daughter then mortgaged their interests in the fund for £10,000, which was paid to the father. Chitty J held that this was a perfectly valid release:

> it appears to me that there is a fallacy in applying to a release of a power of this kind the doctrines applicable to the fraudulent exercise of such a power. There is no duty imposed on the donee of a limited power to make an appointment; there is no fiduciary relationship between him and the objects of the power beyond this, that if he does exercise the power of appointment, he must exercise it honestly for the benefit of an object or the objects of the power, and not corruptly for his own personal benefit; but I cannot see any ground for applying that doctrine to the case of a release of a power; the donee of the power may, or he may not, be acting in his own interest, but he is at liberty, in my opinion, to say that he will never make any appointment under the power, and to execute a release of it.[141]

Obviously, this will only apply if the power is of a type which may be released, and the court finds that the power is not subject to fiduciary duties excluding such a release.

[135] See *Re Christie-Miller's Settlement Trusts* [1961] 1 All ER 855n; *Re Courtauld's Settlement* [1965] 2 All ER 544n.

[136] *Re Christie Miller's Marriage Settlement Trusts* [1961] 1 WLR 462; *A v B* [2016] EWHC 340 (Ch).

[137] [1900] 1 Ch 807. [138] [1965] 2 All ER 544n.

[139] *Fielden v Christie-Miller* [2015] EWHC 87 (Ch) at 39.

[140] [1896] 1 Ch 250. [141] [1896] 1 Ch 250 at 255.

27

Discretionary trusts

1 Introduction

This chapter considers the key features of a discretionary trust. Unlike a fixed trust, which gives defined shares to the beneficiaries, a discretionary trust gives the trustees a discretion as to how to allocate the beneficial interests. When Steven Huntley was drawing up his will in 2009–10, he wanted to provide for his partner and their two children, as well as his three children from previous relationships. However, he was concerned that they might not be capable of managing a large inheritance (his estate was worth £6.9 million when he died in a motor cycle accident in 2011). For this reason he was advised to set up a discretionary trust. He was also advised that this arrangement would allow his private company (the Swift Group of Companies Ltd) to be continued by the trustees without having to distribute the business assets.[1]

2 The nature of discretionary trusts

Discretionary trusts were usefully defined by Warner J in *Mettoy Pension Trustees Ltd v Evans* as:

> cases where someone, usually but not necessarily the trustee,[2] is under a duty to select from among a class of beneficiaries those who are to receive, and the proportions in which they are to receive, income or capital of the trust property.[3]

They are mechanisms by which an owner of property can grant to others the power to allocate a fund among a defined class or group. As in a power of appointment, the allocator has complete discretion as to how the fund should be allocated, either or both in terms of the persons who should receive shares of the fund, and the size of the shares they should receive. However, unlike mere powers of appointment, the allocator is under a mandatory duty to make allocations in accordance with the terms of the trust. The court will intervene to ensure that this duty is discharged.

[1] *Re Huntley Deceased* [2014] EWHC 547 (Ch). The case came to court because his advisers failed to draft the will to accord in full with his wishes.

[2] This exception recognizes the possibility of there being separate management and custodian trustees or of the discretions being conferred on a protector.

[3] [1990] 1 WLR 1587.

3 The flexibility of discretionary trusts

The discretionary trust is, therefore, an extremely flexible mechanism for the distribution of property. It combines all the advantages of the power of appointment in permitting the owner of property not merely to delegate the task of transferring his property to others, but also of delegating the responsibility for deciding how that property should be distributed. Yet it avoids the potential pitfalls of the mere power because the trustees are under a duty to distribute according to the terms of the trust, which is enforceable by the court. This inherent flexibility, coupled with the security of enforcement by the court, has made the discretionary trust ideal as a means of allocating large funds among large potential classes of beneficiaries. For example, in the leading case of *McPhail v Doulton*,[4] Bertram Baden established a trust in 1941 to provide benefits for the staff of Matthew Hall & Co Ltd and their relatives and dependants (see Figure 27.1). Clause 9(a) of the deed stated that:

> The trustees shall apply the net income of the fund in making at their absolute discretion grants to or for the benefit of any of the officers and employees or ex-officers and ex-employees of the company or to any relative or dependants of any such person in such amounts . . . as they think fit.

In 1941 the company employed some 1,300 people. By 1962 the fund contained assets valued at £163,000, which had risen to £463,000 in 1972. Clearly, it was never the intention of Mr Baden that each and every member of the specified class should receive payments from the fund, but that those appointed trustees should have the discretion to select some to benefit. Equally, it was not his intention that the trustees be able to sit idly by and fail to make any allocations at all. The language of the deed clearly indicated an obligation, or

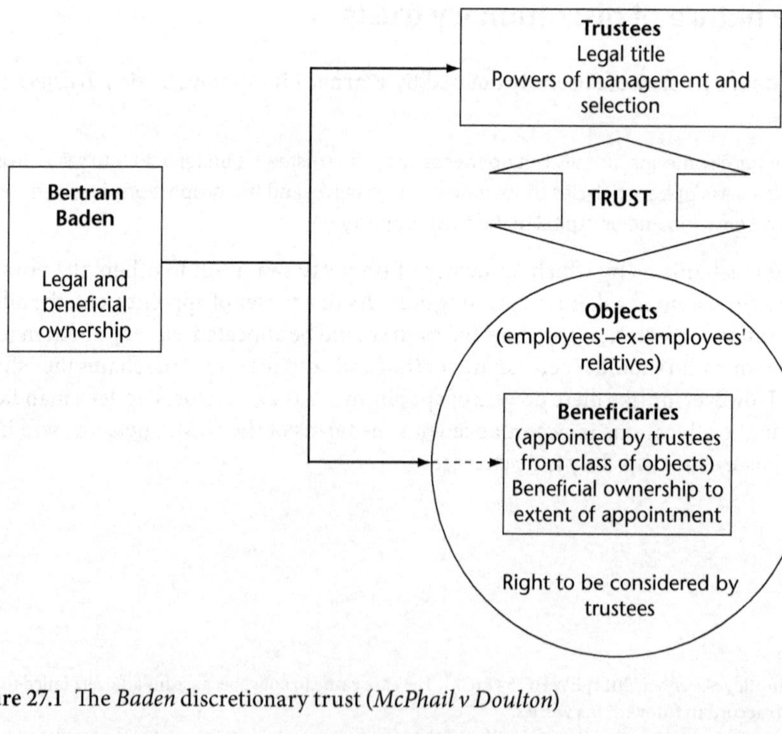

Figure 27.1 The *Baden* discretionary trust (*McPhail v Doulton*)

[4] [1971] AC 424.

duty, to distribute the income of the fund. The House of Lords held that a trust power or, in today's terminology, a discretionary trust, had been created. Although the trustees had complete discretion which particular members of the class specified were to receive shares of the income produced by the fund, they had no freedom to refuse to carry out the trust.

4 The development of the discretionary trust

Although the terminology of the 'discretionary trust' is a more recent development, the underlying concept of an equitable obligation which is discretionary in part while remaining predominantly mandatory is well established and has a strong historical pedigree.[5] In *Brown v Higgs*,[6] Lord Eldon, the Lord Chancellor, held that equitable obligations could not simply be categorized as trusts or powers:

> But there are not only a mere trust and a mere power, but there is also known to this court a power which the party to whom it is given is entrusted and required to execute; and with regard to that species of power the court consider it as partaking so much of the nature and qualities of a trust that, if the person who has that duty imposed upon him does not discharge it, the court will, to a certain extent, discharge the duty in his room and place.[7]

In essence, he was describing what today would be termed a discretionary trust. The older cases often use the phrase 'trust power'. This term has been the source of some confusion, since it is used interchangeably in the cases to describe both a trust implied in default of the exercise of a power of appointment under the principle of *Burrough v Philcox*,[8] and an obligation which would today be characterized as a discretionary trust.

In *Crockett v Crockett*,[9] Lord Cottenham found that a possible construction of a will where a husband left all his property 'at the disposal of his wife, for herself and children', was that she was 'as between herself and her children found a trustee, with a large discretion as to the application of the fund'.[10] This analysis was followed by Sir John Romilly MR in *Hart v Tribe*.[11] Even in the leading case of *McPhail v Doulton*,[12] the House of Lords spoke of the obligation created by Baden's deed as a 'trust power',[13] although when the case returned to the Court of Appeal as *Re Baden's Deed Trusts (No 2)*[14] the term 'discretionary trust' was used. It is important to be alive to the different terminology used.[15]

5 Types of discretionary trusts

There are two types of discretionary trust: 'exhaustive' and 'non-exhaustive'.

(1) Exhaustive discretionary trusts

In an exhaustive discretionary trust the trustees are subject to a duty to distribute the whole of the trust fund, or its income, to the potential beneficiaries. They have no power to decide not to distribute part of the fund. An example of an exhaustive discretionary trust

[5] See also Chapter 2. [6] [1800] 5 Ves 495. [7] [1800] 5 Ves 495 at 570.
[8] [1840] 5 My & Cr 72. [9] [1848] 2 Ph 553. [10] [1848] 2 Ph 553 at 561.
[11] [1854] 18 Beav 215. [12] [1971] AC 424.
[13] Lord Wilberforce did on one occasion refer to 'discretionary trusts': see [1971] AC 424 at 452.
[14] [1973] Ch 9.
[15] See also *Mettoy Pensions v Evans* [1991] 1 WLR 1587, for a useful discussion of the various terminologies used in the cases, and the potential for confusion between trusts and powers.

is found in *Re Locker's Settlement Trusts*,[16] where a discretionary trust was established in favour of a class of individuals, charities, and other institutions. The trustees were regarded as being in breach of trust when they failed to distribute the trust income within a reasonable period of time.[17] An exhaustive discretionary trust will normally arise, as in *Re Gourju's Will Trusts*,[18] when the trustees are not given an express power to retain all or part of the income from the fund.

(2) **Non-exhaustive discretionary trusts**

In a non-exhaustive discretionary trust, the trustees are not obliged to distribute the whole of the trust fund or its income among the class of beneficiaries but may, in their discretion, decide to accumulate it. This is only possible if the trustees are expressly given the power to retain and accumulate the income, or part of the income, from the trust fund by the terms of the trust. *McPhail v Doulton*[19] is an example of a non-exhaustive discretionary trust. The trust deed did not require the trustees to distribute all the income generated by the fund to the employees, ex-employees, relatives, and dependants, but granted them the power to retain and accumulate it.[20] In many ways a non-exhaustive discretionary trust is extremely similar in practice to a fiduciary power. In neither case is the allocator of the fund obliged to distribute the fund or its income to the class of potential objects or beneficiaries. This leads to the question whether there is any real distinction between them.[21] Analytically, a distinction can be drawn on the basis of the nature of the duties owed by the allocator in each case. Under a non-exhaustive discretionary trust, the prime duty of the trustee is to distribute the fund income among the class of beneficiaries, although there is a power to retain and accumulate. Whether the trustee has exercised that power properly is open to the supervision of the court under an objective test, that he must have acted in the best interests of the class of beneficiaries. In the case of a power of appointment, the donee of the power has no prime duty, as it is purely within his discretion whether he allocates the property subject to the power. He owes no objective duties that the court can supervise, but purely a subjective duty to act as he thinks best. Provided he acts genuinely, the court cannot question his decision. This is a fine distinction, but it demonstrates that the non-exhaustive discretionary trust remains in essence a trust, although it is extremely close on the scale of equitable obligations to the fiduciary power. A further distinction is that, under a discretionary trust, the legal title to the trust fund will normally be vested in the trustees, who will thus also be required to invest and manage the trust property. In contrast, a fiduciary power may be held by a person with no rights of ownership to the fund. Thus, in *Mettoy Pension Trustees Ltd v Evans*,[22] a power of appointment over a pension fund surplus was held in a fiduciary capacity by a company which was not simultaneously the trustee thereof. However, in the majority of cases, a fiduciary power will be held by a trustee, since the donee's status as a trustee invests the power with fiduciary characteristics.

[16] [1977] 1 WLR 1323. [17] [1977] 1 WLR 1323 at 1325. [18] [1943] Ch 24.

[19] [1971] AC 424.

[20] Clause 9(b) of the deed creating the Matthew Hall Staff trust fund stated: 'The trustees shall not be bound to exhaust the income of any year or other period in making grants', and granted them a power to invest the undistributed surplus under clause 6(a).

[21] See, for example, Grbich, '*Baden*: Awakening the Conceptually Moribund Trust' [1974] 37 MLR 643.

[22] [1990] 1 WLR 1587.

6 Essential validity of discretionary trusts

A discretionary trust will only be validly created if it satisfies the requirements for the validity of trusts in general. It must have certainty of subject matter and objects, and it must comply with the beneficiary principle. The trust must not exist for a period exceeding the duration of the perpetuity period,[23] must not be capricious, and must not be 'administratively unworkable'.

(1) Certainty of objects

(a) Historical background

We have already looked at the test for certainty of objects. Prior to the leading case of *McPhail v Doulton*,[24] the test was whether a complete list of beneficiaries could be drawn up. The reason for requiring this is that, following the principle well expressed by Lord Eldon in *Morice v Bishop of Durham*,[25] a trust is only valid if the court is able to execute it in the event of a failure by the trustee to carry out their obligation so to do, whether through death, neglect, or refusal. Before *McPhail v Doulton*, it was generally thought that the only method the court could employ to carry out the trust in the event of the trustee's default was to order equal division of the fund between all the potential beneficiaries. Obviously, such equal division would require a complete list of the beneficiaries. However, some early cases had adopted a more flexible approach, holding that the court could exercise its discretion in the event of the trustee's failure. In *Moseley v Moseley*,[26] an estate was held on trust by two trustees for such of the testator's relatives as they should think fit. When the trustees failed to exercise their discretion to allocate the property, the court ordered that it be conveyed into court, rather than divided equally among the class of potential beneficiaries.[27] In *Warburton v Warburton*,[28] trustees held a fund on discretionary trust for the testator's children. The House of Lords ordered that the eldest child be given a double share. In *Hart v Tribe*,[29] a testator's wife held £4,000 on discretionary trust for herself and his children. She refused to award any of the income from the fund for the education and maintenance of his son by another marriage. Sir John Romilly MR directed that the boy receive £30 a year from the fund. Although explicable as a case where the trustees' discretion had not been exercised bona fides, this decision does seem to amount to an exercise of the discretion by the court. In earlier proceedings[30] the Master of the Rolls had indicated that, although the normal means by which the court can execute the trust is equal division between the beneficiaries, this is only one method, and that the court can compel the trustees to exercise their discretion.[31] However, the orthodox position was reiterated in *Gray v Gray*,[32] where Thomas Smith MR held that the only way the court could exercise a discretionary trust where the trustee had failed to do so was by ordering equal division between all the members of the class, and a similar view was taken by Sir Richard Arden in *Kemp v Kemp*.[33] The cases which adopted a more flexible approach were condemned as anomalous by the Court of Appeal in *IRC v Broadway Cottages Trust*.[34] Jenkins LJ asserted the principle that 'a trust for such members of a given

[23] *Re Coleman* [1936] Ch 528. Note that it is possible to vary existing trusts to take advange of new Perpetuity periods—see *Greenwall v Gibbs* [2020] EQHC 1226 (Ch).

[24] [1971] AC 424. [25] [1805] 10 Ves 522 at 539–40. [26] [1673] Cas temp Finch 53.

[27] See also *Clarke v Turner* [1694] Freem Ch 198. [28] [1702] 4 Bro Parl Cas 1.

[29] [1854] 19 Beav 149. [30] *Hart v Tribe* [1854] 18 Beav 215.

[31] See also *Richardson v Chapman* [1760] 7 Bro Parl Cas 318.

[32] [1862] 13 I Ch R 404. [33] [1801] 5 Ves Jr 849. [34] [1955] Ch 20.

class of objects as the trustees shall select is void for uncertainty, unless the whole range of objects eligible for selection is ascertained or capable of ascertainment.'[35] The court rejected the view that it could execute the trust in any way other than by the equal division of the fund among all the potential beneficiaries.[36] It also thought that the trustees could only exercise their discretion properly if they considered every object individually before making a decision.

(b) Criticism of the 'complete list' test

The 'complete list' test applied to discretionary trusts in *IRC v Broadway Cottages Trust*[37] was open to two major criticisms. First, it failed to take account of the developing social function of discretionary trusts. While it might have been appropriate for 'family-style' discretionary trusts, where there was a small class of potential beneficiaries, so that in the event of default by the trustee equal division would be a sensible and fair solution, it was entirely inappropriate for discretionary trusts designed to allocate benefits from a fund among a large class of potential beneficiaries. The 'complete list' test was simply unworkable for trusts such as that established in *McPhail v Doulton*,[38] since it would never be possible to draw up a list of every single individual who fell within the class of employees, ex-employees, and relatives and dependants. The continued application of the 'complete list test' would stagnate the developing social function of the discretionary trust as a means of allocating property. Second, it placed too much emphasis on the distinction between trusts and powers of appointment. An inevitable consequence of the adoption of the complete list test for discretionary trusts was that it became essential to tell if a particular obligation was a trust or a power. If it were characterized as a power, then it would probably be valid, as the test of certainty in *Re Gulbenkian's Settlement Trusts*[39] would apply. If it were characterized as a trust, then the much more demanding complete list test would render it void. This placed an undue significance on the question of characterization, especially since the obligations are in essence very similar to each other. This problem is well illustrated by the history of the litigation in *McPhail v Doulton*.[40] Goff J, at first instance, and the majority of the Court of Appeal, held that a valid power had been created. This was despite the fact that the language creating the obligation was clearly of a mandatory character, and, therefore, the House of Lords unanimously held that it was a discretionary trust. The factor that had influenced the decisions of the lower courts was the problem that, as a result of the *Broadway Cottages*[41] test, to characterize the obligation as a trust would be to render it completely void for uncertainty, as indeed the minority of Lord Hodson and Lord Guest held. It was clearly unsatisfactory that the question of the validity of an obligation should depend upon the fine distinction between powers and discretionary trusts. As Lord Wilberforce observed:

> It is striking how narrow and in a sense artificial is the distinction, in cases such as the present, between trusts or as the particular type of trust is called, trust powers, and powers . . . It is only necessary to read the learned judgment in the Court of Appeal to see that what to one mind may appear as a power of distribution coupled with a trust to dispose of the undistributed surplus, by accumulation or otherwise, may to another appear as a trust for distribution coupled with a power to withhold a portion and accumulate or otherwise dispose of it. A layman and, I suspect, also a logician would find it hard to understand what the difference is.[42]

Given this artificiality, the majority of the House of Lords radically altered the test of certainty applicable to discretionary trusts.

[35] [1955] Ch 20 at 36. [36] [1955] Ch 20 at 31.
[37] [1955] Ch 20, CA. [38] [1971] AC 424. [39] [1970] AC 508.
[40] [1971] AC 424. [41] [1955] Ch 20. [42] *McPhail v Doulton* [1971] AC 424 at 448.

(c) The 'is or is not' test

The effect of the decision of the majority of the House of Lords in *McPhail v Doulton*[43] was briefly summarized by Lord Wilberforce:

> the rule recently fastened upon the courts by *IRC v Broadway Cottages Trust* ought to be discarded and the test for the validity of [discretionary trusts][44] ought to be similar to that accepted by this House in *Re Gulbenkian's Settlement* for powers, namely, that the trust is valid if it can be said with certainty that any given individual is or is not a member of the class.[45]

Thus, it is no longer necessary that it be possible to draw up a 'complete list' of potential beneficiaries. In reaching this conclusion Lord Wilberforce, with whom Lord Reid and Viscount Dilhorne concurred, considered that the Court of Appeal was mistaken in thinking that the duties of the trustees and the powers of intervention by the court required the adoption of the 'complete list test'. In doing so the House of Lords heralded a new attitude to trusts and powers in which primacy is given to the wishes of the settlor.

(2) Administrative unworkability

(a) What does it mean?

Even though a discretionary trust has sufficiently certain objects, it may still be void if it is 'administratively unworkable'. This concept was first proposed by Lord Wilberforce in *McPhail v Doulton*, where he suggested there may be classes where:

> the meaning of the words used is clear but the definition of the beneficiaries is so hopelessly wide as to not form 'anything like a class' so that the trust is administratively unworkable.[46]

He hesitated to give any example, but suggested that a discretionary trust in favour of 'all the residents of Greater London' would fall within the category of administratively unworkable trusts. The principle has been criticized because it is not clear precisely what evil it is seeking to prevent.[47] However, the cases suggest that the sheer size of the class is the most relevant factor. If a class is too vast in number, it is impossible for the trustees to carry out their duty to survey the range of the beneficiaries of the trust in any real sense, and in the event of their default the court would likewise be unable to carry out the distribution of the fund.

(b) Application

In *Re Hay's Settlement Trusts*,[48] Sir Robert Megarry V-C considered obiter that a discretionary trust with a class similar to that of an intermediate power, namely for all the people in the world except for an excluded class, would be administratively unworkable. In *R v District Auditor ex p West Yorkshire Metropolitan County Council*,[49] the Council attempted to create a discretionary trust over a fund of £400,000 in favour of the 'inhabitants of the County of West Yorkshire'. The Council's purpose was to circumvent government legislation which prevented them incurring expenditure prior to their being abolished. The Divisional Court held that, although the class was conceptually certain the

[43] [1971] AC 424. [44] Lord Wilberforce actually used the term 'trust powers'.

[45] [1971] AC 424 at 456.

[46] [1971] AC 424 at 457.

[47] See Harris, 'Trust, Power and Duty' [1971] 87 LQR 31; McKay, '*Re Baden* and the Third Class of Uncertainty' [1974] 38 Conv 269.

[48] [1982] 1 WLR 202.

[49] [1986] RVR 24; Harpum, 'Administrative Unworkability and Purpose Trusts' [1986] CLJ 391.

range of objects, comprising some 2.5 million potential beneficiaries, was so wide as to be 'incapable of forming anything like a class'. It was thus administratively unworkable and void. Drawing from Lord Wilberforce's example of 'all the residents of Greater London', and the facts of this case, it can be surmised that 'administrative unworkability' will only render discretionary trusts void which have a class ranging in the magnitude of millions. Where the line is to be drawn between trusts falling foul of the principle and those which are valid is impossible to predict. It is easier to understand the concept of administrative unworkability in the context of a fixed trust. There, in the case of a small gift to a large class, the costs of ascertainment and distribution could easily take up the whole, or a disproportionately large part, of the fund. With a discretionary trust it must be rare that a fund would be so small that no rational scheme could be devised. However, it is possible that with a small gift to a large class, it might prove impossible to devise any scheme that could have sufficient regard to the interests of the class as a whole, to which the trustees owe fiduciary duties. That would surely then be a case of administrative unworkability. Unworkability could be avoided if, despite the smallness of the gift, the settlor gave some instruction as to the principles upon which the trustees should exercise their discretion.

(3) Capriciousness

A discretionary trust will also be void if it is capricious (see Figure 27.2). This principle was suggested in *Re Manisty's Settlement*[50] in the context of fiduciary powers, when Templeman J indicated that a power in favour of the 'residents of Greater London' might

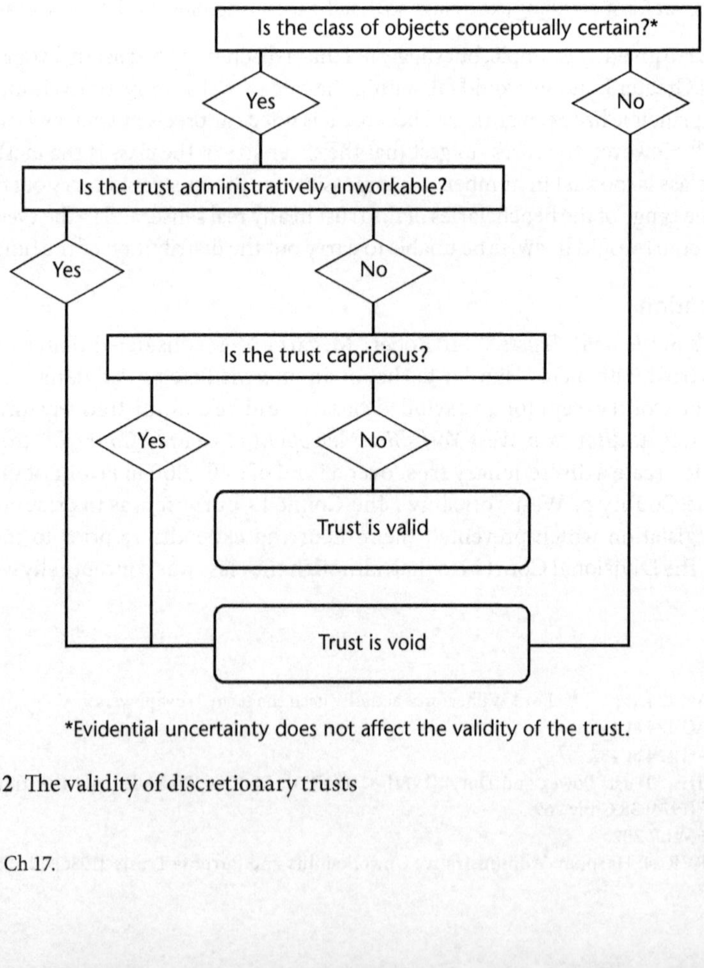

Figure 27.2 The validity of discretionary trusts

[50] [1974] Ch 17.

be capricious. The concept was developed in *Re Hay's Settlement Trusts*,[51] where Sir Robert Megarry V-C suggested that a power in favour of the 'residents of Greater London' would not be void for capriciousness if the donor of the power were, for example, a former mayor of the Greater London Council. The discretionary trust in *R v District Auditor, ex p West Yorkshire Metropolitan County Council*[52] was not regarded as capricious because the Council had every reason to create a fund in favour of its residents. With respect, this probably misses the point. If there is a good reason for failing to recognize a capricious trust, it is surely not that the settlor appeared to have no rational motivation for making the gift, but that the absence of any apparent purpose underlying the discretionary trust makes it impossible to devise a scheme to carry the trust into effect. If this is correct, the rationale is the same as that for administrative unworkability.

(4) **Perpetuities**

The rule against perpetuities, already explained in Chapter 8, applies to discretionary trusts.

7 Rights of beneficiaries of discretionary trusts

(1) **A proprietary interest in the fund?**

In the case of a power of appointment, it is clear that the objects of the power have no proprietary interest in the fund unless an appointment is made in their favour. In the case of a fixed trust, beneficiaries with a vested interest in possession have equitable title to the property held on trust for them, and may compel the trustees to transfer the legal title to them under the rule in *Saunders v Vautier*.[53] The position of the beneficiaries of a discretionary trust is not so clear-cut, and has led some to suggest that they have a form of proprietary right.[54] The rights of the class as a whole are essentially different from the rights of any individual members of the class.

(a) **A proprietary right for the class as a whole**

By analogy with fixed trusts, since a discretionary trust is a mandatory equitable obligation and the trustees must distribute the fund among the beneficiaries, it would seem logical that the equitable title to the property is vested in the class of potential beneficiaries as a whole. This approach was taken in *Re Smith*,[55] where property was held by trustees on discretionary trust for Mrs Aspinall and her three children. Romer J, following the Court of Appeal decision in *Re Nelson*,[56] held that the class as a whole could have come to the trustees and demanded the transfer of the legal title. He suggested that the principle for the class of such a discretionary trust was to 'treat all the people put together just as though they formed one person, for whose benefit the trustees were directed to apply the whole of a particular fund'.[57] However, despite its credentials in logic, this proprietary interest approach was rejected by the House of Lords in *Gartside v IRC*.[58] The case concerned a non-exhaustive discretionary trust in favour of John Gartside and his wife and children. The central question was whether estate duty

[51] [1982] 1 WLR 202. [52] [1986] RVR 24. [53] [1841] Cr & Ph 240.

[54] See *Smith v Michelmores Trust Corporation Ltd* [2021] EWHC 1425 (Ch), where Matthews J considered, obiter, that a right under a discretionary trust might be considered in the nature of a proprietary interest for the purposes of disclaiming a gift—at [68].

[55] [1928] Ch 915. [56] [1928] Ch 920. [57] [1928] Ch 920. [58] [1968] AC 553.

was payable on the trust fund, which had not yet been distributed at the date of John's death. The relevant legislation[59] would render the whole fund liable to estate duty if he was regarded as having an 'interest' in the fund. In these circumstances, the House of Lords held that the deceased beneficiary had no 'interest' in the fund and that estate duty was not payable. To reach this conclusion, it rejected any possibility of a 'group interest' in the fund. Lord Reid said that 'two or more persons cannot have a single right unless they hold it jointly or in common. But clearly objects of a discretionary trust do not have that: they each have individual rights: they are in competition with each other and what the trustees give to one is his alone.'[60] Lord Wilberforce echoed this thinking, stating that although it was correct that a beneficiary had more than a mere hope[61] of a right:

> that does not mean that he has an interest which is capable of being taxed by reference to its extent in the trust's income: it may be a right, with some degree of concreteness or solidity, one which attracts the protection of a court of equity, yet it may still lack the necessary quality of definable extent which must exist before it can be taxed.[62]

The analysis adopted in *Gartside v IRC*[63] was applied to exhaustive discretionary trusts in *Re Weir's Settlement*[64] and *Sainsbury v IRC*.[65] It is arguable that all three decisions were driven by the drafting of the relevant taxing provisions, which would lead to the ludicrous result of taxing the whole trust fund every time an object of a discretionary trust died. As Lord Reid observed in *Gartside*, 'it may be that in 1894, discretionary trusts were not so common that the draughtsman of the legislation must have had them in mind'.[66] In a different context, it is submitted that it is highly likely that a different conclusion would have been reached, and that, despite the authority of the House of Lords, the equitable interest of property subject to a discretionary trust does not remain inchoate, or 'in the air', but vests in the class of potential beneficiaries as a whole. There is support for this view in the approach which is taken in relation to the variation of trusts with the consent of the beneficiaries. In the case of an exhaustive discretionary trust, the class would theoretically be able to demand the transfer of the legal title by the trustees. In reality, this will often be impossible, as the class may be incapable of complete ascertainment.

(b) A proprietary right for individual beneficiaries

Although the class of beneficiaries of a discretionary trust may be regarded as having a collective proprietary entitlement to the fund, it is clear that members of the class cannot claim an individual proprietary entitlement to the fund or any part of the fund unless the trustees exercise their discretion to appoint property in their favour. As Lord Reid observed in *Gartside v IRC*:

> you cannot tell what any one of the beneficiaries will receive until the trustees have exercised their discretion.[67]

[59] Finance Act 1940, s 43(1). [60] [1968] AC 553 at 605–6.

[61] Lord Wilberforce used the Latin word 'spes' in his speech.

[62] [1968] AC 553 at 618. [63] [1968] AC 553.

[64] [1969] 1 Ch 657 at 682. Cross J stated: 'I do not think that Lord Reid was intending to suggest that the distinction [between exhaustive and non-exhaustive discretionary trusts] was relevant to his discussion of the "group theory". Even if the trust is exhaustive and there is no power to withhold income, the objects have individual competing interests, not concurrent interests in the income.'

[65] [1970] Ch 712. [66] [1968] AC 553 at 606. [67] *Gartside v IRC* [1968] AC 553.

(2) **The right to be considered as a potential beneficiary**

The most concrete right that the members of a class of beneficiaries of a discretionary trust possess is the right to be considered as potential recipients from the fund by the trustees.[68] They also have the right to have the trustees exercise their discretion 'bona fides',[69] 'fairly', 'reasonably', or 'properly'.[70]

8 The duties of trustees of discretionary trusts

The prime obligation of the trustee of a discretionary trust is to carry out the terms of the trust and allocate the fund among the class of potential beneficiaries. In the case of an exhaustive discretionary trust, the trustees must allocate the whole of the fund or its income, whereas in the case of a non-exhaustive discretionary trust they have the power to retain and accumulate all or part of the fund or income. The central issues concern the question how the trustees should go about their obligation to allocate in practice.

(1) **Survey of the range of objects**

The trustees of a discretionary trust are subject to a duty to consider the members of the class as potential recipients of benefit from the trust fund. In the case of a trust with a fairly small class of beneficiaries it may be practicable for the trustees to consider the circumstance of each and every member of the class before deciding on any allocations of benefit. However, in the case of discretionary trusts with a large class it is impossible for the trustees to consider the circumstances of each and every member of the class of potential beneficiaries, and Lord Wilberforce, in *McPhail v Doulton*, rejected the need to do so:

> a trustee with a duty to distribute, particularly among a potentially very large class, would surely never require the preparation of a complete list of names, which anyhow would tell him little that he needs to know.[71]

Instead, the trustee has a duty of 'inquiry or ascertainment' so 'in each case the trustees ought to make such a survey of the range of objects or possible beneficiaries as will enable them to carry out their fiduciary duty'.[72]

The requirement that the trustees 'consider' allocations by surveying the range of objects reflects what can reasonably be expected of them in practice. As Sachs LJ observed in *Re Baden's Deed Trusts (No 2)*, 'Assessing in a businesslike way "the size of the problem" is what the trustees are called on to do', and this may sometimes require little more initially than knowing whether the class consists of ten, hundreds, or thousands.[73]

The exact degree of consideration required of the trustees will depend on the type of the discretionary trust concerned. In *McPhail v Doulton*,[74] Lord Wilberforce sought to elucidate what the duty required:

> Any trustee would surely make it his duty to know what is the permissible area of selection and then consider responsibly, in individual cases, whether a contemplated beneficiary was within the power, and whether, in relation to other possible claimants, a particular grant was

[68] *Gartside v IRC* [1968] AC 553 at 606, per Lord Wilberforce.
[69] [1968] AC 553 at 606, per Lord Reid. [70] [1968] AC 553 at 618, per Lord Wilberforce.
[71] [1971] AC 424 at 449. [72] [1971] AC 424 at 457.
[73] [1973] Ch 9 at 20. See also *Re Hay's Settlement Trusts* [1982] 1 WLR 202 at 210, where Sir Robert Megarry V-C considered that the analogous duties of the trustee of a fiduciary power are to: 'consider the range of the objects of the power; and . . . consider the appropriateness of individual appointments'.
[74] [1971] AC 424 at 457.

> appropriate . . . He would examine the field by class and category; might indeed make diligent and careful enquiries, depending on how much money he had to give away and the means at his disposal, as to the composition and needs of particular categories and of individuals within them; decide upon certain priorities or proportions, and then select individuals according to their needs or qualifications.[75]

The duty is, therefore, extremely flexible, and appropriate to the modern usage of discretionary trusts as a mechanism to distribute relatively small funds among selected members of a potentially vast class.

In practical terms, what the duty means is that the trustee must not make an allocation from the fund to an individual beneficiary without first assessing the appropriateness of that allocation in the light of the claims of other possible beneficiaries. It would be inappropriate for the trustees of a fund of £1 million held on an exhaustive discretionary trust for a class of ten beneficiaries to allocate only to three or four individuals without first considering the claims of all the members of the class. In the case of a fund of £1 million to be divided among a class of a hundred thousand, the trustees would not need to consider the case for each member of the class, provided they bear in mind the number of potential claimants from the class and the purposes of the fund when deciding whether to make any individual allocations.

(2) **Allocations only to objects**

The trustees must not allocate the trust fund to persons who do not fall within the class of beneficiaries. Any such allocations will be held void by the court because they fall outside of the terms of the trust,[76] and the trustees will be in breach of trust. If such an allocation is made the beneficiaries may enforce remedies against the trustees[77] and the wrongful recipient of the trust property.[78]

(3) **Expressions of wishes**

A discretionary trust will frequently be accompanied by a letter from the settlor to the trustees setting out the settlor's preferences as to how the trust should be administered. This will not normally be binding on the trustees, but may be binding where the trust instrument so provides.[79] Even an expression of wishes which is not binding in law upon the trustees, may in practice give the settlor de facto control of the trust.[80]

9 Protectors

It has become common practice for trusts, and discretionary trusts in particular, to include the appointment of a protector. The function of the protector depends upon the terms of the trust. The protector may have the right to remove or appoint trustees, to be consulted by the trustees before specified action, be required to consent to any specified action by the trustees, or the right to give directions to the trustees.[81] The protector may

[75] [1971] AC 424 at 449.

[76] See *Smith v Michelmores Trust Corporation* Ltd [2021] EWHC 1425 (Ch), where exercise of a power by discretionary trustees was not to the benefit of the intended object and was also a fraud on a power, as the money paid would benefit the estate and the creditors of the same, rather than the object.

[77] See Chapter 34. [78] See Chapter 37.

[79] *Schmidt v Rosewood Trust Ltd (Isle of Man)* [2003] UKPC 26.

[80] For an example see *Lyon (Alloro Trust) v Revenue & Customs* [2007] UKSPC SPC00616.

[81] See *Re Gubay, Deceased* [2017] EWHC 1225 (Ch).

also have the right to alter the terms of the trust,[82] and to add or remove beneficiaries.[83] The use of devices such as this, with or without expressions of wishes, enormously increases the flexibility of a discretionary trust to achieve a settlor's intentions.

10 Enforcement by the court

(1) Equal division

The rationale for the adoption of the 'complete list' test was that the court could only intervene to enforce the trust by 'equal division' of the fund between the class of potential beneficiaries. While conceding that equal division might be appropriate in 'family trusts' with a limited class, Lord Wilberforce roundly rejected it as wholly inappropriate to large-scale discretionary trusts of the type in issue:

> As a matter of reason to hold that a principle of equal division applies to trusts such as the present is certainly paradoxical. Equal division is surely the last thing the settlor ever intended: equal division among all may, probably would, produce a result beneficial to none . . .[84]

This represents a recognition that the social function of discretionary trusts had evolved to enable property owners to 'confer benefits on deserving cases among large constituencies—in the same sort of way as charitable trusts'.[85] Clearly, there was never any intention by Bertram Baden that every single employee, ex-employee, relative, and dependant should benefit from the fund he had established in their favour, but that the nominated trustees should choose some from that class to receive substantial benefits. The settlor's purpose in creating the fund would be completely defeated if, in the event of the trustees' default, each and every member of the class were to receive an insignificant payment which was far outweighed by the administrative costs of determining the full extent of the class.

(2) Alternatives to equal division

Although 'equal division' might be inappropriate, cases such as *Gray v Gray*[86] and *Kemp v Kemp*[87] suggested that the courts had no alternative. In *McPhail v Doulton*,[88] Lord Wilberforce noted the early cases where the courts had taken a more flexible approach,[89] and concluded that:

> the court, if called upon to execute the [discretionary trust],[90] will do so in the manner best calculated to give effect to the settlor's or testator's intentions . . .

He suggested three alternative means by which the court is able to ensure that the trust is enforced:

> It may do so by appointing new trustees, or by authorising or directing representative persons to the classes of beneficiaries to prepare a scheme of distribution, or even, should the proper basis for distribution appear by itself directing the trustees so to distribute.

[82] As in *Barker v Baxendale Walker Solicitors (a firm)* [2016] EWHC 664 (Ch).

[83] *Schmidt v Rosewood Trust Ltd (Isle of Man)* [2003] UKPC 26.

[84] [1971] AC 424 at 451.

[85] Gardner, *An Introduction to the Law of Trusts* (2nd edn, Oxford University Press 2003), pp 199–200.

[86] [1862] 13 I Ch R 404. [87] [1795] 5 Ves 849. [88] [1971] AC 424 at 457.

[89] [1971] AC 424 at 451. See also *Moseley v Moseley* [1673] Cas temp Finch 53; *Clarke v Turner* [1694] Freem Ch 198; *Warburton v Warburton* [1702] 4 Bro Parl Cas 1; *Richardson v Chapman* [1760] 7 Bro Parl Cas 318, HL.

[90] Lord Wilberforce used the term 'trust powers'.

28

Powers of maintenance and advancement

1 Introduction

Under a trust, a substantial fund is held for Freddy when he reaches the age of twenty-five. Can the fund be used to pay for the costs of going to university when he is only eighteen? The answer will be found in this chapter.

The powers of trustees can be divided into two categories: management powers and distributive powers.[1] Management powers are those which relate to looking after the trust property, for instance, investing a fund or insuring a property. Distributive powers are those which relate to deciding who benefits. Generally the decision as to benefit will have been made by the settlor, by creating a fixed trust, by giving the decision to trustees through a discretionary trust, or by conferring a power of appointment on the trustees or a third party. In addition to this, however, there are some instances where trustees can make a decision as to who benefits from a trust fund, even where not expressly provided for by the settlor. These are the trustees' powers of maintenance and advancement.

Beneficiaries hoping for maintenance or advancements might have one of two different types of interest. The beneficiary might have an already vested interest subject to the rights of a 'remainderman' who will receive the trust property when he dies. This might be expressed as 'a gift on trust for A for life with remainder to B'. Alternatively, the beneficiary might have a contingent rather than a vested interest. This might be expressed 'a gift on trust for A if he qualifies as a dentist'.

2 What are powers of maintenance and advancement?

The trustees' power of maintenance is the power which trustees have to use the income of a fund to meet the living costs of infant beneficiaries who would not otherwise be entitled to receive the income. An example of this might be fee payments out of trust income for the school education of a minor. The power of advancement is the power to make an early payment to a beneficiary who has been given a gift in a trust, but where the right to receive that gift has not yet accrued. An example of this might be a lump sum paid out of the capital of a trust fund so that an adult beneficiary might start a business.

[1] Some books deal with all trustees' powers together. This book does not, since the powers of maintenance and advancement have many similarities with powers of appointment, and trustees' management powers, which are covered in Chapter 30, serve a different function.

3 Changes in the law

The first place to look to see if trustees have powers of maintenance and advancement is the trust deed, which may include express provision. If not, the Trustee Act 1925 grants trustees powers of maintenance[2] and advancement[3] which, following reform by the Inheritance and Trustees' Powers Act 2014, will usually be sufficient. The court also possesses an inherent jurisdiction to provide advancement and maintenance. Reform to the powers of maintenance and advancement followed from two consultation exercises undertaken by the Law Commission.[4] Originally, changes had only been suggested to the statutory trusts that arose on intestacy, but consultation suggested a change to power of trustees of all trusts, including those made by will or during lifetime. This is what was recommended by the Commission[5] and was enacted by the Inheritance and Trustees' Powers Act 2014 which came fully into force on 1 October 2014. Most of the reforms have prospective effect only, but existing trusts may be brought within the scheme under certain circumstances,[6] for example, where a new trust interest is created by a trustee exercising a power of appointment amongst a class of beneficiaries.

4 The trustees' power of maintenance

(1) Express powers of maintenance

A settlor may include express powers of maintenance in the trust instrument. They can expressly direct the trustees as to the terms on which the trust income should be paid out by way of maintenance. However, given the width of the statutory powers, which apply unless there is a contrary intention,[7] it is not usually necessary to do so.[8]

(2) Statutory powers of maintenance

The statutory powers are found in s 31 of the Trustee Act 1925,[9] which clarifies what happens to the income from a trust fund in a number of situations. The section essentially fills gaps in the previous law, so it does not apply where a settlement states expressly what is to happen to the income, or where a person of full age has a vested right to the income. It distinguishes between minors and adults.

(a) Minors

In the absence of express provision in the trust, trustees would not normally be able to pay the income from a trust fund to a minor beneficiary or to another person on the minor's behalf, even if the minor has a vested interest in the income. The Trustee Act 1925, s 31(1)(i),

[2] Trustee Act 1925, s 31; as amended by Inheritance and Trustees' Powers Act 2014, s 8.

[3] Trustee Act 1925, s 32; as amended by the Inheritance and Trustees' Powers Act 2014, s 9.

[4] *Intestacy and Family Provision Claims on Death* (Law Com Consultation Paper No 191, 2009) and *Intestacy and Family Provisions Claims on Death: Sections 31 and 32 of the Trustee Act 1925* (Law Com Consultation Paper No 191 (Supplemental), May 2011).

[5] *Intestacy and Family Provision Claims on Death* (Law Com No 331, 2011).

[6] Inheritance and Trustees' Powers Act 2014, s 10(5).

[7] Trustee Act 1925, s 69(2).

[8] Where express maintenance provisions are inserted, the major issue is normally whether they create fiduciary powers or impose trust obligations—see, for example, *Wilson v Turner* [1883] 22 Ch D 521.

[9] Trustee Act 1925, s 31 replaces the Conveyancing Act 1881, s 43, which itself replaced a provision in Lord Cranworth's Act of 1860.

changes this. It grants the trustees of every trust where property is held for any minor, whether their interest is vested or contingent, the power to apply the whole or the part of the income generated by the relevant part of the fund[10] for his 'maintenance education or benefit'.[11] It will constitute a fraud on the power if it is exercised for the purpose conferring a benefit on someone other than the child, although the proper exercise of the power (for instance to pay school fees) may relieve someone else of an expense.[12] The power is to be exercised solely at the trustees' discretion, though the exercise was required to be 'reasonable' as well as for the benefit of the minor until September 2014.[13] Following the Inheritance and Trustees' Powers Act 2014, for all trusts created after the commencement of that Act, the express requirement of reasonableness is removed, as the words 'as the trustees think fit' replace the original statutory wording.[14]

(b) Adults

An adult with an immediate vested right to the income from a trust has a right to receive it automatically. Section 31(1)(ii) extends the principle to contingent interests by directing that if the beneficiary has reached the age of majority,[15] the trustees are to pay the income to him, until his interest either vests or fails. Payment of such income is not a matter for the trustees' discretion.

(c) Contrary intention

The Trustee Act 1925, s 69(2) makes it clear that the rules in s 31 'apply, if and so far only as a contrary intention is not expressed in the instrument, if any, creating the trust, and have effect subject to the terms of that instrument.' Section 31, therefore, does not apply where there are express provisions in the trust instrument as to what is to happen to the income. A direction in the trust instrument to accumulate the income will be treated as a contrary intention.[16] Thus, in *Re Turner's Will Trusts*,[17] the Court of Appeal held that a beneficiary who was twenty-four years old was not entitled to the income from a fund in which he would obtain a vested interest on attaining the age of twenty-eight years because the settlor had directed that the income be accumulated.[18] In *Re McGeorge*[19] Cross J drew a distinction between an immediate gift on a contingency, which would carry the intermediate income, and an interest which is expressly deferred, which would not. He held that a gift of agricultural land by a testator to his daughter, which was not to take effect until the death of his wife, showed a contrary intention because 'by deferring the enjoyment of the devise until after the widow's death the testator has expressed the intention that the daughter shall not have the immediate income'.[20]

[10] By s 31(4) the same principles are applied to income generated by an annuity vested in a minor and by s 31(2) to unspent income from previous years.

[11] s 31(1)(i).

[12] *Fuller v Evans* [2000] 1 All ER 636.

[13] See *Wilson v Turner* [1883] 22 Ch D 521.

[14] Inheritance and Trustees' Powers Act 2014, s 8(a).

[15] That is, eighteen years of age.

[16] See *Re Watt's Will Trusts* [1936] 2 All ER 1555; *Re Turner's Will Trusts* [1937] Ch 15; *Re Ransome* [1957] Ch 348; *Re Erskine's Settlement Trusts* [1971] 1 WLR 162.

[17] [1937] Ch 15.

[18] Although he had granted the trustees an express power to apply the income for the 'maintenance, benefit and education' of the beneficiaries, and it was the surplus income which was to be accumulated.

[19] [1963] Ch 544.

[20] [1963] Ch 544 at 552–3, per Cross J. He also held that s 31 did not apply because the daughter's interest was not contingent, but rather, vested and subject to being divested.

(d) Subject to prior interests

The payment of income to a beneficiary is 'subject to any prior interests'. Obviously, if property is held on trust for Mabel for life, and on her death for Nathalie (her young daughter), there is no income attributable to Nathalie over which the trustees can use their power because Mabel's life interest gives her the right to the whole of the income.

(e) Gifts carrying intermediate income

On the face of things, the Trustee Act 1925, s 31 appears to give a very broad power of maintenance to trustees. However, it is subject to a limitation. By s 31(3) the powers of maintenance and the duty in respect of adults granted to trustees under s 31(1) are only available if a contingent interest 'carries the intermediate income'. This means that the beneficiary must be entitled not just to the share of the fund given to him or her, but also to any income generated by that part of the fund before the date when his share is paid over to him.[21] For example, the intermediate income might be trust income from the date of death of a testator, until the date of the contingency causing the gift to vest in the beneficiary. This provision has caused the most difficulty in applying the statutory rules. This is partly because the rules relating to entitlement to intermediate income developed separately for real property and personal property, and, although the Law of Property Act 1925, s 175 made an attempt to harmonize the rules, it may not fully have achieved this.

The question is ultimately one of construction. The current approach to interpretation is not to follow strict rules based on previous cases, but to look for 'the meaning of the relevant words in their documentary, factual and commercial context'.[22] Older cases, which take a rule-based approach, may, therefore, need to be viewed with caution. The starting-point nowadays can be taken that a gift carries a right to the intermediate income unless the income has been otherwise allotted.

(i) Vested interests

A person who has a vested interest has the right to the intermediate income, even if the interest (and, therefore, the right to the income) is liable to be divested, unless the income is directed to be applied to someone else.[23] This does not mean that the person is entitled to be paid the income immediately under Trustee Act 1925, s 31, because there may still be a contrary intention excluding the section.

(ii) Discretionary trusts

A beneficiary under a discretionary trust has no individual right to the trust property or its income, and therefore no right to any intermediate income.[24]

(iii) Lifetime contingent gifts

A contingent gift in a settlement created inter vivos carries the right to income, subject to any contrary intention.

[21] [1953] 17 Conv 273 (Ker); PVB, 'Carrying the Intermediate Income' [1963] 79 LQR 184.

[22] *Arnold v Britton* [2015] UKSC 36, [2015] AC 1619 at 15 (a contract case, but applied to a trust instrument in *Barnardo's v Buckinghamshire* [2016] EWCA Civ 1064 at 8–10 and *British Airways Plc v Airways Pension Scheme Trustee Ltd* [2017] EWHC 1191 (Ch) at 408).

[23] *Re McGeorge* [1963] Ch 544 at 552.

[24] *Re Vestey* [1950] 2 All ER 891.

(iv) Contingent gifts by will

It has always been the case that a contingent gift of residuary personal property[25] made by will carries the intermediate income from the date of the testator's death.[26] This was explained in *Re Adams*,[27] where North J stated that since the income was 'undisposed of', it would itself become part of the residue. Law of Property Act 1925, s 175 extends the principle to contingent gifts of specific personal property, and to contingent gifts of real property whether specific or of residue. The section applies unless the income has been otherwise expressly disposed of.[28] The section has been held not to apply to pecuniary legacies.[29]

(v) Pecuniary legacies

Where a will gives a person a contingent right to a fixed sum of money, case law going back three centuries establishes that only the capital amount needs to be paid, and as a general principle there is no right to the intermediate income.[30] There are three exceptions to this principle. First, gifts by fathers to their children. If a pecuniary legacy is left by a father to his child, the gift carries the intermediate income if there is no other fund provided for the child's maintenance,[31] and the contingency is the child attaining the age of majority.[32] The rationale behind this exception is clearly similar to that which reveals itself in the presumption of advancement which rebuts an inference of a resulting trust when a gift is made by a father to his child,[33] namely, the obligation of the father to provide. The exception will also apply when a gift of a contingent pecuniary legacy is made by a person standing in loco parentis to the minor.[34] Second, are gifts made with the intention of providing maintenance. If the will expressly or impliedly indicates that the income be used for the maintenance of the minor, the gift will carry the intermediate income. In *Re Churchill*[35] a gift of a pecuniary legacy to a grandnephew was held to carry the intermediate income where the will directed the trustees at their discretion to pay any part of it 'towards the advancement in life or otherwise for the benefit' of the legatee.[36] It is not necessary that the legacy be contingent upon the attainment of majority.[37] Third, are 'set aside' gifts. Where a pecuniary legacy is set aside by the testator[38] as a segregated fund for his benefit, to be available on the happening of the contingency, the gift will carry the intermediate income.[39]

(f) Undistributed income

(i) Income to be accumulated

Section 31(2) deals with what happens to any income which the trustees decide not to apply for a minor beneficiary's maintenance. The subsection directs that the trustees are to accumulate and invest any such income, and can apply it for the beneficiary's maintenance, as if it were income arising in the current year. If there are still accumulated funds

[25] This includes leasehold property, which ranks as personal property: *Guthrie v Walrond* [1883] 22 Ch D 573; *Re Woodin* [1895] 2 Ch 309.

[26] *Countess of Bective v Hodgson* [1864] 10 HL Cas 656; *Re Taylor* [1901] 2 Ch 134.

[27] [1893] 1 Ch 329.

[28] *Re Reade-Revell* [1930] 1 Ch 52; *Re Stapleton* [1946] 1 All ER 323.

[29] *Re McGeorge* [1963] Ch 544.

[30] *Re George* [1877] 5 Ch D 837, CA; *Re Raine* [1929] 1 Ch 716; *Re McGeorge* [1963] Ch 544.

[31] *Re Moody* [1895] 1 Ch 101; *Re George* [1877] 5 Ch D 837; *Re West* [1913] 2 Ch 345.

[32] *Re Abrahams* [1911] 1 Ch 108.

[33] This was discussed in Chapter 9.

[34] *Re Eyre* [1917] 1 Ch 351.

[35] [1909] 2 Ch 431.

[36] See also *Re Selby-Walker* [1949] 2 All ER 178.

[37] *Re Jones* [1932] 1 Ch 642.

[38] *Re Judkin's Trusts* [1884] 25 Ch D 743.

[39] *Re Medlock* [1886] 54 LT 828; *Re Clements* [1894] 1 Ch 665; *Re Woodin* [1895] 2 Ch 309, CA. Compare also *Re Judkin's Trusts* [1884] 25 Ch D 743.

when the minor reaches the age of majority (or marries, if under that age), these funds must be paid to the beneficiary if the beneficiary has a vested interest in the capital of the fund. If, however, his interest is not vested, or is liable to be determined, he will not be entitled to the accumulated income, and it is added to the capital.[40] One anomalous result of the wording of s 31(2)(i)(b) is that a distinction is drawn between determinable gifts of realty and personalty. The section states that the beneficiary must be entitled to the property from which the income arose 'in fee simple, absolute or determinable, or absolutely'. In *Re Sharp's Settlement Trusts*,[41] it was held that the words 'in fee simple, absolute or determinable' apply only to realty, and the word 'absolute' applies exclusively to 'personalty'. This means that a beneficiary has no entitlement on reaching majority to the accumulated income on a fund of personal property in which he has only a determinable interest. On the facts, a beneficiary who had attained the age of twenty-one was not entitled to the accumulated income from the fund because his contingent interest was liable to be defeated by the exercise of a power of appointment.[42]

(ii) Death of a minor before attaining a vested interest

Where a beneficiary dies before attaining majority (or earlier marriage) and income has been accumulated on his behalf, s 31(2)(ii) provides that the accumulated income should be added to the capital of the fund, and not pass as part of the minor's estate.[43] This provision will not apply if a contrary intention is shown from the trust instrument.[44] Thus in *Re Delamere's Settlement Trusts*,[45] the trustees of a settlement appointed the income from a trust fund to six infant beneficiaries 'in equal shares absolutely'. The Court of Appeal held that this excluded the operation of s 31(2)(ii) and that the infant beneficiaries had indefeasible interests in the accumulated income.

(3) The court's inherent jurisdiction

The court has an inherent jurisdiction to allow trust income to be used for a minor's maintenance,[46] and in exceptional circumstances the court may even allow capital to be so used.[47] The courts have generally refused to allow trust income to be used for a child's maintenance where the father has sufficient means to provide for the child.[48] The width of the general statutory power of maintenance has rendered the court's inherent jurisdiction insignificant.

5 The trustees' power of advancement

(1) Meaning of advancement

A power of maintenance enables the trustees to apply the income generated by a trust fund for the maintenance of the beneficiaries, even where they are not as yet entitled to the capital of the fund. A power of advancement enables the trustees to make what would

40 *Re Sharp's Settlement Trusts* [1973] Ch 331. 41 [1973] Ch 331; [1972] 36 Conv 436 (Hayton).

42 See also *Phipps v Ackers* [1842] 9 Cl & Fin 583; *Re Heath* [1936] Ch 259; *Re Kilpatrick's Policies* [1966] Ch 730; *Brotherton v IRC* [1978] 1 WLR 610.

43 *Re Joel's Will Trusts* [1967] Ch 14. 44 Trustee Act 1925, s 69(2).

45 [1984] 1 WLR 813; [1985] Conv 153 (Griffith).

46 *Wellesley v Wellesley* [1828] 2 Bli 124 at 133–4, per Lord Redesdale.

47 *Ex p Green* [1820] 1 Jac & W 253; *Ex p Chambers* [1829] 1 Russ & M 577; *Robinson v Killey* [1862] 30 Beav 520.

48 *Douglas v Andrews* [1849] 12 Beav 310 at 311.

otherwise be premature transfers to beneficiaries who have future or contingent interests in the trust fund. As Lord Radcliffe observed, in *Pilkington v IRC*, the purpose of a power of advancement is that the trustees can in a proper case:

> anticipate the vesting in possession of an intended beneficiary's contingent or reversionary interest by . . . paying or applying it immediately for his benefit. By so doing they released it from the trusts of the settlement and accelerate the enjoyment of his interest . . .[49]

(2) Express power s of advancement

A settlor may grant the trustees express powers of advancement in the trust instrument.[50] However, since the enactment of a statutory power,[51] modelled on the standard form of such express powers, express powers have only been necessary if a settlor wishes the trustees to have wider powers than those granted by the statute. In the past, this was in fact often to give the trustees power to advance more than half a beneficiary's presumptive share,[52] but this limitation has been removed in all trusts created after the commencement of the Inheritance and Trustees' Powers Act 2014.[53] It is questionable, therefore, how often express powers will be used in the future.

(3) Trustee Act 1925, s 32

(a) Scope of the statutory power of advancement

Section 32(1) grants trustees the power, in their absolute discretion, to make advancements from the capital of a trust fund (except Settled Land Act capital money[54]) for any beneficiary who has an absolute or contingent interest in the fund. Originally, it was only possible to advance capital monies, but the Law Commission recommended an expansion of the wording to avoid the practice where a trustee, wishing to transfer a property asset to the beneficiary under this power, instead had to advance cash to the beneficiary for them to purchase the asset.[55] This alteration of the wording has both prospective and retrospective effect, so that it applies to all trusts, whether created before or after the commencement of the Inheritance and Trustee's Powers Act 2014.[56]

It makes no difference that the beneficiary's contingent interest may at some later date be defeated, for example, by the exercise of a power of appointment, or that the beneficiary's share of the fund may diminish because of an increase in the number of a class to which he belongs.[57] The section introduces some practical limitations on the trustee's power of advancement.

49 [1964] AC 612 at 633. 50 See *Wesley v Chantler* [2018] EWHC 21 (Ch) [9].

51 Trustee Act 1925, s 32, as amended by the Inheritance and Trustees' Powers Act 2014, s 9.

52 See Trustee Act 1925, s 32(1)(a), as originally enacted. The Law Commission found in its second consultation exercise on reform of powers of maintenance that professionally drafted trusts expressly widened this power as a matter of course (see *Analysis of Responses*, paras 5.32–5.50; 8.20–8.28), strengthening the proposal for reform.

53 s 10(3), giving effect to s 9(3)(b), which amends the wording of the Trustee Act 1925, s 32(1)(a) to that effect.

54 Trustee Act 1925, s 32(2). 55 See *Re Collard's Will Trusts* [1961] Ch 293.

56 s 10(2), giving effect to all parts of s 9 (except s 9(3)(b)), which amends all relevant subsections of s 32 to include the application or transfer of property.

57 For example, a trust may grant contingent interests to the grandchildren of the settlor, and the class may subsequently increase with the birth of further children.

(i) Proportion of share which may be advanced

Section 32(1)(a), as we have seen, originally provided that the trustees must not advance to a beneficiary more than a half of his presumptive or vested interest under the fund.[58] This has since been altered in any trust arising after the commencement of the Inheritance and Trustees' Powers Act 2014 to allow the power to be extended to the whole of the beneficiary's share in the trust fund.[59]

(ii) Accounting for advancements in the final distribution

Where a beneficiary is contingently entitled to a share of the trust fund, s 32(1)(b) provides that any property advanced be taken into account in calculating the size of any share to which he becomes absolutely entitled.[60] This obviously prevents unfairness between the beneficiaries.

(iii) Protection of those with a prior interest

Where an advancement would be to the prejudice of those who have a prior life or other interest in the fund, s 32(1)(c) requires that they give consent in writing to any advancement.[61] This protects, for example, a life tenant, who is entitled to the income of the fund during his lifetime. For instance, if property is held on trust for Alice for life, then on trust for her children in equal shares, any advancement to a child will reduce the capital sum invested and consequently reduce Alice's income. Alice's consent to any advancement is, therefore, required.

(b) **The requirement of benefit**

The most important restriction of the trustees' power of advancement is the requirement that the application of capital must be for the 'advancement or benefit' of the beneficiary. The meaning of this phrase was considered by Lord Radcliffe in *Pilkington v IRC*, where he held that the phrase 'advancement and benefit':

> means any use of the money which will improve the material situation of the beneficiary.[62]

The case concerned a proposed advancement of part of the contingent share of an infant beneficiary, Penelope Pilkington. She was entitled to a share of a fund established by her great uncle, provided she reached the age of twenty-one, but the trustees wanted to advance £7,600, to be settled on different trusts in her favour, to avoid death duties. The House of Lords held that this was a proper exercise of the statutory power of advancement, and that there was a benefit to the infant in the avoidance of taxation. Lord Radcliffe observed:

> if the advantage of preserving the funds of a beneficiary from the incidence of death duty is not an advantage personal to that beneficiary, I do not see what is.[63]

It did not matter that the advanced money was to be resettled on different trusts for the infant.[64]

[58] See *Re Marquess of Abergavenny's Estate Act Trusts* [1981] 1 WLR 843; [1982] Conv 158 (Price).

[59] Inheritance and Trustees' Powers Act 2014, s 9(3)(b) removes the phrase 'one-half of' from the Trustee Act 1925, s 32(1)(a) so that it reads that the advancement 'must not, altogether, represent more than the presumptive or vested share or interest of that person in the trust property'.

[60] See *Re Fox* [1904] 1 Ch 480. The Inheritance and Trustees' Powers Act 2014 adds, by s 10(6), s 32(1A) into the Trustee Act 1925 which sets out a requirement to add together all cash and non-cash advancements to find the total amount advanced for this purpose.

[61] The court cannot dispense with the need for consent: *Re Forster's Settlement* [1942] Ch 199. A member of a discretionary class does not need to give consent: *Re Harris's Settlement* [1940] 162 LT 358; *Re Beckett's Settlement* [1940] Ch 279.

[62] [1964] AC 612 at 635. [63] [1964] AC 612 at 640.

[64] *Roper-Curzon v Roper-Curzon* [1871] LR 11 Eq 452; *Re Halstead's Will Trusts* [1937] 2 All ER 57; *Re Ropner's Settlement Trusts* [1956] 1 WLR 902.

A wide range of purposes have been held to be sufficiently beneficial to permit an advancement. In the nineteenth century, typical examples included the provision of an apprenticeship, the purchase of a commission in the army, or an interest in a business.[65] Benefits have included the discharge of the beneficiary's debts,[66] an advancement to a wife who helped her husband set up in business,[67] an advancement to a girl on her marriage,[68] and an advancement to provide for the beneficiary's maintenance and education.[69] In *Re Halstead's Will Trusts*,[70] the court approved an advancement to a man so that he could make provision for his wife and child in the future by settling a sum upon himself for life, and after his death, for his wife for life, and the remainder to his children. Farwell J held that this was within the 'very wide terms in which the word "benefit" has been construed in the past'. The purchases of house and furniture have also been held to be for the benefit of a beneficiary.[71]

In *Re Clore's Settlement Trusts*,[72] the court approved an advancement to enable a contingently entitled beneficiary to make a donation to charity which they felt morally obliged to make. However, in *X v A*,[73] it was held that an advancement of the whole of the trust fund to enable a charitable donation was not of benefit. Hart J reasoned that the extent of the gift meant that the contingently entitled beneficiary would not have their material situation improved by the advancement as required under *Pilkington v IRC*, as the beneficiary would not have been able to meet the moral obligation from their own resources.

(c) Fiduciary nature of the power of advancement

A power of advancement is a fiduciary power, and must, therefore, be exercised by the trustee in a fiduciary manner. In *Re Pauling's Settlement Trusts*,[74] in the context of an express power, the Court of Appeal held that this means that before exercising the power the trustees must 'weigh on the one side the benefit to the proposed advancee, and on the other hand the rights of those who are or may hereafter become interested under the trusts of the settlement'.[75] The trustees are also subject to a duty to ensure that money advanced is applied by the beneficiaries for the purposes for which it was advanced.[76]

(4) The court's inherent jurisdiction

The court possesses an inherent jurisdiction to apply capital[77] for the maintenance or advancement of an infant. For example, in *Clay v Pennington*,[78] the court advanced a sum of £125 to cover the cost of an infant's passage to India.[79]

[65] *Pilkington v IRC* [1964] AC 612 at 634. [66] *Lowther v Bentinck* [1874] LR 19 Eq 166.
[67] *Re Kershaw's Trusts* [1868] LR 6 Eq 322. [68] *Lloyd v Cocker* [1860] 27 Beav 645.
[69] *Re Breed's Will* [1875] 1 Ch D 226; *Re Garrett* [1934] Ch 477. [70] [1937] 2 All ER 57.
[71] *Re Pauling's Settlement Trust* [1964] Ch 303, CA.
[72] [1966] 1 WLR 955. [73] [2006] 1 WLR 741.
[74] [1964] Ch 303. [75] [1964] Ch 303 at 333, per Willmer LJ. [76] [1964] Ch 303 at 334.
[77] *Barlow v Grant* [1684] 1 Vern 255. [78] [1837] 8 Sim 359.
[79] See also *Re Mary England's Estate* [1830] 1 Russ & M 499.

29

Variation of beneficial interests

1 Introduction

What happens if the terms of the trust are no longer appropriate, can the terms of the trust be varied? This may be possible through one of a number of routes. The beneficiaries, providing they are adults and able to consent to a change, can club together and vary the settlor's original plans.[1] They might do so because they find the settlor's conditions burdensome, such as where he has attached age conditions to their interests.[2] Alternatively they might wish to vary the the terms of the trust so that it becomes more tax efficient.[3]

If all the beneficiaries are adults with capacity to consent, the process of variation will be straightforward. It will normally be a private arrangement which will not need to rely on any statutory provisions in order to effect the change. This will not always be the case because the trust will very often contain provisions for the benefit of minors, those without capacity, and the unborn. In this common circumstance, the Variation of Trusts Act allows the court to give consent for those beneficiaries who cannot do it themselves.[4]

(1) **Provisions for variation in the trust**

The starting-point is that once a trust is fully constituted, it is irrevocable and the settlor loses the power to revoke it or to amend its terms.[5] However, it is very common for a trust to include provisions which allow the terms of the trust to be varied by the settlor or by the trustees or by a protector, in each case with or without a requirement of consent by someone else.

(2) **Variation by the beneficiaries**

Where the entirety of the beneficial interests are held by beneficiaries who are identifiable, of full age, and of full mental capacity, those beneficiaries have the ability under the rule in *Saunders v Vautier*,[6] to terminate the trust and to settle the trust funds on new trusts. If they have the consent of the trustees, then the beneficiaries can approve a variation of the trust terms.

[1] *Saunders v Vautier* [1841] Cr & Ph 240. [2] *Goulding v James* [1997] 2 All ER 239.

[3] As Lord Denning MR observed in *Re Weston's Settlements* [1969] 1 Ch 223 at 245: 'Nearly every variation that has come before the court has tax avoidance as its principal object.'

[4] Variation of Trusts Act 1958, s 1(1)(a)–(d). [5] *Paul v Paul* [1882] 20 Ch D 742.

[6] [1841] Cr & Ph 240.

(3) Surrender of a beneficial interest

What amounts to a variation of a trust may be possible where a beneficiary surrenders an interest. For instance, where property is held on trust for Anthea for life, then for her children in equal shares, if Anthea surrenders her life interest, her children will take an immediate interest.

(4) Release of a power

In a similar way, the release of a power of appointment, where this is possible, will have the effect of extinguishing any interests which could be created by the exercise of the power.

(5) Statutory powers of variation

There are some statutory provisions which allow trusts to be varied, notably the Variation of Trusts Act 1958.

(6) Inherent court powers

There are some very limited circumstances in which the courts have an inherent jurisdiction to approve a variation of trust. Where this is the case, the court does not need to rely on statute in order to effect a variation. The court may also approve actions which do not involve a variation, but may have a similar effect, such as authorizing a trustee to ignore trust directions which are illegal.[7] Alternatively, where the terms of the trust benefit unborn children, variation might be permitted on the basis that a person (on the basis of proof by actual evidence) is incapable of having children.[8]

2 Consensual variation

Much of the focus of the case law is inevitably upon difficult circumstances where there are beneficiaries that cannot consent to variation. However, it is important to keep in mind that very often the beneficiaries will be in a position to consent to a variation amongst themselves. The process might be straightforward and consensual.

(1) The primacy of the settlor's intention?

It is a basic principle that a trust must be carried out according to its terms, and that any deviation from them constitutes a breach of trust. In *Re New*, Romer LJ stated that:

> As a rule, the court has no jurisdiction to give, and will not give, its sanction to the performance by the trustees of acts with reference to the trust estate which are not, on the face of the instrument creating the trust, authorised by its terms.[9]

This 'primacy to the settlor's intention' was also expressed by Farwell J in *Re Walker*,[10] where he declined 'to accept any suggestion that the court has an inherent jurisdiction to alter a man's will because it thinks it beneficial'.[11]

[7] Such directions are not binding on the trustee: *Re Beard, Reversionary and General Securities Co Ltd v Hall* [1908] 1 Ch 383.

[8] *Re Westminster Bank Ltd's Declaration of Trust* [1963] 2 All ER 400n, [1963] 1 WLR 820. See also *Re Summer's Trusts* [1874] 30 LT 377; *Re Widdow's Trusts* [1871] LR 11 Eq 408.

[9] [1901] 2 Ch 534 at 544.

[10] [1901] 1 Ch 879 at 885.

[11] Luxton, 'Variation of Trusts: Settlors' Intentions and the Consent Principle in *Saunders v Vautier*' [1997] 60 MLR 719.

(2) The beneficiaries' wishes

Even while the basic principle is that trustees must follow the plans of settlors, it has long been recognized that the beneficiaries of a trust can consent to the execution of the trust in a manner other than that specified by the settlor. A trustee will not be liable for breach of trust if he acts at the request, or with the consent, of the beneficiaries.[12] If the trustees so act and in effect vary the trust by performing it inconsistently with the settlor's intentions, the court will not intervene. At its most dramatic, this enables the beneficiaries to bring the trust to an end. Under the principle of *Saunders v Vautier*,[13] the beneficiaries, provided they are absolutely entitled, sui juris and of age, may call for the legal title to the trust property.[14] In *Re Smith*[15] the beneficiaries of a discretionary trust were held able to compel the trustees to transfer the legal title to them. In *Saunders v Vautier*,[16] Daniel Vautier was the sole beneficiary of a trust of East India stock established by Richard Wright. The settlor directed in the terms of the trust that dividends from the stock be accumulated by the trustees until Daniel attained the age of twenty-five. The court held that as he was solely entitled to the fund, and the accumulation was for his benefit alone, he was entitled to the fund at the age of twenty-one. In effect, primacy was given to the beneficiary's wishes, rather than the settlor's expressed intentions. In *Goulding v James*, Mummery LJ identified the principle embodied in the rule in *Saunders v Vautier*:

> The principle recognises the rights of beneficiaries, who are sui juris and together entitled to the trust property, to exercise their proprietary rights to overbear and defeat the intention of a testator or settlor to subject property to the continuing trusts, powers and limitations of a will or trust instrument.[17]

(3) Limits to consensual variation

The primacy of the beneficiaries' wishes established by *Saunders v Vautier*[18] enables them to vary the beneficial entitlements under a trust. However, their right to do so is subject to severe practical restrictions and is often inadequate to authorize a variation of the beneficial interest. A consensual variation of trust can only take place where there is the unanimous consent of all the actual and potential beneficiaries of the trust, since if any beneficiary fails to give consent the trustees will remain open to liability for breach of trust to any who have not consented. Therefore, consensual variation will not be possible if some of the beneficiaries are minors and unable to give consent, or alternatively unidentifiable or not yet in existence, for example, if the class of beneficiaries includes children as yet unborn, or the future spouses of present beneficiaries. This will often be the case if the trust creates successive interests, as in *Goulding v James*,[19] itself, where the potential beneficiaries of the remainder interest behind a life interest were the (as yet) unborn great-grandchildren of the testator. To overcome these limitations, the law has developed various means by which the court can approve a variation of trust when the beneficiaries are not able to do so themselves.

[12] *Re Pauling's Settlement Trusts* [1964] Ch 303, CA.

[13] [1841] Cr & Ph 240.

[14] See *Re Chardon* [1928] Ch 464; *Re Smith* [1928] Ch 915; *Re Nelson* [1928] Ch 920; *Re Beckett's Settlement* [1940] Ch 279; *Re AEG Unit Trusts (Managers) Ltd's Deed* [1957] Ch 415.

[15] [1928] Ch 915.

[16] [1841] Cr & Ph 240.

[17] [1997] 2 All ER 239 at 247.

[18] [1841] Cr & Ph 240.

[19] [1997] 2 All ER 239 at 247.

3 Variation under the inherent jurisdiction of the court

There are case law based circumstances which have been broadly used to vary trusts in instances where beneficiaries cannot consent. In *Chapman v Chapman*,[20] the House of Lords recognized that in four situations the court possesses an inherent jurisdiction to authorize a variation of the terms of a trust.[21] However, even in these situations, the court has no real jurisdiction to alter the beneficial interests under the trust. Although it can be seen that some of the cases come very close to, or even cross, the borderline, this inherent jurisdiction is broadly administrative rather than substantive. It is also largely of historic interest. In the present day, judges would likely turn first to statute, such as the Variation of Trusts Act 1958, rather than to the inherent jurisdiction.

(1) Conversion jurisdiction

The court has the power to authorize the conversion of property in which an infant has an equitable interest from personalty or realty.[22] Lord Morton emphasized that even this limited jurisdiction was exceptional in nature,[23] and its exercise would in no way affect the infant's beneficial entitlement.[24] The very wide powers of investment now given to trustees mean that this jurisdiction will very rarely be required.

(2) Emergency jurisdiction

The court has jurisdiction to authorize transactions involving the trust property which are not otherwise permitted by the trust if a 'peculiar set of circumstances arises'[25] for which no provision was made in the trust instrument. In one series of cases, the court had approved the sale or mortgage of an infant's property to release funds for the preservation of what was retained where such action was absolutely necessary, for instance, where buildings were in imminent danger of collapse or ruin.[26] Other cases extended this principle to situations where, although there was no absolute necessity, an emergency had arisen which the creator of the trust had not foreseen or anticipated, and where the best interests of the trust required the granting of exceptional authority. In *Re New*,[27] the trust fund consisted of ordinary shares in a private limited company. A company reorganization was proposed in which ordinary shares would be transferred for preference shares and debentures. As the trust instrument did not give the power to invest in such securities, the Court of Appeal authorized the investment acting under their inherent jurisdiction. In *Re Tollemache*[28] the Court of Appeal said that *Re New* 'constitutes the high watermark of the exercise by the court of its extraordinary jurisdiction in relation to trusts', and refused to extend the powers of investment of the trustees to authorize the acquisition of a mortgage which would have enhanced the income of the trust.

Romer LJ in *Re New* emphasized that the variation must be for the 'benefit' of the beneficiaries and where 'the consent of all the beneficiaries cannot be obtained by reason of some of them not being sui juris or in existence.' The court is probably unable, under its

[20] [1954] AC 429. [21] [1954] AC 429 at 445, per Lord Simmonds LC.

[22] See *Earl of Winchelsea v Norcloffe* [1686] 1 Vern 435; *Pierson v Shore* [1739] 1 Atk 480; *Bridges v Bridges* [1752] 12 App Cas 693n; *Inwood v Twyne* [1762] Amb 417; *Lord Ashburton v Lady Ashburton* [1801] 6 Ves 6.

[23] *Re Jackson* [1882] 21 Ch D 786; *Glover v Barlow* [1831] 21 Ch D 788n.

[24] [1954] AC 429 at 451.

[25] *Re New* [1901] 2 Ch 534 at 534, per Romer LJ.

[26] *Re Jackson* [1882] 21 Ch D 786; *Conway v Fenton* [1888] 40 Ch D 512; *Re Montagu* [1897] 2 Ch 8.

[27] [1901] 2 Ch 534. See also *Re Tollemache* [1903] 1 Ch 955, CA. [28] [1903] 1 Ch 955.

inherent jurisdiction, to override or to supply consent on behalf of those who are themselves legally competent to provide it. If limited in this way, the jurisdiction adds nothing to the powers given to the courts by the Variation of Trusts Act 1958.

(3) Maintenance jurisdiction

Where the settlor directed that income from the trust fund should be accumulated for the beneficiaries, the court has the jurisdiction to authorize the advancement of the income to provide for their maintenance. Usually, although not necessarily, this will be in the case of infant beneficiaries.[29] The maintenance jurisdiction does not give the court the power to alter the beneficial interests of the beneficiaries.[30] The statutory powers of advancement and maintenance, as amended by the Inheritance and Trustees' Powers Act 2014, make this power less significant than it was in the nineteenth century and before.

(4) Compromise jurisdiction

The court also has inherent jurisdiction to approve on behalf of those who cannot consent for themselves[31] a compromise agreement between the beneficiaries where there has been a 'genuine dispute' about the extent of the rights of the beneficiaries. Prior to the decision of the House of Lords in *Chapman v Chapman*,[32] this 'compromise jurisdiction' had been given a wide meaning so that it could be used to permit variations in the beneficial interest of the beneficiaries. For example, in *Re Downshire Settled Estates*,[33] the Court of Appeal authorized a scheme restructuring the beneficial interests of a settlement for tax reasons. Evershed MR took the view that 'the word "compromise" should not be narrowly construed so as to be confined to "compromises" of disputed rights'.[34] In his dissenting opinion Denning LJ advocated a very general jurisdiction to vary:

> The jurisdiction is not confined to cases where there is a dispute about the extent of the beneficial interests, nor to cases of emergency or necessity, but extends wherever there is a bargain about the beneficial interests which is for the benefit of the infants or unborn persons.[35]

However, in *Chapman v Chapman*,[36] the House of Lords asserted that the court only has the inherent jurisdiction to approve a compromise altering beneficial interests if there is a 'genuine dispute' as to the beneficial entitlements of the beneficiaries. In essence, this means that the court does not possess any jurisdiction to 'vary' the beneficial entitlement of beneficiaries, but merely a jurisdiction to clarify them when there is a dispute about their extent. In the words of Lord Morton:

> the court's jurisdiction to sanction a compromise in the true sense, when the beneficial interests are in dispute, is not a jurisdiction to alter these interests, for they are still unascertained. If, however, there is no doubt as to the beneficial interests, the court is, to my mind, exceeding its jurisdiction if it sanctions a scheme for their alteration . . .[37]

[29] See *Revel v Watkinson* [1748] 1 Ves Sen 93; *Cavendish v Mercer* [1776] 5 Ves 195n; *Greenwell v Greenwell* [1800] 5 Ves 194; *Errat v Barlow* [1807] 14 Ves 202; *Haley v Bannister* [1820] 4 Madd 275; *Havelock v Havelock* [1881] 17 Ch D 807; *Re Collins* [1886] 32 Ch D 229.

[30] *Chapman v Chapman* [1954] AC 429 at 456, per Lord Morton.

[31] [1954] AC 429 at 457 per Lord Morton, the jurisdiction had been exercised on behalf of 'infants interested under a will or settlement and on behalf of possible after-born beneficiaries'.

[32] [1954] AC 429. [33] [1953] Ch 218. [34] [1953] Ch 218 at 239.

[35] [1953] Ch 218 at 274. [36] [1954] AC 429. [37] [1954] AC 429 at 461.

The decision in *Chapman v Chapman*[38] thus deprived the courts of any real jurisdiction to authorize variations in the beneficial interests under trusts. For example, in *Re Powell-Cotton's Resettlement*,[39] an alleged dispute over an investment clause in the trust instrument was held not to be a 'genuine dispute', and the Court of Appeal refused to authorize a compromise agreement.[40] The restriction of the court's inherent jurisdiction led to the enactment of the Variation of Trusts Act 1958, which gives the court a 'very wide and, indeed, revolutionary discretion'[41] to approve variations of trusts, including the variation of beneficial interests.

(5) A broader jurisdiction?

There is some authority for suggesting that the inherent powers of the court could extend beyond the four situations identified in *Chapman v Chapman*. A lengthy series of cases, reviewed in *Re Duke of Norfolk's Settlement Trusts*,[42] establishes beyond doubt that the court has an inherent jurisdiction to authorize the payment of remuneration to trustees, and even, according to the latter case, increase the level of the remuneration. Fox LJ did not consider this to be inconsistent with the principles expressed in *Chapman v Chapman*, which was primarily concerned with the power of the court to authorize variations in beneficial interests. He said:

> I appreciate that the ambit of the court's inherent jurisdiction in any sphere may, for historical reasons, be irrational and that logical extensions are not necessarily permissible. But I think that it is the basis of the jurisdiction that one has to consider. The basis, in my view, in relation to a trustee's remuneration is the good administration of trusts . . . [I]t is of great importance to the beneficiaries that the trust should be well administered. If therefore the court concludes, having regard to the nature of the trust, to the experience and skill of a particular trustee and to the amounts which he seeks to charge when compared with what other trustees might require to be paid for their services and to all the other circumstances of the case, that it would be in the interests of the beneficiaries to increase the remuneration, then the court may properly do so.[43]

The importance of the case in its immediate context is much reduced because the Trustee Act 2000 now allows trustees to be paid reasonable remuneration for services they provide if they are trust corporations or act in a professional capacity.[44] However, the principle of the case remains valid. The influence of the importance of the good administration of a trust is equally capable of application to administrative arrangements other than remuneration. Nor is authorization of payment for trustees the only instance in which the court enjoys jurisdiction to amend the operating arrangements for trusts. In *Re Ashton's Charity*,[45] followed in *Oldham Borough Council v A-G*,[46] Romilly MR held that, even where there is no applicable statutory authority, the Court of Chancery has a general jurisdiction to authorize the alienation of charity property where the court clearly sees

38 [1954] AC 429. 39 [1956] 1 WLR 23.

40 See also *Allen v Distillers Co (Biochemicals) Ltd* [1974] QB 384; *Mason v Farbrother* [1983] 2 All ER 1078.

41 *Re Steed's Will Trusts* [1960] Ch 407 at 420–1, per Evershed MR.

42 [1981] 3 All ER 220.

43 [1981] 3 All ER 220 at 230. Considerations relevant to approving remuneration were considered by Newey J in *Brudenell-Bruce v Moore* [2014] EWHC 3679 (Ch) at 225–36, where an application was refused.

44 ss 28 to 30. 45 [1856] 22 Beav 288.

46 [1993] 2 All ER 432. See also *Re Parke's Charity* [1842] 12 Sim 329; *Re North Shields Old Meeting House* [1859] 7 WR 541.

that the transaction is for the charity's benefit and advantage. So, in the *Oldham* case, the Court of Appeal was prepared to authorize the sale for building development of a playing field held upon charitable trusts where the proceeds were to be used to acquire a new site with better facilities. Even though it could be argued that this case relates specifically to the courts' charity jurisdiction, it helps, with *Re Duke of Norfolk's Settlement Trusts*, to support the case for holding that the inherent jurisdiction is less constrained than *Chapman v Chapman* might suggest.[47]

4 Miscellaneous statutory powers

(1) Trustee Act 1925, s 57

This provision allows the court to confer additional powers on trustees either generally, or in relation to a specific transaction, where it is expedient to do so.[48] The section is expressly limited to matters of 'the management and administration' of the trust property, and does not enable the variation of beneficial interests under the trust.[49] This distinction is not always easy to maintain in practice. In *Sutton v England*,[50] a scheme to create a sub-trust to benefit US beneficiaries of a family trust shared with UK resident beneficiaries was held by the Court of Appeal to fall within the emergency jurisdiction. This had been refused at first instance, on the basis that, while expedient, conferring the necessary power to partition the trust property to create the sub-trust required an alteration of the beneficial interests of the trust, and was therefore outside the powers conferred under s 57(1). Mummery LJ, while supporting a cautious approach to the intervention of the court in these matters, held that the impact on beneficial interests was permissible because it was incidental to the due management and administration of the trust and it did not alter the nature of the beneficial entitlements.[51]

The section can be used to extend trustees' powers. The section has been used to extend the investment powers of trustees;[52] to amalgamate two funds held on identical trusts;[53] to authorize a sale of a reversionary interest[54] or other trust property where there was no other power of sale[55] or a necessary consent could not be obtained;[56] and to authorize the partition of land[57] and of other trust property.[58] In some cases which come close to trespassing upon the principle that beneficial interests may not be affected, sanction has been given for the release of capital to pay the debts of an income beneficiary, subject to the replacement of the capital on the income beneficiary's death by means of a policy of life assurance.[59]

[47] Compare the dissenting judgment of Lord Denning in *Re Chapman's Settlement Trusts* [1953] Ch 218.

[48] See *Re Beale's Settlement Trusts* [1932] 2 Ch 15; *Re Thomas* [1930] 1 Ch 194; *Re Harvey* [1941] 3 All ER 284; *Re Power* [1947] Ch 572; *Re Cockerell's Settlement Trusts* [1956] Ch 372; *Re Shipwrecked Fishermen and Mariners' Royal Benevolent Society* [1959] Ch 220.

[49] *Re Downshire Settled Estate* [1953] Ch 218.

[50] [2011] 2 P & CR DG15.

[51] [2011] 2 P & CR DG15 at 34–43. Mummery LJ also made reference to *Re Downshire*, where Lord Evershed said that a scheme which had an incidental effect on the beneficial interests was permissible—see at 6.

[52] *Re Shipwrecked Fishermen and Mariners Royal Benevolent Society Charity* [1959] Ch 220; *Mason v Farbrother* [1983] 2 All ER 1078; *Anker-Petersen v Anker-Petersen* [1991] 16 LS Gaz R 32.

[53] *Re Harvey* [1941] 3 All ER 284; *Re Shipwrecked Fishermen and Mariners' Royal Benevolent Society Charity* [1959] Ch 220, not following the inconsistent decision in *Re Royal Society's Charitable Trusts* [1956] Ch 87.

[54] *Re Cockerell's Settlement Trusts* [1956] Ch 372.

[55] *Re Hope's Will Trust* [1929] 2 Ch 136.

[56] *Re Beale's Settlement Trusts* [1932] 2 Ch 15.

[57] *Re Thomas* [1930] 1 Ch 194. This would now be possible under the Trusts of Land and Appointment of Trustees Act 1996.

[58] *Sutton v England* [2011] EWCA Civ 637.

[59] *Re Salting* [1932] 2 Ch 57; *Re Mair* [1935] Ch 562.

In deciding whether approval is 'expedient', the court must consider the interest of the trust estate as a whole.[60] The object of the section is 'to secure that the trust property should be managed as advantageously as possible in the interests of the beneficiaries'.[61]

(2) Settled Land Act 1925, s 64(1)

This section enables the court to authorize 'any transaction affecting or concerning the settled land' by the tenant for life, provided that the transaction is, in the opinion of the court, for 'the benefit of the settled land'. Although limited to settled land, often an aristocratic arrangement setting out the line through which property can descend, this provision allows the court to authorize alterations in beneficial interests, as for example in *Re Downshire Settled Estates*.[62] In that case the motivation for the variation was to avoid estate duty. Since 1996 it has not been possible to create new settlements governed by the Settled Land Act 1925,[63] so this provision is of limited and decreasing importance.

(3) Trustee Act 1925, s 53

This section extends the court's inherent 'maintenance jurisdiction' in favour of infants and gives the court power to order the application of the capital or income from the trust for the 'maintenance, education or benefit of the infant'.[64]

(4) Matrimonial Causes Act 1973

This Act grants the court wide powers to make orders concerning the parties to matrimonial proceedings. By s 24 this includes the powers to order the making of a settlement for the benefit of the 'other party to the marriage and of the children of the family',[65] and to vary the beneficial interests under 'any ante-nuptial or post-nuptial settlement'.[66] This power was exercised by the court to vary a trust in *E v E (Financial Provision)*.[67]

(5) Mental Capacity Act 2005, s 18(1)(h)

This section, which came into force in October 2007,[68] gives the court power to make a settlement on behalf of a person who lacks capacity, and to vary it if any material fact was not disclosed when the settlement was made or if there has been any substantial change in circumstances.

[60] *Re Craven's Estate* [1937] Ch 423.

[61] *Re Downshire Settled Estates* [1953] Ch 218 at 248, per Evershed MR.

[62] [1953] Ch 218. See also *Hambro v Duke of Marlborough* [1994] Ch 158.

[63] The creation of new Settled Land Act settlements is prohibited under the Trusts of Land and Appointment of Trustees Act 1996, s 2(1). Settled Land Act settlements are themselves also variable under the Variation of Trusts Act 1958. See *Duke of Somerset v Fitzgerald* [2019] EWHC 726 (Ch).

[64] See *Re Meux* [1958] Ch 154; *Re Gower's Settlement* [1934] Ch 365; *Re Bristol's Settled Estates* [1964] 3 All ER 939; *Re Lansdowne's Will Trusts* [1967] Ch 603; *Re Heyworth's Contingent Reversionary Interest* [1956] Ch 364.

[65] s 24(1)(a)–(b).

[66] s 24(1)(c)–(d): *C v C (Ancillary Relief: Nuptial Settlement)* [2005] 2 WLR 241; Bennett, 'Variation of Ante and Post Nuptial Settlements' [2007] Fam Law 916.

[67] [1990] 2 FLR 233. See also *Brooks v Brooks* [1996] AC 375; Thomas, 'Divorce and Pension Funds' [1997] Conv 52.

[68] This section replaced a similar provision under the Mental Health Act 1983.

5 The Variation of Trusts Act 1958

(1) Introduction

The Variation of Trusts Act was passed in the aftermath of the decision of the House of Lords in *Chapman v Chapman*,[69] which severely restricted the 'compromise jurisdiction' that the courts had construed to give themselves a wide jurisdiction to vary trusts. The matter was referred to the Law Reform Commission, which concluded that:

> the only satisfactory solution to the problem is to give the court the unlimited jurisdiction to sanction such changes which it in fact exercised in the years preceding the decision in *Chapman v Chapman*.

The subsequently enacted Variation of Trusts Act gives the court a 'very wide discretion'[70] to authorize the variation of trusts, including the adjustment of the beneficial interests thereunder.[71]

The Variation of Trusts Act is not without controversy. By making it easier to vary trusts, it has also made it easier for wealthy families to avoid the payment of tax. The legislation also impacts on trusts established by will. Under contemporary inheritance tax legislation, it has become reasonably common to vary trusts after the death of a settlor so that allocations of property can be distributed in a tax efficient manner, taking advantage of spousal exemptions and the inheritance tax threshold.[72]

Beyond questions of taxation, variation is also sometimes controversial for the straightforward reason that it brings complex family arrangements out into the open. In particular where there are children involved, families sometimes go to great lengths to keep the variation secret. Recently, the courts have limited the possibility of variation behind closed doors, holding that the *prima facie* rule leans in favour of open decision-making.[73]

(2) Scheme of the Variation of Trusts Act

The Variation of Trusts Act operates alongside the principle of consensual variation, by which the beneficiaries can consent to the trust being performed in a manner different to that stipulated by the settlor in the trust instrument. The court is given the power to approve 'any arrangement[74] varying or revoking all or any of the trusts, or enlarging the powers of the trustees of managing or administering any of the property subject to the trusts',[75] on behalf of the categories of persons specified in s 1 who are not able to consent on their own behalf.[76] In this sense, the court acts as a 'statutory attorney'[77] for those who cannot consent for themselves, and it enjoys no power to consent on behalf of persons who are able

[69] [1954] AC 429. [70] *Re Steed's Will Trusts* [1960] Ch 407 at 420–1, per Evershed MR.

[71] The problem of whether an English court might vary a trust governed by a foreign law is examined by Harris in the light of *Charalambous v Charalambous* [2004] EWCA Civ 103; [2005] 121 LQR 16.

[72] Under s 142, Inheritance Tax Act 1984, if the variation within 2 years of the testator's death, the arrangement is treated as if the testator himself effected it.

[73] *V v T* [2014] EWHC 3432 (Ch); *MN v OP* [2019] EWCA Civ 679.

[74] In *Re Steed's Will Trusts* [1960] Ch 407, Evershed MR held that the word 'arrangement' should be given the 'widest possible sense . . . to cover any proposal . . . put forward'. See also *Ridgwell v Ridgewll* [2007] EWHC 2666 (Ch), where Behrens J confirmed this wide interpretation in considering whether the addition of a life interest was an arrangement within s 1.

[75] s 1(1). [76] See *Re Holt's Settlement Trusts* [1969] 1 Ch 100.

[77] *Goulding v James* [1997] 2 All ER 239 at 249, per Mummery LJ.

to consent for themselves.[78] As a safeguard to ensure that the interests of those on whose behalf the court can approve a variation are not prejudiced, the arrangement approved must be for their 'benefit'. Thus the Act achieves flexibility, by allowing trusts to be varied to take account of changing circumstances, while preserving the right of parties who can consent on their own behalf to make their own decisions, and protecting the interests of those who cannot. In *Goulding v James*,[79] Mummery LJ explained the role of the court and the relationship between the statutory jurisdiction and the rule in *Saunders v Vautier*:

> First, what varies the trust is not the court, but the agreement or consensus of the beneficiaries. Secondly, there is no real difference in principle in the rearrangement of the trusts between the case where the court is exercising its jurisdiction on behalf of the specified class under the 1958 Act and the case where the resettlement is made by virtue of the doctrine in *Saunders v Vautier* and by all the adult beneficiaries joining together. Thirdly, the court is merely contributing on behalf of infants and unborn and unascertained persons the binding assents to the arrangement which they, unlike an adult beneficiary, cannot give. The 1958 Act has thus been viewed by the courts as a statutory extension of the consent principle embodied in the rule in *Saunders v Vautier*.[80]

(3) Variation or resettlement?

While the Variation of Trusts Act enables the courts to approve a proposed variation of the allocation of benefit behind a trust, it has been held that the courts do not possess the jurisdiction to approve a 'resettlement' of the trusts. The line between what amounts to a genuine variation and what is a resettlement is hazy.

On one side of the line falls *Re T's Settlement Trusts*.[81] A trust provided that an infant would become entitled to a quarter of the trust income on attaining her majority. The child was irresponsible and immature, and the court's consent was sought to a variation which would transfer her share of the trust fund to new trustees to be held on protective trusts for her life, with remainder to her issue. Wilberforce J held that he did not have jurisdiction to approve this arrangement:

> It is obviously not possible to define exactly the point at which the jurisdiction of the court under the Variation of Trusts Act stops or should not be exercised. Moreover, I have no desire to cut down the very useful jurisdiction which this act has conferred upon the court. But I am satisfied that the proposal as originally made to me falls outside it. Though presented as a 'variation' it is in truth a complete new resettlement. The former trust funds were to be got in from the former trustees and held upon wholly new trusts such as might be made by an absolute owner of the funds. I do not think that the court can approve this.[82]

Similarly, Norris J declined, in *Wright v Gater*, to approve a reordering of the succession rights of a three-year-old because it would probably have amounted to a resettlement: 'Nothing remained of the original statutory trust.'[83]

Re Holt's Settlement[84] falls on the other side of the line. A trust had been created for Mrs Wilson for life, with remainder to her children who attained the age of twenty-one. A variation was proposed under which Mrs Wilson would surrender her life interest in a half of the income in favour of the children, but also to postpone the children's entitlement to

[78] s 1(1) specifically states that the court's power to approve is given irrespective of 'whether or not there is any other person beneficially interested who is capable of assenting thereto'. See also *IRC v Holmden* [1968] AC 685 at 701, per Lord Reid.

[79] [1997] 2 All ER 239 at 247.

[80] [1997] 2 All ER 239 at 247.

[81] [1964] Ch 158.

[82] [1964] Ch 158 at 162.

[83] [2011] EWHC 2881 (Ch) at 16.

[84] [1969] 1 Ch 100.

capital until each child attained the age of thirty.[85] Megarry J felt that this amounted to a genuine variation and not a resettlement:

> It is not, of course, for the court to draw the line in any particular place between what is a variation and what, on the other hand, is a completely new settlement. A line may, perhaps, one day emerge from a sufficiently ample series of reported decisions; but for the present all that is necessary for me to say is whether the particular case before me is on the right side or the wrong side of any reasonable line that could be drawn. In this case I am satisfied that the arrangement proposed falls on the side of the line which bears the device 'Variation'.[86]

Subsequent cases have failed to establish where the line should be drawn. In *Re Ball's Settlement Trusts*, Megarry J laid down a general test to distinguish between 'variations' and 'resettlements', namely, the 'substratum test':

> If an arrangement changes the whole substratum of the trust, then it may well be that it cannot be regarded merely as varying the trust. But if an arrangement, while leaving the substratum, effectuates the purpose of the trust by other means, it may still be possible to regard that arrangement as merely varying the original trusts, even though the means employed are wholly different and even though the form is completely changed.[87]

In *Wyndham v Egremont*,[88] Blackburne J did not find this statement particularly helpful, since it left unanswered what was meant by the 'substratum'. He had been asked to approve a variation of a trust made concerning the ancestral estates around Petworth House in West Sussex. The variation was intended to defer a very considerable tax liability and to ensure that the ancestral estates continued to devolve down the senior male line with the baronies of Egremont and Leconfield. Blackburne J concluded that this was not a resettlement and that he could and should approve it. He referred to a statement of Lord Wilberforce, in a different context (whether a new settlement had been created giving rise to a capital gains tax liability):

> I think that the question whether a particular set of facts amounts to a settlement should be approached by asking what a person, with knowledge of the legal context of the word under established doctrine and applying this knowledge in a practical and common-sense manner to the facts under examination, would conclude.[89]

Applying this test (which can scarcely be considered to be any clearer than the substratum test), Blackburne J concluded that he was being asked to approve only a variation:

> The trustees remain the same, the subsisting trusts remain largely unaltered and the administrative provisions affecting them are wholly unchanged. The only significant changes are (1) to the trusts in the remainder, although the ultimate trust in favour of George and his personal representatives remains the same, and (2) the introduction of the new and extended perpetuity period.[90]

A number of cases have held that extending the trust period is a variation not a resettlement where 'the trusts of each settlement would remain substantially unaltered and the settlement would remain recognizably the same.'[91]

The restriction that the court cannot approve a resettlement is a remaining vestige of the 'primacy of the settlor's intention'.

[85] See also *Goulding v James* [1997] 2 All ER 239, where the Court of Appeal approved a variation in which the life tenant and remainderman agreed that 90 per cent of the trust capital should be divided between themselves, thus defeating the life interest under the trust.

[86] [1969] 1 Ch 100 at 118.

[87] [1968] 1 WLR 899 at 905.

[88] [2009] EWHC 2076 (Ch).

[89] *Roome v Edwards* [1982] AC 279 at 292–3.

[90] [2009] EWHC 2076 (Ch) at 24.

[91] *Pemberton v Pemberton* [2016] EWHC 2345 (Ch) at 28 following *DC v AC* [2016] EWHC 477 (Ch); *Swann v Gibbs* [2020] EWHC 1226 (Ch) at 38. See also *Allfrey v Allfrey* [2015] EWHC 1717 (Ch)—trust period extended, but the same trustees were continuing 'the existing trusts, but with modifications'.

(4) Approval on behalf of whom?

The court may approve a variation of trust on behalf of four groups of persons identified in s 1 of the Variation of Trusts Act 1958. These are categories of people who cannot consent for themselves.

(a) Infancy or incapacity

By s 1(1)(a) the court can consent on behalf of:

> any person having, directly or indirectly, an interest, whether vested or contingent under the trusts who by reason of infancy or other incapacity is incapable of assenting.

The court cannot consent on behalf of adults without disabilities, even if they have only remote interests.[92]

(b) Unidentifiable beneficiaries

By s 1(1)(b) the court may consent on behalf of:

> any person (whether ascertained or not) who may become entitled, directly or indirectly, to an interest under the trusts as being at a future date or on the happening of a future event a person of any specified description or a member of any specified class of persons, so however that this paragraph shall not include any person who would be of that description, or a member of that class, as the case may be, if the said date had fallen, or the said event had happened at the date of the application to the court.

This complicated section is designed to cover the case of beneficiaries who are unidentifiable, in the sense that it is not known who they are because the circumstances that would bring them within the class have not yet occurred. Since they are unidentifiable, they cannot give consent to variations which affect their position, and the court can consent on their behalf. In *Re Clitheroe's Settlement Trust*,[93] for example, a variation of a discretionary trust was approved by the court. The trust was established by Lord Clitheroe in favour of 'the descendants of Sir Ralph Cockayne Assheton [his father] or the spouse of any of them'. Consent was given to a tax advantageous variation by the court under s 1(1)(b) on behalf of any future wife that Lord Clitheroe might have, who would thereby become a beneficiary of the trust. Two features of this section are worthy of special attention.

(i) Persons with an existing contingent interest

The court only has jurisdiction under s 1(1)(b) to grant approval on behalf of persons who 'may become entitled to an interest' under the trust in the future. In *Knocker v Youle*,[94] it was held that this means that the court cannot consent for persons who have a current interest in the trust, no matter how remote, even though it is impracticable to seek their consent. The case concerned a trust created in 1937 in favour of the settlor's daughter, with default clauses that could cause the property to be held on trust for her cousins. As Warner J noted, these were very numerous[95] and some lived in Australia, so that it was not practical to get their approval to a proposed variation. However, he held that he did not have the jurisdiction to grant approval on their behalf because 'a person who has an actual interest directly conferred upon him or her by a settlement, albeit a remote interest, cannot properly be described as one who "may become" entitled to an interest',[96] and is, therefore, not within the scope of s 1(1)(b).

[92] *Christie Miller's Marriage Settlement Trusts* [1961] 1 All ER 855 (Note).

[93] [1959] 1 WLR 1159.

[94] [1986] 1 WLR 934; Riddall, 'Does It or Doesn't It?—Contingent Interests and the Variation of Trusts Act 1958' [1987] Conv 144.

[95] There were seventeen.

[96] [1986] 1 WLR 934 at 937.

(ii) A 'double contingency' test

The second part of the definition in s 1(1)(b) adds a 'proviso'[97] that the court cannot consent on behalf of persons who would have interests in the trust if the event that would render them a beneficiary had in fact occurred at the date of the application. This means that the court only has jurisdiction to approve variation on behalf of persons who become entitled in the event of a 'double contingency'. This perceived 'proviso' was applied in *Re Suffert*.[98] A trust was established for Elaine Suffert for life, with the remainder to such of her issue as she should appoint, and in the event of default to those who would be entitled if she died intestate. She was a spinster, without issue, and had three adult cousins. She sought to vary the trust, one cousin consented, and the approval of the court was sought on behalf of all unascertained persons who might become entitled under the trusts. Buckley J held that he could not grant approval on behalf of the two adult cousins because they fell within the proviso to s 1(1)(b), since if the event under which they would become entitled, namely the death of Elaine Suffert, had occurred at the date of the application, they would have been beneficiaries of the trust. Similarly, in *Re Moncrieff's Settlement Trusts*,[99] a trust was established in favour of Anne Moncrieff, then for such of her issue as she appointed, and in default of appointment, to those entitled on intestacy. The court's approval to a variation was sought on behalf of her adopted son and her next of kin. Buckley J held that there was no jurisdiction to grant approval on behalf of the adopted son, as he fell within the limitation to s 1(1)(b), and would have been entitled at the date of the application if his mother had died. However, the court could consent on behalf of the other next of kin since they would only be entitled on the occurrence of a 'double-contingency', meaning both the death of the mother and the predecease of the adopted son. If the mother alone had died at the date of the application, they would still not have been entitled. *Re Suffert*[100] and *Re Moncrieff's Settlement Trusts*[101] were cited and followed by Warner J in *Knocker v Youle*.[102]

(c) Persons unborn

By s 1(1)(c) the court can consent on behalf of 'any person unborn'. If it is clearly the case that a person is past the age of childbearing and the chance of further beneficiaries arising is an impossible contingency, it is inappropriate to apply to the court to approve a variation under the Variation of Trusts Act. Thus, in *Re Pettifor's Will Trusts*,[103] Pennycuick J refused to approve a variation on behalf of the unborn children of a woman of seventy-eight.

(d) Contingent interests under protective trusts

By s 1(1)(d) the court can consent on behalf of:

> any person in respect of any discretionary interest of his under protective trusts where the interest of the principal beneficiary has not failed or determined.

Protective trusts, sometimes called 'spendthrift' trusts, are normally a type of family trust used to protect a principal beneficiary upon insolvency. Where insolvency occurs, a discretionary trust arises for the the principal beneficiary alongside others, so protecting the principal beneficiary from his creditors. This subsection allows the court to consent on behalf of those wider beneficiaries.

97 [1986] 1 WLR 934 at 937, per Warner J.
98 [1961] Ch 1.
99 [1962] 1 WLR 1344.
100 [1961] Ch 1.
101 [1962] 1 WLR 1344.
102 [1986] 1 WLR 934.
103 [1966] Ch 257.

An important feature of this paragraph is that the court's jurisdiction is not limited to variations which are 'for the benefit' of the person on whose behalf approval is given. If a person falls within the scope of either paras (a)–(c), where the requirement of benefit applies, or para (d), where there is no need to prove benefit, the court may act under para (d).[104]

(5) Avoiding consent

In *A v B*,[105] the need for consent from a large class of potential beneficiaries with remote interests was avoided by the trustees. The court said that the trustees could temporarily release or restrict a power of appointment for the large class, reinstating it as part of the new scheme of variation. This decision was taken in relation to a family trust primarily designed for core beneficiaries and the wider power, which was temporarily surrendered in order to make the variation without consent, was unlikely to ever to be used. Warren J approved this course of action because, although the power was fiduciary, it was being properly exercised to benefit the core beneficiaries.

(6) The requirement of benefit

Under s 1 the court may only grant approval to a scheme of variation on behalf of a person within the categories set out in s 1(1)(a)–(c) if: 'the carrying out thereof would be for the benefit of that person'.

(a) Financial benefit

There is no doubt that the court will grant approval on behalf of persons who would benefit financially from a proposed variation. Converting a terminable interest in income into an absolute interest is an example.[106] Permitting early payment of a contingent interest—beyond the limits in the statutory power of advancement—is another.[107] The financial benefit sought in most cases has been a reduction in tax liability. As Lord Denning MR observed in *Re Weston's Settlement*, 'nearly every variation that has come before the court has tax-avoidance for its principal object'.[108] In *Re Weston's Settlement*,[109] Stamp J did seem to suggest that the court would not sanction 'illegitimate tax avoidance'. He described the proposed variation in a family trust as 'a cheap exercise in tax avoidance which I ought not to sanction, as distinct from a legitimate avoidance of liability to taxation'.[110] However, the Court of Appeal, in *Chapman v Chapman*,[111] had not objected to a variation which had as its prime object the reduction of tax liability. In principle, all attempts to avoid tax, provided they are lawful, should be legitimate and a 'benefit'. This approach was approved and followed in *Ridgwell v Ridgwell*,[112] which concerned variations that sought to defer the date at which any current and future children of the life tenant under a trust fund would obtain a vested interest in the fund. Behrens J, in approving the arrangement, held that the changes would confer a benefit on the current and unborn children, due to the savings in capital gains tax and inheritance tax arising from the variations.[113] The courts may draw a line at 'artificial' tax avoidance, whatever that means.[114]

[104] *Re Turner's Will Trusts* [1968] 1 All ER 321.
[105] [2016] EWHC 340 (Ch) at 22–6.
[106] *Collins v Collins* [2016] EWHC 1423 (Ch).
[107] *CD (A Child) v O* [2004] 3 All ER 780.
[108] [1969] 1 Ch 223 at 245.
[109] [1969] 1 Ch 223.
[110] [1969] 1 Ch 223 at 234.
[111] [1953] Ch 218.
[112] [2007] EWHC 2666.
[113] [2007] EWHC 2666 at 36. There was also a possibility of cheaper life insurance being obtained through the variation.
[114] See *Pitt v Holt* [2013] UKSC 26 at 135.

(b) Non-financial benefits

The courts have also approved variations where the benefit derived is of a social or moral nature. In *Re T's Settlement Trusts*,[115] Wilberforce J held that the advantage of postponing the age at which a minor, who was irresponsible and immature, would become entitled to an interest under the trust was 'the kind of benefit which seems to be within the spirit of the Act'.[116] In *Re Holt's Settlement*,[117] Megarry J granted approval to a variation which deferred the interests of the infant beneficiaries until they attained the age of thirty. He considered that 'the word "benefit" is plainly not confined to financial benefit, but may extend to moral or social benefit',[118] and that it would therefore be a benefit to the children not to receive an income from the trust which would make them independent of the need to work before they had become reasonably advanced in their careers and settled in life. In *Re Remnant's Settlement Trusts*,[119] a family trust contained a forfeiture clause which would forfeit the interests of members of the family who became, or married, Roman Catholics. A variation removing this clause was approved by the court, which found a benefit to the children in that they would no longer be deterred from marrying a Roman Catholic if they so chose, and that the clause could be a source of future family dissension.[120] Facilitating the administration of the trust will also amount to a benefit, so in *Re Seale's Marriage Settlement*,[121] Buckley J approved on behalf of an infant the transfer of a trust to a Canadian trustee where the family had moved permanently to Canada.

(c) Conflicting benefits

The court may be faced with a situation where the proposed variation is beneficial in some ways but disadvantageous in others. For example, there may be great social or moral benefits, but financial disadvantages. In such circumstances the court will weigh the benefits to determine whether the variation is on balance of benefit. In *Re Weston's Settlement*,[122] the court's approval was sought on behalf of the infant beneficiaries of a marriage settlement to a variation which would transfer the trust to Jersey. Although this would produce a financial benefit of some £800,000, the Court of Appeal held that this was outweighed by the social benefits of the children remaining in England. Lord Denning MR explained how he had weighed the different benefits:

> The court should not consider merely the financial benefit to the infants or unborn children, but also their educational and social benefit. There are many things in life more worthwhile than money. One of these things is to be brought up in this our England, which is still 'the envy of less happier lands'. I do not believe it is for the benefit of children to be uprooted from England and transported to another country simply to avoid tax.[123]

This weighing of 'benefit' obviously involves a value judgement on the part of the court of the relative merits of the benefits and disadvantages associated with a proposed variation. In *Ridgwell v Ridgwell*,[124] for example, Behrens J considered that the long-term tax benefits of a proposed variation outweighed any disadvantage of a postponement. In the case, there was an application to create a life interest for a surviving spouse. This interest would postpone interests of certain current and unborn children. However, the postponement

[115] [1964] Ch 158.

[116] [1964] Ch 158 at 162. Wilberforce J held on the facts he did not have the jurisdiction to approve the proposed variation.

[117] [1969] 1 Ch 100. [118] [1969] 1 Ch 100 at 121. [119] [1970] Ch 560.

[120] There was also a financial benefit to the children in having their interests under the trust advanced.

[121] [1961] Ch 574. [122] [1969] 1 Ch 223. [123] [1969] 1 Ch 223 at 245. [124] [2007] EWHC 2666.

would also enable potentially inheritance tax efficient advancements to be made for the benefit of the children.[125] This tax advantage was held to outweigh the disadvantage of the postponement.[126]

(d) Manifest benefit

It is not enough that those on whose behalf the court is asked to grant approval to a proposed variation gain a benefit from the variation. The extent of their benefit must reflect that they are bargaining from a position of strength. This requirement prevents their position being exploited. In *Re Van Gruisen's Will Trusts*,[127] Ungoed Thomas J held that it would not be sufficient for the infants and unborn children on whose behalf he was asked to consent merely to receive the actuarial value of their remainder interest in the trust fund. Instead, the court must make 'a practical and business-like consideration of the arrangement including the total amounts of the advantages which the various parties obtain and their bargaining strength'. On the facts, he held that the share of the infants and unborn did adequately exceed their actuarial value.

(7) A discretion to vary

The Variation of Trusts Act provides that the court 'may if it thinks fit' approve a proposed variation. This clearly gives the court a discretion, and the court is not obliged to approve a variation, even if the requisite element of benefit can be shown. In some recognized circumstances the court will not exercise its discretion to approve a variation.

(a) Fraud on a power

The court will not approve a variation which amounts to a fraud on a power.[128] Megarry J stated the principle in *Re Wallace's Settlements*:

> If it is clear that a fraud on the power is involved, then plainly the court ought to withhold its approval. The power of the court under the Act is a discretionary power exercisable if the court 'thinks fit'; and I cannot conceive that it would be fitting for an arrangement to be approved if that arrangement had been made possible by a manifest fraud on a power, or was in some way connected with such a fraud.[129]

A fraud on a power, it should be remembered, does not require dishonesty, but merely the use of a power for an improper purpose. This can pose a difficulty where a life tenant with a special power of appointment over the remainder interest seeks to exercise the power and to receive a share of capital in return for surrendering the life interest. In *Re Brook's Settlement*[130] Stamp J took a very strict approach and held that if the purpose of the exercise of a power of appointment was that the life tenant should gain a share of the fund, then there was a fraud on the power even though the life tenant may gain a share of the fund lower than the market value of his life interest.[131] However, a more flexible approach was adopted by Megarry J in *Re Wallace's Settlements*,[132] where he approved a variation when there had been an exercise of a power of appointment, even though the life tenant received a share of the fund slightly greater than the actuarial value of her life interest. On the facts, he held that the exercise of the power had been long intended and was for the benefit of the beneficiaries, and therefore there was no fraud.

[125] Inheritance Tax Act 1984, s 3A(5).

[126] [2007] EWHC 2666 at 36. See also *Wright v Gater* [2011] EWHC 2881 (Ch).

[127] [1964] 1 All ER 843n.

[128] See Chapter 26.

[129] [1968] 1 WLR 711 at 717–18.

[130] [1968] 1 WLR 1661.

[131] [1968] 1 WLR 1661 at 1669.

[132] [1968] 1 WLR 711.

(b) Undermining protective trusts

In *Re Steed's Will Trusts*,[133] the Court of Appeal refused to approve a variation which would effectively remove the protective element from a protective trust of property left by a testator to his housekeeper. The Court took the view that the protective element was part of the 'testator's scheme' and it had been his desire and intention that she enjoy that protection.[134]

(c) Relevance of the settlor's intentions

Where the court is requested to grant approval of a variation for persons unable to consent on their own behalf, it is not entitled to refuse a variation which would be for their benefit merely because the variation would contravene the intentions of the original settlor. In such circumstances the intentions and wishes of the original settlor are of 'little, if any, relevance or weight'[135] to the question whether approval should be given. In *Goulding v James*,[136] the testatrix left her residuary estate on trust for her daughter for life, with remainder to her grandson on his attaining the age of forty. It was further provided that if he failed to attain the age of forty the residuary estate should pass to such of his children (i.e. her great-grandchildren) as were living at the date of his death. She had established this trust with the express object of preventing her daughter touching the capital of her estate, because she did not trust her son-in-law. She had postponed her grandson's interest until he was forty because he was presently living with an artistic community in Nantucket and she considered him a 'free spirit' who had not yet settled down. The daughter and grandson sought to vary the trusts under the will so that they would receive a 45 per cent share each of the residuary estate absolutely, with the remaining 10 per cent on trusts for any great-grandchildren. As they were adults, the daughter and grandson were perfectly entitled to agree to such variation, but they sought the approval of the court on behalf of the as yet unborn great-grandchildren. Although the variation was for their benefit, because actuarial valuation showed that the current value of the contingent interest of the great-grandchildren was only 1.85 per cent of the residuary estate, Laddie J held that the court should refuse to exercise its discretion to grant approval because the object of the arrangement was the complete opposite of what the testatrix had intended.[137] However, the Court of Appeal held that approval should have been forthcoming. Mummery LJ held that the testatrix's intentions were all but irrelevant in deciding whether the discretion should be exercised:

> In my judgment the legal position is as follows. (1) The court has a discretion whether or not to approve a proposed arrangement. (2) That discretion is fettered by only one express restriction. The proviso to s 1 prohibits the court from approving an arrangement which is not for the benefit of the classes referred to in (a) (b) or (c). The approval of this arrangement is not prevented by that proviso, since it is plainly the case that it is greatly for the benefit of the class specified in s 1(1)(c).[138]

Ralph Gibson LJ similarly explained that the settlor's original intention was irrelevant:

> Where there is an application under the Variation of Trusts Act 1958 for approval of an arrangement agreed by the beneficiaries, capable of giving assent, it is not clear to me why evidence of the intention of the testator can be of any relevance whatever if it does no more than explain why the testator gave the interests set out in the will and the nature and degree

[133] [1960] Ch 407.

[134] [1960] Ch 407 at 421–2: the purpose of the protection was to prevent the housekeeper being 'sponged upon' by her brothers.

[135] *Goulding v James* [1997] 2 All ER 239 at 251–2, per Mummery LJ.

[136] [1997] 2 All ER 239. [137] [1996] 4 All ER 854. [138] [1997] 2 All ER 239 at 249.

> of feeling with which such provisions were selected. The fact that a testator would not have approved or would have disapproved very strongly does not alter the fact that the beneficiaries are entitled in law to do it and, if it be proved, that the arrangement is for the benefit of the unborn. If, of course, it can be shown that the arrangement put forward constitutes, for example, a dishonest or inequitable or otherwise improper act on the part of one or more of the beneficiaries, then such evidence would clearly be relevant to the question whether the court would 'think fit' to approve it on behalf of a minor or unborn persons. In this case, the evidence of intention of this testatrix seems to me to have been of no relevance.[139]

The decision in *Goulding v James*[140] is at odds with the decision in *Re Steed's Will Trusts*,[141] where the court refused to vary a protective trust because, among other reasons, this was part of the testator's scheme. Likewise, Master Matthews, in approving a new arrangement in *Bathurst v Bathurst*[142] for appointing trustees where the old power of appointment had lapsed on the death of the settler, took account of the arrangement being similar to the provisions which had lapsed in the original trust. Since the power of the court to approve a variation is discretionary, it is hard to see why the testator's motives should be wholly disregarded. On the other hand, treating the court as the 'statutory attorney' for those on whose behalf it consents, its task is not to adjudicate on the merits of the scheme as a whole, but only on its impact on those for whom the court acts as a surrogate. From this point of view, why should those beneficiaries lose the benefits in kind they would receive from a variation unless those benefits are more than compensated by the non-pecuniary benefits of knowing that the testator's wishes have been respected?

(8) Widening powers of investment

The Variation of Trusts Act is not limited to the variation of beneficial interests, but may also be used to vary the powers of the trustees. Before trustees' powers of investment were extended by the Trustee Act 2000, the 1958 Act was used to approve enlarged powers of investment.[143]

(9) Effect of an order to vary

The question has arisen as to how precisely a variation of the beneficial interests under a trust takes place. Does it occur by the order of the court or as a result of the arrangement that is consented to by those who are able, and by the court on those who cannot consent for themselves? The difficulty is not merely theoretical because of the implications of s 53(1)(c) of the Law of Property Act, which requires that a disposition of a subsisting equitable interest 'must be in writing signed by the person disposing of the same'.[144] If the variation is considered a 'disposition',[145] and takes effect as a consequence of the arrangement and not the court order, is it necessary that all those who can consent for themselves do so in writing? Although there is some authority to the contrary,[146] the House of Lords

[139] [1997] 2 All ER 239 at 252.

[140] [1997] 2 All ER 239 at 252, per Mummery LJ. See Luxton, 'Variation of Trusts: Settlors' Intentions and the Consent Principle in *Saunders v Vautier*' (1997) 60 MLR 719.

[141] [1960] Ch 407. [142] [2016] EWHC 3033 (Ch).

[143] See *Mason v Farbrother* [1983] 2 All ER 1078; *Trustees of the British Museum v A-G* [1984] 1 WLR 418; *Steel v Wellcome Custodian Trustees Ltd* [1988] 1 WLR 167. An earlier case, very shortly after the Trustee Investment Act 1961, declined to approve wider investment powers: *Re Kolb's Will Trusts* [1962] Ch 531.

[144] See Chapter 7. [145] *Grey v IRC* [1960] AC 1, HL.

[146] *Re Viscount Hambleden's Will Trusts* [1960] 1 All ER 353n, per Wynn-Parry J.

has held that the variation takes effect through the arrangement and not by the order of the court. The principle was stated by Lord Reid in *IRC v Holmden*:

> Under the Variation of Trusts Act the court does not itself amend or vary the trusts of the original settlement. The beneficiaries are not bound by variations because the court has made the variation. Each beneficiary is bound because he has consented to the variation. If he was not of full age when the arrangement was made he is bound because the court was authorised to act on his behalf and did so by making an order. If he was of full age and did not in fact consent he is not affected by the order of the court and he is not bound. So the arrangement must be regarded as an arrangement made by the beneficiaries themselves. The court merely acted on behalf of or as representing those beneficiaries who were not in a position to give their own consent and approval.[147]

Whether the consenting beneficiaries must comply with s 53(1)(c) was considered by Megarry J in *Re Holt's Settlement*,[148] where he adopted two possible solutions to avoid the difficulty. First, he accepted that the express granting of the power to vary trusts to the courts by Parliament in the Variation of Trusts Act has 'provided by necessary implication an exception from s 53(1)(c)'.[149] Second, if the arrangement is an agreement made for valuable consideration, then because it is specifically enforceable, the 'beneficial interests pass to the respective purchasers on the making of the agreement', by means of a constructive trust.[150] By virtue of s 53(2), writing is, therefore, not required.

[147] [1968] AC 685 at 701; *Re Joseph's Will Trusts* [1959] 1 WLR 1019.

[148] [1969] 1 Ch 100. It is worth noting that *Re Holt's Settlement Trusts* was decided prior to the House of Lords' decision in *Re Holmden's Settlement Trusts* and that Megarry J proceeded on the basis that it was the court order which varied the trusts.

[149] [1969] 1 Ch 100 at 115: Megarry J accepted that this was not the most natural construction and that he was 'straining a little at the wording in the interests of legislative efficiency'.

[150] [1969] 1 Ch 100 at 116, following *Oughtred v IRC* [1960] AC 206, HL.

PART VIII

Managing Trust Property

30. Management and delegation 625
31. Investment 641
32. Appointing and changing trustees 667

30

Management and delegation

1 Introduction

Trusts can serve a variety of functions, one of which is to create more flexibility in deciding who benefits from property than is possible through outright gifts. We have already looked at distributive flexibility in Chapters 24 to 29. The distributive powers given to trustees, donees of powers, and protectors or appointors are very different from trustees' management powers, which we look at in this part of the book. The management powers of trustees are concerned with looking after property or funds (for instance, through choosing and reviewing investments, discussed in Chapter 31). They do not allow the trustees to choose who benefits.

(1) **Trusts with no management powers**

With some kinds of property, such as a valuable painting which it is intended should be kept as a family heirloom, trustees might be directed to hold the property upon trust in its original form without any powers of disposition over the property. The purpose of the trust is to prevent the property—in this case, the painting—from being sold. The trust can be used in a similar fashion to enable shares to be kept unsold for the benefit of future generations of a family, although in this case, the trustees will receive dividend payments from the shareholding which they must pass on to the beneficiaries.

A common form of trust in which the trustee has no powers of disposition or management is a trust of a life insurance policy. When a person takes out a contract of life insurance, under which the insurance company undertakes to pay a sum of money on the death of the person insured, that sum is payable to the personal representatives of the person taking out the insurance contract, and forms part of that person's estate. Since most people taking out this form of life insurance intend their family to benefit from the proceeds of the policy, they may declare that they hold it in trust for their family.[1] The effect of this is that, on their death,[2] the insurance company may make the payment directly to the family members who have been named as beneficiaries,[3] rather than to the personal

[1] A trust arises wherever a policy of life assurance on the life assured is expressed to be made for the benefit of the spouse or children of the insured: Married Women's Property Act 1882, s 11. In other cases, there must be an express intention to create a trust: compare *Re Webb, Barclays Bank Ltd v Webb* [1941] Ch 225 (trust created), and *Re Engelblach's Estate* [1924] 2 Ch 348 (no trust created).

[2] Or, in the case of an endowment policy, the date of maturity, if earlier: see *Re Ioakimidis' Policy Trusts* [1925] Ch 403.

[3] The spouse or children may be identified by name, in which case the proceeds of the policy are payable to their estate even if they predecease the insured: *Cousins v Sun Life Assurance Society* [1933] Ch 126. If the policy is expressed to be for the insured's spouse or children (or both) without naming them, it is construed as being for the benefit of those in that category who survive the insured: *Re Browne's Policy* [1903] 1 Ch 188.

representatives. This can speed up payment. In addition, the proceeds of the policy do not form part of the estate of the deceased for inheritance tax purposes, and are not available to meet any debts which the insured may have owed. This is one of the reasons why, in *Foskett v McKeown*,[4] disappointed investors under a land investment scheme sought to trace their misused funds into an insurance policy taken out by the swindler in trust for his family. The proceeds from the policy would not otherwise have been available to meet their claim.

The disadvantages to the insured of creating a trust are that the insured will no longer be able to vary the terms of the policy without obtaining the consent of the beneficiary.[5] The insured must also act in the responsible way required of a trustee, considering the interests of the beneficiaries, for instance in considering whether to surrender the policy.[6]

(2) **The need for management**

Unlike paintings and fully paid-up insurance policies, some property cannot be left unmanaged: it requires active management. For instance, if land is held on trust, then, unless it is occupied by the beneficiary, the trustee will need to arrange for it to be let in order to produce an income. The trustee will also need to ensure that the rent is paid promptly and that proper steps have been taken to ensure that the property is properly maintained. Indeed, even a painting may need special measures to be taken to ensure that it is properly conserved, and it would be prudent to insure it. The necessary powers of management might be given to, or retained by, the beneficiaries, as is the case with nominee trusts, which were considered in Chapter 25. The powers of management, though, may be conferred upon the trustees holding the title to the property, or in the special case of custodian trusts (also considered in Chapter 25) by a separate group of trustees.

A trust might be created expressly for the purpose of conferring responsibility for active management on the trustees, as in the case of property being left on trust for a young child, or an adult who suffers from mental impairment. In other cases, for instance, where there is complex beneficial entitlement, the need for powers of management might arise incidentally.

2 The extent of management powers

The powers of management conferred upon a trustee are not the same in every case. Quite obviously, the powers of express trustees are likely to differ significantly from those of constructive trustees upon whom a trust has been imposed because of their improper conduct. In the latter case, the question of the trustees' powers rarely arises. They are wrongdoers who are, by definition, acting in breach of duty. How far they are authorized to act is, therefore, unlikely to be in issue.

Even in the case of express trustees, however, the powers of management of the trustees will differ markedly from one situation to another. The first place to look to find the trustee's powers is the trust instrument which, if well drafted, should include most of the powers which a trustee is likely to need. Failing this, powers may be implied by statute or common law. Finally, the court has statutory and inherent powers to authorize management transactions.

[4] [1998] Ch 265.

[5] *Re Schebsman* [1944] Ch 83, CA. The contrary view expressed in *Hill v Gomme* (1839) 5 My & Cr 250 is wrong. If the matter remains in simple contract, then the insured will remain at liberty to vary the policy: *Green v Russell* [1959] 2 QB 226.

[6] *Re Equitable Life Assurance Society of US Policy and Mitchell* (1911) 27 TLR 213.

(1) Express powers

The trust instrument may set out in considerable detail the authority of the trustees. This is particularly likely to be the case with large, professionally drawn trust deeds such as those governing pension funds or unit trusts, or even large family trusts, especially where the assets pose distinctive issues of management.[7] For example, if the property which is held upon trust is a controlling interest in a private company which it is intended should be run by the trustees, or if it consists of an author's moral rights in literary works, it would be prudent and usual for the documents establishing the trust to define in detail the powers of the trustees.

Powers of management may or may not include a power to dispose of the property and to reinvest the proceeds. In the case of a trust for sale (described later in the chapter), the trustees are placed under an express obligation to sell the property and either to distribute or to reinvest the proceeds. Where the trust concerns land, the trustees will, in the absence of any express contrary intention, have both an automatic statutory power to sell the land and to postpone a sale.[8] This does not apply to trusts for sale of other kinds of property, although there can, of course, be an express power to postpone a sale.

(2) Implied powers

There are some cases where powers or duties can be implied from the context of a trust. Where a trust comprising money or quoted stocks and shares contains an express power of investment, but fails to provide express authority for sale for the purpose of reinvestment, it is reasonable to infer this power. The implication might, in some cases, go beyond the implication of a power and impose a duty on trustees.

A power will not be implied if it is inconsistent with the purpose of the trust. Thus, if a charitable trust is established to retain for the public benefit a particular house once owned by a particular historical figure, or a particular building for its architectural merit, then a sale could not take place without altering the terms of the trust 'because after a sale the proceeds or any property acquired with the proceeds could not possibly be applied for the original charitable purpose'.[9]

(3) Statutory powers

Where a trust deed does not set out express powers of management or does not do so comprehensively, and no powers can be implied as a question of fact, the omission may be supplied by statute in one of two ways. First, there are some specific situations in which statutory powers of management are implied. The most notable of these are in trusts of land. Second, there are some general powers which are implied into all trusts by the Trustee Act 1925 and the Trustee Act 2000.

(a) Trusts of land

Since the Trusts of Land and Appointment of Trustees Act 1996, a single form of trust, the 'trust of land', applies to all trusts of land. The Act replaced the two previous types of trust of land (although preserving strict settlement trusts already in existence). The

[7] For example, in *Re Duke of Norfolk's Settlement Trusts* [1982] Ch 610, CA, the trustees had powers of management which enabled them to carry out a substantial redevelopment of the Strand Estate which formed part of the settlement trusts.

[8] Trusts of Land and Appointment of Trustees Act 1996, ss 4, 6, and 8.

[9] *Oldham Borough Council v A-G* [1993] 2 All ER 432 at 439, per Dillon LJ. A similar decision was made in *Re Sir Edward Heath Charitable Trust* [2012] WTLR 1469.

detailed technical rules governing trusts of land will be found in textbooks on land law, and need not detain us here. A few important features of the trusts are, however, worth pointing out.

The trustees of a trust of land will often be the beneficiaries (in most cases of co-owner-ship), but can be specially appointed trustees (as is likely to be the case with land held on behalf of clubs and societies). The Trusts of Land and Appointment of Trustees Act 1996 gives the trustees all the powers of an absolute owner including the power to sell,[10] and a power to retain the property by postponing the sale for an indefinite period.[11] The power to retain applies even to an express trust to sell land, and is not capable of being excluded. There are some special provisions which do not apply to most trusts, and which reflect the reality that many trusts of land result from the beneficiaries combining to make a purchase of land for their own use. In exercising their powers, the trustees are required to consult the beneficiaries of full age and entitled in possession, and to give effect to the wishes of the majority by value, so far as this is consistent with the general interest of the trust.[12]

Beneficiaries with an interest in possession have a prima facie right to occupy the land.[13] Their rights of occupation are subject to the power of the trustees to exclude or restrict them.[14] The courts have jurisdiction to intervene in cases of dispute,[15] jurisdiction which may be needed more frequently than might be suggested by the rules about consultation, since trustees are required to act unanimously, and in cases of dispute a beneficiary who is also a trustee may be reluctant to concur with the majority.

(b) General statutory powers

The Trustee Act 1925 contains a small number of powers of management which are incorporated into all trusts. Additional management powers are conferred on trustees by the Trustee Act 2000. The Trustee Act 2000 also replaces the investment provisions of the 1925 Act with a new investment regime. The investment powers are of sufficient importance to merit a separate chapter.[16]

(i) Sale

The Trustee Act 1925 contains various provisions governing sale which authorize trustees, for instance, to sell either by auction or by private contract.[17] While these provisions extend and expand upon any trust or power which a trustee may have to sell, they do not confer any authority upon the trustees to sell where it has not arisen in some other way. Similarly, the Trustee Act 2000, which extends the investment powers of trustees, does not include any provision authorizing sale except for the purpose of varying an investment.[18] There is therefore no general statutory power of sale except in the case of trusts of land.

(ii) Receipts

By s 14 of the Trustee Act 1925, a trustee may give a receipt in writing 'for any money, securities, or other personal property or effects payable, transferable, or deliverable to him under any trust or power' which is a sufficient discharge to the person making the transfer and which exonerates the transferee from having to enquire into the application of the property by the trustee. This power cannot be excluded by a contrary provision in the trust instrument, if any.[19] If there is more than one trustee, they must all, it seems, concur in the receipt because of the principle that trustees must act unanimously,[20] except

[10] Trusts of Land and Appointment of Trustees Act 1996, s 6. [11] Ibid, s 4.
[12] Ibid, s 11. [13] Ibid, s 12. [14] Ibid, s 13. [15] Ibid, s 14. [16] See Chapter 31.
[17] s 12. [18] What constitutes investment and reinvestment is discussed in Chapter 31.
[19] s 14(3). [20] *Attenborough v Solomon* [1913] AC 76.

where the trust instrument authorizes them to act by a majority[21] or, possibly, individually. Charity and pension trustees are authorized by statute to act by a majority. Where capital money arises on a sale of land held upon trust, a minimum of two trustees are required to give a valid receipt, except where the trustee is a trust corporation.[22]

(iii) Insurance

Trustees had no duty at common law to insure the trust property,[23] nor had they any power to do so. Section 19 of the Trustee Act 1925 conferred a limited power for trustees to take out insurance, and those powers were extended in 1996[24] and again by the Trustee Act 2000, which substituted a new s 19 for the original in the Trustee Act 1925. The new provision authorizes trustees to insure any trust property against the risks of loss or damage due to any event, and to pay the premiums out of the income or capital of the trust funds.[25] In the case of trusts where the beneficiaries are all of full age and capacity and together are absolutely entitled to the trust property, this power to insure is subject to any direction given by those beneficiaries.[26] If any payments are made out under the insurance policy, these payments will be treated as capital belonging to the trust, or may be used to reinstate the property lost or damaged.[27] The statutory duty to take reasonable care applies to the exercise of both the statutory and any express power to insure.[28]

(iv) Compromises

A variety of powers relating to the management of property, including some enabling trustees to enter into a compromise or arrangement concerning a dispute, are contained in the Trustee Act 1925, s 15. In *Re Earl of Strafford (Decd)*,[29] the sixth Earl of Strafford had left his mansion house, Wrotham Park, and his London home, together with most of his personal property, on a complex trust providing for a series of life interests. The trusts had subsequently been varied by transferring the property to Wrotham Park Settled Estates, an incorporated company.[30] There was some confusion as to whether a number of articles, amounting in value to over £170,000, belonged to the Earl of Strafford, and had been settled by him on trust, or whether they belonged to his wife, the Countess. The initial steps in litigation were taken in order to resolve the issue before the beneficiaries under the Countess's will proposed a compromise. The Court of Appeal held that the trustees were permitted by s 15 to agree to this proposed compromise even if other of their beneficiaries objected, and even though it involved a surrender of beneficial interests by those proposing the compromise. Buckley LJ said:

> The language of s 15 is, it appears to me, very wide. It would, I think, be undesirable to seek to restrict its operation in any way unless legal principles require this, for it seems to me to be advantageous that trustees should enjoy wide and flexible powers of compromising and

[21] *Re Butlin's Settlement Trust* [1976] Ch 251; [1976] 2 All ER 483. Charitable trustees may act by a majority even if there is no express stipulation on the trust instrument: *Re Whiteley* [1910] 1 Ch 600 at 608.

[22] Trustee Act 1925, s 14(2), as amended by the Law of Property (Amendment) Act 1926 and the Trusts of Land and Appointment of Trustees Act 1996, Sch 3. See Settled Land Act 1925, s 94(1) and Law of Property Act 1925, s 27(2), as amended and re-enacted by the Law of Property (Amendment) Act 1926.

[23] *Re McEacharn* [1911] 103 LT 900.

[24] By the Trusts of Land and Appointment of Trustees Act 1996.

[25] Trustee Act 1925, s 19(1), as substituted by Trustee Act 2000, s 34. [26] Ibid, s 19(2).

[27] Ibid, s 20. [28] Trustee Act 2000, s 1 and Sch 1, para 5.

[29] [1979] 1 All ER 513.

[30] Subsequently involved in a leading case concerning the award of damages in lieu of an injunction for breach of a restrictive covenant: *Wrotham Park Estate Co v Parkside Homes Ltd* [1974] 2 All ER 321.

> settling disputes, always bearing in mind that such a power, however wide, must be exercised with due regard for the interests of those whose interests it is the duty of the trustees to protect. I see nothing in the language of the section to restrict the scope of the power.[31]

The Court of Appeal held that the compromise could be approved provided that, when considered as a whole, it was for the benefit of all the beneficiaries in accordance with their several interests in the trust property. It is not a requirement of approving a compromise that a claim adverse to the trust would otherwise be certain to succeed.[32] There must, nevertheless, be a genuine dispute.[33] The trustees are also required to comply with the statutory duty to take reasonable care imposed by the Trustee Act 2000, s 1.

(v) Reversionary interests

Trustees are given wide powers under s 22 of the Trustee Act 1925 to enter into arrangements, agreements, and other transactions concerning property to which the trust is entitled but which is not yet vested in the trustees. This would include, for instance, property which was payable to the trustees upon the winding up of a testator's estate. Once again, trustees must comply with the statutory duty to take reasonable care imposed by the Trustee Act 2000, s 1.

(4) **Exceptional authority given by court**

The express powers of trustees, as supplemented by the general and special statutory powers, may not cover every transaction which the trustees consider desirable. There is always the possibility of a situation arising which had not been anticipated: a valuable collection of modern art might, for instance, have started to deteriorate owing to the decomposition of some of the materials. Urgent restoration might be required in order to preserve the collection, yet no source of funds may be available to the trustees. In cases such as these, the trustees could enter into some otherwise unauthorized transaction (such as selling one piece of art to pay for repairs to the others), with the consent of all the beneficiaries. If some of the beneficiaries are unascertainable or unable to consent, or perhaps, where they decline consent, the trustees might need to apply to court for approval for an exceptional transaction. The powers of the court to approve such a transaction are discussed in Chapter 29 since some of the powers are also available to vary beneficial interests.

The inherent jurisdiction of the courts over trusts enables the court to correct obvious minor administrative errors. In *HR Trustees Ltd v Wembley Plc (In Liquidation)*,[34] only four out of five of a pension scheme's trustees had signed an amendment to its rules, despite all five having agreed to the amendment. It was held that the court could cure the defect by the application of the maxim that equity looked on matters as done which ought to be done and, therefore, correct what had been an obvious administrative error. Without this correction the amendment would have been invalid.

3 Delegation by trustees

Traditionally, equity has been reluctant to permit delegation by trustees of their powers in the absence of an express power provided in the trust instrument, but statutory powers of delegation have increasingly been available to trustees. The position for most trusts is now governed by the Trustee Act 2000, which has substantially changed the approach to delegation.

[31] [1979] 1 All ER 513 at 520. [32] *Re Ridsdel* [1947] Ch 597.
[33] *Re Earl of Strafford* [1980] Ch 28; *Chapman v Chapman* [1954] AC 429, CA.
[34] [2011] EWHC 2974 (Ch).

It should be noted that there are two forms of delegation. The trustees, acting together, may decide to delegate collectively a function to an agent. Alternatively, a single trustee may seek, for instance, during a temporary period of absence, to assign his individual functions to a person to exercise on his behalf. This chapter looks first at collective delegation before considering individual delegation, although some elements of the discussion apply to both forms of delegation.

4 Delegation at common law

(1) The general principle: no delegation of trustees' duties

Traditionally, equity took the view that a trustee had no power to delegate his powers to an agent, either individually or collectively. As the Latin maxim expresses it: *delegatus non potest delegare*. This was emphasized by Lord Langdale MR in *Turner v Corney*,[35] which involved a trust where there was an express power of delegation. He stated that:

> trustees who take on themselves the management of property for the benefit of others have no right to shift their duty on other persons; and if they employ an agent, they remain subject to responsibility toward their cestui que trust, for whom they have undertaken the duty.

The rationale for this restriction was that the settlor had placed his confidence in the trustees he had chosen to perform the trust obligations.[36] As Lord Westbury stated in *Robson v Flight*:

> such trusts and powers are supposed to have been committed by the [settlor] to the trustees he appoints by reason of his personal confidence in their discretion, and it would be wrong to permit them to be exercised by [another].[37]

However, in consequence of the evolution of the law, this general principle must now be replaced by the more moderate position stated by Lord Radcliffe in *Pilkington v IRC*:[38] 'the law is not that trustees cannot delegate: it is that trustees cannot delegate unless they have authority to do so'. Thus, the central question is as to the circumstances in which trustees enjoy the authority to delegate their responsibilities.

(2) A limited entitlement to delegate

(a) Delegation in the ordinary course of business

During the eighteenth century, the courts came to accept that, in some circumstances, delegation to an agent was required for reasons of commercial practicality. In *Learoyd v Whiteley*,[39] Lord Watson, therefore, stated a general principle permitting trustees to delegate their functions:

> whilst trustees cannot delegate the execution of the trust, they may . . . avail themselves of the services of others wherever such employment is according to the usual course of business.[40]

[35] [1841] 5 Beav 515. See also *Robson v Flight* [1865] 4 De GJ & SM 608 at 613, per Lord Westbury LC; *Speight v Gaunt* [1883] 22 Ch D 727 at 756, per Lindley LJ.

[36] *Speight v Gaunt* [1883] 9 App Cas 1 at 29, per Lord Fitzgerald.

[37] [1865] 4 De GJ & SM 608 at 613.

[38] [1964] AC 612, HL. See also Jones, 'Delegation by Trustees: A Reappraisal' [1959] MLR 381.

[39] [1887] 12 App Cas 727.

[40] [1887] 12 App Cas 727, 734.

(b) Scope of the right to delegate

The common law power of trustees to delegate within the ordinary course of business did not, however, entitle trustees to delegate all of their functions or duties. The right to delegate extended only in respect of their ministerial acts, in other words those that did not require an exercise of discretion on their part. Trustees were not permitted to delegate their discretions,[41] such as the selection of trust investments,[42] or the decision whether or not to sell[43] or lease[44] trust property. Thus, whilst trustees were able to delegate the implementation of their decisions and the routine administration of the trust, they were required to continue to take all the basic decisions themselves.

(3) Trustees' liability for the acts of their agent

The mere fact that trustees were entitled to appoint an agent, whether because such an appointment was within the ordinary course of business or for reasons of necessity, did not mean that they were free from personal liability for any loss caused by the acts of the agent. Trustees would be personally liable for breach of trust if the agent they appointed was not appropriate, or if they failed to exercise adequate supervision, on the grounds that they had acted other than as reasonably prudent men of business.

(a) Agent employed outside of the scope of his business

A trustee who had legitimately delegated to an agent was liable to the trust if he employed an agent to carry out functions that were outside of the scope of his ordinary business.[45] As Kay J said in *Fry v Tapson*:[46]

> *Speight v Gaunt* did not lay down any new rule, but only illustrated a very old one, viz., that trustees acting according to the ordinary course of business, and employing agents as a prudent man of business would do on his own behalf are not liable for the default of an agent so employed. But an obvious limitation to that rule is that the agent must not be employed out of the ordinary scope of his business. If the trustee employs an agent to do that which is not the ordinary business of such an agent, and he performs that unusual task improperly, and loss is thereby occasioned, the trustee would not be exonerated.[47]

The trustees, who were considering investing trust funds on a mortgage, had delegated the task of selecting a valuer for the land concerned to their solicitors. The solicitors recommended a London surveyor, who did not have local knowledge of the area where the land was situated,[48] and who also had a pecuniary interest in the grant of the mortgage, as he would receive a commission of £75 if the mortgage was granted. He overvalued the property, and the trustees lent £5,000, which was lost when the mortgagor became bankrupt. The trustees were held liable to replace this loss to the trust fund because it was out of the ordinary course of business of solicitors to appoint a valuer.

[41] *Speight v Gaunt* [1883] 9 App Cas 1. This limitation was restated in *Scott v National Trust* [1998] 2 All ER 705 at 717, per Robert Walker J. [42] *Rowland v Witherden* [1851] 3 Mac & G 568.

[43] *Clarke v Royal Panopticon* [1857] 4 Drew 26; *Green v Whitehead* [1930] 1 Ch 38.

[44] *Robson v Flight* [1865] 4 De GJ & SM 608.

[45] See *Re Earl of Litchfield* [1737] 1 Atk 87; *Ghost v Waller* [1846] 9 Beav 497; *Rowland v Witherden* [1851] 3 Mac & G 568; *Re Gasquoine* [1894] 1 Ch 470.

[46] [1884] 28 Ch D 268. [47] [1884] 28 Ch D 268 at 280.

[48] See also *Budge v Gummow* [1872] 7 Ch App 719.

(b) Trustees' duty to supervise agents

Trustees who appointed an agent were under a duty properly to supervise his activities. The standard of care required was that of the ordinary prudence which a man uses in his own business affairs.[49] In *Rowland v Witherden*,[50] for example, trustees had committed the management of a trust fund completely to a solicitor, who had misapplied it. The Lord Chancellor held that the trustees were liable for their failure properly to supervise the solicitor's activities:

> The short result of the case is, that the trustees, instead of themselves seeing to the investment of the trust fund, delegated that duty to their solicitor, who misapplied the money . . . The trustees were bound to satisfy themselves in some way other than by the mere assurances of their solicitor, and by payments made by him as for interest, that the money was really advanced on mortgage. But they did not even require a sight of the mortgage deed, but simply paid the money to their solicitor and implicitly relied on his integrity . . .[51]

Similarly, in *Fry v Tapson*,[52] Kay J held that the trustees would be liable for their acceptance of the valuation 'without attempting to check it'.[53]

5 A statutory right to delegate

The Trustee Act 1925[54] considerably extended the powers of trustees to delegate functions to agents by dispensing with the requirement that the delegation be reasonably necessary or in the ordinary course of business. However, the powers were still relatively restrictive—for instance only ministerial functions could normally be delegated—and the provisions of the Act relating to the liability of trustees where they had delegated a function were obscure to the point of unintelligibility. The leading case on the liability of trustees who had delegated functions to an agent was *Re Vickery*,[55] but even though this was reported in 1931, questions remained about the interpretation both of the statutory provisions and of this case some seventy years later. Few doubted that the position under the Act was unsatisfactory, not least the students who were required to grapple in examinations with the problems created by the statutory provisions or practitioners giving advice on them.[56]

In 1982 the Law Reform Committee considered whether the scope for delegation should be widened to encompass the trustees' discretions as well as ministerial functions, but concluded that the distinction between the delegation of administrative and managerial functions and of their discretions should be maintained.[57] However, in its Consultation Paper in 1999, *Trustees' Powers and Duties*, the Law Commission suggested that the climate of opinion had changed and that trustees should be entitled to delegate the task of managing the trust property to a fund manager, who would be entitled to make investment decisions within the context of an investment policy determined by the trustees:

> We consider that there is no longer any continued justification for the existing restrictions on trustees' powers of collective delegation. The principal objection to the present law is that trustees' powers of investment and certain of their powers of management (such as the

[49] *Munch v Cockerell* [1840] 5 My & Cr 178; *Mendes v Guedalla* [1862] 2 John & H 259; *Speight v Gaunt* [1883] 22 Ch D 727.

[50] [1851] 3 Mac & G 568.

[51] [1851] 3 Mac & G 568 at 574.

[52] [1884] 28 Ch D 268.

[53] [1884] 28 Ch D 268 at 282.

[54] s 23 (now repealed).

[55] [1931]1 Ch 572.

[56] For a lively discussion and summary of the issues, see *Trustees' Powers and Duties* (Law Com Consultation Paper No 146, 1997), Pt IV.

[57] Law Reform Committee, *23rd Report* (Cmnd 8733), para 4.3.

power to sell, lease or mortgage trust property) are regarded in all respects as fiduciary. As such they must be exercised by the trustees alone and are non-delegable. This position was the product of a time when the decisions which trustees had to take were both comparatively straightforward and infrequent. However, it is increasingly unrealistic, given that many of these tasks (particularly in relation to investment) now arise regularly and often require speedy professional advice and execution. We consider that the 'exigencies of business' now justify the delegation of these discretions because adherence to the present restrictions is likely to frustrate the trustees' paramount duty to act in the best interests of the trust.[58]

At around the same time, judicial notice was taken of the difficulty caused by the inability of the trustees to delegate their discretions. In *Scott v National Trust*, Robert Walker J stated:

trustees may not (except in so far as they are authorised to do so) delegate the exercise of their discretions, even to experts. This sometimes creates real difficulties, especially when lay trustees have to digest and assess expert advice on a highly technical matter (to take merely one instance, the disposal of actuarial surplus in a superannuation fund).[59]

It will be seen in Chapter 31 that a major reason for delegating trustee powers is so that an investment manager can be appointed. The pressure to allow trustees to delegate in this manner grew over a long period and flows from a changing understanding of the nature of the role of the trustee. In an article describing a career in legal practice, Francis Barlow charts the slow disappearance of strict settlements of land, which do not normally require high levels of management activity from the trustees, and the emergence of active fund management.[60] As Barlow describes, following the 'Big Bang' of the 1980s, the role of the trustee started to change. Modern trustees might be expected to make use of sophisticated financial products in the City of London. In order to do so, they might delegate to an investment expert.

The ability to delegate reflects changing times. It also reflects the changing nature of the trust. The very word implies, at least to some people, a personal obligation. Once trustees are able to delegate, the 'trust relationship' becomes much less personal. While some settlors have historically chosen trustees precisely because they have a good opinion of their personal character,[61] the ability for trustees to delegate suggests a move away from that interpersonal understanding of the trust. Crucially, the trust also becomes a 'business opportunity' for some. The agent will not act for free. He will charge for his expertise. This means that while an agent will potentially be of considerable advantage to the trust, it is always important to keep in mind that, in some circumstances, more will not always be merrier. The more people involved in the trust and its administration, the more expensive it will be to operate. These expenses will come at a cost to the beneficiaries.

6 The current statutory framework

The Trustee Act 2000 now provides the framework for delegation by trustees. It distinguishes between two principal situations: delegation by charity trustees, and delegation by other trustees. The position the Act takes is much more radical in the latter case than it is in the former. There is also special provision for pension scheme trustees and some other special situations. Although not so described in the Act, the power of delegation conferred on most trustees can conveniently be called the general power of delegation.

[58] Para 5.16. [59] [1998] 2 All ER 705 at 717.

[60] Barlow, 'The Flexibility of Family Trusts' (2013) 19 *Trusts and Trustees* 255.

[61] *Moggridge v Thackwell* (1803) 32 ER 15.

(1) General power of delegation

The approach adopted by the Trustee Act 2000 to most trustees is radically new. Instead of specifying when trustees may appoint agents, the Act confers a general power to delegate any function other than certain non-delegable functions.[62] This is a complete reversal of the previous position.

The functions that *cannot* be delegated by trustees to an agent are:

(a) decisions concerning the distribution of the trust assets;[63]

(b) decisions as to whether costs or fees should be debited to capital or to income;[64]

(c) the appointment of new trustees;[65]

(d) any power to delegate trustee functions or to appoint a nominee or custodian.[66]

In addition, trustees of land who are obliged to consult the beneficiaries before exercising any of their powers may not delegate the obligation to carry out this consultation.[67] Should trustees delegate any function that involves a duty to consult, it must be on terms that enable the trustees to conduct that consultation and to give effect to the wishes of the beneficiaries.[68]

The connecting link between the matters that the trustees cannot delegate is that they are functions that lie at the heart of trusteeship and have a clear fiduciary content.[69] The functions that can be delegated include all ministerial acts (i.e. the implementation of decisions already taken), including the implementation of decisions relating to the distribution of trust funds. However, unlike the previous position, it is also possible for the trustees to delegate functions that may require the exercise of discretions or decisions. For instance, if Andrew and Brenda are appointed as trustees of a valuable collection of antiquarian books, some of which need rebinding, they could delegate to a librarian acquaintance the task of finding a craftsman with the appropriate skills. Similarly, they can delegate their investment functions, including the choice of which investments to make, although there are special rules applying to the delegation of asset management that are considered in Chapter 31.

(2) Delegation in special cases

The general power of delegation described earlier does not apply to charity trustees or to trustees of pension schemes. Instead, charity trustees are allowed to delegate only in a one of three situations listed in the 2000 Act, namely carrying out a decision already made by the trustees, investment functions, and certain functions relating to land. The reason for limiting the powers of charity trustees to delegate is that there are some functions that are so central to the trust that it would not be appropriate for anyone other than the trustees to exercise them.

The general power is also restricted in its application to pension scheme trustees. Pension scheme trustees are not permitted to delegate investment functions under the general power,[70] or to appoint nominees or custodians,[71] although in other respects pension fund trustees may employ the general power of delegation. The reason for excluding the power to delegate investment functions is that there are special provisions dealing with this in the Pensions Act 1995, which contains special safeguards to protect the rights of occupational pension scheme members.

62 Trustee Act 2000, s 11(1) and (2). 63 Ibid, s 11(2)(a). 64 Ibid, s 11(2)(b).
65 Ibid, s 11(2)(c). 66 Ibid, s 11(2)(d). 67 Ibid, s 13(3), (4), and (5). 68 Ibid, s 13(4).
69 See further Chapter 35 for a discussion of the fiduciary duties imposed on trustees.
70 Trustee Act 2000, s 36(5). 71 Ibid, s 36(8).

The general power of delegation does not apply to trustees of authorized unit trusts[72] or to trustees of a common investment scheme or of a common deposit scheme made under the Charities Act 2011.[73]

(3) **Who may be appointed agent**

The trustees have a wide discretion as to whom they may appoint as an agent. They may even appoint one or more of the trustees as agent[74] (for instance, four trustees might wish to delegate to one of their number the task of negotiating the terms of a lease for premises to be occupied by the trust), or a person who has already been appointed as a nominee or custodian.[75] The trustees may not authorize two different people to undertake the same function[76] unless they are appointed to exercise the function jointly. That is a matter of common sense. The trustees are also prohibited from appointing a beneficiary as an agent,[77] even if the beneficiary is also a trustee. This particular restriction does not apply to trusts of land, where under the Trusts of Land and Appointment of Trustees Act 1996, s 9, it is possible for trustees of land to delegate to a beneficiary of full age 'any of their functions as trustees which relate to the land'. This provision would enable trustees of land to delegate the functions relating to the management of the land to the beneficiary who is tenant for life for the time being. It would not permit them to delegate to the beneficiary any function relating to the application of the proceeds from any dealings with the land.

(4) **Terms of agency**

The appointment of an agent by trustees does not have to be in writing, or evidenced in writing, except in the case of the delegation of asset management functions.[78] The terms of the appointment, including the remuneration of the agent, are at the discretion of the trustees[79] (although the amount of the remuneration must be reasonable),[80] with a number of significant caveats. The special restrictions applicable to the delegation of asset management functions are explained in Chapter 31. Another limitation on the power of trustees to set their own terms is that where a function being delegated is subject to any specific duties or restrictions attached to that function, then those duties or restrictions apply to the agent as they would have done to the trustee,[81] although if that restriction relates to obtaining advice, there is no need for the agent to seek advice if he is the kind of person who could have given it to the trustees.[82] For instance, a trust might authorize the trustees to take out insurance on buildings belonging to the trust only after consulting a qualified surveyor or valuer. If the trustees delegate this function to a chartered surveyor, there is no need for that agent to consult another valuer.

There are certain terms relating to the appointment of agents which can be agreed by trustees only if 'it is reasonably necessary for them to do so'.[83] These are the terms:

(a) allowing the agent to appoint a substitute;[84]
(b) exemption clauses limiting the liability of the agent;[85]
(c) terms permitting the agent to act in circumstances giving rise to a conflict of interest.[86]

[72] Ibid, s 37. [73] Ibid, s 38. [74] Ibid, s 12(1). [75] Ibid, s 12(4).
[76] Ibid, s 12(2). [77] Ibid, s 12(3). [78] Ibid, s 15, as discussed in Chapter 31. [79] Ibid, s 14.
[80] Ibid, s 32(2). [81] Ibid, s 13. [82] Ibid, s 13(2). [83] Ibid, s 14(2).
[84] Ibid, s 14(3)(a). [85] Ibid, s 14(3)(b). [86] Ibid, s 14(3)(c).

No definition is given in the Act of what is meant by the words 'reasonably necessary'.[87] Trustees will, therefore, need to act cautiously and to be prepared to demonstrate the basis on which they considered the inclusion of one of these terms to be reasonably necessary. This might be that it was usual business practice for specialists operating in a particular field to require such a provision. The Explanatory Memorandum to the Act provides an example:

> The appointment of a fund manager will often be essential to the efficient and effective management of the assets of the trust. Section 14(3)(a) flows from this. As the standard terms of business of fund managers generally require limits on liability and the ability to act despite a conflict of interest, the ability to appoint a manager would amount to little in practice if trustees were unable to accept such terms.

(5) Liability of agent

It has already been noted that powers and functions delegated to agents are subject to the same conditions and restrictions as applied to that power or function in the hands of the trustees. The Act does not apply any special statutory duty upon agents, so their position is governed by the contractual principles of agency. In most situations these will impose a duty upon the agent to exercise due care and diligence in the exercise of the functions assigned to him. Because these duties arise in contract, the agent's principal liability is to the trustees who appointed him. An unresolved issue is whether there might be some circumstances in which the agent might be directly liable to the beneficiaries, whether under the Contracts (Rights of Third Parties) Act 1999 or under common law or equitable principles arising from interference with the rights of third parties.[88] An analogous situation is where a solicitor negligently draws up a will for a testator, with the result that a beneficiary fails to obtain the benefit intended by the testator. It is now well established that the solicitor owes a duty of care in tort to the beneficiary, which is directly enforceable, in addition to the contractual duty owed to the testator.[89] However, a difference in this situation is that the testator (or his estate), although having a cause of action, has suffered no loss, and it is only if the beneficiary can sue that the wrongdoing solicitor can be held to account. In the case of a trust, any action brought by the trustees against an agent will enlarge the trust assets and so normally benefit the beneficiaries, reducing or even eliminating one of the justifications for conceding a direct cause of action. In addition, if the beneficiaries have a direct cause of action against an agent, it could give rise to potential double jeopardy, a matter that was of concern to the Court of Appeal in *Carr-Glyn v Frearsons*[90] when dealing with an action by a beneficiary under a will. The court in that case was able to resolve the issue by holding that any action by the testatrix's estate could only be complementary to that by the beneficiary: each could sue for their own loss only.

(6) Liability of trustees

(a) Liability in deciding whether or not to delegate

The Trustee Act 2000 adopts the same approach to the liability of trustees as at common law. Essentially trustees are obliged to exercise care in both the appointment and in the supervision of agents. This is achieved by the imposition of the statutory duty of care.

[87] See Hanbury and Martin, *Modern Equity* (18th edn, Sweet & Maxwell 2009), p 608, where it is suggested that these amendments were introduced to permit delegation to fund managers on their standard terms of business.

[88] For a discussion of the liability of third parties who cause loss to a trust, see Chapter 37.

[89] See *Ross v Caunters* [1980] Ch 297; *White v Jones* [1995] 2 AC 207; *Carr-Glyn v Frearsons* [1999] Ch 326.

[90] [1999] Ch 326. See also *Worby v Rosser* [2000] PNLR 140.

The Act says nothing, however, about the duty of trustees in deciding whether or not to delegate. Trustees are, therefore, under no *statutory* duty to exercise due care in deciding whether or not to delegate any of their functions, except in relation to decisions by trustees of land to delegate to a beneficiary.[91] They do not, for instance, need to demonstrate that it was reasonably necessary to delegate, nor that delegation was in the best interests of the beneficiaries. The fact that trustees can delegate even where there is no need to do so has been criticized, on the basis that it is unfair that the trustee should be able to delegate tasks to agents at the expense of the trust which he could easily and reasonably undertake himself. For this reason the Law Reform Committee recommended in their 23rd Report in 1982 that trustees should only be able to charge the trust for the expenses of delegation which were reasonably incurred.[92] This recommendation has not been enacted. There could also be the converse problem, where trustees unreasonably decide to undertake a specialist activity without appointing an agent. It remains to be seen whether the courts will impose a duty of care in such situations on the basis that the trustees are in breach of their general duty to act in the best interests of the beneficiaries.

(b) Duty of care in selection and appointment

Having made a decision to appoint an agent, the trustees are subject to the statutory duty to take reasonable care in selecting the agent, in determining the terms on which the agent is to act, and in preparing the investment policy statement where investment functions are delegated.[93] So, for instance, the trustees would be liable for appointing an agent to sell trust property who did not have the relevant expertise, if this is something that the trustees could reasonably have been expected to discover. Suppose that Stephanie is the trustee of a shop, which had been let to Rufus before Stephanie was appointed as a trustee. She needs to negotiate an increase in the rent under a rent review clause in the lease. Having no experience herself, she appoints a local estate agent to act on the trust's behalf. She fails to ask if he has any experience of dealing with commercial property, and his lack of experience causes a loss because the rent obtained on review is far below the level it should be. Stephanie will be liable for breach of trust.[94]

(c) Duty of care in supervision

The trustees are also under a statutory duty to keep an eye on the activities of the agent by keeping the arrangements for the delegation under review, monitoring the actions of the agent, considering whether to intervene, and taking appropriate action where necessary.[95] Imagine, for instance, that Veronica has employed an antiquarian book specialist to catalogue and value a collection of rare books that she holds on trust. Veronica allows the specialist free access to the collection for this purpose. When a scholar asks to see a book, it is discovered that this book and several others are missing. Veronica takes no action, and it later transpires that the specialist had yielded to temptation by stealing a number of the books, something which would not have happened if his access had been supervised. Veronica could be liable for breach of trust for failure to review the arrangements if it is considered that in the circumstances she failed to exercise reasonable care. The position in this respect is just as it was at common law. For instance, in *Re Lucking's*

[91] Trusts of Land and Appointment of Trustees Act 1996, s 9A (added by Trustee Act 2000, Sch 2).

[92] Law Reform Committee, 23rd report (Cmnd 8733), para 4.6. See Trustee Act 2000, ss 14 and 32, concerning the reasonable remuneration of agents.

[93] Trustee Act 2000, s 1 and Sch 1, para 3.

[94] The agent will be liable for breach of his contractual duty of care.

[95] Trustee Act 2000, ss 21 and 22.

Will Trusts,[96] Mr Lucking was the sole trustee of a trust fund which consisted of a majority shareholding in a private company. He appointed a Lieutenant-Colonel Dewar to manage the company, who sent a blank cheque which Lucking signed. Dewar subsequently misappropriated some £16,000. Cross J held that Lucking was liable for his own breach of trust in failing to supervise the activities of Dewar after he became aware of reasons to doubt his honesty.[97] The standard of care applied was that of *Speight v Gaunt*,[98] namely that the trustee is 'bound to conduct the business of the trust in such a way as an ordinary prudent man of business would conduct a business of his own'.[99] The duty so expressed is effectively the same duty as the statutory duty of care.

(d) Liability for failure to observe restrictions

Where trustees have failed to comply with one of the restrictions on the appointment of agents, for instance, where they have agreed to a clause limiting the liability of the agent where it was not reasonably necessary to do so, the trustees will be in breach of trust. There may also be limitations on the appointment of agents contained in the trust instrument that they are required to observe at pain of committing a breach of trust. The fact that the trustees have exceeded their powers in authorizing a person to act as their agent does not, however, invalidate the appointment.[100] In *Daniel v Tee*,[101] trustees failed to comply with the restrictions on the delegation of asset management functions to an agent (see the discussion of this case in Chapter 31). They were, therefore, liable for any losses resulting from that delegation. However, because the judge held that the trustees would in any event have made the same investment decisions themselves, no loss to the trust had arisen.

(e) Vicarious liability

Where the trustees have exercised due care in the appointment and supervision of an agent, they are not liable merely because the agent does something which causes a loss to the trust. Section 23 of the Trustee Act 2000 exempts trustees who are not personally in breach of the statutory duty of care from what may be called vicarious liability.[102] For instance, in the example given earlier of the theft by a specialist of books from a valuable collection of which Veronica was the trustee, Veronica is not automatically liable, because her agent was dishonest and stole the books. To hold her liable it has to be shown that she did not exercise reasonable care in selecting the specialist (perhaps she should have taken up references from other clients) or that she did not take appropriate action in supervising him.

Section 23 may not be happily worded. It states that 'a trustee is not liable for any act or default of the agent' unless the trustee has failed to comply with the statutory duty 'when entering into the arrangements under which the person acts as agent' or 'when carrying out his duties' of keeping the appointment under review. On a literal interpretation, a trustee who fails to conduct a review at all, rather than carrying out a review badly, would not be liable. This interpretation, however, would undoubtedly be contrary to the policy of the Act, and it is likely that the courts will give the section a purposive interpretation to make trustees liable for unreasonable omissions as well as careless commissions.

[96] [1968] 1 WLR 866. *Bartlett v Barclays Bank Trust Co Ltd (Nos 1 & 2)* [1980] Ch 515 provides another example.

[97] Cross J considered that the statutory protection for trustees then in force gave no indemnity to trustees who were themselves at fault.

[98] [1833] 22 Ch D 727.

[99] [1833] 22 Ch D 727 at 874.

[100] Trustee Act 2000, s 24.

[101] [2016] EWHC 1538 (Ch).

[102] The Law Commission in *Trustees' Powers and Duties* (1997) Law Com Consultation Paper No 146, paras 4.29–4.31 suggests that this description is not particularly helpful or accurate since there is no case in which a trustee has been held vicariously liable. However, the expression accurately conveys the concept of liability for the fault of others, even where there is no personal fault.

(f) Liability of trustees of land for the acts of their agents

Where trustees of land have delegated their functions to a beneficiary under the special power to do so in the Trusts of Land and Appointment of Trustees Act 1996,[103] they are subject to the statutory duty of care in respect of the decision to delegate and in the supervision of the arrangement.[104]

7 Individual delegation

In addition to the trustees acting together to appoint an agent, it is also possible for an individual trustee to delegate by appointing a substitute to exercise all or any of his powers. This was not something that was possible at common law, because of the principle *delegatus non potest delegare*. There is now statutory authority contained in Trustee Act 1925, s 25. As originally enacted, this section permitted delegation only during the absence of a trustee overseas. The section was substantially enlarged by the Powers of Attorney Act 1971 to confer a general authority to delegate trustee functions (including discretions), but only for a period not exceeding twelve months. The current provisions date from the Trustee Delegation Act 1999, which made further minor amendments. Section 25(1) of the Trustee Act 1925 (as amended) provides that:

> Notwithstanding any rule of law or equity to the contrary, a trustee may, by power of attorney,[105] delegate the execution or exercise of all or any of the trusts, powers and discretions vested in him as trustee either alone or jointly with any other person or persons.

The delegation may not exceed twelve months,[106] must be by made by deed,[107] and notice must be given to the other trustees and to the person entitled to appoint new trustees.[108] The purpose of this last requirement is to enable the trustees to consider whether the trustee making the delegation should be replaced. Where a trustee delegates his functions under s 25(1), he remains strictly liable for any losses caused by the agent, as s 25(7) provides that the donor of the power of attorney 'shall be liable for the acts or defaults of the donee in the same manner as if they were the acts or defaults of the donor'. Appointment of an agent under this section is thus a far less satisfactory course of action for a trustee than appointment of an agent under the powers of collective delegation provided by the Trustee Act 2000.

A delegation by means of a power of attorney will, like all such appointments of an agent, lapse should the principal cease to have full mental capacity, but the Trustee Delegation Act 1999[109] permits the power to be executed as a lasting power, which remains valid despite the incapacity of the principal.

103 Trusts of Land and Appointment of Trustees Act 1996, s 9.

104 Trusts of Land and Appointment of Trustees Act 1996, s 9A (inserted by Trustee Act 2000).

105 Discussed in Chapter 3.

106 Trustee Act 1925, s 25(2)(a) (as amended).

107 This is a requirement of all powers of attorney.

108 Trustee Act 1925, s 25(4) (as amended).

109 Trustee Delegation Act 1999, ss 6 and 9. The Act repeals Enduring Powers of Attorney Act 1985, s 3(3), which previously permitted the delegation of trustee functions by enduring power of attorney. See now Mental Capacity Act 2005, Sch 4.

31

Investment

1 Introduction

Of their non-distributive functions, the powers and duties of trustees in relation to investment are undoubtedly the most important.[1] Except in the very simplest of trusts, it is the duty of the trustee to preserve the trust assets over a period for the benefit of a number of beneficiaries. In many cases, the property which is transferred to the trustee is transferred as a fund, rather than as a set of assets which are to be retained in their original form. The trustee is expected to preserve the value of that fund through proper investment. In some cases, such as with unit trusts, and to some extent with pension funds, investment is the primary purpose of the trust.

It is in the context of investment that the concept of the trust fund is at its most apparent. The beneficiaries are entitled to share in the wealth which the trust assets represent. The component parts of that wealth are very much less important to the beneficiaries than its aggregate value. We have already seen how the concept of the fund enables some assets to be disposed of, so that the purchaser acquires the assets free from the trust obligations, with the trust obligations instead resting upon the price paid by the purchaser, or with whatever is purchased with the proceeds of the disposal. This process is known as overreaching.

Not every trust requires investments to be sold and reinvested. The landed aristocrat who leaves the family mansion upon trust for future generations of the family will no doubt hope that the home will be preserved intact.[2] The married couple joining together in the purchase of a matrimonial home will no doubt intend to keep it as their dwelling. Even here, though, the land that constitutes the trust asset will be treated as a fund which can be sold and reinvested: so the new squire can sell some land on the fringe of the estate for building development and invest the proceeds in stocks and shares, or the married couple can up sticks and sell to move to another area where they will buy another house, without in either case dissolving the original trust. The case of land is somewhat special, since the legislature has ensured that trustees of land will always have a power of sale and reinvestment,[3] and there is no general power of sale in relation to property other than land which is vested in trustees.

The issues which have to be addressed in the context of investment are first, when trustees are permitted to dispose of existing trust assets in order to substitute new assets; second, what assets may be substituted for the original ones; and third, the principles

[1] Note that trustees who are conducting investment business must be authorized under s 19 of the Financial Services and Markets Act 2000, or exempted. Breach of this requirement may be a criminal offence, and subject to up to two years' imprisonment.

[2] See *Wyndham v Egremont* [2009] EWHC 2076, where the court approved a variation of trust to enable the Petworth estates to follow the titles to Leconfield and Egremont.

[3] Trusts of Land and Appointment of Trustees Act 1996, s 6.

upon which those investments must be chosen. Overarching these issues is a fundamental question—what is the purpose of investment? It is with that question that we need to begin.

2 The purpose of investment

(1) Even-handedness between beneficiaries

As little as a century ago, one of the more common forms of trust was the family settlement, in which a man of property would settle funds for the benefit of his spouse and children for their lives, with entitlement to the capital then passing to the next generation. The duty of the trustees in such a case was to ensure that the capital was preserved for the benefit of the capital beneficiaries, while an income was produced for the settlor's wife and children. The trustees were obliged to keep a fair balance between the two, except where they had been given other instructions by the settlor. This rule of even-handedness between beneficiaries was at the root of the rule in *Howe v Dartmouth*, although this rule has been abolished in trusts created after 1 October 2013 by the Trusts (Capital and Income) Act 2013.

(2) The purpose of the trust

Not all trusts provide for successive interests, requiring both income generation and preservation of capital. It is possible that a trust will provide for the accumulation of income for a limited period, with a view to conferring a lump sum benefit on a beneficiary at a future date. In such a case, it is of greater importance that the trust fund should produce capital appreciation than that it should provide a large income. For instance, in the case of an endowment fund for a major museum and art gallery, 'the desirability of having an increase of capital value which will make possible the purchase of desirable acquisitions for the museum despite soaring prices does something to justify the greater risks whereby capital appreciation may be obtained'.[4] On the other hand, the investment of a pension fund will require a combination of investments which will provide some measure of protection against the ravages of inflation[5] and of investments which will enable the payment of benefits to pensioners as and when they fall due for payment, bearing in mind always the need to make a judgement which takes account of the risks of the investments in question[6] and which has proper regard to the need for security.[7] It may even be that, in considering investment policy, the trustees will need to have regard to the circumstances of individual beneficiaries. Trustees of land, for instance, may invest or apply trust funds in the purchase of property for occupation by a beneficiary,[8] a decision which can be made only after considering the circumstances of the beneficiaries. Also, in *Nestlé v National Westminster Bank plc*,[9] Staughton LJ thought that it would be appropriate for trustees to take into account the circumstances of the beneficiaries, as, for example, 'if the life tenant is living in penury and the remainderman already has ample wealth'.[10]

[4] *Trustees of the British Museum v A-G* [1984] 1 All ER 337 at 343, per Megarry V-C.
[5] *Mason v Farbrother* [1983] 2 All ER 1078 at 1086–7.
[6] See *Cowan v Scargill* [1985] Ch 270.
[7] See Grosh, 'Trustee Investment: English Law and the American Prudent Man Rule' [1974] 23 ICLQ 748.
[8] Trusts of Land and Appointment of Trustees Act 1996, s 6.
[9] [1993] 1 WLR 1260. [10] [1993] 1 WLR 1260 at 1279.

Expressed in general terms, it can be said that the purpose of investment is to enable the fulfilment of the objectives of the trust. In one of the leading investment cases, Sir Robert Megarry said:

> The starting point is the duty of trustees to exercise their powers in the best interests of the present and future beneficiaries of the trust, holding the scales impartially between different classes of beneficiaries. This duty of the trustees towards their beneficiaries is paramount . . . When the purpose of the trust is to provide financial benefits for the beneficiaries, as is usually the case, the best interests of the beneficiaries are normally their best financial interests. In the case of a power of investment, as in the present case, the power must be exercised so as to yield the best return for the beneficiaries, judged in relation to the risks of the investments in question; and the prospects of the yield of income and capital appreciation both have to be considered in judging the return from the investment.[11]

This statement does not apply only to the exercise by trustees of their powers. The influence of the policy which underlies it can be seen also in the historical approach to trustees' general powers of permitted investment, and in the approach which the courts have in the past adopted in considering extensions to trustees' powers of investment.

3 Powers of disposal

(1) **Assets available for investment**

Except where trustees are under an obligation to make an immediate distribution, the trustees will have assets to invest where the funds they receive are in cash or currency. It would rarely be appropriate for the trustees to retain large quantities of banknotes, uncleared cheques, or similar assets. Where the assets which the trustees receive are already in some form of investment, such as shares in a public company, a landholding, or some other enduring form, then it is less clear whether there is a power or even an obligation to realize those assets for the purpose of reinvestment. There is no general power of sale in a trust (except where it is a trust of land), in the absence of an express provision.

(2) **Trust for sale**

In some trusts, the trustees are placed under an obligation to sell the property in the form in which it is originally received, and either to distribute or to reinvest the proceeds of sale. Such a trust is called a trust for sale. A trust for sale may be imposed expressly by the settlor. Before the Trusts of Land and Appointment of Trustees Act 1996, it was also the statutory form of a trust of land, although that is no longer the case.

A trust for sale may, finally, have arisen under the rule in *Howe v Earl of Dartmouth*, where hazardous or wasting assets, or assets generating no income, and which formed part of a testator's residuary estate, were received by a trustee who is to hold the assets for beneficiaries entitled to successive interests. This rule was abolished, following a recommendation of the Law Commission,[12] for any trust arising after 1 October 2013.[13] Express and statutory trusts for sale are unaffected by this reform.

[11] *Cowan v Scargill* [1985] Ch 270 at 286, per Megarry V-C.

[12] *Capital and Income in Trusts: Classification and Apportionment* (Law Com No 319, 2009), para 6.65.

[13] Trusts (Capital and Income) Act 2013, s 1(2)(a). The trustees retain the power to sell such investments, but are under no duty to do so—s 1(3).

(3) Other powers of sale and reinvestment

A well-drafted trust will have anticipated the desirability of selling trust assets for the purpose of reinvestment, and will have made express provision. Trusts of land governed by the Settled Land Act 1925 confer upon the tenant for life, as trustee of the land, a power of sale,[14] with the proceeds of sale being treated as capital money which, if not otherwise required, is available for reinvestment.[15] Similarly, there is a power of sale[16] and a power indefinitely to postpone sale[17] in the case of trusts of land governed by the Trusts of Land and Appointment of Trustees Act 1996. This includes all trusts of land which are created on or after 1 January 1997, and all trusts of land arising before that date and which are not governed by the Settled Land Act 1925.

Strangely, the Trustee Act 2000, which introduced a new regime for investment of trust funds failed to make clear whether trustees had a power of sale for the purposes of investment. The Act stated in s 3 that 'a trustee may make any kind of investment that he could make if he were absolutely entitled to the assets of the trust', but nowhere does it indicate when a trustee may or must make investments. The Trustee Investments Act 1961, which the Trustee Act 2000 largely replaces, did contain the more explicit statement that 'a trustee may invest any property in his hands, whether at the time in a state of investment or not that and may from time to time vary such investments'.[18] This omission is made all the more puzzling by the fact that s 8 of the Trustee Act 2000 confers a power on the trustees of personalty to purchase a legal estate in land as an investment.[19] In the absence of a general statutory provision, it will be a matter for the proper construction of the trust instrument as to whether the trustees are permitted or expected to invest the trust property. Such a conclusion could readily be reached if the trust assets are to be retained for any length of time, and the conferment of a statutory power of investment could be interpreted as implying a power to sell for the purpose of making an investment.[20] The indications are that the courts are likely to take a broad and common sense view of when property is available for investment. In *Gregson v HAE Trustees Ltd*,[21] Henry Cohen, the founder of the Courts furniture group, set up a family trust in 1960 using company shares, with the intention that a wider family group should benefit from the success of the company. The trustees did not sell the shares and in 2004, when the Courts group collapsed, the shares became worthless. It was held that the shares constituted investments, even though it was not envisaged that they would necessarily be sold. Henry Cohen had not prohibited their sale, and indeed had given the trustees a power to sell them. The trustees should, therefore, have considered whether to diversify the trust's investments. The judge stated:

> It seems to me that on its natural reading 'the investments of the trust' comprise any asset of the trust which happens to be invested, whether it was in that state when originally settled or it came into that state of investment later.[22]

However, as has already been explained, there could be circumstances in which the power of sale is excluded because the trust requires the retention of the assets in a particular

[14] Settled Land Act 1925, s 38. [15] Ibid, s 73.

[16] Trusts of Land and Appointment of Trustees Act 1996, s 6. [17] Ibid, s 4. [18] s 1(1).

[19] In fact, the section allows the purchase of land for purposes other than investment such as for occupation by a beneficiary (s 8(1)(c)) or for any other reason (s 8(a)).

[20] See Trustee Act 1925, s 16(1), which could be interpreted as conferring a power of sale in these circumstances. Compare *Hume v Lopes* [1892] AC 112; *Re Pratt's Will Trust* [1943] Ch 326.

[21] [2008] EWHC 1006 (Ch).

[22] [2008] EWHC 1006 (Ch) at 81 (Robert Miles QC sitting as a deputy High Court judge). The claim for breach of trust failed because the corporate trustees had no assets and the judge held that it was not possible for a beneficiary to make a direct ('dog leg') claim against the directors.

form.[23] Although there are authorities that suggested that there must be a clear exclusion of the statutory investment powers in express terms,[24] these were cases that sought to limit and not to exclude the trustee's powers of investment. It is submitted that the implied statutory power to sell for the purpose of investment does not apply to property that it is the trustee's duty to retain.[25]

4 Authorized investments

(1) Principles

Except in those rare situations where a person is both trustee and beneficiary (as, for instance, in the case of co-ownership trusts of land), a trustee is investing property on behalf of others. This requires an approach to risk which may not be the same as that which might be adopted by a person making investments on his or her own behalf. Whilst an individual may consider it appropriate when making decisions on their own behalf to incur a high degree of risk, this is much less appropriate when dealing with the assets of others. To take an extreme example, a person can choose to gamble with their own money by buying lottery tickets, but this would not be a suitable application of trust funds. A 'turf investment' at the racecourse would not be a trustee investment.

There are two different methods which can be used to limit the investment decisions of trustees to investments which are suitable for trust funds. One is to provide a list of investments which are considered to be sufficiently secure and robust to be used for the investment of trust funds, limiting trustees to making a choice from this menu. The other is to impose a general duty on trustees only to select investments which meet the criteria of suitability. The first approach was at one time the approach adopted in English law, but the Trustee Act 2000 implemented a sea change by sweeping away most of the previous restrictions on investment by trustees and adopting the second approach.

(2) History

The turbulence caused by the bursting of the South Sea Bubble in 1720 was the cause for a serious curtailment by the Court of Chancery of the investments which trustees were permitted to make. From the end of the eighteenth century onwards, it became the rule that a trustee would be liable to bear the deficiency if any loss resulted from making an investment in a way which was not authorized by the settlor or the beneficiaries, and which had gone beyond the range of investments contemplated by the courts or the legislature. Prior to the Trustee Act 2000, the investments authorized by the general law were conservative, placing considerable emphasis on the security of trust funds.

The policy adopted by legislation up to and including the Trustee Investments Act 1961 was to protect beneficiaries by limiting trustees to 'safe' forms of investment. The Trustee Investments Act 1961 adopted a very much more constrained regulation of trustee investments than in some other jurisdictions, notably in North America, where the principal

[23] See the now repealed s 1(3) of the Trustee Investments Act 1961, which stated that the previous statutory provisions are 'exercisable only in so far as a contrary intention is not expressed'.

[24] *Re Rider's Will Trusts* [1958] 1 WLR 974; *Re Burke* [1908] 2 Ch 248; *Re Hill* [1914] WN 132.

[25] Compare Settled Land Act 1925, s 67, under which heirlooms (defined as personal chattels settled so as to devolve with settled land) may be sold only pursuant to an order of the court, even where the purpose of sale is to invest the proceeds. In *Re Hope* [1899] 2 Ch 679 the court refused permission under this section to sell the 'Hope' diamond.

requirement was that in making investments, trustees should act as a prudent man would do when investing on behalf of others.[26] It also lagged substantially behind the practice of well-advised settlors inserting their own express investment powers. This, of course, limited the return that trustees could achieve through investment for the beneficiaries; as safety and high-income yield rarely go hand in hand.

Precisely to avoid the limitations on the powers of investment by trustees, settlors often included an express power of investment in a settlement. The trustees could also obtain the consent of the beneficiaries to investments which would not otherwise be authorized, although this course of action was only available if all the beneficiaries were capable of giving consent. Finally, the trustees could enlarge their investment powers by means of an application to court, either under the Variation of Trusts Act 1958, where the concurrence of the beneficiaries who are capable of consenting, or where this is not practicable, under s 57 of the Trustee Act 1925.

(3) **The new approach**

The new approach to investment has been embraced by the Trustee Act 2000. The approach was described in a Treasury consultation paper.[27] Rather than limit the kinds of investment which trustees can make, it is seen as more sensible to give the trustees more extensive powers of investment in relation to the selection of individual investments. The interests of the beneficiaries are then protected by requiring the trustees to take such expert advice as the nature of the trust requires and by charging them with responsibility to ensure that the portfolio of investments is properly balanced.

This new approach was first adopted by the Pensions Act 1995. This permitted pension fund trustees to make any kind of investment as if they were absolutely entitled to the assets.[28] However, the trustees are required to maintain a statement of investment policy,[29] including information about the policy on risk, expected returns, and realization. The trustees are expected to secure and consider professional advice, to consider the need to maintain a balanced portfolio, and to consider the merits of each individual investment proposed.[30] The same approach has now been adopted by the Trustee Act 2000 as the general principle for most trusts.[31] Trustees are given the same power to invest trust funds, with some narrow exceptions, as if they owned the assets outright. They are, however, subject to an obligation to act in the best interests of the beneficiaries, to consider the need for diversification of investment, to consider the suitability of individual investments, and to take advice where appropriate.

The power of investment conferred by the Trustee Act 2000, described as the 'general power of investment', extends the powers of investment which may have been conferred upon trustees by other statutory provisions or by the trust instrument, but it can be excluded or restricted by the trust instrument or by legislation.[32] The general power of investment applies to existing trusts, not just those created after the passing of the 2000 Act.[33]

[26] See Grosh, 'Trustee Investment: English Law and the American Prudent Man Rule' [1974] 23 ICLQ 748.

[27] 'Investment Powers of Trustees' (May 1996). [28] Pensions Act 1995, s 34. [29] Ibid, s 35.

[30] Ibid, s 36. See also Occupational Pensions Schemes (Investment) Regulations, SI 2005/3378, which set out detailed regulations governing the exercise of the investment powers. There is special provision allowing the trustees to delegate some of these responsibilities: s 34.

[31] The general investment powers do not apply to occupational pension schemes, authorized unit trusts, or certain schemes under the Charities Act 1993: see Trustee Act 2000, ss 36–8. There are special statutory rules applying to these forms of collective investment.

[32] Trustee Act 2000, s 6. [33] Ibid, s 7.

(4) Express powers of investment

(a) Interpretation

The need for express powers of investment is significantly reduced by the general power of investment conferred by Trustee Act 2000. Nevertheless, it is still common practice for professionally drafted trusts to contain express investment powers. The approach to the interpretation of such powers is demonstrated by *Re Harari's Settlement Trusts*.[34] Sir Victor Harari had transferred assets to trustees which fell outside the categories authorized by the general rules for trustees. Under an express provision in the trust deed, it was declared that:

> The trustees shall hold the said investments so transferred to them as aforesaid upon trust that they may either allow the same to remain in their present state of investment so long as the trustees may see fit or may at any time or times realise the said investments and invest the money produced thereby in or upon such investments as to them may seem fit with power to vary or transpose any investments for or into others.

It was argued before the judge that the investments which the trustees could select under this clause were limited to those generally authorized by law (which, of course, at the time were much narrower than they are now), since the clause did not clearly and unambiguously extend the range of investments beyond those permitted by statute. Jenkins J held, however, that the trustees were given a wider power of investment. In his view, he was free to construe the settlement according to what he considered to be the natural and proper meaning of the words used in their context, and he saw no justification for implying any restriction on the wide construction which the words themselves were sufficient to bear.[35]

(b) Limits to investment powers

Although it is clear from *Re Harari's Settlement Trusts*[36] that investment clauses will not be given a restrictive interpretation, there are still pitfalls for the draftsman. If the draftsman seeks to impose a limit on the range of permissible investments, that limit should be clearly and unambiguously expressed. Difficulties have occurred in the past with clauses limiting investments to stocks in 'any British colony or dependency' because of changes in the status of Commonwealth and former Commonwealth countries.[37] A clause authorizing investment in 'blue chip' securities has also been held to be ineffective on grounds of uncertainty.[38]

(c) Meaning of 'investment'

A number of cases have considered what is meant by the word 'investment'. The cases suggest that an application of funds will not be considered to be an investment unless the assets produce an income. It may be that in the light of changing investment practice, a different view would be taken today and that assets expected to produce a capital gain could be considered to be investments even if they were producing no income.[39] Nevertheless, good drafting will make clear that applications in non-income generating assets are

[34] [1949] 1 All ER 430.

[35] See, to similar effect, *Re Peczenik's Settlement* [1964] 2 All ER 339.

[36] [1949] 1 All ER 430.

[37] *Re Maryon-Wilson's Estate* [1912] 1 Ch 55, CA; *Re Brassey's Settlement* [1955] 1 WLR 192; *Re Rider's Will Trusts* [1958] 1 WLR 974.

[38] *Re Kolb's Will Trusts* [1962] Ch 531.

[39] See *Cook v Medway Housing Society* [1997] STC 90 at 98, for support for this view. See, however, *Dominica Social Security Board v Nature Island Investment Co* ([2008] UK PC 19 at 21), referred to in *Dalriada Trustees v Faulds* [2012] 2 All ER 734, where Bean J, although accepting that the statement might be too limited in that it did not include assets acquired with a view to capital gain, held that an unsecured personal loan would not constitute an investment.

permitted. The Universities' Superannuation Scheme Rules (the pension scheme for academic staff within the old universities), for instance, state that the trustee may apply its assets for the purchase of 'investments or property whether producing income or not'.[40]

(d) Loans

In *Khoo Tek Keong v Ch'ng Joo Tuan Neoh*,[41] the Privy Council held that trustees were not authorized to make an unsecured personal loan under a clause which permitted them 'to invest all moneys liable to be invested in such investments as they in their absolute discretion think fit'. Where security is given for the loan, it may be classed as an investment under such a clause and, again, a suitably drafted clause can authorize the application of trust funds in unsecured personal loans.[42]

(5) General power of investment under Trustee Act 2000

(a) Meaning of 'investment'

The general power of investment conferred by the Trustee Act 2000 states that 'a trustee may make any kind of investment that he could make if he were absolutely entitled to the assets of the trust'.[43] The Act does not define what is meant by an investment, and this is therefore something to be resolved by reference to general principles of interpretation. The explanatory note to the Act states that an investment is something which is expected to produce an income or capital return. The case law on the use of the word in express investment clauses shows a narrower interpretation being adopted. In *Re Wragg*,[44] P O Lawrence J held that a clause authorizing investment in 'stocks funds shares and securities or other investments' was wide enough to include the purchase of land that was to be rented out to produce an income. He stated that 'to invest' includes as one of its meanings:

> to apply money in the purchase of some property from which interest or profit is expected and which property is purchased in order to be held for the sake of the income which it will yield.

In *Re Power*,[45] the court considered that the purchase of a house for occupation by a beneficiary was not permitted under a clause providing that:

> All moneys requiring to be invested under this my will may be invested by the trustee in any manner in which he may in his absolute discretion think fit in all respects as if he were the sole beneficial owner of such moneys including the purchase of freehold property in England or Wales.

The reason for this was that land being occupied by a beneficiary would not be generating income, and it could not therefore appropriately be described as an investment.[46] Strict application of this interpretation of the meaning of 'investment' would preclude trustees from purchasing, in the absence of the conferral of an express power in the trust instrument, assets for investment which only have potential to appreciate in capital value but

[40] Rules of Universities' Superannuation Scheme (19 November 2015), r 67.1. See also r 67.2.8, which expressly states that trust monies may 'be applied in any form of investment which may come to be developed, recognised and adopted as a new form of investment in reputable financial circles'.

[41] [1934] AC 529.

[42] *Re Laing's Settlement* [1899] 1 Ch 593. The Rules of Universities' Superannuation Scheme (19 November 2015) state that the trustee may apply funds 'upon such personal credit, with or without security, as the trustee company shall think fit' (r 67.1).

[43] Trustee Act 2000, s 3(1).

[44] [1919] 2 Ch 58.

[45] [1947] Ch 572.

[46] See also *Re Peczenik's Settlement Trusts* [1964] 1 WLR 720.

do not produce any income. This would include the purchase of precious metals, works of art, fine wine, or antiques. Premium bonds would also not be considered an investment.

The reason the Trustee Act 2000 is silent on a definition of 'investment' can be found in the Law Commission report on the powers and duties of trustees that preceded the Act. The Commission expressed the view that avoiding any definition of investment would permit the concept to evolve in ways which might be constrained were a definition to be given.[47] The explanatory notes accompanying the Act state that the power of investment conferred by the Act permits trustees to invest so as to produce an income or capital return, but these do not form part of the Act and cannot be regarded as having overruled the definition of 'investment' in *Re Power*.[48] It would, however, be inconvenient if the word 'investment' in the Trustee Act 2000 were to be interpreted in the same restrictive way. Changing patterns of investment now mean that many applications of funds carry no rights to income. Some companies, for example, adopt a policy of making no declaration of a dividend in order to reinvest profits with the intention of increasing the value of their shares. Similarly, it is possible to purchase units in authorized unit trusts where all income is reinvested rather than being paid out to investors, again with the intention of producing capital growth. It is also possible to purchase capital bonds that are redeemable after a fixed period at a value higher than the purchase price, compensating for the lack of interest by this capital growth. All of these applications of funds generate potential capital growth and can have a place in a properly constructed investment portfolio. It would be unfortunate if trustees were not able to take advantage of them. As has already been indicated, it is possible that were the issue to be addressed today, a court would adopt the view set out in the explanatory memorandum and hold that the expression 'investment' included any application of funds which produced either potential income or potential capital returns.[49]

(b) Traditional investments

There are certain types of investment which undoubtedly fall within the expression 'investment' as used in the Trustee Act 2000. These would include deposits in a bank or building society, the purchase of government stock, and the purchase of shares in publicly quoted companies. All of these forms of investment were permitted by the Trustee Investments Act 1961, which contained the list of authorized trustee investments prior to the enlargement of investment powers given to trustees by the 2000 Act. The 1961 Act was the first Act to allow trustees to invest in company shares. This was a significant step, as a short analysis of different types of investment will indicate.

Where money is invested by deposit with a bank, the bank pays annual or other periodic interest, but undertakes only to return the sum originally deposited when the account is closed. Government stock is not repayable on demand, but is usually repayable at a fixed future date. Again, interest is payable periodically, but when the date for repayment of the stock falls due, it is repaid only at face value. Pending the date of repayment, the price at which the stock is traded will fluctuate in accordance with prevailing market interest rates and the period before redemption. A stock which offers a high fixed rate of interest on its nominal value, compared with market rates, will tend to trade at a premium (i.e. at a higher price than its nominal value), reflecting the advantage of the holder receiving the

[47] *Trustees Powers and Duties* (Law Com Report No 260, 1999), p 22.

[48] [1947] Ch 572.

[49] This view was taken in a different context in *Cook v Medway Housing Society* [1997] STC 90 at 98. See also Hicks, 'The Trustee Act 2000 and the Modern Meaning Of Investment' [2001] 15 TLI 203, for the view that the 'portfolio' theory of investment permits more flexibility.

high income. Conversely, a stock which offers a low rate of nominal interest will tend to trade at a discount against its nominal value, reflecting the low yield of interest.

Shares (also referred to as 'equities') in public companies offer the advantage, compared with fixed interest securities and deposits, of offering the potential for both income and capital growth. The policy of most companies is to pay an annual dividend out of the profits which the company makes, while also retaining assets and profits which will enable the underlying capital value of the company to grow. As the net worth of the company increases, so its stock market value will tend to increase. The shareholder will thus receive an income and hope to participate in capital gains. The stock market can be volatile, particularly in the short term, so that, as investment advisers are required to warn, 'the value of your investment can fall as well as rise'. The share-market crash on 6 February 2018 shows how dramatic the falls can be, with £50 billion wiped off the value of the FTSE 100 top companies in a day, following six days of panic selling which saw £2.9 ($4) trillion wiped off the value of global stock markets.[50] Nevertheless, over the longer term, investments in shares have consistently outperformed bank and building society deposits and purchases of fixed interest securities. The ability of trustees, even in the absence of express extended powers of investment, to invest in shares, has been of considerable importance in enabling astute trustees to produce a reasonable income while providing a good measure of protection against inflation through capital appreciation.

(c) Financial instruments

The relatively recent past has seen an increase in the variety of financial instruments available. Some of these were created expressly for the purpose of providing investment vehicles, whilst others originated as mechanisms to help in managing the risks of exchange rate or share price fluctuations. Some appear to have evolved for purely speculative purposes. It is not clear whether all of these financial instruments would be considered to be investments permitted by the Trustee Act 2000. Some should fall within the meaning of the term, provided that it is not given too narrow an interpretation. Capital bonds, under which a company undertakes to repay a given sum at a fixed date in the future, but without any payment of interest in the meantime, have already been referred to. Since these bonds are sold at a price below their redemption value, the capital gain makes up for the loss of interest. There should be no reason why these capital bonds should not be considered valid trustee investments.

There are other financial instruments which are less readily considered to be investments within the ordinary meaning of the term. This includes, for instance, the so-called 'derivatives'. One form of derivative is the 'future' under which a person commits to the sale or purchase of shares or currency at a given date in the future at a fixed price. The other principal form is the 'option' under which the holder has the right, but not an obligation, to buy (purchase) or sell (put) at a fixed price on a future date. These instruments allow a jeweller, for instance, to reduce the risks of the price of gold going up or down by entering into an advance purchase contract or option. They would allow an exporter who knows that he will receive payment in a foreign currency in a year's time to reduce the risk of currency fluctuation by entering into a contract which effectively fixes the exchange rate. However, they also allow speculators to gamble on whether prices will go up or down.[51] There may be a place for this kind of speculation in some trusts, such as

[50] *The Guardian*, Business: Economics (6 February 2018).

[51] It is also possible to gamble on prices going up or down through 'spread betting', where a gambler stakes money against the future price of a given share. If the share falls within the agreed band or spread of prices at the set date, the betting company pays out on the bet. It is unlikely that any convincing argument could be made that spread betting constitutes an investment within the meaning of the Trustee Act 2000.

pension trusts, and banks were offering dealings in derivatives to private clients with substantial funds to invest. However, since they are extremely risky compared to most other forms of investment, they could well be considered to be outside the scope of authorized investment. Even if they were held to be 'investments' as that term is used in the Trustee Act 2000, a trustee would have to show that a properly informed decision had been made to apply trust funds in this fashion, and that the inherent risks were being managed, for instance by applying only a small part of the fund in this way.

(d) Purchase of land

The general power of investment does not in itself authorize trustees to invest in the purchase of land.[52] Section 8 of the Trustee Act 2000, however, contains authority for trustees (with some exceptions[53]) to purchase land. This extends to all trustees the power to apply trust funds to the purchase of land which was first conferred by statute on trustees of land by the Trusts of Land and Appointment of Trustees Act 1996.[54] There is now no distinction between trustees of land and trustees of personal property in this regard. Trustees may purchase land as an investment, for occupation by a beneficiary or for any other reason. The purchase may be of a legal freehold or leasehold estate in the United Kingdom.[55] Trustees have no statutory authority to purchase land overseas, but the power to acquire such land could be conferred expressly by the trust instrument. Trustees who acquire land under the statutory power conferred by the Trustee Act 2000, s 8, have all the powers of an absolute owner in relation to the land for the purpose of exercising their functions as trustees.[56]

(e) Loans

Trustees have been permitted to invest in loans secured by way of a mortgage over the borrower's land for over one hundred years.[57] The Trustee Act 2000 continues to allow trustees to invest by way of loans secured on land,[58] but there is nothing in the Act which expressly confers any power to make unsecured loans. *Khoo Tek Keong v Ch'ng Joo Tuan Neoh*[59] suggests that unsecured loans would not be considered as investments without some express authority.

(f) Modification of the general power of investment

The general power of investment conferred on trustees by the Trustee Act 2000 is in addition to any express powers which might be conferred upon trustees,[60] but may also be restricted or excluded by an express provision.[61] It goes almost without saying that the general power of investment can be modified by legislation, although, out of an abundance of caution, the Act makes this clear.[62]

[52] Trustee Act 2000, s 3(3).

[53] The power does not apply to trustees of settled land, who have the power to apply trust funds to the purchase of land under the Settled Land Act 1925, ss 73 and 75. Similarly, the power does not apply to occupational pension funds, authorized unit trusts, and certain charity investment funds: Trustee Act 2000, ss 36–8.

[54] s 6.

[55] Or the equivalent of a legal estate in the case of land in Scotland: Trustee Act 2000, s 8(2).

[56] This means, for instance, that trustees are able to grant leases, borrow against the security of the land, carry out building works, and so on.

[57] See Trustee Act 1925, s 8; Trustee Investments Act 2000, Sch 1, Pt II, para 13. Similar provisions appeared in the legislation which these Acts replaced.

[58] Although Trustee Act 1925, s 8 has been repealed, Trustee Act 2000, s 3(3) acknowledges that trustees may make loans secured on land.

[59] [1934] AC 529. The case is referred to above in relation to express powers of investment.

[60] Trustee Act 2000, s 6(1)(a). [61] Ibid, s 6(1)(b). [62] Ibid, s 6(1)(b).

As was indicated earlier, the Act applies to trusts created before the commencement of the Act as well as to those created subsequently.[63] Where a trust instrument contains a phrase such as 'the trustees may invest in any investment authorized by law for the investment of trust property', this will be treated as conferring on trustees the general power of investment, whether the trust was made before or after the 2000 Act.[64] Express provisions contained in trust instruments made before 3 August 1961 (the day on which the Trustee Investments Act 1961 came into operation) are not to be treated as restricting or excluding the general power of investment.[65]

5 Widening of powers of investment

The substantial increase in the investment powers given to trustees by the Trustee Act 2000 should mean that it will be rare that they will consider their powers to be too narrow. However, there may be some instances in which they seek wider investment powers, for instance, permitting the purchase of property overseas, or clarifying whether they are permitted to invest in assets which produce no income. There are a number of ways in which this may be possible.

(1) Power of variation in trust deed

Some trust deeds contain provisions under which alterations or amendments to the deed can be made. For instance, the Universities' Superannuation Scheme Rules provide that the rules can be altered by deed, with certain restrictions concerning maintaining the purpose of the scheme to provide pensions and other benefits for eligible employees, and subject to certain consents.[66]

(2) Variation of trust

Using one of the mechanisms described in Chapter 29, the terms of the trust can be varied. Although this could include the use of the Variation of Trusts Act 1958, the Trustee Act 1925, s 57, also allows changes in investment powers.[67] It has an advantage over the Variation of Trusts Act 1958 in that it does not require the beneficiaries to be consulted or to agree to the enlargement of the investment powers. In *Anker-Petersen v Anker-Petersen*,[68] it was suggested that applications for extending powers of investment were more appropriately brought under s 57 than under the Variation of Trusts Act 1958. This was because it was more realistic for the court to consider the matter on behalf of the beneficiaries as a group rather than individually, as the 1958 Act required. It was observed in *Gelber v Sunderland Foundation* that a benefit of relying upon Trustee Act 1925, s 57 in preference to the Variation of Trusts Act is that, under the Trustee Act, the proposed change is still potentially possible even if it disadvantages some of the beneficiaries.[69]

[63] Ibid, s 7(1).

[64] Ibid, s 7(3). A trust instrument made after the 2000 Act, which stated that trustees could invest in the manner authorized by the Trustee Investments Act 1961 would, however, be treated as limiting the investment powers of trustees to those permitted under the old rules set out in that Act.

[65] Trustee Act 2000, s 7(2).

[66] Rules of Universities' Superannuation Scheme (19 November 2015), r 79. See also *British Coal Corpn v British Coal Staff Superannuation Scheme Trustees Ltd* [1995] 1 All ER 912.

[67] *Mason v Farbrother* [1983] 2 All ER 1078.

[68] [1991] 16 LS Gaz R 32.

[69] [2018] EWHC 2344 (Ch), [12].

(3) Principles on which court grants approval

In a case decided shortly after the passing of the Trustee Investments Act 1961, *Re Kolb's Will Trusts*,[70] it was said that the investment powers in that Act should 'be taken to be prima facie sufficient and ought only to be extended if, on the particular facts, a special case for extending them can be made out'.[71] Subsequent cases departed from that view, and showed a greater willingness to entertain requests for enlarging powers of investment. Thus, in *Mason v Farbrother*,[72] Blackett Ord V-C approved a considerable widening of the powers of investment of the trustees of the Co-operative Wholesale Society pension fund, and in *Trustees of the British Museum v A-G*,[73] Megarry V-C approved the enlargement of the investment powers of the trustees of a museum of international importance. The first case was dealt with under the provisions of the Trustee Act 1925, s 57, and the latter under the Variation of Trusts Act 1958, but there does not seem to have been a difference in approach.[74] Relevant factors included the quality of the advice available to the trustees, and the measures which were to be taken to balance risk and safety. The division of the trust fund into separate parts with different risk profiles was considered to be an important factor in granting approval. In *Steel v Wellcome Custodian Trustees*,[75] Hoffmann J approved almost unfettered investment powers, with no obligation to divide the fund into divisions for the trustees of an extremely large charitable foundation. He had regard to the size of the fund, the eminence and experience of the trustees, and the provisions in the proposed scheme for obtaining advice.

The width of the powers given by the 2000 Act might mean that there would be the same kind of reluctance to entertain an application as happened in *Re Kolb's Will Trusts*. Since the current legislative regime does not require any division of the trust fund, it is unlikely that a court would insist on it if granting enlarged powers, but the factors identified by Hoffmann J would still surely be relevant in deciding whether an extension of powers was appropriate. There are still circumstances, however, in which the courts will exercise their discretion, even after the passing of the Trustee Act 2000. Morgan J, in *Alexander v Alexander*,[76] ordered a sale of land under s 57(1) of the Trustee Act 1925 where no such power existed in the trust instrument. The trustees wanted to sell a cottage which had fallen into such a bad state of repair that it was uninhabitable, but the terms of the trust instrument expressly prohibited sale of the cottage, meaning no such power could be implied.[77] Morgan J held that normally where a transaction 'is expedient within the subsection, the court would exercise its discretion to confer power upon the trustees to effect the transaction'.[78] Though the settlor had expressed his wishes through a prohibition on sale in the trust instrument, he had provided the cottage for occupation by the beneficiaries of the trust, and since the beneficiaries also agreed on the trustee's course of action, there was no reason for the court not to exercise its discretion in the best interests of the beneficiaries.

[70] [1962] Ch 531. [71] [1962] Ch 531 at 540.

[72] [1983] 2 All ER 1078. [73] [1984] 1 All ER 337.

[74] Although in the Trustee Act 1925, s 57 the test for variation is 'expediency', which on a plain reading, cannot be thought to be stringent test. See *Gelber v Sunderland Foundation* [2018] EWHC 2344 (Ch), [11].

[75] [1988] 1 WLR 167. [76] [2011] EWHC 2721 (Ch).

[77] Either under Trusts of Land and Appointment of Trusteees Act 1996, s 6 or the Trustee Act 2000, s 8.

[78] [2011] EWHC 2721 at 33.

6 Theories of investment

(1) The responsibilities of trustees

Foremost amongst the responsibilities of trustees is a requirement to have regard to the fact that they are dealing with money belonging to others and, therefore, have a duty to safeguard it. They must also consider the appropriate balance between capital and income, and the need to protect the trust assets against erosion through inflation. If the trustees are holding only a small fund which they are expected to distribute in the near future, then the principal consideration will be safeguarding the assets in the short term whilst keeping the ability to draw on the fund for the purposes of distribution. Investing the money by way of deposit in a bank might be the simplest and most appropriate way of doing this. However, if the funds are larger and are to be retained for a longer period, then other considerations affecting the choice of investments come into play.

(2) Risk management

The advantage of depositing money with a bank is that the bank undertakes to return the same amount as was deposited with it, together with interest. The depositor runs only a very small risk that if the bank becomes insolvent, it may not be able to meet its obligations in full. That risk is made smaller still by government deposit protection schemes and the general unwillingness of governments to see deposit-taking institutions fail. The disadvantage is that the effect of inflation reduces the purchasing power of the cash sum which the bank returns to the depositor. How then is it possible for an investor to safeguard against inflation? A traditional means of doing this is to purchase company shares, which over the long term can be expected to increase in value in money terms, as well as providing an income through the dividends which the company pays. However, the risks associated with company shares are greater. The company may not flourish: it may be badly managed, or it may be operating in a sector which is generally in decline. In consequence, the risks that a single shareholding will fall in value are much greater than is the case with a bank deposit. The greater potential return from company shares is balanced by a greater element of risk. Trustees are permitted to take risks with trust funds. No investment is entirely risk free. However, it is the function of the trustees to manage the risks so that the balance of risk and profit is appropriate for the nature of the trust.

(3) Investment portfolios

One of the principles of investment policy is that you should not 'put all your eggs in one basket'. By investing in several companies, not just one, there is less chance that all will fail (although equally less chance that all will thrive). The risks are further reduced if the investments are made in different market sectors—for instance, buying shares in companies operating in different fields such as banking, oil distribution, business services, or supplying utilities. Portfolio investment theory is that where an investment fund is large enough, different parts of the fund should be invested in different ways to provide a balance of growth or income potential, and of security and risk. Instead of evaluating the profile or risk of individual investments, what matters is the balance across the portfolio as a whole—higher risks in some parts of the fund may be balanced by lower risks, or compensating considerations, in other parts of the fund. The exact balance will vary according to individual requirements. A pension fund investing for existing pensioners needs to tilt more towards income and security than, say, a trust fund, which is designed to accumulate to pay out a sum to a beneficiary in twenty years' time. The portfolio theory of investment was examined and discussed in *Nestlé v National Westminster Bank plc*.[79]

(4) Trustee Investments Act 1961

The Trustee Investments Act 1961 espoused the portfolio investment theory, but did so in a rigid way. Investments authorized for trustees were divided into three categories, and trustees who wished to invest in the riskier categories were obliged to take advice, and for certain investments (called wider-range investments) to create a separate part of the trust fund. The enlargement of the categories of permitted investment was welcome, but the way in which the Act required trustees to allocate investments was mechanical, cumbersome, and arbitrarily inflexible.[80] Certain aspects of the operation of the Act were rightly described as 'curious'.[81]

(5) Trustee Act 2000

The rigidity and capriciousness of the investment rules in the 1961 Act have been swept away by the 2000 Act. This permits trustees to invest in the way most appropriate for the circumstances of their trust, with none of the arbitrary limitations of the 1961 Act. In reviewing whether trustees have acted properly, the courts are likely to take account of the current theory of portfolio investment.[82]

(6) Total overall return

The return on an investment consists of either or both capital growth and income return. The total return which an investment makes is the combination of both of these elements. If £1,000 is invested in company shares and at the end of the first year of investment the shares have increased in value to £1,100, and the company has paid a dividend of £50, the total overall return on the investment is £150—the sum total of the capital growth and the income. If a person were investing for their own benefit, they might aim to get the best possible overall total return, regardless of the split between capital growth and income. If they need money, they can always cash in part of the investment if the income it produces is insufficient. Conversely, they could reinvest the income if they wanted to see their overall wealth increase. This type of investment approach, known as total return investment theory, potentially delivers a higher rate of return than one that isolates income returns from capital returns, because it removes restrictions from investment choices made by the trustees.[83] It would enable trustees to make investment choices to compensate for unexpected or unbalanced investment returns.

[79] [1993] 1 WLR 1260; Martin, 'Investment Duties: A Victory for Complacency' [1992] 142 NLJ 1279; Kenny, 'Are a Bank Trustee's Fees Performance Related?' [1993] Conv 63; Watt and Stauch, 'Is There Liability for Imprudent Trustee Investment?' [1998] Conv 352.

[80] The Act initially required a division of the trust fund into two equal parts to enable the wider powers of investment to take effect (Trustee Investments Act 1961, s 2(1)), and this was later varied by the Trustee Investments (Division of Trust Fund) Order 1996, SI 1996/845, to permit three-quarters of the fund to be applied in the wider range of investments. Trustees could not choose some other division, such as two-thirds.

[81] *Nestlé v National Westminster Bank Ltd* [1993] 1 WLR 1260 at 1278, per Staughton LJ. See also Legair 'Modern Portfolio Theory: A Primer' [2000] 14 TLI 75.

[82] See further Hicks, 'The Trustee Act 2000 and the Modern Meaning of Investment' [2001] 15 TLI 203.

[83] See *Capital and Income in Trusts: Classification and Apportionment* (Law Com No 315, 2009); Ford, 'Trustee Investment and Modern Portfolio Theory' [1996] 10(4) TLI 102.

Total return investment could be adopted by a trust which has no beneficiaries currently entitled to the income, such as a charitable trust.[84] The trust invests for the best total overall return, and draws down a defined percentage of the fund each year. However, if the trust is one in which a beneficiary is entitled to the income, the strategy could operate unfairly since under current law the income is defined as the return the trust obtains through dividends and interest on its investments. Where there is an income beneficiary, the strategy would therefore only be appropriate where it is expressly envisaged by the trust instrument and a different means of identifying regular periodic sums which should be paid to the 'income' beneficiaries. This might be a fixed sum, possibly index-linked, or a fixed percentage of the value of the fund each year.

7 Duties

(1) **The general duty of care**

There is a substantial body of case law considering the duties of trustees in relation to investment, much of which remains relevant, although the Trustee Act 2000 imposes some statutory duties. The first of these statutory duties is the statutory duty of care. Trustees are required to exercise such care and skill in relation to investments as is reasonable in the circumstances.[85] As is explained elsewhere, a higher standard of care is expected from trustees acting in a professional capacity and where the trustee claims to have special knowledge or experience.[86] This is no more than a statutory restatement of the principles which had been established by the cases, with a clarification of the position of professional trustees. In *Speight v Gaunt*,[87] Lord Blackburn stated that the general duty of trustees was to act honestly and fairly and to take 'all those precautions which an ordinary prudent man of business would take in managing similar affairs of his own'. In *Re Whiteley*[88] Lindley LJ refined this dictum as it applies to investment. He said:

> The duty of the trustee is not to take such care only as a prudent man would take if he had only himself to consider, the duty is rather to take such care as an ordinary prudent man would take if he were minded to make an investment for the benefit of other people for whom he felt morally bound to provide.[89]

Lord Watson on appeal to the House of Lords explained:

> Business men of ordinary prudence may, and frequently do, select investments which are more or less of a speculative character; but it is the duty of a trustee to confine himself to the class of investments which are permitted by the trust, and likewise to avoid all investments of that class which are attended by hazard.[90]

In addition to the specific duties relating to investment, trustees remain subject to their general fiduciary duties in making investment decisions.[91] This means that they should

[84] New statutory powers are conferred on charity trustees to effect total return investments—these are considered later under special considerations for charity investments.

[85] Trustee Act 2000, s 1(1). [86] Trustee Act 2000, s 1(1). [87] [1883] 9 App Cas 1.

[88] [1886] 33 Ch D 347; affd sub nom *Learoyd v Whiteley* [1887] 12 App Cas 727.

[89] [1886] 33 Ch D 347 at 355. [90] [1887] 12 App Cas 727 at 733.

[91] There is widespread concern about how fiduciary duties are interpreted in the context of investment—see Kay, *Final Report on UK Equity Markets and Long Term Decision Making* (November 2012), which was commissioned by the Department for Business and Skills. The Law Commission, as a result, opened a consultation on the fiduciary duties of investment intermediaries. The final report was published on 1 July 2014 (*Fiduciary Duties of Investment Intermediaries*, Law Com No 350), which calls for better guidance on fiduciary duties over legislative reform.

not act in a way which gives rise to a conflict of interest. Thus, in a Canadian case, it was held that the trustees were in breach of trust where they made a loan to a company owned by one of the trustees. Even though this application of the trust funds did not fall outside the investment powers of the trustees, the conflict of interest made the loan an improper investment.[92]

We have already seen that the rule in *Howe v Earl of Dartmouth*, if it has not been superseded by the Trustee Act 2000, may require immediate disinvestment by trustees of hazardous investments received under a residuary testamentary gift which is to be held for beneficiaries with successive interests in trusts arising before the commencement of the Trusts (Capital and Income) Act 2013.[93] However, in accordance with portfolio investment theory, as has already been explained, trustees may be entitled to retain or to make an investment which involves a measure of risk (as most investments inevitably do), provided that the risk involved in that investment is balanced by other elements in the portfolio. That is the tenor of most recent judgments on the investment powers of trustees. In *Nestlé v National Westminster Bank plc*,[94] Hoffmann J said that 'an investment which in isolation is too risky and therefore in breach of trust may be justified when held in conjunction with other investments'. The investment saga of a £3 million testamentary estate in *Daniel v Tee*[95] provides an example of trustees making investments that were too risky. On the basis of advice, the funds had been invested in a 'growth portfolio', which comprised 80 per cent equities and 20 per cent non-equities. In the judgment of Deputy Judge Richard Spearman QC, the decision to opt for this sort of portfolio was one that no trustee, complying with their duties to invest, could reasonably have made.[96]

(2) **The standard investment criteria**

The Trustee Act 2000, s 4, requires all trustees exercising a power of investment, including trustees exercising express investment powers, to have regard to what are described as the 'standard investment criteria'.[97] There are two such criteria. First, the trustees must have regard to the suitability of the investment concerned, and second to the need for diversification. The trustees must have regard to these standard investment criteria both in making investments,[98] and also in periodically reviewing the investments.[99] The responsibilities of trustees in relation to investments are ongoing—they cannot invest funds and then forget them. They must keep the investment portfolio under periodic review. It is also clear that the duty to review extends to investments settled on the trustee at the creation of the trust, as well as investments made by trustees in pursuance of their powers of investment.[100]

When looking at the suitability of investments, the Trustee Act 2000 envisages a two-stage process. The trustees must consider the suitability for the trust of a particular kind of investment. For instance, should the trust invest in purchasing shares in a unit trust? The trustees must then consider the suitability of the particular investment proposed. For instance, having decided that investing in a unit trust would be suitable, which fund manager and which of that manager's investment funds should be selected?

[92] *Re David Feldman Charitable Foundation* [1987] 58 OR (2d) 626.

[93] s 1(2)(a) and (b) disapply the rules of apportionment for 'new trusts' arising on or after 5 October 2013.

[94] [1993] 1 WLR 1260. [95] [2016] EWHC 1538 (Ch).

[96] Ibid, at paras 162–4. The issue of the liability of the trustees is discussed in Chapter 34.

[97] These criteria are not new. They first appeared in the Trustee Investments Act 1961, s 6(1).

[98] Trustee Act 2000, s 4(3). [99] Trustee Act 2000, s 4(1).

[100] See further *Gregson v HAE Trustees Ltd* [2008] EWHC 1006 (Ch) at 83, per Deputy Judge Robert Miles QC.

(3) The need for advice

A further requirement of the Trustee Act 2000 is that trustees must normally take proper advice on investment decisions.[101] The Trustee Investments Act 1961 required trustees always to take advice before making all but a very limited range of investments. This requirement has been changed by the 2000 Act. Trustees can dispense with seeking advice if they reasonably conclude that in all the circumstances it is unnecessary or inappropriate to do so.[102] For instance, the trustees may consider the sums involved to be too small, or they may already have sufficient expertise available to them through fellow trustees or employees of the trust. However, for trustees to dispense with advice requires a conscious decision on the part of the trustees. It would be a breach of trust for trustees to fail to seek advice through oversight, even in a situation where advice was unnecessary, although it is hardly likely in such an instance that any action for breach of trust would be pursued.

'Proper advice' is defined by the Act as 'the advice of a person who is reasonably believed by the trustee to be qualified to give it by his ability in and practical experience of financial and other matters relating to the proposed investment'.[103] The trustees are not obliged to follow the advice which they are given. Their obligation is only to obtain and consider it. They would not be discharging their function if they followed the advice without applying their own minds to it,[104] but equally it would be unwise to disregard the advice without good reason.[105] In *Daniel v Tee*,[106] in pursuing an investment strategy that was too risky, the trustees were acting on the advice of responsibly chosen investment advisers, and were held not to have acted unreasonably in relying on that advice. The trustees may have a claim in negligence against the advisers, but this may be of little value if the advisers are insolvent.[107]

(4) Financial considerations

The object of investment is to produce a financial return from trust assets. The trustees are expected to adopt an investment strategy which has regard to the nature and purpose of the trust. This will affect whether the trustees should be maximizing income, maximizing capital growth, or balancing the two, and what balance there should be between risk and return. Where there are both income and capital beneficiaries, the trustees must seek a balance between high income and capital growth. It has been said that in all but the smallest fund, this will require a high proportion of the trust assets to be invested in company shares.[108] Where an income beneficiary would not be liable to tax on certain kinds of investment, however, this also should be considered by the trustees and would legitimately influence their investment decisions.[109] Because trustees must consider how to achieve a fair and proper balance between all the different classes of beneficiary, they will not be in breach of trust simply because their investment policy has resulted in greater erosion of the real capital value of the trust fund than would have been the case with a different investment strategy. Trustees are not under an absolute obligation to ensure that the capital value of the fund is maintained.[110] For instance, in *Nestlé v National*

[101] Trustee Act 2000, ss 5(1) (new investments) and 5(2) (review of existing investments).

[102] Ibid, s 5(3).

[103] Ibid, s 5(4). A person acting as an investment adviser must be authorized under Financial Services and Markets Act 2000, s 19.

[104] See *Jones v AMP Perpetual Trustee Co NZ Ltd* [1994] 1 NZLR 690.

[105] See *Cowan v Scargill* [1985] Ch 270 at 289 (discussed later).

[106] [2016] EWHC 1538 (Ch).

[107] *Crowden v QBE Insurance (Europe) Ltd* [2017] EWHC 2597 (Comm).

[108] *Nestlé v National Westminster Bank plc* [1993] 1 WLR 1260.

[109] Ibid.

[110] See *Jones v AMP Perpetual Trustee Co NZ Ltd* [1994] 1 NZLR 690.

Westminster Bank plc,[111] the heiress to the chocolate family fortune complained that, had the trustees invested differently, she could have received an inheritance four times greater than was the case. The Court of Appeal held that, although there had been errors of judgement on the part of the trustees, including a misunderstanding of the width of their powers of investment, and a failure to review the investments sufficiently often, there had not been any breach of trust resulting in liability to the heiress. It was also said that even if trustees had acted for the wrong reasons, they would still not be liable if their decision could be justified objectively by other, valid, reasons.[112] The case illustrates the difficulty which the beneficiary faces in seeking to prove a breach of trust in relation to investment by trustees.[113]

(5) **Ethical considerations**

The extent to which trustees may have regard to ethical considerations[114] was explored by Megarry V-C in *Cowan v Scargill*.[115] The National Coal Board pension fund was controlled by both management-appointed and union-appointed trustees. The union-appointed trustees objected to a proposed annual investment plan unless it adopted the policy of withdrawing from overseas investment and from investment in industries in competition with coal. This led to a direct clash between the union-appointed trustees, led by Arthur Scargill—the National Union of Mineworkers General Secretary and a veteran of industrial disputes—and the other trustees, leading to the hearing in court. Eschewing the use of a barrister, Arthur Scargill chose to represent himself in court. Sir Robert Megarry held that the action of the union trustees was unreasonable. The duty of trustees was to optimize the benefits which the beneficiaries would receive. In the vast majority of cases, financial considerations would prevail. There could be rare cases where this was not so.

> Plainly the present case is not one of this rare type of case. Subject to such matters, under a trust for the provision of financial benefits, the paramount duty of the trustees is to provide the greatest financial benefits for the present and future beneficiaries.[116]

Trustees were not to be deflected from this duty to the beneficiaries merely because the policy of seeking the best financial returns conflicted with their personal opinions:

> Trustees may have strongly held social or political views. They may be firmly opposed to any investment in South Africa[117] or other countries, or they may object to any form of investment in companies concerned with alcohol, tobacco, armaments or other controversial products. In the conduct of their own affairs, of course, they are free to abstain from making any such investments. Yet under a trust, if investments of this type would be more beneficial to the beneficiaries than other investments, the trustees must not refrain from making the investments by reason of the views that they hold.[118]

[111] [1993] 1 WLR 1260. [112] See also *Cowan v Scargill* [1985] Ch 270.

[113] See also *Jones v AMP Perpetual Trustee Co NZ Ltd* [1994] 1 NZLR 690, where trustees were held not liable for retaining shares in a falling market; *Daniel v Tee* [2016] EWHC 1538 (Ch), where trustees were not liable for an investment strategy in 80 per cent equities, as they had followed independent advice and the beneficiaries could not prove the loss related to the investment decisions, as the risky threshold of 80 per cent was never actually reached.

[114] See Lord Nicholls, 'Trustees and Their Broader Community; Where Duty, Morality and Ethics Converge' [1995] 9 TLI 71; Luxton, 'Ethical Investments in Hard Times' [1992] 55 MLR 587; Thornton, 'Ethical Investments: A Case of Disjointed Thinking' [2008] CLJ 396.

[115] [1985] Ch 270. [116] [1985] Ch 270 at 288.

[117] This remark was made before the end of apartheid. [118] [1985] Ch 270 at 287.

It was not enough that they were honest and sincere in their cause. The general standard of conduct required of trustees demanded more:

> Honesty and sincerity are not the same as prudence and reasonableness. Some of the most sincere people are the most unreasonable; and Mr Scargill told me that he had met quite a few of them. Accordingly, although a trustee who takes advice on investments is not bound to accept and act on that advice, he is not entitled to reject it merely because he sincerely disagrees with it, unless in addition to being sincere he is acting as an ordinary prudent man would act.[119]

One of the cases which Megarry V-C thought might be exceptional and where ethical or moral considerations could legitimately sway the decision of the trustees was where all the beneficiaries were adults who shared the same moral values who 'might well consider that it was far better to receive less than to receive more money from what they consider to be evil and tainted sources'.[120]

Such a situation arose in *Harries v Church Comrs for England*,[121] which concerned the investment policy of the body controlling the investment funds of the Church of England. The revenue from these funds, together with contributions from parishes, was used to maintain churches and to meet the stipends of the clergy. The Church Commissioners operated an ethical investment policy, under which they chose not to invest in businesses which might be offensive to the Church, including armaments, gambling, tobacco, newspapers, and South Africa.[122] Sir Donald Nicholls V-C considered that these exclusions were appropriate and justified for a religious charity whose members were likely to support such a policy, but he rejected a call by the Bishop of Oxford for a much wider group of exclusions. Even though ethical considerations were legitimate for the Church Commissioners, provided that they left an adequate width of investment, where charity trustees held assets for investments, their principal duty was to seek the maximum return consistent with commercial prudence. If they did not do this, they would not be discharging their duty of furthering the purposes of the trust. If the Church Commissioners used their funds otherwise than for investment, how in the long term could they ensure that the clergy were paid and the Church's buildings maintained?

Trustees might be at risk of negative legal consequences. In *Martin v Edinburgh District Council*,[123] Lord Murray held that trustees were in breach of trust for pursuing a policy of disinvestment in South Africa prior to the end of apartheid 'without considering expressly whether it was in the best interests of the beneficiaries and without obtaining professional advice'. Trustees would only be entitled to adopt a blind policy of this nature where it was expressly permitted or required by the instrument establishing the trust. The decision to exclude a sector of possible investments in a way which 'runs contrary to the best financial indicators available at the time'[124] on political or ethical grounds is what constitutes the breach of trust. It is not relevant that the ethical investments may actually turn out to produce a reasonable return; the decision to invest in them should only have been made if other non-ethical investments were considered and rejected on the basis that they would not yield a greater return.

The legal prohibition against ethical investment has come under pressure in recent years. First, there is an arguable case that ethically based investments have a lower risk profile than other investments, or that in some instances (such as with investments in 'green' technology) that they have greater growth potential, which could justify a decision

[119] [1985] Ch 270 at 289. [120] [1985] Ch 270 at 288. [121] [1993] 2 All ER 300.

[122] A very similar list of exclusions to those given by Megarry V-C in the passage cited earlier.

[123] [1988] SLT 329.

[124] Thornton, 'Ethical Investments: A Case of Disjointed Thinking' [2008] CLJ 396.

by trustees.[125] Second, ethical schemes are much more common than they once were. This is typified by the Local Government Pension Scheme, which is subject to its own statutory framework.[126] It provides benefits for about 5 million past and present employees. Subject to guidance from the Secretary of State,[127] scheme administrators are currently able, if it is thought that their members would be in support, to take some financial risks in the pursuit of ethical investment goals. These risks cannot be 'significant'. Nevertheless, the administrators are allowed more leeway than is permitted by a strict reading of the common law rules.[128]

(6) Periodic review of investments

The duty of trustees in relation to investment is a continuing one. They do not discharge their duty merely by giving proper consideration to the appropriateness of an investment at the time it is made or the asset acquired. They must also consider periodically whether the balance of investment is correct, and whether individual investments are retained. This responsibility is specifically imposed by the Trustee Act 2000, s 4(2), but would in any event apply on general trust principles. In *Bartlett v Barclays Bank Trust Co Ltd (No 2)*,[129] trustees held a controlling shareholding in a property investment company. It was held that they were in breach of trust in failing to review the activities of the company and in permitting the directors to engage in a speculative and inadvisable development scheme. In *Jeffrey v Gretton*,[130] trustees were held to be in breach of the duty to review investments under s 4(2), on the basis that they should have considered selling a Grade II dilapidated property once the life tenant had given up his interest by deed of variation. Instead, the trustees had permitted the life tenant to remain in the property until his death and had, without professional advice, sought to refurbish the property. Mr Justice Blohm QC held that the trustees had failed in their duty to review the investments, as they should not have decided to defer sale as the life tenant had given up his entitlement under the deed of variation, and should have considered professional advice on the financial merits of the plan to retain and refurbish the property.[131]

Provided that the trustees have given proper consideration to whether an investment should be retained, they will not be liable because it can be seen, with the benefit of hindsight, that they made a mistake. In *Re Chapman*[132] the trustees had properly invested in mortgages of agricultural land. The value of the land fell, placing the security of the mortgages at risk. The trustees nevertheless decided to retain them, hoping that the market would improve. Instead, land values fell still further. The Court of Appeal refused to find the trustees liable.

> There is no rule of law which compels the court to hold that an honest trustee is liable to make good loss sustained by retaining an authorized security in a falling market, if he did so

[125] See McCormack, 'Sexy But Not Sleazy: Trustee Investments and Ethical Considerations' [1998] 19 *Company Lawyer* 39, who argues that pursuing an ethical investment policy may not be a poor decision for trustees. This is in relation to ethically managed unit trusts and their relative performance on the stock market (FTSE).

[126] Superannuation Act 1972, s 7; Public Service Pensions Act 2013.

[127] Local Government Pension Scheme (Management and Investment of Funds) Regulations 2016, reg 7(2)(e).

[128] The Secretary of State is able to direct how ethical decisions should taken, but not what those decisions should be in more concrete terms. See *R (on the Application of Palestine Solidarity Campaign and another) v Secretary of State for Housing, Communities and Local Government* [2020] UKSC 16, [31].

[129] [1980] 1 All ER 139.

[130] [2011] WTLR 809.

[131] [2011] WTLR 809 at 69–72. On the facts, though in breach of the duty, no loss had occurred on the market value of the property, which had not increased or decreased over the period in which the ex-life tenant had lived at the property.

[132] [1896] 2 Ch 763.

> honestly and prudently, in the belief that it was the best course to take in the interests of all parties. Trustees acting honesty, with ordinary prudence and within the limits of their trust, are not liable for mere errors of judgment.[133]

It is believed that this will continue to be the case, notwithstanding the omission by the Trustee Act 2000 of s 4 of the Trustee Act 1925, under which trustees were not to be held liable for breach of trust by reason only of continuing to hold an investment which has ceased to be authorized either by the trust instrument or by the general law.

(7) **Special rules for particular investments**

(a) Mortgages of land

In the nineteenth century, before building societies played the major role which they did in the first half of the twentieth century in financing the purchase of residential property, private mortgages were very common and a frequent type of investment for trustees. Modern conditions of inflation, and the ready availability of commercial funds from the building societies and banks, make this form of investment much less popular for trustees, although it still occurs to a limited extent, and is envisaged by the Trustee Act 2000, s 3(3). Special rules used to be provided by the Trustee Act 1925, s 8, for trustees lending on mortgage. These rules protected trustees against liability for advancing too high a proportion of the value of the property if they lent no more than two-thirds of a valuation made by an independent surveyor or valuer. These rules have now been removed by the Trustee Act 2000 so that the question of whether a mortgage transaction was prudent and appropriate must be decided without recourse to any such guidelines.[134] It is not considered advisable for trustees to lend on the security of anything other than a first legal mortgage,[135] although it is possible that a loan on a properly registered second mortgage would not, in itself, be a breach of trust. The trust instrument may, of course, permit a loan on a second mortgage, or even an unsecured loan.

(b) Controlling interest in a company

Trustees who have a shareholding which gives them a controlling interest in a company are expected to take more than a passive interest in the affairs of the company. They should either ensure that one of the trustees is a member of the board (if not an executive director) or, at the very least, they should keep a watching brief lest the company seeks to act in an improvident way.[136]

(8) **Special considerations for charity investment**

(a) Charities Act 2011

The Charities Act 2011, s 96, authorizes the court or the Charity Commission to approve schemes for the establishment of common investment funds where trustees wish to pool the investments of two or more charitable trusts.[137] There should normally be some connection between the participating charities. Section 100 of the Act contains provisions for the establishment of common deposit schemes for charities.[138]

[133] See also *Jones v AMP Perpetual Trustee Co NZ Ltd* [1994] 1 NZLR 690.

[134] See *Re Solomon* [1912] 1 Ch 261; *Re Dive* [1909] 1 Ch 328; *Shaw v Cates* [1909] 1 Ch 389.

[135] See *Chapman v Browne* [1902] 1 Ch 785, CA.

[136] *Re Lucking's Will Trusts* [1967] 3 All ER 726.

[137] For a common investment scheme approved under previous legislation see *Re University of London Charitable Trusts* [1964] Ch 282. Sections 97 to 103 set out the bodies that may participate in and the provisions and powers applicable to such schemes.

[138] ss 101 to 103 set out the bodies that may participate and the provisions applicable to such schemes.

(b) Total return investments

We have already seen that charities may wish to make use of total return investments; to invest so as to obtain the best overall return to the charity and then decide how to allocate the overall return, both capital growth and income. This previously required a Charity Commission scheme to authorize such investments. Since 1 January 2014, charities with a permanent endowment have been allowed to adopt a total returns policy under the Charities Act 2011, s 104A.[139] This follows the passing of the Charities (Total Returns) Regulations 2013, with which charities have to comply before passing and managing a 'total returns' portfolio.

(c) Social investments

Charities, in seeking to achieve their charitable purposes, normally either expend funds in the furtherance of those purposes (e.g. funding research into infectious diseases) or invest in the traditional sense to generate funds to supplement donations and other income to fund future expenditure on charitable purposes (e.g. through purchasing shares in a listed company). It must be thought that where charities do make investments, it is particularly appropriate that they invest ethically.[140] Charities are mission-based organizations and in many cases it would not make sense for them to attempt to bring about social change in their own neighbourhoods but undermine that progress through harmful investments elsewhere. On the other hand, charitable organizations are almost by definition in a constant need of income and low return investments might undermine the interests of their beneficiaries. One attempt to get around this dilemma is through the concept of 'social investments' which match and complement the organization's purposes but do not come at too high a cost in terms of lost income.

The Law Commission launched a consultation paper on 'social investment' by charities.[141] A social investment is one which seeks to achieve both a charitable purpose and an (often limited) financial benefit in one, composite transaction. A good example is a homelessness charity purchasing empty properties to be renovated and let at a low rent, thereby helping the homeless but also achieving a small financial return through rent and the increase in value of the purchased properties. Social investments are not new financial instruments in the sector, but there may be legal barriers to charity trustees making use of them either because of restrictions within charity law (such as the requirement not to provide anything other than incidental private benefits) or concerns within the general scope of trustee investment powers.

Concerns over the width of the statutory investment powers under the Trustee Act 2000, and the dubious position of ethical investments, led the Law Commission to provisionally propose a new statutory power conferring on charity trustees the power to make social investments.[142] This power was introduced by the Charities (Protection and Social Investment) Act 2016, s 15,[143] which came into force on 31 July 2016. A social investment by charities[144] is defined as a 'relevant act'[145] that is carried out 'with a view to both directly

[139] Inserted by the Trusts (Capital and Income) Act 2013, s 4.

[140] See Nobles, 'Charities and Ethical Investment' [1992] Conv 115.

[141] *Social Investment by Charities* (Law Com CP No 216, 2014). The short consultation period opened on 24 April 2014 and closed on 18 June 2014.

[142] Ibid, para 4.12.

[143] Which inserted ss 292A, 292B and 292C into the Charities Act 2011.

[144] The new power does not apply to charities established by, or whose purposes and functions are set out in, legislation, or charities established by Royal Charter. These charities will need to continue to rely on their existing constitutional powers, which will not be affected by this new legislation—see Charities Act 2011, ss 292B(4) and 292B(5).

[145] Charities Act 2011, s 292A(4). This includes the application of property, but also taking on a commitment such as the grant of a guarantee over property.

furthering the charity's purposes and achieving a financial return for the charity'.[146] An application or use of funds or other property achieves a 'financial return' if its outcome is better for the charity in financial terms than expending the whole of the funds or other property in question.[147] The definition is wide and may include some actions which would not ordinarily be thought of as investments.[148]

The exercise of this general power, which can be excluded by the trust instrument,[149] is subject to specific duties on charity trustees. The Law Commission provisionally proposed that the standard investment criteria under the Trustee Act 2000 should not apply to social investments by charities,[150] as they do not sit comfortably with social investments and may 'constitute a trap for the unwary' charity trustee.[151] While trustees must still have regard generally to the standard investment criteria,[152] trustees are obliged to consider whether advice on the proposed social investment ought to be sought, and, if so, to consider that advice.[153] Moreover, trustees are under a specific duty to satisfy themselves that any social investment is in the best interests of the charity in question,[154] which includes consideration of the duration of the investments, the risk, the likely cost, and the expected benefits from following this type of investment.[155] Trustees must also review their charity's social investments from time to time.[156] In conducting the review, the same requirements relating to advice must be followed as if the social investment was being made for the first time.[157]

8 Delegation

(1) Authority to delegate investment management

Investment decisions and their execution are so complex that in many cases it will not be appropriate for trustees to manage the investment of trust funds themselves. This is more likely to be the case where large funds are under investment or where the trustees do not themselves have investment experience. In such cases, the management of the investments might be delegated by the trustees. For instance, as the case of *Cowan v Scargill*[158] illustrated, the National Coal Board pension fund, one of the largest such funds, was not invested directly by the trustees. Instead, it was managed by professional financial advisers on behalf of the trustees, subject to the approval of an annual investment plan giving direction, which was prepared by the advisers for consideration by the board of trustees.

[146] Charities Act 2011, s 292A(2). [147] Charities Act 2011, s 292A(5).

[148] Charity Commission, *Social Investment by Charities—The New Power Introduced by the Charities (Protection and Social Investment) Act 2016: Interim Guidance* (updated 1 August 2016).

[149] Charities Act 2011, s 292B(3). [150] Law Com CP No 216, para 4.27.

[151] Ibid, para. 3.76.

[152] These are nonetheless amended by the Charities (Protection and Social Investment) Act 2016, s 15(2)–(4), which permits social investments to take place for charities by inserting s 4(4) and s 4(5) into the Trustee Act 2000.

[153] Charities Act 2011, s 292C(2)(a) and (b), respectively. This might include legal, financial, or other advice, and could be provided by someone the trustees believe to be comptent to give the necessary advice, including a member of charity staff or volunteers.

[154] Charities Act 2011, s 292C(2)(c).

[155] Charity Commission CC14 *Charities and investment matters: a guide for trustees* (October 2011, updated 1 August 2016).

[156] Charities Act 2011, s 292C(3).

[157] Ibid, s 292C(4), which repeats the advice criteria in s 292C(2)(a) and (b). [158] [1985] Ch 270.

Prior to the Trustee Act 2000, it was not clear whether the delegation of investment management was permitted by general law, so that it was considered wise for a trust instrument expressly to authorize the delegation by trustees of investment management to professional portfolio managers.[159] The Pensions Act 1995 contains provisions enabling trustees to delegate certain of their functions concerning investment subject to a number of safeguards.[160] The Trustee Act 2000 has now extended to all trustees the explicit authority to delegate investment management.[161] This implements a proposal made by the Law Commission.[162] The change has been achieved by authorizing trustees to delegate any function relating to the trust, with certain exceptions.[163] Investment management is one of the functions which can be delegated.[164]

(2) **Conditions**

Where trustees do choose to delegate investment management, or *asset management*, to use the wider phrase used in the Trustee Act 2000, certain conditions must be satisfied. These conditions probably apply even in cases where this is done under an express power in the trust instrument rather than under the statutory power to delegate. First, the delegation to the agent must be in writing, or must be evidenced in writing.[165] Second, the trustees must produce a policy statement in writing, or evidenced in writing, which gives guidance as to how the asset management functions should be exercised.[166] This policy statement should, for instance, indicate what level of risk the trustees consider acceptable, what balance is being sought between income and capital growth, and whether there are any types of investment that should be avoided. Third, the contract with the agent must require the agent to comply with the current policy statement given by the trustees.[167] Fourth, the trustees must exercise reasonable care in the selection of the agent, since the selection of agents is one of the functions to which the statutory duty of care applies.[168]

In addition, the Act specifically imposes on the agent the obligation to have regard to the standard investment criteria, described earlier.[169] However, the agent is dispensed from the need to obtain advice if the agent is the sort of person from whom it would have been proper to seek advice.[170] Thus, where, as will often be the case, the trustees delegate investment management to a professional fund manager (such as an investment bank), the agent does not have to seek advice from other professionals. Professional fund managers will sometimes insist on a limitation of liability, or permission to act where there may be a potential conflict of interest, and the trustees are authorized by the Act to agree to such terms if it is reasonably necessary to do so.[171] The appointment of an agent will be valid notwithstanding any failure by the trustees to comply with the limits relating to the appointment,[172] but the trustees may thereby expose themselves to potential liability for breach of trust. In *Daniel v Tee*[173] a risky investment was made on the advice of a solicitor of the firm, who was not a direct trustee or executor of the testamentary trust. There had been no lawful delegation to this partner, as the requirements of s 15 had not been

159 See Hayton, 'Investment Management Problems' [1990] 106 LQR 88.

160 Pensions Act 1995, s 34.

161 The powers granted in the Trustee Act 2000 do not, therefore, apply to pension trusts.

162 *Trustees Powers and Duties* (Law Com No 260, 1999). This proposal adopts a recommendation of the Trust Law Revision Committee.

163 Trustee Act 2000, s 11.

164 Investment functions are included in the list of functions which can be delegated by trustees of a charitable trust, and are not excluded from the general authority given to other trustees.

165 Trustee Act 2000, s 15(1).

166 Ibid, s 15(2)(a).

167 Ibid, s 15(2)(b).

168 Ibid, s 1 and Sch 1, para 3.

169 Ibid, s 13(1).

170 Ibid, s 13(2).

171 Ibid, s 14(2) and (3).

172 Ibid, s 24.

173 [2016] EWHC 1538 (Ch).

followed. However, as the losses incurred would have taken place even if the delegation had been properly done and as the trustees had involved their fellow partner in good faith, the trustees were not liable for the impermissible delegation of their investment functions.[174]

(3) Supervision and review

Just as the functions of trustees are not completed once they have made the initial investments of the trust fund, so their functions are not completed where they have appointed an agent. The trustees must keep the arrangement under review,[175] they must intervene if necessary by giving directions or terminating the agency,[176] and they must review and revise the investment policy statement.[177]

(4) Related functions

In addition to the delegation of investment management, trustees may also appoint nominees to act on their behalf, custodians to hold documents relating to trust assets or the trust assets themselves, and custodian trustees in whom the trust assets are vested. These arrangements were described in Chapter 25.

[174] Ibid at paras 188–90.
[175] Trustee Act 2000, s 22(1).
[176] Ibid, s 22(1) and (4).
[177] Ibid, s 22(2).

32

Appointing and changing trustees

1 Introduction

The role of trustees is central to the operation of trusts. In most cases they have extensive powers conferred upon them by the trust instrument or by the general law. The way in which they exercise those powers can have a huge impact upon whether or not the objectives of the trust are achieved, and upon the beneficiaries. Choosing the right trustees is, therefore, essential. We look in this chapter at how the original trustees are appointed, and what steps can be taken should the trustees need to be changed through resignation or retirement, or because the settlor or the beneficiaries are no longer content that a trustee should continue in office.

2 The original trustees

(1) Appointment by the settlor

(a) Express trusts

When a trust of property is created, generally the settlor will appoint the initial trustees of the settlement. If they create the trust inter vivos by declaring that they hold the property on trust for the beneficiaries, they will be the trustee. If they transfer the property to a third party subject to a trust, that person will become the trustee. Usually, the deed creating the trust will appoint the trustees. If the trust is testamentary, so that it is only created after their death, the testator will usually nominate the trustees in their will.

(b) Implied trusts

A trust may also come into being without being formally created, for instance, because it is an implied, resulting, or constructive trust. In such cases the trust is imposed on the legal owner of the property, who thereby becomes a trustee. Lord Browne-Wilkinson, in *Westdeutsche Landesbank Girozentrale v Islington London Borough Council*,[1] suggested that the legal owner would only become a trustee in such cases after becoming aware of the trust obligation, or at least of the circumstances affecting his conscience. It is probably better to regard Lord Browne-Wilkinson's comments as intimating that the trustee is not subject to the full fiduciary duties of trusteeship until he is aware of the existence of the trust. The trust exists irrespective of his knowledge in the sense that the property belongs in equity to the beneficiaries. However, the mere fact that there is a 'trust' in this sense does not mean that the trustee will be subject to personal liability for breach of trust if he acts in a manner inconsistent with the existence of the trust.

[1] [1996] AC 669 at 705.

(c) Capacity to act as a trustee

Any legal person with legal capacity, whether an individual or corporation,[2] may act as a trustee. However, the Law of Property Act 1925, s 20, provides that: 'The appointment of an infant to be a trustee in relation to any settlement or trust shall be voidable.' This restriction only applies in respect of express trusts, and if a minor receives property in circumstances that would create a resulting or constructive trust he will become a trustee of the property.[3] However, this will only be possible in the case of personal property, as s 1(6) of the Law of Property Act 1925 provides that an infant cannot hold a legal estate in land. If a minor is appointed trustee of an express trust, there are mechanisms which will enable the minor to be removed from his position and replaced.[4] Special rules are applicable to the appointment of trustees in a charitable trust.[5]

(d) Disclaimer

A person appointed trustee can disclaim the trust at any time before he has accepted it. He may disclaim by deed, although that is not necessary and a disclaimer can be inferred from his conduct.[6] A disclaimer may be set aside if it can be shown that the disclaimer has been procured through undue influence.[7] Resulting and constructive trustees cannot disclaim because the trust is imposed upon them because of their conduct, and once a trust has been accepted, the trustee cannot disclaim.[8] A trustee cannot disclaim part of a trust, and, therefore, acceptance of part will amount to an acceptance of the whole.[9]

(e) A trust will not fail for want of a trustee

If a trust has been validly created by the transfer of the trust property to the trustees, or by the death of the testator who has specified trusts in his will, the trust will not fail if the nominated trustees disclaim the trust, are incapable of acting as trustees,[10] or have predeceased the testator. Equity will not permit a trust to fail for want of a trustee[11] and will seek to carry the settlor's intentions into effect as far as is possible. This principle operates in different ways, depending on whether the trust was created by an inter vivos or testamentary transfer.

(i) Inter vivos transfer of property to trustees upon trust

If the settlor effectively transferred the trust property to trustees by means of an inter vivos conveyance and the trustees disclaim, the trust property will revest in the settlor subject to the trusts. For example, in *Mallott v Wilson*,[12] the settlor transferred land in 1866 to a trustee on trust. When the trustee executed a deed of disclaimer in 1867, it was held that the trust did not fail but that the property was automatically revested in the settlor by operation of law, and that he held the land subject to the trusts that had been validly created.[13] If the settlor has died since the trust was created, the property will revest in his personal representatives, who will again hold it subject to the trusts.

[2] See *A-G v St John's Hospital Bedford* [1865] 2 De GJ & Sm 621; *Re Thompson's Settlement Trust* [1905] 1 Ch 229; *Bankes v Salisbury Diocesan Council of Education Inc* [1960] Ch 631.

[3] See *Re Vinogradoff* [1935] WN 68.

[4] See, for example, Trustee Act 1925, s 36(1).

[5] See Chapter 23.

[6] *Stacey v Elph* [1833] 1 My & K 195; *White v Barton* [1854] 18 Beav 192; *Holder v Holder* [1968] Ch 353.

[7] *Mackay v Wesley* [2020] EWHC 3400 (Ch).

[8] *Re Sharman's Will Trusts* [1942] Ch 311.

[9] *Re Lord and Fullerton's Contract* [1896] 1 Ch 228; *Re Lister* [1926] Ch 149, CA.

[10] See *Re Armitage* [1972] Ch 438.

[11] *Robson v Flight* [1865] 4 De GJ & Sm 608.

[12] [1903] 2 Ch 494.

[13] See also *Jones v Jones* [1874] WN 190.

(ii) Testamentary transfers of property upon trust

If the trust was intended to be created by the testamentary transfer of the trust property to trustees and they predecease the testator, the deceased's personal representatives will hold the property on the terms of the trust that he had intended to create. For example, in *Re Willis*,[14] a testatrix had left property on discretionary trusts for various charities. The trustee, who was to select how the property was to be allocated between the charities, had predeceased her. However, the court held that the trust did not fail but that the fund would vest in her executors and the court would select how the fund should be allocated.[15] Similarly, if the trustee survives the testator but then disclaims the trust, the property will also revest in the settlor's personal representatives, again subject to the trusts.

In either case the trust will not fail and the court has the power to appoint new trustees.[16] However, this principle is subject to the qualification that the trust will fail if the identity of the disclaiming trustee was essential to the trust. In *Re Lysaght (Decd)*,[17] a testator left the residue of her estate to the Royal College of Surgeons to provide scholarships, which were not to be awarded to Jews or Roman Catholics. In these circumstances the RCS, as trustee, refused to accept the trust. Buckley J held that the trust therefore failed, stating that:

> If it is of the essence of a trust that the trustees selected by the settlor and no one else shall act as the trustees of it and those trustees cannot or will not undertake the office, the trust must fail.

In the circumstances, because the gift was charitable and had failed, it was applied cy-près.[18]

(f) Limitation on the number of trustees

Where the trust fund consists of personal property there is no limit on the number of trustees that the settlor may appoint when the trust is created. However, in the case of a trust of land, the property legislation of 1925 restricts the number of persons who may hold the legal title to a maximum of four.[19] This restriction was introduced with the objective of increasing conveyancing efficiency.[20]

Where more than four names appear on the transfer form, the Land Registry will decline to register the transfer until the four who are to act as trustees have been identified, the default position being that the first four named who are willing and able to act should be trustees. It is to be noted that those who are named after the first four persons named as trustees do not automatically become trustees if a vacancy arises, and they will only become a trustee if they are properly appointed by whoever has the authority to appoint replacement trustees. In the context of land, it is also worth noting that although it is possible to have a sole trustee, overreaching of equitable trust interests cannot take place unless there is a payment to two trustees of land.[21] This is the case even where there

[14] [1921] 1 Ch 44. [15] See also *Moggridge v Thackwell* [1803] 7 Ves 36.

[16] *A-G v Stephens* [1834] 3 My & K 347; *Jones v Jones* [1874] 31 LT 535; *Mallott v Wilson* [1903] 2 Ch 494.

[17] [1966] Ch 191; see also *Reeve v A-G* [1843] 3 Hare 191; *Re Lawton* [1936] 3 All ER 378.

[18] See Chapter 22.

[19] Trustee Act 1925, s 34(2). See also Law of Property Act 1925, s 34(2) and (3).

[20] There are a number of very limited exceptions to the principle in s 34(3), primarily being land held on trust for 'charitable, ecclesiastical, or public purposes'.

[21] See Law of Property Act 1925, ss 2 and 27. Overreaching is the process by which interests in the land are transferred to the proceeds of sale, so that, for example, a beneficial interest in land does not bind a purchaser, but is instead expressed as a proportion of the price paid to the vendor. See further Bevan, *Land Law* (3rd edn, OUP 2022) Ch 2.

are two trustees, but one has appointed the other as his attorney so that the attorney is acting in two capacities—on his own behalf and on behalf of the trustee for whom he is attorney.[22]

3 Retirement of trustees

(1) Voluntary retirement of trustees

Once a trustee has been appointed and has taken up his office, he may subsequently wish to retire from the trust. It is possible for the trust to contain an express power permitting retirement, but s 39 of the Trustee Act 1925 provides a general power which is usually adequate:

> Where a trustee is desirous of being discharged from the trust, and after his discharge there will be either a trust corporation or at least two individuals to act as trustees to perform the trust, then, if such trustee as aforesaid by deed declares that he is desirous of being discharged from the trust, and if his co-trustees and such other person, if any, as is empowered to appoint trustees, by deed consent to the discharge of the trustee, and to the vesting in the co-trustees alone of the trust property, the trustee desirous of being discharged shall be deemed to have retired from the trust, and shall, by the deed, be discharged therefrom under this Act, without any new trustee being appointed in his place.

This provision permits the retirement of a trustee without a replacement being appointed, but this will only be possible if at least two trustees, or a trust corporation remain. Where these conditions are not satisfied, a trustee may retire and be replaced under the power contained in s 36 of the Trustee Act 1925, which is considered later in the chapter. Retirement will not protect a trustee from liability for breaches of trust that he committed whilst he was a trustee, and he will be liable for breaches of trust committed after his retirement if he retired to facilitate those breaches.[23]

(2) Compulsory retirement of trustees

Historically, trustees could not be forced to retire by the beneficiaries of a trust, no matter how much the beneficiaries may have wished to have them replaced, and they could only be forcibly removed on grounds of incapacity or maladministration. However, where the beneficiaries are of age and legally competent, it has been seen that they can demand that the trust be brought to an end under the rule in *Saunders v Vautier*.[24] If they wish, they could, therefore, effectively remove the trustees and replace them by settling the property on new trusts. This process may be both costly (including potential liability to additional tax) and inefficient, as it requires a transfer of the legal title to the trust property from the original trustees to the beneficiaries, and then from the beneficiaries to the new trustees. Consequently, the Trusts of Land and Appointment of Trustees Act 1996 introduced a new statutory power enabling the beneficiaries of a trust to require a trustee to retire in circumstances where they could have taken advantage of the rule in *Saunders v Vautier* to achieve the same result. By s 19(2)(a) of the Act, the beneficiaries of a trust may give a written direction to a trustee or trustees to retire from the trust.[25] This right is only

[22] Trustee Delegation Act 1999, s 7. The same applies where the attorney acts for two or more trustees and is not acting with another trustee.

[23] See Chapter 34. [24] [1841] 4 Beav 115.

[25] There must be a written direction—see *Malik v Kettle* [2020] EWHC 2568 (Ch), where an alleged appointment of a trustee was held invalid as this process had not been followed.

exercisable if there is no person nominated for the purpose of appointing new trustees by the trust instrument,[26] and if the beneficiaries of the trust are of full age and capacity and, taken together, are absolutely entitled to the property subject to the trust.[27] This means that the right to direct retirement will not be available where there are infant beneficiaries of the trust, which will often be the case in respect of a discretionary trust. Where a trustee has been directed to retire by the beneficiaries, s 19(3) provides that he will be required to make a deed declaring his retirement and shall be deemed to have retired and be discharged from the trust. However, he will only be required to retire if three conditions are satisfied:

(1) reasonable arrangements have been made for the protection of any rights he has in connection with the trust;[28]
(2) after he has retired there will be either a trust corporation or at least two persons to act as trustees to perform the trust;[29] and
(3) either another person is to be appointed a new trustee on his retirement, or the continuing trustees consent by deed to his retirement.[30]

The power to compulsorily retire trustees under s 19 enables the beneficiaries to defeat the intentions of the settlor, who may have intended that a specific individual act as trustee. This ability to undermine the settlor's express intentions is the inevitable consequence of the rule in *Saunders v Vautier*. A settlor can, however, expressly exclude the right to compulsorily retire trustees under s 19.[31] Where trusts have come into existence before the commencement of the Act, the power to direct retirement can be excluded by the execution of a deed to that effect by the settlor, or surviving settlors, who created the trust.[32] If such a deed is executed, it is irrevocable in effect.[33]

4 Appointing new trustees

(1) The need for new appointments

It is inevitable that in the lifetime of many trusts circumstances may arise where it is necessary to appoint new trustees.

(a) Appointment of additional trustees

It may be necessary or beneficial for the number of original trustees appointed by the settlor to be increased by the appointment of additional trustees. This may be because of the workload that the trustees are experiencing, or for simple reasons of convenience. In the case of land, if the settlor has created a trust for sale with a single trustee it may be necessary to appoint at least one additional trustee (or a trust corporation) so that, if the land is sold, the purchaser can gain the benefit of overreaching.[34]

[26] s 19(1)(a). [27] Trusts of Land and Appointment of Trustees Act 1996, s 19(1)(b).

[28] s 19(3)(b). This would include, for example, unpaid fees and expenses.

[29] s 19(3)(c). This is consistent with s 39 of the Trustee Act 1925.

[30] s 19(3)(d). In the event that the co-trustees refuse to consent to the retirement directed by the beneficiaries, the only means of removal of the trustee will be by order of the court exercising its jurisdiction under s 41 of the Trustee Act 1925. [31] s 21(5).

[32] Trusts of Land and Appointment of Trustees Act 1996, s 21(6). [33] s 21(7).

[34] The Trustee Delegation Act 1999, s 7, makes it clear that the 'two trustee' rule is not satisfied if all of the trustees are represented by a single person acting under a power of attorney, or where the same single person is both a trustee and acts under a power of attorney for the other trustees.

(b) Appointment of replacement trustees

It may be necessary to appoint new trustees as replacements for those who are no longer able to act as such, for example, because of death or mental incapacity, or who have retired from the trust.

(c) Removal of trustees

In some circumstances it may be necessary to remove a trustee from the trust against his will, for example, if he proves to be incompetent or is frustrating the efficient exercise of the trust.

(2) Power to appoint new trustees

Having recognized that there may be a need in some circumstances to appoint new trustees, the central question is how such appointments can be made: who has the power to select and appoint new trustees, and in what circumstances can such powers be exercised?

(a) Express powers

In keeping with the fundamental philosophy that, as far as possible the settlor's intentions will be carried out, the trust deed may contain an express power authorizing the appointment of new trustees by the settlor, by a protector, or by some other person or persons. Older cases suggest that such a power will be strictly construed,[35] although these cases may have been overtaken by more modern principles of interpretation. It remains clear that if an instrument describes a specific method for the appointment of trustees, a failure to comply with this method will be ineffective. So, in *Speechley v Allott*,[36] the purported appointment of trustees by a club at a meeting using a show of hands rather than the secret ballot required by the rules meant that the appointments were invalid. The failure was a matter of substance, not merely of form. There were also other failings of substance in the procedures used. The failure to follow the requirements for the appointment of trustees can be catastrophic, as is illustrated by *Briggs v Gleeds (Head Office)*,[37] since if trustees are not properly appointed, they do not become trustees and none of their purported acts as trustees will be effective.

There is some question whether the donee of such a power can appoint himself as trustee of the settlement. In *Re Skeats' Settlement*,[38] a trust contained an express power granting certain persons the power to appoint 'any other person' to be trustee. They exercised the power to appoint themselves. Kay J held that this was invalid since the power was fiduciary in character and it would thus be 'extremely improper for a person who has a power to appoint or select new trustees to appoint or select himself'.[39] This principle was followed by Kekewich J in *Re Newen*,[40] but was doubted by Buckley J in *Montefiore v Guedalla*,[41] where he stated that:

> On the cases, I am clearly of opinion that it has not been laid down that the appointors are outside the class who can be appointed, although it has been said, and it is a very salutary rule, than an appointor ought not, save in exceptional circumstances, to appoint himself.[42]

However, in *Re Sampson*,[43] Kekewich J considered that the decision in *Montefiore v Guedalla*[44] might require future reconsideration.[45]

35 *Stones v Rowton* [1853] 17 Beav 308; *Re Norris* [1884] 27 Ch D 333.
36 [2014] EWCA Civ 230.
37 [2014] EWHC 1178 (Ch).
38 [1889] 42 Ch D 522.
39 [1889] 42 Ch D 522 at 527.
40 [1894] 2 Ch 297.
41 [1903] 2 Ch 723.
42 [1903] 2 Ch 723 at 725.
43 [1906] 1 Ch 435.
44 [1903] 2 Ch 723.
45 *Re Sampson* concerned a statutory rather than an express power to appoint new trustees.

Express powers are commonplace, even though there are statutory powers modeled on the express powers which had previously been included in trust deeds. If there is an express power providing for the removal of trustees from the trust, s 36(2) of the Trustee Act 1925 applies, which provides:

> Where a trustee has been removed under a power contained in the instrument creating the trust, a new trustee or trustees may be appointed in the place of the trustee who is removed, as if he were dead, or, in the case of a corporation, as if the corporation desired to be discharged from the trust, and the provisions of this section shall apply accordingly, but subject to the restriction imposed by this act on the number of trustees.

(b) **Statutory powers**

There are three important statutory provisions granting the power of appointment of new trustees.

(i) Trustee Act 1925, s 36

This section provides for the appointment of new trustees in a wide range of circumstances by persons either nominated in the trust deed by the settlor, or, in the absence of any such nomination, by the persons provided for by the section. The intervention of the court is not required for appointments made under the power contained in s 36.

(ii) Trustee Act 1925, s 41

This section grants the court a wide power to appoint new trustees either in addition to or in substitution for present trustees. The power is discretionary and may be exercised whenever the court considers it is expedient.

(iii) Trusts of Land and Appointment of Trustees Act 1996, ss 19 and 20

It has already been noted how the Trusts of Land and Appointment of Trustees Act 1996 has introduced a new statutory right enabling the beneficiaries of a trust to direct the compulsory retirement of a trustee. Section 19(2)(b) also grants the beneficiaries the right to direct the appointment of new trustees, and s 20 provides for the appointment of a replacement trustee where a trustee is mentally incapable of acting and there is no person willing and able to appoint a replacement under s 36(1) of the Trustee Act 1925.

5 Trustee Act 1925, s 36

(1) **Appointing substitute trustees**

(a) **The power to appoint substitute trustees**

The Trustee Act 1925, s 36(1) provides:

> Where a trustee, either original or substituted, and whether appointed by a court or otherwise, is dead, or remains out of the United Kingdom for more than twelve months, or desires to be discharged from all or any of the trusts or powers reposed in or conferred on him, or refuses or is unfit to act therein, or is incapable of acting therein, or is an infant, then subject to the restrictions imposed by this Act on the number of trustees–
>
> (a) the person or persons nominated for the purpose of appointing new trustees by the instrument, if any, creating the trust; or
> (b) if there is no such person, or no such person able and willing to act, then the surviving or continuing trustees or trustee for the time being, or the personal representatives of the last surviving or continuing trustee;

may, by writing, appoint one or more other person (whether or not being the persons exercising the power) to be a trustee or trustees in the place of the trustee so deceased, remaining out of the United Kingdom, desiring to be discharged from the trust, and the provisions of this section shall apply accordingly, but subject to the restrictions imposed by this Act on the number of trustees.

(b) Circumstances in which the power may be exercised

Section 36 provides that the power to appoint new trustees may be exercised in seven well-defined circumstances, which cover many of the most likely situations in which new trustees would need to be appointed. It is to be noted that s 36 applies only to trustees and not to personal representatives.[46] An improper appointment not made in compliance with the statutory powers is invalid, so that no substitution takes place and the original trustees remain in office (or their personal representatives).[47]

(i) The trustee is dead

By s 36(8) the power of appointment under s 36(1) is also exercisable where a person who is nominated trustee in a will predeceases the testator. There is some authority[48] that the sections will also be operative in the unlikely event that the settlor attempts an inter vivos transfer to a trustee who is already dead. However, this will only be the case if the dead trustee was one of a number of others who were alive, since an attempt by the settlor to transfer property inter vivos to trustees who are all dead will not create a trust in the first place.

(ii) The trustee remains out of the United Kingdom for more than 12 months

The rationale for this provision was that the limited and slow means of communication and travel would prevent a trustee who was absent from the country from being able to properly carry out the trust business. It is possible under s 25 of the Trustee Act 1925 for a trustee to delegate his managerial functions and discretions by a power of attorney for up to twelve months, for instance, during absence abroad.[49] Today, with such instant means of communication as email, telephone, and fax, and with the availability of rapid air transport, it is questionable whether the absence of a trustee abroad inevitably prevents him from conducting the business of the trust. The absence from the UK must be for a continuous period of twelve months. In *Re Walker*[50] Mr Walker was co-trustee of a settlement with Mrs Walker. He was out of the UK for more than a year from spring 1899, with the exception of one week in London in November 1899. In these circumstances Farwell J held that Mrs Walker could not exercise the power of appointment under what is now s 36(1).[51] The power enables a trustee to be removed against his will, as was held by Danckwerts J in *Re Stoneham's Settlement Trusts*.[52]

(iii) The trustee desires to be discharged from all or any of the trusts or powers reposed in or conferred on him

This provision means that a trustee can be discharged from only part of his trust responsibility, which prior to the Act was only possible through the court.[53]

[46] See *Re Cockburn's Will Trust* [1957] Ch 438; *Re King's Will Trusts* [1964] Ch 542. However, the court has power to appoint a substituted person representative under the Administration of Justice Act 1985, s 50.

[47] See *Jasmine Trustees Ltd v Wells & Hind (A Firm)* [2008] Ch 194 at 216, 52, per Mann J.

[48] See *Re Hadley* [1851] 5 De G & Sm 67.

[49] Discussed in Chapter 30.

[50] [1901] 1 Ch 259.

[51] Previously, Trustee Act 1893, s 10.

[52] [1953] Ch 59.

[53] See *Savile v Couper* [1887] 36 Ch D 520; *Re Moss's Trusts* [1888] 37 Ch D 513.

(iv) The trustee refuses to act

This clearly covers the case where a trustee disclaims the trust.

(v) The trustee is unfit or incapable

This refers to any personal incapacity that would prevent the trustee acting as such. It clearly includes mental incapacity, so in *Re East*[54] the court held that there was a valid exercise of a power to appoint new trustees where one of three co-trustees lost mental capacity.[55] Similarly, in *Re Lemann's Trust*,[56] age and infirmity were considered sufficient 'incapacity'. A trustee will also be considered unfit to act if he is bankrupt, as was held in *Re Wheeler and De Rochow*.[57] It seems that a trustee is not unfit to act merely through absence abroad.[58] However, in *Mesnard v Welford*,[59] a trustee who had been absent in New York for twenty years was held to be incapable of acting for the purposes of an express power of appointment.[60] The cases holding that a trustee resident overseas may be incapable of acting all date from the nineteenth century, and improvements in communications and in the speed of international travel cast their current reliability into doubt.[61] In the case of the dissolution of a corporate trustee, s 36(3) provides:

> Where a corporation being a trustee is or has been dissolved then, for the purposes of this section the corporation shall be deemed to be and to have been from the date of the dissolution incapable of acting in the trusts or powers reposed in or conferred on the corporation.

(vi) The trustee is an infant

Such an eventuality is only likely to arise in respect of a constructive or resulting trust of personal property, since in other cases the appointment of an infant as trustee is void.[62]

(vii) The trustee has been removed under an express power

If the trust instrument includes an express provision for the removal of trustees, any trustee who is so removed may be replaced under the powers of appointment of s 36 as if he were a trustee who had died.[63]

(c) Persons who may exercise the power to appoint new trustees

In addition to defining the circumstances in which new trustees may be appointed, s 36 of the Trustee Act also specifies who is to make any such appointments. The section adopts an order of priority as to who can exercise the power. It emphasizes the settlor's intentions by giving priority to any person nominated for the purpose in the trust instrument, but provides alternative mechanisms for appointment if there is no such person nominated.

54 [1873] 8 Ch App 735. The phrase used at the time was that he became of unsound mind.

55 It is possible for a trustee to execute a lasting power of attorney before becoming of unsound mind that has the effect of delegating to an agent his functions as a trustee of land and which operates in the event of his incapacity: Trustee Delegation Act 1999, s 1. See generally Mental Capacity Act 2005, ss 9–14 for the distinction between enduring powers of attorney (which have been repealed) and lasting powers of attorney (which must be registered to be effective).

56 [1883] 22 Ch D 633.

57 [1896] 1 Ch 315. See also *Re Roche* [1842] 1 Con & Law 306; *Re Hopkins* [1881] 19 Ch D 61.

58 See *Withington v Withington* [1848] 16 Sim 104; *O'Reilly v Alderson* [1849] 8 Hare 101; *Re Harrison's Trusts* [1852] 22 LJ Ch 69; *Re Bignold's Settlement Trusts* [1872] 7 Ch App 223.

59 [1853] 1 Sm & G 426.

60 See also *Re Lemann's Trusts* [1883] 22 Ch D 633, where Chitty J gave the residence of a trustee abroad as one instance of incapacity.

61 See the remarks by Millett J in *Richard v Mackay* [1997] 11 TLI 22.

62 Law of Property Act 1925, s 20.

63 s 36(2).

(i) The person or persons nominated by the trust instrument

By s 36(1)(a), if the settlor has nominated a person or persons in the instrument creating the trust to exercise the power of appointment of new trustees, then it is they who can exercise the power to appoint under s 36(1). Such persons only fall within s 36(1) if they have a general power to make appointments[64] and not a power which is only granted in specific circumstances. In *Re Sichel's Settlements*,[65] the nominated persons were given the power to appoint new trustees in the event of the present trustees becoming 'incapable to act'. Neville J held, following the decision of Kekewick J in *Re Wheeler and De Rochow*,[66] that they were not the appropriate persons to appoint a new trustee where one of the existing trustees was 'unfit' to act. Where several persons are jointly nominated, in the absence of a contrary intention[67] the survivor or survivors cannot exercise the power.[68] In that event, the power to appoint will be exercisable by those indicted in s 36(1). The same result will follow if the nominated persons are incapable of acting, for example because of disagreement.[69]

(ii) The surviving or continuing trustee or trustees

If there are no persons nominated in the trust instrument, or if such persons are unable or unwilling to act, s 36(1)(b) provides that it is the 'surviving or continuing trustee or trustees for the time being' who may appoint new trustees. It has been held that the last surviving or continuing trustee includes a sole trustee.[70] The central difficulty concerns the questions as to who are the 'continuing trustees' where it is intended to remove a trustee who is alive and capable, since it is a basic principle that trustees must act with unanimity. It would prove impossible to remove a trustee against his will if he was to be regarded as a 'continuing trustee' and, therefore, had to be party to the decision to remove and replace him. The position is complicated by s 36(8), which provides that the continuing trustees include 'a refusing or retiring trustee, if willing to act in the execution of the provisions of this section'. This has the effect that a retiring sole trustee or retiring group of trustees are able to appoint their successors, although s 37(1) (c) means that two retiring trustees cannot be replaced by one, not being a trust corporation.[71] Whether a trustee should be regarded as 'refusing or retiring' was considered by Danckwerts J in *Re Stoneham's Settlement Trusts*.[72] He took the general view that a trustee who is being removed from the trust is not retiring and therefore does not fall within the scope of s 36(8):

[64] *Re Walker and Hughes' Contract* [1883] 24 Ch D 698.

[65] [1916] 1 Ch 358.

[66] [1896] 1 Ch 315. However, he did express his disagreement with the decision.

[67] *Re Harding* [1923] 1 Ch 182.

[68] This is subject to the exceptions that the survivors can exercise the power if the property is vested in them (*Re Bacon* [1907] 1 Ch 475), they hold the power as trustees (Trustee Act 1925, s 18(1)), or the power was granted to a class of which two or more members survive (*Jefferys v Marshall* [1870] 19 WR 94).

[69] *Re Sheppard's Settlement Trust* [1888] WN 234. Alternatively, because they cannot be found: *Cradock v Witham* [1895] WN 75.

[70] *Re Shafto's Trusts* [1885] 29 Ch D 247. *Adam and Company International Trustees Ltd v Theodore Goddard (a firm)* [2000] WTLR 349; A Barlow, 'The Appointment of Trustees: A Disappointing Decision' [2003] Conv 15. See also *Jasmine Trustees Ltd v Wells & Hind (A Firm)* [2008] Ch 194, where it was held by Mann J that, in a trust subject to the older version of the wording of s 37(1)(c) existing before 1 January 1997, a company was not to be classed as a trustee, as it was not an 'individual' as required under the old wording of s 37(1)(c). The statutory provision now talks of 'persons' (following amendment by the Trust of Land and Appointment of Trustees Act 1996, Sch 3) and a company is a legal person.

[71] *Adam and Company International Trustees Ltd v Theodore Goddard (a firm)* [2000] WTLR 349; Barlow, 'The Appointment of Trustees: A Disappointing Decision' [2003] Conv 15.

[72] [1953] Ch 59.

> It seems to me, in the absence of any authority which binds me to decide otherwise, that a person who is compulsorily removed from a trust is not a person who retires and is not a retiring trustee.

Similarly, following *Re Coates to Parsons*,[73] he held that a trustee who has been abroad for more than twelve months was not a 'refusing or retiring trustee' within the meaning of s 38, and that, therefore, he was not a 'continuing trustee' and his concurrence was not needed for the appointment of a new trustee.

(iii) The personal representatives of the last surviving or continuing trustee

As a last resort, if there are no nominated persons who can make new appointments and there are no 'surviving or continuing' trustees, the statute pragmatically provides in s 36(1)(a) that the 'personal representatives of the last surviving or continuing trustee' have the power to appoint new trustees.

(d) No one is able to appoint a substitute trustee

In some extreme circumstances, even where there is a jurisdiction to appoint a substitute trustee under s 36 there will be no one who is capable of exercising it. Such a problem is especially likely where property is held by a sole trustee who has become mentally incapable. Since a sole incapable trustee is a surviving trustee, he alone is entitled to exercise the power to appoint a substitute for himself, and yet is incapable of so doing. In such circumstances where the power to appoint under s 36 is moribund, the court may exercise its jurisdiction to appoint new trustees under s 41. The Trusts of Land and Appointment of Trustees Act 1996 has conferred upon the beneficiaries of the trust the right to direct the appointment of a substitute. This jurisdiction is examined later in this chapter.

(2) Appointing additional trustees

(a) The power to appoint additional trustees

The Trustee Act 1925, s 36(6)[74] also provides for the appointment of additional trustees:

> Where, in the case of any trust, there are not more than three trustees—
>
> (a) the person or persons nominated for the purpose of appointing new trustees by the instrument, if any, creating the trust; or
>
> (b) if there is no such person, or no such person able and willing to act, then the trustee or trustees for the time being;
>
> may, by writing appoint another person or other persons to be an additional trustee or additional trustees, but it shall not be obligatory to appoint any additional trustees, unless the instrument, if any creating the trust, or any statutory enactment provides to the contrary, nor shall the number of trustees be increased beyond four by virtue of any such appointment.

(b) Circumstances in which the power may be exercised

Section 36(6) gives the trustee of a trust the option to increase the number of trustees to a maximum of four through the appointment of additional trustees. This power is subject to any express terms in the trust or by statute requiring the number of trustees to be increased.

[73] [1886] 34 Ch D 370.

[74] As amended by Trusts of Land and Appointment of Trustees Act 1996, Sch 3, para 3(11).

(c) Persons who may appoint additional trustees

The mechanisms by which such appointments may be made are almost identical to those adopted under s 36(1).

(i) The person or persons nominated by the trust instrument

Priority is given to the settlor's express intention in the form of persons nominated for the purpose of appointing trustees in the trust instrument. Providing they are willing and able to act, they alone can exercise the power.

(ii) The trustee or trustees for the time being

In the absence of any nominated persons the other trustees, whether a sole trustee or co-trustees, may appoint additional trustees. Obviously, if there are no trustees remaining because of death, the provisions of s 36(1) will operate. A limited power is available to the donee of an unregistered enduring power of attorney[75] or a registered lasting[76] power of attorney to exercise the functions of the trustees to appoint a new trustee if to do so is necessary to ensure that there are two trustees to receive capital money arising from a disposition of land.[77]

(3) Making appointments under s 36

(a) Persons who may be appointed

In the case of substitute appointments, under s 36(1), the persons who may exercise the power can appoint whoever they desire as trustees and it is specifically provided that they may appoint themselves if they wish. However, owing to a slight difference in drafting, persons who are nominated to appoint additional trustees are not specifically permitted to appoint themselves under s 36(6), and, in *Re Power's Settlement*,[78] it has been held that they cannot appoint themselves. Where there are already two trustees, it is not possible for them to retire and to be replaced by a single trustee, unless that trustee is a trust corporation recognized under English law.[79]

(b) Relevance of the beneficiaries' wishes

The person (or persons) entitled to appoint new trustees is under no obligation to consult the beneficiaries of the trust and ascertain their wishes as to who should be appointed. In *Re Brockbank*[80] Vaisey J held that the person entitled to appoint under s 36 could not be compelled to do what the beneficiaries wanted, as the right to appoint belonged solely to those whom it was given by the statute and the court was unwilling to interfere with its exercise.[81] The only means by which the beneficiaries could compel the appointment of the persons they wanted to be trustees would be to put an end to the trust[82] under the rule in *Saunders v Vautier* or to make a direction under the Trusts of Land and Appointment of Trustees Act 1996.[83] The power to make a direction under the 1996 Act does not apply if the person entitled to appoint new trustees was nominated by the trust instrument.

[75] It is no longer possible to create enduring powers of attorney, although existing unregistered powers may still be used, if registered—Mental Capacity Act 2005, Sch 4, Pt 1 para 1.

[76] Added by the Mental Capacity Act 2005.

[77] Trustee Act 1925, s 36(6A)–(6D), as inserted by the Trustee Delegation Act 1999.

[78] [1951] Ch 1074, CA.

[79] See *Adam and Co International Trustees Ltd v Theodore Goddard* (2000) ITELR 634.

[80] [1948] Ch 206.

[81] See also *Re Gadd* [1883] 23 Ch D 134; *Re Higginbottom* [1892] 3 Ch 132.

[82] [1948] Ch 206 at 210.

[83] s 19. This jurisdiction is discussed later in this chapter.

(c) **Formalities of appointment**

The appointment of new trustees, whether substitute trustees under s 36(1) or additional trustees under s 36(6), must be made in writing. However, an appointment made by deed will have the effect of vesting the trust property in the new trustees under s 40 of the Trustee Act 1925, subject to registration of the trustees as legal owners in the case of land and shares.

(d) **Effect of appointment Section 36(7) provides that:**

> Every new trustee appointed under this section as well before as after all the trust property becomes by law, or by assurance, or otherwise vested in him, shall have the same powers, authorities and discretions, and may in all respects act as if he had been originally appointed a trustee by the instrument, if any, creating the trust.

This provision applies equally to the appointment of additional or substitute trustees.

6 Trustee Act 1925, s 41

(1) **The power of the court to appoint new trustees**

Section 41(1) of the Trustee Act 1925 provides:

> The court may, whenever it is expedient to appoint a new trustee or new trustees, and if it is found inexpedient difficult or impracticable so to do without the assistance of the court, make an order appointing a new trustee or new trustees either in substitution for or in addition to any existing trustee or trustees, or although there is no existing trustee.

(2) **Scope of the power under s 41**

This provision gives the court a very wide discretion to appoint trustees, either in substitution for, or in addition to, existing trustees. However, a number of features should be noted.

(a) **Relation to other powers of appointment of trustees**

Appointments will generally only be made under the jurisdiction of s 41 where they cannot be made through the exercise of an express power within the trust instrument, nor under the statutory power granted by s 36 of the Trustee Act 1925.[84]

(b) **'Whenever it is expedient to appoint ... if it is found inexpedient, difficult or impractical so to do without the assistance of the court'**

This double-limbed test sets down the circumstances in which the court may exercise the power of appointment. It must be both expedient for a substitute or additional trustee to be appointed and in some sense, because of the circumstances, the assistance of the court must be necessary. Section 41(1) itself specifies some such circumstances where the jurisdiction may need to be exercised:

> In particular ... the court may make an order appointing a new trustee in substitution for a trustee who lacks capacity[85] to exercise his functions as a trustee or is a bankrupt, or is a corporation which is in liquidation or has been dissolved.

[84] *Re Soulby's Trusts* [1873] 21 WR 256; *Re Gibbon's Trusts* [1882] 45 LT 756; *Re Sutton* [1885] WN 122.
[85] The words were substituted for the original wording of the statute by the Mental Capacity Act 2005.

A number of illustrations can be given of other circumstances in which the power has been exercised. In *Re Smirthwaite's Trust*,[86] the court exercised its statutory power[87] to appoint new trustees when all of the trustees named in the settlor's will had predeceased him. In *Re May's Will Trust*,[88] one of three trustees of a will was in Belgium during the time of the German invasion and had not escaped. It was held that there was no evidence that she was 'incapable of acting' within the meaning of s 36(1) so that she could not be replaced by the continuing trustees, but the court appointed a new trustee under s 41. The court may also act where an express power or the power under s 36 is incapable of being exercised, for example if the donee of an express power is an infant.[89] In *Re Rendell's Trusts*,[90] the court exercised its power to appoint a trustee where one of the surviving trustees was opposed to the appointment.

(c) Removal of trustees against their will

It is clear that s 41 permits the court to remove trustees from the trust against their will. In *Re Henderson* Bennet J stated:

> I do not think that it is open to doubt that on the language of the sub-section the court has jurisdiction to displace a trustee against his will and to appoint a new trustee in substitution for him. Take the case of a trustee who is a convicted felon or a bankrupt whom the beneficiaries desire to have replaced by a new trustee. On the language of the sub-section, in my judgement, the court has a discretion, which it can exercise, if it regards it as expedient so to do, by appointing a new trustee in place of the trustee who has been convicted of felony, or who is a bankrupt ... I do not doubt that the section gives the court jurisdiction in a proper case to appoint new trustees in place of and against the will of an existing trustee. Before exercising that jurisdiction the court must be satisfied that it is expedient to make such an appointment.[91]

He held that a trustee who had refused to retire in place of the Public Trustee should be removed against her will because she had previously agreed to retire but had changed her mind for no reason of substance. This was followed by Roxburgh J, in *Re Solicitor, A*,[92] where a bankrupt solicitor was replaced by the court acting under s 41.

One limitation to the principle that the court can remove a trustee against his will under s 41 is that there must be no dispute as to the facts. This was emphasized by Cotton LJ in *Re Combs*[93] and accepted by Bennet J in *Re Henderson*.[94]

(3) Exercise of the court's discretion

The court's power to appoint under s 41 is discretionary, and it must be satisfied that any appointments are 'expedient'. The way in which the court's discretion should be exercised has arisen in many cases. The principles are in general the same, whatever the basis of the court's discretion, but there are some special considerations which apply to s 41.

(a) Is an appointment expedient?

The question whether an appointment was 'expedient' was raised in *Re Weston's Settlement*,[95] where there was an attempt to move a trust from England to Jersey for tax reasons, and to replace the English trustees with trustees in Jersey. Applications were made under the Variation of Trusts Act 1958 in favour of the infant beneficiaries of the

86 [1871] LR 11 Eq 251. 87 Under the Trustee Act 1850. 88 [1941] Ch 109.
89 *Re Parson's* [1940] Ch 973. 90 [1915] 139 LT Jo 249.
91 [1940] Ch 764 at 767. 92 [1952] Ch 328. 93 [1884] 51 LT 45.
94 [1940] Ch 764. See also *Popoff v Actus Management Ltd* [1985] 5 WWR 660. 95 [1969] 1 Ch 223.

trust and under s 41 for the appointment of new trustees. The court refused to exercise its discretion under either of these provisions. As to s 41, Lord Denning MR said:

> with the appointment of new trustees the Trustee Act 1925 gives no guide. It simply says that the court may appoint new trustees 'whenever it is expedient'. There being no guidance in the statute, it remains for the court to do the best it can.[96]

Several reasons for the refusal of the court to appoint appear from the judgment. First, the proposed move of the trust to Jersey was solely for reasons of tax avoidance. Second, there was a relatively slight connection between the beneficiaries and Jersey. They had lived there for only a short time, and there was a high probability that they would move after the trust had been transferred. As Harman LJ said, they 'cannot be said to have proved that they truly intend to make Jersey their home'.[97] Third, the court referred to the inadequacy of the law in Jersey (at that date) for dealing with trusts. In these circumstances the court refused to appoint trustees, and instead held that 'these are English settlements and they should remain so unless some good reason connected with the trusts themselves can be put forward.'[98]

(b) Should overseas trustees be appointed?

It is unlikely that the reluctance in *Re Weston's Settlement* to appoint overseas trustees would be applied today. At around the same date, in *Re Windeatt's Will Trusts*,[99] the court was willing to approve a scheme for the variation of a trust, including the appointment of new trustees in Jersey, where the family had lived for some nineteen years. Such a strong local connection would probably have made a difference in *Re Weston's Settlement*. Moreover, given the significant improvement in communications, and the increased recognition of trusts overseas, it is likely that the courts would now be more willing to entertain the appointment of trustees.[100] In *Richard v The Hon A B Mackay*,[101] Millett J suggested that where trustees were exercising their own discretion to appoint an overseas trustee and seek merely approval from the court, the court should only need to be satisfied that the decision was 'not so inappropriate that no reasonable trustee could entertain it'. He recognized that social conditions had moved on and that international families with international interests 'are as likely to make their home in one country as in another and as likely to choose one jurisdiction as another for the investment of their capital'. The court should not act in a way that frustrated this.

(c) General principles

The court will not remove a trustee simply because that trustee does not have the confidence of the beneficiaries. In *Fielden v Stephen Christie-Miller*,[102] Sir William Blackburne refused to remove trustees at the request of some of the beneficiaries who thought that they had not acted sufficiently independently, a claim evidenced by the trustees having opposed them in litigation. Sir William commented:

> I do not consider that a trustee's duty of neutrality as between the beneficiaries for whose benefit he holds the trust fund requires him to take no position when his own conduct is called into question.

The replacement of a trustee will normally be the right course of action where there is a genuine conflict of interest on the part of one or more trustees or where the relationship between the trustees, or possibly between the trustees and the principal beneficiaries, has

[96] [1969] 1 Ch 223 at 245. [97] Ibid at 248. [98] Ibid at 284. [99] [1969] 1 WLR 692.
[100] See *Re Beatty's WT (No 2)* [1997] 11 TLI 77; *Richard v Mackay* [1997] 11 TLI 22 (decided 1987).
[101] [1997] 11 TLI 22. [102] [2015] EWHC 2940 (Ch) at 55.

completely broken down. For example, in *James v Williams, Re Weetman (deceased)*,[103] the settlor had created a trust under which 50 per cent of the shares in a family company were to be held on trust for the workforce, with the remainder on trust for the family. There had been a breakdown in the relationship between the family trustees and two other trustees who were regarded by the family as having taken sides against them. It was ordered that those trustees should be replaced. Likewise, in *Brudenell-Bruce v Moore*,[104] Newey J ordered the replacement of a trustee who had made unauthorized claims for payment and who had completely fallen out with the principal beneficiary, even though the lion's share of responsibility for that breakdown could be attributed to the beneficiary. Another trustee with whom the beneficiary had fallen out should remain because relationships between the two were nowhere near as bad.

The main driver in making decisions appears to be the impact which retaining or replacing the trustee will have on the proper administration of the trust. In *Scott v Scott*, the two trustees had fallen out, and each applied for the removal of the other. Deputy High Court Judge Behrens held that the hostility between the two trustees was insufficient to justify a removal unless it was, or might, hinder the administration of the trust. The trustee who should remain had been selected by the settlor, had been a trustee for a number of years, and would be able to deal with potential complexities which the trust might experience in the near future. The other trustee, who should be removed, had made stale and unfounded allegations about the other, and had unreasonably failed to concur in some trust decisions. That trustee's hostility was affecting the welfare of the beneficiaries.[105]

The court, as part of its inherent jurisdiction over trusts, has the power to make a direction as to the manner in which trustees should exercise their powers. That does not involve any replacement of the trustees, who will all be bound by the court order.[106]

(4) Persons the court will appoint trustees

(a) General principles guiding the court's selection

In *Re Tempest*,[107] which concerned the appointment of new trustees under a predecessor to s 41,[108] the Court of Appeal laid down three criteria that the court will apply in exercising its discretion to appoint new trustees. These criteria (which align with the general principles just described for whether a trustee should be removed) were set out by Turner LJ.

(i) Regard to the wishes of the settlor

> First, the court will have regard to the wishes of the persons by whom the trust has been created, if expressed in the instrument creating the trust, or clearly to be collected from it.[109]

(ii) Regard to the interests of the beneficiaries

> Another rule which may, I think, safely be laid down is this—that the court will not appoint a person to be a trustee with a view to the interest of some of the persons interested under the trust, in opposition either to the wishes of the testator or to the interests of the other cestuis que trust. I think so for this reason that it is of the essence of the duty of every trustee to hold an even hand between the parties interested under a trust.[110]

103 [2015] EWHC 1166 (Ch). 104 [2014] EWHC 3679 (Ch).

105 See also *Nwosu v Nwosu* [2018] EWHC 1520 (Ch) (substitute executor appointed, as an impasse had been reached, and the effective administration of the trust would otherwise be impeded).

106 *Crick v Crick* [2015] EWCA Civ 826 at 11. 107 [1866] 1 Ch App 485.

108 Trustee Act 1850. 109 [1866] 1 Ch App 485 at 487. 110 [1866] 1 Ch App 485 at 487.

(iii) Regard to the effective execution of the trust

> A third rule which, I think, may safely be laid down is this—that the court in appointing a trustee will have regard to the question, whether his appointment will promote or impede the execution of the trust, for the very purpose of the appointment is that the trust may be better carried into execution.[111]

(iv) Applying the principles

The Court of Appeal held that the proposed trustee, Mr Petre, should not be appointed. Although there could be no objection to him 'in point of character, position or ability', he fell foul of the rules proposed. First, he was the nominee of the beneficiary of the trust, Charles Tempest, and the testator's intentions had been to exclude him 'from all connection with his estate'. Second, the court considered that he had been:

> proposed as a trustee ... with a view to his acting in the trust in the interests of some only of the objects of it ... and not with a view to his acting as an independent trustee for the benefit of all the objects of the trusts.

In *Alkin v Raymond*,[112] the High Court refused to appoint the testator's daughter to the trust to replace existing trustees on the basis that it was against the wishes of her father as testator and that it would not be effective for the administration of the estate, as it would be difficult for her to hold a reasonably objective balance between the competing claims to the estate.

(b) Persons the court will not normally appoint trustees

There are some persons who, irrespective of their abilities, the court will not normally appoint as trustees because of their relationship to the trust and the likelihood of a conflict of interest. The court will not appoint, except in exceptional circumstances,[113] a beneficiary or a beneficiary's spouse as trustee,[114] nor the solicitor to the life tenant or the solicitor to an existing trustee.[115] Nor, according to a number of cases, will the court appoint a person living abroad unless the trust's property or the beneficiaries are also abroad,[116] although it may be that this attitude is changing.[117]

7 Trusts of Land and Appointment of Trustees Act 1996

(1) Appointment of trustees at the direction of the beneficiaries

It has been seen that ss 36 and 41 of the Trustee Act 1925 provide mechanisms for the appointment of new trustees, whether additional or replacement, in specified circumstances. However, in neither case do the beneficiaries of the trust have the right to require

[111] [1866] 1 Ch App 485 at 488. [112] [2010] WTLR 117.

[113] For example, where no independent person can he found to take up the office: *Ex p Clutton* [1853] 17 Jur 988; *Re Clissold's Settlement* [1864] 10 LT 642; *Re Burgess' Trusts* [1877] WN 87; *Re Parrott* [1881] 30 WR 97; *Re Lightbody's Trusts* [1884] 33 WR 452.

[114] *Ex p Clutton* [1853] 17 Jur 988; *Ex p Conybeare's Settlement* [1853] 1 WR 458; *Re Orde* [1883] 24 Ch D 271; *Re Kemp's Settled Estate* [1883] 24 Ch D 485, CA; *Re Coode* [1913] 108 LT 94.

[115] *Re Kemp's Settled Estates* [1883] 24 Ch D 485 27; *Re Norris* [1884] 27 Ch D 333; *Re Earl of Stamford* [1896] 1 Ch 288; *Re Spencer's Settled Estates* [1903] 1 Ch 75.

[116] *Re Guibert's Trust Estate* [1852] 16 Jur 852; *Re Hill's Trusts* [1874] WN 228; *Re Drewe's Settlement Trusts* [1876] WN 168; *Re Freeman's Settlement Trusts* [1887] 37 Ch D 148; *Re Liddiard* [1880] 14 Ch D 310; *Re Whitehead's Will Trusts* [1971] 1 WLR 833.

[117] See *Re Beatty's WT (No 2)* [1997] 11 TLI 77; *Richard v Mackay* [1997] 11 TLI 22.

the appointment of a specific person as a trustee, as the right to appoint is vested in either other persons (the surviving or continuing trustees, or the personal representatives of the last surviving trustee) or the court. However, the Trusts of Land and Appointment of Trustees Act 1996, s 19, has granted the beneficiaries of a trust the right to direct the appointment of new trustees. Section 19(2)(b) provides that the beneficiaries can give:

> a written direction to the trustees or trustee for the time being (or, if there are none, to the personal representative of the last person who was a trustee) to appoint by writing to be a trustee or trustees the person or persons specified in the direction.

As in the case of the power to direct the retirement of trustees, this right to direct appointment can only be exercised if the beneficiaries would otherwise be entitled to take advantage of the rule in *Saunders v Vautier*[118] because they are of age, legally competent, and collectively entitled to the trust property.[119] The right to direct appointments is also excluded if the trust instrument expressly nominates a person for the purpose of appointing new trustees,[120] or if the right has been expressly excluded.[121] The beneficiaries' right to direct the appointment of new trustees cannot be exercised so as to appoint more than the maximum number of trustees permitted under the Trustee Act 1925.[122]

Problems remain concerning the practical implementation of the beneficiaries' right to direct the appointment of new trustees. Whereas s 19(3) makes clear that a trustee who is directed to retire must do so, there is no equivalent provision requiring the trustees (or the personal representative of the last surviving trustee) to carry into effect a direction to appoint. If the trustees are required to make the directed appointment, it is unclear whether they would be liable if the person nominated by the beneficiaries was unsuitable and the trust suffered a loss in consequence of the appointment. Presumably, the appointing trustees would be exempt from any liability for breach of trust in such circumstances because the appointment would have been made at the unanimous instigation of the beneficiaries.

(2) Appointment of a substitute for a mentally incapable trustee

It has already been noted that, where a trustee has become mentally incapable, the right to appoint a substitute trustee may have become moribund. This may be because the persons enjoying the right to appoint, whether under an express power or under s 36 of the Trustee Act 1925, are unwilling to do so, or because there is no one entitled to appoint a substitute: for example, where there is a sole trustee who has become incapable and the trust instrument does not include an express power of appointment. In order to facilitate the appointment of a substitute without the need for the court to intervene, s 20(2) of the Trusts of Land and Appointment of Trustees Act 1996 (as amended by the Mental Capacity Act 2005) provides that the beneficiaries of the trust may give 'a written direction to appoint by writing the person or persons specified in the direction to be a trustee or trustees in place of the incapable trustee'. The right to give such a direction only arises where a trustee lacks capacity to exercise his functions as trustee,[123] and there is no person who is both entitled and willing and able to appoint a trustee in place of him under s 36(1) of the Trustee Act 1925.[124] The right to direct an appointment in

[118] [1841] 4 Beav 115. [119] s 19(1)(b). [120] s 19(1)(a). [121] s 21(5)–(8).

[122] Trusts of Land and Appointment of Trustees Act 1996, s 19(5).

[123] s 20(1)(a). Capacity is defined under the Mental Capacity Act 2005, ss 1 and 2. [124] s 20(1)(b).

such circumstances is only conferred upon the beneficiaries if they would otherwise be entitled to take advantage of the rule in *Saunders v Vautier*: they are of age, legally competent, and collectively entitled to the trust property.[125] The direction to appoint must be made to either a receiver of the incapable trustee,[126] or a person acting for him under an enduring or lasting power of attorney,[127] or a person with authority to act under the Court of Protection.[128] The beneficiaries' right to direct an appointment under s 20 may be expressly excluded in the trust instrument,[129] or, in the case of a trust created before the commencement of the Act, may be excluded by the execution of a deed to that effect by all the surviving settlors.[130]

8 Appointment of special trustees

A number of statutory provisions provide for the appointment of special trustees.

(1) Judicial Trustees Act 1896

(a) Nature of a judicial trustee

A judicial trustee is a trustee appointed by the court under s 1 of the Judicial Trustees Act 1896. The person appointed a judicial trustee is an officer of the court and is, therefore, subject to its control and supervision. The purpose of appointing a judicial trustee is to ensure the proper execution of the trust, but without incurring the full expense of having the trust administered by the court. This was explained by Jenkins J in *Re Ridsdel*:[131]

> The object of the Judicial Trustees Act 1896 ... was to provide a middle course in cases where the administration of the estate by the ordinary trustees had broken down, and it was not desired to put the estate to the expense of a full administration of the estate ... a solution was found in the appointment of a judicial trustee, who acts in close concert with the court and under conditions enabling the court to supervise his transactions.[132]

Although the judicial trustee may be given special directions by the court, and he may apply for the court's directions in his decisions, the purpose is not to 'reduce the administration of an estate by a judicial trustee to very much the same position as where an estate is being administered by the court and every step has to be taken in pursuance of the court's directions'.[133]

The appointment of a judicial trustee was particularly important prior to the enactment of s 50 of the Administration of Justice Act 1985, since it was the only way that a personal representative could be replaced. Although a judicial trustee is largely in the same position as any other trustee, for example he has the power to compromise claims,[134] he cannot appoint his successor under the provisions of s 36 of the Trustee Act 1925.

[125] s 20(1)(c). [126] s 20(2)(a). [127] s 20(2)(b).

[128] s 20(2)(c) (as amended by the Mental Capacity Act 2005). For details of the Court of Protection, see Mental Capacity Act 2005.

[129] s 21(5). [130] s 21(6). [131] [1947] Ch 597. [132] Ibid at 605.

[133] *Re Ridsdel* [1947] Ch 597. [134] *Re Ridsdel* [1947] Ch 597.

(b) **Appointment of a judicial trustee**

(i) The power to appoint

The Judicial Trustees Act 1896, s 1(1) provides that:

> Where application is made to the court by or on behalf of the person creating or intending to create a trust, or by or on behalf of a trustee or beneficiary, the court may, in its discretion, appoint a person (in this Act called a judicial trustee) to be a trustee, either jointly with any other person or as sole trustee, and if sufficient cause is shown, in place of any existing trustees.

The power to appoint a judicial trustee is therefore purely discretionary. It is also clear that a trustee may be removed against his will and replaced by a judicial trustee. In *Thomas and Agnes Carvel Foundation v Carvel*,[135] Lewison J held that the survivor of two persons who had made mutual wills and his personal representative was a trustee for the purposes of this section:

> As Clauson J made clear in *In re Hagger*[136] the survivor of two persons who make mutual wills is treated as a trustee, and as Lord Camden in *Dufour v Pereira*[137] said the trust binds those who claim under him. Accordingly, in my judgment the survivor and his executor are trustees in the usual sense of that word. A person entitled to enforce the trust thus imposed by law is, in my judgment, a beneficiary. In my judgment, therefore, although a person claiming under the English doctrine of mutual wills is not entitled to make an application under section 50 of the 1985 Act, he is entitled to apply under section 1 of the 1896 Act.[138]

(ii) Persons who may be appointed

Section 1(3) provides that:

> Any fit and proper person nominated for the purpose in the application may be appointed a judicial trustee, and, in the absence of such nomination, an official of the court may be appointed, and in any case a judicial trustee shall be subject to the control and supervision of the court as an officer thereof.

(iii) Remuneration of judicial trustees

Section 1(5) provides that the court may direct that the judicial trustee be remunerated for his services from the trust property.

(2) **Public Trustee Act 1906**

(a) **Nature of the public trustee**

The Public Trustee is a corporation sole which may act as an ordinary trustee, custodian trustee,[139] or judicial trustee.[140] The office was established by the Public Trustee Act 1906, and one main function is to administer small estates. Once appointed, he has the same powers and duties, rights and liabilities as an ordinary trustee.

135 [2008] Ch 395. 136 [1930] 2 Ch 190 at 195.

137 [1769] 21 ER 332. 138 [1769] 21 ER 332 at 404, 29.

139 A custodian trustee holds the property of the trust fund and the documents relating to such property, but leaves the administration of the trust to the managing trustee. See Public Trustee Act 1906, s 4(2).

140 Public Trustee Act 1906, s 2(1).

(b) **Appointment of the public trustee**

(i) Appointment as an ordinary trustee

Section 5(1) provides that the Public Trustee may be appointed trustee of any will or settlement:

> either as an original or as a new trustee, or as an additional trustee, in the same cases, and in the same manner, and by the same persons or court, as if he were a private trustee, with this addition, that, though the trustees originally appointed were two or more, the public trustee may be appointed sole trustee.

This is subject to the limitations that he may decline to accept any trust, although not on the grounds of the small value of the trust fund,[141] that he may not act as the trustee of any trust under a deed of arrangement for the benefit of creditors or as administrator of an insolvent estate,[142] and that he shall not accept any trust exclusively for religious or charitable purposes.[143] The court may order the appointment of the Public Trustee even if the trust instrument prohibits his appointment.[144]

(ii) Appointment as a custodian trustee

Section 4(1) provides that:

> Subject to rules under this Act the public trustee may, if he consents to act as such, and whether or not the number of trustees has been reduced below the original number, be appointed to be custodian trustee of any trust–
>
> (a) by order of the court made on the application of any person on whose application the court may order the appointment of a new trustee; or
> (b) by the testator, settlor or other creator of any trust; or
> (c) by the person having power to appoint new trustees.

(iii) Intestate estates

The Public Trustee holds the estate of a person who dies intestate, pending the appointment of an administrator.[145]

9 The court's inherent jurisdiction

In addition to the statutory power to remove trustees under s 41 of the Trustee Act 1925, the court possesses an inherent jurisdiction to remove trustees in an action begun by writ for the administration or execution of a trust.[146] The overriding consideration seems to be the welfare of the beneficiaries and the trust estate, and it is likely that the general principles described above in relation to the exercise of the court's statutory power under the Trustee Act 1925, s 41 would apply. Some specific guidance was provided by the Privy Council in *Letterstedt v Broers*,[147] where Lord Blackburn said:

[141] s 2(3). [142] s 2(4). [143] s 2(5). [144] s 5(3).

[145] Law of Property (Miscellaneous Provisions) Act 1994, s 14.

[146] *Re Wrightson* [1908] 1 Ch 789; *Re Henderson* [1940] Ch 764.

[147] [1884] 9 App Cas 371.

> The reason why there is so little to be found in the books on this subject is probably that suggested by Mr Davey in his argument. As soon as all questions of character are as far settled as the nature of the case admits, if it appears clear that the continuance of the trustee would be detrimental to the execution of the trusts, even if for no other reason than that human infirmity would prevent those beneficially interested, or those who act for them, from working in harmony with the trustee, and if there is no reason to the contrary from the intentions of the framer of the trust to give this trustee a benefit or otherwise, the trustee is always advised by his own counsel to resign, and does so. If, without any reasonable ground, he refused to do so, it seems to their Lordships that the court might think it proper to remove him ...[148]

The court may act under its inherent jurisdiction even where the facts are in dispute.[149] The inherent jurisdiction was used to remove three trustees against their will in *Clarke v Heathfield (No 2)*.[150] The case concerned a trust fund of money belonging to the National Union of Mineworkers. The three trustees transferred the funds abroad to prevent them being sequestrated as a result of the illegal industrial action by the union. Members of the NUM sought to have the trustees removed by the court. Mervyn Davies J held that the court should exercise its power to remove the trustees under its inherent jurisdiction. A number of factors influenced his decision to remove, including the trustees' refusal to obey orders of the court and that the transfer of the funds abroad rendered them unavailable for the purposes for which they were contributed by the membership of the union.[151]

Removal may also be possible where a trustee puts themselves in a conflict of duty and interest with the trust, as demonstrated in *Manton v Manton*.[152] Here, following a bitter dispute between rival trustees in a family trust, the defendant went to work for a competing business and many clients followed him to the new business. Cooke J stressed that the overriding consideration was the proper administration of the trust, and that it was not necessary to demonstrate proof of loss before the court could act:

> it cannot be necessary to wait and see whether any loss actually results ... in considering whether a trustee should be removed, when the court focuses on the proper administration of the trust and interests of the beneficiaries in securing its proper administration, a breach of duty which puts the trust at risk of loss is highly relevant, whether or not it can be demonstrated that the loss has actually occurred...[153]

There was a real risk to the trust assets and the trust as a result of the defendant's breach of his duty to avoid conflicts of duty and interest, and he was removed. The clear hostility that arose between the parties would not have been enough to warrant such action, unless it could be demonstrated that it would impede the administration of the trust.[154]

A summary of the powers to appoint and move trustees is provided in tabular format in Figure 32.1.

[148] [1884] 9 App Cas 371 at 386.

[149] *Re Chetwynd's Settlement* [1902] 1 Ch 692; *Re Wrightson* [1908] 1 Ch 789; *Re Henderson* [1940] Ch 764.

[150] [1985] ICR 606.

[151] The jurisdiction has also been used in *Bridge Trustees Ltd v Noel Penny Turbines* [2008] EWHC 2054 (Ch), to remove the donee of a fiduciary power against his will. The donee was not a trustee and, therefore, fell outside the jurisdiction of the Trustee Act 1925, s 41.

[152] [2020] EWHC 125 (Ch).

[153] [2020] EWHC 125 (Ch) at [17].

[154] [2020] EWHC 125 (Ch) at [68]–[72]

Circumstances	Relevant power	Exercised by
Initial appointment	Own choice	Settlor/testator; court (if original trustee disclaims the trust, or if the trust would otherwise fail for want of a trustee)
Appointment of additional trustee	Express power	Person nominated
	Trustee Act 1925, s 36(6)	Trustees for the time being
	TOLATA* 1996, s 19	Beneficiaries
Replacement of existing trustee	Express power	Person nominated
	Trustee Act 1925, s 36 (in specified circumstances)	'Surviving or continuing trustees' or personal representatives of last such
	TOLATA 1996, s 19	Beneficiaries
	TOLATA 1996, s 20	Beneficiaries
	(Mentally incapable trustee)	
	Trustee Act 1925, s 41	Court
Retirement without replacement	Trustee Act 1925, s 39	Retiring trustee with consent of others
	TOLATA 1996, s 19	Beneficiaries with consent of remaining trustees
Removal of trustee	Trustee Act 1925, s 36	'Surviving or continuing trustees' or personal representatives of last such
	TOLATA 1996, s 19	Beneficiaries (with consent of remaining trustees if not being replaced)
	Trustee Act 1925, s 41	Court
	Inherent jurisdiction	Court

*Trusts of Land and Appointment of Trustees Act 1996

Figure 32.1 Summary of powers to appoint and remove trustees

PART IX

Controlling Trustees and Fiduciaries

33. Need for control 693
34. Remedies against the trustee for breach of trust 714
35. Fiduciary duties of trustees and other fiduciaries 744
36. Limitation of action 783

33

Need for control

1 The need for control and accountability of trustees

(1) The nature of trusts

Trusts impose legally binding obligations, and powers can be exercised only within the limits set by the instrument in which they are created. We have seen that this requires sufficient certainty for the courts to know what obligations have been imposed, and the bounds within which any discretions or powers may be exercised. But more than this is needed. There have to be mechanisms for controlling trustees or the donees of powers and holding them accountable for their actions.

It will be seen that the prime responsibility for supervising the activities of the trustees falls to the beneficiaries, who are able to complain to the court if they believe the trustees have committed, or are about to commit, a breach of trust. If the beneficiaries are able to apply to the court before the alleged breach has taken place they may obtain an injunction against the trustees to restrain them from committing the contemplated breach. Trustees are also subject to a number of duties which enable the beneficiaries to keep a better check on their activities by entitling them to obtain information which will inform them of the trustees' actions and may enable the beneficiaries to detect breaches of trust. This chapter will consider those duties.

(2) The potential for abuse

It is obvious that whenever one person has the effective control of property but is required to act for the benefit of another, there is a possibility that he will misuse the powers that he holds. For example, a trustee may be tempted to apply the trust property for his own benefit rather than for the benefit of the beneficiaries, or the donee of a special power of appointment may attempt to appoint to someone outside of the class.

(3) The reality of abuse

Human nature being what it is, the law reports are littered with cases where trustees enjoying the responsibility to manage trust property have abused their position and failed to carry out their duties. For example, in *Lipkin Gorman v Karpnale Ltd*,[1] a solicitor misappropriated money from his firm's client account to finance his gambling habit. *Bishopsgate Investment Management Ltd v Maxwell (No 2)*[2] concerned the infamous Maxwell pension fraud. Ian and Kevin Maxwell were directors of a company that held

[1] [1987] 1 WLR 987. [2] [1994] 1 All ER 261.

assets on trust for the pension schemes of companies owned by Robert Maxwell. To support other private companies that Robert Maxwell owned, property was misappropriated from the trust fund. Kevin and Ian, as directors, were responsible for signing transfer forms authorizing the misappropriations. This was a classic case where those who held the management power over the property by virtue of their position as directors and trustees abused their position and were able to apply the property for improper purposes, rather than for the benefit of the pensioners.

(4) **Preventing abuse**

It is often impossible to prevent those who are dishonest from taking advantage of the opportunities for abuse that their position brings, and the crucial question is generally whether an adequate remedy is available when an abuse has taken place. However, the legal system possesses some mechanisms by which to attempt to prevent abuses occurring.

(a) **Supervision and regulation**

The law could introduce methods requiring the ongoing supervision of trustees, by the court or by independent regulators, so that their dealings are scrutinized and the potential for abuse is reduced. This has been done for charitable trusts and pension schemes. However, it would be a Herculean task to introduce regulation for all trusts; nor could it possibly eliminate all opportunities for fraud or poor practice, as some of the examples described in the chapters on charity illustrate.

Generally, abuse occurs because of the dishonesty or incompetence of trustees. The choice of trustee is, therefore, of the utmost importance. At present, there is no general provision disqualifying certain individuals from holding office as trustees, although the Charities Act 2011 does disqualify certain persons from serving as charity trustees. Following the recommendations of the Pension Law Review Committee, which sat under the chairmanship of Professor Roy Goode after the Maxwell scandal, s 29(1) of the Pensions Act 1995 provides that a person is disqualified from being a trustee of any pension trust scheme if he has been convicted of any offence involving dishonesty or deception, is an undischarged bankrupt, or is disqualified to act as a company director.[3] A company cannot serve as trustee of a pension fund if any of its directors are disqualified from acting as trustee under the section.

(b) **The duty to act unanimously**

Obviously, the greatest dangers of abuse arise where the trust property is held and managed by a sole trustee. For this reason, in the context of land, overreaching, which defeats the interests of the beneficiaries of a trust of land, is only permitted by statute where any capital money is paid to or by the direction of at least two trustees.[4] The 'two-trustee' rule has been clarified and strengthened by the Trustee Delegation Act 1999 under which, if one of two trustees has delegated his powers relating to the sale of land to the other trustee, the sole trustee-cum-attorney cannot give a valid receipt without a second person being added as trustee.[5]

[3] Under the Company Directors' Disqualification Act 1986.

[4] Law of Property Act 1925, ss 2 and 27. See also *State Bank of India v Sood* [1997] 1 All ER 169.

[5] Trustee Delegation Act 1999, s 7. The same is true where there are two or more trustees all of whom have delegated their powers to the same agent.

Except in the case of pension fund trusts[6] and charity trusts, co-trustees must generally act unanimously.[7] They cannot act on the basis of a majority decision.[8] The principle was stated by Jessel MR in *Luke v South Kensington Hotel Ltd*:

> There is no law that I am acquainted with which enables the majority of trustees to bind the minority. The only power to bind is the act of [them all].[9]

Illustrations of the application of the requirement of unanimity can be drawn from a number of areas. If one of several co-trustees enters into a contract to sell trust property to a third party, the duty to act unanimously means that the contract cannot be enforced against the trust.[10] Similarly, the trustees must act unanimously in the exercise of their discretions. In *Tempest v Lord Camoys*,[11] one of two trustees wished to exercise their discretion to purchase land with the trust property, but the other trustee refused to concur in the purchase. The Court of Appeal held that, as the refusing trustee had properly exercised his discretion, the court could not interfere and the purchase could not take place as the trustees were not unanimous. However, in *Messeena v Carr*,[12] Lord Romilly MR held that there was no breach of trust where a discretion was exercised by one of two trustees and the other 'approved and sanctioned what was done'. A receipt which is given for money by only one of two trustees will be ineffective to discharge the payor unless this is done by way of an express term in the trust instrument. Hence, in *Lee v Sankey*,[13] a firm of solicitors was held not to have been discharged when it paid over the proceeds of a testator's real estate and was given a receipt by one of the two trustees of the will, who misappropriated the money and died insolvent.

In some undefined but exceptional circumstances it may be that the duty to act unanimously will not apply. In *Nicholson v Smith*,[14] for example, it was held that notice of the intention to renew a lease by one of two trustees was sufficient.

(c) Deterrence and remedies

Rather than supervising trustees so as to prevent abuse occurring, equity has put in place powerful remedies that are available when an abuse occurs, which, therefore, act to deter those who might consider abusing their position. If the remedies available to the beneficiaries of a trust operate to deprive a trustee of any gain made through abuse of his position, this will act as a disincentive to abuse in the first place. Some abuses, particularly the misappropriation of trust property, also constitute criminal offences, in which case the possibility of criminal conviction will also act as a deterrent.

2 The means of control

(1) Criminal sanctions

Some measure of control over the conduct of trustees is provided by the general criminal law. In particular, if a trustee misappropriates trust property he will be guilty of theft. The Theft Act 1968 defines theft in s 1(1):

> A person is guilty of theft if he dishonestly appropriates property belonging to another with the intention of permanently depriving the other of it.

[6] Pensions Act 1995, s 32 provides that trustees of an occupational pension scheme may make decisions by a majority.

[7] The trust instrument may specify circumstances in which the trustees do not need to be unanimous.

[8] See *Leyton v Sneyd* [1818] 8 Taunt 532; *Tempest v Lord Camoys* [1882] 21 Ch D 571, CA; *Astbury v Astbury* [1898] 2 Ch 111; *Boardman v Phipps* [1967] 2 AC 46. HL.

[9] [1879] 11 Ch D 121 at 125.

[10] *Naylor v Goodall* [1877] 47 LJ Ch 53.

[11] [1882] 21 Ch D 571.

[12] [1870] LR 9 Eq 260.

[13] [1873] LR 15 Eq 204.

[14] [1882] 22 Ch D 640.

'Property belonging to another' is defined in s 5(2) to include property held on trust so that 'where property is subject to a trust, the persons to whom it belongs shall be regarded as including any person having a right to enforce the trust, and an intention to defeat the trust shall be regarded accordingly as an intention to deprive of the property any person having that right'. Thus, the trustee, or anyone else who misappropriates the trust property, will be guilty of theft.[15] However, although the prospect of a conviction for theft may serve as a deterrent to abuse, it does not restore the trust property to the beneficiaries, which is often their prime concern.

(2) **Supervision by the court**

Every trust is technically under the jurisdiction and the supervision of the court. However, in practice, the court does not exercise a day-to-day function of supervising the activities of trustees, ensuring that they do not abuse their powers and that they carry out their duties properly. The court is dependent on the beneficiaries of the trust to bring complaints regarding the trustees' conduct to their attention. If the beneficiaries approach the court before a trustee acts improperly, it will be able to issue an injunction to restrain the proposed breach of trust. Where a breach has already occurred, the beneficiaries will be awarded an appropriate remedy.

Even though it does not act as a day-to-day watchdog over trustees, the court serves the very important function of setting the standard of probity that trustees are required to observe in their dealings, by which their conduct will be tested if a claim is made against them by the beneficiaries. The higher the standard of care that is required, the greater the probability that the trustee will not be able to gain by abusing his position, and the greater the deterrent effect. Traditionally, the courts have set extremely high standards for the conduct of trustees, and the remedies available border on the draconian.

(a) **The fiduciary position of the trustee**

Trustees stand in a fiduciary position to the beneficiaries of the trust. This means that they are always expected to act in the interests of the beneficiaries, with the implication that they are not permitted to take advantage of their position for their own benefit. As such, they owe a duty of exclusive loyalty to the beneficiaries. Trustees are not the only persons deemed fiduciaries in equity. Those occupying positions of trust and responsibility for the affairs of others, such as company directors, agents, and partners, are also regarded as fiduciaries. Equity imposes a rigid rule that a fiduciary must not benefit by virtue of his position, which thus acts as a safeguard to ensure that there is no possibility that he is abusing it. A fiduciary will be forced to disgorge any profits that he may have made in breach of his fiduciary duty by making restitution of them to the persons to whom the duty was owed. We consider this topic in Chapter 35.

(b) **The standard of care expected of trustees**

Equity imposes an objective standard of care on the way that trustees carry out their duties. In some cases a statutory duty to take reasonable care applies; in all others trustees are expected to act with the standard of care of an ordinary prudent man of business who is acting on behalf of someone else.[16] If the trustee fails to exercise the requisite standard of care or fails to carry out his duties or acts outside of his powers or the terms of the trust,

[15] See *Re A-G's Reference (No 1 of 1985)* [1986] QB 491; [1986] 102 LQR 486; [1986] 45 CLJ 367 (Gearty); [1986] 136 NLJ 913 (Smart); [1987] Conv 209 (Martin).

[16] *Speight v Gaunt* [1883] 9 App Cas 1, HL; *Bartlett v Barclay's Bank Trust Co Ltd* [1980] Ch 515.

he will have committed a breach of trust and will be liable to compensate the beneficiaries for any loss caused by his breach.

(3) Supervision by the beneficiaries

As the court cannot supervise the activities of every trustee, the prime responsibility for such supervision falls to the beneficiaries of the trust. They are expected to monitor the trustee's activities, and to complain to the court if there is any breach of fiduciary duty or breach of trust. It is entirely appropriate that this burden should fall to them, as they are the very people who are most interested in the proper performance of the trust. It is they who will be most anxious to ensure that the trustee carries out his duties properly, that trust property is not misapplied, and that the trustee does not use his position to his own advantage at their expense. A number of principles, which have been examined earlier in this book, confirm that the beneficiaries are the persons primarily responsible for the supervision of the trustees.

(a) Beneficiary principle

The beneficiary principle, examined in Chapter 24, is predicated on the understanding that the beneficiaries are primarily responsible for supervising the trustees. The very reason equity requires a trust to have identifiable legal persons as beneficiaries is that in the absence of such a beneficiary, no one possesses the necessary locus standi to apply to the court in the event of a breach by the trustees, and there is no one in whose favour the court can decree specific performance of the trust.[17]

(b) Beneficiaries' entitlement to information

As we see later, the beneficiaries of a trust are entitled to receive information from the trustees which will allow the latter to be held accountable for their management of the trust.

(c) Beneficiaries may approve breaches of trust

Whilst it might be expected that trustees are subject to an absolute obligation to carry out the terms of a trust as specified by the original settlor, this is not in fact the case. If the beneficiaries consent to the trustees acting otherwise than in accordance with the terms of the trust, then they will not attract liability for their breach. Trustees may vary the terms of the trust with the consent of the beneficiaries, or even bring the trust to an end.[18] The courts have no jurisdiction to step in and prevent a breach of trust which is made with the full consent of all the beneficiaries, even if this defeats the intentions of the settlor.

(d) Beneficiaries entitled to seek remedies

Where a trustee has abused his powers or position the trustees may come to the court to seek a remedy. There are a variety of remedies that may be available to them, each of which will be examined in detail in the following chapters.

(i) Compensation for breach of trust

Where trustees have committed a breach of trust, the beneficiaries are prima facie entitled to recover compensation from them for any loss the trust has sustained as a result of the breach. The remedy of damages for breach of trust is purely personal against the

[17] *Morice v Bishop of Durham* [1804] 9 Ves 399; *Bowman v Secular Society Ltd* [1917] AC 406; *Re Astor's Settlement* [1952] Ch 534; *Re Shaw* [1957] 1 WLR 729.

[18] *Saunders v Vautier* [1841] Cr & Ph 240.

trustee, and will, therefore, be ineffective if the trustee is insolvent. The nature and scope of the remedy for breach of trust is considered in Chapter 34.

(ii) Account of profits for breach of fiduciary duty

If the trustee has made an unauthorized profit for himself by allowing his duty and his personal interest to conflict, he will be in breach of his fiduciary duty and the beneficiaries will be able to recover from him any profit that he has made. The nature and scope of the equitable duty to account for profits received in breach of fiduciary duty is considered in Chapter 35.

(iii) Proprietary remedies

If the trustee who has committed a breach of trust or made an unauthorized profit is insolvent, any personal remedies of the beneficiaries will be rendered largely ineffective. They will merely rank amongst the trustee's general creditors. However, if they can show that the trustee has property amongst his assets which was trust property, or if he has assets which can be shown to be the product of trust property by application of the rules of tracing, the beneficiaries will be able to claim those assets as belonging to the trust. They will not fall to be considered as comprising part of his general assets, and, in effect, the trust will gain priority over the interests of the general creditors. The availability of proprietary remedies, and the rules used to identify trust property, are considered in Chapter 38.

(iv) Remedies against strangers to the trust

Where a breach of trust involves third parties who are strangers to the trust, the beneficiaries may have both personal and proprietary remedies against them. If such a stranger has received and retained property that was misappropriated from the trust, the beneficiaries will be able to assert their equitable entitlement to it unless he had acquired it as a bona fide purchaser for value without notice of the existence of the trust. This is also the case if he can be shown to have property amongst his assets which is the product of trust property he received by the rules of tracing. If, however, he received property from the trust but has subsequently dissipated it, or its proceeds, he may yet be liable to account to the trust for the value of the property he received. In addition, a stranger who has not himself received trust property, but who has dishonestly assisted the trustees in a misappropriation of trust property, may also be liable to compensate the trust for the value of the misappropriated property. The remedies available to the beneficiaries against strangers to a trust are considered in Chapter 37.

(e) Effectiveness of supervision by the beneficiaries

It is obvious that the beneficiaries of a trust have a strong vested interest in ensuring that it is properly carried out according to its terms, and that the trustees do not abuse their position. However, the effectiveness of their supervision depends upon the nature of the trust. In the case of a small family trust, where the trustees and the terms of the trust are well known to the beneficiaries, such scrutiny is likely to be close and effective. In the case of large modern trust funds, with many thousands of beneficiaries and millions of pounds of assets, the beneficiaries are not in a position to scrutinize the day-to-day conduct of the trustees, both because of the enormity of the task, and the complexity of the situations involved. In such circumstances it is not realistic to expect the beneficiaries effectively to supervise the trustees' performance of their duties. To take the Maxwell pension fraud as an example: could the employees entitled to pensions realistically be expected to scrutinize the dealings of the directors of the companies holding the assets on trust so as to prevent the wrongful transfer of trust assets to the Maxwell private companies? Another limitation is that the trustees' misconduct often only comes to light after the event, when it is too late to prevent it, and when the beneficiaries' remedies may be all but ineffective because of the trustees' insolvency and because the trust property has been dissipated. Both these problems demonstrate the limitation of the effectiveness of supervision by the beneficiaries, and emphasize the importance of appointing appropriate persons to act in that capacity.

(4) **Statutory regulation**

It has already been noted that certain trusts are subject to statutory regulation, including trusts used as publicly available investment vehicles, pension funds, and charitable trusts. The statutory regime for charitable trusts is set out in Chapter 20.

3 The duty to exercise discretions properly

(1) **The duties of trustees relating to the exercise of discretion**

Where trustees have discretion as to how the trust property should be managed or allocated, they must exercise their discretion properly. It is not for the courts to force the trustees to reach a particular conclusion in the exercise of their discretion, but they will intervene if the trustees exercise their discretion improperly or improperly fail to exercise it. In *Tempest v Lord Camoys*,[19] Jessel MR said:

> It is settled law that when a [settlor] has given a pure discretion to trustees as to the exercise of a power, the court does not enforce the exercise of the power against the wish of the trustees, but it does prevent them from exercising it improperly.[20]

(2) **The trustees' duty to consider exercising a discretion**

Trustees are under a duty to consider whether they should exercise any discretion that they hold with regard to the trust property, even though the court cannot compel how the discretion should be exercised. These principles were applied in *Tempest v Lord Camoys*. Mr Fleming, one of the trustees, had properly considered the exercise of his discretion and had refused to invest the trust property in land or to raise money by way of a mortgage. As Brett LJ said:

> there was undoubtedly an absolute discretion in the trustees as to what land they should purchase. Mr Fleming has not refused to exercise the power at all, but has objected to purchase this particular property. It needs no authority to induce us to hold that if a discretion is given to trustees as to what property they should purchase the Court will not take it out of their hands.[21]

In *Turner v Turner*,[22] the court set aside deeds of appointment which had been exercised by the trustees on the grounds that, although they appeared to be valid, the trustees had not even read them. In effect, there had been no real consideration whether or not the power should be exercised. In *Klug v Klug*,[23] a trustee had refused to concur in an advancement because the beneficiary (her daughter) had married without her consent. Neville J held that the court would intervene to direct the payment because the trustee 'has not exercised her discretion at all'.

[19] [1882] 21 Ch D 571. [20] [1882] 21 Ch D 571 at 578. [21] [1882] 21 Ch D 571.
[22] [1984] Ch 100. [23] [1918] 2 Ch 67.

(3) Relevance of the beneficiaries' wishes

Where the trustees of a trust hold discretionary powers it is they alone who must decide whether or not to exercise the discretion. Except in respect of a trust of land,[24] trustees are not subject to an obligation to consult their beneficiaries before they exercise their discretions, nor are they obliged to follow beneficiaries' wishes. In *Re Brockbank*[25] Vaisey J refused to compel a trustee to exercise his power to appoint new trustees under s 36 of the Trustee Act 1925[26] in the manner demanded by the beneficiaries and other trustees. He emphasized the discretionary nature of the power:

> The power of nominating a new trustee is a discretionary power, and, in my opinion is no longer exercisable and, indeed, can no longer exist if it has become one of which the exercise can be dictated by others.

This statement no longer holds completely true following the Trusts of Land and Appointment of Trustees Act 1996, which gives beneficiaries a limited authority to direct the appointment of new trustees.[27] However, the proposition set out remains accurate in respect of other trustee discretions, even in situations where the beneficiaries can call for the appointment of new trustees or bring the trust to an end under the rule in *Saunders v Vautier*.[28] The beneficiaries cannot dictate how the trustees should exercise their discretion.

(4) Improper exercise of discretion

(a) General principles

Given that the courts will intervene if trustees exercise, or threaten to exercise, their discretion improperly, the question naturally arises as to the circumstances in which an exercise will be regarded as improper. The difficulty, similar to that faced in the judicial review of administrative decisions, is that the court does not act as the judge of whether trustees make the 'right' decision. The court will only interfere in limited circumstances. This was explained by Lord Truro LC in *Re Beloved Wilkes' Charity*:

> it is to the discretion of the trustees that the execution of the trust is confided, that discretion being exercised with an entire absence of indirect motive, with honesty of intention, and with a fair consideration of the subject. The duty of supervision on the part of the court will thus be confined to the question of the honesty, integrity, and fairness with which the deliberation has been conducted, and will not be extended to the accuracy of the conclusion arrived at . . .[29]

However, it is clear that trustees do not enjoy an absolute discretion.

There are circumstances in which the court will be prepared to intervene.

(b) Fraudulent exercise

The court will clearly intervene if it can be shown that a discretion was exercised fraudulently.[30]

[24] Trusts of Land and Appointment of Trustees Act 1996, s 11. Stevens and Pearce, *Land Law* (5th edn, Sweet & Maxwell 2013), Ch 13.

[25] [1948] Ch 206.

[26] See Chapter 32.

[27] See Chapter 32. Trusts of Land and Appointment of Trustees Act 1996, ss 19–21 enable the beneficiaries of a trust to direct the trustees to make appointments, or compel retirements, if they would otherwise be able to bring the trust to an end under the rule in *Saunders v Vautier*.

[28] [1841] 4 Beav 115.

[29] [1851] 3 Mac & G 440.

[30] *Cloutte v Storey* [1911] 1 Ch 18.

(c) Improper motives

The court will intervene if the trustee exercises or refuses to exercise the power for irrelevant and extraneous motives. For example, in *Klug v Klug*;[31] the court intervened where one of two trustees refused to exercise her discretionary power of advancement[32] in favour of her daughter because she had married without her consent. In the Irish case of *Tomkin v Tomkin*,[33] a valuable house and land near Dublin had been left under a family trust. The trustee, who was also a beneficiary, had a power to postpone sale. T C Smyth J held that the trustee 'by deliberate inaction, was content to let matters lie so that at a future date he could more conveniently acquire the trust property without having explored or realised its development potential'. He also allowed members of his family to occupy the property without payment of rent. It was held that the trustee was in breach of trust for acting as if he were the sole owner, and for disregarding the interests of the other beneficiaries. The judge indicated that the property should be sold.

(d) Failure to take account of relevant matters

The ability of the court to intervene and impugn an exercise of the trustees' discretion was recognized by the House of Lords in *Dundee General Hospital Board of Management v Walker*,[34] where Lord Reid stated:

> If it can be shown that the trustees considered the wrong question, or that, although they purported to consider the right question they did not really apply their minds to it or perversely shut their eyes to the facts or that they did not act honestly or in good faith, then there was no true decision and the court will intervene.[35]

This statement raises the possibility that the courts might be prepared to intervene and annul a decision on which trustees were simply misdirected or in error, rather than acting fraudulently or improperly. A number of cases, establishing a doctrine known as the rule in *Re Hastings-Bass*,[36] took the view that decisions of trustees which were demonstrated to be erroneous could be annulled.

(e) The rule in *Re Hastings-Bass*

The rule *in Re Hastings-Bass* was reviewed by the Supreme Court in *Pitt v Holt*.[37] The case involved two conjoined appeals in which the court was asked to set aside decisions of trustees which had attracted unforeseen tax disadvantages. The Court of Appeal[38] had held that the law had taken a 'seriously wrong turn' and that the court should 'reverse that error and put the law back on the right course.'[39] The Supreme Court affirmed this ruling, but held that in one case the decision of the trustees could be reversed on the grounds of mistake. The view of the Supreme Court (confirming the Court of Appeal decision) was

[31] [1918] 2 Ch 67. This is one possible explanation of the case. Another is that the discretion had not even been considered.

[32] See Chapter 28. [33] 1998/6924P (8 July 2003). [34] [1952] 1 All ER 896.

[35] [1952] 1 All ER 896 at 905. This formulation was cited with approval by Robert Walker J in *Scott v National Trust* [1998] 2 All ER 705 at 717–18.

[36] [1975] Ch 25. The view of the Supreme Court was that the doctrine actually originated in *Mettoy Pension Trustees Ltd v Evans* [1990] 1 WLR 1587.

[37] [2013] UKSC 26. See Pearce, 'Beyond *Pitt v Holt*: The Final Word on *Re Hastings-Bass* or Merely a New Chapter?' [2014] Denning LJ 170; Colebrook, '"Get out of jail free" card: the courts' offer of assistance to errant trustees' [2013] Denning LJ 211.

[38] [2011] EWCA Civ 197. This was a conjoined appeal from the earlier decisions in *Pitt v Holt* [2010] EWHC 45 (Ch) and *Futter v Futter* [2010] EWHC 449 (Ch).

[39] [2011] EWCA Civ 197, per Longmore LJ at 227. By contrast Deputy Bailiff Birt, in the Jersey case of *In the Matter of the Green GLG Trust* [2002] JLR 571 at 25–8, considered that the rule in *Re Hastings-Bass* was 'entirely consistent with precedent and principle'.

that the circumstances in which a decision of trustees could be set aside was significantly narrower than the first instance decisions applying the rule in *Re Hastings-Bass* had suggested. A decision of trustees would be void where the trustees acted beyond their powers ('excessive execution').[40] On the other hand, where a decision was within the powers of the trustees, it could be set aside as improperly made (or held voidable for 'inadequate deliberation') only where there had been a breach of duty on the part of the trustees.[41] Where the trustees 'have been given, and have acted on, information or advice from an apparently trustworthy source, and what the trustees purport to do is within the scope of their power' the only remedies would be for mistake (if applicable) or an action in negligence against the provider of the advice. An intermediate situation was where a discretion had been exercised fraudulently (for an improper purpose), where there was problematic[42] Court of Appeal authority,[43] which might need to be revisited, that the exercise of the power was void rather than merely voidable.

The rule in *Re Hastings-Bass* appeared to have become what some had described as a 'get out of jail free' card, in which, where a decision had been made that proved with hindsight to be disadvantageous (often because of the tax liabilities which it generated), the trustees and the beneficiaries could collude together to reverse the decision. The decision in *Pitt v Holt* significantly limits the rule and exposes trustees to greater jeopardy for incorrect decisions.[44] The decision may have led, however, to an increase in the number of cases based on mistake,[45] or seeking rectification.[46]

(f) Excessive execution

Examples of excessive execution which will deprive an act of trustees of any effect would include a failure by trustees to act unanimously or the use of the wrong instrument to make a purported transfer. Similarly, going beyond the scope of a discretion or power (which should logically include an administrative power—as Bean J appeared to indicate in *Dalriada Trustees v Faulds*[47]), for instance, by making an appointment to a person who is not within the class of beneficiaries, will also be cases of excessive execution. Since a power of advancement can be used only to benefit an eligible beneficiary, a purported advance which fails to do so will also be an instance of excessive execution and so void.[48]

The potentially serious impact of an act of trustees being void is illustrated by *Briggs v Gleeds (Head Office)*.[49] Owing to an error, a number of deeds over a period of over a decade were not properly executed, including critically, the 'deed' appointing new trustees of a pension scheme. The new 'trustees' made a number of decisions relating to the scheme. Newey J held that because the instruments had not been correctly executed, they were wholly ineffective. He acknowledged that this would have a range of unfortunate consequences, including excluding some employees from benefits and conferring a windfall on others, and increasing the deficit in the scheme by around £45 million.

[40] [2013] UKSC 26 at 60, 80, and 93. [41] [2013] UKSC 26 at 41, 73, and 93.

[42] [2013] UKSC 26 at 62. [43] *Cloutte v Storey* [1911] 1 Ch 18.

[44] Given that what is alleged is a breach of trust, it is for a beneficiary to 'grasp the nettle' ([2011] EWCA Civ 197, per Lloyd LJ at 130) and bring the action for breach of fiduciary duty. It would be rare for trustees to bring such actions.

[45] But see *Dukeries Healthcare Ltd v Bay Trust International Ltd* [2021] EWHC 2086 (Ch). In the context of an artificial tax avoidance scheme, a claimant had not fully considered documents and so had a cavalier attitude to risk. While the claimant, as a lay person, could not be expected to fully understand the trust documents, the judge was still not prepared to find a mistake.

[46] Douglas, 'Misuse of Rectification in the Law of Trusts' [2018] 134 LQR 138.

[47] [2012] 2 All ER 734 at 58.

[48] Lloyd LJ in the Court of Appeal [2011] EWCA Civ 197 at 66; *Roadchef (Employee Benefits Trustees) Limited v Hill* [2014] EWHC 109 (Ch) at 110–23. [49] [2014] EWHC 1178 (Ch).

(g) Inadequate deliberation

According to Lloyd LJ in the Court of Appeal in *Pitt v Holt*, the breach of duty required to make a decision voidable needs to be a breach of a fiduciary duty. This was confirmed by the Supreme Court. Fiduciary duty in this context must mean more than the breach of a duty of loyalty, and extend to a failure to take account of a material factor (such as the criteria for the exercise of a power,[50] or the fiscal consequences of a decision), or to consider an irrelevant matter.[51] Failing to consider a matter which was unlikely to have had an impact on a decision will be insufficient to justify the court's intervention.[52] Where trustees have with due care sought and acted upon professional advice from a competent adviser, they will not be in breach of fiduciary duty if the advice turns out to be incorrect.[53] The remedy of the beneficiaries would then be a claim for breach of duty against the advisers. Lloyd LJ accepted:

> that this distinction makes potentially vulnerable an act done by trustees who fail to take any advice, whereas the same act done in the same circumstances by trustees who take advice which proves to be incorrect is not vulnerable.[54]

The Supreme Court did not require, as a condition of relief by the courts, that it must be shown that the trustees would have acted differently had they been properly informed.[55] It was felt that a more flexible approach might be required.[56] Whether to afford relief is subject to the discretion of the court, a discretion which can be subject to terms,[57] and which is unlikely to be exercised if prejudice would thereby be caused to third parties.

(h) Capriciousness

Re Manisty's Settlement[58] suggests that the court will intervene if trustees exercise a discretion capriciously. Templeman J stated that:

> The court may also be persuaded to intervene if the trustees act 'capriciously', that is to say, act for reasons which I apprehend could be said to be irrational, perverse or irrelevant to any sensible expectation of the settlor; for example, if they chose a beneficiary by height or complexion or by the irrelevant fact that he was a resident of Greater London.

(i) Unreasonableness

There have been some cases in which the courts appear to have been willing to interfere with the exercise of a discretion by trustees merely on the grounds that it can be considered as unreasonable. For example, in *Re Roper's Trust*,[59] Fry J considered that the court could intervene if the trustees had 'not exercised a sound discretion'.[60] In contrast, cases from the mid-twentieth century favour the view that the court will not intervene merely on the grounds that the exercise was unreasonable if it was made in good faith.[61] In the Scottish case of *Dundee General Hospitals v Walker*,[62] the trustees had accepted that the

[50] *Roadchef (Employee Benefits Trustees) Limited v Hill* [2014] EWHC 109 (Ch) at 107. For criticism of the use of breach of fiduciary duty in this context, see Nolan, 'Fiduciaries and Their Flawed Decisions' [2013] 129 LQR 469.

[51] This was the interpretation adopted by Proudman J in *Roadchef (Employee Benefits Trustees) Limited v Hill* [2014] EWHC 109 (Ch) at 105.

[52] *Re Prudential Staff Pension Scheme* [2011] EWHC 960 (Ch).

[53] See *Daniel v Tee* [2016] EWHC 1538 (Ch).

[54] [2011] EWCA Civ 197 at 128.

[55] See *Sieff v Fox* [2005] 1 WLR 3811 at 119 (a decision of Lloyd LJ before *Pitt v Holt*).

[56] [2013] UKSC 26 at 91–2.

[57] [2013] UKSC 26 at 91–2.

[58] [1974] Ch 17.

[59] [1879] 11 Ch D 272.

[60] See also *Re Hodges* [1878] 7 Ch D 754; *Re Lofthouse* [1885] 29 Ch D 921, CA.

[61] See *Re Steed's Will Trusts* [1960] Ch 407 at 418.

[62] [1952] 1 All ER 896.

test for the exercise of their discretion was whether it was reasonable, but the House of Lords doubted that this was appropriate. Lord Normand concluded:

> I desire to reserve the question whether the trustee's decision was open to question on any other grounds save that it was dishonest, or that it involved a trespass beyond the limits of what was committed to them by the [settlor]. [I]t is one thing to say that the trustees must honestly discharge their trust and keep within the bounds of the powers and duties entrusted to them, and quite another to say that they must not fall into errors which other persons, including a court of law, might consider unreasonable.[63]

The possible breadth of the revised *Hastings-Bass* principle, as explained by the Supreme Court in *Pitt v Holt*, would permit intervention in some cases where trustees have acted unreasonably, but a level of unreasonableness amounting to perversity is likely to be required. In *Edge v Pensions Ombudsman* Scott V-C, in speaking of the basis on which a court would review pension trustees' decisions, said:

> The judge may disagree with the manner in which the trustees have exercised their discretion, but unless they can be seen to have taken into account irrelevant, improper or irrational factors, or unless their decision can be said to be one that no reasonable body of trustees properly directing themselves could have reached, the judge cannot intervene.[64]

The judge indicated that: 'Their exercise of the discretionary power cannot be set aside simply because a judge . . . thinks it was not fair'.[65] Similarly, in *British Airways Plc v Airways Pension Scheme Trustee Ltd*,[66] Morgan J said, in reviewing the decisions of pension trustees, which it was alleged had been made perversely or irrationally, or taking into account irrelevant considerations:

> I have expressed no view on the merits of the decisions made. In accordance with clear authority, the merits of the decisions in this case are for the trustees and not for the court.

(j) Compelling action

According to Park J in *Breadner v Granville-Grossman*,[67] there is a substantial distinction 'between on the one hand, the courts declaring something which the trustees have done to be void, and, on the other hand, the courts holding that a trust takes effect as if the trustees had done something which they never did at all'. He considered that he had no jurisdiction to treat as effective the purported exercise of a power outside the time limits for its exercise where the trustees had made a mistake about the last date for its exercise. The power in that instance was a mere power, which in his view lapsed when the time limit expired. Fiduciary powers may be treated differently by the courts. It was recognized in *McPhail v Doulton*[68] that there were various ways in which the courts could secure the performance of discretionary trusts, and those methods may be equally applicable to fiduciary powers. They include directing the trustees to act in a particular way. For instance, in *Klug v Klug*,[69] the court ordered a payment to be made to a beneficiary despite the improper refusal of one trustee to concur in the decision; and in *Mettoy Pension Trustees Ltd v Evans*,[70] Warner J was prepared to exercise a fiduciary power himself where there was no other person able to do so by reason of a conflict of interest. Also, in *Bridge Trustees Ltd v Noel Penny Turbines*,[71] Purle QC felt able to invoke the court's inherent

[63] [1952] 1 All ER 896 at 901. See also *Re Gulbenkian's Settlement Trusts* [1970] AC 508.
[64] [1998] Ch 512 at 534. [65] [1998] Ch 512 at 535. [66] [2017] EWHC 1191 (Ch) at 633.
[67] [2000] 4 All ER 705 at 723. [68] [1971] AC 424. [69] [1918] 2 Ch 67.
[70] [1990] 1 WLR 1587. [71] [2008] EWHC 2054 (Ch).

jurisdiction to replace an ex-trustee[72] of a pension trust for failure to exercise a fiduciary power to distribute surplus assets vested in him under the terms of the pension scheme.

(k) Continued life in the *Hastings-Bass* rule?

The decision in *Pitt v Holt*, and its emphasis on the need for trustees to be in breach of duty for the *Hastings-Bass* rule to apply, has largely stopped the number of recorded cases seeking to put aside a decision of trustees. However, there may still be cases where it is in the interests of trustees to acknowledge a breach of trust in order to have a decision reversed: the consequence of reversing an improper decision might negate any loss for which the trustees would otherwise be liable.[73]

4 Are trustees required to give reasons for their decisions?

(1) No duty to give reasons

The basic rule was stated by Harman LJ in *Re Londonderry's Settlement*:[74]

> trustees exercising a discretionary power are not bound to disclose to their beneficiaries the reasons actuating them in coming to a decision.

This statement accords with a long line of authorities establishing that trustees, who have decided either to exercise or not to exercise their discretion, are under no duty to provide the beneficiaries with reasons for their decision.[75] The absence of a requirement to give reasons for a decision is well illustrated in *Re Beloved Wilkes' Charity*.[76] The case concerned a trust to provide for the education of a boy from one of three named parishes, or, if there was no suitable candidate from those parishes, a boy from any parish. The trustees decided to use the funds to support a boy, Charles Joyce, who was outside of the parish. Their exercise of the discretion was challenged on the grounds that there was a suitable boy, William Gale, from within the parishes. Lord Truro LC held that the trustees were under no duty to disclose the 'particulars' of why they had exercised the discretion in that way, and that there was no ground for imputing bad motives to the trustees from the affidavits.

(2) Justification for the rule

The main justification for the non-disclosure principle is that it is considered to be in the best interests of the decision-making process that it should be confidential.[77] In *Re Londonderry's Settlement*,[78] Salmon LJ provided an explanation:

> So long as the trustees exercise [the power] bona fide with no improper motive, their exercise of the power cannot be challenged in the courts—and their reasons for acting as they did are, accordingly, immaterial. This is one of the grounds for the rule that trustees are not obliged

[72] If the donee had remained a trustee, the court would have been able to use the power to remove trustees under Trustee Act 1925, s 41.

[73] See *Roadchef (Employee Benefits Trustees) Limited v Hill* [2014] EWHC 109 (Ch).

[74] [1965] Ch 918 at 928.

[75] *Re Gresham Life Assurance Society, ex p Penney* [1872] 8 Ch App 446; *Breakspear v Ackland* [2008] EWHC 220 (Ch); *Edge v Pensions Ombudsman* [1998] Ch 512 at 534. See also *Wilson v Law Debenture Trust Corpn* [1995] 2 All ER 337.

[76] [1851] 3 Mac & G 440.

[77] *Breakspear v Ackland* [2008] EWHC 220 (Ch).

[78] [1965] Ch 918, CA.

> to disclose to beneficiaries their reasons for exercising a discretionary power. Another ground for this rule is that it would not be for the good of the beneficiaries as a whole, and yet another that it might make the lives of trustees intolerable should an obligation rest upon them. Nothing would be more likely to embitter family feelings and the relationship between the trustees and members of the family, were the trustees obliged to state their reasons for the exercise of the powers entrusted to them. It might indeed well be difficult to persuade any persons to act as trustees were a duty to disclose their reasons, with all the embarrassment, arguments and quarrels that might ensue, added to their present not inconsiderable burdens.[79]

Similar sentiments have been expressed by Briggs J in *Breakspear v Ackland*.[80] The judge held that a beneficiary under a discretionary family settlement should not be provided with disclosure of a 'wish letter' in which the settlor had given non-binding guidance to the trustees. Briggs J conducted an extensive overview of authorities (including the Australian and Jersey decisions) and academic commentary relating to the *Londonderry* principle and concluded:

> Such confidentiality serves the due administration of family trusts both because it tends to reduce the scope for litigation about the rationality of the exercise by trustees of their discretions, and because it is likely to encourage suitable trustees to accept office, undeterred by a perception that their discretionary deliberations will be subjected to scrutiny by disappointed or hostile beneficiaries, and to potentially expensive litigation in the courts.[81]

The letter of wishes supported an inherently confidential process and should, therefore, itself be confidential.[82]

(3) **Trustees voluntarily provide reasons**

Although there is no obligation on the trustees to give reasons for decisions regarding the exercise of their discretion, if they do choose to give reasons this may reveal grounds for the court to intervene. As Lord Truro LC said in *Re Beloved Wilkes' Charity*:

> If, however, as stated by Lord Ellenborough in *R v Archbishop of Canterbury*,[83] trustees think fit to state a reason and the reason is one which does not justify their conclusion, then the Court may say that they have acted by mistake and in error, and that it will correct their decision; but if, without entering into details, they simply state, as in many cases it would be most prudent and judicious for them to do, that they have met and considered and come to a conclusion, the Court has then no means of saying that they have failed in their duty, or to consider the accuracy of their conclusion[84]

(4) **Where beneficiary has a legitimate expectation**

While there has been no general relaxation of the rule that beneficiaries are not entitled to be informed by trustees of their reason for a decision, in *Scott v National Trust*,[85] Robert Walker J suggested that where the beneficiaries of a trust enjoy a legitimate expectation

[79] [1965] Ch 918, CA at 936–7.

[80] [2009] Ch 32. See Griffiths, 'An Inevitable Tension? The Disclosure of Letters of Wishes' [2008] Conv 322; Fox, 'Disclosure of a Settlor's Wish Letter in a Discretionary Trust' [2008] 67 CLJ 252. See also *Dawson—Damer v Taylor Wessing LLP* [2017] EWCA Civ 74, where *Breakspear v Ackland* was cited with approval.

[81] [2009] Ch 32 at 51, 54.

[82] [2009] Ch 32 at 52 [58]. The same conclusion was reached in Australia (*Hartigan Nominees Ltd v Rydge* [1992] 29 NSWLR 405) and Jersey (*Re Rabaiotti's 1989 Settlement* [2001] WTLR 953).

[83] [1812] 15 East 117. [84] [1851] 3 Mac & G 440. [85] [1998] 2 All ER 705.

that a discretion will be exercised in their favour, they may be entitled to be given the reasons for a change of policy. He stated:

> If (for instance) trustees (whether of a charity, or a pension fund, or a private family trust) have for the last ten years paid £1,000 per quarter to an elderly, impoverished beneficiary of the trust it seems at least arguable that no reasonable body of trustees would discontinue the payment, without any warning, and without giving the beneficiary the opportunity of trying to persuade the trustees to continue the payment, at least temporarily. The beneficiary has no legal or equitable right to continued payment, but he or she has an expectation. So I am inclined to think that legitimate expectation may have some part to play in trust law as well as in judicial review cases.[86]

It has yet to be seen how far such a principle may be taken in the context of private trusts. However, it might perhaps have led to a different result in *Wilson v Law Debenture Trust Corpn plc*,[87] where it was held that pension trustees were not required to disclose their reasons for reversing a policy that they had pursued in the preceding years concerning the transfer of a fund surplus.

5 Information about the trust

(1) Documents required for accountability

Although it has long been held that trustees cannot be obliged to disclose their reasons for making a discretionary decision, it has always been the case that they have been obliged to provide information to the beneficiaries such as the trust accounts showing how the trust funds are invested and how they have been distributed. Trustees are under a duty to keep a copy of the trust instrument, other essential trust documents, and accounts of the trust funds. These are the most basic records required for accountability. In *Pearse v Green*,[88] Plumer MR said: 'It is the first duty of an accounting party, whether an agent, trustee, a receiver or executor to be constantly ready with his accounts.'[89] Master Matthews, commenting on a more recent statement of a similar sentiment, observed that what this means is 'that every beneficiary, whether in possession or in reversion, was entitled to an accounting, and to see the documents which justified this.'[90] Exactly which documents this might require would vary from case to case and—depending on the nature and scale of the trust—would not necessarily require the kind of accounts which might be drawn up by a professional accountant.

(2) Obligation to disclose

Beneficiaries are not entitled to see every document retained by a trustee, even if it relates to the trust. What is now considered to be the authoritative basis for disclosure was set out by the Privy Council in *Schmidt v Rosewood Trust Ltd*,[91] replacing an older and now discredited approach. Broadly, the old approach sought to categorize the types of documents which could be prima facie released upon the request of a beneficiary.[92] The newer approach, which continues to evolve in the courts, starts from the position that the judge has a discretion as to whether or not documents might be released. The same principles

[86] [1998] 2 All ER 705 at 718. [87] [1995] 2 All ER 337. [88] [1819] 1 Jac & W 135.
[89] See also *Clarke v Lord Ormonde* [1821] Jac 108; *Springett v Dashwood* [1860] 2 Giff 521.
[90] *Royal National Lifeboat Institution v Headley* [2016] EWHC 1948 (Ch) at 12.
[91] [2003] 2 AC 709. [92] See *Breakspear v Ackland* [2009] Ch 32, [23].

would readily apply to a request for information by a protector,[93] although, as Henderson J observed in *Davidson v Seelig*:

> There is little, if any, existing authority on the rights of joint protectors to obtain information and documents from the trustees of their settlements, and I accept this is an area where the law may be expected to develop.[94]

(a) A beneficial right to disclosure of trust documents?

The beneficiaries of a trust were historically regarded as enjoying the entitlement to access to trust documents on the basis of their proprietary right in the trust property. In *O'Rourke v Darbishire*,[95] Lord Wrenbury explained:

> The beneficiary is entitled to see all trust documents because they are trust documents and because he is a beneficiary. They are in this sense his own. The proprietary right is a right to access to documents which are your own.[96]

(b) Supervisory jurisdiction

The traditional proprietary rationale for the disclosure of trust information has at least two problems: it can at times conflict with the rule that trustees cannot be obliged to disclose reasons for discretionary decisions; and it does not explain what information should be provided to the objects of discretionary trusts. The first problem led the Court of Appeal, in *Re Londonderry's Settlement*, to a circular reasoning in attempting to explain why some documents held by trustees were not 'trust documents'.[97] An artificial attempt at classification emerged,[98] defining which documents should be prima facie released as trust documents and which should not on the basis that they were merely documents in the hands of the trustees. The second problem is more fundamental and relates to discretionary objects, as found in the modern discretionary trust. The underlying conceptual issue is that the objects of a discretionary trust become beneficiaries only if a distributive decision is made in their favour; until that point they can therefore have no proprietary interest in the trust documents. The Privy Council, in *Schmidt v Rosewood Trust Ltd*,[99] addressed these issues. The case concerned an appeal from the Isle of Man by the object of a power of appointment under a trust who sought access to the trust documents. The Privy Council rejected the contention that an object of a power of appointment could not obtain disclosure of trusts documents because he did not have a proprietary interest under the trust. Instead the court took as the starting point that trusts are subject to the supervision of the courts, and to make that supervision effective, the beneficiaries or potential beneficiaries must have access to sufficient information. The right to seek disclosure of trust documents was an aspect of the inherent jurisdiction of the court to

93 This is a role which has been considered to have developed in about the 1990s. See *JSC Mezhdunarodniy Promyshlenniy Bank v Pugachev* [2017] EWHC 2426 (Ch) at 348. The protector will ensure trustees are carrying through the trust in accordance with their mandate.

94 [2016] EWHC 549 (Ch) at 63.

95 [1920] AC 581.

96 [1920] AC 581 at 626–7.

97 [1965] Ch 918 at 938. Salmon LJ appears to suggest that a document is a trust document because the trustee is entitled to see it, but that he is entitled to see it because it is a trust document in which he has a proprietary right.

98 See *Breakspear v Ackland* [2009] Ch 32, [20].

99 [2003] 2 AC 709; Davies, 'Integrity of Trusteeship' [2004] 120 LQR 1. Hayton argues that the courts should take a lead from this decision and regard it as appropriate to insist on pension trustees providing reasons for their decisions: 'Pension Trusts and Traditional Trusts: Drastically Different Species of Trusts' [2005] Conv 229.

supervise the administration of trusts. On this basis a beneficiary will not enjoy an absolute right to disclosure of trust documents, as the court may exercise its inherent jurisdiction so as to limit disclosure. Lord Walker stated:

> no beneficiary (and least of all a discretionary object) has any entitlement as of right to disclosure of anything which can plausibly be described as a trust document. Especially when there are issues as to personal or commercial confidentiality, the court may have to balance the competing interests of different beneficiaries, the trustees' themselves and third parties. Disclosure may have to be limited and safeguards may have to be put in place. Evaluation of the claims of a beneficiary (and especially of a discretionary object) may be an important part of the balancing exercise which the court has to perform on the materials placed before it.[100]

The case did not require the Privy Council to decide whether the object of the power of appointment in question should be entitled to the disclosure sought, as this was remitted to the High Court of the Isle of Man for further consideration. The Privy Council did not provide comprehensive guidance as to the circumstances in which a request for disclosure might be denied. However, it did suggest that limits and safeguards may have to be put in place where there are issues of personal confidentiality and a need to balance the competing interests of different beneficiaries, the trustees, and third parties.[101]

The new supervisory approach, as it is starting to develop in the courts, gives judges a wider discretion. It does not attempt to classify sets of documents to which the beneficiary might have a proprietary right. This can be seen from *Breakspear v Ackland*,[102] a case in which Briggs J was called upon to decide whether the non-binding 'wish letter' of a settlor should be revealed to beneficiaries. Such a letter, accompanying a trust and expressing the settlor's hopes as to how it might be carried out, cannot intuitively be thought to be a 'trust document' in any proprietary sense.[103] Yet the beneficiaries were able to obtain disclosure. The judge stated that after a reinterpretation of existing case law,[104] the decision called for, 'the exercise of a discretion rather than the adjudication upon a proprietary right.'[105] A similar permissive and discretionary approach can be seen in *Lewis v Tamplin*.[106] In that case, a group of beneficiaries sought a substantial array of documents, apparently concerned that there had been a breach of trust. HHJ Paul Matthews found that without the presence of special reasons directing him away from assisting the beneficiaries, then a broad range of documents should be released.[107] The case adds a further and important nuance to the law, as he held that it was not necessary for all the beneficiaries to act and consent together in order to achieve disclosure.[108] It follows from this reasoning is that, even in circumstances where the beneficiaries are in conflict amongst themselves, then documents might still be released.

(c) Voluntary disclosure

Even in cases where the trustees cannot be compelled to provide information to beneficiaries, they may be permitted to do so if they consider that it is in the best interests of the trust.[109]

[100] [2003] 2 AC 709 at 734 [67].

[101] See also *Foreman v Kingstone* [2004] 1 NZLR 841, for further examination of the circumstances in which the court may refuse to limit disclosure of trust documents to beneficiaries.

[102] [2009] Ch 32.

[103] See *Countess Bathurst v Kleinwort Benson (Channel Islands) Trustees Ltd* [2007] WTLR 959, [117]. Compare: *Re Rabaiotti's Settlements* [2000] WTLR 953.

[104] *O'Rourke v Darbishire* [1920] AC 581; *Re Londonderry's Settlement* [1965] Ch 918.

[105] *Breakspear v Ackland* [2009] Ch 32, [52].

[106] *Lewis v Tamplin* [2018] EWHC 777 (Ch).

[107] Ibid [43].

[108] Ibid [45].

[109] *Breakspear v Ackland* [2009] Ch 32 at 67.

(d) Ban on disclosure

Is it possible for a settlor to restrict the information which the trustees can provide to beneficiaries? Briggs J thought, in *Breakspear v Ackland*,[110] that such a fetter would not be lawful. The Supreme Court of Bermuda addressed the question in *Re Application for Information about a Trust*,[111] an appeal from Bermuda. There was an express provision in a trust deed that the trustees could provide information to the beneficiaries only with the consent of the protector, who was the principal beneficiary. There was a family feud between the protector and another beneficiary, who was entitled to around one-third of the trust fund. The protector had instructed the trustees to release no information at all. The court held that a ban on providing information which purported to exclude the court's supervisory jurisdiction would be void because it would impact upon the accountability of trustees for the irreducible core obligations inherent in a trust. Otherwise, the court would have regard to the restriction of providing information when exercising its supervisory jurisdiction. In this case the family dispute meant that the mechanism was not working as the settlor must have intended, and disclosure of key information, subject to appropriate safeguards, was ordered.

(e) Disclosable information

Although the *Schmidt* case adopts a flexible approach in which there is no category of trust document which all beneficiaries have an absolute right to see, it does recognize that trustees have a duty to provide information enabling beneficiaries to ascertain their rights, provided that a claimant has established a sufficiently strong basis that they have an interest in the trust.[112] Subject to the caveat that other considerations may operate, some of the older cases on disclosure provide a guide to the information which trustees can normally be expected to disclose. These hold that beneficiaries, unless there are special considerations, will be entitled to copies of the governing instruments, and to be told who the trustees are and given their addresses.[113] In addition, most beneficiaries, including the objects of a discretionary trust,[114] will be entitled (at their own expense[115]) to see the trust accounts. In *Low v Bouverie*,[116] Lindley LJ said the trustees must: 'give all his cestui que trust, on demand, information with respect to the mode in which the trust fund has been dealt with, and where it is'.

(f) Compelling disclosure

There might seem to be a disjuncture between the older cases which spoke of an obligation to disclose, and the *Schmidt* approach that disclosure is primarily about the supervisory jurisdiction of the court, but the two positions are not really in conflict. Trustees who unreasonably fail to provide information which a court believes should be disclosed expose themselves to being liable to pay the costs of any application to the court to enforce the performance of his duty of disclosure.[117] A trustee in doubt about what to disclose can apply to the court for directions.

110 [2009] Ch 32. 111 [2013] 16 ITELR 85.

112 See *Birdseye v Roythorne & Co* [2015] EWHC 1003 (Ch) at 24–5.

113 *Re Murphy's Settlements* [1998] 3 All ER 1, a case where the settlor was required to provide this information to the objects of a discretionary trust.

114 *Chaine-Nickson v Bank of Ireland* [1976] IR 393.

115 See *Ottley v Gilby* [1845] 8 Beav 602; *Kemp v Burn* [1863] 4 Giff 348; *Re Watson* [1904] 49 Sol Jo 54.

116 [1891] 3 Ch 82 at 99.

117 As in *Royal National Lifeboat Institution v Headley* [2016] EWHC 1948 (Ch); *Re Skinner* [1904] 1 Ch 289.

(3) **Obligation to disclose not unconditional**

Even before *Schmidt* it was recognized that the right to information was not unconditional. In *Low v Bouverie*, a beneficiary who was entitled to a life interest sought information about any incumbrances on his interest as a prelude to obtaining a loan secured on his life interest. Lindley LJ said[118] that trustees were not required to provide this information. His reason was that: 'It is no part of the duty of a trustee to assist his cestui que trust in selling or mortgaging his beneficial interest and in squandering or anticipating his fortune.' In modern parlance it would be said that the information which the beneficiary was seeking was not required as part of making the trustees accountable.

(a) **Advice**

The duty of the trustees is simply to provide the beneficiaries with information, not to provide them with advice. As Megarry V-C said in *Tito v Waddell (No 2)*:

> trustees . . . are under a duty to answer inquiries by the beneficiaries about the trust property . . . But that is a far remove from saying that trustees have a duty to proffer information and advice to their beneficiaries; and I think the courts should be very slow to advance along the road of imposing such a duty. I say nothing about what may be kindly or helpful; I deal only with a duty for the breach of which the trustees may be held liable in equity.[119]

(b) **Relevant considerations**

Potter J, in the New Zealand case of *Foreman v Kingstone*,[120] summarized the factors which she thought could be derived from the judgment of the Board in *Schmidt* as matters that may be taken into account by the court in the exercise of its supervisory jurisdiction:

(a) whether there are issues of personal or commercial confidentiality;
(b) the nature of the interests held by the beneficiaries seeking access;
(c) the impact on the trustees, other beneficiaries and third parties;
(d) whether some or all of the documents can be withheld in full or redacted form;
(e) whether safeguards can be imposed on the use of the trust documentation (for example, undertakings, professional inspection, etc) to limit any use of the documentation beyond that which is legitimate; and
(f) whether (in the case of a family trust) disclosure would be likely to embitter family feelings and the relationship between the trustees and beneficiaries to the detriment of the beneficiaries as a whole.

Taking just one example, in a trust in favour of 'any charity in New Zealand', the trustees could be expected to react more positively to a request for information from a charity which had already received a distribution than another charity making a random request.

(4) **Other routes to disclosure**

Documents which a trustee is not required to disclose under trust law principles may still be subject to disclosure in a subject access request under the Data Protection Act 2018,[121] or as part of the disclosure requirements in court proceedings.

[118] [1891] 3 Ch 82 at 99. [119] [1977] Ch 106 at 242–3. [120] [2004] 1 NZLR 841 at 90.
[121] *Dawson-Damer v Taylor Wessing LLP* [2017] EWCA Civ 74.

(5) **Reform required?**

The rule that trustees are not obliged to provide reasons for their decisions may mean that it is almost impossible for the beneficiaries to challenge a decision because they do not have sufficient evidence to sustain a claim that the trustees acted dishonestly, took irrelevant matters into consideration, or failed to take account of all relevant factors. For example, in *Re Beloved Wilkes' Charity*,[122] one suggestion was that the trustees had chosen Charles Joyce rather than William Gale because Joyce was the brother of a clergyman who had been in contact with one of the trustees, who was also a clergyman. Without a comprehensive statement of the trustees' deliberations and reasons, it was impossible to demonstrate that the discretion had been improperly exercised. In the contrasting case of *Klug v Klug*,[123] a daughter was able to show that her mother had acted improperly because she had letters where she had made clear that she would not exercise the discretion, because of her daughter marrying contrary to her wishes.

Thus, the present law creates an inherent inconsistency. While equity seeks to prevent trustees acting improperly, it also fails to provide the beneficiaries with the right to know how decisions were reached so as to enable them to be subjected to proper scrutiny. This inconsistency runs deeper than this. Where a beneficiary takes legal action to challenge the exercise of a discretion, it is likely that he will be able to force the trustees to disclose their reasons. As Robert Walker J observed in *Scott v National Trust*:

> If a decision taken by trustees is directly attacked in legal proceedings, the trustees may be compelled either legally (through discovery or subpoena) or practically (in order to avoid adverse inferences being drawn) to disclose the substance of the reasons for their decision.[124]

However, it is submitted that the real need for reasons arises before any question relating to an exercise of discretion is brought to court. At present, the beneficiary is required to decide whether there are sufficient grounds to mount a legal challenge to an exercise of discretion—and to provide evidence to support this claim—while remaining in the dark as to the real reasons for it. In some circumstances the facts themselves may prima facie indicate that the discretion was wrongly exercised, but in many cases there may be no such external indications. In such circumstances the presumption that, in the absence of evidence to the contrary, a trustee has exercised his discretion properly, operates so as to present an insurmountable obstacle to effective scrutiny of the trustees' decision-making. The problems facing beneficiaries were well captured in a submission of counsel for the plaintiffs in *Wilson v Law Debenture Trust Corpn plc*,[125] where he argued that the trustee of a pension scheme was:

> in fact bound to give reasons for the exercise of discretions conferred upon the trustee by the relevant trust instrument because it would be unreasonable that members of the scheme who had bought their interests should not be able to see that the trustee has exercised its discretion properly–which they cannot see in the absence of reasons given for the trustee's actual exercise of its discretion.[126]

In contrast to the reluctance of equity to oblige trustees to provide reasons for their decisions, the law relating to the scrutiny of decision-making by public bodies has developed rapidly over the past fifty years, including the emergence of a duty to give reasons for decisions.[127] There is a strong case for a similar principle to apply to at least some trusts, such

[122] [1851] 3 Mac & G 440. [123] [1918] 2 Ch 67. [124] [1998] 2 All ER 705 at 719.

[125] [1995] 2 All ER 337. [126] [1995] 2 All ER 337 at 348, summarized by Rattee J.

[127] See *Padfield v Minister of Agriculture, Fisheries and Food* [1968] AC 997; *R v Secretary of State for the Home Department, ex p Doody* [1994] 1 AC 531; *R v Secretary of State for the Home Department, ex p Fayed* [1997] 1 All ER 228.

as pension schemes, where the beneficiaries have helped to generate the trust funds, even if the case is less compelling for family trusts.

This distinction is certainly inherent in *Breakspear v Ackland*,[128] where Briggs J deliberately left open the question of whether the principle of immunity applied outside the family trusts context.[129]

(6) **Audit**

There is no general duty on trustees to have the trust accounts audited. However, a number of statutory provisions permit either the trustees or the beneficiaries to obtain an audit of the accounts. The Trustee Act 1925, s 22(4) enables the trustees in their absolute discretion to have the trust account audited once every three years, or more frequently if the nature of the trust or any dealings make it reasonable. The costs of such an audit may be met from the capital and income of the trust property. The Public Trustee Act 1906, s 13(1) enables any trustee or beneficiary to apply for an audit of the trust accounts provided (unless the court gives leave) that no other audit has taken place in the previous twelve months. This section has been described as an 'exceedingly drastic enactment'[130] as it establishes the right to an audit. However, if an improper application is made, the applicant may be ordered to bear the costs of the audit.[131]

Audits may also be required by the trust instrument or by regulation applying to certain types of trust. For instance, the Pensions Act 2004 imposes special requirements for periodic actuarial valuations,[132] and charities are under special duties to provide audit information to the Charity Commission under the Charities Act 2011.

[128] [2009] Ch 32.
[129] [2009] Ch 32 at 52, 58.
[130] *Re Oddy* [1911] 1 Ch 532, per Parker J.
[131] *Re Oddy* [1911] 1 Ch 532; *Re Utley* [1912] 106 LT 858.
[132] s 224.

34

Remedies against the trustee for breach of trust

1 Introduction

Trusts impose obligations on the trustees, and the trustees can be held liable for breach of trust if their failure to meet the obligations imposed upon them causes a loss. The duties of trustees fall into three main categories.[1] First, there is an obligation to act within the 'four corners' of the trust. If the trust is for the benefit of Kamal's children, the trustees are not permitted to make dispositions in favour of anyone who is not one of Kamal's children. Similarly, if the trust is to retain an asset, the trustees normally have no power to sell it. Secondly, in relation to the performance of many of their duties, trustees are under a duty to act prudently, or in modern language, with reasonable skill and care. This applies where trustees choose to delegate, and in relation to the exercise of their powers of investment. Finally, some of the duties of trustees are fiduciary: they owe duties of loyalty to their beneficiaries. These three categories can overlap: see Figure 34.1. In addition to this, there may be some specific requirements (this is the case in relation to the exercise of investment powers) on the exercise by trustees of some of their functions. For example, trustees of land are expected to consult the beneficiaries about the exercise of their

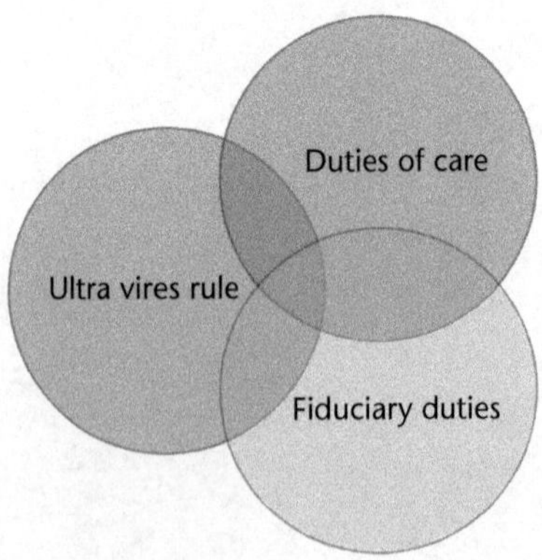

Figure 34.1 Types of duty owed by trustees

[1] A slightly different classification is suggested by Tipping J in *Bank of New Zealand v New Zealand Guardian Trust Co Ltd* [1999] 1 NZLR 664 at 687, cited by Lord Toulson in *AIB v Redler* [2014] UKSC 58 at 60. That classification confuses the nature of the duty with the effect of a breach.

powers. The defence of limitation, relating to the period of time within which a claimant can bring a case, is discussed in Chapter 36.

The duties and obligations imposed on trustees are enforceable by the beneficiaries against the trustees. The nature of such liability for breach of trust is, as we shall see, personal, so that trustees are liable to make good any losses to the trust property from their own pockets.

2 Meaning of breach of trust

(1) General definition

It is difficult to provide a simple definition of a breach of trust. Sir Robert Megarry V-C was unwilling to attempt any 'comprehensive definition of a breach of trust' in *Tito v Waddell (No 2)*,[2] but referred to two American definitions that had found approval in the courts. First, Pomeroy's *Equity Jurisprudence*[3] states that 'every omission or violation by a trustee of a duty which equity lays on him is a breach of trust'. Second, Professor Scott states that a trustee 'commits a breach of trust if he violates any duty which he owes as trustee to the beneficiaries'.[4] These two definitions demonstrate that the essence of a breach of trust is the failure of the trustees properly to carry out the duties expected of them. Their duties may be either expressly required of them by the trust deed creating the trust or imposed by the general principles of equity. Trustees can be liable for breach of trust for both their acts and their omissions.

(a) Acting inconsistently with the trust (ultra vires)

Trustees do not have power or authority to do anything that they wish. Their powers and authority are limited. If they exceed the boundaries of their powers and authority, then their actions will constitute a breach of trust.[5] The concept is essentially the same as the public law and company law concept of ultra vires, although there are very few cases where that term has been used in relation to breaches of trust.[6] Other cases[7] have used the expression excessive execution, but that is a very much more limited concept, since it is normally associated only with the exercise of powers of appointment. Where a trustee acts ultra vires, by exceeding his powers or by acting inconsistently with the general law, there will be a breach of trust.[8] As Lord Walker said in *Futter v Revenue and Customs*: 'That can be seen as a form of strict liability in that it is imposed regardless of personal fault.'[9]

So, for example, a trustee will commit a breach of trust if he sells property when he has no power of sale.[10] Similarly, if the trustees of a discretionary trust allocate the trust property to a person outside the class of potential beneficiaries, they will also be acting in

[2] [1977] 3 All ER 129. He regarded such an attempt as a 'perilous task' (at 247).

[3] As adopted by Corpus Juris Secundum [1955] vol 90, pp 225 and 228, para 247.

[4] *Scott on Trusts* (3rd edn, Little, Brown & Co. 1967), vol 3, p 1605, para 201.

[5] *Pye v Gorges* [1710] Prec Ch 308; *Mansell v Mansell* [1732] 2 P Wms 678; *Charitable Corpn v Sutton* (1742) 9 Mod Rep 349; *Clough v Bond* [1838] 3 My & Cr 490; *Harrison v Randall* [1851] 9 Hare 397; *Reid v Thompson and M'Namara* [1851] 2 I Ch R 26; *Dance v Goldingham* [1873] 8 Ch App 902.

[6] See *Pitt v Holt* [2011] EWCA Civ 197 at 72, 161, and 231; *Edge v Pension Ombudsman* [1999] EWCA Civ 2013; *Breadner v Granville-Grossman* [2000] EWHC Ch 224 at 91.

[7] See *Futter v Revenue and Customs* [2013] UKSC 26 at 60. This was an appeal from the Court of Appeal decision in *Pitt v Holt*.

[8] *Adair v Shaw* [1803] 1 Sch & Lef 243; *Collier v M'Bean* [1865] 34 Beav 426.

[9] See *Futter v Revenue and Customs* [2013] UKSC 26 at 80.

[10] *Perrins v Bellamy* [1899] 1 Ch 797. Both this and the next example were given by Lord Walker in *Futter v Revenue and Customs* [2013] UKSC 26 at 79.

breach of trust.[11] In *Lloyds TSB Bank Plc v Markandan & Uddin (A Firm)*,[12] a firm of solicitors held mortgage loan funds on trust from a bank 'until completion'. They were duped into paying out the money to a fictitious firm acting for a fictitious buyer as part of a fraudulent scheme. It was held that this was a breach of trust because the purported sale was a nullity, and 'completion' as defined in the terms of the trust had not therefore taken place.

It may seem hard on trustees who are duped like this that they are in breach of trust for acting inconsistently with the terms of the trust. They are liable for the breach notwithstanding that they have acted with reasonable care, or even that they have taken, and acted upon, apparently competent professional advice.[13] This is because acting on professional advice is a defence to an allegation of lack of care, but does not permit something which is unauthorized. However, *Daniel v Tee*[14] suggests an interesting twist. In that case it was alleged that trustees had improperly delegated their investment decisions. The judge held that was not the case, but even if it were, the trustees would still have followed the professional advice and made the same investment decisions. Any improper delegation, therefore, caused no loss. In addition, the apparently draconian strict liability may be tempered by Trustee Act 1925, s 61 (considered later in this chapter) which allows a court to grant relief where trustees have acted with reasonable care.[15]

(b) Duties of care

In relation to some of their responsibilities, trustees are not strictly liable, but are required to act with reasonable care or prudence. If they fail to fulfil their duties to the trust through neglect or omission, they will commit a breach of trust.[16] Historically, the standard of care required of trustees was the objective standard of the 'ordinary prudent man of business', a description contained in the leading case of *Speight v Gaunt*.[17] As Brightman J said in *Bartlett v Barclays Bank Trust Co Ltd*:[18]

> The cases establish that it is the duty of a trustee to conduct the business of the trust with the same care as an ordinary prudent man of business would extend towards his own affairs.[19]

It is suggested that this formulation of the duty of a trustee is simply an expression, using the language of the Victorian era, of a duty to take reasonable care.[20] This interpretation is

[11] *National Trustees Co of Australasia Ltd v General Finance Co of Australasia Ltd* [1905] AC 373.

[12] [2012] EWCA Civ 65.

[13] *Futter v Revenue and Customs* [2013] UKSC 26 at 80; *National Trustees Co of Australasia Ltd v General Finance Co of Australasia Ltd* [1905] AC 373.

[14] [2016] EWHC 1538 (Ch).

[15] See *Lloyds TSB Bank Plc v Markandan & Uddin (A Firm)* [2012] EWCA Civ 65 at 52 and 61 (duped solicitors did not act with reasonable care); another almost identical decision to the same effect is *Santander UK v RA Legal Solicitors* [2014] EWCA Civ 183. Compare *Nationwide Building Society v Davisons Solicitors* [2012] EWCA Civ 1626 (solicitors acted reasonably).

[16] *Charitable Corpn v Sutton* [1742] 9 Mod Rep 349; *Lord Montfort v Lord Cadogan* [1810] 17 Ves 485; *Moyle v Moyle* [1831] 2 Russ & M 710; *Taylor v Tabrum* [1833] 6 Sim 281; *Clough v Bond* [1838] 3 My & Cr 490; *Fenwick v Greenwell* [1847] 10 Beav 412; *Dix v Burford* [1854] 19 Beav 409; *Stone v Stone* [1869] 5 Ch App 74; *Jefferys v Marshall* [1870] 19 WR 94; *Re Brogden* [1888] 38 Ch D 546, CA; *Evans v London Co-operative Society* [1976] *The Times*, 6 July; *Bartlett v Barclays Bank Trust Co Ltd* [1980] Ch 515.

[17] [1883] 9 App Cas 1. [18] [1980] Ch 515 at 531.

[19] *Re Speight* [1883] 22 Ch D 727; affd sub nom *Speight v Gaunt* [1883] 9 App Cas 1; *Learoyd v Whiteley* [1887] 12 App Cas 727, HL; *Re Godfrey* [1883] 23 Ch D 483; *Re Chapman* [1896] 2 Ch 763, CA; *Re Lucking's Will Trusts* [1967] 3 All ER 726, [1968] 1 WLR 866.

[20] However, even in the twenty-first century, there have been judicial references to duties based on prudence and diligence: see *Richards v Wood* (27 February 2014, unreported, CA (Civil Division)); *AIB Group (UK) plc v Mark Redler & Co Solicitors* [2013] EWCA Civ 45 at 12 (referring to a duty to be prudent, but including within this duty the trustees' duties in relation to investment which are subject to the statutory duty to take reasonable care); compare *Englewood Properties Ltd v Patel* [2005] 3 All ER 307 (vendor of land under duty as constructive trustee to take reasonable care of the land).

reinforced by observations which suggest that the standard of the 'ordinary prudent man of business' can vary according to the context. Thus it has been said that a higher standard of care is demanded of professional trustees,[21] such as a trust corporation because of 'the special care and skill which it professes to have'.[22]

The duty of care demanded of trustees in respect of the performance of some of their duties has now been placed on a statutory footing. Section 1(1) of the Trustee Act 2000 provides that:

> Whenever the duty under this subsection applies to a trustee, he must exercise such care and skill as is reasonable in the circumstances, having regard in particular–
>
> (a) to any special knowledge or experience that he has or holds himself out as having, and
> (b) if he acts as trustee in the course of a business or profession, to any special knowledge or experience that it is reasonable to expect of a person acting in the course of that kind of business or profession.[23]

This statutory duty of care applies to certain specific situations which are outlined in Sch 1 to the Trustee Act 2000. These include the exercise of the power of investment, review of the trust investments, obtaining advice about trust investments, the exercise of powers in relation to land (including the power to acquire land), and the appointment of agents, custodians, or nominees. Newey J has observed:

> None of those appearing before me suggested that there is a difference of significance between the statutory and common law duties of care. The Law Commission itself expressed the view that its proposals for a new statutory duty of care probably represented 'no more than a codification of the existing common law duty'.[24]

The statutory duty adds little if anything to the concept of the 'prudent' trustee, although it clarifies that 'express regard should be had to the particular skills and position of the trustees, and to the circumstances of the trust.'[25] Most of a trustee's functions are governed by a duty to act prudently or with reasonable care.

If a trustee has failed to exercise the required standard of care, and loss is caused to the trust, he will be liable for breach of trust. For example, in *Re Lucking's Will Trusts*,[26] a trustee was held liable for his failure adequately to supervise the management of a company in which the trust held a controlling interest. Similarly, in *Bartlett v Barclays Bank Trust Co Ltd (No 2)*,[27] a bank was held liable for its failure to supervise two land development projects undertaken by a company of which the bank held 99.8 per cent of the shares as trustee for the Bartlett Trust.[28] The investment proved imprudent and hazardous and wholly unsuitable for a trust. It may not always be easy to determine whether a trustee's breach

[21] *Nestle v National Westminster Bank* [1992] EWCA Civ 12, applying the view of the Radcliffe Committee on the Powers and Duties of Trustees (Cmnd 8733), para 2.15.

[22] *Bartlett v Barclays Bank Trust Co Ltd* [1980] Ch 515 at 531, per Brightman J. See also *Re Waterman's Will Trusts* [1952] 2 All ER 1054.

[23] Detailed statutory duties have also been imposed on company directors under Pt 2, Ch 10, of the Companies Act 2006, including a duty to exercise due care, skill, and diligence under s 174, which are of relevance where the directors act as trustees. This largely replicates the same duty as that applicable to trustees, with the realization that higher standards may be required of professional directors than of lay trustees. Hence, s 174(2)(a) holds that the duty is one of a reasonably diligent person with the 'the general knowledge, skill and experience that may reasonably be expected of a person carrying out the functions carried out by the director in relation to the company'.

[24] *Brudenell-Bruce v Moore* [2014] EWHC 3679 (Ch) at 93. See *Trustees' Powers and Duties* (Law Com No 260, 1999) at 2.35.

[25] *Trustees' Powers and Duties* (Law Com No 260, 1999) at 4.24.

[26] [1967] 3 All ER 726; [1968] 1 WLR 866.

[27] [1980] Ch 515.

[28] See also *Armitage v Nurse* [1997] 2 All ER 705 at 716.

was one of commission or omission, as was seen in *Bishopsgate Investment Management Ltd v Maxwell (No 2)*,[29] but the distinction may be important, especially as to the issue of causation.

(c) Fiduciary duties

Trustees are fiduciaries, and as such owe duties of loyalty to their beneficiaries. The duties include not acting in ways which put personal interest above the interests of the beneficiaries (such as making a personal profit), keeping confidences entrusted to them, and maintaining a fair balance between the interests of different classes of beneficiary. Just because a trustee is a fiduciary does not mean that all a trustee's duties are fiduciary, and it is possible for people who are not trustees (such as agents) to be fiduciaries. Unfortunately, the limits of fiduciary duties are not clearly defined, which can lead to a lack of clarity about the boundary between fiduciary duties and duties of care.[30] Fiduciary duties are so important that they are considered in Chapter 35.

(d) Other duties

Some duties of trustees are hard to categorize. In *Re Merchant Navy Ratings Pension Fund*,[31] it was held that trustees have a duty to promote the purpose for which a trust was created. This can be expressed as a duty to put the interests of the beneficiaries first, but this is not an unqualified principle, for instance in pension schemes the interests of the employer are also relevant. This, being essentially a duty of loyalty, is probably best described as a fiduciary duty, but it will be relevant to interpreting the trust instrument and to evaluating whether trustees have acted reasonably.

(e) Exemption clauses

(i) Exemption clauses are in principle permissible

While trustees are subject to the general duty to act with reasonable care or the prudence of an ordinary man of business, the trust instrument may specifically exclude their liability for conduct that was not dishonest.[32] Even the new statutory duty of care introduced by s 1 of the Trustee Act 2000 may be expressly excluded by the trust instrument.[33] In *Armitage v Nurse*[34] the Court of Appeal considered the efficacy of a clause in a trust instrument which provided that:

> No trustee shall be liable for any loss or damage which may happen to Paula's fund or any part thereof or the income thereof at any time or from any cause whatsoever unless such loss or damage shall be caused by his own actual fraud.

The Court of Appeal held that, in principle, exemption clauses could be valid, that this clause was valid, but that there was a limit on how far an exoneration clause could go.

[29] [1994] 1 All ER 261.

[30] See *Futter v Revenue and Customs* [2013] UKSC 26, where the Supreme Court said that a breach of fiduciary duty is required to enable a trustee's decision to be avoided for inadequate deliberation, despite the fact that an obligation to consider a decision is a duty of care.

[31] [2015] EWHC 448 (Ch).

[32] Some groups of trustees, such as pension trustees, may not exclude their liability for a breach of trust in this way—Pensions Act 1995, s 33. This includes trustees of unit trusts (Financial Services and Markets Act 2000, s 253) and trustees of debenture trusts (Companies Act 2006, s 750).

[33] Sch 1, para 7.

[34] [1998] Ch 241; Pollard and Walsh, 'Exclusion Clause in Trust Deed Validly Excludes Liability for Gross Negligence' [1997] 11 TLI 52; McBride, 'Trustee Exemption Clauses' [1998] CLJ 33.

(ii) Irreducible core values

The limit which Millett LJ applied to exemption clauses was that there was an irreducible minimum core set of values attached to trusteeship, and no exemption clause could go so far as to cut into this core. This core included an obligation to act without fraud. However, he held that the irreducible core did not include the obligation to act without negligence:

> But I do not accept the further submission that these core obligations include the duties of skill and care, prudence and diligence. The duty of the trustee to perform the trusts honestly and in good faith for the benefit of the beneficiaries is the minimum necessary to give substance to the trusts, but in my opinion it is sufficient.[35]

He, therefore, held that a clause, like the one he was considering, restricting liability to actual fraud, was effective to exclude a trustee from liability for loss or damage to the trust property 'no matter how indolent, imprudent, lacking in diligence, negligent or wilful he may have been, so long as he has not acted dishonestly'.[36]

Subsequent cases support the view taken in *Armitage v Nurse*.

(iii) Liability for fraud

Common precedents for exclusion or exoneration clauses exempt trustees for all liability except their actual fraud.[37] The question therefore arises of what constitutes fraud in this context. Millett LJ suggested that if a trustee acted in a way which he did not honestly believe was in the interests of the beneficiaries, he would be acting fraudulently. Further elucidation has been given by the Court of Appeal in *Walker v Stones*.[38] The central issue concerned the application of an exclusion clause which purported to protect trustees from liability arising other than through 'wilful fraud or dishonesty'. The Court of Appeal held that the test for dishonesty could not be limited to an inquiry into the subjective state of mind of the trustee, but included an irreducible objective standard.[39] How the standard was to be applied would vary from case to case and could take into account whether a trustee was acting in a professional capacity, and whether the trustee had put his own interests above those of the beneficiaries.[40] Giving the judgment of the court, Sir Christopher Slade held that the exclusion clause must be interpreted so as to 'take account of the case where the trustee's so-called "honest belief", though actually held, is so unreasonable that, by any objective standard, no reasonable solicitor trustee could have thought that what he did or agreed to was for the benefit of the beneficiaries'.[41] Summarizing the result of the case, Lewison J, in *Fattal v Walbrook Trustees (Jersey) Ltd*,[42] put forward a number of propositions. A trustee will not be considered to have acted dishonestly simply because he has committed a deliberate breach of trust. This could be done without dishonesty. What is required to show dishonesty in the case of a professional trustee is that he is a trustee who has committed a deliberate breach of trust, and:

(a) Who knows that the deliberate breach is contrary to the interests of the beneficiaries; or
(b) Who is recklessly indifferent whether the deliberate breach is contrary to their interests or not; or

35 [1998] Ch 421 at 253–4.

36 [1998] Ch 421 at 251. Trustees of pension funds cannot exclude liability for breach of the duty of skill and care in the performance of investment functions: Pensions Act 1995, s 33.

37 See *Fattal v Walbrook Trustees (Jersey) Ltd* [2010] EWHC 2767 (Ch) at 73.

38 [2001] QB 902.

39 Applying the test of dishonesty adopted by the House of Lords in *Royal Brunei Airlines Sdn Bhd v Tan* [1995] 3 All ER 97, and by the Court of Appeal in *Twinsectra Ltd v Yardley* [1999] Lloyd's Rep Bank 438.

40 [2001] QB 902 at 939, and *Fattal v Walbrook Trustees (Jersey) Ltd* [2010] EWHC 2767 (Ch) at 82.

41 [2001] QB 902 at 939.

42 [2010] EWHC 2767 (Ch). See also *Newgate Stud Company v Penfold* [2004] EWHC 2993 (Ch).

(c) Whose belief that the deliberate breach is not contrary to the interests of the beneficiaries is so unreasonable that, by any objective standard, no reasonable professional trustee could have thought that what he did or agreed to do was for the benefit of the beneficiaries.[43]

Lewison J considered that the test for dishonesty derived from *Walker v Stones* had not been changed by cases considering the meaning of dishonesty in the context of dishonest assistance in breach of trust.[44]

In the most straightforward cases, the allegation of dishonesty will be made against an ordinary natural person. But it is also possible to bring a case against a corporate trustee. Where this route is taken, the claimant will identify directors, officers, and employees of the incorporated organization. The claimant should strive to show that these people had knowledge of the fraud early on in his case.[45]

(iv) Gross negligence

Millett LJ addressed the argument in *Armitage v Nurse* that it was not possible to exempt a trustee from liability for gross negligence.[46] He considered that the argument was without foundation, even though such a distinction was made in Scotland. In English law, in his view, 'we regard the difference between negligence and gross negligence as merely one of degree.' His view that it is possible to exclude liability for gross negligence has been followed by Behrens J in *Re Clapham (Decd)*,[47] and, in *Spread Trustee Company Ltd v Hutcheson*,[48] the Privy Council held by a majority that English law (and therefore also, in the view of the majority, Guernsey law until amended by statute on this point) permits an exemption clause to exclude liability for gross negligence. The view that there is no distinction between ordinary negligence and gross negligence apart from a vituperative epithet[49] is not, however, universally held. Gross negligence (in the slightly different context of defining the term when used in a contract) has been defined by a Supreme Court judge in Ireland as 'something flagrantly and conspicuously wrong, and conduct undertaken with actual appreciation of the risks involved, or in serious disregard of, or with indifference to an obvious risk, akin to recklessness'.[50] If gross negligence should properly be defined in this or a similar way, it casts doubt on the reasoning of the Court of Appeal in *Armitage v Nurse* that it would be irrational to distinguish between liability for negligence and liability for gross negligence.

(v) Protection of voluntary trustees

There is an irony in the operation of exoneration clauses in that the people most likely to require them are professional trustees. Unpaid lay trustees are less likely to be aware of the benefit of an exemption clause. In this context, *Barnsley v Noble*[51] is of interest. Although the case turns on the interpretation of a particular clause in standard form, it shows a willingness to be beneficent towards non-professional trustees. Sir Terence Etherton C rejected the interpretation proposed by counsel for the claimant, observing that accepting it would have the effect of 'depriving an honest and conscientious non-professional trustee, who

43 [2010] EWHC 2767 (Ch) at 81.

44 *Fattal v Walbrook Trustees (Jersey) Ltd* [2010] EWHC 2767 (Ch).

45 *Sofer v SwissIndependent Trustees SA* [2020] EWCA Civ 699 at [32].

46 An argument made in Matthews [1989] Conv 42.

47 [2005] EWHC 3387 (Ch).

48 [2011] UKPC 13. See Shearman and Pearce, 'Exempting a Trustee for Gross Negligence' [2011] Denning LJ 181–91.

49 *Grill v General Iron Screw Collier Company* [1866] LR 1 CP 600 at 612 (Willes J).

50 O'Donnell J in *ICDL GCC Foundation FZ-LLC v European Computer Driving Licence Foundation Ltd* [2012] IESC 55 at 16. The majority of the court adopted a slightly different formulation requiring proof that the defendant has 'to a significant extent, been negligent': see Fennelly J at 142.

51 [2016] EWCA Civ 799.

acted without a particular provision of the trust deed in mind, of the benefit of the exoneration clause even though the breach of trust was entirely unconscious or accidental'.[52]

(vi) Reform

Millett LJ, in *Armitage v Nurse*,[53] expressed the opinion that trusts exemption clauses had gone too far, with the result that professional trustees were able to exclude liability even for gross negligence despite charging for their services and in circumstances where they would not dream of excluding liability for ordinary professional negligence. However, he thought that it was for Parliament to deny them effect, even though it may be noted that a minority of the Privy Council in *Spread Trustee Company Ltd v Hutcheson*[54] thought that before *Armitage v Nurse* it was not clear that an exemption clause could have applied to gross negligence.[55] In *Re Clapham (Decd)*,[56] Behrens J also observed that this was an area of law 'ripe for reform'.

The Law Commission conducted a review of the operation of trustee exemption clauses[57] and issued a final report in 2006.[58] The Law Commission found that it was relatively common to find express provision for exclusion of liability in modern trust instruments and that professional trustees have come to rely on them as a means of affording protection from liability for breach of trusts. Thus, it rejected an absolute prohibition on all trustee exemption clauses on the grounds that denying settlors all power to modify or restrict the extent of the obligations and liabilities of trustees would undermine the flexibility and adaptability of the trust relationship. However, while many professional trustees considered such clauses to be a necessary component of modern trust practice, and the inclusion of an exclusion clause is likely to lead to lower liability insurance premiums, the Law Commission had originally considered that there was a very strong case for some regulation of trustee exemption clauses. More particularly, it proposed that professional trustees should not be able to rely on clauses which exclude their liability for breach of trust arising from negligence, and that in so far as professional trustees may not exclude liability for breach of trust, that they should not be permitted to claim indemnity from the trust fund. There was little support for this approach in the consultation exercise, and the Law Commission abandoned proposing legislative intervention.[59] Instead, it proposed that trustee exemption clauses should be regulated by rules of good practice agreed by the professional and regulatory bodies,[60] and that, where an exemption clause seeks to limit liability for negligence for paid trustees, such steps must be taken as are reasonable to inform the settlor of the meaning and effect of the clause.[61] Breach of any of the rules would not lead to damages for breach of trust, but breach of discipline. It is striking that Guernsey and Jersey have both legislated to prevent exemption clauses applying to trustee liability for gross negligence,[62] and this strongly suggests that the Law Commission may have been too timid in its approach.[63]

[52] Ibid at 51. [53] [1998] Ch 241 at 256. [54] [2011] UKPC 13.

[55] See also Hayton, 'The Irreducible Core Content of Trusteeship' in Oakley, *Trends in Contemporary Trust Law* (Clarendon Press 1997); McCormack, 'The Liability of Trustees for Gross Negligence' [1998] Conv 100.

[56] [2005] EWHC 3387 (Ch) at 89. [57] *Trustee Exemption Clauses* (Law Com No 171, 2003).

[58] *Trustee Exemption Clauses* (Law Com No 301, 2006).

[59] It appears other legislative enactments regulating the use of exemption clauses are inapplicable in the trust context—see *Baker v J E Clark Co (Transport) UK Ltd* [2006] EWCA Civ 464 at 21, where Tuckey LJ held that the Unfair Contract Terms Act 1977 did not apply to trustee exemption clauses.

[60] *Trustee Exemption Clauses* (Law Com No 301, 2006), para 7.2. [61] Ibid, para 6.65.

[62] See *Spread Trustee Company Ltd v Hutcheson* [2011] UKPC 13.

[63] See Kenny, 'Conveyancer's Notebook: The Good, the Bad and the Law Commission' [2007] Conv 103 at 103–8. See also Delaney, 'Trustee Exemption Clauses—Proposals for Regulation in Ireland' [2009] Tru LI 89 at 99, where she concluded that there 'is a strong case for some form of statutory regulation, and the Law Commission's earlier assertion that the current legal position is too deferential to professional trustees in particular is one that has commanded support from both academics and members of the judiciary'.

(f) Breach of trust in the context of constructive and resulting trusts

Whereas the trustees of an express trust are liable for breach of trust, the position of a trustee of a resulting or constructive trust is more complex. The essential difference relates to the nature of the duties of such trustees, since in many cases they will not be expected to perform the ordinary functions of express trustee such as the investment of the trust fund. As Millett LJ observed in *Lonrho plc v Al-Fayed (No 2)*:

> It is a mistake to suppose that in every situation in which a constructive trust arises the legal owner is necessarily subject to all the fiduciary obligations and disabilities of an express trustee.[64]

The primary duty of a constructive trustee is often simply to preserve the trust property for the benefit of the beneficiaries, and to ensure that it is not dissipated. If the trust property is dissipated by the trustee he may be liable to compensate the beneficiaries for their loss, i.e. the value of the trust property. A person held liable as a constructive trustee for knowingly receiving trust property will be under the same custodial duties as if the trust had been a voluntarily assumed express trust.[65] However, it appears that a constructive trustee will only be personally liable in this way if, at the relevant time, he was consciously aware of his obligations as a trustee, or of the factors that gave rise to the imposition of a trust. In *Westdeutsche Landesbank Girozentrale v Islington London Borough Council*, Lord Browne-Wilkinson stated:

> Since the equitable jurisdiction to enforce trusts depends upon the conscience of the holder of the legal interest being affected, he cannot be a trustee of the property if and so long as he is ignorant of the facts alleged to affect his conscience, i.e. until he is aware that he is intended to hold the property for the benefit of others in the case of an express trust, or, in the case of a constructive trust, of the factors which are alleged to affect his conscience.[66]

While the precise import of this analysis is somewhat obscure, the best interpretation is probably that although someone may become a trustee unknowingly, he cannot be held personally liable for any breach of trust, or breach of fiduciary duty, if he was unaware of the fact that he was such a trustee, or of the circumstances making him a trustee. Thus, a third party who is improperly given trust property becomes a constructive trustee of it (subject to the defence of being a bona fide purchaser), and the beneficial interest of the beneficiaries is preserved. However, the fact that he is a trustee does not mean that he will attract personal liability for breach of trust if he dissipates the property in circumstances where he was unaware of the constructive trust. In *Bristol and West Building Society v Mothew*, Millett LJ adopted this analysis as a summary of the practical outworking of Lord Browne-Wilkinson's comments:

> In *Westdeutsche Landesbank Girozentrale v Islington London Borough Council* Lord Browne-Wilkinson expressly rejected the possibility that a recipient of trust money could be personally liable, regardless of fault, for any subsequent payment away of the moneys to third parties even though, at the date of such payment, he was ignorant of the existence of any trust.[67]

(2) Nature of liability for breach of trust

(a) Trustees are personally liable

The liability of a trustee for a breach of trust is a personal liability, and any remedy is available only against the trustee as an individual, and not against any specific assets. If the

64 [1992] 1 WLR 1 at 12.

65 *Arthur v Attorney General of the Turks and Caicos Islands* [2012] UKPC 30 at 34–7.

66 [1996] AC 669.

67 [1996] 4 All ER 698 at 716. See also *Statek Corp v Alford* [2008] EWHC 32, discussed in Chapter 37.

trustee in breach has died, his personal liability continues against his estate.[68] There may be separate remedies in relation to any assets retained by the trustee or in the hands of a third party, and different remedies are also available for breach of fiduciary duty. These other remedies are considered in Chapters 35, 37, and 38.

(b) Trustees are liable only for their own breaches of trust

Trustees are only liable for their own breaches of trust and not for the breaches of their co-trustees.[69] However, where several trustees are liable for a breach of trust they are jointly and severally liable. Thus, in *Bishopsgate Investment Management Ltd v Maxwell (No 2)*,[70] Kevin and Ian Maxwell, who had both signed transfers misappropriating assets held on trust for the pensions of the employees of Maxwell-owned companies, were jointly and severally liable for their breaches. Joint and several liability means that the beneficiary can recover the entire loss to the trust from any one of the trustees alone.[71] Even where the beneficiary has obtained a judgment against all the trustees he may choose to execute it against any one.[72] As Leach MR stated in *Wilson v Moore*:[73] 'all parties to a breach of trust are equally liable; there is between them no primary liability'.

Although the beneficiaries may be able to recover the entire loss suffered by the trust from just one of the trustees in breach, that trustee may be able to recover a contribution to the damages he has had to pay from his fellow trustees.[74]

(c) Breaches before appointment

A trustee is not liable for breaches of trust which were committed before his appointment.[75] On appointment he is obliged to make reasonable inquiries to ensure that the trust affairs are in order,[76] but, except in so far as a discrepancy appears, he 'is entitled to assume that everything has been duly attended to up to the time of his becoming trustee'.[77] However, if he does discover such a breach he should take proceedings against the former trustees responsible.

(d) Liability after retirement

Retirement does not save a trustee from liability for breaches of trust committed while he was a trustee. He will also be liable if he retired to enable a breach of trust to take place. The principle was stated by Kekewich J in *Head v Gould*:

> in order to make a retiring trustee liable for a breach of trust committed by his successor you must shew, and shew clearly, that the very breach of trust which was in fact committed was not merely the outcome of the retirement and new appointment, but was contemplated by the former trustee when such retirement and appointment took place.[78]

The key factor which renders a retired trustee liable is the fact that he was fully aware of, and connived in, the subsequent breach of trust.

(e) Trustees not vicariously liable for each other

The Trustee Act 2000 repealed a contentious provision in the Trustee Act 1925 (s 30(1)), which addressed the issue of when trustees would be liable for the acts of other trustees.

68 See *Fry v Fry* [1859] 27 Beav 144.

69 *Townley v Sherborn* [1634] J Bridg 35.

70 [1994] 1 All ER 261, CA.

71 *Walker v Symonds* [1818] 3 Swan 1; *Re Harrison* [1891] 2 Ch 349; *McCheane v Gyles (No 2)* [1902] 1 Ch 911.

72 *A-G v Wilson* [1840] Cr & Ph 1; *Fletcher v Green* [1864] 33 Beav 426.

73 [1833] 1 My & K 126 at 146.

74 Discussed later in the chapter.

75 *Re Strahan* [1856] 8 De GM & G 291.

76 *Harvey v Oliver* [1887] 57 LT 239; *Re Lucking's Will Trusts* [1968] 1 WLR 866.

77 *Re Strahan* [1856] 8 De GM & G 291 at 309, per Turner LJ.

78 [1898] 2 Ch 250 at 273–4.

It did not replace it, with the effect that trustees will be liable for losses caused by other trustees only when they themselves are in breach of trust, for instance by concurring in an ultra vires decision, or by wrongly failing to act to prevent another trustee committing a breach of trust.

(f) Election between compensatory and restitutionary remedies

It will be seen that in some circumstances beneficiaries may have more than one remedy. For instance where a trustee has improperly used trust property for his own purposes and made a profit, the beneficiary may be able to pursue both an action for the loss caused to the trust by the breach (equitable compensation), and an action to deprive the trustee of the profit (a claim for restitution based on unjust enrichment). These remedies are not cumulative. In *Tang Man Sit (Decd) v Capacious Investments Ltd*,[79] the Privy Council held that the remedies of compensation for breach of trust and restitution where a trustee has breached his fiduciary duty are alternative, and that the beneficiaries must elect between them to prevent double recovery. The case concerned a planned joint venture for the development of land. The defendant provided land for the development, which was funded by the plaintiff company. It was agreed that the defendant would assign legal title to sixteen of the houses built to the plaintiffs. It was held that this created a trust of the houses for the plaintiff, but in breach of trust the title was never assigned by the defendants. Over a period of years, the defendant let the houses to tenants and received a profit of some HK$2m in the form of rent. The plaintiffs claimed that they were entitled to an equitable account of these profits on the grounds that they were unauthorized remuneration received by the defendant trustee in breach of its fiduciary duty, and also damages for breach of trust for the rent that they could have obtained from the houses if they had been assigned at the appropriate time, a sum which was assessed at HK$17m. The defendant had paid HK$1.8m to the plaintiffs by way of account of the profit received, and the plaintiffs subsequently sought the damages due. The defendant argued that by accepting the account of profits the plaintiffs had made an irrevocable election between the restitutionary and compensatory remedies. The Privy Council held that in the circumstances no election had been made, so that the plaintiffs were entitled to recover full damages, less the HK$1.8m they had already received. The Privy Council stated that:

> Faced with alternative and inconsistent remedies a plaintiff must choose, or elect, between them. He cannot have both.[80]

3 Compensation for breach of trust

(1) General principles

(a) A compensatory remedy

The remedy for breach of trust is essentially compensatory.[81] When a breach has been committed the trustee responsible is liable to compensate the trust (rather than an

[79] [1996] AC 514. See Stevens, 'Election between Alternative Remedies' [1996] RLR 117; Birks, 'Inconsistency between Compensation and Restitution' [1996] 112 LQR 375.

[80] [1996] 1 All ER 193 at 197 (Lord Nicholls).

[81] See Oakley, 'The Liberalising Nature of Remedies for Breach of Trust' in Oakley, *Trends in Contemporary Trust Law* (Clarendon Press 1997), pp 219–30; Capper, 'Compensation for Breach of Trust' [1997] Conv 14; Sealy, 'Mortgagees and Receivers—A Duty of Care Resurrected and Extended' [2000] 59 CLJ 31; Birks and Rose (eds), *Restitution and Equity, Vol 1: Resulting Trusts and Equitable Compensation* (Routledge 2000).

individual beneficiary[82]) for all the loss flowing directly or indirectly from the breach.[83] As Street J said in *Re Dawson*:

> the trustee is liable to place the trust estate in the same position it would have been in if no breach had been committed.[84]

In some cases, for example, *Target Holdings Ltd v Redferns*,[85] this compensation has been described as 'restitution' of the trust estate.[86] However, this usage is likely to cause confusion. As a legal term of art, restitution is the response which consists in a defendant giving up to the claimant any gains made through unjust enrichment.[87] A trustee in breach of trust may not have received any personal gain, in which case it is impossible to regard him as 'enriched'. The trustee is required to compensate the trust for the loss it has sustained in consequence of his conduct, not to return an enrichment he has received. As Lord Browne-Wilkinson observed in *Target Holdings Ltd v Redferns*:

> in the case of a breach of such a trust involving the wrongful paying away of trust assets, the liability of the trustee is to restore to the trust fund, often called the trust estate, what ought to have been there.[88]

(b) **Causation**

A trustee who has acted in breach is only liable to compensate the trust for loss which was caused by his breach. If there is no causal link between the breach and the loss, the trustee will not be liable. This is clear from the decision of the Court of Appeal in *Bishopsgate Investment Management Ltd v Maxwell (No 2)*.[89] This case arose out of the infamous Robert Maxwell pension fraud. Robert Maxwell had conducted a fraud on a massive scale, which included misappropriating pension funds held by the plaintiff company of which Ian Maxwell was a director. Ian Maxwell, as a director, had signed transfers to Robert Maxwell's private companies beneath the signature of his brother, Kevin, and had also signed blank transfers. He had made no inquiry about the transactions and had signed the transfers because his brother had done so. The plaintiff obtained summary judgment against him. Ian Maxwell appealed on the basis that the plaintiff had not shown that his inactivity had caused the loss. The Court of Appeal made it clear that where a fiduciary has committed a breach of duty by omission, the plaintiff claiming damages must prove that the omission caused the loss, in the sense that compliance would have prevented the damage.[90] However, the court held that this was not a case where the breach was in the nature of an omission, but that the breach was simply the improper transfer of the shares to Robert Maxwell Group plc. Causation was thus clearly established and the summary judgment was upheld.

The requirement of causation was considered at length by the House of Lords in *Target Holdings Ltd v Redferns*.[91] The case concerned a complex mortgage fraud. Mirage Properties Ltd agreed to sell properties in Birmingham to Crowngate Developments Ltd,

[82] *Re X Trust* [2013] WTLR 731 (Royal Court of Jersey).

[83] *Bateman v Davis* [1818] 3 Madd 98; *Lander v Weston* [1855] 3 Drew 389; *Knott v Cottee* [1852] 16 Beav 77; *Re Miller's Deed Trusts* [1978] LS Gaz R 454; *Bartlett v Barclays Trust Co Ltd* [1980] Ch 515. See also Baxter, 'Trustees' Personal Liability and the Role of Liability Insurance' [1996] Conv 186.

[84] [1966] 2 NSWLR 211 at 215.

[85] [1996] 1 AC 421.

[86] [1996] 1 AC 421 at 434, per Lord Browne-Wilkinson. See also Hanbury and Martin, *Modern Equity* (18th edn, Sweet & Maxwell 2009), which describes the liability as 'restitutionary' (at p 685).

[87] Birks, *Introduction to the Law of Restitution* (Clarendon Press 1985), pp 9–27.

[88] [1996] 1 AC 421 at 434.

[89] [1994] 1 All ER 261.

[90] [1994] 1 All ER 261 at 264, per Hoffmann LJ.

[91] [1996] 1 AC 421, [1996] 112 LQR 27 (Rickett); [1996] LMCLQ 161 (Nolan); [1997] Conv 14 (Capper); [1995] 9 TLI 86 (Ulph). See also [1998] 114 LQR 214 (Sir Peter Millett).

a company owned by Mr Kohli and Mr Musafir, for £775,000. To execute the fraud, Kholi and Musafir arranged for the purchase to be made through two intermediary companies they owned (first Panther Ltd and then Kholi & Co), so that it appeared that the sale to Crowngate was for a consideration of £2 million. Crowngate applied to Target Holdings for a loan of £1.7 million, and employed Redferns as their solicitors. The loan application was supported by a £2 million valuation of the properties made by a firm of estate agents. The loan was paid into Redferns' client account on 28 June 1989, without any express instructions as to the release of the funds. On 29 June £1.25 million was transferred to the account of Panther in Jersey, although at this stage the contract for the purchase of the properties had not yet been entered, and it was not until July that the contracts and mortgages in favour of Target were executed. Subsequently, the value of the properties dropped sharply and Target sought to recover their loss.

Any action against the estate agents, who had carried out the valuation, was of little value because they were in liquidation. Target therefore sought to recover its loss (allowing for the amount recovered from the sale of the property) from Redferns. Target applied for summary judgment. There was no doubt that the transfer of funds before the contracts for sale and the mortgages had been entered had constituted a breach of trust. The only question for the court was whether Redferns had any defence. Warner J at first instance held that Redferns had an arguable defence. The Court of Appeal, by a majority, disagreed. It held that once a breach of trust was established, the trustee was obliged to make good the deficiency in the trust fund, and the rules about remoteness of damage applicable to contract claims had no application.[92] Ralph Gibson LJ delivered a powerful dissenting judgment, in which he held that Warner J had been correct to refuse to give Target final judgment. He took the view that there was an arguable defence that the breach had not caused the loss. Although he felt that Target was likely to succeed, he held that it was arguable that it would have gone ahead with the transaction in any event, relying on the valuation of the properties by the estate agents, and that in such circumstances the breach of trust by Redferns would not have been the cause of the loss.

Redferns appealed to the House of Lords, which, agreeing with Ralph Gibson LJ, held that Target was not entitled to final judgment. Lord Browne-Wilkinson stated the underlying principle as follows:

> there does have to be some causal connection between the breach of trust and the loss to the trust estate for which compensation is recoverable, viz the fact that the loss would not have occurred but for the breach.[93]

He went on to conclude that, on the assumption that the transaction would have gone ahead irrespective of the breach of trust, the breach had not been the cause of the loss suffered:

> Target has not demonstrated that it is entitled to any compensation for breach of trust. . . . Target obtained exactly what it would have obtained had no breach occurred, ie a valid security for the sum advanced.[94]

In the course of his judgment he rejected Target's argument that Redferns were under an immediate duty to restore the trust fund, holding that in a commercial conveyancing

[92] Referring to *Clough v Bond* [1838] 3 My & Cr 490; *Re Dawson* [1966] 2 NSWLR 211; *Alliance and Leicester Building Society v Edgestop Ltd* [1994] 2 All ER 38; *Bishopsgate Investment Management Ltd v Maxwell (No 2)* [1994] 1 All ER 261, CA.

[93] [1996] 1 AC 421 at 434. See also *Re Miller's Deed Trusts* [1978] LS Gaz 454; *Nestlé v National Westminster Bank plc* [1994] 1 All ER 118.

[94] [1996] 1 AC 421 at 440.

context a client has no right to have the solicitor's client account reconstituted after the transaction is completed.[95] He also rejected the argument that the quantum of compensation was to be fixed at the date that the alleged breach occurred. Instead he held:

> The quantum is fixed at the date of judgment, at which date, according to the circumstances then pertaining, the compensation is assessed as the figure then necessary to put the trust estate or the beneficiary back into the position it would have been in had there been no breach.[96]

Despite concluding that Target had not proved causation, the House of Lords was doubtful whether Redferns would ultimately be able to show that their breach had not caused the loss. Lord Browne-Wilkinson summarized:

> There must be a high probability that, at trial, it will emerge that the use of Target's money to pay for the purchase from Mirage and the other intermediate transactions was a vital feature of this transaction . . . If the moneys made available by Redfern's breach of trust were essential to enable the transaction to go through, but for Redfern's breach of trust Target would not have advanced any money. In that case the loss suffered by Target by reason of the breach of trust will be the total sum advanced to Crowngate less the proceeds of the security.[97]

In conclusion, the decision of the House of Lords in *Target Holdings Ltd v Redferns* requires a claimant seeking compensation when trust property has been transferred contrary to the terms of the trust (or in the case of a bare trust, contrary to the instructions of the beneficiary) to demonstrate that, but for the alleged breach of trust, he would not have suffered the loss sustained. Conversely, the defendant can escape liability by demonstrating that the loss would have been sustained even if the breach had not occurred. The decision was subject to criticism, but it was affirmed without qualification by the Supreme Court in *AIB Group (UK) Plc v Mark Redler & Co Solicitors*.[98] The Supreme Court in *AIB* also took the view that damages in a case like *Target Holdings* should be limited to that which would have been recoverable in contract, because the trust was 'part of the machinery for the performance of a [commercial] contract'.[99]

By way of qualification to this general proposition, there may be circumstances in which the burden of proof shifts to the defendant. In *Bristol and West Building Society v May, May & Merrimans (No 1)*[100] Chadwick J held that where a solicitor had made a warranty or misrepresentation to a mortgagee which the solicitor knew[101] to be misleading there was no need for the claimant to answer the 'what if' question:

> It would, as it seems to me, be a strange principle of equity which allowed a solicitor who, in breach of the duty of good faith owed to his client, had given a warranty which he knew to be false with the intention that the client should act upon it, to say, in answer to a claim for compensation in respect of loss which had resulted from the client relying on the warranty and acting as he intended, that the client must establish that he would not have so acted if he had been told the true facts. After all, a common reason for giving a warranty which the warrantor knows to be false is the fear that, without the false warranty, the lender will refuse to proceed. If it were not for that fear the warrantor would have no reason to withhold the truth. [W]here a fiduciary has failed to disclose material facts, he cannot be heard to say, in answer to a claim for equitable compensation, that disclosure would not have altered the decision to proceed with the transaction.[102]

[95] [1996] 1 AC 421 at 436. [96] [1996] 1 AC 421 at 437. [97] [1996] 1 AC 421 at 440–1.

[98] [2014] UKSC 58; [2015] AC 1503. See the discussion of the cases in *Main v Giambrone & Law* [2017] EWCA Civ 1193.

[99] [2015] AC 1503 at 71, per Lord Toulson, similarly at 137, per Lord Reed.

[100] [1996] 2 All ER 801; Alcock, 'Limiting Contractual and Tortious Damages' [1997] LMCLQ 26.

[101] Or must be taken to have known. [102] [1996] 2 All ER 801 at 825–6.

He held that this approach was supported by the earlier decision of the Privy Council in *Brickenden v London Loan & Savings Co*,[103] which he considered had not been overruled by the House of Lords in *Target Holdings Ltd v Redferns*.

(c) Liability only for loss caused by the breach

The cases dealing with the liability of a solicitor for releasing mortgage funds without authority show that the liability extends only to the loss caused by the breach and does not include other losses arising from entering into the mortgage.[104] There is no reason to think that the rule is not of general application to other breaches of trust. Where the transaction was induced by fraud, and would not have been made but for the fraud, then compensation will be based on the direct losses caused by the transaction,[105] but this is simply a case of applying the ordinary rules about causation.[106]

(d) Liability and the extent of professional involvement

Judges in equity have recently adopted a principle from the ordinary common law of negligence. Applying what has come to be known as the *SAAMCo* principle,[107] the extent of liability for loss is linked to the extent to which a professional took control of their client's affairs. A distinction by Lord Sumption in *BPE Solicitors v Hughes Holland* is whether the professional is: 'guiding the whole decision-making process,'[108] or, 'contributed a limited part of the material on which his client will rely . . . .'[109]

In *Main v Giambrone & Law*,[110] a case involving equitable principles, Jackson LJ considered the application of the *SAAMCo* principles in the context of breaches of duty, leading to lost deposits. The breach was by a firm of Italian lawyers involved in a failed luxury holiday home development in Calabria. The scheme collapsed amongst dramatic, albeit unproven, allegations that the whole project was a money laundering operation used by the IRA and Italian Mafia to recycle the proceeds of IRA criminal activities. The *SAAMCo* principle did not limit liability in the particular case. The firm had assumed significant influence over the transaction. This meant that the loss was, 'clearly in the scope of Giambrone's duty.'[111]

By contrast, in *Liv Bridging Finance Ltd v EAD Solicitors LLP*,[112] a firm of solicitors was acting for a short term loan provider. A solicitor at the firm, named Mr Gorman, paid away loan monies for the purchase of properties on Merseyside. He did so, in breach of trust, without first ensuring that the loans were protected by an effective first legal charge on the properties. The schemes into which the loans were paid appear to have been fraudulent, and so the loan provider lost the money advanced. Halliwell J found that the firm of solicitors should compensate the loan provider. However, in an application of the *SAAMCo* principles, the loan company was able to recover only those losses within the ambit of the firm's specific duty to obtain a charge. There could be no wider recovery for the loan provider.

[103] [1934] 3 DLR 465. [104] *Swindle v Harrison* [1997] 4 All ER 705.

[105] Ibid; Elliott, 'Restitutionary Compensatory Damages for Breach of Fiduciary Duty?' [1998] RLR 135.

[106] *Collins v Brebner*, 26 January 2000 (CA) at 57–64.

[107] Named after *South Australia Asset Management Corporation v York Montagu Ltd* [1997] AC 191, a well-known common law liability case turning on the extent of liability for the negligent valuation of property in circumstances where there had been a general fall in property values.

[108] *BPE Solicitors v Hughes Holland* [2017] UKSC 21, [40].

[109] *BPE Solicitors v Hughes Holland* [2017] UKSC 21, [41]. [110] [2017] EWCA Civ 1193.

[111] *Main v Giambrone & Law* [2017] EWCA Civ 1193 at [86].

[112] [2020] EWHC 1590 (Ch) at [35].

The *SAAMCo* principles have very recently been reviewed and nuanced by the Supreme Court.[113] In *Manchester Building Society v Grant Thornton UK LLP*,[114] a case concerning the tortious common law liability of an accountancy firm, the Supreme Court emphasized that there is 'spectrum' of liability-causing circumstances. Their Lordships were keen to stress that the test is no longer conceived in 'either/or' terms. So, on the basis of this reasoning, it has become harder for professionals to 'box off' liability through a claim that they had only a limited role in relation to their client's loss-making decisions.

(e) Obligation to restore the trust fund

In some cases, rather than paying compensation to the beneficiaries (who can only be entitled to individual pecuniary compensation if they are absolutely entitled to the fund),[115] the appropriate measure of compensation will be to restore to the trust fund what it has lost.[116] This would be the case, for instance, where a trust is continuing, especially if it is a complex family trust where the loss suffered by individual beneficiaries is hard to assess.[117] Depending on the nature of the breach, this may be the same compensation as would be payable through common law damages for breach of contract, but that will not necessarily be the case.[118]

(f) Remoteness and foreseeability of loss

Although *Target Holdings Ltd v Redferns (a firm)*[119] and *AIB Group (UK) Plc v Mark Redler & Co Solicitors*[120] demonstrate a need to establish causation in order to render a trustee liable to compensate for breach of trust, the further question arises whether, where such causation is established, a trustee is liable for all the loss which flows from his breach, directly or indirectly, or whether some principle of remoteness operates to limit his liability to such losses as were reasonably foreseeable as a result of the breach. Traditionally it has been held that the trustee's liability is not mitigated by such principles as remoteness of damage.[121] Indeed, in *Target Holdings Ltd v Redferns* itself,[122] the House of Lords held that the common law principle of remoteness of damage has no application to liability where trust property was wrongly transferred by the trustee in breach of the terms of the trust. Lord Browne-Wilkinson stated:[123]

> If specific restitution of the trust property is not possible, then the liability of the trustee is to pay sufficient compensation to the trust estate to put it back to what it would have been had the breach not been committed. Even if the immediate cause of the loss is the dishonesty or failure of a third party the trustee is liable to make good that loss to the trust estate if, but for the breach, such loss would not have occurred. Thus the common law rules of remoteness of damage and causation do not apply.

113 In the twinned cases of *Manchester Building Society v Grant Thornton UK LLP* [2021] UKSC 20 and *Khan v Meadows* [2021] UKSC 21.

114 [2021] UKSC 20.

115 *AIB v Redler* [2015] AC 1503 at 100.

116 See the discussion in Dawson, 'Corporate Rescue by the Upright Rescuer—A Trap for the Unwary' [2016] *Insolvency Intelligence* 82.

117 *Brudenell-Bruce v Moore* [2014] EWHC 3679 (Ch) at 242–51.

118 *Main v Giambrone & Law* [2017] EWCA Civ 1193 at 63.

119 [1996] AC 421.

120 [2015] AC 1503. See the discussion of the cases in *Main v Giambrone & Law* [2017] EWCA Civ 1193.

121 Underhill and Hayton, *Law Relating to Trusts and Trustees* (16th edn, LexisNexis 2003), p 855.

122 [1996] 1 AC 421.

123 [1996] 1 AC 421 at 434. For criticism of this position, see: *Bank of New Zealand v New Zealand Guardian Trust Co Ltd* [1999] 1 NZLR 213; affd [1999] 1 NZLR 664; *Collins v Brebner* [2000] Lloyd's Rep PN 587; Elliott, 'Remoteness Criteria in Equity' [2002] 65 MLR 588.8.

(g) Other limits on loss

Causation in the 'but for' sense is not the only limit on a trustee's liability for loss. In *Novoship (UK) Limited v Nikitin*,[124] it was said that, in addition, '[c]ommon sense . . . also plays its part in determining the extent of equitable compensation.' Again, in *Hughes-Holland v BPE Solicitors*, Lord Sumption, delivering the decision of the Supreme Court, said:

> the relevant filters [on liability] are not limited to those which can be analysed in terms of causation. Ultimately, all of them depend on a developed judicial instinct about the nature or extent of the duty which the wrongdoer has broken.[125]

The operation of these filters or limits on liability in the context of trustees' duties has yet to be clearly explained, but they are likely to be used to limit the simple operation of the 'but for' causation test. One filter to which Lord Sumption refers, that could be of relevance in relation to trustees, is the 'familiar example' of effective or substantial causation.

(h) Accounting for tax liability

The rule that tax liability is to be taken into account when calculating damages for personal injury in tort[126] is not applied, and, in *Re Bell's Indenture*,[127] it was held that a trustee should restore the value of misappropriated property to the trust without allowance for the tax that would have had to be paid on it by the trust if it had not been misappropriated.

(2) Investment

Trustees now have much wider powers of investment than used to be the case, so it will now be rare for a trust to hold or to make an unauthorized investment. However, where a trustee does purchase an unauthorized investment, he will be liable for any loss resulting from the purchase which will be the amount by which those investments have fallen in value[128] or for the difference between the value of the investments actually made and those which should have been purchased or retained.[129] In the same way, if a trustee retains unauthorized investments he will be liable to the beneficiaries for any loss that the trust suffers as a result. The measure of loss will be the amount that the investments could have realized if they had been sold at the proper time, less the value that they actually realized.[130]

Even where trust funds have been invested in permitted investments, under Trustee Act 2000, s 5, a trustee is under duty to review the investments of the trust and to obtain and consider proper advice about whether they should be varied. If he fails to fulfil this duty, or fails to exercise the requisite duty of reasonable care, he will be liable to compensate the trust for the resulting loss. The Trustee Act 1925, ss 8 and 9, contains some special rules relating to investments made by lending on the security of a mortgage (a common form of trustee investment in the Victorian era, but now very rare).

(3) Assessing compensation

(a) Date for assessing compensation

In *Target Holdings Ltd v Redferns*,[131] it was held that the quantum of equitable compensation payable in respect of a breach of trust is to be assessed not at the date that the

[124] [2014] EWCA Civ 908; [2015] 1 QB 499 at 108.
[125] [2017] 3 All ER 969 at 20.
[126] *British Transport Commission v Gourley* [1956] AC 185, HL.
[127] [1980] 1 WLR 1217.
[128] *Knott v Cottee* [1852] 16 Beav 77.
[129] *Re Massingberd's Settlement* [1890] 63 LT 296.
[130] *Fry v Fry* [1859] 27 Beav 144. See also *Jaffray v Marshall* [1994] 1 All ER 143.
[131] [1996] 1 AC 401.

breach occurred, but at the date of judgment. The House of Lords overruled the decision in *Jaffray v Marshall*,[132] where it had been held that a trustee who committed an ongoing breach of trust by failing to restore trust property to the trust fund was required to compensate the beneficiaries on the basis of the property's value at the date on which the action was brought.

(b) Subsequent events

Since the purpose of equitable compensation is to restore any loss caused by the breach, if as a result of events subsequent to the breach the loss is mitigated or reversed, those events will be taken into account. Thus, in *Target Holdings*, it was relevant that the mortgage security had been obtained, albeit later than should have been the case. Equally, in *Hulbert v Avens*,[133] where trustees incurred a penalty by not paying tax on time, but made a profit by favourably investing the money that should have been used for tax, the profit was to be set against the penalty, and the trustees could be held liable only for the difference. Again, in *AIB Group (UK) Plc v Mark Redler & Co Solicitors*,[134] a firm of solicitors carelessly failed to discharge a prior loan on a remortgage. In consequence, the lending bank obtained only a second charge. This was a breach of trust since the solicitors had not complied with the terms of their authority. The borrower defaulted and the bank was unable to recover its loan in full. The Supreme Court held that the solicitors were only liable for the extent to which the bank would have recovered more if it had received the first charge; most of their loss was attributable to the property being worth less than it had expected.

(c) Offsetting losses and gains

(i) The general rule

It is a basic principle that each breach of trust is to be treated independently of the trustee's other activities. A loss suffered by the trust as a result of a breach in one transaction cannot be offset against a gain achieved for the trust in another. The trustee remains liable for the loss caused by his breach, irrespective of the gain. This principle was accepted in *Bartlett v Barclays Bank Trust Co Ltd (No 2)*,[135] where Brightman J stated:

> The general rule . . . is that where a trustee is liable in respect of distinct breaches of trust, one of which resulted in a loss and the other in a gain, he is not entitled to set the gain against the loss, unless they arise in the same transaction.[136]

This rule was applied in *Dimes v Scott*,[137] where the trustees of a settlement created on the death of Captain Piercey in 1802 failed to sell an investment in the East India Company, which they had been directed to convert into money by the Captain's will. The trustees paid the full income received (10 per cent per annum) to the life beneficiary. Under the (now abolished) rule in *Howe v Dartmouth*,[138] the life tenant was only entitled to a 4 per cent return on the value of the investment as income. When the unauthorized investment was realized in 1813, the proceeds were used to purchase Consols. As the price of the Consols had fallen since the date of the testator's death, they were able to purchase more than they would have been able to at that time. It was held that the gain to the beneficiaries of the extra Consols could not be offset against the trustees' liability for excessive payments made to the life tenant while the unauthorized investment was retained.

132 [1994] 1 All ER 143. 133 [2003] EWHC 76 (Ch). 134 [2015] AC 1503.

135 [1980] Ch 515; [1980] Conv 155 (Shindler); [1983] Conv 127 (Pearce and Samuels).

136 [1980] Ch 515 at 538. See also *Adye v Feuilleteau* [1783] 3 Swan 84n; *Robinson v Robinson* [1848] 11 Beav 371; *Wiles v Gresham* [1854] 2 Drew 258.

137 [1828] 4 Russ 195. 138 [1802] 7 Ves 137.

(ii) Distinct breaches of trust

The rule preventing any set-off between losses and gains only applies if there are distinct, independent breaches of trust. If the breaches occur in the course of one indivisible transaction then any gain will be taken into account. This provides an adequate explanation for *Fletcher v Green*.[139] Here the trustee of a settlement committed a breach of trust by lending money on a mortgage which proved insufficient security. When the security was realized the money was invested in Consols, which rose in value, producing a gain of £251. The court held that this gain must be set off against the trustee's liability for the failure of the security.

(iii) Set-off in exceptional circumstances

In *Bartlett v Barclays Bank Trust Co Ltd (No 2)*,[140] the general principle that there should be no set-off between gains and losses flowing from a breach of trust was reaffirmed, although without enthusiasm. However, on the specific facts, Brightman J did permit the defendant bank to set off the gain that had been made in one investment in breach of trust against a loss made in another. A company owned by the trust made two investments in property development schemes which were wholly inappropriate, and the bank was liable for having failed adequately to supervise the operations of the company. On one project, the 'Old Bailey Project', the company lost £580,000 capital and a great deal of income. On another project, the 'Guildford Development', which was entered under exactly the same policy of investment, the company made a profit of some £271,000. Brightman J held that this profit could be offset against the liability of the bank for the loss incurred by the Old Bailey Project. However he failed to provide an adequate explanation of why the set-off was permitted. Having stated the general principle, he continued:

> the relevant cases are not altogether easy to reconcile. All are centenarians and none is quite like the present. The Guildford development stemmed from exactly the same policy and (to a lesser degree because it proceeded less far) exemplified the same folly as the Old Bailey project. Part of the profit was in fact used to finance the Old Bailey disaster. By sheer luck the gamble paid off handsomely, on capital account. I think it would be unjust to deprive the bank of this element of salvage in the course of assessing the cost of the shipwreck. My order will therefore reflect the bank's right to an appropriate set-off.[141]

Despite the fact that the developments took place under the same policy, it cannot be said that they were effectively part of the same transaction so as not to be 'distinct' breaches of trust.

(iv) A new approach?

It is hard to reconcile the decision in *Bartlett v Barclays Bank Trust Co Ltd (No 2)* with *Dimes v Scott*, and, indeed, the facts of the latter case seem a better illustration of connected losses and gains than the former. Brightman J showed no enthusiasm for the general rule, and was astute to find a basis for distinguishing his own decision in order to achieve justice between the parties. The approach to the assessment of compensation adopted by the House of Lords and the Supreme Court in *Target Holdings* and *AIB v Redler* is consistent with this. Lord Browne-Wilkinson emphasized that beneficiaries should only be able to recover what they had actually lost:

> Equitable compensation for breach of trust is designed to achieve exactly what the word compensation suggests: to make good a loss in fact suffered by the beneficiaries and which, using hindsight and common sense, can be seen to have been caused by the breach.[142]

[139] [1864] 33 Beav 426. [140] [1980] Ch 515. [141] [1980] Ch 515 at 538.

[142] [1996] AC 421 at 163. This reasoning was approved in *AIB v Redler* [2015] AC 1503 at 73, 105, and 111.

It may be that if the Supreme Court has the opportunity to review the decision in *Dimes v Scott*, it will conclude that common sense requires that a realistic, rather than a purist, approach should be taken to balancing profits and losses made by trustees in breach.

(4) **Interest**

Where a trustee is liable to compensate the trust for loss caused by his misapplication of trust property, the trust is also entitled to recover interest on the sum misapplied. The rationale for this was explained by Buckley LJ in *Wallersteiner v Moir (No 2)*:

> It is well established in equity that a trustee who in breach of trust misapplies trust funds will be liable not only to replace the misapplied principal fund but to do so with interest from the date of the misapplication. This is on the notional ground that the money so applied was in fact the trustee's own money and that he has retained the misapplied trust money in his own hands and used it for his own purposes.[143]

The court assumes that the trustee has retained the misapplied property and has, therefore, had the opportunity to earn interest on it. A number of cases have considered the rate of interest which should be payable. Ultimately, the determination of the appropriate rate of interest is a matter for the discretion of the court, and decisions have taken account of factors such as the Bank of England base rate,[144] other relevant interest rates,[145] and the character,[146] conduct or fault of the trustee.[147]

The most generous approach, seen in *Watson v Kea Investments Limited*,[148] is to award a rate reflecting a 'growth fund' index. This will be very costly for the defendant as they will be required to pay over interest at a rate indexed with successful professional investments. In *Watson*, McCombe LJ held this to be 6.5 per cent. Such an approach reflects a business-world reality in circumstances where the claimant would have, as a matter of fact, invested the funds in a profitable scheme. Compound interest might also be charged in an appropriate case, for instance where the trustee has been fraudulent or made personal use of the money.[149] It may even be that there is now a general principle that compound interest should be paid truly to reflect the beneficiaries' loss.[150]

4 **Defences to liability for breach of trust**

Even if a trustee has committed a breach of trust which has caused loss to the trust, it is not inevitable that he will be required to pay equitable compensation to the trust. A number of defences are available to trustees which may wholly or partially protect them from liability. A trustee who is unclear whether a proposed action will constitute a breach may

143 [1975] QB 373 at 397.

144 *Wallersteiner v Moir (No 2)* [1975] QB 373, 508n; *Belmont Finance Corpn Ltd v Williams Furniture Ltd (No 2)* [1980] 1 All ER 393, CA; *O'Sullivan v Management Agency and Music Ltd* [1985] QB 428, CA.

145 *Guardian Ocean Cargoes Ltd v Banco do Brasil (No 3)* [1992] 2 Lloyd's Rep 193; *Bartlett v Barclays Bank Trust Co Ltd (No 2)* [1980] Ch 515 at 547.

146 *Re Evans (Decd)* [1999] 2 All ER 777 (non-professional administrator of a small estate charged interest at the lower end of the possible range).

147 *A-G v Alford* [1855] 4 De GM & G 843 (fraudulent trustee expected to pay a higher rate of interest).

148 [2019] EWCA Civ 1759.

149 *Wallersteiner v Moir (No 2)* [1975] QB 373; *Piety v Stace* [1799] 4 Ves 620; *Heathcote v Hulme* [1819] 1 Jac & W 122; *Brown v Sansome* [1825] M'Cle & Yo 427; *Jones v Foxall* [1852] 15 Beav 388; *Penny v Avison* [1856] 3 Jur NS 62; *Re Davis* [1902] 2 Ch 314.

150 *Wallersteiner v Moir (No 2)* [1975] QB 373 at 388.

apply to the court for directions.[151] This can be particularly useful where trustees face a difficult problem, for instance, in situations such as when dealing with potential claims from victims of abuse by the late Jimmy Savile.[152]

(1) Beneficiaries' consent or concurrence

(a) General principles

A beneficiary cannot complain of a breach of trust by a trustee to which he consented, or in which he actively concurred or passively acquiesced.[153] As Wilmer LJ stated in the context of an advance of trust property made by a trustee bank to the beneficiaries in breach of trust in *Re Pauling's Settlement Trusts*:

> if the bank can establish a valid request or consent by the advanced beneficiary to the advance in question, that is a good defence on the part of the bank to the beneficiary's claim, even though it can be plain that the advance was made in breach of trust.[154]

The case concerned a marriage settlement created in 1919 on the marriage of Violet Pauling and Commander Younghusband. The trustees were the bank Coutts & Co. By an express provision of the trust deed, the trustees had the power to advance up to one-half of the beneficiaries' presumptive share under the trust for their advancement or absolute use. The family consistently lived beyond its means, and Violet's current account with the trustees was often overdrawn. Between 1948 and 1954, a number of advancements were made to the children of the marriage, Francis, George, Anne, and Anthony, who were all of age by 1951, ostensibly for such purposes as improvements to their homes and the purchase of furniture. The money advanced was generally paid into Violet's overdrawn current account. The children subsequently complained that the bank had acted in breach of trust in making these advancements.

In respect of a number of advances, the Court of Appeal held that the bank was not liable because the beneficiaries had validly consented to the advances being made, with full knowledge that the money would be applied to reduce their mother's overdraft.

If a trustee wishes to avoid liability completely, he must have gained the consent of all the beneficiaries of the trust. If only some had consented, the remainder will retain the right to maintain an action against him for his breach (but only for their share of the loss).

(b) Requirements for relief from liability

(i) The beneficiary must be of age

A beneficiary must have reached the age of majority for his consent to a breach of trust to be effective to protect the trustee from liability. The consent of a minor is ineffective.[155] However, a minor who fraudulently misrepresents his age to persuade trustees to pay trust money over to him will not be permitted to deny that his consent was effective because of his age.[156]

[151] *Cotton v Brudenell-Bruce, Earl of Cardigan* [2014] EWCA Civ 1312. For a categorization of situations where this can be done see *Public Trustee v Cooper* [2001] WTLR 901.

[152] *National Westminster Bank Plc v Lucas* [2014] EWCA Civ 1632.

[153] *Walker v Symonds* (1818) 3 Swan 1; *Stafford v Stafford* [1857] 1 De G & J 193; *Chillingworth v Chambers* [1896] 1 Ch 685, CA.

[154] [1964] Ch 303 at 335.

[155] *Adye v Feuilleteau* [1783] 3 Swan 84n; *Lord Montfort v Lord Cadogan* [1816] 19 Ves 635; *Wilkinson v Parry* [1828] 4 Russ 272; *March v Russell* [1837] 3 My & Cr 31.

[156] *Overton v Banister* [1844] 3 Hare 503; *Wright v Snowe* [1848] 2 De G & Sm 321.

(ii) The beneficiary has no other incapacity

If the beneficiary is under any incapacity that would invalidate his consent a trustee remains liable.[157] Therefore, a beneficiary who is of age but under a mental incapacity cannot give an effective consent to a breach of trust. In *Re Pauling's Settlement Trusts*,[158] one son, Francis, was a schizophrenic, but it was held that his mental condition was not sufficiently serious to render his consent invalid.[159]

(iii) The beneficiary must have freely given consent

Only the freely given consent of a beneficiary will be sufficient to protect a trustee from liability. In *Re Pauling's Settlement Trusts*,[160] it was held that the trustees could not rely on the beneficiaries' consent where it was given while the children were acting under the undue influence of their parents. It was only when they were 'emancipated' from parental control that their consent was effective. However, in such circumstances, a trustee will only be liable 'if he knew, or ought to have known that the beneficiary was acting under the undue influence of another'.[161]

(iv) The beneficiary must have given informed consent

A trustee will only be protected if the beneficiary's consent to the breach of trust was an informed consent.[162] The principle was stated by Wilberforce J, at first instance, in *Re Pauling's Settlement Trusts*:

> the court has to consider all the circumstances in which the concurrence of the cestui que trust was given with a view to seeing whether it is fair and equitable that, having given his concurrence, he should afterwards turn round and sue the trustees: that subject to this, it is not necessary that he should know that what he is concurring in is a breach of trust, provided that he fully understands what he is concurring in . . .[163]

This principle was also adopted by Harman J in *Holder v Holder*[164] and Goff LJ in *Re Freeston's Charity*.[165]

(v) The beneficiary need not have benefited from the breach

In *Fletcher v Collis*,[166] it was held that a trustee will be protected from liability where a beneficiary has consented to the breach even if he did not obtain any personal benefit from that breach.[167]

(2) **Breach subsequently condoned by the beneficiaries**

A trustee is similarly protected from liability if, after a breach has been committed, the beneficiaries condone it, release him from liability, or indemnify him. This principle is subject to the same qualifications as apply to the rule that a trustee is not liable to a beneficiary who has consented to a breach of trust: i.e. the condoning or releasing beneficiary

[157] *Crosby v Church* [1841] 3 Beav 485; *Mara v Manning* [1845] 2 Jo & Lat 311; *Fletcher v Green* [1864] 33 Beav 426.

[158] [1961] 3 All ER 713 at 731–2; on appeal [1964] Ch 303 at 347–8.

[159] See Mental Capacity Act 2005, which provides a presumption of capacity in relation to a transaction, unless it can be proved otherwise.

[160] [1964] Ch 303. [161] [1964] Ch 303 at 338, per Willmer LJ.

[162] There must be a full and frank disclosure by the trustee. See *Phipps v Boardman* [1964] 2 All ER 187.

[163] [1961] 3 All ER 713 at 730. [164] [1968] Ch 353. [165] [1979] 1 All ER 51.

[166] [1905] 2 Ch 24.

[167] See also *Re Pauling's Settlement Trusts* [1961] 3 All ER 713 at 730; *Allen v Rea Brothers Trustees Ltd* [2002] WTLR 625.

must be of age;[168] the condoning or releasing beneficiary must not be under any other incapacity; the beneficiary must freely condone the breach or release the trustee from liability;[169] the beneficiary must have known what he was condoning or from what he was releasing the trustee. Condonation obtained through undue influence will be of no effect. As Westbury LC stated in *Farrant v Blanchford*:[170]

> Where a breach of trust has been committed from which a trustee alleges that he has been released, it is incumbent on him to show that such release was given by the cestui que trust deliberately and advisedly, with full knowledge of all the circumstances, and of his own rights and claims against the trustee . . .[171]

(3) **The discretion of the court to grant relief from liability**

(a) **Trustee Act 1925, s 61**

Trustee Act 1925, s 61,[172] confers upon the court a general discretion to grant a trustee relief from liability for breach of trust. The section provides:

> If it appears to the court that a trustee, whether appointed by the court or otherwise, is or may be personally liable for any breach of trust . . . but has acted honestly and reasonably, and ought fairly to be excused for the breach of trust and for omitting to obtain the direction of the court in the matter in which he committed such breach, then the court may relieve him either wholly or in part from personal liability for the same.

This section clearly grants a wide discretion to the court, both as to whether a trustee should be relieved at all and, if so, the extent to which he should be relieved.[173] This enables the court to take account of the circumstances in which the breach occurred and to assess the culpability of the trustee in the light of them. However, the starting point of the law is that a trustee is prima facie liable even for honest technical breaches of trust, and the burden falls to the trustee to demonstrate that he should be granted relief.[174]

(b) **Preconditions for the grant of relief under s 61**

An obvious precondition is that the trustee must be in breach and seeking to be excused from that breach. So, in *Sleight v Callin*,[175] HH Judge Klein noted directly that a defendant was unable to use s 61 to resist her ordinary obligation, as a trustee, to pay over sums to a beneficiary.[176] Section 61 allows a trustee to be excused from liability, not to be excused from run-of-the-mill performance of the trust. Beyond that fundamental point, the courts have emphasized that the discretion conferred by s 61 is not to be exercised on the basis of strict and narrow interpretations. As Byrne J observed in *Re Turner*:[177]

[168] *Wade v Cox* [1835] 4 LJ Ch 105; *Parker v Bloxam* [1855] 20 Beav 295.

[169] Westbury LC stated in *Farrant v Blanchford* that a trustee must be able to show that the beneficiary 'gave the release freely and without pressure or undue influence or any description'. See also *Lloyd v Attwood* [1859] 3 De G & J 614; *Reade v Reade* [1881] 9 LR Ir 409.

[170] [1863] 1 De GJ & Sm 107 at 119.

[171] See also *Ramsden v Hylton* [1751] 2 Ves Sen 304; *Hore v Becher* [1842] 12 Sim 465; *Pritt v Clay* [1843] 6 Beav 503; *Thomson v Eastwood* [1877] 2 App Cas 215, HL; *Re Garnett* [1885] 31 Ch D 1, CA.

[172] Trustee Act 1925, s 61, re-enacts s 3 of the Judicial Trustees Act 1896, and many of the cases discussed here consider the effect of s 3.

[173] Davies, 'Section 61 of the Trustee Act 1925: Deus Ex Machina?' [2015] Conv 379, laments the lack of principled guidance and comments: 'it is still not entirely clear what needs to be shown for claims for relief under s.61 to succeed.'

[174] *Re Stuart* [1897] 2 Ch 583; *Santander UK v RA Legal Solicitors* [2014] EWCA Civ 183.

[175] [2021] EWHC 1050 (Ch). [176] Ibid at [121]. [177] [1897] 1 Ch 536 at 542.

> It would be impossible to lay down any general rules or principles to be acted on in carrying out the provisions of the section, and I think that each case must depend on its own circumstances.[178]

However, for the court even to consider relief, the trustee must show that he had acted 'honestly and reasonably' and that he 'ought fairly to be excused'. Although there is little authority, some consideration has been given to the meaning of these requirements.

(i) 'Honesty'

It is clear that a trustee cannot be granted relief from liability if he has acted dishonestly.[179] However, as Kekewich J observed in *Perrins v Bellamy*,[180] in a large majority of cases where a breach of trust has been committed, the trustee will not have acted dishonestly and the real question will concern whether the trustee had acted 'reasonably':

> The legislature has made the absence of all dishonesty a condition precedent to the relief of the trustee from all liability. But that is not the grit of the section. The grit is in the words 'reasonably, and ought fairly to be excused for the breach of trust'. . .[181]

(ii) 'Reasonably'

A trustee will only be granted relief from liability if he had acted reasonably. As Kekewich J pointed out in *Perrins v Bellamy*,[182] this means that the trustees must have 'acted reasonably in their breach of trust'. It will, therefore, be very hard for a trustee to gain relief if the very basis of his breach of trust was that he had failed to observe the appropriate standard of care expected of a trustee.[183] For example, in *Bartlett v Barclays Bank Trust Co Ltd (No 2)*,[184] the bank was liable because they had failed adequately to supervise the management of the company owned by the trust. Since the very grounds of their liability was their negligence, they could not be said to be entitled to relief under s 61 as they had not acted 'reasonably'. Gross J, in *The Mortgage Business plc v Conifer & Pines Solicitors & Essex Solicitors*,[185] said:

> those much better versed in this area than me do take the view that even under Section 61 a person found liable for a breach of trust which involves lack of reasonable care can nonetheless satisfy a court that he acted reasonably. It may seem odd, but there it is.

It would be very odd indeed, and oxymoronic, if a person who had failed to exercise reasonable care could still be said to have acted reasonably.[186] However, the context was that Gross J was dealing in that case with solicitors who had admitted to negligence by paying out mortgage funds before completion. That kind of breach of trust, of course, is a

[178] See also *Re Pauling's Settlement Trusts* [1964] Ch 303 at 359, per Upjohn LJ: 's 61 is purely discretionary, and its application necessarily depends on the particular facts of each case.'

[179] There is no direct guidance on the meaning of this, but the meaning in other contexts, such as in relation to exoneration clauses, may be relevant: see *Walker v Stones* [2001] QB 902 (the absence of any reasonable belief).

[180] [1898] 2 Ch 521. See, however, *Re Clapham* [2005] EWHC 3387 (Ch), where, in the case of a wrongful payment out of the trust funds by the trustee, it was confirmed that the section does not apply where the mistaken actions of the trustee have been grossly negligent.

[181] [1898] 2 Ch 521 at 527–8. For a more contemporary statement to the same effect, see Patten LJ in *P&P Property Limited v Owen White & Caitlin LLP* [2018] EWCA Civ 1082 at [105].

[182] [1898] 2 Ch 521 at 529.

[183] The appropriate standard of care will either be the new statutory duty of care under s 1 of the Trustee Act 2000 or, if this does not apply, the common law standard of the 'ordinary prudent man of business'.

[184] [1980] Ch 515.

[185] [2009] EWHC 1808 (Comm).

[186] Although just this possibility is anticipated by Companies Act 2006, s 1157(1).

breach of an absolute duty to act within the limits of the authority to disperse funds, and a breach can, therefore, occur without negligence. In these kinds of case, it is quite possible for a breach of trust to have been committed even where a trustee has acted reasonably.[187] However, the Court of Appeal has said very clearly in *Santander UK v RA Legal Solicitors*[188] that where a breach of trust is based on negligence, it is highly unlikely that the trustee could be considered to have acted reasonably. A trustee will not be considered to have acted reasonably if he did not follow usual accepted practice without good reason. For instance, in *Re Stuart*,[189] a trustee who had invested money on a mortgage did not follow the procedure set out in what is now s 8 of the Trustee Act 1925.[190] Although Stirling J held that this 'was not necessarily fatal' to the application of s 61, the legislature had laid down a standard by which the trustee was to be judged. He concluded that, if the trustee had been dealing with his own money, he would not have advanced the mortgage without further precautions.[191]

Cases where solicitors have been caught up by a mortgage fraud and have paid out mortgage funds without authority provide useful illustrations. In some of the cases, the solicitors have ignored warning signs or failed to carry out normal checks.[192] They cannot then be said to be acting reasonably. By contrast, the careful, conscientious, and thorough solicitor, who conducts the transaction by the book and acts honestly and reasonably in relation to it in all respects but still does not discover the fraud may still be held to have been in breach of trust for innocently parting with the loan money to a fraudster. He is, however, likely to be treated mercifully by the court on his section 61 application.[193]

Solicitors who have complied with best practice in most respects, even if there may be some immaterial minor respects in which they have lapsed, are much more likely to be held to have acted reasonably[194]—'the requisite standard is that of reasonableness not of perfection.'[195] In *Santander UK v RA Legal Solicitors*,[196] the Court of Appeal held that whilst it was wrong to apply a rigid or mechanistic approach, there were a number of factors relevant to deciding whether a solicitor had acted reasonably: the extent to which recognized best or usual conveyancing practice had been adopted; the materiality or relevance of any lapses, having regard particularly to their causative connection with the loss; and the seriousness of any departure from good practice (regardless of its causative impact). In that case the number and seriousness of the solicitors' failings meant that they could not be considered to have acted reasonably, in the view of Briggs LJ, even if the sophistication of the fraud to which they were subject was such that it would have been committed even if they had taken all reasonable care.[197] Etherton LC agreed, but placed more weight on the materiality of the breaches by the solicitors. He was prepared to contemplate that even despite unreasonable conduct a trustee could convince the court that his or her unreasonable conduct did not materially contribute to the opportunity for the loss or did not materially increase the risk of such loss,[198] in which case the court could consider exercising a discretion to exculpate the trustee under s 61.

[187] See *Re Turner* [1897] 1 Ch 536; *Re Stuart* [1897] 2 Ch 583; *Re Dive* [1909] 1 Ch 328; *Shaw v Cates* [1909] 1 Ch 389; *Re Mackay* [1911] 1 Ch 300.

[188] [2014] EWCA Civ 183 at 31–2.

[189] [1897] 2 Ch 583.

[190] Then s 4 of the Trustee Act 1888 and s 8 of the Trustee Act 1893.

[191] [1897] 2 Ch 583 at 591–2.

[192] As in *Lloyds TSB Bank Plc v Markandan & Uddin (A Firm)* [2012] EWCA Civ 65, [2012] 2 All ER 884 for reasons given at 60. See also *Purrunsing v A'Court & Co (a firm)* [2016] EWHC 789 (Ch).

[193] [2012] EWCA Civ 65 at 61.

[194] As in *Nationwide Building Society v Davisons Solicitors* [2012] EWCA Civ 1626.

[195] [2012] EWCA Civ 1626 at 48.

[196] [2014] EWCA Civ 183 at 20–32.

[197] [2014] EWCA Civ 183 at 96–102.

[198] [2014] EWCA Civ 183 at 110.

The Trustee Act 1925, s 61, applies to professional as well as non-professional trustees.[199] However, in the case of a 'professional trustee', or a paid trustee[200] the courts have held that a higher standard of care is expected,[201] and they are more reluctant to grant relief under s 61. As the Court of Appeal said in *Re Pauling's Settlement Trusts*:

> Where a banker undertakes to act as a paid trustee of a settlement created by a customer, and so deliberately places itself in a position where its duty as trustee conflicts with its interest as a banker, we think that the court should be very slow to relieve such a trustee under [s 61].[202]

Conversely, the courts have shown greater sympathy to lay trustees. In *Iles v Iles*,[203] a lay trustee, who was also a beneficiary, did not realize that she should have been paying some of the income from the rent on trust property to her daughter. Briggs J held that (at least initially) she had acted reasonably. He took into account:[204]

> her complete lack of business experience . . . and the absence of any indication to a lay person with that degree of inexperience from reading the 1992 Declaration of Trust (without its Schedule) that she was accountable to her daughter for rent from a defined part of the Forge between 2000 and 2004.

Another relevant factor is whether the trustee sought and acted on professional advice. In *Ward-Smith v Jebb*,[205] a lay trustee was held to have acted unreasonably for failing to seek legal advice on a technical question about the eligibility of a potential beneficiary; in contrast, in *Re Evans*,[206] it was a factor in holding a lay trustee had acted reasonably that she had taken advice from her solicitors.

(iii) 'Ought fairly to be excused'

Most cases dealing with s 61 focus on the question of reasonable conduct and often assume that if this is established, relief should follow almost as of course. As Kekewich J observed in *Perrins v Bellamy*:

> I venture to think that, in general and in the absence of special circumstances, a trustee who has acted 'reasonably' ought to be relieved, and that it is not incumbent on the Court to consider whether he ought 'fairly' to be excused, unless there is evidence of a special character showing that the provisions of the section ought not to be applied in his favour.[207]

However, he recognized in a later case (*Davis v Hutchings*[208]) that there might be circumstances where a trustee who had acted both honesty and reasonably ought not to be relieved from liability. This was a case where the trustees gave a share of the trust fund to their solicitor, who claimed that he was the assignee of the share. They failed to investigate his title, which would have revealed that the assignment was subject to the plaintiff's charge over the share. Kekewich J held that there was no justification for the trustees being 'let off'.[209] This appears to be an exercise of discretion, but the case can perhaps be

[199] In *Re Pauling's Settlement Trusts* [1964] Ch 303 at 338, the Court of Appeal said that 'it would be a misconstruction of the section to say that it does not apply to professional trustees'; and (at 356) Wilmer LJ said that 'all of us are agreed that in the very special circumstances of this case the bank should be accorded some relief notwithstanding the fact that they were professional trustees paid for their services'.

[200] *Santander UK plc v RA Legal Solicitors* [2014] EWCA Civ 183 at 30.

[201] *National Trustees Co of Australasia Ltd v General Finance Co of Australasia Ltd* [1905] AC 373; *Bartlett v Barclays Bank Trust Co Ltd* [1980] Ch 515.

[202] [1964] Ch 303 at 339. [203] [2012] EWHC 919 (Ch). [204] [2012] EWHC 919 (Ch) at 49.

[205] [1964] 108 Sol Jo 919. [206] [1999] 2 All ER 777.

[207] [1898] 2 Ch 521 at 529.

[208] [1907] 1 Ch 356. But see *Re Allsop* [1914] 1 Ch 1, where the Court of Appeal, while accepting that *Davis v Hutchings* may have been right on its facts, rejected the wider dicta of Kekewich J.

[209] [1907] 1 Ch 356 at 365.

better explained on the grounds that the trustees' conduct was unreasonable because of the failure to investigate title, an obvious precaution. It is undoubtedly the case that the court has a discretion as to whether to grant relief. As Evershed MR said in *Marsden v Regan*, having found that the trustee had acted honestly and reasonably:

> There still remains the question: Ought she fairly to be excused? That is the most difficult point of all. But it is essentially a matter within the discretion of the judge . . .[210]

The best judicial guidance on the exercise of the discretion is given by Briggs LJ in *Santander UK plc v RA Legal Solicitors*.[211] He pointed out that granting relief impacted upon the beneficiary of the trust. The primary cause of a loss in the case of mortgage fraud were the actions of the fraudsters, but the affected beneficiary might be either an institutional lender with deep pockets or insurance against the risk or an individual purchaser whose life savings were on the line.

> Relief under section 61 is often described as an exercise of mercy by the court. In my judgment the requirement to balance fairness to the trustee with a proper appreciation of the consequences of the exercise of the discretion for the beneficiaries means that this old-fashioned description of the nature of the section 61 jurisdiction should be abandoned. In this context mercy lies not in the free gift of the court. It comes at a price.[212]

(c) The extent of relief

If the court finds that the conditions for granting relief are met, the extent to which the trustee may be relieved is a matter for the discretion of the court. Section 61 provides that the trustee may be relieved 'wholly or in part'. In *Re Pauling's Settlement Trusts*,[213] one breach of trust by the bank involved the advance of £2,600 to Francis and George to pay off a debt owed by their mother secured on her life interest, known as the 'Hodson Loan'. In return, the mother assigned to them life policies with a surrender value of £650, on which she promised to continue to pay the premiums, and which would pay £3,000 on her death. There was a division between the members of the Court of Appeal as to the extent to which the bank should be relieved of liability in respect of this transaction. The majority found that, in the circumstances, the bank had acted honestly and reasonably, but that it should only be relieved to the extent of the surrender value of the policies which had been assigned to them. Willmer J, dissenting, held that they should be relieved from all liability:

> whereas my brethren think that the bank should be relieved only in part, I take the view that if relief is to be accorded to all, it should be accorded in full. I can see no logical reason for stopping short of relief in full.[214]

In *Re Evans (Decd)*,[215] a lay trustee, after taking advice from her solicitor, had taken out insurance cover for a potential claim for a beneficiary she had not been in contact with for years and who she thought was probably dead. When the beneficiary later turned up, the insurance policy was insufficient to cover the interest due on his share. The judge granted partial relief against liability to pay interest.

210 [1954] 1 WLR 423 at 435. See also *Re Wightwick's Will Trusts* [1950] Ch 260.
211 [2014] EWCA Civ 183.
212 [2014] EWCA Civ 183 at 34.
213 [1964] Ch 303.
214 [1964] Ch 303 at 356.
215 [1999] 2 All ER 777.

5 Contribution and indemnity where a trustee is liable

Although a trustee may be liable to the beneficiaries for breach of trust without any defence, in some circumstances, he may be entitled to a contribution or indemnity from his co-trustees, or from the beneficiaries of the trust, which will have the practical effect of partially or completely alleviating his obligation to provide equitable compensation.

(1) Indemnity from co-trustees

As was noted earlier, trustees who together commit a breach of trust are jointly and severally liable for that breach. However, in some circumstances, a trustee may be entitled to receive a full indemnity from liability for his breach from his fellow trustees.

(a) Co-trustee acted fraudulently

Where one of several trustees acts fraudulently, the others are entitled to a complete indemnity from liability. In *Re Smith*[216] two trustees invested in debentures. One, who was also the tenant for life of the settlement, invested because he believed that this would increase his income from the trust, while the other invested because he had received a bribe to do so. Kekewich J held that, because of his dishonesty, the bribed trustee alone was liable.

(b) Co-trustee is a professional

A trustee may be entitled to an indemnity if his co-trustee was a professional whose advice he could reasonably be expected to rely on. This has most often been the case where a co-trustee was a solicitor.[217] In *Re Partington*[218] the two trustees of a settlement invested in a mortgage which was an improper investment for the trust. Stirling J held that Mr Allen, who was a solicitor, was liable to indemnify his co-trustee, Mrs Partington, because she had 'been misled by her co-trustee by reason of his not giving her full information as to the nature of the investments which he was asking her to advance the money upon'. For an indemnity the trustee must have acted purely on the basis of reliance on the solicitor trustee. In *Head v Gould*[219] Kekewich J said that there was no right to an indemnity merely because a co-trustee is a solicitor when the trustee 'was an active participator in the breach of trust complained of, and is not proved to have participated merely in consequence of the advice and control of the solicitor'.[220]

(c) Co-trustee has personally benefited from the breach of trust

The general principle was considered by the Court of Appeal in *Bahin v Hughes*.[221] Cotton LJ said that a trustee is entitled to an indemnity from his co-trustee either when they are both liable to the beneficiary because the co-trustee got trust money into his own hands and made use of it[222] or 'against a trustee who has himself got the benefit of the breach of trust'.[223] Where the trustee has retained the funds, he must, as a matter of 'obvious' equity, return them. The position is less clear where the trustee has not retained the funds.[224] Where the trustee is also a beneficiary, and has benefited by the breach of trust,

216 [1896] 1 Ch 71.

217 See *Lockhart v Reilly* [1856] 25 LJ Ch 697; *Bahin v Hughes* [1886] 31 Ch D 390, CA.

218 [1887] 57 LT 654.

219 [1898] 2 Ch 250.

220 [1898] 2 Ch 250 at 265.

221 [1886] 31 Ch D 390.

222 See *Thompson v Finch* [1856] 25 LJ Ch 681.

223 [1886] 31 Ch D 390 at 396.

224 *City Index Ltd v Gawler* [2007] EWCA Civ 1382.

he is liable to indemnify his co-trustees to the extent of his beneficial interest. The principle was stated by Kay J in *Chillingworth v Chambers*:

> the weight of authority is in favour of the holding that a trustee who, being also a [beneficiary], has received, as between himself and his co-trustee, an exclusive benefit by the breach of trust, must indemnify his co-trustee to the extent of his interest in the trust fund, and not merely to the extent of the benefit which he has received.[225]

The trustees of a will invested in mortgages which proved to provide insufficient security. Chillingworth had also become a beneficiary, and the purposes of the investment had been to produce a higher rate of interest from the trust property, which was for his benefit. The court held that the deficit of £1,580 was to be made good from Chillingworth's beneficial interest, and that Chambers was indemnified from liability. If the trustee-beneficiary's interest is insufficient to cover the total loss, the trustees will be equally liable for the remaining loss.

(2) **Contribution from co-trustees**

The Civil Liability (Contribution) Act 1978 gives the court a wide discretion to apportion liability between trustees who are jointly and severally liable for breach of trust.[226] Section 1(1) states the general principle of contribution:

> any person liable in respect of any damage suffered by another person may recover contribution from any other person liable in respect of the same damage (whether jointly with him or otherwise).

The general discretion of the court is found in s 2(1):

> in any proceedings for contribution under s 1 the amount of the contribution recoverable from any person shall be such as may be found by the court to be just and equitable having regard to the extent of that person's responsibility for the damage in question.

The court can, therefore, reflect the respective blameworthiness of co-trustees in the extent to which they permit contribution. Under s 2(2) the court has the power to find that a trustee is exempt from making contributions to his co-trustee, or that a trustee is entitled to a complete indemnity from his co-trustee.

(3) **Indemnity from a beneficiary**

As has already been noted, a trustee will not incur any liability for a breach of trust to a beneficiary who consented to it, or subsequently concurred in it. The trustee remains liable to any beneficiaries who did not so consent or concur. However, the trustee may be entitled to be indemnified from the beneficial interest of any beneficiary who requested or consented to the breach.

(a) **The court's inherent jurisdiction**

If a trustee commits a breach of trust at the instigation or the request of a beneficiary the court has the power, under its inherent jurisdiction, to impound the beneficiary's beneficial interest to indemnify the trustee for any liability he might incur.[227] There is no

[225] [1896] 1 Ch 685 at 707.

[226] s 6(1) makes clear that the statute applies to damage caused by breach of trust. *Friends' Provident Life Office v Hillier Parker May & Rowden (a firm)* [1997] QB 85; *Dubai Aluminium Co Ltd v Salaam* [2003] 2 AC 366; *Charter plc v City Index Ltd* [2008] Ch 313; Virgo, 'Contribution Revisited' [2008] 67 CLJ 254.

[227] *Booth v Booth* [1838] 1 Beav 125; *Lincoln v Wright* [1841] 4 Beav 427; *Raby v Ridehalgh* [1855] 7 De GM & G 104; *Bentley v Robinson* [1859] 9 I Ch R 479; *Sawyer v Sawyer* [1885] 28 Ch D 595, CA; *Ricketts v Ricketts* [1891] 64 LT 263; *Chillingworth v Chambers* [1896] 1 Ch 685.

need for the request or instigation to be made in writing.[228] However, the trustee will not be entitled to an indemnity unless the beneficiary knew the facts of what was happening. Where the beneficiary has not requested or instigated the breach of trust but merely consented to it, the trustee may still be entitled to an indemnity from his beneficial interest. This will only be the case if the consent was given in writing and the beneficiary gained a personal benefit from the breach.[229] The indemnity will only extend to the amount of that benefit.[230]

(b) Trustee Act 1925, s 62

This section grants the court a wide discretion to impound the beneficial interest of a beneficiary who has instigated, requested, or consented in writing to a breach of trust.

In *Re Pauling's Settlement Trusts (No 2)*,[231] Wilberforce J stated that the purpose of the section was to extend the courts' inherent jurisdiction, and, in *Bolton v Curre*,[232] Romer J said that the forerunner to s 62[233] 'was intended to enlarge the power of the court as to indemnifying trustees, and to give greater relief to trustees, and was not intended and did not operate to curtail the previously existing rights and remedies of trustees, or to alter the law except by giving greater power to the court'. It has been held that the requirement of writing applies only to a beneficiary's consent,[234] and the court may impound the beneficiary's interest under s 62, where there has been instigation or a request irrespective of the absence of writing. The court will only impound the beneficiary's interest if he had sufficient knowledge. In *Re Somerset* Smith LJ stated:

> upon the true reading of this section, a trustee in order to obtain the benefit conferred thereby, must establish that the beneficiary knew the facts which rendered what he was instigating, requesting or consenting to in writing a breach of trust.[235]

It is not necessary that he actually know that those facts amount to a breach of trust.[236] In *Re Pauling's Settlement Trusts (No 2)*,[237] Wilberforce J held that the protection of the section was available not only to existing trustees of the trust but also to former trustees who had since retired from the trust or been replaced. The only requirement is that the person seeking the indemnity was a trustee at the time of the breach.

(c) Contributory negligence

It was held at first instance in *Lloyds TSB Bank v Markandan & Uddin*[238] that the Law Reform (Contributory Negligence) Act 1945 is not applicable, either directly or by analogy, to reduce a claim against a trustee to reflect the extent to which the claimant's own fault has directly or directly contributed to the loss.[239] The judge (Roger Wyand QC) said:

> Section 61 of the Trustee Act gives limited relief to trustees where the trustees have acted reasonably and honestly. It could have provided for the conduct of the beneficiary to be taken into account as the Defendant here wishes. It did not and it is not for the Court to extend the law in a way that was not done by the legislature.

[228] *Griffiths v Hughes* [1892] 3 Ch 105; *Mara v Browne* [1895] 2 Ch 69.

[229] *Booth v Booth* [1838] 1 Beav 125; *Chillingworth v Chambers* [1896] 1 Ch 685.

[230] *Raby v Ridehaigh* [1855] 7 De GM & G 104.

[231] [1963] Ch 576.

[232] [1895] 1 Ch 544 at 549.

[233] Trustee Act 1888, s 6; repeated by the Trustee Act 1893, s 45.

[234] *Griffiths v Hughes* [1892] 3 Ch 105; *Re Somerset* [1894] 1 Ch 231.

[235] [1894] 1 Ch 231.

[236] The best view is that the beneficiary must understand what he is doing and the legal effect of the indemnity. See *Sofer v SwissIndependent Trustees SA* [2020] EWCA Civ 699 at [61].

[237] [1963] Ch 576.

[238] [2010] EWHC 2517.

[239] No appeal was made against this part of the decision: see [2012] 2 All ER 884 at 55.

35

Fiduciary duties of trustees and other fiduciaries

1 Introduction

As we have seen in the last chapter, the duties of trustees fall into several categories: the duty to act within the four corners of the trust, the duty to exercise care and skill in the performance of most of their functions, and the duty to show loyalty to their beneficiaries. This chapter looks at the last of these three types of duty. The duty of loyalty is owed by most trustees, but a similar duty is also imposed upon others who hold certain positions of trust and confidence, such as agents and company directors. The duty requires the fiduciary to put the interests of the principal above their own, not to put themselves in a position of a potential conflict, nor to receive any secret payment, profit, or commission. For instance, a football manager who takes a personal 'backhander' when a player is transferred for a substantial fee could be subject to equitable remedies to deprive the manager of all the gains made through his or her corrupt behaviour, as well as facing potential criminal proceedings and the loss of their post. In one of the leading cases on breach of fiduciary duty,[1] an agent was paid commission on the sale of the Monte Carlo Grand Hotel both by the seller and by the buyer. The agent had failed to disclose to the buyer that it was being paid a double commission. This was held to be in breach of the agent's duty to act in the buyer's best interests, and the agent was obliged to account for the whole of the €10 million secret commission which had been received, even including that part which the controller of the company had paid in tax to the US Treasury.[2] Limitation, relating to the time period in which a claimant can bring a case with regard to unauthorized profits is discussed in Chapter 36.

2 Fiduciary relationships

(1) Fiduciary duties and fiduciary relationships

There is a degree of circularity in identifying when fiduciary duties are owed.[3] A fiduciary is a person who owes fiduciary duties to another, but whether they can be characterized as a fiduciary depends upon whether they owe fiduciary duties. The essence of fiduciary

[1] *FHR European Ventures LLP v Mankarious* [2014] UKSC 45.

[2] *FHR European Ventures LLP v Mankarious* [2016] EWHC 359 (Ch).

[3] See Conaglen, 'The Nature and Function of Fiduciary Loyalty' [2005] 121 LQR 452; Hilliard, 'The Flexibility of Fiduciary Doctrine in Trust Law: How Far Does It Stretch in Practice?' [2009] TLI 119.

duties is that they are duties of loyalty. As Millett LJ said in *Bristol and West Building Society v Mothew*,[4] in a passage later approved by the Supreme Court in *Pitt v Holt*:[5]

> A fiduciary is someone who has undertaken to act for or on behalf of another in a particular matter in circumstances which give rise to a relationship of trust and confidence. The distinguishing obligation of a fiduciary is the obligation of loyalty. The principal is entitled to the single-minded loyalty of his fiduciary . . . .

In deciding whether a person is a fiduciary, the central question is whether their position imposes upon them duties of loyalty.

(2) **The trustee as a fiduciary**

Trustees are the paradigm example of fiduciaries.[6] By virtue of their office,[7] trustees are subject to a range of onerous negative obligations in equity, which are designed to prevent them from abusing their position by acting in their own interests at the expense of the interests of his beneficiaries. The powers of trustees give them both great flexibility and opportunity for abuse. The trustee who controls the property can use it for his own advantage, for example, by selling himself the trust property at an undervalue. Fiduciary duties are imposed on trustees to prevent them from gaining personal advantages at the expense of the beneficiaries.

(3) **Types of fiduciary relationship**

The fiduciary relationship has been described as 'one of the most ill-defined, if not altogether misleading terms in our law'.[8] It has also been said that 'there are few legal concepts more frequently invoked but less conceptually certain than that of the fiduciary relationship'.[9] As Frankfurter J said in the American case *SEC v Chenery Corpn*:[10]

> To say that a man is a fiduciary only begins analysis; it gives direction to further inquiry. To whom is he a fiduciary? What obligations does he owe as a fiduciary? In what respect has he failed to discharge these obligations? And what are the consequences of his deviation from duty?[11]

It is important to recognize that a fiduciary relationship may arise in a number of ways. In *LAC Minerals Ltd v International Corona Resources Ltd*,[12] a decision of the Canadian Supreme Court, Wilson J distinguished between relationships which in their very nature are fiduciary, and those which take on a fiduciary character because of the particular relationship between the parties:

> It is . . . my view of the law that there are certain relationships which are almost per se fiduciary, such as trustee and beneficiary, guardian and ward, principal and agent, and that where such relationships subsist they give rise to fiduciary duties. On the other hand, there are relationships which are not in their essence fiduciary, such as the relationship brought into being

[4] [1998] Ch 1 at 18. [5] [2013] UKSC 26.

[6] See Goff and Jones, *The Law of Unjust Enrichment* (8th edn, Sweet & Maxwell 2011), Ch 38; Oakley, *Constructive Trusts* (3rd edn, Sweet & Maxwell 1997), Ch 3; Finn, *Fiduciary Obligations* (Law Book Company 1977); Shepherd, 'Towards a Unified Concept of Fiduciary Relationships' [1981] 97 LQR 51.

[7] *Keech v Sandford* [1726] Sel Cas Ch 61; *Price v Blakemore* [1843] 6 Beav 507.

[8] Finn, *Fiduciary Obligations* (Law Book Company 1977), p 1.

[9] *LAC Minerals Ltd v International Corona Resources Ltd* [1989] 61 DLR (4th) 14 at 26, per La Forest J.

[10] 518 US 80 [1943] at 85–6.

[11] Cited by the Privy Council in *Re Goldcorp Exchanges Ltd* [1994] 2 All ER 806.

[12] [1989] 61 DLR (4th) 14.

by the parties in the present case by virtue of their arm's length negotiations towards a joint venture agreement, but this does not preclude a fiduciary duty from arising out of specific conduct engaged in them or either of them within the confines of the relationship.[13]

(a) Relationships fiduciary per se

English law has never provided a comprehensive definition of fiduciary relationships. Instead, certain relationships, because of their very nature, have come to be regarded as fiduciary. This obviously allows for flexibility as circumstances and commercial practice change. As Finn has stated, a fiduciary 'is, simply, someone who undertakes to act for or on behalf of another in some particular matter or matters'.[14] In the unusual case of *Reading v A-G*[15] the House of Lords held that an army sergeant who had used his uniform to enable lorries smuggling spirits and drugs to pass through army checkpoints was a fiduciary, and, therefore, he was obliged to account to the Crown for the money he had received from the smugglers for his services. In the Court of Appeal, Asquith LJ had attempted a summary of the characteristics of a fiduciary relationship:

> a fiduciary relationship exists (a) whenever the plaintiff entrusts to the defendant property . . . and relies on the defendant to deal with such property for the benefit of the plaintiff or purposes authorised by him, and not otherwise, and (b) whenever the plaintiff entrusts to the defendant a job to be performed and relies on the defendant to procure for the plaintiff the best terms available . . .[16]

This description encompasses most trusts, but the relationship of trustee and beneficiary is not the only one that is characterized as fiduciary by equity. Other relationships held to be fiduciary include: principal and agent;[17] mortgagee and mortgagor;[18] solicitor and client;[19] partners and co-partners;[20] company directors and the company;[21] holders of an

[13] [1989] 61 DLR (4th) at 16.

[14] Finn, *Fiduciary Obligations* (Law Book Company 1977), p 201.

[15] [1951] AC 507.

[16] [1949] 2 KB 232 at 236.

[17] *De Bussche v Alt* [1878] 8 Ch D 286; *Kirkham v Peel* [1880] 43 LT 171; *Lamb v Evans* [1893] 1 Ch 218, CA; *New Zealand Netherlands Society Oranje Inc v Kuys* [1973] 1 WLR 1126, PC; *Imageview Management Ltd v Jack* [2009] EWCA Civ 63; *FHR European Ventures LLP v Mankarious* [2011] EWHC 2308 (Ch); [2014] UKSC 45.

[18] *Farrars v Farrars Ltd* [1888] 40 Ch D 395, CA.

[19] *Re Hallett's Estate* [1880] 13 Ch D 696, CA; *McMaster v Byrne* [1952] 1 All ER 1362; *Brown v IRC* [1965] AC 244, HL; *Oswald Hickson Collier Co v Carter-Ruck* [1984] AC 720n; *Swindle v Harrison* [1997] 4 All ER 705; *Logstaff v Birtles* [2002] 1 WLR 470. In *Conway v Ratiu* [2006] 1 All ER 571, the Court of Appeal said, contra Lord Millett in *Prince Jefri Bolkiah v KPMG (a firm)* [1999] 2 AC 222, that the fiduciary relationship of a solicitor to his client is distinct from the contractual obligations arising under his retainer. As such the fiduciary duty is not necessarily to be found or confined to the terms of the contractual retainer, so that the fiduciary relationship may outlive the contractual solicitor/client relationship. See also *Hilton v Barker Booth and Eastwood (a firm)* [2005] 1 All ER 651 at 28–9, per Lord Walker; *Cobbetts LLP v Hodge* [2009] EWHC 786.

[20] *Bentley v Craven* [1853] 18 Beav 75; *Aas v Benham* [1891] 2 Ch 244; *Thompson's Trustee in Bankruptcy v Heaton* [1974] 1 WLR 605. See also *Holiday Inns Inc v Yorkstone Properties (Harlington)* [1974] 232 *Estates Gazette* 951.

[21] *Sinclair v Brougham* [1914] AC 398; *Regal (Hastings) v Gulliver* [1967] 2 AC 134n; *Selangor United Rubber Estates Ltd v Craddock* (No 3) [1968] 1 WLR 1555; *Industrial Development Consultants Ltd v Cooley* [1972] 1 WLR 443; *Cowan de Groot Properties Ltd v Eagle Trust plc* [1992] 4 All ER 700; *Item Software (UK) Ltd v Fassihi* [2004] EWCA 1244; *O'Donnell v Shanahan* [2009] EWC Civ 751. See Berg, 'Fiduciary Duties: A Director's Duty to Disclose His Own Misconduct' [2005] 121 LQR 213. The duties of directors have been codified in the Companies Act 2006.

office of the Crown and the Crown;[22] and pawnbroker and pawnor.[23] The essence of all these relationships is that one person occupies a position in which he has a duty to act on behalf of another, thereby enjoying the potential to abuse his position by acting for his own interests. They are relationships in which there is an inherent element of 'trust and confidence'[24] between the parties.

Whether or not a relationship is said by judges to be fiduciary is an important matter. In *Lehtimäki v Cooper*,[25] the Supreme Court found, for the first time, that a member of a charitable company was in a fiduciary relationship to the objects of the company. This discovery of a fiduciary relationship allowed the court to direct how the member should use his vote in a company dispute. So, the fiduciary relationship can be understood as a part of the judicial 'tool kit'. Where it is found to exist, the courts gain a tool to intervene.

(b) **Fiduciary duties arising within relationships not fiduciary per se**

The majority of commercial relationships cannot be characterized as fiduciary per se,[26] as the parties simply bargain with each other at arm's length for their own best advantage. However, the specific nature of a particular relationship may bring about a fiduciary relationship between the parties. This was the case in *LAC Minerals Ltd v International Corona Resources Ltd*,[27] where two companies were negotiating at arm's length about the possibility of a joint venture to exploit minerals from land over which the plaintiff company (LAC) owned mining rights. The defendants learnt from the negotiations that adjacent land was also likely to include mineral deposits. The defendants then purchased the adjacent land, defeating a competing bid from the plaintiffs, and developed a mine alone. Although the relationship between the defendants and the plaintiffs was not fiduciary per se, the Supreme Court held that fiduciary duties were owed because the defendants had received confidential information from the plaintiffs in the course of the negotiations. In *A-G v Blake*,[28] Lord Woolf MR similarly suggested that a fiduciary relationship arises whenever information is imparted by one person to another in confidence,[29] although he noted that in the majority of cases such information will be imparted in the context of a relationship which is already fiduciary.

In contrast, in *Re Goldcorp Exchange Ltd (In Receivership)*,[30] the Privy Council held that a relationship had remained exclusively commercial so that it had not become fiduciary. The company sold customers gold and other precious metals as 'non-allocated metal' that was held for them by the company free of charge. Customers were entitled to take physical delivery of the metal by giving seven days' notice, at which point it would be appropriated from the metal that the company held in bulk. It was argued that the company stood in a fiduciary relationship to the customers, but the Privy Council held that their relationship was purely contractual. As Lord Mustill explained:

> No doubt the fact that one person is placed in a particular position vis-à-vis another through the medium of a contract does not necessarily mean that he does not also owe fiduciary duties to that other by virtue of being in that position. But the essence of a fiduciary relationship is

[22] *Reading v A-G* [1951] AC 507; *A-G v Guardian Newspapers Ltd (No 2)* [1990] 1 AC 109; *A-G for Hong Kong v Reid* [1994] 1 All ER 1, PC; *A-G v Blake* [1998] 1 All ER 833.

[23] *Mathew v TM Sutton Ltd* [1994] 4 All ER 793; *Hurstanger v Wilson* [2007] EWCA Civ 299.

[24] *Conway v Raitu* [2006] 1 All ER 571 at 71, per Auld LJ.

[25] [2020] UKSC 33. See Picton, '*Lehtimäki v Cooper*: Duty and Jurisdiction in Charity Law' (2021) 84 MLR 383–93.

[26] See Oakley, 'The Liberalising Nature of Remedies for Breach of Trust' in Oakley, *Trends in Contemporary Trust Law* (Sweet & Maxwell 1997), pp 230–3.

[27] (1989) 61 DLR (4th) 14. [28] [1998] 1 All ER 833. [29] [1998] 1 All ER 833 at 842.

[30] [1994] 2 All ER 806. See also *Khodai v Tamimi* [2009] EWCA Civ 1109 (relationship between lender and borrower).

> that it creates obligations of a different character from those deriving from the contract itself. Their Lordships have not heard in argument any submission which went beyond suggesting that by virtue of being a fiduciary the company was obliged honestly and conscientiously to do what it had by contract promised to do . . . It is possible, without misuse of language to say that the customers put faith in the company, and that their trust has not been repaid. But the vocabulary is misleading; high expectations do not necessarily lead to equitable remedies.[31]

The case of *Sinclair Investment Holdings SA v Versailles Trade Finance Ltd*[32] provides an example of a commercial relationship giving rise to a fiduciary status, and of the core content of a fiduciary relationship. The facts as alleged were that Mr Cushnie was a director and had a substantial interest in companies within the Versailles Group. The Versailles Group inflated its turnover through dishonest dealings, and as a result, Mr Cushnie was able to sell his shareholding at a profit, repay a mortgage on a property he owned, and sell it for £8.6 million. One of the Group's victims was Sinclair, which was seeking to recover from Mr Cushnie the money that had been misappropriated. It was argued that he stood in a fiduciary position in relation to the claimants. A company director is not normally a fiduciary for people dealing with the company, even where he makes personal representations,[33] but the Court of Appeal held that the pleadings in the case contained an arguable case that Mr Cushnie had undertaken a duty of loyalty to Sinclair so as to make him a fiduciary.[34] According to Arden LJ:

> if it is alleged that a person who does not fall within the usual categories of a fiduciary relationship, such as trustee and director, made manifest his intention to enter into a fiduciary relationship—that is, to undertake to the other a duty of loyalty—there would be a sufficient pleading of fiduciary relationship.[35]

The fiduciary did not need to receive the claimant's property, but in her view:

> In a case such as this, it seems to me to be necessary that the fiduciary relationship should be with respect to an item of property, and that requirement explains why a fiduciary relationship may be specific and govern only part of a party's relationship with another.[36]

That condition would have been satisfied in this case because there was an express term that Sinclair's funds were to be held on trust if they were not used for trading.

(c) Exceptions to the general rule

Even in a relationship which would normally be characterized as fiduciary, the courts may find that on the facts no fiduciary duties are owed. While most trustees will be fiduciaries, it is hard to see, for example, how a resulting trustee who is unaware that property has been acquired in their name could be considered to owe duties of loyalty to the purchaser or transferor. Similarly, in *Independent Trustee v GP Noble Trustees*,[37] a husband used pension trust funds to pay financial provision to his divorced wife under a court order which was later revoked. Since, on the finding of the Court of Appeal, this was to be treated as a transfer without consideration, the wife was accountable to the pension fund for any sums which she retained. Lloyd LJ considered that it would be appropriate to

[31] [1994] 2 All ER 806 at 821–2.

[32] [2005] EWCA Civ 722. See Panesar, 'The Nature of Fiduciary Liability in English Law' [2007] Conv 2, 11–12.

[33] See *Hageman v Holmes* [2009] EWHC 50 (Ch), where a fiduciary obligation was not imposed on a director in relation to a deed of covenant, on the basis that the rights between the relevant parties were contractual only.

[34] In *Schenk v Cook* [2017] EWHC (QB) 144 at 87, a fraudster owed fiduciary duties because he held himself out as an attorney at law providing financial advice to 'provide a veneer of trustworthiness'.

[35] [2005] EWCA Civ 722 at 20. [36] [2005] EWCA Civ 722 at 21. [37] [2012] EWCA Civ 195.

describe the wife as a constructive trustee holding the funds on trust for the beneficiaries under the pension fund trusts, although 'she would have been under no relevant duty as regards the money until she had notice of the interest of the beneficiaries.'[38] In some cases, even where the trustee is aware the property is held on trust, the circumstances may negate the existence of a fiduciary duty. In *Janus Capital Management LLC v Safeguard World International Ltd*,[39] it was held that where property is held on a bare trust to the order of the principal, the trustee is not a fiduciary.[40]

(d) Employees

Whether an employee owes fiduciary duties to an employer depends upon the nature of the employee's responsibilities: there has to be much more than simply an ordinary employment relationship. It is easy to accept that a financial controller holds a position in which it would be not just a breach of contract, but also a breach of fiduciary duty to use his position to divert company funds into his own account.[41] Similarly, it would be hard to defend a claim for breach of fiduciary duty against a university professor or school teacher who sold an advance copy of an examination paper to a student. However, will an employee be prevented from doing work in their own time because of fiduciary duties owed to their employer? The starting-point is that a contract of employment does not automatically give rise to fiduciary duties. As Moses LJ said in *Helmet Integrated Systems v Tunnard*:

> It is commonplace to observe that not every employee owes obligations as a fiduciary to his employer. An employee owes an obligation of loyalty to his employer but he will not necessarily owe that exclusive obligation of loyalty, to act in his employer's interest and not in his own, which is the hallmark of any fiduciary duty owed by an employee to his employer. The distinguishing mark of the obligation of a fiduciary, in the context of employment, is not merely that the employee owes a duty of loyalty but of single-minded or exclusive loyalty.[42]

Likewise, in *University of Nottingham v Fishel*,[43] Elias J said:

> the essence of the employment relationship is not typically fiduciary at all. Its purpose is not to place the employee in a position where he is obliged to pursue his employer's interests at the expense of his own ... in determining whether a fiduciary relationship arises in the context of an employment relationship, it is necessary to identify with care the particular duties undertaken by the employee, and to ask whether in all the circumstances he has placed himself in a position where he must act solely in the interests of his employer.

The employee is not required to devote all his or her time to the employer's business, and is free to exploit for their own benefit the general fund of skill, knowledge and expertise they have acquired. Thus, in *Tunnard*, it was held that there was no breach of fiduciary duty when a salesman for a company selling firefighters' helmets designed his own helmet, then resigned in order to market it on his own account. He was not employed as a designer, and he only marketed his own helmet after the end of his employment. Similarly, in *Fishel*, a university scientist was encouraged by his employers to conduct overseas research work. He did some paid research projects in working time. This was held to be in breach of contract because he had not obtained prior approval, as his contract required. However, it was not a breach of fiduciary duty, because he was not under a specific duty to secure the work for the university.

Conversely, Dr Fishel was held to be in breach of fiduciary duty when he used university staff for whom he was responsible to help him carry out his externally paid work. This was

[38] [2012] EWCA Civ 195 at 81. [39] [2016] EWHC 1355 (Ch). [40] [2016] EWHC 1355 (Ch) at 248.
[41] *LS Systems v Scott* [2015] EWHC 1335 (Ch).
[42] [2007] IRLR 126 at 36. [43] [2000] ICR 1462.

because 'he was in my view clearly putting himself where there was a potential conflict between his specific duty to the University to direct the embryologists to working the interests of the University, and his own financial interest in directing them abroad.'

The fiduciary duties owed by an employee depend on the nature of the responsibility the employee has, not upon seniority. In *National Grid v McKenzie*,[44] a relatively junior project engineer was responsible for the negotiation of contracts for services to be rendered to National Grid and the approval of charges made. He took a personal commission on some contracts. He was held liable to account for these commissions to his employer, even though there was no proof of loss, and he could not enter any contracts of behalf of the company without a countersignature. The important aspect of his position was that he was able to influence how and where contracts were placed. According to Norris J:

> The correct description of Mr McKenzie is that he was an employee who (in certain limited respects) owed fiduciary duties: it is a mis-description to call him 'a fiduciary' and an error to treat him as a trustee.[45]

Similarly, in *Airbus Operations Ltd v Withey*,[46] a middle manager at Airbus was responsible for supervising certain sub-contractors. He did not select the sub-contractors nor could he influence the sums they were paid, since payments were on a fixed price tariff. He gave out-of-office-hours advice to one sub-contractor, for which he was paid. There was no evidence that Airbus had been affected financially, or that the sub-contractor's work was below standard, but the judge found that the sub-contractor received more Airbus work than would have been the case if it had not paid Withey a commission from the profits it made. It was held that Withey owed fiduciary duties to Airbus and was liable to account for all the payments he received, even though he had put in valuable out-of-hours work for the sub-contractor. The judge explained that in finding a breach of fiduciary duty, 'care must be taken not automatically to equate the duties of good faith and loyalty, or trust and confidence, with fiduciary obligations.'[47] These duties could be purely contractual. The question was whether, in the light of the particular duties undertaken by the employee, 'he has placed himself in a position where he must act solely in the interest of his employer.'[48] In this instance, Withey could exercise considerable influence in the choice of sub-contractors, and the judge found that he had used this to give preference to the sub-contractor from which he received a commission. The secrecy about the commission, and the fact that the level exceeded a normal daily rate for the work provided in return, confirmed the breach of fiduciary duty.

(e) Company directors

Directors of companies owe fiduciary duties to the company whilst they are in post, and to a certain degree these duties continue after they leave office.[49] This will be considered later in relation to the exploitation of opportunities.

(4) Some caveats

There are a few cautionary observations which are worth making about fiduciary relationships.

[44] [2009] EWHC 1817 (Ch).
[45] [2009] EWHC 1817 (Ch) at 26.
[46] [2014] EWHC (QB) 1126.
[47] [2014] EWHC (QB) 1126 at 96.
[48] Ibid at 97.
[49] *Sybron Corpn v Rochem Ltd* [1984] Ch 112; *Canadian Aero-Services v O'Malley* [1973] 40 DLR (3d) 371; *Agip (Africa) Ltd v Jackson* [1990] Ch 265. See Koh, 'Once a Director, Always a Fiduciary?' [2003] 62 CLJ 403, for a consideration whether a director continues to be a fiduciary even after he ceases to be a director of the company.

(a) Not all duties owed by a fiduciary are fiduciary duties[50]

As Lord Browne-Wilkinson observed in *Henderson v Merrett Syndicates Ltd*,[51] the phrase 'fiduciary duties' is a dangerous one, giving rise to a mistaken assumption that all fiduciaries owe the same duties in all circumstances. In *Bristol and West Building Society v Mothew*,[52] Millett LJ commented:

> The expression fiduciary duty is properly confined to those duties which are peculiar to fiduciaries and the breach of which attracts legal consequences differing from those consequent upon the breach of other duties. Unless the expression is so limited it is lacking in practical utility. In this sense it is obvious that not every breach of duty by a fiduciary is a breach of fiduciary duty.[53]

He held that it was inappropriate to apply the expression fiduciary to the obligation of a trustee to use proper skill and care in the discharge of his duties. Thus a solicitor acting in a house purchase owes a fiduciary duty to act in the best interests of the client, but there is also a contractual duty to exercise care and skill in the investigation of title, and a duty to act in accordance with the client's instructions in relation to any funds held on the client's behalf in the solicitor's client account. Similarly, we have seen in regard to employees, that a fiduciary duty may be found to apply only to part of a relationship. Care must be taken to separate these responsibilities:

> English law maintains a clear distinction, grounded in principle rather than the accidents of history, between equitable duties owed by fiduciaries and any duties that they might also owe at common law.[54]

The nature of the duties owed by any individual requires a careful examination of the relevant contractual terms (where this is applicable) and 'the scope of the fiduciary duties, if any, can only properly be determined against the full factual matrix'.[55]

(b) Fiduciary duties in other contexts

The concept of fiduciary duty is used in other contexts, such as in relation to undue influence. It should not be assumed that this automatically imposes a duty of loyalty. So, the presumption of undue influence where a patient makes a gift by will in favour of the medical practitioner providing them with medical care does not necessarily entail fiduciary duties of loyalty with which we are presently concerned.

(c) Presumptions can be displaced

As we have seen, even where a relationship (such as trustee and beneficiary) is one in which fiduciary duties are presumed, the specific facts may displace that presumption.

(d) Artificial use of fiduciary relationships

La Forest J in the Canadian Supreme Court case *LAC Minerals Ltd v International Corona Resources Ltd*[56] said that one usage of the term 'fiduciary':

> stems, it seems, from a perception of remedial inflexibility in equity. Courts have resorted to fiduciary language because of the view that certain remedies, deemed appropriate in the

[50] See Austin, 'Moulding the Content of Fiduciary Duties' in Oakley, *Trends in Contemporary Trust Law* (Sweet & Maxwell 1997).

[51] [1995] 2 AC 145 at 206.

[52] [1996] 4 All ER 698; Nolan, 'Multiple Duties and Multiple Employment' [1997] CLJ 39.

[53] [1996] 4 All ER 698 at 710.

[54] *O'Keefe v Caner* [2017] EWHC 1105 (Ch) at 96, per Keyser QC sitting as a High Court judge.

[55] *Courtwood Holdings SA v Woodley Properties Ltd* [2016] EWHC 1168 (Ch) at 34 (Asplin J).

[56] [1989] 61 DLR (4th) 14.

> circumstances, would not be available unless a fiduciary relationship was present. In this sense, the label fiduciary imposes no obligations, but is rather merely instrumental or facilitative in achieving what appears to be the appropriate result.

He referred by way of illustration to *Chase Manhattan Bank NA v Israel-British Bank (London) Ltd*[57] The plaintiff bank paid \$1m to the defendant bank by mistake, having forgotten that they had previously made an identical payment. Goulding J held that as a consequence of the mistaken payment, the defendant bank had become a fiduciary of the plaintiff bank, so that the \$1m was held on constructive trust for them. By means of this reasoning, the plaintiff could maintain a proprietary claim to \$1m in the assets of the defendant, which was insolvent, thus negating the value of any personal right to restitution at common law on the grounds of mistake. La Forest J regarded this case as an example of the statement quoted above. It was not that the relationship between the banks was genuinely 'fiduciary', as they were simply businesses operating at arm's length. Rather, the relationship was characterized this way merely to facilitate the availability of tracing. In *Westdeutsche Landesbank Girozentrale v Islington London Borough Council*,[58] Lord Browne-Wilkinson considered that, while the decision in *Chase Manhattan* could be regarded as rightly decided, the reasoning of Goulding J was erroneous. He considered that a constructive trust was constituted not by the mere receipt of the mistaken payment, but by the fact that the bank to whom the payment had been made knew of the mistake within two days of their receipt of the money:

> Although the mere receipt of the moneys, in ignorance of the mistake, gives rise to no trust, the retention of the moneys after the recipient bank learned of the mistake may well have given rise to a constructive trust.[59]

However, it is submitted that even this reasoning does not adequately explain the creation of an equitable proprietary interest in the money mistakenly paid. The central question should focus rather on the proprietary effects of the mistaken payment. If the mistake was sufficient to prevent property in the money passing to the payee, then the payee will hold it subject to an immediate constructive trust from the moment that it was received. He may not become a fiduciary for the payor until he becomes aware that the mistake had been made and he was conscious of the circumstances giving rise to the constructive trust. The mere fact that he becomes aware of a mistake rendering him subject to a personal obligation to make restitution should neither make him a fiduciary of the payor nor subject the money in his hands to a constructive trust.

3 Fiduciary duties

(1) Core content

The leading case on the content of fiduciary duties is *Bristol and West Building Society v Mothew*,[60] where Millett LJ identified the core content of the fiduciary duty:

> The distinguishing obligation of a fiduciary is the obligation of loyalty. The principal is entitled to the single-minded loyalty of his fiduciary. This core liability has several facets: a fiduciary must act in good faith; he must not make a profit out of his trust; he must not place himself in a position where his duty and his interest may conflict; he may not act for his own benefit or the benefit of a third person without the informed consent of his principal. This is not intended to be an exhaustive list, but it is sufficient to indicate the nature of fiduciary obligations.[61]

[57] [1981] Ch 105. [58] [1996] AC 669. [59] [1996] AC 669 at 715. [60] [1998] Ch 1.
[61] [1998] Ch 1 at 18. See also *A-G v Blake* [1998] 1 All ER 833 at 842, per Lord Woolf MR.

Although this list may not be comprehensive, it is difficult to find other facets to add. One of the few is probably the duty of trustees 'to promote the purpose for which the trust was created', sometimes expressed as a duty to act in the best interests of the beneficiaries[62] and to act even-handedly between the interests of different beneficiaries.[63] It is also important to note that the precise content of specific fiduciary relationships will vary. In *A-G v Blake* Lord Woolf MR stated:

> There is more than one category of fiduciary relationship, and the different categories possess different characteristics and attract different kinds of fiduciary obligations.[64]

(2) **Duration**

The duration of the core fiduciary duty of loyalty is also determined by the context of the relationship in which the fiduciary duty arose. The mere fact that a person once occupied a fiduciary position does not necessarily mean that they will be subject to a lifelong duty of loyalty. *A-G v Blake* concerned the nature of the fiduciary duties of a former secret service agent. George Blake had served as a member of the security services from 1944 until 1960. In 1951 he had become an agent for the Soviet Union. He was arrested and imprisoned, but escaped to live in Moscow. The Crown sought to recover the profits derived from his autobiography, written after leaving Britain, on the grounds that the publication was in breach of fiduciary duty. The Court of Appeal held that, although Blake's employment had rendered him subject to a fiduciary duty, his fiduciary duties did not endure beyond the termination of his employment. Lord Woolf MR explained:

> We do not recognise the concept of a fiduciary obligation which continues notwithstanding the determination of the particular relationship which gives rise to it . . . A former employee owes no duty of loyalty to his former employer. It is trite law that an employer who wishes to prevent his employee from damaging his legitimate commercial interests after he has left his employment must obtain contractual undertakings from his employee to this effect. He cannot achieve his object by invoking the fiduciary relationship which formerly subsisted between them.[65]

Against this, there are situations in which a fiduciary duty will continue. In *The Northampton Regional Livestock Centre Company Ltd v Cowling*,[66] the partner in a firm of property consultants was held liable for breach of fiduciary duty to a third party even after having left the partnership, because the breach related to a continuing transaction begun whilst a partner. As we see later, company directors may also be liable for breach of duty in relation to maturing business opportunities which they exploit after leaving office.

4 Abuse of position

(1) **Fiduciaries owe a duty of exclusive loyalty**

As Millett LJ indicated, in *Bristol and West Building Society v Mothew*,[67] a fiduciary owes a duty of exclusive loyalty to his principal. This duty of loyalty applies to prevent the fiduciary abusing his position. It operates to deter fiduciaries from acting in breach and to provide restitution for the principal if a breach is committed. Where the fiduciary is a

[62] *Re Merchant Navy Ratings Pension Fund* [2015] EWHC 448 (Ch) at 228 (Asplin J).

[63] The duty to maintain a fair balance between different groups is considered to be a fiduciary duty in the context of public law: see *Prescott v Birmingham Corporation* [1955] Ch 210.

[64] [1998] 1 All ER 833 at 842.

[65] [1998] 1 All ER 833 at 841–2.

[66] [2015] EWCA Civ 651 at 74 (this involved liability to a third party after the end of a partnership, but the principles should be the same).

[67] [1998] Ch 1.

trustee, the potential for abuse of position arises because the trustee may use his powers of management over the trust property for his own benefit rather than in the best interest of the beneficiaries. This danger was recognized in early cases. In *Keech v Sandford*,[68] a trustee held the lease of a market on trust for an infant. When the lease came to an end, the lessor refused to renew it to the trust, and the trustee took it personally. King LC held that the trustee could not take the lease for himself and noted the danger of the trustee abusing his position at the expense of the interests of the beneficiary:

> I very well see, if a trustee, on the refusal to renew, might have a lease for himself, few trust estates would be renewed to the [beneficiary].

Similarly, if the trustee wishes to sell part of the trust property he may be tempted to sell it to himself at an undervalue. In his capacity as trustee his duty would be to gain the best possible price for the beneficiaries, but as an individual, he would obviously wish to obtain the lowest price to enjoy the best bargain for himself. As trustee he would be both the purchaser, who offers a price, and the seller, who agrees to the price, it would be easy for him to abuse his position so that he benefits at the expense of the beneficiaries by selling to himself at an undervalue.[69]

In *Item Software (UK) Ltd v Fassihi*,[70] the Court of Appeal held that a fiduciary was under a duty to disclose his own misconduct to his principal, even though he had not obtained any unauthorized profit. However, this decision has been criticized,[71] and it remains unclear whether such an extension of the fiduciary duty is consistent with earlier authorities.[72]

(2) **The difficulty of weighing motives**

If a trustee does act in circumstances where it could be suggested that he had abused his position to gain a personal benefit, it may be impossible to weigh his true motives: i.e. whether he was in fact allowing his own interests to prevail over those of the beneficiaries. As Lord Eldon LC observed in *Ex p James*,[73] 'no court is equal to the examination and ascertainment' of these facts. Indeed, because of the practical impossibility of discovering a fiduciary's true motives, equity has taken the very strict view that a fiduciary is liable to account for any profits he makes whenever there was an objective possibility of a conflict between his interests and his duty.[74] There is no need to demonstrate that the fiduciary acted with the subjective intention of benefiting himself at the expense of the beneficiaries. This is a blunt instrument applied in the beneficiaries' favour. As Lord Herschell stated in *Bray v Ford*:

> It is an inflexible rule of a Court of Equity that a person in a fiduciary position . . . is not, unless otherwise expressly provided, entitled to make a profit; he is not allowed to put himself in a position where his interest and duty conflict.[75]

We will see that the duty of exclusive loyalty imposed by a fiduciary duty is not absolute, and that there are circumstances where fiduciaries are allowed to benefit from their position, for instance, because they have obtained the full informed consent of their principal.

[68] [1726] Sel Cas Ch 61.

[69] See *Holder v Holder* [1968] Ch 353; *Re Thompson's Settlement* [1986] Ch 99; *O'Donnell v Shanahan* [2009] EWCA Civ 751.

[70] [2004] EWCA 1244; Conaglen, 'Directorial Disclosure' [2005] 64 CLJ 48.

[71] See Berg, 'Fiduciary Duties: A Director's Duty to Disclose His Own Misconduct' [2005] 121 LQR 213.

[72] See *Horcal Ltd v Gatland* [1984] BCLC 549 at 554, per Robert Goff LJ.

[73] [1803] 8 Ves 337 at 345.

[74] See *Regal (Hastings) Ltd v Gulliver* [1967] 2 AC 134n; [1942] 1 All ER 378, HL; *Boardman v Phipps* [1967] 2 AC 46, HL.

[75] [1896] AC 44.

5 Unauthorized remuneration

(1) General principle

As a general rule, a trustee is not entitled to receive remuneration for his work[76] unless authorized by the trust deed appointing him, or by statute.[77] The rationale for this principle was stated by Lord Normand in *Dale v IRC*:

> it is not that reward for services is repugnant to the fiduciary duty, but that he who has the duty shall not take any secret remuneration or any financial benefit not authorized by the law. . . or by the trust deed under which he acts[78]

This statement makes clear that the bar on remuneration is not absolute, so that properly authorized remuneration may be retained by the trustee. In the modern commercial world, where the majority of trusts are administered by professional trustees, the general principle still stands, but it has been recognized that there are other competing objectives. As Fox LJ observed in *Re Duke of Norfolk's Settlement Trusts*:

> the court has to balance two influences which are to some extent in conflict. The first is that the office of trustee is, as such, gratuitous; the court will accordingly be careful to protect the interests of the beneficiaries against claims by the trustees. The second is that it is of great importance to the trust that the trust should be well administered.[79]

To balance these objectives the courts have a wide inherent jurisdiction to permit trustees to receive remuneration.

(2) Reimbursement of trustee's expenses

Even though some trustees may not seek to claim expenses, as trustees, they are entitled to the reimbursement of any expenses incurred by them in the work of the trust.[80] Section 31(1)(a) of the Trustee Act 2000 provides that a trustee is entitled to be reimbursed from the trust funds for 'expenses properly incurred by him when acting on behalf of the trust'.

(3) Authorized remuneration

Trustees may be entitled to remuneration in a number of ways.

(a) Trust instrument

Trustees may be entitled to remuneration under the trust instrument.[81] Such provisions are extremely common, and professional trustees will only act if the trust deed contains such a provision. The authorization may be for an honorarium (a payment for holding office) or for payment for actual services rendered.

[76] Bishop and Prentice, 'Some Legal and Economic Aspects of Fiduciary Remuneration' [1983] 46 MLR 289.

[77] *How v Godfrey and White* [1678] Cas temp Finch 361; *Bonithon v Hockmore* [1685] 1 Vern 316; *Robinson v Pett* [1734] 3 P Wms 249; *Re Ormsby* [1809] 1 Ball & B 189; *Taylor v Taylor* [1843] 4 Dr & War 124; *Re Barber* [1886] 34 Ch D 77; *Re Bedingfield* [1887] 57 LT 332; *Barrett v Hartley* [1866] LR 2 Eq 789; *Re Accles Ltd* [1902] WN 164.

[78] [1954] AC 11 at 27.

[79] [1982] Ch 61 at 79.

[80] *Stott v Milne* [1884] 25 Ch D 710; *Re Chapman* [1894] 72 LT 66, CA; *Hardoon v Belilios* [1901] AC 118; *Holding and Management Ltd v Property Holding and Investment Trust plc* [1990] 1 All ER 938, CA; see also *Boardman v Phipps* [1967] 2 AC 46, HL, where the fiduciary received payment 'on a liberal scale' for his work and skill in obtaining a profit for himself and the trust.

[81] *Webb v Earl of Shaftesbury* [1802] 7 Ves 480; *Willis v Kibble* [1839] 1 Beav 559; *Public Trustee v IRC* [1960] AC 398, HL; *Space Investments Ltd v Canadian Imperial Bank of Commerce Trust Co (Bahamas) Ltd* [1986] 1 WLR 1072, PC.

(b) Statute

Section 29 of the Trustee Act 2000 provides that, in the absence of an express entitlement in the trust instrument, a trust corporation, or a professional trustee who is not a sole trustee,[82] is entitled to receive reasonable remuneration for any services provided on behalf of the trust. Such a professional trustee will only be entitled to reasonable remuneration if 'each other trustee has agreed in writing that he may be remunerated for the services'. It should be noted that different rules apply to the remuneration of the trustees of a charitable trust.[83]

Other statutory provisions govern the remuneration of certain specialized trustees. Trustees of charitable purpose trusts may be remunerated if the four sets of conditions set out in s 185 of the Charities Act 2011 are met, one of which is that remuneration is clearly in the interests of the charity.[84] The Public Trustee may charge fees fixed by the Treasury,[85] as might anybody appointed as a custodian trustee.[86] The court may grant remuneration to a person appointed a judicial trustee.[87] If the court appoints a corporation to be a trustee, then it may authorize the corporation to receive remuneration for its services.[88]

Section 28 of the Trustee Act 2000 provides that trustees who are acting in a professional capacity are entitled to receive payment for their services on behalf of the trust even if those services are capable of being provided by a lay trustee.

(c) Inherent jurisdiction of the courts

The court enjoys an inherent jurisdiction to authorize a trustee to receive remuneration, both in respect of work already done and for future work.[89] However, as Lord Goff recognized in *Guinness plc v Saunders*,[90] this jurisdiction is irreconcilable with the rule that a trustee is not entitled to remuneration for services rendered by him to the trust except as expressly provided in the trust deed. He, therefore, held that the exercise of the jurisdiction should be 'restricted to those cases where it cannot have the effect of encouraging the trustees in any way to put themselves in a position where their interests conflict with their duties as trustees'.

The scope of the inherent jurisdiction was examined in *Re Duke of Norfolk's Settlement Trusts*.[91] The Court of Appeal accepted 'without doubt' that the court possesses an inherent jurisdiction to authorize the payment of remuneration to trustees, both in the case of prospective trustees for future services and in the case of an unpaid trustee who has already accepted office and has embarked on his fiduciary duties on a voluntary basis. It also held that the court had the jurisdiction to increase the level of remuneration to which a trustee was entitled under the trust instrument. Fox LJ indicated the factors that the court should take into account in exercising this jurisdiction:

> If therefore the court concludes, having regard to the nature of the trust, the experience and skill of a particular trustee and to the amounts which he seeks to charge when compared with what other trustees might require to be paid for their services and to all the other circumstances of the case, that it would be in the interests of the beneficiaries to increase the remuneration, then the court may properly do so.[92]

[82] s 29(1), (2). [83] ss 28(3), 29(1), (2), and 30 of the Trustee Act 2000.

[84] Guidance on the use of these powers may be found in Charity Comm, CC11 *Trustee Expenses and Payments* (March 2012).

[85] *Re Masters* [1953] 1 WLR 81.

[86] Public Trustee Act 1906, s 9, as amended by the Public Trustee (Fees) Act 1957 and subsequent orders.

[87] Public Trustee Act 1906, s 4(3). [88] Judicial Trustees Act 1896, s 1(5).

[89] *Brown v Litton* [1711] 1 P Wms 140; *Re Masters* [1953] 1 All ER 19; *Re Worthington* [1954] 1 WLR 526; *Re Jarvis* [1958] 2 All ER 336; *Boardman v Phipps* [1967] 2 AC 46, HL; *Re Duke of Norfolk's Settlement Trusts* [1982] Ch 61, CA; *O'Sullivan v Management Agency and Music Ltd* [1985] QB 428, CA.

[90] [1990] 1 All ER 652 at 667.

[91] [1982] Ch 61; [1981] 40 CLJ 243 (Ockleton); [1982] 45 MLR 211 (Green); [1982] 98 LQR 181 (PVB); [1982] Conv 231 (Hodkinson); [1982] 126 Sol Jo 195 (Fox).

[92] [1982] Ch 61 at 79.

(d) Solicitor-trustees

A solicitor-trustee who acts in legal proceedings on behalf of the trust, himself, and his co-trustees, or himself and his beneficiaries, is entitled to receive the usual costs under the rule in *Cradock v Piper*.[93] In *Re Worthington*,[94] Upjohn J said that this rule was 'exceptional, anomalous and not to be extended'.[95]

6 Purchase of trust property by trustees

The court is keen to ensure that fiduciaries do not gain any advantage by exploiting their position at the expense of those for whose benefit they are supposed to be acting. One of the most obvious dangers is that the trustee, who has control over the trust property, will sell it to himself at an undervalue. A similar difficulty is that the trustee may use the advantages of his position to purchase the beneficial interest from the beneficiaries at an undervalue. Equity has applied two rules, or presumptions, which are designed to prevent the trustee abusing his position. They were summarized by Megarry V-C in *Tito v Waddell (No 2)*:

> there are two separate rules. The self-dealing rule is that if a trustee sells the trust property to himself the sale is voidable by any beneficiary ex debito justitiae,[96] however fair the transaction. The fair-dealing rule is that if a trustee purchases the beneficial interest of any of his beneficiaries, the transaction is not voidable ex debito justitiae, but can be set aside by the beneficiary unless the trustee can show that he has taken no advantage of his position and has made full disclosure to the beneficiary, and that the transaction is fair and honest.[97]

These two rules therefore differ in their sphere of operation and standard of liability.

(1) The self-dealing rule

(a) Application of the self-dealing rule

The self-dealing rule[98] applies when a trustee or a person in an analogous position purchases property from the trust. As Arden MR stated in *Campbell v Walker*:

> Any trustee purchasing the trust property is liable to have the purchase set aside, if in any reasonable time the [beneficiary] trust chooses to say, he is not satisfied with it.[99]

The self-dealing rule does not apply to a person who has no trust relationship with the property,[100] but it does apply to a trustee who has retired from the trust with the object of buying trust property[101] and to a trustee who has recently retired.[102] However, in *Re Boles*

[93] [1850] 1 Mac & G 664; *Lincoln v Windsor* [1851] 9 Hare 158; *Broughton v Broughton* [1855] 5 De GM & G 160; *Whitney v Smith* [1869] 4 Ch App 513; *Pince v Beattie* [1863] 9 Jur NS 1119; *Re Corsellis* [1887] 34 Ch D 675; *Re Worthington* [1954] 1 All ER 677.

[94] [1954] 1 WLR 526.

[95] [1954] 1 WLR 526 at 529.

[96] This means as of right, or literally 'by obligation of justice'. In other words, it is a remedy which the court has no discretion to refuse.

[97] [1977] Ch 106.

[98] See McPherson J, 'Self-dealing Trustees', in Oakley, *Trends in Contemporary Trust Law* (Sweet & Maxwell 1997).

[99] [1800] 5 Ves 678 at 680.

[100] In *Hollis v Rolfe* [2008] EWHC 1747 (Ch), it was held there was no breach of the rule against self-dealing by a trustee joining with her co-trustees in transferring the property to her ex-husband, who had no trust relationship with the property.

[101] *Spring v Pride* [1864] 4 De GJ & Sm 395; *Re Mulholland's Will Trusts* [1949] 1 All ER 460.

[102] *Wright v Morgan* [1926] AC 788.

and British Land Co's Contract,[103] it was held that it did not apply where a trustee had retired for twelve years. It will have no application against trustees with no active duties to perform[104] or who have disclaimed the trust.[105] The rule will not catch a transaction completed by a trustee if the contract was entered before he became a fiduciary.[106] There can be an issue as to whether a person has taken office as a trustee. In *Holder v Holder*,[107] Victor Holder was named as an executor in the will of his father, Frank. Victor was the tenant of one of the two farms, 'Lower Farm', included in the estate. He renounced his executorship to enable him to buy the farm, although beforehand he had performed some minor acts in the administration of the estate, including signing a few cheques for trivial sums and endorsing a few insurance policies. He subsequently purchased the farm at public auction. His brother sought to have the sale set aside on the basis that he had, as executor, purchased trust property. The Court of Appeal held that although the purported renunciation of his executorship was technically ineffective, he had never assumed the duties of an executor and had not interfered in any way with the administration of the estate. He had not, therefore, been in the position of both vendor and purchaser of the farm, and the sale was not set aside.[108]

The potentially draconian operation of the self-dealing rule is illustrated by *Kane v Radley-Kane*.[109] The defendant was the administratrix of her husband's estate and stepmother to his three sons. He had died intestate, leaving amongst his assets shares in a software company that were valued at £50,000 at the date of his death. Since the entire estate was worth only £93,000, and the defendant was entitled by statute to a legacy of £125,000, she transferred the shares into her own name. Some three years later, she sold them for £1,131,438. The plaintiff, one of her stepsons, sought a declaration that the transaction by which the defendant had appropriated the shares to herself was rendered void by the self-dealing rule. Sir Richard Scott V-C held that the self-dealing rule applied to the transaction. As the transaction was not expressly or impliedly authorized by statute, and the beneficiaries had not consented to it, it was held to be void. The proceeds of sale were, therefore, to be treated as part of the assets of the state and the defendant entitled merely to the legacy of £125,000.

(b) Standard required by the self-dealing rule

From the earliest cases the self-dealing rule has been applied strictly, and the courts have been unwilling to enter into any consideration of whether the trustee in fact abused his position. An affected transaction is liable to be set aside whenever a trustee has purchased trust property, no matter whether the purchase was to all intents and purposes fair. As Lord Eldon LC stated in *Ex p James*:

> This doctrine as to purchase by trustees, assignees, and persons having a confidential character, stands more upon general principle than upon the circumstances of any individual case. It rests upon this: that the purchase is not permitted in any case, however honest the circumstances; the general interests of justice requiring it to be destroyed in every instance.[110]

[103] [1902] 1 Ch 244. [104] *Parkes v White* [1805] 11 Ves 209. [105] *Stacey v Elph* [1833] 1 My & K 195.

[106] *Vyse v Foster* [1874] LR 7 HL 318; *Re Mulholland's Will Trusts* [1949] 1 All ER 460; *Newman v Clarke* [2016] EWHC 2959 (Ch); [2017] 4 WLR 26.

[107] [1968] Ch 353.

[108] This explanation of the case was preferred by Vinelott J in *Re Thompson's Settlement* [1986] Ch 99. See also *In Plus Group Ltd v Pyke* [2002] 2 BCLC 201; [2003] 62 CLJ 42 (Koh), where the Court of Appeal held that a company director was not in breach of his fiduciary duties by competing with the company in circumstances where he had been wholly excluded from the management of the company such that his position was entirely nominal.

[109] [1999] Ch 274. [110] [1803] 8 Ves 337 at 344.

The law has adopted a strict objective approach that whenever a trustee is both vendor and purchaser the transaction may be set aside. Thus, even a purchase by a trustee at public auction can be set aside by the beneficiaries.[111] In *Wright v Morgan*,[112] the Privy Council held that a sale of land to the trustee at a price fixed by independent valuers must be set aside.

Some doubt was cast upon this strict application of the self-dealing rule by the Court of Appeal in *Holder v Holder*.[113] Sachs LJ took the view that there was no longer any need for the court to be shackled by a rigid rule of an irrebuttable presumption 'which stems from the alleged inability of a court to ascertain the state of mind of a trustee',[114] and that it should be treated merely as a rule of practice. Danckwerts LJ seemed, similarly, to take the view that the rule was a matter for the discretion of the judge. However, in *Re Thompson's Settlement*,[115] Vinelott J seemed to prefer to view the decision in *Holder v Holder* as turning on the fact that the brother had never acted as executor in a way which could be taken to amount to acceptance of a duty to act in the interests of the beneficiaries under the will. He affirmed the more traditional approach:

> The principle is applied stringently in cases where a trustee concurs in a transaction which cannot be carried into effect without his concurrence and who also has an interest or owes a fiduciary duty to another in relation to the same transaction. The transaction cannot stand if challenged by a beneficiary, because in the absence of an express provision in the trust instrument the beneficiaries are entitled to require that the trustees act unanimously and that each brings to bear a mind unclouded by any contrary interest or duty in deciding whether it is in the interests of the beneficiaries that the trustees concur in it.[116]

The application of a strict approach was also supported by Sir Richard Scott V-C in *Kane v Radley-Kane*, where he stated that it was 'a general and highly salutary principle of law that a trustee cannot validly contract with himself[117] and cannot exercise his trust powers to his own advantage'.[118]

(c) Exceptions to the self-dealing rule

We have seen that the self-dealing rule does not apply to rights acquired by a person before becoming a trustee.[119] The self-dealing rule will not apply if the trust instrument authorizes the trustee to purchase trust property.[120] Similarly, if the beneficiaries consent to the purchase, they cannot subsequently have it set aside. The court also possesses the discretion to permit a purchase,[121] probably even retrospectively.[122] Where land is subject to a strict settlement,[123] s 68 of the Settled Land Act 1925 provides that the tenant for life of settled land may purchase the property. An appropriately worded exoneration clause may exempt a trustee from the consequences of the breach of the rule.[124]

[111] *Whichcote v Lawrence* [1798] 3 Ves 740; *Campbell v Walker* [1800] 5 Ves 678; *Dyson v Lum* [1866] 14 LT 588.

[112] [1926] AC 788. [113] [1968] Ch 353. [114] [1968] Ch 353 at 402.

[115] [1986] Ch 99. [116] [1986] Ch 99 at 115.

[117] Evans-Lombe J suggested in *Hollis v Rolfe* [2008] EWHC 1747 (Ch) at 176, that the impossibility of a person contracting with himself is a separate 'primitive self-dealing' rule which applies to all persons regardless of the existence of a trust or fiduciary relationship.

[118] [1998] 3 All ER 753 at 757.

[119] See also *Spiro v Glencrown Properties Ltd* [1991] Ch 537.

[120] *Sargeant v National Westminster Bank plc* [1990] 61 P & CR 518. An example is *AAZ v BBZ* [2016] EWHC 3234 (Fam).

[121] *Farmer v Dean* [1863] 32 Beav 327. [122] *Mills v Mills* [2015] EWHC 1522 (Ch).

[123] Following the introduction of the trust of land in the Trusts of Land and Appointment of Trustees Act 1996, no new strict settlements can be created, but existing settlements will continue.

[124] As in *Barnsley v Noble* [2016] EWCA Civ 799; [2017] Ch 191.

(d) Remedies of the beneficiary

Where trust property has been acquired by a trustee in contravention of the self-dealing rule, the transaction is voidable at the option of the beneficiaries. If the trustee has resold the property, he will be required to make restitution to the trust of any profits he made.[125] If he has retained the property, the beneficiary may insist that it is re-conveyed to the trust, or a new sale may be ordered. There is no explicit limitation period which applies to these claims, and transactions have been set aside as long as twelve years after they were made.[126]

(2) The fair-dealing rule

The fair-dealing rule applies where a trustee purchases the beneficial interest from one or more of the beneficiaries. Since such a transaction is the result of negotiation between the trustee and the beneficiary, there is less risk that the trustee will exploit his position. Equity, therefore, adopts a less strict approach than under the self-dealing rule. Transactions entered in violation of the fair-dealing rule are voidable by the beneficiary unless the trustee can show that he has not taken any advantage by virtue of his position.[127] The onus in this respect is on the trustee.[128] The rule was stated by Lord Eldon in *Coles v Trecothick*:

> a trustee may buy from the [beneficiary], provided that there is a distinct and clear contract, ascertained to be such after a jealous and scrupulous examination of all the circumstances, proving that the [beneficiary of the] trust intended the trustee should buy; there is no fraud, no concealment, no advantage taken, by the trustee of information acquired by him in the character of trustee.[129]

In *Thomson v Eastwood*,[130] Lord Cairns stated that a court of equity would examine such a transaction and 'ascertain that value paid by the trustee, and will throw upon the trustee the onus of proving that he gave full value, and that all information was laid before the [beneficiary] when it was sold'.

There is no reason in principle why an appropriately worded provision in a trust instrument or an exoneration clause should not modify the operation of the self-dealing rule.[131]

7 Bribes and secret commissions

Bribes and secret commissions received by a fiduciary are the most egregious examples of breaches of fiduciary duty: they are clear examples of where there is a potential conflict of interest. Remedies, which we will explore later, operate to deprive the fiduciary of the benefit of receiving a bribe. The same remedies are available in respect of undisclosed commissions received by a fiduciary.[132] For instance, a trustee who recommended that the trust used a firm of stockbrokers who paid him a commission was obliged to account for this to the trust.[133] Such payments may be permitted by the trust or by the agreement of

[125] *Hall v Hallet* [1784] 1 Cox Eq Cas 134; *Ex p James* [1803] 8 Ves 337.

[126] *Brudenell-Bruce v Moore* [2012] EWHC 1024 (Ch).

[127] *Clarke v Swaile* [1762] 2 Eden 134; *Coles v Trecothick* [1804] 9 Ves 234; *Randall v Errington* [1805] 10 Ves 423; *Morse v Royal* [1806] 12 Ves 355; *Sanderson v Walker* [1807] 13 Ves 601; *Dover v Buck* [1865] 5 Giff 57.

[128] *Sharma v Farlam Ltd* [2009] EWHC 1622 (Ch) at 169. [129] [1804] 9 Ves 234.

[130] [1877] 2 App Cas 215. [131] See *Barnsley v Noble* [2016] EWCA Civ 799.

[132] *A-G for Hong Kong v Reid* [1994] 1 All ER 1; Pearce, 'Personal and Proprietary Claims Against Bribees' [1994] LMCLQ 189; *FHR European Ventures LLP v Cedar Capital Partners LLC* [2014] UKSC 45, Pearce, 'Bribes, Secret Commissions and the Monte Carlo Grand Hotel' [2014] 26 Denning LJ 274.

[133] *Williams v Barton* [1927] 2 Ch 9.

the principal. In the Monte Carlo Grand Hotel case,[134] detailed later in this chapter, it was unsuccessfully argued by an agent who negotiated the sale of the hotel that the principal had given informed consent to the agent being paid substantial commissions both by the seller of the hotel and the purchaser.

8 Incidental profits

The remedies depriving a fiduciary of profits do not apply just to payments which are obviously corrupt, but also to other unauthorized profits which the fiduciary receives as a result of holding their position. The rationale for this rule was clearly expressed by Lord Herschell in *Bray v Ford*:

> It is an inflexible rule of a court of equity that a person in a fiduciary position, such as the respondent, is not, unless otherwise expressly provided, entitled to make a profit; he is not allowed to put himself in a position where his interest and his duty conflict. It does not appear to me that this rule is as has been said, founded upon principles of morality. I regard it rather as based on the consideration that, human nature being what it is, there is danger, in such circumstances, of the person holding a fiduciary position being swayed by interest rather than by duty, and thus prejudicing those whom he was bound to protect. It has, therefore, been deemed expedient to lay down this positive rule.[135]

The concept of conflict of interest, which the rule aims to prevent, was explained by Lord Cranworth LC in *Aberdeen Rly Bros v Blaikie*:[136]

> And it is a rule of universal application, that no one, having such duties to discharge, shall be allowed to enter into engagements in which he has, or can have, a personal interest conflicting, or which possibly may conflict, with the interests of those whom he is bound to protect.[137]

(1) **Renewal of an existing arrangement**

A trustee who renews for himself a lease which was previously held on trust for the beneficiaries will hold the lease on trust for them. This rule was applied in *Keech v Sandford*.[138] The trustee held the profits of Romford market on trust for a minor. When the lease expired, the landlord refused to renew the lease to the trust. Instead, he renewed the lease to the trustee personally. King LC held that the lease should be assigned by the trustee to the infant and that he should account for the profits he had made. He recognized that it 'may seem hard that the trustee is the only person of all mankind who might not have the lease', but justified the result in the light of general policy considerations:

> it is very proper that the rule should be strictly pursued, and not in the least relaxed; for it is very obvious what would be the consequences of letting trustees have the lease, on refusal to renew to [the beneficiary].[139]

The principle of *Keech v Sandford* applies only where a lease owned by a trust is renewed to a fiduciary. In *Re Biss*[140] a man rented premises for his business. When he died his widow,

[134] *FHR European Ventures LLP v Cedar Capital Partners LLC* [2014] UKSC 45.

[135] [1896] AC 44 at 51.

[136] [1854] 2 Eq Rep 1281.

[137] See also *Richardson v Chapman* [1760] 7 Bro Parl Cas 318, HL; *Phayre v Peree* [1815] 3 Dow 116, HL; *Shallcross v Oldham* [1862] 2 John & H 609; *Bennett v Gas Light and Coke Co* [1882] 52 LJ Ch 98; *Lagunas Nitrate Co v Lagunas Syndicate* [1899] 2 Ch 392; *Costa Rica Rly Co v Forwood* [1901] 1 Ch 746; *Re Thomson* [1930] 1 Ch 203.

[138] [1726] Sel Cas Ch 61.

[139] [1726] Sel Cas Ch 61 at 62.

[140] [1903] 2 Ch 40.

who was the administratrix of his estate, continued the business with the help of their adult son. The landlord refused to renew the lease to the widow but granted it to the adult son. It was held that the son did not hold the lease on trust for the estate because he did not stand in a fiduciary relationship with the estate. He was, therefore, under no personal incapacity to take the benefit, the renewal was not an accretion to the original term, and it had not been renewed to him until there had been an absolute refusal by the landlord to renew to the administratrix for the estate.

In *Don King Productions Inc v Warren*,[141] the principle of *Keech v Sandford* was applied by analogy to the renewal of a contract held on trust for a partnership to one of the partners in a personal capacity. The case concerned a partnership established between boxing promoters Don King and Frank Warren in 1994. The partnership was subsequently dissolved in 1997. On the basis that partners stand in a fiduciary relationship, the Court of Appeal held that the entire benefit of any management or promotion agreements concluded by a partner after the date of the dissolution but before the conclusion of the winding up of the partnership affairs with a boxer with whom he already has such an agreement would be held on trust for the partnership.

(2) Purchase of a freehold reversion

The principle of *Keech v Sandford* has been extended to include the purchase by a trustee of the freehold reversion of land leased to the trust. Until recently there were doubts whether the rule operated in the same absolute manner. In *Protheroe v Protheroe*,[142] the rule was applied strictly to a husband who purchased the freehold reversion of a house he held on trust jointly with his wife, but earlier cases suggested that the rule would only apply if the lease was renewable to the trust by law or custom.[143] However, it was applied without any such qualification in *Thompson's Trustee in Bankruptcy v Heaton*,[144] where a partner had purchased the freehold reversion of a farm that was a partnership asset. Following *Protheroe v Protheroe*,[145] Pennycuick V-C held that:

> it is also well established that where someone holding a leasehold interest in a fiduciary capacity acquires the freehold reversion, he must hold that reversion as part of the trust estate.[146]

Thompson's Trustee in Bankruptcy v Heaton was cited with approval by the Court of Appeal in *Don King Productions Inc v Warren*,[147] suggesting that the rule will be applied equally strictly where a trustee acquires the freehold reversion.

(3) Remuneration received as a director

Where the trust assets include company shares, the trustees control the associated voting rights at company meetings. If the trustees exploit this power to appoint themselves as directors of the company they will be liable to account for any remuneration they thereby receive. The position was considered in *Re Macadam*,[148] where the trustees of a will were

[141] [2000] Ch 291.

[142] [1968] 1 WLR 519; (1968) 32 Conv 220 (Crane); [1968] 31 MLR 707 (Jackson); [1968] 84 LQR 309 (Megarry).

[143] *Re Lord Ranelagh's Will* [1884] 26 Ch D 590; *Phillips v Phillips* [1885] 29 Ch D 673, CA; *Longton v Wilsby* [1897] 76 LT 770; *Bevan v Webb* [1905] 1 Ch 620; *Phipps v Boardman* [1964] 1 WLR 993 at 1009; [1969] Conv (NS) 161 (Cretney).

[144] [1974] 1 WLR 605.

[145] [1968] 1 WLR 519.

[146] [1968] 1 WLR 519 at 521.

[147] [2000] Ch 291 at 340.

[148] [1946] Ch 73. See also *Re Francis* [1905] 74 LJ Ch 198; *Re Orwell's Will Trusts* [1982] 1 WLR 1337.

granted the power to appoint two directors of a company. They duly appointed themselves and received remuneration for their services. Cohen J held that they were accountable to the trust for the remuneration they had received, and stated the general principles that apply:

> I think the root of the matter really is: did [the trustee] acquire the position in respect of which he drew the remuneration by virtue of his position as trustee? In the present case there can be no doubt that the only way in which the plaintiffs became directors was by the exercise of the powers vested in the trustees of the will. Although the remuneration was remuneration for services as director of the company, the opportunity to receive that remuneration was gained as a result of the exercise of a discretion vested in the trustees, and they had put themselves in a position where their interest and duty conflicted.[149]

The converse conclusion from this reasoning is that trustees are not accountable for any remuneration received from a directorship if they did not in fact use their position to obtain it.[150] Thus, in *Re Dover Coalfield Extension Ltd*,[151] it was held that a trustee would be able to retain remuneration received from a directorship to which he had been appointed before becoming a trustee, as it would not have been obtained by use of his position. In *Re Gee*[152] it was held that a trustee who is elected to a directorship would be entitled to retain any remuneration he received if he would still have been elected a director even if the trust shares he controlled had been voted against him, since he would not then have obtained his position through the use of the trust share. However, he would not be protected from liability merely because he abstained from using the trust shares.

Trustees will not be liable to make restitution if the trust instrument permits them to appoint themselves directors and receive remuneration.[153] The court also possesses an inherent jurisdiction to permit trustees to retain remuneration they receive as directors on a similar basis to the inherent jurisdiction accepted in *Re Duke of Norfolk's Settlement Trusts*.[154] Goulding J considered that the court would permit a trustee 'to retain reasonable remuneration for effort and skill applied by him in performing the duties of the directorship over and above the effort and skill ordinarily required of a director appointed to represent the interests of a substantial shareholder'.[155]

Russell J held that the commission received was to be treated as part of the trust estate.

(4) **Competition**

If the trust assets include a business the trustee must not set up in competition. In *Re Thomson*[156] Clauson J held that it would be a breach of fiduciary duty for a trustee of a yacht-broking business to set up independently as a yacht-broker because he would have been 'entering into an engagement in which he would have a personal interest conflicting or which possibly might conflict with the interests of those he was bound to protect'.[157] The rationale for this decision may be the relatively specialized nature of the yacht-broking business, where it was inevitable that brokers would be in competition with each other. In *Aas v Benham*[158] it was held that there was no breach of fiduciary duty where a member of a partnership of shipbrokers formed a company to build ships. The two operations would

149 [1946] Ch 73 at 82. 150 *Re Lewis* [1910] 103 LT 495. 151 [1907] 2 Ch 76.
152 [1948] Ch 284. 153 *Re Llewellin's Will Trusts* [1949] Ch 225. 154 [1979] Ch 37.
155 [1979] Ch 37 at 162–3. 156 [1930] 1 Ch 203. 157 [1930] 1 Ch 203 at 216.
158 [1891] 2 Ch 244; *Moore v M'Glynn* [1894] 1 IR 74.

not be in competition. In *In Plus Group Ltd v Pyke*,[159] Sedley LJ considered that a director of a company could not simply become involved with a competing third party without the consent of the company because of his fiduciary duty,[160] although on the facts of the case he held that the fiduciary duty had not been breached.

9 Opportunities

A fiduciary is liable to make restitution to his principal if he obtains a profit by exploiting an opportunity that rightfully belonged to his principal. A fiduciary who exploits such an opportunity for his own benefit without the authorization of his principal will be liable to account even where the principal could not have taken advantage of the opportunity himself.[161]

(1) Company directors

(a) General principle

The equitable duties of directors have been codified in the Companies Act 2006.[162] Hence, by s 175(1):

> A director of a company must avoid a situation in which he has, or can have, a direct or indirect conflict of interest that conflicts, or possibly may conflict, with the interests of the company.

The director must also not exploit any property, information, or opportunity,[163] and it is immaterial whether the company could take advantage of it.[164] Although this is a codification, cases before the Act remain relevant, although the Act signals one significant difference in that a mere potential for conflict of interest is not sufficient: the director's duties are not infringed if the situation complained of cannot reasonably be regarded as likely to give rise to a conflict of interest.[165] In *Cook v Deeks*,[166] three of the four directors of a company who were negotiating for a contract to construct a railway took the contract for themselves in their private capacity so as to exclude the fourth director. The Privy Council held that this amounted to a breach of their fiduciary duty, and that they were liable to account to the company for the profits they made from the transaction. In the leading case, *Regal (Hastings) Ltd v Gulliver*,[167] a company that owned cinemas wanted to acquire two other cinemas in Hastings. To enable the company to achieve this objective it formed a subsidiary with 5,000 shares. The company was financially only able to take up 2,000 of the shares in the subsidiary. Since the owner of the cinemas refused to sell them unless the share capital was completely taken up, the directors of the company purchased

[159] [2002] 2 BCLC 201; Grantham, 'Can Directors Compete with the Company?' [2003] 66 MLR 109.

[160] Rejecting dicta to the opposite effect in *London and Marshonaland Exploration Co Ltd v New Mashonaland Exploration Co Ltd* [1891] WN 165.

[161] See *Regal (Hastings) Ltd v Gulliver* [1967] 2 AC 134n; [1942] 1 All ER 378; *Industrial Development Consultants Ltd v Cooley* [1972] 1 WLR 443; *Boardman v Phipps* [1967] 2 AC 46, HL; *O'Donnell v Shanahan* [2009] EWCA Civ 751.

[162] This followed from recommendation of the Law Commission in *Company Directors: Regulating Conflicts of Interest and Formulating a Statement of Duties* (Law Com No 261, 1999).

[163] See *Goldtrail Travel Ltd (In Liquidation) v Aydin* [2016] EWCA Civ 371 (director paid personally for agreement for five-year seat commitment by a tour operating company to an airline).

[164] Companies Act 2006, s 175(2). [165] Companies Act 2006, s 175(4)(a).

[166] [1916] 1 AC 554. [167] [1967] 2 AC 134n; [1942] 1 All ER 378.

the remaining 3,000 shares and the deal went ahead. The company was subsequently sold and the directors made a profit of £2 16s 1d on each of the shares they had taken up. The House of Lords held that the directors were accountable to the purchasers of the company for the profit they had made on the shares because they had obtained it by reason of their fiduciary position. As Lord Russell of Killowen concluded:

> The directors standing in a fiduciary relationship to Regal ... and having obtained these shares by reason and only by reason of the fact that they were directors of Regal and in the course of the execution of that office, are accountable for the profits which they have made out of them.[168]

It made no difference that the company could not have taken up the opportunity itself for lack of finance, nor that the directors had acted bona fides without fraud.[169]

(b) **Liability after ceasing to hold office**

There have been a number of cases in which company directors have been held liable for breach of fiduciary duty in respect of maturing business opportunities even after they have ceased office. The principles were authoritatively summarized by the Court of Appeal in *Foster Bryant Surveying Ltd v Bryant*.[170] The court pointed out that a director was free to resign, and was not a fiduciary in this respect, whatever the impact on the company. Their fiduciary obligations did not normally continue after ceasing to hold office, and:

> After ceasing the relationship by resignation or otherwise a director is in general (and subject of course to any terms of the contract of employment) not prohibited from using his general fund of skill and knowledge, the 'stock in trade' of the knowledge he has acquired while a director, even including such things as business contacts and personal connections made as a result of his directorship.

Despite this, directors could be liable for a breach of fiduciary duty after ceasing to hold office where they exploited a maturing business opportunity. The basis for this liability was that the opportunity belonged to the company. Liability would arise:

> where the resignation may fairly be said to have been prompted or influenced by a wish to acquire for himself any maturing business opportunities sought by the Company and where it was his position with the Company rather than a fresh initiative that led him to the opportunity which he later acquired ... In considering whether an act of a director breaches the preceding principle the factors to take into account will include the factor of position or office held, the nature of the corporate opportunity, its ripeness, its specificness and the director's relation to it, the amount of knowledge possessed, the circumstances in which it was obtained and whether it was special or indeed even private, the factor of time in the continuation of the fiduciary duty where the alleged breach occurs after termination of the relationship with the Company and the circumstances under which the breach was terminated, that is whether by retirement or resignation or discharge.

The operation of these principles is illustrated by an earlier case, *Industrial Development Consultants Ltd v Cooley*.[171] Neville Cooley was the managing director of Industrial Development Consultants Ltd, a company that provided construction consultancy services. He entered into negotiations on behalf of the company with the Eastern Gas Board for a contract to build new depots. The Board refused to enter into a contract with the

[168] [1942] 1 All ER 378 at 389.

[169] For a review of the authorities in this area, see *Ultraframe (UK) Ltd v Fielding* [2005] EWHC 1638 (Ch), where Lewison J preferred the dissenting opinion of Lord Upjohn in *Boardman v Phipps* [1967] 2 AC 46 at 124 that there must be a realistic possibility of conflict of duty and interest for the duty to be breached.

[170] [2007] EWCA Civ 200 at 8. [171] [1972] 1 WLR 443.

company because of their policy of not employing development companies, but they offered a contract to Cooley in his personal capacity, which he accepted. He then gained release from his position as managing director by representing that he was suffering from a serious illness. Roskill J held that Cooley was liable to account for the profit he had gained from the contract because in entering it he had allowed his duty and his interests to conflict.

In *O'Donnell v Shanahan*,[172] a company had, though it was not part of its normal business, agreed to procure finance and advise a particular investor who was interested in purchasing a development company. The deal did not proceed beyond valuation reports, but the defendant directors, who ran a property development partnership on the side, procured the property deal for themselves and a third party and did not pay the company commission. Rimer LJ held that the directors had exploited an opportunity that they obtained only through the company. It did not matter that property development was not in the company's normal course of business; the opportunity should have been disclosed so that the company could decide where or not to exploit it itself.

(c) **Authorized opportunities**

Although directors are prima facie liable to make restitution of any profit they receive by appropriating an opportunity belonging to their company, they will be protected from liability if they were authorized to take up the opportunity. This seems to be the correct analysis of the decision of the Privy Council in *Queensland Mines Ltd v Hudson*.[173] Hudson was the managing director of Queensland Mines, a company that was investigating the possibility of mining iron ore in Tasmania. Two licences were obtained from the Tasmanian government, but the company was not able to start mining operations because of lack of finance. Instead, Hudson resigned as managing director and exploited the licences himself, eventually selling them to an American company from which he received royalties on the ore mined. The company argued that he should account for the profits he had made, but the Privy Council held that he was not liable. As Lord Scarman observed, the difficulty of the case lay 'not in the formulation of the law but in the analysis of the facts'.[174] On the facts the Privy Council concluded that by 1962, the board of directors, 'fully informed as to all the relevant facts, had reached a firm decision to renounce all interest in the exploitation of the licence and had assented to Mr Hudson taking over the venture for his own account'. The basis of the decision thus seems to be that the directors had decided that the company would not take up the opportunity, and that Hudson was therefore free to take it up himself. The objection that only a shareholders' meeting can give authority[175] is resolved by the Companies Act 2006 which states that there will be no conflict of duty and interest if the matter in question has been authorized by the directors.[176]

(2) **Trustees**

Since a trustee is a fiduciary vis-à-vis the beneficiaries of the trust, he will similarly act in breach of duty if he takes personal advantage of opportunities that properly belong to the trust. For example, if a trust includes shares amongst its assets, and a rights issue

172 [2009] EWCA Civ 751.

173 [1978] 18 ALR 1; Sullivan, 'Going it Alone—*Queensland Mines v Hudson*' [1979] 42 MLR 711. See also *Island Export Finance Ltd v Umunna* [1986] BCLC 460; *In Plus Group Lyd v Pyke* [2002] 2 BCLC 201.

174 [1978] 18 ALR 1 at 3.

175 Sullivan, 'Going it Alone—*Queensland Mines v Hudson*' [1979] MLR 711. See also *Prudential Assurance Co v Newman Industries (No 2)* [1980] 2 All ER 841 at 862; *Shaker v Al-Bedrawi* [2002] 4 All ER 835.

176 Companies Act 2006, s 175(4)(b). The conditions for the exercise of effective authorization are contained in ss 175(5) and (6), and 180.

is proposed, the trustees cannot purchase the shares offered under the rights issue for themselves unless authorized to do so by the beneficiaries. If they do purchase the shares without authorization they will be held on constructive trust for the beneficiaries.

(3) **Other fiduciaries**

Fiduciaries other than company directors and trustees will also be held liable to account for any unauthorized profits they receive through exploiting an opportunity belonging to their principal. This can be seen from the leading case of *Boardman v Phipps*.[177] A trust had been established by Charles Phipps on behalf of his wife for life, and after her death, for his four children. The trustees were his widow, daughter, and a professional trustee. One asset of the trust was a 27 per cent holding in a private company, Lester & Harris Ltd. Thomas Boardman was the solicitor to the trust and the Phipps family. Boardman and one of the beneficiaries, Thomas Phipps, were unhappy with the way that the company was being run and decided that the only way to protect the trust asset was to acquire a controlling interest in the company. Boardman suggested this to the managing trustee, who made it clear that he was against the trustees buying such a controlling interest and that, without applying to the court, they had no power to do so. Boardman and Phipps, having informed two of the trustees but not the third, who was the testator's elderly widow, subsequently purchased a controlling interest in the company. They then capitalized some of the company's assets, making a profit of some £47,000 for the trust and £75,000 for themselves. One of the other beneficiaries, John Phipps, claimed that they should account for this profit to the trust. By a bare majority the House of Lords held that Boardman was liable to account. He had stood in a fiduciary relationship to the trust and, although he had acted honestly throughout, in exploiting the opportunity, there had been a possibility of a conflict between his duty and his interest.

10 **Use of confidential information**

A fiduciary who makes use of confidential information[178] belonging to his principal will be liable for any profit that he makes,[179] and the fact that an employee is entrusted with confidential information may be enough to make that person a fiduciary.[180] In *A-G v Guardian Newspapers Ltd (No 2)*,[181] the House of Lords held that the *Sunday Times* was liable to account for the profits made by its publication of extracts of *Spycatcher*, a book written by a former member of the British security services, who stood in a fiduciary relationship to the Crown, and which contained confidential information.[182] In *Peter Pan Manufacturing Corpn v Corsets Silhouette Ltd*,[183] the defendant company's designer was shown a sample copy of the design of a new brassiere in confidence by the plaintiff company. When the defendants subsequently manufactured it Pennycuick J ordered that they account for their profits. Liability on the basis of the exploitation of confidential information was also established in the Canadian case of *LAC Minerals Ltd v International*

[177] [1967] 2 AC 46, HL.

[178] See Glover, 'Is Breach of Confidence a Fiduciary Wrong?' [2001] 21 LS 595.

[179] *York and North Midland Rly Co v Hudson* [1853] 16 Beav 485; *Kirkham v Peel* [1881] 44 LT 195.

[180] *Triplex Safety Glass Co Ltd v Scorah* [1938] Ch 211; *British Celanese Ltd v Montcrieff* [1948] Ch 564; *British Syphon Co v Homewood* [1956] 1 WLR 1190; *A-G v Guardian Newspapers Ltd (No 2)* [1990] 1 AC 109, HL; *A-G v Blake* [1998] 1 All ER 833.

[181] [1990] 1 AC 109.

[182] See Jones, 'Breach of Confidence after *Spycatcher*' [1989] CLP 49.

[183] [1964] 1 WLR 96.

Corona Resources Ltd.[184] LAC received confidential information from Corona during the course of negotiations with a view to establishing a joint venture to exploit minerals from land owned by Corona, which indicated that adjacent land was also likely to contain mineral deposits. LAC subsequently purchased the adjacent land in their own right, and exploited the minerals themselves. The Supreme Court held that there was a fiduciary relationship between the parties, and that LAC should hold the land on constructive trust for Corona because of their breach of confidence.[185]

The exploitation of confidential information provides a further possible explanation for the decision in *Boardman v Phipps*.[186] In the course of negotiations for the purchase of the majority shareholding in the company, Boardman, while purporting to act as the trust solicitor on the business of the trust, received essential information about the value of the company's assets and the prices at which shares had recently changed hands. This information enabled him to put forward his offer for the majority shareholding. Lord Hodson and Lord Guest held that Boardman was accountable for the profit he made because he had acquired the shares using this confidential information, which they considered to be trust property. However, Lord Cohen took the view that the information that had been obtained was not 'property in the strict sense'[187] and decided the case on the basis of the rule in *Regal (Hastings) Ltd v Gulliver*,[188] and Lord Upjohn rejected the argument that the information was to be regarded as part of the trust assets.[189]

The duty not to profit from confidential information only subsists for so long as the information received retains its confidential status. Once it has entered the public sphere, the obligation of confidentiality no longer subsists. Thus, in *A-G v Blake*,[190] the Court of Appeal held that a former spy was not in breach of any fiduciary duty when he had published an autobiography that contained information concerning his work which had entered the public sphere prior to publication. Lord Woolf MR commented:

> The duty to respect confidence is also a fiduciary duty, but it subsists only as long as the information remains confidential.[191]

This was subsequently confirmed by the House of Lords.[192] It has also been held that a third party who receives confidential information disclosed by a fiduciary in breach of his duty is not automatically liable to account for any profits resulting from his exploitation of that information. In *Satnam Ltd v Dunlop Heywood & Co Ltd*,[193] a development company owned an option to purchase a site that was determinable by the site owners if it went into receivership. The company of surveyors acting for the development company subsequently told a rival developer that their client had been placed into receivership and that the local authority was favourable towards development. On the basis of this information, the rival developers purchased the site. While the surveyors had clearly breached their fiduciary duty in revealing this confidential information, the Court of Appeal held that the rival developers did not hold the land acquired on constructive trust for the original developers, nor were they liable to account for their profits. Nourse LJ, giving the

184 [1989] 61 DLR (4th) 14.

185 Tang argues that there was no justification for a constructive trust in *LAC Minerals v International Corona Resources*: 'Confidence and the Constructive Trust' (2003) 23 LS 135.

186 [1967] 2 AC 46, HL.

187 [1967] 2 AC 46 at 103. Note that in *Crown Dilmun plc v Sutton* [2004] 1 BCLC 468 it was accepted that confidential information was not property. However, it may have a market value, and can, indeed, be sold on the market—see *Douglas v Hello! Ltd (No 3)* [2008] 1 AC 1.

188 [1967] 2 AC 134n; [1942] 1 All ER 378.

189 [1967] 2 AC 46 at 127–8.

190 [1998] 1 All ER 833 at 842.

191 [1998] 1 All ER 833 at 842.

192 [2000] 4 All ER 385.

193 [1999] 3 All ER 652.

judgment of the court, explained that mere knowledge of a breach of fiduciary duty was insufficient to render a person who was not himself a fiduciary a constructive trustee. He held that the third party would only have been liable to make an account of profits if it had acted dishonestly.

11 Liability for breach of fiduciary duty

In most instances, the courts have applied what Lord Herschell has described as an 'inflexible rule of equity,'[194] and do not require the principal to demonstrate that the fiduciary in fact permitted his duty and his interest to conflict. Instead, a fiduciary will be liable to account if there was a mere possibility that his duty and his interests would conflict. The adoption of such a strict approach has attracted criticism. While in the majority of cases a fiduciary who has profited from his position will have acted dishonestly and without regard for the interest of his principle, in some cases, a fiduciary who received a profit may have been entirely innocent of any wrongdoing or fraudulent conduct, especially if he exploited an opportunity which his principal could not have exploited, or where the danger of a conflict of interest had been so remote that there was no realistic possibility that such a conflict had occurred. In such cases it may seem questionable whether the fiduciary should be liable to make restitution of his profits. Such difficulties were evident in *Boardman v Phipps*,[195] the facts of which were discussed earlier. The House of Lords consistently emphasized that Boardman and his colleague had been entirely innocent of any misconduct. Lord Cohen, for example, said that their integrity was 'not in doubt' and that they had acted 'with complete honesty throughout'.[196] However, it nevertheless held that Boardman was required to make restitution of the profits he had received. Given the success of the defendants' venture, which it must be remembered also resulted in a considerable profit for the trust, the plaintiff was, as Lord Cohen observed, a 'fortunate man in that the rigour of equity enables him to participate in the profits'.[197]

(1) The rationale for strict liability

Despite the potential for unfairness in some cases, English law has not in most cases required proof of turpitude. In *Regal (Hastings) Ltd v Gulliver*,[198] Lord Russell of Killowen stressed that the fiduciary was required to give up the profit he had made irrespective of his honesty:

> The rule of equity, which insists on those, who by use of a fiduciary position make a profit, being liable to account for that profit, in no way depends on fraud, or absence of bona fides; or upon such questions or considerations as whether the profit would or should otherwise have gone to the plaintiff, or whether the profiteer was under a duty to obtain the source of the profit for the plaintiff, or whether he took a risk or acted as he did for the benefit of the plaintiff, or whether the plaintiff has in fact been damaged or benefited by his action. The liability arises from the mere fact of a profit having, in the stated circumstances, been made. The profiteer, however honest and well intentioned, cannot escape the risk of being called upon to account.[199]

In reaching this conclusion, he drew upon the language of Lord King LC in *Keech v Sandford*,[200] and of Lord Eldon LC in *Ex p James*,[201] who had said that the self-dealing

[194] [1896] AC 44 at 51. [195] [1967] 2 AC 46. [196] *Bray v Ford* [1967] 2 AC 46 at 104.
[197] [1967] 2 AC 46 at 104. [198] [1942] 1 All ER 378. [199] [1942] 1 All ER 378 at 386.
[200] [1726] Sel Cas Ch 61. [201] [1803] 8 Ves 337.

rule 'rests upon this: that the purchase is not permitted in any case however honest the circumstances'. In *Guinness plc v Saunders*,[202] the House of Lords held that a company director who had received an unauthorized payment of £5.2 million was liable to account to his company because he had allowed his duty and his interest to conflict, even though he had acted in complete good faith throughout.[203]

A divergence of views was apparent in the House of Lord in *Boardman v Phipps*,[204] as to the degree of likelihood of a real conflict of interest required to render a fiduciary liability to account. It was alleged that Boardman had allowed his duty and his interest to conflict by purchasing a controlling interest in a company partially owned by the trust while there was a possibility that, as the trust solicitor, he could be called upon by the trustees to advise whether it would be wise for them to seek to acquire the power to pursue a similar investment. Lord Upjohn, dissenting, took the view that a fiduciary should only be required to disgorge his profits where there had been a 'real sensible possibility' of a conflict of interest. In the circumstances, he considered that the possibility of a conflict was simply too remote to render Boardman liable:

> The relevant rule for the decision of this case is the fundamental rule of equity that a person in a fiduciary capacity must not make a profit out of his trust which is a part of the wider rule that a trustee must not place himself in a position where his duty and his interest may conflict. It is perhaps most highly against trustees or directors in the celebrated speech of Lord Cranworth LC in *Aberdeen Rly Bros v Blaikie Bros*, where he said: 'And it is a rule of universal application, that no one, having such duties to discharge, shall be allowed to enter into engagements in which he has, or can have, a personal interest conflicting, or which possibly may conflict, with the interests of those whom he is bound to protect.' The phrase 'possibly may conflict' requires consideration. In my view it means that the reasonable man looking at the relevant facts and circumstances of the particular case would think that there was a real sensible possibility of conflict; not that you could imagine some situation arising which might, in some conceivable possibility in events not contemplated as real sensible possibilities by any reasonable person, result in a conflict.[205]

He, therefore, concluded that Boardman had not acted in breach of his duty because there had been no 'real sensible possibility' of a conflict of interest, and that he should not be required to disgorge his profits.

In contrast, the majority of the House of Lords held that the remoteness of the possibility of a genuine conflict of interest was irrelevant to the liability of a fiduciary. Lord Cohen,[206] Lord Hodson, and Lord Guest cited with approval the statement of principle of Lord Russell in *Regal (Hastings) Ltd v Gulliver*.[207] As Lord Hodson observed:

> No doubt it was but a remote possibility that Mr Boardman would ever be asked by the trustees to advise on the desirability of an application to the court in order that the trustees might avail themselves of the information obtained. Nevertheless, even if the possibility of conflict is present between personal interest and the fiduciary position the rule of equity must be applied.[208]

In consequence of the decision of the majority in *Boardman v Phipps*, English law imposes a very strict liability for breach of fiduciary duty so that a fiduciary is liable to account for profits he has received whenever there was a mere possibility, no matter how remote, that his duty and his interest might conflict.

[202] [1990] 2 AC 663. [203] [1990] 2 AC 663 at 710, per Lord Goff.

[204] [1967] 2 AC 46. [205] [1967] 2 AC 46 at 124.

[206] Who had read the speeches to be delivered by Lord Hodson and Lord Guest and agreed in substance with them.

[207] [1967] 2 AC 134n; [1942] 1 All ER 378. [208] [1967] 2 AC 46 at 111.

A number of arguments can be put forward in defence of the strict liability of fiduciaries. First, it should be remembered that a fiduciary is only required to make restitution of *unauthorized* profits. He is able to protect himself from liability by full disclosure of his proposed activities to his principal, which in the case of a trust will mean the beneficiaries. If the principal consents or acquiesces in the conduct disclosed, the fiduciary will not be held accountable for any profits he receives thereby. However, where a fiduciary fails to fully disclose his intended course of action to his principal, it is not unfair to presume that he was acting in a manner that he did not expect would be condoned. Second, it has already been noted that it is impossible to conduct an inquiry into the subjective motives that influenced a fiduciary's conduct to determine whether a genuine conflict of interest occurred.[209] The court can only look to the objective reality of external appearances, and the mere possibility of such a conflict triggers a remedial response in favour of the principal. This ensures that a situation can never arise where the fiduciary does in fact profit from a breach of his duty. Third, it has to be remembered that the rule has implications beyond any immediate case in point. It operates to deter fiduciaries who may consider abusing their position. This has been described as the prophylactic function of the rule: equity does not wait to see whether the principal has suffered any detriment as a result of the fiduciary's conduct but imposes a duty which will hold the fiduciary accountable if he might have been tempted to sacrifice the interests of the beneficiary.[210] This prophylactic approach appeared to be to the fore in the reasoning of the House of Lords in *Guinness plc v Saunders*,[211] where Lord Goff emphasized that the court must not act in a manner that would provide any encouragement to trustees to put themselves in a position where their duty would conflict with their personal interests.

(2) **Amelioration of the consequences of strict liability**

While the adoption of a strict liability to make restitution of unauthorized profits may sometimes be perceived to operate unfairly against an honest fiduciary, such unfairness may partially be alleviated at the remedial stage. Whereas, prima facie, a fiduciary in breach will be required to disgorge the entirety of the profit he received, in some circumstances, the courts have held that a fiduciary may be permitted to retain a proportion for himself.[212] The exercise of such relief is akin to the inherent jurisdiction to authorize a trustee to retain past remuneration, and to recoup his expenses from the trust. For example, in *Boardman v Phipps*,[213] the majority of the House of Lords held that although Boardman was liable to account for the profits he had received, he should enjoy an allowance to represent his work and skill, which had contributed substantially to the making of the profit. This allowance was to be calculated 'on a liberal scale'.

It remains unclear, however, whether the allowance granted in *Boardman v Phipps* included any share of the profits made, or whether it was intended solely to reflect the expenses he had incurred. In *O'Sullivan v Management Agency and Music Ltd*,[214] the

[209] *Ex p James* [1803] 8 Ves 337.

[210] Birks, *Introduction to the Law of Restitution* (Clarendon Press 1985), pp 332–3, 339–43.

[211] [1990] 2 AC 663.

[212] In *Warman International v Dwyer* [1995] 128 ALR 201, the High Court suggested that where a fiduciary had acted in breach of his duty in the context of a business rather than through the receipt of a specific asset, it may well be inappropriate and inequitable to compel the errant fiduciary to account for the whole of the profit of his conduct of the business or exploitation of the principal's goodwill over an indefinite period of time. In such a case it might therefore be appropriate to allow the fiduciary a proportion of the profits, depending upon the particular circumstances.

[213] [1967] 2 AC 46.

[214] [1985] QB 428.

court expressly permitted a fiduciary to retain a share of the profit it had received. An exclusive management contract between a musician and a management company was set aside on the grounds of undue influence. The Court of Appeal held that while the company was required to account for the profits that it had received under contract, it should be permitted to retain an allowance of reasonable remuneration for their skill and labour. This allowance explicitly included a small share of the profits made. The principle was stated by Fox LJ:

> Once it is accepted that the court can make an appropriate allowance to a fiduciary for his skill and labour I do not see why, in principle, it should not be able to give him some part of the profit of the venture if it was thought that justice as between the parties demanded that.[215]

The allowance is, therefore, entirely within the court's discretion, and on the facts it was held that a profit element should be included to recognize the contribution that the company had made to the singer's success, but that this would be less than the profit they might have made if the contract had been properly negotiated in the first place to reflect disapprobation of their conduct in obtaining the contract through undue influence.[216]

The stated objective was to 'achieve substantial justice between the parties'.[217] It might be thought that this would provide a way of adjusting the harsh consequences of the strict approach taken in *Boardman v Phipps*.[218] However, *Guinness plc v Saunders*,[219] suggests that the courts will be unlikely to award a share of the profits to directors or trustees who allow their duty and their interests to conflict. The case concerned a director, Mr Ward, who received £5.2 million under a contract he had entered into to provide his services to help with a takeover bid. He was held liable to account for this money because he had acted in breach of fiduciary duty and had not disclosed his interest to the company board. The question arose whether he should receive any allowance for the services he had performed. The House of Lords held that he should not. Lord Goff analysed the rationale for the award of an allowance on a liberal scale in *Boardman v Phipps*[220] and concluded:

> The decision has to be reconciled with the fundamental principle that a trustee is not entitled to remuneration for services rendered by him to the trust except as expressly provided in the trust deed. Strictly speaking, it is irreconcilable with the rule so stated. It seems to me therefore that it can only be reconciled with it to the extent that the exercise of the equitable jurisdiction does not conflict with the policy underlying the rule. As I see it, such a conflict will only be avoided if the exercise of the jurisdiction is restricted to those cases where it cannot have the effect of encouraging trustees in any way to put themselves in a position where their interests conflict with their duties as trustees.[221]

The allowance in *Boardman v Phipps* was, therefore, justified because of the 'equity underlying Mr Boardman's claim', and, as such, it would not provide any encouragement to trustees to put themselves in a position where their duties as trustees conflicted with their interests. In the case of Mr Ward, remuneration would be inappropriate because he had agreed to provide his services in return for a substantial fee and 'was most plainly putting himself in a position in which his interests were in stark contrast with his duty as a director'.[222] The exercise of the discretion to award an equitable allowance for skill and effort is limited to 'exceptional' or 'unusual' circumstances.[223]

215 [1985] QB 428 at 468.

216 [1985] QB 428 at 469, per Fox LJ: 'the defendants must suffer . . . because of the circumstances in which the contracts were procured.'

217 [1985] QB 428 at 469, per Fox LJ. 218 [1967] 2 AC 46. 219 [1990] 2 AC 663, HL.

220 [1967] 2 AC 46. 221 [1990] 2 AC 663 at 701. 222 [1990] 2 AC 663 at 702.

223 *Global Energy Horizons Corporation v Gray* [2015] EWHC 2232 (Ch) at 130.

(3) **Proof of wrongdoing?**

There are some indications that the English courts wish to move away from the strict liability advocated in *Boardman v Phipps*,[224] although in some cases, they are constrained by the strength of authority.[225] The rules for finding a company director in breach of fiduciary duty after ceasing to hold office require an exercise of judgment in which wrongdoing appears to be an element. *In Plus Group Ltd v Pyke*,[226] Sedley LJ suggested that a company director would not commit a breach of fiduciary duty by serving a competing company without consent if he had been treated unfairly. In *Murad v Al-Saraji*,[227] Clarke, Arden, and Jonathan Parker LJJ all expressed a desire to soften the position of the law on fiduciary liability where a fiduciary had acted without concealment, but felt unable to do so. The question was not discussed by the Supreme Court in *FHR European Ventures LLP v Cedar Capital Partners LLC*.[228] Academic opinion remains divided on the subject, with some commentators welcoming a potential relaxation of strict liability,[229] while others feel that the strictness of the rules serves a useful purpose.[230]

(4) **Conclusion**

It might be thought that, in practice, there is very little difference between the two standards of liability propounded by the House of Lords in *Boardman v Phipps*.[231] Lord Upjohn's 'real sensible possibility' of a conflict of interest test will exclude only those cases where it seems there is absolutely no danger of the beneficiaries in fact being prejudiced by the fiduciary's conduct. It is an objective test, and, therefore, there is still no need to inquire into actual motives, and it is sufficiently harsh to serve as an adequate deterrent to trustees who might contemplate abusing their position. However, although Lord Upjohn's test has much to commend it, and it has found favour with academic commentators,[232] the strict approach that a fiduciary will be liable to account whenever there was a mere possibility of a conflict of interest, no matter how remote or unlikely the circumstances, represents the present position of English law. This, in the context of company law, has been said to raise 'the fiduciary "no-conflict" rule from pragmatic prophylaxis to something far more

[224] [1967] 2 AC 46. [225] *Guinness v Saunders* [1990] 2 AC 663.

[226] [2002] 2 BCLC 201. Grantham argues that this is inconsistent with the strict duty imposed on fiduciaries: (2003) 66 MLR 109.

[227] [2005] EWCA Civ 959, CA; McInnes, 'Account of Profits for Breach of Fiduciary Duty' [2006] LQR 11; *Ultraframe (UK) Ltd v Fielding* [2005] EWHC 1638 (Ch) (where Lewison J expressed his support for an approach based on a realistic possibility of conflict of interest, in preference to the strict approach).

[228] [2014] UKSC 45.

[229] See, for example, Panesar, 'The Nature of Fiduciary Liability in English Law' [2007] Conv 2, 11–19: 'whilst the strict liability rule was justified in the context of some of the nineteenth century cases where evidential issues prevented the court from ascertaining the intention of the fiduciary, in modern cases it is questionable whether such an approach is justified. There is much to be said for recent judicial calls for recognition that it is not appropriate to apply laws decided in a wholly different context to a different kind of situation.'

[230] See, for example, Samet, 'Guarding the Fiduciary's Conscience—A Justification of a Stringent Profit-Stripping Rule' (2008) OJLS 763, arguing that allowing the fiduciary to argue that he acted as an honest person would, therefore, be more than a mere decrease in its overall deterrent effect. The strict no-profit rule prevents manipulation.

[231] [1967] 2 AC 46.

[232] Jones, 'Unjust Enrichment and the Fiduciary's Duty of Loyalty' (1968) 84 LQR 472; Finn, *Fiduciary Obligations* (Law Book Company 1977), pp 130–68. It is also arguably the basis of the rule relating to directors duties in s 175(4)(a) of the Companies Act 2006.

draconian'.[233] The only way that the fiduciary can avoid liability, no matter how honest he may have been, is by ensuring that his profit-making activities are authorized by his principal following full disclosure.

12 Remedies for breach

There are several potential consequences to a breach of fiduciary duty in addition to the possible criminal and contractual consequences.

(1) Compensation for loss suffered

In many cases, the fiduciary in breach will have made a profit. Then, the appropriate remedy will be to remove that profit from them. Yet in other circumstances, there might be no profit. Worse, the fiduciary might actually have caused a loss to their principal. In such circumstances, the fiduciary must compensate for that loss. The obligation to pay equitable compensation for breach of fiduciary duty is a purely personal remedy.

If a fiduciary commits a breach of duty their principal will be entitled to recover equitable damages to compensate them for any loss they have suffered.[234] Where the fiduciary was a trustee their breach will probably have constituted a breach of trust, entitling the beneficiaries to receive compensation. The right to receive equitable compensation for breach of fiduciary duty will also arise even where the fiduciary was not also a trustee.[235] The principal will be entitled to recover such compensation as would put them in the position they would have been in if the wrong had not been committed.[236]

To establish the right to compensation, the principal must demonstrate that the alleged breach of fiduciary duty caused the loss sustained. In *Swindle v Harrison*,[237] Mrs Harrison mortgaged her house in order to enable her son to purchase and restore a hotel. Her solicitors helped to obtain further bridging finance, but did not disclose that they would receive a commission on it. The hotel business was unsuccessful and the solicitors sought possession. Mrs Harrison counterclaimed that she was entitled to receive equitable compensation for the equity she had lost in her home on the grounds that the solicitors had committed a breach of their fiduciary duty. The Court of Appeal held that the solicitors had breached their duty by failing to make full disclosure of the circumstances and that they were, therefore, liable to compensate her for any loss suffered. However, the essential issue was whether her loss had been caused by the breach. The Court of Appeal concluded that she would have completed the transaction anyway, so that the breach of fiduciary duty was not the cause of the loss.

In this context, *Auden McKenzie (Pharma Division) Ltd v Patel*[238] is of interest. A director had misappropriated funds through sham invoices. In his defence, the director

[233] Gower and Davies, *Principles of Modern Company Law* (9th edn, Sweet & Maxwell 2012) at p 601. They argue that the operation of the rules essentially gives companies a right of first refusal on opportunities seen by directors as worth pursuing. Looking to the facts of *O'Donnell v Shanahan* [2009] EWCA Civ 751, this could happen even where the business opportunity was incidental to the company's main business.

[234] Compensation for loss is a fundamental feature of equitable compensation. This is true even while the courts have not always maintained a clear line between loss-based and gains-based remedies. See, e.g., *Interactive Technology Corporation Limited v Jonathan Ferster* [2018] EWCA Civ 1594, 15.

[235] See, e.g., *Auden McKenzie (Pharma Division) Ltd v Patel* [2019] EWCA Civ 2291.

[236] See Conaglen, 'Equitable Compensation for Breach of Fiduciary Dealing Rules' [2003] 119 LQR 246.

[237] [1997] 4 All ER 705; Tjio and Yeo, 'Limited Liability for Breach of Fiduciary Duty' [1998] 114 LQR 181; Elliott, 'Restitutionary Compensatory Damages for Breach of Fiduciary Duty?' [1998] RLR 135. See also Sir Peter Millett, 'Equity's Place in the Law of Commerce' [1998] 114 LQR 214.

[238] [2019] EWCA Civ 2291.

claimed that he would have paid out the value in dividends had it not been for his sham. It followed that the sham invoices had in fact caused no real loss to the company. The Court of Appeal held that this line of hypothetical argument was sustainable in law.

(2) **Transparency about commissions**

A fiduciary receiving commissions from a third party must always tell his clients about the arrangement. This prevents them from being 'secret profits'. It is a matter of good faith, but it is not always necessary to explain the precise nature of the relationship to the clients. This is illustrated by the facts of *Medsted Associates Ltd v Canaccord Genuity Wealth (International) Ltd*[239] Medsted was an introducing broker. In this role, it introduced clients, to whom it was a fiduciary, to a firm named Collins Stewart. Medsted received a share of commission paid by the clients to Collins Stewart.

Contrary to a contract, Collins Stewart 'cut out' Medsted and dealt directly with certain clients. The High Court held that Collins Stewart was in breach of its obligation not to circumvent Medsted.[240] If the judge had gone no further, *Medsted* would have been an ordinary case in contract. However, the judge took an extra step. Teare J also found that because Medsted was in a fiduciary relationship with its clients it should have precisely explained the profits that it made from the arrangement. Disapproving of the fact that Medsted had not been entirely transparent in relation to the commissioning arrangement, Teare J awarded only nominal damages on public policy grounds. He said that the court ought not to assist Medsted in a breach of duty.

The case as it was decided in the High Court raised the prospect that unless a fiduciary had been entirely clear with the principal about commissions from third parties, then that fiduciary would not be able to rely on the courts to recoup them. Medstead appealed and the High Court decision was reversed.

On appeal, Medsted was awarded substantive damages. The Court of Appeal held that while there is a duty to inform the principal of commissions, there was not necessarily a duty to inform them of the precise nature of the arrangement. This was particularly the case where the principal was a sophisticated investment client who did not obviously need the protection of the court. This reasoning charts a middle ground where the necessary level of transparency will be dependent, case-by-case, on the nature of the business circumstances in which the commission was arranged.

(3) **Accounting for the unauthorized receipts**

A fiduciary who has received a bribe or a secret commission or made unauthorized profits will be required in equity to account for these gains or receipts to the principal.[241] The liability of a fiduciary to account for a profit made from his position does not depend upon the principal having suffered any loss,[242] and can apply even where the breach of fiduciary duty has conferred 'a substantial windfall benefit' on the principal.[243] This is because 'the breach of duty does not consist in the making of a profit by the fiduciary, but in the

[239] [2019] EWCA Civ 83.

[240] *Medsted Associates Ltd v Canaccord Genuity Wealth (International) Ltd* [2017] EWHC 1815 (Comm).

[241] A remedy might also be available even where there is no fiduciary relationship. For example, the relationship might be merely contractual. See *Wood v Commercial First Business Ltd* [2021] EWCA Civ 471 at [47].

[242] *Akita Holdings Ltd v Attorney General of The Turks and Caicos Islands* [2017] UKPC 7 at 17. See also *Novoship (UK) Ltd v Nikitin* [2014] EWCA Civ 908; Campbell [2015] Conv 160.

[243] *The Northampton Regional Livestock Centre Company Ltd v Cowling* [2015] EWCA Civ 651 at 1.

keeping of it for himself.'[244] He is obliged to pay over to his principal a sum of money equivalent to the amount of profit received, though not necessarily the actual money (or its proceeds) which comprised the profit. The breach need not be the direct cause of the receipt, but there must be a sufficient connection between the breach and the profit in order to bring the equitable remedy into play.[245]

The obligation to account operates as a personal remedy and can be justified on the principles of restitution or unjust enrichment.[246] The proprietary remedy considered later might be more attractive where the fiduciary has invested the sums received at a profit, or where the fiduciary is insolvent, but the personal remedy might be more advantageous where the receipts can no longer be traced, or the investments made with them have fallen in value.[247] In a case where the value of the property acquired has both risen and fallen in value, the court has some flexibility in assessing the value required to do justice in the circumstances.[248] The relevant date for the assessment of the quantum of the personal remedy is the date that the profit was received. The principal will only be entitled to recover the actual or net profit that was received by the fiduciary.[249]

(4) **Proprietary remedies**

(a) The debate about proprietary remedies

The courts have consistently held that a proprietary remedy is available for breach of fiduciary duty where the fiduciary has misappropriated property to which the principal already has a legal title. For example, in *Agip (Africa) Ltd v Jackson*,[250] a company was defrauded by its chief accountant, Zdiri, who altered the name of the payees of genuine payment orders so that they were payable to dummy companies he had created. Millett J held that as the accountant was a fiduciary of the company by virtue of his senior position and responsibility, the misappropriated money was held on constructive trust by the recipient dummy companies, and Agip was enabled to trace it. The money paid to such companies was not previously subject to a trust but had been the absolute property of the company. Similarly, in *Brinks Ltd v Abu-Saleh (No 3)*,[251] Rimmer J held that gold bullion that had been stolen was subject to a constructive trust in favour of its corporate owners because the robbery had been carried out with the assistance of a security guard who stood in a fiduciary relationship. Cases supporting the imposition of a trust in a wider range of circumstances go at least as far back as *Keech v Sandford*,[252] where the court held that a lease that had been renewed to a trustee in his personal capacity, rather than on behalf of the trust, should be assigned to the infant beneficiary. This suggests that the

244 *Novoship (UK) Limited v Nikitin* [2014] EWCA Civ 908 at 104; *Schenk v Cook* [2017] EWHC 144 (QB) at 86. See also Mitchell, 'Stewardship of Property and Liability to Account' [2014] Conv 215 and Millett, 'Bribes and Secret Commissions Again' [2012] CLJ 582.

245 *Parr v Keystone Healthcare Ltd* [2019] EWCA Civ 1246 at 18.

246 See Goff and Jones, *The Law of Unjust Enrichment* (8th edn, Sweet & Maxwell 2011), Ch 6; Birks, *Introduction to the Law of Restitution* (Clarendon Press 1985), pp 313–57; Burrows, *The Law of Restitution* (2nd edn, Butterworths 2002), pp 493–508; [1989] CLJ 302 (Jackman).

247 *A-G for Hong Kong v Reid* [1994] 1 All ER 1.

248 *Global Energy Horizons Corporation v Gray* [2015] EWHC 2232 (Ch) at 143.

249 *Patel v London Borough of Brent* [2003] EWHC 3081.

250 [1990] Ch 265; [1992] 4 All ER 385; Birks [1989] 105 LQR 528; Millet [1991] 107 LQR 71; [1991] Ch 547; [1992] 4 All ER 451; Harpum [1991] 50 CLJ 409; Goulding [1992] Conv 367; Swadling [1992] All ER Rev, 258–65.

251 [1995] *The Times*, 23 October; Stevens, 'Delimiting the Scope of Accessory Liability' [1996] Conv 447.

252 [1726] Sel Cas Ch 61.

infant enjoyed an equitable entitlement to the lease from the moment that the trustee had acquired it. The trustee was also obliged to account for the profits he had received in the meantime. This account of profits is also explicable on the basis that the lease was always the property of the trust.

Against this, there are other cases, most notably *Lister v Stubbs*, which have rejected the notion that unauthorized profits received by a fiduciary are always held on a constructive trust. More recently, the Court of Appeal held in *Sinclair Investments (UK) Ltd v Versailles Trade Finance Ltd (In Administration)*,[253] that the general rule was that the only remedy was personal, 'unless the asset or money is or has been beneficially the property of the beneficiary or the trustee acquired the asset or money by taking advantage of an opportunity or right which was properly that of the beneficiary.'[254]

In many other cases the courts have not clearly identified the remedy awarded. The problem was stated clearly in the Australian High Court by Gibbs J in *Consul Development Pty Ltd v DPC Estates Pty Ltd*:

> The question whether the remedy which the person to whom the duty is owed may obtain against the person who has violated the duty is proprietary or personal may sometimes be one of some difficulty. In some cases the fiduciary has been declared a trustee of the property which he has gained by his breach; in others he has been called upon to account for his profits and sometimes the distinction between the two remedies has not . . . been kept clearly in mind.[255]

(b) The Monte Carlo Grand Hotel case

In the Monte Carlo Grand Hotel case (*FHR European Ventures LLP v Cedar Capital Partners LLC*[256]), the Supreme Court gave a clear and unequivocal answer to the question of when a proprietary remedy is available for breach of fiduciary duty.[257] Cedar Capital Partners had been engaged both by FHR, a consortium wishing to buy the Monte Carlo Grand Hotel and by the owners. Cedar did not disclose to the consortium that it was receiving a commission of €10 million from the sellers. By the time the case reached the Supreme Court, it was not disputed that Cedar was in breach of fiduciary duty to FHR. The question was simply what remedy was available. The Supreme Court held that the general rule was that any benefit acquired by an agent as a result of his agency and in breach of his fiduciary duty is held on trust for the principal.[258] Lord Neuberger, delivering the judgment of the court, said that the case law did not provide a definitive answer to the question, although the majority of the cases supported the view of the Supreme Court. Those which supported a contrary view[259] were all open to criticism and should be treated as overruled. The view adopted by the Supreme Court had the merit of simplicity, and was supported by a number of policy considerations. Amongst these, particularly stringent rules were justified in relation to bribes and secret commissions, which undermined trust in the commercial world.

[253] [2011] EWCA Civ 347. [254] [2011] EWCA Civ 347 at 88. [255] [1975] 5 ALR 231 at 249.

[256] [2014] UKSC 45. The case is referred to in the text as the Monte Carlo Grand Hotel case. See Gummow, 'Bribes and Constructive Trusts' [2015] 131 LQR 21; Whayman, 'Proprietary Remedy Confirmed for Bribes and Secret Commissions' [2014] Conv 518.

[257] Elizabeth Houghton argues that the solution is too blunt, and a rule with some flexibility would have been preferable: 'Equity's New Darling and the Pitfalls of Remedial Absolutism' (2016) T&T 956.

[258] [2014] UKSC 45 at 35.

[259] Including *Metropolitan Bank v Heiron* [1880] 5 Ex D 319 and *Lister & Co v Stubbs* [1890] 45 Ch D 1 and cases applying those decisions. This includes the Court of Appeal decision in *Sinclair Investments (UK) Ltd v Versailles Trade Finance Ltd (In Administration)*, where the leading judgment was given by Lord Neuberger before his elevation to the Supreme Court. The Supreme Court also disapproved of the decision in *Tyrrell v Bank of London* [1862] 10 HL Cas 26.

(c) An end to the debate?

Before the Monte Carlo Grand Hotel case there had been a debate, 'revealing "passions of a force uncommon in the legal world"',[260] about the circumstances in which a bribe or secret commission would be held on trust. The decision of the Supreme Court now answers that question definitively. Although the rule described by the Court applies to agents, that was because the case involved an agent. There is no reason to think that the rule does not apply equally to all fiduciaries since Lord Neuberger drew support from the fact that this is the case in other Commonwealth legal jurisdictions.[261] Equally, the Supreme Court described the rule so broadly that it is not confined just to bribes or secret commissions, but to all unauthorized benefits received by a fiduciary. This view has been adopted at first instance.[262]

(d) Advantages of a proprietary remedy

Proprietary remedies have an advantage over personal remedies when the defendant is insolvent and there are identifiable assets which are held on constructive trust for the claimant. Another advantage of the proprietary remedy is that it enables the proceeds of an unauthorized benefit to be traced into other assets which they have been used to acquire.[263] In *A-G for Hong Kong v Reid*,[264] Reid received bribes exceeding NZ$2.5m in the course of his work as a public prosecutor in Hong Kong. Part of this money was used to purchase three freehold properties in New Zealand. The Privy Council considered that, since Reid had acted in breach of his fiduciary duty, he held the money he received on constructive trust for the Crown. Since the houses were the traceable proceeds of the bribes received, they were also held on trust for the Crown. In *The Federal Republic of Brazil v Durant International Corporation*,[265] which is considered more fully in relation to tracing,[266] proprietary claims were made in relation to assets acquired through a money laundering exercise using bribes received by the Mayor of Sao Paulo. In the Monte Carlo case itself, it was held in subsequent litigation[267] that because some of the secret commission received by Cedar had been used to pay the deposit on the purchase of a house by Mankarious (the beneficial owner of Cedar), the claimants were entitled to a proportionate share in that property. They were also entitled to a share in life insurance policies proportionate to the premiums which the secret commission had financed.[268]

(e) Remaining issues

(i) No surviving assets

It is a basic rule of trusts law that, for a trust to exist, there must be identifiable trust property. If a fiduciary has disposed of all the unauthorized benefits, a proprietary claim must inevitably fail. It was held in subsequent litigation in the Monte Carlo Grand Hotel case that no proprietary claim could be made in respect of money spent on legal fees, stamp

[260] Pill LJ in the Court of Appeal [2014] Ch 1 at 61, quoted by Lord Neuberger [2014] UKSC 45 at 29. For the debate, see previous editions of this textbook and the articles cited by Lord Neuberger at 29. See also Pearce, 'Personal and Proprietary Claims Against Bribees' [1994] LMCLQ 189.

[261] *FHR European Ventures LLP v Cedar Capital Partners LLC* [2014] UKSC 45 at 45.

[262] *Global Energy Horizons Corporation v Gray* [2015] EWHC 2232 (Ch) at 143.

[263] See *The Northampton Regional Livestock Centre Company Ltd v Cowling* [2015] EWCA Civ 651 at 97, where it was suggested that this might obviate the need to claim compound interest where the property improperly acquired had been put to profitable use.

[264] [1994] 1 All ER 1; Allen, 'Bribes and Constructive Trusts: *A-G of Hong Kong v Reid*' [1995] 58 MLR 87.

[265] [2015] UKPC 35. [266] Chapter 38.

[267] *FHR European Ventures LLP v Mankarious* [2016] EWHC 359 (Ch).

[268] Applying the principle established by *Foskett v McKeown* [2001] 1 AC 102.

duty, and property renovations.[269] No proprietary claim can be made in respect of a claim for equitable compensation, or the joint and several liability of a partner who is held liable for benefits received by another member of the firm[270] because in neither case is the action one to strip a fiduciary of sums received on behalf of the principal.

(ii) Difficulties in assessing benefit

According to the Monte Carlo Grand Hotel case, all benefits received by a fiduciary in breach of duty are held on constructive trust. Assessing that benefit in a case involving bribes (such as *A-G for Hong Kong v Reid*[271]) or where a fixed commission has been paid (like the €10 million in the Monte Carlo Grand Hotel case) is relatively easy. In other cases, it could be much more difficult, and the question can arise as to what is held on trust. A fiduciary who sets up in business in competition to the fiduciary's principal is accountable only for the profits, not the whole proceeds of the business. The trust should, therefore, apply only to the profits, but the calculation of profits can be notoriously difficult. In *Boardman v Phipps*,[272] Lord Boardman learnt of a profitable investment opportunity through his position as solicitor to a trust. He used his own money to acquire shares in the private company concerned. The House of Lords decided that he was liable as a constructive trustee of the profits, but it also affirmed the decision of the High Court, which had declared that there was a constructive trust of the whole shareholding (no doubt ameliorated by an allowance for the cost of acquisition).[273]

(iii) Agent permitted to mix funds

The terms under which an agent operates may permit the agent to collect funds on behalf of the principal without there being a trust.[274] In *Nelson v Rye*,[275] the manager of a musician had agreed to receive all the income arising from his client's activities, and to account annually to him for the income received, less his agreed commission and expenses. Laddie J held that in these circumstances the manager was a constructive trustee of any income he had failed to pay to his client in accordance with their agreement, citing with approval an academic article authored by Sir Peter Millett.[276] Somewhat ironically, in *Paragon Finance plc v Thakerar & Co*,[277] Millett LJ suggested that *Nelson v Rye* had been wrongly decided, and that the income wrongly retained could not have been held on constructive trust for the client. Millett LJ explained that, in his opinion, the nature of the agency agreement had rendered it impossible to establish a constructive trust:

> Unless I have misunderstood the facts or they were very unusual it would appear that the defendant was entitled to pay receipts into his own account, mix them with his own money, use them for his own cash flow, deduct his own commission, and account for the balance to the plaintiff only at the end of the year. It is fundamental to the existence of a trust that the trustee is bound to keep the trust property separate from his own and apply it exclusively for the benefit of the beneficiary. Any right on the part of the defendant to mix the money which he received with his own and use it for his own cash flow would be inconsistent with the existence of a trust.[278]

269 *FHR European Ventures LLP v Mankarious* [2016] EWHC 359 (Ch).
270 *The Northampton Regional Livestock Centre Company Ltd v Cowling* [2015] EWCA Civ 651 at 96.
271 [1994] 1 All ER 1. 272 [1967] 2 AC 46. 273 [1967] 2 AC 46 at 117.
274 *Re D&D Wines International Ltd (In Liquidation); Angove Pty Ltd v Bailey* [2016] UKSC 47.
275 [1996] 2 All ER 186. 276 'Bribes and Secret Commissions' [1993] RLR 7.
277 [1999] 1 All ER 400. 278 [1999] 1 All ER 400 at 416.

The logic described here is impeccable so far as it applies to authorized transactions. It was applied by the Court of Appeal in *Attorney-General's Reference (No 1 of 1985)*.[279] A pub manager employed by a brewery, who was required, under his contract, to sell only beer supplied by the brewery, purchased his own barrels of beer, sold them in the pub, and retained the proceeds. He was acquitted of theft for a number of reasons, one of which was that he was liable for breach of fiduciary duty only for the profit element.

> The profit element . . . remained part of a mixed fund. Therefore there never was a moment at which [the manager] was trustee of a definite fund. It follows that there never was a moment when the employers had any proprietary interest in any of the money. The money did not belong to another. There was therefore no theft.[280]

It is possible, although uncertain, that after the Monte Carlo Grand Hotel case, a distinction should be made between authorized receipts and unauthorized profits, with a constructive trust applying only to the latter. A problem which would then arise is that, if as was the case in *Nelson v Rye*, there is only an obligation to account at the year-end, it is only after this date that it will be possible to quantify the amount of any secret profit. Until then there would be no specifically identifiable asset which could form the subject-matter of the constructive trust.

(iv) Indirect benefits

In *Sinclair Investments (UK) Ltd v Versailles Trade Finance Ltd (In Administration)*,[281] a fiduciary made profits by inflating the value of shares he owned by creating a false pattern of trading ('cross-firing') using funds (of which TPL, an investment intermediary, was the beneficiary) applied in breach of trust. The Court of Appeal reached the conclusion that he was obliged to account for these profits because 'there was undoubtedly a close commercial causal connection between Mr Cushnie's misuse of the funds in respect of which he owed fiduciary duties to TPL, and the money which he made on the sale of the shares.'[282] Following the Monte Carlo Grand Hotel case, such profits would now be considered to be held on a constructive trust. Similarly, in the Monte Carlo case, Mr Mankarious had financed the deposit on a house purchase using funds derived from the secret commission received by his company. It was held that he could not retain any profits he made from the share he had acquired in the house, even that part funded by means of a mortgage.

(f) The evil of bribery

The decision in the Monte Carlo Grand Hotel case was explicitly influenced by the evil of bribery and secret profits. The same is true of the earlier Privy Council decision in *A-G of Hong Kong v Reid*,[283] As Lord Templeman observed:

> Bribery is an evil practice which threatens the foundation of any civilised society. In particular, bribery of policemen and prosecutors brings the administration of justice into disrepute.[284]

The seriousness of the wrong to be addressed was one of the things which justified the adoption of the general rule about imposing a constructive trust. However, dishonesty is not a requirement for the imposition of remedies for breach of fiduciary duty, as was emphasized by the House of Lords in *Boardman v Phipps*. Fiduciaries who transgress the rules will be subject to a constructive trust in relation to any specifically identifiable

[279] [1986] 1 QB 491. [280] [1986] 1 QB 491 at 506.
[281] [2011] EWCA Civ 347. [282] [2012] Ch 453 at 51.
[283] [1994] 1 All ER 1. [284] [1994] 1 All ER 1 at 4.

benefits even if they have acted entirely in good faith. This may be seen as an appropriate way of signaling that fiduciary duties are not to be taken lightly.[285] If, conversely, the remedy is seen as excessive,[286] other means will have to be found to limit its impact.

(5) **Choice of remedies**

We have seen that a variety of remedies are available for injured principals or beneficiaries. These may be added to where the fiduciary is also in breach of trust or in breach of contract. The injured claimant is free to choose whichever remedy is most advantageous, and, indeed, may opt for more than one remedy provided that this does not result in double recovery. The way in which remedies can work together is demonstrated by *FHR European Ventures LLP v Mankarious*,[287] in which, in implementing the Supreme Court decision, it was held that proprietary remedies were available in respect of those assets acquired using the secret commission, and personal remedies to account were available in respect of funds which had been dissipated.

Where remedies are alternatives, the claimant must make an election between them.[288] For instance, the claimant must choose whether to recover the sums received by the fiduciary, or seek compensation for the loss caused by the breach. Once this election has been made, it is binding.[289]

(6) **Dog's leg claims**

The directors of corporate trustees will not be liable to beneficiaries for a breach of trust or breach of directors' duty of care owed to the trustee company. Such claims, referred to as 'dog's leg claims', arise where the trustee company has no assets to meet a claim, but the directors do, and a beneficiary of a trust seeks to make the directors liable for breach of a duty of care owed to the company, which as it comprises trust property, makes them liable to the beneficiary. This arose in *Gregson v HAE Trustees Ltd*,[290] where Ms Gregson argued that the trust company, HAE Trustees Ltd, was in breach of the duty to diversify investments of the trust settlement. The trust investments had become worthless, and the trust company had no other assets. Mrs Gregson, therefore, sued the directors. She argued that the duties of the directors were directed to avoid losses to the trust, and, by analogy to advisers such as solicitors, claims against the directors formed part of the trust property itself. In rejecting Ms Gregson's claim, Deputy Judge Robert Miles QC held that the fiduciary duties owed by directors were owed to the company, not to the beneficiaries.[291] Moreover, he held that to allow such a claim 'would for all practical purposes, circumvent the clear and established principle that no direct duty is owed by the directors to the

[285] See the sentiments of Lawrence Collins J in *Daraydan Holdings Ltd v Solland International Ltd* [2004] EWHC 622 at 86.

[286] See some of the vociferous criticism of *Reid*: Crilley, 'A Case of Proprietary Overkill' [1994] RLR 57; Tang, 'Confidence and the Constructive Trust' [2003] 23 LS 135; Penner, 'The Difficult Doctrinal Basis for the Fiduciary's Proprietary Liability to Account for Bribes' [2012] 18 T&T 1000; Virgo, 'Profits obtained in breach of fiduciary duty: personal or proprietary claim?' [2011] 70 CLJ 502.

[287] [2016] EWHC 359 (Ch).

[288] *Tang Man Sit (Decd) v Capacious Investments* [1996] AC 514. See Stevens, 'Election between Alternative Remedies' [1995] RLR 117; Birks, 'Inconsistency between Compensation and Restitution' (1996) 112 LQR 375.

[289] *Interactive Technology Corp Ltd v Ferster* [2017] EWHC 217 (Ch).

[290] [2008] EWHC 1006 (Ch); Court, '*Gregson v HAE Trustees Ltd*: It's a Dog's Life' [2008] PCB 298; Nolan, 'Shopping for Defendants: Worthless Trust Companies and Their Directors' [2008] 67 CLJ 472.

[291] [2008] EWHC 1006 (Ch) at 58. The fiduciary duties of directors have been codified under the Companies Act 2006, and operate according to existing legal principles—s 170(3). The statutory duty on directors to exercise reasonable care, skill, and diligence is found in s 174.

beneficiaries'.[292] However there are a number of ways in which a company director may be exposed to personal liability. First, as in *Prest v Petrodel Resources Ltd*,[293] it may be found that the company, although on its face having title to property vested in it, is not entitled to the beneficial ownership. Second, a company director who instigates or assists a breach of trust may be personally liable for dishonest assistance in breach of trust (see *Royal Brunei Airlines v Tan*[294]). Third, in exceptional circumstances a director may assume direct fiduciary duties to people dealing with the company: this was the case in *Sinclair Investments (UK) Ltd v Versailles Trade Finance Ltd*.[295] Fourth, where proprietary remedies are available against a company, these can be enforced against any recipient of the property except a bona fide purchaser for value without notice (this is possibly one of the reasons why the Supreme Court was willing to grant a proprietary remedy in the Monte Carlo Grand Hotel case).[296] Finally, even where a director has parted with assets received from a company in breach of trust or fiduciary duty, the director may be personally liable if it would be unconscionable for him, given his knowledge of the circumstances, not to make recompense to the disappointed beneficiaries.

13 Defences to an action for breach of fiduciary duty

(1) Conduct authorized by trust instrument

We have already seen that behaviour which would otherwise be a breach of fiduciary duty (for instance, acquiring assets from the trust in contravention of the self-dealing rule) may be permitted by the terms of the trust, or that the fiduciary may be protected by an appropriately phrased exoneration clause.

(2) Conduct authorized by principal

Conduct which would otherwise amount to a breach of fiduciary duty may be permitted by the principal. In the Monte Carlo Grand Hotel case, Cedar and Mr Mankarious had failed to obtain informed consent from the purchaser of the hotel for being paid a commission by the seller. This is what made the commission secret and in breach of fiduciary duty. The fiduciary will only be able to rely on consent or acquiescence if full disclosure has been made of the intended course of conduct.[297] In *Boardman v Phipps*,[298] the House of Lords accepted that if Boardman had acted with the consent of the trustees and beneficiaries, he would not have been in breach of fiduciary duty and would not therefore have been liable to account for the profits he had received.[299] However, he had failed to obtain the consent of one of the trustees,[300] and had not sought the approval of the plaintiff beneficiary. By contrast, in *Queensland Mines Ltd v Hudson*,[301] a company director who had taken up an opportunity initially offered to the company was not held liable to account for his profits because he had acted after full disclosure to the other directors.

[292] [2008] EWHC 1006 (Ch) at 46. [293] [2013] UKSC 34. [294] [1995] 2 AC 378.

[295] [2005] EWCA Civ 722; [2011] EWCA Civ 347. See Panesar, 'The Nature of Fiduciary Liability in English Law' [2007] Conv 2, 11–12.

[296] *FHR v Cedar Capital Partners LLC* [2014] UKSC 45; Pearce, 'Bribes and Secret Commissions' [2014] 26 Denning LJ 274.

[297] *SPL Private Finance (PF1) IC Ltd v Arch Financial Products LLP* [2014] EWHC 4268 (Comm) at 182.

[298] [1967] 2 AC 46. [299] [1967] 2 AC 46 at 93, per Viscount Dilhorne.

[300] Who was, incidentally, suffering from senile dementia.

[301] [1978] 18 ALR 1; Sullivan, 'Going it Alone— *Queensland Mines v Hudson*' (1979) 42 MLR 711.

36

Limitation of action

1 Introduction

This chapter considers the defence of limitation in regard to an action for compensation for breach of trust, which is governed by the Limitation Act 1980. It also considers those provisions as they apply to actions against fiduciaries who have received an unauthorized profit, which has proved more difficult because the legislation does not make any express provision for such claims.

Despite their importance, the current limitation rules[1] have been described by the Law Commission as 'unfair, complex, uncertain and outdated'.[2] The rules are contained in the Limitation Act 1980, but there are gaps which the courts have had to grapple with. Limitation periods are different for different categories of action, such as contract or tort claims,[3] but we are concerned here with the provisions affecting trusts more specifically.

2 Limitation of action for breach of trust

We turn first to the limitation periods for breach of trust.

(1) General principle

The general principle contained in the Limitation Act 1980 is that most claims are subject to a six-year limitation period. The same limitation period applies to most claims for breach of trust,[4] but there are two important exceptions, examined later. It is now taken as the starting-point (although this was not always so) that all claims are subject to a limitation period of six years unless there is some other statutory provision.[5] It has also been suggested that the courts may have jurisdiction to disallow a defence based on limitation where it considers the defence to be an abuse of process.[6] It would require exceptional circumstances for it to be inequitable to allow a limitation defence.

It is important to know when the date of action accrues, which is considered below in relation to trusts. The importance of the six-year period, and the need for caution in

[1] See Birks and Pretto (eds), *Breach of Trust* (Bloomsbury Hart 2002), Chs 11 and 12.

[2] *Limitation of Actions* (Law Com No 270, 2001), para 1.5.

[3] Limitation Act 1980, ss 2–4A (tort), ss 5–7 (contract). There has been important litigation in this area—see, for example, *Elliot v Hattens Solicitors (a firm)* [2021] EWCA Civ 720 (CA) (concerning when the limitation period starts to run in negligence cases).

[4] Limitation Act 1980, s 21(3).

[5] *Gwembe Valley Development Company Ltd v Koshy* [2003] EWCA Civ 1048.

[6] *Pakistan v Prince Mukkaram Jah, His Exalted Highness the 8th Nizam of Hyderabad* [2016] EWHC 1465 (Ch) at [113–15].

considering when the period starts to run, was effectively illustrated by the Supreme Court in *Matthew v Sedman*.[7] This concerned a claim, in negligence and breach of trusts,[8] against the respondent trustees, now replaced by the appellant trustees, for failure to bring action against a company in which the trust had a major shareholding and for which a right of action had accrued following misleading information and a suspension of trading.[9] The issue here was whether, where a cause of action accrues at, or on the expiry of, the midnight hour at the end of a day (a 'midnight deadline'), the following day counts towards the calculation of the limitation period. On the facts, a claim had been issued by the appellants via claim form on Monday 7 June 2017, but Friday 3 June 2011 was the day which commenced immediately after the expiry of the midnight deadline for bringing a claim. If Friday 3 June was included in the limitation period, then the action would be statute barred under the limitation period. If it was not counted, then the action would be within the six year period.[10] It is established practice when counting the date at which the limitation period of an action starts to accrue, fractions of a day can be excluded, so where the cause of action accrues part way through a day (e.g. 12 noon), then that whole day may be excluded from the calculation for limitation purposes, and the counting of the period starts on the next calendar day.[11] The Supreme Court held, as an exception to this general rule, that where a cause of action accrues at the very start of a day following midnight, that day should be included in the calculation of the limitation period. This is because the action begins at, and not after, midnight.[12] The appellants were, therefore, out of time.

(2) **Two exceptions**

(a) **Trustee was party to fraud**

The Limitation Act 1980, s 21(1)(a) provides that there is no limitation period to an action by the beneficiary 'in respect of any fraud or fraudulent breach of trust to which the trustee was a party or privy'.[13] Fraud in this context almost certainly means dishonesty[14] rather than simply a conscious breach of trust.[15] The exception will only apply if the trustee himself was involved in the fraud.[16] In *Thorne v Heard*,[17] the trustees allowed a solicitor who was acting for them to retain the proceeds of sale of trust property, which he then fraudulently applied to his own use. The Court of Appeal held that the plaintiff's action was barred by the Statute of Limitations and that the case did not fall within the exception because the fraud was that of the solicitor and not of the trustees, who were, therefore, neither party nor privy to the fraud.

[7] [2021] UKSC 19.

[8] On appeal to the Supreme Court, a claim in contract was also added.

[9] The company had in fact been declared insolvent, and action was under a scheme of arrangement, which is a court-sanctioned agreement between a company and its creditors.

[10] The weekend was excluded, because the action needed to be started by claim form, and that was not possible over a weekend period.

[11] See, for example, *Gelmini v Moriggia* [1913] 2 KB 549; *Dodds v Walker* [1981] 1 WLR 1027.

[12] [2021] UKSC 19 per Lord Stephens at [46]–[49].

[13] This used to be the general rule for all actions for breach of trust. See *North American Land and Timber Co Ltd v Watkins* [1904] 1 Ch 242; affd [1904] 2 Ch 233, CA.

[14] See Millett LJ in *Armitage v Nurse* [1998] Ch 241.

[15] The meaning attributed to the provision included deliberate but not dishonest breach of trust in *Re Sale Hotel and Botanical Gardens Co* [1897] 77 LT 681. See also *Vane v Vane* [1873] 8 Ch App 383; *North American Land and Timber Co Ltd v Watkins* [1904] 2 Ch 233, CA.

[16] *Williams v Central Bank of Nigeria* [2014] UKSC 10; *Madoff Securities International Ltd v Raven* [2013] EWHC 3147 (Comm) at 384.

[17] [1894] 1 Ch 599.

(b) Trustee who retains trust property in his hands

Section 21(1)(b) provides that there is no limitation period to an action by the beneficiary 'to recover from the trustee trust property or the proceeds of trust property in the possession of the trustee, or previously received by the trustee and converted to his use'. There is no requirement here that the trustee be guilty of fraud. The action lies, owing to the mere fact that the trustee still holds trust property or its proceeds, in his hands. The exception was applied in *Re Howlett*,[18] where a trustee occupied trust property without paying any occupational rents to the beneficiary. Danckwerts J held that the beneficiary could recover occupation rent from the trustee even after the limitation period had expired because the situation fell within the exception. The trustee should have obtained a rent from the property, and since he had not done so, he 'must be considered as having it in his own pocket at the material date'.[19] If the trust property has been dissipated by the trustee, for example if it has been lost,[20] spent on the maintenance of an infant beneficiary,[21] or applied in the discharge of a debt,[22] the exception will not apply. The Supreme Court has held that company directors will fall within the scope of this provision if they misdirect company funds in a way which gives them a personal benefit.[23]

(3) Constructive trusts

The two exceptions to the six-year limitation period apply to actions for breach of trust. The 1980 Act defines the terms trusts and trustees by reference to the definition found in the Trustee Act 1925 and, therefore, includes express trustees, personal representatives, and trustees holding property on implied or constructive trusts.[24] Millett LJ, in a much praised analysis in *Paragon Finance plc v DB Thackerar & Co*,[25] thought that it was relevant in this context to divide constructive trustees into two categories: the first where the trust relationship arose prior to the breach through a voluntary assumption of fiduciary responsibilities; the second where the constructive trust was imposed 'as a direct consequence of the unlawful transaction which is impeached by the plaintiff'. These two situations have been described as Class 1 and Class 2 constructive trusts, respectively. That distinction was affirmed by the Supreme Court in *Williams v Central Bank of Nigeria*,[26] which confined Class 2 constructive trusts to the two types of accessory liability, knowing receipt of trust property, and dishonest assistance in breach of trust. Class 1 constructive trusts (examples would include *Quistclose* trusts, trusteeship *de son tort*, or the position of a company director[27]) are subject to the same limitation regime as express trusts.[28] Class 2 constructive trusts (i.e. accessory liability) are not, so even where dishonesty is involved, the normal six-year limitation period applies.[29]

[18] [1949] Ch 767. See also *James v Williams* [2000] Ch 1.

[19] [1949] Ch 767 at 778.

[20] *Re Tufnell* [1902] 18 TLR 705; *Re Fountaine* [1909] 2 Ch 382.

[21] *Re Page* [1893] 1 Ch 304; *Re Timmis* [1902] 1 Ch 176.

[22] Even when the trustee was a partner in the bank to which the debt was owed. See *Re Gurney* [1893] 1 Ch 590.

[23] *Burnden Holdings (UK) Limited v Fielding* [2018] UKSC 14.

[24] Trustee Act 1925, s 68(17). It has also been held to include fiduciary agents: *Burdick v Garrick* [1870] 5 Ch App 233; company directors: *Re Lands Allotment Co* [1894] 1 Ch 616, CA; a mortgagee in respect of the proceeds of sale: *Thorne v Heard* [1895] AC 495; but not a trustee in bankruptcy: *Re Cornish* [1896] 1 QB 99; nor the liquidator of a company in voluntary liquidation: *Re Windsor Steam Coal Co (1901) Ltd* [1928] Ch 609.

[25] [1999] 1 All ER 400.

[26] *Williams v Central Bank of Nigeria* [2014] UKSC 10.

[27] *Yong v Panweld Trading Pte Ltd* [2012] SGCA 59; 15 ITELR 445 (Singapore Court of Appeal).

[28] See, for example, *Dalkilic v Pekin* [2021] EWHC 219 (Ch) at [336]–[337].

[29] For the reasons for this, see *Williams v Central Bank of Nigeria* [2014] UKSC 10.

(4) Breach of fiduciary duty

There has been some uncertainty about the limitation periods (if any) applicable to claims for breach of a fiduciary duty since such claims are not expressly mentioned in the Limitation Act 1980.[30] However, applying the principle that all actions are subject to a six-year limitation period unless there is an express provision to the contrary,[31] it has now become clear that actions based on breach of fiduciary duty must normally be brought within six years of the breach.[32] In *Coulthard v Disco Mix Club Ltd*,[33] this conclusion was reached by analogy with the limitation period applying to a common law action for damages.[34] Where the claim against the fiduciary is for a liability which falls within the description of a Class 1 constructive trustee, the exceptions for fraud and the retention of trust property will apply.[35]

(5) Postponing the start of the limitation period

(a) 'The date on which the right of action accrued'

Section 21(3) (setting out the general limitation period for breaches of trust) provides that 'for the purposes of this subsection, the right of action shall not be treated as having accrued to any beneficiary entitled to a future interest in the trust property until the interest fell into possession.' This means that time does not begin to run against a remainderman, or beneficiary with a reversionary interest, until his interest has fallen into possession.

(b) Fraud

Section 32(1) provides that the date from which the Limitation Act shall run may be postponed to a date later than the date of the cause of action where either:

(a) the action is based upon the fraud of the defendant; or
(b) any fact relevant to the plaintiff's right of action has been deliberately concealed from him by the defendant; or
(c) the action is for relief from the consequences of a mistake.

In these three cases the period of limitation does not begin to run 'until the claimant has discovered the fraud, concealment or mistake (as the case may be) or could with reasonable diligence have discovered it.' Discovery of the alleged fraud means discovery of the precise deceit which the claimant alleges has been perpetrated on them.[36] A claimant will have discovered a fraud when he is aware of sufficient material properly to be able to plead it.[37] On the issue of what amounts to 'reasonable diligence':

> The question is not whether the claimant *should* have discovered the mistake sooner, but whether he *could* with reasonable diligence have done so. The burden of proof is on the claimant. He must establish on the balance of probabilities that he *could not* have discovered the

[30] *A-G v Cocke* [1988] Ch 414; *Nelson v Rye* [1996] 2 All ER 186; Stevens, 'Too Late to Face the Music? Limitation and Laches as Defences to an Action for Breach of Fiduciary Duty' [1997] Conv 225.
[31] *Gwembe Valley Development Company Ltd v Koshy* [2003] EWCA Civ 1048.
[32] *Seaton v Seddon* [2012] EWHC 735 (Ch); *Page v Hewetts Solicitors* [2013] EWHC 2845 (Ch).
[33] [2000] 1 WLR 707. [34] *Paragon Finance v DB Thakerar & Co* [1998] EWCA Civ 1249.
[35] *Seaton v Seddon* [2012] EWHC 735 (Ch); *Kleanthous v Paphitis* [2011] EWHC 2287 (Ch).
[36] *Barnstaple Boat Co Ltd v Jones* [2007] EWCA Civ 727; *Cunningham v Ellis* [2018] EWHC 3188 Comm at [87].
[37] *Law Society v Sephton and Co* [2004] EWCA Civ 1627 at [110]; *OT Computers Ltd v Infineon Technologies AG* [2021] EWCA Civ 501 at [26].

> mistake without exceptional measures which he could not reasonably have been expected to take.[38]

The test for reasonable diligence is how a person carrying on a business of the relevant kind would act, on the assumption that he or she desired to know whether or not (s)he had made a mistake, if (s)he had adequate but not unlimited staff and resources and was motivated by a reasonable but not excessive sense of urgency.[39]

It has been held that this section applies to actions against trustees.[40] Section 32(2) extends the postponement of the running of time to include cases of deliberate breach 'in circumstances in which it is unlikely to be discovered for some time'. The breach will not be deliberate unless the defendant knows that what he is doing amounts to a breach of trust.[41]

(6) **Claims to the personal estate of a deceased person**

The Limitation Act 1980 s 22(1)(a) provides that:

> No action in respect of any claim to the personal estate of a deceased person or to any share or interest in any such estate (whether under a will or on intestacy) shall be brought after the expiration of twelve years from the date on which the right to receive the share or interest accrued.

Since a personal representative may also be a trustee, the question has arisen whether in such circumstances the six-year limitation period in s 21(3) or the twelve-year period in s 22(1)(a) should apply. Under the preceding legislation,[42] it was essential to determine whether the personal representative had become a trustee. If he had, then the six-year period would displace the twelve-year period.[43] The prevailing view seems to be that under the Limitation Act 1980 the period of twelve years will apply to all actions concerning the personal estate of a deceased person, whether or not the personal representative became a trustee.[44]

(7) **Actions for account**

Where someone has obtained a benefit to which they are not entitled, or has incurred an expense which should be payable by another, an account in equity may be ordered. An account may be ordered, for instance, where equitable co-owners are entitled to share the

[38] *FII Group Test Claimants v HMRC* [2020] UKSC 47 at [203] per Lords Reid and Hodge, approving the observations of Millet LJ in *Paragon Finance plc v DB Thakerar & Co* [1998] EWCA Civ 1249.

[39] *FII Group Test Claimants v HMRC* [2020] UKSC 47 at [207]. See *Boyse (International) Ltd v Natwest Markets* [2021] EWHC 1387 (Ch), where the High Court granted summary judgment in favour of two banks on the basis that the claimant trust company was statute barred as a reasonably diligent person would have been alert to a fraudulent LIBOR scheme on the surrounding evidence at the time of action.

[40] *Beaman v ARTS Ltd* [1949] 1 KB 550, CA; *Kitchen v Royal Air Forces Association* [1958] 1 WLR 563; *Phillips-Higgins v Harper* [1954] 1 QB 411; *Bartlett v Barclays Bank Trust Co Ltd* [1980] Ch 515; *Boyse (International) Ltd v Natwst Markets* [2021] EWHC 1387 (Ch).

[41] *Cave v Robinson Jarvis & Rolf* [2003] 1 AC 384.

[42] Real Property Limitation Act 1874, s 8; Trustee Act 1888, s 8.

[43] See *Re Swain* [1891] 3 Ch 233; *Re Timmis* [1902] 1 Ch 176; *Re Richardson* [1920] 1 Ch 423, CA; *Re Oliver* [1927] 2 Ch 323; *Re Diplock* [1948] Ch 465, CA; affd sub nom *Ministry of Health v Simpson* [1951] AC 251, HL.

[44] See, in support of this view, *Re Loftus* [2007] 1 WLR 591; Preston and Newsom, *Limitation of Actions* (4th edn, Longman 1989), p 51.

occupation of residential property, but only one of them has been paying the bills,[45] or where land held by co-owners has been let or exploited for profit.[46] An account is not in itself a substantive remedy, and will normally be accompanied by an order to pay compensation or some other substantive remedy. The purpose of account is to find what is due, not to compel its payment. As Richards J said in *Barnett v Cregg*:

> An order for an account may be made against a person who holds or has held money or other property for another in a fiduciary capacity, most obviously as a trustee. It is the means by which the beneficial owners of the fund can ascertain the manner in which the fund has been administered and applied, and it may provide the basis for proceedings to recover trust property or for personal remedies against the trustee or others.[47]

The Limitation Act 1980, s 23, prescribes that the time limit for actions for an account are the same as the time limits applicable to the claim which is the basis of the duty to account. This can include breach of trust or breach of fiduciary duty, for both of which the normal limitation period is six years.

(8) **Reform of limitation**

The Law Commission recommended sweeping reform of the limitation period applicable to claims for a remedy for a wrong in its Report, *Limitation of Actions*,[48] which, if they had been implemented, would have simplified and radically altered the limitation period applicable to actions for breach of trust. The Law Commission proposed the introduction of a single core limitation regime applicable to all claims. This would have consisted of a primary limitation period of three years, starting from the date on which the claimant knows, or ought reasonably to know (a) the facts which give rise to the cause of action; (b) the identity of the defendant; and (c) if the claimant has suffered injury, loss, or damage or the defendant has received a benefit, that the injury, loss, damage, or benefit was significant. This primary limitation period would have been supplemented by a long-stop limitation period of ten years, starting from the date of the accrual of the cause of action, or from the date of the act or omission which gives rise to the cause of action. It was proposed that this core regime should apply to all claims for breach of trust and claims to recover trust property,[49] and to claims for breach of fiduciary duty.[50] No distinction would have been made between fraudulent and non-fraudulent breaches of trust,[51] nor would a special limitation period have operated where the claimant was bringing a claim to recover property against his or her trustee.[52] A special rule would have operated in the case of a claim for the recovery of property held on a bare trust so that the cause of action shall not accrue unless and until the trustee acts in breach of trust.[53] In 2002, the then Government accepted the Law Commission's recommendations in principle, subject to further consideration of certain aspects of the report. However, on 19 November 2009, the Government announced to the House of Commons that it would not be taking the reforms forward.

[45] *Leake v Bruzzi* [1974] 1 WLR 1528; *Leigh v Dickeson* [1884] 15 QBD 60. See also *Henderson v Eason* [1851] 17 QB 701 at 721, per Parke B.

[46] *Henderson v Eason* [1851] 17 QB 701; *Job v Potton* [1875] LR 20 Eq 84; *Jacobs v Seward* [1872] LR 5 HL 464.

[47] [2014] EWHC 3080 (Ch) at [62].

[48] Law Com No 270, (2001).

[49] Law Com 270, para 4.94.

[50] Law Com 270, para 4.95.

[51] Law Com 270, paras 4.97–4.101.

[52] Law Com 270, paras 4.102–4.106.

[53] Law Com 270, para 4.105.

3 Laches

Actions for breach of trust were not originally subject to any period of limitation, for reasons explained in *Williams v Central Bank of Nigeria*.[54] However, if a claimant delayed bringing his action, the court might have considered that it was inequitable for him to succeed, and would therefore protect the defendant from liability. The doctrine was explained by the Privy Council in *Lindsay Petroleum Co v Hurd*:

> the doctrine of laches in courts of equity is not an arbitrary or a technical doctrine. Where it would be practically unjust to give a remedy, either because the party has, by his conduct, done that which might fairly be regarded as equivalent to waiver of it, or where by his conduct and neglect he has, though perhaps not waiving that remedy, yet put the other party in a situation in which it would not be reasonable to place him if the remedy were afterwards to be asserted, in either of these cases, lapse of time and delay are most material.[55]

Laches[56] can only be used as a defence 'if in all the circumstances it would be unconscionable for a party to be permitted to assert his beneficial right'.[57]

(1) Relation to statutory limitation periods

In *Re Pauling's Settlement Trusts*,[58] Wilberforce J held that there was no room for the operation of the equitable doctrine of laches because 'there was an express statutory provision providing a period of limitation'.[59] The Court of Appeal, in *Re Loftus*,[60] took the view that the remark applied only to instances where there was a statutory limitation period, and that in cases where no limitation period applied (trustees guilty of fraud or retaining trust property), the doctrine of laches was preserved by Limitation Act 1980, s 36.[61] This position is confirmed by the Supreme Court decision in *Adamson v Paddico (267) Ltd*.[62]

(2) How the doctrine operates

Although it was not a direct decision on the doctrine, the Supreme Court said in *Adamson v Paddico (267) Ltd*[63] about laches that it 'generally requires (a) knowledge of the facts [by the claimant], and (b) acquiescence, or (c) detriment or prejudice [to the defendant]'. In *Patel v Shah*,[64] the Court of Appeal said that:

> The inquiry should require a broad approach, directed to ascertaining whether it would in all the circumstances be unconscionable for a party to be permitted to assert his beneficial right.

Laddie J was somewhat more forthcoming about relevant considerations in *Nelson v Rye*.[65] He stated that there were no defined hurdles over each of which a litigant must struggle before the defence is made out,[66] and instead identified a number of main factors which should be taken in to account by the court:

> The courts have indicated over the years some of the factors which must be taken into consideration in deciding whether the defence runs. Those factors include the period of the

[54] [2014] UKSC 10. [55] [1874] LR 5 PC 221 at 239–40. [56] The word is pronounced 'lay cheese'.

[57] *Zumax Nigeria Ltd v First City Monument Bank Plc* [2017] EWHC 2804 (Ch) at 236; *Re Loftus, decd* [2006] EWCA Civ 1124 at 42–7.

[58] [1961] 3 All ER 713. [59] [1961] 3 All ER 713 at 735. Affirmed by the Court of Appeal [1964] Ch 303.

[60] [2007] 1 WLR 591 at 41, per Chadwick LJ. [61] See also *Patel v Shah* [2005] EWCA Civ 157 at 22.

[62] [2014] UKSC 7 at 30–2. [63] [2014] UKSC 7 at 34. [64] [2005] EWCA Civ 157.

[65] [1996] 2 All ER 186; Stevens, 'Too Late to Face the Music? Limitation and Laches as Defences to an Action for Breach of Fiduciary Duty' [1997] Conv 225.

[66] [1996] 2 All ER 186 at 200.

delay, the extent to which the defendant's position has been prejudiced by the delay, and the extent to which the prejudice was caused by the actions of the plaintiff.[67]

(3) Knowledge of the right of action

It is unlikely that the doctrine of laches will prevent a claimant from bringing an action unless the claimant had knowledge of the rights he failed to pursue. In *Lindsay Petroleum Co v Hurd*,[68] the Privy Council stated that 'in order that the remedy should be lost by laches or delay, it is . . . necessary that there should be sufficient knowledge of the facts constituting the title to relief.'

(4) Length of delay

There is no set length of time that will cause the court to apply the doctrine of laches. Instead, the court must determine whether, given the circumstances, it would be inequitable to allow the claim to succeed. Very short periods, if not accompanied by acts of acquiescence by the claimant, will not be sufficient. In *Lindsay Petroleum Co v Hurd*,[69] the Privy Council held that a delay of fifteen months was insufficient, as was a delay of two-and-a-quarter years in *Re Sharpe*.[70] In *Weld v Petre*,[71] in the context of the redemption of a mortgage, the Court of Appeal suggested a period of twenty years, therefore, holding that a delay of eighteen years and four months was 'not of itself sufficient to disentitle the plaintiffs to relief'.[72]

(5) Prejudice to the defendant

The doctrine of laches operates very closely with the principle of acquiescence. As the Privy Council noted in *Lindsay Petroleum Co v Hurd*,[73] equity will grant relief where to allow the claimant his remedy would be practically unjust because he has 'by his conduct, done that which might fairly be regarded as equivalent to a waiver'.

While the authorities recognize that the defence may apply where the only action (or rather, inaction) on the part of the claimant has been a prolonged period of silence or inactivity,[74] the mere fact of a delay in commencing proceedings is not usually sufficient to give rise to the defence of laches. As Laddie J observed in *Nelson v Rye*:

> I accept that mere delay alone will almost never suffice, but the court has to look at all the circumstances and then decide whether the balance of justice or injustice is in favour of granting the remedy or withholding it. If substantial prejudice will be suffered by the defendant, it is not necessary to prove that it was caused by the delay. On the other hand, the plaintiff's knowledge that the delay will cause such prejudice is a factor to be taken into account.[75]

[67] [1996] 2 All ER 186 at 201. See also *Mills v Partridge* [2020] EWHC 2171 (Ch) at [117].

[68] [1874] LR 5 PC 221 at 241.

[69] [1874] LR 5 PC 221.

[70] [1892] 1 Ch 154. In *Bunn v BBC* [1998] 3 All ER 552; Lightman J refused to grant an injunction preventing a television broadcast because it had been delayed until the last minute. This would not, however, have affected any remedy in damages for the alleged breach of confidence.

[71] [1929] 1 Ch 33 at 54–5.

[72] [1929] 1 Ch 33 at 55, per Lawrence LJ.

[73] [1874] LR 5 PC 221 at 239–40.

[74] *Lindsay Petroleum Co v Hurd* [1874] LR 5 PC 221; *Erlanger v New Sombrero Phosphate Co* [1878] 3 App Cas 1218; *Brooks v Muckleston* [1909] 2 Ch 519.

[75] [1996] 2 All ER 186 at 201.

In *Fisher v Brooker*,[76] (in which one of the composers of Procol Harum's 'A Whiter Shade of Pale' sought to enforce his authorship after a delay of over thirty years), Lord Neuberger said:

> Although I would not suggest that it is an immutable requirement, some sort of detrimental reliance is usually an essential ingredient of laches, in my opinion.[77]

The House of Lords in that case did not think that the delay, in itself, was a bar to equitable relief. There were no evidential problems and any prejudice on the part of the defendants was balanced by the fact that they had not had to account for royalties to the composer until he indicated that he intended to enforce his rights.[78]

4 Limitation of action against unauthorized profits

It has proved more difficult to apply the provisions of the Limitation Act 1980 to actions against fiduciaries who have received an unauthorized profit, because the legislation does not make any express provision for such claims. Instead, provisions designed primarily with express trusts in mind have had to be interpreted so as to provide a limitation period for actions for breach of fiduciary duty and the concomitant constructive trusts of unauthorized profits which arise from them. The relevant principles have been considered and clarified by a number of decisions, but uncertainty remains.[79]

The major turning point came in *Gwembe Valley Development Company Ltd v Koshy*, where Mummery LJ confirmed that all actions are subject to a six-year limitation period unless there is express provision to the contrary:

> [I]t is possible to simplify the court's task when considering the application of the 1980 Act to claims against fiduciaries. The starting assumption should be that a six-year limitation period will apply—under one or other provision of the Act, applied directly or by analogy—unless it is specifically excluded by the Act or established case-law. Personal claims against fiduciaries will normally be subject to limits by analogy with claims in tort or contract . . . By contrast, claims for breach of fiduciary duty, in the special sense explained in Mothew, will normally be covered by section 21. The six-year time limit under section 21(3) will apply, directly or by analogy, unless excluded by subsection 21(1)(a) (fraud) or (b).[80]

The case concerned a company director who had received undisclosed profits from a contract with the company. The court held that his position meant that he had had 'trustee-like responsibilities' in the exercise of his powers of management of the property of the company and in dealing with the application of its property, and that therefore the claim for an account was within the scope of s 21. Since he had acted dishonestly in breaching his fiduciary duty, s 21(1)(a) applied to exclude the six-year limitation period, and he was not entitled to any defence of limitation. The decision had been followed at first instance[81]

[76] [2009] 1 WLR 1764.

[77] [2009] 1 WLR 1764 at 64.

[78] See also *Dalkilic v Pekin* [2021] EWHC 219 (Ch) at [323]–[333], in a case involving ownership of shares in a burger manufacturing company, Bacon J held that there had been no 'material prejudice' caused by delay in bringing action, despite allegations that memories of events had dimmed as a result of delay and that pertinent documentation was alleged to have been destroyed.

[79] *Bristol and West Building Society v Mothew* [1998] Ch 1; *Paragon Finance plc v DB Thackerar* [1999] 1 All ER 400; *Cia De Seguros Imperio v Heath (REBX) Ltd* [2001] 1 WLR 112; *JJ Harrison (Properties) Ltd v Harrison* [2002] BCLC 162; *Gwembe Valley Development Company Ltd (In Receivership) v Koshy* [2003] EWCA Civ 1048; *Re Loftus* [2007] 1 WLR 591; *Seaton v Seddon* [2012] EWHC 735 (Ch); *Page v Hewitts Solicitors* [2013] EWHC 2845 (Ch).

[80] [2003] EWCA Civ 1048 at 111.

[81] *Seaton v Seddon* [2012] EWHC 735 (Ch); *Page v Hewetts Solicitors* [2013] EWHC 2845 (Ch).

and was confirmed in *First Subsea Ltd v Balltec Ltd*,[82] where the Court of Appeal would have applied the six-year limitation period in s 21 to a breach of fiduciary duty by a non-executive company director who had entered into a competing contract were it not for the finding of fraud by the trial judge, which lifted that limitation period. A six-year limitation period was applied in *Creggy v Barnett.*[83] Creggy had set up an offshore company for Barnett as part of a tax avoidance scheme, and was a signatory to a bank account held by the company. Creggy misused his position to make large payments to a third party. This was a breach of fiduciary duty for which Creggy would have been liable if the claims against him had not been time limited.

There remains a question about the exception in s 21(1)(b) which provides that there is no limitation period for an action 'to recover from the trustee trust property or the proceeds of trust property in the possession of the trustee, or previously received by the trustee and converted to his use . . .'. The Supreme Court has held in *Burnden Holdings (UK) Ltd v Fielding*[84] that company directors are to be treated as though they are trustees of the company's assets, so that no limitation period applies where they misapply company funds in a way which generates a personal gain.[85] That is now clear, but since it is now the general rule that the gains from breach of fiduciary duty are held on constructive trust, does this make a fiduciary a trustee for the purposes of s 21(1)(b)? The answer is uncertain, unless the gains were made from a pre-existing proprietary base (such as in *Burnden Holdings (UK) Ltd v Fielding*). Although it was not necessary to deal with this point in *First Subsea Ltd v Balltec Ltd*, the court said:

> The provisions of s.21(1)(b) in respect of the property of the company have no application to cases like *Gwembe* where there is no misappropriation or receipt of pre-existing company property but only a breach of duty which gives rise to a constructive trust over (for example) the secret profit. This is because in such cases the director is not a trustee virtute officii in respect of the profit. He has no proprietary relationship with what he acquires other than as the recipient of the proceeds of his breach of duty. He is not therefore in the terms of s.21(1)(b) in possession of trust property.[86]

The Supreme Court's decision in *Burnden Holdings (UK) Ltd v Fielding*[87] changes this result in the case of company directors, but does not alter the logic of the statement as it relates to other fiduciaries. The odd result may be that, whilst the proprietary remedy for breach of fiduciary duty no longer makes any distinction between breaches involving an existing proprietary base and those which do not, the distinction may remain relevant for the purposes of limitation.

The start of the limitation period is postponed where there has been concealment by the defendant.[88] It has been suggested that in a very exceptional situation the doctrine of estoppel could operate where there are 'circumstances in which it would be inequitable for a defendant to take a limitation point, and that the court would then prevent him from doing so.'[89] The equitable doctrine of laches will be available where a claim to an account

[82] [2017] EWCA Civ 186. [83] [2016] EWCA Civ 1004. [84] [2018] UKSC 14.

[85] [2018] UKSC 14 per Lord Briggs at [19]–[23].

[86] [2017] EWCA Civ 186 at 59. [87] [2018] UKSC 14.

[88] Limitation Act 1980, s 32 applied to breach of fiduciary duty in *Gresport Finance Ltd v Battaglia* [2016] EWHC 964 (Ch).

[89] *High Commissioner for Pakistan v Prince Mukkaram Jah, His Exalted Highness the 8th Nizam of Hyderabad* [2016] EWHC 1465 (Ch) at 114, citing *Chagos Islanders v The Attorney General and Her Majesty's British Indian Ocean Territory Commissioner* [2004] EWCA Civ 997 at 46.

is not subject to a statutory limitation period, in which case it may protect a fiduciary from unduly delayed proceedings if it would be inequitable to allow them to proceed, for example because he would suffer substantial prejudice or detriment. However, there is debate as to whether the defence of laches will be available where s 21(1) of the Limitation Act 1980 applies. In *Gwembe Valley Development Co Ltd v Koshy*, the Court of Appeal held that the defence of laches was not available as a defence to the action for dishonest breach of fiduciary duty, as the defence of laches was not available where s 21(1) applies.[90] This has since been doubted in *Re Loftus*,[91] where it was suggested that the equitable doctrine was not excluded under cases coming within s 21(1) of the Limitation Act 1980. Chadwick LJ, on reprising earlier authorities, concluded:

> If the court were saying, in the *Gwembe Valley* case, that there is no scope for a defence of laches or acquiescence in a case where the 1980 Act prescribes no period of limitation, I would respectfully disagree; although, of course, if that proposition were binding upon me I would have no choice but to apply it. But the court did not say that in terms; and, because I think the proposition obviously wrong, I am not persuaded that the court intended to be understood as endorsing it.[92]

It would appear that Chadwick LJ's position is the better view.

[90] [2003] EWCA Civ 1048 at 140.

[91] [2007] 1 WLR 591 at 41, per Chadwick LJ.

[92] [2007] 1 WLR 591 at 40.

PART X

Recovering Trust Property

37. Remedies against strangers to the trust 797
38. Tracing 831

37

Remedies against strangers to the trust

1 Introduction

A company has the right to sell airline tickets, provided that it keeps the money received in a special account on trust for the airline. A company director uses this money as if it belonged to the company.[1] The company is in breach of trust, but does the airline have a remedy against the director? The answer is yes. In some circumstances a person who is not a trustee—a stranger to the trust—can be held liable. The law in this area used to be difficult and complex, but it has been made increasingly straightforward by some judicial developments.

2 When can strangers be liable?

(1) Relationship to remedies against trustees

Chapters 34 and 35 have examined the remedies that beneficiaries may pursue against a trustee who acts in breach of trust or in breach of his fiduciary duty. However, if a trustee commits a breach of trust which involves a third party who was not a trustee, either as a participant in the breach or as the recipient of trust property transferred to him in breach of trust, the beneficiaries of the trust may be entitled to pursue remedies against the stranger. The third party is termed a 'stranger to the trust' because he was not a trustee and, therefore, was not subject to any obligations prior to his involvement in the breach. Remedies against third parties may prove more attractive to the beneficiaries than the remedies against the trustee in breach. The availability of remedies against a stranger to the trust will be especially important if the trustee is insolvent, thus rendering direct remedies against him ineffective. There may be other remedies against a third party, for instance the trustees may have an action for breach of contract or in tort against an adviser who has given negligent advice.[2]

(2) Personal and proprietary claims

A stranger can be liable either because the stranger holds property which is still subject to a trust, or for doing something which is considered to be so wrong that equity requires the individual to pay compensation. Proprietary claims would be available in the first of

[1] These were the facts in *Royal Brunei Airlines v Tan* [1995] 2 AC 378.

[2] See *Royal Brunei Airlines v Tan* [1995] 3 All ER 97 at 108.

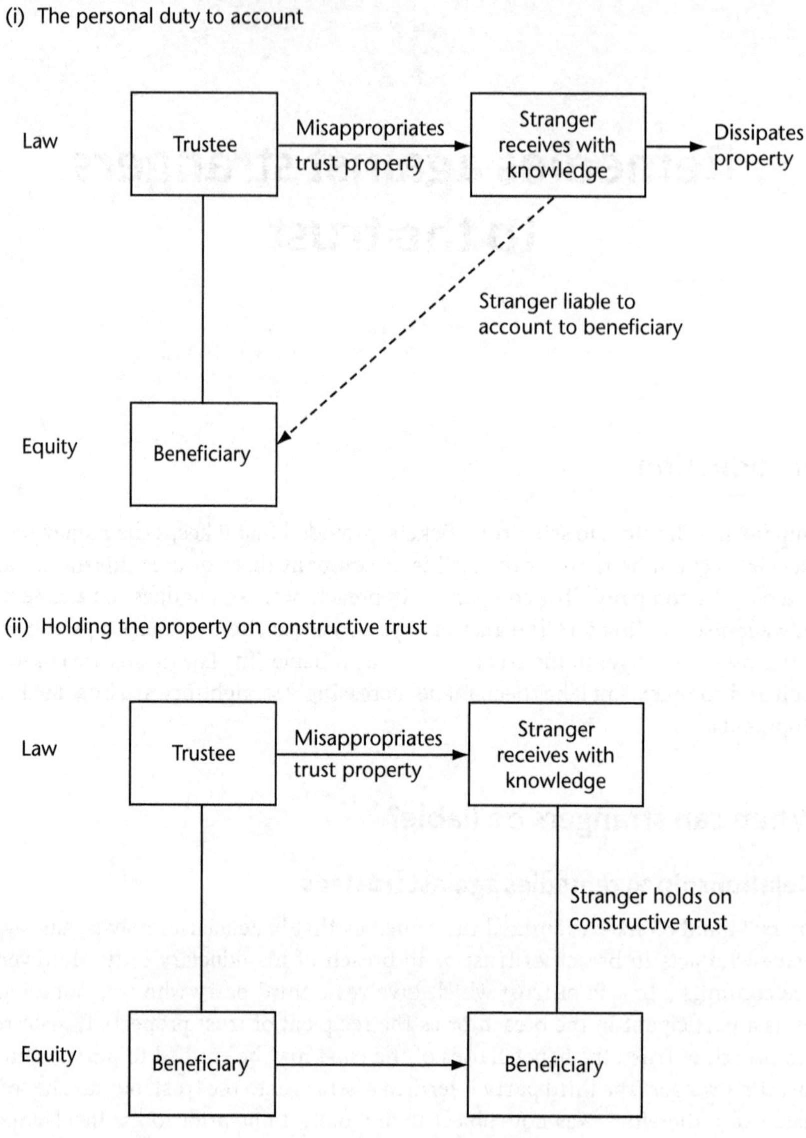

Figure 37.1 The contrast between personal and proprietary claims

these two situations; personal claims in the second (see Figure 37.1). For instance, if the trustee of a Van Gogh painting gives it in breach of trust to his friend Marlene, the beneficiaries can recover the painting from Marlene. If Marlene was a participant in a scheme with the trustee to steal the painting, which can no longer be found, then Marlene could be held personally liable to the beneficiaries for her dishonest conduct. In this chapter we consider only the ways in which a stranger to a trust can be held personally liable. The rules for tracing trust property in the hands of a stranger are set out in the next chapter.

(a) Proprietary claims

Claims to recover the trust property where it can still be identified do not require the proof of any fault. This is true even when the property has been converted into a different form, for instance, if Marlene had sold the Van Gogh painting and invested the proceeds. The defence available to an innocent recipient is that equitable claims cannot be pursued against a bona fide purchaser for value without notice.[3] Marlene, of course, in the example above, is not an innocent recipient for valuable consideration.

Re Diplock[4] contains an example of a successful proprietary claim against innocent volunteers who received property in breach of trust. The executors of Caleb Diplock had wrongfully distributed his residuary estate among various charities. Since the charities were innocent volunteers who had not provided valuable consideration, they received the money subject to the pre-existing equitable interests of the beneficiaries to whom it should have been allocated. His next of kin were, therefore, able to claim from the charities any assets that could be shown to represent the trust property by the rules of tracing.

If the stranger who receives trust property in breach of trust has disposed of it, retaining nothing of the original property or its proceeds, the property is said to have been dissipated. Once the trust property has been dissipated it is no longer possible for the beneficiaries to maintain any proprietary claim against the stranger who had received it. However, the stranger may still be subject to a personal liability to make restitution of the value of the property he had received in breach of trust.

(b) **Personal claims**

Where a stranger has participated in the commission of a breach of trust, but has not received any trust property, there is no property which the beneficiaries can claim to recover. Similarly, if a stranger did receive trust property, but it has been dissipated so that no traceable proceeds remain, the beneficiaries cannot enjoy any proprietary claim. They will be confined to a personal action for equitable compensation, unless they can rely upon some other common law breach of contract or tort. If the stranger has only partially dissipated the trust property he received, or it is traceable into assets that have fallen in value, a personal action may also be preferred, as the stranger will be liable to restore the value of the trust property. The stranger is often said to be 'liable to account as a constructive trustee' even though there is no property which the stranger holds on trust. In *Polly Peck International plc v Nadir (Asil) (No 2)*,[5] Scott LJ described this remedy as 'the in personam constructive trust claim'. The personal nature of the claim can also be seen from cases such as *Re Montagu*[6] and *Lipkin Gorman v Karpnale Ltd*,[7] which are considered later in the chapter. The equitable liability to account as a constructive trustee is essentially fault-based, so that a stranger will only be liable on proof of the requisite degree of fault.

(3) **Types of stranger liability**

The circumstances in which a stranger may be held liable as a 'constructive trustee' were identified by Lord Selbourne LC in *Barnes v Addy*:

> those who create a trust clothe the trustee with a legal power and control over the trust property, imposing on him a corresponding responsibility. That responsibility may no doubt be extended in equity to others who are not properly trustees, if they are found either making themselves trustees de son tort, or actually participating in any fraudulent conduct of the trustee to the injury of the [beneficiary]. But, on the other hand, strangers are not to be made constructive trustees merely because they act as agents of trustees in transactions within their legal powers, transactions, perhaps of which the Court of Equity may disapprove, unless those agents receive and become chargeable with some part of the trust property, or unless they assist with knowledge in a dishonest and fraudulent design on the part of the trustees . . .[8]

[3] The doctrine of notice was discussed in Chapter 1. [4] [1948] Ch 465, CA.
[5] [1992] 4 All ER 769 at 781. [6] [1987] Ch 264; [1992] 4 All ER 308.
[7] [1992] 4 All ER 331; [1987] 1 WLR 987. [8] [1874] 9 Ch App 244 at 251–2.

More modern terminology is now used to describe the three circumstances in which a stranger will be held liable.

(a) Trustee de son tort

Where a stranger who had not been appointed as a trustee takes it upon himself to act as a trustee and deals with the trust property accordingly, he will be held liable for any breach of trust that was committed just as if he were in fact a properly appointed trustee.

(b) Dishonest assistance in a breach of trust

Where a stranger dishonestly participates in a breach of trust committed by the trustees, he will be liable to account personally as a constructive trustee for any loss suffered by the trust.

(c) Unconscionable receipt of trust property

Where a stranger receives trust property, knowing that it is trust property, he will be liable to account as a constructive trustee to the trust for the value of the property received.

(4) Liability is fault-based

Apart from the category of trustees de son tort, the other two situations in which a stranger can be held liable as a constructive trustee are based upon fault. The stranger is held liable to the trust for acting wrongfully. The imposition of liability on strangers requires a balance between protecting the interests of beneficiaries and facilitating ordinary business and commercial transactions. Solicitors or bankers may temporarily be in possession of trust property as part of the normal process of trust management and delegation, but this does not necessarily mean that if their conduct is inconsistent with the terms of the trust they should be liable as constructive trustees, as where they honestly follow instructions from the trustees. Similarly, commercial companies may come into contact with trustees and trust funds as part of everyday commerce. They may make attractive defendants to beneficiaries in a breach of trust action, as they have deep pockets, but if they were to be held to account too readily, this could deter them from dealing with trust funds and inhibit the normal operations of trade or business.

(5) What kind of constructive trustee?

While the liability of a stranger to a trust has historically been termed 'liability to account as a constructive trustee' the language of constructive trusteeship has been subjected to criticism on the grounds of artificiality. In *Paragon Finance plc v Thakerar & Co*, Millett LJ considered the use of the phrase unfortunate:

> In such a case the expressions 'constructive trust' and 'constructive trustee' are misleading, for there is no trust and usually no possibility of a proprietary remedy; they are 'nothing more than a formula for equitable relief': *Selangor United Rubber Estates Ltd v Craddock (No 3)*[9] per Ungoed Thomas J.[10]

While this is certainly true in respect of the liability of a stranger who has dishonestly assisted in a breach of trust, it is questionable whether the criticism applies equally forcefully to the liability of strangers who have dealt with the trust property as a trustee de son tort, or who have knowingly received and misapplied trust property. In such cases the

[9] [1999] 1 All ER 400 at 409. [10] [1968] 2 All ER 1073 at 1097.

stranger is liable to account because of his direct relationship with the trust property.[11] In *Dubai Aluminium Co Ltd v Salaam*,[12] Lord Millett suggested that the terminology 'accountable in equity' should replace the terminology 'accountable as a constructive trustee'.[13] This has not been adopted in subsequent decisions. Nevertheless, caution needs to be exercised when encountering the phrase 'constructive trustee'. It is to be remembered, whatever the phrasing, that the remedy is a personal liability to account by the stranger. It is also important to note what type of constructive trust the court is employing. The matter came before the Supreme Court in *Williams v Central Bank of Nigeria*,[14] in the context of which limitation period applied to trustees de son tort, dishonest assistors, and those in knowing receipt of trust property. The court distinguished between constructive trustees who had a relationship with the trust property before the behaviour for which they were held liable, and those who became constructive trustees only because of their wrongdoing.

(6) **A multiplicity of remedies**

One of the difficulties in approaching stranger liability is placing the actions in context with the other remedies available to beneficiaries where there has been a breach of trust and trust property has been misapplied. The key to understanding is to recognize that actions for dishonest assistance and for knowing receipt are independent of and additional to the remedies available against the trustee and any remedies to recover any trust property which is still identifiable.

3 Trustees de son tort

(1) **Definition**

A person who has not been appointed a trustee but intermeddles in the administration of a trust by taking it upon himself to act as if he were a trustee will be held liable as if he were in fact a properly appointed trustee. He is known as a trustee de son tort, or a de facto trustee.[15] The principle was explained by Smith LJ in *Mara v Browne*:

> if one, not being a trustee and not having authority from a trustee, takes upon himself to intermeddle with trust matters or to do acts characteristic of the office of trustee, he may thereby make himself what is called in law a trustee of his own wrong—i.e. a trustee de son tort, or, as it is also termed a constructive trustee.[16]

(2) **What makes someone a trustee de son tort?**

The principle that an intermeddling stranger may become a trustee de son tort is an application to the law of trusts of the principle that anyone who takes it upon himself to act in a fiduciary capacity will be treated and held accountable as if he in fact held the fiduciary position he assumed. Thus, a person who takes it upon himself to act as an

[11] See Martin, 'Recipient Liability after *Westdeutsche*' [1998] Conv 13.

[12] [2003] 2 AC 366.

[13] [2003] 2 AC 366 at 404 [142].

[14] [2014] UKSC 10.

[15] See *Henchley v Thompson* [2017] EWHC 225 (Ch) at 1.

[16] [1896] 1 Ch 199 at 209. See also *Selangor United Rubber Estates Ltd v Cradock (No 3)* [1968] 2 All ER 1073 at 1095, per Ungoed-Thomas J.

executor[17] or as an agent for another will be held liable to account to his principal just as if he had been properly appointed.[18] *Blyth v Fladgate*[19] is an illustration. Solicitors to a trust, after the death of all the trustees, lent trust funds on a mortgage which proved to be inadequate security for the loan. Since the trustees were already dead, the solicitors could not be acting as agents; they had instead assumed responsibility as trustees and were liable for the inadequacy of the investment. The important characteristic of this case is that the solicitors did not act merely as agents; they went beyond the responsibilities of an agent 'by doing acts characteristic of a trustee and outside the duties of an agent.'[20]

To become a trustee de son tort it is necessary that the defendant should have 'effectively [taken] on the role of a trustee',[21] or 'intended to assume the obligations of an actual trustee',[22] rather than acted in a more limited capacity (or as a burglar[23]). Kekewich J in *Re Barney*[24] went further and suggested that more was required than intermeddling. He said that it was essential to the character of a trustee that 'he should have trust property actually vested in him, or so far under his control that he has nothing to do but require that . . . it should be vested in him', and that 'if that is true of a trustee properly appointed, why is it not also true of a trustee de son tort'.[25] That remark does not take account of the complexity of some modern trusts, where the assets may be held by separate custodian trustees; it is suggested that the restriction is overstated.

(3) **Remedies**

In *Soar v Ashwell*, Lord Esher MR took the view that an intermeddling stranger must be treated, and therefore held liable, as if he were a properly appointed trustee:

> Where a person has assumed, either with or without consent, to act as a trustee of money or other property . . . a Court of Equity will impose upon him all the liabilities of an express trustee . . .[26]

The trustee de son tort is expected to act within the terms of the trust, and to act with the care and skill of a validly appointed express trustee. In *Blyth v Fladgate*,[27] the partners of a firm of solicitors who had become trustees de son tort were held liable to the trust for the loss caused by an improper investment. It should also not be forgotten that the beneficiaries may have proprietary claims to any trust assets vested in the trustee de son tort. Trustees de son tort are treated in the same way as express trustees for the purposes of limitation periods.[28]

[17] *Haastrup v Okorie* [2016] EWHC 12 (Ch); *Haastrup v Haastrup* [2016] EWHC 3311 (Ch).

[18] See *Lyell v Kennedy* [1889] 14 App Cas 437, HL; *English v Dedham Vale Properties Ltd* [1978] 1 WLR 93.

[19] [1891] 1 Ch 337.

[20] *Williams-Ashman v Price and Williams* [1942] Ch 219 per Bennett J explaining the rationale of *Mara v Browne* [1896] 1 Ch 199, CA. See also *Jasmine Trustees Ltd v Wells & Hind (A Firm)* [2007] EWHC 38 (Ch) (appointment of new trustees was invalid on the facts, so invalidly appointed trustees were trustees de son tort).

[21] *Daniel v Tee* [2016] EWHC 1538 (Ch). (The defendant conceded that this was the case.)

[22] *High Commissioner for Pakistan in the United Kingdom v Prince Mukkaram Jah, His Exalted Highness the 8th Nizam of Hyderabad* [2016] EWHC 1465 (Ch) at 130.

[23] *Haastrup v Okorie* [2016] EWHC 12 (Ch) at 62.

[24] [1892] 2 Ch 265.

[25] [1892] 2 Ch 265 at 272–3.

[26] [1893] 2 QB 390 at 394.

[27] [1891] 1 Ch 337.

[28] *Williams v Central Bank of Nigeria* [2014] UKSC 10 at 9.

4 Dishonest assistance in breach of trust

(1) Definition

Where a trustee commits a breach of trust, he will be personally liable to compensate the trust for any loss suffered in consequence of his breach.[29] His liability is a primary liability, as he was subject to the trust obligations. However, equity will also hold liable a stranger who assists a trustee in committing a breach of trust. This secondary, accessory, liability may provide the only effective remedy for the beneficiaries if the trustee is insolvent.

The rationale for the imposition of accessory liability against strangers to a trust was examined by the Privy Council in *Royal Brunei Airlines Sdn Bhd v Tan*,[30] where Lord Nicholls stated:

> Beneficiaries are entitled to expect that those who become trustees will fulfil their obligations. They are also entitled to expect, and this is only a short step further, that those who become trustees will be permitted to fulfil their obligations without deliberate intervention from third parties. They are entitled to expect that third parties will refrain from intentionally intruding in the trustee-beneficiary relationship and thereby hindering a beneficiary from receiving his entitlement in accordance with the terms of the trust instrument. There is here a close analogy with breach of contract. A person who knowingly procures a breach of contract, or knowingly interferes with the due performance of a contract, is liable to the innocent party. The underlying rationale [of accessory liability] is the same.[31]

(2) The need for fault

Accessory liability requires fault as on the part of the defendant. For example, in *Lipkin Gorman v Karpnale Ltd*,[32] Cass, a partner in a firm of solicitors, had used money from the firm's client account to finance his gambling habit. As well as seeking a remedy against the club in which the money had been spent, the firm claimed that the bank at which the client account was held was liable as an accessory to the partner's breach of trust. The manager of the bank, which also held Cass's personal account, had been aware that Cass had been cashing cheques at the casino and had warned him that his gambling was not controlled. At first instance it was held that the bank had sufficient knowledge of Cass's misuse of funds to render it liable to account for the money that had been misappropriated. The claim against the bank was, however, subsequently dismissed by the Court of Appeal[33] on the grounds that the bank had not been sufficiently aware that a breach of trust was being committed. Thus, there is a clear element of fault required on the part of the third party before constructive trusteeship is imposed, and it is in determining the degree of fault required that most of the difficulties have arisen in the case law. It is now settled law that accessory liability arises when there has been a dishonest assistance in a breach of trust.

(3) A personal remedy

A stranger who acts as an accessory to a breach of trust will generally only be subject to a personal liability to account to the trust for the loss suffered in consequence of the breach. Ordinarily he will not have received any trust property, and consequently the

[29] See Oakley, 'The Liberalising Nature of Remedies for Breach of Trust' in Oakley, *Trends in Contemporary Trust Law* (1996, OUP), pp 239–47; Elliott and Mitchell, 'Remedies for Dishonest Assistance' [2004] 67 MLR 16.

[30] [1995] 2 AC 378; [1995] 111 LQR 545 (Harpum); [1995] Conv 339 (Halliwell); [1995] 54 CLJ 505 (Nolan); [1995] RLR 105 (Stevens); [1996] LMCLQ 1 (Birks); [1996] 112 LQR 56 (Gardner); [1997] 60 MLR 443 (Berg).

[31] [1995] 2 AC 378 at 387.

[32] [1992] 4 All ER 331; [1987] 1 WLR 987.

[33] [1992] 4 All ER 409.

beneficiaries will be unable to identify any assets in his hands that could be the subject of a proprietary claim.[34] The remedy is compensatory, not restitutionary. Since the stranger did not receive any trust property he was not enriched at the expense of the beneficiaries by his assistance. By definition, restitution is only available to reverse an unjust enrichment. This was recognized by the Privy Council in *Royal Brunei Airlines Sdn Bhd v Tan*:

> Liability as an accessory is not dependent upon receipt of trust property, It arises even though no trust property has reached the hands of the accessory. It is a form of secondary liability in the sense that it only arises where there has been a breach of trust.[35]

The extent of liability of the accessory is considered to be joint and several with that of the trustee for any loss caused to the trust.[36] However, where a profit has arisen from the breach, the stranger is only liable for his own share of the profit, not that of the trustee.[37]

(4) **Requirements of accessory liability**

A stranger will only be held liable as an accessory to a breach of trust if four requirements are satisfied: the existence of a trust or fiduciary relationship; breach of that trust or relationship; assistance by the stranger in the breach; dishonesty on the part of the stranger. These requirements have undergone some transformation. They were first identified by Peter Gibson J in *Baden Delvaux v Société Générale*[38] but were subjected to significant revision by the Privy Council in *Royal Brunei Airlines Sdn Bhd v Tan*. As we shall see, subsequent developments suggest that the second requirement might need to be rephrased.

(a) **The existence of a trust or fiduciary relationship**

Accessory liability began as a secondary liability where there had been a breach of trust. By definition, that required a trust to exist, as in *Royal Brunei Airlines v Tan*. The plaintiff airline used a firm to act as their agents for the sale of tickets. Under the contract between the parties, the firm agreed to hold any money received from the sale of tickets on trust for the airline until it was paid over. The defendant was the founder and principal shareholder of the firm. In breach of the terms of the contract the firm, authorized by the defendant, used money received from ticket sales for its own purposes. On the insolvency of the firm the airline claimed that the defendant was liable to account as an accessory to the breach of trust that had been committed by the firm. In these circumstances there was clearly an express trust, thus opening the possibility of accessory liability.

Accessory liability has been extended to strangers assisting the breach of other fiduciary relationships. In *Selangor United Rubber Estates v Craddock (No 3)*,[39] the directors of the company were treated as having sufficient control of the company's property for an action as an accessory to be run against them. There may even be no need for there to be property. In *JD Wetherspoon Plc v Van de Berg & Co Ltd*,[40] an action was brought in

[34] However, many of the cases concern banks or other financial organizations where the trust property has passed through their hands. See, e.g., *Lipkin Gorman v Karpnale Ltd* [1987] 1 WLR 987; *Agip (Africa) Ltd v Jackson* [1990] Ch 265.

[35] [1995] 3 All ER 97 at 99–100. This is considered further later in the chapter under knowing receipt.

[36] *Ultraframe (UK) Ltd v Fielding* [2007] WTLR 835; *Novoship (UK) Ltd v Mikhaylyuk* [2012] EWHC 3586 at 98, per Christopher Clarke J.

[37] See Ridge, 'Justifying the Remedies for Dishonest Assistance' [2008] 124 LQR 445.

[38] *Baden, Delvaux and Lecuit v Société Générale pour Favoriser le Dévelopement du Commerce et de l'Industrie en France SA* [1983] BCLC 325.

[39] [1968] 2 All ER 1073; see also *FHR European Ventures LLP v Cedar Capital Partners LLC* [2014] UKSC 45 (secret profits made by a fiduciary).

[40] [2009] EWHC 639.

respect of allegations of breach of fiduciary duty by a company engaged to find new pubs for the Wetherspoon chain. The claims included allegations of accessory liability. Peter Smith J stated:[41]

> In my view in a case for accessory liability there is no requirement for there to be trust property. Such a requirement wrongly associates accessory liability with trust concepts . . . Accessory liability does not involve a trust. It involves providing dishonest assistance to somebody else who in a fiduciary capacity has committed a breach of his fiduciary duties.

In the event that he was wrong about this point, he was willing to find that confidential information could be treated as property for the purpose of the claim. The logic of the decision is sound, and it has been followed at first instance,[42] and in the Court of Appeal.[43]

(b) A breach of trust

Existing case law suggests that a stranger will only be liable as an accessory if there has been a breach of trust or fiduciary duty in the primary relationship. In *Baden Delvaux v Société Générale*,[44] Peter Gibson J had held that a stranger would only be liable if the trustee had assisted in a dishonest and fraudulent design of the trustees.[45] In *Royal Brunei Airlines v Tan*,[46] the defendant, therefore, claimed that he should not be liable as an accessory because the firm, which had misused money held on trust, had not acted fraudulently or dishonestly.[47] A trustee may commit a breach of trust innocently or negligently. The Privy Council rejected the defendant's argument and held that there was no need to demonstrate that the trustee had acted dishonestly or fraudulently.[48] All that was required was a breach of trust, irrespective of whether it had been committed honestly or dishonestly. A stranger will, therefore, be liable as an accessory if he acted with a sufficient degree of personal fault, irrespective of the degree of fault of the trustee in breach:

> what matters is the state of mind of the third party sought to be made liable, not the state of mind of the trustee. The trustee will be liable in any event for the breach of trust, even if he acted innocently, unless excused by an exemption clause in the trust instrument or relieved by the court. But *his* state of mind is essentially irrelevant to the question whether the *third party* should be made liable to the beneficiaries for the breach of trust. If the liability of the third party is fault-based, what matters is the nature of his fault, not that of the trustee. In this regard dishonesty on the part of the third party would seem to be a sufficient basis for his liability, irrespective of the state of mind of the trustee who is in breach. It is difficult to see why, if the third party dishonestly assisted in a breach, there should be a further prerequisite to his liability, namely that the trustee also must have been acting dishonestly. The alternative view would mean that a dishonest third party is liable if the trustee is dishonest, but if the trustee did not act dishonestly that of itself would excuse a dishonest third party from liability. That would make no sense.[49]

41 [2009] EWHC 639 at 518.

42 *Goldtrail Travel Ltd (In Liquidation) v Aydin* [2014] EWHC 1587 (Ch) (reversed on other grounds [2017] UKSC 57).

43 *Novoship (UK) Ltd v Mikhaylyuk* [2014] EWCA Civ 908 at 91–3.

44 *Baden, Delvaux and Lecuit v Société Générale pour Favoriser le* Développement *du Commerce et de l'Industrie en France SA* [1983] BCLC 325.

45 This position was also supported in *Barnes v Addy* [1874] 9 Ch App 244 and *Belmont Finance Corpn Ltd v Williams Furniture Ltd* [1979] Ch 250.

46 [1995] 2 AC 378.

47 The Privy Council held that, in fact, the company had acted dishonestly since the state of mind of the defendant could be imputed to it: [1995] 2 AC 378 at 393.

48 The Privy Council relied on earlier authorities to reach this conclusion: *Fyler v Fyler* [1841] 3 Beav 550; *A-G v Leicester Corpn* [1844] 7 Beav 176; *Eaves v Hickson* [1861] 30 Beav 136.

49 [1995] 2 AC 378 at 385 (emphasis added).

Similarly, there is no requirement that the original breach of trust (or fiduciary duty) to itself cause loss for a dishonest third party to be held liable.[50] There is no need for the defendant to have known of the existence of the trust or to be aware what the concept of a trust in English law means.[51]

Whilst no case yet goes this far, it is possible that in future a stranger could be held liable for dishonestly causing loss even if the trustee is not liable, for instance because of a valid exoneration clause, or even because the trustee has not broken any duty. For instance, an investment adviser could potentially be held liable for dishonest assistance where the adviser has persuaded a trustee (who has acted within the trust provisions and with reasonable care) to make an investment in an investment scheme known by the adviser to be fraudulent.

(c) Assistance

A stranger will only be liable as an accessory if he in fact assisted the commission of a breach of trust or breach of fiduciary duty. Peter Smith J in *JD Wetherspoon plc v Van de Berg & Co Ltd*[52] observed that 'in most cases the breach can only occur as a result of the activities of the assistor'. In *Royal Brunei Airlines Sdn Bhd v Tan*,[53] the defendant had authorized the use of trust money by the firm for its ordinary business purposes, including the paying of salaries and expenses and keeping its bank overdraft down. He had clearly assisted in the commission of the breach. However, where it cannot be shown that the stranger has assisted the breach of trust, there will be no grounds for any accessory liability. In *Brinks Ltd v Abu-Saleh (No 3)*[54] the defendant's husband had couriered some of the proceeds of the Brinks-Matt gold robbery to Switzerland. It was claimed that the defendant had knowingly assisted in a breach of trust by accompanying her husband on his trips so as to give the impression that they were enjoying a family holiday, thus cloaking the illegal nature of his activities and making it easier for him to cross borders. Rimer J held that she had not in fact assisted the breach of trust, and that she was not, therefore, liable to account for the £3 million her husband had couriered. He held that she had not participated in the breach because she was not party to the couriering agreements entered into by her husband, and he had carried out all elements of the couriering exercise. Her only role had been to provide him with company on the long and tiring drives. In essence, Rimer J seems to have held that a stranger will only be liable as an accessory if he participates in the breach by performing positive acts of assistance. Mere passive acquiescence in the activity alleged to constitute a breach of trust will accordingly be insufficient to establish liability. It is submitted that this reasoning is unduly narrow, and that a person should be liable as an accessory whenever his or her conduct passively encourages the commission of a breach of trust, provided that it was dishonest. Support for the view that passive assistance will be sufficient is given by *Adelaide Partnerships Ltd v Danison*.[55] Mr Danison ran a fraudulent investment scheme, the proceeds from which were paid into an account on which his wife was a signatory. The judge held the wife was liable for dishonest assistance:

> It is an obvious help to the setting up of a fraudulent scheme such as this that the fraudster should have available destination accounts to which the money can be transferred or

[50] See *Madoff Securities International Ltd (In Liquidation) v Raven* [2013] EWHC 3147 at 340, per Popplewell J, where a defendant tried to escape potential liability for dishonest assistance on the basis that the original breach of trust had caused no loss.

[51] See *Barlow Clowes v Eurotrust* [2006] 1 All ER 333.

[52] [2009] EWHC 639 at 518. [53] [1995] 2 AC 378.

[54] [1995] *The Times*, 23 October; Stevens, 'Delimiting the Scope of Accessory Liability' [1996] Conv 447; Oakley, 'Is Knowledge Still a Prerequisite of the Imposition of "Accessory Liability"'? [1996] 10 TLI 53.

[55] [2011] EWHC 4090 (Ch).

> through which it can be laundered, which served the purpose of frustrating, or impeding at least, the tracing of those funds from the account to which the victims of the fraud initially pay it. It would be very helpful to such a fraudster to have an account which was not, immediately at least, traceable to his name, but under what he might regard as friendly control.[56]

(d) Dishonesty

We have already seen that the equitable liability of a stranger as an accessory to a breach of trust is fault-based.[57] It operates as a species of equitable wrong, similar to a common law tort. Much of the debate over the years has concerned the degree of fault that must be demonstrated before an assistor will be held liable as an accessory. Prior to *Royal Brunei Airlines Sdn Bhd v Tan*,[58] this debate was couched in the language of 'knowledge'. In some cases it had been held that a stranger would be liable as a knowing assistor if he had participated in a breach of trust without any actual knowledge but in circumstances where he had been negligent in not realizing, or discovering, that he was assisting a breach of trust.[59] However, increasingly it came to be held that a higher standard of fault than mere negligence was required to establish accessory liability;[60] that the assistor must have acted with 'dishonesty'.[61] This higher threshold for liability was adopted by the Court of Appeal in *Lipkin Gorman v Karpnale Ltd*[62] and *Polly Peck International plc v Nadir (Asil) (No 2)*.[63] In *Royal Brunei Airlines Sdn Bhd v Tan*,[64] the Privy Council held that accessory liability was founded upon the dishonesty of the assistor.[65] Lord Nicholls explained why the requirement of dishonesty was to be preferred to that of knowledge:

> To inquire . . . whether a person dishonestly assisted in what is later held to be a breach of trust is to ask a meaningful question, which is capable of being given a meaningful answer. That is not always so if the question is posed in terms of knowingly assisted. Framing the question in the latter form all too often leads one into tortuous convolutions about the sort of knowledge required, when the truth is that knowingly is inapt as a criterion when applied to the gradually darkening spectrum where the differences are of degree and not kind.[66]

In *Twinsectra Ltd v Yardley*,[67] the House of Lords confirmed that dishonesty was the necessary condition for the imposition of accessory liability, thus affirming the decision in *Royal Brunei Airlines Sdn Bhd v Tan*.

[56] [2011] EWHC 4090 (Ch) at 58.

[57] *Twinsectra v Yardley* [2002] 2 All ER 377 at 107, per Lord Millett.

[58] [1995] 2 AC 378.

[59] *Selangor United Rubber Estates Ltd v Cradock (No 3)* [1968] 1 WLR 1555; *Karak Rubber Co Ltd v Burden (No 2)* [1972] 1 WLR 602; *Rowlandson v National Westminster Bank Ltd* [1978] 1 WLR 798; *Baden, Delvaux and Lecuit v Société Générale pour Favoriser le Développement du Commerce et de l'Industrie en France SA* [1983] BCLC 325.

[60] See, for example, *Agip (Africa) Ltd v Jackson* [1990] Ch 265; Sir Peter Millett, 'Tracing the Proceeds of Fraud' [1991] 107 LQR 71; affd [1991] Ch 547; [1992] 4 All ER 451; Harpum, 'Equitable Liability for Money Laundering' [1991] 50 CLJ 40; Goulding, 'Equity and the Money Launderers' [1992] Conv 367; Nolan, 'Knowing Assistance—A Plea for Help' [1992] 12 LS 332; See also *Eagle Trust plc v SBC Securities Ltd* [1992] 4 All ER 488; *Cowan de Groot Properties Ltd v Eagle Trust plc* [1992] 4 All ER 700 at 754.

[61] Birks, 'Misdirected funds again' [1989] 105 LQR 528.

[62] [1992] 4 All ER 409; [1989] 1 WLR 1340.

[63] [1992] 4 All ER 769 at 777, per Scott LJ.

[64] [1995] 2 AC 378.

[65] *Royal Brunei Airlines v Tan* was followed by the Court of Appeal in *Satnam Ltd v Dunlop Hetwood Ltd* [1999] 3 All ER 652 and applied in *Cigna Life Insurance New Zealand Ltd v Westpac Securities Ltd* [1996] 1 NZLR 80.

[66] [1995] 2 AC 378 at 391.

[67] [2002] 2 AC 164; [2002] 10 RLR 112 (Rickett); [2002] Con 303 (Kenny) and 387 (Thompson); [2002] 16 TLI 165 (Penner); [2003] Con 398 (Andrews); [2004] 120 LQR 208 (Yeo). See also *Barlow Clowes v Eurotrust* [2006] 1 All ER 333.

(5) The test for 'dishonesty'

Defining what is meant by dishonesty initially proved problematic, although it is now 'clearly established'[68] that the test first set out in *Royal Brunei Airlines Sdn Bhd v Tan* is the applicable standard.

(a) Dishonesty judged objectively

In *Royal Brunei Airlines v Tan*, Lord Nicholls was at pains to explain that dishonesty provided an objective criterion for assessment of the defendant's conduct:

> [I]n the context of the accessory liability principle acting dishonestly, or with a lack of probity, which is synonymous, means simply not acting as an honest person would in the circumstances. This is an objective standard. At first sight this might seem surprising. Honesty has a connotation of subjectivity, as distinct from the objectivity of negligence. Honesty, indeed, does have a strong subjective element in that it is a description of a type of conduct assessed in the light of what a person actually knew at the time, as distinct from what a reasonable person would have known or appreciated. Further, honesty and its counterpart dishonesty are mostly concerned with adverting conduct, not inadvertent conduct. Carelessness is not dishonesty. Thus for the most part dishonesty is to be equated with conscious impropriety.[69]

He held that these inherently subjective characteristics of dishonesty did not mean that individuals were free to set their own standards. Honesty is not an optional scale, with higher and lower values according to the moral standards of each individual. A person who knowingly appropriates a person's property will not escape a finding of dishonesty simply because he sees nothing wrong in such behaviour.[70] He considered that in the majority of circumstances there would be little difficulty identifying how an honest person would behave. For example, he stated:

> Unless there is a very good and compelling reason, an honest person does not participate in a transaction if he knows it involves a misapplication of trust assets to the detriment of the beneficiaries. Nor does an honest person in such a case deliberately close his eyes and ears, or deliberately not ask questions, lest he learn something he would rather not know, and then proceed regardless.[71]

He also indicated that any assessment of dishonesty would have to be contextual, taking account of the circumstances of the transaction which constituted a breach of trust and the personal attributes of the assistor, including his experience and intelligence,[72] and that strangers should not generally be liable as assistors if they had acted negligently.[73] Strangers who owe a duty of care to the trust (for example, advisers, consultants, bankers, and agents) are liable in tort if they fail to exercise reasonable skill and care, and there is no compelling reason to impose any additional liability in equity.

(b) A wrong turn

In *Twinsectra Ltd v Yardley*,[74] the House of Lords subjected the comments of Lord Nicholls to careful scrutiny in order to identify the essential elements of dishonesty, and made comments that appeared to require a subjective awareness of wrongdoing on the part of the defendant, a criterion which aligned with the test then applied in the criminal law. Lord Hutton identified three ways in which the standard of dishonesty may be applied, the third of which he described as the 'combined test'. The majority of the House of Lords

[68] *Ivey v Genting Casinos (UK) Ltd (t/a Crockfords)* [2017] UKSC 67 at 62; *Group Seven Ltd v Notable Services LLP* [2019] EWCA Civ 614.

[69] [1995] 2 AC 378 at 389. [70] Ibid at 389. [71] Ibid at 389.

[72] Ibid at 391. [73] Ibid at 392. [74] [2002] 2 AC 164.

held that the combined test explained by Lord Hutton should be adopted as the standard of dishonesty necessary for the imposition of accessory liability. This required:

> that before there can be a finding of dishonesty it must be established that the defendant's conduct was dishonest by the standards of reasonable and honest people and that he himself realised that by those standards his conduct was dishonest.[75]

Lord Hutton was influenced by the criminal law test, to the same effect, set out in *R v Ghosh*.[76] He may also have been troubled by the consequences for the defendant in that case, a solicitor, of a finding of dishonesty. In *Twinsectra Ltd v Yardley*, the defendant solicitor was held not to have acted dishonestly. The claimant lenders had advanced £1 million to a firm of solicitors subject to an undertaking that the money would be retained until it was applied in the acquisition of property by the borrower, Yardley. In breach of this undertaking the firm of solicitors subsequently paid the money to Leach, another solicitor who was acting for Yardley in respect of the transaction. Leach then failed to ensure that the money was utilized solely for the acquisition of property in accordance with the undertaking, and Yardley used £358,000 for other purposes. At first instance Carnwath J held that Leach had not acted dishonestly, although he had been 'misguided'. While he had been aware of all the facts he had 'simply shut his eyes to the problems' and had considered it a matter for the other solicitors whether he could release the money to his client. The Court of Appeal held that Leach had acted dishonestly because he had shut his eyes to the rights of *Twinsectra*, but that decision was reversed by the House of Lords. The majority held that Leach had not acted dishonestly. The crucial question was whether 'Leach realized that his action was dishonest by the standards of responsible and honest solicitors'.[77] The trial judge had held that he did not realize that other solicitors would consider his conduct to be dishonest. Lord Millett dissented in favour of the adoption of a purely objective test which does not require the defendant to have realized that he was acting dishonestly. In Lord Millett's view, the only subjective elements were findings of fact as to the defendant's experience, intelligence, and actual state of knowledge of the breach of trust.

(c) Clarification

The test adopted by the majority of the House of Lords in *Twinsectra Ltd v Yardley* appeared to mean that a defendant would not be regarded as dishonest if he had acted dishonestly according to the objective standards of honest men, but had personally set himself a different standard of honesty such that he was not consciously aware that his conduct would be regarded as dishonest by ordinary standards. The question came to the Privy Council again in *Barlow Clowes International Ltd v Eurotrust International Ltd*.[78] The central issue in this case was whether liability on the basis of dishonesty required the court to conduct an inquiry into the defendant's views as to what the ordinary standards of honesty would be, so as to then determine whether he had consciously reflected that he was transgressing them. The Judicial Committee, which had a membership which overlapped with that of the Lords in *Twinsectra*, retreated from the suggestion that *Twinsectra* had sought to apply a different test from that set out in *Royal Brunei Airlines*. The explanation could be interpreted as an exercise in verbal gymnastics.[79] Lord Hoffmann stated that, although some

[75] [2002] 2 AC 164 at 27.

[76] [1982] QB 901. See Thompson, 'Criminal Law and Property Law: An Unhappy Combination' [2002] Con 387.

[77] [2002] 2 AC 164 at 49, per Lord Hutton. See also at 20, per Lord Hoffmann.

[78] [2006] 1 All ER 333; Ryan, '*Royal Brunei* Dishonesty: Clarity at Last?' [2006] Conv 188.

[79] See Conaglen and Goymour, 'Dishonesty in the Context of Assistance—Again' [2006] 65 CLJ 18, who suggest this is judicial 'sleight of hand'. See also Yeo, 'Dishonest Assistance: Restatement from the Privy Council' [2006] LQR 171.

of the comments made in *Twinsectra Ltd v Yardley* might have contained an 'element of ambiguity', they had not intended to be different from the principles stated in *Royal Brunei Airlines Sdn Bhd v Tan*.[80] Lord Hoffmann explained that Lord Hutton had not intended to impose a requirement that the defendant must have had reflections about what the normally accepted standards of conduct were. He further indicated that his own comments in *Twinsectra Ltd v Yardley*, that a dishonest state of mind meant 'consciousness that one is transgressing ordinary standards of honest behaviour',[81] were only intended 'to require consciousness of those elements of the transaction which make participation transgress ordinary standards of honest behaviour'.[82] They did not, therefore, 'also require him to have thought about what those standards were'.[83] The Privy Council therefore accepted the following statement of the trial judge as a correct statement of the law:

> Although a dishonest state of mind is a subjective mental state, the standard by which the law determines whether it is dishonest is objective. If by ordinary standards a defendant's mental state would be characterised as dishonest, it is irrelevant that the defendant judges by different standards.[84]

The majority did not concede that *Twinsectra* had been wrongly decided, or contained an inaccurate statement of the test for dishonesty, they simply sought to reinterpret it as if it had been a direct application of the test in *Royal Brunei Airlines v Tan*.

(d) Problems with the clarification

The clarification of the test for dishonesty given in *Barlow Clowes v Eurotrust*[85] did not fully resolve the issue because it, and *Royal Brunei Airlines v Tan*, were Privy Council decisions which, under the rules of precedent then applicable, could not prevail over the House of Lords decision in *Twinsectra*.[86] Since *Barlow Clowes* did not purport to disagree with *Twinsectra*, but only to interpret or explain it, lower courts were able to adopt the *Barlow Clowes* explanation of *Twinsectra*, thus applying the original *Royal Brunei Airlines* test of dishonesty. Thus, in *Abou-Rahmah v Abacha*,[87] Arden LJ confirmed that all that was required to impose liability was the defendant's knowledge of facts which would be judged dishonest applying normal standards of honest conduct. She said:

> the *Barlow Clowes* case gives guidance as to the proper interpretation to be placed on it as a matter of English law. It shows how the *Royal Brunei* case and the *Twinsectra* case can be read together to form a consistent corpus of law.[88]

A similar view was taken in other cases. Peter Smith J in *AG of Zambia v Meer Care & Desai*,[89] a case concerning a complex international fraud involving the corrupt spending of huge sums by the former President of Zambia and the actions of a solicitor in handling various tainted transactions through his client account, concluded, following a formulation by Lord Clarke MR, writing extrajudicially:[90]

> the test for dishonest assistance is an objective one, but an objective one which takes account of the individuals in questions characteristics . . . It is a test which requires the Court to assess

[80] [1995] 2 AC 378. [81] [2002] 2 AC 164 at 20. [82] [2006] 1 All ER 339 at 16.

[83] [2006] 1 All ER 339 at 16. [84] Ibid at 10. [85] Ibid 333.

[86] This rule of precedent has been modified by *Willers v Joyce (Re: Gubay (deceased) No 2)* [2016] UKSC 44. See criticism by Mirfield, 'A novel theory of Privy Council precedent' [2017] LQR 133.

[87] [2006] EWCA Civ 1492. See Lee, 'Dishonesty and Bad Faith after *Barlow Clowes: Abou-Rahmah v Abacha*' [2007] JBL 209; Ryan, '*Royal Brunei* Dishonesty: A Clear Welcome for *Barlow Clowes*' [2007] Conv 168. See also *Statek Corp v Alford* [2008] EWHC 32 (Ch).

[88] [2006] EWCA Civ 1492 at 68. [89] [2007] EWHC 952.

[90] 'Claims Against Professionals: Negligence, Dishonesty and Fraud' [2006] 22 *Professional Negligence* 70/85.

> the individual's conduct according to an objective standard of dishonesty. In doing so the Court has to take into account as to what the individual knew; his experience, intelligence and reasons for acting as he did. Whether the individual was aware that his conduct fell below the objective standard is not part of the test.[91]

(e) Confirmation of the test for dishonesty

Confirmation that the test for dishonesty in this context was that set out in *Royal Brunei Airlines v Tan* was given unequivocally and authoritatively[92] by the Court of Appeal in *Starglade Properties Ltd v Nash*.[93] It was held that the deliberate removal of the assets of an insolvent company in order to defeat the legitimate claims of creditors was 'not in accordance with the ordinary standards of honest commercial behaviour' and the director responsible was therefore dishonest.[94] That decision has been treated as conclusive of the issue and applied, where the question could not be avoided,[95] in subsequent cases,[96] even when the matter has been disputed.[97] The Supreme Court has now confirmed in *Ivey v Genting Casinos (UK) Ltd (t/a Crockfords)*[98] that the approach taken in *Starglade Properties Ltd v Nash*[99] was correct.

The *Crockfords* case did not involve dishonest assistance, but an allegation of cheating in a game of punto banco baccarat. A professional gambler, with an assistant, had asked the croupier to turn the cards being used so that (unknown to the croupier) it was possible to tell (from minute differences in the pattern on the backs of the cards) which were high value and which were low value when the same pack of cards was used a second time. This edge-sorting technique gave the gambler an advantage which the Supreme Court held to be cheating, so that Crockfords was within its rights in refusing to pay him the £7.7 million he claimed as his 'winnings'. The Supreme Court considered that if dishonesty had to be proved, this had been done, even though the gambler asserted that he had done nothing wrong. The Supreme Court stated that the test for certainty in both civil and criminal cases was that:

> the fact-finding tribunal must first ascertain (subjectively) the actual state of the individual's knowledge or belief as to the facts. The reasonableness or otherwise of his belief is a matter of evidence (often in practice determinative) going to whether he held the belief, but it is not an additional requirement that his belief must be reasonable; the question is whether it is genuinely held. When once his actual state of mind as to knowledge or belief as to facts is established, the question whether his conduct was honest or dishonest is to be determined by the fact-finder by applying the (objective) standards of ordinary decent people. There is no requirement that the defendant must appreciate that what he has done is, by those standards, dishonest.[100]

By aligning the test of dishonesty in criminal cases, the Court has resolved one of the tensions between what had previously been different approaches in civil and criminal cases. It has subsequently been followed by the Court of Appeal on *Group Seven Ltd v Notable Services LLP*,[101] where an accountant member, Mr Landman, in a multi-disciplinary

[91] [2007] EWHC 952 at 357.
[92] *Breitenfeld UK Ltd v Harrison* [2015] EWHC 399 (Ch) at 82 (Norris J).
[93] [2010] EWCA Civ 1314.
[94] [2010] EWCA Civ 1314 at 39.
[95] *Breitenfeld UK Ltd v Harrison* [2015] EWHC 399 (Ch) at 82.
[96] See, for example, *Novoship (UK) Ltd v Mikhaylyuk* [2012] EWHC 3586 (Comm); *SPL Private Finance (PF2) IC Ltd v Farrell* [2015] EWCA Civ 1004.
[97] *Group Seven Ltdr v Nasir* [2017] EWHC 2466 (Ch) at 415.
[98] [2017] UKSC 67.
[99] [2010] EWCA Civ 1314; [2011] Lloyd's Rep FC 102.
[100] [2017] UKSC 67 at 74.
[101] [2020] Ch 129.

solicitors firm, was held liable for dishonest assistance for permitting monies from a client account to be used as part of a fraudulent money laundering scheme. The Court of Appeal stressed the importance of the objective nature of the dishonesty test as highlighted in *Ivey*:

> [T]he defendant's actual state of knowledge and belief as to the relevant facts forms a crucial part of the first stage of the test for dishonesty set out in *Tan*. But once the relevant facts have been ascertained, including the defendant's state of knowledge or belief as to the facts, the standard of appraisal which must then be applied to those facts is a purely objective one. The court has to ask itself what is essentially a jury question, namely where the defendant's conduct was honest or dishonest according to the standard of ordinary decent people.[102]

The facts of this case are considered below.

(6) **Markers of dishonesty**

In *Starglade Properties Ltd v Nash*,[103] the Court of Appeal indicated that dishonesty could be equated with acting in a way which was 'not in accordance with the ordinary standards of honest commercial behaviour.' Other cases have offered some guidance as to characteristics of dishonest behaviour. In *Breitenfeld UK Ltd v Harrison*,[104] a company director of ForgeMet, in breach of fiduciary duty, diverted work to a company run by his son John and daughter-in-law Gemma, who also worked for ForgeMet. The judge held them liable for dishonest assistance, even though they had claimed to have done nothing wrong:

> they knew that what they were doing was not proper having regard to Mr Harrison's duties to ForgeMet. People who hold honest beliefs about the desirability of a particular course of commercial activity do not cloak that activity in secrecy and conceal it from the owners of the business they are employed to serve. John Harrison and Gemma Harrison did not act as honest people would act: and their consciences told them that they were engaged in transactions in which they could not honestly participate, so they acted secretly.[105]

Recently, in *Burns v Burn & Ors*,[106] the court held that the defendant members of a firm had no real prospect of defending a claim that they had dishonestly assisted in a breach of trust involving the dissipation of the claimant's pension monies. The defendants ought to have known that the use to which they said the pension funds had been put was improper as it was outside the terms of the investment contemplated by a brochure they themselves had produced. It was no defence to rely on their subjective beliefs that they were acting honestly.[107]

Turning a 'blind eye'[108] to circumstances that suggest that funds have an illegitimate source will also be an indicator of dishonesty, even though it might also be explained as incompetence. In *Group Seven Ltd v Notable Services LLP*, Group Seven Ltd invested €100m with a company AIC, which had been set up to defraud Group Seven. AIC purported to lend the money to Larn Ltd, a company owned by one of the fraudsters, Mr Nobre. The money was paid into Notable Services' client account on trust for Larn Ltd. This was a

102 [2020] Ch 129 at [58]. 103 [2010] EWCA Civ 1314.

104 [2015] EWHC 399 (Ch). 105 [2015] EWHC 399 (Ch) at 84.

106 [2021] EWHC 75 (Ch), a decision that may be more notable for the fact that it confirms that the court will grant summary judgment in an appropriate case, even where serious allegations of dishonesty were made and contested.

107 [2021] EWHC 75 (Ch) at [51].

108 Also referred to as Nelsonian knowledge after the famous story of Admiral Horatio Nelson having once deliberately failed to acknowledge the order of the commander of the fleet by putting a telescope to the eye which he had lost in an earlier naval battle—see the discussion in *Stanford International Bank Ltd v HSBC Bank Plc* [2020] EWHC 2232 (Ch).

money laundering scheme, and by the time it was discovered some €15m had been paid out of Notable's account on the instructions of Mr Nobre, actioned by Mr Landman, who worked at Notable. Mr Landman also received a personal payment of £170,000 from the same account. Police action stopped the fraud and €88m was returned. The present action concerned whether Mr Landman as a third party to the trust for dishonest assistance of the remaining €12m and through unconscionable receipt of the personal payment,

At first instance, Morgan J found that Mr Landman was liable for unconscionable receipt for the personal payment of £170,000,[109] but was not liable for the balance of the laundered money (€12m) as he did not have the requisite knowledge that the transactions were dishonest. The Court of Appeal, in reversing the decision held that the question was whether Mr Landman had 'consciously decided to refrain from taking any step to confirm the true state of affairs for fear of what he may have discover'.[110] The test to be applied required two conditions to be satisfied:[111]

> [T]he imputation of blind-eye knowledge requires two conditions to be satisfied. The first is the existence of a suspicion that certain facts may exist, and the second is a conscious decision to refrain from taking any step to confirm their existence.[112]

It was held that Morgan J had erred in his approach to assessing Mr Landman's knowledge on the facts, in the importance attached to his receipt and concealment of the personal funds. In consequence, Mr Landman must have turned a blind eye having had clear suspicions that the money was not at Larn Ltd's free disposal and not followed them up from fear of what he may discover.

In *Natwest Markets plc v Bilta (UK) Ltd*,[113] the Court of Appeal revisited what was required for blind-eye knowledge. This case, which involved fraud in spot trading of carbon credits, amounting to over £44 million lost revenue for the HMRC,[114] saw the Court of Appeal order a retrial of a dishonest assistance claim on the basis that the High Court failed to consider key evidence in reaching its findings, which were thrown into further doubt by the nineteen months delay in the handing down of the lower court's judgment. In considering the test for dishonesty and blind-eye knowledge as applied by the trial judge, Asplin, Anders, and Birss LJJ reviewed the decision in *Group Seven*, in particular some obiter statements that in principle 'belief' as required by *Ivey* may include suspicion which in and of itself falls short of blind-eye knowledge. The Court of Appeal confirmed that it is not enough that the defendant merely suspects something to be the case, or that he negligently refrains from making further inquiries. The state of a person's mind is a question of fact, and suspicions of all types and degrees of probability may form part of it, and thus form part of the overall picture to which the objective standard of dishonesty is to be applied.[115] They concluded:

> [*Group Seven*] goes no further than confirming that the honesty of a person's conduct falls to be considered objectively in the light of all relevant material including their state of mind. The court went on to find that, on the basis of the trial judge's findings as to the state of the defendant's actual knowledge of the relevant facts, the inescapable conclusion was that he had blind-eye knowledge that the recipient was not beneficially entitled to the money

[109] The requirements of claims in unconscionable receipt are considered later in this chapter.

[110] [2020] Ch 129 at [101].

[111] Following the guidance of the House of Lords in *Manifest Shipping & Co Ltd* [2003] 1 AC 469.

[112] [2020] Ch 129 at [59].

[113] [2021] EWCA Civ 680.

[114] This involved exploiting the VAT-free status of inter EU member states imports and exports. A good description of the schemes, and the linked 'carousel' fraud involving third parties, is provided at [2021] EWCA Civ 680 [4]–[13].

[115] [2021] EWCA Civ 680 at [132].

[96]–[101]. The defendant's whole course of conduct was objectively dishonest, because no reasonable and honest person who knew those facts would have done what he did to facilitate the payment. The case was therefore one of actual knowledge of facts which, objectively assessed, constituted a breach of trust.[116]

(7) **Remedies**

Where a claimant successfully proves dishonest assistance, the remedies available are either equitable compensation for any loss suffered,[117] or an account of profits made by the assister.[118] The claimant can normally elect between these two, but the Court of Appeal said in *Novoship (UK) Limited v Nikitin*:[119]

> We consider that where a claim for an account of profits is made against one who is not a fiduciary, and does not owe fiduciary duties . . . the court has a discretion to grant or withhold the remedy . . . One ground on which the court may withhold the remedy is that an account of profits would be disproportionate in relation to the particular form and extent of wrongdoing.

5 Proprietary remedies for receipt in breach of trust

Where property has been disposed of in breach of trust or fiduciary duty, but is still identifiable in its original or a substituted format, the beneficiaries of the trust will be able to assert their proprietary rights to those assets. This does not require any proof of fault on the part of the recipient. It is also possible, in some cases, for a common law action for unjust enrichment to be asserted where the claimant has legal title (perhaps as trustee) to the misappropriated assets. The equitable rights require the continuing existence of the property in the hands of the defendant; the common law action can be pursued, subject to any change of position on the part of the recipient, even where the recipient no longer has the property. The application of the rules for these no-fault claims are explained in Chapter 38 on tracing.

6 Liability for unconscionable receipt

(1) **The basis of liability**

The potential personal liability of recipients of trust property has long been recognized, but one aspect has caused particular difficulty. After much debate about the level of knowledge required to find a defendant liable, this is now characterized as receipt in circumstances where it would be unconscionable to retain the benefit of the receipt, or unconscionable receipt in short. For this reason, this head of liability, previously given the label 'knowing receipt' is more descriptively entitled 'unconscionable receipt'.[120]

[116] [2021] EWCA Civ 680 at [133].

[117] *Goldtrail Travel Ltd (In Liquidation) v Aydin* [2016] EWCA Civ 371; [2016] 1 BCLC 635.

[118] See *Group Seven Ltd v Notable Services LLP* [2020] Ch 129; *Novoship (UK) Limited v Nikitin* [2014] EWCA Civ 908 at 84, and the cases cited by Longmore LJ at 71. See Campbell, 'The Honest Truth about Dishonest Assistance' [2015] Conv 160.

[119] [2014] EWCA Civ 908 at 119.

[120] See *Group Seven Ltd v Notable Services LLP* [2020] Ch 129; *Akita Holdings Ltd v The Honourable Attorney General of The Turks and Caicos Islands (Turks and Caicos Islands)* [2017] UKPC 7 at 6; *Benedetti v Sawiris* [2013] UKSC 50 at 3.

A leading statement of the requirements for liability sets out three elements:

> the plaintiff must show, first, a disposal of his assets in breach of fiduciary duty; secondly, the beneficial receipt by the defendant of assets which are traceable as representing the assets of the plaintiff; and thirdly, knowledge on the part of the defendant that the assets received are traceable to a breach of fiduciary duty.[121]

This statement, although approved by the Court of Appeal, is misleading in some respects, which need to be explored later. It could be taken to suggest that the defendant needs still to be in possession of the claimant's assets. If that were the case, this head of liability would serve only a very limited purpose because a proprietary claim could be made to those assets. The main value in this head of liability is that it can be pursued even when the recipient no longer has the claimant's assets, for instance, because they have been passed on or dissipated.

(2) **A form of unjust enrichment?**

Liability for unconscionable receipt has been described as a form of unjust enrichment.[122] The stranger is held liable because he has received something to which he is not entitled and because it would be unjust to retain the benefit of the receipt. The measure of liability, achieved through the equitable remedy of account, is to give restitution to the trust not what the trust has lost, but what the stranger has gained, including, it seems, any profits made through the receipt.[123] The categorization of unconscionable receipt as unjust enrichment is not universally accepted. There are differences in the operation of the rules for each form of liability. In particular, the common law rules on unjust enrichment do not require proof of fault or unconscionable conduct. There is a potential overlap.[124]

(3) **Misapplication of trust assets**

Hoffmann LJ, in the passage quoted above in *El Ajou*, said that 'the plaintiff must show, first, a disposal of his assets in breach of fiduciary duty'.[125] Liability for unconscionable receipt is only available where funds have been misapplied in breach of trust or fiduciary duty. Without an initial trust or fiduciary duty 'it is difficult, if not impossible' to see how a case for unconscionable receipt can be made out.[126] The property need not have been subject to an existing trust: the diversion of company funds by a director in breach of fiduciary duty will be sufficient.[127] Liability will only arise where funds have been misapplied. If a disposition of company (or trust) funds has been validly made, 'questions of "knowing receipt" ... do not arise.'[128]

[121] Hoffmann LJ in *El Ajou v Dollar Land Holdings Plc* [1994] 1 All ER 685, 700 approved by the Court of Appeal in *Bank of Credit & Commerce International v Akindele* [2000] EWCA Civ 502.

[122] *Twinsectra Ltd v Yardley* [2002] 2 AC 164 at 105 (Lord Millett, dissenting). See also *Otkritie International Investment Management Ltd v Urumov* [2014] EWHC 755 (Comm) at 9.

[123] *Akita Holdings Ltd v The Honourable Attorney General of The Turks and Caicos Islands* [2017] UKPC 7 at 11, following the judgment of Longmore LJ in *Novoship (UK) Ltd v Mikhaylyuk* [2015] QB 499.

[124] See, for instance, *Clegg v The Estate & Personal Representatives of Andrew Gregory Pache* [2017] EWCA Civ 256; *Clydesdale Bank Plc v Stoke Place Hotel Ltd* [2017] EWHC 181 (Ch).

[125] *El Ajou v Dollar Land Holdings Plc* [1994] 1 All ER 685, 700.

[126] *Gabriel v Little* [2013] EWCA Civ 1513 at 46.

[127] *Belmont Finance Corporation Limited v Williams Furniture Limited (No 2)* [1980] 1 All ER 395.

[128] *Criterion Properties v Stratford UK Properties* [2004] 1 WLR 1846, [2004] UKHL 28 at 4. Applied in *Madoff Securities International Ltd v Raven* [2013] EWHC 3147 (Comm) at 368.

In most cases the receipt of the property will occur as a result of the breach of trust or fiduciary duty. However, this is not essential. Brightman J, in *Karak Rubber Co Ltd v Burden (No 2)*, made clear that liability is based on the wrongful use of trust property in a manner which is inconsistent with the trust: one situation in which liability can occur is therefore where a person 'receives trust property knowing it to be such but without breach of trust, and subsequently deals with it in a manner inconsistent with the trusts.'[129]

(4) Beneficial receipt by the defendant

(a) Factual requirement of receipt

It goes almost without saying that liability for unconscionable receipt requires the person charged to have in fact received the trust property, unlike the liability of a dishonest accessory, where receipt of property is not a requirement. What constitutes receipt in this context is not entirely clear. Some situations will be clear-cut. Where a casino owed money for a gambling debt is paid money which the gambler has embezzled from a trust fund, it would undoubtedly be considered a recipient for the purposes of liability if the other conditions are met. A 'fence' engaged in a money laundering activity by paying misappropriated cheques through his personal bank account would similarly be considered a recipient.[130] In *Group Seven Ltd v Notable Services LLP*,[131] (described earlier), Mr Landman had received £170,000 from the trust fund as a negotiated fee for his assistance in allowing Notable's bank account to be used for fraud and was held liable for unconscionable receipt despite an attempt to disguise the personal payment by having it received by a nominee.[132] It would also be a sufficient basis for liability (if the other conditions are met) if the property could have been traced to the hands of the stranger if they had retained it.[133] On the other hand, where rights were abandoned without being converted into other property, there was nothing to found a claim.[134] A vesting of legal or equitable title in the recipient is not necessary, since having control over the property appears to be sufficient.[135]

(b) Beneficial receipt

In some of the case law, it is suggested that property must be acquired or retained by the recipient for his own use and benefit, so that an agent would not be liable for recipient liability.[136] Indeed, Millett J (as he then was), in *Agip v Jackson*, suggested that a bank would normally not be liable for unconscionable receipt, as it would be acting de facto as the agent of its customers.[137] The application of *Agip v Jackson* was doubted by Lord Justice Moore-Bick in *Uzinterimpex JSC v Standard Bank plc*,[138] but on the facts there was sufficient receipt, as the account in question the bank had set up was a transaction account

[129] [1972] 1 WLR 602 at 632.

[130] See *Statek Corporation v McNeill Alford & Anor* [2008] EWHC 32; *Adelaide Partnerships v Danison* [2011] EWHC 4090 (Ch) at [56–7].

[131] [2020] Ch 129.

[132] [2020] Ch 128 at [87]–[95], approving the approach of Morgan J in relation to unconscionable receipt.

[133] *El Ajou v Dollar Land Holdings plc (No 2)* [1995] 2 All ER 213.

[134] *Forester Maurice Labrouche v Frey* [2016] EWHC 268 (Ch) at 276.

[135] See, for example, *Karak Rubber Co Ltd v Burden (No 2)* [1972] 1 WLR 602.

[136] See *Williams-Ashman v Price & Williams* [1942] 1 Ch 219, and, in support, *Twinsectra v Yardley* [2002] 2 AC 164 at 105, per Lord Millett. See also *Adelaide Partnerships Ltd v Danison* [2011] EWHC 4090 (Ch).

[137] [1990] Ch 265. In fact, Millett J suggested that it was only where a bank reduced an overdraft that this was seen as them acting for their own benefit so that they could be liable for receipt.

[138] [2008] EWCA Civ 819 at 39–40.

to allow the recipient bank to claim fees and expenses, and was clearly for the benefit of the bank, not a customer. If receipt as an agent cannot give rise to liability, but receipt on one's own account can, there would be a difference between an auctioneer selling antique furniture held on trust and a second-hand dealer who buys and resells. The exoneration of agents from liability could be justified on the basis that a person is not enriched by the receipt of funds for which they are accountable as an agent, but it may equally unduly limit the operation of personal liability for unconscionable receipt. In many cases there will be an alternative claim for dishonest assistance.

On a related point, it is clear that the property received by the defendant must be property in respect of which the claimant still has an equitable right. In *Byers v Samba Financial Group*,[139] Fancourt J dismissed a claim by an investment company and its creditors to hold a defendant bank liable for knowing receipt of trust property consisting of shares in a number of banks. This was on the basis that, pursuant to Saudi Arabian law which governed the transfer, beneficial ownership passed to the defendant bank. Fancourt J said that '[it] is the essence of such a claim that the beneficiary asserts that the recipient as, or had, the beneficiary's property'.[140]

(5) **Fault**

(a) Liability is based on conscience

Hoffmann J's third requirement was 'knowledge on the part of the defendant that the assets received are traceable to a breach of fiduciary duty.'[141] The stranger's liability is rooted in equitable notions of conscience. Unless the stranger was aware that the property he received was subject to a trust, he was entitled to treat it as his own, for example, by disposing of it, consuming it on services which leave no traceable end product, or transferring it to others. His conscience will only be affected if he knew that the property was subject to a trust, in which case he will have become subject to an obligation to preserve it for the beneficiaries. As Lord Browne-Wilkinson stated in *Westdeutsche Landesbank Girozentrale v Islington London Borough Council*:

> Since the equitable jurisdiction to enforce trusts depends upon the conscience of the holder of the legal interest being affected, he cannot be a trustee of the property if and so long as he is ignorant of the facts alleged to affect his conscience, i.e. until he is aware that he is intended to hold the property for the benefit of others in the case of an express or implied trust, or, in the case of a constructive trust, of the factors which are alleged to affect his conscience.[142]

(b) The current position

There has been considerable debate over many years about what level or kind of knowledge is required to make a defendant liable. The leading case is *Bank of Credit & Commerce International v Akindele*.[143] In this case the liquidators of BCCI claimed that an investor was liable to account for over $16m, which he had received in performance of an investment agreement he had entered with a company controlled by the BCCI group, purportedly to buy and sell shares in BCCI, which was alleged to have been a sham. Although the

[139] [2021] EWHC 60 (Ch). [140] [2021] EWHC 60 (Ch) at [116].

[141] Hoffmann LJ in *El Ajou v Dollar Land Holdings Plc* [1994] 1 All ER 685, 700 approved by the Court of Appeal in *Bank of Credit & Commerce International v Akindele* [2000] EWCA Civ 502.

[142] [1996] AC 669 at 705.

[143] [2001] Ch 437. See Barkehall-Thomas, '"Goodbye" Knowing Receipt. "Hello" Unconscientious Receipt' [2001] 21(2) OJLS 239.

agreement was not found to have been a sham, the payments were held to have been procured in consequence of a fraudulent breach of fiduciary duty by the directors of BCCI, so that they were impressed with a constructive trust. As such the investor had received trust property. The Court of Appeal held, however, that he was not personally liable to account for the trust money he had received, because he had not acted 'unconscionably'. He had not been aware of the internal arrangements within BCCI that had rendered the payment a breach of fiduciary duty. Nourse LJ rejected previous attempts to provide a categorization of different types of knowledge or notice and proposed a new generalized test of liability:

> I have come to the view that, just as there is now a single test of dishonesty for knowing assistance, so ought there to be a single test of knowledge for knowing receipt. The recipient's state of knowledge must be such as to make it unconscionable for him to retain the benefit of the receipt.[144]

(c) The previous debate

The ruling in *Akindele* sought to put an end to a long debate over what kind of fault is needed for liability. Previous cases were sometimes inconsistent, and often equivocal.

(i) Strict liability

Most cases held that some degree of fault was required. As Lord Browne-Wilkinson stated in *Westdeutsche Landesbank Girozentrale v Islington London Borough Council*:

> unless [the recipient of trust property] has the requisite degree of knowledge he is not personally liable to account as trustee.[145]

It was rarely argued that liability should be strict (i.e. require no proof of fault), (although Lord Millett took this position in a dissenting opinion in *Twinsectra v Yardley*[146]). There is one case, normally treated as exceptional, in which strict liability was applied as the basis for recipient liability. In *Re Diplock*[147] the Court of Appeal held that charities which had mistakenly received money from an estate, because the executors had erroneously believed that a valid charitable bequest had been made, were personally liable to account to the estate for the property they had received, irrespective of the fact that they had acted entirely innocently. The liability of the charities was affirmed by the House of Lords in *Ministry of Health v Simpson*.[148]

This imposition of a strict liability to account as a constructive trustee, has not found favour in subsequent decisions.[149] It has been confined to claims involving the administration of estates, or analogous circumstances. Even in *Ministry of Health v Simpson*,[150] Lord Simonds was careful to limit the principle to the administration of an estate. He started his judgment with a warning that it was 'important in the discussion of this question to remember that the particular branch of the jurisdiction of the Court of Chancery with which we are concerned relates to the administration of assets of a deceased person'.[151]

144 [2000] 4 All ER 221 at 235.

145 [1996] AC 669 at 707. In support of this proposition he cited *Re Diplock* [1948] Ch 465 and *Re Montagu's Settlement Trusts* [1987] Ch 264.

146 [2002] 2 All ER 377. Lord Millett has also argued extrajudicially that recipient liability should be strict—see, for example, his comments in a book review, 'Landmark Cases in the Law of Restitution' [2007] 123 LQR 159 at 164–5.

147 [1948] Ch 465.

148 [1951] AC 251.

149 See the comments of Nourse LJ in *BCCI Ltd v Akindele* [2000] 4 All ER 221 at 236.

150 [1951] AC 251.

151 [1951] AC 251 at 265.

Subsequent cases have extended the personal liability imposed in *Re Diplock*[152] to circumstances analogous to the administration of estates.[153] In *Butler v Broadhead*[154] and *Re J Leslie Engineers Co Ltd (in liquidation)*,[155] it was held that there was sufficient analogy between the position of the executor of an estate and the liquidator of a company to entitle a creditor to recover from overpaid contributories in a winding-up. However, the claim did not succeed in either case,[156] and there has been no general extension of the principle to all trust situations.

The strict liability of the recipients in *Re Diplock* was also ameliorated by a requirement that the claimants first exhaust their personal remedies against the executors who had wrongly paid the charities. The Court of Appeal stated:

> Since the original wrong payment was attributable to the blunder of the personal representatives, the right of the unpaid beneficiary is in the first instance against the wrongdoing executor or administrator; and the beneficiary's direct claim in equity against those overpaid or wrongly paid should be limited to the amount which he cannot recover from the party responsible.[157]

As the Court observed, this may mean that in some circumstances the whole amount will have to be recovered from the innocent volunteers, for example if the executors are insolvent, have acted under a court order, or are protected by s 27 of the Trustee Act 1925.[158]

The strict liability imposed in *Re Diplock* has left the law in a state of confusion. On the one hand, strict liability would, to some extent, mirror the developing common law doctrine of unjust enrichment. On the other hand, the imposition of a strict liability to account as a constructive trustee is inconsistent with the general emphasis on fault as the justification for the remedy. In any event, the scope of the liability is extremely limited if other remedies against the blundering executor must be exhausted first. Moreover, the development of unjust enrichment means that the *Re Diplock* equitable accounting rule will rarely be needed. It used to be the case that the common law action for money had and received was only available for mistakes of fact.[159] Recovery is now possible for mistakes of law.[160] The executors in *Re Diplock* had paid money to persons they believed were legally entitled to receive because of their misconstruction of the relevant law, but were unable to claim repayment themselves. However, now that the barrier preventing recovery of money paid under a mistake of law has been removed, the executors would have a direct claim, subject to the defence of change of position.[161]

(ii) Degrees of knowledge

The fault required as the footing for liability has often been expressed as 'knowledge,' and this terminology was utilized by Lord Browne-Wilkinson in *Westdeutsche Landesbank Girozentrale v Islington London Borough Council*.[162] A scale of the knowledge that a

152 [1948] Ch 465.

153 See also Smith, 'Unjust Enrichment, Property and the Structure of Trusts' [2000] 116 LQR 412.

154 [1975] Ch 97.

155 [1976] 1 WLR 292.

156 In *Butler v Broadhead*, the claim was barred by the Companies Act, and in *Re J Leslie Engineers Co Ltd* the creditors exhausted their claim against the liquidators.

157 [1948] Ch 465 at 503.

158 Trustee Act 1925, s 23, provides that the personal representatives may gain protection where they advertise their intention to distribute in the *Gazette* and a newspaper.

159 See *Barclays Bank v W J Simms* [1980] QB 677; *Rover International Ltd v Cannon Film Sales Ltd (No 3)* [1989] 1 WLR 912, CA; *Lipkin Gorman v Karpnale Ltd* [1991] 2 AC 548, HL.

160 *Kleinwort Benson Ltd v Lincoln City Council* [1999] 2 AC 349; [1998] 4 All ER 513.

161 *Lipkin Gorman v Karpnale Ltd* [1991] 2 AC 548.

162 [1996] AC 669 at 707.

recipient might have possessed was provided by Peter Gibson J in *Baden Delvaux v Société Général*.[163] Having considered all the previous decisions, and drawing heavily from the doctrine of notice operating in the context of land conveyancing, including the definition of constructive notice provided in s 199 of the Law of Property Act 1925, he identified five classes of knowledge:[164] (i) actual knowledge; (ii) wilfully shutting one's eyes to the obvious; (iii) wilfully and recklessly failing to make such inquiries as an honest and reasonable man would make; (iv) knowledge of circumstances which would indicate the facts to an honest and reasonable man; and (v) knowledge of circumstances which would put an honest and reasonable man on inquiry.

Although there is some correlation between knowledge and fault, equating the two is potentially confusing and misleading. Peter Gibson J's analysis shows that the concept of knowledge for these purposes includes not only facts that the recipient of trust property actually knew but also facts that he could or should have known. Subsequent cases have sought to distinguish between knowledge of types (i)–(iii) and knowledge of types (iv) and (v). The former can be described as things that a person knows, pretends not to know, or refuses to know. They are rooted in some degree of conscious moral culpability on the part of the recipient, whereas knowledge of types (iv) and (v) derive from his negligence or inadvertence. Paraphrased differently, the question then becomes one of the degree of culpability required, rather than the extent of knowledge, although the link between the two remains.

(iii) Negligence of the recipient

Some English cases[165] have held that a stranger should be liable to account as a constructive trustee if he received trust property with knowledge of any of the five types identified in *Baden Delvaux*,[166] including mere negligence. In *El Ajou v Dollar Land Holdings plc*,[167] Millett J (who later advocated strict liability) suggested, albeit obiter, that liability could be founded upon something less than dishonesty:

> I am content to assume, without deciding, that dishonesty or want of probity involving actual knowledge (whether proved or inferred) is not a precondition of liability; but that a recipient is not expected to be unduly suspicious and is not to be held liable unless he went ahead without further inquiry in circumstances in which an honest and reasonable man would have realised that the money was probably trust money and was being misapplied[168]

Until the judgment of the Court of Appeal in *BCCI (Overseas) Ltd v Akindele*,[169] it was generally thought that the criteria of negligence had been rejected in favour of a requirement of conscious wrongdoing. However, Nourse LJ, while rejecting the formulation of a test of liability in terms of 'knowledge' in favour of a generalized requirement of 'unconscionability', held that dishonesty was not a 'necessary ingredient of liability in knowing receipt'.[170] He approved those authorities favouring liability on the basis of the lower threshold of 'constructive knowledge', which thus favours the adoption of a negligence standard.[171]

[163] *Baden, Delvaux and Lecuit v Société Général pour Favoriser le Développement du Commerce et de l'Industrie en France SA* [1983] BCLC 325.

[164] [1983] BCLC 325 at 407, considered at 408–21.

[165] *Selangor United Rubber Estates v Cradock (No 3)* [1968] 1 WLR 1555; *Karak Rubber Co Ltd v Burden (No 2)* [1972] 1 All ER 1210; *Rowlandson v National Westminster Bank Ltd* [1978] 3 All ER 370; *Belmont Finance Corpn v Williams Furniture Ltd* [1979] 1 All ER 118, CA.

[166] [1983] BCLC 325. [167] [1993] 3 All ER 717. [168] [1993] 3 All ER 717 at 739.

[169] [2000] 4 All ER 221. [170] Ibid at 231.

[171] This included a series of New Zealand cases, where all five categories of *Baden Delvaux* knowledge had been held sufficient to give rise to liability—see, for example, *Westpac Banking Corpn v Savin* [1985] 2 NZLR 41; *Nimmo v Westpac Banking Corpn* [1993] 3 NZLR 218.

It would almost certainly be wrong to interpret these English cases as accepting that 'mere' negligence will be sufficient to ground liability. The language of Millett J in *El Ajou* falls short of accepting that mere negligence would be sufficient. At the least he would have required awareness of circumstances that create a probability of wrongdoing. Similarly, Nourse LJ in *BCCI (Overseas) v Akindele* did not suggest that mere negligence should be enough for liability; he cited with approval the statements of Megarry V-C in *Re Montagu's Settlement Trusts* requiring conscious impropriety and did consider that an element of fault was necessary. Moreover, this view is consistent with other authorities in which negligence was held to be insufficient, which have not been overruled. This accords with the view that commercial parties in particular should not be burdened by the imposition of personal liability for receipt of trust property unless they are at fault. Indeed, in *Cowan de Groot Properties v Eagle Trust*,[172] Knox J pointed out that the duty of the directors of a purchasing company is to buy as cheaply as they can.[173] This, after all, fits the philosophy of profit: buy cheap and sell dear. In the view of Knox J, it would be unduly onerous to impose upon directors of a company a positive duty to inquire into the reasons for a sale to them at a bargain price. His view is supported by *Eagle Trust plc v SBC Securities Ltd*,[174] where Vinelott J emphasized that the doctrines of constructive notice had developed 'in the field of property transactions' and that the courts had been particularly reluctant to extend the doctrine of constructive notice to cases where moneys are paid in the ordinary course of business to the defendant in discharge of a liability.[175]

There is, therefore, no real authority if favour of the proposition that 'mere negligence' is sufficient for liability. The lowest test suggested is that the circumstances should have been such that a reasonable and honest recipient would have made further enquiries.

(iv) Conscious wrongdoing

Before *Akindele*, *Re Montagu's Settlement Trusts*[176] was one of the leading cases on unconscionable receipt. The tenth Duke of Manchester had sold a number of paintings which were hanging in the ancestral home. He had forgotten that they were included in a trust he had created in 1923. The question was whether his estate was liable in knowing receipt for the sums he had received from the sales, but later spent. Megarry V-C found that the Duke was not aware when he sold the paintings that they were subject to the trust, although he had access to that information. He held that the Duke of Manchester should only be held liable to account for the value of the paintings sold in breach of trust if he had acted with 'want of probity'. He considered that knowledge stemming from negligence would not establish sufficient fault to justify liability:

> knowledge is not confined to actual knowledge, but includes at least knowledge of types (ii) and (iii) in the *Baden* case . . . for in such cases there is a want of probity which justifies imposing a constructive trust . . . Whether knowledge of the *Baden* types (iv) and (v) suffices for this purpose is at best doubtful; in my view it does not, for I cannot see that the carelessness involved will normally amount to a want of probity.[177]

He referred to authorities decided prior to *Baden Delvaux*, where it had been held that negligence was insufficient to give rise to a constructive trust,[178] and emphasized that the requirement of 'knowledge' was essentially different from the concept of 'notice' used to

[172] [1992] 4 All ER 700 at 761. [173] Ibid at 761. [174] [1992] 4 All ER 488. [175] Ibid at 507.

[176] [1987] Ch 264; [1992] 4 All ER 308; [1986] Harpum 102 LQR 267 and Harpum [1987] 50 MLR 217; Hayton [1987] CLJ 385.

[177] [1987] Ch 264 at 285.

[178] *Carl-Zeiss-Stifung v Herbert Smith & Co (No 2)* [1969] 2 Ch 276; *Competitive Insurance Co Ltd v Davies Investments Ltd* [1975] 1 WLR 1240.

determine whether equitable property rights had been defeated. Subsequent cases followed the approach of Megarry V-C. In *Lipkin Gorman v Karpnale Ltd*,[179] Alliott J held that 'want of probity is the key aspect in the approach the court should take'.[180] This was affirmed by the Court of Appeal.[181] In *Eagle Trust plc v SBC Securities Ltd*,[182] Vinelott J reiterated that in the context of a commercial transaction:

> to make a defendant liable as a constructive trustee, it must be shown that he knew, in one of the senses set out in categories (i) (ii) and (iii) of Peter Gibson J's analysis in *Baden*, that the moneys were misapplied.[183]

In *Cowan de Groot Properties v Eagle Trust*,[184] Knox J similarly held that it was essential for a plaintiff to demonstrate that the recipient of trust property had knowledge within categories (i), (ii), and (iii).[185] *Re Montagu* was also endorsed by Lord Browne-Wilkinson in *Westdeutsche Landesbank Girozentrale v Islington London Borough Council*[186] and by Knox J in *Hillsdown Holdings plc v Pensions Ombudsman*.[187]

(v) Dishonesty

While *Re Montagu* held that liability to account as a constructive trustee would only be imposed against a conscious wrongdoer, the standard of liability could also be expressed as a requirement of dishonesty. In *Agip (Africa) Ltd v Jackson*,[188] Millett J warned against an 'over refinement or a too ready assumption that categories (iv) and (v) are necessarily cases of constructive notice only' and suggested that the 'true distinction is between honesty and dishonesty', which is essentially a jury question.[189] As was discussed above, in the context of liability of a stranger as an accessory to a breach of trust, the Privy Council has adopted dishonesty as the touchstone of liability in preference to knowledge.[190] In the context of the liability of a recipient of trust property, it is arguable that dishonesty is synonymous with the want of probity identified in *Re Montagu*. Both terms were used by the Court of Appeal in *Carl-Zeiss-Stifung v Herbert Smith & Co (No 2)*,[191] and the requirement of dishonesty was applied by the Court of Appeal in *Twinsectra Ltd v Yardley*.[192]

Using a test of dishonesty would apply the same test to dishonest assistance and unconscionable receipt, and for that reason might appear attractive.[193] However, there are arguments against: (1) it would deprive recipient liability of most of its value since there will be very few cases which, if dishonesty is required, could not be recast as dishonest assistance; (2) where a stranger has had the benefit of wrongfully acquired funds, the use of a less rigorous criterion for liability than dishonesty is justified; and (3) if dishonesty is required, the gulf between unconscionable receipt, the line of cases following *Re Diplock*, and the no-fault common law rules on unjust enrichment

179 [1992] 4 All ER 331; [1987] 1 WLR 987.

180 [1992] 4 All ER 331 at 349.

181 [1992] 4 All ER 409 at 420, per May LJ.

182 [1992] 4 All ER 488.

183 [1991] BCLC 438 at 509.

184 [1992] 4 All ER 700.

185 Ibid at 760. He also held that if it was necessary to have regard to knowledge of types (iv) and (v) that there still was no knowledge on the facts.

186 [1996] AC 669 at 707. See also *Hillsdown Holdings plc v Pensions Ombudsman* [1997] 1 All ER 862.

187 [1997] 1 All ER 862 at 902–3.

188 [1990] Ch 265; [1992] 4 All ER 385 at 405.

189 See also *Metall und Rohstoff AG v Donaldson Lufkin & Jenrette Inc* [1990] 1 QB 391 at 474; *Polly Peck International plc v Nadir (No 2)* [1992] 4 All ER 769 at 781–2.

190 *Royal Brunei Airlines v Tan* [1995] 2 AC 78; *Barlow Clowes v Eurotrust* [2006] 1 All ER 333.

191 [1969] 2 All ER 367.

192 [1999] Lloyd's Rep Bank 438; [2000] 59 CLJ 444 (D Fox).

193 See, for example, *Re Hampton Capital Ltd* [2015] EWHC 1905 (Ch) at [67]; *Niru Battery Manufacturing Company v Milestone Trading Ltd* [2003] EWCA Civ 1446 at [157].

becomes even wider. As was noted earlier, the requirement of dishonesty was rejected by the Court of Appeal in *BCCI (Overseas) v Akindele* in favour of a requirement of 'unconscionability'.

(vi) Unconscionability

In *BCCI (Overseas) v Akindele*,[194] the Court of Appeal sought to cut through the Gordian knot of the debate about 'knowledge' by the introduction of a new test of 'unconscionability'. That new test has been applied in subsequent decisions, but it is highly questionable whether this new approach is any clearer than what it preceded. The use of the test of unconscionability has been eschewed in other areas because of its vague and uncertain meaning. It fails to resolve the significant question whether 'conscious wrongdoing', as understood by Megarry V-C in *Re Montagu's Settlement Trusts*,[195] is required for a successful action, or whether some species of negligence is sufficient to found a claim. The adoption of unconscionability as the test indeed reopens the possibility that something akin to negligence on behalf of the recipient may be sufficient to impose liability. To put it in other language, there may be times when it is unconscionable for the recipient to receive the trust property, not because of what he knew or ought to have known, but because of what could have been discovered had the transaction been conducted differently and a different range of information had been disclosed. The test could even conceivably make liability appropriate in other circumstances where there is no kind of knowledge whatsoever, but where the recipient can be considered, for instance, to have been unfairly enriched.[196]

Nourse LJ himself noted that the test of unconscionability would not avoid 'difficulties of application', although he felt that it would 'avoid those difficulties of definition and allocation to which the previous categorizations have led'.[197] While Nourse LJ appears to acknowledge the difficulties associated with the adoption of 'knowledge' as a criterion for liability, he reintroduces them by requiring the court to determine if the recipient's 'state of knowledge' would render it unconscionable to retain the benefit. Moreover, it is difficult to see how the test of unconscionability differs from that of dishonesty in practice, particularly as Nourse LJ found on the facts that the investor had not acted 'unconscionably' on the basis that he had not acted dishonestly.[198] Since (as noted earlier) Nourse LJ dismissed dishonesty as an essential ingredient of recipient liability, he must have intended unconscionability to mean something different, but he gives no guidance as to what that difference is. This gives considerable weight to Lord Nicholls' assertion in *Royal Brunei Airlines v Tan* that 'if unconscionable means something different, it must be said that it is not clear what that something different is'.[199] What appears to have happened is that the Court of Appeal found a way of dodging the debate about the kind of fault needed by expressing the test in terms at such a high level of generalization that it cannot be disputed. The vague concept of 'unconscionability' is so malleable that it provides no clear limits, understandable by both the courts and recipients, as to when personal liability may be imposed for improper receipt of trust property.

[194] [2000] 4 All ER 221; Stevens, 'No New Landmark—An Unconscionable Mess in Knowing Receipt' [2001] RLR 99.

[195] [1987] Ch 264.

[196] Which is the way in which the test of unconscionability operates in relation to the equitable jurisdiction to set aside voluntary transactions.

[197] [2000] 4 All ER 221 at 236.

[198] Ibid at 236, 238.

[199] [1995] 3 All ER 97 at 108.

(d) **What is unconscionable?**

(i) Unconscionability confirmed but not explained

The application of 'unconscionability' to provide the requisite fault for imposing liability has been followed in subsequent cases, though they have done little to help define the boundaries of how the test will operate in practice.[200] Some cases have referred to or applied the requirement of unconscionability without explaining it.[201]

(ii) Does unconscionability equate with dishonesty?

Some cases appear to have equated unconscionability with dishonesty. For instance, in *Haque v Raja*, Henderson J rejected a claim for unconscionable assistance because the only basis pleaded was dishonesty, which 'is entirely speculative in nature, and unsupported by any firm evidence. It provides far too slender a basis upon which to found a charge of this gravity.'[202] Similarly, when Popplewell J was dealing with the fallout from the failure of a Ponzi scheme[203] in *Madoff Securities International Ltd (In Liquidation) v Raven*,[204] one of the issues was whether a Mrs Kohn, who had received over $27m in the course of fifteen years for research conducted by her on behalf of the investment company and for personal introductions to clients and others, was obliged to repay the sums. Having found that the payments had been properly made, and that there was no breach of fiduciary duty by the directors in making them, any claim to knowing receipt necessarily failed for want of a breach of trust or fiduciary duty. However, Popplewell J opined that:

> Mrs Kohn's knowledge was not such as to render receipt and retention of the payments unconscionable. They were no more than reasonable remuneration for services legitimately provided by her and she acted honestly in relation to them in all material respects.[205]

In *Arthur v The Attorney General of the Turks & Caicos Islands*,[206] the Privy Council said: 'Knowing receipt in the *Akindele* sense is . . . not merely absence of notice but unconscionable conduct amounting to equitable fraud. It is a classic example of lack of bona fides.'

(iii) Grounds for suspicion

Other cases have held that liability does not require dishonesty. In *Adelaide Partnerships Ltd v Danison*,[207] the Deputy High Court Judge said that the mental standard was less than dishonesty, 'But it still, in my view, requires knowledge of the commission of a breach of trust' or 'if he had shut his eyes to circumstances of obvious suspicion.' A similar test was applied in *Re Hampton Capital Ltd*, where the judge equated the change of position defence to a claim for unjust enrichment with unconscionability in the *Akindele* sense, and concluded that the defence was not available because the defendant 'knew enough to have reasonable grounds for suspecting the money paid to him after the first

[200] *City Index Ltd v Gawler* [2008] Ch 313 (CA). See Gardner, 'Moment of Truth for Knowing Receipt' [2009] LQR 20. The majority applied *Akindele*. Arden LJ seemed to consider the case to be one of unjust enrichment.

[201] *Hollis v Rolfe* [2008] EWHC 1747 (Ch) at 174; *Horler v Rubin* [2011] EWHC 453 (Ch); *Ecology Support Services Ltd v Hellard* [2017] EWHC 160 (Ch) at 38.

[202] [2016] EWHC 1950 (Ch) at 52.

[203] This is a fraudulent investment scheme in which high returns are promised on investments, but the returns are paid for using funds provided by new investors. In this case some $17 billion dollars was owing at the collapse of the scheme.

[204] [2013] EWHC 3147 (Comm). [205] [2011] EWCA Civ 347 at 373. [206] [2012] UKPC 30 at 40.

[207] [2011] EWHC 4090 (Ch) (Judge Cooke) at 70.

£125,000 to be stolen'.[208] Other cases have similarly taken the view that dishonesty does not need to be shown and that the test for change of position is the same as for unconscionable receipt.[209]

(iv) Negligence enough?

One case goes further still. In *Independent Trustee Services Ltd v GP Noble Trustees Ltd*,[210] a freezing order had been made to protect pension funds which had been improperly invested, a contributing factor being the alleged dishonesty of two directors. Lewison J had to deal with an application to vary the order on the application of a defendant company that had received some of the funds and wanted a relaxation to enable it to pay for its legal defence. Without stating what the test was, Lewison J expressed his view that there was an arguable case that the defendant had been dishonest, but added that: 'It is also clear from *BCCI v Akindele* that a lower threshold than dishonesty will suffice to impose liability for knowing receipt'.[211] Some of his remarks suggest that negligence would be sufficient, and he made a number of comments about the defendants having notice of the breach of trust because the investments for which the payments were made were manifestly bad.[212] The test for unconscionable receipt was not discussed when the case was considered by the Court of Appeal.[213] In *Otkritie International Investment Management Ltd v Urumov*,[214] Eder J said 'in certain circumstances a defendant will be liable if he fails to make reasonable enquiries about the circumstances of the receipt.'[215]

(v) The Baden categorization

There are other cases again which have used the *Baden* categorization. In *Armstrong GmbH v Winnington Networks Ltd*,[216] the judge said:

> In my judgment, the position, in a commercial context, can be summarised as follows:
>
> (1) *Baden* types (1) to (3) knowledge on the part of a defendant render receipt of trust property 'unconscionable'. It is not necessary to show that the defendant realised that the transaction was 'obviously' or 'probably' in breach of trust or fraudulent; the possibility of impropriety or the claimant's interest is sufficient.
>
> (2) Further *Baden* types (4) and (5) knowledge also render receipt 'unconscionable' but only if, on the facts actually known to this defendant, a reasonable person would either have appreciated that the transfer was probably in breach of trust or would have made inquiries or sought advice which would have revealed the probability of the breach of trust.[217]

This passage was referred to and followed by Morgan J in *Group Seven Ltd v Notable Services LLP*.[218] In a Court of Appeal decision, made not long after *Akindele*, it was said that actual knowledge was not essential, but what else might suffice to impose liability was left unclear.[219]

[208] [2015] EWHC 1905 (Ch) (George Bompas QC) at 65.

[209] For instance, *Otkritie International Investment Management Ltd v Urumov* [2014] EWHC 191 (Comm).

[210] [2009] EWHC 161 (Ch). [211] Ibid at 16. [212] [2009] EWHC 161 (Ch) at 17.

[213] *Independent Trustee Services Ltd v GP Noble Trustees Ltd* [2012] EWCA Civ 195.

[214] [2014] EWHC 191 (Comm). [215] Ibid at 81.

[216] [2013] Ch 156. [217] [2013] Ch 156 at 132.

[218] [2018] EWHC 2466 (Ch) at 477, reasoning expressly approved by the Court of Appeal [2020] Ch 129 at [95].

[219] *Criterion Properties Plc v Stratford UK Properties* [2002] EWCA Civ 1783/1883.

(e) Knowledge and notice

There is conflicting opinion on the relationship between knowledge for current purposes and the equitable doctrine of notice. Megarry V-C cautioned in *Re Montagu's Settlement Trusts*:

> It should be remembered that the doctrine of purchaser without notice and constructive trust are concerned with matters which differ in important respects. The former is concerned with the question whether a person takes property subject to or free from some equity. The latter is concerned with whether or not a person is to have imposed upon him the personal burdens and obligations of trusteeship.[220]

He thought that liability for unconscionable receipt should not be based on concepts of notice. In *Eagle Trust plc v SBC Securities Ltd*,[221] Vinelott J held that the level of enquiry that purchasers of land are expected to make should not be transposed to other types of business deal. He applied instead the criterion of whether there was commercially unacceptable conduct in the particular context involved, an approach approved in *Royal Brunei Airlines v Tan*.[222]

What might initially appear as a different view was taken by Lord Sumption in *Credit Agricole Corporation and Investment Bank v Papadimitriou*.[223] In his view:

> Whether a person claims to be a bona fide purchaser of assets without notice of a prior interest in them, or disputes a claim to make him accountable as a constructive trustee on the footing of knowing receipt, the question what constitutes notice or knowledge is the same.[224]

In that case, Robin Symes, an art dealer who had shared a home and a life with Christo Michailidis, dishonestly sold an art collection which belonged to Christo's father and mother. The proceeds were channelled through bank accounts via a complex arrangement involving a loan from the defendant bank repaid through the improperly acquired funds. It was (oddly) conceded that the bank was still in possession of some of the funds. Was the bank obliged to pay them to Christo's family? Since the bank had given value, it would have a defence to a proprietary claim if it was a bona fide purchaser without notice. The view of the court was that the banking arrangements were so unusual, and so lacking in commercial purpose, that they were indicative of wrongdoing[225] or gave serious cause to question the propriety of the transaction,[226] and the bank was not, therefore, a bona fide purchaser without notice. The court did not need to address knowing receipt because the local court's rejection of this claim was not appealed. Lord Sumption's remarks, however, are clearly the result of careful deliberation and should not be dismissed lightly. They are consistent with the view expressed in *Arthur v The Attorney General of the Turks & Caicos Islands*[227] that Sir Robert Megarry's views should be taken to provide a gloss on the application of the doctrine of notice:

> Knowledge, in the knowing receipt sense, means not merely notice, but, in accordance with *Akindele*, such knowledge as to make the recipient's conduct unconscionable and to give rise to equitable fraud.[228]

The doctrine of notice is, therefore, relevant, but with the caveat that in everyday commercial transactions where the rigorous procedures for the investigation of title to land are not involved, the markers of impropriety have to be much clearer. There is an elegance

220 [1987] Ch 264 at 272–3; [1994] 4 All ER 308 at 320.
221 [1992] 4 All ER 488. 222 [1995] 3 All ER 97 at 107.
223 [2015] 2 All ER 974. See Pearce, 'When must a bank repay stolen funds?' [2015] Conv 521.
224 [2015] 2 All ER 974 at 33. 225 The formulation of Lord Sumption.
226 The formulation of Lord Clarke. 227 [2012] UKPC 30. 228 [2012] UKPC 30 at 36.

in aligning the doctrine of notice with the test for unconscionable receipt: it means that a person who has given value for property is equally liable for the receipt whether they are still in possession of the funds or not.

(f) Knowledge and companies

Where a company is used as a façade or device to conceal the wrongdoing of a controller, the controller can be held liable for knowing receipt by the company,[229] and '[a] company which is used as a façade to channel misappropriate funds will be treated as being no better placed than the company's controller.'[230]

(g) Personal attributes

The personal attributes of the defendant are considered relevant in claims for dishonest assistance,[231] and it would be odd if that were not the case also for unconscionable receipt. In *Re Clasper Group Services Ltd*,[232] it was held that in determining whether a defendant had the requisite knowledge the court must take his personal 'attributes'[233] into account. Whereas a mature and experienced person might be held to have had sufficient knowledge, an innocent and inexperienced person might not. The case concerned a seventeen-year-old boy employed by his father's company who was given a cheque for £2,000 by his father a month before the company went into voluntary liquidation. He paid it into his bank account and then lent £3,000 from the account to another company that his father had acquired. Warner J held that, bearing in mind the youth, low intelligence, and inexperience of the boy, he did not have sufficient knowledge affecting his conscience to justify the imposition of a constructive trust.

Even if personal attributes are relevant, an experienced businessman will not avoid a finding of unconscionable knowledge because, although they were aware of the facts, they were not aware of the legal consequences of being a constructive trustee.[234]

(h) Where now?

It cannot easily be said that the test for liability for 'knowing or unconscionable receipt' is clear. There remains much confusion between knowledge, notice, and fault, none of which is resolved by the use of the inherently vague notion of unconscionability. If *Akindele* was intended to settle, once and for all, what needs to be shown to make a person liable for unconscionable receipt, it has singularly failed. What is meant by unconscionability remains to be explored. Most cases dealing with the issue are first instance cases, and express inconsistent and sometimes opposing views about what needs to be shown. The decisions of higher courts do not provide unequivocal guidance. The most that can be said is that the test probably lies somewhere between proof of fraud and gross negligence. It may be that there is value in leaving the criterion vague since, as Carnwath LJ said in *Criterion Properties Plc v Stratford UK Properties*: 'the purpose of the new formulation was to give greater flexibility for the application of common sense in commercial situations'.[235] Against this, flexibility equates to uncertainty. What is needed, it is suggested, is an authoritative review of the existing case law in the Supreme Court, and the

229 *The Law Society of England and Wales v Habitable Concepts Ltd* [2010] EWHC 1449 (Ch) at 20 (Norris J).

230 *Otkritie International Investment Management Ltd v Urumov* [2014] EWHC 191 (Comm) at 67, and [167]; *Trustor AB v Smallbone (No 2)* [2001] 1 WLR 1177; *Petrodel Resources Ltd v Prest* [2013] 3 WLR 1.

231 *Royal Brunei Airlines Sdn Bhd v Tan* [1995] 3 All ER 97 at 107.

232 [1989] BCLC 143.

233 Following Lawson J in *International Sales and Agencies Ltd v Marcus* [1982] 3 All ER 551 at 558.

234 *FHR European Ventures LLP v Mankarious* [2016] EWHC 359 (Ch) at 67.

235 [2002] EWCA Civ 1783/1883 at 31.

establishment of a clear and coherent set of boundaries on unconscionability or a replacement test providing greater clarity. Until then, this remains a difficult area on which to advise clients, which is an issue that needs to be resolved.

(6) Time of knowledge or fault

Brightman J, in *Karak Rubber Co Ltd v Burden (No 2)*,[236] made clear that liability is based on the wrongful use of trust property in a manner which is inconsistent with the trust. He identified three possible variants, Firstly, where a person knowingly receives trust property in breach of trust. Secondly, where a person receives trust property without notice of the trust and subsequently deals with it in a manner inconsistent with trust of which she has become aware. Finally, where a person receives trust property knowing it to be such but without breach of trust, and subsequently deals with it in a manner inconsistent with the trusts.

A recipient of trust property will only be held liable to account as a constructive trustee if he had the requisite level of knowledge or fault when he received it or disposed of it. A recipient of trust property will not, therefore, be liable to account if he had been aware of the existence of the trust before he received the property, but had honestly forgotten that it was subject to a trust at the time that it was received. Thus, in *Re Montagu's Settlement Trusts*,[237] Megarry V-C held that the tenth Duke of Manchester was not liable to account for the value of the trust chattels he had received, because he had not been aware of the existence of the trust at the date that he had received them. He explained:

> If a person once has clear and distinct knowledge of some fact, is he treated as knowing that fact for the rest of his life, even after he has genuinely forgotten all about it? . . . it seems to me that a person should not be said to have knowledge of a fact that he once knew if at the time in question he has genuinely forgotten all about it, so that it could not be said to operate on his mind any longer.[238]

He suggested a cautious approach, stating that the court should be slow to conclude that what was once known had been forgotten. Conversely, in *Sheridan v Joyce*,[239] a trustee loaned trust money in breach of trust. The recipient, Fair, did not initially know that the money was trust money, but later discovered it was. The Court of Chancery of Ireland held that he had become a constructive trustee of the money as soon as he had become aware of the facts. It should not be forgotten, though, that a person who has acquired property as a bona fide purchaser for value without notice is able to rely on that defence, even if they subsequently discover the existence of a trust.

(7) Causal link

Hoffmann LJ's criteria in *El Ajou v Dollar Land Holdings plc* for unconscionable receipt included 'knowledge on the part of the defendant that the assets he received are traceable to a breach of fiduciary duty'.[240] We have looked at the requirement of knowledge, but this criterion also requires that the defendant has received assets derived from the breach of trust or fiduciary duty.[241] There must, in other words, be a causal link between the assets received by the defendant and the breach of duty.[242] The requirement flows from the nature of liability: 'After all, receipt of trust property is the gist of the action.'[243]

[236] [1972] 1 WLR 602. [237] [1987] Ch 264. [238] [1987] Ch 264 at 284.
[239] [1844] 1 Jo & Lat 401. [240] [1994] 2 All ER 685 at 700g.
[241] See *Clydesdale Bank Plc v Stoke Place Hotel Ltd* [2017] EWHC 181 (Ch) at 166, where this meant that a claim would be less than damages for conspiracy.
[242] *Ecology Support Services Ltd v Hellard* [2017] EWHC 160 (Ch) at 37.
[243] *Novoship (UK) Limited v Nikitin* [2014] EWCA Civ 908 at [89].

(8) **Remedies**

Provided that there is no double recovery, liability for unconscionable receipt can be used in tandem with proprietary claims based on tracing and liability for dishonest assistance.[244]

(9) **Limitation**

The Supreme Court held in *Williams v Central Bank of Nigeria*[245] that a person who is liable for knowing or unconscionable assistance is not treated as a trustee for the purposes of the Limitation Act 1980, but subject to the ordinary limitation period of six years.

7 Mapping a way through personal stranger claims

What follows in Figures 37.2 and 37.3 is a tabular synopsis of how to apply the tests for personal liability for dishonest assistors and knowing recipients of trust property. It is intended as an aid only, and the relevant law has already been discussed in the rest of this chapter in detail.

(1) **Stranger who assists in a breach of trust**

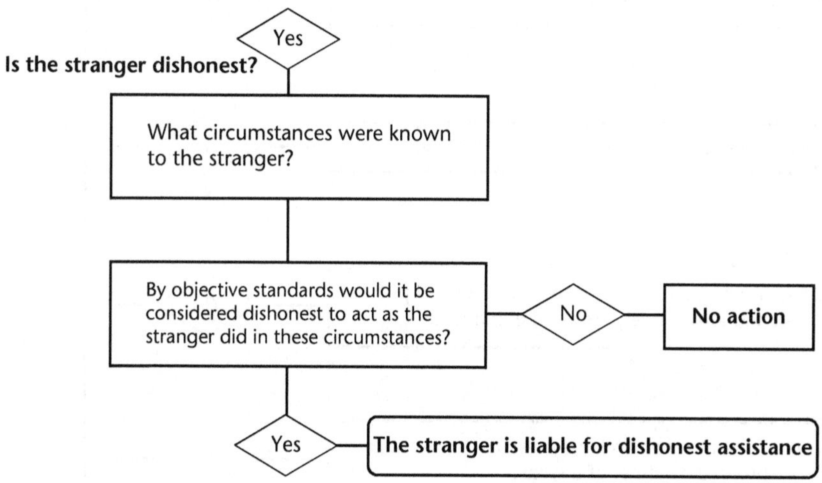

Figure 37.2 Dishonest assistance

[244] *Adelaide Partnerships Ltd v Danison* [2011] EWHC 4090; *FHR European Ventures LLP v Mankarious* [2016] EWHC 359 (Ch).

[245] [2014] UKSC 10.

(2) **Stranger who receives trust property in breach of trust**

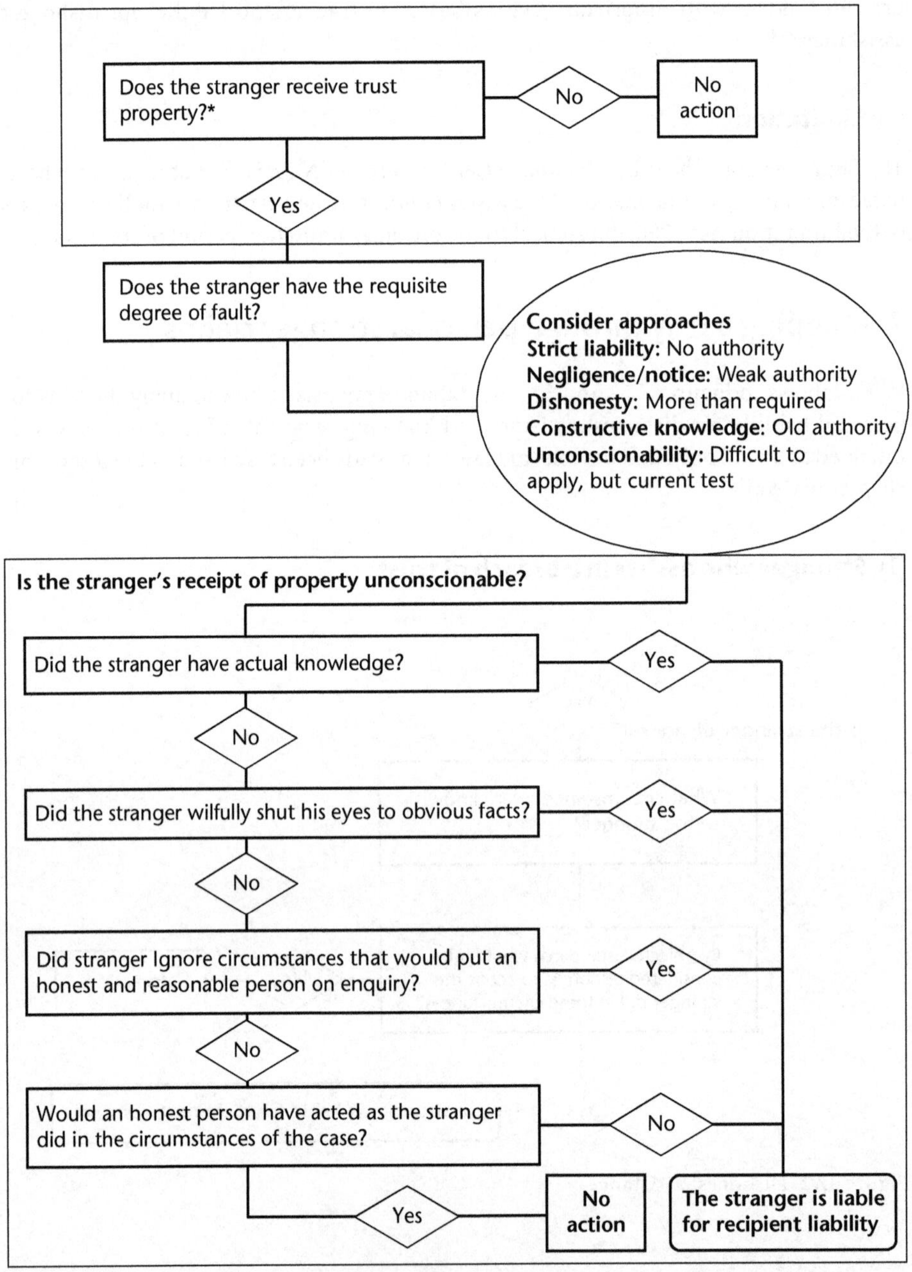

*Receipt needs control (and benefit) of the property.

Figure 37.3 Recipient liability

38

Tracing

1 Introduction

A corrupt mayor takes bribes for placing public contracts. He launders the proceeds by giving them to his wife, who (unaware of the source of the funds) uses them to purchase investment property. Other bribes are laundered through a network of companies. Some of the bribes are used to purchase investment properties overseas. Can the investment properties be recovered by the city corporation? We saw in Chapter 35 that a principal has a proprietary claim to bribes received by a fiduciary. Does that claim extend to assets acquired through those bribes which are now in third-party hands? This chapter considers the process of tracing, in other words the ways in which a person who is entitled to property can continue to assert a claim to the property even if it is now in the hands of someone else, or even if it has been mixed with other property.

2 What is tracing?

(1) Tracing is a process by which property is identified

(a) Following the original property

Tracing describes the process by which the law allows the original owner of property to identify and claim as his assets in the hands of a third party.[1] For instance, if a trustee (Tim) holds 1,000 Royal Mail shares on trust for Billy and, in breach of trust, transfers them to his daughter Dolly as an eighteenth birthday gift, tracing is the process by which Billy can assert his rights against Dolly. That form of tracing is known as 'following', because the asset is in its original form.

(b) Tracing substitute property

If Tim, instead of giving the shares directly to Dolly, had sold them and given the cash proceeds to Dolly as a gift, tracing could still apply. Billy will be unable to claim the shares back (unless the buyer was aware that they were held on trust), but he could claim the money as representing the shares. He could also have used tracing against Tim himself if Tim had sold the shares and bought a car with the proceeds. In *Foskett v McKeown*, one of the leading modern cases on tracing, Lord Millett distinguished between 'following' and 'tracing' as follows:

> Following is the process of following the same asset as it moves from hand to hand. Tracing is the process of identifying a new asset as the substitute for the old.[2]

[1] For extensive considerations of tracing see Birks (ed), *Laundering and Tracing* (Clarendon Press 1995); Smith, *The Law of Tracing* (Clarendon Press 1997).

[2] [2001] 1 AC 102 at 127; Stevens, 'Vindicating the Proprietary Nature of Tracing' [2001] Conv 94; Grantham and Rickett, 'Tracing and Property Rights: The Categorical Truth' [2000] 63 MLR 905; Berg, 'Permitting A Trustee To Retain A Profit' [2001] 117 LQR 366; Sir Robert Walker, 'Tracing after *Foskett v McKeown*' [2000] RLR 573; Jaffey, 'Tracing, Property and Unjust Enrichment' [2000] 14 Tru LI 194.

Where the property concerned is intangible property, it may not always be easy to discern the difference between the original property changing hands and new property being created in substitution for the old.[3] Fortunately, the distinction is rarely important. For convenience, the word 'tracing' is often used in this chapter to describe both following and tracing.

(c) There must be property to follow or trace

Since tracing and following are proprietary concepts, they can only be used if there was initially and there remains (in its original or any substituted form) an asset or property to which claim can be made. As Christopher Clarke J said in *Yugraneft v Abramovich*:[4]

> In order to be able successfully to trace property it is necessary for the claimant, firstly, to identify property of his, which has been unlawfully taken from him ('a proprietary base'); secondly, that that property has been used to acquire some other new identifiable property. The new property may then have been used to acquire another identifiable asset ('a series of transactional links'). Thirdly, the chain of substitutes must be unbroken.

The property need not be physical property; it could be intangible. In *Armstrong v Winnington*,[5] Deputy High Court Judge Stephen Morris QC held that European Union Allowances (EUAs)—carbon trading units of account—had the necessary characteristics set out in *National Provincial Bank v Ainsworth*[6] to be recognized as intangible property. The same would be true of other legally constructed, but transferable rights such a milk quotas or possibly taxi licences, although in the latter case the need to satisfy requirements of suitability may introduce too great a personal element. The requirement that there must be property to trace is extended by the process of reverse or backwards tracing, which may permit misappropriated funds to be traced in equity into an asset acquired before the trust property was received.[7]

Tracing can be understood as a process of investigation and as such, it requires positive evidence about misappropriation and substitutions. For this reason, the court has extensive powers to order the disclosure of documents and evidence. If appropriate, such an order will normally be accompanied by an attempt to prevent the property from being dissipated such as a freezing order barring access to the relevant property. These orders can be made very early in proceedings, although the defendant can also resist them in the court in the hope of bringing about a delay.[8]

(d) Mixing

Tracing is possible in the simple situations described earlier. It can also be used in more complex situations, where property held on trust for one beneficiary has been mixed up with property held on trust for other beneficiaries (for instance with an investment fraud), or where a trustee has mixed trust funds with his own.

[3] *Armstrong DLW GmbH v Winnington Networks Ltd* [2012] 3 All ER 425 at 67.

[4] [2008] EWHC 2613 (QBD) at 349.

[5] *Armstrong DLW GmbH v Winnington Networks Ltd* [2012] 3 All ER 425.

[6] [1965] AC 1175 at 1247–8.

[7] *The Federal Republic of Brazil v Durant International Corporation* [2015] UKPC 35; *Foskett v McKeown* [1998] Ch 265 (Court of Appeal).

[8] See *CPOD SA v de Holand Jr* [2020] EWHC 1247 (Ch); *Mediterranean Reffineria Sicilliana Petroli SpA v Mabanaft GmbH* [1978] 12 WLUK 11.

(e) Breach of trust

It is easy to forget that in most, if not all, cases of tracing or following, the trustee will have acted in breach of trust and will personally be liable. Tim should not give trust property to his daughter (unless she is entitled as a beneficiary) and will personally be liable to Billy for the loss this causes.

(2) Why use tracing?

Tracing is resorted to most frequently when the trustee is insolvent, so that a personal claim is of limited value.[9] It can also be used where a profit has been made using funds or property which originally belonged to the trust so that a claim to the property itself would be more valuable than a personal claim for damages.[10]

(3) Tracing at common law and in equity

Despite the extent to which legal and equitable rules have been harmonized, a distinction continues (at least at present) to be made between the legal and equitable rules governing tracing. While the common law rules have little application beyond the most simple of dealings with property, the equitable rules are considerably more generous and facilitate tracing through more complex transactions. The rules in equity have developed particularly to trace property through mixed funds. The equitable rules also have a moral dimension, operating more harshly against a wrongdoer who misappropriates property than against an innocent party.

(4) Tracing and claiming

Tracing is merely a process that enables an owner of property to identify assets as representing his original property. As such, the process of tracing does not itself determine the rights that the original owner may assert in any assets identified by the rules of tracing. Tracing is not therefore a remedy but a mechanism. However, tracing provides a foundation for the assertion of a right or a remedy. The original owner may seek to assert a proprietary right to any assets identified through tracing. Alternatively, he may seek a purely personal remedy requiring that the holder of the identified assets make restitution of the value of the property he has received. The assertion of an appropriate remedy in respect of assets identified through rules of tracing has been termed 'claiming'.[11] This purpose and nature of tracing was explained by Lord Millett in *Foskett v McKeown*:

> Tracing is thus neither a claim nor a remedy. It is merely the process by which a claimant demonstrates what has happened to his property, identifies its proceeds and the persons who have handled or received them, and justifies his claim that the proceeds can properly be regarded as representing his property.[12]

Whether an original owner will be able to assert a proprietary claim to any assets identified by the tracing process as representing his property will depend upon a number of factors, including the nature of his interest in the original asset, and whether any intervening defences negate his ability to claim. Where he can assert a proprietary claim his right of ownership is, in effect, preserved into the exchange product of his original property.

[9] See Oakley, 'Proprietary Claims and Their Priority in Insolvency' [1995] CLJ 377.

[10] *Re Tilley's Will Trust* [1967] Ch 1179; *Jones (FC) & Sons v Jones* [1996] 4 All ER 721; *Foskett v McKeown* [2001] 1 AC 102.

[11] See Smith, *The Law of Tracing* (Clarendon Press 1997), pp 284–369.

[12] [2001] 1 AC 102 at 128.

This chapter will provide a reminder of the importance of tracing as a process for dealing with trust property, and then examine in turn the rules of tracing at common law and in equity, and then the ensuing claiming rights of an original owner who has been able to identify assets which represent his original property.

(5) **Tracing and trust property**

The prime obligation of trustees is to allocate the trust property to those entitled to it under the terms of the trust. If they misappropriate the trust property and transfer it to third party strangers to the trust, they will clearly have acted in breach. However, if the trustees are insolvent, any remedy that the beneficiaries might be able to maintain against them for breach of trust will be useless as a means of restoring the trust fund. In such circumstances the beneficiaries may instead seek a remedy against the stranger who received the trust property. A stranger who has received trust property may be liable as a constructive trustee, and the beneficiaries may be able to pursue either proprietary or personal remedies against him. This section briefly considers the proprietary remedies available to recover the property in the recipient's hands.

(a) **Proprietary remedies against a stranger who has received trust property**

Where property is subject to a pre-existing trust, the beneficiaries are already entitled to the equitable ownership of the trust property. They enjoy a proprietary interest in the trust fund that is capable of enduring through changes in the legal ownership. While the trustees are able to transfer the legal title to the trust property, mere transfer of the legal title does not defeat the interests of the beneficiaries. Thus, if trust property is transferred by trustees to a stranger in breach of trust, the beneficiaries may be able to assert a proprietary interest in such of the property (or its traceable proceeds) as remains in the hands of the stranger. If the stranger is insolvent, any assets identifiable in his hands as representing the trust property will continue to belong to the trust in equity, and they will not therefore be available to satisfy the claims of his creditors.

(b) **Applying proprietary remedies**

A stranger who receives trust property transferred in breach of trust will not gain priority over the equitable interests of the beneficiaries unless he was a bona fide purchaser for value without notice. The interests of the beneficiaries will, therefore, be preserved if the stranger was a volunteer who had provided no consideration in return for receipt of the trust property, irrespective of whether he was aware of the existence of the trust or not. If the stranger had provided valuable consideration, the interests of the beneficiaries will only be preserved if he purchased the property with notice that it was subject to a trust. In essence, the burden falls to the recipient of trust property to demonstrate that his conscience was not affected so as to require him to observe the trust. He will only be able to do this if he can satisfy all the elements of the equitable doctrine of notice.

(i) Stranger was a volunteer

A stranger who receives trust property as an innocent volunteer will hold it subject to the beneficiaries' pre-existing equitable interest, irrespective of whether he had knowledge that it was trust property. The beneficiaries will be able to demand that he returns it or its traceable proceeds. As Lord Browne-Wilkinson observed in *Westdeutsche Landesbank Girozentrale Bank v Islington London Borough Council*:

> Even if the [third party recipient] is not aware that what he has received is trust property [the beneficiary] is entitled to assert his title in that property.[13]

[13] [1996] AC 669 at 707.

The preservation of the beneficiaries' proprietary rights to the trust property is not, therefore, determined by the fault of the recipient, and it provides extremely important protection of their interests. In *Re Diplock*[14] the executors of a will transferred a testator's residuary estate to charities in the belief that valid charitable bequests had been made. As the recipient charities were innocent volunteers, who had provided no consideration in return for the gifts received, the Court of Appeal held that beneficiaries under the will were entitled to recover any trust property, or its traceable proceeds, remaining in their hands. Where the recipient of trust property was an innocent volunteer, the beneficiaries' proprietary interests therein will be preserved in any asset identifiable in his hands by the rules of tracing, but he will not be subject to a personal liability to account as a constructive trustee. As Megarry V-C explained in *Re Montagu's Settlement Trusts*:

> Suppose... a trustee transfers trust property to a person who takes it in all innocence, believing that he is entitled to it as a beneficiary... He cannot claim to be a purchaser for value without notice, for he is a mere volunteer. If when the truth emerges he still has the property he must restore it, whereas if he no longer has either the property or its traceable proceeds, he is under no liability, unless he has become a constructive trustee.[15]

As was noted in the previous chapter, liability as a constructive trustee is imposed only if the stranger had received the trust property with the requisite degree of fault. The position of an innocent volunteer who has received trust property without fault, therefore, clearly highlights the dichotomy between the proprietary and personal remedies which may be available against a stranger who receives trust property.[16]

(ii) Stranger provided valuable consideration

A stranger who acquires trust property for valuable consideration will still hold it subject to the pre-existing equitable interest of the beneficiaries if, at the time he acquired it, he had sufficient knowledge that it was trust property to affect his conscience. He is not protected by the equitable doctrine of notice and must yield priority to the beneficiaries. If he still possesses the property received (or its traceable proceeds) he will hold it on constructive trust for the beneficiaries. The beneficiaries' equitable interests will be preserved if the purchaser acquired the trust property with actual, implied, or constructive notice of the existence of the trust. Such constructive notice includes notice of everything that he would have known about the property if he had made all the inspections and investigations expected of a reasonably prudent man of business.[17] As Millett J stated in *Macmillan Inc v Bishopsgate Investment Trust plc*:

> In English law notice ... includes not only actual notice (including wilful blindness or contrived ignorance, where the purchaser deliberately abstains from an inquiry in order to avoid learning the truth) but also constructive notice, that is to say notice of such facts as he would have discovered if he had taken proper measures to investigate them.[18]

This amounts to a negligence standard, so that a purchaser will be affixed with constructive notice if he negligently failed to realize that the property was trust property. It is important to note that, while this negligence standard of constructive notice is sufficient to prevent a purchaser acquiring trust property free from the equitable interest of the beneficiaries, it may be insufficient to fix the purchaser with a liability to account

[14] [1948] Ch 465, CA. [15] [1987] Ch 264 at 271.

[16] See Birks, *Introduction to the Law of Restitution* (Clarendon Press 1985), pp 411–12 and 439–47.

[17] See types (iv) and (v) of knowledge categorized by Peter Gibson J in *Baden Delvaux and Lecuit v Société Générale pour Favoriser le Développement du Commerce et de l'Industrie en France SA* [1983] BCLC 325. See also *Northern Bank Ltd v Henry* [1981] IR 1.

[18] [1995] 3 All ER 747 at 769.

as a constructive trustee for the property he received. As Megarry V-C observed in *Re Montagu's Settlement Trusts*:

> one has to be very careful to distinguish the notice that is relevant in the doctrine of purchase without notice from the knowledge that suffices for the imposition of a constructive trust.[19]

This view that different standards might apply may no longer reflects current thinking. In *Credit Agricole Corp and Investment Bank v Papadimitriou*[20] (discussed later), the Privy Council suggested that—at least in the context of commercial financial transactions—the test would be the same. Although the doctrine of constructive notice might seem to place a very heavy burden upon a purchaser of property to satisfy himself that it was not subject to a trust, in reality, the extent of inquiries necessary to discharge that burden will vary with the nature of the property concerned and the circumstances of the transaction. While a purchaser of land is required to make comprehensive investigations into the title of the vendor, there has been a reluctance to carry a similarly onerous requirement into commercial transactions, where the speed of transfer does not permit such extensive pre-acquisition inquiries.[21] In *Macmillan Inc v Bishopsgate Investment Trust plc*,[22] Millett J was reluctant to impose an onerous duty to investigate title to shares offered for sale, when commercial custom and practice did not require close investigation of the transferor's title. He, therefore, held that banks which had acquired shares which were held on trust for the plaintiff, having been wrongly transferred as part of the attempt to support the ailing Maxwell business empire, were not affixed with constructive notice, because they had not acted with actual knowledge or suspicion that the transferee was not the beneficial owner.[23] In *El Ajou v Dollar Land Holdings plc (No 1)*,[24] he had cautioned that a commercial party was not expected to be unduly suspicious.[25]

(iii) Stranger was a bona fide purchaser

Where trust property is received by a stranger to the trust who was a bona fide purchaser for value without knowledge of the existence of the trust (whether actual or constructive), the stranger will acquire the property free from any interests of the beneficiaries. They will no longer be able to maintain any proprietary claim to the erstwhile trust property (or its proceeds) in the stranger's hands, as equitable title has validly passed to the purchaser free from their interest. This does not affect the possibility of pursuing personal remedies.

(6) **The nature of the tracing process**

(a) **Tracing and restitution**

There has been a great deal of debate as to the conceptual nature[26] of tracing.[27] Traditionally, tracing was understood to form part of the law of property, and to operate

[19] [1987] Ch 264; [1992] 4 All ER 308 at 324–5, citing the Court of Appeal in *Re Diplock* [1948] Ch 465 at 478–9.

[20] [2015] UKPC 15.

[21] See *Manchester Trust v Furness* [1895] 2 QB 539; *Greer v Downs Supply Co* [1927] 2 KB 28.

[22] [1995] 3 All ER 747.

[23] [1995] 3 All ER 747 at 780–1. See Gegal, 'Cross-Border Security Enforcement, Restitution and Priorities', Ch 7 in Rose (ed), *Restitution and Banking Law* (Bloomsbury 1998), pp 112–19.

[24] [1993] 3 All ER 717. [25] Ibid at 739.

[26] See Birks, 'Mixing and Tracing: Property and Restitution' [1992] 45 CLP 69; Moriarty, 'Tracing, Mixing and Laundering' in Birks (ed), *Laundering and Tracing* (Clarendon Press 1995), pp 73–94; Smith, *The Law of Tracing* (Clarendon Press 1997); Birks, 'On Taking Seriously the Difference Between Tracing and Claiming' [1997] 11 TLI 2; Smith, 'Unjust Enrichment, Property and the Structure of Trusts' [2000] 116 LQR 412; Burrows, 'Proprietary Restitution: Unmasking Unjust Enrichment' [2001] 117 LQR 412.

[27] Including in the courts. See *Armstrong DLW GmbH v Winnington Networks Ltd* [2012] 3 All ER 425 at 62–98.

by preserving title to property through substitutions and mixtures. However, some academics have argued that the tracing process should be understood as part of the law of restitution.

Restitution is the response which consists of a defendant giving up to a claimant an unjust enrichment that he has received at the claimant's expense. Generally, restitution will be effected by means of a personal remedy, so that the defendant will be ordered to pay to the claimant a sum of money equivalent to the enrichment he has received. In his seminal work *Introduction to the Law of Restitution*, Professor Birks classified this remedy as 'restitution in the first measure', and the measure of the restitution is the 'value received', i.e. the extent to which the defendant was unjustly enriched. However, he has argued that restitution will sometimes be effected by means of a proprietary remedy, so that the defendant is forced to give up to the claimant any property in his hands which represents the enrichment he received. This is termed 'restitution in the second measure', and the measure of restitution is the 'value surviving' in the defendant's hands.[28] Tracing is regarded merely as a process by which 'value surviving' is identified. This is not a matter of mere semantics as this analysis has important consequences for understanding of the tracing process.

This restitutionary analysis cuts to the very heart of the nature of tracing. Traditionally, tracing has been understood to operate by descent of title, or 'vested interest'. A claimant is entitled to trace because he initially had title to property, which title he is able to follow into mixtures and exchange products because it was never lost. This analysis is rejected by Birks because of the perceived danger of a 'geometric multiplication'[29] in the claimant's wealth as he gains interests in all the exchange products for his property as well. For example, if a trustee takes £5,000 from the trust and purchases a diamond ring, which he sells for £10,000, and then purchases a car with the money, the beneficiary could have equitable title to the ring, the car, and the £10,000 in the hands of the seller of the car, all at the same time (although he will be required to elect between these rights to prevent double recovery). As an alternative to this 'vested interest' approach, Professor Birks has argued that the original owner of property has only a 'power in rem which he can bring down on assets that by the rules of tracing are identified as the surviving enrichment'.[30] The original owner has no proprietary rights to any mixed fund or to assets purchased out of a mixed fund, but only a 'power to crystallize such a right'.[31]

In his later work, Professor Burrows has also argued that tracing operates to prevent unjust enrichment. He asserts that the tracing of rights into substitute assets cannot be explained on a proprietary basis:

> Ownership of a pig can explain ownership of the piglets but does not explain why P can be said to own the horse that D has obtained in substitution for the pig stolen from P. To reason from one to the other is to apply a very tempting but, in truth, fictional notion of property.[32]

In his view, where a substitution occurs the owner of the original property is given a new title to reverse the unjust enrichment of the third party who has substituted it. Unmasking the underlying principle of unjust enrichment thus opens the door to consideration

[28] Birks, *Introduction to the Law of Restitution* (Clarendon Press 1985), pp 75–98 and 358–401.

[29] Birks, *Introduction to the Law of Restitution* (Clarendon Press 1985), p 394. See also Burrows, *The Law of Restitution* (2nd edn, Clarendon Press 2002), p 92.

[30] See Birks, 'Mixing and Tracing: Property and Restitution' [1992] 45(2) CLP 69 at 89–95.

[31] Birks, *Introduction to the Law of Restitution* (Clarendon Press 1985), p 393. See also *Re J Leslie Engineers Co Ltd* [1976] 1 WLR 292.

[32] 'Proprietary Restitution: Unmasking Unjust Enrichment' [2002] 117 LQR 412 at 418. See also Rotherham, 'The Metaphysics of Tracing: Substituted Title and Property Rhetoric' [1996] 34 Osgoode Hall LJ 321.

whether the act of substitution should automatically entitle an original owner to obtain title to the new asset. However, it can be countered that it is well established in English law that an original owner has an automatic right to claim entitlement to assets which are substituted for his property. Given that 'unjust enrichment' and 'property' are both legal constructs it is just as legitimate for a legal system to characterize such an automatic entitlement as an aspect of property as it would be to characterize it as unjust enrichment. The same goes for the conventions by which one determines the ownership of piglets produced by a pig.

In his final work before his untimely death, Professor Birks reiterated his long-held view that tracing is merely a power on the part of an owner to vest a currently traceable substitute in himself, not a right, although he acknowledged that this view is not uncontroversial.[33]

(b) Tracing as a proprietary process

It is submitted that the relegation of tracing to a mere process without proprietary implications is unduly reductionist and at odds with both authority and principle.[34] While tracing is sometimes used only as a basis for making a personal claim, the process of tracing is intrinsically proprietary in nature. Stephen Morris QC, in *Armstrong v Winnington*,[35] considered that some claims could be treated as 'proprietary restitutionary claims', because they had a proprietary base, but this confusingly and unnecessarily elides the distinct concepts of descent of title with the principles of unjust enrichment.[36] The leading cases concerning the right to trace at common law and in equity support the view that tracing operates by 'descent of title', or by way of charge, another proprietary concept.[37] This is illustrated by *Lipkin Gorman v Karpnale Ltd*, the leading case concerning common law tracing, where money had been wrongly taken from the client account of a firm of solicitors. Lord Goff held that the implication of the firm tracing the money was that it remained 'their property at common law'.[38] In *Jones (FC) & Sons (a firm) v Jones*,[39] the Court of Appeal similarly held that money was traceable at common law because the recipient had not obtained title to it. In *Foskett v McKeown*, which concerned the tracing of trust property in equity, the House of Lords clearly stated that the tracing process was to be viewed as part of the law of property, rather than restitution. Lord Millett explained:

> The transmission of a claimant's property rights from one asset to its traceable proceeds is part of our law of property, not of the law of unjust enrichment. There is no 'unjust factor' to justify restitution (unless 'want of title' be one, which makes the point). The claimant

[33] Birks, *Unjust Enrichment* (2nd edn, Oxford University Press 2005), p 198. See also Hedley and Halliwell (eds), *The Law of Restitution* (Butterworths 2002), p 58.

[34] See *Westdeutsche Landesbank Girozentrale v Islington London Borough Council* [1996] AC 669 at 709, where Lord Browne-Wilkinson stated in respect of Professor Birks' argument that unjust enrichment would give rise to an automatic resulting trust: 'First, the argument elides rights in property (which is the only proper subject matter of a trust) into rights in "the value transferred". A trust can only arise where there is defined property: it is therefore not consistent with trust principles to say that a person is a trustee of property which cannot be defined. The same argument applies to the right to trace in equity. It can only subsist in respect of identified property which is held on trust for the person tracing and not in respect of some abstract concept of value.'

[35] *Armstrong DLW GmbH v Winnington Networks Ltd* [2012] 3 All ER 425 at 88–91. See Smith, 'The Vindication of an Owner's Rights to Intangible Property' [2013] 7 JIBFL 412.

[36] The term proprietary restitutionary claim is normally used where the proprietary right is created (for instance by way of a constructive trust) to reverse unjust enrichment, but did not exist prior to the claim.

[37] See *Re Hallett's Estate* [1880] 13 Ch D 696 and the judgment of Robert Walker J in *El Ajou v Dollar Land Holdings plc (No 2)* [1995] 2 All ER 213, who suggested (at 223) that: 'tracing claims depend not on equitable ownership as such but on the concept of an equitable charge'.

[38] [1992] 4 All ER 512 at 529. [39] [1997] Ch 159.

> succeeds if at all by virtue of his own title, not to reverse unjust enrichment. Property rights are to be determined by fixed rules and settled principles, they are not discretionary. They do not depend upon ideas of what is 'fair, just or reasonable'. Such concepts, which in reality mask decisions of legal policy, have no place in the law of property. A beneficiary of a trust is entitled to a continuing beneficial interest not merely in the trust property but in its traceable proceeds also, and his interest binds every one who takes the property or its traceable proceeds except a bona fide purchaser for value without notice.[40]

Professor Burrows[41] considers this affirmation of the proprietary nature of tracing to have been unfortunate. He argues that it is a fiction to say that a claimant is given ownership of traced property because his or her ownership of the original property continues through the substitute property, and he argues that the truth is that the claimant may be given a new title to the traced property to reverse the defendant's unjust enrichment at the claimant's expense.[42] However, the rules of tracing, which will be examined later, have evolved specifically to identify property. Their one object is to identify specific assets in which the claimant has a continuing proprietary interest. This is evident from rules such as the 'lowest intermediate balance', which prevents tracing into money added later to an account which has been depleted, because that additional money is not in equity the property of the claimant. Similarly, the limitation that property will not be traced into the hands of a bona fide purchaser for value without notice demonstrates that the basis is descent of title. Tracing is impossible in such circumstances, because the proprietary chain is broken at the point where the equitable interest is defeated. The right of a claimant to take advantage of any increase in value of assets identified by the rules of tracing also points to the proprietary nature of the tracing process.[43]

It is questionable whether the supposed fear of 'geometric multiplication' of the claimant's property is justified in practice. The danger is only apparent at common law in consequence of the principle *nemo dat quod non habet*.[44] The well-established limitation that the common law cannot trace into a mixed fund itself prevents such 'geometric progression'. In equity, 'geometric multiplication' is curtailed by the principle that the right to trace is lost as against a bona fide purchaser for value. Geometric multiplication is also inhibited by the principle that a claimant cannot recover twice for the same loss.[45] Geometric multiplication provides a claimant with a choice of trails of ownership from among which he can choose. It is therefore no more of a problem than other situations in which a claimant has a choice of remedies, as for example where the purchaser of a defective product can choose to sue either the manufacturer in tort or the retailer for breach of contract.

40 [2001] 1 AC 102 at 127. Similar sentiments were also expressed by Lord Browne-Wilkinson at 109. Earlier cases supporting the proprietary nature of tracing in equity include: *Sinclair v Brougham* [1914] AC 398; *Re Diplock* [1948] Ch 465; *Chase Manhattan Bank NA v Israeli-British Bank (London) Ltd* [1981] Ch 105; *Agip v Jackson* [1992] 4 All ER 451. For criticism of such a proprietary understanding of the tracing process, see Burrows, 'Proprietary Restitution: Unmasking Unjust Enrichment' [2001] 117 LQR 412.

41 Burrows, *The Law of Restitution* (2nd edn, Butterworths 2002), p 81. See also Burrows, 'Proprietary Restitution: Unmasking Unjust Enrichment' [2001] 117 LQR 412 and Birks, 'Property, Unjust Enrichment, And Tracing' [2001] 54 CLP 231.

42 See also Rotherham, 'Tracing Misconceptions in *Foskett v McKeown*' [2003] RLR 57.

43 See also the arguments of Grantham and Rickett, 'Property Rights as a Legally Significant Event' [2003] 62 CLJ 717.

44 On a literal translation, 'no one gives what he does not have'; this is interpreted to mean that no person may give a better title to property than he enjoys himself.

45 *Van Zuylen v Whiston-Dew & Anor* [2021] EWHC 2219 (Ch) at [298].

(c) The debate continues

The previous section has argued that continuing proprietary interests are at the heart of tracing. However, this is now much more difficult to argue for a closely connected cousin of tracing, equitable subrogation. In *Bank of Cyprus UK Ltd v Menelaou*,[46] the Supreme Court was divided, but the majority of the Court was clear that a claim in unjust enrichment could lead to a proprietary remedy.[47] Subrogation is the process by which a claimant is permitted to 'step into the shoes' of a third party so that the third party's rights are transferred to the claimant. So for example in equity, if a defendant pays off a charge on property secured to a third party, the claimant might benefit from a transfer of the third party's rights over the property.

In the mortgage lending context, on a traditional approach, proprietary subrogation might only be available to a claimant lender seeking a transfer of rights where that lender's own money had been used to discharge a prior security. This would represent a logic of continuing proprietary interests. In *Menelaou*, a different approach was taken. In the case, Mr Parris and his wife Donna Menelaou (parents of Melissa Menelaou) owned Rush Green Hall, subject to a mortgage to the bank of £2.2 million. They decided to downsize, and found a purchaser for £1.9 million and a new house, Great Oak Court. Purchase was agreed before informing the bank, which reluctantly agreed, subject to repayment to it of £750,000 and a charge over the new property (bought for £875,000 in name of Melissa, who was unaware of the agreement to mortgage it to the bank). This was a transfer of the charge rather than a payment of the bank's own money. The solicitors, for some reason, forged the mortgage by Melissa, who was registered as owner subject to a charge to the bank. It was conceded that the mortgage was unenforceable. However, the Supreme Court held that Melissa held subject to an obligation to pay the bank £750,000 on the basis of unjust enrichment remedied by proprietary subrogation. In the decision, the bank was subrogated to a lien (i.e. a claim by a creditor against property) which the vendors of Great Oak Court had prior to receiving payment from the parents. The bank stepped into the shoes of a third party vendors and the relevant rights were transferred to it. This put the bank in a very similar position to the rights it would have enjoyed if the mortgage had been properly effected.

In order to come to this proprietary remedy, the majority did not require a continuing proprietary interest in the proceeds of sale of Rush Green Hall. The subrogration was possible as a response to unjust enrichment by itself. Only Lord Carnwath relied exclusively on finding a continuing proprietary interest in the proceeds of sale as being the basis for subrogration to proprietary rights.[48] Viewed in the light of the previous discussion, the case does seem to be part of a general drift away from a traditional continuing proprietary interest approach. Even if the conceptual basis—i.e. the mechanism through which a claim in unjust enrichment led to a proprietary remedy—of *Menelaou* might be thought to be in need of further clarification, *Menelaou* does show a direction of judicial travel in a context closely related to tracing.

Another case which seems to challenge the proprietary, or descent of title, approach to tracing is *National Bank Trust v Yurov*.[49] In that High Court decision, a corrupt banker

[46] [2015] UKSC 66.

[47] Ibid [96]. See for general analysis on the broad implications of this case: Buckingham and Chambers, 'Subrogation, the straightjacket of unjust enrichment and legal taxonomy *Bank of Cyprus UK Ltd v Menelaou* [UKSC 66] 3 Conv 219. Compare: Lord Sumption in *Lowick Rose LLP v Swynson* Ltd [2017] UKSC 32 at [29] where he implied that subrogation connected to unjust enrichment might be a contained circumstance without wider doctrinal ramifications.

[48] *Bank of Cyprus UK Ltd v Menelaou* [2015] UKSC 66 at [140].

[49] [2020] EWHC 1779 (Comm).

named Sergey Belyaev had transferred £5 million into a bond fund, hoping to pass all ownership to his wife. This was part of an attempt at 'judgment proofing'—i.e. keeping the value out of the hands of a court that might require him to pay damages. He was unsuccessful in that task, and although it was held that he had successfully gifted some of the value so that it had become dissipated, the remainder was found to be owned by Belyaev and his wife in 50 per cent shares.

The court attempted to impose a charging order on the value. In this enforcement context in relation to a judgment for damages, there was no question of proprietary tracing. It was accepted that the claimant bank did not have an original proprietary interest in the fund. However, the court expressly said that it was using a tracing process to assess the scope and character of its charging order. Denying the wife's claim that Belyaev's portion of the value had already been spent on legal fees and living expenses, the judge used a tracing analysis to find that the value had been depleted proportionately. The judge described this approach as 'experimental'[50] as an example of tracing being used in a non-proprietary context. It will be interesting to see if future judges follow the lead in future.

Despite pressure on the proprietary principle it cannot be thought to have been abandoned by the courts. In *Forester Maurice Labrouche v Frey & Ors*,[51] Asplin J affirmed the proprietary basis of tracing process. The facts are extremely complex, and the decision long,[52] but the essence of the case, for present purposes, was as to whether a trustee had relinquished 'founders rights'[53] under a Liechtenstein foundation, and whether these could be traced into another entity. Asplin J underlined the basis of tracing:

> It is not in dispute that: tracing involves a process of attribution, not causation and that the law deems one asset to represent another, usually through the identification of 'transactional links'; and that the focus is on attributing the value in one asset to the value in another.[54]

In dismissing the tracing claim, Asplin J upheld the proprietary basis of tracing:

> To put the matter another way, in my judgment, any proprietary element in the Founder's Rights cannot be traced into either the Newin's assets or beneficial interests because there is no evidence that that proprietary element, if any, was transferred or transformed into a different asset held by Newin. The Founder's Rights merely ceased to exist.[55]

While debate may continue over the legal basis of tracing, it is used frequently, and with increasing sophistication, to protect trust assets.

3 Tracing and claiming at common law

(1) Common law tracing through clean substitutions

It is well established that the common law rules of tracing are capable of following the ownership of property through a clean substitution, in other words, through an exchange which did not involve any mixing of the original property being traced with other

[50] Ibid at [37]. [51] [2016] EWHC 268 (Ch).

[52] See Furness QC et al, 'Where Different Legal Systems Collide: The Decision in *Labrouche v Frey & Ors* [2016] EHWC 268 (Ch)' [2016] T&T 741.

[53] These were certain rights, recognized by Swiss law, in a company.

[54] [2016] EWHC 268 (Ch) at 268.

[55] Ibid at 277. An argument that reverse tracing could deal with dissipation of the founders rights was also rejected—reverse tracing is considered later in this chapter.

property.[56] This was established in the leading early case, *Taylor v Plumer*.[57] Sir Thomas Plumer had entrusted a stockbroker, Walsh, with money for investment in Exchequer bills. Walsh instead misappropriated the money and used it to purchase bullion and American bonds. He was apprehended and surrendered the property. The central issue was whether the bullion and bonds were rightly the property of Sir Thomas, or of Walsh's trustee in bankruptcy. Lord Ellenborough held that the money which Sir Thomas had given to Walsh could be traced into the bullion and securities, and that they were properly the property of Sir Thomas. He stated the principle:

> It makes no difference in reason or law into what other form, different from the original, the change may have been made . . . for the product or the substitute for the original thing still follows the nature of the thing itself . . .

(2) **Common law tracing of tangible property into a mixed bulk**

Alongside tracing property through clean substitutions, the common law is also able to trace tangible property which is mixed with identical property so as to create a bulk. Where such mixing occurs, the owners of the goods which have been mixed become tenants in common of the whole in the proportions which they have contributed to it.[58] In *Indian Oil Corpn Ltd v Greenstone Shipping Co SA (Panama) (The Ypatianna)*,[59] an owner's crude oil was mixed with other crude oil belonging to a shipowner, which was already on board a vessel. Staughton J held that the owner was entitled to trace his oil into the bulk. In *Glencore International AG v Metro Trading International Inc (No 2)*,[60] Moore-Bick J extended this principle to a situation where oil was blended with oil of a different grade or specification, with the result that a new product was produced. The original owner was held able to trace his oil into the mixture, identifying a proportion in the new blend which takes account of both the quantity and the value of the oil contributed to the new bulk. However, the right to trace will be lost where tangible property is not merely mixed to form a bulk but is consumed in the manufacture of an entirely new product so as to lose its identity altogether. Thus, in *Borden (UK) Ltd v Scottish Timber Products Ltd*,[61] it was not possible to trace resin which was, with the authority of the owner, mixed with other materials so as to manufacture chipboard. The result might have been different if the mixing had not been by consent.[62] Where tangible property is mixed so as to form a bulk, the rights of the original owner will vary depending upon whether the mixing was wrongful or innocent, and whether the property can be divided between the parties.

[56] See Worthington, *Proprietary Interests in Commercial Transactions* (Oxford University Press 1996), pp 133–44; Smith, *The Law of Tracing* (Clarendon Press 1997), pp 162–74; Matthews, 'The Legal and Moral Limits of Common Law Tracing', in Birks (ed), *Laundering and Tracing* (Clarendon Press 1995), pp 23–72; Burrows, *The Law of Restitution* (2nd edn, Butterworths 2002), pp 83–93; [1966] 7 WALR 463 (Scott); [1976] 92 LQR 360 (Goode); [1976] 40 Conv (NS) 277 (Pearce); [1979] 95 LQR 78 (Khurshid and Matthews); [1997] LMCLQ 65 (Band).

[57] [1815] 3 M & S 562. It has been argued that this case has been fundamentally misinterpreted.

[58] *Spence v Union Marine Insurance Co* [1868] LR 3 CP 427. [59] [1988] QB 345.

[60] [2001] 1 Lloyd's Rep 284. [61] [1981] Ch 25.

[62] See Smith [2013] 7 JIBFL 412, who distinguishes between specification (mixtures which create a new thing, like the chipboard in *Borden*), accession (adding a minor component to a dominant asset, like painting a car), and true mixtures which are capable of separation.

(3) Common law tracing of money through mixed funds

While *Taylor v Plumer*[63] demonstrates that the common law can trace property through clean substitutions, it also established the limitation that the common law is incapable of tracing money through a mixed fund. Lord Ellenborough stated that it was only possible to follow assets where they are able to be 'ascertained' to represent the original property, and that such ascertainment becomes impossible 'when the subject is turned into money, and mixed and confounded in a general mass of the same description'.

Subsequent cases have thus held that the common law cannot trace money through a mixed fund.[64] Say, for example, that an agent holds shares on behalf of his principal. If the agent sells the shares and uses the proceeds to purchase a diamond ring, the common law can trace his property into the ring. However, if the agent sells the shares and then mixes the proceeds with money of his own to create a mixed fund (for instance by paying it into his personal bank account) and then uses money from the fund to purchase the ring, the common law can no longer trace because of the mixing which has taken place. The rationale for this limitation was said by Lord Ellenborough to be a difficulty of fact, not law. Money has no earmark and, therefore, cannot be distinguished within a mixed fund, whereas 'money in a bag, or otherwise kept apart from other money', is ear-marked and so outside of the limitation.

The limitation was accepted by the Court of Appeal in *Banque Belge Pour l'Etranger v Hambrouck*.[65] The case concerned a man who obtained cheques by fraud from his employers, which were paid into his bank account. He then passed the money to his mistress, Mlle Spanoghe, who paid it into her bank account. The Court of Appeal held that it was possible to trace the money at common law into Mlle Spanoghe's account. Previously it had been thought that the common law would not trace money into a bank account at all, but the Court held that, following the equity case *Re Hallett's Estate*,[66] there was nothing to prevent it examining the details of a bank account.[67] The mere fact that the money had been paid into a bank account did not itself cause a failure of the means of ascertainment.[68] However, in granting the claim, the Court stressed that there had been no mixing of the money in the bank accounts concerned. If there had been mixing, then it seems that common law tracing, unlike equitable tracing, would not have been available.[69] Similarly, in *Lipkin Gorman v Karpnale Ltd*,[70] common law tracing was only possible because the defendants had conceded that there had been no mixing of the misappropriated money.

It is important to note that while the common law is incapable of tracing money *through* a mixed fund, it is capable of tracing money *into* a mixed fund so as to establish that the recipient is subject to a personal remedy based on the receipt of that property.

(4) Common law tracing through the banking system

While the common law is prima facie capable of tracing money through a bank account, provided that it remains unmixed, later cases have found that tracing is not possible at common law where money has been transferred between bank accounts and the means

[63] [1815] 3 M & S 562.

[64] See *Re Diplock* [1948] Ch 465 at 519–20; *Agip (Africa) Ltd v Jackson* [1990] Ch 265; *El Ajou v Dollar Land Holdings plc* [1993] BCLC 735; *Bank Tejarat v Hong Kong and Shanghai Banking Corpn* [1995] 1 Lloyd's Rep 239; *Jones (FC) & Sons v Jones* [1997] Ch 159.

[65] [1921] 1 KB 321. [66] [1880] 13 Ch D 696.

[67] See *Jones (FC) & Sons v Jones* [1997] Ch 159, where money was traced at common law into a bank account.

[68] As Atkin LJ graphically said: 'But if in 1815 the common law halted outside the banker's door, by 1879 equity had the courage to lift the latch, walk in and examine the books . . . I see no reason why the means of ascertainment so provided should not now be available both for common law and equity proceedings.'

[69] [1921] 1 KB 321 at 336, per Atkin LJ; at 330, per Scrutton LJ. [70] [1991] 2 AC 548.

of exchange has inevitably involved some element of mixing.[71] In *Agip (Africa) Ltd v Jackson*,[72] the claimant firm was defrauded by its chief accountant, Zdiri. He altered the names of the payee on genuine payment orders in favour of dummy companies he had created. One payment of $518,000 was made to a dummy company, Baker Oil Services Ltd, who held an account at a branch of Lloyds Bank in London. On receiving the payment order, Agip's bankers telegraphed instructions to Lloyds Bank Overseas Division to credit the account of Baker Oil at their London branch with a corresponding amount. At the same time, their correspondent bank in New York debited their account and credited Lloyds Bank's correspondent bank in New York. The next day the money was transferred from the Baker Oil account to the account of the defendants, who were a firm of accountants in the Isle of Man. All but $45,000 was then paid out. There had been no mixing of the money in the Baker Oil account. At first instance Millett J held that Agip could not trace the money at common law. One reason for this denial focused on the nature of the transfer. He held that:

> The money was transmitted by telegraphic transfer. There was no cheque or any equivalent. The payment order was not a cheque or its equivalent . . . Nothing passed between Tunisia and London but a stream of electrons. It is not possible to treat the money as received by Lloyds Bank of London, or its correspondent bank in New York, as representing the proceeds of the payment order or of any other physical asset previously in its hands . . .[73]

This argument was rejected by the Court of Appeal, where Fox LJ took the view that it did not matter that the transfer had been by order rather than cheque.[74] More significantly, however, Millett J had held that the claimants were not entitled to trace at common law because the money must have been mixed with other money when the transfer took place through the New York clearing system between Agip and Lloyds' correspondent banks. This reasoning was supported by the Court of Appeal,[75] and tracing at common law was thus prevented.

Similar reasoning was employed in *Bank Tejarat v Hong Kong and Shanghai Banking Corpn (CI) Ltd*,[76] where the claimant had paid the defendants DM3.4m via the Frankfurt clearing system. Tuckey J applied the principle identified in *Agip (Africa) Ltd v Jackson* and held that, as the claimant's money would inevitably have become mixed with other money through the Frankfurt deutschmark clearing system, it was impossible to trace the money at common law into the hands of the defendants.[77] The claimant's claim to personal restitution at common law by way of an action for money had and received, therefore, failed.

In both cases the inadequacy of the common law rules of tracing required the claimants to turn instead to equity, asserting that the misappropriated money was subject to a trust and that the respective defendants were liable on the grounds of knowing assistance.[78] It is argued that the refusal to allow common law tracing on the grounds of inevitable mixing during the process of transfer of funds involves an unduly literalistic analysis of

[71] See Smith, *The Law of Tracing* (Clarendon Press 1997), pp 249–62.

[72] [1990] Ch 265; [1992] 4 All ER 385; Birks, 'Misdirected Funds Again' [1989] 105 LQR 528; Sir Peter Millett, 'Tracing the Proceeds of Fraud' [1991] 107 LQR 71; [1991] Ch 547; [1992] 4 All ER 451; Harpum, 'Equitable Liability For Money Laundering' [1991] 50 CLJ 409; Goulding, 'Equity and the Money Launderers' [1992] Conv 367; Swadling, 'The Law of Restitution' [1992] All ER Rev 258–65.

[73] [1990] Ch 265 at 399.

[74] [1992] 4 All ER 451 at 465.

[75] [1992] 4 All ER 451 at 465, per Fox LJ.

[76] [1995] 1 Lloyd's Rep 239; Birks, 'Tracing Misused *Bank Tejarat v Hong Kong and Shanghai Banking Corp*' [1995] 9 TLI 91 and 'Persistent Problems in Misdirected Money' [1996] LMCLQ 1.

[77] [1995] 1 Lloyd's Rep 239 at 245.

[78] Now dishonest assistance: *Royal Brunei Airlines v Tan* [1995] 2 AC 378.

the tracing process. Whenever transfers occur between banks, whether by virtue of an electronic transfer or a cheque which is presented through the clearing system, it is not as if the specific money held in the account from which the funds are drawn is transferred to the bank holding the account into which it is to be paid. Where money is held in a bank account, the nature of the relationship between the bank and its customer is one of debtor and creditor, so that there is no real connection between the balance in an account and any specific money as such. Where money is debited from one account and credited to another, there should simply be an evidential presumption that the money represented thereby has passed from one account to the other. The means of transfer operative between the banks holding the accounts should not prevent that inference.

Unless such an inference is operative there is no reason why the common law should ever be able to trace into or through a bank account. The mere transfer of money between accounts held at different domestic banks is effected through the clearing system and yet this does not seem to have prevented common law tracing. In *Jones (FC) & Sons (a firm) v Jones*,[79] the partner of the claimant firm drew cheques totalling £11,700 on a joint account at the Midland Bank, which were paid into an account opened in the name of his wife with a firm of commodity brokers. She then received cheques for £50,760 from the commodity brokers, which she paid into a deposit account. The Court of Appeal held that the firm's trustee in bankruptcy should be entitled to trace at common law and that it was not necessary to take account of the reality of the clearing system which lay behind the transaction. Millett LJ stated that:

> Accordingly, the trustee can follow the money in the joint account at Midland Bank, which had been vested by statute in him, into the proceeds of the three cheques which Mrs Jones received from her husband. The trustee does not need to follow money from one recipient to another or follow it through the clearing system; he can follow the cheques as they pass from hand to hand. It is sufficient for him to be able to trace the money into the cheques and the cheques into their proceeds.[80]

If this reasoning is correct (and it is suggested that it is, since it reflects the reality of banking practice), there is equally no reason why the court should have been concerned with the means of transfer through the clearing system in *Agip (Africa) Ltd v Jackson* and *Bank Tejarat v Hong Kong and Shanghai Banking Corpn (CI) Ltd*. Surely it is enough to identify a debit from one account echoed by a corresponding receipt by another. This is as much a swap of one chose in action for another as if a cheque had physically changed hands. Millett LJ seems to lay great stress upon the presence of a physical cheque, which would suggest a return to his argument in *Agip (Africa) Ltd v Jackson*[81] that the common law cannot trace through an electronic transfer, which was rejected by the Court of Appeal.[82] Some clarification has been provided in relation tracing funds through interbank transfers. *Credit Agricole Corp and Investment Bank v Papadimitriou*[83] was a complex, inter-family money-laundering case. For many years until his death in 1999, Christo Michailidis had shared a home and life with Robin Symes, a dealer in modern art. Less than a year after Christo's death, Symes sold an art collection which the Gibraltar courts found belonged to Christo's father and mother. When Christo's family found out about the sale, they began proceedings to recover the proceeds. The collection had been sold by Symes to an art deco dealer for $15 million; around $10 million of the proceeds had then

[79] [1997] Ch 159. [80] [1997] Ch 159 at 169. [81] [1990] Ch 265; [1992] 4 All ER 385.

[82] In *SmithKline Beecham v Apotex Europe Ltd* [2007] Ch 71, Jacobs LJ considered that the *Jones* case was a clear example of constructive trusteeship and therefore equitable tracing would have been available. If true, this would, of course, solve the issue, as will be demonstrated later in the chapter.

[83] [2015] UKPC 13. See Pearce, 'Case Note: When must a bank repay stolen funds?' [2015] Conv 51.

been laundered through a network of companies controlled by Symes. One claim made against the bank was a proprietary claim based on equitable tracing, and this was the issue heard on appeal.

In the Privy Council, it was not in dispute that the bank had received funds that originated from the sale, despite a complex money-laundering scheme that had been designed to obscure this. One significant aspect of the scheme concerned an international, inter-bank transfer, made between the defendant bank and another. The Privy Council did not question whether the funds could be traced, and the case therefore provides useful confirmation that, in equity at least, tracing is not inhibited or prevented by inter-bank transfers where the only evidence of funds moving is for one account to be debited and another to be credited.

The nature of a bank account is also another cause for difficulty in relation to common law tracing. As has been noted, the relationship between banker and customer is one of debtor and creditor. In *R v Preddy*,[84] a criminal case concerning mortgage fraud, the House of Lords held that where money was debited from one account and paid into another account, the second account holder had not obtained the property of the first account holder so as to render him liable to conviction for theft under s 15(1) of the Theft Act 1968.[85] Lord Goff explained:

> The question remains . . . whether the debiting of the lending institution's bank account, and the corresponding crediting of the bank account of the defendant or his solicitor, constitutes obtaining of that property. The difficulty in the way of that conclusion is simply that, when the bank account of the defendant (or his solicitor) is credited, he does not obtain the lending institution's chose in action. On the contrary that chose in action is extinguished or reduced pro tanto,[86] and a chose in action is brought into existence representing a debt in an equivalent sum owed by a different bank to the defendant or his solicitor. In these circumstances it is difficult to see how the defendant thereby obtained property belonging to another, ie to the lending institution.
>
> Professor Sir John Smith has suggested that 'Effectively, the victim's property has been changed into another form and now belongs to the defendant. There is the gain and equivalent loss which is characteristic of, and perhaps the substance of, obtaining'.[87] But even if this were right, I do not for myself see how this can properly be described as obtaining property belonging to another. In truth the property which the defendant has obtained is the new chose in action constituted by the debt now owed to him by his bank, and represented by the credit entry in his own bank account.[88]

If this analysis is correct, it appears to remove any ability of the common law to trace money through bank accounts. If the increased balance in the credited account cannot be identified with the corresponding reduction in the balance of the debited account, then it is untraceable into that account. This is fundamentally inconsistent with the decision of the Court of Appeal in *Jones (FC) & Sons (a firm) v Jones*,[89] where it was held that the money credited to Mrs Jones' account belonged at law to the firm from whose account it had been debited. It is equally inconsistent with *Banque Belge Pour l'Etranger v Hambrouck*.[90] Even though the claimants were seeking a personal remedy, their right to restitution was dependent upon establishing that the defendant had received their money into her bank account. It is also suggested that it is inconsistent with the judgment of the House of Lords

[84] [1996] AC 815; Fox, 'Property Rights and Electronic Funds Transfers' [1996] LMCLQ 456.
[85] Obtaining property by deception. [86] Meaning 'reduced as far as it can go'.
[87] [1995] Crim LR 564, 565–6.
[88] [1996] AC 815 at 834. [89] [1997] AC 159. [90] [1921] 1 KB 321.

in *Lipkin Gorman v Karpnale Ltd*,[91] where Lord Goff held that the claimant firm of solicitors was entitled to trace money misappropriated from their client account:

> There is in my opinion no reason why the solicitors should not be able to trace their property at common law in that chose in action, or in any part of it, into its products, ie cash drawn by Cass from their client account at the bank. Such a claim is consistent with their assertion that the money so obtained by Cass was their property at common law.[92]

It would be utterly illogical if the firm were permitted to trace if Cass withdrew cash from their client account, and presumably also if he subsequently paid the cash into his own bank account, but not if he arranged for a direct transfer of money from their client account to his own bank account. Yet this would seem to be the implication of the decision in *R v Preddy*.[93] The ramifications of this case for the ability to trace through bank accounts at common law have yet to be fully considered by the courts.[94] However, the decision prompted statutory reform of the law of theft to ensure that defendants who received mortgage funds by fraud would be guilty of an offence.[95]

(5) **Criticism of the common law rules of tracing**

While the authorities have consistently held that the common law is incapable of tracing property through a mixed fund, this limitation has been subject to much criticism. The very origins of this limitation have been challenged by Lionel Smith, who has argued that, in *Taylor v Plumer*,[96] the common law court was in fact considering the equitable rules of tracing, with the implication that there was therefore no reason for the common law to consider itself limited in subsequent cases.[97] While this misunderstanding was acknowledged by Millett LJ in *Jones (FC) & Sons (a firm) v Jones*,[98] he made clear that this alone did not permit the overthrow of the settled common law principle which had emerged despite the misunderstanding.[99]

Even though the limitation cannot be eliminated merely because of historical misunderstanding of *Taylor v Plumer*,[100] it is open to objections on its own terms. It appears to be rooted in the perception that the common law cannot identify property in a mixed fund but, as commentators have pointed out,[101] there is no reason why the common law cannot recognize joint title to a mixed fund through a tenancy-in-common. This possibility was recognized in *Spence v Union Marine Insurance Co Ltd*,[102] where bales of wool were mixed and it was not possible to identify their owners because the identifying marks had been lost in a shipwreck. The court held that there was a tenancy-in-common.

There appears to be no rational justification for treating money differently. The consequence has been to force claims to mixed funds to be made in equity. To enable equitable tracing claims to succeed where there is no express trust, the courts may have been tempted to expand the circumstances in which constructive trusts will be found. It is questionable whether the expansion of equitable rights and interests in the commercial field is appropriate.[103] The common law rules of tracing have also restricted the availability of common

[91] [1991] 2 AC 548. [92] [1991] 2 AC 548 at 574. [93] [1996] AC 815.

[94] For comment on the implications of *R v Preddy* in the context of tracing, see Fox, 'Property Rights and Electronic Funds Transfers' [1996] LMCLQ 456.

[95] Theft (Amendment) Act 1996.

[96] [1815] 3 M & S 562.

[97] Smith, 'Tracing in *Taylor v Plumer*: Equity in the Court of King's Bench' [1995] LMCLQ 240.

[98] [1997] AC 159. [99] [1997] AC 159 at 169. [100] [1815] 3 M & S 562.

[101] Pearce, 'A Tracing Paper' [1976] Conv (NS) 277. [102] [1868] LR 3 CP 427.

[103] E.g. *Re Goldcorp Exchange* [1995] 1 AC 74; *Westdeutsche Landesbank Girozentrale v Islington London Borough Council* [1996] AC 669.

law restitution through the action for money had and received, since it cannot be demonstrated that a defendant was enriched by the receipt of the claimant's property where it has passed through a mixed fund. Thus, in *Bank Tejarat v Hong Kong and Shanghai Banking Corpn (CI) Ltd*,[104] the claimant's claim for common law restitution on the grounds of mistake failed because it was not able to trace its money into the hands of the defendants because it had become mixed in the Frankfurt clearing system. At present it is impossible to utilize the equitable rules of tracing to found a common law claim to restitution.[105]

There is no basis in principle, or in practice, for emasculating the common law rules by prohibiting tracing through a mixed fund. If the common law rules were to develop so as to enable such tracing, there would be less need for an inappropriate expansion of equity and fiduciary relationships into the commercial sphere. In *Jones (FC) & Sons (a firm) v Jones*,[106] Millett LJ expressed dissatisfaction with the present position:

> There is no merit in having distinct and different tracing rules at law and in equity, given that tracing is neither a right nor a remedy but merely the process by which the plaintiff establishes what has happened to his property and makes good his claim that the assets which he claims can properly be regarded as representing his property. The fact that there are different tracing rules at law and in equity is unfortunate though probably inevitable, but unnecessary differences should not be created where they are not required by the different nature of legal and equitable doctrines and remedies. There is, in my view, even less merit in the present rule which precludes the invocation of the equitable tracing rules to support a common law claim; until that rule is swept away unnecessary obstacles to the development of a rational and coherent law of restitution will remain.[107]

In *Foskett v McKeown* he reiterated his dissatisfaction with the current position in the House of Lords, and stated:

> Given its nature, there is nothing inherently legal or equitable about the tracing exercise. There is thus no sense in maintaining different rules for tracing at law and in equity. One set of tracing rules is enough . . . There is certainly no logical justification for allowing any distinctions between them to produce capricious results in cases of mixed substitutions by insisting on the existence of a fiduciary relationship as a precondition for applying equity's tracing rules. The existence of such a relationship may be relevant to the nature of the claim which the plaintiff can maintain, whether personal or proprietary, but that is a different matter.[108]

However, given that the case involved a straightforward situation where a trustee had misappropriated trust property, and that the equitable tracing rules were therefore undoubtedly available, he concluded that it was not the occasion to explore the relationship between equitable and common law tracing rules further. His comments are, therefore, strictly obiter, and the traditional dichotomy between the rules of tracing in equity and at common law remains intact, albeit on notice of impending demise.[109]

(6) Claiming at common law

It has been seen that the common law enables legal owners to trace their property through clean substitutions, and to trace tangible property into a mixed bulk. Once the tracing process has identified assets which represent the original property, the original

[104] [1995] 1 Lloyd's Rep 239; [1995] 9 TLI 91 (Birks).

[105] See *Jones (FC) & Sons v Jones* [1997] AC 159 at 169–70, per Millett LJ.

[106] [1997] Ch 159. [107] [1997] Ch 159 at 169–70. [108] [2001] 1 AC 102 at 128.

[109] See, however, *Shalson v Russo* [2005] Ch 281 at 314, 104, where Rimer J opined that the distinction between common law and equitable tracing remained, despite obiter comments to the contrary by Lord Millett in *Foskett v McKeown* [2001] 1 AC 102 at 129.

owner may be able to assert a claim thereto. The original owner may be entitled to assert a proprietary right, or he may be entitled to claim restitution, which is a personal remedy.

(a) Claiming assets which are the product of a clean substitution

Common law tracing through clean substitutions operates on the basis of the preservation of the claimant's title to the property being traced. The claimant had legal title before any clean substitutions took place, and such substitutions are not able to deprive him of his title. Except in the case of currency (banknotes and coins), to which special rules apply,[110] even a bona fide purchaser will not take free from the claimant's original title because his legal title is good against the world and cannot be defeated. This seems to have been the rationale of *Taylor v Plumer*,[111] where Lord Ellenborough said that Sir Thomas had simply 'repossessed himself of that, of which . . . he had never ceased to be the lawful proprietor'. In *Lipkin Gorman v Karpnale Ltd*, where a solicitor had taken money for gambling from the client account of his firm, Lord Goff held that the firm could trace at common law:

> There is in my opinion no reason why the solicitors should not be able to trace their property at common law in that chose in action [the client account], in any part of it, into its product, ie cash drawn by Cass from their client account at the bank. Such a claim is consistent with their assertion that the money so obtained by Cass was their property at common law.[112]

Historically, except for land, the common law did not possess adequate remedies to enable the claimant to vindicate his proprietary entitlement to assets identified as representing his original property. As Professor Goode[113] has pointed out, until changed by statute,[114] the common law was only ever able to offer a personal remedy in damages for detinue or conversion. However, in some older cases, the owner was able to recover his property through self-help,[115] and more recent cases have now established beyond doubt that an original owner may claim legal title to any assets identified by the rules of tracing.[116]

Where a legal owner can identify assets in the hands of a third party as representing his original property, he will be entitled to claim them as his own.[117] In *Lipkin Gorman v Karpnale Ltd*,[118] Lord Goff stated that the legal owner of property was entitled to trace or follow his property into its product. This principle was applied by the Court of Appeal in *Jones (FC) & Sons (a firm) v Jones*,[119] where the defendant had received money drawn from the bank account of a firm which had committed an act of bankruptcy before it had been adjudicated bankrupt. The money was invested in an account held by a firm of commodity brokers which dealt in potato futures. The investment was highly successful and

[110] See Fox, 'Bona Fide Purchase and the Currency of Money' [1996] CLJ 547; Fox, 'The Transfer of Legal Title to Money' [1996] RLR 60.

[111] [1815] 3 M & S 562.

[112] [1991] 2 AC 548; at 529, [1992] 4 All ER 512; [1991] Lloyd's MCLQ 473 (Birks); [1991] 107 LQR 521 (Watts); [1992] Conv 124 (Halliwell); [1992] 55 MLR 377 (McKendrick); [1992] 45(2) CLP 69 (Birks).

[113] Goode, 'The Right to Trace and Its Impact in Commercial Transactions' [1976] LQR 360.

[114] Torts (Interference with Goods) Act 1977, s 3, replacing the Common Law Procedure Act 1854, s 78, entitles the court to order the delivery of goods.

[115] As in *Taylor v Plumer* [1815] 3 M & S 562.

[116] See *Jones (FC) & Sons v Jones* [1997] AC 159.

[117] *Armstrong DLW GmbH v Winnington Networks Ltd* [2012] 3 All ER 425 at 88–92. Stephen Morris QC considered this to be a proprietary restitutionary claim, although this confuses the historic distinction between proprietary claims and restitutionary claims.

[118] [1991] 2 AC 548 at 573.

[119] [1997] Ch 159; Andrews and Beatson, 'Common Law Tracing: Springboard or Swan Song?'; Fox, 'Common Law Claims to Substituted Assets' [1997] CLJ 30. See also Davern, 'Common Law Tracing, Profits and the Doctrine of Relation Back' [1997] RLR 92–6.

the account contained almost five times as much money as had been initially invested. The Court of Appeal held that, as the firm could trace the money at common law into the account with the brokers, its trustee in bankruptcy was entitled to the money in the account (which had been paid into court). Beldam LJ stated:

> There is now ample authority for the proposition that a person who can trace his property into its product, provided the product is identifiable as the product of his property, may lay legal claim to that property.[120]

Where an owner is entitled to claim specific assets at common law he will be entitled to take advantage of any appreciation in value which they have experienced.

(b) Claiming assets where tangible property has been mixed

The common law permits the tracing of tangible property into a mixed bulk. Where a mixed bulk has been created, the rights of an original owner will vary depending upon whether the bulk can be separated into proportionate shares representing the assets of the contributors.

(i) Claiming where the bulk can be divided into proportionate shares

Where the bulk is capable of division, a contributor will be entitled to claim the proportionate share which represents his original property, and of which he is a tenant-in-common. Such division will usually be possible if the property is fungible in nature, such as when it consists of grain, oil, or wine.[121] The principle was stated by Staughton J in *Indian Oil Corpn Ltd v Greenstone Shipping Co SA (Panama) (The Ypatianna)*:

> where B wrongfully mixes the goods of A with goods of his own, which are substantially of the same nature and quality, and they cannot in practice be separated, the mixture is held in common and A is entitled to receive out of it a quantity equal to that of his goods which went into the mixture, any doubt as to that quantity being resolved in favour of A.[122]

(ii) Claiming where the bulk cannot be divided into proportionate shares

In contrast, where property was wrongfully mixed to form a bulk that cannot be divided into the proportionate shares of the contributors, the original owner will be entitled to claim the entire bulk. The right to claim the entire bulk in such circumstances was recognized by the House of Lords in *Foskett v McKeown*,[123] on the grounds that the wrongdoer is entitled to claim only what he can prove is his own. Such circumstances are admittedly likely to be rare, but Lord Millett referred to the Canadian case of *Jones v De Marchant*[124] by way of example. In that case, a husband had wrongfully used eighteen beaver skins belonging to his wife, together with four skins of his own, to have a fur coat made up, which he gave to his mistress. Since the skins could no longer be separated, it was held that the wife was entitled to ownership of the entire coat. If the amalgamation of two products to make a new one had been carried out with consent, then any claim to the original materials or to the new product would be lost.[125]

(c) Claiming personal restitution at common law

The process of tracing may also provide a foundation for a personal claim to restitution. Where property is misappropriated or misdirected, a recipient will be treated as having been unjustly enriched. The extent of his enrichment is the value of the property that he

120 [1997] Ch 159 at 171.

121 *Foskett v McKeown* [2001] 1 AC 102 at 133, per Lord Millett.

122 [1988] QB 345, 371.

123 [2001] 1 AC 102.

124 [1916] 28 DLR 561.

125 *Borden (UK) Ltd v Scottish Timber Products Ltd* [1981] Ch 25.

had received. If he has received, but subsequently dissipated, misappropriated property, then a proprietary claim will not be available because there is no longer any specifically identifiable asset. As Lord Lane CJ observed in *A-G's Reference (No 1 of 1985)*,[126] there can be no proprietary remedy unless there is an asset which can be 'identified as a separate piece of property'. The original owners may, however, be entitled to claim personal restitution from the recipient: a claim that because the recipient had been enriched by the receipt of the property, he must compensate the original owner to that extent. A personal restitutionary claim may also be more advantageous to an original owner than a proprietary claim, even where the property has not been dissipated, if the assets which represent his property have subsequently fallen in value, since the measure of restitution will be determined by the value of the property at the point of receipt. However, such a personal remedy will only be more advantageous in practice if the recipient is solvent and able to discharge the obligation to make restitution.

The liability of a person who has received property belonging to another to make restitution at common law is strict, subject to the availability of the defence of change of position. The role of common law tracing as a foundation for a personal liability to make restitution is evident in *Lipkin Gorman v Karpnale Ltd*,[127] where a solicitor had misappropriated money from his firm's client account in order to finance his gambling at the Playboy Club. His firm sought to recover restitution from the club of the misappropriated money it had received. The firm could not make a proprietary claim to any assets in the club's hands as none could be identified which were the product of the money received. The common law rules would not permit tracing once the money had become mixed with other money of the club. However, the rules of common law tracing did establish that the club had received money which belonged to the firm, and thus entitled the firm to maintain the common law action for money had and received. As Lord Goff explained:

> It is well established that a legal owner is entitled to trace his property into its product, provided that the latter is indeed identifiable as the product of his property . . . Before Cass drew upon the solicitor's client account at the bank, there was of course no question of the solicitor's having any legal property in any cash lying at the bank. The relationship of the bank with the solicitors was essentially that of debtor and creditor; and since the client account was at all material times in credit, the bank was the debtor and the solicitors were its creditors. Such a debt constitutes a chose in action, which is a species of property; and since the debt was enforceable at common law, the chose in action was legal property belonging to the solicitors at common law. There is in my opinion no reason why the solicitors should not be able to trace their property at common law in that chose in action, or in any part of it, into its product, ie cash drawn by Cass from their client account at the bank. Such a claim is consistent with their assertion that the money obtained by Cass was their property at common law . . . it further follows, from the concession made by the respondents,[128] that the solicitors can follow their property into the hands of the respondents when it was paid to them at the club.[129]

Thus, the firm's ability to trace the money drawn from the client account into the hands of the club, via the activities of the misappropriating solicitor, was vital to the establishment of their entitlement to restitution by way of an action for money had and received. Lord Goff stressed that the firm's claim was not proprietary, although it was founded upon the receipt of property.[130]

[126] [1986] QB 491 at 506. [127] [1991] 2 AC 548.

[128] The respondents had conceded that if it could be shown that the firm enjoyed legal title to the money from the client account in the hands of the solicitor, then that title was not defeated by mixing of that money with other money in his hands.

[129] [1991] 2 AC 548 at 572–3. [130] [1991] 2 AC 548 at 572.

4 Tracing and claiming in equity

(1) The scope of equitable tracing

Whereas the common law rules of tracing have remained restricted, equity developed rules which are much more flexible. There is no barrier preventing the tracing of equitable proprietary interests through a mixed fund. The rules, which originated in the context of the misappropriation of property subject to an express trust, are derived from evidential presumptions which enable the court to determine whether property has survived through mixing, and whether any assets purchased with money from a mixed fund can be said to represent property contributed to the mixture. The equitable rules are particularly designed to deal with mixing of funds in a bank account. By necessity they are rough and ready and not overly sophisticated. The presumptions on which they are founded also take account of the moral blameworthiness of the parties whose funds have been mixed. If a mixed fund consists of misappropriated trust property and the property of the wrongdoing trustee, the rules operate harshly against the wrongdoer. In contrast, if the mixture is comprised of misappropriated trust property and that of an innocent volunteer, they seek to achieve a fair balance between the two innocent parties.

(2) The right to trace in equity

Equitable tracing is not available in every situation in which property has been misappropriated or misapplied. Historically, equity has taken the view that tracing is only possible where there was an initial fiduciary relationship. While the language of a fiduciary relationship in this context is somewhat imprecise and opaque,[131] what is really required is that the property sought to be traced was subject to a trust and thus belonged to the claimant in equity.

(a) The requirement of a fiduciary relationship

The present position of the English cases is that an initial fiduciary relationship is a prerequisite of the right to trace in equity. This was reaffirmed in *Westdeutsche Landesbank Girozentrale v Islington London Borough Council*.[132] While the House of Lords overruled the earlier decision of *Sinclair v Brougham*,[133] Lord Browne-Wilkinson was at pains to stress that this did not amount to a rejection of the requirement of a fiduciary relationship, since the House of Lords was not wishing to cast any doubt on the principles of tracing established in the later case of *Re Diplock*.

In *Re Diplock*[134] charities had wrongly received payments of £203,000 under a will. The next of kin were held entitled to trace the money in equity into the charities' hands, because the executors clearly stood in a fiduciary relationship to the estate. The Court of Appeal had examined the judgments of the House of Lords in *Sinclair v Brougham*[135] and concluded that a fiduciary relationship was a prerequisite to tracing in equity. Lord Greene MR stated:

> Lord Parker and Lord Haldane both predicate the existence of a right of property recognised by equity which depends upon there having existed at some stage a fiduciary relationship of some kind (though not necessarily a positive duty of trusteeship) sufficient to give rise to

[131] See Chapter 35.

[132] [1996] AC 669. In *Dublin Corpn v Building and Allied Trade Union* [1996] 1 IR 468 the Irish Supreme Court doubted that *Sinclair v Brougham* was authority for the proposition that a fiduciary relationship was a prerequisite of equitable tracing.

[133] [1914] AC 398. [134] [1948] Ch 465. [135] [1914] AC 398.

> the equitable right to trace property. Exactly what relationships are sufficient to bring such an equitable right into existence for the purposes of the rule which we are considering is a matter which has not been precisely laid down. Certain relationships are clearly included; eg trustee (actual or constructive) and cestui que trust; and 'fiduciary' relationships such as that of principal and agent . . .[136]

In *Sinclair v Brougham*, a building society had operated an ultra vires banking business. The case concerned the rights of the depositors who had invested their money with the bank when the building society had become insolvent. The House of Lords held that they were not entitled to claim restitution at common law through the action for money had and received, which would have meant that they would have stood as creditors in the insolvency and they would have ranked pari passu with the other general creditors of the society. At that time the right to restitution was said to be founded upon an implied contract to repay money had and received. The House of Lords held that, since the building society had acted ultra vires in conducting the banking business, any contract to repay the depositors would also have been ultra vires and was, therefore, void and unenforceable. Since this would have the consequence that the depositors would have no entitlement to claim as creditors in the insolvency, the House of Lords held that the building society had received their deposits as a fiduciary and that they were entitled to trace their money in equity into its remaining assets. In subsequent cases, the implied contract theory was rejected as artificial, and the right to restitution is now available through the autonomous cause of action in unjust enrichment. In *Westdeutsche Landesbank Girozentrale v Islington London Borough Council*,[137] the House of Lords therefore held that, if the same facts had arisen for decision today, the depositors would have been entitled to personal restitution on the grounds that the building society had been unjustly enriched by the receipt of their deposits when there had been a total failure of consideration because their promise to repay was ultra vires and void. There would therefore be no need to trace in equity and, in as far as the House of Lords had found that the deposits were held on trust for the depositors by the building society so as to be traceable in equity, it was overruled.

Other cases also support the view that a fiduciary relationship is an essential prerequisite for equitable tracing.[138] While in *Foskett v McKeown*,[139] Lord Millett considered that there was no logical justification for insisting upon the existence of a fiduciary relationship as a precondition for applying equity's tracing rules, the requirement was not overruled because the case concerned a straightforward case of the misappropriation of trust money.

Where trust property has been misappropriated or misdirected, the essential requirement of a fiduciary relationship will be satisfied. The trustee stood in a fiduciary relationship vis-à-vis the beneficiary who is seeking to trace in equity. However, the fiduciary relationship need not have existed prior to the misappropriation or misdirection of the property concerned, since the circumstances of the misappropriation or misdirection may themselves give rise to a fiduciary relationship entitling the original owner to trace in equity. In *Chase Manhattan Bank NA v Israeli-British Bank (London) Ltd*,[140] Chase Manhattan paid the Israeli-British Bank $1m. Owing to a clerical error, the same amount was paid again later the same day. The Israeli-British bank became insolvent, and Chase Manhattan sought to trace the second mistaken payment money into its assets. Although they would clearly have had a personal action for restitution of the sum paid by mistake, it was essential that they could maintain a proprietary claim, because they would

[136] [1948] Ch 465 at 540. [137] [1996] AC 669.

[138] *Agip (Africa) Ltd v Jackson* [1992] 4 All ER 451 at 466 (Foxx LJ); *Boscawen v Bajwa* [1995] 4 All ER 769 at 777 (Millett LJ).

[139] [2001] 1 AC 102 at 128–9. [140] [1981] Ch 105.

otherwise merely rank among the general creditors. However, the banks were two commercial organizations, dealing with each other at arm's length, and as such they did not stand in a fiduciary relationship, nor was the money paid subject to a pre-existing trust. Despite this, Goulding J held that the very fact that the payment had been made by mistake brought about a fiduciary relationship that entitled Chase Manhattan to trace. He stated his rationale:

> a person who pays money to another under a factual mistake retains an equitable property in it and the conscience of that other is subjected to a fiduciary duty to respect his proprietary right.[141]

However, this decision was subjected to criticism by the House of Lords in *Westdeutsche Landesbank Girozentrale v Islington London Borough Council*,[142] where Lord Browne-Wilkinson stated that he could not agree that the mere fact that the payment had been made by mistake meant that the payor retained the equitable interest in the money paid when it had not previously been subject to a trust.[143] Although the judge's reasoning was doubted, Lord Browne-Wilkinson felt that the case may have been rightly decided:

> The defendant bank knew of the mistake made by the paying bank within two days of the receipt of the moneys. The judge treated this fact as irrelevant but in my judgement it may well provide a proper foundation for the decision. Although the mere receipt of the moneys, in ignorance of the mistake, gives rise to no trust, the retention of the moneys after the recipient bank learned of the mistake may well have given rise to a constructive trust.[144]

Nonetheless, it is suggested that this reasoning is spurious. If the mistaken payment effected a transfer of the ownership of the money to the payee when it was received, there is no reason why a trust should have been imposed when the bank discovered that a mistake had occurred. The bank was clearly subject to an obligation to make restitution at common law, but the mere fact that it should have to make restitution does not generate a constructive trust. While the equitable obligation to account has been held to give rise to a constructive trust because of the operation of the maxim that equity treats as done that which ought to be done, there is no equivalent principle at common law. Instead, the crucial question should focus on the proprietary consequences of the mistaken payment at the moment it was made, in other words, whether the mistake prevented title in the money passing to the payee. Lord Goff indicated that a fundamental mistake might prevent the beneficial interest in property passing to a payee.[145]

The requirement of an initial fiduciary relationship has been subject to significant criticism, both on the grounds that it is not supported in authority and that it is not justified in principle.[146] The major criticism is that the requirement is artificial, the courts being willing to find, or 'discover',[147] a fiduciary relationship whenever they feel that tracing is justified, as in *Chase Manhattan Bank NA v Israeli-British Bank (London) Ltd*.[148] For this reason, Goff and Jones suggested in an earlier edition of their seminal text that whether tracing (which they call a 'restitutionary proprietary claim') should be available should 'depend on whether it is just, in the particular circumstances of the case, to impose a

[141] [1981] Ch 105 at 119. [142] [1996] AC 669. [143] Ibid at 714.

[144] Ibid at 715. [145] Ibid at 690.

[146] See Televantos, 'Losing the Fiduciary Requirement for Equitable Tracing Claims' [2017] LQR 492; Goff and Jones, *The Law of Restitution* (6th edn, Sweet & Maxwell 2002), pp 104–6; Birks, *Introduction to the Law of Restitution* (Clarendon Press 1985), pp 377–85; Pearce, 'A Tracing Paper' [1976] 40 Conv 277. It is argued that *Sinclair v Brougham* [1914] AC 398 did not require an initial fiduciary relationship and that the case was misunderstood by the Court of Appeal in *Re Diplock* [1948] Ch 465.

[147] Goff and Jones, *The Law of Restitution* (6th edn, Sweet & Maxwell 2002), p 105. [148] [1981] Ch 105.

constructive trust on, or an equitable lien over, particular assets . . .'.[149] However, this proposal is equally unsuitable because of its arbitrary nature and it has not been maintained in subsequent editions, where it is regretted that the courts have not taken opportunities which have been presented to overrule the requirement.[150] Televantos suggests that 'if tracing is about vindicating property rights, there is no justification for requiring a claimant bringing an equitable tracing claim to do anything more than prove the existence of a property right and the fact of substitution'.[151] This conclusion comes from an alternative review of the authorities discussed above, which suggests that the courts are not bound by the requirement to find a fiduciary relationship for a tracing claim in equity to succeed. The key, in his view, is whether the property has been disposed of without the authority of the holder(s) of the legal and equitable title.

In practice, it seems that the requirement of a 'fiduciary relationship' is less of a limitation than some critics have suggested. It is the commercial situations which have generated the most difficulty. However, even in the commercial context the requirement is easily circumvented. As Millett J observed in *Agip (Africa) Ltd v Jackson*,[152] it is 'readily satisfied in most cases of commercial fraud, since the embezzlement of a company's funds almost invariably involves a breach of fiduciary duty on the part of one of the company's employees or agents'.[153] Although he noted the criticism, he felt that it was not for a court of first instance to reconsider the requirement, and as has been seen the Court of Appeal merely reasserted it.[154]

(b) Equitable ownership of the property traced

While it is true that the requirement of a fiduciary relationship has not prevented tracing in practice, the language is confusing because it conceals the true basis of equitable tracing. Equity is not concerned with the presence of a fiduciary relationship per se, but rather with the identification of a trust. A person will only be entitled to trace property in equity of which he was the equitable owner. Where trust property was misappropriated or misdirected, the beneficiaries are entitled to trace the trust property which belongs to them in equity. Where the property of an absolute owner is misappropriated or misdirected, he will only be entitled to trace if the circumstances of the misappropriation or misdirection gave rise to a trust in his favour.[155] An alternative analysis of tracing was propounded by Pearce, who argued that equitable tracing should be available whenever there is a 'continuing right of property recognised in equity', which would recognize the possibility of using equity to trace beneficial ownership.[156] If the circumstances do not disclose a transfer of equitable beneficial ownership, the recipient should be obliged to give effect to the owner's continuing proprietary interest. Professor Birks has adopted the argument that equitable tracing should be available whenever there is a sufficient 'proprietary base'. By this he means that:

> the circumstances of the original receipt by the defendant must be such that, either at law or in equity, the plaintiff retained or obtained the property in the matter received by the defendant, and then continued to retain it until the moment at which the substitution or intermixture took place.[157]

[149] Goff and Jones, *The Law of Restitution* (3rd edn, Sweet & Maxwell 1987), p 79.

[150] Goff and Jones, *The Law of Restitution* (6th edn, Sweet & Maxwell 2002), pp 104–6. In this edition, Goff and Jones argue that the comments of the House of Lords in *Foskett v McKeown* [2001] 1 AC 102 that 'there is no sense in maintaining different rules for tracing at law and in equity' lead to the conclusion that the courts should no longer insist on a fiduciary relationship before a claimant can trace in equity.

[151] Televantos, 'Losing the Fiduciary Requirement for Equitable Tracing Claims' [2017] LQR 492, p 512.

[152] [1992] 4 All ER 385.

[153] [1992] 4 All ER 385 at 402.

[154] [1992] 4 All ER 451.

[155] See *Westdeutsche Landesbank Girozentrale v Islington London Borough Council* [1996] AC 669 at 706, per Lord Browne-Wilkinson.

[156] [1976] 40 Conv 275.

[157] Birks, *Introduction to the Law of Restitution* (Clarendon Press 1985), p 378.

The trust analysis of the right to trace in equity was supported by the Privy Council in *Re Goldcorp Exchange Ltd (in receivership)*.[158] The customers who had purchased 'non-allocated metal' were not entitled to trace their purchase money into the bulk of metal held by the company because they could not be shown to have any equitable proprietary interest in it arising through the contract of sale.[159]

It is submitted that there is a strong argument for permitting equitable tracing to be employed wherever property has changed hands in circumstances where there has been no transfer of the equitable beneficial interest. However, such a development would not lead to any significant practical change in the operation of equitable tracing, since there is such a close connection between equitable ownership and a fiduciary relationship that the two terms could almost be seen to be synonymous. This much is admitted by Birks:

> the requirement of a fiduciary relationship is, in this context one and the same as the requirement of an undestroyed proprietary base . . . a plaintiff who wants to assert an equitable proprietary interest in the surviving enrichment must show facts such that the property in the original receipt did not pass at law and in equity to the recipient. If he can show such facts, so that, at least in equity, he retained the property in the res, he will, after identifying the surviving enrichment, be able to raise an equitable proprietary interest in those different assets. Where such facts are shown, the relationship between him and the recipient can, rightly, be described as 'fiduciary' in that it will resemble the relationship between cestui que trust and trustee.[160]

While the continuing proprietary interest analysis may be little more than an alternative label for the present search for a 'fiduciary relationship', it has the definite merit of de-mythologizing the process because it is a more accurate and precise description of what the court is looking for. That said, the mere fact that a different label is used does not answer the difficult questions as to the circumstances in which a trust will arise so as to justify tracing in equity.

(c) Circumstances in which it will be possible to trace in equity

(i) Misappropriation of trust property by a trustee

Equitable tracing will always be available against a trustee who has wrongfully misappropriated trust property, because the beneficiary retains his equitable title to the trust property. Thus equitable tracing was permitted in *Foskett v McKeown*,[161] where a trustee had wrongfully used trust money to pay the premiums due under his insurance policy.

(ii) Receipt of trust property by a stranger to a trust

Where property subject to a trust is transferred to a stranger in breach of trust, the beneficiary will be entitled to trace the trust property into the hands of the stranger unless he was a bona fide purchaser for value without notice, in which case the beneficiary's equitable title will be defeated.

(iii) Profits received by a fiduciary in breach of duty

It now appears clear that unauthorized profits received by a fiduciary are held on constructive trust for his principal, so that the principal will be entitled to trace them in equity.[162]

[158] [1994] 2 All ER 806.

[159] See Birks, 'Establishing a Proprietary Base' [1995] RLR 83. Compare *El Ajou v Dollar Land Holdings plc (No 2)* [1995] 2 All ER 213, where Robert Walker J suggested that tracing depends on the concept of an equitable charge and not equitable ownership.

[160] Birks, *Introduction to the Law of Restitution* (Clarendon Press 1985), p 381.

[161] [2001] 1 AC 102.

[162] See *FHR European Ventures LLP v Cedar Capital Partners LLC* [2014] UKSC 45, and the discussion of this issue in Chapter 35.

(iv) Stolen or misappropriated property

In *Lipkin Gorman v Karpnale Ltd*,[163] Lord Templeman approved Australian authorities which hold that a thief does not gain title to his property, but holds it on trust. He cited with approval O'Connor J in *Black v S Freedman & Co*:

> Where money has been stolen, it is trust money in the hands of the thief and he cannot divest it of that character. If he pays it over to another person, then it may be followed into that person's hands. If, of course, that other person shows that it has come to him bona fides for valuable consideration, and without notice, it then may lose its character as trust money and cannot be recovered . . .[164]

In *Westdeutsche Landesbank Girozentrale v Islington London Borough Council*,[165] Lord Browne-Wilkinson also held that theft would generate a constructive trust sufficient to give rise to the right to trace in equity. He considered whether a resulting trust would arise when a thief stole a bag of coins:

> I agree that the stolen moneys are traceable in equity. But the proprietary interest which equity is enforcing in such circumstances arises under a constructive, not a resulting, trust. Although it is difficult to find clear authority for the proposition, when property is obtained by fraud equity imposes a constructive trust on the fraudulent recipient; the property is recoverable and traceable in equity . . . Money stolen from a bank account can be traced in equity.[166]

This principle would have been sufficient to justify tracing in equity in *Agip (Africa) Ltd v Jackson*[167] without having to find that the accountant, Zdiri, was a fiduciary. He was simply a thief who never gained title to the money he misappropriated, so it was possible to follow it into Baker Oil's account and beyond. The principle that a constructive trust arises from the fraudulent receipt of property was applied to establish a right to trace by Lawrence Collins J in *Commerzbank Aktiengesellschaft v IMB Morgan plc*,[168] where a stockbroker in Nigeria had received money into its accounts which had been obtained as a result of fraud.

It may be noted that, although the authorities now support the view that the thief holds on trust, it is an unusual kind of trust since, so far as the property originally stolen is concerned, the thief does not normally have legal title. This is always the case where tangible property is stolen, and may even be the case in relation to certain intangible property, such as money.[169] Because of this unusual characteristic, there is much to be said for the view that the right to trace exists because of the continuing equitable proprietary rights of the true owner, rather than because of the existence of a trust in the conventional sense.

(v) Payments made under a void contract

An area of controversy is whether a payment made under a contract void ab initio is traceable in equity.[170] It had been argued that such a payment would give rise to a resulting trust in favour of the payor, thus entitling him to trace the payment into the assets of

[163] [1991] 2 AC 548; [1992] 4 All ER 512. [164] [1910] 12 CLR 105. [165] [1996] AC 669.

[166] [1996] AC 669 at 716. The following cases were cited in favour of this proposition: *Stocks v Wilson* [1913] 2 KB 235; *R Leslie Ltd v Sheill* [1914] 3 KB 607; *Bankers Trust Co v Shapira* [1980] 1 WLR 1274; *McCormick v Grogan* [1869] LR 4 HL 82. The proposition has been doubted in a number of subsequent authorities, including *Halifax Building Society v Thomas* [1996] Ch 217; *Paragon Finance v DB Thakerar* [1999] 1 All ER 400; *Shalson v Russo* [2003] WTLR 1165; *Sinclair Investment Holding SA v Versailles Trade Finance Ltd* [2005] EWCA Civ 722.

[167] [1990] Ch 265; affd [1992] 4 All ER 451. [168] [2004] EWHC 2771.

[169] Where intangible property is obtained by fraud, legal title may pass to the thief, as, for instance, if shares or registered land are registered in his name.

[170] See Worthington, *Proprietary Interests in Commercial Transactions* (Oxford University Press 1996), pp 148–61.

the payee. However, this analysis was comprehensively rejected by the House of Lords in *Westdeutsche Landesbank Girozentrale v Islington London Borough Council*,[171] where it was held that money paid under a void interest rate swap agreement was not subject to a resulting trust. Lord Goff stated:

> there is no general rule that the property in money paid under a void contract does not pass to the payee; and it is difficult to escape the conclusion that, as a general rule, the beneficial interest in the money likewise passes to the payee.[172]

The House of Lords reversed the decision of the Court of Appeal[173] that a resulting trust had arisen, and overruled *Sinclair v Brougham*.[174] It, therefore, seems that it will generally be impossible to trace money paid under a void contract in equity and that the payor will be confined to seeking restitution at common law. However, Lord Browne-Wilkinson did seem to suggest that a trust would be imposed if the recipient of the payment was aware of the invalidity of the contract so as to affect his conscience and justify the imposition of a constructive trust, and that such a trust could arise even after receipt if the payee became aware of the invalidity while the payment was still identifiable in his hands.

(vi) Payments made under a voidable contract

In *El Ajou v Dollar Land Holdings plc (No 1)*,[175] Millett J held that a resulting trust arose when a payment had been made under a voidable contract. The case concerned a fraudulent share-selling scheme operated by three Canadians. The claimants' money was invested in the scheme after their agent was bribed to invest in it. The proceeds were eventually invested in a property development project carried on with the defendants, Dollar Land Holdings. The claimants sought to recover their money from the defendants. Millett J held that although they could not trace at common law, because the money had been mixed, they could trace in equity because there was a fiduciary relationship between them and their agent, who was bribed. However, Millett J went on to consider the position of other victims of the fraud who had not invested through a fiduciary and concluded that they too would be entitled to trace:

> Other victims, however, were less fortunate. They employed no fiduciary. They were simply swindled. No breach of any fiduciary obligation was involved. It would, of course, be an intolerable reproach to our system of jurisprudence if the plaintiff were the only victim who could trace and recover his money. Neither party before me suggested that this is the case; and I agree with them. But if the other victims of the fraud can trace their money in equity it must be because, having been induced to purchase the shares by false and fraudulent misrepresentations, they are entitled to rescind the transaction and revest the equitable title to the purchase money in themselves, at least to the extent necessary to support an equitable tracing claim . . .[176]

[171] [1996] AC 669. [172] [1996] AC 669 at 690.

[173] [1994] 1 WLR 938; [1994] RLR 73 (Swadling). Dillon LJ had adopted the following conclusion: 'Since, contrary to the expectation of the parties, the swap transaction and contract are, and were from the outset, ultra vires and void, the purpose for which the £2.5 million was paid by the bank to the council has wholly failed, and the £2.5 million has, from the time the council received it, been held on a resulting trust for the bank.'

[174] [1914] AC 398.

[175] [1993] BCLC 735; revsd [1994] BCLC 464, CA. See also *Daly v Sydney Stock Exchange* [1986] 160 CLR 371; *Lonrho plc v Fayed (No 2)* [1992] 1 WLR 1; *Halifax Building Society v Thomas* [1996] Ch 217. See Worthington, *Proprietary Interests in Commercial Transactions* (Oxford University Press 1996), pp 161–8.

[176] [1993] BCLC 735 at 753.

While this neatly emphasizes that the essence of the right to trace is not a fiduciary relationship per se but the need to demonstrate an equitable proprietary interest, the judgment of the Privy Council in *Re Goldcorp Exchange Ltd (in receivership)*[177] casts doubt upon the proposition. The purchasers of 'non-allocated metal' argued that they were entitled to rescind the contract on the grounds of misrepresentation. Although they had not in fact rescinded their contracts, the Privy Council suggested that even if they had they would not have been entitled to an equitable proprietary right. As Lord Mustill explained:

> even if this fatal objection could be overcome, the argument would, in their Lordships' opinion, be bound to fail. While it is convenient to speak of the customers 'getting their money back' this expression is misleading. Upon payment by the customers the purchase moneys became, and rescission or no rescission remained, the unencumbered property of the company. What the customers would recover on rescission would not be 'their' money, but an equivalent sum . . .[178]

In the light of *Westdeutsche Landesbank Girozentrale v Islington London Borough Council*,[179] it seems that the mere fact that a contract is avoided will not give rise to a trust entitling a payor to trace in equity.[180]

(vii) Payments made by mistake

As has already been seen in *Chase Manhattan Bank NA v Israeli-British Bank (London) Ltd*,[181] it was held that a payor was entitled to trace in equity a payment caused by his mistake of fact. However, it remains unclear why equitable tracing was permitted. In *Westdeutsche Landesbank Girozentrale v Islington London Borough Council*,[182] Lord Browne-Wilkinson doubted that the payor could be said to have retained the equitable title to his money when it was not subject to a trust prior to the payment, and the payee had not known at the moment that the payment was made that the payor was acting under a mistake. He seemed to suggest that a trust only arose because the payee became aware of the mistake two days later, thus affecting his conscience and leading to the imposition of a trust. This analysis has been subject to criticism,[183] and, as was noted earlier, the true question should be whether the payee received good title to the money paid at the moment that it was transferred to him. If so, no trust arises, and, while the recipient may be required to make restitution of the amount of the payment, the payor should not be entitled to trace. Tracing should only be possible if the money was paid under a mistake of fact so fundamental as to prevent property passing. The real difficulty is in identifying mistakes sufficiently fundamental to prevent property passing. As Robert Goff J said in *Barclays Bank Ltd v W J Simms*,[184] in the majority of cases property will pass in payments made under a mistake of fact.[185] In *Re Goldcorp Exchange Ltd*,[186] the Privy Council emphasized that the mistake in *Chase Manhattan* was a mistake whereby one party mistakenly made the same payment twice.[187] In *Westdeutsche* Lord Goff suggested that only a fundamental mistake of fact might prevent the equitable interest in money passing to a payee.[188] In *Bainbridge & Anor v Bainbrige*,[189] a case concerning mistaken transfers of farm land which triggered unexpected and stringent tax consequences the proceeds of the transfers had been used to purchase new land. Since the buyers of the new land had

177 [1994] 2 All ER 806. 178 [1994] 2 All ER 806 at 825–6. 179 [1996] AC 669.

180 See also *Criterion Properties plc v Stratford UK Properties LLC* [2004] 1 WLR 1846.

181 [1981] Ch 105. 182 [1996] AC 669.

183 Birks, 'Trusts Raised to Avoid Unjust Enrichment: The *Westdeutche* Case' [1996] RLR 3, 21–3.

184 [1980] QB 677. 185 See Swadling, 'Restitution for No Consideration' [1994] RLR 73.

186 [1994] 2 All ER 806. 187 [1994] 2 All ER 806 at 826.

188 [1996] AC 669 at 690. 189 [2016] EWHC 898 (Ch).

acted in good faith, any claim to the land had to be based on identifying it through the tracing process as a substitute for the land sold, as there was no claim to recession of the contract. Master Matthews, relying on a dictum from Behrens J in *Pearce v Beverley*[190] suggested that a tracing claim by mistake could succeed:

> In my judgment this shows that it is not only in cases of fraudulent misrepresentation that the idea of 'proprietary base by avoidance' and the tracing process can be prayed in aid. The principle is wide enough to cover other vitiating factors too. In my judgment it extends to cases of mistake, and it is therefore open to the Claimants in the present case to make a claim to the new land.

(3) **Equitable tracing through clean substitutions**

Where trust property has been exchanged for other property, the beneficiaries are entitled to trace into the exchange product. Thus, if a trustee uses £5,000 of trust money to purchase a diamond ring for that price, the beneficiaries will be able to trace their equitable ownership into the ring.

(4) **Equitable tracing of tangible property into a mixed bulk**

If the trust property consists of tangible property, for example if it is a quantity of crude oil, it is possible that the trustee may wrongfully allow the trust property to be mixed with other property so as to form a bulk. In such circumstances, by analogy with the common law rules, the beneficiaries would be entitled to trace the trust property into the bulk, and they would be entitled to a share of the equitable ownership proportionate to their contribution.[191]

(5) **Equitable tracing of money through a mixed fund**

More difficult problems present themselves if misappropriated trust property is mixed with other property so that it can no longer be identified as such. Assets purchased from the mixed fund cannot then be regarded as solely the product of the trust property. Unlike the rules of tracing at common law, the equitable rules of tracing permit the trust property to be traced through a mixed fund of money and into assets acquired from it. *Foskett v McKeown*[192] involved just such a situation. The case concerned a Mr Murphy, who in 1986 had taken out a unit-linked life insurance policy, which provided for the payment of a death benefit of £1 million. The proceeds of the life insurance policy were written in trust for the benefit of his children. The initial annual premiums due under this policy were paid by Mr Murphy using his own money. However, the premiums due in 1989 and 1990 were paid using money from a bank account which he held on trust for the customers of a company he controlled which had contracted to buy land on their behalf in Portugal. In 1991 Mr Murphy committed suicide, and the death benefit was paid. The question at issue was whether the beneficiaries were entitled to trace their misappropriated money into the proceeds of the policy. The House of Lords held, by a bare majority, that the beneficiaries were entitled to a share of the proceeds proportionate to the contribution of the trust

190 [2013] EWHC 2627 (Ch), where he held that a transaction has been tainted by undue influence and a tracing claim was permissible.

191 *Foskett v McKeown* [2001] 1 AC 102 at 141.

192 [2001] 1 AC 102.

money to the payment of the premiums. Lord Millett explained that the beneficiaries were able to trace their trust money into the insurance policy itself, and thence into the proceeds of the policy:

> It is, however, of critical importance in the present case to appreciate that the purchasers do not trace the premiums directly into the insurance money. They trace them first into the policy and thence into the proceeds of the policy. It is essential not to elide the two steps. In this context, of course, the word 'policy' does not mean the contract of insurance. You do not trace the payment of a premium into the insurance contract any more than you trace a payment into a bank account in to the banking contract. The word 'policy' is here used to describe the bundle of rights to which the policyholder is entitled in return for the premiums. These rights, which may be very complex, together constitute a chose in action, viz the right to payment of a debt payable on a future event and contingent upon the continued payment of further premiums until the happening of the event. That chose in action represents the traceable proceeds of the premiums; its current value fluctuates from time to time. When the property matures, the insurance money represents the traceable proceeds of the policy and hence indirectly of the premiums. It follows that, if a claimant can show that premiums were paid with his money, he can claim a proportionate share of the policy.[193]

Foskett v McKeown involved a somewhat unusual mixture of funds in the form of the payment of premiums of an insurance policy. More commonly, misappropriated funds will become mixed in a bank account. Equity has developed special rules to determine whether trust property can be traced through a mixture of funds in a bank account.

(6) Equitable tracing of money through the banking system

The difficulty of identifying whether substitutions have taken place where money has passed through the banking system has been considered in the chapter in relation to the common law. The difficulties which were expressed by Millett J in *Agip (Africa) Ltd v Jackson*[194] have never been raised in relation to tracing in equity, and *Credit Agricole Corp and Investment Bank v Papadimitriou*[195] provides assurance, should it be needed, that equitable tracing is possible through complex inter-bank transactions and through the international bank clearing system. Any lingering doubts must also have been dispelled by *The Federal Republic of Brazil v Durant International Corporation*.[196] An additional difficulty is whether and how mixed funds should be treated: where, for instance, a trustee takes funds from a trust account and pays them into a personal account which already has a credit balance. While equity is capable of tracing property through a mixed fund, the process of identification can be extremely complex where money has become mixed with funds in a bank account. The rules that have evolved are simply rough and ready presumptions which operate to determine whether any remaining balance, or property purchased, can be identified as the product of the trust money. They operate differently depending upon whether the mixture consisted of trust money and the money of the wrongdoing trustee, or the money of the trust and of another innocent party, for example money misappropriated from another trust. The rules emerged in the last century, and they are only really appropriate for simple bank accounts.

193 [2001] 1 AC 102 at 134.
194 [1992] 4 All ER 385.
195 [2015] UKPC 13. See Pearce, 'Case Note: When must a bank repay stolen funds?' [2015] Conv 51.
196 [2015] UKPC 35.

(a) Mixture of the trust property and the trustee's own property

Where a wrongdoing trustee has mixed trust property with his own property in a bank account, the rules operate harshly against him. If the mixed fund has been partially dissipated, any remaining balance, or assets acquired from the account, are presumed to belong to the trust. The burden is on the wrongdoer to show that the asset or balance represents his own money.[197] In *Sinclair Investments v Versailles Trade Finance*,[198] part of the defence to a tracing claim was that the money claimed had become irretrievably mixed with the defendant's own funds. Lord Neuberger MR dismissed this bluntly:[199]

> I do not see why . . . a proprietary claim should be lost simply because the defaulting fiduciary, while still holding much of the money, has acted particularly dishonestly or cunningly by creating a maelstrom. Where he has mixed the funds held on trust with his own funds, the onus should be on the fiduciary to establish that part, and what part, of the mixed fund is his property.

Where the account balance has been reduced by withdrawals which have been dissipated, the court will presume that the remaining balance represents the trust property and that the wrongdoer's own money has been dissipated. The wrongdoer will not be permitted to assert that it represents his own money and that the money he has spent and dissipated was the trust money. As Millett LJ stated in *Boscawen v Bajwa*:

> A trustee will not be allowed to defeat the claim of his beneficiaries by saying that he has resorted to trust money when he could have made use of his own.[200]

This presumption was applied in *Re Hallett's Estate*. A solicitor, who was a trustee of his own marriage settlement, was entrusted with money by a client for investment. He paid money from the trust and his client's money into his bank account, which also contained some of his own money. He made various payments out, which had been dissipated. On his death, the account contained enough money to satisfy the claims of the trust and the client, but not his other creditors. The central question was whether the money in the account could be said to be the property of the trust and client, in which case they would gain priority over the general creditors. The Court of Appeal held that the trustee must be presumed to have spent his own money first, and to have preserved the trust monies. Lord Walker, in *Re Lehman Bros International (Europe)*,[201] evocatively described the process this way:

> Client money held temporarily in a house account does not, in the eyes of trust law, 'swill around', but sinks to the bottom in the sense that when the firm is using money for its own purposes it is treated as withdrawing its own money from a mixed fund before it touches trust money.

If the presumption adopted in *Re Hallett's Estate* were absolute, it would produce an anomalous result if the wrongdoing trustee purchased assets from the account and then dissipated the remaining balance. The trustee would be able to claim that the assets had been acquired with his own money, since he was deemed to spend this first. In consequence, the presumption that the trustee withdraws and spends his own money first is not absolute but a specific application of the general maxim that 'everything is presumed against a wrongdoer'. Whatever the circumstances and the order of events, the wrongdoer is presumed to have acted so as to preserve the trust money. Thus, assets acquired before the remaining balance of the account was dissipated may be claimed to represent the trust property. As Millett LJ stated in *Boscawen v Bajwa*:

> if the beneficiary asserts that the trustee has made use of the trust money there is no reason why he should not be allowed to prove it.[202]

[197] *Lupton v White* [1808] 15 Ves 432. [198] [2011] 4 All ER 335. [199] At 138.
[200] [1995] 4 All ER 769 at 778. [201] [2012] 3 All ER 1 at 65. [202] [1995] 4 All ER 769 at 778.

Hence in *Re Oatway*,[203] where application of the presumption in *Re Hallett's Estate* would have worked an injustice, exactly the opposite presumption was applied, namely that the trustee had spent the trust money first. Lewis Oatway was a solicitor and the trustee of a will. He misappropriated £3,000 from the trust and paid this into a bank account, where it was mixed with his own money. He purchased Oceana shares for £2,137 using money from the account. At the time that he purchased them there would have been enough of his own money in the account to purchase the shares. After the purchase, he dissipated the balance of the account and died insolvent, leaving the shares, now valued at £2,474. If the rule in *Re Hallett* were applied, the shares would have been purchased with his money, and, therefore, form part of his general assets. However, Joyce J held that the shares were to be regarded as the product of the trust money. Having examined the rule in *Re Hallett's Estate* he concluded:

> It is, in my opinion, equally clear that when any of the money drawn out has been invested, and that investment remains in the name or under the control of the trustee, the rest of the balance having been afterwards dissipated by him, he cannot maintain that the investment which remains represents his own money alone, and that what has been spent and can no longer be traced and recovered was the money belonging to the trust.[204]

The contrasting decisions in *Re Hallett's Estate*[205] and *Re Oatway*[206] are not in conflict with each other, but are applications of a general principle that the trustee is estopped from asserting that he has preserved his own money at the expense of trust funds. It has been described as 'cherry picking' since the beneficiaries are allowed to choose the most beneficial construction of what has happened.[207] This rule works to the advantage of the beneficiaries of the trust, but it must be remembered that it acts to the detriment of the general creditors, who will inevitably receive a lower dividend from the insolvency. It is questionable whether this priority is always just.

In most cases where tracing is argued the claimant is trying to salvage a small part of what they have lost as a result of a trustee's wrongdoing. What would happen where a trustee mixes his own money with trust funds and then makes a profitable purchase, but leaves enough money in the mixed account to satisfy the claims of beneficiaries? It has been argued that in such a case, both beneficiary and trustee should share the profits.[208] This was addressed in *Turner v Jacob*.[209] Mrs Turner put money to which her daughter (Mrs Jacob) was entitled into a deposit account. A number of withdrawals were made which reduced the balance to around £10,000. The balance in the account never subsequently fell below this level, but there were a significant number of deposits and withdrawals, including withdrawals to support the purchase of two houses. Patten J considered that Mrs Jacob could not claim that the money to which she had a claim had been used to purchase either of the houses:

> It seems to me that in a case (such as the present) where the trustee maintains in the account an amount equal to the remaining trust fund, the beneficiary's right to trace is limited to that fund. It is not open to the beneficiary to assert a lien against an investment made using monies out of the mixed account unless the sum expended is of such a size that it must have included trust monies or the balance remaining in the account after the investment is then expended so as to become untraceable.[210]

203 [1903] 2 Ch 356. 204 [1903] 2 Ch 356 at 360.
205 [1880] 13 Ch D 696. 206 [1903] 2 Ch 356.
207 *Dyson Technology Ltd v Curtis* [2010] EWHC 3289 (Ch) (20 September 2010) at 20.
208 Birks, *Introduction to the Law of Restitution* (Clarendon Press 1985), p 370.
209 [2006] EWHC 1317 (Ch).
210 [2006] EWHC 1317 (Ch) at 102. Mrs Jacob was the residuary beneficiary under her mother's will. A personal claim by Mrs Jacob against her mother would have reduced the value of the residuary estate, which also included the proceeds of selling the first house to be purchased. Mrs Jacob claimed to be entitled to a proportion of the value of the second house to be purchased, which her mother had left in her will to her husband.

(b) Property of trusts or innocent volunteers mixed

The harsh presumptions which operate against a wrongdoer who has mixed trust property with his own are not applied where trust property has been mixed with that of other trusts or other innocent volunteers. In such a case, the rules reflect the moral blamelessness of the parties whose money has been mixed, and they aim to do substantive justice between them. For over a century, the preferred method of distribution has been what is called 'pari passu' distribution, or, in colloquial English, 'share and share alike'.

(i) Ponzi schemes

A very common type of investment fraud is known as a Ponzi scheme, named after the Italian crook who ran such a scam. An example is described in *Madoff Securities International Ltd v Raven*.[211] For over twenty years before his confession, Bernard Madoff took billions of dollars from 'investors' through his New York company, Bernard L Madoff Investment Securities LLC. He purported to run the investment advisory business as a legitimate and highly successful business with impressive returns. Flaux J said:

> the reality was that the investment advisory business made no material investments at all. Clients' money was pooled in a single account at JP Morgan and treated by Mr Madoff and his associates as his own. He would pay 'profits' or 'redemptions' to clients ostensibly by way of return on their investment, but in reality this consisted of other clients' money, the Ponzi scheme being funded by a constant influx of funds. However, in December 2008, requests for redemptions by customers nervous at the financial crisis and the collapse of Lehman Brothers exceeded the amount of funds deposited by new customers and the scheme collapsed. The customers of the investment advisory business had between them lost about US$ 19.5 billion.

In cases such as this, the remaining funds are able to meet only a fraction of the sums due to investors. How should they be returned?

(ii) Individually identifiable assets

Where assets can specifically be linked to an individual investor, the investor can lay claim to that specific asset. For instance, in *Russell-Cooke Trust Co v Prentis*,[212] a solicitor ran a secured investment scheme in which some investors' payments were linked to specific mortgage loans. Lindsay J held that where this link was established, the investor was entitled to that specific asset.

(iii) Assets not capable of individual allocation

It will often be the case that it is not possible to identify a link to a specific asset, or where there are several claims to a single asset. This would be so if a dishonest solicitor has put clients' money into his client account, but has improperly withdrawn money for his own purposes, or where there are some unallocated assets acquired with the deposits made by investors in a Ponzi scheme. Three ways of allocating the assets have been identified.

(iv) Pari passu allocation

Pari passu allocation works by identifying the proportion which each individual contribution has made to the total value of the valid claims, and then distributing the available assets in the same proportions. So, if £50,000 of Joey's money was paid by a Ponzi scheme fraudster into an empty 'investment account' in July, the next month £100,000 of

[211] [2011] EWHC 3102 (Comm).

[212] [2003] 2 All ER 478. See also *Re Diplock* [1948] Ch 465, where some of the funds were specifically identifiable.

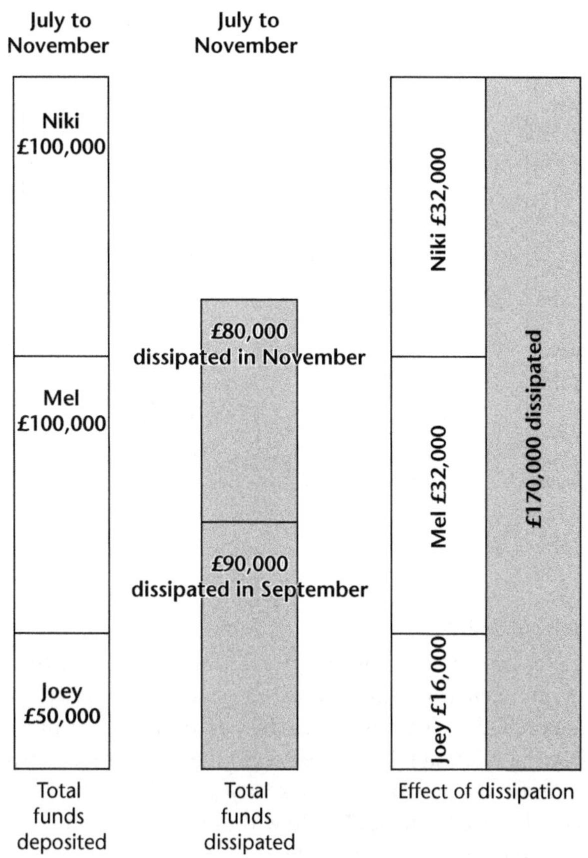

Figure 38.1 Pari passu allocation

Melanie's money was paid in, and, in September, the fraudster withdrew £90,000 for his own use, the remaining £60,000 would be shared as to one-third by Joey and two-thirds by Melanie. If in October, and before the fraud was discovered, the fraudster paid in another £100,000 from Nikita, and in November took another £80,000 from the account, the remaining £80,000 would be shared as to one-fifth by Joey (since that is the proportion he contributed to the total of £250,000 originally invested), two-fifths by Melanie (since that is the share she contributed) and two-fifths by Nikita. The shares would, therefore, be worth £16,000, £32,000, and £32,000, respectively: see Figure 38.1.

(v) Rolling charge allocation

Pari passu allocation divides assets using a global calculation—that is, it looks only at the total invested and the total available for distribution. A more sophisticated method, known as the rolling charge or North American method, recalculates shares every time a transaction occurs. So if the facts were as described earlier, in July, the whole fund would belong to Joey. After Melanie's money was deposited, the fund would belong one-third to Joey and two-thirds to Melanie. In September the withdrawal would make those shares of a reduced pot of £60,000, so the addition of Nikita's money would reduce Joey's share to £20,000 of the £160,000 total, or one-eighth; Melanie would have a share of two-eighths (one-quarter); and Nikita's share would be five-eighths. The fraudster's withdrawal in November would leave those shares worth £10,000, £20,000, and £50,000, respectively. It can be seen that the system is complicated and requires detailed records: see Figure 38.2.

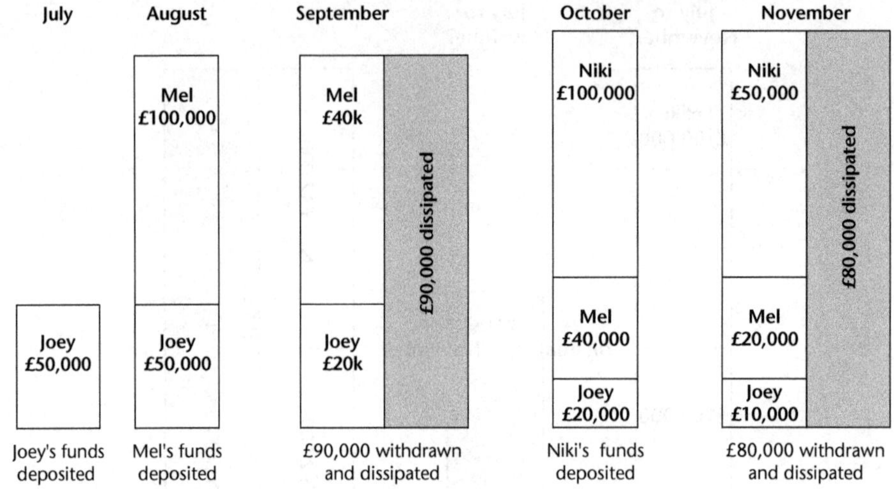

Figure 38.2 Rolling charge allocation

(vi) 'First in, first out' allocation

The final type of allocation applies the tag, 'first in, first out'. It was the method adopted in *Clayton's case*[213] and hence has been named the rule in *Clayton's case*. Under this rule it is presumed that money is paid out of a current account in the same order in which it had been paid in. If this rule is applied to the Ponzi scheme fraudster's investment account described earlier (and there are good reasons why it would *not* be applied in this situation), the effect would be that of the £170,000 withdrawn and dissipated by the fraudster, the first £50,000 would be treated as having been taken from Joey, the next £100,000 from Melanie, and the last £20,000 from Nikita. As a consequence only Nikita would receive anything, and Nikita's share would be the whole remaining £80,000, with neither Joey nor Melanie receiving anything: see Figure 38.3.

(vii) Which method of application to use?

The rule in *Clayton's case* was applied in a number of cases in the nineteenth century.[214] However, the case has been so rarely applied since to innocent beneficiaries of a breach of trust, possibly the only reported example being *Re Diplock* in 1948,[215] that one judge has said that 'it might be more accurate to refer to the exception that is, rather than the rule in, *Clayton's case*.'[216] The main reason why the rule is applied so rarely is that it is not perceived as operating fairly between innocent beneficiaries. Leggatt LJ, in *Barlow Clowes International Ltd (in liquidation) v Vaughan*,[217] described the rule as 'capricious, arbitrary and inapposite'. The judicial approach has not been directly to challenge the rule, but to find ways of avoiding its application.

In *Barlow Clowes International Ltd v Vaughan*, the Court of Appeal was faced with the consequences of the collapse of the Barlow Clowes investment company in Gibraltar. Depositors had paid into investment plans, but the money had been misapplied, and the

[213] [1816] 1 Mer 572.

[214] See *Re Hallett's Estate* [1880] 13 Ch D 696 (Fry J); *Hancock v Smith* [1889] 41 Ch D 456; *Re Stenning* [1895] 2 Ch 433; *Mutton v Peat* [1899] 2 Ch 556.

[215] *Re Diplock* [1948] Ch 465, CA.

[216] Lindsay J in *Russell-Cooke Trust Co v Prentis* [2003] 2 All ER 478 at 55.

[217] [1992] 4 All ER 22 at 46. See Fox, 'Legal Title as a Ground of Restitutionary Liability' [2000] RLT 465.

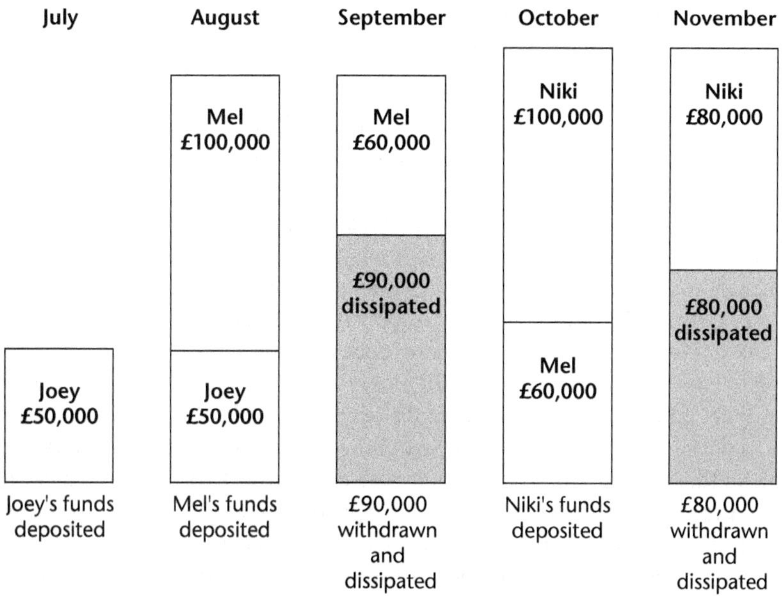

Figure 38.3 'First in, first out' allocation

company was left owing some £115 million to investors, with assets far less than that amount. Some investors argued that the rule in *Clayton's case* should be applied, with the consequence that the late investors would recover virtually all their money, leaving the early investors with nothing. After a wide-ranging examination of the authorities, the court held that the rule was well established and that it was not open to the Court of Appeal to overrule it. As Dillon LJ observed:

> the decisions of this court establish and recognise a general rule of practice that *Clayton's case* is to be applied when several beneficiaries' moneys have been blended in one bank account and there is a deficiency. It is not . . . for this court to reject that long established general practice.[218]

There are four ways in which the courts have avoided applying the rule in *Clayton's case*. First, the rule was originally devised to regulate the banker–client relationship, so that a line could be drawn under old ledger entries. That was a purpose far removed from the relationship between innocent beneficiaries. The rule has been held applicable only to active running bank accounts (like a current account, where there are regular deposits and withdrawals), and not to other types of account like deposit accounts,[219] or to disentangling transactions involving other property.[220] Second, the application of *Clayton's case* is not possible if the state of records is such that it would be impossible or impracticable to apply.[221] Third, it has been said that the rule will give way to even the slightest contra-indication.[222] Fourth, the courts have declined to apply the rule where it would result in injustice. This last reason is the principal reason why the Court of Appeal, in *Barlow Clowes*, felt free to depart from applying the rule. The principles governing the application of the rule were summarized by Woolf LJ:

> The rule need only be applied when it is convenient to do so and when its application can be said to do broad justice having regard to the nature of the competing claims . . . It is not

[218] [1992] 4 All ER 22 at 33.
[219] *Sinclair v Brougham* [1914] AC 398; *Re Diplock* [1948] Ch 465, CA.
[220] *Re Goldcorp Exchange Ltd* [1995] 1 AC 74.
[221] *Re Eastern Capital Futures Ltd* [1989] BCLC 371.
[222] *Barlow Clowes International Ltd (in liquidation) v Vaughan* [1992] 4 All ER 22.

> applied if this is the intention or presumed intention of the beneficiaries. The rule is sensibly not applied when the cost of applying it is likely to exhaust the fund available for the beneficiaries.[223]

On the facts, it was held that the rule would not be applied because the investment fund was regarded by the investors as a common pool, and that they should share pari passu in what remained because they had experienced a common misfortune. It would have been wholly inequitable to apply the rule in *Clayton's case*, which would have meant some investors recovering everything to the exclusion of the rest, who would recover nothing. Subsequent cases have continued to reject the application of the rule.[224] In *Russell-Cooke Trust Co v Prentis*,[225] Lindsay J declined to apply the rule to victims of a common misfortune because it would operate unfairly. Lawrence Collins J also refused to apply the rule in *Commerzbank Aktiengesellschaft v IMB Morgan plc*,[226] where money obtained by fraud had been paid into the account of a firm of stockbrokers, where it had become mixed so that it was not possible to identify any part of the funds as belonging to a particular client. He held that the rule would be 'impracticable and unjust' to apply, and held that the balance in the account should be divided in proportion among the clients (pari passu).

The rolling charge or North American method of allocation 'appears never to have been applied in England'[227] and has been expressly rejected twice. In the *Barlow Clowes* case, Woolf LJ accepted that the solution could have advantages over a distribution pari passu, but considered that the complications made it impracticable to apply in the circumstances of that case.[228] In *Russell-Cooke Trust Co v Prentis*,[229] Lindsay J noted this rejection and added that the method was inappropriate because it was 'complicated and may be expensive to apply'. Rimer J suggested in *Shalson v Russo*[230] that the rolling charge rule was preferable to the pari passu method, but noted that the cost and expense of assembling the necessary evidence would often be prohibitive. The consequence is that the pari passu method of allocation is universally, or almost universally, the method of distribution adopted.[231]

(c) The lowest intermediate balance

Whether a fund consists of a mixture of trust money with the wrongdoer's own, or the money of an innocent volunteer, if money has been dissipated from the account and then further money is paid into the account, the trust has no claim to any of that other money. The trust is limited to what is known as the lowest intermediate balance, because it is impossible that anything in the account above that figure represents trust property. The operation of this rule is seen in *Roscoe v Winder*.[232] A wrongdoer misappropriated some £455, which he paid into his own bank account. After a few days the balance was reduced to £25, though by his death, it had risen to £358. It was held that a charge could only extend over the £25. Sargant J explained this on the basis that the principle of *Re Hallett's*

223 [1992] 4 All ER 22 at 39.

224 See also the discussion of the rule in *Re French Caledonia Travel* [2004] 22 ACLC 498; [2003] NSWSC 1008; Conaglen, 'Contests between Rival Beneficiaries' [2005] 64 CLJ 45.

225 [2003] 2 All ER 478; Conaglen, 'Contests between Rival Beneficiaries' [2005] 64 CLJ 45.

226 [2004] EWHC 2771.

227 *Steele v Steele* [2001] All ER (D) (Ferris J). This was a family case involving a question of ownership of funds in a joint account. The judge applied the presumption in such cases that the funds are owned jointly.

228 [1992] 4 All ER 22 at 39.

229 [2003] 2 All ER 478, 57.

230 [2005] Ch 281, 150.

231 See, for example, *Charity Commission v Framjee* [2015] 1 WLR 16.

232 [1915] 1 Ch 62.

Estate[233] could only apply to money which came from the trust fund: any increase in the balance above the lowest intermediate balance must have come from other sources. If the subsequent payments in had been specifically intended to replenish the trust funds, then the trust would be entitled to a charge over them because this would be expressly imposing upon the later payment a trust equivalent to the trust which rested on the previous balance.[234] The rule preventing tracing beyond the lowest intermediate balance was reaffirmed by the Court of Appeal in *Bishopsgate Investment Management v Homan*.[235]

(d) Bank trustee depositing trust money with itself

The situations described earlier have all involved cases where a trustee has mixed trust money with either his own or that of innocent volunteers in bank accounts. However, given that banks may themselves act as trustees, they may deposit trust money with themselves. If they then become insolvent, the question may arise as to whether the beneficiaries can trace the money in the hands of the bank. This issue was considered by the Privy Council in *Space Investments Ltd v Canadian Imperial Bank of Commerce Trust Co (Bahamas) Ltd*[236] The case concerned a bank, the Mercantile Bank Trust Co Ltd, which was the trustee of various settlements. The trust instruments contained clauses permitting the trustee to open and maintain savings accounts with any bank, including itself. The bank deposited trust money with itself, and then became insolvent. The question was whether the beneficiaries were entitled to trace the trust money into the bank accounts and, therefore, gain priority over the other unsecured creditors of the bank. The Privy Council held that they were not entitled to do so because the deposit was entirely lawful and not in breach of trust. The beneficiaries were to be treated like all the other depositors of the bank, who were restricted to proving in the liquidation as unsecured creditors for the amount that ought to have been credited to their accounts at the date of liquidation. However, the Privy Council considered that the position would have been different if the bank trustee had misappropriated the trust money and had acted in breach of trust by depositing the trust property with itself. In such circumstances the beneficiaries would be entitled to an equitable charge over all the assets of the bank. Lord Templeman explained the Board's reasoning:

> A bank in fact uses all deposit moneys for the general purposes of the bank . . . in these circumstances it is impossible for the beneficiaries interested in trust money misappropriated from their trust to trace their money to any particular asset belonging to the trustee bank. But equity allows the beneficiaries, or a new trustee appointed in place of an insolvent bank trustee to protect the interests of the beneficiaries, to trace the trust money to all the assets of the bank and to recover the trust money by the exercise of an equitable charge over all the assets of the bank.[237]

This accorded the beneficiaries priority over all the unsecured creditors of the bank. This was justified by the Board on the grounds that the settlor and beneficiaries of the trust had never accepted the risks involved in the possible insolvency of the bank, whereas the

[233] [1880] 13 Ch D 696.

[234] Sargant J took the view that if the account was a separate trust account then, the mere fact of a payment in would be sufficient indication of an intention to substitute the additional moneys (see e.g. *Re Hughes* [1970] IR 237), but there was no such intention in the case of a payment into a general trading account.

[235] [1995] 1 All ER 347; Smith, 'Tracing, "Swollen Assets" and the Lowest Intermediate Balance: *Bishopsgate Investment Management Ltd v Homan*' [1994] 8 TLI 102. See also *British Columbia v National Bank of Canada* [1994] 119 DLR (4th) 669.

[236] [1986] 1 WLR 1072. [237] [1986] 1 WLR 1072 at 1974.

unsecured other creditors had voluntarily accepted that risk. In conclusion, the distinction between the beneficiaries' position where the deposit was authorized and where it was not was justified on the basis that:

> Equity . . . protects beneficiaries against breaches of trust. But equity does not protect beneficiaries against the consequences of the exercise in good faith of powers conferred by the trust instrument.[238]

This decision has been criticized, since in effect it enables the beneficiaries to maintain a security interest over assets that could not possibly be the product of the trust property.[239] In *Re Goldcorp Exchange Ltd*,[240] the Privy Council referred to *Space Investments* and the criticisms which had been levelled at the judgment, but concluded that:

> In the present case it is not necessary or appropriate to consider the scope and ambit of the observations in *Space Investments* or their application to trustees other than bank trustees . . .

The exact scope and application of the principle therefore awaits further judicial clarification.

An odd decision in this context is *Credit Agricole Corp and Investment Bank v Papadimitriou*,[241] where the claimants succeeded in establishing a proprietary claim even though there appeared to be no surviving property. Symes sold a misappropriated art collection in the spring of 2000. The laundering process was fully executed over the next two years, and on 13 August 2001, the funds held in Gibraltar (which were the funds to which the claimants could assert their rights) were transferred to London to pay off a loan facility on which Symes had drawn. By the end of August 2001, there were no longer any identifiable assets to which the claimants' rights could attach. In this case the claimants only brought their claim against the bank in 2004, by which time there was no credit remaining in the account. The claim surprisingly succeeded. Some potential reasons to explain this are explored by Pearce,[242] who concludes that the most likely possibility is that it was a pragmatic decision. The Privy Council felt the bank was liable for knowing receipt of trust property received in breach of trust and was therefore 'content to find liability notwithstanding the flaw in the claim pursued on appeal'. This is very much a case that, on this point, deserves no more than to be confined to its facts in the future.

(7) Tracing into assets acquired prior to misappropriation

The question has arisen whether misappropriated money can be traced in equity into an asset acquired before the trust property was received.[243] If Janette, as trustee, borrows money to buy a yacht and then repays that loan with money taken from a trust, can the beneficiaries of that trust, Boris and Bertha, trace into the yacht? There has been no substitution of the trust property for the yacht, as it was purchased before the trust money was used. Instead, in a standard analysis, Janette has used trust money to discharge a debt (repay the loan), so the property has been dissipated, leaving Boris and Bertha with no action to trace the trust fund. The process necessary to trace the yacht has been described as 'backward tracing' or 'reverse tracing'. In *Bishopsgate Investment Management v*

[238] [1986] 1 WLR 1072.

[239] Goode, 'Ownership and Obligation in Commercial Transactions' [1987] 103 LQR 433.

[240] [1994] 2 All ER 806. [241] [2015] UKPC 13.

[242] Pearce, 'Case Note: When must a bank repay stolen funds?' [2015] Conv 51.

[243] Sir Peter Millett, 'Law of Restitution (Publication Review)' [1995] 111 LQR 517; Oliver, 'The Extent of Equitable Tracing' [1995] 9 TLI 78; Oakley, 'Propriety Claims and Their Priority in Insolvency' [1995] 54 CLJ 377.

Homan,[244] Dillon LJ was willing to accept that in some circumstances trust money could be traced into a pre-acquired asset. The first instance judge had suggested that tracing would be possible if property had been acquired with borrowed money, by way of either loan or overdraft, and there was an inference that when the borrowing was incurred it was the intention that it should be repaid[245] with the misappropriated money. He considered that the beneficiary would be entitled to a charge over the asset acquired provided that the connection between the misappropriation and the asset was sufficiently proved. In contrast, Leggatt LJ entirely dismissed the possibility of such reverse tracing:

> there can be no equitable remedy against an asset acquired *before* misappropriation of money takes place, since ex hypothesi it cannot be followed into something which existed and so had been acquired before the money was received and therefore without its aid.[246]

In *Foskett v McKeown*,[247] in the Court of Appeal, Scott V-C expressed the opinion that it should be possible to trace into assets acquired with borrowed money if the trust money was used to repay the borrowing and it had always been the intention that the trust money would be used to acquire the asset. This was on the basis that equity looks to the substance, not the form, of transactions.

In *Relfo Ltd v Varsani*,[248] the Court of Appeal had to consider the availability and existence of reverse tracing as part of a knowing receipt claim into what amounted to a money-laundering scheme of inter-bank transfers. These transfers had not occurred simultaneously or in chronological order, so a claim to reverse tracing was necessary to identify the fee. Arden LJ held that reverse tracing was possible in these situations. Much weight was given to counsel's submissions on *Agip (Africa) Ltd v Jackson*,[249] also cited with approval by the Court of Appeal in *Foskett v McKeown*,[250] that 'monies held on trust can be traced into other assets even if those other assets are passed on before the trust monies are paid to the person transferring them, provided that that person acted on the basis that he would receive reimbursement for the monies he transferred out of the trust funds.'[251] It followed that:

> The decision in *Agip* demonstrates that in order to trace money into substitutes it is not necessary that the payments should occur in any particular order, let alone chronological order. As Mr Shaw submits, a person may agree to provide a substitute for a sum of money even before he receives that sum of money. In those circumstances the receipt would postdate the provision of the substitute. What the court has to do is establish whether the likelihood is that monies could have been paid at any relevant point in the chain in exchange for such a promise. I see no reason in logic or principle why this particular way of proving a substitution should be limited to payments to or by correspondent banks.[252]

Further support for the existence and utility of reverse or backwards tracing has been provided by the Privy Council[253] in *The Federal Republic of Brazil v Durant International Corporation*.[254] Like previous decisions, this case involved tracing the proceeds of wrongdoing through a complex web of bank accounts. The mayor of Sao Paulo in Brazil (Paulo

[244] [1995] 1 All ER 347. [245] [1995] 1 All ER 347 at 351.

[246] [1995] 1 All ER 347 at 355. In support, see Conaglen, 'Difficulties with Tracing Backwards' [2011] 127 LQR 432.

[247] [1997] 3 All ER 392 at 409.

[248] [2014] EWCA Civ 360. See Watterson, 'Recovering Misapplied Corporate Assets from Remoter Recipients' [2014] 73 CLJ 496. [249] [1990] 1 Ch 265. [250] [1997] 3 All ER 392 at 409.

[251] [2014] EWCA Civ 360 at 63. [252] Ibid.

[253] The status of Privy Council decisions as precedents was considered in *Willers v Joyce* [2016] UKSC 44. Mirfield, 'A Novel Theory of Privy Council Precedent' [2017] LQR 1.

[254] [2015] UKPC 35; Bloomfield, 'An Exploration of Backwards Tracing: Doctrine, Theory and Practice' [2017] 23 T&T 227; Turner, 'Tracing to and Fro' [2016] CLJ 462.

Maluf) took bribes which were laundered through a bank account (Chanini) and two companies (Durant and Kildare) controlled by Maluf and his son. Most of the money was clearly traceable, but Maluf argued that it was not possible to trace some of the money because Chanini had paid Durant before the bribe was received. Maluf also argued that the lowest intermediate balance rule should be applied, which would have the same effect. In rejecting both of Maluf's arguments, the Privy Council accepted that backward tracing is available where a claimant can establish:

> a coordination between the depletion of the trust fund and the acquisition of the asset which is the subject of the tracing claim, looking at the whole transaction, such as to warrant the court attributing the value of the interest acquired to the misuse of the trust fund.[255]

Evidence of this co-ordination would be 'likely to depend on inference from the proved facts, particularly since in many cases the testimony of the trustee, if available, will be of little value'.[256]

It is clear from the Privy Council decision that there is a strong policy element to the existence of backward tracing,[257] as 'the development of increasingly sophisticated and elaborate methods of money laundering, often involving a web of credits and debits between intermediaries, makes it particularly important that a court should not allow a camouflage of interconnected transactions to obscure its vision of their true overall purpose and effect'.[258] The decision has led to developments of the reverse tracing doctrine in New Zealand.[259] Popplewell J contemplated, but on the facts rejected, reverse tracing through a co-ordinated set of transactions in *ORB arl v Ruhan*.[260] Similarly, in *Re D'Eye (Thomas v Mariner Properties Ltd)*,[261] Registrar Baister held that a sequence of payments of bank money were in fact contemporaneous on an analysis of the facts, but, had they not been, he saw no problem in holding that backwards tracing could apply on the basis of a coordinated scheme, citing both *Ralfo* and *Brazil v Durant*.

It seems clear, barring a decision of the Supreme Court to the contrary, that backwards or reverse tracing is now a viable action to be pleaded in relation to tracing assets through complicated payment schemes, at least where the requirements of a coordinated scheme can be established. This is an evolution, not revolution of the tracing process, and is a modern day example of equitable principles working to prevent inequitable conduct obscuring the legitimate identification of funds from trusts.

(8) The limits of equitable tracing

While the right to trace in equity is not lost merely because the property becomes mixed with other property, there are circumstances in which it will no longer be possible to identify assets as representing the original property.

255 Ibid at 40. 256 Ibid.

257 See Turner, 'Case Comment: Tracing to and Fro' [2016] CLJ 462, who argues that the *Brazil v Durant* case is not about reverse tracing, but instead decides that 'the assets into which a claimant may trace because they "represent" an original asset or its traceable proceeds are defined by the scope of the transaction, unlimited by accidents of the order and timing of the events by which the transaction is performed.'

258 [2015] UKPC 35 at 38. Scott V-C's observations in *Foskett v McKeown* about substance over form received express approval.

259 See Fong, 'Case Comment: Tracing Backwards through Mortgage Payments' [2017] LQR 389, which considers *The Fish Man Ltd (in Liquidation) v Hadfield* [2016] NZHC 1750, [2017] NZAR 1198 and *Intext Coatings Ltd v Deo* [2016] NZHC 2754, [2017] NZAR 47.

260 [2016] EWHC 850 (Comm). See also *Forester Maurice Labrouche v Frey & Ors* [2016] EWHC 268 (Ch), where a claim was rejected on the basis that the property interest had been dissipated.

261 [2017] BPIR 1174.

(a) Bona fide purchaser

It is not possible to trace trust property into the hands of a bona fide purchaser for value without notice. In such circumstances the equitable ownership of the property is entirely defeated, and the purchaser receives the absolute ownership thereof.[262] The beneficiaries may, however, be able to trace into the consideration provided by the purchaser, since this will represent the proceeds of the property. There are two components to the defence.

(i) For value

An interesting question fell to be determined by the Court of Appeal in *Independent Trustee v GP Noble Trustees*.[263] A wife (Mrs Morris) had obtained an order for financial provision in divorce proceedings. This required her husband to pay her more than £1 million. Unbeknown to Mrs Morris, her (by now ex-) husband made this payment using funds which he had misappropriated from pension trusts. If this was where matters had rested, Mrs Morris would have been able to defend any claim for the recovery of these funds by the pension fund trustee by asserting her position as a bona fide purchaser for value without notice. She was unaware of the illegitimate source of the funds, and the satisfaction of the court order meant that she provided value. However, matters did not rest in this way. Still ignorant of her ex-husband's fraud, Mrs Morris discovered from her children that Mr Morris was enjoying a standard of living inconsistent with the assets which he had disclosed to the divorce court. Mrs Morris, therefore, successfully applied to have the financial provision order set aside so that she could make a claim for a higher sum. Before the new hearing could take place, Mr Morris was found guilty of dishonest assistance in breach of trust and knowing receipt of trust funds. Could Mrs Morris retain the sums which she had already been paid? The Court of Appeal held that she could not. By having the financial provision order set aside, she had provided no value in return for the funds she had received and could no longer claim to be a bona fide purchaser for value, regardless of any lack of knowledge on her part. She was, therefore, accountable to the pension fund for any sums she still had in her hands, and for the traceable proceeds of any money of which she had disposed.

(ii) Without notice

The question of what amounts to notice defeating a claim to be a bona fide purchaser in relation to the knowing receipt of trust property was considered in *Sinclair Investments v Versailles Trade Finance*.[264] Banks had been repaid loans with money which had been derived from a complex fraud. The issue was whether the banks had notice of the illegitimate source of the funds. Part of the problem in many cases like this is that there can be growing suspicions of wrongdoing: at what point do those suspicions amount to notice? The starting point in commercial transactions is that parties are entitled to proceed on the assumption that they are dealing with honest men.[265] The first hint of a suspicion does not amount to notice,[266] nor does knowledge of a claim connote notice of a right.[267] Knowing the facts does not automatically equate to knowledge of the legal consequences. A person should only be treated as appreciating the legal consequences where he actually

[262] It was suggested in *Armstrong GmbH v Winnington Networks Ltd* [2012] 3 All ER 425 at 101 that the defence might also operate to 'clear' a legal claim, but this is contrary to a well-established principle. It may be that the defence to a restitutionary claim based on change of position could operate in the same way.

[263] [2012] 3 All ER 210.

[264] [2011] 4 All ER 335.

[265] See *Macmillan Inc v Bishopsgate Investment Trust plc (no 3)* [1995] 3 All ER 747 at 782–3, per Millett J.

[266] [2011] 4 All ER 335 at 101.

[267] Ibid at 108.

knew them, or ought reasonably to have known them.[268] It is essentially a question for the judge at what point 'a reasonable and honest person in the position of the banks, with all their experience and available sources of advice, should have known, done, and appreciated, as well as what they actually knew, did, and appreciated'.[269] What amounts to constructive notice might vary in different situations[270] and will not be established until it is shown that 'the facts known to the defendant made it imperative for him to seek an explanation, because in the absence of an explanation it was obvious that the transaction was probably improper.'[271]

(b) Dissipation

Once property and its proceeds have been dissipated, or used up, tracing is impossible because there is clearly no asset that represents the original property. The principle was stated by the Court of Appeal in *Re Diplock*:

> The equitable remedies presuppose the continued existence of the money either as a separate fund or as part of a mixed fund or as latent in property acquired by means of such a fund. If, on the facts of any individual case, such continued existence is not established, equity is as helpless as the common law itself.[272]

Therefore, beneficiaries would be unable to trace if a trustee used trust property to pay for a meal which he consumed or a foreign holiday which he has taken, as no asset would remain. Similarly, if the property has been used to discharge a debt, nothing would be left that could be said to represent the trust property.[273] A debt is a chose in action and once it has been paid it ceases to exist. There is no longer a relationship of debtor and creditor. In *Re Diplock*,[274] the Court of Appeal held that it was not possible to trace trust money wrongfully transferred to two charities which had used it to discharge debts. In *Re Tilley's Will Trusts*,[275] it was held that it was not possible to trace money paid into an overdrawn bank account, because such payment only goes to reduce the amount of the overdraft, which is simply a debt owed by the customer to the bank. The inability to trace money paid into an overdrawn account was also accepted by the Court of Appeal in *Bishopsgate Investment Management Ltd v Homan*[276] and by the Privy Council in *Re Goldcorp Exchange*.[277] This was also the position in *Moriarty v Atkinson*.[278] A yacht brokering company received client funds to finance the purchase of new boats. Some of these funds were paid into the client account and were found to be held subject to a trust. Most, however, was paid into the company's current account that was always in debit. The Court of Appeal held that there was no trust in respect of these sums as the purchase money 'was effectively used to reduce the company's liability with the bank and it effectively disappeared so that there was never any fund on which a proprietary claim could operate'.[279] The Court did not accept that the undertaking of the company to pay the money into the client account was sufficient to impose a trust on a different account from the one into which the money had been paid.[280] *Credit Agricole Corp and Investment Bank v Papadimitriou*[281] suggests that

[268] Ibid at 104. [269] Ibid at 101. [270] At 106–7.

[271] At 108, adopting a statement by Millett J in *Macmillan Inc v Bishopsgate Investment Trust plc (no 3)* [1995] 3 All ER 747 at 782–3.

[272] [1948] Ch 465 at 521.

[273] For an alternative view, see Smith, 'Tracing into the Payment of a Debt' [1995] 54 CLJ 290.

[274] [1948] Ch 465. [275] [1967] Ch 1179.

[276] [1995] Ch 211; Gullifer, 'Recovery of Misappropriated Assets: Orthodoxy Re-established?' [1995] LMCLQ 446.

[277] [1995] 1 AC 74. See also *Boscawen v Bajwa* [1995] 4 All ER 769 at 775; *PMPA v PMPS* (27 June 1994, unreported) [1995] RLR 217, HC of Ireland.

[278] [2008] EWCA Civ 1604. [279] Ibid at 15, per Lord Neuberger. [280] Ibid at 16–21.

[281] [2015] UKPC 13.

repayment of a debt may give rise to a proprietary claim against the bank which received the funds, but (as considered above) this aspect of the decision is both unexplained and hard to justify.

Nevertheless, where a beneficiary's money is used in breach of trust to discharge a *secured* debt the beneficiary will be entitled to be subrogated to the position of the secured creditor and therefore able to recover the amount of the discharged loan from the debtor. This was considered in *Boscawen v Bajwa*.[282] Money was held on trust by a solicitor for the Abbey National, which had advanced it intending that it be used to complete the purchase of a house owned by Mr Bajwa which was subject to a charge in favour of the Halifax. In breach of trust, the money was used to redeem the charge but the purchase fell through. The Court of Appeal held that the Abbey National's money could be traced into the discharge of the debt and that they should be subrogated to the position of the Halifax, which had been the creditor of the legal charge. Millett LJ explained that the Abbey National was entitled to subrogation because they had intended to retain the beneficial interest in its money unless and until that interest was replaced by a first legal mortgage on the property[283] and that in the circumstances, Mr Bajwa could not claim that the charge had been redeemed for his benefit as this would be unconscionable.[284] While subrogation may provide some answer to the problem of dissipation where money has been used to discharge a debt, it will only operate to the claimant's advantage if the debt was secured. Despite these authorities supporting the view that it is impossible to trace into an overdrawn bank account, in *Foskett v McKeown*,[285] Scott V-C considered that it remained an open question whether it was possible to trace into assets acquired from an overdrawn bank account:

> The availability of equitable remedies ought, in my view, to depend upon the substance of the transaction in question and not upon the strict order in which associated events happen . . . I would wish, for my part, to make it clear that I regard the point as still open and, in particular, that I do not regard the fact that an asset is paid for out of borrowed money with the borrowing subsequently repaid out of trust money as being necessarily fatal to an equitable tracing claim by the trust beneficiaries. If, in such a case, it can be shown that it was always the intention to use the trust money to acquire the asset, I do not see why the order in which the events happen should be regarded as critical to the claim.[286]

In *Re Diplock*[287] the Court of Appeal suggested that the use of trust property to improve a house where the improvement added no value to the house, or even caused a loss in value, would amount to a dissipation preventing tracing. In such circumstances there is nothing to trace, because 'the money will have disappeared leaving no monetary trace behind.' If the property has been dissipated, the only possible remedy will be a personal remedy against the trustee for breach of trust, or if it was received by a stranger who is liable to account for its value as a constructive trustee because he acted dishonestly.

(c) Unascertained goods

It is not usually possible to trace in equity into unascertained goods, because the purchaser does not gain title to those goods under the contract of sale until they have been separated from the bulk. This was so held in *Re London Wine Co (Shippers) Ltd*[288] and by

[282] [1995] 4 All ER 769; Birks, 'Tracing, Subrogation and Change of Position' [1995] 9 TLI 124; Mitchell, 'Subrogation, Tracing and the *Quistclose* Principle' [1995] LMCLQ 451; Andrews, 'Tracing and Subrogation' [1996] 55 CLJ 199; Oakley, 'The Availability of Proprietary Remedies' [1997] Conv 1.

[283] [1995] 4 All ER 769 at 782. [284] Ibid at 784. [285] [1997] 3 All ER 392.

[286] Ibid at 409. In support of this proposition he cited *Agricultural Credit Corpn of Saskatchewan v Pettyjohn* [1991] 79 DLR (4th) 22 and Smith, 'Tracing into the Payment of a Debt' [1995] 54 CLJ 290.

[287] [1948] Ch 465 at 547. [288] [1975] 126 NLJ 977.

the Privy Council in *Re Goldcorp Exchange Ltd*[289] In the latter case, a company dealing in precious metals sold customers 'non-allocated metal' which the company stored as a bulk on their behalf. The customers were entitled to physical delivery of the metal on seven days' notice. The company became insolvent and, after the payment of the secured creditors, there would be nothing left for the customers who had bought 'non-allocated metal'. The customers claim to a proprietary right to the gold failed. One reason was that the customers had purchased unascertained goods and that title, including equitable title, would not pass until the goods were ascertained by the seller from the bulk. Clearly, there could be a declaration of trust on behalf of the purchaser of unascertained goods by the seller, but on the facts the Privy Council held that was not the intention of the company:

> The company cannot have intended to create an interest in its general stock of gold which would have inhibited any dealings with it otherwise than for the purpose of delivery under the non-allocated sale contracts.[290]

It follows that if trust property is used to purchase unascertained goods, there will be no possibility of tracing into the bulk unless the relationship is such that it can be shown that there was a trust in favour of the purchaser.[291]

(d) **Inequitable to trace**

In *Re Diplock*[292] the Court of Appeal considered that there should be no tracing if an innocent volunteer has used trust property to improve land. To impose a charge over the land for the increase in value in such circumstances would not, in the court's view, produce an equitable result.[293] The reason for this is that a charge is enforceable by sale, and the result is that the innocent volunteer could be compelled to sell his land. This limitation may perhaps be seen as an example of the general defence of change of position, which was recognized by the House of Lords in *Lipkin Gorman Ltd v Karpnale*.[294] Whether it will be inequitable to trace will depend on the circumstances of each case. *Re Diplock*[295] concerned charities who were innocent volunteers. As Goff and Jones suggest,[296] the result might have been different if the innocent volunteer had been a rich banker who had used trust money wisely to increase the value of his country house, and he has ample liquid assets to discharge any charge over the house without having to sell it. It may now be the case that the Trusts of Land and Appointment of Trustees Act 1996 contains sufficient safeguards to protect the innocent volunteer against the unfair pursuit of a claim to an interest in land through the rules of tracing.

(9) **Claiming in equity**

Once the equitable tracing process has identified assets which represent the original trust property, the beneficiaries may be able to assert a claim thereto. The potential claims available to beneficiaries in equity are wider than at common law. Depending upon the precise circumstances, the beneficiaries may be able to assert either a proprietary claim to the assets identified, an equitable lien to restore the trust fund, or a personal claim to restitution.

289 [1994] 2 All ER 806.

290 [1994] 2 All ER 806 at 815.

291 See *Hunter v Moss* [1994] 3 All ER 215.

292 [1948] Ch 465.

293 [1948] Ch 465 at 546–8. The inability to trace where money has been expended on maintaining or improving land was accepted by Lord Browne-Wilkinson in *Foskett v McKeown* [2001] 1 AC 102 at 109. Where property is used for such purposes, he considered that it would 'at most' give rise to a proprietary lien to recover the money expended.

294 [1991] 2 AC 548.

295 [1948] Ch 465.

296 Goff and Jones, *The Law of Restitution* (6th edn, Sweet & Maxwell 2002), p 111.

(a) Claiming assets identified as representing the original trust property

Where assets have been identified as representing the original trust property, the beneficiaries may wish to claim a proprietary entitlement to them by asserting their equitable ownership. The ability to make such a claim will be especially important if the person who possesses the assets is insolvent, since this will gain the beneficiaries priority over their other creditors. Beneficiaries may also wish to assert a proprietary claim in order to take advantage of any rise in value of the assets identified.[297] A proprietary claim may, therefore, enable them to gain a windfall benefit. In *Foskett v McKeown*,[298] Lord Millett considered that if A misappropriates B's money and uses it to buy a winning ticket in the lottery, B is entitled to claim the winnings.

(i) Claiming assets that were cleanly substituted for the trust property

It has long been established that where trust property has been misappropriated, the beneficiaries will be entitled to claim any assets which can be identified as the product of a clean substitution.[299] Lord Millett explained as follows:

> The simplest case is where a trustee wrongfully misappropriates trust property and uses it exclusively to acquire other property for his benefit. In such a case the beneficiary is entitled *at his option* either to assert his beneficial ownership of the proceeds or to bring a personal claim against the trustees for breach of trust and enforce an equitable lien or charge on the proceeds to secure restoration of the trust fund. He will normally be able to exercise the option in the way most advantageous to himself.[300]

(ii) Claiming assets that were acquired from a mixed fund

Prior to *Foskett v McKeown*, a distinction appears to have been drawn between the rights of beneficiaries where assets were acquired from a mixed fund consisting of the trust property and the property of another innocent party, and where they had been acquired from a mixed fund consisting of the trust property and the property of the wrongdoing trustee. Where the mixed fund had consisted of the trust property and the property of another innocent party, for example another trust or an innocent volunteer, the assets acquired would be shared pari passu and the beneficiaries would be entitled to claim a share of the equitable ownership proportionate to their contribution. However, where the mixed fund consisted of the misappropriated trust property and the property of the wrongdoing trustee, it was thought that the beneficiaries were not able to claim a proportionate share of any assets acquired. Instead, they were limited to claiming an equitable lien over the property to secure the restoration of the trust fund. This distinction originated with the judgment of Jessel MR in *Re Hallett's Estate*,[301] and was applied by Scott V-C in the Court of Appeal in *Foskett v McKeown*.[302] However, in the House of Lords, Lord Millett held that no such distinction was to be drawn between the right of beneficiaries to claim a proportionate share of assets acquired from a mixed fund:

> In my view the time has come to state unequivocally that English law has no such rule. It conflicts with the rule that a trustee must not benefit from his trust. I agree with Burrows that the beneficiary's right to elect to have a proportionate share of a mixed substitution necessarily

[297] Some earlier cases, such as the decision of the House of Lords in *Sinclair v Brougham* [1914] AC 398, suggested that a beneficiary was not able to assert a proprietary claim so as to take advantage of an increase in the value of the property. However, this was questioned in *Re Tilley's Will Trusts* [1967] 1 Ch 1179, and, in *Foskett v McKeown* [2001] 1 AC 102, the House of Lords finally held definitively that beneficiaries are entitled to gain the advantage of an increase in value of assets acquired from the trust property.

[298] [2001] 1 AC 102.

[299] *Re Hallett's Estate* [1880] 13 Ch D 696.

[300] [2001] 1 AC 102 at 130.

[301] [1880] 13 Ch D 696.

[302] [1998] Ch 265.

> follows once one accepts, as English law does (i) that a claimant can trace in equity into a mixed fund and (ii) that he can trace unmixed money into its proceeds and assert ownership of the proceeds.
>
> Accordingly, I would state the basic rule as follows. Where a trustee wrongfully uses trust money to provide part of the cost of acquiring an asset, the beneficiary is entitled at his option either to claim a proportionate share of the asset or to enforce a lien upon it to secure his personal claim against the trustee for the amount of the misapplied money.[303]

(iii) Claiming assets where tangible property has been mixed to form a bulk

If the trust property consists of tangible property that has been mixed so as to form a physical bulk, the beneficiary will be entitled to claim a share of the equitable ownership of the bulk proportionate to his contribution. In the event that pro rata division is impossible, the beneficiary will be entitled to take the whole bulk.[304] However, given the greater ability of equity to facilitate the co-ownership of property through the medium of a trust, it is much less likely that such a situation will arise than at common law.

(b) Enforcing an equitable lien

Beneficiaries are able to claim a proportionate share of assets acquired from a mixed fund that included the trust property. In many cases, this proprietary claim will prove most advantageous to the beneficiaries, since it will enable them to gain priority over other general creditors in the event of an insolvency, or to take advantage of any increase in value of the assets. Such a proprietary claim will not, however, be advantageous if the assets acquired from the mixed fund have fallen in value, since a proprietary claim will force the beneficiaries to bear a rateable share of the loss. In order to protect the beneficiaries in such circumstances, they are entitled to choose to claim to enforce an equitable lien against the mixed fund to secure their personal claim against the trustee to have the trust fund restored. The availability of such a lien was recognized in *Re Hallett's Estate*.[305] In *Foskett v McKeown*, the House of Lords asserted a general rule that a beneficiary has the right to elect between claiming a proportionate share of an asset acquired from a mixed fund and enforcing an equitable lien. However, Lord Millett explained that a lien will only be available where the mixed fund consisted of the trust property and the wrongdoing trustee's own property, and not where the mixed fund consisted of the property of equally innocent parties:

> Innocent contributors, however, must be treated equally inter se. Where the beneficiary's claim is in competition with the claims of other innocent contributors, there is no basis upon which any of the claims can be subordinated to any of the others. Where the fund is deficient, the beneficiary is not entitled to enforce a lien for his contribution; all must share rateably in the fund. The primary rule in regard to a mixed fund, therefore, is that gains and losses are borne by the contributors rateably. The beneficiary's right to elect instead to enforce a lien to obtain repayment is an exception to the primary rule, exercisable where the fund is deficient and the claim is made against the wrongdoer and those claiming through him.[306]

Thus if a trustee misappropriates £5,000 from a trust fund and mixes it with £5,000 of his own money and purchases shares for £10,000, the beneficiaries will be able to either claim half of the equitable interest in the shares or enforce a lien for £5,000 against the shares. If the shares have risen in value to £12,000, the assertion of a proportionate proprietary

303 [2001] 1 AC 102 at 131.

304 *Foskett v McKeown* [2001] 1 AC 102 at 132, per Lord Millett.

305 [1880] 13 Ch D 696.

306 [2001] 1 AC 102 at 132.

interest will be more advantageous. If they have fallen in value to £8,000, the enforcement of a lien will ensure that the trust fund is fully restored, and that the beneficiaries do not have to bear the consequences of the wrongdoer's poor investment.

(c) Claiming personal restitution in equity

Where trust property has been misapplied and dissipated so that there are no longer any assets remaining which can be identified as its traceable proceeds, the beneficiaries will not be able to assert a proprietary claim. However, they may be able to claim personal restitution from a stranger who received the trust property. In this context the rules of tracing operate as a process by which it can be established that a stranger had in fact received trust property. This was recognized by Millett LJ in *Boscawen v Bajwa*:

> Tracing properly so-called . . . is neither a claim nor a remedy but a process. Moreover, it is not confined to the case where the plaintiff seeks a proprietary remedy; it is equally necessary where he seeks a personal remedy against the knowing recipient or knowing assistant.[307]

The personal liability of a stranger who has received trust property to make restitution was considered in the previous chapter. As was seen, unlike at common law, the mere fact of receipt alone is presently insufficient to generate a personal liability to make restitution in equity. The equitable liability to account as a knowing recipient of trust property requires that the recipient has such a state of knowledge that it would be 'unconscionable' for the benefit of receipt to be retained.

(d) Choice of remedy

The Supreme Court confirmed in *Test Claimants in the Franked Investment Income Group Litigation v Revenue and Customs Commissioners*[308] that where more than one remedy is available to a claimant, the claimant is 'free to choose the remedy that best suits his case'.[309] This is a general principle of English law.[310]

[307] [1995] 4 All ER 769 at 776. [308] [2012] 3 All ER 909. [309] Lord Hope at 21.
[310] See Lord Walker at 41 and *Deutsche Morgan Grenfell Group v IRC* [2006] UKHL 49.

Index

Please note that page references to Figures will be followed by the letter 'f', to Tables by the letter 't'

abuse of position
duty of exclusive loyalty 753–4
potential for abuse 693
preventing 694–5
reality of abuse 693–4
accessory liability requirements *see* breach of trust; dishonesty
accountability of trustees
abuse
duty to act unanimously 694–5
preventing 694
reality of 693–4
deterrence and remedies 695
documentation 707
duty to exercise discretions properly 699–705
information provision 707–13
need for 693–5
whether required to give reasons 705–7
see also control of trusts/trustees; duties and obligations of trustees; trustees
accumulations, excessive 186
acquiescence, perpetual injunctions 91
actions
for account 787–8
common law 4–5
knowledge of right of action 790
administration
cy-près schemes 499
fusion of 9
Strong v Bird, rule in 159
administrative unworkability 142, 543, 564
application 587–8
meaning 587
admissibility of evidence 210–11
advancement, powers of 599–602
accounting for advancements in the final distribution 601
benefit requirement 601–2
express powers of advancement 600
fiduciary nature 602
meaning of advancement 599–600
proportion of shares 601
protection of those with a prior interest 601
statutory power of advancement 600–1
see also maintenance powers
advancement, presumption of
admissibility of evidence 221
alternative explanations 219–20
cohabiting partners 218
defining 201
evidence of an illegal purpose 221
family relationships other than father and son 218
father and child 216
husband and wife 216–17
inferences of intention 219
mother and child 217
nature of 215
no intention to make gift but wish to retain interest in property 219–20
pending abolition 215–16
persons standing in loco parentis 216
same-sex marriages 218
strength of 218–19
when applicable 216–17
when inapplicable 217–18
wife and husband 218
see also presumed resulting trusts
affirmation 74
agency
agent employed outside scope of business 632
automatic termination 63
and equity 64
liability of agent 637
mandate 65
and ownership 64–5
permission to mix funds 779–80
powers of attorney/lasting powers of attorney 63–4
relationship 62–3
terms of 636–7
trustees' duty to supervise agents 633
trustees' liability for acts of agent 632–3, 640
who may be appointed as agent 636
see also delegation
alienation 16, 558
of charity property 608–9
conditions restricting 189
allocation of assets
assets not capable of individual allocation 864
beneficial interests 241
corporate receipts, reform 549
delegation 48–9
'first in, first out' allocation 866, 867f
individually identifiable assets 864
made only to genuine beneficiaries 125
obligation to allocate 30
para passu 864–5
rolling charge allocation 865
altruism 61
amateur sport, advancement
evolution of promotion 450–1
not all amateur sports clubs charitable 451
statutory extension of promotion 451
ameliorative waste 102
***American Cyanamid* guidelines, interlocutory injunctions** 95, 96
'balance of convenience' 96–7
other special factors to take into consideration 97–8
prohibitory injunction involved 99
'real prospect of trial' 98
'serious question to be tried' 96
see also interlocutory injunctions
animal welfare 455–6
care of particular animals 539–40
exceptions to the beneficiary principle 455, 539–41
Performing and Captive Animals Defence League 456

animal welfare (*cont.*)
public benefit 474
vivisection 477
annuities, pension schemes 53
anticipatory performance 80
anti-suit injunctions 102–3
Anton Pillar orders 109
see also search orders
appeals, interlocutory injunctions 99
appointment, powers of
administrative unworkability 564
bare/mere power 31
duties of donee of a mere power 567–9
beneficial entitlement and ownership 14, 536
capriciousness 563–4
certainty 129–30
of objects 126
certainty of objects 563
classification by donee's duties
bare/mere power 562
fiduciary powers 562
classification by mode of exercise 563
classification by the nature of the class
general powers 561
hybrid powers 562
special powers 561
compared with powers of trustee 27
delegation of allocation 49
distinguishing from powers of attorney 29
donor/donee of a power 15
duties of donee of a mere power 567–9
duty not to delegate the exercise of the power 567
no duty to consider the width of the field 567
no duty to exercise 567
duty not to exercise fraudulently 567–9
duty to consider the appropriateness of appointments 574
exercise of
contracts to exercise 566
defective exercise 565
duty not to delegate 567
duty not to exercise excessively 567
duty not to exercise fraudulently 567–9
effect of valid exercise 566
excessive 566
formalities 564–5
protectors 565
failure to exercise a mere power 569–72
demonstrating a general intention 571
express gift in default of appointment 570
implied trust in default 570–2
juridical nature of the implied trust in default 571–2
no express gift over in default 570
failure to exercise the power 576–7
fiduciary *see* fiduciary duties and powers
hybrid 34, 562
made without due consideration 575–6
modern trusts 14–15
nature of 560–3
no direct control of property 28
objects of powers 34, 563
release of 577–80
rights of objects of powers 563
testamentary power, contracts to exercise 81
validity of 563–4
see also appointment of trustees
appointment of trustees
additional trustees 671, 677–8
breach of trust before 723
custodian trustees 687
at direction of the beneficiaries 683–4
duty of care 638
express powers 672–3
formalities 679
inherent jurisdiction of court 687–8
judicial trustees 685–6
need for new appointments 671–2
new/substitute trustees 671–3
mentally incapable trustees 684–5
no one able to appoint 677
person nominated by trust instrument 676
persons exercising power to appoint 675–7
property management 30
original trustees 667–70
Public Trustee Act 1906 686–7
public trustees 686, 687
removal 672, 687–8
remuneration of judicial trustees 686
replacement trustees 672
by the settlor 667–70
special trustees 685–7
statutory powers 673
substitute trustees 673–7
circumstances in which power exercised 674–5
death of trustee 674
power to appoint 673–4
surviving or continuing trustee 676–7
Trustee Act 1925, s 36 673–9
making appointment sunder 678–9
persons who may be appointed 678
relevance of beneficiaries' wishes 678
Trustee Act 1925, s 41 679–83
court discretion 680–2
general principles 681–2
overseas trustees appointed 681
persons court will appoint 682–3
persons court will not normally appoint 683
power of court to appoint 679
removal of trustees against their will 680
scope of power 679–80
whether appointment expedient 680–1
Trusts of Land and Appointment of Trustees Act 1996, ss 19 and 20 683–5
see also retirement of trustees
arbitration, contracts referring to 81
arts, culture, heritage or science: advancement 449–50
assets
assurances 321
available for investment 643
chargeable 58
clubs and societies *see* clubs and societies
collective investment fund, forming 27
company 27
family home 271
floating charge over 27, 399
held for mixed purposes 358
individually identifiable 864
misapplication of 815–16
non surviving 778–9
not capable of individual allocation 864
rolling charge allocation 865

tracing 850
acquired prior to misappropriation 870–2
assets identified as representing the original trust property 877–88
'first in, first out' allocation 866, 867f
individually identifiable 864
not capable of individual allocation 864
pari passu allocation 864–5
product of a clean substitution 849–50
where tangible property mixed 842, 850, 860
trust fund 26, 27
unit trusts 53
see also allocation of assets
assignment
contract to assign 558–9
direct assignment 557–8
equitable interest, dealing with 557–8
assurance 319–25
active 320
by agreement 324–5
ambiguity, resolving 321
and common intention 315, 324
and false representations 323–4
grant of future rights, relating to 322–3
interpreting 325
not required to have been intended to be acted upon 323
passive 322
precision 320–1
specific assets 321
unspecific 340
by whom 325
see also proprietary estoppel
attestation, wills 383
clause 384
Attorney-General
regulation and control of charitable trusts 511–12
supervision of trustees' obligations 32
authority, powers conferring 28–9
authorized investments 645–52
express powers
interpreting 647
limits to investment powers 647
meaning of 'investment' 647–8
financial instruments 650–1
history 645–6
limits to powers 647
loans 648, 651
meaning of 'investment' 647–9
modification of the general power of investment 651–2
new approach 646
principles 645
purchase of land 651
traditional investments 649–50
Trustee Act 2000, general power under 648–52
see also investment(s)
automatic resulting trusts 195, 196, 200–1, 221
and constructive trusts 238
gaps in beneficial ownership 225–6
interpreting gifts to individuals for purposes 226–7
'out and out' transfers 227–9
pension fund surplus 229
resulting trust for whom 229

bank accounts/deposits
arrangements without trusts 59
banknotes, transfer of 45
Council of Mortgage Lenders, standard terms 237n327
Quistclose trusts 236
resulting trusts 220, 223
banking system, tracing of money through
at common law 843–7
in equity 861–70
see also tracing
bankruptcy 50–1
see also trustee in bankruptcy
bare powers
of appointment 31
capriciousness 564
release of 577–80
bare trusts
delegation of management responsibilities 48
directions by beneficiaries 177–9
as a form of fixed trust 551–2
hiding identity of true property owner 44
bargaining opportunity, loss of 93
bargains, enforcement (constructive trusts) 250–4
alternatives to constructive trusts 253–4
mutual wills 252
Pallant v Morgan equity 252–3, 254
specifically enforceable contract to sell property 250
third party, promise involving 250–2
see also constructive trusts
beneficial interests
allocation of 241
constructive trusts 397–400
date of accrual under a secret trust 415–16
declared, failure of 225–6
dispositions of subsisting equitable interests 183
express trusts declaring 278
failure to declare 225
as a mere interest in personam 33
method of quantification 314
need for quantification 313
overreaching 48
as a proprietary interest in rem 33–4
quantifying 313–14
see also variation of beneficial interests
beneficial ownership *see* ownership
beneficiaries of trusts
approval of breach of trust 697
bankruptcy 50–1
beneficial entitlement
appointment, powers of 536
ascertainable immediately or in the future 555
to defined interests 555–6
discretionary trusts 536
divestment 537
equitable ownership 14
fixed trusts 535–6
to information 697
and ownership 535–7
Saunders v Vautier principle, applying 556
unidentified beneficiaries 536
vested or contingent 555–6
beneficial principle 125
as cestui que trust 13
choosing who benefits 535–49
compared with property owners 34
direction by beneficiary of a bare trust 177–9
duties owed to 32
enforcement of trust obligations 32

beneficiaries of trusts (*cont.*)
entitled to seek remedies 697–8
equitable ownership of trust property 10
even-handedness between 546–8, 549
express trusts 141
gaps in beneficial ownership 225–6
gifts with no obvious beneficiary 361
informed consent of all 31
non-existent 225
options upon tracing and following 27–8
overriding the terms of the trust by 32
personal claims against trustee 28
potential, right to be considered as 591
primary trust, terms of 50–1
proprietary entitlement 28, 33, 590–1
receipt of trust income and income tax 57
remedies, constitution of trusts 143
residuary beneficiary 545
rights of 27, 28
discretionary trusts 589–91
equitable trust obligations 32–4
mutual wills 397–9
semantic clarity 126
settlor contracting with 165–6
should not manage the property 50
size of class 484
supervision by 697–9
unable to manage the property 49
unidentified 536
valuable consideration given by 156
variation of beneficial interests by 603
volunteer, of an incompletely constituted trust 156–7

beneficiary principle
application of 538–9
certainty of objects 125, 141, 544–5
contravention of 226
criticism 543–4
exceptions to
animal welfare 455, 539–41
anomalous 455
charitable trusts 421, 429, 431, 510
graves and monuments, maintenance of 540–1
policy limitations on purpose trusts 541
purposes benefiting an identifiable class 541–3
saying masses for the dead 541
express trusts 141
gifts for non-charitable purposes 355
invalidity 546
Quistclose trusts 231
rationale for 537–8
resulting trusts 226, 232
supervision by beneficiaries 697
trust cannot be enforced by court 538
trust will violate the rule against perpetuity 538
without beneficiaries there is no owner 537–8

benefit requirement *see* public benefit

Benjamin orders 133–4

bills of exchange 147

bona fide purchaser
doctrine of notice 19
misappropriated property 55
stranger as 836
for value 873
without notice 873–4

bona vacantia (ownerless property) 374, 377

bonus shares 549

breach of contract 102
see also contracts

breach of covenant
breach of negative covenant 98–9
common law remedies 165
damages for 93, 165
specific performance 83

breach of fiduciary duty
account of profits 698
accounting for unauthorized receipts 775–6
bribes 780–1
compensation for loss suffered 774–5
conflict of interest 770
defences to an action for 782
indirect benefits 780
liability for 769–74
limitation of action 786
rationale for strict liability 769–71
remedies 774–82
choice of remedy 781
dog's leg claims 781–2
proprietary 776–81
transparency about commissions 775
unauthorized gains 56
see also fiduciary duties and powers

breach of trust
acting inconsistently 715–16
before appointment 723
approval by beneficiaries 697
beneficiaries' consent or concurrence 734–5
compensation *see* compensation for breach of trust
constructive trusts 722
contribution and indemnity where trustee liable 741–3
contributory negligence 743
court discretion to grant relief 736–40
extent of relief 740
fairness 739–40
honesty 737
reasonableness 737–9
defences to liability 733–40
dishonest assistance 803–14
accessory liability requirements 804–7
assistance 806–7
defining 803
dishonesty 807, 808–12
existence of a trust or fiduciary relationship 804–5
fault, need for 803
personal remedy 803–4
duty of care 716–18
election between compensatory and restitutionary remedies 724
exemption clauses 718–21
failing to act with objective standard of care 31
fiduciary duties and powers 718
and fiduciary duties of trustees 31
fraud, liability for 719–20
general definition 715–22
indemnity from co-trustees 741–2
informed consent 735
injunctions 103
joint stock companies 60
liability of trustees for 28, 31, 722–3
limitation of action 783–8
constructive trusts 785

exceptions 784–5
general principle 783–4
trustee party to a fraud 784
trustee retaining trust property in his hands 785
meaning 715–24
nature of liability 722–4
by omission 31
overreaching 48
own breaches, trustee liable for 723
personal benefit from 741–2
requirements for relief from liability 734–5
resulting trusts 722
specific performance, obstacle to ordering 82
subsequently condoned by beneficiaries 735–6
tracing 833
trustees not vicariously liable for each other 723–4
trustees personally liable 722–3
unauthorized acts 31
unauthorized disposal 48
breach of warranty of authority 64
bribes 760–1, 780–1
British Social Attitudes survey 269
Browne-Wilkinson, Nicholas C. H. (Lord) 19, 29, 34, 67n8, 121, 126, 134, 137, 145, 149, 189, 195, 198, 200, 204, 206, 209, 223, 224, 238–9, 241, 260, 302, 312, 313, 314, 330–1, 334–5, 492, 667, 722, 725, 726, 729, 732, 751, 752, 817, 818, 819–20, 822, 834, 838n34, 839n40, 852, 854, 857, 858, 859, 876n293
building contracts, contracts requiring constant supervision 82–3
building societies 62
burden of a covenant, freehold land 17
burden of proof
rectification 77
reliance 326
secret trusts 408–9
business
agent employed outside scope of 632
contracts to carry on 80–1
see also ordinary course of business
capital gains tax (CGT) 57, 613, 616
defining 58
and trusts 58
capital transfer tax 58
capriciousness 142, 563–4, 588–9, 703
certainty
choosing who benefits 535
conceptual 126, 137
evidential 128–9
Hague Convention on the Law Applicable to Trusts 115
of intention to create a trust
contagious uncertainty 137
express trust, requirements 141
language used 116–17
meaning of requirement 116–17
precatory words 117–18, 120, 138
'sham' intention 118–20
lack of intention to create a trust
evidence, importance of 120–1
no trust without intention 120
something other than a trust intended 120
no single test for all trusts
appointment, powers of 129–30
discretionary trusts 129n83, 130–1
fixed trusts 127–9
individual ascertainability test, problems with 131–3
of objects
beneficiary principle 125, 141, 544–5
charitable trusts 429
class definition 125
'complete list' ('class ascertainability') test 128, 130, 131, 133, 136, 586
conceptual certainty 126, 137
discretionary trusts 585–7
evidential certainty 127
express trusts 141
fixed trusts 556
general considerations 125
Gulbenkian test 130, 131, 133, 136, 137
mutual wills 395
powers of appointment 563
trusts, powers and gifts 126
of subject matter
contagious uncertainty 137
contract to create a trust 124
definition of trust too vague 123
future property 123–4
mechanism allowing property to be identified 123
mutual wills 395
no specific property identified 121
requirement of certainty 121–4
trust can only exist in relation to specific property 121, 141
trust of a share of a larger bulk 122–3
trust property not earmarked or segregated 121–2
and uncertainty 125
three certainties 115, 141
of words 115, 116, 126, 131
see also decision; McPhail v Doulton; uncertainty
cestui que trust 13, 537n13, 539, 631, 710, 711, 735, 736, 856
cestui que use 11, 12
CGT *see* capital gains tax (CGT)
Chancellor
emergence of judicial role 5
and equity in eighteenth and nineteenth centuries 7
as Keeper of the Great Seal 5
as lawyer 6
Chancery Courts
charities, history 423
as courts of conscience 5–6
as courts of equity 6
and definition of equity 4, 5
equitable remedies 66
equity administered by 5
jurisdiction to award damages 86
limited reform of jurisdiction 7
maxims of equity 23
motivation for emergence of 5
origins of equity 5
primacy of 6

Chancery Courts (*cont.*)
reform of personnel 7
'use,' development of 11
charitable gifts
amalgamation with other charities 501–2
benignant construction in cases of ambiguity 468
for charitable purposes 51–2
contested 372–3
Equality Act 2010 and public benefit 486
failure of
application cy-près 503–5
charities that had never existed 505
charity by association 504–5
cy-près doctrine 494–5, 500–6
gifts to specific institutions or bodies 504
gifts with an underlying general charitable intention 504
incorporated charities 502–3
initial 494–5, 500–6
subsequent 499–500
testamentary rules, criticism 505–6
unincorporated charities 502
whether charity actually failed 501–3
in wills 494–5, 499–506
gifts for purposes 421
interpreting 467–70
ordinary rules of construction 468
for purposes 421
purposes must be exclusively charitable 467–8, 488–9
to religious leaders 444
to specific institutions or bodies 504
statutory amendment 468
with an underlying general charitable intention 504
unincorporated charities 502
wills
initial failure 500–6
subsequent failure 499–500
see also charitable purposes; charitable trusts; charities; gifts; wills
charitable incorporated organization (CIO) 426
charitable purposes 432–70
amateur sport, advancement 450–1
animal welfare 455–6
arts, culture, heritage or science: advancement 449–50
beneficial to the community 457–8
categories 433–5
catch-all category 434, 435
changing 495
Charitable Trusts (Validation) Act 1954 470
Charitable Uses Act 1603 433
citizenship or community development, advancement 446–8
beneficial to the community 457–8
conjunctions 469
defence and rescue services, promoting efficiency 457
and defining charitable trusts 432–5
development by analogy 458–9
educational advancement 439–41
efficiency of charities, promoting 448
environmental protection or improvement, advancement 453–4
failure 494
gifts for 51–2
health/saving of lives 444–6
human rights, conflict resolution and equality 451–3
locality, trust for benefit of 470
merit requirement, artistic works 449–50
monuments 449
need, relief of 453–4
new 434, 435, 436t
cy-près doctrine 506–8
recognising 458–60
overseas 460
Pemsel case (1891) 434, 441, 449, 472, 473
poverty prevention or relief 436–9
preservation of ability to develop 433
promotion of restorative justice 434
reform and cy-près application 493–4
religion, advancement of 441–4
statutory definition of 'charity' 432–3
without an analogy 459–60
charitable trusts
beneficiary principle, exceptions to 421, 429, 431, 510
charity proceedings
any person interested in the charity 513–15
consent of the Charity Commission 515
court jurisdiction 515
cy-près application 237
defining, when a trust is charitable 432
exception to beneficiary principle 429
in favour of a defined charitable object 426
Gift Aid 430
gifts for charitable purposes 51–2
in name of Crown 427
origins 423
political objects 461–7
private 510–11
privileges enjoyed by 428–31
certainty of objects 429
as to essential validity 429–30
financial 430, 431
perpetuity 429–30
public benefit 430
purpose trusts 429
whether justified 430–1
public benefit *see* public benefit
regulation and control 510–31
Attorney-General 511–12
Charity Commission 511, 513, 516–31
Charity Governance Code 531
charity proceedings 513–15
Code of Fundraising Practice 531
control of charity trustees 527–9
Crown 511
Fundraising Regulator 530–1
good governance 530–1
Human Rights Act 530
judicial review of charity decisions 529–30
local authorities 529
Olive Cook scandal 530–1
other regulators 515–16
regulatory system 511–16

supervision of trustees' obligations 31
see also charitable gifts; charitable purposes; Charity Commission
charities
alienation of property 608–9
all charitable institutions treated similarly 427
and altruism 428
by association 504–5
charitable and benevolent giving 545–6
mechanisms for 426–7
Charities Act 2011 662
continuing importance 425–6
defining
Charity Commission role 434–5
development of definition by analogy 433
legal meaning 421
statutory definition 432–3
discretionary trusts in favour of charitable objects 426
efficiency, promoting 448
exempt 525
extent of charitable sector 422
failure of
application cy-près 503–5
charities that had never existed 505
charity by association 504–5
cy-près doctrine 494–5, 500–6
gifts to specific institutions or bodies 504
gifts with an underlying general charitable intention 504
incorporated charities 502–3
unincorporated charities 502
whether charity actually failed 501–3
finance 422–3
fiscal privileges of charitable status 485
forms 421
general charitable intention 503, 504
'heads' of 434
history 423–4
incorporated 502–3
influence 421–2
insolvent 503
investment 662–4
judicial review of decisions 529–30
legal structure 495
legitimate political activity by 463–5
medical and healthcare 444–5
misdescribing 495
negative perceptions 428
NHS, implementing 424
non-existence of 505
outright gifts to charitable organizations 426
preservation of ability to develop charitable purposes 433
and the public 423
regulation and control 427
relevance of previous law 433
role and status 421–31
social investments 448, 663–4
in society 421–6
Statute of Charitable Uses (1601) 424, 445
'spirt' and 'intendment' 458
total return investments 663
trusteeship, voluntary principle 423
trusts in favour of defined charitable objects 426
unincorporated 502
unity of charity 427
unpaid trustees 423
volunteers 423
see also charitable purposes; charitable trusts; unincorporated associations
Charities Register 523, 524–5
Charity Commission 427
categories of charitable purpose
Charitable Uses Act 1603 433
Pemsel case (1891) 434, 441, 449, 473
role of Commission in defining 'charity' 434–5
challenges in regulation 516–21
changing regulatory approaches 520–1
threat from terrorist financing and money laundering 518–19
charitable and benevolent giving 546
and charity scandals 517–18
and clubs and societies 368
control of charity trustees
disqualification 527–8
duties of charity trustees 528–9
'Cup Trust' scandal 517–18, 521
duties and powers 521–4
annual report 521
control of charity trustees 527–9
duty to maintain a register of charities 523
extension of powers 522
to give advice to charity trustees 523–4
good governance, ensuring 530–1
Human Rights Act 530
judicial review of decisions 529–30
local authorities and charities 529
Official Custodian, designating 524
power to act for protection of charities 522–3
power to institute inquiries 521–2
duty to inform regarding desirability of bringing legal proceedings 523
functions 516
funding from 520
jurisdiction 513
and negative perceptions of charities 428
and outright gifts 426
on poverty 437–8
public benefit, guidance on 471, 472–3
assessing benefit 476, 478
Equality Act 2010 486
'personal nexus' rule (public benefit) 480, 481, 482
on reform of charitable purposes 493
regulation and control of charitable trusts 427, 510
challenges in regulation 516–21
changing regulatory approaches 520–1
regulatory system 511
Strategic Review (2011) 520
structure 516
supervision of trustees' obligations 32
see also charitable purposes; charitable trusts; charities
charity proceedings
any person interested in the charity 513–15

charity proceedings (*cont.*)
consent of the Charity Commission 515
court jurisdiction 515
Charity Tribunal 525, 526
charity trustees, control of 527–9
chattels
constitution of trusts 147
co-ownership and trusts 46
donatio mortis causa (DMC) 162
ownership, transfer of 45
cheques
constitution of trusts 147
function 147
misappropriated 816
obtaining by fraud 843
tracing and claiming 845
uncleared 643
chose in action, trusts of a promise 167
citizenship or community development, advancement
civic responsibility and good citizenship 447
corporate responsibility 447
ethical standards in business, promoting 447
promotion of community capacity-building 447
rural or urban regeneration 446–7
volunteering/voluntary sector 447–8
civic responsibility and good citizenship 447
civil partners 387
claims of civil partners 374
division between spouse and issue 375–6
and family home 267, 269, 270, 271
lack of civil partner 374
methods of making provision after death 371
with no issue 375
personal chattels, inheriting 374, 375
and void civil partnerships 375
see also same-sex relationships
Civil Society Futures 425–6
claiming and tracing 833–4, 852–79
assets product of a clean substitution 849–50
assets where tangible property mixed 842, 850, 860
bulk cannot be divided into proportionate shares 850
at common law 848–51
enforcing an equitable lien 878–9
in equity 852–79
assets acquired from a mixed fund 877–8
assets cleanly substituted for trust property 877
assets identified as representing the original trust property 877–88
choice of remedy 879
circumstances in which possible to trace 856–60
clean substitutions 860
equitable ownership of traced property 855–6
fiduciary relationship requirement 852–5
mixture of trust property and trustee's own property 862–3
of money, through a mixed fund 860–1
payments made by mistake 859–60
personal restitution 879
property of trusts or innocent volunteers mixed 864–8
right to trace 852–60
scope of equitable tracing 852
tangible property into a mixed bulk 860
through banking system 861–70
personal restitution at common law 850–1
where bulk divided into proportionate shares 850
clean hands principle 24, 92, 343
clean substitutions 841–2, 860
product of 849–50
clubs and societies 353–68
amateur sports clubs 451
asset holding and management problem 354–61
gifts to members 355–6
limits to the mutual contract theory 357–60
mutual contract theory 356–7
purpose trust theory 354–5
assets
held for mixed purposes 358
members not having control of 358
associate members 358
and Charity Commission 368
critique 367–8
dissolution
incorporated bodies 361
restrictions on dissolving the society 357
surplus funds on 362–7
unincorporated associations 361–4
expulsion from 104
forms of unincorporated association 61, 354–7
gifts
conditions attached to 359–60
made subject to rules of association 356
to members 355–6
with no obvious beneficiary 361
purpose trust theory 354–5, 356
holding of property by 54–5
incorporated 353, 362
loss of social amenity 368
members
contractual rights 365
gifts to 355–6, 359–60
lack of identifiable membership 358–9
last surviving members of an association 365–6
members' clubs 55, 354
not having control of assets 358
mutual contract theory 356–7
associations without mutual contract status 360–1
doubting 366–7
limits to 357–60
mandate theory 361
proprietary clubs 353, 362
societies that are not unincorporated associations 354
surplus funds on dissolution 362–7
incorporated or proprietary clubs 362
unincorporated associations 362–4
windfall gains 367–8
winding up by members 362
see also unincorporated associations
codicil 384, 385, 388, 405

cohabiting partners 218, 270, 271
criticism of current law 348
methods of making provision after death 371
rights before sale 294–5
rights on sale
registered land 295–6
unregistered land 295
sole legal owner
registered land 295–6
unregistered land 295
see also family home
Coke, Sir Edward 6
collective investment
investment clubs 52
lottery syndicates 52
National Lottery 52, 206, 218, 423
trust fund 27
unit trusts 52–3
common injunctions 6, 8
common intention
agreement
express, amounting to a declaration of trust 308
must be operative 308
not imputed 308–9
on shares not essential 308
and assurance 315, 324
detrimental reliance 286, 287, 288–9, 305, 306
examples 307–8
express 312
inferred 313
seen as an artificial exercise 347
common intention constructive trusts
ambit 248
application beyond the family home 307
cohabiting partners, rights of 348
common intention 307–9, 313, 315
conduct, common intention inferred from
contributions after the date of purchase 309
contributions towards mortgage payments 310
direct contribution to the purchase price 309
financial contribution alone insufficient 311
indirect contributions 309–10
knowledge of both parties 311
relating to the expected interest 312–13
criteria developed 305
criticism 314–15
development of 305–7
examples 249
Jones v Kernott (2011) 274–5
leading cases 273
and proprietary estoppel 249, 313
quantifying the beneficial interest 313–14
reliance or detriment 311–13
rationale 312
where express common intention 312
Rosset reformulation 305–6
common intention inferred from conduct 306
deficiencies 314–15
detrimental reliance 306
express common intention 306
impact of dual approach 306
invented agreement 314
quantification 306
significant change 275–6
Stack v Dowden (2007) 273–4, 278
traditional use 305
underlying theory 249
see also family home; proprietary estoppel
common law
agency 64
delegation at 631–3
equitable remedies ameliorating 66–7
equitable remedies supporting 66
and equity
historical divide 10
origins of 4–5
relationship 6
history and emergence 4
incompletely constituted trusts, remedies for
actions by the trustee 166–7
settlor contracted with beneficiary 165–6
settlor covenanted or contracted only with the trustee 166
significance 165
trusts of a promise 167–9
joint tenancy, preference for 47
marriage 270
origins of equity 4–5
powers of attorney recognized at 29n9, 64
priority between competing legal rights 23
remoteness of vesting, preventing 187
tracing at 833, 841–51
banking system 843–7
claiming 848–51
clean substitutions 841–2, 849–50
criticism 847–8
mixed funds 843
of tangible property, into a mixed bulk 842, 850, 860
Community Amateur Sports Clubs (CASCs) 450, 451
companies
assets 27
controlling interest in 662
dissolution of incorporated bodies 361
incorporation 60, 61, 129, 354
charities 502–3
independent legal status 60
joint stock 59–60, 554n19
not-for-profits 61
open-ended investment companies (OEICs) 60–1
public 59
share register 146, 154, 178, 552
subscribers 61–2
unconscionability 827
see also directors
compensation
awards 334
breach of fiduciary duty 774–5
for breach of trust *see* compensation for breach of trust
see also specific performance
compensation for breach of trust 724–33
accounting for tax liability 730
assessing 730–3
causation 725–8
compensatory remedy 724–5
date for assessing 730–1
distinct breaches 732
foreseeability of loss 729
general principles 724–30
interest 733
investment 730
liability and extent of professional involvement 728–9
liability only for loss caused by breach 728

compensation for breach of trust (*cont.*)
new approach 732–3
obligation to restore trust fund 729
offsetting losses and gains 731–3
other limits on loss 730
remoteness 729
set-off in exceptional circumstances 732
subsequent events 731
supervision by beneficiaries 697–8
see also breach of trust; liability of trustees
'complete list' ('class ascertainability') test, certainty of objects 128, 130, 131, 133, 136, 586
compromise jurisdiction 607–8
conceptual certainty 126
concurrent ownership of property
joint tenancy 46, 47
successive 47
tenancy-in-common 46, 47
trusts and co-ownership 46–7
conditional and determinable interests 185
conditions precedent 191
conditions subsequent 191–2
conditions void as contrary to public policy 189–91
conditions void for uncertainty 188–9
determinable interests 192
distinguishing conditional and determinable gifts 192
effect of an invalid condition 191–2
ways of qualifying a gift 188
conduct, common intention inferred from
contributions after the date of purchase 309
contributions towards mortgage payments 310
direct contribution to the purchase price 309
financial contribution alone insufficient 311
indirect contributions 309–10
confidential information 767–9
conflict resolution/ reconciliation, advancement 452
consideration
agreements made without 81–2
necessity of, in mutual wills 392
see also valuable consideration
constitution of trusts 139–69
cases illustrating effective declaration
by conduct 145
loose conversation 144
overarching intention to create a trust 145–6
words of gift by settlor to himself 144–5
words repeated over a period of time 144
effective declaration, requirements 143
enforcement of trusts *see* enforcement of trusts
'equity will not assist a volunteer,' exceptions to rule 157–64
donatio mortis causa (gift on account of death) 160–4
importance of exceptions 157–8
Strong v Bird, rule in 158–60
express trusts, requirements 141–2
formalities 143–4
fully constituted trusts 142, 143, 154, 415f
incompletely constituted trusts 142
remedies of beneficiary 143
transfer, constituting the trust by 146–54
bills of exchange 147
chattels 147
cheques 147
constitution through coincidental receipt by trustee 152–4
copyrights 147
equitable interests 147
requirements for effective transfer 146–7
where registration required 148–52
valid trust, two ways of creating
declaration of self as trustee 139–40
transfer of property on trust to trustees 140–1
constructive trusts
alternatives to 253–4
arising when 30, 396–7
and automatic resulting trusts 238
beneficial interests and rights 397–400
breach of trust 722
common intention *see* common intention constructive trusts
court imposed 196
date of creation 395
defining 238–9
executors 252
family home 30
imposition of 335
institutional 239
justice and good conscience 240
mutual wills 252, 395, 396–7
'new model' 258–60, 348
personal liability to account 241–2
preventing benefit from crime
death, property acquired by crime causing 243–6
jurisdiction to grant relief from forfeiture 246–7
principle that no criminal may benefit 242–3
property obtained by theft 243
reform of forfeiture rule 248
property subject to 397
and proprietary estoppel 316–17
remedial constructive trusts 261, 262
rationale for imposing 390–1
remedial 239–40
beyond unjust enrichment 256–7
defining 254
development of 255–6
difficulties 257–8
and 'new model' constructive trust 258–60, 348
prospects in England 260–3
rescission of voluntary dispositions 67
and resulting trusts 196, 197–8, 304
role
allocation of beneficial interests 241
misappropriated property 241
personal liability to account 241–2
preservation of pre-existing equitable interests 241

receipt of an unauthorized profit by a fiduciary 241
search for a coherent theory 240
secret trusts characterised as 418
trust affecting property 397
trusts arising by implication 141
when used 238

consumer protection regime 73–4
contagious uncertainty 137–8
contempt of court 25, 88, 89, 100, 108
threat of imprisonment 6, 78, 87

contracts
arbitration, referring to 81
building 82
to carry on a business 80–1
contrary to public policy 83
to create a trust 124
to exercise a testamentary power of appointment 81
general law of 54
illegal 83
immoral 83
insurance 70
invalidity of 858
land 78
mutual contract theory 356–7
mutual wills
absence of any contract 392–3
breach of contract by revocation 393
necessity of a contract 391–2
necessity of, in mutual wills 391–2
partnership 81
PMA 146
prior to and following 11 May 2000 166
promise, contractually binding 59–60, 120
requiring constant supervision 82–3
rescission of 67, 70–1
results vs. activities 82–3
setting aside 71
specific performance 78–83
specifically enforceable contract to sell property 179–81, 250
terms insufficiently precise 83
to transfer goodwill 81
uberrimae fidei 70
unique personal property, sale of 78
unlawful 83
void 857–8
voidable 858–9
see also breach of contract

contributory negligence 743
control of trusts/trustees
court supervision 696–7
criminal sanctions 695–6
duty to exercise discretions properly 699–705
duties of trustees 699
improper exercise of 700–5
relevance of beneficiaries' wishes 700
fiduciary position of trustee 696
improper exercise of discretion
capriciousness 703
compelling action 704–5
excessive 702
failure to take into account relevant matters 701
fraudulent exercise 700
general principles 700
inadequate deliberation 703
motives 701
rule in *Re Hastings-Bass* 701–2, 705
unreasonableness 703–4
information provision 707–13
means of control 695–9
need for 693–5
statutory regulation 699
supervision by court 696–7
whether required to give reasons 705–7
see also accountability of trustees

conversion jurisdiction 606
co-ownership
acquisition in joint names 202–3
and concurrent ownership 46
equitable, unit trusts as form of 52
family home 283
joint legal ownership 283
proprietary rights 16
and trusts 46–7
see also concurrent ownership of property; joint tenancy; tenancy-in-common

copyright 104, 124, 147, 175, 241n20, 441, 567
corporate receipts 548–9
corporate responsibility 447
co-trustees
acting fraudulently 741
contribution from 742
indemnity from 741–2
personal benefit from breach of trust 741–2
professionals 741

Court of Common Pleas 4
Court of Protection 64, 685
courts
approval for variations on behalf of beneficiaries 32
concurrent jurisdiction of the Charity Commission 513
of conscience 5–6
constructive trusts imposed by 196
directions by 166–7
exceptional authority given by 630
inherent jurisdiction of *see* inherent jurisdiction of court
lasting power of attorney supervised by 64
orders unlikely to be ineffective 91
refusal of injunctions 91
restructuring of system 7
single court replacing pre-existing duality of courts 8
undertakings to 88
see also Chancery Courts; Court of Appeal; Court of Appeals in Chancery; Court of Common Pleas; Court of Protection; Senior Courts

creation of trust
evidence 120–1
express intention 141

crime
financial 45
prevention of benefit from
death, property acquired by crime causing 243–6
jurisdiction to grant relief from forfeiture 246–7
principle that no criminal may benefit 242–3
property obtained by theft 243
reform of forfeiture rule 248
terrorism *see* terrorism
theft, property obtained by 243

Crown
charitable trusts in name of 427
ownerless property reverting to after death 374, 377
parens patriae of charity 511
prerogative of 4
surplus funds going to 367
as a trustee 28
and unity of charity 427
custodian trusts 52, 553–4
trustees 687
cy-près doctrine 493–509
changes in charitable purposes 495
charitable gifts in wills
initial failure 494–5, 500–6
subsequent failure 499–500
whether charity actually failed 501–3
charitable purposes 493–4, 495
charity, failure of
application cy-près 503–5
charity by association 504–5
gifts to specific institutions or bodies 504
gifts with an underlying general charitable intention 504
incorporated charities 502–3
unincorporated charities 502
whether charity actually failed 501–3
choosing new charitable purposes 506–8
circumstances triggering administrative schemes 499
Charities Act 2011, s 62 496–500
historic triggers 496
ongoing reform 499
statutory amendment 498
defining 'cy-près' 493
failure
of charitable appeals 508–9
types of 494–5
general charitable intent 495
interpretation, problems of 495
outside will context 494
schemes 506–8
wills context 493
see also charitable gifts; charitable purposes; charitable trusts; charities; wills
damages
assessment of 86
breach of covenant 165
expectation loss 77
gain-based 93
good working rule, as to timing of award 92
inadequate as remedy 88–9
jurisdiction to award 86
in lieu of perpetual injunction 92–3
in lieu of specific performance 86
loss of a bargaining opportunity 93
measure of 93–4
negotiating 93
nominal only, entitlement to 79
quantification difficult 79
reliance loss 77
Shelfer tests 93
undertaking in
freezing injunctions 108
interlocutory injunctions 99
search orders 111
when awarded 92–3
see also injunctions; interlocutory injunctions; perpetual injunctions; remedies; specific performance
Davies, Sir Mervyn 111, 576, 688
Deakin Report (1996) 424
death
claims to personal estate of deceased person 787
Crown, ownerless property reverting to following 374, 377
of donor, property surviving 159–60
of first testator 396
fully secret trusts 405
gift to take effect on 208–9
imminent, contemplation of 160–1
intention of donor continuing until 159
of minor 599
of principal 63
property acquired by crime, causing 243–6
aiding and abetting suicide 245
forfeiture of entitlement by survivorship 246
forfeiture of entitlement on victim's intestacy 246
forfeiture of entitlement under victim's will 245
jurisdiction to grant relief from forfeiture 246–7
manslaughter 243, 244, 245, 246
principle that no criminal may benefit 242–3
reform of forfeiture rule 248
rights under pre-existing trusts 246
unlawful killing 244n34
violence used or threatened 243–5
property rights expiring on 369
saying masses for the dead 541
of secret trustee 410–11
Strong v Bird, rule in 159–60
of survivor, constructive trust arising on 396–7
of trustee 674
see also donatio mortis causa (DMC); intestacy; wills
deception 71, 527, 694, 846n85
declaration of trust
beneficial interests
declaration not made 225
failure of 225–6
by conduct 145
effective, requirements for 143
by conduct 145
loose conversation 144
overarching intention to create a trust 145–6
words of gift by settlor to himself 144–5
words repeated over a period of time 144
express agreement amounting to 308
inter vivos declarations of trust
sub-trusts 173–4
trusts of land 170–3
trusts of personal property 173
perpetual injunctions 94–5
self as trustee 139–40
subsidiary trust 559
sub-trust 173–4
will, declaration of trust by 174
deemed disposals, capital gains tax (CGT) 58
defence and rescue services 457

defences
breach of fiduciary duty 782
breach of trust 733–40
laches 24
rectification 77
specific performance 84–5
defined interests *see* fixed trusts
delay
defeating of equity 24
detrimental reliance 91
length of 790
perpetual injunctions 91
rescission 74–5
specific performance 85
delegation
of allocation 48–9
at common law 631–3
conditions, investment management 665–6
current statutory framework 634–40
general power of 635
general principle 631
individual 640
investment management 664–5
liability of trustees for acts of agent 632–3
limited entitlement to delegate 631–2
management powers 630–1
no delegation of trustees' duties 631
in ordinary course of business 631
powers of appointment 567
reasons of convenience 48
scope of right 632
in special cases 635–6
statutory right to delegate 633–4
vulnerable individuals, providing for 49–51
see also agency; management powers
demergers 549
Denning, Lord Alfred Thompson 'Tom' (Lord) 7, 9, 22, 98n333, 99–100, 108n461, 109, 110, 130, 135, 182, 240, 245, 257, 258, 259, 260, 261, 302n28, 305, 311, 330, 335, 339, 348, 607, 609n47, 616, 681
detriment
acquisition of new land by claimant 329
or change of position 328
detrimental reliance 330, 332
equivocal actions 330–1
improvement of claimant's own land 329
improvement of legal owner's land 329
knowledge of legal owner 332
and legal owner
improvement of land 329
knowledge of 332
personal disadvantage 330
and public benefit, balancing 477
redressing 338–9
or reliance 311–13
requirement of 328
types 329–30
and unconscionability 328
weighing against derived benefits 331–2
working without adequate remuneration 330
see also proprietary estoppel
detrimental reliance
common intention 286, 287, 288–9, 305, 306
common intention constructive trusts 305
delay and acquiescence 91
evidence 289n121, 289n122
express trusts 279
family home 285, 286, 287, 288–9, 297, 306, 312
laches 791
proprietary estoppel 330, 332
quantifying shares 290n127
remedial constructive trusts 263
and unconscionability 152
diminished responsibility 245
Diplock, Kenneth (Lord) 9, 95, 96, 97, 207, 218–19, 226, 259, 262, 302, 304–5, 309, 505n86
directors
authorized opportunities 766
fiduciary relationships 750
general principles 764–5
joint stock companies 59
liability after ceasing to hold office 765–6
remuneration 27, 762–3
see also companies
disclaimer by secret trustee
after death of testator 411
revocation of acceptance 410–11
disclosure of information 707–13
see also information disclosure
discretionary trusts 581–93
allocation obligation 30
alternatives to equal division 593
beneficial entitlement 536
beneficiaries, rights of 589–91
proprietary interest in the fund 589–90
blurring of distinctions 38
certainty
no single test for all trusts 130–1
of objects 129n83, 130–1
certainty of objects 585–7
court enforcement 593
delegation of allocation 49
development 583
duties and obligations of trustees
allocations only to objects 592
expressions of wishes 592
survey of range of objects 591–2
duties of trustees 591–3
early development of equitable obligations akin to 36–7
enforcement by court 593
equal division 593
even-handedly, duty to act 546–7
evolution of intermediate obligations 36, 37
exhaustive 39, 583–4
failure 133
fiduciary duties and powers 31
fiduciary powers 579
flexibility 582–3
historical background 585–6
individual ascertainability test, problems with 131
invalidity 142
maintenance powers 597
vs. mere powers 43
nature of 581
non-exhaustive 39, 41n47, 584
power conferred on a trustee, whether 43
proprietary rights
class as a whole 589–90
individual beneficiaries 590–1
right to be considered as a potential beneficiary 591
and protective trusts 50
protectors 592–3
tax rates 57
types 583–4
validity 585–9
administrative unworkability 587–8

discretionary trusts (*cont.*)
capriciousness 588–9
certainty of objects 585–7
'complete list' test, criticism 586
'is or is not' test 587
perpetuities, rule against 589
discrimination 190, 452–3
prohibition of 191, 486
religious 486
dishonest assistance 803–14
accessory liability requirements 804–7
assistance 806–7
defining 803
dishonesty 807, 808–12
existence of a trust or fiduciary relationship 804–5
fault, need for 803
personal remedy 803–4
dishonesty 807
clarification 809–10
judged objectively 808
markers 812–14
problems with clarification 810–11
remedies 814
test for 808–12
confirmation 811–12
and unconscionability 824
unconscionable receipt, liability for 822–3
disposal of trust property
overreaching 48
powers *see* disposal powers
without authority 27
disposal powers 643–5
dispositions
defining 175–6
scope 175–6
of subsisting equitable interests 174–84
exceptions to need for writing 177–84
meaning of 'disposition' 175–6
scope of disposition 175–6
'signed by the person disposing of the same or his agent' 177
'or by will' 177
'in writing' 177
writing requirement 174–7
distributive powers 594, 625
divestment 537
divorce 270
and family home 293–4
revocation of wills 388
DMC *see* donatio mortis causa (DMC)
doctrine of notice
acting in good faith (bona fides) 19
actual notice 20
concept 18–19
constructive notice, rules on 20–1
destruction of equitable proprietary interests by 21
and doctrine of constructive notice 821
legal title 19–20
operation of 19
protection of bona fide purchaser for value 33
protection of equitable interests 47–8
purchase for value 19
requirements of equitable doctrine 19
without notice requirement 20
see also equitable proprietary rights; proprietary rights; trust deeds; trust instrument
documentation
accountability 707
incorporated
clearly identified in the will 384
in existence at date of will 384
referred to in the will 384
rectification of 17
mistake 75
unilateral instruments 76–7
see also trust deeds
dominion, delivery of in a DMC 162–3
donatio mortis causa (DMC)
conditional and revocable 161
contemplation of imminent death 160–1
critique 164
delivery of dominion 162–3
methods of making provision 370
property which cannot be subject to 163–4
requirements 160–3
subject matter 163
see also constitution of trusts; death; gifts
double dominium (duality of ownership) 10
duress, undue influence 71
duties and obligations of trustees
allocation of trust property 30
charity trustees
duty to apply for registration 528
duty to have an annual audit 529
duty to keep accounts 528
duty to prepare an annual report 529
duty to prepare annual accounts 528
to consider exercising a discretion 699
dependent upon trust terms 28
discretionary trusts
allocations only to objects 592
expressions of wishes 592
survey of range of objects 591–2
duty to exercise discretions properly 699–705
exclusive loyalty, strict duty of 31
investment 654, 656–64
management of trust property 30
mandatory character 30–1
reasons for decisions
justification for rule 705–6
legitimate expectation 706–7
no duty to give 705
voluntary provision of reasons 706
to supervise agents 633
see also equitable trust obligations; liability of trustees; trustees
duty of care 638–9, 656–7
breach of trust 716–18
standard of care 697–7

easement 17n61, 66, 101
defining 94n310
grant of 334
education
advancement 441
arts and culture 449
broad concept of 439
craftsmanship, encouraging 439
Independent Schools Council 472
industrial training and professional bodies 439–40
public benefit 474, 487–8
teaching 439
truly educational value 440

trusts for advancement of 439–41
worthy of charitable status 440
Eldon, Lord 7, 36–7, 163, 215, 392, 572, 583, 585, 754, 758, 760, 769–70
emergency jurisdiction 606–7, 609
employment relationships 103
endowment policies 52n33
enforcement
of constructive bargains 250–4
of fiduciary powers 39
specifically enforceable contract to sell property 179–81, 250
of trusts *see* enforcement of trusts
enforcement of trusts
beneficiaries, rights of 32
beneficiary principle 538
discretionary trusts 593
doctrine of notice 47–8
fully constituted trusts 155
hybrid obligations 37
incompletely constituted trusts 155–7
indirect 157
secret trusts
arising outside of testator's will 413–14, 415f
fraud prevention 412–13
English law
methods of making provision after death 371
rejection of 'new model' constructive trust 259
remedial constructive trusts, prospects for *see* remedial constructive trusts
resulting trusts 195
environmental protection or improvement, advancement 453–4
equal division, trust for 593
equality and diversity, promotion of 452–3
equitable interests
constitution of trusts 147
disclaimers 176
doctrine of notice 18, 19–20
fixed trusts 557–9
overreaching 48
pre-existing, preservation of 241
priority between 18
protecting 47–8
subsisting, dispositions of 174–84
exceptions to need for writing 177–84
meaning of 'disposition' 175–6
scope of disposition 175–6
'signed by the person disposing of the same or his agent' 177
'or by will' 177
'in writing' 177
writing requirement 174–7
see also beneficiaries of trusts
equitable ownership *see* ownership
equitable property rights *see* doctrine of notice; equitable proprietary rights; proprietary rights
equitable proprietary rights
destruction by doctrine of notice 21
doctrine of notice
acting in good faith (bona fides) 19
actual notice 20
concept 18–19
constructive notice, rules on 20–1
destruction of equitable proprietary interests by 21
and doctrine of constructive notice 821
legal title 19–20
operation of 19
purchase for value 19
requirements 19
without notice requirement 20
priority between equitable interests 18
equitable remedies 22, 66–111
ameliorating the common law 66–7
enforcing equitable obligations 67
mutuality 83–4
rectification
burden of proof 77
common mistake 75–6
defences to 77
mistake in written document 75
requirements for 75–7
of unilateral instruments 76–7
unilateral mistake 76
rescission
limitations on availability 74–5
for misrepresentation 70–1
for mistake 67–70
for undue influence 71–3
specific performance 77–86
supporting the common law 66
where equity intervenes 66–7, 77–8
see also remedies
equitable rights
corresponding to legal 17
proprietary, without a legal equivalent 17
see also legal rights; rights
equitable trust obligations 26–43
allocation of trust property 30
beneficiaries, rights of 32–4
classification 34–42
blurring of distinctions 38–40
blurring of traditional categories of trust and power 38–40
contemporary 38
distinguishing between trusts and powers 34–5
enforcing fiduciary powers 39
evolution of intermediate obligations 36–7
McPhail v Doulton decision 26, 37–8
pension schemes 40
traditional categorization 35–6
content of, under the trust 30
discretion not exercised 43
discretionary extreme 42
early developments akin to discretionary trusts 36–7
equitable remedies enforcing 67
express intention to impose 29
fiduciary powers 31–2
hybrid 36, 37
implied intention to impose 29
imposed 29–30
intermediate
evolution of 36–7
recognition 26
intermediate points on scale 42
liability of trustees for breach of trust 31
to manage the trust property 30
mandatory character 30–1
mandatory expressions, whether used 43
mandatory extreme 42

equitable trust obligations (*cont.*)
objects of powers of appointment 34
pension schemes 27, 40
power conferred on a trustee, whether 43
powers conferring authority 28–9
practical guide to interpretation 42–3
rights and duties, determining 40–1
scale of 35, 39f, 41–2
source of 29–30
traditional categorization
limitations of 35–6
trust or power 35
trusts combined with powers 36
trust as species of 28
trust fund 26–8
trust power 43
trusts subject to 28–32
equitable waste 102
equity 3–25
and agency 64
challenging the law 6
Chancery Courts as courts of 6
character of jurisdiction 5–6
and common law
historical divide 10
origins of equity 4–5
relationship 6
concept 4
creativity of 22
defects 7
and durability of proprietary rights 18–21
in the eighteenth and nineteenth centuries 7
equality 23, 24
establishing
assurance 319–25
detriment 328–32
essence of proprietary estoppel 317
reliance 325–8
unconscionable conduct 317–19
fairness in 4
filling the gap 273
fusion of law with *see* fusion of law and equity
impact on everyday lives 3
intervention by 66–7, 77–8
Judicature Acts 1873 and 1875 4
as justice of God 4
layperson's understanding 4
legal definition 4, 5
maxims of equity *see* maxims of equity
mere equities 17–18, 21
minimum equity approach 257
origins 4–10
Pallant v Morgan equity 252–3, 254
prevailing of 6
primacy of 7, 8
and property management 44–65
reforms 7
satisfying
appropriate remedy 336–43
range of remedial responses 332
types of award 332–6
supremacy 8
tracing in 833, 852–79
assets acquired prior to misappropriation 870–2
assets acquired from a mixed fund 877–8
assets cleanly substituted for trust property 877
assets identified as representing the original trust property 877–8
bank trustee depositing trust money with itself 869–70
banking system, tracing of money through 861–70
bona fide purchaser 873–4
choice of remedy 879
circumstances in which possible to trace 856–60
and claiming 833–4, 852–79
clean substitutions 860
enforcing an equitable lien 878–9
equitable ownership of traced property 855–6
fiduciary relationship 852–5
limits of equitable tracing 872–6
lowest intermediate balance 868–9
method of application 866–8
misappropriation of trust property by a trustee 856
mixed funds 860–1
mixture of trust property and trustee's own property 862–3
of money, through a mixed fund 860–1
payments made by mistake 859–60
payments under a void contract 857–8
payments under a voidable contract 858–9
personal restitution 879
profits received by a fiduciary in breach of duty 856
property of trusts or innocent volunteers mixed 864–8
receipt of trust property by a stranger to a trust 856
right to trace 852–60
rule in *Clayton's case* 866
scope of equitable tracing 852
of tangible property, into a mixed bulk 842, 850, 860, 878
and transfer of ownership 45–6
see also 'equity will not assist a volunteer' rule
'equity will not assist a volunteer' rule
constitution of trusts 150
exceptions to 157–64
donatio mortis causa (gift on account of death) 160–4
importance of exceptions 157–8
Strong v Bird, rule in 158–60
incompletely constituted trusts 156
remedies of beneficiary 143
specific performance 81
'equity's darling' 19
estate duty 58, 148, 589–90, 610
estate in fee simple 11
estates
feudal system of land holding 11
parallel doctrine 11
see also estate duty; fee simple, estate in; testate and intestate succession
estoppel *see* proprietary estoppel
even-handedly, duty to act 546–8
bonus shares 549
cash payments 549
corporate receipts received as a 'windfall' by the trust 548–9
demergers 549
and discretionary trusts 546–7

general duty 546
investment 642
reform of the allocation of corporate receipts 549
and successive interests
apportionment between income and capital 548
corporate receipts received as a 'windfall' by the trust 548–9
duty to convert investments 547–8
evidence
admissibility of 210–11, 221
altering of wills 384
creation of trust 120–1
detrimental reliance 289n121, 289n122
illegal purposes test 221
of intention, lack of 197
intention of gift 208
intention of loan 209–10
quality of 210
real possibility of destruction of 110
evidential certainty 127, 128–9
executors 355, 540, 758, 799, 818, 819
and constitution of trusts 156, 168
constructive trusts 252
donatio mortis causa (DMC) 160
joint 159
and mutual wills 389, 390
presumed resulting trusts 211
and probate 373
testamentary transfers 669
tracing 835, 852
exemption clauses 718–21
fraud 719–20
reform 721
voluntary trustees 720–1
exhaustion
discretionary trusts 39, 583–4
of a fund 237
trust fund not exhausted 226
expectation loss 77
expectations
criticism of analysis 338
excessive 340–1
financial remedies, explaining 337–8
fulfilment of claimant's 'reasonable expectation' 336–7
what was promised 337
express trusts
administrative unworkability 142
appointment of trustees by settlor 667
beneficiaries 141
capacity 142
capriciousness 142
constitution 141
express intention to create 141
family home
declaring beneficial interests 278
functions of trusts 277–8
not declaring beneficial interests 279
subsequent variation of shares 278–9
when trusts created 277
formalities 141–2
and proprietary estoppel 279
Quistclose trusts as 233
requirements 141–2
secret trusts characterised as 417–18
settlor creating 29
trust property 141
see also implied trusts

failure
beneficial interests 225–6
of charitable appeals 508–9
of charities and charitable gifts
application cy-près 503–5
charitable purposes 494
charities that had never existed 505
charity by association 504–5
cy-près doctrine 494–5, 500–6
gifts to specific institutions or bodies 504
gifts with an underlying general charitable intention 504
incorporated charities 502–3
initial failure 494–5, 500–6
subsequent failure 499–500
testamentary rules, criticism 505–6
unincorporated charities 502
whether charity actually failed 501–3
in wills 494–5, 499–506
cy-près doctrine 494–5, 500–6
discretionary trusts 133
exercise of mere power of appointment 569–72
gifts for purposes 421
not allowed by equity 31
to observe restrictions 639
public benefit test 473
Quistclose trusts, purpose in 236
secret trusts 409
specific charitable purpose 226
of trust, for uncertainty of subject matter 125
of trustees to exercise fiduciary power 577
fair-dealing rule 760
fairness
breach of trust 739–40
common intention constructive trusts 309
in equity 4
even-handedly, duty to act 549
fair balance between beneficiaries 546
family home 281, 291, 293, 294, 309, 341, 348, 350
proportionality 341
see also even-handedly, duty to act; unfairness
false representations 323–4
family home
acquisition in sole legal owner cases
express agreement 287–8
inferred from conduct 288–9
and civil partnerships 267, 269, 270, 271
common intention constructive trusts
application beyond the family home 307
common intention 307–9, 347
criteria developed 305
development of 305–7
Jones v Kernott (2011) 274–5
leading cases 273
Rosset reformulation 305–6
significant change 275–6
Stack v Dowden (2007) 273
traditional use 305
constructive trusts 30
criticism of current law 346–9
current approach to legal issues 273–6
acquisition and quantification 276

family home (*cont.*)
applying 280–94
common intention
constructive trusts 273–5
criticisms 346–7
equity fills the gap 273
features 276
focus on family home 276
intention of the parties 276
deserted wife's right to occupy 17–18
detrimental reliance 285, 286, 287, 288–9, 297, 306, 312
equity of deserted wife 297
evolution of rights in 297–315
deserted wife's equity 297
proprietary interest in the home 298
resulting trusts 298–304
exclusion of abusive spouse from 66
express agreement 287–8
express trusts
declaring beneficial interests 278
functions 277–8
not declaring beneficial interests 279
rebutting the presumptions 283
starting-point 283
subsequent variation of shares 278–9
when created 277
fairness 281, 291, 293, 294, 309, 348, 350
gender imbalance 348
and inheritance tax 58
injunctions, rights protected by 104
interests in 273–96
express trusts 277–9
Jones v Kernott (2011) 273–6, 278, 280–4, 288, 291, 297
proprietary rights, practical impact 294–6
significant change 275–6
Stack v Dowden (2007) 273, 276, 278–86, 288, 290–2, 297
intestacy 376
joint legal ownership 283
legal response to disputes 271
ownership
by a company or third party 290
joint legal ownership 283, 284
sole legal ownership/title *see below*
proprietary estoppel *see* proprietary estoppel
proprietary rights
practical impact 294–6
rights of cohabitant before sale 294–5
purchase price contributions
direct 299
discount against purchase price 300–1
general household expenses 301
impact of excluding mortgage contributions 300
incidental expenses 301
mortgage contributions not referable to agreement 300
mortgage repayments 299–300
otherwise explained as gifts 302
otherwise explained as loans 301–2
repairs or renovation 301
quantifying beneficial interests 313–14
quantifying shares 290–4
basis of quantification 290–1
comparison with divorce 293–4
express intention 290
inferring and imputing intention 290
relevant factors 291–2
quantifying the interest 302–4
constructive trusts subsuming resulting trusts 304
utilizing constructive trust analysis 303–4
rebutting the presumptions 283–90
acquisition in sole legal owner cases 287–9
cultural factors 289
express agreement 287–8
express trusts 283
joint legal title 284
ownership by company or third party 290
sole legal title 284–7
reform attempts 344–6
resulting trusts
continuing role for 280–1
evolution of rights in family home 298–304
fate of 282–3
property other than the family home 281–2
rejection of analysis 280
social and legal context 267–71
sole legal ownership/title 283
acquisition 287–9
original approach 284
registered land 295–6
revised approach 284–7
rights on sale 295–6
unregistered land 295
see also cohabiting partners; marriage; proprietary estoppel
fee simple, estate in 11, 317, 332–3, 337, 599
fee simple absolute in possession (freehold) 19n73
transfer of 340
fee tail 11n34
feoffees 11, 12
feudal system of land holding 11
fiduciary duties and powers 572–3, 752–3
abuse of position 753–4
see also abuse of position
advancement, powers of 602
and agency 64
appointments made without due consideration 575–6
breach of fiduciary duty 769–74
bribes 760–1
classification by donee's duties 562
confidential information, use of 767–9
considering whether to exercise the power 574
core content 752–3
court supervision 575–7
different duties in different contexts 574–5
difficulty of weighing motives 754
discretionary trusts 579
of donee 574–5
duration 753
duty of exclusive loyalty 753–4
duty to consider the appropriateness of appointments 574
duty to consider the range of objects 574
enforcement 39
failure of trustees to exercise 577
failure to exercise the power 576–7

fair-dealing rule 760
incidental profits 761–4
injunctions for breach 67
opportunities 764–7
company directors 764–6
trustees 766–7
other contexts 751
purchase of trust property by trustees 757–60
receipt of an unauthorized profit by a fiduciary 241
release of powers 577–80
authorization to release 579
consequences of release 577–9
and fraud on a power 580
means of release 580
mere powers 578
mere powers with a trust in default of appointment 578–9
no authorization to release 579
secret commission 760–1
self-dealing rule *see* self-dealing rule
trustee as fiduciary 745
trustees subject to 31
unauthorized renumeration 755–7
see also agency; fiduciary relationships

fiduciary relationships 744–52
artificial use 751–2
company directors 750
employees 749–50
exceptions to general rule 748–9
fiduciary per se 746–7
not fiduciary per se 747–8
tracing and claiming in equity 852–5
types 745–50
see also fiduciary duties and powers

Financial Action Task Force (FATF) 519

financial compensation 334

financial instruments 650–1, 663

First-Tier Tribunal (Charity) 525–7

fixed trusts 550–9
allocation obligation 30
beneficial entitlement
ascertainable immediately or in the future 555
to defined interests 555–6
and ownership 535–6
Saunders v Vautier principle, applying 556
vested or contingent 555–6
certainty of objects 556
for equal division 128
equitable interest, dealing with 557–9
contract to assign 558–9
direct assignment 557–8
directions to trustees to hold on trust 558
subsidiary trust, declaration 559
evidential certainty 128–9
example 550, 551f
execution and performance 556–7
in favour of a class 128, 550
for identified individual 127–8
mandatory 38
nature of 550, 551f
Saunders v Vautier, rule in 536
trusts combined with powers 36
unequal shares 128
uses of
bare trusts 551–2
concurrent interests 555
consecutive interests 555
custodian trusts 52, 553–4
nominee trusts 552–3, 626
non-trustee custodians 554
when certainty required 129

flexibility
discretionary trusts 582–3
freezing injunctions 108
interlocutory injunctions 95
trusts 26, 37

floating charges 27, 399

'floating trust' 398–9
use of property subject to 399–400

forfeiture of entitlement
aiding and abetting suicide 245
'deemed predecease rule' recommended to replace 248
jurisdiction to grant relief from 246–7
reform of rule 248
by survivorship 246
trials and convictions 245
on victim's intestacy 246
under victim's will 245
violence, used or threatened 244, 245
see also constructive trusts

formalities 170–84
absence of, defence to specific performance 84
appointment of trustees 679
constitution of trusts 143–4
constructive trusts 184
declarations of trust by will 174
dispositions of subsisting equitable interests 174–84
exceptions to need for writing 177–84
writing requirement 174–7
express trusts 141–2
inter vivos declarations of trust 170–4
limitations on additional formalities 565
powers of appointment, exercise of 563–4
required by terms of the power 565
resulting trusts 184

fraud
breach of trust 719–20
co-trustees 741
'fraud on the power' 31, 618
improper exercise of discretion 700
limitation of action 786–7
power of appointment, duty not to exercise fraudulently 567–9
appointor intends to secure a personal benefit 569
bargain with the appointee 568–9
benefit for a person not an object of the power 569
powers of appointment 567–9
release of fiduciary powers 580
secret trusts, enforcing to prevent 412–13
setting aside transactions for 17
trustee party to 784
wills, capacity to make 380

freedom of expression 99

freehold land, equitable proprietary rights 17

freehold reversion, purchase of 762

freezing injunctions
appointment of a receiver 108
defining 106
enforcement principle 106
flexibility 108
history 108–9
known as 'Mareva' injunctions 106
nature of 106
operation of 107–8

freezing injunctions (*cont.*)
standard form 107
undertaking in damages 108
when granted 106–7
friendly societies 62
Friends of Three Faiths Forum 453
fully constituted trusts 142, 154, 415f
defining 143
enforcing 155
see also constitution of trusts
fully secret trusts 402
acceptance 406–7
communication
of both the fact and terms of trust 404–5
of the extent of the trust 405
to joint trustees 405–6
made before the death of testator 405
failure 409
intention 404
secret trustee predeceasing the testator 410
funded pension schemes 53, 229
fusion of law and equity
fusion of administration 9
Judicature Acts 1873 and 1875, effect 8–9
single coherent body of law 9–10
single court replacing pre-existing duality of courts 8
in substance 9

Gift Aid 430
gifts
on account of death *see* donatio mortis causa (DMC)
ambiguous 199
to be applied for purposes 51
bills of exchange 147
carrying intermediate income 597–8
certainty of objects 126
for charitable purposes 51–2
cheques 147
contingent 597–8
contributions otherwise explained as 302
deathbed *see* donatio mortis causa (DMC)
distinguishing conditional and determinable gifts 192
evidence of intention 208
express trusts 570
imperfect 156
inter vivos, intention to make 159
interpreting to individuals for purposes 226–7
lack of intention to make 198–9
lifetime 370, 380
no obvious beneficiary 361
outright gifts to charitable organizations 426
presumption against 202
for purposes 421
recalling as unconscionable 150–1
secret trusts 401–2
subject to a condition 134–5
to take effect on death 208–9
to unincorporated associations *see* clubs and societies; unincorporated associations
ways of qualifying 188
words of, by settlor to himself 144–5
see also charitable gifts
good conscience concept 19
Goodman Committee (1976) 459
goodwill 771n212
of a business 107n437
contracts to transfer 81
graves, maintenance of 540–1, 544
gross negligence 720, 721

habeas corpus 6
Hale, Brenda Marjorie (Baroness) 89, 274, 275, 346
in *Jones v Kernott* 280, 281–2, 283n81, 284–5
in *Stack v Dowden* 277, 279, 284–5, 287n107, 290, 291, 292
half-secret trusts 402
communication 407–8
failure 409
secret trustee predeceasing the testator 410
harassment 105
alleged sexual harassment 427n47
hardship 5, 70, 437
to children 294
financial 438, 454, 513
specific performance 84, 85
health advancement
analogous and ancillary purposes 446
imposition of fees or charges for treatment 445–6
medical and healthcare charities 444–5
public benefit 474
saving lives 446
High Court of Justice, and Judicature Acts 1873 and 1875 7
Higher Education Funding Council for England 511
human rights
advancement of human rights, conflict resolution and equality 451–3
broad category 451
conflict resolution/reconciliation 452
religious/racial harmony, equality and diversity 452–3
and Charity Commission 442
conditions void as contrary to public policy 190, 191
trusts with political objects 461
hybridity, enforcement of hybrid obligations 37

illegality
acts by strangers 806
clean hands principle 24
conditions 188
contracts 83
drugs 275
fox hunting 543n68
hiding identity of true property owner 45
illegal purposes 211–15
change, contextualizing 213–14
critique 462n263, 466, 475
evidence 221
impact upon old reliance rule 212–13
majority decision 212
multi-factorial approach 211–12, 214
Patel v Mirza (2017) 211–14
policy considerations 214
presumed resulting trusts 213
problem of 211
special cases 214–15
transactions 214
types of illegal purpose 221n202
immigration 97
industrial action 688
and specific performance 83

- trust directions 604
- unlawful killing 243, 244n34, 245

immoral contracts 83

implied trusts
- appointment of trustees by settlor 667
- in default 570–2
- juridical nature 571–2
- *see also* express trusts

inalienability, rule against 188, 355, 429, 538
- charitable trusts 429
- rule against perpetuities 186–7
- unincorporated associations 355

incapacity 614, 675
- breach of trust 735
- mentally incapable trustees 684–5
- *see also* powers of attorney

incidental profits 761–4
- competition 763–4
- purchase of a freehold reversion 762
- remuneration received as a director 762–3
- renewal of existing arrangement 761–2

income tax
- avoiding by use of trusts 57–8
- defining 57
- rates of 57
- receipt of trust income by beneficiaries 57
- taxable income 57
- and trusts 57

incompletely constituted trusts
- common law remedies
  - actions by the trustee 166–7
  - directions by court 166–7
  - settlor contracted with beneficiary 165–6
  - settlor covenanted or contracted only with the trustee 166
  - significance 165
  - trusts of a promise 167–9
- defining 142
- enforcing 155–7
- valuable consideration, beneficiaries given 156
- volunteer beneficiaries 156–7
- *see also* constitution of trusts

incorporated clubs and societies 353

Incorporated Council of Law Reporting 459

incorporation of company 60, 61, 129, 354

indemnities
- from beneficiaries 742–3
- from co-trustees 741–2

individual ascertainability test 131–3

infancy 614, 675

information disclosure
- about trust 707–13
- advice 711
- ban on 710
- beneficial entitlement 697
- beneficial right to disclose 708
- to Charity Commission 523
- compelling 710
- disclosable 710
- documents required for accountability 707
- non-disclosure principle 705
- obligation not unconditional 711
- obligation to disclose 707–10
- reform 712–13
- routes to 711
- supervisory jurisdiction 708–9
- voluntary 709

inherent jurisdiction of court
- advancement, powers of 602
- breach of trust, remedy 742–3
- constructive trusts 512
- cy-près doctrine 496, 499
- fiduciary duties and powers 756
- indemnities from beneficiaries 742–3
- information provision 709
- maintenance powers 595, 599
- removal of trustees 687–8
- remuneration of trustees 756
- variation of beneficial interests 604, 606–9
  - broader understanding 608–9
  - compromise jurisdiction 607–8
  - conversion jurisdiction 606
  - emergency jurisdiction 606–7, 609
  - maintenance jurisdiction 607, 610
- *see also* courts; jurisdiction

inheritance tax (IHT)
- chargeable transfers 58
- defining 58
- exempt transfers 58
- history 58
- operation of 58
- transfers of value, charged on 58
- and trusts 58–9

injunctions 86–111
- anti-enforcement 103
- anti-suit injunctions 102–3
- common 6
- ex parte 88
- failure to comply with 87
- freezing *see* freezing injunctions
- history 86–7
- interlocutory *see* interlocutory injunctions
- mandatory 87, 90–1, 99–100, 103
- maxims of equity 25
- nuisance 66
- perpetual *see* perpetual injunctions
- power to grant 87
- privacy protection 105
- prohibitory 87
- quia timet 88, 100–1
- rights protected by
  - anti-suit injunctions 102–3
  - breach of contract 102
  - breach of trust 103
  - employment relationships 103
  - expulsion from clubs and societies 104
  - family matters 104
  - harassment 105
  - intellectual property rights 104
  - nuisance 102
  - planning permission 105
  - restrictive covenants 86, 103, 514
  - trespass 101–2
  - waste 102
- superinjunctions 22, 87, 88, 105, 105n415
- undertakings to court 88
- uses of 86
- without notice 88

insolvency
- avoiding effects of 56
- charitable companies 503
- *see also* bankruptcy; winding up

institutional constructive trusts 239, 254

institutional resulting trusts 223–4

insurance, rescission of contracts 70

intellectual property rights 111
- copyright 104, 124, 147, 175, 241n20, 441

intention/intentionality
advancement, presumption of 219
ascertaining 120
assumed intention and beneficial interests 314
certainty of intention 116–21
contagious uncertainty 137
to create a trust 116–20
express trusts 141
lack of intention to create a trust 120–1
common intention constructive trusts *see* common intention constructive trusts
to create a trust
language used 116–17
meaning of requirement 116–17
precatory words 117–18, 120, 138
'sham' intention 118–20
of donor, continuing until death 159
equitable trust obligations, imposing 29
evidence of
gifts 208
loans 209–10
express intention to create a trust 141
family home
express intention 290
inferring and imputing intention 290, 315
limited bases for inferring intention 315
quantification of beneficial interests 314
significant change 276
fully secret trusts 404
importance of 196
inter vivos gift, making 159
lack of intention to create a trust
evidence, importance of 120–1
no trust without intention 120
something other than a trust intended 120
maxims of equity 25
no evidence of 197
not every trust arising due to 55
powers of appointment 571
resulting trusts 196, 197
intention of transferor 198
lack of intention to make a gift 198–9
presumed intention of parties 198
of settlors 604, 619–20
'sham' intention 118–20
inter vivos declarations of trust
sub-trusts 173–4
trusts of land 170–3
trusts of personal property 173
inter vivos gift 58, 159, 162
interim injunctions 88
interlocutory injunctions
American Cyanamid guidelines 95, 96–8, 99
approach on appeal 99
breach of negative covenant 98–9
flexibility 95
freedom of expression 99
general principles governing 95–100
granted where 87–8
libel 99, 100
mandatory 99–100
third parties, impact on 100
trade disputes 100
undertaking in damages 99
when to grant 95–6
intestacy 373–7
claims of surviving spouse or civil partner 374
Crown, property going through 374
division between spouse and issue 375–6
forfeiture of entitlement by 246
'hotchpot' doctrine 376
inheritance principles 374
issue and no spouse or civil partner 375
lack of spouse or civil partner 374
Law Commission 373
matrimonial home 376
order of inheritance amongst remoter relatives 376
partial 371, 376
per stirpes principle 375
problems raised by including only blood relations 377
and relatives 374
rules 373–6
secret trusts 403
statutory legacy 375, 376
see also death; wills
invalidity
absence of writing 418
beneficiary principle 546
of contracts 858
discretionary trusts 142
effect of an invalid condition 191–2
of trusts 119–20
see also validity
investment clubs 52
investment trusts 60
investment(s) 641–66
assets available for 643
authorized *see* authorized investments
authorized investments 645–52
charity, special considerations for 662–4
compensation for breach of trust 730
controlling interest in a company 662
delegation 664–5
disposal powers 643–5
duties of trustees 656–64
advice, need for 658
ethical considerations 659–61
financial considerations 658–9
general duty of care 656–7
periodic review 661–2
property management 30
even-handedness between beneficiaries 642
investment portfolios 654–5
mortgages of land 662
other powers of sale and reinvestment 644–5
power of variation in trust deed 652
principles of which court grants approval 653
purpose 642–3
related functions 666
responsibilities of trustees 654
risk management 654
social 448, 663–4
special rules for particular investments 662
standard criteria 657
supervision and review 666
terminology 60
theories 654–6
total overall return 655–6
trust for sale 643
Trustee Act 2000 655
Trustee Investments Act 1961 655

trustees' powers of disposition over 27
unit trusts, rights of investors in 53
widening of powers 652–3
IPRs *see* intellectual property rights
Ireland, legal right share 371

joint stock companies 59–60, 554n19
joint tenancy 46, 47
methods of making provision after death 370
mutual contract theory 357
secret trusts 403
see also tenancy-in-common
joint venture trusts 252
Judicature Acts 1873 and 1875
effect 8
fusion of law and equity 8–10
legal definition of equity 4
operation of s 25(11) of Supreme Court of Judicature Act 1873 8
procedural implications of the reforms 8
restructuring court system 7
supremacy of equity enshrined 8
Supreme Court of Judicature Act 1873, s 25 8
uniform jurisdiction given to Senior Court judges 8
judicial review, charity decisions 529–30
jurisdiction
of Chancery Courts, limited reform 7
Charity Commission 513
charity proceedings 515
compromise 607–8
conversion 606
damages awards 86
emergency 606–7, 609
equity, character of 5–6
forfeiture rule, reform of 248
inherent jurisdiction of court *see* inherent jurisdiction of court
maintenance powers 599
uniform, given to Senior Court judges 8

King's Bench 4
King's Council 4, 5
King's Court 4

laches
detrimental reliance 791
equitable defence of 24
limitation of action 789–91
doctrine 789–90
knowledge of right of action 790
prejudice to defendant 790–1
statutory limitation periods 789
land
of claimant 329
constitution of trusts 144
constructive notice, rules on 20–1
contracts 78
improvement 329
mortgages of 662
new, acquisition by claimant 329
ownership of
legal 329, 332–3, 335
shared 308, 555
social legal ownership 295–6
transfer of 164, 332–3, 335
trusts and co-ownership 47
purchase money resulting trusts 206–7
purchase of 651
registered 295–6
transfer of an undivided share 333
unregistered 20, 48, 295
voluntary transfers of 204–5
see also trusts of land
Land Registry 44, 45, 48, 146, 149, 171, 214
limitation on number of trustees 669–70
transfer, constituting the trust by 146, 149
law
correcting 5
equity challenging 6
equity following 23
fusion with equity *see* fusion of law and equity
prevailing of, where equities equal 23
single coherent body of 9–10
see also common law
Law Commission 546, 633–4, 638
on breach of trust 717, 721
on charities and charitable trusts 446, 467, 508, 509, 526, 527
on constructive trusts 242–3
on cy-près triggers 499
and duty to act even-handedly 548
exemption clauses 721
and family home 270–1, 345–6
and incompletely constituted trusts 164
and intestacy 373
on investments 663–4, 669
on limitation of action 783, 788
on political purposes test 466
and presumed resulting trusts 213
and reform of forfeiture rule 248
and rule against perpetuities 185, 187
on wills 319, 369, 370n7, 373, 377–81
attestation 383
evidence of intention 386
rectification 387
suggestion for a dispensing power 387
Law Reform Commission 611
Law Reform Committee 633
Lawson, F. H. 15, 16
lease, grant of 333
legal ownership *see* ownership
legal personality 51n28, 61, 62
clubs and societies 54, 353
independent 354, 502
mutual societies 61
separate 354
legal rights
vs. equitable 18
equitable rights corresponding to 17
Ireland 371
proprietary 18
see also equitable rights; rights
legitimate expectations
charitable purposes 470
reasons for decisions 706–7
trusts protecting 55
Letters of Administration 158, 159, 373
liability of agent 637
liability of strangers 799–800
liability of trustees
for acts of agent 632–3
breach of trust *see* breach of trust; compensation for breach of trust
in deciding whether or not to delegate 637–8
duty of care in selection and appointment 638
duty of care in supervision 638–9

liability of trustees (*cont.*)
failure to observe restrictions 639
personal liability to account 241–2
trustees of land for acts of agents 640
vicarious liability 639
see also breach of trust; duties and obligations of trustees
libel 99, 100
life insurance policies 370, 778
lifetime gift 370, 380
maintenance powers 597
lifetime trust 370
limitation of action
actions for account 787–8
breach of fiduciary duty 786
breach of trust 783–8
constructive trusts 785
exceptions 784–5
general principle 783–4
trustee party to a fraud 784
trustee retaining trust property in his hands 785
claims to personal estate of deceased person 787
fraud 786–7
laches 789–91
doctrine 789–90
knowledge of right of action 790
length of delay 790
prejudice to defendant 790–1
statutory limitation periods 789
postponing start of limitation period 786–7
reform 788
rescission 75
unauthorized profits, against 791–3
unconscionable receipt, liability for 829
loans
authorized investments 651
evidence of intention 209–10
investment 648
purchase price contributions 301–2
trust of unused loan funds 230
locus standi 31, 34
Lord Cairns' Act 92
lottery syndicates 52

***McPhail v Doulton* decision (equitable)**
and blurring of distinctions 38
and blurring of traditional categories of trust and power 39
categorization of trust or power 35
delegation of allocation 49
and enforcing fiduciary powers 39
equitable obligations 26
evolution of intermediate obligations 36
individual ascertainability test 131
limitations of traditional categorization 36
rights and duties, determining 40, 41
scale of equitable obligations 41
as a twentieth-century watershed 37–8
see also equitable trust obligations
maintenance jurisdiction 607, 610
maintenance powers
adults 596
and allocation of trust property 30
categories of 594
contingent gifts 597–8
contrary intention 596
death of a minor before attaining a vested interest 599
defining 594
discretionary trusts 597
express 595
gifts carrying intermediate income 597–8
income to be accumulated 598–9
inherent jurisdiction of court 599
legal changes 595
lifetime contingent gifts 597
minors 595–6
pecuniary legacies 598
statutory 595–9
subject to prior interests 597
of trustees 595–9
undistributed income 598–9
vested interests 597, 599
see also advancement powers
management of trust property *see* property management
management powers
delegation by trustees 630–1
express 627
extent of 626–31
implied 627
need for management 626
statutory 627–30
compromises 629–30
exceptional authority given by court 630
general 628–30
insurance 629
receipts 628–9
reversionary interests 630
sale 628
trusts of land 627–8
trusts with no powers 625–6
see also delegation
mandate
agency 65
theory 361
mandatory injunctions 87, 103
general principles governing 90–1
interlocutory 99–100
manifest disadvantage 71
manslaughter 243, 245, 246
motor 244n35
voluntary or involuntary 244
'Mareva' injunctions *see* freezing injunctions
marriage
advancement, presumption of 216–17, 218
common law 270
conditions restraining 189–90
and emancipation of women 269
equity of deserted wife 297
null and void 225
occupation rights 17–18
polygamous 375
revocation of wills 387
same-sex 218
surviving spouse
claims of 374
division between spouse and issue 375–6
lack of 374
method of making provision for 371
with no issue 375
personal chattels, inheriting 374, 375
void 375
see also cohabiting partners; family home; same-sex relationships
Master of the Rolls 585
matrimonial home *see* family home
maxims of equity
clean hands principle 24

conduct of claimant 24
delay defeats equity 24
equality is equity 24
equity acting in personam 25
equity follows the law 23
equity will not suffer a wrong to be without a remedy 23
he who seeks equity must do equity 24
imputing intention to fulfil an obligation 25
looking to the intent rather than the form 25
non-binding nature 22
regarding as done that which ought to be done 25
where equities are equal, the first in time prevails 23
where equities are equal the law prevails 23

medical and healthcare charities 444–5

Megarry, Sir Robert 54n44, 80, 86, 100, 116, 177, 180–1, 182, 183, 195, 200, 229n266, 231, 364n63, 365, 404, 409, 413, 503, 504, 505n86, 514, 564, 574, 576, 587, 589, 591n73, 613, 617, 618, 621, 643, 653, 659, 660, 711, 715, 757, 821, 822, 823, 826, 828, 835, 836

members' clubs 55, 354

mental capacity, loss of 63

mere equities 17–18, 21

mere interest in personam 33

mere powers 131, 562, 564
of appointment 31
blurring of distinctions 38
vs. discretionary trusts 43
with a trust in default of appointment 578–9, 581

misappropriated property 55–6, 241

misrepresentation
innocent 70
meaning 70
representation of fact 70
rescission of contracts 70–1
rescission of voluntary dispositions for 71
specific performance 84

mistake
common 75–6
rectification 75–6
requirements for 69
rescission for
contracts 67
difficulties with current principles 70
only part of transaction affected 70
Pitt v Holt (2013) 68, 70
requirements 69
taxation 69
voluntary transactions 67–70
specific performance 84
unilateral 76
in written document 75
see also rectification; rescission

mixed funds, tracing of money through 843

money laundering 45, 428, 528, 728, 778, 812, 813, 816, 846, 871, 872
and terrorist financing 518–19

money purchase schemes 53

monuments 449, 468, 540–1

mortgages
contributions not referable to agreement 300
Council of Mortgage Lenders, standard terms 237n327
equitable rights corresponding to legal 17
impact of excluding mortgage contributions 300
repayments 299–300

murder 245

mutual contract theory 356–7
associations without mutual contract status 360–1
doubting 366–7
gifts with no obvious beneficiary 361
limits to
assets held for mixed purposes 358
charitable unincorporated associations 360
conditions attached to gifts to unincorporated associations 359–60
lack of identifiable membership 358–9
members not having control of the assets 358
restriction on dissolving the society 357
mandate theory 361
see also clubs and societies

mutual societies 61–2, 422

mutual wills
constructive trusts 252, 395, 396–7
date of execution 395
date of first testator's death 396
doctrine 389–90
establishing
absence of any contract 392–3
additional evidence of agreement 394–5
breach of contract by revocation 393
certainty of subject and objects 395
identical wills, mere fact of 393–4
necessity of a contract 391–2
necessity of consideration 392
standard of proof 393
operation of 395–7
practical problem 389
rationale for imposition of a constructive trust 390–1
see also wills

mutuality, specific performance 79, 83–4

Nathan Report (1952), charities 424, 516

National Council for Voluntary Organizations 424

National Lottery 52, 206, 218, 423

National Trust 422, 450, 453, 514, 529, 530

natural justice, rules of 104

need, relief of 453–4
examples 454
interests of social welfare 455
public benefit 474
recreational facilities, provision 454–5

negligence
contributory negligence 743
gross negligence 720, 721
liability of draftsman for 388
unconscionable receipt, liability for 820–1, 825
undue influence 71

Neuberger, David (Lord) 92–3, 122–3, 213, 214–15, 263, 278, 280, 281, 300, 304n42, 320, 321, 324, 349, 503, 777, 778, 791, 862

New Zealand
'new model' constructive trust 260
reverse tracing doctrine 872

nominee trusts 552–3, 626

***non est factum* doctrine** 67

non-marital heterosexual relationships *see* cohabiting partners
notice *see* doctrine of notice
notice(s)
power of attorney 64
see also doctrine of notice
nuisance
injunctions 66, 86, 93, 102
suspension of 94
noise 102
public or private 86, 102

objects, certainty of
beneficiary principle 125, 141, 544–5
charitable trusts 429
class definition 125
'complete list' ('class ascertainability') test, certainty of objects 128, 130, 131, 133, 136, 586
conceptual certainty 126, 137
discretionary trusts 130–1, 585–7
evidential certainty 127
express trusts 141
fixed trusts 556
general considerations 125
Gulbenkian test 130, 131, 133, 136, 137
individual ascertainability test 131–3
mutual wills 395
powers of appointment 563
trusts, powers and gifts 126
whether a single test for 136
obligations *see* duties and obligations of trustees; equitable trust obligations
occupancy right 333–4, 337
family home 17–18, 297
proprietary estoppel 333–4
occupational pension schemes 646n31
OEICs *see* open-ended investment companies (OEICs)
open-ended investment companies (OEICs) 60–1
ordinary course of business
delegation in 631, 633
doctrine of constructive notice 821
trust fund 27
trustees' liability for acts of agent 632
overlord, feudal system 11
overreaching 48, 177n47, 296, 641, 669, 671, 694
ownership
absolute legal owner 140
and agency 64–5
beneficial, gaps in
declared beneficial interests fail 225–6
essential requirements of trust not satisfied 226
failure to declare beneficial interests 225
non-existent beneficiary 225
specific charitable purpose, failure of 226
trust fund not exhausted 226
beneficiaries of trusts and beneficial entitlement 14, 535–7
position of 33
concurrent 46–7
duality of 10
elements 16
equitable 14, 29
constitution of trusts 143
and legal ownership 9, 10, 29
sub-trust created by 29n10
of traced property 855–6
family home 269
by a company or third party 290
joint legal ownership 283, 284
sole legal ownership 283, 284–7, 295–6
hiding identity of true property owner 44–5
imposition of trust obligations 29
of land
legal 329, 332–3, 335
shared 308, 555
transfer of 164, 332–3, 335
trusts and co-ownership 47
legal
constitution of trusts 143
electronic 147
and equitable ownership 9, 10, 29
family home 283
improvement of land 329
joint 283
knowledge of 332
proprietary rights 18
sole 283
title 29
transfer of 332–3
trustee as legal owner 10, 13–14
ownerless property reverting to after death 374, 377
property 16
and proprietary rights 15
resulting trusts 199
retention of 199
separation of 10–11
single outright owner 47
successive 47
transferring 45–6
trusts 13–14
unincorporated associations, capability of owning 354
see also title
Oxfam 422, 426, 463
Charity Commission inquiry into sexual scandal cover-up (Haiti, 2010) 465, 510, 517, 518, 521

***Pallant v Morgan* equity** 252–3, 254
parental duties
advancement, presumption of 216, 217
conditions affecting 190
partnership contracts 81
partnerships, contracts 81
pecuniary legacies 598
Pension Law Review Committee 694
Pension Protection Fund 54
pension schemes
annuities 53
approved schemes 53
defined benefit/contribution 53
equitable trust obligations 27, 40
executive pension plan 53n39
funded 53, 229
occupational 646n31
pension fund surplus 54, 229
special characteristics 54
trusts 53, 54
winding up 367
performance doctrine 25
permissive waste 102
perpetual injunctions
acquiescence 91
clarity of order 89
clean hands principle 92
court order unlikely to be ineffective 91
damages
an inadequate remedy, where 88–9
in lieu 92–3
measure of 93–4
when awarded 92–3

declarations 94–5
delay 91
general principles governing 88–95
grant of as discretionary 90–1
granted where 87
infringement of claimant's rights 89
mandatory 90–1
prohibitory 90
refusal by court 91
suspension of 94

perpetuities, rule against
beneficiary principle 538
complexity 188
excessive accumulations 186
remoteness of vesting 185–6
perpetuity rules before 6 April 2010 187
perpetuity rules on or after 6 April 2010 187–8
rule against inalienability 186–7
rules 185–7

personal disadvantage, detriment 330

'personal nexus' rule (public benefit)
continued relevance 481–2
criticism 481
impact 480–1
meaning 479, 480
and poor relations 482
scope 482
unsatisfactory state of current law 485

personal property
contracts for sale 78
co-ownership and trusts 46
inter vivos declarations of trust 173
purchase money resulting trusts 206
voluntary transfers of 203

personal representatives 163, 361, 389, 494, 625, 668, 669, 674, 684, 785, 819
inheritance principles 374
intestacy rules 374, 376
of last surviving or continuing trustee 677
and probate 373
proving lack of will, in intestacy 373–4

personal rights 10, 28, 33, 557
vs. proprietary rights 16

personal service contracts 80, 103, 146

planning permission 16, 93, 105

policy limits 185–92
conditional and determinable interests 185
conditions void as contrary to public policy 189–91
conditions void for uncertainty 188–9
distinguishing conditional and determinable gifts 192
effect of an invalid condition 191–2
ways of qualifying a gift 188
rule against perpetuities
complexity 188
remoteness of vesting rules 187–8
rules 185–7

political objects, trusts with 461–7
ancillary political activities 463
application of the restriction 462–3
critique of political purposes test 466–7
furthering the interests of a political party 461
legitimate political activity by charities 463–5
lobbying before a general election 465
meaning of 'political objects' 461–2
procuring a reversal of government policy, decision or authorities 462
procuring changes in the laws 461–2

Ponzi schemes 864

portfolio investment theory 654, 655, 657

poverty
clothing provision for children 437
contextual meaning 437–8
and destitution 437
'going short' 437
legal concept 437
meaning 436–8
meaning of 'relief' or 'prevention' 438–9
prevention 436–9, 483
public benefit to relieve 483, 490
purposes of prevention, examples 439
relief, trusts for 436–9

power of attorney
and equitable obligations 29
lasting
certification of instrument 64
creation of 63–4
need for 63
notice to named persons 64
supervision by court 64
uses of 63

powers
acting outside terms of the power 29
of advancement *see* advancement, powers of
authority conferred by 28–9
certainty of objects 35, 126, 131, 136–7
created inter vivos 36
distributive 594, 625
'fraud on the power' 31
hybrid 34
individual ascertainability test, problems with 131
investment 647
of maintenance *see* maintenance powers
management *see* management powers
purely discretionary 34
and trusts
combination of 36
disposition, powers of 27
distinguishing between 34, 115
and enforcing fiduciary powers 39
fiduciary duties and powers 31
functional similarity 34
limitations of traditional categorization 35–6
trust or power 35
see also appointment, powers of

precatory words 117–18, 120, 138

presumed resulting trusts 195
advancement, presumption of
admissibility of evidence 221
alternative explanations 219–20
defining 201
evidence of an illegal purpose 221
inferences of intention 219
nature of 215
pending abolition 215–16
strength of 218–19
when applicable 216–17
when inapplicable 217–18

presumed resulting trusts (*cont.*)
alternatives to
evidence a gift was intended 208
gift to take effect on death 208–9
classic presumption 201–3
acquisition in joint names 202–3
against gifts 202
provider of purchase money 202
evidence
admissibility of 210–11, 221
gifts intended 208
of illegal purpose 221
loan intended 209–10
quality of 210
executors 211
illegal purposes 211–15
change, contextualizing 213–14
evidence 221
impact upon old reliance rule 212–13
majority decision 212
multi-factorial approach 211–12, 214
Patel v Mirza (2017) 211–14
policy considerations 214
presumed resulting trusts 213
problem of 211
special cases 214–15
transactions 214
purchase money resulting trusts 205–7
rebutting the presumption of resulting trust 207–11
admissibility of evidence 210–11
alternatives to a resulting trust 208–10
quality of evidence 210
voluntary transfers of land 204–5
voluntary transfers of personal property 203
primary trust
for intended recipients 231
lack of 232
for a purpose 231–2
terms of 50–1
see also Quistclose trusts
privacy orders 105
privacy protection *see* injunctions
privilege against self-incrimination 111
privity of contract
equitable proprietary rights 17
incompletely constituted trusts 157n89
probate 371
profits
account of 698
incidental 761–4
personal 31, 718
private 471, 475, 487
profit-making ventures 445–6, 774
taxable 430n67
unauthorized *see* unauthorized profit
windfall 397
prohibitory injunctions 87, 90
promise
of assurance 266
'balance of cost,' pension schemes 53
by banks 59
contractually binding 59–60, 120
by deed 108
falling short of an agreement 263
of future benefit/conduct 258, 259
incomplete constitution of trusts 96, 118
mere promise to create a trust 77
nominal consideration 108
principle of 265
remedial constructive trusts 213
resulting trusts 176
of settlors 96, 108, 109, 118, 143
third parties 202–4
third parties, involving 250–2
'trust of a promise' 118n60, 120–1
incompletely constituted trusts 167–9
where reasonable to rely on 263
property management
arrangements without trusts 59–65
beneficiaries of trusts
inability to manage the property 49
should not manage the property 50
clubs and societies, property holding by 54–5
collective investment 52–4
delegation
beneficiary should not manage the property 50
beneficiary unable to manage property 49
management functions 48
equitable interests, protecting 47–8
and equity 44–65
gifts
to be applied for purposes 51
for charitable purposes 51–2
ownership
hiding identity of true property owner 44–5
sharing 46–7
trustees' duties and obligations 30
property/trust property
acquired by a crime causing death
aiding and abetting suicide 245
forfeiture of entitlement by survivorship 246
forfeiture of entitlement on victim's intestacy 246
forfeiture of entitlement under victim's will 245
jurisdiction to grant relief from forfeiture 246–7
manslaughter 243, 244, 245, 246
principle that no criminal may benefit 242–3
reform of forfeiture rule 248
rights under pre-existing trusts 246
unlawful killing 244n34
violence used or threatened 243–5
acquisition in joint names 202–3
allocation 30
beneficial interests and constructive trusts 397
cannot be subject to a donatio mortis causa 163–4
capacity of trustee to deal with 28
ceasing to exist 125
certainty of subject matter
contract to create a trust 124
definition of trust too vague 123
future property 123–4
mechanism allowing property to be identified 123

no specific property identified 121
requirement of certainty 121–4
trust can only exist in relation to specific property 121, 141
trust of a share of a larger bulk 122–3
trust property not earmarked or segregated 121–2
and uncertainty 125
crimes concerning
causing death 243–6
theft 243
defining 15
equitable rights corresponding to legal 17
express trusts 141
future 123–4
holding by clubs and societies 54–5
identical interests in 24
immovable 107
legal title *see* legal title
mechanism allowing identification 123
misappropriated 55–6, 241
misdescription 85
movable 107
no specific property identified 121
not earmarked or segregated 121–2
not subject to 'equity will not assist a volunteer' rule 163–4
ownership 16
product of trust property will also be trust property 27
purchase by trustees 757–60
residuary interest distinguished from future property 124
rights in 16
specific, trust only existing in relation to 121
specifically enforceable contract to sell 179–81, 250
substance rather than form of transactions 17
surviving death of donor 159–60
tangible 842
tracing *see* tracing
transfer on trust to trustees 140–1
transferring ownership of 45–6
trust fund, belonging to 27

proprietary clubs 353
proprietary estoppel
assurances *see* assurances
awards 332–6
composite remedy 334–5
financial compensation 334
grant of a lease 333
grant of easement 334
imposition of a constructive trust 335
no remedy 335–6
occupancy right 333–4
transfer of legal ownership of land 332–3
transfer of undivided share of land 333
and common intention constructive trusts 249, 313
and constructive trusts 262, 316–17
remedial constructive trusts 261, 262
defining 316
detriment
acquisition of new land by claimant 329
or change of position 328
detrimental reliance 330, 332
equivocal actions 330–1
improvement of claimant's own land 329
improvement of legal owner's land 329
knowledge of legal owner 332
personal disadvantage 330
redressing 338–9
requirement of 328
and unconscionability 328
weighing against derived benefits 331–2
working without adequate remuneration 330
and detrimental reliance 306
distinguishing constructive trusts 317
equity, establishing
assurance 319–25
based on unconscionable conduct 317–19
detriment 328–32
essence of proprietary estoppel 317
equity, satisfying
appropriate remedy 336–43
range of remedial responses 332
types of award 332–6
essence of 317
expectations
criticism of analysis 338
excessive 340–1
financial remedies, explaining 337–8
fulfilment of claimant's 'reasonable expectation' 336–7
what was promised 337
and express trusts 279
and indirect contributions 299
interests in family home 296
land contracts 78
nature of 316–17
quantification of beneficial interests 314
reliance
burden of proof 326
as a causal connection 326
establishing 326–7
reasonableness 328
requirement 325
remedies
award, principles governing 336
bars to a remedy 343
composite approach 339
fulfilment of claimant's 'reasonable expectation' 336–7
multifactorial approach 340–3
redressing detriment 338–9
untrammelled discretion 339–40
unconscionable conduct 317–19
broader understanding 318–19
strict criteria ('five probanda') 317–19
three requirements 319
underlying principles 313n92
unregistered land 295
see also common intention; common intention constructive trusts; constructive trusts; family home; remedies

proprietary rights
beneficial interests in rem 33–4
beneficiaries, entitlement of 28, 33
defining 15–16
discretionary trusts
class as a whole 589–90
individual beneficiaries 590–1

proprietary rights (*cont.*)
right to be considered as a potential beneficiary 591
durability 18–21
equitable *see* equitable proprietary rights
equitable interests as 48
essential characteristic 16
family home 298
legal 18
mere equities 21
misappropriated property 55
and other rights in property 16
and ownership 15, 16
vs. personal rights 16
strangers to trust 797–9, 814, 834
subsidiary rights 16
see also property/trust property
protective trusts
primary trust, terms of 50–1
secondary, terms of 51
Public Accounts Committee 518
public benefit
abstract public goods 474
alternatives to 483–5
class of beneficiaries, size of 484
fiscal privileges of charitable status 485
purpose of trust 484–5
assessing
balance of benefit and detriment 477
controversial nature of 476
hybrid approach, considering 478
modern conditions 478–9
objective assessment 477
view of the public 476–7
whether always measuring objectively 477–8
balance of benefit and detriment 477
benefit aspect 473
benefit may be direct or indirect 474–5
form of benefit may be practical or intangible 474
recognized as charitable 475
relating to aims of charity 475–6
Charity Commission guidance 471, 472–3
concept 430, 476
consequences of failing 473
current law, unsatisfactory state 485
defining 473–90
alternative approach to public benefit 483–5
assessing benefit 476–9
benefit aspect 473, 474–6
impact of conditions or restrictions on benefit 485–8
non-charitable benefits, must be incidental 488–90
public aspect 479–83
unsatisfactory state of current law 485
gun and rifle clubs 479
impact of conditions or restrictions on benefit
arbitrary restrictions not permitted 486–7
assumption that benefits available to all in need 485
'class within a class' not permitted 487
Equality Act 2010 486
excluding the less well-off 487–8
Oppenheim test 485
some restrictions may be justified 485–6
indirect 475–6
non-charitable benefits, must be incidental
'exclusively charitable' rule 467–8, 488–9
incidental private or non-charitable benefits 489
severance of non-charitable elements 490
particular circumstances 490–2
poverty relief 490
practical impact 471–3
proof of need for 477
public aspect 473
'personal nexus' rule *see* 'personal nexus' rule (public benefit)
poor relations 482–3
poverty prevention 483
sufficiently large group 479–80
public benefit test
when applicable 471
where applicable 472
regulatory tool 471
of religion 490–2
when self-evident 490
Public Guardian 63
public nuisance 86, 102
public policy, conditions void as contrary to
conditions affecting parental duties 190
conditions restraining marriage 189–90
conditions restraining religion 190
conditions restricting alienation 189
impact of legislation and changes in social attitudes 191
purchase money resulting trusts 205–7
instalment payments 206
land purchase 206–7
nature of contributions 207
provider of purchase money 202
purchase of personal property 206
size of beneficial share 207
purchase price contributions
direct 299
discount against purchase price 300–1
general household expenses 301
impact of excluding mortgage contributions 300
incidental expenses 301
mortgage contributions not referable to agreement 300
mortgage repayments 299–300
otherwise explained as gifts 302
otherwise explained as loans 301–2
repairs or renovation 301
see also family home
purpose trusts 537–45
beneficiary principle 537–41
gifts to unincorporated associations 354–5, 356
non-charitable 187
policy limitations on 541
and privileges enjoyed by charitable trusts 429
purposes benefiting an identifiable class 541–3
administratively unworkable class 543
application to unincorporated association 542
rule in *Re Denley's Trust Deed* 542, 543

'Red Cross' Trusts 545
theory 354–5
see also charitable trusts

quia timet injunctions 88, 100–1
***Quistclose* trusts**
beneficiary principle 231
case 230–1
criteria needed
existence of trust compatible with terms of business 235
failure of purpose 236
high level of certainty 235
money advanced for a specific purpose 234
money kept in separate bank account 236
money not at free disposal of recipient 234–5
unused funds to be returned 235
express trust 233
finding 236–7
mandate, whether 233
nature of 231–2
primary trust
for intended recipients 231
lack of 232
for a purpose 231–2
as quasi-trust 233
resulting trust throughout 232–3
sui generis situation 233
trust of unused loan funds 230
see also resulting trusts

Radcliffe Commission (1956) 431
reasonableness
fulfilment of claimant's 'reasonable expectation' 336–7
reliance 328
receipts *see* unconscionability
receiver appointment 39n41, 108
recreational facilities, provision 454–5
rectification
burden of proof 77
common mistake 75–6
defences to 77
of documents 17
mistake in written document 75
requirements for 75–7
of unilateral instruments 76–7
unilateral mistake 76
of wills 387
regeneration, rural or urban 434, 446–7, 448
reliance
or detriment 311–13
proprietary estoppel
burden of proof 326
as a causal connection 326
establishing 326–7
reasonableness 328
requirement 325
reliance loss 77
religion
advancement of 441–4
not merely belief 444
conditions restraining 190
equal treatment 443–4
faith healers 441–2
gifts to religious leaders 444
Jainism 443
Jedism 443
meaning 442–3
Pemsel case (1891) 441
public benefit of 490–2
purposes ancillary to 444
religious organizations and gifts to members 355
religious/racial harmony, equality and diversity 452–3
sects and cults 444
spiritual or non-secular 443
remedial constructive trusts 239–40
beyond unjust enrichment 256–7
defining 254
detrimental reliance 263
development of 255–6
difficulties 257–8
'new model' constructive trust 258–60, 348
no single coherent theory 257
promises 213
and proprietary estoppel 261
prospects for, in England
changing environment 262–3
judicial attitudes 260–1
revival of controversy 261–2
range of remedial responses 256
restitutionary cause of action 255
uncertainty as to cause of action 257
uncertainty as to remedy 257–8
remedial trusts
commercial transactions 55
restitutionary resulting trusts 221
remedies
abuse of position 695
appropriate, determining 336–43
award, principles governing 336
composite approach 339
fulfilment of claimant's 'reasonable expectation' 336–7
multifactorial approach 340–3
redressing detriment 338–9
untrammelled discretion 339–40
awards 334–5
appropriate remedy 336–43
principles governing 336
beneficiaries entitled to seek 697–8
breach of fiduciary duty 774–82
advantages of a proprietary remedy 778
choice of remedy 781
dog's leg claims 781–2
Monte Carlo case 777, 780
proprietary 776–81
common law 4–5, 165–9
composite 334–5
dishonesty 814
election between compensatory and restitutionary remedies 724
equitable *see* equitable remedies
incompletely constituted trusts
actions by the trustee 166–7
settlor contracted with beneficiary 165–6
settlor covenanted or contracted only with the trustee 166
significance 165
trusts of a promise 167–9
lack of 335–6
liability of strangers 797
maxims of equity 23
multifactorial approach
excessive expectations 340–1
other factors 341–3
proportionality 341
quasi-bargains 340
unspecific assurances 340
proprietary 698
advantages of 778
breach of fiduciary duty 776–81

remedies (*cont.*)
proprietary estoppel
award, principles governing 336
bars to a remedy 343
composite approach 339
fulfilment of claimant's 'reasonable expectation' 336–7
multifactorial approach 340–3
redressing detriment 338–9
untrammelled discretion 339–40
remedial constructive trusts 257–8
self-dealing rule 760
strangers to trust, against 698, 797–829
tracing 834–6
trustees de son tort 802
unconscionable receipt, liability for 829
unjust enrichment 222
remoteness of vesting rules 185–8
removal of trustees 672, 687–8
against their will 680
remuneration
authorized 755–7
entitlement to 755–6
expenses 755
inadequate 330
trust deeds 755, 756
trustees 27
unauthorized 755–7
repairing covenants 82
contracts requiring constant supervision 82–3
reputation, injunctions to protect 105
rescission
affirmation 74
of contracts
for misrepresentation 70–1
for mistake 67
limitations on availability
affirmation 74
delay 74–5
restitutio in integrum impossible 74
third-party rights 74
for misrepresentation 70–1
for mistake
contracts 67
difficulties with current principles 70
only part of transaction affected 70
Pitt v Holt (2013) 68, 70
requirements 69
taxation 69
voluntary transactions 67–70
restitutio in integrum impossible 74
setting aside transactions for 73–4
for undue influence 17, 71–3
actual undue influence 71
meaning 71
presumed undue influence 71–2
third parties 72–3
of voluntary transactions/ dispositions
for misrepresentation 70–1
for mistake 67–70
see also rectification
residuary interest 124
restitutio in integrum 74
restitution, and **tracing** 836–8
restitutionary trusts *see* remedial trusts
restrictive covenants 86, 103, 514
resulting trusts 195–237
alternatives to 208–10
evidence gift was intended 208
evidence loan was intended 209–10
gift to take effect on death 208–9
arising when 29
automatic *see* automatic resulting trusts
breach of trust 722
concept 223
and constructive trusts 196, 197–8, 304
contribution to the purchase price, family home 299–302
defining 195
distinguishing 196–8
extinguishing 181–4
family home
continuing role for 280–1
contribution to the purchase price 299–302
contributions otherwise explained as gifts 302
evolution of rights in 298–304
fate of resulting trusts in 282–3
general principles 299
original acquisition method 298
property other than 281–2
quantifying the interest 302–4
rejection of analysis 280
institutional 223–4
intention, importance of 196
presumed *see* presumed resulting trusts
promises 176
purchase money resulting trusts 205–7
Quistclose trusts *see Quistclose* trusts
rationale for
automatic resulting trusts 200–1
intention of transferor 198
lack of intention to make a gift 198–9
presumed intention of parties 198
retention of ownership 199
unjust enrichment 199–224
rebutting the presumption
admissibility of evidence 210–11
alternatives to a resulting trust 208–10
quality of evidence 210
rejection of 222–3
rescission of voluntary dispositions 67
restitutionary 221
resulting in operation 196
unincorporated associations
members' subscriptions 362–3
outside legacies and donations 363
proceeds of entertainments and collecting boxes 363–4
unjust enrichment 199–200
autonomous cause of action 222
institutional resulting trust 223–4
operating to reverse 221–4
rejection of resulting trust 222–3
remedy 222
restitutionary resulting trusts 221
why trusts result 196
retirement of trustees
compulsory 670–1
liability after 723
voluntary 670
reversionary interests 630
revocation of wills
breach of contract 393
destruction 388
methods 387–8

new will or document in form of a will 388
revival of rushed will 388
revocability 387

rights
equitable *see* equitable rights
human *see* human rights
personal *see* personal rights
proprietary *see* proprietary rights
protected by injunctions 101–2
subsidiary 16

risk management 654

***Rochefoucauld v Boustead*, rule in** 171–2, 418

Rudden, B. 15, 16

rule against perpetuities *see* perpetuities, rule against

rural regeneration *see* regeneration, rural or urban

same-sex relationships 218, 270
see also civil partnerships

satisfaction doctrine 25

***Saunders v Vautier*, rule in**
fixed trusts 536, 556
overriding the terms of the trust 32
unit trusts, rights of investors in 53

***Schmidt v Rosewood* decision**, and blurring of traditional categories of trust and power 26, 40

search orders 109–11
defining 109
no real harm to defendant 110
preconditions to grant of 109–10
privilege against self-incrimination 111
protection for defendant
application to vary or discharge 111
damages, undertaking in 111
items to be removed 111
search in presence of defendant 111
service and explanation by a solicitor 110
times of service 111
real possibility evidence will be destroyed 110
serious potential damage 109
strong prima facie case 109

secondary trusts 50
terms 51

secret commission 760–1

secret trusts 401–18
acceptance 406–7
revocation before death of testator 410–11
arising on intestacy 403
arising when 401, 403
burden of proof 408–9
characterised as constructive trusts 418
characterised as express trusts 417–18
communication
of both the fact and terms of trust 404–5
of the extent of the trust 405
fully secret trusts 404–6
half-secret trusts 407–8
to joint trustees 405–6
must be consistent with will 408
must be made before death of testator 405
must be made before execution of will 407–8
creation, requirements for 403
date of accrual of beneficial interest 415–16
death or disclaimer of secret trustee 410–11
enforcement, justifying 411–14
arising outside of testator's will 413–14, 415f
to prevent fraud 412–13
failure 409
features 401
fully secret 402, 404–7, 409, 410
gifts 401–2
half-secret 402, 407–8, 409, 410
and hiding identity of true property owner 45
joint tenancy 403
juridical nature 417–18
problems associated with modern theory 416–17
secret trustee
death following testator 410
death or disclaimer 410–11
disclaimer after death of testator 411
predeceasing the testator 410
revocation of acceptance 410–11
whether benefiting from a secret trust 411
standard of proof 409
types 402–3
see also wills

self-dealing rule 757–60
application of 757–8
exceptions to 759
remedies of beneficiary 760
standard required 758–9

Senior Courts
damages, jurisdiction to award 86
injunctions, power to grant 87
Judicature Acts 1873 and 1875 7, 8
privilege against self-incrimination 111
uniform jurisdiction given to judges 8

settlors
appointment of trustees by 667–70
capacity to act as trustee 668
disclaimer 668
express trusts 29, 667
implied trusts 667
inter vivos transfer to trustees 668–9
limitation on the number of trustees 669–70
testamentary transfers of property 669
trust will not fail for want of trustee 668–9
fixed trusts 30
income tax avoidance 57–8
incompletely constituted trusts, remedies for
contracting with the beneficiary 165–6
covenanting or contracting only with trustee 166
intention of 604, 619–20
owners as 140
promise of 96, 108, 109, 118, 143

severance
excessive exercise of power 566
joint tenancy 46, 170
of non-charitable elements in a trust 490

shares
advancement powers 601
agreement not essential 308
attempted transfers of 150–1
bonus 549
corporate receipts received as a 'windfall' by the trust 548–9
CREST system, registration through 147
joint stock companies 59, 60

shares (*cont.*)
open-ended investment companies (OEICs) 60–1
quantification of, in family home
basis of quantification 290–1
comparison with divorce 293–4
express intention 290
inferring and imputing intention 290
relevant factors 291–2
requirements for effective transfer 146–7
share certificates 146, 147, 154, 220, 554
share register of company 146, 154, 178, 552
and specific performance 83
subsequent variation, express trusts 278–9
tenancy-in-common 46
tracing and claiming 850
trust fund 27
Shelter 424
Simonds, Gavin (Lord) 166, 355, 433, 818
social investment, charities concerned with 448
social investments 448, 663–4
solicitor-trustees 757
specific performance 77–86
absence of necessary formalities 84
agreements made without consideration 81–2
anticipatory performance 80
breach of covenant 83
claimant in breach 82
contracts
to carry on a business 80–1
to exercise a testamentary power of appointment 81
land 78
partnership 81
of personal service 80
referring to an arbitration 81
requiring constant supervision 82–3
sale of unique personal property 78
to transfer goodwill 81
damages
claimant entitled only to nominal damages 79
in lieu 86
quantification difficult 79
defences 84–5
delay 85
effect of order 86
hardship 84, 85
misdescription of property 85
misrepresentation by plaintiff 84
mistake 84
mutuality 79, 83–4
obstacles to ordering 81–3
practical unavailability of market substitutes 79
statutory rights to 79
where available 78–80
where unavailable 80–1
see also damages
sports *see* amateur sport, advancement
springboard principle, perpetual injunctions 89
standard of proof
civil 387, 409
mutual wills 393
secret trusts 409
strangers to trust
bona fide purchaser 836
constructive trustee 800–1
dishonest assistance in breach of trust 800, 803–14
illegal acts by 806
personal claims 799
proprietary claims 797–9, 814, 834
providing valuable consideration 835–6
remedies against 698, 797–829
proprietary 814
tabular synopsis of claims 829, 830f
trustees de son tort 800, 801–2
types of stranger liability 799–800
unconscionable receipt, liability for 814–29
basis of 814–15
beneficial receipt by the defendant 816–17
causal link 828
conscience, liability based on 817
conscious wrongdoing 821–2
current position 817–18
degrees of knowledge 819–20
dishonesty 822–3
factual requirement of receipt 816
fault 817–28
knowledge and companies 827
knowledge and notice 826–7
limitation of action 829
misapplication of trust assets 815–16
negligence 820–1, 825
previous debate 818–23
remedies 829
strict liability 818–19
time of knowledge or fault 828
unjust enrichment 815
as volunteers 834–5
when liable 797–801
relationship to remedies against trustees 797
see also third parties
strict liability
amelioration of the consequences 771–2
proof of wrongdoing 773
rationale for 769–71
***Strong v Bird*, rule in** 158–60
donee must have been granted administration 159
donor's intention continuing until death 159
intention to make an inter vivos gift 159
property surviving death of donor 159–60
subject matter, certainty of
contagious uncertainty 137
contract to create a trust 124
definition too vague 123
future property 123–4
mechanism allowing property to be identified 123
mutual wills 395
no specific property identified 121
requirement of certainty 121–4
trust can only exist in relation to specific property 121, 141
trust of a share of a larger bulk 122–3
trust property not earmarked or segregated 121–2
and uncertainty 125
subpoena 712
subsidiary rights 16
subsidiary trust 559
sub-trusts
created by equitable owner 29n10
inter vivos declarations of trust 173–4

succession 369–400
intestacy *see* intestacy
methods of making provision 369–73
civil partnerships 371
cohabiting partners 371
contested gifts to charities 372–3
donatio mortis causa (DMC) *see* donatio mortis causa (DMC)
in English law compared with other jurisdictions 371
family and dependents 371–3
intestacy *see* intestacy
joint tenancy 370
lifetime gift 370
lifetime trust 370
nominations and expressions of wishes 370–1
surviving spouse 371
wills *see* wills
probate 371, 373
property rights expiring on death 369
successive ownership 47
suicide, aiding and abetting 245
superinjunctions 87, 88, 105
and creativity of equity 22
Trafigura 105n415
supervisory jurisdiction 129, 135, 512–13, 560, 708
abuse, preventing 694
control of trustees 696–7
duty of care 638–9
fiduciary duties and powers 575–7
information 708–9
surplus funds
dissolution of clubs and societies 362–7
animal welfare 365–6
charitable unincorporated associations 366
funds going to Crown 367
identifying the members 365
incorporated or proprietary clubs 362
last surviving member of an association 365–6
members' contractual rights 365
special cases 366
unincorporated associations 362–4, 366
pension schemes 54, 229
survivorship
constructive trust arising on death 396–7
date of first testator's death 396
floating trust by survivor 399–400
forfeiture of entitlement by 246
joint tenancy 46
mutual contract theory 356
see also under civil partners; marriage

tangible property 842, 850, 860
taxation
accounting for tax liability 730
artificial avoidance schemes 69
capital gains tax (CGT) 57, 58, 613, 616
capital transfer tax 58
charitable trusts 430
evasion of 56n58
Gift Aid 430
and hiding identity of true property owner 44, 45
income tax 57–8
inheritance tax (IHT) 58–9
legitimate avoidance 56
pension schemes funded from 53
and rescission for mistake 69
Special Commissioners for Income Tax 477
stamp duty 179
tax avoidance 12, 56
tax-planning 12
value added tax 430
tenancy-in-common 46, 47
see also joint tenancy
tenure 11, 269
terrorism 45, 474, 528
Home Affairs Committee on Counter Terrorism 519
threat from terrorist financing and money laundering 518–19
testate and intestate succession *see* death; intestacy; wills
theft, property obtained by 243
third parties
conflict with transferor 172–3
innocent 108
interlocutory injunctions, impact of 100
primary, terms of 50–1
promise 202–4, 250–2
protective trusts 50
rescission
limitations on availability 74
for undue influence 72–3
undue influence 72–3
wrongdoing by and rights of beneficiaries 28
see also strangers to trust
title
equitable 29
legal 19–20, 28
declaration of self as trustee 139–40
family home 284–9
joint 284, 296
sole 284–9
separation of 13
transfer of 148–9
see also ownership
tracing
applying proprietary remedies 834–6
assets
acquired prior to misappropriation 870–2
assets identified as representing the original trust property 877–88
bulk cannot be divided into proportionate shares 850
clean substitutions 849–50
'first in, first out' allocation 866, 867f
individually identifiable 864
not capable of individual allocation 864
pari passu allocation 864–5
product of a clean substitution 849–50
tangible property mixed 842, 850, 860
where tangible property mixed 842, 850, 860
breach of trust 833
at common law 833, 841–51
banking system 843–7
claiming 848–51
clean substitutions 841–2, 849–50
criticism 847–8
mixed funds 843
personal restitution 850–1
personal restitution, claiming 850–1
where bulk divided into proportionate shares 850
debate 840–1
defining 831–41

tracing (*cont.*)
in equity 833–4, 852–79
assets acquired prior to misappropriation 870–2
assets identified as representing the original trust property 877–88
bank trustee depositing trust money with itself 869–70
banking system, tracing of money through 861–70
bona fide purchaser 873–4
choice of remedy 879
circumstances in which possible to trace 856–60
and claiming 833–4, 852–79
clean substitutions 860
enforcing an equitable lien 878–9
equitable ownership of traced property 855–6
fiduciary relationship 852–5
limits of equitable tracing 872–6
lowest intermediate balance 868–9
method of application 866–8
misappropriation of trust property by a trustee 856
mixed funds 860–1
mixture of trust property and trustee's own property 862–3
of money, through a mixed fund 860–1
payments made by mistake 859–60
payments under a void contract 857–8
payments under a voidable contract 858–9
personal restitution 879
profits received by a fiduciary in breach of duty 856
property of trusts or innocent volunteers mixed 864–8
receipt of trust property by a stranger to a trust 856
right to trace 852–60
rule in *Clayton's case* 866
scope of equitable tracing 852
of tangible property, into a mixed bulk 842, 850, 860, 878
executors 835, 852
limits of equitable tracing 872–6
bona fide purchaser 873–4
dissipation 874–5
inequitable to trace 876
unascertained goods 875–6
mixing 832
nature of process 836–41
proprietary 838–9
restitution and tracing 836–8
as process by which property identified 831–3
following original property 831
property to follow or trace 832
tracing substitute property 831–2
property of trusts or innocent volunteers mixed 864–8
proprietary process 838–9
reasons for use 833
and restitution 836–8
stranger was a volunteer 834–5
and trust property
applying proprietary remedies 834–6
proprietary remedies against a stranger 834
and trustee in bankruptcy 842, 845, 850
trade disputes 100
trade unions 104, 440
transactions
authorized 48
commercial 147
illegal purposes test 214
investigation of validity 21
only part affected, in mistake 70
setting aside 17
unconscionable bargains 73–4
undue influence 72
substance rather than form of 17
voluntary *see* voluntary transactions/dispositions
transfer, constituting the trust by 146–54
constitution through coincidental receipt by trustee 152–4
ineffective transfers and declaration 154–5
past the point of no return 148–50
requirements for effective transfer
land 146
shares 146–7
where registration required
Pennington v Waine principle 150, 151, 152
recalling the gift would be unconscionable 150–1
reinterpreting unconscionability 150–1
transfer past the point of no return 148–50
transferor 'doing everything within his power' 148
see also constitution of trusts
transfers of value 58, 224
trespass 609, 704
award of damages 92
on Forestry Commission land 91
judicial legislation 349
prohibitory injunctions 90
rights protected by injunctions 101–2
suspension of injunctions 94
trust deeds 145, 358, 463, 579, 584, 595, 627, 647, 710
breach of trust 715, 721, 734
express powers 672
maintenance powers 595
power of variation in 652
remuneration 755, 756
'sham' intention 118, 119
statutory provisions 673
trust for sale 643
trust fund
accretions and substitutions 27
assets forming 27
concept 26–7
and following 27–8
maintaining integrity of 30
not exhausted 226
and powers of appointment 34
product of trust property will also be trust property 27
restoration of 729
tracing and following trust property 27–8
see also assets
trust instrument
appointment of trustees 676
authorized remuneration 755
rectification 77
'royal lives' clause 187
trust property *see* property/trust property
trust terms *see* terms of trust

trustee in bankruptcy
constructive trusts 785n24
primary trusts 50
protective trusts 50
secondary trusts 51
and terms of primary trust 50–1
tracing 842, 845, 850
trustees
actions at the initiative of 167
advice to charity trustees from Charity Commission 523–4
coincidental receipt, constitution through 152–4
Crown as 28
custodian 52, 553
death of 674
declaration of self as 139–40
desiring to be discharged 674–5
expenses 755
incompletely constituted trusts 166–7
as infants 675
joint 405–6
as legal owners 10, 13–14, 28
limitation on the number of 669–70
loss to trust caused by 67
maintenance powers 595–9
opportunities 766–7
original 667–70
powers *see* powers
purchase of trust property by 757–60
refusing to act 675
retirement of
compulsory 670–1
voluntary 670
remaining out of the UK for more than 12 months 674
removal 675
remuneration 27
retirement of *see* retirement of trustees
role 28
selection 638
settlor covenanted or contracted only with 166
special, appointment of 685–7
standard of care 696–7
transfer of property on trust to 140–1
trustees of the settlement 28
unfit or incapable 675
voluntary 720–1
voluntary principle of trusteeship 423
see also accountability of trustees; appointment of trustees; control of trusts/trustees; co-trustees; duties and obligations of trustees; liability of trustees
trustees de son tort 800
causes 801–2
defining 801
remedies 802
trusts
arising when 29
arrangements without 59–65
of the benefit of a covenant 167
and capital gains tax 58
certainty
of intention 116–21
no single test for all trusts 127–33
of objects 125–37
of subject matter 121–5
see also certainty
concept 28
contract to create 124
and co-ownership 46–7
development of 12–13
duality of ownership 10
emergence of 11–13
equitable obligations, subject to 28–32
failure 125
feudal system of land holding 11
flexibility 26, 37
floating 398, 399–400
impact 14
and income tax 57
intention to create
language used 116–17
meaning of requirement 116–17
overarching 145–6
precatory words 117–18, 120, 138
'sham' intention 118–20
invalidly created 119–20
lack of intention to create
evidence, importance of 120–1
no trust without intention 120
something other than a trust intended 120
modern 13–14
origins 11
ownership
beneficiary as equitable owner 14
trustee as legal owner 10, 13–14
pension schemes 53, 54
and powers
distinguishing between 34, 115
and enforcing fiduciary powers 39
functional similarity 34
limitations of traditional categorization 35–6
overview 34–5
trust combined with 36
trust or power 35
see also appointment, powers of
pre-existing, rights under 246
purpose 10, 28
'Red Cross' Trusts 545
separation of management from its enjoyment 14
separation of ownership, importance 10–11
separation of title under 13
as sui generis 'proprietary obligation' 28
and tax planning 56–9
'use,' development of 11–12
variation of 652
void 51, 468
see also trustees
trusts of a promise 118n60, 120–1
incompletely constituted trusts 167–9
trusts of land
inter vivos declarations of trust
conflict between transferor and third party beneficiaries 172–3
formalities required 170–1
Rochefoucauld v Boustead, rule in 171–2
liability of trustees for acts of agent 640
management powers 627–8

unanimity requirement 676, 695
unauthorized profit
breach of fiduciary duty 56
breach of trust 31
limitation of action against 791–3
receipt by a fiduciary 241
remedies 67
trust fund 27
unauthorized receipts 775–6
unauthorized remuneration 755–7

uncertainty
conditions void for 188–9
contagious 137–8
of objects, whether a single test for 136
remedial constructive trusts
cause of action 257
remedy for 257–8
resolving
alternative test for powers 136–7
ascertainment 133–4
'Benjamin orders' 133
conditional gifts 134–5
mechanism for 134–5
see also certainty
unconscionability
Baden categorization 825
confirmed but not explained 824
and detriment 152, 328
and dishonesty 824
imposed trust obligations 29–30
liability for unconscionable receipt 814–29
and negligence 825
proprietary estoppel, based on unconscionable conduct 317–19
broader understanding 318–19
strict criteria ('five probanda') 318
three requirements 319
recalling a gift as unconscionable 150–1
reinterpreting 150–1
setting aside unconscionable bargains 73–4
strangers to trust, remedies against 800
unconscionable receipt, liability for 814–29
basis of 814–15
beneficial receipt by the defendant 816–17
causal link 828
conscience, liability based on 817
conscious wrongdoing 821–2
current position 817–18
degrees of knowledge 819–20
dishonesty 822–3
factual requirement of receipt 816
fault 817–28
grounds for suspicion 824–5
knowledge and companies 827
knowledge and notice 826–7
limitation of action 829
misapplication of trust assets 815–16
negligence 820–1, 825
negligence of recipient 820–1
personal attributes 827
previous debate 818–23
remedies 829
strict liability 818–19
time of knowledge or fault 828
unjust enrichment 815
see also unfairness
undue influence
actual 71
duress 71
examples 71–2
meaning 71
presumed 71–2
rebutting 72
rescission for 71–3
setting aside transactions for 17
third party influence 72–3
wills, capacity to make 380
unfairness 69, 84, 526, 601, 769, 771
see also fairness; unconscionability
unilateral instruments, rectification of 76–7
unincorporated associations
absence of an independent legal personality 354
charitable 360
defining 354
dissolution 361–2
surplus funds on 362–7
gifts
conditions attached to 359–60
considered as valid 354–5
cy-près doctrine 502
to members 355–6
subject to rules of association 356
mutual contract theory 356–7
ongoing reform to cy-près triggers 499
purpose trust theory 354–5
purpose-based understanding of 355
purposes benefiting an identifiable class 542
resulting trusts
members' subscriptions 362–3
outside legacies and donations 363
proceeds of entertainments and collecting boxes 363–4
societies not seen as 354
surplus funds on dissolution 362–7
current approach 364
resulting trusts 366–7
unincorporated associations *see* unincorporated associations
whether capable of owning property 354
see also charities; clubs and societies
unit trusts
assets 53
collective investment 52–3
and pension schemes 53
trust fund, concept of 27
unjust enrichment
autonomous cause of action 222
bargains, enforcement (constructive trusts) 254
principles 199
rationale for resulting trusts 199–200
rejection of resulting trust 222–3
and remedial constructive trusts 256–7
remedy for 222
resulting trusts operating to reverse 221–4
institutional resulting trust 223–4
rejection of resulting trust 222–3
remedy for unjust enrichment 222
restitutionary resulting trusts 221
resulting trusts and unjust enrichment 224
see also resulting trusts
unlawful contracts 83
unlawful killing 243, 244n34, 245
unreasonableness 703–4
urban regeneration *see* regeneration, rural or urban
'use'
development of, in emergence of a trust 11–12
Statute of Uses 12, 13
'use upon a use' 13

validity
appointment, powers of 563–4, 566
charitable trusts 429–30
discretionary trusts 585–9
administrative unworkability 587–8
capriciousness 588–9
certainty of objects 585–7
'complete list' test, criticism 586
'is or is not' test 587
perpetuities, rule against 589
fully constituted trusts 142
purpose trust theory 354–5, 356
valid trust, two ways of creating
declaration of self as trustee 139–40
transfer of property on trust to trustees 140–1
see also invalidity
valuable consideration
constitution of trusts 156
doctrine of notice 19
provided by stranger 835–6
stranger a bona fide purchaser 836
variation of beneficial interests 603–21
approval 32, 614–16
benefit requirement 616–18
conflicting benefits 617–18
consensual
avoiding consent 616
beneficiaries' wishes 605
limits to 605
primacy of settlor's intention 604
contingent interests 615–16
'double contingency' test 615
persons with an existing contingent interest 614
under protective trusts 615–16
discretion to vary
fraud on a power 618
undermining protective trusts 619
'double contingency' test 615
financial benefit 616
incapacity 614
infancy 614
inherent court jurisdiction 604, 606–9
broader understanding 608–9
compromise jurisdiction 607–8
conversion jurisdiction 606
emergency jurisdiction 606–7, 609
maintenance jurisdiction 607, 610
manifest benefit 618
Matrimonial Causes Act 1973 610
Mental Capacity Act 2005, s 18(1)(h) 610
miscellaneous statutory powers 609–10
non-financial benefits 617
persons unborn 615
protective trusts 615–16
undermining 619
provisions for 603
release of powers 604
Settled Land Act 1925, s 64(1) 610
spendthrift trusts 615
statutory powers 604
surrender of beneficial interest 604
Trustee Act 1925, s 53 610
Trustee Act 1925, s 57 609
unidentifiable beneficiaries 614–15
Variation of Trusts Act 1958
approval 614–16
avoiding consent 616
benefit requirement 616–18
conflicting benefits 617–18
'double contingency' test 615
effect of an order to vary 620–1
financial benefit 616
infancy or incapacity 614
manifest benefit 618
non-financial benefits 617
persons unborn 615
persons with an existing contingent interest 614
relevance of settlor's intentions 619–20
scheme of 611–12
unidentifiable beneficiaries 614–15
variation or resettlement 612–13
widening powers of investment 620
wishes of beneficiaries 605
see also beneficial interests; beneficiaries of trusts
venture capital funds 60
vicarious liability 639
void contracts, payments under 223, 857–8
void trusts
graves and monuments, maintenance of 468
pure purpose 51
voidable contracts, payments under 858–9
voluntary transactions/dispositions
rescission of
for misrepresentation 71
for mistake 67–70
voluntary waste 102
volunteer
charities 423
'equity will not assist a volunteer' rule
constitution of trusts 150
donatio mortis causa (gift on account of death) 160–4
exceptions to 157–64
importance of exceptions 157–8
incompletely constituted trusts 156
specific performance 81
Strong v Bird, rule in 158–60
incompletely constituted trusts, volunteer beneficiaries 156–7
stranger as 834–5
volunteering/voluntary sector 447–8
vulnerable individuals, providing for
beneficiary should not manage the property 50
beneficiary unable to manage property 49
protective trusts 50–1

Walker, Robert (Lord) 38, 40, 262n182, 275, 280, 281, 285, 319, 320, 321, 323, 324–5, 328, 340, 341, 430, 514, 529, 634, 706–7, 709, 712, 715, 838n37, 856n159, 862
waste 102, 105n415
Wellcome Trust 422
Wilberforce, Richard (Lord) 16, 33, 35, 38–41, 54n51, 84, 86, 141, 153, 182, 363, 364n11, 391, 429, 492, 502n95, 503, 510n13, 513, 514, 516, 518–20, 538, 539, 542, 657, 667, 671, 841

wills 377–88
altering 384–5, 388
attestation 383, 384
capacity to make
age 378
black letter rules 379
fraud 380
golden rule 380
lifetime gifts 380
no fixed standard of testamentary capacity 379
perversity of will 379
presumption of capacity 379
reform 379
'sound mind, memory and understanding' 378–9
testamentary capacity test 378–9
undue influence 380
charitable gifts
initial failure 494–5, 500–6
subsequent failure 499–500
communication requirements 407–8
contingent gifts 598
cy-près doctrine 493
declaration of trust by 174
destruction 388
dispensing power, Law Commission's suggestion for 387
evidence of intention 386
execution
attestation 383
half-secret trusts 407–8
identical wills among husband and wife 382
'intended . . . to give effect to the will' 382
qualification to be a witness 383
'signed by the testator' 381–2
statement 381
witnesses 382–3
'in writing' 381
forfeiture of entitlement by 245
general charitable intention 503
half-secret trusts 407–8
incorporated document
clearly identified in the will 384
in existence at date of will 384
referred to in the will 384
interpretation 385–6
lapse 386
liability of draftsman for negligence 388
new will or codicil 385
obliteration of words 385
principles 385–6
proving, by Probate Registry 371
rectification 387
revocation
destruction 388
methods 387–8
mutual wills 393
revival of rushed will 388
revocability 387
setting aside 71
will itself, alterations on 385
will 'speaks from death' 385
winding up
clubs and societies 362
joint stock companies 59
witnesses, wills 382–3
Wolfenden Report (1978), charities 424
women
emancipation of 269
equality 453
equity of deserted wife 17–18, 297
gender imbalance 348
married 13, 297
Women's Institutes 455
Woodfield Report (1987), charities 516
words 35, 43
actual words used 338
ambiguous 126
certainty of 115, 116, 126, 131
general 251
of gift by settlor to himself 144–5, 155
loose conversation 144
meaning attached to 134
obliteration of, in wills 385
policies 168
precatory 117–18, 120, 138
repeated over a period of time 144
in statutes 124, 172, 176
trust instrument 130
in wills 383, 385
writing requirement
absence of writing and invalidity 176, 418
dispositions of subsisting equitable interests 174–84
'an equitable interest . . . subsisting at the time of disposition' 177
exceptions to need for writing 177–84
extinguishing a resulting trust 181–4
meaning of 'disposition' 175–6
scope of disposition 175–6
'signed by the person disposing of the same or his agent' 177
'or by will' 177
'in writing' 177
exceptions to need for writing
direction by beneficiary of a bare trust 177–9
specifically enforceable contract 179–81
writs 6
categories 5
at common law 4–5